W9-BAP-837
$29.00
8747
GEORGIA BOOK STORE
659-0959
$30.00

THE LEGAL ENVIRONMENT OF BUSINESS

SECOND EDITION

THE LEGAL ENVIRONMENT OF BUSINESS

SECOND EDITION

RATE A. HOWELL
The Ohio State University

JOHN R. ALLISON
University of Texas, Austin

N. T. HENLEY
Georgia State University

The Dryden Press
Chicago New York Philadelphia San Francisco Montreal Toronto
London Sydney Tokyo Mexico City Rio de Janeiro Madrid

Acquisitions Editor: Mary Fischer
Project Editor: Holly Crawford
Design Supervisor: Jeanne Calabrese
Production Supervisor: Diane Tenzi
Permissions Editor: Doris Milligan
Director of Editing, Design, and Production: Jane Perkins

Cover Photography and Design: Nina Lisowski
Copy Editor: Charlene Posner
Indexer: Richard Ruane
Compositor: G&S Typesetters, Inc.
Text Type: 10/12 Sabon

Howell, Rate A.
The legal environment of business.

Includes index.
1. Industrial laws and legislation—United States.
2. Trade regulation—United States. 3. Commercial law
—United States. 4. Industry—Social aspects—United
States. I. Allison, John Robert, 1948–
II. Henley, N. T. (Nathaniel T.) III. Title.
KF1600.H68 1987 346.73′07 86-4503
ISBN: 0-03-008369-9 347.3067

Printed in the United States of America
789-039-987654321

Address orders:
383 Madison Avenue
New York, NY 10017

Address editorial correspondence:
One Salt Creek Lane
Hinsdale, IL 60521

CBS COLLEGE PUBLISHING
The Dryden Press
Holt, Rinehart and Winston
Saunders College Publishing

PREFACE

The first edition of our *Legal Environment of Business* text was published in January 1984, in response to the increased offerings of legal environment courses in business schools as alternatives to traditional business law courses. (These offerings appear under a number of titles at the undergraduate and graduate levels: The Legal Environment of Business, Business and Government, Business and the Legal System, and Business and Society, to name but a few.) Because the text found widespread acceptance in that market, this second edition retains the basic format and approach of its predecessor.

Several significant changes and additions, nonetheless, have been made to keep the text abreast of current developments in the dynamic areas of law that collectively fall within the legal environment spectrum. Not only do these properly convey an air of currency and relevance of the subject to our students but, additionally, they ensure that the text continues to meet the standards of Legal Environment of Business courses as set forth by the American Assembly of Collegiate Schools of Business (AACSB).

The most significant changes and additions are the following:

- Addition of a new chapter, The Legal Environment of International Business.

- Comprehensive updating of the three employment chapters, including expanded coverage of the "comparable worth" doctrine.
- Complete rewriting of the Vertical Price Fixing and Vertical Territorial and Customer Restrictions (now renamed Vertical Nonprice Restrictions) sections in the antitrust area.
- Expanded coverage of joint ventures in the Horizontal Restraints of Trade chapter, also in the antitrust area, including a new section on research and development joint ventures.
- Amplified discussion of the religion and free speech clauses of the First Amendment in the chapter on Constitutional Law, as they apply to business managers, with emphasis upon recent U.S. Supreme Court decisions in this area.
- Expanded coverage of the subjects of Contracts and Sales in Chapter 8, Business Law—Selected Topics.
- Update of the "intent to monopolize" discussion of Section 2 of the Sherman Act in Chapter 10, including the addition of the *Aspen Ski* case.

In addition to the above, several changes of a more general nature have been made. For example, a number of other chapters have undergone a broad updating, especially those on the subjects of business's influence on the legal process, consumer protection law, and environmental law. Second, in response to users' suggestions, recent cases have been added to the Questions and Problems at chapter ends throughout the text. (The Questions and Problems have proved to be a valuable catalyst for class discussions, and their usefulness is even more enhanced with these additions.)

As noted earlier, the strengths of the first edition—the basic format and conceptual approach—have been completely retained. The following is a brief description of that format and approach.

Structure: The text is again divided into three parts. Part I, Business and the Legal System, examines the fundamental nature, structure, and processes of our legal system. It also examines in some depth the various sources of our rules of law. Part II, Business and the Regulatory Environment, presents several common rationales for government regulation and then examines various federal and state laws that impose constraints on business activities. Part III, Business and Society, provides a thorough treatment of business responsibilities to larger segments of society. Many of these responsibilities are specified by law, and some of the pertinent laws are regulatory in nature. Other responsibilities, however, are less clearly defined and are thus more of an ethical or moral nature.

Writing Style: We have continued to be mindful of the fact that we are writing this text *for students*. Thus we have not attempted to create a legal reference work, or to expound on topics of our own particular interest, at the expense of a coherent and balanced textbook. Similarly, we have continued to use a lucid, readable writing style. Legal jargon is used only when absolutely necessary, and in those instances it is fully explained. We have also avoided the vice of "rule-stating." Rather than merely setting forth rule after rule, we have provided explanation, background, illustration, and analysis of relevant legal principles.

Coverage: Our topical treatment continues to be evenly balanced. This means that we have tried to align the depth and breadth of our treatment of a given topic with the professional consensus regarding that topic's relative importance. Similarly, a proper balance has been struck between the theoretical and the practical. Ample theoretical foundation is provided, and then is supported by practical illustrations. We have continued to be careful not to go too far in either direction: that is, the theory does not delve into the arcane, and the practical does not overemphasize the "how to" aspect.

Case Presentation: Cases are included at pertinent points in each chapter, rather than being lumped together at chapter ends. We continue to present the facts of each case in our own words for the purpose of clarity. Following the summary of facts is the court's opinion, which has—in every case—been edited judiciously to maintain a reasonable length and to focus the student's attention on those points being illustrated. At the same time, we have not over-edited; enough of the opinion is presented to enable the student to participate in the court's analysis, to obtain a sense of the judicial process, and to consider relevant policy implications.

Teaching Aids: This edition is again accompanied by complete instructional support materials. The *Instructor's Manual*, prepared by the authors, includes a test bank of objective and brief essay questions by Thomas Brierton of Northern Illinois University. The *Study Guide* has been written by Dan Bertozzi, Jr., of California Polytechnic State University. Additionally, a Newsletter which we have prepared is available from The Dryden Press; this will be updated periodically.

Once again we are grateful to the many people whose assistance was invaluable in the preparation of this edition. In addition to those who have prepared the ancillary materials, noted above, we owe special thanks to Robert Prentice, of the University of Texas at Austin, for the updating of his original chapter on Securities Regulation. We are similarly indebted to E. Ray Lanier for his preparation of the chapter on the Legal Environment of International Business. Our thanks also go to several colleagues at other institutions who participated in a survey designed by The Dryden Press to assess the strengths and weaknesses of the first edition. They are: Dr. Randy Abbott, Southwest State University; Ronald Bird, Meredith College; Rene Cone, University of North Carolina; Richard Finkley, Governors State University; Susan Grady, University of Massachusetts; David Hoch, University of Southwestern Louisiana; Louise Holcomb, Gainesville Junior College; Louis E. Katz, Youngstown State University; John Michael, Texas Christian University; Gary Nickelson, Texas Christian University; Margaret Noteman, University of North Carolina; Dr. Sheelwant B. Pawar, Idaho State University; Marvin Segal, College of DuPage; John H. Shannon, Seton Hall University; Katie Simmons, Gainesville Junior College; Burke T. Ward, Villanova University; Daniel Warner, Western Washington University; Clint Wood, Delta State University.

Additionally, we thank the following reviewers of the second edition manuscript: Thomas Brierton, Northern Illinois University; W. Arthur Graham, University of Montana; E. C. Hipp, Clemson University; Neal A. Phillips, University of Delaware; Robert T. Rhodes, Texas Christian University; Kent Royalty, St. Cloud State University.

Finally, we wish to thank Mary Fischer, acquisitions editor, and Holly Crawford, project editor, for their critical roles in developing and producing this second edition.

Rate A. Howell, *Columbus, Ohio*

John R. Allison, *Austin, Texas*

N. T. Henley, *Atlanta, Georgia*

September 1986

CONTENTS

Business and the Legal System

PART I

C·H·A·P·T·E·R 1

NATURE AND SOURCES OF LAW

Introduction to Legal Environment

This book is about the legal environment of business—or, perhaps more descriptively, about the legal environment within which all businesses in this country must operate. While the term "legal environment" has no precise boundaries, any course in this area will almost certainly possess the following elements:

An overview of law and our legal system, in general.

An examination of the primary lawmaking and adjudicatory processes—including those of our administrative agencies.

A substantial emphasis upon the role that economic, social, and political forces play in the shaping of legal rules.

A preponderant emphasis upon the broad area of "government regulation"—that is, upon those specialized bodies of law that impact most directly upon businesses (such as consumer protection law, securities regulation law, and the antitrust laws).

These elements alone should convey the idea that the legal environment is a real force in the business world and is extremely dynamic, undergoing changes in both substance and procedure much more rapidly than do the traditional bodies of law. Additionally, other dimensions of the business and law relationship lend further breadth and fascination to the subject.

First are the many governmental programs or actions that have a substantial impact upon the business world (even though the actions themselves are not regulatory in the true sense of the word). The adoption of a "tight money" policy by the Federal Reserve Board is one example falling within this category. While such a policy is designed to combat inflationary pressures generally, rather than to eliminate undesirable practices within a particular industry, the practical effect of such a policy upon some kinds of businesses can be dramatic. Thus, in the early 1980s, the 20 percent interest rates that resulted in part from anti-inflationary actions of the FRB dried up consumer demand for new homes and automobiles to such an extent that many contractors and new car dealers found themselves in financial difficulty, through no fault of their own.

A second characteristic of regulatory law is that some political administrations have favored more stringent regulation of business than others. Administrations favoring such regulation have not only pushed for enactment of new regulatory statutes to create rights and duties that did not exist earlier (such as the Equal Employment Opportunity Act of 1972), but have also directed administrative agencies (such as the Federal Trade Commission) to enforce the existing regulatory statutes with increased vigor. By contrast, late in the Carter administration initial steps were taken towards the lessening of government regulation in limited areas, and a considerable number of more sweeping actions in this direction have been taken during the two Reagan terms of office. (Two examples: the policy of the Justice Department not to contest a number of significant business mergers that would certainly have been challenged under the antitrust laws by earlier administrations, and the continuing deregulation of the banking and airline industries.)

In this regard, however, one caveat is worthy of note at the outset: despite the recent trend toward the lessening of some regulatory activity, the conclusion is inescapable that *the overall regulation of business by both the federal and state governments will continue at a very significant level in the years ahead.*

A Glimpse of Things to Come

If one may paint the "legal environment of business" picture with a very broad brush, it can be said that the subject breaks down into two segments. The first consists of an *overview of law* in general, having to do with such matters as the nature and sources of law; the roles played by the courts (and administrative agencies) in the implementation of the legal rules; and the primary lawmaking processes—the formulation of case law by the courts, the fashioning of statutory law by Congress and the state legislatures, and the promulgation of regulations by administrative agencies. These matters and others of a similar nature are covered in Part I.

The legal environment of business
Source: Reprinted by permission: Tribune Media Services

The other segment is comprised of those somewhat narrower bodies of law that are specifically *regulatory in nature*—that is, are tailored to limit anticompetitive business structures and behaviors, to govern the labor-management relationship, and to protect the rights of buyers of consumer products and of investors. All of these areas are examined in Parts II and III.

Before proceeding with a general overview of the nature and purposes of law, however, brief references to three cases are made to give the reader a more graphic view of the kinds of issues that we discuss throughout the text.

The Case of the Unhappy Homebuyers

In 1972 a construction company contracted to build a house for an Illinois couple for $71,000. Before moving in, the buyers discovered a number of substantial defects which, they claimed, caused the house to be uninhabitable. They therefore refused to accept the house and sued the builder for $19,000, the amount they had paid him while the house was being built. In this case, the first of its kind to reach the highest court in the state, the Illinois Supreme Court ruled that a builder's contract carried with it an implied warranty of habitability—that is, a promise *in the eyes of the law* that the building would be reasonably fit for use as a residence, even though no such promise appeared in the written contract itself. Accordingly, the buyers recovered their money.[1]

[1] *Petersen v. Hubschman Construction Co., Inc.*, 389 N.E.2d 1154 (1979).

Capsule Comment: In this case we have an illustration of judicial lawmaking—the making of rules *by the courts* on a case-by-case basis (in certain areas of the law) if they feel that existing principles will not bring about a satisfactory result. While the Illinois Supreme Court conceded that its decision represented "a distinct departure from accepted principles of real estate law," it said that homebuyers needed warranty protection under modern day conditions, where the buyer is usually not knowledgeable about construction practices, has little or no opportunity to inspect work as it is being done, and thus is forced to rely upon the integrity of the builder.

The Case of the Irate Pipeline Workers

In 1972 Alaska passed a statute requiring all companies engaged in construction of the Trans-Alaska pipeline to hire qualified Alaskan residents in preference to nonresidents. (Alaskan residents were defined as persons who had resided in the state for a minimum period of one year prior to their seeking employment.) When this law was challenged by a number of nonresident job applicants who were refused employment, the U.S. Supreme Court ruled that the terms of the statute were so sweeping in scope and application as to violate the "privileges and immunities" clause of the U.S. Constitution. Accordingly, the statute was invalidated.[2]

Capsule Comment: Here we are exposed to two additional elements found within the legal environment scene. First is the fact that *state legislatures* occasionally pass statutes designed to remedy particular evils operating upon the states' economies—in this instance, the high unemployment of Alaskan residents caused in part by the influx of workers from the "lower forty-eight." Secondly, we learn that such statutes (indeed, all statutes) are subject to *constitutional scrutiny*—that is, an examination by the courts, when a proper challenge is made, to determine whether or not they are in conformity with all applicable constitutional provisions.

The Case of the Overzealous Advertiser

In advertising campaigns beginning in 1921, the Warner-Lambert Company had continuously represented its Listerine mouthwash to be "effective in ameliorating, preventing and curing colds and sore throats." The Federal Trade Commission, acting under its statutory authority to prohibit business practices which it determined to be unfair or deceptive, challenged the truthfulness of these representations in a complaint filed against the company in 1972. In 1975, after hearings in which it was conclusively proven

[2] *Hicklin v. Orbeck*, 437 U.S. 518 (1978). A further look at this case, and especially the court's reasoning, is taken in Chapter 5.

that the claims were in fact untrue, the FTC issued a cease and desist order banning such advertising. Additionally, the order required future Warner-Lambert advertisements to contain the statement that "Listerine will not prevent or cure colds or sore throats, and Listerine will not be beneficial in the treatment of cold symptoms or sore throats." This statement was to appear in the next ten million dollars' worth of Listerine advertising. Thereafter, when Warner-Lambert challenged the order in the courts on the ground that the FTC lacked the authority to impose such a requirement, the highest court to hear the case—a U.S. court of appeals—ruled that the order was valid, thus agreeing with the FTC's contention that the "corrective advertising" requirement was reasonably necessary to counteract misstatements that had been made over such a long period of time.[3] When Warner-Lambert appealed this ruling to the U.S. Supreme Court, that court in effect approved the court of appeals' decision by refusing to hear the appeal.

Capsule Comment: Legislative bodies, such as Congress and the state legislatures, often pass statutes that grant limited regulatory powers to **administrative agencies**. Such agencies are sometimes given authority to regulate an entire industry (such as the trucking industry) or an activity common to many businesses (such as the issuance of corporate stocks and bonds). This case gives us an introductory exposure to the actions of a federal agency in but one of the cases coming before it. It also illustrates the fact that many regulatory cases brought by administrative agencies are initially heard and decided by the agencies themselves, rather than being initiated in the courts. (The subject of administrative agencies is covered in depth in Chapter 6.)

We turn now to an introductory overview of the nature, sources, and classifications of law, for the remainder of this chapter.

What Is Law?

Ever since the law began to take form, scholars have spent impressive amounts of time and thought analyzing its purposes and defining what it is and what it ought to be—in short, fitting it into a philosophical scheme of one form or another. While space does not permit inclusion of even the major essays in which these philosophers defend their respective views, their conclusions provide us with useful observations about the nature of law. Consider, for example, the following:

We have been told by Plato that law is a form of social control, an instrument of the good life, the way to the discovery of reality, the true reality of the social structure; by Aristotle that it is a rule of conduct, a contract, an ideal of reason, a rule of decision, a form of order; by Cicero that it is the agreement of reason and nature, the distinction between the just and the un-

[3] *Warner-Lambert v. FTC*, 562 F.2d 749 (1977).

just, a command or prohibition; by Aquinas that it is an ordinance of reason for the common good, made by him who has care of the community, and promulgated [thereby]; by Bacon that certainty is the prime necessity of law; by Hobbes that law is the command of the sovereign; by Spinoza that it is a plan of life; by Leibniz that its character is determined by the structure of society; by Locke that it is a norm established by the commonwealth; by Hume that it is a body of precepts; by Kant that it is a harmonizing of wills by means of universal rules in the interests of freedom; by Fichte that it is a relation between human beings; by Hegel that it is an unfolding or realizing of the idea of right.[4]

Although these early writers substantially agreed as to the general purposes of law—the insuring of an orderliness to all human activity—their definitions of the term seem to vary considerably.

Today there is still no single definition of **law** that has universal or official acceptance, largely because legal authorities in this country have also differed as to which elements of the law are of primary importance.[5] *A traditional view* often limits the term to those legal rules and principles in place in a given state at a given time. The American Law Institute, for example, states that "Law is the body of principles, standards and rules which the courts . . . apply in the decision of controversies coming before them."[6] In contrast, we find an *environmental definition* as follows: "Law is a dynamic process, a system of regularized, institutionalized procedures for the orderly decision of social questions, including the settlement of disputes."[7]

For educational purposes both of these approaches have merit; the rules or processes alone are but part of the picture. In Part I we follow the environmental approach to law, which places major emphasis upon the judicial processes—the law-making and adjudicatory processes. (At the same time, however, a limited exposure to rules of law will be afforded by the actual court cases used to illustrate these processes.) Parts II and III continue this blend. While the emphasis in these parts will be placed on selected regulatory rules and regulations themselves, the merits of the environmental approach will be preserved in two ways: first, by examining the conditions that necessitated the regulation, and second, by noting how regulatory rules must change in order to adapt to evolving business practices.

---

[4] Huntington Cairns, *Legal Philosophy from Plato to Hegel* (Baltimore: Johns Hopkins University Press, 1949).

[5] For example, Roscoe Pound, one of America's most eminent legal scholars, concluded that there were no less than twelve different concepts of "law."

[6] *Restatement, Conflict of Laws 2d*, § 4. American Law Institute Publishers. Copyright 1971. Reprinted with the permission of The American Law Institute.

[7] James L. Houghteling, Jr., *The Dynamics of Law* (New York: Harcourt Brace Jovanovich, 1963).

Law and Order

Implicit in Plato's observation that law is "a form of social control" is the possibility that there may be other forms—as, indeed, there are.[8] In any society, there is an ordering of things. If priorities between competing groups or individuals are not established by law, history demonstrates that they will be established by bare political or economic power—or, in extreme situations, by sheer physical force. When force is involved, it may derive from a central authority (as was true in Nazi Germany in the 1930s) or from group or individual action. An example of group action occurred in this country in the late 1800s around Virginia City, Montana Territory. Because of the remoteness of the area, federal authorities were powerless to enforce U.S. statutes, and widespread lawlessness ensued. Finally, vigilante committees were formed, whose members summarily hung some of the more notorious—albeit colorful—outlaws in 1877. The principle of the rule of law, with its emphasis on broad considerations of fairness and the orderly settling of disputes, is generally felt to be so superior to the alternatives that today it is the concept upon which the governments of all civilized nations are based.

The Nature of Legal Rules

Legal rules come in all shapes and sizes. Some are rather narrow orders, statutes, or regulations (as exemplified by those in the three capsule cases earlier in this chapter). But some other important legal principles or prohibitions are phrased in much broader language, especially those found in our state and federal constitutions (for instance, "The citizens of each State shall be entitled to all privileges and immunities of the several states.") We shall therefore broadly define *legal rules* as all standards of human conduct, established and enforced by government officials. This definition, in addition to emphasizing the broad aspect of the law, also makes it clear that the rules must derive from the state. Thus, although the rules or standards that result from religious beliefs or membership in professional or social organizations may affect one's conduct in given situations, they do not qualify as legal rules.

Requisites of a Legal System

In order for a legal system to function properly, particularly within a democratic government such as ours, it must command the respect of the great majority of people governed by it. In order to do so, the legal rules which

[8] The term *control* should be interpreted broadly here to avoid laying undue emphasis upon the negative, or restrictive, aspect of law. To be sure, every legal system does contain criminal statutes that absolutely prohibit certain kinds of activity, as well as other rules that impose duties upon individuals in particular situations. But most of the rules and principles that comprise the Anglo-American system of law are devoted to the creation and preservation of rights and liberties of the individual.

comprise it must, as a practical matter, possess certain characteristics. They must be (1) relatively certain, (2) relatively flexible, (3) known or knowable, and (4) apparently reasonable.

In the following chapters we consider these requirements more fully and determine the extent to which our legal system satisfies them. For the moment, we give brief descriptions of each of the four.

Certainty

One essential element of a stable society is reasonable certainty about its laws, not only at a given moment but over long periods of time. Many of our activities, particularly business activities, are based on the assumption that legal principles will remain stable into the foreseeable future. If this were not so, chaos would result. For example, no television network would enter into a contract with a professional football league, under which it was to pay millions of dollars for the right to televise league games, if it were not reasonably sure that the law would compel the league to live up to its contractual obligations or to pay damages if it did not. And no lawyer would advise a client on a contemplated course of action without similar assurances.

Because of these considerations, the courts and legislatures (and to a somewhat lesser extent, administrative agencies) are generally reluctant to overturn principles that have been part of the law for any appreciable period of time.[9]

Flexibility

In any nation, particularly a highly industrialized one such as the United States, societal changes occur with accelerating (almost dismaying) rapidity. Each change presents new legal problems that must be resolved without undue delay. This necessity was recognized by Justice Cardozo when he wrote that "the law, like the traveler, must be ready for the morrow."[10]

Some problems are simply the result of scientific and technological advances. Prior to Orville and Wilbur Wright's day, for example, it was a well-established principle that landowners had unlimited rights to the airspace above their property, any invasion of which constituted a **trespass**—a wrongful entry. But when the courts became convinced that the flying machine was

---

[9] This is not to say, of course, that the law is static. In the area of products liability, for example, the liability of manufacturers for injuries caused by defective products is much more extensive than it was twenty-five years ago. But even this enlargement of liability, and of similar changes in other areas, resulted from a series of modifications of existing principles rather than from an abrupt reversal of them.

[10] Benjamin N. Cardozo, *The Growth of the Law* (New Haven: Yale University Press, 1924), pp. 19–20.

here to stay, the utter impracticality of this view became apparent and owners' rights were subsequently limited to a "reasonable use" of their airspace.

Other novel problems result from changing methods of doing business or from shifting attitudes and moral views. Recent examples of the former are the proliferating use of the business franchise and of the general credit card. Attitudinal changes include such fundamental questions as to what the proper ends of government should be—for example, the extent to which safety standards should be imposed upon the automobile industry, and the circumstances (if any) in which abortions should be permitted.

Of course, some of the problems that confront the state and federal governments require solutions that are more political than legal in nature. This is particularly true where large numbers of the citizenry are faced with a common problem, such as the inability of many elderly persons to pay for proper health care, and where the alleviation of the problem may well be thought to constitute a legitimate function of either the state or federal government. The passage by Congress of the so-called Medicare Act of 1964 is an example of an attempted solution at the federal level of this particular problem.

Regardless of political considerations, however, the fact remains that there are many problems (particularly those involving disputes between individuals and between individuals and business firms) that can be settled only through the judicial processes—that is, by one of the parties instituting legal action against the other. The duty to arrive at a final solution in all such cases falls squarely upon the courts, no matter how novel or varied the issues.

Knowability

One of the basic assumptions underlying a democracy—and, in fact, almost every form of government—is that the great majority of its citizens are going to obey its laws voluntarily. It hardly need be said that obedience requires a certain knowledge of the rules, or at least a reasonable means of acquiring this knowledge, on the part of the governed. No one, not even a lawyer, "knows" all the law or all the rules that comprise a single branch of law; that could never be required. But it is necessary for persons who need legal advice to have access to experts on the rules—lawyers. It is equally necessary that the law be in such form that lawyers can determine their clients' positions with reasonable certainty in order to recommend the most advantageous courses of action.

Reasonableness

Most citizens abide by the law. Many do so even when they are not in sympathy with a particular rule, out of a sense of responsibility, a feeling that it is their civic duty, like it or not; others, no doubt, do so simply through fear of

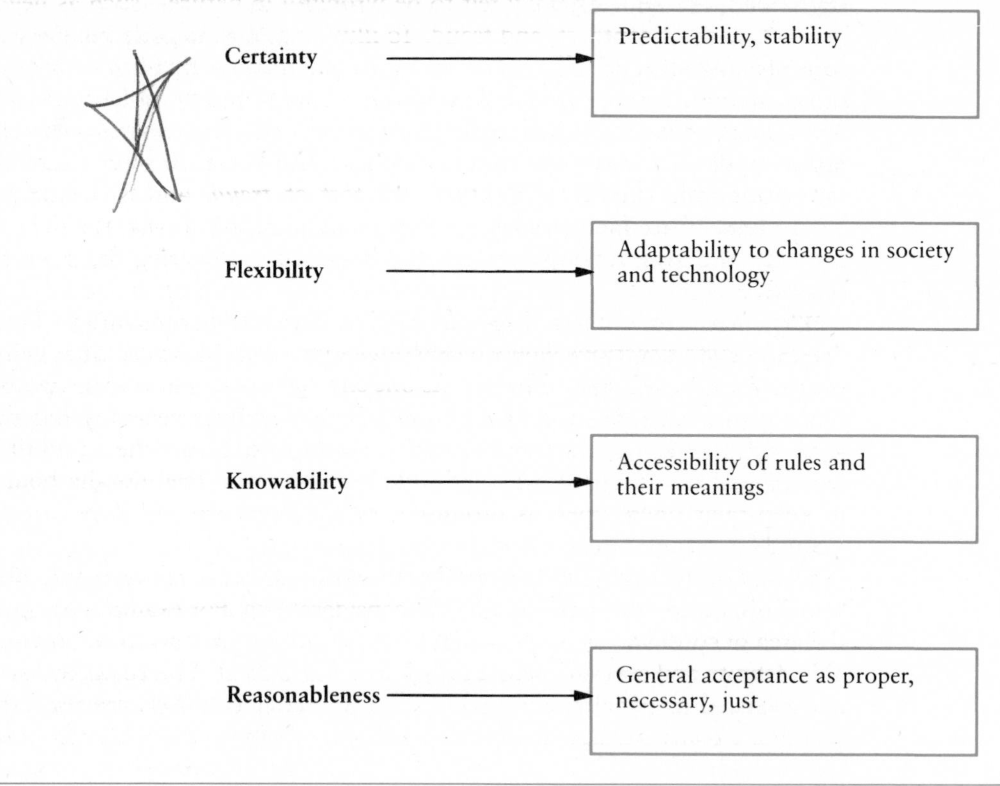

Figure 1.1 Requisites of a Properly Functioning Legal System

getting caught if they don't. But by and large the rules have to appear reasonable to the great majority of the people if they are going to be obeyed for long. The so-called Prohibition Amendment, which met with such wholesale violation that it was repealed in 1933, is the classic example of a rule lacking widespread acceptance. Closely allied with the idea of reasonableness is the requirement that the rules reflect, and adapt to, changing views of morality and justice. Figure 1.1 summarizes the qualities a legal system must possess to function properly.

Law, Morals, and Justice

Law and Morals

Although the terms *law* and *morals* are not synonymous, legal standards and moral standards parallel one another more closely than many people believe. For example, criminal statutes prohibit certain kinds of conduct that are clearly "morally wrong"—murder, theft, arson, and the like. And other rules of law impose civil liability for similar kinds of conduct which, though not crimes, are also generally felt to be wrongful in nature—such as negligence, breach of contract, and fraud. To illustrate: S, in negotiating the sale of a race horse to B, tells B that the horse has run an eighth of a mile in fifteen seconds on several occasions within the past month. In fact, the animal has never been clocked under eighteen seconds, and S knows this. B, believing the statement to be true, purchases the horse. In such a case S's intentional misstatement constitutes the tort of *fraud*, and B—assuming he can prove these facts in a legal action brought against S—has the right to set aside the transaction, returning the horse and recovering the price he has paid.

Why, then, are the terms *law* and *morals* not precisely synonymous? First, there are some situations where moral obligations may be perceived as being greater than those imposed by law. As one example, a person who has promised to keep an offer open for a stated period of time generally has the legal right, under contract law, to withdraw the offer before the stated time has elapsed. Yet many persons who make such offers feel morally bound to keep their offers open as promised, even though the law does not require this.

Second, many rules of law are based upon practical requirements that have little or no relationship to moral considerations. For example, again in the area of contract law, courts uniformly require agreements to be "reasonably definite and certain" before they will enforce them. This requirement is not imposed to penalize wrongdoers, but is rather based on the practical fact that a court is simply unable to determine whether a particular contract has been breached if it is not reasonably sure what each party has obligated himself or herself to do under its terms. Similarly, state statutes that prohibit foreigners who live outside the United States from owning farmlands within such states are based more upon economic and political grounds than on moral considerations—for example, the fear that such ownership would unduly drive up land prices or would be yet another menace to our traditional concept of locally owned, family-based farms.

Law and Justice

The relationship between law and justice is similar to that between law and morals. In the vast majority of cases, legal rules produce results that are "just"—fair and reasonable, given the nature of the controversies that have to be resolved. Where this is not so to any substantial extent, the rules are usually changed or exceptions to them are made. Yet it must be conceded that even long-standing legal rules occasionally bring about results that are perceived by many people to be questionable or "downright wrong." Without attempting to defend the law in all such instances, some cautions should nevertheless be voiced.

First, there is never complete agreement as to what is just; there are always some decisions that are just to some people but not to others. And even if there were unanimity of opinion—a perfect justice, so to speak—the fact-patterns presented by some cases are such that it is simply impossible to attain this end.[11]

In some situations, for example, a legal controversy may arise between two honest persons who dealt with one another in good faith, as sometimes occurs in the area of "mutual mistake." Take this case: S contracts to sell land to B for $40,000, both parties mistakenly believing that a General Motors plant will be built on adjoining land. When B learns that the plant will not be built, he refuses to go through with the deal. If a court rules that the mistake frees B of his contractual obligations, the result might be quite unjust as far as S is concerned. And if it rules otherwise, the decision might seem quite unfair to B. Yet a decision must be made, one way or the other.

Second, in some instances it is fairly clear who is right and who is wrong, but the situation has progressed to the point where it is impossible, either physically or legally, to put the "good" person back into the original position. These "bad check" cases will illustrate: A buys a TV set from Z, giving Z her personal check in payment. If the check bounces, it is clear that Z should be allowed to recover the set. But what if the TV has been destroyed by fire while in A's hands? Here the most the law can do is give Z a *judgment* against A—an order requiring A to pay a sum of money to Z equal to the amount of the check, which A may or may not be financially able to do. Or suppose that A had resold the TV to X before Z learned that the check had bounced. Would it not be unfair to permit Z to retake the set from X, an innocent third party?

Another aspect of the law and justice relationship is the fact that a rule designed to eliminate an evil in one area may in operation produce questionable side effects in another area. Consider, for example, the passage by Congress of the Foreign Corrupt Practices Act in 1977, designed for the laudable purpose of prohibiting American companies from bribing foreign officials when seeking to make sales overseas. A scant three years later, testimony in U.S. Senate hearings indicated not only that the law often made it impossible for American firms to compete with foreign companies who were free of this restriction, but also that the law had adversely affected this nation's balance of trade payments to the extent of several billions of dollars.

Because of these considerations and others discussed later, the most that the law can seek to accomplish is the bringing about of *substantial* justice, both in the adjudication of specific controversies and in efforts to alleviate broader social and economic problems.

---

[11] *Fact-pattern* refers to the proven acts of each party that have led up to a particular controversy, together with the circumstances surrounding such acts. In cases commenced in the courts the facts are usually determined by the jury but occasionally by the court—the judge; in cases initiated before administrative agencies, the facts are determined by administrative law judges.

The Law—Processes and Products

As we have already briefly noted, a major objective of Part I is the examination of the *processes by which law is created.* The major processes are (1) the formulation of rules by the courts, (2) enactment and interpretation of statutes, (3) interpretation and application of constitutional provisions, and (4) promulgation of rules and regulations by administrative agencies. We will examine these processes in some depth in subsequent chapters. In the meantime, however, certain basic characteristics of each should be recognized.

Formulation of Rules by the Courts

There are some areas of law where the creation of basic principles has been left essentially to the courts—the judges—as they settle individual cases coming before them. One of the best examples is in our contract law, where, over the years, the courts have decided such matters as what constitutes an offer, an acceptance, a substantial breach of contract, and the like. The product of this process—the rules resulting from it—is called **common law** or **case law.** This type of law, and the unique manner in which it has adjusted to changing social and economic conditions, is discussed further in Chapter 3.

Enactment and Interpretation of Statutes

In most areas of law today legislative bodies—state legislatures or Congress—have prescribed the rules by the enactment of statutes. Typical examples are the corporation laws of the various states, and such federal laws as the Civil Rights Act of 1964 and the Tax Reform Act of 1984. Law that is promulgated in this fashion is **statutory law**; and, unlike common law, is set forth in the applicable state and federal codes.

Once a statute is passed, a further process—judicial interpretation—is usually required. While the meaning of the typical statute may be quite clear in regard to most situations, cases are always arising that involve novel or narrow fact-patterns which do indeed present arguable points as to what the legislature really intended as to those particular situations by passing the act in question. Only when the courts settle such specific controversies does the precise legal meaning of a statute come about.

Take, for example, this situation. A state statute prohibits the building of any "structure" over 100 feet in length outside municipalities without approval of the county commissioners. A farmer erects a 150-foot turkey shed, with a roof consisting of a series of one-foot by two-inch planks separated by six inches of airspace, without such approval; thereafter, legal action is brought by the county asking for its removal. Should the court construe the term "structure" so broadly as to include sheds of the sort involved here, in which case removal would be ordered? Or did the legislature, perhaps, really mean to require commissioners' approval only in the case of the construction of "buildings," in which event the statute might have no applicability to the construction of sheds? Forces that prompt legislative bodies to pass statutes, and factors that are examined by the courts in searching for the slippery thing called "legislative intent," are treated in Chapter 4.

Interpretation of Constitutions

The role that constitutional law plays in the legal environment of business is important to us for two reasons. First, the federal Constitution contains guidelines that set forth the powers of the state and federal governments—for instance, so-called police powers are generally reserved to the states, while the primary power to regulate interstate commerce is delegated to the federal government. Thus, if a state statute (such as one prescribing maximum tractor-trailer lengths) is found by a court to unduly burden interstate commerce, the state has attempted to exercise power that it does not possess, and the law is invalid.

Second, even if a state or the federal government passes a statute in an area that it unquestionably has the power to regulate, the statute still must be in conformity with other constitutional guarantees—for example, the statute must afford "due process" to all persons subject to it, and must not deny them the "equal protection of the laws." Because these clauses and others are not defined in the Constitution, the courts, especially the federal courts, must interpret them on a continuing case-by-case basis. (The principle that all state and federal laws in conflict with the federal Constitution are *void* was established by the U.S. Supreme Court in the case of *Marbury v. Madison*, 1 Cranch 137, 2 L.Ed. 60, 1803.)

Rulemaking by Agencies

Administrative agencies, such as the federal Securities and Exchange Commission and the state public utility commissions, are often created and empowered by statute to regulate areas of business or to oversee other governmental programs, which, for one reason or another, cannot be effectively regulated by the courts or legislatures. The issuance and enforcement of rules and regulations by such agencies is our fourth major law-making process and is covered in depth in Chapter 6.

Some Classifications of Law

While the law-making and adjudicatory processes are the major concern in Part I, the products that result from the law-making process—the rules themselves and the bodies of law which they make up—must not be overlooked. At the outset, particularly, it is useful to recognize some of the more important *classifications of law*.

Subject-Matter Classification

One way of classifying all the law in the United States is on the basis of the subject matter to which it relates. If one were to view the entire spectrum of the law, the following list of branches of law or subjects would be a representative group:

Agency law	Family law
Antitrust law	Labor law
Commercial paper	Partnerships
Constitutional law	Property
Consumer protection	Sales
Contracts	Securities regulation
Corporation law	Taxation
Criminal law	Torts
Environmental protection	Wills and estates

Two initial observations may be made about this classification.

1. The rules that comprise the subjects of agency, contracts, and torts are still largely made up by the courts of the various states on a case-by-case basis. Thus these may be described as *common-law* subjects. By contrast, corporation law, criminal law, sales law, and taxation are *statutory* subjects—governed by comprehensive state or federal statutes. The remaining subjects are made up largely of *administrative agencies* rules, for instance, environmental protection and securities regulation (however, the rules of consumer protection law are mixed in nature).

2. Ranked on the basis of their relevance to the business world, the subjects fall into three categories. First are those areas of law that are almost entirely business related—antitrust law, consumer protection law, and labor law are examples. In the second category are those broader subjects that have substantial application to many business activities but which have equal applicability to relationships between individuals. Constitutional law, contracts, sales, and torts all fall in this middle category. The third grouping is made up of those subjects that obviously have little or no application to the business world—family law and wills and estates. The last two chapters in Part I survey those areas of law in the second category, while Parts II and III are devoted entirely to the high-relevance subjects of the first category.

Federal and State Law

Another way of classifying all law in this country is on the basis of the governmental unit from which it arises. On this basis, all law is either **federal law** or **state law.** (We are using the term "state law" broadly to include rules of subdivisions of the state, such as city ordinances.)

As was briefly noted earlier, the U.S. Constitution specifically enumerates certain areas of activity that are to be controlled exclusively or at least essentially by the federal government, such as maintenance of the armed forces and regulation of interstate commerce. Federal rules of law relating to these areas primarily arise from two sources: acts of Congress, and the rules and regulations promulgated by federal agencies. Because the list of areas within the jurisdiction of the federal government is not a lengthy one, most bodies of law are, in fact, promulgated by the several states. Thus there are, strictly speaking, fifty bodies of contract law, fifty bodies of corporation law, fifty bodies of motor vehicle law, and so on. But, fortunately, this is not as bewildering as it appears, because the rules that comprise a given branch of law in any state substantially parallel those that exist in the other states, particularly in regard to the common-law subjects.

Common Law (Case Law) and Statutory Law

The term *common law* has several different meanings. It sometimes is used to refer only to the judge-made rules in effect in England at an early time—the "ancient unwritten law of England." It sometimes is also used to refer only to those judge-made rules of England that were subsequently adopted by the states in this country. In this text, however, we define the term more broadly to mean *all the rules and principles currently existing in any state, regardless of their origin, that result from judicial decisions in those areas of law where legislatures have not enacted comprehensive statutes*. This type of law, examined further in Chapter 3, is frequently referred to as case law, judge-made law, or unwritten law.

The term *statutory law*, by contrast, is generally used to refer to the state and federal *statutes* in effect at a given time—that is, rules which have been formally adopted by legislative bodies rather than by the courts. When *statutory law* is used in contrast to *common law*, it also embraces state and federal constitutions, municipal ordinances, and even treaties. Statutory law is frequently referred to as written law in the sense that once a statute or constitutional provision is adopted, its exact wording is set forth in the final text as passed—though the precise meaning, we should recall, is still subject to interpretation by the courts. (The subjects of statutory law and judicial interpretation are covered in Chapter 4.)[12] Figure 1.2 summarizes the major distinctions between common law and statutory law.

Civil and Criminal Law

Civil Law: The most common types of controversies are civil actions—that is, actions in which the parties bringing the suits (the plaintiffs) are seeking

[12] Today, with but one or two narrow exceptions, all federal law is statutory; in other words, there is no general federal common law. State law, on the other hand, is comprised of both common and statutory law, with the latter making up the lion's share.

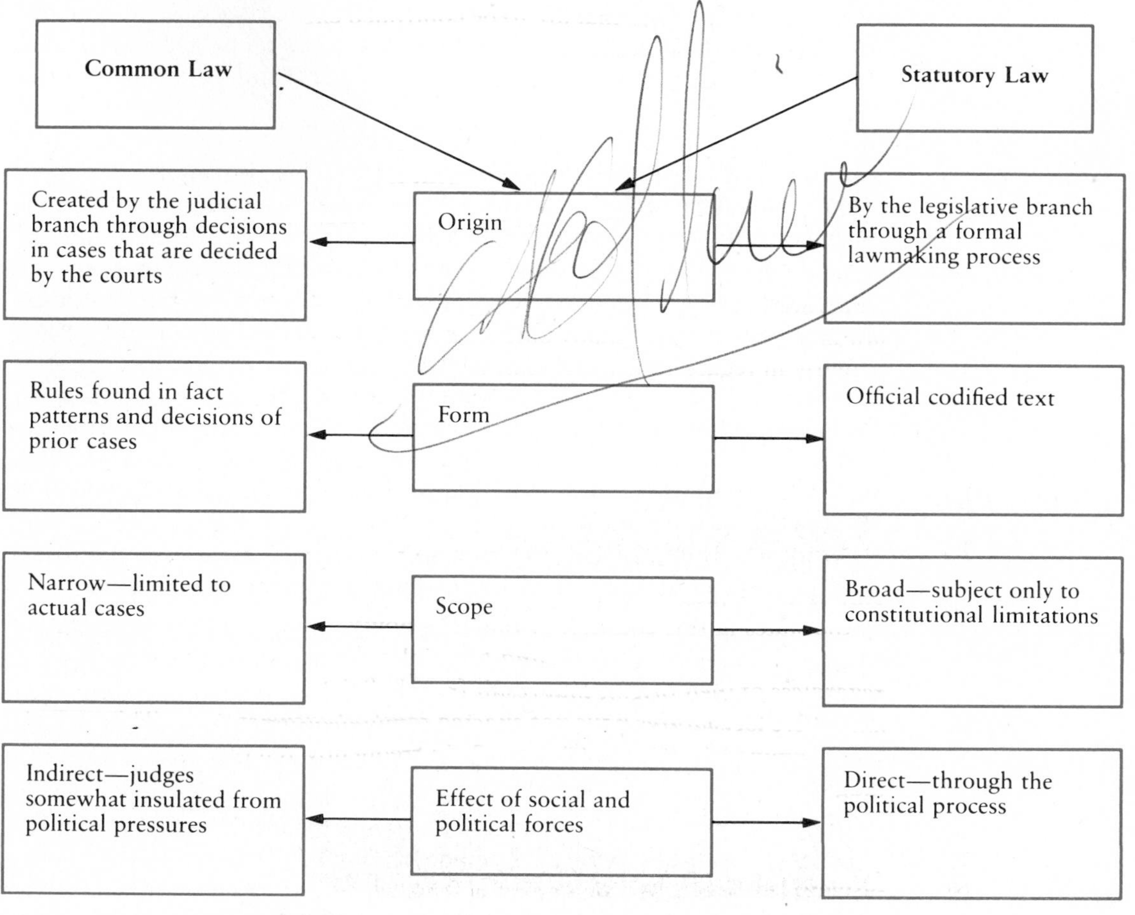

Figure 1.2 Major Differences in Common and Statutory Law

to enforce private obligations or duties against the other parties (the defendants). **Civil laws,** then, are all those laws which spell out the rights and duties existing between individuals (including, of course, business enterprises). Contract law, tort law, and sales law all fall within the civil category.

The usual remedy which the plaintiff is seeking in a civil suit is **damages**—a sum of money roughly equivalent to the loss which he or she has suffered as a result of the defendant's wrong. Thus if the X Company reneges on its contract to sell 10,000 bushels of corn to the Y Company for $22,500, with the result that the Y Company has to pay a third party $25,000 for the same quantity, the Y Company is entitled to $2,500 damages plus incidental damages, if any (such as additional storage or trucking costs resulting from the X Company's breach of contract). Another civil remedy is the **injunction,** a court decree ordering the defendant either to perform a particular act which he or she has the legal duty to perform or to refrain from performing a particular act which he or she has no right to perform. In any event, in a civil suit the plaintiff is simply seeking to have his or her injury redressed rather than seeking to have the defendant punished by the imposition of a fine or by imprisonment.

Criminal Law: Criminal law, in contrast to civil law, is comprised of those statutes by which a state or the federal government prohibits specified kinds of conduct, and which additionally provides for the imposition of *fines or imprisonment* upon persons convicted of violating them. Criminal suits are always brought by the government whose law is allegedly violated—for example, *State of Wyoming v. Olson* or *United States v. Fry*. Case titles such as these do not always denote criminal actions, however, because the state and federal governments, like other litigants, can be parties to civil suits. Such suits might arise, for example, where a state is suing a construction company for damages arising out of its failure to complete a road building project, or where a taxpayer is seeking to recover an alleged overpayment of income taxes from the state.

While any incursion into the vast area of criminal law is essentially outside the scope of this text, three observations are nonetheless in order.

1. In enacting criminal statutes, a state is saying that there are certain activities so inherently inimical to the public good that they must be flatly prohibited. Such statutes, then, simply provide the very minimum standards of conduct to which all persons must adhere. There are other standards of conduct above this level which the law also requires in certain situations, but one who fails to meet these higher standards is normally liable only in a civil action to the person who suffers a loss as a consequence of this wrong. To illustrate: X acts in a negligent (careless) manner and injures Y while doing so. While Y is entitled to recover damages from X in a civil suit because of the wrong that has occurred, the wrong is not of such a nature that the state could bring a criminal action against X.[13]

2. In addition to the nature of the liability that is imposed, criminal suits also differ from civil suits in another significant respect. In a criminal action (which is always brought by the state) it is necessary that the state's case be proved "beyond a reasonable doubt," whereas in civil actions the plaintiff—the person bringing the suit—need prove his or her allegations only by "a preponderance of the evidence." Because the defendant—the accused—in almost every case is able to raise *some* doubts regarding questions of fact (for example, was the defendant the driver or a passenger in a car causing the death of a pedestrian), the evidence in a criminal action may leave

[13] Some wrongful acts are of a dual nature, subjecting the wrongdoer to both criminal and civil penalties. For example, if X steals Y's car, the state could bring a criminal action against X, and Y could also bring a civil action to recover damages arising from the theft.

enough doubt in the jury's mind that it must return a verdict in favor of the defendant. The same evidence in a civil suit, however, might support a verdict in favor of the plaintiff.[14]

3. Except for the most serious crime of treason, crimes are either **felonies** or **misdemeanors**, depending upon the severity of the penalty which the statute prescribes. The definition of *felony* differs somewhat from state to state, but it is usually defined as any crime where the punishment is either death or imprisonment, as in the case of murder, arson, or rape. *Misdemeanors* are all crimes carrying lesser penalties.

It is probably safe to say that most of the law that comprises the "legal environment of business" falls within the civil law category. This is because administrative agencies ordinarily can issue only "cease and desist" orders to companies which are found to have violated their rules and regulations, and much of the enforcement activity of the agencies ends at this point.

This is not to say, by any means, that businesses (or their officers) never can incur criminal liability. For example, the violation of the Sherman Act is a federal crime. This act, which is the basic statute forbidding monopolies and unreasonable restraints of trade, expressly provides that violation of its terms constitutes a felony and further provides that guilty corporations may be fined as much as $1 million; individuals are subject to fines of up to $100,000 and three years' imprisonment or both.[15] And some federal agencies, though having no criminal enforcement authority, may refer the results of their investigations to the Justice Department for possible prosecution by that department if they feel that a criminal violation has occurred. The Securities and Exchange Commission is one such agency. Figure 1.3, on page 22, outlines major differences between civil and criminal law.

Public and Private Law

Some branches of law deal more directly with the relationship that exists between the government and the individual than do others. On the basis of the degree to which this relationship is involved, law is occasionally classified as public law or private law.

When an area of law is directly concerned with the government-individual relationship, it falls within the **public law** designation. Subjects that are most clearly of this nature are criminal law, constitutional law, and administrative law. Since **criminal laws** consist of acts that are prohibited by a government itself, the violation of which is a "wrong against the state," such laws more directly affect the government-individual relationship than do

[14] This type of problem, particularly the role of the jury in civil suits, is examined in some detail in the next chapter.

[15] Civil suits under the Sherman Act are also possible. For a comprehensive discussion of this act, see Chapters 11 and 12.

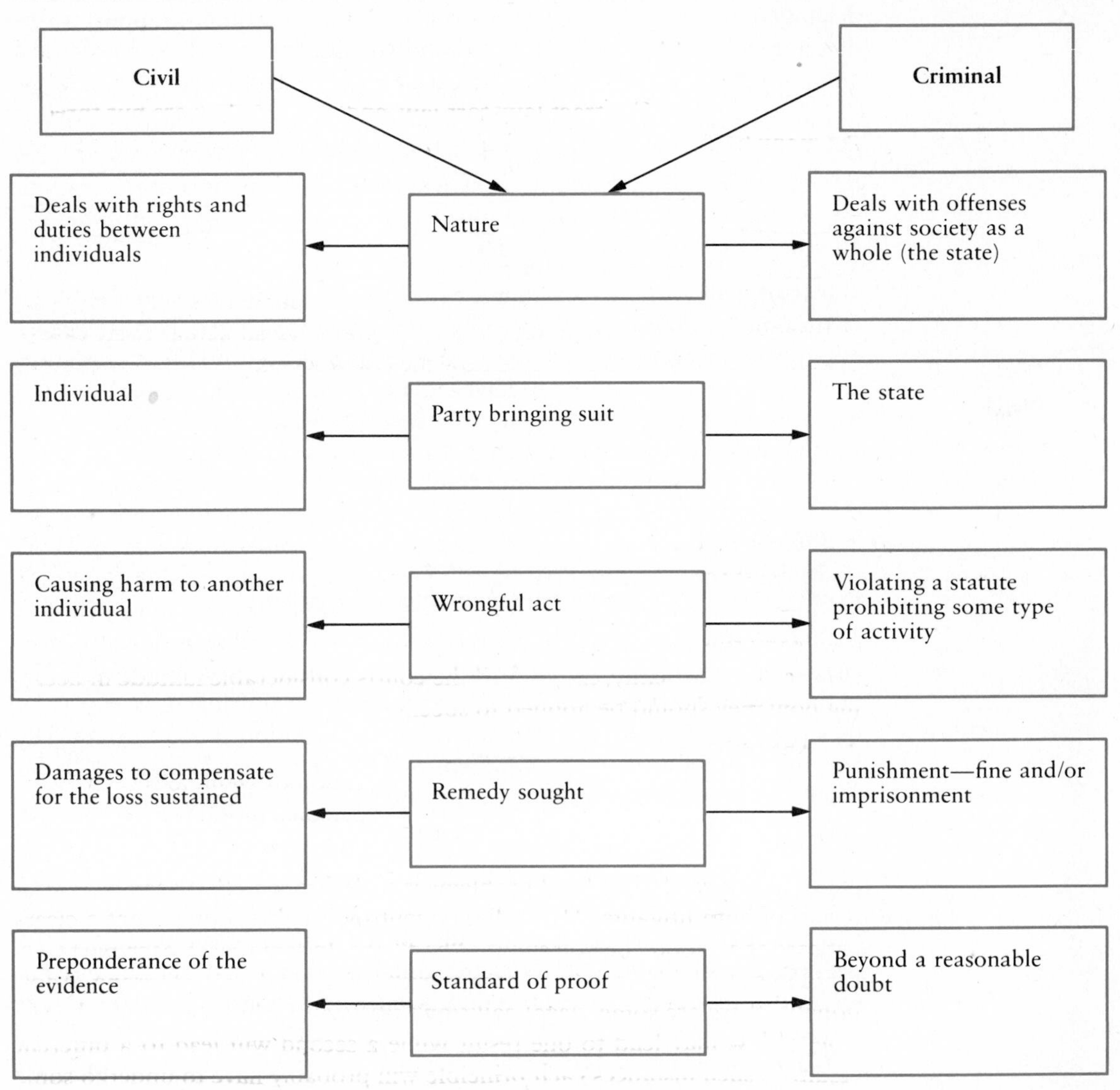

Figure 1.3 Major Differences in Criminal and Civil Law

any of the other laws. To the extent that our federal Constitution contains provisions substantially guaranteeing that certain rights of the individual cannot be invaded by federal and state government activities, the subject of **constitutional law** falls within the same category. **Administrative law**—comprised of the principles that govern the procedures and activities of government boards and commissions—is of a similar nature in that such agencies are also concerned with the enforcement of certain state and federal statutes (and regulations promulgated thereunder) against individual citizens.

Other areas of law, which are primarily concerned with the creation and enforcement of rights of one individual versus another, fall within the **private law** category. Contract law, tort law, and property law are but three of the many branches of law that are almost exclusively devoted to the spelling out of private obligations.[16]

Some Misconceptions About the Law

We conclude this chapter with a brief reference to some widely held misconceptions about our legal system and an exposure to an actual court case—just the first of many to illustrate how the law works in "real life" situations.

The Myth of the One Right Answer

It is widely believed that in any given fact-pattern there is one "correct" legal answer to the problem it presents. This is true in a good many situations but certainly not as often as many persons believe. The chief reasons for divergent legal opinions are quite explainable.

1. Many rules are expressed in rather general terms so as to fit varying situations. Consequently, they afford the courts considerable latitude in deciding how they should be applied to specific situations.

2. The ultimate legal processes are in the hands of individuals, the judges, whose application of rules is always subject, to some extent, to their individual economic and political philosophies and personal moral beliefs. The law, therefore, is not an exact science and never will be.[17]

3. The nature of most legal problems is such that something can be said in behalf of both litigants. The ordinary controversy does not present a clear-cut case of a "good" person suing a "bad" one. In some cases, each party has acted in good faith; in others, each is guilty of some degree of wrong. Additionally, there are some "legal collision" situations, where one general principle of law may lead to one result while a second will lead to a different result. In such instances each principle will probably have to undergo some modification when applied to particular cases, with results that are not always harmonious.

---

[16] While every state is indeed concerned that all its laws be properly enforced, including those of the private law areas, the state concern or involvement in such areas is distinctly secondary to the interests of the litigants themselves.

[17] It is sometimes said that the law is a "social science." While this view seemingly (and wrongly) ascribes to the principles of the social studies a precision and certainty equal to those of the physical sciences, the label is perhaps acceptable to the extent that the rules of law do apply to and are concerned with all human activities.

The Myth of the Expensive Lawyer

The belief is sometimes expressed, usually with great feeling, that an individual or firm who is financially able to employ top-flight legal counsel is virtually "above the law." While it is undeniably true that a person who employs a competent lawyer will in general experience fewer legal problems than would otherwise be the case, this does not support the broad proposition that such a person can flout our legal rules at will. The average attorney is competent enough that his or her client will fare well under the law when the rules support the client; when the rules do not, the client will usually incur liability under them, no matter how skilled the counsel may be. (The conviction of a number of President Nixon's aides on obstruction of justice charges growing out of the Watergate affair and the bribery convictions of several Congressmen in the FBI-conducted "Abscam" operation in 1981 are two of the more notable examples in support of the latter proposition.)

The Myth of Judicial Eccentricity

The feeling is sometimes expressed that the law is not based on common sense—that its rules are so esoteric and arbitrary, and the judges and lawyers so preoccupied with them, that the results are not in keeping with reality or with what a reasonable person would expect. This indictment, in very large measure, is false. Cases invariably present practical problems for the courts, and the courts keep the practical considerations in mind in choosing the rules that apply.

Take, for example, this situation. C, a contractor, agrees to build a house according to certain specifications for O, the owner, for $60,000. When the house is completed, by which time O has paid $36,000, O discovers that the family room is 10 inches shorter than the plans specified. O refuses to make further payments for this reason, whereupon C brings suit to recover the balance of $24,000.

Now, as far as contract law is concerned, the principle is well established that a person who breaches his or her contract is not permitted to recover anything from the other party. The question here is: Should that rule be applicable to this specific situation, where that would mean that C would not recover any of the balance? The practical person might well say, "I wouldn't think so—where the defect is so slight, it would seen unfair for C to suffer a loss of $24,000." The law reaches the same conclusion; under a view known as the **doctrine of substantial performance**, a person in C's position is usually permitted to recover most of the unpaid balance (even though he did, technically, breach the contract).

The foregoing does not mean, of course, that the law is perfect or that startling or unfair decisions never occur. But by and large the unreasonable result occurs with much less frequency than reports in the news media would indicate; and even in such cases, the possibility usually exists that an appellate court will subsequently repair much of the damage.

The Valley Fever Case

In order for students to adequately understand actual court cases, they must have some familiarity with our court systems and procedures, covered in the next chapter. For this reason, a major emphasis on reported cases necessarily will have to await this groundwork. Because there are, however, some practical advantages in introducing real-life situations as early as possible, the case below is presented at this point.

Only three prefatory comments seem necessary in view of the simple fact-pattern that is presented.

1. This is a "negligence" action. This means that the plaintiff (Crim) is contending that the defendant company (International Harvester), while demonstrating its products at its proving grounds, *failed to use due care* in protecting him from (or in warning him about) a health hazard at the site.[18]

2. In a negligence action, it is ordinarily for the jury to decide whether the defendant did or did not use *due care* in the fact-pattern presented—that is, did or did not exercise the care that "a reasonable, prudent person" would have exercised in similar circumstances.

3. Whenever a judgment is entered by the trial court, the losing party may appeal the case to a higher court; in so doing, such party—the appellant—must allege that one or more errors were made during the trial of the case. The appellate court's job is then a limited one—to determine, from an examination of the record of the case, whether any of the appellant's claims of error is correct. If error is found, the judgment is reversed and the case is usually *remanded* (sent back to the trial court for further proceedings); if there is no error, the judgment is *affirmed*. In this case, defendant/appellant claimed (a) that the trial court erred in its interpretation of Arizona case law, and (b) that the jury's verdict was not supported by the evidence presented at the trial.

With these thoughts in mind, let us examine the nature of Rex Crim's complaint against the International Harvester Company. A number of comments immediately follow the decision of the higher court to clarify certain procedural and mechanical aspects of the case.

Crim v. International Harvester Company

U.S. Court of Appeals, Fifth Circuit 646 F.2d 161 (1981)

In January of 1977 International Harvester brought a large number of its dealers from around the country to Phoenix, Arizona, to see a demonstration of the International Scout, a new four-wheel-drive vehicle that was designed and brought out to compete against American Motors' Jeep. One of the dealers was Rex Crim, plaintiff, of Henderson, Texas.

The site of the demonstration was the International Harvester proving grounds, located in desert valley land outside Phoenix. At the end of the day-

[18] The subject of negligence, which is but one of a number of kinds of wrongs known as *torts*, is covered more fully in Chapter 8. For now, we can say that negligence is essentially synonymous with "carelessness."

long affair, Crim and the other dealers test drove the Scout in desert tracks laid out for the occasion, at which time large quantities of dust were stirred up.

A few weeks after Crim returned home, he was hospitalized with coccidioidomycosis—a flu-like disease commonly known as valley fever. This is a disease caused by spores found on the surface of desert soil or in the air when the soil is disturbed by human activity. (While some forms of valley fever are mild, others are serious; for example, the "disseminate" form—where the disease spreads to areas outside the lungs—produces a 50 percent mortality rate.)

After a long hospitalization, during which time it was determined that Crim's disease was the disseminate form, Crim brought this suit to recover damages in a U.S. District Court in Texas, claiming that International Harvester was negligent in failing to warn him of, and in failing to protect him from, the possibility of contracting valley fever. The trial judge instructed the jury that under Arizona law an owner or occupier of land (here, International Harvester) is liable for physical harm caused to an invitee (Crim) by a condition on the premises if three conditions are met:

1. He knows or by the exercise of ordinary care would have discovered the condition, and should realize that it involves an unreasonable risk of harm to invitees.

2. He should expect that invitees will not discover or realize the danger, or will fail to protect themselves against it.

3. He fails to exercise reasonable care to protect them against the danger.

Under these instructions the jury found in favor of Crim and awarded him $55,000 damages.

International Harvester appealed this judgment to the proper U.S. Court of Appeals, and in its appeal made two basic contentions. First, International Harvester claimed that under a recent Arizona decision it did *not* owe a duty to warn Crim of the specific hazard of valley fever, and that the trial court's instructions were thus incorrect. And, second, International Harvester contended that even if it did owe a duty to exercise reasonable care to protect Crim, the evidence at the trial was insufficient to support the jury's finding that International Harvester knew, or should have known, of the risk that existed. (*Note*: only those portions of the higher court's decision applicable to these two contentions are set forth below.)

Suttle, Judge:

. . . [First,] the standard of care that Arizona courts expect landowners or occupiers of land to show to business invitees is derived from Section 343 of Restatement (Second) Torts. The district court's charge to the jury . . . was based on Section 343 [and was thus proper]. Nevertheless, International Harvester [refers us to the case of] *Randolph v. Arizona Board of Regents* (505 P.2d 559) in which an Arizona appellate court held that . . . the University of Arizona does not have a duty to warn prospective students about valley fever. . . .

The case now before the court simply does not entail the same policy considerations as *Randolph*. International Harvester is not a state university soliciting thousands of applicants from across the country to move to Arizona for their education. Rather, International Harvester is a private business inviting employees and business associates to testing grounds for the express purpose of test-driving Scout vehicles in the desert. This activity exposes the participant to an intense concentration of stirred-up dust which . . . greatly increases the chances of contracting valley fever in its disseminated form. [Therefore] we hold that . . . private businesses that bring business invitees to Arizona . . . for the specific purpose of engaging in human activity on their land that guarantees exposure to intense concentrations of dust [do owe to such invitees the duty to warn or to protect against hidden dangers].

[Second,] International Harvester . . . contends that the jury had no evidence from which to conclude (1) that International Harvester knew of, or by the exercise of ordinary care would have discovered, the unreasonable risk of harm, and (2) that International Harvester failed to exercise reasonable care to protect Crim. *Both contentions are without merit.* [Emphasis added.]

Crim produced ample evidence on the knowledge issue. He tendered evidence of newspaper publicity, television documentary coverage, and literature that was readily available to the public. Furthermore, two managers of the International Harvester proving grounds testified they knew about valley fever, as did the local doctor who acted as International Harvester's Medical Examiner.

Likewise, the jury certainly had evidence before it from which to conclude that International Harvester did not exercise reasonable care upon the facts of this case. According to International Harvester's evidence, Arizona landowners do not, as a rule, warn or try to protect visitors from exposure to valley fever spores. But the jury was not presented with the question of what steps any reasonable landowner would take to protect any visitor. Here the issue was what steps a reasonable *business* would have taken to warn or protect *invitees* brought from [outside] regions to engage in a particular risky activity. [Emphasis added.] Also, the jury could have concluded from the conflicting evidence that protective masks worn in the heavy dust would filter out the infectious spores. In fact, for over 15 years International Harvester itself has furnished respirators to its heavy-equipment operators who test earth-moving machines at the proving grounds. [Thus] there was sufficient . . . evidence for the jury to find that International Harvester did not act reasonably in not warning Crim or providing him with a protective mask. . . .

Judgment affirmed.

★★★

Comment:

1. Since this is our first case, a few comments about the mechanics of case reporting are in order.

a. The opinion, written by Judge Suttle, is that of the appellate court—in this instance, the U.S. Court of Appeals, Fifth Circuit. (The decision that is quoted in almost every case in this text is that of an appellate court—the highest court to have heard the case. In the rare instance where a case has been selected where there was no appeal, the decision is that of the trial court and is noted as such.)

b. Ellipses (. . .) appearing in an opinion indicate portions that have been deleted by the authors. Deletions are made to eliminate redundancy, or to exclude issues that are not relevant to points that the case has been selected to illustrate. Except for deletions and bracketed author comments, the statements of the higher court are presented verbatim.

c. General principles of law that appear in appellate court decisions are frequently followed by references to earlier cases as sources of such principles. The names of these cases have, in general, been deleted by the authors for easier reading. (However, if the ruling of an earlier case has special applicability to the case being decided—such as *Randolph v. Arizona Board of Regents* on p. 26—its name will be retained.)

2. In regard to procedural matters presented by this case, the following should be noted.

a. The plaintiff, Crim, was able to commence his suit in a federal trial court, rather than a state court, because he and the defendant company were citizens of different states.[19] That is why the appellate court in this case was also a federal court (the U.S. Court of Appeals, Fifth Circuit, which hears appeals from judgments of federal district courts located in Texas, as here, and in five other southern states).

b. Because no federal law was applicable to the case, both the trial and appellate courts correctly looked to the law of Arizona, the state where the wrong occurred, in order to determine the rights and duties of the parties. (That explains the reference to the Randolph case, noted earlier.)

3. A word of caution. It is imperative for readers to acquire the ability to determine the *precise* issue or issues posed by a case, so that they will not leap to unwarranted general conclusions. Can we say, for example, that the instant case establishes the principle that landowners or occupiers are necessarily liable for injuries occurring on their property? Very clearly, the case does not stand for that principle at all. Rather, it enunciates the narrower rule that the landowner or occupier is liable *only if* there is some evidence of negligence on his or her part. Thus, in the instant case, if valley fever had been a rare disease, or if there was little medical data indicating that infectious spores were concentrated in dusty areas, International Harvester would probably not have been held liable.

Questions and Problems

1. In two cases reaching the U.S. Supreme Court in 1985, the United States—through action by the Solicitor General—asked the court to overrule its controversial 1973 decision in *Roe v. Wade*, 410 U.S. 113. (In that case the Court held that a Texas statute making it a crime for anyone to have an abortion within the state, ex-

---

[19] The subject of federal jurisdiction is discussed more fully in Chapter 2.

cept where the abortion was done "upon medical advice for the purpose of saving the mother's life," violated the Due Process clause of the U.S. Constitution.) In effect, this controversial ruling "legalized" abortion to the extent that it gave pregnant women the absolute right to an abortion during the first trimester of their pregnancies, if they so desired.

Leaving aside the precise constitutional question that is raised (which is noted briefly in Chapter 5), do you generally agree with the 1985 position of the United States? In other words, do you feel—because of religious beliefs or moral principles—that a duly-enacted state "anti-abortion" statute (such as the Texas statute), ought not be set aside by the federal courts in the absence of a federal statute mandating such a result? Discuss.

2. In the "Case of the Unhappy Homebuyers," briefly described on pp. 5 and 6, would you say that the rule of law applied by the Illinois Supreme Court falls in the "public law" category or in the "private law" category? Explain.

3. The law that falls within the "government regulation of business" category (such as our consumer protection laws, environmental protection regulations, and antitrust law) was obviously felt at one time to be essentially beneficial to the well-being of our country. Yet, particularly in the last several years, much of this type of law has come in for severe criticism from many quarters. What do you think are the chief reasons for this criticism? Explain.

4. If X and Y make a contract and X later refuses to go through with the deal, having no reason to do so, we say that X's conduct is a *wrong* but is not a *crime*. Why is it not a crime?

5. For some years, the Washington Interscholastic Activities Association had a rule that prohibited girls from participating on high school football teams in the state. When this rule was challenged by parents of two girls who wanted to go out for football, the Supreme Court of Washington had to decide whether the rule violated a provision of the state constitution. (*Darrin v. Gould*, 540 P.2d 882, 1975.) Leaving aside the precise legal question that was posed, do you think that the rule is a good one? Discuss.

6. What are the main advantage and the main danger that result from the requirement that legal rules be essentially certain in nature? Explain.

7. Mrs. P sues the D Church to recover damages for injuries sustained when she tripped on a loose stair tread on church premises. For many years prior to this suit, the courts of the state had followed the rule that nonprofit organizations, such as churches, shall not be liable in such situations even where the injury is the result of their own carelessness. If the court hearing the case of *Mrs. P v. The D Church* is now asked to *overrule* that principle:

a. Which of the four basic requirements (or characteristics) of an effective legal system would cause the court the most difficulty in granting Mrs. P's request for a change in the law?

b. Which of the other basic requirements might cause the court to be sympathetic to arguments that the law ought to be changed?

8. In the "valley fever" case at the end of the chapter, the higher court, in a portion of the decision that does not appear, seemed to say that the scope of International Harvester's duty to its dealers was, to some extent, affected by the fact that most of the dealers (including Crim) were brought into Arizona from other parts of the country. What bearing, in your opinion, might this fact have on International Harvester's liability? Explain.

C·H·A·P·T·E·R 2

COURT SYSTEMS

Legal rules and principles take on vitality and meaning only when they are applied to real-life controversies between real persons, when the rules are *applied to facts:* when, for example, a particular plaintiff is successful or unsuccessful in his or her attempt to recover a specific piece of land from a particular defendant, or where one company is successful or unsuccessful in recovering damages from another company as a result of an alleged breach of contract on the latter company's part. But the fitting of rules to facts—the settling of legal controversies—does not occur automatically. This process, which we call the process of **adjudication**, has to be in somebody's hands; that "somebody" is the state and federal courts that hear the thousands of cases that arise every year.[1] As Figure 2.1 indicates, rules and facts come together in the adjudication process, leading to a decision.

---

[1] In addition to the state and federal trial courts, many administrative agencies (such as the Federal Trade Commission) also hear certain kinds of controversies—usually those in which the agency is contending that a company has violated the agency's own rules or regulations. (The general subject of administrative agencies, including the role that they play in the adjudicatory process, is covered in Chapter 6.)

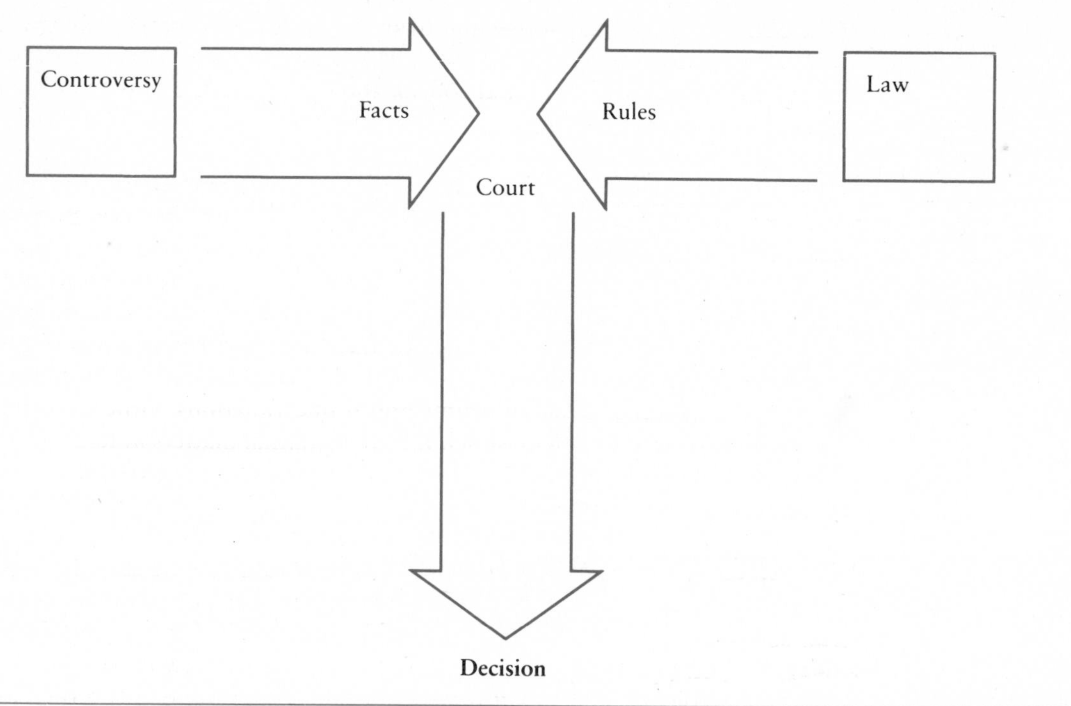

Figure 2.1 The Process of Adjudication

The primary reason, then, for looking at the courts and the work that they do is to gain an overall awareness of this important legal process. There is, however, another reason for doing so. In the following chapters many actual cases are presented. The reader is given the basic facts of a particular controversy, the judgment entered by the trial court on the basis of those facts, and excerpts of the appellate court's decision in affirming or reversing the trial court's judgment. Obviously, some familiarity with court systems and the judicial processes will facilitate one's understanding of the legal significance of each step in these proceedings.

In this chapter, then, we take a brief look at the state and federal court systems, some problems of jurisdiction arising thereunder, and the functions of the trial and appellate courts.

Court Systems

As a result of our federal system of government, we live under two distinct, and essentially separate, sovereign types of government—the state governments and the federal government. Each has its own laws and its own court system. For this reason, it is necessary to examine both systems in order to acquire an adequate knowledge of the court structures within which controversies are settled.

The Typical State System

While court systems vary somewhat from state to state, most state courts fall into three general categories. In ascending order, they are (1) courts of limited jurisdiction, (2) general trial courts, and (3) appellate courts (which frequently exist at two levels).

Courts of Limited Jurisdiction: In every state some trial courts have *limited jurisdiction*; that is, they are limited as to the kinds of cases they can hear.[2] These courts include justice of the peace courts, municipal courts, traffic courts, probate courts, and domestic relations courts. While such courts actually decide a majority of the cases that come to trial, we substantially are going to eliminate them from further consideration because they are not courts of general jurisdiction. Many of them deal with minor matters, such as the handling of small claims and traffic violations. Others (such as the probate courts) deal with much more substantial matters in terms of the amount of money involved; but even these courts are limited to cases of *very specialized subject matter*.

General Trial Courts: The most important cases involving state law, and the ones we will be most concerned with hereafter, commence in the *general trial courts*. These are courts of "general jurisdiction"; they are empowered to hear all cases except those expressly assigned by statute to the "minor" courts discussed above. Virtually all important cases involving contract law, criminal law, and corporation law, for example, originate in the general trial courts.[3] In some states these courts are called "district courts," in others "common pleas courts," and in still others "superior courts" (the latter being something of a misnomer). Whatever the specific name, such a court normally exists in every county of every state.

Appellate Courts: All states have one or more *appellate courts*, which hear appeals from judgments entered by the courts below. In many states there is only one such court, usually called the "supreme court," but in the more populous states there is a layer of appellate courts interposed between the trial courts and the supreme court. Ohio, for example, has twelve intermediate appellate courts, each of which hears appeals on a geographical basis. That is, appeals from judgments of common pleas courts in one section of the state go to a particular intermediate court, while appeals arising from another cluster of counties go to a different intermediate court. There are from three to six justices in the various appellate districts, depending upon the population of the counties within their respective jurisdictions (though actual appeals are heard by only three judges, in virtually all cases).

---

[2] Here *jurisdiction* means the legal power to act.

[3] These courts may occasionally be referred to hereafter simply as *state trial courts*, to distinguish them from federal trial courts. When this is done, reference is being made to the trial courts of *general jurisdiction* rather than to the minor trial courts.

The Federal Court System

Article III, Section 1 of the U.S. Constitution provides that "the judicial power of the United States shall be vested in one Supreme Court, and in such inferior courts as the Congress may from time to time ordain and establish." The numerous federal courts that exist today by virtue of this section can, at the risk of oversimplification, be placed into three main categories similar to those of the state courts: (1) specialized courts, (2) general trial courts (district courts), and (3) appellate courts—the courts of appeal and the Supreme Court.

Specialized U.S. Courts: Some federal courts have limited jurisdiction, such as the U.S. Tax Court, the U.S. Court of Military Appeals, and the recently created U.S. Claims Court. While these courts frequently deal with important matters, we are eliminating them from further consideration (as we did the similar state courts) because of their specialized nature.

General Trial Courts: The basic courts having general jurisdiction within the federal system are the *U.S. district courts*, sometimes called federal trial courts. Most federal cases originate in these courts.

Congress has created ninety-four judicial districts, each of which contains one federal district court. Ninety-one of these, including one for the District of Columbia, are located in the U.S. proper, with the remaining three in Puerto Rico, Guam, and the Virgin Islands. (An additional federal district court for the Canal Zone was closed in March of 1982 by federal legislation implementing the Panama Canal Treaty of 1977.)

The federal districts, with the exceptions noted above, essentially are based upon state lines. The less populated states have only one federal district court within their boundaries, while most of the remaining states have two (the U.S. District Court for Northern Iowa and the U.S. District Court for Southern Iowa, for example). Several states have three such courts, and California, New York, and Texas have four each. In any event, every square foot of land in this country and its territories is, geographically speaking, within the jurisdiction of one U.S. district court.

The Appellate Courts: Above the district courts are two levels of *federal appellate courts*—the U.S. courts of appeal and, above them, the U.S. Supreme Court. There are thirteen U.S. courts of appeal. Eleven of these, located in "circuits" across the country, have jurisdiction to hear appeals from the district courts located in the states within their respective boundaries. For example, the 9th U.S. Court of Appeals in San Francisco hears appeals from decisions of district courts within the states of Alaska, Arizona, California, Hawaii, Idaho, Montana, Nevada, Oregon, and Washington. Each of these eleven courts also hears appeals from federal administrative agencies' rulings.

The jurisdiction of the remaining two courts of appeal is somewhat different from that of the others. The U.S. Court of Appeals for the District of

Columbia hears appeals from the federal district court located in the district, as well as appeals from rulings of federal agencies that are issued there. The other appellate court is the U.S. Court of Appeals for the Federal Circuit, which was created when Congress enacted the Federal Courts Improvement Act of 1982. (That act also eliminated two older, specialized federal courts, the U.S. Court of Claims and the U.S. Court of Customs and Patent Appeals, and created another court, the U.S. Claims Court.) The major jurisdiction of this newest court of appeals is to hear all patent appeals from Patent and Trademark Office boards throughout the country and appeals from decisions of the new U.S. Claims Court, which is the trial court in which most monetary claims against the federal government originate.

Appeals from judgments of the U.S. courts of appeal, like appeals from judgments of the state supreme courts that present federal questions, can be taken to the U.S. Supreme Court. That court, however, actually hears only a small percentage of such appeals, because review by the highest court is usually not a "matter of right"—that is, the U.S. Supreme Court usually has no legal obligation to review the judgment.[4] Rather, parties who seek a review normally must petition the Supreme Court for a **writ of certiorari**, and the court has absolute discretion in deciding which of these cases are sufficiently important to warrant the granting of certiorari.[5] In most instances certiorari is denied; in a typical year the Court hears only about 155 of the approximately 5,500 appeals that are made.

Some Observations

The typical state court system and the federal system can be diagrammed as in Figure 2.2 (p. 36). Several general comments can be made about this diagram.

1. The basic trial courts are the U.S. District Courts and the state general trial courts; all courts above this level are appellate courts.

2. Trial courts must settle questions of both *fact* and *law*, while appellate courts rule on questions of law only. Questions of fact are "what happened" questions: for instance, did the defendant corporations expressly or impliedly agree not to sell goods to the plaintiff? Questions of law, by contrast, are "what is the rule applicable to the facts?" (Much more is said about the fact-law distinction later in this chapter.)

3. While a majority of the decisions of the trial courts are not appealed, a good many are. Hereafter we are concerned primarily with the *decisions of*

---

[4] Appeal as a matter of right does exist in very limited kinds of cases. For example, the U.S. Supreme Court *must* hear appeals in cases in which a state supreme court has ruled a federal statute to be unconstitutional, and cases in which a federal court of appeals has invalidated a state statute on the ground that it violated a provision of the U.S. Constitution.

[5] A *writ of certiorari* is an order of a higher court requiring a lower court to forward to it the records and proceedings of a particular case.

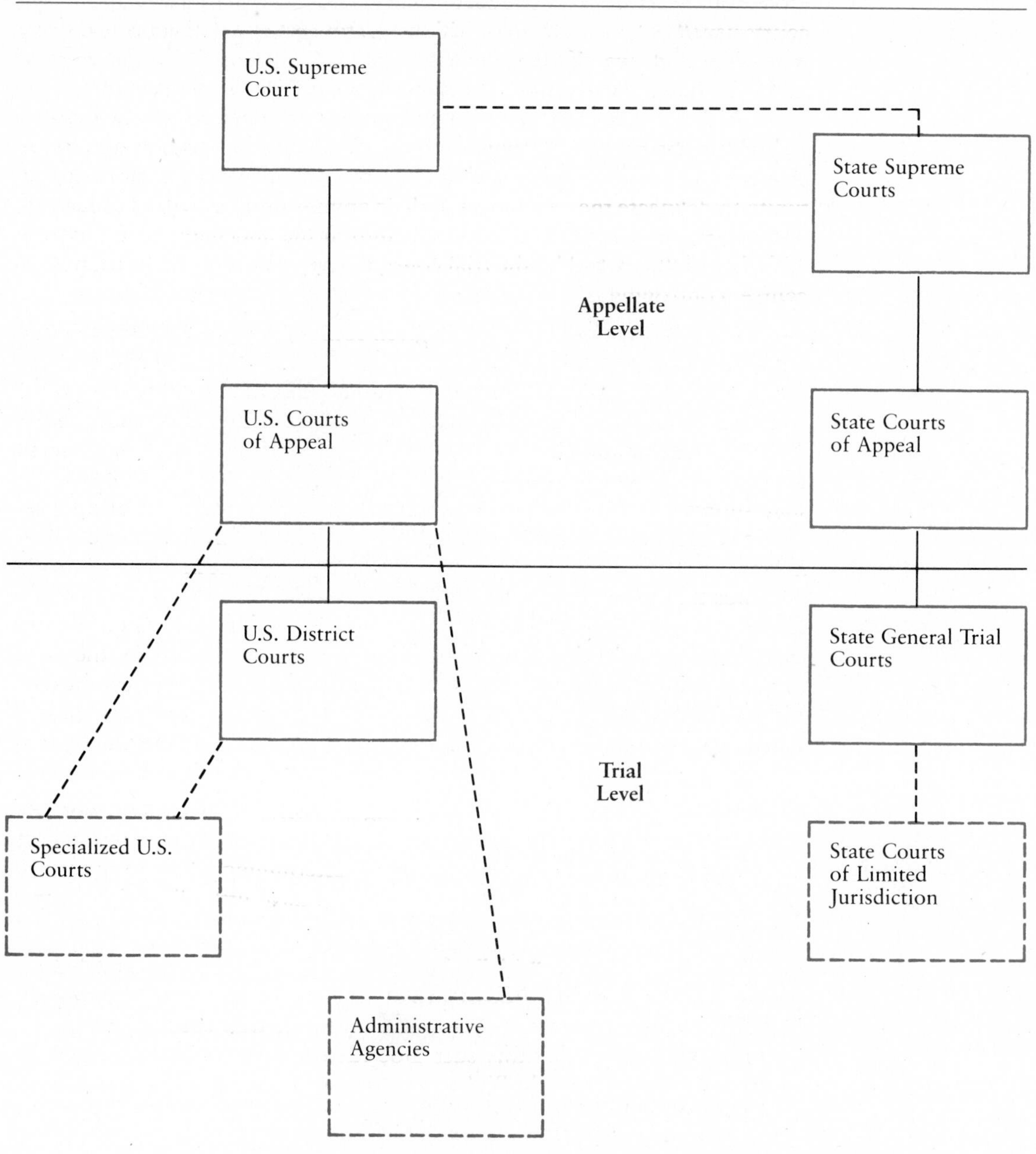

Figure 2.2 **The Federal and State Court System**

the appellate courts. There are several basic reasons for this. First, state trial courts usually enter a judgment without writing a formal opinion as to their reasoning; and, even if there is such an opinion, it is normally not reported (published). Appellate courts, on the other hand, normally do write opinions which are reported, and access to them is available to anyone wishing to look up the rulings of law involved. Second, appellate courts have more time to adequately research the law than do trial judges—and more opportunity to delineate the legal issues in their opinions for the benefit of lawyers and others who may read them. And, third, if the appellate court disagrees with the result reached by the trial court, the appellate court's decision is, of course, controlling.

4. Once a case is initiated within a given court system, it will normally stay within that system until a final judgment is reached. Thus, if a case is properly commenced in a state court of general jurisdiction, any appeal from the trial court's judgment must be made to the next higher state court rather than to a federal appellate court. And if a case reaches the highest court in the state, its judgment is final. In other words, on matters of state law, the state supreme courts are indeed supreme.[6] However, judgments of state supreme courts in cases that present "federal questions" are appealable. To illustrate: a plaintiff initiates an action in a state trial court in which he or she contends that a particular state statute violates the **due process** clause of the federal Constitution, and the defendant does not ask for the case to be removed to the federal courts. If the case is ultimately heard by the state supreme court, the loser may ask the U.S. Supreme Court to review the correctness of the judgment by petitioning that court for certiorari. (For a further discussion of federal questions and removal, see "Problems of Jurisdiction" later in this chapter.)

5. Supreme courts in those states having an intermediate level of appellate courts—state courts of appeal—generally have wide discretion, somewhat akin to that of the U.S. Supreme Court, in determining which appeals they will hear. The supreme courts of other states have little discretion in this matter.

6. With regard to the "title" of an appealed case, the state and federal courts follow somewhat different rules. In most state courts, the original plaintiff's name appears first—just as it did in the trial court. Suppose, for example, that Pink (plaintiff) sues Doe (defendant) in a state trial court, where the case is obviously *Pink v. Doe.* If the judgment of the trial court is appealed, the rule followed by most state courts is that the title of the case remains *Pink v. Doe* in the appellate courts, no matter which party is the **appellant** (the one bringing the appeal). In the federal courts, on the other

[6] The normal terminology is being used here. In a few states, however, the "supreme court" label is given to an intermediate appellate court, with the highest court in the state bearing some other name. The court of last resort in the state of New York, for example, is the Court of Appeals of New York.

hand, the appellant's name appears first. Under this rule, if Doe (defendant) loses in a U.S. district court and appeals to a U.S. court of appeals, the title of the case will be *Doe v. Pink* in the higher court. For this reason, when one sees a case in a federal appellate court so entitled, one cannot assume that Doe was the party who originated the action in the trial court. That determination must be made by referring to the facts of the case as set forth in the decision of the appellate court.

The "Style" of Case Reporting: As has been noted, the decisions of the appellate courts are published in chronologically numbered volumes. Most states have a dual system of reporting. When a state supreme court renders a decision, its opinion is printed in full both in "official reports," which are authorized by the state, and in a "regional reporter" published by the West Publishing Company, called the National Reporter System. Under the West system, the reports of state courts are grouped on a geographical basis under these headings: Atlantic (A.), Southeastern (S.E.), Northeastern (N.E.), Northwestern (N.W.), Southern (S.), Southwestern (S.W.), and Pacific (P.). For example, decisions of the courts of Iowa, Michigan, Minnesota, Nebraska, North Dakota, South Dakota, and Wisconsin appear in the Northwestern reports.

The volume and page numbers that appear after the title of a case comprise its "citation." Thus a case entitled *Schupak v. McDonald's System, Inc.*, 200 Neb. 485, 264 N.W.2d 827, will be found in volume 200 of the official Nebraska reports at page 485, and in volume 264 of the second series of the National Reporter System for states in the Northwestern area at page 827. (Only the citations of the West system are given for cases in this text, since a number of states have dispensed with the publication of their official reports.)

Problems of Jurisdiction

In order for a court to settle a particular controversy, it is necessary for it to have "**jurisdiction** over the case."[7] This means that it must have jurisdiction of both the *subject matter* involved in the suit, and, in most cases, jurisdiction of the *person* (the individual or company) against whom the suit is being brought. If a trial court should enter a judgment in a particular case and, on appeal, the higher court finds that either of these kinds of jurisdiction was lacking, the judgment of the trial court is void—of no effect whatever.

Subject-Matter Jurisdiction

As we have already seen, some courts in both the state and federal systems are sharply limited as to the kinds of cases they can hear. Within a state system, for example, probate courts are normally empowered to hear only

[7] As earlier, *jurisdiction* means the legal power to act, especially to hear and decide controversies.

those cases involving decedents' estates and guardianship proceedings; they clearly have no authority to hear ordinary breach of contract cases. Other courts, those of general jurisdiction, have much broader powers; they can hear all types of cases except the relatively few that by statute must originate in the specialized courts. Within a given court system, then, the subject-matter jurisdiction of the several courts is essentially clear.

Occasionally, however, cases will arise that present a more difficult problem, involving the lines of demarcation between the jurisdiction of the *state* courts and the *federal* courts. This occurs because while most cases must begin only in the state courts or only in the federal courts, some cases can be commenced in either court system. A brief look at jurisdictional rules is thus necessary.

Subject Matter: State versus Federal Jurisdiction

Under federal law, certain kinds of cases must be brought in the federal courts. Typical of such cases are those arising in the areas of bankruptcy, copyright and trademarks, admiralty, and federal criminal actions. As to these types of cases, the federal courts are said to have "exclusive jurisdiction."

As to all other controversies, the general rule is that *all cases must be commenced in the state courts* except those which present a **federal question** or involve **diversity of citizenship.** Since most controveries do not involve such matters, the great majority of cases do, in fact, originate in the state courts. Nevertheless, the rule does make it necessary to understand the terms "federal question" and "diversity of citizenship" in order to become familiar with the most common kinds of cases heard by the federal courts.

Federal Questions: A federal question exists in any suit where the plaintiff's case—**cause of action**—is based in whole or in part upon a *federal statute* or upon a provision of the *U.S. Constitution* or a *U.S. treaty*. Once it is shown that a federal question is involved in a particular case, the federal courts have jurisdiction of that case regardless of the amount in controversy—the amount of money the plaintiff is seeking or the value of the right that the plaintiff is asserting. (For many years, plaintiffs in some federal question cases could bring their suits in the federal courts only if the amount in controversy was over $10,000. In 1981, however, Congress eliminated this requirement by statute.)

The federal and state courts have **concurrent jurisdiction** in all federal question cases except for those where federal courts have exclusive jurisdiction. In other words, except for cases arising in the areas of bankruptcy, copyright and trademarks, admiralty, and federal criminal law, plaintiffs in federal question cases have the choice of commencing their actions in the federal court system *or* the appropriate state system. (As a matter of practice, where concurrent jurisdiction exists, most suits are brought in the federal courts. And, if the plaintiff does commence the action in a state court, federal removal statutes grant the *defendant* the "right of removal"—the right to have the case transferred to the federal courts.) Thus federal question cases are heard by state courts only in the exceptional instance where the cases are filed there initially and the defendants do not exercise the right of removal.

Diversity of Citizenship: Under one section of the U.S. Constitution, the federal courts are authorized to hear cases in which the plaintiff and defendant *are citizens of different states*, even though no federal question is involved. By virtue of federal legislation that implements this section, however, a second requirement must be met: the amount in controversy must exceed $10,000 in all cases. (Suits between citizens of different states involving lesser amounts, therefore, can be initiated only in the state courts.)

At first glance, it may seem illogical that diversity cases are permitted to be brought in the federal courts, since no questions of federal law are presented by such cases. There is a reason for this extension of federal jurisdiction, however, and it is succinctly stated as follows: "Diversity jurisdiction was created to alleviate fears that an out-of-state litigant might be subject to local bias in the courts of the state where his adversary resided, and to afford suitors the opportunity, at their option, to assert their rights in the federal rather than the state courts."[8]

Regardless of whether the fears of local bias are the motivation, it is true that a substantial percentage of the 60,000-odd cases that are filed in the federal courts each year are, in fact, based solely on "diversity" grounds. It is also true that in some cases, particularly those in which several parties are involved, the question of whether diversity exists is so complex as to be outside the scope of this text. Nevertheless, the following examples will illustrate the basic rules as they apply to suits brought *between individuals*.

Case 1. X, a citizen of Michigan, seeks to enforce a $15,000 promissory note against Y, a citizen of Wisconsin residing in Madison. X's suit can be brought in the U.S. District Court for Western Wisconsin, if he so desires.

Case 2. P, a citizen of Ohio, is injured in Indianapolis when her car is negligently struck by a car driven by D, a citizen of Indiana residing in Indianapolis. If P files suit against D in the U.S. District Court for Southern Indiana, asking (in good faith) for damages in excess of $10,000, that court has jurisdiction of the case.

Case 3. W and X, citizens of Nebraska, seek to recover $50,000 in damages from Y, a citizen of Nebraska, and Z, a citizen of Wyoming, the case arising out of an alleged breach of contract. Here diversity is lacking, since

---

[8] 36 C.J.S., Federal Courts, § 55, Copyright 1960 by West Publishing Co.

there are citizens of Nebraska on both sides of the case; this suit could not, therefore, be heard by a federal court.

In diversity cases, as in many federal question cases, the federal and state courts again usually possess concurrent jurisdiction. Thus the plaintiffs in Cases 1 and 2 above could have brought their actions in *state* courts in Wisconsin and Indiana, respectively, had they wished to do so. And, had they done so, it should be further noted that the defendants could *not* have had the cases transferred to the federal courts. This is because the right of removal in diversity cases, under the removal statutes mentioned earlier, exists only if the defendant is not a citizen of the state in which the suit is brought. (More specifically: in Case 1, if suit were brought in the Wisconsin state courts, defendant Y could not have the case transferred because he is a citizen of Wisconsin. Similarly, in Case 2, if suit were brought in the Indiana courts, defendant D could not have the case transferred because he is a citizen of Indiana.) By contrast, the right of removal *would* exist in the following situation: P, a Nevada citizen, has a cause of action against D, a Utah citizen. P brings suit in a Nevada state court against D, and P has D served with a summons while D is vacationing in Reno. Because D is not a citizen of Nevada, he may have the case removed to the federal district court in Nevada.

Insofar as suits involving corporations are concerned, these too may be brought in federal courts if diversity exists and if the "over $10,000" requirement is met. However, a corporation, unlike an individual, may be a citizen of two different states at the same time. This results from the rule that, for diversity purposes, a corporation is a citizen of the state in which it is incorporated, *and* a citizen of the state in which it has its principal place of business, if the principal place of business is in a state other than the state of incorporation. Thus, if X, a citizen of Maine, is suing the Y Company, which is incorporated under the laws of Delaware, X could not bring the action in a federal court if the Y Company had its principal place of business in Maine. In other words, diversity is lacking here since plaintiff and defendant are both citizens of Maine.

The case below is typical of those in which a federal court must decide whether or not a *federal question* is presented.

Pavolini v. Bard-Air Corporation

U.S. Court of Appeals, Second Circuit
645 F.2d 144 (1981)

John Pavolini was a commercial pilot for Bard-Air Corporation, a charter air carrier certified by the Federal Aviation Agency (FAA) to provide transportation of persons and property over certain designated air routes in New York and adjacent states.

During June, 1979, Pavolini discovered that the aircraft he and four other Bard-Air pilots were assigned to fly were unsafe and did not comply with FAA regulations. He reported the violations to James Knight, Bard-Air's director of operations and vice-president, but Knight took no action to correct them.

Following Knight's orders, Pavolini piloted air taxi flights on August 14, 20, and 23, 1979, which caused him to exceed flight and duty time limitations set by the FAA. Knight also ordered Pavolini to falsify flight records to show that the August 14 flight was within the FAA duty time limitations. Pavolini refused to falsify the record, and reported this violation to the FAA.

Thereafter Pavolini reported additional violations of safety regulations to the FAA. When Knight learned of these reports, he summarily fired Pavolini. (Following an investigation, the FAA found that Pavolini's charges were true, and it accordingly levied a fine against Bard-Air.)

After Pavolini was unable to get employment as a pilot because of his discharge, he brought this action in a federal court against Bard-Air for damages for loss of wages, mental distress and anguish, alleging that his discharge violated the Federal Aviation Act of 1958 and the First and Fourteenth Amendments of the U.S. Constitution. The trial court rejected these contentions, ruling that the suit presented no federal question, and dismissed the action. Pavolini appealed.

Feinbert, Chief Judge:

. . . The main issue on appeal is whether the district court correctly concluded that there is no implied cause of action under [the Federal Aviation Act of 1958] for wrongful discharge. We agree with the conclusion of the district court, and we affirm the judgment dismissing the complaint. . . .

Pavolini first argues that an implied cause of action exists under the Federal Aviation Act in favor of a pilot discharged for reporting violations of safety provisions to the FAA. . . . [For a plaintiff to win in such a case,] there must be a duty [imposed by a federal law,] the violation of which has caused the injury, before we reach the question whether a private remedy exists to redress the injury. Pavolini's claimed injuries were allegedly caused by his discharge, but *the Act does not require an air carrier to continue to employ an employee for any reason, nor does the Act prohibit a carrier from discharging an employee for reporting safety violations to the FAA.* [Emphasis added.]

It is true that the statute commands the Administrator of the FAA "to promote safety of flight of civil aircraft in air commerce by prescribing" and enforcing standards, rules and regulations . . . "as will best tend to reduce or eliminate the possibility of, or recurrence of, accidents in air transportation." . . . And we can assume on this record that Bard-Air has violated the Act in several respects. But nevertheless, this is an action seeking redress for loss of employment and Pavolini's injury does not flow, in a legal sense, from Bard-Air's failure to obey any statutory requirement or from a violation of any statutory prohibition. Under the circumstances, it is not necessary to consider further [Pavolini's claim that the Federal Aviation Act gives him an implied cause of action].

Pavolini also argues that his termination for reporting the violations deprived him of his constitutional right to freedom of speech under the First and Fourteenth Amendments. However, before Pavolini can recover for alleged violations of [these] amendments, he must establish that his discharge by Bard-Air was "state action." Plaintiff relies principally on extensive governmental regulation of the air transport industry to support his claim that Bard-Air was performing a public function. But regulation, without more, is insufficient to treat the discharge by Bard-Air as action by the state; further, we reject the notion that because the FAA may have in some indirect way approved of plaintiff's reporting a safety violation, the discharge was thereby transformed from private conduct to state action. In the absence of state action, plaintiff's constitutional claims fail.[a]

In light of the above, we reluctantly conclude that there is no proper basis for federal jurisdiction here. Since federal courts are courts of limited jurisdiction, Pavolini's remedy, if any, lies in the state courts, which have traditionally exercised jurisdiction over controversies between employers and employees. [Emphasis added.] . . . We believe that it is unfortunate that a federal court cannot provide recourse to an employee fired for reporting violations of federal safety regulations. We are well aware that Pavolini was in a difficult situation, facing a loss of his job on the one hand and a potential loss of lives on the other; he should be commended for placing public safety over private concerns. We certainly have no desire to encourage retaliation by employers against their employees who, having failed to obtain voluntary compliance, turn to the appropriate federal agency charged with insuring safety in an effort to prevent injury or death. But we are mindful that we do not sit as a legislature. Congress has in the past acted to protect against retaliation federal employees who "blow the whistle" on violators of the law [in limited circumstances, but such protection is not applicable to this particular controversy]. In view of what has occurred here, Congress may well wish to consider protecting in an appropriate way those who help prevent the loss of life from improper operation or maintenance of aircraft.

The judgment of the district court is affirmed.

★ ★ ★

Jurisdiction of the Person

A court does not have the power to hear a case simply because its subject matter, the general nature of the proceeding, falls within its jurisdiction. A second type of jurisdiction—jurisdiction over *the person of the defendant* (or, in some cases, property of the defendant)—must also be present. In other words, while subject-matter rules determine the court system that may hear a case, jurisdiction of person rules determine the *particular trial court* within that system where the case must be commenced. In this regard, a

[a]The requirement that Pavolini show that the free speech interference complained of was interference by the state, as distinguished from interference by a private person or corporation, results from the language of the constitutional amendments themselves. The First Amendment provides, in part, that "*Congress* shall make no law . . . abridging the freedom of speech," and the Fourteenth Amendment provides, in part, that "No *state* shall make or enforce any law which shall abridge the privileges and immunities of Citizens of the United States." [Emphasis added.] These amendments are discussed more fully in Chapter 5.

distinction between "actions in personam" and "actions in rem" must be noted.

Actions in Personam: The great majority of civil suits are actions *in personam*—that is, actions in which the plaintiff is seeking to hold the defendant liable on a personal obligation. Three of the most common examples are the following:

1. P sues D to recover damages (that is, a sum of money) arising out of a *breach of contract* on D's part.

2. P sues to recover damages for *personal injuries* that D has wrongly inflicted upon him.

3. P sues D to recover a *debt* that is owed by the D Company.

Whenever a plaintiff brings an action *in personam* against an individual, as in cases 1 and 2 above, he or she must demonstrate to the court that it has "jurisdiction of the defendant's person." While the laws of the various states differ to some extent, this usually can be done only by showing (1) that the *defendant's residence* is within the territorial jurisdiction of the court, and that the summons was either personally served on the defendant there or left with some other adult at that residence, or (2) if the defendant's residence is elsewhere, that he or she was *personally served* with the summons while within the court's territorial jurisdiction. Since the second of these is often difficult to accomplish, and impossible if the defendant remains outside the jurisdiction, the result in practice is that the plaintiff must normally commence suit in a court of the state where the defendant lives, wherever that may be.

Where the defendant is a corporation, special rules apply. A court in a given state can clearly exercise *in personam* jurisdiction over any corporation that is incorporated or maintains its principal offices in that state. In addition to these introductory rules, special statutes permit actions against out-of-state corporations (and individuals) in limited circumstances.[9]

Actions in Rem: In some actions the plaintiff is seeking merely to enforce a right against certain *property* that is owned by the defendant or in which the defendant claims an interest. Such suits are *actions in rem*, and can be

[9] Because of the difficulty and expense involved in suing an out-of-state resident, all states have adopted "long-arm statutes" of one kind or another, which permit some types of actions to be brought against out-of-state residents in the *plaintiff*'s home state. One typical statute, for example, provides in essence that any nonresident who "engages in business" in the state is thereby giving his consent to be sued in that state by any person who has a claim against him arising out of the transaction of such business. In such an action the plaintiff need only have the service of process (the complaint and summons) be made on the secretary of state in the plaintiff's state in order to acquire jurisdiction on the nonresident defendant. Additionally, all states have similar statutes providing that nonresidents who operate motor vehicles within their borders are thereby appointing a designated state official, such as the secretary of state or director of the department of motor vehicles, to be their agent for the purpose of being sued if they are involved in an accident while in the state.

brought in any court within whose territorial jurisdiction the property—the "res" or thing—is located.

The typical case is the mortgage foreclosure action, which can be illustrated as follows. X, a Kentucky resident, owns an apartment building in Ohio with a $35,000 mortgage on it held by an Ohio bank. If X defaults on the mortgage payments, the bank can bring a mortgage foreclosure action in Ohio in the common pleas court of the county where the building is located. (Under the laws of most states relating to such actions, the bank need only publish notices of the suit in a newspaper in order to bring X's interest in the property within the jurisdiction of the court, in which case service upon X is said to be made "by publication," as distinguished from "personal service.")

In the next case—an *in personam* action brought in Oklahoma against several out-of-state corporations—the U.S. Supreme Court pays particular attention to the constitutional principles raised by such actions.

Harry and Kay Robinson purchased a new Audi automobile from Seaway Volkswagen (hereafter referred to as "Seaway") in Massena, N.Y., in 1976. The following year the Robinson family left New York for a new home in Arizona. As they passed through Oklahoma another car struck their Audi in the rear, causing a fire that severely burned Mrs. Robinson and her two children.

The Robinsons subsequently brought this products-liability action against four defendants in an Oklahoma trial court, claiming that their injuries resulted from defective design and placement of the Audi's gas tank and fuel system. The defendants were the automobile's manufacturer, Audi NSU Auto Union Aktiengesellschaft (Audi); its importer, Volkswagen of America, Inc. (Volkswagen); its regional distributor, World-Wide Volkswagen Corp. (World-Wide); and the retail dealer, Seaway.[a]

Defendants World-Wide and Seaway entered special appearances in the Oklahoma trial court, claiming that it did not have jurisdiction over them. When the trial court ruled that it *did* have jurisdiction, the defendants appealed that ruling to the Supreme Court of Oklahoma. That court, for reasons appearing in the decision below, affirmed the trial court's ruling. World-Wide and Seaway then appealed to the U.S. Supreme Court. (Woodson, whose name appears in case title, was the trial court judge.)

White, Justice:

The issue before us is whether, consistently with the Due Process Clause of the Fourteenth Amendment, an Oklahoma court may exercise *in personam* jurisdiction over a nonresident automobile retailer and its wholesale distributor in a

[a] The driver of the car which collided with the Robinsons' car does not figure in this particular litigation.

products-liability action, when the defendants' only connection with Oklahoma is the fact that an automobile sold in New York to New York residents became involved in an accident in Oklahoma. . . .

The facts presented to the District Court showed that World-Wide is incorporated and has its business office in New York. It distributes vehicles, parts, and accessories, under contract with Volkswagen, to retail dealers in New York. Seaway, one of these retail dealers, is incorporated and has its place of business in New York. Insofar as the record reveals, Seaway and World-Wide are fully independent corporations whose relations with each other and with Volkswagen are contractual only.

Respondents [the Robinsons and Woodson] *adduced no evidence that either World-Wide or Seaway does any business in Oklahoma, ships or sells any products to or in that State, has an agent to receive process there, or purchases advertisements in any media calculated to reach Oklahoma.* [Emphasis added.] In fact, . . . there was no showing that any automobile sold by World-Wide or Seaway has ever entered Oklahoma with the single exception of the vehicle involved in the present case.

Despite the apparent paucity of acts between petitioners [World-Wide and Seaway] and Oklahoma, . . . the Supreme Court of Oklahoma held that personal jurisdiction over the petitioners was authorized by Oklahoma's "long-arm" statute . . .[b] We reverse.

The Due Process Clause of the Fourteenth Amendment limits the power of a state court to render a valid personal judgment against a nonresident defendant. A judgment rendered in violation of due process is void in the rendering State and is not entitled to full faith and credit elsewhere. Due process requires that the defendant be given adequate notice of the suit, and be subject to the personal jurisdiction of the court. In the present case it is not contended that notice was inadequate; the only question is whether these particular petitioners were subject to the jurisdiction of the Oklahoma courts.

As has long been settled, and as we reaffirm today, a state court may exercise personal jurisdiction over a nonresident defendant only so long as there exist "minimum contacts" between the defendant and the forum state. The concept of minimum contacts, in turn, can be seen to perform two related, but distinguishable, functions. It protects the defendant against the burdens of litigating in a distant or inconvenient forum. And it acts to ensure that the States, through their courts, do not reach out beyond the limits imposed on them by their status as coequal sovereigns in a federal system.

The protection against inconvenient litigation is typically described in terms of "reasonableness" or "fairness." We have said that the defendant's contacts with the forum State must be such that maintenance of the suit "does not offend traditional notions of fair play and substantial justice." The relationship be-

---

[b]That statute provided, in essence, that Oklahoma courts could exercise personal jurisdiction over any person who causes "tortious injury" in Oklahoma by acts committed outside the state if such person "regularly does or solicits business" in Oklahoma, or "derives substantial revenue from goods used or consumed" in Oklahoma.

tween the defendant and the forum must be such that it is "reasonable to require the corporation to defend the particular suit which is brought there." Implicit in this emphasis on reasonableness is the understanding that the burden on the defendant, while always a primary concern, will in an appropriate case be considered in light of other relevant factors, including the forum State's interest in adjudicating the dispute; the plaintiff's interest in obtaining convenient and effective relief; . . . the interstate judicial system's interest in obtaining the most efficient resolution of controversies; and the shared interest of the several States in furthering fundamental substantive social policies.

The limits imposed on state jurisdiction by the Due Process Clause, in its role as a guarantor against inconvenient litigation, have been substantially relaxed over the years. . . . Nevertheless, we have never accepted the proposition that state lines are irrelevant for jurisdictional purposes, nor could we, and remain faithful to the principles of interstate federalism embodied in the Constitution. [While] the economic interdependence of the States was foreseen and desired by the Framers [of the Constitution] . . . the Framers also intended that the States retain many essential attributes of sovereignty, including, in particular, the sovereign power to try causes in their courts.

[The Court here quoted several constitutional principles adopted in prior jurisdictional-dispute cases, and continued]: Thus the Due Process Clause "does not contemplate that a State may make binding a judgment *in personam* against an individual or corporate defendant with which the State has no contacts, ties, or relations." Even if the defendant would suffer minimal or no inconvenience from being forced to litigate before the tribunals of another State; even if the forum State has a strong interest in applying its law to the controversy; even if the forum State is the most convenient location for litigation, the Due Process Clause, acting as an instrument of interstate federalism, may sometimes act to divest the State of its power to render a valid judgment.

Applying these principles to the case at hand, we find . . . a total absence of those affiliating circumstances that are a necessary predicate to any exercise of state-court jurisdiction. Petitioners carry on no activity whatsoever in Oklahoma. They close no sales and perform no services there. They avail themselves of none of the privileges and benefits of Oklahoma law. They solicit no business there either through salespersons or through advertising reasonably calculated to reach the State. Nor does the record show that they regularly sell cars at wholesale or retail to Oklahoma customers or residents or that they indirectly, through others, serve or seek to serve the Oklahoma market. In short, respondents seek to base jurisdiction on one, isolated occurrence and whatever inferences can be drawn therefrom: the fortuitous circumstance that a single Audi automobile, sold in New York to New York residents, happened to suffer an accident while passing through Oklahoma.

It is argued, however, that because an automobile is mobile by its very design and purpose, it was "foreseeable" that the Robinsons' Audi would cause injury in Oklahoma. Yet "foreseeability" alone has never been a sufficient benchmark for personal jurisdiction under the Due Process Clause. . . .

If foreseeability were the criterion, a local California tire retailer could be forced to defend in Pennsylvania when a blowout occurs there; a Wisconsin seller of a defective automobile jack could be haled before a distant court for damage caused in New Jersey; or a Florida soft-drink concessionaire could be summoned to Alaska to account for injuries happening there.[c] Every seller of chattels would in effect appoint the chattel [the product] his agent for service of process. . . . We are unwilling to endorse a . . . principle [that would bring about such a result].

When a corporation "purposefully avails itself of the privilege of conducting activities within the forum State" it has clear notice that it is subject to suit there. . . . Hence if the sale of a product of a manufacturer or distributor . . . is not simply an isolated occurrence, but arises from the efforts of the manufacturer or distributor to serve the market for its products in other States, it is not unreasonable to subject it to suit in one of those States. . . .

But [because such efforts are lacking in this case], there is no . . . basis for Oklahoma jurisdiction over World-Wide or Seaway. . . .

Reversed.

★★★

"Conflict of Laws" Questions: In any case brought in either a state or federal court and based solely upon state law, there is always the possibility that one of the parties will claim that the law of one state is applicable, while the other party will contend that the law of a different state is controlling. (This is especially true, as one might imagine, in the diversity cases initiated in the federal courts.)

The following example illustrates the nature of the problem. O, a citizen of Ohio, makes a contract in Indiana with I, a citizen of Illinois, with the contract calling for performance by I to be rendered in Texas. If I thereafter refuses to carry out his part of the bargain and is sued by O in a federal court in Illinois, it may well be that the court will have to decide whether the entire dispute is to be settled by the law of just one of the four states or whether certain points of dispute will be governed by the law of one state and other issues by the law of a second state.

In general, the courts of each state have been free to formulate their own rules by which "choice of law" questions are to be settled within their respective jurisdictions. The rules that have been devised in each state therefore comprise that state's **conflict of laws** rules. And, fortunately, it can be said that the rules adopted by the several states in this area of law are essentially—though not entirely—uniform. In regard to the application of contract law, for example, it is generally held that the *validity* of a contract is to be determined by the law of the state in which the contract was made, while questions having to do with *performance* of the contract are governed by the law of the state in which performance is to take place.

[c]The court here is referring to fact-patterns of three prior cases, in all of which it held that plaintiffs could *not* bring suit in the states in which the accidents occurred.

In the area of tort law, there is a split of authority insofar as the basic rules are concerned. A number of states still adhere to the traditional view that the law of the state in which the tort occurred is controlling. Under this view, if A should sue B in a negligence action in a Delaware court to recover damages resulting from an automobile accident occurring in New Jersey, determination of B's negligence would be on the basis of New Jersey law. Today, however, most courts have adopted a different rule. Under it, the courts apply the law of the state having the "most significant relationship" to the case; the place where the tort occurred, therefore, is not necessarily controlling. Thus, in the prior example, if A were a passenger in the car driven by B and both were Delaware residents, and if the car was registered in Delaware, and if the journey was not for the purpose of carrying on business in New Jersey, Delaware law would probably be applied.

Law, Equity, and Remedies

In the remainder of this chapter we will examine the major steps in the process of adjudication, paying particular attention to the roles played by the trial and appellate courts in that process. We will see that in all legal controversies the plaintiff is asking for a **remedy**—an order addressed to the defendant, requiring that person to do (or not to do) a particular act. A remedy, then, is "the means by which a plaintiff's right is enforced, or the violation of a right is prevented, redressed, or compensated."[10] All remedies are either "legal" or "equitable" in nature, a fact that can be explained only by a brief glimpse at the development of the early court systems in England.

Courts of Law

After the Norman conquest of England some nine hundred years ago, a nationwide system of courts was established. This was accomplished when the first Norman kings designated individuals throughout the country to be their personal representatives in the settling of certain kinds of legal controversies.

These early courts, which were called royal courts or king's courts, *were sharply limited as to the kinds of remedies they could grant.* Essentially, they could grant relief only in cases where the plaintiff was asking for (1) money damages, (2) the possession of real estate, or (3) the possession of personal property.

In settling the disputes within their limited jurisdiction, the courts made up their own rules as they went along, based largely on the customs and moral standards then prevailing, plus their own ideas of what kinds of conduct were "just" in particular situations. The formulation of rules in this

---

[10] *Black's Law Dictionary*, Revised Fifth Edition, Copyright 1979 by West Publishing Co.

manner, a process that continues today in some branches of law, gave birth to the common law. The courts ultimately became *courts of law*, and the remedies which they granted in the three types of controversies that they could hear were *remedies at law*.

Courts of Equity

While this system introduced a uniformity to the settling of disputes, controversies began to arise when plaintiffs sought remedies *other than those that the courts of law could grant*. Rebuffed by these courts, they frequently petitioned the king for relief. Most of the petitions were ruled on by the king's secretary, the chancellor, who granted relief when he thought the plaintiff's claim was a fair one. Out of the rulings of successive chancellors arose a new body of "chancery" rules and remedies for cases outside the jurisdiction of the courts of law.

Finally, a system of chancery courts, known as *courts of equity*, evolved. Thus it was that two systems of courts (each with different judges) and two bodies of rules—law and equity—existed concurrently. A plaintiff wanting a legal remedy brought an **action at law** in a court of law; a plaintiff wanting some other relief brought an **action in equity** in an equity court.

The two primary remedies that a court of equity could grant were the **injunction** and the **decree of specific performance.**

The Injunction: If a plaintiff brought an action in a king's court asking that the defendant be ordered to refrain from doing a particular act, his request had to be denied. For example: if P asked the court to order D to stop grazing cattle on land belonging to P, the court could only grant damages for the past injury done to the land; it did not have the power to prevent such trespasses in the future. In such a case, P's only hope was that the chancellor, whose power to grant relief was not so circumscribed, would feel that his request was justified and would order the defendant to stop performing the wrongful act—a order that today is called the *injunction*. (In later years, as courts of equity became established, actions for injunctive relief were commenced directly in those courts.)

The Decree of Specific Performance: The foregoing is also applicable to cases in which a plaintiff was asking for a *decree of specific performance*—an order commanding the defendant to live up to the terms of a contract made with the plaintiff. Courts of law could not do this; all they could do was order the defendant to pay the plaintiff a sum of money (damages) to compensate the plaintiff for losses suffered as a result of the breach of contract. Courts of equity, on the other hand, were empowered to issue a decree of specific performance when they felt that awarding damages would be an inadequate remedy—that is, in those exceptional situations where a sum of money would not, in their opinion, adequately recompense the plaintiff

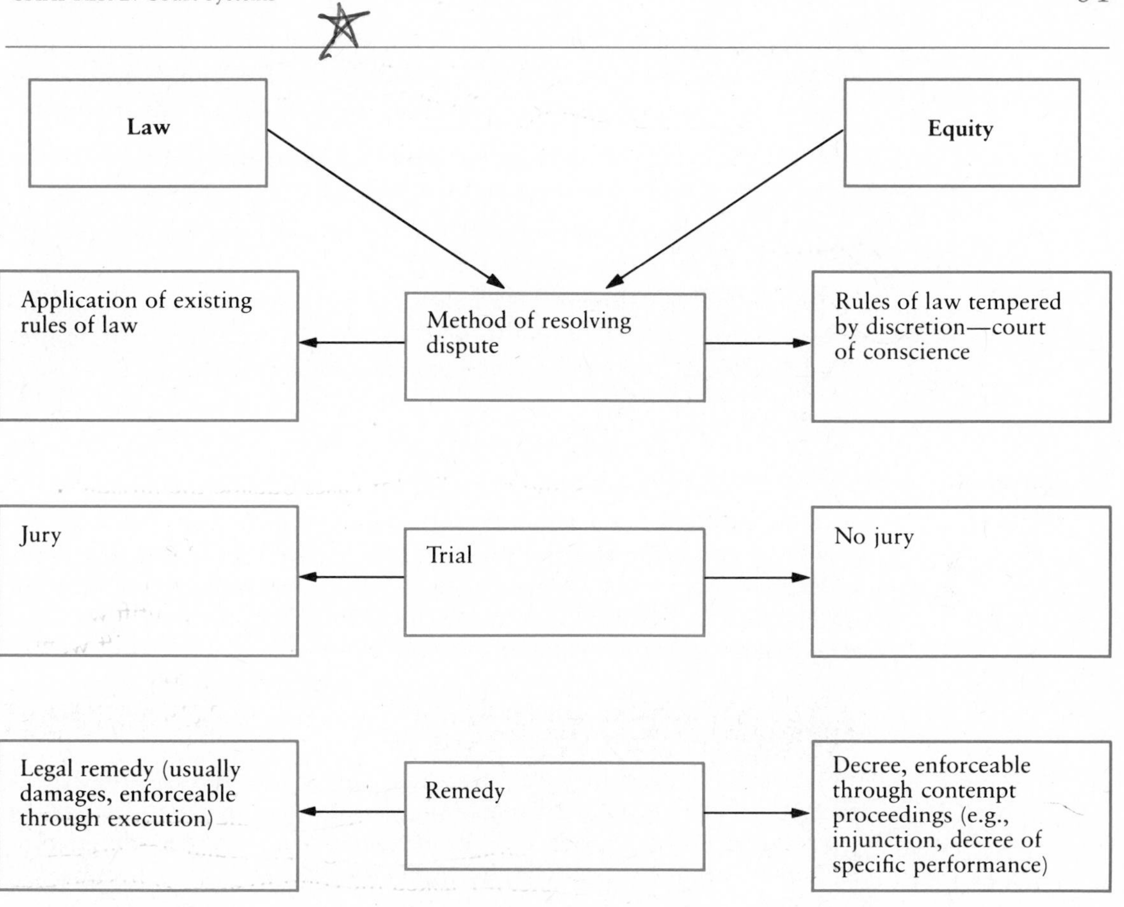

Figure 2.3 Major Differences in Law and Equity

for the loss of services promised by the defendant or for the property the defendant had contracted to convey. (The awarding of damages, however, is the normal remedy in breach of contract suits. Only in exceptional cases, involving highly unique services or property, is specific performance granted.)[11]

The Present Scene

While the distinction between legal and equitable remedies as diagrammed in Figure 2.3 persists today, there has been a "fusion" of law and equity courts in virtually all states. This means that courts of law and equity, as

[11] Other common equitable actions, in addition to those asking for injunctions and decrees of specific performance, are (1) divorce actions, (2) mortgage foreclosure suits, and (3) actions for an accounting, brought by one member of a partnership against another.

such, have been eliminated. Instead, the basic trial courts in the state and federal systems are empowered to hear both legal and equitable actions.

Today, the basic distinctions between the two kinds of actions are these:

1. Whether an action is one at law or in equity depends solely upon the *nature of the remedy* that the plaintiff is seeking.

2. There is *no jury* in an equitable action. Questions of both fact and law are decided by the court—the trial judge.

3. Proceedings in equitable actions are *less formal* than those at law, particularly in regard to the order in which witnesses' testimony can be presented and the determination of admissibility of their evidence.

Resolution of Disputes

Out-of-Court Settlements

Most disputes are settled without resort to the courts. In many instances the sums involved are too small to justify taking legal action, and in others the parties may come to a satisfactory compromise. And, even where substantial amounts are involved, one of the parties may choose to forgo a legal remedy simply to preserve the other's goodwill.

Arbitration Agreements

Another method of settling a dispute is through an **arbitration agreement**, a procedure that is being used increasingly in the business world today. In these agreements, the parties to a dispute agree that it will be submitted to one or more arbitrators of their choice and that the arbitrator's decision will be binding.

Compared to litigation, voluntary arbitration has several advantages: (1) disputes can be settled more quickly, (2) arbitrators can be chosen who have special expertise in the particular business practices that are the subject of the controversy, (3) the proceedings are relatively informal, and (4) the cost is ordinarily less than if the cases go to court.

Generally, there are two kinds of arbitration agreements: agreements to submit and submission agreements. *Agreements to submit* are usually part of a larger contract (such as a collective bargaining agreement) and provide that future disputes arising out of the contract will be submitted to arbitration. *Submission agreements* are agreements to submit existing disputes to arbitration.

While the legal validity of arbitration agreements used to be subject to considerable doubt, most of this has been resolved. A federal statute, for example, now makes such written agreements involving interstate commerce "valid, irrevocable, and enforceable, save on such grounds as exist at law or in equity for the revocation of any contract." Many states also have arbitration statutes; but because these vary in detail, the relevant statute of a state should be examined before any agreement of arbitration is entered into.

Mediation

Mediation is a method of resolving a dispute by bringing in a third party, the *mediator*, whose role is largely to narrow the issues, facilitate communication between the parties, and suggest possible compromises. Mediation thus differs from arbitration largely in the fact that while a mediator may make recommendations at various stages of the negotiations, he or she cannot impose a final settlement that is binding upon the parties.

While mediation can be useful in virtually any kind of dispute, it has traditionally been used most often in settling of international disputes and, in the United States, in the labor-management area. In that regard, mention should be made of the Federal Mediation and Conciliation Service, a federal agency whose primary role is to facilitate the negotiation of collective bargaining agreements between unions and companies in interstate commerce.

Recent Developments

In recent years several additional methods of dispute resolution have been increasingly successful. Two of these merit special mention.

The *Magnusson-Moss Warranty Act*, a federal statute passed in 1975, facilitates the settlement of disputes between the buyers of *consumer products*—such as television sets and automobiles—and their manufacturers. It does this, first, by encouraging manufacturers to set up "informal dispute settlement mechanisms" within their companies to handle customer complaints. Where a manufacturer has created such an office, consumers must use the informal procedures afforded by that office in order to settle their disputes before they can resort to court action. Secondly, where the informal procedures prove unsuccessful, both the Federal Trade Commission and the attorney general may seek injunctions against any manufacturer who has been found to violate any provision of the act.

The newest and most innovative method for settling commercial disputes is a technique known as the *minitrial*. In this process, lawyers for corporations in a dispute present summaries of their respective companies' positions to a "neutral advisor" (with top executives of the firms usually present). The basic purpose of the advisor is to narrow the issues and to advise the parties how a court would probably rule on them in the event of litigation. After the minitrial, the executives meet (without the presence of their lawyers) in an effort to negotiate a settlement—an effort that has proven to be successful in a high percentage of cases.

A chief advantage of the minitrial is the speed with which disputes are settled, with the resultant cost savings to the parties; the typical minitrial is completed the same day it begins. Additionally, the process exposes executives of each company to the claims of its antagonist, and also gives the executives a greater hand in reaching a settlement than if the case had gone to trial. One of the most publicized controversies involving use of the minitrial was a three-way dispute between the National Aeronautics and Space Administration (NASA), a consortium of companies called the Space Communications Company (a prime contractor for construction of a $1.5 billion satellite system for NASA), and TRW, Inc., a prime subcontractor on the project, who contended it was entitled to an additional $100 million for the construction of certain components of the system. After three years of pretrial litigation—with no settlement yet in sight—the parties reached an agreement after a minitrial that lasted less than a month (with an estimated savings of over $1 million in additional legal fees).

Settlement by Litigation

Despite increasing use of the various dispute-resolution processes outlined above, the fact remains that thousands of cases *are* initiated in the courts every year. It is only through the adjudication of these controversies by the courts that the implementation of the rules of law really takes place.[12]

While the trial and appellate courts are both concerned with the same general goal, the orderly settling of legal disputes, their basic responsibilities differ to a significant degree. As was noted earlier, the trial courts must decide disputed questions of fact and then select the rules of law applicable thereto.[13] The appellate courts, by contrast, are concerned exclusively with settling questions of law. They decide whether the rulings of the trial court, about which the appellant is complaining, were correct. With these observations before us, we will now examine the processes by which the two levels of courts perform their duties.

The Trial Courts: Pretrial Proceedings

Pretrial proceedings consist of two stages, the *pleading stage* and the *discovery stage*. We now look at each of these steps briefly.

The Pleading Stage

The typical suit is commenced by the plaintiff, through an attorney, filing a **complaint** (or petition) with the court having jurisdiction of the case. At the same time, the plaintiff asks the court to issue a summons to the defendant, notifying that person that a complaint is on file.[14] The defendant then has a

---

[12] Again, a reminder that the settlement of controversies by *administrative agencies* is examined in Chapter 6.

[13] While the rulings of the trial courts are appealable, the importance of their work can hardly be overstated. It is on their determination of the facts that the precise legal issues are framed, and most of their decisions are final. (That is, a majority of the judgments of the trial courts are not, in fact, appealed.)

[14] In the usual actions, actions *in personam*, the officer delivering the summons (such as a deputy sheriff) must either serve the summons on the defendant personally or leave it with some adult at the defendant's residence.

prescribed period of time in which to file a response of some sort, normally an **answer**, to the complaint. After that has been done, the plaintiff can file a *reply* to the answer. The complaint, answer, and reply make up the *pleadings* of a case, the main purpose of which is to permit the court and the parties to ascertain the actual points in issue.

The Complaint: The complaint briefly sets forth the plaintiff's version of the facts and ends with a "prayer" (request) for a certain remedy based on those facts. Its primary purpose is to notify the defendant that a claim is being asserted against him or her based on certain *allegations* of fact.

The Answer: The defendant usually responds to the complaint by filing an *answer* (or, in circumstances to be noted later, a "motion to dismiss"). In the typical case the defendant will disagree with one or more allegations of fact set forth in the complaint, and the answer will indicate the specific points of disagreement. For example, three allegations in a complaint growing out of an automobile accident may be (1) that the defendant was the driver of a car that collided with the plaintiff's on a certain date, (2) that defendant's car was to the left of the center line at the time of impact, and (3) that defendant was driving negligently at the time. Depending upon the particular circumstances, the defendant might deny the first allegation (on which the others are obviously based), claiming that he was merely a passenger in the car, which was being driven by someone else. Or the defendant might admit allegations (1) and (2) but deny allegation (3), claiming that he was directed to drive left of center by a police officer who was investigating a prior accident at the scene. In either event, the answer would raise *questions of fact*, which would have to be settled at the trial.

The answer also permits the defendant to raise *affirmative defenses*—legal points that will absolve the defendant of liability even if his or her version of the facts is proven wrong. For example, the defendant in the above case may deny that he was driving negligently, and, in addition, may allege that plaintiff was himself guilty of contributory negligence; if this is true, it will free defendant of liability under the law of most states even if it is later established in the trial court that he was driving in a negligent manner at the time of the accident.

Motion to Dismiss: If a defendant contends that he or she is not legally liable even if the plaintiff's allegations of fact are true, defendant will file a *motion to dismiss* instead of an answer. Technically this is called a "motion to dismiss for the reason that the complaint states no cause of action": the complaint fails to state a legally recognizable claim. For example, if the D Company, a retailer, cut down two trees in front of its place of business in spite of protests from P, a neighboring retailer, and if P sued the D Company to recover damages, the D Company might well file such a motion in response to P's complaint. In such a case, assuming that the felling of the trees did not violate any municipal ordinance or rule of the local planning commission, the D Company had a perfect right to remove the trees; thus the motion to dismiss will be "sustained" by the court and the suit will be ended at that point. (A trial court's ruling on such a motion, however, may always be appealed to a higher court. If such court rules that a motion to dismiss should have been overruled rather than sustained, then the case will be sent back to the trial court for further proceedings.)[15]

Two further points should be noted.

1. By filing a motion to dismiss on the ground that no cause of action is stated, the defendant does not admit that the plaintiff's version of the facts is correct. Rather, he is simply saying that even if the facts are as stated, plaintiff has no basis under the law for bringing the suit. Thus, if the motion is overruled, the defendant is permitted to raise questions of fact during the trial.

2. Such motions always raise a question of law: Assuming that the facts are as alleged in the complaint, does plaintiff have a cause of action? If the trial judge says no, the motion to dismiss is granted and that ends matters, as far as proceedings in the trial court are concerned. On the other hand, if the trial judge rules that the complaint *does* state a cause of action, the motion is overruled and the defendant must file an answer. The case then continues in the trial court.

The Reply: If the defendant raises new matter—additional facts—in his answer, then the plaintiff must file a reply. In this pleading plaintiff will either deny or admit the new facts alleged in the answer. (In some cases, after all the pleadings and supporting documents have been filed, if the court concludes that neither the facts nor inferences that can be drawn from those facts are in dispute, the court may enter a **summary judgment** in favor of the one party or the other, depending upon the law that is applicable to such facts. Ordinarily, however, there *are* disputed questions of fact and any request for a summary judgment is refused; in such instance the case then proceeds to trial.)

The Discovery Stage

In early years, cases moved directly from the pleading stage to the trial stage. This meant that each party, going into the trial, had little information as to the specific evidence that the other party would rely on in presenting his case. Trial proceedings, as a result, often became what was commonly de-

[15] The terminology used in referring to this particular type of "motion to dismiss" follows the rules of civil procedure that have, in recent years, been adopted by many states. The earlier name for this same pleading device—the **demurrer**—continues to be used in a number of states, however. In such states, what has been said here in regard to the motion to dismiss applies with equal force to the demurrer.

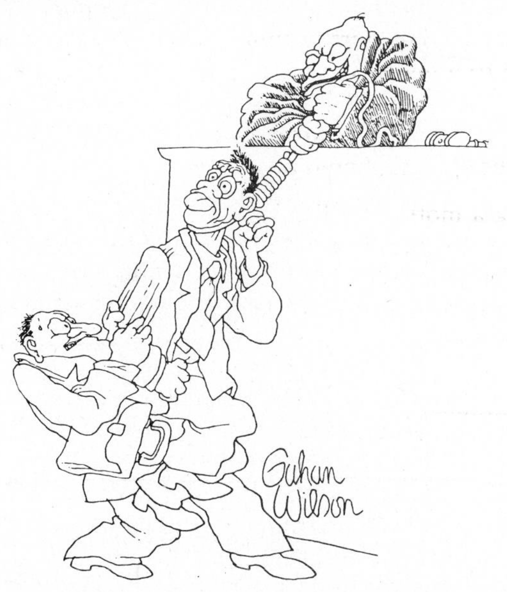

A lawyer must forcefully protect the rights of the client.

Source: Reprinted by permission of The Putnam Publishing Group, from . . . AND THEN WE'LL GET HIM! by Gahan Wilson. Copyright © 1978 by Gahan Wilson.

scribed as a "cat and mouse" game, with the parties often bringing in evidence that surprised their opponents.

The undesirability of these proceedings was finally perceived by lawyers and judges, with the result that the Federal Rules of Civil Procedure, adopted in 1938, provided means (called "discovery proceedings") by which much of the evidence that each party was going to rely on in proving his or her version of the facts would be fully disclosed to the other party before the case came on for trial. The most common discovery tools recognized by these federal rules, which have now been essentially adopted by the states, are *depositions, interrogatories,* and *requests for production of documents.*

A deposition is testimony of a witness that is taken outside of court. Such testimony is given under oath, and both parties to the case must be notified so that they can be present when the testimony is given, and thus have the opportunity to cross-examine the witness.

Interrogatories are written questions submitted by one party to the other, which he or she must answer under oath. Use of this device is a primary way by which the questioning party may gain access to evidence that otherwise would be solely in the possession of his adversary.

A demand for documents permits a party to gain access to those kinds of evidence—such as business records, letters, and hospital bills—which are in the possession of the other party. Under modern rules of civil procedure the party seeking the documents has the right to possess them for the purposes of inspection and reproduction.

The Trial Courts: Trial Proceedings

The Trial Stage

Unless a controversy is settled by a judgment on the pleadings (such as the granting of a motion to dismiss), or unless the parties settle out of court, a case will eventually come on for trial. There a jury may be impaneled, evidence presented, a verdict returned, and a judgment entered in favor of one of the parties.

Impaneling a Jury: In any civil action in which the plaintiff is asking for a remedy at law, questions of fact are often resolved by a jury. However, a jury can be "waived" (dispensed with) if this is agreeable to both parties. In such instances the court decides questions of both fact and law. While waiver of a jury is increasingly common in civil actions today, there are still many actions where at least one of the parties demands a jury trial. The remainder of this discussion thus assumes the presence of a jury.

The names of prospective jurors are drawn from a list of those who have been selected for possible duty during the term. Each prospective juror is questioned by the attorneys in an effort to make sure that the jury will be as impartial as possible. If questioning indicates that a particular person would probably not be capable of such impartiality, he or she can be **challenged for cause**. Prospective jurors can be challenged, for example, if it is shown that they have a close friendship with one of the parties or the party's attorney, a financial interest in the case, or a bias resulting from any other aspect of the action. Any prospective juror disqualified for cause is excused, and another takes his or her place and is questioned in like fashion. This preliminary examination of prospective jurors is called the ***voir dire*** examination.

When there are no more challenges for cause, the attorney for each party has a limited number of **peremptory challenges.** Such challenges permit the attorney to have a juror removed arbitrarily, without assigning a reason for doing so. Once the number of prospective jurors who have survived both kinds of challenges reaches the number required by law to hear the case, they are sworn in and the case proceeds. (Traditionally the number of jurors has been twelve, but in recent years many states have reduced the number to eight, or even fewer, in civil actions.)

Order of Presentation of Proof: After the opening statements, the case is presented by the plaintiff, who has the **burden of proof** (the duty to prove the facts alleged in the complaint). The plaintiff attempts to meet this burden by calling witnesses whose testimony supports his or her version of the facts.

After each of the plaintiff's witnesses is examined by the plaintiff's attorney ("direct examination"), the defendant's attorney can "cross-examine" the witness for the purpose of discrediting the person's testimony on as many points as possible. For example, a cross-examination might divulge (1) that pertinent facts in the direct examination were omitted, (2) that a witness's powers of observation were poor, or (3) that the witness stood to benefit financially if the plaintiff won a judgment.

The Rules of Evidence: Before proceeding to the next steps in the trial of a case, a brief mention of *evidence* is necessary. As a practical matter, one of the most crucial steps in a lawsuit is the establishment of the facts—a final determination as to what actually happened. An early English judge said, "Without a known fact, it is impossible to know the law on that fact."[16] And unless a litigant can convince the jury that his or her version of the facts is correct, the case may very well collapse at the outset.

Because the findings of fact play such an important role in the outcome of a case, it is imperative that the jury determine the facts on the basis of the most reliable testimony possible—testimony that is relevant, unbiased, and based on direct observations of the witnesses. *The primary purpose of the rules of evidence is to exclude testimony that lacks these characteristics.* (With an exception to be noted later, the jury's findings of fact are conclusive. This means that an appellate court, in determining the propriety of a rule of law applied by a lower court, must normally accept the jury's version of the facts as being correct.)

While the rules of evidence are so numerous and so complex as to preclude any balanced survey of the subject here, it is possible to examine briefly three of the most common kinds of testimony that the rules ordinarily remove from the jury's consideration—assuming that timely objection to such testimony is made by counsel during the trial proceedings. That is, if improper testimony is elicited from a witness by the attorney for one of the parties, and the opposing counsel does *not* make a formal challenge by "objecting" to it at that time, such testimony is normally permitted to become part of the record.[17]

Irrelevant Testimony: If a witness is asked a question that can have no possible bearing on the facts in issue, the opposing counsel may enter an objection on the basis that the answer would be "irrelevant." In a personal injury suit, for example, such matters as the defendant's religious beliefs, or the

[16] C. J. Vaughan, *Bushel's Case*, Jones (T.), 1670.

[17] Actions brought in the federal courts are governed by the Federal Rules of Evidence which Congress adopted in 1975. The rules of evidence that are applicable to actions in state courts are adopted by the various state supreme courts, and the rules vary somewhat from state to state. However, the federal rules are generally acknowledged as representing the most "modern view" of evidentiary rules and are increasingly being adopted by the state courts.

fact that he was convicted of a charge of negligent driving several years earlier, would have no bearing on the instant case. Objections to such testimony would be "sustained" by the court. And, in a land condemnation suit brought by a state against the corporation that owns the land (where the primary issue is the present value of the property being taken), testimony by the state as to the price that the corporation paid for the land ten years earlier would be irrelevant. Similarly, in the same kind of suit, the amount of insurance carried by the corporation on buildings on the land is also ruled by the courts to be irrelevant, because it is common knowledge that buildings are often either underinsured or overinsured.

Hearsay: It is essential that the jury have before it direct evidence—testimony based on the witnesses' *personal knowledge and observation* of facts and circumstances surrounding the issues being litigated. Evidence not of this type is called "hearsay" and is usually excluded. Thus if an issue in a particular case is whether a trucker delivered a shipment of goods to the X Company on a certain day, witness W (a jogger in the vicinity at the time) could testify that he saw packages being unloaded from a truck on the day in question. But neither W nor any other witness would be allowed to testify that he was *told by a third party* (Z), that Z saw goods being unloaded on the day in question.[18]

There are, however, many exceptions to the hearsay rule; that is, many admissions of out-of-court statements where experience has shown the statements to be generally reliable, and where there is a "necessity" for admission of the statement. For example, *business records* may usually be introduced in evidence by the person having custody of such records if the record was made "in the usual course of business," and if the record was made at or near the time of the act or transaction which it records.

Opinion: Sometimes a witness is asked for, or volunteers, information about a matter he or she believes to be true but of which the person actually has no personal knowledge. Such testimony, calling for the *opinion* of the witness, is normally excluded. For example, a witness could testify that the defendant's car was weaving back and forth on a highway, but if he further testified—on the basis of that observation alone—that the defendant was "obviously drunk," a motion to strike that part of the testimony would be sustained. Not only does the witness lack personal knowledge as to the *cause* of the defendant's erratic behavior, but the statement also constitutes a "conclusion of fact"—an inference that the jury, rather than a witness, is to draw from the evidence presented.

[18] Hearsay is essentially defined as any assertion (made either orally or in writing) by a person who is not in court—a person who is not subject to cross-examination—which assertion is offered to prove the fact asserted. Thus the hearsay rule excludes many kinds of offered testimony in addition to what witnesses were told by others, such as statements in newspapers and books (unless they are "learned treatises") and those made by TV newscasters.

Opinion testimony is not always excluded. On technical matters that lie outside the knowledge of ordinary jurors it is frequently necessary that qualified experts be permitted to state their opinions as an aid to the jury's determination of the probable facts. Thus a physician may give an opinion as to the cause of a death or an engineer as to the cause of a bridge collapsing. And, additionally, courts have discretion to permit opinions of lay witnesses (nonexperts) on a number of issues—the speed of a car or a third party's emotions at a particular time, for instance.

A word about "presumptions": Experience has shown that the existence of some facts is, in the ordinary course of events, so likely to be attended by other facts that a jury, upon proof of the first fact or set of facts, can justifiably assume that such other facts also exist, even though direct proof of them is lacking. For example, it is common knowledge that a very high percentage of U.S. mail actually reaches the addressee; hence, once it is proven that X in fact mailed a letter to Y, the jury can reasonably infer (or presume) that the letter was actually delivered to Y's address (in the absence of convincing evidence to the contrary). Thus it is not always necessary that each and every fact in issue be established by the introduction of direct evidence.

Motion for a Directed Verdict: After all the plaintiff's evidence has been presented, it is likely that the defendant's attorney will make a motion for a **directed verdict**. By doing so, the attorney is contending that plaintiff has failed to prove his or her case—that is, either plaintiff has failed to introduce evidence tending to prove one or more allegations of fact necessary to the case or the evidence on such points was too weak to present a jury question. Normally the plaintiff's evidence is not this defective, and the motion is denied. The defendant's attorney then presents his or her witnesses, and each is cross-examined by the plaintiff's attorney.

After all the evidence is in, both parties may make motions for a directed verdict, each claiming that the evidence he or she has presented is so conclusive that the court should find the facts in his or her favor *as a matter of law*. Normally the evidence is not that conclusive; the motions are thus denied and the questions of fact left to the jury.

A Jury Question: In determining whether the evidence justifies the granting of a motion for a directed verdict, one rule of thumb is usually followed. If the court is of the opinion, from the evidence presented, that "reasonable minds could not differ" as to the facts, then—and only then—the court can grant a motion for a directed verdict. Otherwise, as is normally the case, the question must be left to the jury.

The case of *U.S. v. Douglas Aircraft Co.* is typical of those in which a trial judge must decide whether he or she may make a ruling as to a particular fact as a matter of law.[19] In that suit, the U.S. sought to recover for damage

---

[19] 169 F.2d 755 (1948).

done to a government plane parked at a Los Angeles airport when it was struck by a taxiing Douglas plane. After all the evidence was in, the U.S. asked the court to rule as a matter of law that the Douglas pilot was guilty of negligence. The trial court refused, and submitted the question to the jury, instead, which found that the Douglas pilot was *not* negligent under the circumstances. On appeal by the U.S., the higher court ruled that the issue of negligence was properly left to the jury (reasonable minds could differ on the question) in view of the fact the evidence showed (1) that the Douglas pilot zigzagged his plane while taxiing, in order to enlarge his field of vision, and (2) that the government plane was difficult to see because it was camouflaged in brown tones, it was parked against a ridge of brown hills, and the field was covered with haze at the time of the collision.

Instructions: When a case is submitted to the jury, the court instructs it about the law applicable to the various findings of fact which it might make. For example, the judge might tell the jury: "If you find that defendant flatly told plaintiff he was not going to perform his contract with plaintiff, then this is a breach of contract for which defendant will be liable in damages; but if you find that defendant's statement was more in the nature of a request for additional time within which to perform, indicating a willingness to perform as contracted in the event the request was rejected, this will not constitute a breach of contract on defendant's part."

The next case shows how extremely important it is that the trial court's instructions spell out the obligations and rights of both parties, fully and completely, and thus adequately reflect all of the rules of law that are applicable to the controversy.

Pearce v. Motel 6, Inc.
Court of Appeals of Washington, Division 2
Wash.App., 624 P.2d 215 (1981)

This was a negligence action brought by Flo Pearce against Motel 6, Inc., the owner and operator of the national chain of motels of that name.

On July 5, 1976, Mrs. Pearce and her husband checked into defendant's motel at Fife, Washington, on the outskirts of Tacoma, while on vacation from their home in California. That evening Mrs. Pearce was injured when she slipped and fell as she entered the shower stall in the bathroom of her motel room. Mrs. Pearce thereafter brought this action against the defendant corporation to recover damages.

Plaintiff's primary allegation was that defendant was negligent in not furnishing mats or by not applying some form of nonskid surface preparation to its shower floor pans.

Testimony at the trial indicated that defendant had not supervised construction of the motel, but had acquired it after construction had been completed. Testimony also showed that the shower stalls used were common to those found on the market at the time that the Fife facility was constructed.

An expert witness called by plaintiff testified that the stalls had been cleaned and maintained in such a manner that the fiberglass and Gel-Coat finish had retained the same shine, smoothness, and luster as the product had possessed when originally installed. The expert further testified, however, that the fiberglass industry since that time had improved its methods of constructing fiberglass shower stalls, and that the newer stall floors were more slip resistant than the earlier ones. Evidence was also produced which indicated that at the time of the accident at least two surface preparations were on the market which could have been applied to the early model ("smooth surface") pans to achieve a degree of slip resistance similar to that of the newer shower stalls, and that defendant had not used either of these products.

In addition to the two shower floor preparations, the plaintiff's expert testified to a comparison he had made between the Fife unit's shower stall and a shower stall found in a new Motel 6 unit in Tumwater, Washington (a facility that, unlike the Fife facility, was built under the defendant's supervision). The gist of that testimony was that the shower stalls in the newer Tumwater motel, having been built by the use of the more modern techniques, were considerably more slip resistant than those at Fife. This comparison was apparently made for the purpose of showing that defendant was aware of both the dangers of and alternatives to the smooth surface shower floors.

The defendant's evidence was, essentially, that no similar accidents had occurred during the five years that it had owned the Fife facility, and that it had not received any complaints about the safety of the shower stalls during that time.

The jury found defendant guilty of negligence under instructions appearing in the higher court's opinion, and returned a verdict in favor of plaintiff for $35,000. The court accordingly entered judgment for plaintiff in that amount.

On appeal, defendant made two basic arguments: (1) that plaintiff's evidence of negligence was so weak that it should not have been submitted to the jury, and (2) that the trial court's instruction as to the duties owed by a motel to its guests was erroneous.

Reed, Chief Judge:

. . . We have serious misgivings about the relevance of much of plaintiff's evidence. Plaintiff's expert seemed to [base] his opinion primarily upon his comparison of the relative safety of the Fife and Tumwater facilities. It is, of course, not enough to say that shower A is more or less dangerous than shower B. No evidence was offered that the Fife unit did not meet industry standards. However, plaintiff described the shower pan surface as "slick as ice," and plaintiff's expert characterized it as constituting a "significant hazard potential for a slip and fall." [Thus,] we believe the evidence, while not strong, was enough to create a jury issue as to defendant's awareness of the condition and the relatively inexpensive means for correcting it. . . .

[The court then discussed the question as to the correctness of the trial judge's instruction on negligence as follows]:

[The] trial court gave, as its only instruction defining the duty or duties owed by defendant to plaintiff, the following:

The operator of a motel owes to a person who has an express or implied invitation to come upon the premises in connection with that business, a duty to exercise ordinary care for his safety. This includes the exercise of ordinary care to maintain in a reasonably safe condition those portions of the premises which such person is expressly or impliedly invited to use or which he might reasonably be expected to use.

The trial court refused, however, to give defendant's proposed instruction which read as follows:

A hotel/motel operator is liable for physical harm caused to its guests by a condition of the premises if, but only if, it
(a) knows or by the exercise of reasonable care would discover the condition and should realize that it involves an unreasonable risk of harm to such guests, and
(b) should expect that they will not discover or realize the danger, or will fail to protect themselves against it, and
(c) fails to exercise reasonable care to protect them against the danger.

As applied to plaintiff's basic theory that the shower as originally constructed and maintained was a dangerous instrumentality which defendant could have rendered safe by utilizing methods currently available, the proposed instruction was a correct statement of the law governing the case. The failure to give the instruction precluded defendant from meaningfully presenting its case and from arguing its theories of defense to the jury and consequently of a fair trial. In [a prior case], this court said:

Basic in the law of negligence is the tenet that the duty to use care is predicated upon knowledge of danger, and the care which must be used in any particular situation is in proportion to the actor's knowledge . . . of the danger to another in the act to be performed. . . .
Generally speaking, the possessor of land is liable for injuries to a business visitor caused by a condition encountered on the premises only if he (a) knows or should have known of such condition and that it involved an unreasonable risk; (b) has no reason to believe that the visitor will discover the condition or realize the risk; and (c) fails to make the condition reasonably safe or to warn the visitor so that the latter may avoid harm.

Plaintiff argues that defendant was entitled to no more than the general instruction which was given and was able effectively to argue its defenses to the jury. We do not agree. First, nowhere was the jury told that before it could find defendant had breached its duty of due care to plaintiff, it must find that *defendant knew or should have known* the shower facility presented *an unreasonable risk of harm*. Second, nowhere was the jury advised that *defendant's duty was tempered by what it could reasonably expect its guests would perceive for themselves*, e.g., that fiberglass shower floors become slippery when wet. [Emphasis added.] . . . In short, the failure to give defendant's proposed instruction virtually rendered defendant [liable] upon a finding only that the shower fixture was unreasonably dangerous, [even if plaintiff knew or should have been aware of the danger]. . . .

Reversed and remanded for a new trial.

★ ★ ★

After the Verdict: After the jury has returned its verdict, the court enters a judgment in conformity with it. Thereafter, as we have seen, the party against whom the judgment was entered may move for a new trial, alleging that certain errors occurred. If this motion is overruled by the trial court, the loser can then appeal the judgment to a higher court.

There is also one other possibility. After a verdict has been returned, the losing party may ask the court to disregard the verdict and enter a judgment in his or her favor; this is done by making a motion for **judgment notwithstanding the verdict,** often called a judgement n.o.v. If the court feels that reasonable people could have reached a verdict *only* in favor of the party who has made the motion, rather than the verdict which was actually returned, it will grant the motion. (Such a motion is granted only in exceptional circumstances, and the correctness of such a ruling can be appealed by the party against whom the judgment is entered.)

The Appellate Courts

An Overview

The work of the higher courts in ruling on appeals differs considerably from that of the trial courts.[20] In the first place, appellate courts are concerned only with *questions of law*—that is, whether the rulings of the trial court, of which the appellant complains, were legally correct. Second, intermediate appellate courts normally are comprised of three or more judges, while the highest court in a state usually has five or seven justices. This obviously brings to bear *more judicial experience* on the points in issue than can be afforded by the single trial judge. Third, since only questions of law are in issue, there is *no reintroduction of evidence and thus no jury*. The questions of law are settled on the basis of the record in the lower court, together with consideration of the opposing parties' briefs (written arguments) and oral arguments as to the correctness of the rulings in question. As a result, unlike the rulings of the trial court, which must be made during "the heat of battle," the decisions of the appellate courts can be made in a detached and unhurried manner.

---

[20] All appellate courts have *some* "original jurisdiction"; that is, certain exceptional cases can be properly commenced in them. However, we are not here concerned with the work of the appellate courts in such situations.

Questions of Law

Many different kinds of "questions of law" are presented by the cases in the remainder of this text. The most common of these questions arises where the appellant is claiming that errors were made by the trial court in (1) admitting or excluding evidence during the trial, (2) ruling on motions, particularly on motions for a directed verdict, (3) stating the law in instructions to the jury (as indicated in the *Motel 6* case), and (4) interpreting state or federal statutes.

Effect of Error

If the appellate court is of the opinion that an alleged error did occur and that it conceivably could have affected the outcome of the case, the lower court's judgment will be reversed (set aside), and normally the case will be *remanded* (sent back) to the trial court for a new trial. The reason for the remanding is that most errors are of such a nature that the higher court cannot be positive the verdict or judgment would have gone for the other party had the error not occurred. For example, if it were determined that the trial court erred in admitting hearsay testimony of one witness, it is possible that the verdict and judgment would still have been entered for the same party who won in the lower court even if the testimony had been excluded.

Some judgments, however, are reversed outright, with no further proceedings being necessary. This is particularly true where the rule of law that the trial court has applied to the established facts is simply contrary to the law then existing in that state. In such a situation the appellate court will apply the correct rule of law and enter final judgment accordingly.

Setting Aside a Verdict

In most cases each party is able to introduce some evidence tending to prove that his or her version of the facts is correct, and it is for the jury (or the court, in the absence of a jury) to determine which testimony is the more convincing. As we have seen, the appellate courts are normally bound by the jury's verdict; that is, they must accept the jury's version of the facts *with one major exception.*

To guard against the possibility that a jury will make a finding of fact that is totally unwarranted, an appellant can always contend that one or more findings of fact were "unsupported by the evidence." This presents an additional *question of law* for the appellate court, and the court can reverse the judgment (necessitating a new trial) if it agrees with the appellant's contention. If a jury makes a finding of fact that is unsupported by any evidence, the verdict obviously can be set aside. Such an instance, however, occurs but rarely.

Much more common are situations where one party introduces substantial evidence tending to prove the existence of a certain fact, and the other party introduces some, but perhaps weaker, evidence to the contrary. If the jury bases its verdict on the lesser or weaker evidence, the party whose evidence was ignored will very likely ask the appellate court to set the verdict aside on the general ground that it is contrary to the evidence.

In the great majority of such appeals, the higher courts let the verdicts stand. Two of the more important reasons for this are (1) the jury, not the higher court, actually observed the demeanor of the witnesses during their testimony, and are thus more qualified to evaluate the testimony, and (2) the trial judge, who also observed the witnesses, would probably have set the verdict aside had he or she believed that it was not sufficiently supported by the evidence.

Because of these considerations, then, the courts of many states permit the verdict to stand as long as there is "any credible (believable) evidence to support it," or, in other states, as long as the evidence is "not inherently improbable or inherently unbelievable." Under these rules, a verdict supported by any credible evidence will probably not be set aside even if the evidence is "vague, weak, or unsatisfactory."

Some states follow a different rule: a verdict can be set aside if it is "not supported by the preponderance or weight of the evidence." Even under this view, however, the setting aside of a verdict is exceptional because of what is meant by **weight** and **preponderance**. Testimony of just one witness can constitute the weight or preponderance of the evidence if the testimony is unbiased, positive, and persuasive, even though others testify to the contrary. For example, statements like the following frequently appear in court decisions: "The 'preponderance' of the evidence is not determined by the number of witnesses, but by the greater *weight of the evidence*, which does not necessarily mean the greater number of witnesses, but [rather upon the witnesses'] opportunity for knowledge, information possessed, and [their] manner of testifying. . . ."[21]

The following case is typical of those presenting the "insufficient evidence" claim.

Ford Motor Credit Company v. Jackson
Court of Civil Appeals of Alabama
347 So.2d 992 (1977)

Willie Jackson, a laborer for a pecan company, bought a new Mercury Marquis automobile from a Pensacola, Alabama, dealership in July of 1974. At that time he was 56 years old, uneducated, unable to read, and able to write only his name.

The price of the car was approximately $8,500, and as a down payment Jackson paid $300 cash and traded in a 1972 car for which he received a $1,736 credit. The purchase agreement provided that he would pay the balance of the purchase price in 36 monthly installments of $230.75. After the sale, the dealer assigned the agreement to Ford Motor Credit Company (Ford).

[21] *Garver v. Garver*, 121 P. 165 (1912).

In March of 1975 a Ford representative—wearing a badge and carrying a gun—repossessed the automobile from Jackson because he was allegedly behind in his payments. Jackson then brought this action in early 1976 to recover damages for "wrongful conversion," claiming that he was not behind in his payments and that Ford did not, therefore, have the right to retake the automobile.[a]

Prior to the trial, Jackson signed a deposition in which he testified that he had made "five or six payments" on the automobile. He further stated that he was unable to remember if he had made the first payment in July or August of 1974; that payments were due on the 15th of the month; and that he didn't have any receipts for his payments because he "had gotten upset after the car was taken and had thrown everything away."

At the trial Jackson testified that he had made the first payment on July 15, and that he made his payments by certified check or money order. He also produced receipts for three of his payments, and said that other receipts were in the car when it was repossessed. He also testified that he "knew" he had sent eight payments, and that "I probably sent nine." Jackson also admitted that the payment he made in February, 1975, was late. (It was this payment which Ford refused to accept and which triggered the repossession.)

Ford's evidence was "directly opposed" to Jackson's. Ford's collection supervisor testified that Jackson made only five payments, and that the money order for the sixth payment was not accepted because of "the delinquency of his account." His testimony was supported by records maintained by his department.

The jury returned a verdict for Jackson in the amount of $2,536. Ford, contending that the verdict was not supported by the evidence, then made a motion for a "judgment notwithstanding the verdict," or, in the alternative, for a new trial. The trial court denied this motion, and Ford appealed.

Holmes, Judge:

. . . Alabama law with regard to the granting of a motion for judgment notwithstanding the verdict is clear. The motion should not be granted if there is any conflict in the evidence for the jury to resolve. Moreover, the existence of such evidence is to be determined by the scintilla rule.[b]

Ford contends the evidence adduced at trial does not constitute a scintilla of evidence that Jackson was not in arrears. Ford states that where testimony of a witness is incredible, unbelievable, or inherently improbable, it has to be disregarded as without probative value [without legal weight].

---

[a]The tort of conversion (or "wrongful conversion," as used here) may be generally defined as the unauthorized taking of one person's goods by another.

[b]Under the Alabama scintilla rule, a case must go to the jury if the evidence (or reasonable inferences therefrom) "furnishes a mere gleam, glimmer, spark, the least particle, the smallest trace or scintilla of evidence" in support of the theory of the party who has produced such evidence.

Albeit Ford's statement of the legal principle is valid, the principle has no applicability to this case. We believe that the cases upon which Ford has relied are distinguishable from that presently before this court. [The court here briefly examined those cases. In one, involving an accident at a railroad crossing, where there was "objective," undisputed evidence as to the train's low speed and high visibility as it approached the crossing, testimony of the plaintiff (as to the length of time that he had in avoiding the train) was rejected by the trial court, the court saying that "a simple mathematical calculation" based on the objective facts showed that plaintiff's testimony could not possibly be true. And, in a second case, where the defendant testified that she had earned more than $60,000 before her seventeenth birthday by selling newspaper clippings in Mobile, Alabama, in the early 1900s, the trial court properly excluded that testimony from the jury's consideration, saying that it was "so unrealistic that no credit" should be given to it. The court then continued]:

In this case [however], we have testimony which neither can be disproven through application of objective facts nor which is so inherently improbable or unreasonable as to be without probative value as a matter of law.

[Insofar as the dispute as to the number of payments is concerned], Jackson merely testified that he had made the payments in question. Although his testimony on direct and cross-examination was contradictory, such contradictions in this instance do not make the testimony unbelievable as a matter of law so as to require reversal by this court. *The question of which part of Jackson's testimony was believable was for the jury.* [Emphasis added.]

Ford also contends that [in any event] Jackson failed to establish a . . . case of conversion [because] Jackson admitted that he made a late payment in February and failed to make a payment in March of 1975. Under the security agreement he executed with Ford, such action on his part would constitute default and entitle Ford to possession of the car. Hence, Ford [argues that it clearly had] a superior right to the car.

We cannot agree. Jackson [in other testimony] stated that he made eight payments, the first one having been in July of 1974 [and that he "always kept one month ahead"]. Under this view of the evidence, the payment rejected by Ford in February would have been for March [in which case the rejection was wrongful]. Thus, one reasonable interpretation of the evidence disclosed that Jackson was not in default, had a superior right to possession, and consequently did establish a . . . case of conversion. Ford's contentions with respect to the sufficiency of the evidence are, therefore, without merit. . . .

Judgment affirmed.

★★★

Analysis of the Adjudicative Processes

A good many criticisms are made of the manner in which controversies are settled under our present legal system. Many of these have to do with the general nature of the "adversary system," the role of the jury, and the selection and performance of judges.

The Adversary System

Most legal disputes are settled through *adversary proceedings*, where the parties meet face to face (legally speaking) with each permitted to contest the allegations of fact and points of law raised by the other. The attorney for each party determines how to prove that his or her client's version of the facts is correct, and each researches the law to find legal principles upon which to base the client's case. The parties themselves thus frame the issues, and the judge simply rules on the issues that are presented.

It is sometimes said that the adversary system puts an undue premium on the relative effectiveness of the competing attorneys and too greatly limits the trial judge's role in the outcome of the case. Overall, these criticisms are probably not as valid as they seem.

In the first place, the skill of the competing lawyers is usually equal enough for each party to be able to introduce the evidence and to present rules of law in support of his or her position. Additionally, the rules of procedure and evidence, and the normal desire of the trial judge to see that each party has a fair opportunity to "have a say," place certain limits on the practical advantage that one party might have in a case where his or her counsel is markedly more able than the other litigant's counsel.

The Role of the Jury

Many weaknesses, real or imagined, are attributed to the jury's role in the adjudicative processes, including the following: (1) jurors cannot understand the complex issues that are presented; (2) jurors are too likely to be influenced by the personalities of the attorneys rather than by objective considerations; and (3) given the rules of law applying to the various alternative findings that they may return, juries frequently ignore or overemphasize evidence in order to bring in a verdict in favor of a party for whom they have sympathy or against a party for whom they have animosity.

Supporters of the jury system, on the other hand, feel that most of these criticisms are not, in general, supported by the facts. First, in many cases there are only one or two controlling issues, and these are quite understandable to the average person. Second, verdicts can be set aside if they are clearly based on "passion or prejudice," in addition to the other grounds mentioned earlier. And, third, there is substantial agreement among judges and trial lawyers that jurors generally take their duties seriously and perform them conscientiously.

Performance of the Judges

The overall performance of a legal system obviously depends to a great extent upon the character and competence of its judges. For this reason, particularly, it is distressing to note that the judges of this country have, as a class, come in for rather heavy criticism over the years. While some of this criticism may be unjustified, there is considerable evidence that the performance of a significant percentage of our judges (though certainly not a majority) can be characterized as barely adequate, or worse.

Three factors are chiefly responsible. First, judges' salaries are often lower than the income that can be earned in private practice by topnotch attorneys. Second, in the United States, persons who aspire to a career in the judiciary are not required to take special training or to go through an apprenticeship of a year or two on an appeals court, as is the case in many other countries. And, third, the judges of our state courts have traditionally been elected. This has frequently resulted in the nomination of candidates by the political parties on the basis of their party service and loyalty rather than on ability and experience. And, once elected, incumbent judges have not easily been dislodged even when their performance is mediocre or worse.

In recent years, in an effort to alleviate the shortcomings resulting from the election of judges, over thirty states and the District of Columbia have adopted some form of "merit plan" selection of judges. While these plans vary to some extent, they all are based on the idea that when a judicial vacancy occurs, a judicial nominating commission develops a list of three to five persons whom they feel to be the best qualified persons for the job. (These commissions are nonpartisan in nature, and are usually comprised equally of lawyers and nonlawyers.) The list of names is submitted to the governor, who selects one person to fill the vacancy. Thereafter, appointees must indicate before their terms of office expire whether they wish to stand for another term. If so, the appointee runs unopposed in the next general election, with the voters simply indicating whether they are satisfied with the performance rendered during the first term of office. If the appointee loses on this vote, the appointive process then begins anew.

Questions and Problems

1. Owens, a Wyoming citizen, is owed $100,000 by St. Pierre, a Nebraska citizen residing in Omaha. Owens files a suit to recover the debt in a Wyoming state court (the District Court, Laramie County, in Cheyenne, Wyoming), and thereafter has a summons served on St. Pierre while St. Pierre is in Cheyenne attending the Frontier Days rodeo. When the case comes on for trial, St. Pierre files a motion asking that the case be removed to the federal courts (the U.S. District Court for the State of Wyoming). Must the state court grant the removal request? Why or why not?

2. Gatch was an employee of a radio station (Arrow Broadcasting) who brought suit against Hennepin Broadcasting to recover $8,000 damages, alleging that Hennepin interfered with his contract with Arrow and that this interference constituted a wrong under Minnesota law. (Gatch was a Minnesota resident, and Hennepin was a Minnesota corporation.) When Gatch filed this suit in a Minnesota state court, Hennepin asked that it be removed to the federal courts, claiming that a *federal question* was presented in view of the fact that Hennepin was subject to the rules and regulations of the Federal Communications Commission. Do you agree that this fact raises a federal question? Why or why not? (*Gatch v. Hennepin Broadcasting*, 349 F.Supp. 1180, 1972.)

3. The State of Washington brought suit against the International Shoe Company, a Delaware corporation, to recover unpaid contributions to the state unemployment compensation fund. The suit was brought in a state court in Washington, and the state (plaintiff) initiated the action by serving a notice of assessment on a salesman of the company in Washington and by mailing a copy of the assessment to the company's principal place of business in St. Louis.

In the trial court, the company contended that the Washington courts could not have *in personam* jurisdiction over it in view of the fact that it was incorporated in Delaware, had no offices in Washington, and maintained no warehouses or stores in the state. (In other words, the company contended that its contacts with the state were so slight that it would be contrary to "due process of law" for it to litigate the case in Washington.)

The trial court ruled that it constitutionally did have jurisdiction, in view of the fact that the company employed thirteen salesmen who lived in the state, and that these salesmen often rented sample rooms in retail business buildings for the purpose of soliciting orders from buyers in the state. (Any orders were submitted to the company in St. Louis, which shipped directly to the buyer in Washington.) The Supreme Court of Washington agreed with the trial court, and the company appealed to the U.S. Supreme Court. Do you think that that court should agree with the lower courts' holding that the company had a sufficient "presence" in the state to permit it to be sued in Washington? Explain why or why not. (*International Shoe Co. v. Washington*, 326 U.S. 310, 1945.)

4. While taking a shortcut across the back of the Gomez Company's property one evening, North is injured when he falls into an unguarded excavation. When North brings a negligence action against Gomez in the proper state court to recover damages, that court applies the rule that a trespasser cannot hold a landowner liable even if it (landowner) is guilty of negligence, and dismisses the action. North appeals the decision to the state supreme court, which affirms the rule of nonliability. In this case, is the ruling of the state supreme court final—i.e., if North were to appeal to the U.S. Supreme Court, would it refuse to consider the case? Why or why not?

5. California has a "long arm" statute which provides, in essence, that any out-of-state resident who drives an automobile within the state is thereby giving his consent to be sued in the California courts if he is involved in an accident while in the state. (The statute further provides that the employer of the driver, if any, may also be sued in the California courts.)

With this statute in effect, Hall (a California resident) was struck by a car driven in California by a Nevada resident. The driver, an employee of the State of Nevada, was in California on official state business, and was driving a car owned by the State of Nevada at the time of the accident. Hall thereafter sued the driver and the State of Nevada in a California court to recover damages.

At the trial, the State of Nevada contended that there were several constitutional reasons why it could not be sued in such an action. The gist of the state's argument was that the state courts of one state (here, California) did not have jurisdiction over it. In other words, Nevada contended that the courts of one state do not have the power to determine the liability of a sister state. Basing your answer on the limited exposure to the subject of jurisdiction that we have experienced so far, do you think Nevada's argument is a good one? Discuss. (*Nevada v. Hall*, 99 S.Ct. 1182, 1979.)

6. Hayden Building Associates (HBA) makes a contract with Fry in Iowa City, Iowa, under the terms of which HBA is to build an oil refinery for Fry in Kansas City, Missouri, for $2 million. Later HBA refuses to do the work, whereupon Fry sues it in an Iowa court for damages for breach of contract. At the trial, as a defense, HBA contends that the contract was invalid under Missouri law because it did not comply with one section of a Missouri statute applicable to construction contracts. (HBA did concede, however, that the contract was clearly valid under Iowa law.) Is HBA correct in its contention that the validity of the contract is governed by Missouri law in view of the fact that the performance of the contract was to take place in Missouri? Why or why not?

7. Batchoff was injured by a negligent driver, Stortz. Batchoff sued Stortz *and* the owner of the car (Craney), claiming that Stortz was Craney's agent at the time of the accident. In support of this contention, Batchoff testified that, prior to the accident, he heard Craney ask Stortz to take the car from Billings, Montana, to Butte for him, and that Craney told Batchoff that he could ride along.

Craney, on the other hand, produced witnesses who testified that Craney had loaned his car for the day to a friend, U.S. Senator Wheeler. Craney also produced evidence that Batchoff (plaintiff) had testified in a prior proceeding before a state industrial board that it was Stortz, not Craney, who told Batchoff that he could ride along on the trip. The jury believed Batchoff's testimony, and Craney was thus held liable on the agency theory.

Craney appealed to the Montana Supreme Court, contending in effect that his evidence was better than Batchoff's; that the jury was thus wrong in its verdict; and that the verdict should be set aside. Do you agree with this contention? Explain what rule or rules the higher court should follow in answering this question. (*Batchoff v. Craney*, 172 P.2d 308, 1946.)

8. Mrs. Hunt was burned when she brushed her hand across the surface of a stove that (unknown to her) had just been demonstrated in a Montgomery Ward store in Greensboro, North Carolina. The stove was of a new "counter-top" style, where the heat came from "spiderweb" lines in the smooth glass top, rather than from conventional burners. Montgomery Ward's primary defense was that it had exercised due care (was not negligent) in view of the fact an employee had placed a large "HOT" sign on the back surface of the stove immediately after the demonstration, which Mrs. Hunt apparently did not see.

Before the case went to the jury, Montgomery Ward asked the court to rule, as a matter of law, that (a) it had exercised due care under the circumstances, or, in the alternative, that (b) Mrs. Hunt was guilty of contributory negligence. The trial court refused this request and left both questions to the jury, which returned a verdict for Mrs. Hunt. (It found Montgomery Ward to be negligent and Mrs. Hunt not negligent.) Do you think the trial court was correct in sending these questions to the jury? And, if so, do you think that the verdict was supported by the evidence? Discuss. (*Hunt v. Montgomery Ward*, 272 S.E.2d 357, 1980.)

C·H·A·P·T·E·R 3

COMMON LAW

In Chapter 1 we indicated that there are several basic processes by which law is made: (1) the formulation of rules by the courts—the judges—in deciding cases coming before them in those areas of law where no statutes apply; (2) the enactment and interpretation of statutes; (3) the interpretation and application of constitutional provisions; and (4) the promulgation of rules and regulations by administrative agencies. In this chapter we examine the first of these lawmaking processes—the formulation of *common law* (or case law) by the courts.

In the discussion of the early king's courts in England, we saw that they largely made up the law on a case-by-case basis. If, for example, a plaintiff asked for damages for breach of contract in a situation where the defendant denied that a contract ever existed, the court had to spell out the nature of a contract—that is, specify the minimum elements which the court felt must exist in order for it to impose contractual liability on the defendant. Similarly, if a defendant admitted making the contract in question but sought to escape liability for reasons of illness or military service, the court had to decide what kinds of defenses ought to be legally recognizable—defenses that should free the defendant from his or her contractual obligations.

Over a period of time, then, as more and more cases were settled, a rudimentary body of contract law came into being. Thereafter, when other cases arose involving contractual matters, the courts quite naturally looked to the earlier cases to see what principles of law had been established. The same procedure was followed in many other branches of law, and the legal rules that arose in this manner constituted the **common law**, or case law, of England.

In fashioning common-law principles, the English courts laid great stress on the customs, morals, and forms of conduct that were generally prevailing in the community. Additionally, where such factors were not well established or where the rules led to questionable results, the judges' personal feelings as to what kinds of conduct were just and fair, or were "right or wrong," undoubtedly entered the picture.

The Current Scene

The common-law rules that had developed in England were, of course, the law of our early colonies. And, when those colonies achieved statehood, they adopted those rules as a major part of their respective bodies of law. In subsequent years, as the territories became states, they too adopted the common law in one of three ways. Some of these states' *constitutions* contained an express provision that "the common law of England shall remain in force" except where clearly abrogated by the legislature, and another group of states adopted *statutes* to the same effect. And, in the remaining states that did not adopt such formal expressions of intent, the common law was adopted judicially—by the courts themselves. Thus, at one time, the major portion of the law of all states (with the exception of Louisiana) was common law in nature.[1]

Gradually, however, the state legislatures began to pass increasing numbers of statutes, with the result that today most branches of the law are statutory in nature. For example, all states now have comprehensive statutes governing the areas of corporation law, criminal law, tax law, municipal corporations, and commercial law. Some of these statutes have been based largely on the common-law principles that were in effect earlier. Others, however, have been passed to create bodies of rules that did not exist previously, or that expressly overrule common-law principles.

Despite the ever increasing amount of statutory law in this country (which we examine in some detail in the next chapter), *several branches of law today are still essentially common law in nature in forty-nine of our states*—particularly the subjects of *contracts*, *torts*, and *agency*. In these areas, where the legislatures have not seen fit to enact comprehensive statutes, the

---

[1]Louisiana continues to be governed by the *civil-law* (as distinguished from common-law) system of law. Under such a system, adopted by most European countries, virtually all law is "codified"—that is, statutory.

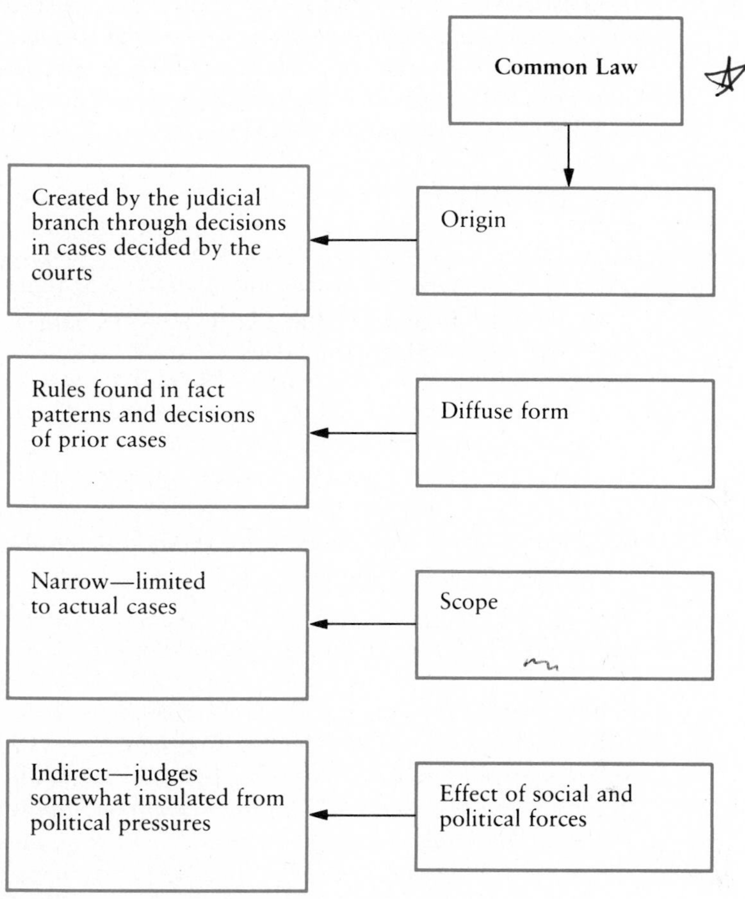

Figure 3.1 Common Law

courts still settle controversies on the basis of judge-made or case law—the rules formulated by the courts in deciding earlier cases over the years, as illustrated in Figure 3.1. (While many of these rules had their origin in England, as has been indicated, our definition of common law also includes those additional rules that have originated in the state courts in this country.)

An Overview

The primary purpose of this chapter is to examine selected cases in which appellate courts have been called upon to affirm, modify, or overrule common-law views that have been adopted earlier. As a preface to the narrower issues presented by these cases, however, a more sweeping view of the common law (and the role played by the judges who fashion it) is useful. This broader view will first be sketched out by brief observations by one of this country's most noted legal scholars on the *role of the judge* in analyzing existing case law. Following this, a complementary view on the *general purposes of common law* is supplied by excerpts from an opinion in a case decided by one of our state supreme courts.

Role of the Judge

Benjamin N. Cardozo was a judge of the Court of Appeals of New York from 1913 to 1932, and an associate justice of the U.S. Supreme Court from 1932 until his death in 1938. While on the court of appeals he wrote on a wide variety of legal topics, and during his early tenure on that court he gave a series of lectures at the Yale School of Law. In these lectures, which were published in book form in 1921, Cardozo contended that four "directive forces" shaped the law, and especially the common law, as follows: (1) philosophy (logic); (2) history; (3) custom; and (4) social welfare (or sociology).

In his first lecture, on the role of philosophy in the law, Cardozo briefly commented on the special tasks of the judge in interpreting statutes and constitutions, and then continued:

We reach the land of mystery when constitution and statute are silent, and the judge must look to the common law for the rule that fits the case. . . . The first thing he does is to compare the case before him with the precedents, whether stored in his mind or hidden in the books. . . . Back of precedents are the basic juridical conceptions which are the postulates of judicial reasoning, and farther back are the habits of life, the institutions of society, in which those conceptions had their origin, and which, by a process of interaction, they have modified in turn. . . . If (precedents) are plain and to the point, there may be need of nothing more. **Stare decisis** *is at least the everyday working rule of the law. . . .*[2]

Early in that same lecture, however, Cardozo cautioned that the finding of precedent was only part of the judge's job, and indicated how the law must grow beyond the early precedents, in these words:

The rules and principles of case law have never been treated as final truths, but as working hypotheses, continually retested in those great laboratories of the law, the courts of justice. . . . In [the] perpetual flux [of the law,] the problem which confronts the judge is in reality a twofold one: he first must extract from the precedents the underlying principle, the ratio decidendi *(the ground of decision); he must then determine the path or direction along which the principle is to move and develop, if it is not to wither and die. . . .*

The directive force of a principle may be exerted along the line of logical progression; this I will call the rule of analogy or the method of philosophy;

---

[2] *Stare decisis* means, literally, "to stand by decisions." The concept is revisited later in this chapter.

along the line of historical development; this I will call the method of evolution; along the line of the customs of the community; this I will call the method of tradition; along the lines of justice, morals and social welfare, the mores *of the day; and this I will call the method of sociology. . . .*[3]

Role of the Common Law

Some observations on the scope and purposes of common law are found in the decision in the case below, which involves the **contributory negligence** doctrine. Under that doctrine, which was a firmly established part of the common law of this country for many years, a defendant in a negligence action was entirely freed of liability if he or she were able to prove that the plaintiff—the person seeking damages as a result of an injury—was *also* guilty of negligence that contributed to the injury.

While this doctrine brought about results that were acceptable in most instances, some legal writers in rather recent years felt that the application of the rule was unfair in the case where the negligence of the plaintiff was clearly less than the negligence of the defendant. In such instances, these critics felt that the plaintiff ought to be granted *some* damages despite his or her negligence.

Accordingly, these commentators proposed that a doctrine of **comparative negligence** should be applied in such situations. The gist of this doctrine is that a jury in a negligence action (or judge, if there is no jury) shall first "add up" the negligence on the parts of both parties. Then, if the jury finds that the plaintiff's negligence is less than that of the defendant, a proportionate recovery by the plaintiff shall be allowed.[4] To illustrate: if the jury finds that plaintiff's damages were $10,000, and further finds that one-third of the negligence arose from the plaintiff's conduct and two-thirds from the defendant's actions, plaintiff will be allowed a recovery of $6667.

On the basis of this introductory distinction between the two doctrines, let us examine the "social and economic factors" which the Supreme Court of Florida felt should be examined in deciding whether the contributory negligence rule should be abandoned.

Hoffman v. Jones
Supreme Court of Florida
280 So.2d 431 (1973)

William Jones was killed in Brevard County, Florida, when the car he was driving collided with a truck driven by an employee of the Pav-A-Way Corporation. Jones's wife, as administratrix of his estate, thereafter brought this action for damages against Hoffman, the truck driver, and Pav-A-Way, alleging that Hoffman was driving negligently at the time of the accident. Hoffman and Pav-A-Way defended on the ground that Jones was also guilty of negligence.

---

[3] Cardozo, *The Nature of the Judicial Process* (1921). Excerpts are used by permission of the Yale University Press.

[4] The subject of comparative negligence is discussed further in Chapter 8.

The jury in the trial court found: (1) that Hoffman was guilty of negligence; (2) that Jones was guilty of negligence; and (3) that Jones's negligence was less than that of Hoffman, the defendant truck driver. On the basis of these facts the trial court, following the contributory negligence rule that had been uniformly applied in earlier Florida cases, dismissed the action.

On appeal by the estate, the court of appeal held that the *comparative negligence* rule should have been applied, which would permit a recovery by the estate. In subsequent proceedings the defendants raised the question whether a court of appeal (an intermediate state court) had the authority to set aside a precedent that had been established many years earlier by the state supreme court. Accordingly, the court of appeal "certified" (formally presented) this question to the Florida Supreme Court: "Whether or not the Court should replace the contributory negligence rule with the principles of comparative negligence?"

Adkins, Judge:

The . . . contributory negligence rule has uniformly been followed by the courts of the State [for many years]. The District Court of Appeal attempted, therefore, to overrule all precedent of this Court in the area of contributory negligence and to establish comparative negligence as the proper test. In so doing, the District Court has exceeded its authority. [The court here examined a number of cases in support of the principle that a court of appeal could not bring about such a change of law "on its own," so to speak, and then continued]:

Prior to answering the question certified, we must also consider our own power and authority to replace the rule of contributory negligence with that of comparative negligence. *It has been suggested that such a change in the common law of Florida is properly within the province only of the Legislature, and not that of the courts. We disagree.* [Emphasis added.]

The rule that contributory negligence is an absolute bar to recovery was—as most tort law—a judicial creation, and it was [first judicially adopted in this state in 1886].

[The court here noted the origin of the contributory negligence rule in England in the 1700s, traced the acceptance of the rule by a number of states in this country, and then continued]:

All rules of the common law are designed for application to new conditions and circumstances as they may be developed by enlightened commercial and business intercourse, and are intended to be vitalized by practical application in advanced society. One of the most pressing social problems facing us today is the automobile accident problem, for the bulk of tort litigation involves the dangerous instrumentality known as the automobile. . . .

Contemporary conditions must be met with contemporary standards which are realistic and better calculated to obtain justice among all of the parties involved, based upon the circumstances applying between them at the time in question. [Emphasis added.] The rule of contributory negligence as a complete bar to recovery was imported into the law by judges. Whatever may have been the historical justification for it, today it is almost universally regarded as unjust and inequitable to vest an entire accidental loss on one of the parties whose negligent conduct combined with the negligence of the other party to produce the loss. If fault is to remain the test of liability, then the doctrine of comparative negligence, which involves apportionment of the loss among those whose fault contributed to the occurrence, is more consistent with liability based on a fault premise. . . .

The . . . absolute-bar theory of contributory negligence . . . has been abolished in almost every common law nation in the world, including England, its country of origin, . . . and [a substantial number of states in this country].

One reason for the abandonment of the contributory negligence theory is that the initial justification for establishing the complete defense is no longer valid. . . . Contributory negligence was adopted to protect the essential growth of industries, particularly transportation. . . . Modern economic and social customs, however, favor the individual, not industry. . . . We find [therefore] that none of the justifications for denying any recovery to a plaintiff who has contributed to his own injuries to any extent, has any validity in this age.

Perhaps the best argument in favor of the movement from contributory to comparative negligence is that the latter is simply a more equitable system of determining liability and a more socially desirable method of loss distribution. The injustice which occurs when a plaintiff suffers severe injuries as the result of an accident for which he is only slightly responsible, and is thereby denied any damages, is readily apparent. . . . *Therefore, we now hold that a plaintiff in an action based on negligence will no longer be denied any recovery because of his contributory negligence.* [Emphasis added.]

[Rather,] if it appears from the evidence that both plaintiff and defendant were guilty of negligence which was, in some degree, a legal cause of the injury to the plaintiff, this does not defeat the plaintiff's recovery entirely. The jury in assessing damages would in that event award to the plaintiff such damages as in the jury's judgment the negligence of the defendant caused to the plaintiff. In other words, the jury should apportion the negligence of the plaintiff and the negligence of the defendant; then, in reaching the amount due the plaintiff, the jury should give the plaintiff only such an amount apportioned with his negligence and the negligence of the defendant. [The court here gave some further guidelines as to how the new rule should be applied in varying circumstances, and concluded]:

The certified question having now been answered [in the affirmative], this cause is remanded to the [trial court] for a new trial.

★★★

Common Law— The Doctrine of *Stare Decisis*

The heart of the common-law process lies in the inclination of the courts generally to follow precedent—to stand by existing decisions. This policy, as we were told by Cardozo, is referred to as the doctrine of *stare decisis*. Under this approach, when the fact-pattern of a particular controversy is established, the attorneys for both parties search for earlier cases involving similar fact-patterns in an effort to determine whether applicable principles of law have been established. If this research produces a number of similar cases (or even one) within the state where a rule has been applied by the appellate courts, the trial court will ordinarily feel constrained to follow the same rule in settling the current controversy. (But, as we have already seen in *Hoffman v. Jones*, this does not mean that the courts are reluctant to abandon a precedent if it produces clear injustice under "contemporary conditions.)"

The basic strength of the doctrine of *stare decisis* is that it brings relative certainty to the law. As a principle is applied to more and more cases presenting the same (or substantially similar) issues, attorneys can be increasingly confident that the rule will be followed in the future and can advise their clients on this basis. And, to a somewhat lesser extent, the well-established principles become increasingly known to the general populace.

The case that follows is particularly valuable because it shows the strong inclination of the courts to follow an established principle even though its wisdom or fairness is open to question. Since the basis of this suit—the subject of fraud—is discussed in some detail in Chapter 8, we need only say here that, in essence, **fraud** is the intentional misleading of one person by another, as a result of which the innocent party suffers a loss of some sort (usually of an economic nature).

In this case, the purchasers of a tract of land in Massachusetts sued the seller to recover damages, alleging that the seller intentionally misrepresented the number of acres the tract contained. As a defense, the seller relied upon two earlier Massachusetts cases which had adopted the view that such misrepresentations did not constitute fraud if the actual boundaries of the land in question were pointed out to the purchaser prior to the time of the sale. This view apparently is based on the theory that the buyer, in such a situation, does not suffer a loss or "injury." The primary question is whether the highest court in Massachusetts should follow its earlier pronouncements in these cases.

Mabardy et al. v. McHugh et al.
Supreme Judicial Court of Massachusetts
88 N.E. 894
(1909)

Plaintiffs, Mabardy and others, purchased a tract of land from defendants after being told by one of the defendants that the tract contained sixty-five acres. Plaintiffs later learned that the tract actually contained forty and three-fourths acres, and they brought this action to recover damages on the ground that defendants' misrepresentation as to the acreage constituted fraud. At the trial, two primary issues were presented—one a question of fact and the other a question of law.

On the question of fact, the defendants contended that they had shown the boundaries of the land to the plaintiffs before the contract was made; the plaintiffs denied this. Before the case was submitted to the jury, the defendants raised the question of law by asking the trial judge to instruct the jury that if it believed the defendants' evidence as to the showing of the boundaries, then

"Gorgeous day! Puts one in the mood for a landmark decision."

Precedent is an important part of the American legal system.
Source: Drawing by Ed Fisher; © 1981 *The New Yorker* Magazine, Inc.

under the existing case law of Massachusetts "the misrepresentations as to the acreage would be of no consequence"—would not constitute fraud—even if the defendants knew their representations were untrue.

The trial judge so instructed the jury, the jury returned a verdict for the defendants (finding that the boundaries were shown), and judgment was entered for defendants. Plaintiffs appealed.

Rugg, Justice:

. . . The correctness of this instruction is challenged. It is in exact accordance with the law as laid down in *Gordon v. Parmelee*, 2 Allen, 212, and *Mooney v. Miller*, 102 Mass. 217. The facts in the case at bar are similar in all material respects to these cases. An attempt is made to distinguish [the present case from the earlier cases] on the ground that the present plaintiffs are Syrians, ignorant of our language, and that hence a trust relation existed between them and the defendant. But whatever else may be said of this contention, two of their own countrymen, who were thoroughly familiar with our language, acted as interpreters for them. [Thus,] *in effect, the contention of the plaintiffs amounts to a request to overrule these two cases.* They have been cited with approval in *Roberts v. French*, 26 N.E. 416, and as supporting authorities, without criticism, in other opinions. The court, however, has refused to apply the rule of those judgments to other facts closely analogous. This court in recent years, by pointed language and by conclusions reached, has indicated a plain disposition not to extend legal immunity for the falsehood of vendors in the course of negotiations for sales beyond the bounds already established [by *Gordon* and *Mooney*].

This judicial attitude perhaps reflects an increasingly pervasive moral sense in some of the common transactions of trade. While the science of jurisprudence is not, and under present conditions cannot be, coextensive with the domain of morality, nor generally undertake to differentiate between motives which mark acts as good or bad, yet it is true, as was said by Mr. Justice Brett in *Robinson v. Mollett*, L.R. 7 H.L.C. 802, that "the courts have applied to the mercantile business brought before them what have been called legal principles, which have almost always been the fundamental ethical rules of right and wrong." This is only a concrete expression of the broader generalization that law is the manifestation of the conscience of the commonwealth.

In many other jurisdictions the rule of *Gordon v. Parmelee* and *Mooney v. Miller* has not been followed, and false representations as to area of land, even though true boundaries were pointed out, have been held actionable [that is, fraudulent].

Other cases, apparently opposed to the Massachusetts rule, on examination prove to go no further than to decide that misrepresentations as to area, when there is no evidence that boundaries were shown, constitute deceit. This is the substance of the latter part of the instruction given in the superior court, and is the law of the commonwealth. . . .

If the point [as to the correctness of the instruction] was now presented for the first time, it is possible that we might be convinced by the argument of the plaintiffs and the great weight of persuasive authority in its support. *But there is something to be said in support of the two earlier decisions now questioned.* [Emphasis added.] A purchase and a sale of real estate is a transaction of importance and cannot be treated as entered into lightly. People must use their own faculties for their protection and information, and cannot assume that the law will relieve them from the natural effects of their heedlessness or take better care of their interests than they themselves do. Thrift, foresight and self-reliance would be undermined if it was the policy of the law to attempt to afford relief for mere want of sagacity. It is an ancient and widely, if not universally, accepted priniciple of the law of deceit, that, where representations are made respecting a subject as to which the complaining party has at hand reasonably available means for ascertaining the truth and the matter is open to inspection, if, without being fraudulently diverted therefrom, he does not take advantage of this opportunity, he cannot be heard to impeach the transaction on the ground of the falsehoods of the other party. This rule in its general statement applies to such a case as that before us. It is easy for one disappointed in the fruits of a trade to imagine, and perhaps persuade himself, that the cause of his loss is the deceit of the other party, rather than his own want of judgment.

It is highly desirable that laws for conduct in ordinary affairs, in themselves easy of comprehension and memory, when once established, should remain fast. *The doctrine of* stare decisis *is as salutary as it is well recognized.* [Emphasis added.] While perhaps it is more important as to far-reaching juridical principles that the court should be right, in the light of higher civilization, later and more careful examination of authorities, wider and more thorough discussion and more mature reflection upon the policy of the law, than merely in harmony with previous decisions, *it is nevertheless vital that there be stability in the courts in adhering to decisions deliberately made after ample consideration.* [Emphasis added.] Parties should not be encouraged to seek re-examination of determined principles and speculate on a fluctuation of the law with every change in the expounders of it. As to many matters of frequent occurrence, the establishment of some certain guide is of more significance than the precise form of the rule. It is likely that no positive rule of law can be laid down that will not at some time impinge with great apparent severity upon a morally innocent person. The law of gravitation acts indifferently upon the just and the unjust. A renewed declaration of law, that is already in force, supported by sound reason and not plainly wrong, in the long run probably works out substantial justice, although it may seem harsh in its application to some particular case. These considerations are regarded as so weighty by the House of Lords that it cannot overrule any of its own decisions.

The conclusion is that we do not overrule the decisions whose soundness has been debated at the bar, although we do not extend their scope, but confine them strictly to their precise point, namely, that where the seller of real estate shows upon the face of the earth its true boundaries and does not fraudulently dissuade full examination and measurement, and the estate is not so extensive or of such character as to be reasonably incapable of inspection and estimate, and there is no relation of trust between the parties, the purchaser has no remedy for a misrepresentation as to the area alone. . . .

Judgment affirmed.

★ ★ ★

Choice of Precedent

The application of *stare decisis* raises little difficulty where the facts of the earlier cases are virtually identical to those of the case under discussion, and where one rule has been uniformly followed (as in the case of *Mabardy v. McHugh*). In many situations, however, while a number of prior cases have involved similar fact-patterns, the courts have applied different rules to each. In other words, they have distinguished some cases from others, feeling that the fact-patterns of the cases were sufficiently dissimilar to justify the varying decisions.

This is unquestionably one of the problems arising under the doctrine of *stare decisis:* the decided cases are frequently so similar on the facts that it is an extremely close question as to how far distinctions can honestly be made—or should be made—by the courts. Critics claim that this is a weakness of the doctrine, in that it produces a degree of uncertainty in the law—the very condition that it is designed to eliminate. Be that as it may, this also contains an element of strength, for it affords the courts some latitude in choosing which rule of law will bring about the most desirable result in a specific controversy.

The following case clearly indicates the nature of the problem. It is also significant in two other respects. First, the reasoning of the majority of the Court of Appeals of New York has been widely (though not universally) followed in other states in negligence cases brought against manufacturers. Second, the issue presented by it permits some observations about the impact of changing social and economic considerations on the law's evolution.

The case raises the question of whether a plaintiff can, on the negligence theory, recover damages from a careless manufacturer where the plaintiff did not purchase the defective goods directly from the manufacturer. Prior to 1900, and for some years thereafter, the general rule in New York and many other states was that the plaintiff could not, that the only recourse was to bring an action against the person from whom the goods were purchased.

This rule of nonliability was partly based on both social and economic considerations. From a social standpoint, cases involving this question were relatively few because manufacturing was in its infancy in this country. Thus the refusal to award damages did not affect large numbers of people. And from an economic standpoint, the courts were reluctant to adopt a rule of liability that might impose serious economic hardship on young and financially struggling manufacturers.

By the time this case was heard, both these conditions had changed to some extent. And, perhaps for other reasons as well, the New York courts had begun to recognize certain exceptions to the general rule, dating as far back as the *Winchester* case in 1853. With these observations in mind, let us see how Justice Cardozo and his colleagues viewed the cases that arose between 1853 and 1916 in determining which rules should be applicable to MacPherson's action against the Buick Motor Company.

MacPherson v. Buick Motor Co.
Court of Appeals of New York
111 N.E. 1050 (1916)

The Buick Motor Company, defendant, manufactured an automobile and sold it to a retail dealer. MacPherson, plaintiff, purchased it from the dealer and was subsequently injured when the car collapsed. The collapse was due to the "crumbling" of the wooden spokes of one of the car's wheels while MacPherson was driving it. He brought this action against Buick, contending that it had manufactured the car negligently.

Defendant denied the claim of negligence on the ground that the defective wheel was made by another manufacturer, the Imperial Wheel Company, from whom defendant had purchased it. Additionally, defendant contended that it had no liability to plaintiff even if it were negligent, for the reason that no contractual relationship existed between it and plaintiff.

There was evidence tending to prove that the wood in the wheel was defective, that a reasonable inspection by Buick would have disclosed the defect, and that Buick omitted any inspection of the purchased wheels. The trial court instructed the jury that if it believed this evidence, and if it felt that Buick's care was less than that which a manufacturer should reasonably have exercised, then Buick was guilty of negligence. The court further instructed the jury that, in such event, Buick would be liable to plaintiff despite the fact there was no privity of contract (relationship) between it and plaintiff.

Under these instructions, the jury returned a verdict for plaintiff. An intermediate court, the Appellate Division of the Supreme Court, affirmed the judgment of the trial court, and Buick appealed to the highest court in New York State.

Cardozo, Justice:

. . . The question to be determined is whether the defendant owed a duty of care and vigilance to any one but the immediate purchaser. . . .

[Cardozo at this point examined five earlier negligence cases, in each of which the defendant sought to escape liability on the ground that the plaintiff was a "remote party"—that is, that plaintiff did not deal directly with the defendant. In the first of these, *Thomas v. Winchester*, liability was imposed, because of the unusual danger that resulted from the negligence. In the remaining cases, the question was whether the "Thomas rule" was applicable. The court discussed the five cases as follows:]

The foundations of this branch of the law, at least in this state, were laid in *Thomas v. Winchester*, 6 N.Y. 397 (1853). A poison was falsely labeled. The sale was made to a druggist, who in turn sold it to a customer. The customer recovered damages from the seller who affixed the label. "*The defendant's negligence,*" *it was said*, "*put human life in imminent danger.*" [Emphasis added.] A poison falsely labeled is likely to injure any one who gets it. Because the danger is to be foreseen, there is a duty to avoid the injury. Cases were cited by way of illustration in which manufacturers were not subject to any duty irrespective of contract. The distinction was said to be that the manufacturers' conduct (in those cases), though negligent, was not likely to result in injury to any one except the purchaser. We are not required to say whether the chance of injury was always as remote as the distinction assumes. The principle of the distinction is for present purposes the important thing.

Thomas v. Winchester became quickly a landmark of the law. *In the application of its principle there may at times have been uncertainty or even error. There has never in this state been doubt or disavowal of the principle itself.* [Emphasis added.] The chief cases are well known, yet to recall some of them will be helpful. *Loop v. Litchfield*, 42 N.Y. 351 (1870), is the earliest. It was the case of a defect in a small balance wheel used on a circular saw. The manufacturer pointed out the defect to the buyer, who wished a cheap article and was ready to assume the risk. The risk can hardly have been an imminent one, for the wheel lasted five years before it broke. In the meanwhile the buyer had made a lease of the machinery. It was held that the manufacturer was not answerable to the lessee. *Loop v. Litchfield* was followed in *Losee v. Clute*, 51 N.Y. 494, the case of the explosion of a steam boiler (in which a manufacturer was again held not to be answerable to a remote plaintiff). That decision has been criticized (*Thompson on Negligence, 233; Shearman & Redfield on Negligence, 117*); but it must be confined to its special facts. It was put upon the ground that the risk of injury was too remote. The buyer in that case had not only accepted the boiler, but had tested it. The manufacturer knew that his own test was not the final one. The finality of the test has a bearing on the measure of diligence owing to persons other than the purchaser.

These early cases suggest a narrow construction of the [Thomas] rule. Later cases, however, evince a more liberal spirit. First in importance is *Devlin v. Smith*, 89 N.Y. 470. The defendant, a contractor, built a scaffold for a painter. The painter's servants were injured. The contractor was held liable. He knew that the scaffold, if improperly constructed, was a most dangerous trap. He knew that it was used by the workmen. He was building it for that very purpose. Building it for their use, he owed them a duty, irrespective of his contract with their master, to build it with care.

From *Devlin v. Smith* we pass over intermediate cases and turn to the latest case in this court in which *Thomas v. Winchester* was followed. That case is *Statler v. Ray Mfg. Co.*, 195 N.Y. 478. The defendant manufactured a large coffee urn. It was installed in a restaurant. When heated, the urn exploded and injured the plaintiff. We held that the manufacturer was liable. We said that the urn "was of such a character inherently that, when applied to the purposes for which it was designed, it was liable to become a source of great danger to many people if not carefully and properly constructed."

It may be that Devlin v. Smith *and* Statler v. Ray Mfg. Co. *have extended the rule of* Thomas v. Winchester. *If so, this court is committed to the extension.* [Emphasis added.] The defendant argues that things imminently dangerous to life are poisons, explosives, deadly weapons—things whose normal function it is to injure or destroy. But whatever the rule in *Thomas v. Winchester* may once have been, it has no longer that restricted meaning. A scaffold is not inherently a destructive instrument. It becomes destructive only if imperfectly constructed. A large coffee urn may have within itself, if negligently made, the potency of danger, yet no one thinks of it as an implement whose normal function is destruction. . . . We have mentioned only cases in this court. But the rule has received a like extension in our courts of intermediate appeal. . . . We are not required at this time either to approve or to disapprove the application of the rule that was made in each of these cases. It is enough that they help to characterize the trend of judicial thought. . . .

We hold then, that the principle of Thomas v. Winchester *is not limited to poisons, explosives, and things of like nature, implements of destruction. If the nature of a thing is such that it is reasonably certain to place life and limb in peril when negligently made, it is then a thing of danger.* [Emphasis added.] Its nature gives warning of the consequences to be expected. If to the element of danger there is added knowledge that the thing will be used by persons other than the purchaser, and used without new tests, then, irrespective of contract, the manufacturer of this thing of danger is under a duty to make it carefully.

That is as far as we are required to go for the decision of this case. There must be knowledge of a danger, not merely possible, but probable. It is possible to use almost anything in a way that will make it dangerous if defective. That is not enough to charge the manufacturer with a duty independent of his contract. Whether a given thing is dangerous may be sometimes a question for the court and sometimes a question for the jury. There must also be knowledge that in the usual course of events the danger will be shared by others than the buyer. Such knowledge may often be inferred from the nature of the transaction. But it is possible that even knowledge of the danger and of the use will not always be enough. The proximity or remoteness of the relation is a factor to be considered. We are dealing now with the liability of the manufacturer of the finished product, who puts it on the market to be used without inspection by his customers. *If he is negligent, where danger is to be foreseen, a liability will follow.* [Emphasis added.]

We are not required, at this time, to say that it is legitimate to go back to the manufacturer of the finished product and hold the manufacturer of the component parts. . . . We leave that question open. We shall have to deal with it when it arises. . . .

From this survey of the decisions, there thus emerges a definition of the duty of a manufacturer which enables us to measure this defendant's liability. Beyond all question, the nature of an automobile gives warning of probable danger if its construction is defective. This automobile was designed to go 50 miles an hour. Unless its wheels were sound and strong, injury was almost certain. It was as much a thing of danger as a defective engine for a railroad. The defendant knew the danger. It knew also that the car would be used by persons other than the buyer. This was apparent from its size; there were seats for three persons. It was apparent also from the fact that the buyer was a dealer in cars, who bought to resell. The maker of this car supplied it for the use of purchasers from the dealer just as plainly as the contractor in *Devlin v. Smith* supplied the scaffold for use by the servants of the owner. The dealer was indeed the one person of whom it might be said with some approach to certainty that by him the car would not be used. Yet the defendant would have us say that he was the one person whom it was under a legal duty to protect. The law does not lead us to so inconsequent a conclusion. *Precedents drawn from the days of travel by stagecoach do not fit the conditions of travel today. The principle that the danger must be imminent does not change, but the things subject to the principle do change.* [Emphasis added.] They are whatever the needs of life in a developing civilization require them to be. . . .

Judgment affirmed.

★★★

Additional Precedent Problems

A second problem, quite different from that of the *MacPherson* case, is presented when there are few or no cases within the state involving the precise issue currently being raised. In such instances, the court has relatively free choice in deciding what rule of law should be applicable. If a particular precedent has been widely established in other states in similar cases, the court will no doubt seriously consider its adoption, but it is under no obligation to do so.

A third possibility is that of a "split of authority"—where some states have adopted one rule and others a contrary rule. Such situations exist in several areas of contract law, one illustration of which involves the right of a minor to disaffirm (cancel) a contract and recover payments made to the other party. For example: M, a minor, purchases a car from X for $1,000. Six months later, while he is still under the age of eighteen, M offers to return the car to X and demands the return of his $1,000. X refuses, citing the fact that the car has depreciated $400 while in M's hands. In such a case, many states hold the minor liable for the depreciation, permitting M to recover only $600. However, many other states do *not* charge the minor with the depreciation, and in those jurisdictions he is entitled to recover the full $1,000 regardless of the condition of the car. In such a situation, an appellate court of a state which has not previously been faced with the issue is at liberty to decide which rule to adopt, or even to reject both views in favor of another.

A fourth possibility, considerably more unlikely than the others, is that little or no authority exists in any state on the issue at hand. Here the court may be asked to draw analogies from existing principles applicable to somewhat different situations, or it may simply prefer to fashion a rule of law based on its own ideas of justice and fair dealing.

Overruling a Precedent

One possible danger inherent in a slavish adherence to the doctrine of *stare decisis* is the possibility that a "bad" rule will become so embedded in the law that it will bring about undesirable results for many years to come.[5] (A rule could be bad either because it produced a result that was of doubtful wisdom at the outset or because it was based upon conditions that had changed in later years.)

While the danger does exist, it is not very great. In the first place, most of the decisions in precedent-setting cases are, in fact, supported by some degree of logic. The courts that settle these issues, like others, normally search for a rule that brings about a reasonable result—one that is not clearly bad. And, especially in recent years, appellate courts have felt increasingly free to modify or discard earlier rules if they feel that changes in social views or economic conditions require them to do so.

The case that follows presents a situation where the original reasons for the rule no longer exist, and the court is called upon to decide whether this

[5] This possibility is perhaps the kind of thing that Justice Frankfurter had in mind when he quoted T. H. Huxley's statement that "a theory survives long after its brains are knocked out." *Massachusetts Bonding and Insurance Co. v. U.S.*, 352 U.S. 128 (1956).

is a sufficient ground for reversal of the precedent. While it cannot be said that all courts will (or should) abandon a precedent in the light of changing economic conditions, the Supreme Court of Pennsylvania advances powerful arguments as to why this ought to be done when the changes are substantial in nature.

Flagiello v. Pennsylvania Hospital
Supreme Court of Pennsylvania
208 A.2d 193
(1965)

read
for Wed Jan. 21

Mrs. Flagiello, a patient in the Pennsylvania Hospital in Philadelphia, fell and broke an ankle while being moved by two of its employees. She brought this action against the hospital to recover damages, alleging that the employees were guilty of negligence. The defendant hospital moved for a judgment on the pleadings, contending that under the case law of Pennsylvania, it was well established that a charitable institution was not responsible for the wrongs of its employees. The trial court sustained this motion and entered judgment for defendant. Plaintiff appealed to the Supreme Court of Pennsylvania.

Musmanno, Justice:

. . . The hospital has not denied that its negligence caused Mrs. Flagiello's injuries. It merely announces that it is an eleemosynary institution, and, therefore, owed no duty of care to its patient. It declares in effect that it can do wrong and still not be liable in damages to the person it has wronged. It thus urges a momentous exception to the generic proposition that in law there is no wrong without a remedy. From the earliest days of organized society it became apparent to man that society could never become a success unless the collectivity of mankind guaranteed to every member of society a remedy for a palpable wrong inflicted on him by another member of that society. In 1844 Justice Storrs of the Supreme Court of Connecticut crystallized into epigrammatic language that wise concept, as follows: "An injury is a wrong; and for the redress of every wrong there is a remedy; a wrong is a violation of one's right; and for the vindication of every right there is a remedy." *Parker v. Griswold*, 17 Conn. 288.

[The court addressed itself to several specific arguments advanced by the defendant to support its contention that charitable institutions were not, and should not be, subject to the general rule stated above. One of these arguments was that, on economic grounds alone, the imposition of liability on charitable institutions would be financially ruinous to them. The court rejected this argument, noting first that, as a general rule, a defendant is never permitted to escape liability as to valid claims solely on the ground that an entry of a judgment against him would be financially burdensome to him, or might even force him into bankruptcy. The court also noted that the rule of immunity as to charitable institutions originated in this country at a time when most of their patients paid nothing for the services they received, and that the rule was an effort by the courts to preserve the meager assets of such institutions. Judge Musmanno further observed that conditions have now changed; that so-called charitable hospitals operate on the same basis as ordinary business establishments; that in 1963 "the fees received from patients in the still designated charitable hospitals in

Pennsylvania constituted 90.92 percent of the total income of such hospitals," and that the plaintiff did, in fact, pay defendant $24.50 a day for services rendered her. On these facts, the court rejected defendant's claim of immunity based on financial considerations. The court then turned to the remaining major contention of the defendant, specifically, that the rule of immunity as to charitable hospitals was so firmly established in the case law of Pennsylvania, including cases decided by the Pennsylvania Supreme Court, that, under the doctrine of *stare decisis*, the rule could not now be abandoned by the courts. In that regard Judge Musmanno, in a lengthy examination of cases, concluded that the immunity doctrine originated in an early English case that was soon overruled there, that the American courts seemed to adopt the rule of that case blindly, without examining the validity of the reasons ostensibly underlying it, and further noted that approximately half the states in this country have now rejected the doctrine of immunity. The court then continued:]

Failing to hold back both the overwhelming reasons of rudimentary justice for abolishing the doctrine, and the rising tide of out-of-state repudiation of the doctrine, the defendant hospital and the Hospital Association of Pennsylvania fall back for defense to the bastion of *stare decisis*. It is inevitable and proper that they should do so. Without *stare decisis*, there would be no stability in our system of jurisprudence.

Stare decisis channels the law. It erects lighthouses and flys the signals of safety. The ships of jurisprudence must follow that well-defined channel which, over the years, has been proved to be secure and trustworthy. But it would not comport with wisdom to insist that, should shoals rise in a heretofore safe course and rocks emerge to encumber the passage, the ship should nonetheless pursue the original course, merely because it presented no hazard in the past. The principle of *stare decisis* does not demand that we follow precedents which shipwreck justice. . . .

There is nothing in the records of the courts, the biographies of great jurists, or the writings of eminent legal authorities which offers the slightest encouragement to the notion that time petrifies into unchanging jurisprudence a palpable fallacy. [Emphasis added.] As years can give no sturdiness to a decayed tree, so the passing decades can add no convincing flavor to the withered apple of sophistry clinging to the limb of demonstrated wrong. There are, of course, principles and precepts sanctified by age, and no one would think of changing them, but their inviolability derives not from longevity but from their universal appeal to the reason, the conscience and the experience of mankind. No one, for instance, would think of challenging what was written in Magna Charta, the Habeas Corpus Act or the Bill of Rights of the Constitution of the United States. . . .

While age adds venerableness to moral principles and some physical objects, it occasionally becomes necessary, and it is not sacrilegious to do so, to scrape away the moss of the years to study closely the thing which is being accepted as authoritative, inviolable, and untouchable. The Supreme Court of Michigan said sagaciously in the case of *Williams v. City of Detroit*, 364 Mich. 231, that "it is the peculiar genius of the common law that no legal rule is mandated by the doctrine of *stare decisis* when that rule was conceived in error or when the times and circumstances have so changed as to render it an instrument of injustice."

The charitable immunity rule proves itself an instrument of injustice and nothing presented by the defendant shows it to be otherwise. In fact, the longer the argument for its preservation the more convincing is the proof that it long ago outlived its purpose if, indeed, it ever had a purpose consonant with sound law. "Ordinarily, when a court decides to modify or abandon a court-made rule of long standing, it starts out by saying that 'the reason for the rule no longer exists.' In this case, it is correct to say that the 'reason' originally given for the rule of immunity never did exist." *Pierce v. Yakima Valley Hospital Ass'n*, 260 P.2d 765.

A rule that has become insolvent has no place in the active market of current enterprise. *When a rule offends against reason, when it is at odds with every precept of natural justice, and when it cannot be defended on its own merits, but has to depend alone on a discredited genealogy, courts not only possess the inherent power to repudiate, but, indeed, it is required, by the very nature of judicial function, to abolish such a rule.* [Emphasis added.]

We, therefore, overrule *Michael v. Hahnemann*, 404 Pa. 424, and all other decisions of identical effect, and hold that the hospital's liability must be governed by the same principles of law as apply to other employers. . . .

Reversed and remanded.

★★★

Precedent and Public Policy

We have seen that the formulation of common law requires a court to sift and examine prior cases in order to determine whether one rule of law has generally been adhered to in similar situations. If it has, the court in most instances can apply that rule without considering in detail whether it is good for the populace as a whole—that is, whether it brings about a result that is good public policy. This is so because most established rules of law are, in fact, based upon public policy considerations.

Occasionally, however, after a precedent has been discovered, a court will refuse to apply it in a particular case—or may even overrule it—for the reason that such application would, in its opinion, bring about essentially harmful results in future years. In such instances the rule is said to be "contrary to public policy." Insofar as the formulation of common-law rules in each state is concerned, the highest state court determines that state's public policy—defined as the "community common sense and common conscience" in an early case.[6]

In that case, a Mrs. Kinney was employed by a railroad as a car cleaner only after she agreed, by contract, not to hold the railroad liable for dam-

[6] *Pittsburgh, C., C. & St. L. Ry. Co. v. Kinney*, 115 N.E. 505 (1916).

ages in case she was injured on the job by the railroad's negligence. An injury later occurred; when she brought suit, the railroad relied on the "freedom of contract" principle as its defense—specifically, that plaintiff knew of the release clause at the time of contracting and was legally free to agree to such a release if she wished to do so. The Ohio Supreme Court, while reaffirming the freedom of contract principle generally, ruled against the railroad. It held that in this instance the release clause was contrary to public policy and therefore invalid as a defense.

In describing the harmful effects that would result if it gave effect to the clause, the court said:

If a contract between employer and employee, whereby the employee assumes all risks no matter how negligent the employer may be, must be upheld by courts as a valid contract, the enormous increase in industrial casualties, the loss of life and limb that would suddenly and inevitably follow, would be almost inconceivable. We would have a veritable army of crippled unfortunates and maimed dependents, deprived of life's joys and blessings, filling our almshouses as paupers and charges upon the state's financial resources, entailing a burdensome system of taxation. Wholly apart from the higher humanitarian questions involved, the increased burden thus placed upon the state for charitable purposes would be, in and of itself sufficient to affect contracts of this character with a vital public interest. Courts should not hestitate to hold such contracts wholly null and void.

Selected Change-of-Law Issues

The cases of *Hoffman v. Jones* and *Flagiello v. Pennsylvania Hospital* have already presented situations in which common-law precedents were abandoned for one reason or another. We conclude our discussion of case law with a brief look at two additional, somewhat more business-related, controversies in which the courts have, in rather recent years, reexamined traditional concepts.

The Implied Warranty of Habitability

There has been much litigation over the years arising out of sales of new homes which the buyers subsequently found to be defective. The prevailing view for many years in this country was that the disappointed buyer could recover damages from the seller or builder on only two theories: fraud and breach of express warranty.

This view afforded the buyer little relief in many instances. In order to recover on the fraud theory the buyer generally had to prove that the seller made a false statement about the condition of the property which the seller knew to be false when he or she made it, or that the seller concealed a defect which he or she was aware of at the time of contracting. In many cases the buyer was unable to sustain this burden of proof (even where the seller may actually have been guilty of deception to some extent), and thus the buyer recovered nothing.

Buyers who proceeded on the express warranty theory often ran into similar difficulties. While a buyer who sued on this theory did not have to prove fraud (deception) on the part of the seller, he or she did have to prove that the seller made a clear-cut warranty (a statement of fact about the property) which turned out to be untrue. In this situation, too, the buyer was often unable to prove that a specific warranty was ever made (or, if one were made, that it covered the particular defect that the buyer was complaining of).

Except in those cases where the buyer's claim of fraud or breach of express warranty was proven, the age-old defense of *caveat emptor* ("let the buyer beware") completely freed the seller of liability. By the mid-1960s, however, the supreme courts of some states made "new law" by recognizing another theory—the implied warranty of habitability—under which the disappointed buyer might be granted a recovery. The reasons underlying this judicially-created rule (which today has been recognized by most courts) are set forth in the opinion in the following case.

Theis v. Heuer
Supreme Court of Indiana
280 N.E.2d 300 (1972)

Mr. and Mrs. Theis, plaintiffs, purchased a new home in Evansville, Indiana, from the builder, James Heuer. After taking possession, they found that several inches of water and sewage collected in the basement after hard rains, which was caused by the improper positioning of sewer lines and drainage tile around the residence. The plaintiffs then brought this action to recover damages from Heuer.

Because there was no warranty in the sales contract covering this defect, plaintiffs brought this action on two theories: (1) negligence, and (2) breach of an *implied warranty* that the home was fit for human habitation. The trial court ruled that, under Indiana case law, a builder was not liable on the negligence theory to a home buyer who had taken possession and further ruled (for reasons appearing in the decision below) that a home builder did *not* guarantee it to be inhabitable; accordingly, it dismissed the action. Plaintiffs appealed this ruling to an intermediate court of appeals, which held that a builder *could* be held liable on both the *negligence and implied warranty theories*. The defendant/builder then appealed this ruling to the state's highest court.

The Supreme Court of Indiana, in a one-paragraph decision, adopted the opinion of the intermediate court "as its own," and accordingly ordered that opinion to be published in full. [*Note:* only that part of the intermediate appeals court's decision dealing with the imposition of implied warranty liability is set forth below.]

Sharp, Judge:

. . . The [trial court relied] very heavily upon the decision of *Tudor v. Heugel*, 178 N.E.2d 442 (1961). In [that case] the purchaser of the home brought suit against both the vendor-builder and the realtor who had sold the home . . . for various defects including a defective drainage system. . . . This court . . . in *Tudor* clearly held that the doctrine of *caveat emptor* applies to ordinary real estate transactions, and that neither the seller nor the realtor could be held liable where there was no allegation that either [party] made false representations concerning the new house being sold or express warranties pertaining thereto.

We might engage in some meaningless logic chopping in an attempt to distinguish this case from *Tudor*. However, we believe *that in the context of the development of the law in the intervening decade since 1961 that* Tudor *represents bad law and should be overruled.* [Emphasis added.] Neither this court nor our own Supreme Court are wedded to a wooden concept of *stare decisis* which causes adherence to past decisions when the reason for such decisions no longer exists.

The rule of caveat emptor [applied by the trial court] has been severely criticized. For example, in *Humber v. Morton*, 426 S.W.2d 554 (1968), the Supreme Court of Texas stated:

The caveat emptor rule as applied to new houses is an anachronism patently out of harmony with modern home buying practices. It does a disservice not only to the ordinary prudent purchaser but to the industry itself by lending encouragement to the unscrupulous, fly-by-night operator and purveyor of shoddy work. . . .

In overruling *Tudor* we look to a modern trend of well-reasoned authority. In *Wawak v. Stewart*, 449 S.W.2d 922 (1970), the Supreme Court of Arkansas stated:

Twenty years ago one could hardly find any American decision recognizing the existence of an implied warranty in a routine sale of a new dwelling. Both the rapidity and the unanimity with which the courts have recently moved away from the harsh doctrine of caveat emptor *in the sale of new houses are amazing, for the law has not traditionally progressed with such speed.*

Yet there is nothing really surprising in the modern trend. The contrast between the rules of law applicable to the sale of personal property and those applicable to the sale of real property was so great as to be indefensible. One who bought [an item] as simple as a walking cane or kitchen mop was entitled to get his money back if the article was not of merchantable quality. But the purchaser of a $50,000 home ordinarily had no remedy even if the foundation proved to be so defective that the structure collapsed into a heap of rubble. . . .

[The court then cited with approval a 1966 case in which the Idaho Supreme Court imposed implied warranty liability on the builder of a new home. The court in that case said]:

The implied warranty of fitness does not impose upon the builder an obligation to deliver a perfect house. No house is without defects, and defects susceptible of remedy ordinarily would not warrant rescission [i.e., cancellation]. But major defects which render the house unfit for human habitation and which are not readily remediable, entitle the buyer to rescission and [damages]. . . .

We therefore [rule] that *Tudor v. Heugel* [holding that a home builder does not impliedly warrant it to be fit for human habitation] can no longer be considered the law of this State. . . .

Judgment of the trial court is reversed, and [the case is remanded to it for further proceedings].

★★★

The Tort of Wrongful Discharge[7]

Employment agreements fall into two categories, insofar as their duration is concerned: *fixed term* contracts and contracts *at will*. The fixed-term agreement, as the name implies, refers to contracts that run for a specified period of time (such as January 1, 1985, to December 30, 1986). At-will relationships, by contrast, are those in which both the employer and the employee have the right to terminate the agreement at any time.

Fixed-term contracts give employees substantial protection, because these agreements can be terminated by employers only "for cause"—for instance, excessive absenteeism or embezzlement on the part of the employee. An employee discharged *without* cause can thus sue for damages for breach of the employment contract.

The at-will relationship, by contrast, gives the employee no such protection. The traditional at-will rule has been that the employer may terminate the relationship at any time, for cause or for no cause at all. In most instances this traditional doctrine has not been unfair to the employee, because he or she knows from the inception of the agreement that there is no guarantee as to the duration of the relationship.

Over the years, however, a recurring problem in the at-will area has presented itself: the discharge of the employee for reasons that are either totally unrelated to the employment relationship or for other reasons that seem to be grossly unfair to the employee. In these cases, *the clear, traditional doctrine has been that the employer's right to terminate is absolute*. Under this view, for example, an employee who is discharged for testifying in an administrative proceeding brought by the government against his or her employer has no "cause of action" against the employer—that is, cannot recover damages from the employer—even though his or her testimony was entirely truthful and was given during a lawful administrative hearing.

Because of results of this sort, a growing number of courts have recently fashioned an exception to the at-will doctrine which is essentially that an employee *may* recover damages for *wrongful termination* (or "abusive discharge") (1) where the reason for the discharge contravenes a clear public policy of the state, or (2) where the discharge results from malice or other

---

[7] A tort is a "civil wrong"—any conduct a court feels to be violative of another's rights even though the conduct is not necessarily criminal in nature. Basic principles of tort law are discussed in Chapter 8.

improper motive on the part of the employer. A discharge of the employee for refusing to obey the employer's request to avoid jury duty would be a tort falling within the public policy category,[8] and a discharge of a married woman for refusing to "be nice" and to "go out" with her foreman is a wrongful motive example.[9]

Tameny v. Atlantic Richfield Company, 610 P.2d 1330 (1980), is representative of those newer cases which permit a discharged employee, in limited circumstances, to recover damages under the "abusive discharge" tort theory. There the plaintiff, Tameny, was discharged by Atlantic Richfield (Arco) allegedly because he refused to "threaten and cajole" independent service station dealers to adhere to Arco's price-pegging scheme—a scheme that violated the Sherman Antitrust Act. Although Tameny's employment with Arco was an at-will relationship, the Supreme Court of California awarded him damages on the tort theory. The court reviewed a number of cases in other states in which recovery had been allowed, and summarized them as follows:

These recent decisions demonstrate a continuing judicial recognition of the fact, enunciated by this court more than 35 years ago, that the days when a servant was practically the slave of his master have long since passed. In the last half century the rights of employees have not only been proclaimed by a mass of legislation touching upon almost every aspect of the employer-employee relationship, but the courts have likewise evolved certain additional protection at common law. . . . This development at common law shows that the employer is not so absolute a sovereign of the job that there are not limits to his prerogative. One such limit at least is the present case. The employer cannot condition employment upon required participation in unlawful conduct by the employee. An employer [who demands that the employee commit a criminal act to further its interests] violates a basic duty imposed by law upon all employers, and thus an employee who has suffered damages as a result of such discharge may maintain a tort action for wrongful discharge against the employer.[10]

Questions and Problems

1. In a case reaching the Wisconsin Supreme Court in 1985 (*Koback v. Crook*, 366 N.W. 2d 857), the court was asked to decide an issue that has become increasingly common in recent years. The precise question is whether a social host who gra-

---

[8] *Nees v. Hocks*, 532 P.2d 512 (1975).

[9] *Monge v. Beebe Rubber Company*, 316 A.2d 549 (1974). This case was exceptional in that the court viewed the employer's wrongful discharge as a breach of contract, rather than a tort. (A scholarly critique of these theories is found in an article by John D. Blackburn, Associate Professor of Finance, The Ohio State University, "Restricted Employer Discharge Rights," *American Business Law Journal* 17, no. 4, Winter 1980.)

[10] A fuller presentation of this case appears in Chapter 21, with emphasis upon those portions of the court's decision that deal with the moral and ethical obligations of employers generally.

tuitously serves a drink to an intoxicated guest—knowing that the guest is to be driving home soon—should, under common-law negligence principles, be held liable to a third party who is struck by the intoxicated driver while he or she is en route home. (Some states have statutes which determine the issue of liability, but other states—including Wisconsin—do not. And, in those states without applicable statutes, the state supreme courts have reached conflicting results.) If you were a judge on the Wisconsin Supreme Court, would you be in favor of imposing liability on the basis of common-law principles? That is, do you feel that the serving of a drink to an intoxicated guest is an act of carelessness, and that it should be reasonably foreseeable to the host that the guest might be involved in an automobile accident on the way home? Discuss.

2. Contract Packers leased a number of trucks from Hertz Truck Leasing and Rental Service of Jersey City, N.J. The brakes on one of the trucks failed, which resulted in an accident that injured a Contract Packers' employee, Cintrone. Cintrone then brought suit for damages against Hertz, the lessor.

Cintrone's case was essentially based on the "implied warranty" theory—the theory that Hertz, simply by the act of leasing the truck, thereby impliedly warranted (guaranteed) that the trucks were reasonably fit for operation on the highway, and that this warranty was breached because a truck with defective brakes is not fit for highway use. Hertz's defense was that, under a New Jersey statute, the implied warranty theory applied to *sales* of goods (such as cars and trucks), and neither the statute nor the principle behind the statute had ever been applied in New Jersey to *lessors* of cars and trucks.

Cintrone's response to this defense was twofold: (a) that since the liability of lessors in New Jersey was based on common-law rules rather than on any statute, the New Jersey courts had the authority to impose implied warranty liability on lessors even though this was contrary to existing precedent in the state, and (b) that the same public safety considerations that justified imposing implied warranty liability on new car sellers ought also to justify the imposition of such liability on commercial leasing companies. Do you feel that either or both of these contentions are valid? Discuss. (*Cintrone v. Hertz Truck Leasing and Rental Service, Inc.*, 212 A.2d 769, 1965.)

3. Mrs. Maddux was injured when the car she was riding in was struck by a car driven by Donaldson, and, almost immediately thereafter, by a second car driven by Bryie. When Mrs. Maddux sued the two negligent drivers, the facts of the case were such that it was impossible to determine which of her injuries were caused by the first collision and which by the second collision. At the time of the suit, the Michigan common-law rule was that, in such a case, neither defendant could be held liable for any damages; accordingly, the trial court dismissed Mrs. Maddux's action. She then appealed to the Supreme Court of Michigan, claiming that the rule of nonrecovery was too unfair to an injured plaintiff. Do you agree with this contention? If so, what do you think a better rule would be? (*Maddux v. Donaldson*, 108 N.W.2d 33, 1961.)

4. Tuttle, a barber in a small town in Minnesota, alleged that Buck, a banker, had set up a rival barbershop in town for the sole purpose of putting Tuttle out of business. Because there were no prior cases in the U.S. on this subject, the trial court had to decide whether such conduct on the part of Buck constituted a wrong in the eyes of the law (thus making Buck liable in damages). Among other things, Buck contended that his action was lawful because there was no common-law rule prohibiting conduct of this sort. Assuming that there was no existing common-law rule, do you think that the court should therefore enter judgment in favor of Buck, or do you think the court could—and should—make new law by declaring Buck's conduct to be unlawful? Explain your reasoning. (*Tuttle v. Buck*, 119 N.W. 946, 1909.)

5. Mr. Henningsen bought a new Plymouth from his local New Jersey dealer, who had purchased it from the manufacturer, Chrysler Corporation. Ten days later Mrs. Henningsen was injured when the steering gear failed and the car ran into a brick wall. In Mrs. Henningsen's suit against Chrysler, she alleged that a manufacturer, by putting its products into the stream of commerce, impliedly warrants (guarantees) that they are "merchantable"—reasonably fit for ordinary use—and further alleged that in this case the car was *not* merchantable because of the steering defect.

As a defense, Chrysler contended that the common-law rule in New Jersey (the rule of prior cases) was to the effect that a manufacturer was liable on the breach of warranty theory only to a person who purchased the car *directly* from the manufacturer. On the basis of that rule, Mrs. Henningsen would lose, since the car was purchased from a dealer rather than from Chrysler. (a) Do you think the existing common-law rule should be changed to permit a subsequent buyer (such as the Henningsens) to hold Chrysler liable? (b) What would the reasons be for and against such a change? (*Henningsen v. Bloomfield Motors, Inc.*, 161 A.2d 69, 1960.)

6. In a number of cases, the supreme court of State X had adopted the rule that a seller of land who overstated the *value of the land* to a prospective buyer was not guilty of fraud, even if he or she knew that the true market value of the land was much lower than the figure stated to the buyer. (The reasoning of the court, in these cases, was that the value of any property is merely a matter of opinion and that the buyer should realize this.) After this rule is adopted, a new case reaches the supreme court, in which the buyer of land claims that the seller was guilty of fraud when he—the seller—intentionally misrepresented the *rental value* of the property. (Seller told Buyer, an out-of-state resident who had never seen the land, that "it can readily be rented for $100 a month," a statement that proved to be false.) If the supreme court felt that the seller in such a case should be made to pay damages on the theory that he was guilty of fraud, would the court have to overrule the prior decisions, or do you think that the facts of the new case are sufficiently different so as to permit the court simply to apply a different rule to it? Explain your reasoning. (*Cahill v. Readon*, 273 P.653, 1928.)

7. Anne DeMarco, a minor, was injured in a Publix Super Market store in Miami, Florida, when a soft drink bottle exploded. (Her father, Carl, was an employee of Publix.) After the accident, Publix's insurance company paid for Anne's medical expenses, but refused to pay additional damages for pain, suffering, and inconvenience. When her father subsequently brought suit against Publix to recover such additional damages, Publix told DeMarco he would be discharged if he did not withdraw the suit. DeMarco refused, and his employment was terminated.

DeMarco then brought *this* action for damages against Publix, contending that his discharge under the circumstances was a wrongful one. Do you agree with DeMarco that this is a situation where the "wrongful discharge" exception ought to be applied? Why or why not? (*DeMarco v. Publix Super Markets, Inc.*, 360 So.2d 134, 1978.)

C·H·A·P·T·E·R 4

STATUTORY LAW

While a significant portion of our law is still common-law in nature, most of our federal and state law today results from the enactment of statutes by legislative bodies—formally adopted rules which collectively comprise our *statutory law*, the second of the major sources of law.[1] All states, for example, have comprehensive statutes governing such subjects as corporation law, criminal law, and motor vehicle law. Similarly, at the federal level, sweeping statutes in the areas of antitrust law, labor law, and securities regulation have been in place for many years. And examples of more recent (and narrower) federal statutes are the Consumer Product Safety Act of 1972, the Bankruptcy Reform Act of 1978, the Chrysler Loan Guarantee Act of 1979, and the Steelmaking Facilities Clean Air Act of 1981. Figure 4.1 summarizes the origin, form, scope, and effect of statutory law.

---

[1]The term "statutory law," when broadly used in contrast to "common law," includes not only laws passed by legislative bodies but, additionally, U.S. treaties, the federal and state constitutions, and municipal ordinances. In this chapter, however, the term is used in its more customary sense, referring only to acts of the state legislatures and of Congress.

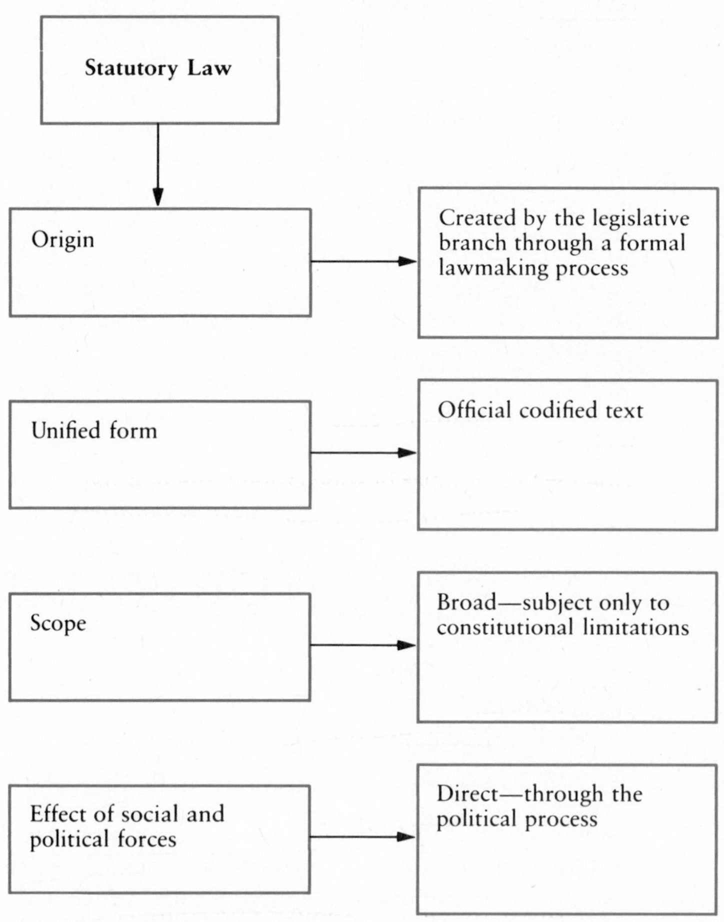

Figure 4.1 Statutory Law

A Profile of Our Federal and State Statutory Law

In this chapter our first objectives are to examine the reasons for the existence of statutory law, to become acquainted with the basic rules that delineate the jurisdictions of the federal and state governments, and to note the contrasts between statutory and common law. We will then turn our attention to the closely related area of statutory interpretation—the process by which the courts spell out the precise meaning of statutes that are applicable to the particular cases coming before them—and conclude with a summary of selected state statutes that are of special significance to the business community.[2] As a backdrop for a better understanding of the issues that are ad-

[2] The salient federal statutes are discussed in detail in Parts II and III of the text.

dressed in this chapter, however, a brief description of the vast scope of our statutory law is first in order.

The United States Code

All of the acts of Congress currently in effect (referred to as "federal legislation") comprise the U.S. Code—a compilation of statutes so numerous that it is twenty-one volumes in length. Insofar as its structure is concerned, the code is divided into fifty major areas called "Titles," with each title further being divided into "Chapters" and sometimes "Subchapters," with each chapter and subchapter in turn being comprised of the individual code provisions called "Sections."

Title 16 of the code, for example, entitled "Conservation," is made up of thirty-eight chapters consisting of Sections 1 through 1912. Chapter 1, "The National Parks, Military Parks, Monuments, and Seashores," is divided into a number of subchapters, the first having to do with general provisions relative to the creation and administration of the National Park Service, with subsequent subchapters applicable to the individual parks—for instance, Subchapter 5, "Yellowstone" (consisting of Sections 21 through 40) and Subchapter 6, "Sequoia and Yosemite" (Sections 41 through 79). The ensuing thirty-seven chapters of Title 16 bear such names as "The National Forests," "Wild and Scenic Rivers," and "Fishing Conservation and Management."

Other representative titles of the U.S. Code are the following:

Title 5—Government Organization and Employees

Title 10—The Armed Forces

Title 11—Bankruptcy

Title 18—Crimes and Criminal Procedure

Title 20—Education

Title 22—Food and Drugs

Title 29—Labor

Title 42—The Public Health and Welfare

The State Codes

Each state code is a compilation of all state statutes ("state legislation") covering those areas of law which are constitutionally subject to state regulation. The structure of the typical state code is very similar to that of the U.S. Code, with the largest divisions consisting of titles that are further broken down into smaller chapter and section segments. Some of the representative titles of the Indiana Code, for example, are the following:

Title 4—State Administration

Title 9—Motor Vehicles

Title 20—Education

Title 23—Business and Other Transactions

Title 24—Trade Regulation, Consumer Sales, and Credit

Title 26—Commercial Law

Title 28—Financial Institutions

Title 35—Criminal Law

Statutory Law—The Rationale

There are many reasons for the existence of statutory law, three of which deserve special mention. First, one of the primary functions of any legislative body is to adopt measures having to do with the *structure and day-to-day operation* of the government of which it is a part. Thus many federal statutes are of the "nuts and bolts" variety relating to such matters as the operation of the federal court system, the Internal Revenue Service, and the administration and employment rules of the U.S. Civil Service Commission. In similar vein, many state statutes relate to such matters as the property tax laws, the operation of school systems, and the setting forth of powers of municipalities within their borders.

Second, many activities are of such a nature that *they can hardly be regulated by common-law principles* and the judicial processes. In the area of criminal law, for example, it is absolutely essential for the general populace to know what acts are punishable by fine and imprisonment; the only sure way to set forth the elements of specific crimes is through the enactment of federal and state criminal statutes. Similarly, the activities of corporations are so complex and so varied that they do not lend themselves to judicial regulation. Few judges, for example, have either the expertise to deal with such questions as the conditions under which the payment of corporate dividends should be permitted, or the time to deal with the spelling out of such conditions on a case-by-case basis. Thus the only practical way to deal with these and other problems is by the drafting of detailed statutes which, in total, make up the comprehensive corporation laws of the states.

The third function of a legislature is to expressly change (or even overrule) common-law rules where it believes such modifications are necessary, and—even more commonly—to enact statutes to *remedy new problems* to which common-law rules do not apply. Thus a state legislature might pass a statute making nonprofit corporations (such as hospitals) liable for the wrongs of their employees to the same extent as are profit-making corporations, thereby reversing the early common-law rule of nonliability for such employers. Or a legislature, aware of increasing purchases of its farmlands by foreign citizens—a situation not covered by common-law rules—might re-

"Take the Kentucky Fried Chicken stamps. You'll love the glue . . . it's made with their secret blend of herbs and spices!"

Legislative solutions to modern problems require considerable creativity on the part of lawmakers.
Source: Reprinted by permission: Tribune Media Services.

act to this perceived evil by passing a statute placing limits on the number of acres aliens may own or inherit. (Over twenty states today have such statutes, and approximately ten have passed laws that prohibit aliens who live outside the U.S. from owning *any* farmlands within these states' borders.)

The Federal/State Relationship, Generally

Under our system of dual sovereignty, fifty-one primary governments exist in this country—the federal government and the fifty state governments. This situation requires that the powers of the federal and state governments be delineated to prevent overlapping areas of authority. The basic lines of demarcation are found in the federal Constitution, where the powers of the federal government are spelled out in Section 8 of Article 1. Of the numerous powers, the following are of particular importance:

The Congress shall have Power
To lay and collect Taxes, Duties, Imposts and Excises, to pay the Debts and provide for the common Defense and general Welfare of the United States; . . .
To borrow Money on the Credit of the United States;
To regulate Commerce with foreign Nations, and among the several States, and with the Indian Tribes;
To establish an uniform Rule of Naturalization, and uniform Laws on the subject of Bankruptcies throughout the United States;

To coin Money, regulate the Value thereof, and of foreign Coin, and fix the Standard of Weights and Measures; . . .
To establish Post Offices and post Roads;
To promote the Progress of Science and useful Arts, by securing for limited Times to Authors and Inventors the exclusive right to their respective Writings and Discoveries;
To constitute Tribunals inferior to the supreme Court; . . .
To declare War, grant Letters of Marque and Reprisal, and make Rules concerning Captures on Land and Water;
To raise and support Armies, but no Appropriation of Money to that Use shall be for a longer Term than two Years;
To provide and maintain a Navy;
To make Rules for the Government and Regulation of the land and naval forces;
To provide for calling forth the Militia to execute the Laws of the Union, suppress Insurrections and repel Invasions;
To provide for organizing, arming, and disciplining, the Militia, and . . .
To make all Laws which shall be necessary and proper for carrying into Execution the foregoing Powers, and all other Powers vested by this Constitution in the Government of the United States, or in any Department or Officer thereof.

Under Section 8, the powers that appear therein have been expressly granted by the states to the federal government and are thus referred to as the "delegated" or "enumerated" powers. All other powers (called "reserved") rest in the state governments.

The subject-matter limitations appearing in Section 8 are the prime sources of the federal and state governmental jurisdictions, going to the very essence of their respective powers. For this reason, they are often discussed under the subject of Constitutional Law (which is covered in the following chapter). However, because acts of Congress and the state legislatures are valid only when addressed to subjects within their respective jurisdictions, the delegated powers of Section 8 have such a direct relationship to the subject of statutory law that they will, instead, be examined here—with particular emphasis being given to the **commerce clause**.

General Observations

By and large, the lines of demarcation between the authority of the federal and state governments are quite clear. Most of the powers delegated to the federal government under Section 8—such as the power to operate post offices and to maintain the various armed forces—involve such clearcut activities that no state could claim to possess any regulatory powers over them.

By the same token, the powers reserved to the states are also, in general, clearly established. Virtually all of the powers of a given state spring from the state's **police power**—a term referring to the state's inherent authority to regulate the health, safety, morals, and general welfare of its people.[3] Statutes relating to the operation of motor vehicles, the manufacture and sale of intoxicating liquors, and the state criminal statutes obviously fall within the police power, since they are directly involved with matters of health, safety, and morals. Typical statutes based upon the "general welfare" component of the police power are those that regulate such matters as marriage and divorce, the inheritance of property, and the landlord-tenant relationship. (The power to enact zoning laws also falls within the police power category, but the legislatures normally delegate this power to their cities; thus most zoning regulations are, in fact, found in municipal ordinances and regulations of municipal zoning commissions.)

The Commerce Clause

As noted, most of the federal powers are so delineated that states rarely enact legislation infringing upon these powers. Thus federal and state confrontations in these areas are relatively rare.

By contrast, the scope of Congress's regulatory powers under the commerce clause—and the related question of the extent to which states' regulatory powers might affect interstate commerce—have raised serious federal and state jurisdictional issues over the years. We will briefly examine here the basic principles of law applicable to these questions.

Federal Regulation of Interstate Commerce

Commerce: The clause granting to Congress the power "to regulate Commerce with foreign Nations, and among the several States" was at first construed very narrowly by the courts. Under this view, the commerce which was subject to federal regulation was basically limited to the activities of companies who bought or sold goods that were actually transported across state lines and the transportation companies that moved such goods. In a 1918 case, for example (*Hammer v. Dagenhart*, 247 U.S. 251), the U.S. Supreme Court held that a federal law prohibiting the interstate transportation of goods made in factories that employed children was inapplicable to such companies because manufacturing was an internal state activity and thus not within the commerce clause.

In subsequent cases, however, the highest court rejected the early approach. The rule today is that all phases of production of goods and services constitute **interstate commerce** where an appreciable portion of the final goods or services do, in fact, enter interstate commerce. Under this view,

[3] The taxation power is the only major power not falling within the police power; this is because it is a "granted" rather than an "inherent" power (i.e. the power to tax is granted by the state constitutions).

most manufacturing activities clearly constitute commerce. Along similar lines, the U.S. Supreme Court held in *Mandeville Farms v. Sugar Company*, 334 U.S. 219 (1948), that the growing of sugar beets by California farmers was interstate commerce in view of the fact that the growing phase was subsequently followed by two other phases—refining and distribution—which ultimately resulted in the refined sugar being shipped across state lines in appreciable quantities.

Activities Affecting Commerce: The jurisdiction of the federal government has been broadened even further by the courts' view today that Congress may not only regulate interstate commerce, but, additionally, all business activities that have "an appreciable effect" on interstate commerce. As one example of this approach, the U.S. Supreme Court held in *Heart of Atlanta Motel v. United States*, 379 U.S. 241 (1964), that a motel in Atlanta, Georgia, was subject to the Civil Rights Act of 1964, a federal statute prohibiting discrimination in places of public accommodation, even though all of its operations were conducted solely within the state and all of its employees were Georgia citizens. The court ruled, first, that the movement of persons from state to state constituted "commerce," and, second, that the motel's operations substantially affected interstate commerce in view of the fact that three-fourths of its clients were interstate travelers.

A more recent example of cases that have further broadened the commerce clause scope is that of *McLain v. Real Estate Board of New Orleans*, 100 S.Ct. 502 (1980). In that case the issue was whether a number of New Orleans real estate firms and trade associations had violated the federal antitrust laws by entering into several price-fixing contracts. The lower federal courts dismissed the action, ruling that the defendants' actions were "purely local" in nature and thus not subject to the antitrust laws. The U.S. Supreme Court reversed, finding that the indirect effects of the defendants' activities were sufficiently related to interstate commerce as to justify the conclusion that the federal laws *did* apply to such activities. This finding of sufficient effect—a "not insubstantial effect"—was based primarily on the fact that (1) significant amounts of money lent by local banks to finance real estate purchases came from out-of-state banks, and (2) most of the mortgages taken by the local banks were "physically traded" by them to financial institutions in other states.

As a result of these broadened views, there are very few business activities today whose activities are so completely local (*intra*state) in nature as to be outside the scope of federal regulation under the commerce clause.

The State Governments and Interstate Commerce

A major purpose of the commerce clause was to free interstate commerce from the possibility that the individual states would impede such commerce by erecting economic barriers against out-of-state goods. This purpose has been substantially achieved.

The implied prohibition against state regulation of interstate commerce found in the commerce clause does not, however, mean that *all* state regulations—statutes and rulings of state agencies—affecting interstate commerce are necessarily invalid. A primary reason for this lies in the fact that Congress has passed comprehensive statutes governing some subject areas of interstate commerce, narrower statutes in other subject areas, and no statutes at all in the remaining areas. As a result, state regulations are often legally applicable to persons or firms who are in interstate commerce (or whose activities affect interstate commerce) and who are, therefore, also subject to federal regulation. This is particularly true where the state regulations are based on the "health and safety" components of the state police power.

While it is difficult to categorize all of the cases in which the state regulations may or may not be valid in this area of the law, most of the cases fit into three broad categories.

Preemption: If a federal statute or other regulation applicable to an area of interstate commerce shows, in the opinion of the court, an intent by Congress that the federal government shall have exclusive domain over the subject matter or the specified activities, then it is said that the federal government has "preempted the field." In such instances, under the supremacy clause of the constitution, *all state regulations are void* to the extent that they affect such subject matter or activities.[4] In other words, where preemption exists, the rule is that the state regulation is invalid not only where it conflicts with the federal regulation, but, additionally, is invalid even if it is "not in direct conflict" with the federal regulation.

Preemption may be either express or implied. Express preemption occurs where the federal statute or regulation expressly provides that the federal government shall have sole jurisdiction over the subject matter, and implied preemption occurs where the federal regulation applicable to a given area is, in the opinion of the court, so comprehensive and complete that an attempt to preempt is presumed—even though the statutes or other regulations do not contain a preemption provision.

Two cases in this area are instructive. In *Fidelity Savings & Loan Association v. de la Cuesta*, 458 U.S. 141 (1982), the legality of a California law which generally prohibited the enforcement of "due-on-sale" clauses in mortgages taken by federal savings and loan associations was in issue.[5] In that case, the U.S. Supreme Court held that the regulations of the federal Home Loan Bank Board—which permitted the enforcement of such clauses

[4]The "supremacy clause" is found in Section 1 of Article VI of the U.S. Constitution, which provides that "This Constitution, and the laws of the United States which shall be made in pursuance thereof . . . shall be the supreme law of the land."

[5]A due-on-sale clause is a provision in a mortgage which, in effect, prohibits a homeowner from selling his or her mortgaged home and allowing the buyer to *assume* the existing mortgage. The buyer, therefore, must instead *refinance* the property through a lending institution (usually at a higher interest rate).

in all instances—showed a clear intent on the part of the board to preempt the field in regard to such subject matter. Accordingly, the California law was void. The highest court, while failing to characterize the preemption as express or implied, based its ruling in part on the board's preface to its regulations, in which it stated that due-on-sale provisions of federal savings and loan associations shall be governed "solely by federal law."

Another typical case is that of *Campbell v. Hussey*, 368 U.S. 297 (1961), in which case the U.S. Supreme Court ruled that a Georgia law requiring "type 14" tobacco grown in Georgia be identified with a white tag was invalid under the preemption doctrine. The court based its ruling on the fact that a federal statute setting up a federal tobacco grading system provided that "factors of a geographical nature" could not be reflected in the grading scale adopted by the U.S. Department of Agriculture, and that the federal grading system was so comprehensive as to impliedly preempt the entire field of tobacco grading.

Although many other instances of federal preemption do exist, it should be cautioned that the courts are reluctant to find an implied preemption unless such an intent is overwhelmingly clear. Thus, in the many cases in which it is claimed that an implied preemption exists, the claim is more often rejected than accepted by the courts, in which instances the state regulation is upheld.

Limited Federal Regulation: When federal statutes are applicable to a certain area of interstate commerce but the legislation is not comprehensive enough to constitute a preemption, state statutes affecting the area are constitutional as long as they do not "conflict" with the federal regulation. In other words, if compliance with the state regulation does not violate any of the federal rules, and if compliance does not "unduly burden" interstate commerce, the regulation is valid. *State of Washington v. Sterling Theatres Company*, 394 P. 2d 226 (1964) is one of many cases falling within this category. There the Washington State Supreme Court ruled that a state antitrust law (a "little Sherman" act) did not conflict with the provisions of the Sherman Act, the federal antitrust law, and hence the provisions of the state law *were* applicable to the defendants, a number of motion picture exhibitors and distributors who entered into a conspiracy prohibited by the state act. On the other hand, if the state regulation does conflict with the federal, the state regulation again, under the supremacy clause, is void.

Absence of Federal Regulation: When a state statute affects an area of interstate commerce in which federal regulation is entirely lacking, the state regulation is normally valid, subject to two important limitations: (1) the regulation must further a legitimate local (state) interest, and (2) the regulation again must not "unduly burden"—unreasonably interfere with—interstate commerce. In determining whether the burden is undue, on the one hand, or "merely incidental," on the other, the courts balance the purpose of the state regulation (the importance of the interest being protected) against the magnitude of its effect on interstate commerce.

In this regard, state statutes passed under the "public safety" component of the police power are more likely to be upheld than are other statutes because they usually meet the legitimate local interest requirement. However, even public safety statutes and regulations are often set aside under the unreasonable burden test. For example, in *Southern Pacific Co. v. Arizona*, 325 U.S. 761 (1945), the U.S. Supreme Court held that a state statute limiting the length of passenger trains to fourteen cars and freight trains to seventy cars had "such an adverse effect" upon interstate rail operations that the statute was unconstitutional under the commerce clause. And in *Kassel v. Consolidated Freightways Corp.*, 455 U.S. 329 (1981), the highest court set aside an Iowa statute barring use of trucks longer than sixty feet on the state's interstate highways on the same grounds. The unreasonable burden finding was based on (1) testimony that compliance with the statute would cost interstate trucking companies more than $12 million per year, and (2) evidence that the commonly-used sixty-five-foot units were no more likely to be involved in traffic accidents than the smaller units.

In recent years state "economic legislation" passed under the general welfare segment of the police power has been increasingly common. The state regulations involved in the next two cases raise both the legitimate local interest and the undue burden issues, there being no serious claim that federal preemption existed in either case.

Exxon Corp. v. Governor of Maryland
U.S. Supreme Court
437 U.S. 117
(1977)

During the 1973 nationwide oil shortage, evidence was produced indicating that out-of-state oil producers and refiners were favoring their company-operated gasoline stations in Maryland at the expense of independently operated stations. Responding to this evidence, the Maryland legislature passed a statute which, among other things, prohibited producers and refiners from operating retail gasoline stations in the state.

Exxon Corporation, a refiner who sold much of its gasoline to wholesalers and independent retailers in Maryland, also sold substantial quantities of gasoline through thirty-six retail stations that it owned in the state. Exxon, joined by Phillips, Shell, Gulf, and three smaller refiners, challenged the constitutionality of the statute. They contended that the statute violated both the due process and commerce clauses of the U.S. Constitution. The federal trial court agreed with these contentions, but the federal Court of Appeals reversed that judgment and ruled that the statute was valid. The oil companies appealed to the U.S. Supreme Court.

Stevens, Justice:

. . . As brought out during the trial, the salient characteristics of the Maryland retail gasoline market are as follows: Approximately 3,800 retail service stations sell over 20 different brands of gasoline. However, no petroleum products are produced in Maryland, and the number of stations actually operated by a refiner or an affiliate is relatively small, representing about 5 percent of the total number of Maryland retailers. . . .

[The court then held that statute did not violate the due process clause, saying that "(t)he evidence presented by the refiners may cause some doubt on the wisdom of the statute, but it is, by now, absolutely clear that the Due Process Clause does not empower the judiciary 'to sit as a superlegislature to weigh the wisdom of legislation.'. . . Appellants argue that (the statute) is irrational and that it will frustrate rather than further the State's desired goal of enhancing competition. But . . . this argument rests simply on an evaluation of the economic wisdom of the statute, and cannot override the State's authority to 'legislate against what are found to be injurious practices in their internal commercial and business affairs.'"[a] The court then turned to the contention that the statute violated the Commerce Clause of the Constitution].

Appellants argue that the divestiture provisions of the Maryland statute violate the Commerce Clause in three ways: (1) by discriminating against interstate commerce; (2) by unduly burdening interstate commerce; and (3) by imposing controls on a commercial activity of such an essentially interstate character that it is not amenable to state regulation.

Plainly, the Maryland statute does not discriminate against interstate goods, nor does it favor local producers and refiners. Since Maryland's entire gasoline supply flows in interstate commerce and since there are no local producers or refiners, such claims of disparate treatment between interstate and local commerce [are] meritless. Appellants, however, focus on the retail market, arguing that the effect of the statute is to protect in-state independent dealers from out-of-state competition. They contend that the divestiture provisions "create a protected enclave for Maryland independent dealers." As support for this proposition, they rely on the fact that the burden of the divestiture requirements falls solely on interstate companies. But this fact does not lead, either logically or as a practical matter, to a conclusion that the State is discriminating against interstate commerce at the retail level.

As the record shows, there are several major interstate marketers of petroleum that own and operate their own retail gasoline stations. These interstate dealers, who compete directly with the Maryland dealers, are not affected by the Act because they do not refine or produce gasoline. In fact, the Act creates no barriers whatsoever against interstate independent dealers; it does not prohibit the flow of interstate goods, place added costs upon them, or distinguish between in-state and out-of-state companies in the retail market. The absence of any of these factors distinguishes this case from those in which a State has been found to have discriminated against interstate commerce. [The court then turned to the oil companies' second argument.]

Appellants argue [that the statute] impermissibly *burdens* interstate commerce [by pointing to] evidence in the record which indicates that, because of the divestiture requirements, at least three refiners will stop selling in Maryland, and which evidence also supports their claim that the elimination of company-operated stations will deprive the consumer of certain special services [provided

[a] More will be said about the due process clause in the next chapter.

by company-operated stations]. Even if we assume the truth of both assertions, neither warrants a finding that the statute impermissibly burdens interstate commerce.

Some refiners may choose to withdraw entirely from the Maryland market, but there is no reason to assume that their share of the entire supply will not be promptly replaced by other interstate refiners. The source of the consumers' supply may switch from company-operated stations to independent dealers, but interstate commerce is not subjected to an impermissible burden simply because an otherwise valid regulation causes some business to shift from one interstate supplier to another.

[After ruling against the oil companies on their first two arguments, the court also rejected their contention that the sale of gasoline at retail was of such an interstate nature that it could not be regulated by a state. On this point the court said, "This Court has only rarely held that the Commerce Clause itself preempts an entire field from state regulation, and then only when a lack of national uniformity would impede the flow of interstate goods. The evil that appellants perceive in this litigation is not that the several states will enact differing regulations, but rather that they will all conclude that divestiture provisions are warranted. The problem thus is not one of national uniformity (and we cannot, therefore) conclude that the States are without power to regulate in this area." Finding the statute to be constitutional, the court affirmed the judgment of the court of appeals.]

★★★

Hunt v. Washington State Apple Advertising Commission
U.S. Supreme Court
432 U.S. 333 (1977)

For many years prior to this dispute, Washington State had maintained a stringent, mandatory apple inspection program designed to protect and enhance the reputation of Washington apples. The program was administered by the state's Department of Agriculture, and required all apples shipped in interstate commerce to be tested under strict quality standards and graded accordingly. In all cases, the Washington State grades were the equivalent of, or superior to, the comparable grades and standards adopted by the U. S. Department of Agriculture (USDA).[a] Compliance with the inspection scheme cost the state's growers approximately $1 million each year.

In addition to the inspection program, the state legislature sought to enhance the market for Washington apples through the creation of a state agency, the Washington State Apple Advertising Commission, charged with the duty of promoting and protecting the state's apple industry. Among its activities were the promotion of Washington apples in both domestic and foreign markets through advertising, market research, and analysis, and scientific research into the uses, development, and improvement of apples.

[a]Because this case had to do with the legality of the North Carolina regulatory statute, rather than with the right of Washington State to establish its *grading system*, it was not contended in any of the proceedings that the Washington State grading system was preempted by the U.S. Department of Agriculture system.

In 1972 the North Carolina Board of Agriculture adopted an administrative regulation, unique in the fifty states, which required all closed containers of apples shipped into the state to display either the applicable USDA grade or a notice indicating no classification. *State grades were expressly prohibited.* In addition to its obvious consequence—prohibiting the display of Washington State apple grades on containers of apples shipped into North Carolina—the regulation presented the Washington apple industry with a marketing problem of potentially nationwide significance. This arose from the fact that Washington apple growers annually had been shipping approximately 500,000 closed containers of apples into North Carolina, stamped with the applicable Washington State variety and grade. Furthermore, prior to the adoption of the North Carolina resolution, it had been the Washington State apple industry's practice to purchase these containers preprinted with the various apple varieties and grades, prior to harvest. After these containers were filled with apples of the appropriate variety and grade, they were placed in cold-storage warehouses until shipped after February 1 of each year.

Since the ultimate destination of the apples was unknown at the time that they were placed in storage, compliance with North Carolina's unique regulation would have required Washington growers to obliterate the printed labels on containers shipped to North Carolina, thus giving their product a damaged appearance. Alternatively, they could have changed their marketing practices to accommodate the needs of the North Carolina market: repack apples to be shipped to North Carolina in containers bearing only the USDA grade or store the estimated portion of the harvest destined for that market in such special containers. As a last resort, they could discontinue the use of the preprinted containers entirely. None of these costly options was attractive to the industry. Moreover, if a number of other states followed North Carolina's lead, the resultant inability to display the Washington grades could force Washington growers to abandon the state's expensive inspection and grading system which their customers had come to know and rely on over the sixty years of its existence.

With these problems confronting the industry, the Washington State Apple Advertising Commission (the Commission) petitioned the North Carolina Board of Agriculture to amend its regulation to permit the display of state grades. An administrative hearing was held on the question, but no relief was granted. In fact, North Carolina hardened its position shortly thereafter by *enacting the regulation into law.* The statute read as follows:

All apples sold, offered for sale or shipped into this State in closed containers shall bear on the container, bag or other receptacle, no grade other than the applicable U.S. grade or standard or the marking 'unclassified,' 'not graded' or 'grade not determined.'—N.C. Gen. Stat. § 106-189.1 (1973).

The Commission once again requested an exemption which would have permitted the display of both the U.S. and Washington State grades on their shipments to North Carolina, but this request was also denied.

The Commission then brought this action in a U.S. District Court in North Carolina against Hunt, Governor of North Carolina, and the North Carolina

Board of Agriculture, the state agency charged with enforcement of the statute, contending that the statute violated the Commerce Clause of the United States Constitution. That court, for reasons appearing below, agreed with the Commission and granted an injunction prohibiting North Carolina from enforcing the statute. Defendants appealed to the U.S. Supreme Court.

Burger, Justice:

. . . We turn to the appellants' claim [the claim of Hunt and the North Carolina board] that the District Court erred in holding that the North Carolina statute violated the Commerce Clause insofar as it prohibited the display of Washington State grades on closed containers of apples shipped into the State. Appellants do not really contest the District Court's determination that the challenged statute burdened the Washington apple industry by increasing its costs of doing business in the North Carolina market and causing it to lose accounts there. Rather, they maintain that any such burdens on the interstate sale of Washington apples were *far outweighed by the local benefits* flowing from what they contend was a valid exercise of North Carolina's inherent police powers designed to protect its citizenry from fraud and deception in the marketing of apples. [Emphasis added.]

Prior to the statute's enactment, appellants point out, apples from 13 different States were shipped into North Carolina for sale. Seven of those States, including the State of Washington, had their own grading systems which, while differing in their standards, used similar descriptive labels (*e.g.*, fancy, extra fancy, etc.). This multiplicity of inconsistent state grades, as the District Court itself found, posed dangers of deception and confusion not only in the North Carolina market, but in the Nation as a whole. The North Carolina statute, appellants claim, was enacted to eliminate this source of deception and confusion by replacing the numerous state grades with a single uniform standard. Moreover, it is contended that North Carolina sought to accomplish this goal of uniformity in an evenhanded manner as evidenced by the fact that its statute applies to all apples sold in closed containers in the State without regard to their point of origin. Nonetheless, appellants argue that the District Court gave "scant attention" to the obvious benefits flowing from the challenged legislation and to the long line of decisions from this Court holding that the States possess "broad powers" to protect local purchasers from fraud and deception in the marketing of foodstuffs.

As the appellants point out, not every exercise of state authority imposing some burden on the free flow of commerce is invalid. Although the Commerce Clause acts as a limitation upon state power even without congressional implementation, our opinions have long recognized that,

> *in the absence of conflicting legislation by Congress, there is a residuum of power in the state to make laws governing matters of local concern which in some measure affect interstate commerce or even, to some extent, to regulate it.*—Southern Pacific Co. v. Arizona ex rel. Sullivan, *325 U.S. 761, (1945)*. . . .

By the same token, however, *a finding that state legislation furthers matters of legitimate local concern, even in the health and consumer protection areas, does not end the inquiry.* [Emphasis added.] Such a view . . . would mean that the Commerce Clause of itself imposes no limitations on state action [except in the rare case where a state admittedly intended to discriminate against interstate goods]. Rather, when such state legislation comes into conflict with the Commerce Clause's overriding requirement of a national "common market," we are confronted with the task of effecting an accommodation of the competing national and local interests. We turn to that task.

As the District Court correctly found, the challenged statute has the practical effect of not only burdening interstate sales of Washington apples, but also discriminating against them. This discrimination takes various forms. The first, and most obvious, is the statute's consequence of *raising the costs of doing business in the North Carolina market for Washington apple growers and dealers, while leaving those of their North Carolina counterparts unaffected.* [Emphasis added.] As previously noted, this disparate effect results from the fact that North Carolina apple producers, unlike their Washington competitors, were not forced to alter their marketing practices in order to comply with the statute. They were still free to market their wares under the USDA grade or none at all as they had done prior to the statute's enactment. Obviously, the increased costs imposed by the statute would tend to shield the local apple industry from the competition of Washington apple growers and dealers who are already at a competitive disadvantage because of their great distance from the North Carolina market.

Second, the statute has the effect of *stripping away from the Washington apple industry the competitive and economic advantages it has earned for itself through its expensive inspection and grading system.* [Emphasis added.] The record demonstrates that the Washington apple-grading system has gained nationwide acceptance in the apple trade. Indeed, it contains numerous affidavits from apple brokers and dealers located both inside and outside of North Carolina who state their preference, and that of their customers, for apples graded under the Washington, as opposed to the USDA, system because of the former's greater consistency, its emphasis on color, and its supporting mandatory inspections. Once again, *the statute had no similar impact on the North Carolina apple industry and thus operated to its benefit.* [Emphasis added.]

Third, by prohibiting Washington growers and dealers from marketing apples under their State's grades, the statute has a leveling effect which insidiously operates to the advantage of local apple producers. As noted earlier, the Washington State grades are equal or superior to the USDA grades in all corresponding categories. Hence, with free market forces at work, Washington sellers would normally enjoy a distinct market advantage vis-à-vis local producers in those categories where the Washington grade is superior. However, because of the statute's operation, Washington apples which would otherwise qualify for and be sold under the superior Washington grades will now have to be marketed under their inferior USDA counterparts. *Such "downgrading" offers the North Carolina apple industry the very sort of protection against competing out-of-state products that the Commerce Clause was designed to prohibit.* [Emphasis added.] At worst, it will have the effect of an embargo against those Washington apples in the superior grades as Washington dealers withhold them from the North Carolina market. At best, it will deprive Washington sellers of the market premium that such apples would otherwise command.

Despite the statute's facial neutrality, the Commission suggests that its discriminatory impact on interstate commerce was not an unintended byproduct and there are some indications in the record to that effect. The most glaring is the response of the North Carolina Agriculture Commissioner to the Commission's request for an exemption following the statute's passage in which he indicated that before he could support such an exemption, he would "want to have the sentiment from our apple producers *since they were mainly responsible for this legislation being passed*. . . . " Moreover, we find it somewhat suspect that North Carolina singled out only closed containers of apples, the very means by which apples are transported in commerce, to effectuate the statute's ostensible consumer protection purpose when apples are not generally sold at retail in their shipping containers. However, we need not ascribe an economic protection motive to the North Carolina Legislature to resolve this case; we conclude that the challenged statute cannot stand insofar as it prohibits the display of Washington State grades even if enacted for the declared purpose of protecting consumers from deception and fraud in the marketplace.

When discrimination against commerce of the type we have found is demonstrated, the burden falls on the State to justify it both in terms of the local benefits flowing from the statute and the unavailability of nondiscriminatory alternatives adequate to preserve the local interests at stake. North Carolina has failed to sustain that burden on both scores. [Emphasis added.]

The several States unquestionably possess a substantial interest in protecting their citizens from confusion and deception in the marketing of foodstuffs, but the challenged statute does remarkably little to further that laudable goal at least with respect to Washington apples and grades. The statute, as already noted, permits the marketing of closed containers of apples under *no* grades at all. Such a result can hardly be thought to eliminate the problems of deception and confusion created by the multiplicity or differing state grades; indeed, it magnifies them by depriving purchasers of all information concerning the quality of the contents of closed apple containers. Moreover, although the statute is ostensibly a consumer protection measure, it directs its primary efforts, not at the consuming public at large, but at apple wholesalers and brokers who are the principal purchasers of closed containers of apples. And those individuals are presumably the most knowledgeable individuals in this area. Since the statute does nothing at all to purify the flow of information at the retail level, it does little to protect consumers against the problems it was designed to eliminate. Finally, we note that any potential for confusion and deception created by the Washington grades[b] was not of the type that led to the statute's enactment. Since Washington

[b]Indeed, the District Court especially indicated in its findings of fact that there had been no showing that the Washington State grades had caused any confusion in the North Carolina market.

grades are in all cases equal or superior to their USDA counterparts, they could only "deceive" or "confuse" a consumer to his benefit, hardly a harmful result.

In addition, it appears that nondiscriminatory alternatives to the outright ban of Washington State grades are readily available. For example, North Carolina could effectuate its goal by permitting out-of-state growers to utilize state grades only if they also marked their shipments with the applicable USDA label. In that case, the USDA grade would serve as a benchmark against which the consumer could evaluate the quality of the various state grades. If this alternative was for some reason inadequate to eradicate problems caused by state grades inferior to those adopted by the USDA, North Carolina might consider banning those state grades which, unlike Washington's, could not be demonstrated to be equal or superior to the corresponding USDA categories. Concededly, even in this latter instance, some potential for "confusion" might persist. However, it is the type of "confusion" that the national interest in the free flow of goods between the States demands be tolerated.

The judgment of the District Court is affirmed.

★ ★ ★

Procedural Requirements

All state constitutions (and, to a lesser extent, the federal Constitution) contain provisions about the manner in which statutes shall be enacted. As a general rule, acts that do not conform to these requirements are void.

For example, virtually all state constitutions provide that revenue bills "shall originate in the House of Representatives," a requirement that also appears in the federal Constitution. Three other requirements normally appearing in state constitutions (1) restrict the enactment of "special" or "local" laws,[6] (2) require that the subject of every act be set forth in its title, and (3) prohibit a statute (including amendments) from embracing more than one subject. Additionally, all constitutions prescribe certain formalities in regard to the enactment processes themselves, such as specific limitations on the time and place of the introduction of bills, limitations on the amendment of bills, and the requirement that bills have three separate readings before final passage. The rules of the U.S. House of Representatives and Senate generally impose similar requirements on Congressional actions, with one notable variation: Senate rules (unlike those of the House) permit bills originating there to carry amendments that are unrelated to the subject of the bill to which they are attached.

These kinds of provisions, while appearing to be unduly technical, actually serve meritorious purposes. For example, while legislatures normally strive to pass statutes of general application, it is necessary that some laws

[6] "A special or local law is one that, because of its restrictions, can operate on or affect only a portion of the citizens, or a fraction of the property embraced within a classification created thereby." 82 C.J.S., Statutes, § 14, Copyright © 1953 by West Publishing Co.

operate only upon certain classes of persons or in certain localities of a state. Such special or local laws are valid only if the basis of their classification is reasonable; two of the purposes of the constitutional provisions mentioned above are to insure such reasonableness and to guarantee that the classes of persons covered be given notice of the consideration of the bill prior to its passage. Similarly, the purpose of requiring that the subject of an act be expressed in its title is to insure that legislators voting on a bill are fully apprised of its subject, thereby guarding against the enactment of "surprise" legislation. And the purpose of the requirement that a bill contain one subject is to prevent the passage of omnibus bills (those that bring together entirely unrelated, or incongruous, matters).

Requirement of Certainty

All statutes are subject to the general principle of constitutional law that they be "reasonably definite and certain." While the Constitution itself does not expressly contain such a provision, the courts have long taken the view that if the wording of a statute is such that persons of ordinary intelligence cannot understand its meaning, then the statute violates the due process clause of the Constitution and is thus invalid. (The courts are saying that a government that has charged a citizen with the violation of an ambiguous statute has thereby *denied that citizen the due process of law.*) In such an instance, it is said that the statute is "unconstitutionally vague."

As a practical matter, the majority of statutes that are challenged on the ground of vagueness or uncertainty are upheld by the courts. This is because most statutes are, in fact, drafted carefully and because the courts are extremely reluctant to declare a statute unconstitutional if they can avoid doing so. Thus, if the wording of a statute is subject to two possible but conflicting interpretations, one of which satisfies constitutional requirements and the other of which does not, the former interpretation will be accepted by the courts if they can reasonably do so.

Two examples will indicate the usual approaches taken by the courts. In the case of *McGowan v. State of Maryland*, 366 U.S. 420 (1960), it was held that a statute permitting Sunday sales of "merchandise essential to, or customarily sold at, or incidental to the operations of bathing beaches and amusement parks" was reasonably definite, and thus valid. There the court said that people of ordinary intelligence would be able to know what kinds of commodities were referred to by the act "as a matter of ordinary commercial knowledge, or by simply making an investigation at any bathing beach or amusement park" within the state. On the other hand, in the case of *Day v. Anderson*, 362 P.2d 137 (1961), a Wyoming statute that restricted the use of pleasure boats to streams having "an average flow for the month of July in excess of 1,000 cubic feet per second" was held to be invalid, the court saying that there was no reasonable way in which prospective boaters could determine which rivers and streams were excluded by such a provision.

Statutory Law and Common Law—A Contrast

Statutory law and common law differ in several significant respects. The most obvious of these are the *processes* by which each comes into being and the *form* of each after it becomes operative.

Processes and Form

Legislative acts become law only after passing through certain formal steps in both houses of the state legislatures or of Congress and, normally, by subsequent approval of the governor or the president. The usual steps are (1) introduction of a bill in the house or senate by one or more members of that body; (2) referral of the bill to the appropriate legislative committee, where hearings are held; (3) approval of the bill by that committee and perhaps others; (4) approval of the bill by the house and senate after full debate; and (5) signing of the bill by the executive (or a legislative overriding of an executive veto). At each of these stages the opponents of the bill are given considerable opportunity to raise objections, with the result that the bill may be voted down or may pass only after being substantially amended. *Common-law rules*, by contrast, are creatures of the judicial branch of government; they are adopted by the courts for settling controversies in those areas of law where the legislature has not spoken.

As a result of these differences, the products of the two processes—the rules themselves—are significantly different. A *statute* has an official text, usually drafted in specific terms, which becomes part of the state or federal code. *Common-law rules*, on the other hand, tend to be more general in nature and can be determined ony by examining the fact-patterns and decisions of the prior cases in which they have been applied.

In addition to these obvious contrasts between the two types of law, there are others that are equally significant. We will note these briefly.

Social and Political Forces That Shape the Law

The social and political forces within a state have a greater and more evident impact on statutory law than on common law. Judges are somewhat more insulated from such pressures than are legislatures. Additionally, the steps required in the enactment of statutes enable representatives of vocal special interest groups (who are frequently at odds with one another) to attract considerable publicity to their causes. And, of course, the raw political power that each is able to exert upon the legislators plays a significant, though not always controlling, part in the final disposition of a bill. (In this regard, it is impossible to overlook the role played by lobbyists and political action committees, "PACs," a topic that is examined in detail in Chapter 7.)

Legislative Options

While judges are required to settle controversies that come before them, legislatures generally have no duty to enact legislation. Thus legislatures have the option of refraining from the passage of laws where there is little public sentiment for them or where competing groups are so powerful that inaction is, politically, the better part of valor.

Legislative Scope

Subject only to the relatively few constitutional limitations placed upon it, the legislative power to act is very broad. Thus legislatures are not only free to enact statutes where case law is nonexistent, but they also can pass statutes that expressly overrule common-law principles. Examples of the latter are those statutes involving the legality of married women's contracts. Under English and early American common law, it was firmly established that married women lacked the capacity—the legal ability—to contract, and thus any agreements they entered into while married had no effect. Today, all states have enacted statutes that generally confer upon married women the same rights to contract as those enjoyed by other citizens.

As for jurisdictional scope, legislatures have the power to pass broad statutes encompassing all aspects of a given subject, whereas the courts can "make law" only in deciding the cases that come before them. Every state, for example, has comprehensive corporation acts, in which virtually all aspects of corporate activities, from incorporation procedures to dissolution procedures, are specified in detail. Similarly, every state has an all-encompassing criminal code, within which the criminal offenses in the state are defined.

Statutory Interpretation

We have seen that legislative bodies make law whenever they enact statutes. By doing so, they formally state what kinds of conduct they are requiring or prohibiting in specified situations and what results they expect from the passage of these laws on the rights and duties of affected parties.

But the true scope and meaning of a particular statute is never known with precision until it is formally construed by the courts in settling actual disputes arising under it. This searching for legislative intent, which usually necessitates a **statutory interpretation**, is thus another major source of our law.

Interpretation: A Necessary Evil?

Whenever a dispute arises where one or both of the parties is basing his or her case upon the wording of a particular statute, one might think that the court's job would be mechanical in nature; that is, once the facts were established, a careful reading of the statute would make it clear what result the legislature intended in such a situation. While this is often true, there are many instances in which it is not.

To bring the nature of the problem into sharper focus, consider the following situation. X flies a stolen airplane from one state to another and is convicted under a U.S. statute that makes the interstate movement of stolen motor vehicles a federal crime. In this statute, a motor vehicle is defined as "an automobile, automobile truck, automobile wagon, motorcycle, or any other self-propelled vehicle not designed for running on rails." Is an airplane a "motor vehicle" under this law? The problem is that the words of the statute are broad enough to embrace aircraft if they are given a literal interpretation; yet it is at least arguable that Congress did not really intend such a result. (The U.S. Supreme Court answered no to the question, with Justice Holmes saying that the term *vehicle* is "commonly understood as something that moves or runs on land, not something which flies in the air"—though he did admit that "etymologically the term might be considered broad enough to cover a conveyance propelled in the air.")[7]

The "Plain Meaning" Rule

The primary source of legislative intent is, of course, the language that comprises the statute itself. In the relatively rare case where a court feels that the wording of an act is so clear as to dictate but one result, and that the result is not "patently absurd," the consideration of other factors is unnecessary. If, for example, a state statute provides that "every applicant for examination and registration as a pharmacist shall be a citizen of the United States," a state pharmacy board would have to refuse to process the application of an alien even though he or she may have *applied for* U.S. citizenship as of the date of the pharmaceutical examination.[8] In cases of this sort (and occasionally in others where the language is somewhat less precise) the courts say that the statute possesses a **plain meaning** and that interpretation is thus unnecessary.

Aids to Interpretation

Most statutes, however, do not easily lend themselves to the "plain meaning" rule. This is true (1) because laws are usually drafted so as to contain an element of "deliberate imprecision," the legislature intending thereby to afford the courts some latitude in their application, and (2) because very few words (even in statutes that are highly restricted in scope) are susceptible to but one meaning. Thus in the majority of cases the courts recognize that some degree of *interpretation* is necessary and that a consideration of factors beyond the express language of a particular clause is advisable, if not mandatory, in determining the precise legislative intent.

At the outset, the court must give weight to prior judicial interpretations, if relevant. It will also look for guidance from (1) examination of the law's **textual context**, which involves reading the statute as a whole rather than concentrating solely upon the language of the disputed clause; (2) examina-

---

[7] *McBoyle v. United States*, 283 U.S. 25 (1931).

[8] *State v. Dame*, Supreme Court of Wyoming, 249 p.2d 156 (1952).

tion of the statute's **circumstantial context**—that is, identification of the problem that prompted its enactment; and (3) reference to the law's "legislative history"—an examination of the reports of the legislative committees through which the bill passed prior to its final adoption.

Illustrating the *textual context* approach is a case in which the defendant was convicted of violating a section of a California statute which provided that "every person who loiters about any school or public place at or near which children attend or normally congregate is a public vagrant," subject to fine and imprisonment. On appeal, defendant contended that the statute was unconstitutionally vague in that its terms literally prohibited loitering for reasonable purposes as well as for unlawful ones. The Supreme Court of California rejected this contention because the preceding section of the statute provided that "every person who annoys or molests a child under the age of 18 is a vagrant," subject to fine and imprisonment. Viewed in that light, the court held that the section under which defendant was convicted meant only to prohibit loitering where the purpose was to molest or annoy a child, and that it was therefore constitutionally definite.[9]

In the first of the following cases a Virginia court felt that the plain-meaning rule was applicable, and in the second the U.S. Supreme Court ruled that interpretation of a federal statute was necessary—even though its language *seemed* to be perfectly clear. (As you read these decisions, see if you agree with the widely differing approaches that were utilized.) The third case—one that brought national attention to the newly-discovered snail darter—presents a hybrid situation, where the U.S. Supreme Court seemed to say that the words of the statute were perfectly clear, yet felt it necessary to refer to a number of outside factors in order to reinforce the result that it reached under the plain meaning approach.

Temple v. City of Petersburg

Supreme Court of Appeals of Virginia
29 S.E.2d 357 (1944)

For over one hundred years prior to 1942, the City of Petersburg, Virginia, had maintained the Peoples Memorial Cemetery, which was located within the city limits. In 1942 the city purchased a tract of 1.01 acres of land adjacent to the cemetery with the intention of re-interring in it bodies which would have to be exhumed in order to permit the widening of a road that ran along another side of the cemetery.

The Temples, complainants, owned a home on St. Andrews Street in Petersburg, directly across the street from the newly acquired tract. Soon after they learned of the purchase, the Temples filed a bill in equity against the city asking that it be restrained from carrying out its plan to use the land for cemetery purposes.

Complainants relied on Section 56 of the Virginia Code, which provided in part as follows: "No cemetery shall be hereafter established within the corporate limits of any city or town; nor shall any cemetery be established within

[9] *California v. Huddleson*, 40 Cal.Rptr. 581 (1964).

two hundred and fifty yards of any residence without the consent of the owner of the legal and equitable title of such residence. . . . "

The trial court ruled that Section 56 did not prohibit the enlargement of an existing cemetery, and refused to issue an injunction. The Temples appealed.

Gregory, Justice:

. . . We are called upon to ascertain the proper meaning of the statute, and to decide whether or not it has been violated by the city. Specifically the controversy concerns the meaning to be given to the word, "established," used therein. The appellants maintain that under the statute the enlargement of an existing cemetery, such as is sought here, in reality is the establishment of a cemetery, while the appellee contends that to enlarge an existing cemetery is not the establishment of a cemetery and, therefore, constitutes no violation of the statute. . . .

The principle and determinative issue to be determined in this case is whether or not the proposed enlargement of Peoples Memorial Cemetery, by the additional 1.01 acre tract, is prohibited by section 56 of the Code.

The appellants most strongly contend that the word, "established," as used in the statute, means "located," and that the evil intended to be inhibited is the location of a cemetery in a city or town upon ground not previously dedicated for cemetery purposes, or the location of a cemetery within 250 yards of a residence, whether by enlargement or otherwise. They contend that the purpose of the statute is to protect residences and lands from the ill effects growing out of close proximity to a cemetery. They further contend that it is unreasonable to say that residences and lands are to be protected against the "establishment" of cemeteries, but are not to be protected against the encroachment or enlargement of existing cemeteries; that the evil created by one is equally as real as that created by the other.

The position of the appellee is that the word "established" has such a clear and precise meaning that no question of statutory construction arises; that the statute provides that no cemetery shall be "hereafter established" in a city or town, and that this language does not mean that a cemetery already established shall not be hereafter enlarged. To hold otherwise [appellee contends], would be not to construe the statute, but in effect, to amend it.

It is elementary that the ultimate aim of rules of interpretation is to ascertain the intention of the legislature in the enactment of a statute, and that intention, when discovered, must prevail. *If, however, the intention of the legislature is perfectly clear from the language used, rules of construction are not to be applied. We are not allowed to construe that which has no need of construction.* [Emphasis added.]

If the language of a statute is plain and unambiguous, and its meaning perfectly clear and definite, effect must be given to it regardless of what courts think of its wisdom or policy. In such cases courts must find the meaning within the statute itself. . . .

In *Fairbanks, etc. Co. v. Cape Charles*, 131 S.E. 439, the court says: "Under the distribution of powers by the Constitution, it is the function of this court to interpret and not to enact laws. The latter power belongs to the Legislature alone."

The word "established" is defined in *Webster's New International Dictionary*, 2nd Ed., 1936, thus: "To originate and secure the permanent existence of; to found; to institute; to create and regulate;—said of a colony, a State or other institutions."

Just why the Legislature, in its wisdom, saw fit to prohibit the establishment of cemeteries in cities and towns, and did not see fit to prohibit enlargements or additions, is no concern of ours. Certain it is that language could not be plainer than that employed to express the legislative will. From it we can see with certainty that while a cemetery may not be established in a city or town, it may be added to or enlarged without running counter to the inhibition found in section 56. We are not permitted to read into the statute an inhibition which the Legislature, perhaps advisedly, omitted. Our duty is to construe the statute as written.

If construction of the statute *were* necessary and proper in this case, we would be forced to the same conclusion. Even if it be assumed that there is ambiguity in the language in section 56, the legislative history of its enactment and a consideration of Code sec. 53, a related statute, would remove all doubt as to what the legislature intended by its language in section 56.

Code sec. 53 affords a complete answer to the question of legislative intent in the use of the word "established" in section 56, for the former section makes a distinction between "establish" and "enlarge" in these words: "If it be desired at any time to establish a cemetery, for the use of a city, town, county, or magisterial district, or to enlarge any such already established, and the title to land needed cannot be otherwise acquired, land sufficient for the purpose may be condemned. . . . "

The foregoing language, taken from section 53, completely demonstrates that the Legislature did not intend the words "establish" and "enlarge" to be used interchangeably, but that the use of one excluded any idea that it embraced or meant the other. As used, they are mutually exclusive. To enlarge or add to a cemetery is not to establish one within the meaning of section 56.

The language of the statute being so plain and unambiguous, and the intention and meaning of the Legislature so clear, we hold that the City of Petersburg has not violated Code sec. 56, and the decree accordingly should be affirmed.

Affirmed.

★★★

Holy Trinity Church v. United States
United States Supreme Court
143 U.S. 457
(1892)

In February of 1885 Congress passed a statute designed to prohibit the importation of foreigners and aliens under contracts to perform labor and service in the United States. The most important section of the act was as follows:

Be it enacted by the Senate and House of Representatives of the United States of America in Congress assembled, That from and after the passage of this act it shall be unlawful for any person, company, partnership, or corporation, in any manner whatsoever, to prepay the transportation, or in any way assist or encourage the importation or migration of any alien or aliens, any foreigner or foreigners, into the United States, its Territories, or the District of Columbia, under contract or agreement . . . made previous to the importation or migration of such alien or aliens, foreigner or foreigners, to perform labor or service of any kind in the United States, its Territories, or the District of Columbia.

In 1887 the Holy Trinity Church of New York City made a contract with one Warren, a pastor then living in England, under the terms of which he was employed to serve as its pastor. Pursuant to that contract, Warren immigrated to the United States and assumed his pastoral duties. Soon thereafter the United States instituted this action against the church to recover the fine provided by the federal statute.

In the Circuit Court of Appeals, the defendant church contended that Congress, by passing the act of 1885, did not intend to prohibit the kind of contract involved in the instant case. The court rejected that contention and found the church guilty. The church appealed to the United States Supreme Court.

Brewer, Justice:

. . . It must be conceded that the act of the corporation is within the letter of this section, for the relation of rector to his church is one of service, and implies labor on the one side with compensation on the other. Not only are the general words labor and service both used, but also, as it were to guard against any narrow interpretation and emphasize a breadth of meaning, to them is added "of any kind;" and, further, as noticed by the Circuit Judge in his opinion, the fifth section, which makes specific exceptions, among them professional actors, artists, lecturers, singers and domestic servants, strengthens the idea that every other kind of labor and service was intended to be reached by the first section. While there is great force to this reasoning, we cannot think Congress intended to denounce with penalties a transaction like that in the present case. *It is a familiar rule that a thing may be within the letter of the statute and yet not within the statute, because not within its spirit, nor within the intention of its makers.* [Emphasis added.] This has often been asserted, and the reports are full of cases illustrating its application. This is not the substitution of the will of the judge for that of the legislator, for frequently words of general meaning are used in a statute, words broad enough to include an act in question, and yet a consideration of the whole legislation, or of the circumstances surrounding its enactment, or of the absurd results which follow from giving such broad meaning to the words, makes it unreasonable to believe that the legislator intended to include the particular act. . . .

[The Court then cited several cases illustrating the application of the above rule. In one of these, *United States v. Kirby*, 7 Wall. 482, the defendant was charged with violating a federal statute that made it a crime "to knowingly and wilfully obstruct the passage of the mail, or any driver or carrier of the same." The defendant, a Kentucky sheriff, admitted that he "obstructed" a mail carrier, one Farris, while the latter was on duty, but defended on the ground that the obstruction occurred solely as the result of his arresting Farris under a warrant that was issued by a Kentucky court after Farris had been indicted on a murder charge. The U.S. Supreme Court held that the arrest of Farris was not, under the circumstances, a violation of the statute. In its opinion the court said: "All laws should receive a sensible construction. General terms should be so limited in their application as not to lead to injustice, oppression or an absurd consequence. It will always, therefore, be presumed that the legislature intended exceptions to its language which would avoid results of this character. The reason of the law in such cases should prevail over its letter." . . . The court then turned its attention to the case at bar, and continued:]

Among other things which may be considered in determining the intent of the legislature is the title of the act. We do not mean that it may be used to add to or take from the body of the statute, but it may help to interpret its meaning. . . .

Now, the title of this act is, "An act to prohibit the importation and migration of foreigners and aliens under contract or agreement to perform labor in the United States, its Territories and the District of Columbia." Obviously the thought expressed in this reaches only to the work of the manual laborer, as distinguished from that of the professional man. No one reading such a title would suppose that Congress had in its mind any purpose of staying the coming into this country of ministers of the gospel, or, indeed, of any class whose toil is that of the brain. *The common understanding of the terms labor and laborers does not include preaching and preachers; and it is to be assumed that words and phrases are used in their ordinary meaning.* [Emphasis added.] So whatever of light is thrown upon the statute by the language of the title indicates an exclusion from its penal provisions of all contracts for the employment of ministers, rectors and pastors.

Again, another guide to the meaning of a statute is found in the evil which it is designed to remedy; and for this the court properly looks at contemporaneous events, the situation as it existed, and as it was pressed upon the attention of the legislative body. The situation which called for this statute was briefly but fully stated by Mr. Justice Brown when, as District Judge, he decided the case of *United States v. Craig*, 28 Fed. Rep. 795:

The motives and history of the act are matters of common knowledge. It had become the practice for large capitalists in this country to contract with their agents abroad for the shipment of great numbers of an ignorant and servile class of foreign laborers, under contracts, by which the employer agreed, upon the one hand, to prepay their passage, while, upon the other hand, the laborers agreed to work after their arrival for a certain time at a low rate of wages. The effect of this was to break down the labor market, and to reduce other laborers engaged in like occupations to the level of the assisted immigrant. The evil finally became so flagrant that an appeal was made to Congress for relief by the passage of the act in question, the design of which was to raise the standard of foreign immigrants, and to discountenance the migration of those who had not sufficient means in their own hands, or those of their friends, to pay their passage.

It appears, also, from the petitions, and in the testimony presented before the committees of Congress, that it was this cheap unskilled labor which was making the trouble, and the influx of which Congress sought to prevent. It was never suggested that we had in this country a surplus of brain toilers, and, least of all, that the market for the services of Christian ministers was depressed by foreign competition. Those were matters to which the attention of Congress, or of the people, was not directed. *So far, then, as the evil which was sought to be remedied interprets the statute, it also guides to an exclusion of this contract from the penalties of the act.* [Emphasis added.] . . .

[The court then quoted from reports on the bill by the Senate Committee on Education and Labor, and the Committee of the House, which seemed to express their opinion that the terms *labor* and *service* meant only "manual labor" and "manual service." The court then concluded:]

We find, therefore, that the title of the act, the evil which was intended to be remedied, the circumstances surrounding the appeal to Congress, the reports of the committee of each house, all concur in affirming that the intent of Congress was simply to stay the influx of this cheap unskilled labor. . . .

Judgment reversed.

★★★

Tennessee Valley Authority v. Hill
U. S. Supreme Court
437 U.S. 153
(1978)

The Tennessee Valley Authority (TVA), a wholly owned public corporation of the United States, began construction of the Tellico Dam and Reservoir project in 1967 on the Little Tennessee River just southwest of Knoxville. Tellico was a multipurpose regional development project, designed to generate electricity, to provide flatwater recreation and flood control, and to improve economic conditions in the area. When fully operational, the dam would impound water covering 16,500 acres of valuable and productive farmland.

From the beginning, the project was plagued by lawsuits brought by local landowners and conservationist groups. During the early years of construction this litigation delayed work on the project from time to time, but during these years Congress continued to fund the project and by early 1973 it was nearly completed—after the expenditure of $29 million. In late 1973 the last injunction that had held up completion of the project was dissolved by a federal court when it ruled that TVA's final environmental impact statement satisfied the requirements of the National Environmental Policy Act of 1960 (EPA).

About the time of this action of the federal court, however, a discovery was made in the waters of the Little Tennessee that gave the opponents of the Tellico project new life—the finding of a previously unknown species of perch, the snail darter, by a University of Tennessee ichthyologist. As far as was known at that time (and throughout the years that this particular action was in the courts), the snail darter lived only in that portion of the Little Tennessee River that would be completely inundated by the reservoir created as a consequence of the Tellico Dam's completion.

The discovery of the snail darter brought into play another federal statute—the Endangered Species Act of 1973 (ESA). **That act, among other things, authorized the Secretary of the Interior to declare species of animal life "endangered" and to identify the "critical habitat" of these creatures. When a species or its habitat was so listed, the following portion of § 7 of the act became effective:**

The Secretary [of the Interior] shall review other programs administered by him and utilize such programs in furtherance of the purposes of this chapter. All other Federal departments and agencies shall, in consultation with and with the assistance of the Secretary, utilize their authorities in furtherance of the purposes of this chapter by carrying out programs for the conservation of endangered species and threatened species listed pursuant to section 1533 of this title and by taking such action necessary to insure that actions authorized, funded, or carried out by them do not jeopardize the continued existence of such endangered species and threatened species or result in the destruction or modification of habitat of such species *which is determined by the Secretary, after consultation as appropriate with the affected States, to be critical.*—16 U.S.C. § 1536 (1976 ed.) [Emphasis added.]

In January of 1975 Hill and others petitioned the Secretary of the Interior to list the snail darter as an endangered species. After receiving comments from various interested parties, the secretary acceded to this request. The secretary, in making the formal listing, found that "the impoundment of waters behind the Tellico Dam would result in the total destruction of the snail darter's habitat"—a finding based on the testimony of experts indicating that searches in more than sixty watercourses had failed to find other populations of snail darters.

Subsequently, the secretary (acting under § 7) declared that "all Federal agencies must take such action as is necessary to insure that actions authorized, funded, or carried out by them do not result in the destruction or modification of this critical habitat area." Thereafter, Hill and the other petitioners brought this action in late 1975 in a U.S. District Court in Tennessee, seeking an injunction that would enjoin completion of the dam and impoundment of the reservoir on the ground that these actions would violate the ESA by directly causing the extinction of the snail darter.

The basic question in the district court was whether Congress, by enacting § 7 of the ESA, meant for the act to apply to *virtually completed* projects. The plaintiffs argued that the language of § 7 plainly applied to all projects, completed or not, and that the issuance of an injunction was thus mandatory. The court rejected this argument, primarily for two reasons: (1) the fact that the issuance of an injunction would result in a $53 million loss to the government, and (2) the fact that the ESA "was passed seven years after construction on the dam had commenced, and that Congress had continued appropriations for Tellico with full awareness of the snail darter problem." Assessing these factors, and noting further that the project was over 80 percent completed, the

court *refused to issue an injunction.* It concluded with these words: "At some point in time a federal project becomes so near completion and so incapable of modification that a court of equity should not apply a statute enacted long after inception of the project, [and where such application would] produce an unreasonable result."

The plaintiffs appealed this decision to a U.S. Court of Appeals, which, for reasons appearing below, reversed the district court's judgment and issued a *permanent injunction* halting all activity on the project. TVA appealed to the U.S. Supreme Court.

Burger, Chief Justice:

. . . We begin with the premise that operation of the Tellico Dam will either eradicate the known population of snail darters or destroy their critical habitat. . . . Starting from the above premise, two questions are presented: (a) would TVA be in violation of the Act if it completed and operated the Tellico Dam as planned? and (b) if TVA's actions would offend the Act, is an injunction the appropriate remedy for the violation? For the reasons stated hereinafter, we [agree with the Court of Appeals] that *both questions must be answered in the affirmative.* [Emphasis added.]

It may seem curious to some that the survival of a relatively small number of three-inch fish among all the countless millions of species extant would require the permanent halting of a virtually completed dam for which Congress has expended more than $100 million. The paradox is not minimized by the fact that Congress continued to appropriate large sums of public money for the project, even after congressional Appropriations Committees were apprised of its apparent impact upon the survival of the snail darter. We conclude, however, that the explicit provisions of the Endangered Species Act require precisely that result.

One would be hard pressed to find a statutory provision whose terms were any plainer than those in § 7 of the Endangered Species Act. [Emphasis added.] Its very words affirmatively command all federal agencies "to *insure* that actions *authorized*, *funded*, or *carried out* by them do not *jeopardize* the continued existence" of an endangered species or "*result* in the destruction or modification of habitat of such species. . . ." 16 U. S. C. § 1536 (1976 ed.) [Emphasis added.] This language admits of no exception. Nonetheless, petitioner urges, as do the dissenters, that the Act cannot reasonably be interpreted as applying to a federal project which was well under way when Congress passed the Endangered Species Act of 1973. To sustain that position, however, we would be forced to ignore the ordinary meaning of plain language. It has not been shown, for example, how TVA can close the gates of the Tellico Dam without "carrying out" an action that has been "authorized" and "funded" by a federal agency. Nor can we understand how such action will "*insure*" that the snail darter's habitat is not disrupted. Accepting the Secretary's determinations, as we must, it is clear that TVA's proposed operation of the dam will have precisely the opposite effect, namely the *eradication* of an endangered species.

Concededly, this view of the Act will produce results requiring the sacrifice of the anticipated benefits of the project and of many millions of dollars in public funds. But examination of the language, history, and structure of the legislation under review here indicates beyond doubt that Congress intended endangered species to be afforded the highest of priorities.

[The court here made an exhaustive review of federal conservation statutes enacted in 1966 and 1969, and also of changes in the bill that eventually was passed as the ESA of 1973, and concluded from this review that the commands of § 7 were clearly meant to be mandatory in nature. For example, the court noted that one draft of the bill simply required government agencies to use their authorities to further the ends of the act "insofar as is practicable," and that this limitation was deleted in the final bill.

[The court also noted testimony of the House manager of the bill, who stated in part that "It appears that the whooping cranes of this country . . . are being threatened by Air Force bombing activities along the gulf coast of Texas. Under existing law, the Secretary of Defense has some discretion as to whether or not he will take the necessary action to see that this threat disappears. . . . Once this bill is enacted, the Secretary of Defense *would be required to take the necessary steps*. . . ."]

It is against this legislative background that we must [conclude] that . . . the totality of congressional action makes it abundantly clear that the result we reach today [that the trial court was correct in issuing the injunction] is wholly in accord with both the words of the statute and the intent of Congress. The plain intent of Congress in enacting this statute was to halt and reverse the trend towards species extinction, whatever the cost. . . .

One might dispute the applicability of these examples [such as the cessation of the Air Force practice bombing] to the Tellico Dam by saying that in this case the burden on the public through the loss of millions of unrecoverable dollars would greatly outweigh the loss of the snail darter. But neither the Endangered Species Act nor Article III of the Constitution provides federal courts with authority to make such fine utilitarian calculations. On the contrary, the plain language of the Act, buttressed by its legislative history, shows clearly that Congress viewed the value of endangered species to be "incalculable." Quite obviously, it would be difficult for a court to balance the loss of a sum certain—even $100 million—against a congressionally declared "incalculable" value, even assuming we had the power to engage in such a weighing process, which emphatically we do not. . . .[a]

[a] The court here referred to testimony of fish and wildlife scientists indicating concern about the "unknown uses" that endangered species might have, and about the "unforeseeable place such creatures may have in the chain of life on this planet." A House subcommittee report, for example, stated: "The value of this genetic heritage [which some governmental activities now threaten] is, quite literally, incalculable. . . . Who knows, or can say, what potential cures for cancer or other scourges, present or future, may lie locked up in the structures of plants which may yet be undiscovered, much less analyzed? . . . Sheer self-interest impels us to be cautious. . . ."

[The court then rejected TVA's argument that Congress, by continuing to appropriate money for Tellico Dam after enactment of the ESA in 1973, *impliedly repealed* the 1973 act insofar as the Tellico project was concerned. In this regard the court said]:

To find a repeal of the Endangered Species Act under these circumstances would surely do violence to the cardinal rule . . . that repeals by implication are not favored. . . . When voting on appropriations measures, legislators are entitled to operate under the assumption that the funds will be devoted to purposes which are lawful and not for any purpose forbidden. Without such assurance, every appropriations measure would be pregnant with prospects of altering substantive legislation, repealing by implication any prior statute which might [clearly] prohibit the expenditure. Not only would this lead to the absurd result of requiring Members to review exhaustively the background of every authorization before voting on an appropriation, but it would [also violate House Rule XXI (2) and Rule 16.4 of the Standing Rules of the Senate]. . . .

Judgment [of the U.S. Court of Appeals is] affirmed.[b]

★★★

Selected State Statutes

Most of the broad areas of governmental regulation of business are based upon federal statutes, and the remainder of this text is largely devoted to an analysis of these statutes and the administrative agencies that implement them. Nonetheless, before leaving the general subject of statutory law, several state statutes of particular relevance to the business world also deserve special mention.

The Uniform Commercial Code

This statute is especially significant to business persons (1) because it is a dramatic illustration of one way changes in law can occur in response to shortcomings that exist in prior law; (2) because the statute governs eight commercial law subjects; and (3) because it has been adopted by all states except Louisiana, which has adopted Articles 1, 3, 4, and 5 only. To see what the **Uniform Commercial Code** is and why it came about, a brief look at the past is necessary.

Historical Background: By the latter part of the nineteenth century, there was considerable variety among the laws of the states applicable to business transactions within their borders. As interstate commerce increased, it became increasingly imperative that the bodies of law governing commercial transactions be made as uniform as possible.

[b]Subsequent to this decision, Congress amended the act to specifically permit the completion of the Tellico project.

To achieve this goal, the states in 1890 organized a continuing body called the Conference of Commissioners on Uniform State Laws. Commissioners, appointed by the state governors, were recognized experts in the various fields of commercial law—judges, law professors, and practicing attorneys, for the most part.

The hope was that if the conference drafted model acts from time to time that would ultimately govern all commercial transactions, and if these were adopted by the legislatures of all the states, the law applicable to business transactions would be uniform throughout the country. Two of the most important model acts, drafted about 1900, were the Uniform Sales Act (USA) and the Uniform Negotiable Instruments Law (NIL). Several other model acts of narrower scope, such as the Uniform Warehouse Receipts Act, were also subsequently drawn up.

The hope of total uniformity was never completely realized, for two reasons. First, a few states did not adopt the major acts, the USA and the NIL, and an even larger number failed to adopt the other model acts. Second, even though many states did enact a given uniform statute, the judicial interpretation of certain sections of the act sometimes differed from state to state. (Another problem that came to light subsequently was that many of the uniform acts, drafted and adopted in the early 1900s, were badly out of date by 1940. This was particularly true of the NIL, some provisions of which had little application to banking practices that evolved thirty or forty years after it was written.)

In 1941, in the light of these conditions, the National Conference of Commissioners on Uniform State Laws and the American Law Institute joined forces in an effort to draft a single "modern, comprehensive, commercial code, applicable throughout the country," covering eight areas of commercial law. For the next ten years, hundreds of legal experts in these selected areas worked on the project, which was completed in 1952.

The code was first adopted by Pennsylvania, in 1953. Thereafter, the New York and Massachusetts legislatures recommended that certain changes be made, and the drafters incorporated these modifications in the 1958 edition. A 1962 official edition, bringing about minor changes, was subsequently published; and it is this version (with minor changes made in 1972) that forty-nine of the states have since adopted.

Coverage: The code, commonly referred to as the UCC, consists of ten articles, or chapters:

Article 1 General Provisions

Article 2 Sales

Article 3 Commercial Paper

Article 4 Bank Deposits and Collections

Article 5 Letters of Credit

Article 6 Bulk Transfers

Article 7	Warehouse Receipts, Bills of Lading, and Other Documents of Title
Article 8	Investment Securities
Article 9	Secured Transactions; Sales of Accounts, Contract Rights, and Chattel Paper
Article 10	Effective Date and Repealer

Some Observations on the UCC: The eight substantive areas of law covered by the code are found in Articles 2 through 9. (Article 1 covers only introductory matters. Article 10 simply lists the section numbers of prior statutes of the adopting state, which heretofore covered those areas of law encompassed by the code and which are expressly repealed to eliminate statutory conflict.) From the business student's standpoint, the two most important chapters of the code are Articles 2 and 3.

Article 2 consists of 104 sections that govern virtually all aspects of the law of sales. This article supplants the sales law that was in effect prior to the adoption of the code, which in most states was the old Uniform Sales Act. (A brief survey of the law of sales appears in Chapter 8.)

Article 3, Commercial Paper, supplants the earlier Uniform Negotiable Instruments Law, which had at one time been adopted in all the states. Its eighty sections govern such matters as the rights and obligations of the makers of notes and the drawers of checks and drafts, and the rights and duties of holders and indorsers of all types of negotiable instruments.

Articles 4 through 8 deal with more specialized situations, such as the duties that exist between depositary and collecting banks and the resolution of problems resulting from the issuance and transfer of bills of lading and other documents of title. Article 9 is a lengthy chapter covering all kinds of secured transactions that were formerly governed by separate—and frequently dissimilar—state statutes on chattel mortgages, conditional sales, and other devices by which a creditor might seek to retain a security interest in goods that were physically in the possession of a debtor.

Deceptive Trade Practices Acts

Most states have statutes bearing this name or one similar to it which specifically forbid specified kinds of business conduct. The typical deceptive trade practices act, for example, prohibits merchants from "passing off" (representing and selling) their goods or services as those of another; from representing goods as being new if they are reclaimed, used, or second-hand; and from disparaging the goods or services of competitors by false representations of fact in regard to such goods or services. Additionally, the typical statute also prohibits such practices as "advertising goods or services with the intent not to sell them as advertised," and the making of "false statements of fact concerning the reasons for, or the amounts of, price reductions."

Business Organization Acts

All states have comprehensive statutes applicable to the formation and operation of business partnerships and corporations. Insofar as partnership law is concerned, forty-seven states have adopted a statute known as the **Uniform Partnership Act** (UPA). The UPA governs almost all aspects of the partnership form of organization, beginning with the definition of a partnership—"an association of two or more persons to carry on as co-owners a business for profit"—and a list of tests to be used in determining whether or not a particular relationship legally constitutes a partnership (to be applied in situations where a formal, written partnership agreement is lacking). The act also covers such matters as the relationship between partners and persons dealing with the partnership, including the partners' liability to creditors; the relations of partners to one another; the property rights of partners; and the rules that apply to the dissolution and "winding up" of the business. Thus the resolution of almost every partnership problem is controlled by the UPA. A second statute, the **Uniform Limited Partnership Act** (ULPA), has also been adopted by forty-eight states, under which partnerships may be formed with one or more partners having limited liability, in contrast to the unlimited (personal) liability that partners in ordinary partnerships have for partnership debts. (The subject of partnerships is discussed further in Chapter 9.)

Turning to the corporate form of business organization, the first observation to be made is that the corporation is said to be a "creature of statute." What this means is that corporations can not exist unless permitted to do so by an applicable statute (normally a state statute), and unless the requirements of that statute are met. All states do, in fact, have *general corporation statutes* which permit, and govern, the formation and operation of corporations.[10]

The various state corporation laws are not entirely uniform. This results from the fact that while over half of the states have patterned their laws on the Model Business Corporation Act, the remaining states have not. However, even the statutes of the states in the latter category parallel the provisions of the model act in many major respects, so that in general the corporation laws of the various states are essentially similar in nature.

In any event, the state corporation acts prescribe the formal steps to be taken in the formation of a corporation and set forth a number of matters that must be included in the corporation's "articles of corporation." The typical statute also contains provisions relative to shareholders' meetings, the voting rights of shareholders, and the duties and liabilities of directors.

---

[10] The federal government can also charter corporations insofar as it is "necessary and proper" for carrying out other express federal powers. Examples of federally chartered corporations are the national banks and the Tennessee Valley Authority. Additionally, as we see later, many federal regulatory statutes (such as the securities and labor laws) weigh heavily upon the operations of corporations. Nonetheless, the organization and operation of corporations are still largely matters of *state law*.

Additionally, the usual statute contains many sections applicable to such matters as the issuance and cancellation of stock shares, restrictions upon the corporation's right to pay dividends, and the circumstances in which directors may make distributions to its shareholders out of assets known as the "capital surplus" of the corporation. (The subject of corporations is also discussed further in Chapter 9.)

Questions and Problems

1. Colorado passed a statute that (among other things) made it unlawful for automobile manufacturers to "induce or coerce" Colorado new car dealers into accepting delivery of unordered automobiles and trucks. General Motors, which annually shipped into Colorado more than $100 million worth of automobiles, challenged the statute in the federal courts, contending that it imposed an unreasonable burden on interstate commerce. Colorado replied that the statute was merely a reasonable protection of its local dealers' businesses. Do you agree with the state's defense? Why or why not? (*General Motors v. Blevin*, 144 F.Supp. 381, 1956.)

2. California has a statute, the Unruh Civil Rights Act, which provides in part that "All persons within the jurisdiction of this state are free and equal, and no matter what their sex . . . are entitled to the full and equal accommodations, advantages, facilities, privileges, or services in all business establishments of every kind whatsoever." In a recent case reaching the California Supreme Court, *Koire v. Metro Car Wash*, 707 P.2d 195 (1985), the issue was whether bars and car washes which offered "Ladies' Day" discount prices were in violation of the act. The action was brought against a bar and several car washes by a male who had to pay a fee to enter the bar (while females were admitted free), and who had to pay higher prices at the car washes than their female customers paid. A primary defense of the defendant bar was that, in an earlier case, the California Supreme Court ruled that discriminatory business practices did *not* violate the act if the discrimination existed for the purpose of achieving "socially desirable goals" of the state. (Under that principle, the California court in that case held that the state had such a "compelling societal interest" in insuring housing for the elderly that apartment owners could lawfully offer accommodations to elderly tenants at reduced rentals.) The bar's contention was that its Ladies' Night encouraged more women to attend the bar, thereby promoting more "interaction" between the sexes, and that this was a "socially desirable goal" of the state. Do you think the court should accept this argument? Why or why not?

3. Arizona passed a "Train Limit Law" that made it unlawful for railroads to operate passenger trains of more than fourteen cars and freight trains of more than seventy cars within the state. The avowed purpose of the statute was to reduce the number of accidents attributed to the operation of longer trains. When the Southern Pacific Railroad was found to have operated trains over the maximum limit, Arizona brought this action to recover criminal penalties imposed by the law. The railroad defended on the ground that the law was a clear violation of the commerce clause of the U.S. Constitution. The trial court agreed with this contention, finding little evidence that the law contributed to safety, and further finding that the law substantially burdened interstate freight and passenger operations.

The Arizona Supreme Court found the law to be *constitutional*, despite its effects on commerce, saying that it "bore a reasonable relationship to the safety and health" of Arizona citizens; the railroad appealed this decision to the U.S. Supreme Court. On the questions of safety and effect on commerce, what *additional information* do you think that court might want in order to reach a decision? Explain. (*Southern Pacific Co. v. Arizona*, 325 U.S. 761, 1945.)

4. Identify three significant types of limitations on the legislative powers of Congress and the state legislatures.

5. A student demonstrator and four labor pickets were convicted in the Hamilton County Municipal Court, Ohio, of violating a Cincinnati ordinance making it a criminal offense for three or more persons to assemble on a sidewalk "and there conduct themselves in a manner annoying to persons passing by." On appeal to the U.S. Supreme Court the five contended that the ordinance was unconstitutionally vague (that it was so vague that it violated the due process clause). Do you agree with this contention? Discuss. (*Coates v. Cincinnati*, 402 U.S. 611, 1971.)

6. When the language of a statute does not fall clearly within the plain-meaning rule, what other facts or circumstances do the courts look to in order to determine legislative intent?

7. Johnson, a teenaged boy living in North Carolina, owned a motorcycle. After the motorcycle's original headlight became very weak, he and a friend taped a five-cell flashlight to the handlebars and that evening, with both boys on the motorcycle, they had a collision with an automobile. In ensuing litigation, the car owner pointed out that a North Carolina statute required every motorcycle to have a "headlamp," and he contended that the flashlight was not a headlamp. If you were a judge on the North Carolina Supreme Court hearing the case on appeal, what steps would you take in deciding whether the flashlight was a headlamp under the statute? What result? (*Bigelow v. Johnson*, 277 S.E. 2d 347, 1981.)

8. A city ordinance required that operators of coin-operated amusement machines be licensed, and provided that the chief of police was to determine whether an applicant has any "connections with criminal elements." The city manager, after receiving the report of the chief of police and reports from the building inspector and the city planner, would then decide whether to issue the license. (If the application were denied, the applicant could then petition the city council for a license.) In a legal case brought by a rejected applicant, the contention was made that the licensing ordinance was *unconstitutionally vague* because of the "connections with criminal elements" language. Do you think this contention is correct? Why or why not? (*City of Mesquite v. Aladdin's Castle, Inc.*, 102 S.Ct. 1070, 1982.)

C·H·A·P·T·E·R 5

CONSTITUTIONAL LAW

In the preceding chapter on statutory law, two major aspects of constitutional law were touched upon—the fact that the U.S. Constitution prescribes the basic structure and lawmaking authority of the federal government, and an examination of the scope of the federal government's power to regulate interstate commerce. (Additionally, it was noted that the U.S. Constitution is indeed the law of the land—i.e., that all state and federal laws must be in conformity with its stated provisions, such as the "due process of law" clause.)

In this chapter we will briefly survey the broader *nature and purposes* of the U.S. Constitution, and then devote major attention to the broad area of *constitutional interpretation*, the judicial process by which the Constitution, in the words of Justice Oliver Wendell Holmes, is "afforded a little play in its joints."[1]

---

[1] *Bain Peanut Co. v. Pinson*, 282 U.S. 499 (1931).

The Constitution—Nature and Purposes

Leaving aside for the moment the rights of the individual and the businessperson that are protected by our constitutional guarantees, the U.S. Constitution has two major purposes:

1. It prescribes the organization of the federal government, in addition to its jurisdiction.
2. It sets forth the authority of the legislative, executive, and judicial branches of that government.

Organization and Jurisdiction

As one might expect, many constitutional provisions are devoted to the organization and operation of the federal government. Article I, for example, governs such matters as the establishment of the House of Representatives and the Senate, the manner of selection of representatives and senators, and the steps necessary for the enactment of bills into law. Article II governs all aspects of the election of the President (including the role of the electoral college), and Article III provides for the establishment and operation of the federal courts.

Insofar as the jurisdiction of the federal government is concerned, we noted earlier, while examining the limitations on the powers of state legislatures, the specific powers that are delegated to the federal government by Section 8 of Article I of the Constitution. In addition to the regulation of interstate commerce, certainly the major powers are these: to raise and support armies and a navy; to levy taxes to pay the debts and provide for the "common defense" and "general welfare" of the country; and to make all other laws "necessary and proper" for the carrying out of the delegated powers. Under the rather bland general welfare clause Congress has, in fact, enacted some of its most ambitious programs; creation of the costly social security system and construction of the federal interstate highway system are but two of the most notable of such programs. The far-reaching authority that Congress possesses under this clause comes not only from its broad wording, but additionally from the view of the U.S. Supreme Court that Congress's judgment that a particular program furthers the general welfare of the nation will not be overruled unless that judgment is "arbitrary, or clearly wrong."

Legislative, Executive, and Judicial Authority

The framers of the Constitution, drawing upon the ideas of Blackstone and Montesquieu, felt it imperative that the powers of the legislative, executive, and judicial branches be essentially separate from one another. This separation of powers is substantially brought about under the Constitution; and, by and large, the jurisdiction of each branch is clearly spelled out. It is obvious, for example, that Congress—the legislative arm—cannot grant new trials at the request of disappointed litigants; such power rests solely with the judiciary. Conversely, the courts cannot engage in legislative functions, such as the determination of minimum wage rates. Nevertheless, some problem areas have arisen from time to time regarding the jurisdiction of the respective branches. We will briefly discuss three of these areas.

1. While the power of the Supreme Court to reverse decisions of the lower courts has never been questioned, its power to review the propriety of *legislative* and *executive actions* was, for a time, in doubt. The Constitution does not expressly grant such authority to the court, and it was not until the case of *Marbury v. Madison*, 5 U.S. 137, in 1803 that the court simply assumed that authority, in view of the fact that the Constitution provided no other method for the resolution of certain issues. Today, by virtue of that case, the authority of the court under its "right of judicial review" to inquire into the constitutionality of actions of the other two branches of government is well established.

2. Problems occasionally arise when one branch of government attempts to *delegate its authority* to an officer or agency of another branch. For example, Congress sometimes passes legislation creating a particular agency or commission—a body normally within the executive arm of government—and indicating the general nature of the rules and regulations that it wishes the agency or commission to promulgate. Such statutory delegations of authority by Congress may be challenged in the courts, however, and if a particular statute is found to lack reasonably definite standards governing the rules and regulations that are to be promulgated by the agency, the statute will be declared an "unconstitutional delegation of legislative authority," and the regulations will thus be void. In the 1930s, with the rapid proliferation of federal agencies, the courts were quick to strike statutes down on this ground unless the statutory limitations upon the agencies were clear and definite. Soon thereafter, however, the courts began to accept rather general standards or limitations, thus upholding the statutes and the regulations issued under them.

One of the first cases reflecting this change of view—an increased deference to the actions of administrative agencies—was that of *Yakus v. United States*, 321 U.S. 414 (1944). There Yakus was charged with selling beef at prices above those established by regulations of the Office of Price Administration, a federal wartime agency. In that case the U.S. Supreme Court held that the act creating the agency, the Emergency Price Control Act, was constitutionally valid, saying that "the standards prescribed by the Act are sufficiently definite and precise to enable Congress, the courts, and the public to ascertain whether the Administrator, in fixing the designated prices, has conformed to those standards." (The standards referred to were (1) the act's statement of purposes—to stabilize prices and to prevent speculative, unwarranted, and abnormal increases in prices and rents, and (2) the statutory requirement that the price-fixing regulations of the agency were to be essentially based upon the prices of goods and rents existing between October 1 and October 14, 1941.)

3. Another problem area involves the powers of the presidency in relation to those of the judicial and legislative branches. A case in the first category is that of *United States v. Nixon*, 418 U.S. 683 (1974), which arose out of a criminal action against several of President Nixon's staff members as a result of their alleged obstruction of justice activities in the "Watergate coverup." When the U.S. district court hearing the criminal cases demanded—at the request of the special prosecutor—that President Nixon produce tapes and documents involving specified communications between him and his staff members, he refused to do so on the ground that the doctrine of executive privilege immunized the office of the presidency against such orders from the judicial branch of government. In the action brought by the U.S. to compel the president to produce the tapes and documents, the U.S. Supreme Court ruled that "neither the doctrine of separation of powers nor the need of confidentiality of high-level communications" could insulate the presidency from such demands where (a) the communications did not involve diplomatic or national security matters, and (b) where the demands were necessary to an important governmental process, in this case the prosecution of important criminal cases in the courts. Accordingly, the request for the materials was upheld, and the president acceded to it.

Turning to the subject of executive orders, it is well established that the power of the president to issue such orders comes only from the U.S. Constitution and federal statutes. Thus such orders (which are orders to officers and administrative agencies within the executive branch) are lawful where they merely direct the manner in which acts of Congress shall be implemented. On the other hand, if executive orders are issued in the absence of congressional action, such orders—except when issued in wartime or other true emergency situations—are likely to be voided by the courts.

Youngstown Sheet and Tube Co. v. Sawyer, below, is one of the landmark cases in this area of the law.

Youngstown Sheet and Tube Co. v. Sawyer
U.S. Supreme Court
72 S.Ct. 863
(1952)

In the latter part of 1951 a dispute arose between the nation's major steel mills and their employees over terms and conditions to be included in their new collective bargaining agreement. Lengthy negotiations proved fruitless, and the employees' representative, United Steelworkers of America, C.I.O., gave notice of an intent to strike when the existing bargaining agreements expired on December 31.

The Federal Mediation and Conciliation Service then intervened in an effort to get labor and management to agree. When this and other efforts were unsuccessful, President Truman issued Executive Order No. 10340, which directed the secretary of commerce to take possession of most of the country's steel mills and keep them running. The indispensability of steel as a compo-

nent of substantially all weapons and other war materials then being used by the armed forces in Korea led the president to believe that the work stoppage would immediately jeopardize the nation's national defense and that government seizure of the mills was necessary in order to assure the continued availability of steel.

The secretary of commerce immediately issued his own orders, calling upon the presidents of the various seized companies to serve as operating managers for the United States. They were directed to carry on their activities in accordance with regulations and directions of the secretary. The next morning the president sent a message to Congress reporting his action. He sent another message twelve days later, and Congress took no action thereon.

Obeying the secretary's orders under protest, the companies brought proceedings against him in the U.S. district court. Their complaints charged that the seizure was not authorized by an act of Congress or by any constitutional provisions. The district court was asked to declare the orders of the president and the secretary invalid and to issue preliminary and permanent injunctions restraining their enforcement. Opposing the motion for preliminary injunction, the United States asserted that a strike disrupting steel production for even a brief period would so endanger the well-being and safety of the nation that the president had "inherent power" to do what he had done—power "supported by the Constitution, by historical precedent, and by court decisions."

The district court held against the government on all points and issued a preliminary injunction restraining the secretary from "continuing the seizure and possession of the plants . . . and from acting under the purported authority of Executive Order No. 10340." On the same day, April 30, the U.S. Court of Appeals stayed the injunction, and the U.S. Supreme Court "granted certiorari" (agreed to review the lower courts' proceedings).

Black, Justice:

We are asked to decide whether the President was acting within his constitutional power when he issued an order directing the Secretary of Commerce to take possession of and operate most of the Nation's steel mills. . . .

Two crucial issues have developed: First. Should final determination of the constitutional validity of the President's order be made in this case which has proceeded no further than the preliminary injunction stage? Second. If so, is the seizure order within the constitutional power of the President?

I

[In regard to the first question, the Court ruled that under the compelling circumstances that existed, an inquiry into the constitutional questions at this stage was proper. The Court then addressed itself to the second question.]

II

The President's power, if any, to issue the order must stem either from an act of Congress or from the Constitution itself. [Emphasis added.] There is no statute that expressly authorizes the President to take possession of property as he did here. Nor is there any act of Congress to which our attention has been directed from which such a power can fairly be implied. Indeed, we do not understand the Government to rely on statutory authorization for this seizure. There are two statutes which do authorize the President to take both personal and real property under certain conditions [the Selective Service Act of 1948 and the Defense Production Act of 1950]. However, the Government admits that these conditions were not met and that the President's order was not rooted in either of the statutes. The Government refers to the seizure provisions of one of these statutes [§ 201 (b) of the Defense Production Act] as "much too cumbersome, involved, and time-consuming for the crisis which was at hand."

Moreover, the use of the seizure technique to solve labor disputes in order to prevent work stoppages *was not only unauthorized by any congressional enactment; prior to this controversy, Congress had refused to adopt that method of settling labor disputes.* [Emphasis added.] When the Taft-Hartley Act was under consideration in 1947, Congress rejected an amendment which would have authorized such governmental seizures in cases of emergency. *It is clear that if the President had authority to issue the order he did, it must be found in some provisions of the Constitution.* [Emphasis added.] And it is not claimed that express constitutional language grants this power to the President. The contention is that presidential power should be implied from the aggregate of his powers under the Constitution. Particular reliance is placed on provisions in Article II which say that "the executive Power shall be fully executed"; and that he "shall be Commander in Chief of the Army and Navy of the United States."

The order cannot properly be sustained as an exercise of the President's military power as Commander in Chief of the Armed Forces. The Government attempts to do so by citing a number of cases upholding broad powers in military commanders engaged in day-to-day fighting in a theater of war. Such cases need not concern us here. *Even though "theater of war" be an expanding concept, we cannot with faithfulness to our constitutional system hold that the Commander in Chief of the Armed Forces has the ultimate power as such to take possession of private property in order to keep labor disputes from stopping production. This is a job for the Nation's lawmakers, not for its military authorities.*[a] [Emphasis added.]

Nor can the seizure order be sustained because of the several constitutional provisions that grant executive power to the President. In the framework of our Constitution, the President's power to see that the laws are faithfully executed refutes the idea that he is to be a lawmaker. The Constitution limits his functions in the lawmaking process to the recommending of laws he thinks wise and

[a]Because the Korean conflict was considered by the president to be a "police action" rather than a war, the court's decision was not based on the war powers of the president.

the vetoing of laws he thinks bad. And the Constitution is neither silent nor equivocal about who shall make laws which the President is to execute. The first section of the first article says that "All legislative powers herein granted shall be vested in a Congress of the United States. . . ." After granting many powers to the Congress, Article I goes on to provide that Congress may "make all Laws which shall be necessary and proper for carrying into Execution the foregoing Powers and all other Powers vested by this Constitution in the Government of the United States, or in any Department or Officer thereof."

The President's order does not direct that a congressional policy be executed in a manner prescribed by Congress—it directs that a presidential policy be executed in a manner prescribed by the President. [Emphasis added.] The preamble of the order itself, like that of many statutes, sets out reasons why the President believes certain policies should be adopted, proclaims these policies as rules of conduct to be followed, and again, like a statute, authorizes a government official to promulgate additional rules and regulations consistent with the policy proclaimed and needed to carry that policy into execution. The power of Congress to adopt such public policies as those proclaimed by the order is beyond question. It can authorize the taking of private property for public use. It can make laws regulating the relationships between employers and employees, prescribing rules designed to settle labor disputes, and fixing wages and working conditions in certain fields of our economy. *The Constitution did not subject this law-making power of Congress to presidential or military supervision or control.* [Emphasis added.]

It is said that other Presidents without congressional authority have taken possession of private business enterprises in order to settle labor disputes. But even if this be true, Congress has not thereby lost its exclusive constitutional authority to make laws necessary and proper to carry out the powers vested by the Constitution "in the Government of the United States, or in any Department or Officer thereof."

The founders of this Nation entrusted the law-making power to the Congress alone in both good and bad times. It would do no good to recall the historical events, the fears of power and the hopes for freedom that lay behind their choice. Such a review would but confirm our holding that this seizure order cannot stand.

The judgment of the District Court is affirmed.

★★★

Comment: The principles of law that were clarified in this opinion were used as a starting point in the decision of the U.S. Supreme Court in a much more recent case involving the constitutionality of executive orders, *Dames & Moore v. Regan*, 453 U.S. 654 (1981). That case arose out of the seizure of the American Embassy in Iran in 1979, after which President Carter declared a national emergency under the International Emergency Economic Powers Act (IEEPA) and froze all property owned by the Iranian Government in the U.S. Thereafter, Dames & Moore—an engineering firm which was owed over $3 million by the Government of Iran and the Atomic Energy

Organization of Iran for engineering work performed in that country—brought suit in a U.S. district court against these parties and a number of Iranian banks seeking payment of the debt. When this action was commenced, the court authorized prejudgment attachments of certain of the Iranian assets on behalf of Dames & Moore in the event they were successful in getting a judgment in the case.

In January of 1981, while this case and others were pending, a hostage release agreement was reached between the U.S. and Iran, under the terms of which the U.S. was obligated among other things to terminate all litigation against the Government of Iran. To implement that part of the agreement, President Carter issued a number of executive orders that suspended cases still pending against Iran, and nullified attachments and judgments already obtained prior to the agreement. (Under the agreement, claims in the suspended suits were to be arbitrated by a special claims tribunal.)

Dames & Moore then brought this action against Secretary of the Treasury Regan, to whom the orders were addressed, contending that the president had no authority to nullify existing judicial attachments or to suspend claims that were being litigated in the courts. The U.S. Supreme Court rejected this contention, finding presidential authority in two federal statutes, IEEPA (mentioned above) and the Hostage Act of 1868. IEEPA provided, in part, that "the President may, [under this act] investigate, regulate, . . . nullify, void, prevent or prohibit, any acquisition, holding . . . or dealing in, or exercising any right, power or privilege with respect to, . . . any property in which any foreign country or a national has any interest; by any person, or with respect to any property, subject to the jurisdiction of the United States." Further, the court held that the Hostage Act indicated a "Congressional willingness that the President have broad discretion when responding to the hostile acts of foreign sovereigns."

Constitutional Interpretation

Some provisions of the Constitution are so precise that they need little or no judicial interpretation. Such a clause is found in Section 2 of Article I, which provides in part that "no person shall be a representative who shall not have attained to the age of twenty-five years. . . . "

Many other provisions, on the other hand—particularly those that place limitations upon the powers of the state and federal governments—were deliberately drafted in general terms. The reason for this, of course, is that the drafters of any constitution cannot anticipate the exact problems that may arise fifty or a hundred years hence. Thus they must phrase government limitations and prohibitions in language which will afford the courts some leeway in applying them to specific controversies in later times and in foreseeable circumstances.

In the remainder of this chapter we examine some of the problems inherent in the area of constitutional interpretation, with particular emphasis on the clauses that create and protect the basic rights of the individual and the business firm by placing limits on government power. To indicate at the outset the kinds of problems we will discuss, consider the due process clause. The Fifth Amendment provides, in part, that no person shall "be deprived of life, liberty, or property without due process of law."[2] But nowhere in the Constitution is *due process* defined. Thus the courts—called upon to review the propriety of a government action that results in the taking of life, liberty, or property—are given a wide range in determining whether the action conformed to this constitutional mandate.

Similarly, other clauses guarantee that the citizens of each state shall be entitled to the "privileges and immunities" of citizens of the other states, and forbid the making of laws "respecting an establishment of religion" and those "abridging the freedom of speech." These clauses, too, must be interpreted on a case-by-case basis.

Some Preliminary Observations

We will see how the courts (and especially the U.S. Supreme Court) have interpreted some of the most important constitutional clauses in varying circumstances. First, however, mention should be made of several generalizations that underlie the whole area of constitutional interpretation.

Necessity for Challenge: The Constitution is not "self-executing." Thus, when the government passes or takes action under a statute that may exceed its constitutional powers, the persons or firms who are aggrieved thereby must normally challenge the action in the courts. In other words, constitutional phrases are interpreted by the courts only when actual controversies require them to do so.

Power of Judicial Review: The Supreme Court has virtually unlimited power to decide which appeals it will hear. Where an appeal presents a basic constitutional question, review is normally granted. But most controversies present less significant questions; thus, of the approximately 5,500 appeals that are filed with the Court each year, it usually agrees to hear only about 155. In the rejected cases the judgments of the lower courts stand.

Judicial Restraint: While the Supreme Court theoretically possesses unlimited discretion in the area of constitutional interpretation, it is in fact subject to several restraints. Chief among these is the principle of **judicial self-restraint**—the philosophy that controversies must be settled, insofar as possible, in conformity with previously established principles. This does not mean that previous interpretations are never overturned; we shall see in sub-

[2]In those portions of the Constitution that we are concerned with, the terms "persons" and "citizens" include business organizations unless otherwise noted.

sequent cases that marked changes in interpretation occasionally do come about. It does mean that, barring compelling circumstantial changes, the rules of prior cases will normally be followed. Judicial self-restraint also imposes an implied duty on the justices to subordinate their personal economic and political beliefs to previously established interpretations (although, as we will see later, such factors can never be eliminated entirely from the interpretative processes).

Closely allied with the principle of judicial restraint is the rule or policy known as the "presumption of constitutionality"—the strong inclination of the courts to *uphold* a statute that is claimed to be unconstitutional, unless the arguments against its constitutionality are clear and persuasive. Thus, in cases where the arguments against the statute are not that cogent—where the arguments for and against the statute are rather evenly balanced—the courts usually will find the statute to be constitutional.

Sources of Constitutional Guarantees: Insofar as the structure of the Constitution is concerned, the various provisions that guarantee the basic personal, property, and political rights of the individual do not all spring from the same source. Some of these provisions are found in the Constitution proper, some in the first ten Amendments (the so-called Bill of Rights), and some in later amendments—particularly the Fourteenth Amendment.

The U.S. Supreme Court interprets our constitution. The highest courts of other nations may or may not perform this function.

Source: From *Running a Muck* by John Caldwell. Used by permission of *Writer's Digest Books*.

Scope of Constitutional Guarantees: The limitations upon governmental actions that are found in the First Amendment literally apply only to the federal government. That amendment, for example, commences with these words: "Congress shall make no law respecting an establishment of religion," followed, as we see later, by an enumeration of additional rights that are protected against infringement. It would thus appear that *state* statutes or other actions limiting these rights would be permissible. However, the U.S. Supreme Court, by judicial interpretation, has taken the view that any such state actions are also invalid on the ground that such actions violate another constitutional provision, the "due process" clause of the Fourteenth Amendment (which we examine later). The effect of this interpretation, then, is that neither Congress *nor the states* can limit the freedoms set forth in the First Amendment.

Interpretation of Selected Provisions

We now turn our attention to a number of problems of interpretation that some of the more important constitutional clauses have posed for the courts over the years, beginning with two clauses found in the Constitution proper. The remainder of the chapter focuses on selected provisions of the constitutional amendments.

Full Faith and Credit

Section 1 of Article IV of the Constitution provides in part that "Full faith and credit shall be given in each State to the public acts, records, and judicial proceedings of every other State." The import of this section is quite clear: the courts of one state must recognize judgments and other public actions of its sister states. Thus a business firm that obtains a valid judgment against a debtor in one state may enforce that judgment in the courts of any other state in which that debtor's property may be located. The full faith and credit clause is, however, subject to a number of limitations. For example, if the court that entered the judgment originally did not have jurisdiction of the defendant, the courts of other states will not recognize the judgment. And the courts in a state in which a foreign judgment is sought to be enforced will not enforce that judgment if it violates the public policy of that state.

Privileges and Immunities

Section 2 of Article IV of the Constitution provides, in part, that "The citizens of each State shall be entitled to all privileges and immunities of the several states." The basic import of this clause is that, in general, a state can not discriminate against citizens of another state solely because of their foreign citizenship. Thus a state cannot prohibit travel by nonresidents within its borders, nor can a state deny nonresident plaintiffs access to its court system.

The privileges and immunities clause is, however, subject to many judicially imposed limitations. For example, a state law may—within reasonable limits—subject nonresidents to certain limitations if the law involves protection of a matter of "legitimate local interest." Therefore a state statute may provide that in letting contracts for the construction of public buildings, preference may be given to raw materials or products produced within that state. Similarly, because state universities are essentially supported by taxation of residents, and also because of the interest that residents have in such schools, the charging of higher tuition for nonresident students does not violate the privileges and immunities clause.[3] And since corporations are *not* "citizens" within the meaning of this clause, nonresident corporations can be subject to higher tax rates than those applicable to domestic corporations. (Such rates cannot, however, be so high as to be "confiscatory" in nature—that is, enacted largely as a punishment for the privilege of doing business—or be so onerous as to effectively exclude nonresidents from doing business within the state, for such taxation would likely violate both the due process and commerce clauses of the Constitution.)

In the following case, the U.S. Supreme Court was called upon to determine whether an Alaskan statute violated the privileges and immunities clause.

Hicklin v. Orbeck
U.S. Supreme Court
437 U.S. 518
(1978)

Alaska passed a statute in 1972 (known as "Alaska Hire") for the avowed purpose of reducing unemployment within the state. The key provision of the statute required all employers engaged in specific lines of work to hire qualified Alaskan residents in preference to nonresidents. The types of employment covered by the act were, for the most part, activities relating to "oil and gas leases, and easements or right-of-way permits for oil or gas pipeline purposes." To implement the act, persons who had resided in the state for a minimum period of one year were furnished "resident cards" as proof of their preferred status.

Hicklin and others, plaintiffs, were nonresidents who had worked on the Trans-Alaska pipeline for short periods until late 1975, when the act was first enforced. In 1976, when plaintiffs were refused employment on the pipeline, they brought this action against Orbeck, the state official charged with enforcement of Alaska Hire, contending that the act violated the privileges and immunities clause. The Supreme Court of Alaska, by a vote of three to two, held that the law was constitutional. Plaintiffs appealed.

[3] *Johns v. Redeker*, 406 F2d 878 (1969). (The U.S. Supreme Court in effect affirmed this decision by denying certiorari.)

Brennan, Justice:

. . . The Privileges and Immunities Clause . . . establishes a norm of comity that is to prevail among the States with respect to their treatment of each other's residents. . . . Appellants' appeal to the protection of this Clause is strongly supported by this Court's decisions holding violative of the Clause state discrimination against nonresidents seeking to ply their trade, practice their occupation, or pursue a common calling within the State. For example, in [an early case this Court] . . . recognized that a resident of one State is constitutionally entitled to travel to another State for purposes of employment free from discriminatory restrictions in favor of state residents imposed by the other State.

Again, [in] *Toomer v. Witsell*, 334 U.S. 385 (1948), the leading exposition of the limitations the Clause places on a State's power to bias employment opportunities in favor of its own residents, [this Court] invalidated a South Carolina statute that required nonresidents to pay a fee 100 times greater than that paid by residents for a license to shrimp commercially in the three-mile maritime belt off the coast of that state. The Court reasoned that although the Privileges and Immunities Clause "does not preclude disparity of treatment in the many situations where there are perfectly valid independent reasons for it, it does bar discrimination against citizens of other States where there is no substantial reason for the discrimination beyond the mere fact that they are citizens of other States." A "substantial reason for the discrimination" would not exist, the Court explained, "unless there is something to indicate that noncitizens constitute a peculiar source of the evil at which the statute is aimed.". . .

Even assuming that a State may validly attempt to alleviate its unemployment problem by requiring private employers within the State to discriminate against nonresidents—an assumption made at least dubious [by prior cases]—it is clear under the *Toomer* analysis that Alaska Hire's discrimination against nonresidents cannot withstand scrutiny under the Privileges and Immunities Clause. For although the Statute may not violate the Clause if the State shows [in the words of *Toomer*] "something to indicate that noncitizens constitute a peculiar source of evil," *certainly no showing was made on this record that nonresidents were a peculiar source of the evil [that] Alaska Hire was enacted to remedy, namely, Alaska's uniquely high unemployment.* [Emphasis added.] What evidence the record does contain indicates that the major cause of Alaska's high unemployment was not the influx of nonresidents seeking employment, but rather the fact that a substantial number of Alaska's jobless residents—especially the unemployed Eskimo and Indian residents—were unable to secure employment either because of their lack of education and job training or because of their geographical remoteness from job opportunities. The employment of nonresidents threatened to deny jobs to Alaska residents only to the extent that jobs for which untrained residents were being prepared might be filled by nonresidents before the residents' training was completed.

Moreover, even if the State's showing is accepted as sufficient to indicate that nonresidents were "a peculiar source of evil," *Toomer* compels the conclusion that Alaska Hire nevertheless fails to pass constitutional muster, [because] the discrimination the Act works against nonresidents does not bear a substantial relationship to the particular "evil" they are said to present. Alaska Hire simply grants all Alaskans, regardless of their employment status, education, or training, a flat employment preference for all jobs covered by the Act. A highly skilled and educated resident who has never been unemployed is entitled to precisely the same preferential treatment as the unskilled, habitually unemployed Arctic Eskimo enrolled in a job-training program. If Alaska is to attempt to ease its unemployment problem by forcing employers within the State to discriminate against nonresidents—again, a policy which [itself] may present serious constitutional questions—the means by which it does so must be more closely tailored to aid the unemployed the Act is intended to benefit. Even if a statute granting an employment preference to unemployed residents or to residents enrolled in job-training programs might be permissible, Alaska Hire's across-the-board grant of a job preference to all Alaskan residents clearly is not. . . . [For these reasons,] Alaska Hire cannot withstand constitutional scrutiny.

Judgment reversed.

★★★

First Amendment; Freedom of Religion

The First Amendment provides: "Congress shall make no law respecting an *establishment of religion*, or *prohibiting the free exercise thereof*; or abridging the freedom of speech, or of the press; or the right of the people peaceably to assemble, and to petition the Government for a redress of grievances." (Emphasis added.) Our freedom of religion guarantee—the basis of the so-called "separation of church and state" doctrine—is thus created by two distinct clauses, the establishment clause and the free exercise clause. Before examining each of these briefly, several observations are in order. First, while these clauses sometimes overlap (that is, may prohibit the same kinds of governmental actions or interference in particular cases), they basically create two separate—and different—guarantees. Second, the rights guaranteed by these clauses are not absolute; that is, governmental statutes or actions that are otherwise lawful and which affect or limit religious practices only incidentally are constitutional.[4] And, third, the controversies that present freedom of religion issues are usually not business-related; rather, the most common cases involve such matters as the constitutionality of Christmas programs in public schools and the expenditure of public funds to assist the activities of parochial schools. (Be that as it may, the establishment and free exercise clauses *do* impose significant limitations upon some

Courts are adamant about this.

[4]The U.S. Supreme Court, for example, has repeatedly held that a statute does not violate the establishment clause, even though it may have some religious impact, if three criteria are met: (a) the statute must have a "secular" (nonreligious) legislative purpose, (b) the primary effect of the statute must "neither advance nor inhibit" religion, and (c) the statute does not foster "excessive governmental entanglement" with religion.

kinds of governmental actions that relate to the business world, as will be seen below.)

The Establishment Clause: The basic import of the establishment clause is quite clear. The federal government is, of course, prohibited from establishing an official religion, and—as we have seen—the state governments, under judicial interpretation of the due process clause, are subject to the same prohibition. Of even more practical significance, perhaps, is the general principle which has evolved from the case law to the effect that neither the federal government nor the state governments can enact legislation or adopt regulations favoring one religious group over another, or favoring all religious groups over nonreligious ones.

Many close cases have arisen in this area. For example, the case of *Engel v. Vitale*, 370 U.S. 421, decided in 1962, presented the question of whether an action of the New York State Board of Regents, which authorized the recitation of a short prayer in public schools, violated the establishment clause. The U.S. Supreme Court ruled that it did, even though the prayer was nondenominational in nature and recitation by the students was on an entirely voluntary basis.[5] The court said, in part, that "the constitutional prohibition against laws respecting an establishment of a religion must at least mean that in this country it is no part of the business of government to compose official prayers for any group of the American people to recite as a part of a religious program carried on by any government." The court based its conclusion to a great extent upon the "historical fact that governmentally established religions and religious persecutions go hand in hand," and inferred that the regents' action, if sanctioned, might be the foot-in-the-door that could lead to broader state intervention in the future. (In a related case the U.S. Supreme Court held in 1985 that an Alabama statute permitting a moment of silence in the public schools "for meditation or voluntary prayer" also violated the establishment clause.[6] The majority opinion was based largely on the ground that the statute was clearly intended to promote religion; the decision, therefore, had no application to those statutes of a number of other states which permit a moment of silence "for meditation" only.)

A different type of state involvement was presented by *Estate of Thornton v. Caldor, Inc.* 105 S. Ct. 2914, also decided by the U.S. Supreme Court in 1985. There a state statute which was meant to aid the observance of religious practices ran afoul of the establishment clause. In that case, an employee of the defendant corporation, a Presbyterian, was discharged when

[5] The prayer composed by the regents was as follows: "Almighty God, we acknowledge our dependence upon Thee, and we beg Thy blessings upon us, our parents, our teachers, and our Country."

[6] *Wallace v. Jaffree*, 105 S. Ct. 2479. Official U.S. Supreme Court Reports citation not available at time of printing.

he refused to work on Sundays. He then brought a wrongful discharge action against the employer, basing his suit on a Connecticut statute which read as follows: "No person who states that a particular day of the week is observed as his Sabbath may be required by his employer to work on such day. An employee's refusal to work on his Sabbath shall not constitute grounds for his dismissal." The Supreme Court of Connecticut entered judgment for the employer, agreeing with its contention that the statute violated the establishment clause. The U.S. Supreme Court affirmed, noting first that the statute "imposes on employers and employees an absolute duty to conform their business practices to the particular religious practices of the employee by enforcing observance of the Sabbath the employee unilaterally designates. The State thus commands that the Sabbath religious concerns automatically control over all secular interests of the employer or those of other employees who do not observe a Sabbath. . . ." The court continued, "There is no exception under the statute for special circumstances, such as the Friday Sabbath observer employed in an occupation with a Monday through Friday schedule—a school teacher, for example," and, moreover, "there is no exception when honoring the dictates of Sabbath observers would cause the employer substantial economic burdens or when the employer's compliance would require the imposition of significant burdens on other employees required to work in place of Sabbath observers." The court concluded: "This unyielding weighting in favor of Sabbath observers over all other interests contravenes a fundamental principle of the Religion Clauses, so well articulated by Judge Learned Hand [in an early case]: 'The First Amendment gives no one the right to insist that in pursuit of their own interests others must conform their conduct to his own religious necessities.'"[7]

The Free Exercise Clause: The general thrust of this clause is to guarantee to all persons the right of religious belief and the freedom to practice their beliefs free of governmental interference. Although freedom of religion controversies involving the business world are more often based on the establishment clause than the free exercise clause, the latter clause is nonetheless significant in this area.

Two cases help to illustrate this significance. One involved the legality of a state fair commission's "booth rule," which required all persons and organizations who wished to solicit contributions at the state fair to restrict their solicitations to designated booths on the fair grounds. When this rule was challenged by members of the Baltimore Chapter of Krishna Consciousness, the commission defended on the ground that the rule was justified by public safety considerations. The appellate court, a U.S. court of appeals, held that the rule violated the free exercise clause in view of the commission's failure

[7] Employee claims of religion-based discrimination are most commonly resolved under Title VII of the Civil Rights Act of 1964. For a discussion of applicable sections of this statute, see "Accommodation of Religious Practices" material in Chapter 15.

to produce sufficient evidence that unrestrained solicitations would result in "serious disruption" of fair activities.[8] The second case, in an area that has produced considerable litigation, involved the constitutionality of a state board's refusal to grant unemployment compensation to a foundry employee, Thomas, who refused to accept a job transfer to a division of the company that manufactured military tank components. Thomas, a member of Jehovah's Witnesses, told his employer that such work violated his religious beliefs and requested a re-transfer to his old job. When this request was refused, Thomas quit and subsequently filed a claim for unemployment compensation with the appropriate state board. The board rejected his claim, ruling that Thomas's termination of employment due to his religious beliefs was not a "good cause" termination (a requirement under state law for compensation eligibility), and he appealed this ruling in the state courts. The Supreme Court of Indiana upheld the board's action, accepting the state's argument that the payment of benefits would constitute excessive governmental entanglement with religion. The U.S. Supreme Court reversed, holding that the board's refusal to award benefits violated Thomas's free exercise rights. The court said, in part, "When the state conditions receipt of an important benefit upon conduct proscribed by a religious faith, or where it denies such a benefit because of conduct mandated by religious belief, thereby putting substantial pressure on the adherent to modify his behavior and violate his beliefs, an [unconstitutional] burden exists [and] the infringement upon free exercise is . . . substantial."[9]

As indicated by language in the Maryland state fair decision, governmental actions that are based upon public health, safety, or general welfare considerations may be valid under the free exercise clause even though the actions result in some limitation upon the practices of a religious group or groups. The so-called *blue laws*—statutes and ordinances that limit or prohibit the carrying on of specified business activities on Sundays—are a case in point. Although several states have repealed their blue laws in recent years (and this trend is likely to continue), such laws, in the appreciable number of states that have retained them, are generally held to be constitutional on the ground that their primary purpose is the furtherance of legitimate social or economic ends, and their inhibiting effect upon religious practices is only of an incidental nature. The case of *Braunfeld v. Brown*, 366 U.S. 599 (1961), is an example of such a view. There a Pennsylvania statute prohibited the retail sale of clothing and home furnishings, among other items, on Sundays. Its constitutionality was challenged by members of the Orthodox Jewish Faith whose beliefs required them to abstain from all work and trade from Friday nights until Saturday nights, and who, therefore, customarily opened their stores on Sundays. The U.S. Supreme Court, in holding that the statute did not violate the free exercise clause, said:

---

[8] *Edwards v. Maryland State Fair and Agricultural Society*, 628 F.2d 282 (1980).

[9] *Thomas v. Review Board of Indiana Employment Security Division*, 450 U.S. 707 (1981).

If the purpose or effect of a law is to impede the observance of one or all religions or is to discriminate invidiously between religions, that law is constitutionally invalid. . . . But if the State regulates conduct by enacting a general law within its power, the purpose and effect of which is to advance the State's secular [non-religious] goals, the statute is valid despite its indirect burden on religious observances. . . . We cannot find a State without power to provide a weekly respite from all labor and, at the same time, to set aside one day of the week apart from the others as a day of rest, repose, recreation and tranquility. . . .

First Amendment; Free Speech

Few peoples of the world enjoy more so-called political rights than citizens of the United States. Many of these rights spring directly from the first ten Amendments to the Constitution. Of these, none is given more sweeping protection by the courts than the right of free speech, which comes—as we have seen—from that part of the First Amendment providing that "Congress shall make no law . . . abridging the freedom of speech." As a result of this protection, citizens can, in general, criticize public officials and the laws of their government free of governmental interference.

The free speech guarantee has been interpreted in so many different situations that its precise effect is especially difficult to summarize briefly. Nonetheless, several general observations are possible.

First, this guarantee—while generally interpreted broadly by the courts—is still subject to certain limitations (as is true of all of our other constitutional guarantees). Justice Holmes illustrated this succinctly years ago in his observation that the freedom of speech clause does not sanction a false cry of "fire" in a crowded theater. Furthermore, free speech does not permit one to make false and defamatory statements about another. Thus, if A falsely tells B that C, an attorney, was disbarred at one time, C may recover damages from A in a slander action.[10] Similarly, state and federal statutes that make it a crime to disseminate obscene materials are constitutional (if their definitions of "obscenity" are in conformity with those of the U.S. Supreme Court). And it is well established that "the constitutional guarantees do not permit unrestricted utterances or publication of remarks or literature which is seditious or hostilely subversive, (or) which advocate violent, forceful or terroristic changes (in government)."[11]

Second, the principle is often expressed in the cases that "the law abhors prior restraints." What this means is that, because of the extreme importance attached by the courts to the free speech guarantee, the courts will

---

[10] The subject of slander, which is one type of tort, will be considered further in Chapter 8.

[11] 16 *Am Jur 2d, Constitutional Law* §349 (Lawyers Co-operative Publishing Co., Rochester, New York; Bancroft-Whitney Company, San Francisco, California, 1964.)

ordinarily hold prior restraints to be unconstitutional. Thus if a city council refuses to issue a permit for a rally or some other assembly of a particular group where unpopular speeches may be made, and if the group challenges the action in court, the clear tendency of the courts is to strike down the council's refusal on free speech grounds, rather than support the banning of the assembly. The inclination of the courts, then, is to *permit* the assembly, dealing with any unlawfulness that might grow out of it (such as injuries or destruction of property) to be redressed in subsequent civil actions brought against the wrongdoers themselves. The same approach generally is applicable where a local court issues an injunction against a similar gathering, and where the injunction is attacked in court. (Of course, as indicated earlier, the refusal to issue a permit, or the issuance of an injunction, may be *upheld* in the relatively rare case where a reviewing court is satisfied that the probability of force and violence—if the assemblage were to be held—is indeed very high.)

Third, symbolic (nonverbal) speech is given substantial protection by the courts today. For example, in one case reaching the U.S. Supreme Court, that court had to deal with a regulation adopted by a Des Moines school administrator prohibiting students from wearing black armbands in protest against the Vietnam War. The court ruled that the ban violated the free speech clause, where there was no showing that the wearing of the armbands had disrupted normal school activities.[12] Similarly, the free speech guarantee generally protects expressions espoused by peaceful picketing, although the number of pickets and the places of picketing are subject to reasonable regulation by the courts.

Last, "commercial speech" is being given increasing protection by the courts. In earlier years it was generally held that such speech (for example, statements in advertisements) was not protected by the First Amendment, but today that position is eroding. Thus, in cases arising in 1975 and 1976, the U.S. Supreme Court struck down two restrictive Virginia statutes, saying that they violated the free speech guarantee. The statute in the first case made it a misdemeanor for anyone to publish an advertisement which encouraged or prompted the performance of abortions, and the second declared it to be "unprofessional conduct" for a pharmacist to advertise the prices of prescription drugs. And in *First National Bank v. Belotti*, 435 U.S. 765 (1978), the highest court ruled unconstitutional a Massachusetts statute that prohibited corporations from spending money to influence "the vote on any question submitted to the voters, other than one materially affecting any of the property, business, or assets of the corporation." (A further discussion of this case appears in Chapter 7.)

The Shopping Center Issue: In recent years a number of cases have arisen involving the constitutionality of regulations of privately-owned shopping

[12] *Tinker v. Des Moines School District*, 393 U.S. 503 (1969).

centers and malls, which typically prohibit "soliciting, speech-making, and the seeking of signatures on petitions" on their premises. For discussion purposes, these cases fall into three general categories.

In several cases decided prior to 1972, the U.S. Supreme Court generally held that such restrictions violated the free speech clause of the First Amendment of the U.S. Constitution. The basis of this view was that shopping centers and malls, though privately owned, were the "functional equivalent" of public property. Accordingly, the restrictions issued by the property owners were considered to be the equivalent of *state* action, and therefore prohibited by the First Amendment.[13]

In cases decided in 1972 and subsequently, however, the U.S. Supreme Court substantially rejected this view, ruling first that a private shopping center *could* constitutionally prohibit the distribution of anti-war leaflets on its premises.[14] And in *Hudgens v. NLRB*, 424 U.S. 507 (1976), the high court upheld the right of a shopping center's owners to prohibit the picketing of its stores. In that case the court expressly overruled the pre-1972 cases, ruling that the actions of the owners of shopping centers were *not* state action. As a result, shopping center restrictions are generally valid today as far as the Federal Constitution is concerned.

A third group of cases has, in recent years, presented a different question: whether shopping center restrictions might possibly violate the free speech provisions of *state* constitutions. In those states whose free speech provisions are "more expansive" than those of the U.S. Constitution, the answer is yes.

The leading case in this area is *PruneYard Shopping Center v. Robins*, 447 U.S. 74 (1980), where a group of high school students set up a card table in the shopping center's central area and asked passersby to sign petitions opposing a United Nations resolution against "Zionism." These activities were stopped by a security guard, who told them that they were violating PruneYard regulations. When these regulations were challenged, the U.S. Supreme Court held that the regulations—while presumably valid under the U.S. Constitution—*violated the free speech language of the California Constitution.* The Court first noted the broad language of Article 1, § 2 of the California Constitution, which provided that "Every person may freely speak, write and publish his or her sentiments on all subjects, being responsible for the abuse of this right. A law may not restrain or abridge liberty of speech or press." The high court, agreeing with the conclusion reached by the California Supreme Court, then said that its reasoning in the *Lloyd* and *Hudgens* cases (which upheld the regulations under the Federal Constitution) "does not limit the authority of [a] State to . . . adopt in its own Constitution individual liberties more expansive than those conferred by the Federal Constitution." (The result reached in *PruneYard* could, of

---

[13] *Amalgamated Ford Employees Union Local 590 v. Logan Valley Plaza*, 391 U.S. 308, was the leading case on this point.

[14] *Lloyd Corporation v. Tanner*, 407 U.S. 551 (1972), was the first of these.

course, come about only in those states whose free speech provisions are similar to the language of the California Constitution. And even in such states, the *PruneYard* view is not always followed.)[15]

Due Process of Law (fairness)

The Fifth Amendment, applicable to the federal government, provides in part that "No person shall . . . be deprived of life, liberty, or property without due process of law," and the Fourteenth Amendment contains a clause imposing the same limitation upon state action.

The primary purpose of the due process clauses, as they have been interpreted by the courts, is to prevent the federal and state governments from depriving individuals of certain basic rights in an unfair or arbitrary manner. While life, liberty, and property can be taken in certain circumstances, the main thrust of the due process clause—and the case law that has resulted under it—is that such deprivation should occur only by virtue of judicially acceptable proceedings. The underlying philosophy is aptly summed up in this statement:

"Due process of law" implies at least a conformity with natural and inherent principles of justice, and forbids that one man's property, or right to property, shall be taken for the benefit of another, or for the benefit of the state, without compensation, and that no one shall be condemned in his person or property without an opportunity of being heard in his own defense.[16]

The guarantee springing from this clause extends to both criminal and civil proceedings. In the area of criminal law, a person who has been convicted of a crime may be successful in having the conviction set aside under the due process clause if the statute allegedly violated was so vague as to fail to prescribe "a reasonable standard of guilt." The case of *City of Columbus v. Thompson*, 25 Ohio St.2d 25 (1971), is one such example. There a Columbus "suspicious persons" ordinance was challenged. The ordinance defined a suspicious person as one "who wanders about the streets or other public ways or who is found abroad at late or unusual hours of the night without any visible or lawful business and who does not give satisfactory account of himself."

---

[15] The highest courts of Massachusetts, Pennsylvania, and Washington, for example, have essentially followed the *PruneYard* decision, while those of Connecticut and North Carolina have not. (The decision of the trial court in the Connecticut case, *Cologne v. Westfarms Associates*, 442 A.2d 471 (1982), striking down the mall restrictions under the broad language of the Connecticut Constitution, appeared in the first edition of this text. The Supreme Court of Connecticut subsequently reversed, saying that "a court of this state may [not] direct that the rights of free speech and petition in our state constitution may be expressed upon private property consisting of a large regional shopping center, contrary to the wishes of its owners.") (469 A.2d 1201, 1984.)

[16] *Holden v. Hardy*, 169 U.S. 366 (1898).

The Ohio Supreme Court, in setting aside the conviction of Thompson, held that the ordinance violated the due process clause in that it "leaves the public uncertain as to the conduct it prohibits" and "leaves judges and jurors free to decide, without any legally fixed standards, what is prohibited and what is not in each particular case." (And even where a conviction occurs under a statute whose language *is* reasonably precise, it may be set aside under the due process clause if the accused can show that the trial proceedings were so arbitrarily conducted as to deprive the person of a fair opportunity to present a defense.)

Turning to the area of civil proceedings, we find that the due process clause is upheld as zealously as in criminal cases. For example, if a condemnation statute provides that the value of land taken from a private citizen shall be "conclusively determined" by an appointed board—thereby depriving the landowner of the right to contest the determination in the courts—it quite certainly violates the due process clause. Similarly, tax statutes may, in some circumstances, violate the due process clause. For example, while the courts generally construe the clause in favor of tax laws, statutes which impose taxes that are clearly shown to be confiscatory or discriminatory have been held to constitute the taking of property without due process of law.

In this general area, the courts require that there be both "procedural" due process and "substantive" due process. While the distinction is often a fuzzy one, procedural due process demands that the *proceedings* under which a statute or rule is carried out be fair, while substantive due process requires that the actual *provisions* of the statute or rule also be fair and reasonable. To illustrate the difference: the rules of a medical school specifying the kinds of misconduct that are grounds for dismissal may be clear and based on reason, thereby satisfying the substantive due process requirement. Nevertheless, a student who is dismissed under the rules may be successful in court in having the dismissal set aside if he or she can show, for example, that the dismissal hearing was held without reasonable notice or in an arbitrary fashion, that he or she was not adequately permitted to refute the charges made, or that no appeal of the decision to higher school authorities was permitted. In any of these instances the requirement of *procedural* due process was probably not met.

The first of the following cases presents a due process question in a general setting, while the second involves a state action that had a direct impact upon a specified class of persons in the business world.

Valdez v. City of Ottawa
Appellate Court of Illinois, Third District
434 N.E.2d 1192 (1982)

In early May, 1979, Valdez left his Pontiac LeMans automobile on the shoulder of Frontage Road in Ottawa, Illinois, after it "conked out." Shortly thereafter the Ottawa Police Department placed a sticker on the car, saying that it would be towed unless moved.

The car remained on the shoulder about a week, at which time the police department authorized Kammerer's Auto Wrecking to tow the vehicle away and store it on their property. Mrs. Valdez, after learning from a friend that

the car was at Kammerer's, asked them if she could take possession of it. Kammerer's told her that the $70 towing fee would have to be paid first, and since the Valdezes could not afford the fee the car remained in Kammerer's possession.

Six weeks later Kammerer's requested a disposition permit from the police department. After a police officer failed to reach the Valdezes by phone, the police department issued the permit, and Kammerer's destroyed the car in late July.

Valdez then brought this action against the city and Kammerer's for damages for loss of the vehicle, contending that the city did not afford him due process when it seized the car and permitted its destruction without notice. The trial court rejected this contention, ruling that the plaintiff had left his car unattended for such a long time that he had constructive (theoretical) notice that the police would tow the car. Accordingly, the court entered a summary judgment for defendants, and Valdez (referred to as "plaintiff" in the decision below) appealed.

Alloy, Justice:

. . . The principal issue in this appeal is whether the defendants violated the plaintiff's constitutional rights when they seized [his] automobile without giving [him] prior notice of the seizure. The Fourteenth Amendment provides that:

All persons born or naturalized in the United States, and subject to the jurisdiction thereof, are citizens of the United States and of the State wherein they reside. No State shall make or enforce any law which shall abridge the privileges or immunities of citizens of the United States; nor shall any State deprive any person of life, liberty, or property, without due process of law; nor deny to any person within its jurisdiction the equal protection of the laws. . . .

Due process is not an inflexible standard and does not require a trial-type hearing in every conceivable case of government impairment of private interest. Nonetheless, due process requires that, at a minimum, . . . deprivation of life, liberty or property by adjudication be preceded by notice and an opportunity for hearing appropriate to the nature of the case. The notice must be reasonably calculated to convey the necessary information and to afford the interested parties a reasonable time for a hearing. Those parties must be given notice and an opportunity before the deprivation takes place, unless there exists extraordinary circumstances requiring immediate action to protect a valid governmental interest. Furthermore, there is no question that ownership of an automobile and continued access to it is a property interest within the protection of the Fourteenth Amendment, and whether the deprivation will be permanent or temporary is immaterial. Towing a car without prior notice [subject to exceptions noted later] is a violation of due process rights.

In the case at bar, the defendants invaded the constitutional rights of the plaintiff when it seized, towed and refused to relinquish the auto before payment of a towing fee. The City does not seriously contest the necessity for due process when it seizes and tows vehicles. The question, therefore, is whether the defendants gave the plaintiff adequate notice that the car would be towed, or whether an extraordinary situation existed necessitating immediate seizure and removal of the vehicle.

On the latter question, there is no evidence in the record that the plaintiff's auto posed any substantial danger to traffic as it rested on the shoulder of the road. . . . The road is near an International Harvester plant and the Hines Lumber Company, indicating that high speed travel is unusual. The car was parked completely on the shoulder. The fact that the police saw no need to disturb the car for at least one week is a strong indication that no emergency existed.

The City places primary reliance on the trial court's finding that the plaintiff had constructive notice of the possible seizure and tow. The City argues the plaintiff should have known that if he left the car on the shoulder of the road long enough, the police would tow it away. [The City also contends that] the tow sticker the police attached to the car is additional evidence of the plaintiff's notice. *This argument is without merit.* [Emphasis added.] The auto was currently registered and the police had the plaintiff's name and address. Notice must be reasonably calculated to actually apprise the property owner of the opportunity to contest the government's proposed action. If the plaintiff's residence is readily and easily available, as is true here, the City may not rely on fortuitous or constructive notice to satisfy the Due Process Clause. At a minimum, notice by certified or registered mail would have been appropriate in the instant case.

This does not necessarily mean the State may never remove a vehicle before giving the owner notice. Clearly there are circumstances where a vehicle may be parked in a manner that endangers public safety or impedes efficient movement of traffic. For example, a vehicle may be blocking traffic, parked on a snow route during a snow emergency or standing on the shoulder of an interstate highway for a prolonged period of time. It is not possible or desirable to detail every conceivable situation in which an automobile may be towed without prior notice to the owner. The guiding principle must always be whether or not the vehicle, as it stands, jeopardizes public safety by either creating an unsafe condition or significantly hindering the efficient movement of traffic. The towing of parked vehicles that do not fall within these categories without pre-tow notice and opportunity for a hearing violates the Fourteenth Amendment to the Constitution.

[Furthermore,] if an auto is towed without prior notice to the owner, due process requires prompt notice and an opportunity to a hearing before the government makes any disposition of the vehicle. Additionally, the owner must have an opportunity to contest the seizure and tow before he can be required to pay any charges or fees. *Stypmann v. City & County of San Francisco*, 557 F.2d 1338, 1977. In the case at bar, therefore, the defendants violated the plaintiff's right to due process when they destroyed his automobile without any notice, even if immediate seizure and tow was proper. . . .

The trial court's finding of summary judgment in favor of the defendants is reversed and the case is remanded for trial.

★★★

New Motor Vehicle Board of California v. Orrin W. Fox Co.
U.S. Supreme Court
439 U.S. 96
(1978)

California passed the Automobile Franchise Act in 1973. The purpose of the act was to protect the equities of existing automobile dealers by prohibiting automobile manufacturers from adding dealerships to the market areas of their existing franchisees (dealers) where the effect of such intrabrand competition would be injurious to the existing franchisees and to the public interest. To enforce this prohibition, the act requires an automobile manufacturer who proposes to establish a new retail automobile dealership in the state, or to relocate an existing one, first to give notice of such intention to the California New Motor Vehicle Board (the board) and to each of its existing franchisees in the same "line-make" of automobile located within the "relevant market area," which is defined as "any area within a radius of 10 miles from the site of the potential new dealership."

If any existing franchisee within the market area protests to the board within fifteen days, the board is required to hold a hearing within sixty days to determine whether there is good cause for refusing to permit the establishment or relocation of the dealership. The board is also required to inform the franchisor, upon the filing of a protest, that a protest has been filed, "that a hearing is required . . . and that the franchisor *shall not establish or relocate the proposed dealership until the board has held a hearing*, . . . nor thereafter, if the board [determines] that there is good cause for not permitting such dealership." [Emphasis added.] Violation of the statutory requirements by a franchisor is a misdemeanor, and grounds for suspension or revocation of a license to do business.

In May of 1975 the Orrin W. Fox Company signed a franchise agreement with General Motors to establish a new Buick dealership in Pasadena. In December of that same year Muller Chevrolet agreed with General Motors to transfer its existing Chevrolet franchise from Glendale to La Canada, California. The proposed establishment of Fox and the relocation of Muller were protested by existing Buick and Chevrolet dealers, respectively.

The board responded, as required by the law, by notifying Fox, Muller, and General Motors that the protests had been filed and that therefore they were not to establish or relocate the dealerships until the board held the required hearings, nor thereafter in the event that the board determined there was good cause for not permitting such dealerships.

Before the board could hold hearings on either protest, Fox, Muller, and General Motors brought suit in the U.S. District Court for the Central District of California challenging the constitutionality of the statute. Their primary contention was that the clause in the statute immediately suspending the dealer's right to relocate upon receipt of the notice of protest, prior to a hearing, constituted a violation of procedural due process guaranteed by the Fourteenth Amendment of the Constitution. The district court agreed with this contention, and the board appealed to the U.S. Supreme Court. (The board was able to make a direct appeal to the highest court, under applicable federal rules, because the district court that heard the matter was comprised of three judges, instead of the usual single judge.)

Brennan, Justice:

. . . The disparity in bargaining power between automobile manufacturers and their dealers prompted Congress and some 25 States to enact legislation to protect retail car dealers from [various] perceived abusive and oppressive acts by the manufacturers.[a] California's version is its Automobile Franchise Act. . . .

The appellees [Fox, Muller, and General Motors] argue that the state scheme deprives them of their liberty to pursue their lawful occupation without due process of law. Appellees contend that absent a prior individualized trial-type hearing, they are constitutionally entitled to establish or relocate franchises while their applications are awaiting Board determination. Appellees' argument rests on the assumption that General Motors has a due process protected interest right to franchise at will—which asserted right survived the passage of the California Automobile Franchise Act.

The narrow question before us, then, is whether California may, by rule or statute, temporarily delay the establishment or relocation of automobile dealerships pending the Board's adjudication of the protests of existing dealers. . . .

We disagree with the [district court's holding that California may not do so]. Even if the right to franchise had constituted a protected interest when California enacted the Automobile Franchise Act, California's Legislature was still constitutionally empowered to enact a general scheme of business regulation that imposed reasonable restrictions upon the exercise of the right. "The fact that a liberty cannot be inhibited without due process of law does not mean that it can under no circumstances be inhibited." [Citation.] At least since the demise of the concept of "substantive due process" in the area of economic legislation, this Court has recognized that "legislative bodies have broad scope to experiment with economic problems." States may, through general ordinances, restrict the commercial use of property, and the geographical location of commercial enterprises. Moreover, "certain kinds of business may be prohibited; and the right to conduct a business, or to pursue a calling, may be conditioned. . . . Statutes prescribing the terms upon which those conducting certain businesses may contract, or imposing terms if they do enter into agreements, are within the state's competency." [Citations.]

In particular, the California Legislature was empowered to subordinate the franchise rights of automobile manufacturers to the conflicting rights of their franchisees where necessary to prevent unfair or oppressive trade practices. "The due process clause is not to be so broadly construed that the Congress and state legislatures are put in a straightjacket when they attempt to suppress business and industrial conditions which they regard as offensive to the public welfare." [*Lincoln Union v. Northwestern Co.*, 335 U.S. 525, 1949.] . . .

Further, the California Legislature had the authority to protect the conflicting rights of the motor vehicle franchisees through customary and reasonable procedural safeguards, i.e., by providing existing dealers with notice and an

---

[a] The federal law referred to, the Automobile Dealers' Day in Court Act, was not involved in this action.

opportunity to be heard by an impartial tribunal—the New Motor Vehicle Board—before their franchisor is permitted to inflict upon them grievous loss. States may, as California has done here, require businesses to secure regulatory approval before engaging in specified practices. [The court here cited cases in which this principle was applied to pharmacies, billboard permits, securities registration, and milk inspection.]

These precedents compel the conclusion that the District Court erred in holding that the California Legislature was powerless temporarily to delay appellees' exercise of the right to grant or undertake a Buick or Chevrolet dealership and the right to move one's business facilities from one location to another without providing a prior individualized trial-type hearing. . . .

Reversed.

★★★

Equal Protection of the Laws

Section 1 of the Fourteenth Amendment, in its entirety, is as follows: All persons born or naturalized in the United States and subject to the jurisdiction thereof, are citizens of the United States and the State wherein they reside. No State shall make or enforce any law which shall abridge the privileges or immunities of citizens of the United States, nor shall any State deprive any person of life, liberty, or property, without due process of law; *nor deny to any person within its jurisdiction the equal protection of the laws.* [Emphasis added.] The general import of this clause is to forbid a legislature to enact laws imposing legal duties on certain classes of persons that are not imposed on others.

The equal protection clause, however, does not prohibit *all* class legislation. Occasionally problems are created by one class of persons (such as a particular type of retail establishment) which by reason of the nature of their business or the size of their operation may be subject to restrictions that are not necessary for others. Such class legislation, as viewed by the courts, does not offend the equal protection clause as long as the classification is based on reasonable and rational factors.[17]

Literally, the equal protection clause applies only to the state governments. However, the Supreme Court has taken the view that *federal* statutes which arbitrarily treat one class of persons differently from other classes also violate the due process clause of the Fifth Amendment. The effect of this

[17] While the rational basis test is used in most instances in determining the constitutionality of a statute's classification, in limited circumstances—usually not involving business cases—a different test is applied. Where a classification is considered to be a "suspect classification," that is, based on such matters as race, religion, or alienage, the classification must pass the "strict scrutiny" test. Under this test, the statute will be held to be unconstitutional unless the state can show that there are "compelling" reasons why it should be upheld. In circumstances where the strict scrutiny test is applied, then, a statute is more likely to be held unconstitutional than where the rational basis test is used.

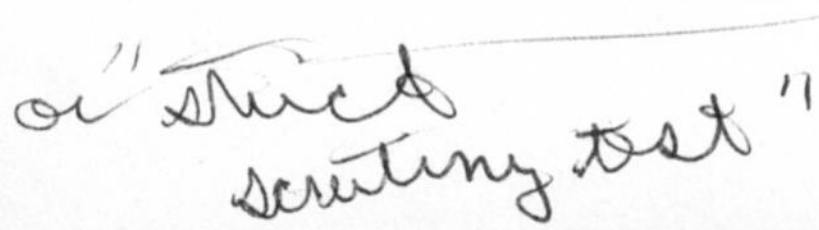

interpretation is to extend the equal protection clause to actions of the federal government as well as those of the state governments.

In the now-celebrated case of *Brown v. Board of Education*, 347 U.S. 483 (1954), the U.S. Supreme Court was called upon to consider the constitutionality of state statutes that required the segregation of public school students on the basis of their color. Prior to this decision the court had applied the "separate but equal" doctrine to somewhat similar cases—that is, the court held that state regulations of this nature were not unconstitutional if the facilities afforded the minority members were equal to those afforded the majority race. The Supreme Court reversed this precedent in *Brown*, saying that the classification and segregation was inherently unreasonable—and thus in violation of the equal protection clause—to matter how adequate the minority facilities might be. (Today, thirty years after this decision, some school boards and federal courts across the nation are still struggling to devise desegregation plans in conformity with this and subsequent decisions of the Supreme Court in this area.) On the other hand, in *Foley v. Connelie*, 435 U.S. 291 (1978), the Supreme Court held that a New York statute requiring state police officers to be U.S. citizens *was* reasonable, and thus did not violate the equal protection clause.

Turning to the business world, there are also significant numbers of cases in which legislation is similarly challenged under the equal protection clause. Typical of these is *Vigeant v. Postal Telegraph Cable Co.*, 157 N.E. 651 (1927), where the highest court of Massachusetts struck down a statute making telegraph companies (but not similar companies) absolutely liable to any person injured by falling poles or wires. The court said, "A classification for the purpose of establishing liability with respect to persons injured by poles and wires without fault, which singles out telegraph companies but excludes telephone companies, electric light, heat and power companies, does not stand on a reasonable basis."

We conclude this chapter by examining two equal protection cases decided by the U.S. Supreme Court in recent years.

Minnesota v. Clover Leaf Creamery Co.
U.S. Supreme Court
101 S.Ct. 715 (1981)

In 1977 the Minnesota legislature enacted a statute banning the retail sale of milk in plastic nonreturnable, nonrefillable containers, but permitting such sale in other nonreturnable, nonrefillable containers, such as paperboard milk cartons. The purpose of the law was set out in § 1:

The legislature finds that the use of nonreturnable, nonrefillable containers for the packaging of milk and other milk products presents a solid waste management problem for the state, promotes energy waste, and depletes natural resources. The legislature therefore . . . determines that the use of nonreturnable, nonrefillable containers for packaging milk and other milk products should be discouraged and that the use of returnable and reusable packaging for these products is preferred and should be encouraged.

The Clover Leaf Creamery Company, a Minnesota dairy that owned equipment for producing plastic nonreturnable milk jugs, six other companies that produced or leased such equipment, and a plastics industry trade association challenged the statute in a state district court on the ground that it violated the equal protection and due process clauses of the U.S. Constitution, and also unreasonably burdened interstate commerce. That court, after extensive hearings as to the act's probable consequences, concluded that the act would not accomplish the legislative purposes. The court further found that, contrary to the statement of purposes, the "actual basis" for the act was promotion of "the economic interests of certain segments of the dairy and pulpwood industries at the expense of the economic interests of other segments of the dairy industry and the plastics industry." The court therefore declared the act to be *null and void*, basing its judgment on the equal protection and due process clauses of the U.S. Constitution, and on its conclusion that the act unreasonably burdened interstate commerce.

On appeal by the state to the Minnesota Supreme Court, that court disagreed with the trial court's conclusion that the act would not accomplish the legislative purposes. It did, nonetheless, agree with the trial court that the act *violated the equal protection and due process clauses*, so it affirmed the trial court's judgment. The state appealed to the U.S. Supreme Court. (*Note*: Only that part of the Supreme Court's decision dealing with the equal protection issue appears below.)

Brennan, Justice:

. . . The parties agree that the standard of review applicable to this case under the Equal Protection Clause is the familiar "rational basis" test. Moreover, they agree that the purposes of the Act cited by the legislature—promoting resource conservation, easing solid waste disposal problems, and conserving energy—are legitimate state purposes. Thus, the controversy in this case centers on the narrow issue *whether the legislative classification between plastic and nonplastic nonreturnable milk containers is rationally related to achievement of the statutory purposes*. [Emphasis added.]

The State identifies four reasons why the classification between plastic and nonplastic nonreturnables is rationally related to the articulated statutory purposes. If any of the four substantiates the Act's claim, we must reverse the Minnesota Supreme Court and sustain the Act.

First, the State argues that the elimination of the popular plastic milk jug will encourage the use of environmentally superior containers. There is no serious doubt that the plastic containers consume energy resources and require solid waste disposal, nor that refillable bottles and plastic pouches are environmentally superior. Citing evidence that the plastic jug is the most popular, and the gallon paperboard carton the most cumbersome and least well regarded package in the industry, the State argues that the ban on plastic nonreturnables will buy time during which environmentally preferable alternatives may be further developed and promoted.

[The court here referred to arguments in the Minnesota legislature when the bill was being considered that the hope was that ultimately a returnable system could be developed that would eliminate the use of paperboard containers as well as plastic ones, and that the bill would, in the meantime, at least prohibit widespread adoption of the newer plastic containers while a returnable system was being readied. The court then continued]:

We find the State's approach fully supportable under our precedents. This Court has made it clear that a legislature need not "strike at all evils at the same time or in the same way," and that a legislature "may implement its program step-by-step, adopting regulations that only partially ameliorate a perceived evil and deferring complete elimination of the evil to future regulations." [Citations.] The Equal Protection Clause does not deny the State of Minnesota the authority to ban one type of milk container conceded to cause environmental problems, merely because another type, already established in the market, is permitted to continue in use. . . .

Second, the State argues that its ban on plastic nonreturnable milk containers will reduce the economic dislocation foreseen from the movement toward greater use of environmentally superior containers. The State notes that plastic nonreturnables have only recently been introduced on a wide scale in Minnesota, and that, at the time the legislature was considering the Act, many Minnesota dairies were preparing to invest large amounts of capital in plastic container production [that would be lost if a completely returnable system were ultimately developed]. Moreover, the State explains, to ban both the plastic and the paperboard nonreturnable milk container at once would cause an enormous disruption in the milk industry because few dairies are now able to package their products in refillable bottles or plastic pouches. Thus, by banning the plastic container while continuing to permit the paperboard container, the State was able to prevent the industry from becoming reliant on the new container, while avoiding severe economic dislocation. The Minnesota Supreme Court did not directly address [the "economic dislocation" argument of the State], but we find it supported by our precedents, as well. [Citations.]

[The court then turned to the third question, whether the act would or would not help to conserve energy. While the court noted that there was a sharp conflict in the evidence on this point, it ruled that the legislature's judgment that it would conserve energy should not be set aside, in these words]: The Minnesota Supreme Court may be correct that the Act is not a sensible means of conserving energy. But we reiterate that it is up to legislatures, not courts, to decide on the wisdom of legislation. Since in view of the evidence before the legislature, the question is at least debatable, the Minnesota Supreme Court erred in substituting its judgment for that of the legislature.

[The court then accepted the state's fourth equal protection argument, the contention that the act would ease the state's solid waste disposal problem. The court further held that the act neither violated the due process clause nor imposed an undue burden on interstate commerce. It thus found the act to be constitutional, and reversed the judgment of the Minnesota Supreme Court.]

★★★

Zobel v. Williams
U.S. Supreme Court
457 U.S. 55
(1982)

The 1967 discovery of large oil reserves on state-owned land in the Prudhoe Bay area of Alaska resulted in a windfall to the state.[a] The state, which had a total budget of $124 million in 1969, before the oil revenues began to flow into the state coffers, received $3.7 billion in petroleum revenues during the 1981 fiscal year. This income will continue, and most likely grow for some years in the future. Recognizing that its mineral reserves, although large, are finite and the resulting income will not continue in perpetuity, the state took steps to assure that its current good fortune will bring long-range benefits. To accomplish this, Alaska in 1976 adopted a constitutional amendment establishing the Permanent Fund into which the state must deposit at least 25 percent of its mineral income each year. The amendment prohibits the legislature from appropriating any of the principal of the fund, but permits use of the fund's earnings for general governmental purposes.

In 1980, the legislature enacted a dividend program to distribute annually a portion of the fund's earnings directly to the state's adult residents. Under the plan, *each citizen eighteen years of age or older receives "one dividend unit" for each year of residency subsequent to 1959, the first year of statehood.* The statute fixed the value of each dividend unit at $50 for the 1979 fiscal year; a one-year resident would thus receive one unit, or $50, while a resident of Alaska since it became a state in 1959 would receive twenty-one units, or $1,050. The value of a dividend unit will vary each year depending on the income of the Permanent Fund and the amount of that income the state allocates for other purposes. The state now estimates that the 1985 fiscal year dividend will be nearly four times as large as that for 1979.

Ronald and Patricia Zobel, residents of Alaska since 1978, brought this suit in 1980 challenging the dividend distribution plan as violative of their right to equal protection guarantees and their constitutional right to migrate to Alaska, to establish residency there, and thereafter to enjoy the full rights of Alaska citizenship on the same terms as all other citizens of the state.

The Alaska trial court granted summary judgment in the Zobels' favor, holding that the plan violated the rights of interstate travel and equal protection. The Alaska Supreme Court reversed, upholding the statute. The Zobels appealed to the U.S. Supreme Court.

Burger, Chief Justice:

. . . Appellants established residence in Alaska two years before the dividend law was passed. The distinction they complain of is not one which the State makes between those who arrived in Alaska after the enactment of the dividend distribution law and those who were residents prior to its enactment. *Appellants instead challenge the distinctions made within the class of persons who were residents when the dividend scheme was enacted in 1980.* [Emphasis added.] The distinctions appellants attack include the preference given to persons who were residents when Alaska became a State in 1959 over all those who have arrived

[a] This statement of facts is taken from the opinion of the U.S. Supreme Court.

since then, as well as the distinctions made between all . . . residents who settled in Alaska at different times during the 1959 and 1980 period.

When a State distributes benefits unequally, the distinctions it makes are subject to scrutiny under the Equal Protection Clause of the Fourteenth Amendment. Generally, a law will survive that scrutiny if the distinction it makes rationally furthers a legitimate state purpose. Some particularly invidious distinctions are subject to [the] more rigorous [strict scrutiny test]. [The court here ruled that it need not decide whether the law should be tested under the strict scrutiny approach, as the appellants contended, for the reason that if the law "cannot pass even the minimal [rationality] test, we need not decide whether any enhanced scrutiny is called for."]

The State advanced and the Alaska Supreme Court accepted three purposes justifying the distinctions made by the dividend program: (a) creation of a financial incentive for individuals to establish and maintain residence in Alaska; (b) encouragement of prudent management of the Permanent Fund; and (c) apportionment of benefits in recognition of undefined "contributions of various kinds, both tangible and intangible, which residents have made during their years of residency."

As the Alaska Supreme Court apparently realized, the first two state objectives . . . are not rationally related to the distinctions Alaska seeks to make between newer residents and those who have been in the State since 1959. Assuming [for the sake of argument] that granting increased dividend benefits for each year of continued Alaska residence might give some residents an incentive to stay in the state in order to reap increased dividend benefits in the future, the State's interest is not in any way served by granting greater dividends to persons for their residency during the 21 years prior to the enactment.

Nor does the State's purpose of furthering the prudent management of the Permanent Fund and the state's resources support retrospective application of its plan to the date of statehood. On this score the state's contention is straightforward:

"As population increases, each individual share in the income stream is diluted. The income must be divided equally among increasingly large numbers of people. If residents believed that twenty years from now they would be required to share permanent fund income on a per capita basis with the large population that Alaska will no doubt have by then, the temptation would be great to urge the legislature to provide immediately for the highest possible return on the investment in riskier ventures."

The State similarly argues that equal per capita distribution would encourage rapacious development of natural resources. Even if we assume that the state interest is served by increasing the dividend for each year of residency beginning with the date of enactment, is it rationally served by granting greater dividends in varying amounts to those who resided in Alaska during the 21 years prior to enactment? We think not.

The last of the State's objectives—to reward citizens for past contributions—alone was relied upon by the Alaska Supreme Court to support the retrospective application of the law to 1959. However, that objective is not a legitimate state purpose. [The court here referred to an earlier case in which it had held that the "past contributions" argument would not sustain a classification that distinguished between new and old residents, the court saying there that acceptance of the past contributions argument "would permit the State to apportion all benefits and services according to the past tax or intangible contributions of its citizens. The Equal Protection Clause prohibits such an apportionment of state services." . . .][b]

If the States can make the amount of a cash dividend depend on length of residence, what would preclude varying university tuition on a sliding scale based on years of residence—or even limiting access to finite public facilities, eligibility for student loans, for civil service jobs, or for government contracts by length of domicile? Could States impose different taxes based on length of residence? Alaska's reasoning could open the door to state apportionment of other rights, benefits and services according to length of residency. It would permit the states to divide citizens into expanding numbers of permanent classes. Such a result would be clearly impossible. . . .

Accordingly, the judgment of the Alaska Supreme Court is reversed. . . .[c]

★★★

Questions and Problems

1. The Montana Fish and Game Commission adopted a regulation in 1976 that set the price of combination hunting licenses at $30 for residents and $225 for nonresidents. (A combination license permitted the taking of one elk, one deer, one black bear, and a specified number of game birds.) This regulation was challenged by nonresident hunters, who contended that it violated the privileges and immunities clause of the U.S. Constitution. The State of Montana contended, among other things, that the interest of Montana residents in the wildlife within its borders was a matter of state protection, and that this interest was substantial enough to justify the regulation. Do you think the U.S. Supreme Court agreed with this defense? Why or why not? (*Baldwin v. Fish and Game Commission of Montana*, 436 U.S. 371, 1978.)

2. The aviation commissioner for the City of Chicago adopted regulations which severely restricted the distribution of literature and solicitation of contributions at city airports. Among other things, the regulations (1) provided that persons who wished to do these things had to register with airport officials daily between 9 and 9:30 a.m.; (2) provided that distribution and solicitation could be carried on only in specified public areas of the airports; and (3) prohibited the solicitation by more than one person from each group at a time. These regulations were challenged by a religious group on the ground that they violated the free speech guarantee of the Constitution. Which, if any, of the above regulations do you feel did violate that clause? Explain. (*International Society for Krishna Consciousness, Inc. v. Rockford*, 585 F.2d 263, 1978.)

3. An Illinois criminal statute provided that violators would be subject to a fine and imprisonment for a specified period of time. It also provided that if a convicted per-

[b] "Such a power in the States could produce nothing but discord and mutual irritation, and they very clearly do not possess it." *The Passenger Cases*, 7 How. 283 (1849).

[c] Subsequent to this decision, Alaska enacted a law granting a flat $1000 to all men, women, and children who had lived in the state for six months.

son had no money to pay the fine, he was required to stay in prison for a longer time in order to "work off" the fine. Do you think that this statute might violate the equal protection clause? Explain. (*Williams v. Illinois*, 399 U.S. 235, 1970.)

4. A national bank in Ohio was charged with violating a federal criminal law that prohibited national banks from making loans to political candidates who were running for office in specified elections. At the trial, the bank contended that the federal law violated the equal protection clause of the Constitution in that it applied to national banks and not to a number of other lending institutions. What additional factors, if any, would you want to examine in order to determine whether the bank's contention is correct? How would these factors help you in determining whether the law's classification was a reasonable one? (*U.S. v. First National Bank*, 329 F.Supp. 1251, 1971.)

5. An Arizona Motor Vehicle Safety Responsibility law provided for the suspension of a driver's license when a judgment for personal injuries was entered against the driver, and where the judgment was not satisfied (paid). The law also provided that even if the driver went into bankruptcy, the discharge in bankruptcy did not relieve the driver from the license suspension. A driver challenged this statute under the Supremacy Clause of the federal Constitution, contending that the statute was contrary to certain provisions of the National Bankruptcy Act. (The Supremacy Clause provides, in effect, that state statutes that conflict with federal statutes are unconstitutional.) The State of Arizona argued that even if there were a conflict, it was justified for the reason that the purpose of the statute was "the protection of the public using the highways from financial hardship that may result from the use of automobiles by financially irresponsible persons," and that this purpose was clearly within the police power of the state. Does this argument save the statute? Why or why not? (*Perez v. Campbell*, 91 S.Ct. 1704, 1971.)

6. Today, the basic standards required by the due process clause of the Constitution are fairly clear, despite the fact that nowhere in the Constitution is this clause defined. What is the explanation for this relative clarity?

7. A motorist was convicted of two traffic offenses in a mayor's court, and the convictions were affirmed by the state's supreme court. He appealed this judgment to the U.S. Supreme Court. He contended that he had been denied a trial before "a disinterested and impartial judicial officer as guaranteed by the Due Process clause," in view of the fact that a major part of the village's income was derived from the fines, costs, and fees imposed by the mayor's court. Do you believe that the appellant's contention is valid? Explain. (*Ward v. Village of Monroeville*, 34 L.Ed.2d 265, 1972.)

8. By what reasoning has the U.S. Supreme Court come to the conclusion that at least some of the provisions in the first ten Amendments to the Constitution apply to the state governments as well as to the federal government?

C·H·A·P·T·E·R 6

ADMINISTRATIVE LAW AND PROCESS

In the preceding chapters we have examined the traditional concepts of law; the common law rules that have developed from custom or judicial decision; statutory law from legislative enactment; and the law that is created when the courts are called upon to interpret the statutes. In this chapter we take a look at what has become our most far-reaching and rapidly developing branch of the law, that which derives from the rules and regulations promulgated by the myriad administrative agencies created by the legislative branch at both federal and state levels, to perform functions that the executive and legislative branches are no longer able to carry out effectively. Administrative law is therefore the law of the administrative process. It governs the powers and procedures of administrative agencies and includes the law of judicial review of agency action by the courts. It consists of and includes the other branches of law discussed in earlier chapters plus agency made law.

Agencies (the term refers here to a governmental authority other than the legislative, executive, or judicial branches) may also be called boards, commissions, authorities, offices, and by other names. But, regardless of the label, the administrative arms of the government perform all the functions of the three constitutional branches. They make law by promulgating rules, regulations, and standards; they enforce that law by exercise of the powers conferred upon them by the legislative branch; and they interpret it by conducting hearings when their procedures call for and permit inquiry and judicial determination in specific cases. They routinely investigate, prosecute, and adjudicate.

Allocation of powers to the various agencies is by no means uniform. That is, each agency may be somewhat unique and possess whatever authority is necessary to perform the functions assigned to it by Congress. The Federal Trade Commission, for example, has considerable prosecutorial authority; the Occupational Safety and Health Administration is concerned with investigating; and the Social Security Administration primarily adjudicates the millions of claims for benefits of one kind or another.

Here we examine the role of the administrative agency in regulating the economy and bringing order to our social system by handling such administrative tasks as granting licenses, levying and collecting taxes, establishing rates to be charged by the transportation industry, determining a fair rate of return for the many public utilities firms, and distributing assistance to those in need in an equitable and socially acceptable manner. It is appropriate to examine administrative law as a logical forerunner to the ensuing sections that deal specifically with the elements that make up the legal environment of business because the impact of administrative agencies upon business, big and small, is far greater than the effect felt by the workings of the judicial system. The percentage of businesses and individuals who find themselves directly involved with the judicial system is extremely small. Yet all of us, either as businesspersons or as individuals, find ourselves increasingly regulated by hundreds of administrative agencies at both the federal and state levels. We therefore have a vital need to know how the system came about, how it functions, and whether or not it has legitimacy.

Small businesses can be overwhelmed by government regulation.
Source: Reprinted by permission: Tribune Media Services.

In the chapters that follow we look at some of the more powerful agencies and examine a few of the areas in which they exercise their power, areas which, for the most part, make up the legal environment in which business must operate. Here, however, we focus on the administrative process with emphasis on the more important functions performed by agencies. These functions, as noted earlier, include rulemaking and adjudicating, both subject to judicial review—an important concept also discussed because of the role it plays as a safeguard against arbitrary official action. We explore the avenues of relief available to those who may be wronged by arbitrary or capricious administrative action or who may seek redress for injury inflicted by the government through its administrators. We begin with a brief discussion of the legitimacy of the administrative agency—its authority to make law that touches our everyday personal and business endeavors.

The Need Emerges

As America grew and prospered and the industrial revolution effected the change from a primarily agrarian to an industrial society, it became evident in the late nineteenth century that the **laissez-faire** attitude of government would have to be abandoned. Some degree of regulation became necessary and desirable as the early giants of industry began to use their strength in ways not felt to be in the best interest of free and open trade and commerce. Consequently, in 1887 and 1890 the Interstate Commerce Act and the Sherman Act, respectively, were passed to curb certain monopolistic practices that were considered to be detrimental to interstate commerce. When those laws and their enforcement fell short of accomplishing what Congress had intended, there followed in 1914 the Clayton and Federal Trade Commission Acts.

A comprehensive scheme of government regulation was thus instituted and has grown and become more complex with each passing year. Agencies were created as problems were seen to exist and as it became evident that solution or control of the problems were to be found in appropriate regulatory legislation. The agency or arm of the government was legislated into existence to administer the law. The tremendous growth of radio brought forth the Federal Communications Commission (FCC); aviation gave us the Federal Aviation Authority (FAA) and the Civil Aeronautics Board (CAB); the stock market crash of 1929 resulted in the Securities and Exchange Commission (SEC); and our concern for the environment and a search for ways to prevent continued pollution gave rise to the National Environmental Policy Act and its administrative arm, the Environmental Protection Agency (EPA).

As technology in manufacturing and marketing and in nearly every facet of American life became more advanced, a greater degree of skill and expertise in a greater number of areas was needed to control and regulate what had become a highly complex industrial and commercial society. Complete and efficient administration by the legislative and executive branches was no longer possible. The country, its government, and its problems had outgrown the capability of the legislature and executive to regulate. Consequently, administrative agencies came into existence as instruments of regulation and, considered collectively, are often referred to as the "fourth branch of the Government."

Legislative Delegation of Lawmaking Power

While the creation of an administrative agency may provide the solution to an apparent problem it may also cause problems for those whose conduct it is designed to regulate. Consequently, the actions of various agencies and administrators in the early stages of administrative history have been called into question. The most logical basis for challenge was found to be the separation of powers doctrine of the Constitution. That document provides in Article I, Section 1 that "All legislative Powers herein granted shall be vested in a Congress of the United States, which shall consist of a Senate and House of Representatives." And Section 8 of Article I provides that the Congress shall have power to make all laws which shall be necessary and proper. It does not provide that Congress may delegate its lawmaking power to an administrative body it has created to deal with a specifically defined problem. Therefore, rules and regulations promulgated by agencies, having the force and effect of law, were early challenged as resulting from an unconstitutional delegation of legislative power. However, in only two Supreme Court cases have the challengers been successful.

These cases, *Panama Refining Co. v. Ryan*, 293 U.S. 388 (1935) and *A.L.A. Schechter Poultry Corp. v. United States*, 295 U.S. 495 (1935), both involved delegation by Congress to the President of powers to regulate certain aspects of commerce and industry. In each case the court was of the opinion that, while delegation was often necessary if the government was to function efficiently, such delegation must at the same time provide discernible standards and guidelines so that the power delegated can be properly channeled along the lines Congress had in mind. In the *Panama* case the Court spoke of delegation running riot, and in *Schechter* Justice Cardozo, in a concurring opinion, referred to the delegated power as not being canalized "within banks that keep it from overflowing. It is unconfined and vagrant. . . . This is delegation running riot. No such plenitude of power is susceptible of transfer."

Since 1935, however, delegations by Congress have consistently been given the approval of the courts. The legislative branch has become more adept at providing standards and guidelines, and perhaps more importantly, the delegating legislation has increasingly provided procedural safeguards to limit and direct the discretionary power to be exercised by the administrator. The ultimate safeguard, on which we will have more to say, is the role of the courts in curbing administrative arbitrariness through strict judicial scrutiny, the availability of judicial review of administrative action. The following case, decided by the Supreme Court of Pennsylvania but embodying principles applicable at all levels of government, is a good example of the resolution of a challenge to the constitutionality of delegation.

Tosto v. Pennsylvania Nursing Home Loan Agency
Supreme Court of Pennsylvania
331 A.2d 198
(1975)

Concerned with the inability of many nursing homes to provide safe and healthy accommodations for their residents, the State of Pennsylvania in 1974 enacted a Nursing Home Loan Agency Law, 62 P.S. 1521.101 *et seq.* A section of the law created the Pennsylvania Nursing Home Loan Agency authorized "to make loans to nursing homes for repair, reconstruction and rehabilitation . . . in order that such nursing homes may meet State and Federal Safety Standards. . . ." Plaintiff Tosto filed a taxpayer's suit seeking to enjoin the operation of the law, alleging a variety of constitutional defects among which was that the delegation of power by the Pennsylvania legislature to the Nursing Home Loan Agency lacked standards and guidelines, thus leaving too much to the discretion of that agency. The Supreme Court of Pennsylvania assumed plenary jurisdiction after the parties had filed motions for judgment on the pleadings.

Roberts, Justice:

. . . This is a taxpayer's suit seeking to enjoin the operation of the recently enacted Nursing Home Loan Agency Law. . . . Plaintiff filed his complaint in the Commonwealth Court alleging a variety of constitutional defects. Defendants petitioned this Court to assume jurisdiction, which we did by per curiam order on October 25, 1974. The parties, after stipulating that no issues of fact existed to be tried, have filed motions for judgment on the pleadings. We determine that judgment should be awarded to defendants.

The N.H.L.A.L. stems from legislative concern with the inability of many nursing homes to provide safe and healthy accommodations for their residents. Pursuant to article VIII, section 7(a) (3) of the Constitution, P.S., the Legislature submitted to the voters the question whether they "favor the incurring of indebtedness by the Commonwealth of $100,000,000 for use as loans to repair, reconstruct and rehabilitate nursing homes in order to meet standards for health and safety?" The program was approved by referendum on May 21, 1974.

Section 201 of the Law creates the Pennsylvania Nursing Home Loan Agency composed of six ex officio members from the executive departments and three gubernatorial appointees. . . . Section 301 provides:

All nursing homes meeting applicable State and Federal regulations, with the exception of Life Safety Code, for the acceptance of Medicaid patients shall be eligible to apply for loans from the Nursing Home Loan Agency under provisions of this act.

Funds for the loans are to be provided by a sale by competitive bidding of general obligation bonds (not exceeding $100,000,000) backed by the credit of the Commonwealth. . . . The Law creates a sinking fund for payment of interest and principal. . . . The sources of the sinking fund are funds received in repayment of loans to nursing homes and appropriations by the Legislature. . . .

Plaintiff next contends that the N.H.L.A.L. involves an unconstitutional delegation of legislative power in violation of article II, section 1 of the Constitution. He invokes the so-called nondelegation rule which, as a "natural corollary" of article II, section 1, "requires that the basic policy choices involved in 'legislative power' actually be made by the Legislature as constitutionally mandated." More specifically, the rule demands that, when the Legislature delegates policy-making discretion to administrative agencies, it must make the "basic policy choices" which will serve as standards to guide and restrain the exercise of discretion. . . .

Plaintiff argues that the Legislature did not provide standards in the N.H.L.A.L. He points to various sections of the Law which grant the agency policymaking discretion without, he contends, adequate standards. In this he is mistaken. The entire Law reveals that the agency's policy decisions must be directed to the effectuation of the Legislature's basic policy of assisting nursing homes that do not comply with the Life Safety Code and are unable to achieve compliance through private sources of financing, which assistance is to be given with prudence for protection of the loan fund. This pervasive general policy is clearly sufficient to satisfy the constitutional requirement that "basic policy choices" be made by the Legislature. But the Law goes even further. It provides very specific definitions of pivotal statutory terms and detailed guidelines for certain important agency decisions. We have no doubt that the standards requirement has been satisfied.

More importantly, the N.H.L.A.L. provides numerous procedural guidelines for protection against administrative arbitrariness and caprice. For example, the agency is required to establish criteria for use in determination of priority among applicants and eligibility for loan refinancing and to develop a standard form for loan applications. The use of neutral, generally applicable criteria and forms is an important safeguard against the arbitrariness of ad hoc decision making. In addition, section 203 (2) of the Law provides that the promulgation of rules and regulations by the agency must be in accordance with the Commonwealth Documents law, assuring regularity and due notice in administrative policymaking.

The Legislature has provided adequate standards and guidelines for the guidance and restraint of administrative discretion. We reject plaintiff's contention as meritless. . . .

We have examined the N.H.L.A.L. and the constitutional defects which plaintiff perceives. We conclude that they are meritless. Judgment on the pleadings is therefore entered for defendants.

★★★

Lawmaking by Administrative Agencies

The authority of an agency to make law is typically determined by the statute that created the agency. For example, the Occupational Safety and Health Act of 1970 (OSHA) provides that the Secretary of Labor is authorized to " . . . set mandatory occupational safety and health standards applicable to businesses affecting interstate commerce. . . ." And, with regard to inspections, investigations and recordkeeping, the Secretary shall " . . . prescribe such rules and regulations as he may deem necessary to carry out (their) responsibilities under this Act, including rules and regulations dealing with the inspection of an employer's establishment."[1] As can be seen, this is a broad delegation of power to the Secretary of Labor, appearing to leave to his or her discretion the adoption of standards, rules, and regulations that will have tremendous effect on an employer covered by OSHA: the sanction for willful or repeated violations is a civil penalty of up to $10,000 for each violation; if convicted of a willful violation that results in the death of an employee the employer can be fined not more than $10,000 or imprisoned up to six months or both; and for a second such offense the penalties are doubled. Thus, the standards, rules, and regulations promulgated by the administrator have the force and effect of law, for Congress has so provided in the enabling act, OSHA in this instance.

But, as is increasingly the case, while Congress confers broad powers on the agency it also specifies the procedures to be used by the agency in developing its laws. Under OSHA, when the Secretary of Labor determines that a rule should be promulgated he or she may appoint an advisory committee of not more than fifteen members to assist in developing the proposed rule. The makeup of the committee in each case is such that interested and affected employers and employees may express their viewpoints and insures that there are members who are knowledgeable in the area being considered. This committee makes its recommendations to the Secretary within ninety days of its appointment.

If an advisory committee has been used the proposed and recommended rule is then published in the *Federal Register* and interested persons are given the opportunity to submit written data or comments on the proposed rule. An interested person may also object to the proposed rule and request a public hearing on the objections; the Secretary would then publish in the *Federal Register* a notice of the rule being objected to and specify a time and place for the hearing. The proposed rule or standard is thereby subject to more careful scrutiny than with the mere submission of written data and comments. In either case, the final rule, the effect of which is to promulgate, modify, or revoke a safety or health standard, is issued. Its effective date is usually delayed a period sufficient to permit affected employers and employees to familiarize themselves with its terms, and to facilitate compliance.

The Administrative Procedure Act

The rulemaking procedures of OSHA were prescribed by the statute. However, they illustrate the two basic models for rulemaking contained in the Administrative Procedure Act of 1946 (APA). The submission of written

[1] OSHA is referred to and discussed in this chapter as a representative administrative agency. A more comprehensive discussion of its functions as an arm of the Labor Department is found in Chapter 14.

data and comments by interested persons is the informal, or notice-and-comment, model. The public hearing method, often required and used even though no objection to a proposed rule has been made, is the formal, or on-the-record, model. Section 553 of the APA provides for general notice of proposed rulemaking to be published in the *Federal Register*, with interested persons being given an opportunity to participate by submitting written data, views, or arguments with or without opportunity for oral presentation—the informal method.

However, when rules are required by statute to be made on the record after opportunity for an agency hearing, Sections 556 and 557 apply and the formal model is used. This is, in effect, a trial type of hearing or adjudication, with interested persons given the opportunity to appear personally to testify and to cross-examine the agency's witnesses. A formal record is kept of the proceedings, and all decisions become a part of the record. The findings and conclusions of the agency must be stated and the resulting rule or regulation must be substantiated by evidence spread on the record. The hearing procedure is similar to that used in a non-jury, federal civil trial.

The Administrative Procedure Act had its origins in the thirties, the New Deal era of President Roosevelt's administration. During that period new and powerful agencies were created to handle the programs designed to promote economic recovery. Those who were already concerned about the size of the bureaucracy became even more so and were increasingly vocal in expressing their alarm. Consequently, in 1939 a committee was appointed by the attorney general to investigate the need for procedural reform in the field of administrative law. Based on this committee's very detailed report, Congress in 1946 enacted the APA, which has done much for uniformity of administrative procedures, insures participation in the process by those most affected, and emphasizes the role of the courts as an integral part of the administrative process by providing for judicial review of administrative action.[2]

At the state level, the National Conference of Commissioners on Uniform State Laws has drafted a Model State Administrative Procedure Act that has been adopted in its entirety by twenty-seven states and in part by several others. The model act follows the basic structure and format of the Federal APA but is considerably shorter and not nearly as comprehensive in prescribing coverage and procedures for hearings.

[2] With regard to the courts' supervisory function in reviewing agency actions, Judge Harold Leventhal said: "The process thus combines judicial supervision with a salutary principle of judicial restraint, an awareness that agencies and courts together constitute a 'partnership' in furtherance of the public interest, and are 'collaborative instrumentalities of justice.' The court is in a real sense part of the total administrative process, and not a hostile stranger to the office of first instance." (*Greater Boston Television Corp. v. FCC*, 444 F.2d 841, D.C.Cir.1970.)

Agency Adjudication—The Right to Be Heard

Agency action often results in controversy. We have seen that the rules made by agencies quite frequently involve what may amount to adversary proceedings. The agency-creating statutes often anticipate such problems and provide for public hearings on proposed rules. And the Administrative Procedure Act, Sections 556 and 557, specifies on-the-record, trial-type hearings when the formal model of rulemaking is used by an agency. Our primary concern here, however, is with the *application* of agency-made law. What procedural safeguards are available when an individual or a business wishes to challenge the application of a rule or regulation to his or her particular situation or set of circumstances? Suppose, for example, that an employer has been cited by an OSHA inspector for violation of a safety or health standard. If the employer in good faith believes that the citation is improper and knows that corrective action would involve considerable expense, can he or she contest the citation? Is there a forum where the employer can present a genuine difference of opinion—in other words, is there a right to be heard before an impartial decision maker? Or, in another case, may an applicant for a license, having been denied, appear personally before the licensing authority and argue his or her right to the license? May the unsuccessful applicant call witnesses, cross-examine opposing (the agency's) witnesses, and be assured of a decision based on the evidence that has been presented and made a part of the record? Answers to these questions of course depend upon the workings of constitutional due process and its applicability to administrative procedures. The Fifth Amendment to the Constitution prohibits the taking of life, liberty, or property, without due process of law. It is on this ground that many decisions of public administrators have been challenged. The claim is asserted that the agency has, by its action, deprived the claimant of some property right without first affording a trial-type hearing with all the elements of procedural due process.

Procedural Due Process

A leading case is *Goldberg v. Kelly*, 397 U.S. 254 (1970), in which the welfare benefits of certain New York recipients were terminated without an opportunity for an evidentiary hearing. In affirming a District Court decision for the welfare recipients, Justice Brennan stated: "It is true, of course, that some governmental benefits may be administratively terminated without affording the recipient a pre-termination evidentiary hearing. But we agree with the District Court that when welfare is discontinued, only a pre-termination evidentiary hearing provides the recipient with procedural due process."

While the court did not determine whether entitlement to welfare benefits was a right or merely a privilege, it did note that such benefits are a matter of statutory entitlement for persons qualified to receive them. Six years later, in a case similar to *Goldberg v. Kelly*, the court seemed to put to rest the "right

v. privilege" approach. The case should be viewed as providing some insight into the administrative workings of one of the largest and busiest agencies, the Social Security Administration.

Mathews v. Eldridge
U.S. Supreme Court, 424 U.S. 319 (1976)

Respondent Eldridge was awarded Social Security disability benefits in 1968. In March, 1972, he received a questionnaire from the state agency charged with monitoring his medical condition to determine if he remained eligible for disability payments. Eldridge completed the form indicating that there had been no improvement in his condition. The state agency then obtained reports from his physician and a psychiatric consultant and determined that Eldridge's disability no longer existed. Upon being advised of this decision and that he had the right to request reconsideration within six months, Eldridge filed a district court suit seeking immediate reinstatement of his benefits, claiming that he had been deprived of due process since no pretermination hearing had been held. That is, the decision to terminate his benefits had been based solely upon his response to a questionnaire and other information obtained by the agency *ex parte*—by one side only. The district court held that the administrative procedures by which the secretary had terminated Eldridge's benefits abridged his right to procedural due process and the Court of Appeals for the Fourth Circuit affirmed. Both courts held that Eldridge should have received an evidentiary hearing prior to termination of his benefits. The state agency appealed to the U.S. Supreme Court.

Powell, Justice:

. . . The issue in this case is whether the Due Process Clause of the Fifth Amendment requires that prior to the termination of Social Security disability benefit payments the recipient be afforded an opportunity for an evidentiary hearing. . . .

Procedural due process imposes constraints on governmental decisions which deprive individuals of "liberty" or "property" interests within the meaning of the Due Process Clause of the Fifth or Fourteenth Amendment. The Secretary does not contend that procedural due process is inapplicable to terminations of Social Security disability benefits. He recognizes, as has been implicit in our prior decisions . . . that the interest of an individual in continued receipt of these benefits is a statutorily created "property" interest protected by the Fifth Amendment. . . . Rather, the Secretary contends that the existing administrative procedures, detailed below, provide all the process that is constitutionally due before a recipient can be deprived of that interest.

This Court consistently has held that some form of hearing is required before an individual is finally deprived of a property interest. . . . Eldridge agrees that the review procedures available to a claimant before the initial determination of ineligibility becomes final would be adequate if disability benefits were not terminated until after the evidentiary hearing stage of the administrative process.

The dispute centers upon what process is due prior to the initial termination of benefits, pending review.

In recent years this court increasingly has had occasion to consider the extent to which due process requires an evidentiary hearing prior to the deprivation of some type of property interest even if such a hearing is provided thereafter. In only one case, *Goldberg v. Kelly,* 397 U.S., at 266–271, has the Court held that a hearing closely approximating a judicial trial is necessary. In other cases requiring some type of pretermination hearing as a matter of constitutional right the Court has spoken sparingly about the requisite procedures. . . .

Accordingly, resolution of the issue whether the administrative procedures provided here are constitutionally sufficient requires analysis of the governmental and private interests that are affected. . . . More precisely, our prior decisions indicate that identification of the specific dictates of due process generally requires consideration of three distinct factors: First, the private interest that will be affected by the official action; second, the risk of an erroneous deprivation of such interest through the procedures used, and the probable value, if any, of additional or substitute procedural safeguards; and finally, the Government's interest, including the function involved and the fiscal and administrative burdens that the additional or substitute procedural requirement would entail. . . .

The continuing-eligibility investigation is made by a state agency acting through a "team" consisting of a physician and a nonmedical person trained in disability evaluation. The agency periodically communicates with the disabled worker, usually by mail—in which case he is sent a detailed questionnaire—or by telephone, and requests information concerning his present condition, including current medical restrictions and sources of treatment, and any additional information that he considers relevant to his continued entitlement to benefits. . . .

Whenever the agency's tentative assessment of the beneficiary's condition differs from his own assessment, the beneficiary is informed that benefits may be terminated, provided a summary of the evidence upon which the proposed determination to terminate is based, and afforded an opportunity to review the medical reports and other evidence in his case file. He also may respond in writing and submit additional evidence. . . .

The state agency then makes its final determination, which is reviewed by an examiner in the SSA Bureau of Disability Insurance. . . . If, as is usually the case, the SSA accepts the agency determination it notifies the recipient in writing, informing him of the reasons for the decision, and of his right to seek *de novo* reconsideration by the state agency. . . . Upon acceptance by the SSA, benefits are terminated effective two months after the month in which medical recovery is found to have occurred. . . .

If the recipient seeks reconsideration by the state agency and the determination is adverse, the SSA reviews the reconsideration determination and notifies the recipient of the decision. He then has a right to an evidentiary hearing before an SSA administrative law judge. . . . The hearing is nonadversary, and the SSA is not represented by counsel. As at all prior and subsequent stages of the administrative process, however, the claimant may be represented by counsel or other spokesmen. . . . If this hearing results in an adverse decision, the claimant is entitled to request discretionary review by the SSA Appeals Council. . . . and finally may obtain judicial review. . . .

Despite the elaborate character of the administrative procedures provided by the Secretary, the courts below held them to be constitutionally inadequate, concluding that due process requires an evidentiary hearing prior to termination. In light of the private and governmental interests at stake here and the nature of the existing procedures, we think this was error.

Since a recipient whose benefits are terminated is awarded full retroactive relief if he ultimately prevails, his sole interest is in the uninterrupted receipt of this source of income pending final administrative decision on his claim. His potential injury is thus similar in nature to that of the welfare recipient in *Goldberg*. . . .

Only in *Goldberg* has the Court held that due process requires an evidentiary hearing prior to a temporary deprivation. It was emphasized there that welfare assistance is given to persons on the very margin of subsistence:

> *The crucial factor in this context—a factor not present in the case of . . . virtually anyone else whose government entitlements are ended—is that termination of aid pending resolution of a controversy over eligibility may deprive an* eligible *recipient of the very means by which to live while he waits.*

Eligibility for disability benefits, in contrast, is not based upon financial need. Indeed, it is wholly unrelated to the worker's income or support from many other sources, such as earnings of other family members, workmen's compensation awards, tort claims awards, savings, private insurance, public or private pensions, veterans' benefits, food stamps, public assistance, or the "many other important programs, both public and private, which contain provisions for disability payments affecting a substantial portion of the work force. . . ."

An additional factor to be considered here is the fairness and reliability of the existing pretermination procedures, and the probable value, if any, of additional procedural safeguards. Central to the evaluation of any administrative process is the nature of the relevant inquiry. . . . In short, a medical assessment of the worker's physical or mental condition is required. This is a more sharply focused and easily documented decision than the typical determination of welfare entitlement. In the latter case, a wide variety of information may be deemed relevant, and issues of witness credibility and veracity often are critical to the decision-making process. *Goldberg* noted that in such circumstances "written submissions are a wholly unsatisfactory basis for decision."

By contrast, the decision whether to discontinue disability benefits will turn, in most cases upon "routine, standard, and unbiased medical reports by physician specialists". . . concerning a subject whom they have personally examined. In *Richardson* the Court recognized the "reliability and probative worth of written medical conclusions" when the "specter of questionable credibility and veracity is not present.". . . To be sure, credibility and veracity may be a factor in the ultimate disability assessment in some cases. But procedural due process rules are shaped by the risk of error inherent in the truthfinding process as applied to the generality of cases, not the rare exceptions. The potential value of an evidentiary hearing, or even oral presentation to the decisionmaker, is substantially less in this context than in *Goldberg*. . . .

In striking the appropriate due process balance the final factor to be assessed is the public interest. This includes the administrative burden and other societal costs that would be associated with requiring, as a matter of constitutional right, an evidentiary hearing upon demand in all cases prior to the termination of disability benefits. The most visible burden would be the incremental cost resulting from the increased number of hearings and the expense of providing benefits to ineligible recipients pending decision. . . . The parties submit widely varying estimates of the probable additional financial cost. We only need say that experience with the constitutionalizing of government procedures suggests that the ultimate additional cost in terms of money and administrative burden would not be insubstantial. . . .

But more is implicated in cases of this type than ad hoc weighing of fiscal and administrative burdens against the interests of a particular category of claimants. The ultimate balance involves a determination as to when, under our constitutional system, judicial-type procedures must be imposed upon administrative action to assure fairness. . . . The judicial model of an evidentiary hearing is neither a required, nor even the most effective, method of decisionmaking in all circumstances. The essense of due process is the requirement that "a person in jeopardy of serious loss (be given) notice of the case against him and opportunity to meet it." *Joint Anti-Fascist Comm. v. McGrath*, 341 U.S., at 171–172. . . . In assessing what process is due in this case, substantial weight must be given to the good-faith judgments of the individuals charged by Congress with the administration of social welfare programs that the procedures they have provided assure fair consideration of the entitlement claims of individuals. . . . This is especially so where, as here, the prescribed procedures not only provide the claimant with an effective process for asserting his claim prior to any administrative action, but also assure a right to an evidentiary hearing, as well as to subsequent judicial review, before the denial of his claim becomes final. . . .

We conclude that an evidentiary hearing is not required prior to the termination of disability benefits and that the present administrative procedures fully comport with due process.

The judgment of the Court of Appeals is reversed.

★★★

Statutory Hearings

The opportunity to be heard or to contest the decision of an administrator is increasingly provided for by the statute governing the agency or by the agency's procedures for enforcing the statute. Under OSHA, an employer who has been cited for a violation and notified of a penalty has fifteen days within which to notify the Secretary of Labor that he wishes to contest the citation or the proposed penalty. The Occupational Safety and Health Act establishes an Occupational Safety and Health Review Commission. It is to this commission that notices of contest are directed for the scheduling (docketing) of the statutory hearing. The commission is an independent federal agency. It is not connected in any way with the Department of Labor or OSHA. There are three commission members who are appointed by the president for six-year terms. Hearings are conducted, or presided over, by forty-three administrative law judges who have career tenure.[3] The judges' decisions are reviewed by the commission members who have the authority to change those decisions. The review commission has comprehensive rules of procedure that, as is the case with other rules and regulations of agencies, are published in the Code of Federal Regulations. The purpose of the procedures is to insure that evidentiary, due process, trial-type hearings are conducted when called for.

The federal Administrative Procedure Act does not require a trial-type hearing in any case except for the removal of an administrative law judge. It does, however, as was earlier noted, call for formal rulemaking and formal adjudication when another statute provides for action to be determined on the record after opportunity for hearing. Consequently, whether or not a party is entitled to a trial-type hearing is primarily a question of the nature of the right or interest that has been affected by the administrative agency's action. There is, of course, no list of sets of circumstances that demand procedural due process hearings. However, numerous decisions by the courts have established trends and principles. A high school student may have a right to a public education and should not be expelled or suspended for disciplinary reasons without a hearing, *Goss v. Lopez*, 419 U.S. 565 (1975). But a medical school student can be dismissed without a formal hearing for academic reasons when her progress had been subjected to repeated review by authorities, *Board of Curators of the University of Missouri v. Horowitz*, 435 U.S. 78 (1978). In the absence of a statutory right to a hearing, each case will be decided on its own facts with particular attention given to the nature of the right or interest that would be affected.

Judicial Review

Perhaps the greatest single safeguard against improper administrative action, involving both rulemaking and adjudication, is the availability of judicial review. Judicial review is often provided for by the statute that created the agency. Further, the Administration Procedure Act provides that: "A person suffering legal wrong because of agency action, or adversely affected

[3] There are 1,114 administrative law judges assigned to federal agencies to conduct hearings. Of that number, in addition to the 43 assigned to OSHRC, 700 are assigned to the Social Security Administration; 118 to the National Labor Relations Board; and 80 are assigned to the Department of Labor.

or aggrieved by agency action within the meaning of a relevant statute, is entitled to judicial review thereof." With regard to the scope of judicial review, Section 706 provides, in part:

To the extent necessary to decision and when presented, the reviewing court shall decide all relevant questions of law, interpret constitutional and statutory provisions, and determine the meaning or applicability of the terms of an agency action. The reviewing court shall—

(1) compel agency action unlawfully withheld or unreasonably delayed; and

(2) hold unlawful and set aside agency action, findings, and conclusions found to be—

(A) arbitrary, capricious, an abuse of discretion, or otherwise not in accordance with law . . .

A specific enabling statute, the Occupational Safety and Health Act, provides that: "Any person adversely affected or aggrieved by an order of the Commission issued . . . may obtain a review of such order in any United States court of appeals for the circuit in which the violation is alleged to have occurred or where the employer has its principal office, or in the Court of Appeals for the District of Columbia Circuit, by filing in such court within sixty days following the issuance of such order a written petition praying that the order be modified or set aside. . . ."

While judicial review is by no means an automatic procedure, and in fact may be precluded by the statute in a particular case, the courts consider it an important doctrine. In a 1971 case, *Environmental Defense Fund, Inc. v. Ruckelshaus*, 439 F.2d 584, Chief Judge Bazelon stated:

To protect these interests from administrative arbitrariness, it is necessary, but not sufficient, to insist on strict judicial scrutiny of administrative action. For judicial review alone can correct only the most egregious abuses. Judicial review must operate to ensure that the administrative process itself will confine and control the exercise of discretion. Courts should require administrative officers to articulate the standards and principles that govern their discretionary decisions in as much detail as possible. Rules and regulations should be freely formulated by administrators, and revised when necessary. Discretionary decisions should more often be supported with findings of fact and reasoned opinions. When administrators provide a framework for principled decision-making, the result will be to diminish the importance of judicial review by enhancing the integrity of the administrative process, and to improve the quality of judicial review in those cases where judicial review is sought.

However, in reviewing administrative action the courts will generally accept the facts as determined by the agency and are reluctant to substitute their judgment for that of the agency experts. And the U.S. Supreme Court has recently reaffirmed its position that administrative agency decisions not to take enforcement actions are not ordinarily reviewable in the federal courts.

Death-row inmates in Texas and Oklahoma had claimed that the Food and Drug Administration had acted illegally in refusing to investigate the safety and effectiveness of drugs used in lethal injections. A D.C. Circuit panel agreed with the inmates but the high court reversed stating that agency decisions not to bring enforcement actions are like prosecutors' decisions not to bring criminal cases. Such agency decisions, said the court, are "presumptively unreviewable." *Heckler v. Chaney*, 105 S.Ct. 1649 (1985).

Certain statutes confer on the administrator complete discretion to act and, in effect, preclude judicial review. For example, in the area of veterans' affairs, the applicable statute, 38 U.S.C.A. Section 211 (a), provides:

> *On and after October 17, 1940 . . . the decisions of the Administrator (of Veterans' Affairs) on any question of law or fact under any law administered by the Veterans' Administration providing benefits for veterans and their dependents or survivors shall be* final and conclusive and no other official or any court of the United States shall have power or jurisdiction to review *any such decision by an action in the nature of mandamus or otherwise.* [Emphasis added.]

Under OSHA, a cutoff of judicial review is provided for. If, after being cited for a violation, the employer fails to file a notice of contest within the prescribed fifteen days, the citation and any assessment of penalty becomes a final order and not subject to review by any court or agency.

A petitioner seeking judicial review must prove to the court's satisfaction:

1. That he or she has completely exhausted the administrative remedies. That is, the administrative procedures must have been given a chance to work. If this requirement has been met there is an official record for the courts to review.

2. That he or she has standing to sue. The petitioner must prove that the administrative action complained of, if left to stand, will cause *injury in fact*. Cases prior to 1970 considered injury to involve a monetary loss. However, recent cases grant standing on the basis of noneconomic loss and a substantial probability that the petitioning party will be adversely affected by governmental action.

3. That the matter is ripe for review. In the administrative process this generally means that a final order has been issued by the agency, an order the courts can review.

Despite what may seem to be formidable hurdles, a determined petitioner, with the help of resourceful and diligent counsel, can usually have a day in court.

Relief against Improper Official Action

The hundreds of government agencies, with millions of employees, in administering their particular sectors and discharging their responsibilities must make important decisions that affect the individual and business alike. Not infrequently a decision may be wrong; it may cause harm or damage to those individuals or businesses against whom the decision operates. Or, as has often been the case, a government employee may act negligently or intentionally and cause physical harm. When these incidents occur to what extent is the government liable? Can it be sued as would be a private party who commits the same kind of act? Can the government employee be sued as though he or she were a private individual? The answers to these questions are not clear, but considerable law on the subject has evolved in recent years.

Sovereign Immunity

The doctrine of sovereign immunity, simply stated, prevents suits against the government unless the government consents to such suits. Therefore, if the government, as a defendant, invokes the doctrine the plaintiff is effectively left without a remedy. The origins of the doctrine in this country are not clear, but it was obviously brought over from England, where the sovereign could do no wrong. As a practical matter, effective and decisive government would be seriously hampered if the government could be sued at will. Or, as Justice Holmes stated in *Kawanakakoa v. Polyblank*, 205 U.S. 349 (1907), " . . .there can be no legal right as against the authority that makes the law on which the right depends."

The doctrine is for the most part judge-made and has stood as a formidable barrier to those seeking redress for wrongs committed by the government or its agents. And, in general, the doctrine is equally applicable at the state and municipal levels of government. Suppose, for example, that a county school bus is driven negligently and is involved in an accident causing considerable personal injury and property damage to plaintiff. The driver of the school bus is of course personally liable for his or her tortious act. But, in all probability, the driver is judgment proof, that is, a wage earner with insufficient assets to pay a substantial money judgment. Under basic rules of agency, the driver's employer, the county, can be held liable for the torts of its employees. However, the county may invoke sovereign immunity and refuse to be sued, thus leaving plaintiff to suffer a loss caused by another.

The Federal Tort Claims Act

The doctrine of sovereign immunity is being eroded or limited at all levels. The Federal Tort Claims Act of 1946[4] is a broad statutory waiver of governmental immunity to lawsuits. Under the act the United States "shall be liable, respecting the provisions of this title relating to tort claims, in the same manner and to the same extent as a private individual under like cir-

[4]Substantive provisions at 28 U.S.C.A. Sections 2671–2680.

cumstances." The government by this act assumes liability for the tortious conduct of its employees. The act does, however, contain several exceptions, specific circumstances in which the government will not be liable. There is no liability if the tort claim is based upon the exercise or performance or the failure to exercise or perform a discretionary function or duty on the part of the agency or federal employee. And there is no liability even though the discretion may have been abused. Discretionary functions by an official are those that require the exercise of judgment or discretion as opposed to the so-called ministerial functions, routine duties prescribed by law.

Neither is the government liable if the tort action is based on certain intentional torts such as assault, battery, libel, slander, and others. Consequently, should an OSHA inspector commit an assault and battery upon a shop owner who wanted to deny entry to inspect, the government would not be liable. However, following a particularly serious incident involving forced entry and unauthorized search at the wrong address by federal narcotics agents, Congress in 1974 amended the act to permit the government to be sued for assault, battery, false imprisonment, false arrest, abuse of process, or malicious prosecution by a federal investigative or law enforcement officer.

State Liability for Torts

At the state level, sovereign immunity has been waived to some extent by statute for specific areas or functions of government and, in some states, completely by court decision. In California, for example, in *Muskopf v. Corning Hospital District*, 359 P.2d 457 (1961), Justice Traynor said:

Thus, in holding that the doctrine of governmental immunity for torts for which its agents are liable has no place in our law we make no startling break with the past but merely take the final step that carries to its conclusion an established legislative and judicial trend.

In Michigan, *Williams v. Detroit*, 111 N.W.2d 1 (1961), the court held that: "From this date forward the judicial doctrine of governmental immunity from ordinary torts no longer exists in Michigan." And, more recently, the South Carolina Supreme Court, in a 3–2 decision, held that: "Sovereign immunity can no longer be tolerated in this state. . . . A doctrine which issues from the maxim, 'the king can do no wrong,' is antagonistic to American democracy and, now that whatever may have justified its adoption has passed, should be abolished." *McCall by Andrews v. Batson*, 329 S.E.2d 741 (S.C. 1985).

An example of legislative abolishment of sovereign immunity is found in a Washington statute that provides:

The State of Washington, whether acting in its governmental or proprietary capacity, shall be liable for damages arising out of its tortious conduct to the same extent as if it were a private person or corporation.

While well over half the states have abolished sovereign immunity, at least in part, several continue to hold the line making it difficult for a plaintiff to obtain a money judgment against the state or its subdivisions. But, as Justice Traynor indicated, the trend is toward the waiver of sovereign immunity by either legislative or judicial action.

Liability of Government Officials

There may be no problem in connection with recovering damages from a government official if, in the conduct of his or her private affairs, he or she is careless and causes damage to a plaintiff. The public official should, and would, be liable just as any other private citizen. However, a problem for plaintiff is created when the tortious act arises out of the official's performance of governmental duties. The question is then whether or not the official may claim official immunity from lawsuit.[5]

In general, law enforcement officers enjoy a qualified immunity. That is, if the conduct of which they are accused was the result of their having acted in good faith and with probable cause, they should not be liable. They may plead good faith and probable cause in their defense. Certain officials are entitled to absolute immunity. Judges, for example, are not liable for acts committed within their jurisdictions even though such actions may have been malicious or corrupt. The reason for granting absolute immunity to judges is to insure the sanctity and independence of the judiciary. Prosecutors enjoy the same sort of absolute immunity and, in the administrative process, so do agency attorneys and administrative law judges. However, other public officials may be held accountable for their invasions of other's rights.

The following case illustrates the principles just discussed. The opinion of the Court in this case is very lengthy and only the portions appropriate to our limited discussion of immunity have been extracted. However, the case should be read in its entirety for its complete review of the evolution of the immunity of public officials at all levels.

Butz v. Economou
U.S. Supreme Court
438 U.S. 478
(1978)

Respondent Economou, and others, filed suit against a number of federal officials in the Department of Agriculture claiming that they had instituted an investigation and administrative proceeding against him in retaliation for his criticism of that agency. Economou's company was at one time registered with the Department of Agriculture as a commodity futures commission merchant. The administrative proceeding out of which this case arose resulted when the

[5] A proposed amendment to the Federal Tort Claims Act would provide an exclusive remedy against the United States in actions based on acts or omissions of United States employees. Such an amendment, not supported by the American Bar Association and opposed by the American Civil Liberties Union, would confer absolute immunity on government officials. (H.R.24,1696, S.1775)

department issued a complaint alleging that Economou willfully failed to maintain the minimum financial requirements prescribed by the department. A finding of such failure would be cause for suspension or revocation of Economou's registration.

Respondent, during the administrative proceeding, filed suit in federal district court seeking initially to enjoin the administrative proceedings. Unsuccessful in this regard, he filed an amended complaint seeking damages against the secretary and assistant secretary of agriculture; the judicial officer and chief hearing examiner of the department; several officials of the Commodity Exchange Authority; the department attorney who had prosecuted the enforcement proceeding; and several auditors who had investigated his company or were witnesses in the administrative proceeding against him.

The district court, relying on *Barr v. Matteo*, 360 U.S. 564 (1959), a landmark case, held that the individual defendants would be entitled to immunity if they could show that "their alleged unconstitutional acts were within the outer perimeter of their authority and discretion." The district court so found and dismissed the amended complaint.

The Court of Appeals for the Second Circuit reversed the district court's judgment of dismissal with regard to the individual defendants reasoning that *Barr v. Matteo* was not the last word in the evolving area of immunity of officials of the executive branch. The court of appeals would make no distinction between suits against state officials under 42 U.S.C., Section 1983 (the Civil Rights Act) and suits against federal officials under the Constitution. It in effect ruled that the individual defendants in this case were entitled to only a qualified immunity. The Supreme Court granted *certiorari*.

White, Justice:

. . . This case concerns the personal immunity of federal officials in the Executive Branch from claims for damages arising from their violations of citizens' constitutional rights. Respondent filed suit against a number of officials in the Department of Agriculture claiming that they had instituted an investigation and an administrative proceeding against him in retaliation for his criticism of that agency. . . .

The complaint stated that prior to the issuance of the administrative complaints respondent had been "sharply critical of the staff and operations of Defendants and carried on a vociferous campaign for the reform of Defendant Commodity Exchange Authority to obtain more effective regulation of commodity trading." The complaint also stated that, some time prior to the issuance of the February 19 complaint, respondent and his company had ceased to engage in activities regulated by the defendants. The complaint charged that each of the administrative complaints had been issued without the notice or warning required by law; that the defendants had furnished the complaints "to interested persons and others without furnishing respondent's answers as well"; and that following the issuance of the amended complaint, the defendants had issued a "deceptive" press release that "falsely indicated to the public that (respondent's) financial resources had deteriorated, when Defendants knew that their statement was untrue and so acknowledge(d) previously that said assertion was untrue." . . .

The defendants moved to dismiss the complaint on the ground that "as to the individual defendants it is barred by the doctrine of official immunity. . . ." The defendants relied on an affidavit submitted earlier in the litigation by the attorney who had prosecuted the original administrative complaint against respondent. He stated that the Secretary of Agriculture had had no involvement with the case and that each of the other named defendants had acted "within the course of his official duties." . . .

The single submission by the United States on behalf of petitioners is that all of the federal officials sued in this case are absolutely immune from any liability for damages even if in the course of enforcing the relevant statutes they infringed respondent's constitutional rights and even if the violation was knowing and deliberate. Although the position is earnestly and ably presented by the United States, we are quite sure that it is unsound and consequently reject it. . . .

Although it is true that the Court has not dealt with this issue with respect to federal officers, we have several times addressed the immunity of state officers when sued under 42 U.S.C., Section 1983 for alleged violations of constitutional rights. These decisions are instructive for present purposes.

Pierson v. Ray, 386 U.S. 547 (1967), decided that § 1983 was not intended to abrogate the immunity of state judges which existed under the common law and which the Court had held applicable to federal judges. . . . *Pierson* also presented the issue "whether immunity was available to that segment of the executive branch of a state government that is . . . most frequently exposed to situations which can give rise to claims under § 1983—the local police officer." *Scheuer v. Rhodes*, 416 U.S., at 244–245. Relying on the common law, we held that police officers were entitled to a defense of "good faith and probable cause," even though an arrest might subsequently be proved to be unconstitutional. We observed, however, that "(t)he common law has never granted police officers an absolute and unqualified immunity, and the officers in this case do not claim that they are entitled to one."

In *Scheuer v. Rhodes*, *supra*, the issue was whether "higher officers of the executive branch" of state governments were immune from liability under § 1983 for violations of constitutionally protected rights. There, the Governor of a State, the senior and subordinate officers of the state National Guard, and a state university president had been sued on the allegation that they had suppressed a civil disturbance in an unconstitutional manner. We explained that the doctrine of official immunity from § 1983 liability, although not constitutionally grounded and essentially a matter of statutory construction, was based on two mutually dependent rationales:

(1) the injustice, particularly in the absence of bad faith, of subjecting to liability an officer who is required, by the legal obligations of his position, to exercise

discretion; (2) the danger that the threat of such liability would deter his willingness to execute his office with the decisiveness and the judgment required by the public good.

The opinion also recognized that executive branch officers must often act swiftly and on the basis of factual information supplied by others, constraints which become even more acute in the "atmosphere of confusion, ambiguity, and swiftly moving events" created by a civil disturbance. Although quoting at length from *Barr v. Matteo*, we did not believe that there was a need for absolute immunity from § 1983 liability for these high-ranking state officials. Rather the considerations discussed above indicated:

(I)n varying scope, a qualified immunity is available to officers of the executive branch of government, the variation being dependent upon the scope of discretion and responsibilities of the office and all the circumstances as they reasonably appeared at the time of the action on which liability is sought to be based. It is the existence of reasonable grounds for the belief formed at the time and in light of all the circumstances, coupled with good-faith belief, that affords a basis for qualified immunity of executive officers for acts performed in the course of official conduct.". . .

Having determined that the plaintiff is entitled to a remedy in damages for a constitutional violation, the court then must address how best to reconcile the plaintiff's right to compensation with the need to protect the decisionmaking processes of an executive department. Since our decision in *Scheuer* was intended to guide the federal courts in resolving this tension in the myriad factual situations in which it might arise, we see no reason why it should not supply the governing principles for resolving this dilemma in the case of federal officials. The Court's opinion in *Scheuer* relied on precedents dealing with federal as well as state officials, analyzed the issue of executive immunity in terms of general policy considerations, and stated its conclusion, quoted *supra*, in the same universal terms. The analysis presented in that case cannot be limited to actions against state officials. . . .

We therefore hold that, in a suit for damages arising from unconstitutional action, federal executive officials exercising discretion are entitled only to the qualified immunity specified in *Scheuer*, subject to those exceptional situations where it is demonstrated that absolute immunity is essential for the conduct of the public business. . . .

Although a qualified immunity from damages liability should be the general rule for executive officials charged with constitutional violations, our decisions recognize that there are some officials whose special functions require a full exemption from liability. . . .

[With regard to other defendants the court said]:

There can be little doubt that the role of the modern federal hearing examiner or administrative law judge within this framework is "functionally comparable" to that of a judge. His powers are often, if not generally, comparable to those of a trial judge: He may issue subpoenas, rule on proffers of evidence, regulate the course of the hearing, and make or recommend decisions. More importantly, the process of agency adjudication is currently structured so as to assure that the hearing examiner exercises his independent judgment on the evidence before him, free from pressures by the parties or other officials within the agency. Prior to the Administrative Procedure Act, there was considerable concern that persons hearing administrative cases at the trial level could not exercise independent judgment because they were required to perform prosecutorial and investigative functions as well as their judicial work . . . and because they were often subordinate to executive officials within the agency. . . . Since the securing of fair and competent hearing personnel was viewed as "the heart of formal administrative adjudication," . . . the Administrative Procedure Act contains a number of provisions designed to guarantee the independence of hearing examiners. . . . They may not perform duties inconsistent with their duties as hearing examiners. . . . When conducting a hearing . . . a hearing examiner is not responsible to, or subject to the supervision or direction of, employees or agents engaged in the performance of investigative or prosecution functions for the agency. . . . Nor may a hearing examiner consult any person or party, including other agency officials, concerning a fact at issue in the hearing, unless on notice and opportunity for all parties to participate. . . . Hearing examiners must be assigned to cases in rotation so far as is practicable. . . . They may be removed only for good cause established and determined by the Civil Service Commission after a hearing on the record. . . . Their pay is also controlled by the Civil Service Commission.

In light of these safeguards, we think that the risk of an unconstitutional act by one presiding at an agency hearing is clearly outweighed by the importance of preserving the independent judgment of these men and women. We therefore hold that persons subject to these restraints and performing adjudicatory functions within a federal agency are entitled to absolute immunity from damages liability for their judicial acts. Those who complain of error in such proceedings must seek agency or judicial review. . . .

We believe that agency officials must make the decision to move forward with an administrative proceeding free from intimidation or harassment. Because the legal remedies already available to the defendant in such a proceeding provide sufficient checks on agency zeal, we hold that those officials who are responsible for the decision to initiate or continue a proceeding subject to agency adjudication are entitled to absolute immunity from damages liability for their parts in that decision.

We turn finally to the role of an agency attorney in conducting a trial and presenting evidence on the record to the trier of fact. We can see no substantial difference between the function of the agency attorney in presenting evidence in an agency hearing and the function of the prosecutor who brings evidence before a court. In either case, the evidence will be subject to attack through cross-examination, rebuttal, or reinterpretation by opposing counsel. Evidence which is false or unpersuasive should be rejected upon analysis by an impartial trier of fact. If agency attorneys were held personally liable in damages as guarantors of the quality of their evidence, they might hesitate to bring forward some witnesses or documents. . . . We therefore hold that an agency attorney who arranges for the presentation of evidence on the record in the course of adjudication is absolutely immune from suits based on the introduction of such evidence.

There remains the task of applying the foregoing principles to the claims against the particular petitioner-defendants involved in this case. Rather than attempt this here in the first instance, we vacate the judgment of the Court of Appeals and remand the case to that court with instructions to remand the case to the District Court for further proceedings consistent with this opinion. *So ordered.*

★★★

Opening Up the Government

Access to Government Records

The Freedom of Information Act of 1966, with significant amendments in 1974, is codified as section 552 of the Administrative Procedure Act. Prior to its enactment it was extremely difficult for a private citizen to obtain and examine government-held documents. The agency from which the information was requested could deny the applicant on the grounds that he or she was not properly and directly concerned or that the requested information should not be disclosed because to do so would not be in the public interest. Under FOIA, any person may reasonably describe what information is sought and the burden for withholding information is on the agency. A response is required of the agency within ten working days after receipt of a request, and denial by the agency may be appealed by means of an expeditable federal district court action. There are of course exemptions—nine specific areas to which the disclosure requirements do not apply. That is, if the information concerns certain matters, the agency is not required to comply with the request. The nine exemptions apply to matters that are:

1. Secret in the interest of national defense or foreign policy
2. Related solely to internal personnel rules and practices of an agency
3. Exempted from disclosure by statute
4. Trade secrets and commercial or financial information obtained from a person and privileged or confidential
5. Inter-agency or intra-agency memoranda or letters
6. Personnel and medical files, the disclosure of which would constitute an invasion of personal privacy
7. Certain investigatory records compiled for law enforcement purposes
8. Related to the regulation or supervision of financial institutions
9. Geological and geophysical information and data, including maps, concerning wells

With regard to the exemptions, Chief Judge Bazelon had this to say in *Soucie v. David*, 448 F.2d 1067 (D.C.Cir.1971):

The touchstone of any proceedings under the Act must be the clear legislative intent to assure public access to all governmental records whose disclosure would not significantly harm specific governmental interests. The policy of the Act requires that the disclosure requirements be construed broadly, the exemptions narrowly.

The Government in the Sunshine Act

A further effort to open up the government is provided by the 1976 Government in the Sunshine Act, codified as section 552b of the Administrative Procedure Act. The purpose of the Act is to assure that " . . . every portion of every meeting of an agency shall be open to public observation." There are, however, exceptions to the open meeting requirement. If the meeting qualifies for one of ten specified exemptions and the agency by majority vote decides to do so, the meeting may be closed to the public. The exemptions of the Act are similar to the nine provided for in the FOIA but are not identical.

At the state level, most have passed some form of open meetings laws. There is considerable diversity, but the common purpose is to permit the public to view the decision-making process at all stages.

Understanding the System

There is much criticism of the "fourth branch of government" but it is, and has been for some time, a fact of American economic and social life. Any study of the subject must accept it for what it is and not be sidetracked by utopian feelings of how it should be. The following excerpt from the excellent work of James O. Freedman states quite succinctly the role of administrative law in our society and its influence in shaping the legal environment of business.

By the time of the nation's bicentennial in 1976, the federal administrative process had achieved a considerable status. It embraced more than sixty independent regulatory agencies as well as perhaps several hundred administrative agencies located in the executive departments. Administrative agencies exercised regulatory responsibilities in scores of important and sensitive areas. The decisions rendered by the federal administrative agencies were many times the number rendered by the federal courts and probably affected the lives of more ordinary citizens more pervasively and more intimately than the decisions of the federal courts. In virtually every relevant respect, the administrative process has become a fourth branch of government, comparable in the scope of its authority and the impact of its decision-making to the three more familiar constitutional branches.

The United States thus has increasingly become an administrative state. Americans have sought to understand the implications of this fact for the character of American democracy, the nature of American justice, and the quality of American life. These implications have often been troubling—even though the administrative process had deep historical roots, even though its growth has been gradual and evolutionary, and even though that growth has occurred only by deliberative acts of democratic choice. If the United States is to realize the promise and respect the limitations of the administrative process, the quest for understanding its implications must be regularly renewed. . . .[6]

Questions and Problems

1. Select a business or profession that one might choose to engage in, and identify and describe the functions of the administrative agencies to which the business or profession would be subject.

2. What recourse is available against an elected official whose performance in office is something less than had been expected by his constituency? Are there any means of controlling or removing an administrative official who was appointed to the position and who does not have to answer to the electorate at the polls?

3. A South Carolina statute created a board of corrections to manage its penal institutions. It also provided for employment of a director of the prison system, and further provided that it was unlawful "for any person to furnish any South Carolina prisoner with any matter declared by the Director to be contraband"—items that inmates could not possess. A person convicted of giving an inmate prohibited property contended that this statute was constitutionally invalid in that it contained no standards which would guide the Director in making up the list of contraband articles. (In other words, it was contended that the statute was unconstitutional because it gave arbitrary authority to the Director in this regard.) Do you think this is a valid objection? Explain. (*Cole v. Manning*, 125 S.E.2d 62, 1962.)

4. In 1966, because of a shortage of railroad cars, the Interstate Commerce Commission began an investigation to determine whether to increase the per diem rate charged railroads who, having used cars belonging to other companies (a common practice), were slow in getting them back to the owning railroad or into the stream of commerce. The increased charge would be an incentive to the user railroad to get the box car off its lines and back into actual use. After obtaining written submissions on boxcar use and demand from the nation's railroads, the commission adopted a rule that established additional incentive per diem charges on an across-the-board basis for all railroads. Several of the affected carriers objected and requested oral hearings based on language of the Interstate Commerce Act that authorizes the ICC to make rules after "a hearing." The challenging railroads maintained that the term "hearing" required that the ICC make rules "on the record" as in Section 553(c) of the Administrative Procedure Act. That is, the commission should have permitted oral testimony, cross-examination of its witnesses, and oral argument. Does Congress's use of the term "hearing" in the Interstate Commerce Act mandate formal, on-the-record rulemaking procedures for the ICC? (*U.S. v. Florida East Coast Railway Co.*, 410 U.S. 224, 1973 and *U.S. v. Allegheny-Ludlum Steel Corp.*, 406 U.S. 742, 1972.)

5. Whether or not a person is entitled to a due process hearing often depends upon the "right" or "privilege" involved. Should an individual have the right to a hearing before his or her parole is revoked? Is liberty a right or a privilege? Should the parole revocation process provide for a due process hearing including written notice, disclo-

---

[6] James O. Freedman, *Crisis and Legitimacy: The Administrative Process and American Government* (Cambridge University Press, 1978).

sure of evidence against the parolee, and the opportunity to present witnesses and documentary evidence? (*Morrissey v. Brewer*, 408 U.S. 471, 1972.)

6. Students in a Florida junior high school were administered "paddlings" for disciplinary reasons. They brought an action for damages and other relief claiming that paddling is cruel and unusual punishment and that they should have had notice and a hearing before the paddlings were given. Is the right not to be paddled within the Fourteenth Amendment's protection as "life, liberty or property?" (*Ingraham v. Wright*, 430 U.S. 651, 1977.)

7. In 1966 the comptroller of the currency issued a rule that permitted national banks to make data processing services available to other banks and to bank customers. This rule was challenged by a firm whose sole business was selling data processing services to businesses generally. Respondent comptroller asserted as a defense that petitioners lacked "standing to sue." If one definition of standing is injury in fact, are the petitioners, the data processing company, likely to obtain reversal of a district court dismissal of their suit? Would the fact that section 4 of the Bank Service Corporation Act provides that "(n)o bank service corporation may engage in any activity other than the performance of bank services for banks" influence your decision? (*Association of Data Processing Service Organizations, Inc. v. Camp*, 397 U.S. 150, 1970.)

8. Mineral King Valley, in the Sierra Nevada Mountains of California, while once the site of extensive mining operations, is now used almost exclusively for recreational purposes. It is a part of Sequoia National Forest and is maintained and administered by the U.S. Forest Service. In response to demands for more skiing facilities the Forest Service invited bids from private developers for the construction and operation of a ski resort that would double as a summer recreation facility. Walt Disney Enterprises was the successful bidder and submitted a plan for a $35 million complex. Representatives of the Sierra Club, a group of environmentalists, brought an action for the purpose of stopping the Mineral King project. Their claim was that the complex would drastically change the aesthetics and ecology of the area and would impair the enjoyment of the park for future generations. Does the Sierra Club have standing to sue? Can they be surrogates for future generations? Or must they allege and prove present specific elements of damage to Sierra Club members? (*Sierra Club v. Morton*, 405 U.S. 727, 1972.)

9. The mother of a "somewhat retarded" teenager petitioned a Circuit Court of Indiana for approval to have the daughter sterilized. The judge approved the petition on the same day and the sterilization was performed, the daughter being told that her appendix was being removed. Two years later the girl married, discovered that she was barren and the reasons therefor, and brought an action for damages against the judge. Is she likely to recover damages? Did the judge overstep his jurisdiction? (*Stump v. Sparkman*, 435 U.S. 349, 1978.)

10. A California couple agreed to provide a foster home for a juvenile offender who had been paroled by penal authorities. The placement officer of the California Youth Authority failed to warn the couple that the boy had "homicidal tendencies." The juvenile attacked his foster mother with a butcher knife, causing serious injuries, and she sued the state in tort. The Youth Authority asserted sovereign immunity in defense. What factors would the Supreme Court of California consider in reviewing the case if the lower court had granted summary judgment for the state? (*Johnson v. California*, 447 P.2d 352, 1968.)

C·H·A·P·T·E·R 7

BUSINESS'S INFLUENCE ON THE LEGAL PROCESS

Government regulation has been a fact of American business life for many years, with concern often expressed by business that there is too much regulation. Consequently, each succeeding political administration has promised to lighten the load for over-regulated business, and some progress has been made toward deregulation in specific areas—energy, the airlines, and occupational safety and health are current examples. However, American business is fully aware that campaign promises by political candidates can be somewhat illusionary and each year must allocate a sizable portion of its operating budget to the education of managers who will conduct business in a regulatory environment. Ideally, business, while recognizing that government regulation is a fact of economic life, would like to limit the scope of regulation to that which is accepted as necessary, reasonable, and beneficial to society but which, at the same time, permits efficient and profitable operations.

Reasonable regulation can result only when there is an understanding of the interaction between government and business and the role each plays in the regulatory process. The government's part—that is, how it recognizes a problem and creates an agency to solve or regulate it—was explored in Chapter 6 and receives more coverage in subsequent chapters dealing with specific areas of importance to government, business, and society. The role of business as it interacts with the government is not so clearly defined. Nevertheless, business has assumed a substantial role in shaping its legal environment by assuring that its voice is heard when legislation or rules and regulations affecting it are being considered. In this chapter, we look at a few of the ways in which business exercises its influence. These include participation in the agency rulemaking process, direct and grass roots lobbying and advocacy advertising, and the formation and use of political action committees (PACs).

Participation by Business in Agency Rulemaking

Government regulatory bodies—administrative agencies—are necessarily diverse; they vary widely in the nature of the functions performed as each carries out the mandate given to it by the Congress to regulate a specific sector of business or society. As we learned in Chapter 6, some agencies distribute welfare assistance and subsidies of one kind or another. Others, such as the Federal Trade Commission, play a primarily prosecutorial role, enforcing government prohibitions against activities inimical to fair trade and open competition. For the most part, however, agencies regulate. Typically, the administrator (the head of the agency, no matter what the title may be) is given the power by Congress to adopt such rules and regulations as the administrator shall deem necessary for the discharge of his or her functions. The resulting rules and regulations will obviously impact on the sector of the economy, or specific businesses, the agency was created to regulate. Consequently, those affected businesses will want, and should have, some influence on the nature of the regulatory measures being devised by the agency; interested parties should have an opportunity to participate in the rulemaking process. For example, the automobile industry would be vitally concerned with safety standards being considered by the Secretary of Transportation. It would therefore want to be represented at the standard-setting procedure to ensure that a proposed standard is attainable at a reasonable cost to the industry and to the consumer. Participation in rulemaking is usually provided for in the statute that created the agency and, in any case, is spelled out in the Administrative Procedure Act (APA). The APA, as noted in Chapter 6, requires that all interested parties be given an opportunity to express their views on proposed rules, by submission of written comment or by personal appearance, before a final rule is adopted. Obviously, those who will be subject to the rule are interested parties and should have a voice in determining what kind of rule it should be and how it should be applied. They should have the opportunity to criticize and suggest changes as the rule evolves and, in fact, assist the agency by providing expert advice.

The role of "interested party" is invariably assumed by the particular business to be affected by proposed rules or regulations. Considerable effort and expense will often be directed by the business toward influencing the outcome of agency rulemaking proceedings. The extent to which business is successful in having its say will often determine the degree of administrative burden and, perhaps more importantly, the cost to industry of the resulting rule or regulation. Two cases serve to illustrate how an affected industry or business (an interested party) was able to influence the outcome of agency rulemaking proceedings.

In 1964 the Surgeon General's Advisory Committee Report on cigarette smoking was issued. The Federal Trade Commission immediately issued a notice of proposed rulemaking for the establishment of trade regulation rules for the advertising and labeling of cigarettes. The notice was published in the *Federal Register* as required, and copies were sent to interested parties. These included all known cigarette manufacturers, public health officials, physicians, consumer organizations, and members of Congress. The proceeding, as is often the case, became adversary in nature with the tobacco industry lined up against most others. Nevertheless, the tobacco industry, through its trade association, the Tobacco Institute, was well represented at the proceeding and tried, albeit unsuccessfully, to convince the FTC that proof of the hazards of cigarette smoking was not conclusive. The FTC eventually adopted a rule requiring warnings on packages of cigarettes and in advertising that smoking is dangerous to human health. However, the effective date of the rule was postponed when Congress intervened. The tobacco industry with an effective lobbying effort was able to transfer the problem to Congress. Today, as evidence of the serious health hazards of smoking continues to mount, the industry is not finding it easy to influence the rulemaking process. The Surgeon General's 1985 campaign for stronger warnings on tobacco products has been successful and the warning now reads: Smoking Causes Lung Cancer, Heart Disease, Emphysema, And May Complicate Pregnancy.

In another case, the National Highway Traffic Safety Administration, a division of the Department of Transportation, published notice of rulemaking regarding the information that should be *permanently* molded into retreaded pneumatic tires. The agency's position and rule, Safety Standard No. 117, would require that eight items of information be permanently molded into all retreaded tires. A vitally interested party, the National Tire Dealers and Retreaders Association, had maintained at the informal rulemaking procedure that many of the items did not relate to safety. Further, the association had conducted an experiment which indicated that the permanent molding would be only 80 percent effective and would increase the cost of each retread by $2.50, or 30 percent. When Standard No. 117 was issued, the agency choosing to reject the association's arguments, the association sought and was granted judicial review. Basing its decision on the facts presented at the rulemaking proceeding, the court vacated parts of the standard, leaving as a requirement those items that did relate to safety and which could be permanently molded into a retread. The tire business was thus able to influence the adoption of a rule with which it could live.

Lobbying

Direct Lobbying

Lobbying can be defined as activity aimed at influencing public officials, particularly members of the legislature, to ensure the passage (or defeat) of legislation that would affect the lobbyist. Lobbyists come in all shapes and sizes and assume for themselves various titles; their main, if not sole, objective is to exert influence and bring pressure to bear on behalf of their clients. Such clients may be any of a large spectrum of special-interest groups that include business, labor, environmentalists, consumers, minorities, professional organizations, and various citizen groups. Targets of the lobbyists' efforts are public officials and lawmakers who make government policy and who enact the law needed to carry out the policy. More specifically, the professional lobbyist is employed and paid by the special-interest group to influence pending legislation. At the rulemaking level, administrators and agency staffs are similarly subjected to pressure from representatives of the sector over which the particular agency may have regulatory power.

While most lobbyists are paid to accomplish the results desired by their special-interest principal, any person who exerts efforts of any kind to influence the legislative process may be termed a lobbyist. This is true even though such a person and his or her principal are motivated only by social or ideological considerations. For example, members of Mothers Against Drunken Drivers (MADD) are lobbyists. The group's special interest is in getting state legislatures to impose greater penalties on those convicted of driving under the influence. Its goals are the same as are those of the professional lobbyists who represent the National Rifle Association or the American Medical Association: the influence of legislation and the shaping of public policy.

There was some early concern over how to handle the favor-seekers and pressure groups that could be expected to frequent the halls of Congress. The right to lobby derives, at least implicitly, from the First Amendment to the Constitution—freedom of speech and the press and the right of the people peaceably to assemble and to petition the government for redress of grievances. The problem was how to control the pressure groups while at the same time insuring the right of the citizens to petition. Early concern for the sanctity of the political process would seem to be justified, since there were several instances of bribery and vote-buying in early administrations.

For example, in 1795 four companies of land speculators were organized to buy some thirty-five million acres of Georgia's western lands for a total of $500,000. A bill was introduced in the Georgia legislature authorizing the sale and was passed as a result of considerable bribery and fraud. Reluctant legislators were bribed with land, slaves, barrels of rice, and money. A chief lobbyist for the speculators was James Gunn, a United States senator from Georgia. At the next election, having learned of the sale, the irate Georgians ousted the entire legislature. (For the legal implications of this situation, see *Fletcher v. Peck*, Supreme Court of the U.S., 1810.10 U.S. [6 Cranch] 87, 3 L.Ed. 162. Georgia's subsequent attempted revocation of the 1795 grant was held to be invalid even though widespread bribery had been involved in the 1795 sale.)

At the federal level, when Nicholas Biddle's second National Bank came under fire in 1833 and congressional battle lines were drawn, Daniel Webster, then a senator from Massachusetts (later to serve on two occasions as secretary of state), wrote this confidential letter to Biddle: "Sir. Since I have arrived here, I have had an application to be concerned, professionally, against the Bank, which I have declined, of course, although I believe my retainer has not been renewed, or REFRESHED as usual. If it is wished that my relation to the Bank should be continued, it may be well to send me the usual retainers." The day after Webster's greatest oratorical effort on behalf of the bank, Biddle handed him $10,000. He received a total of $32,000 from the bank while it was under fire in the Senate.

By the middle of the nineteenth century, the value of U.S. manufactured goods reached one billion dollars, thus exceeding the value of farm products. With the shift from an agricultural to an industrial economy, lobbying intensified. In 1852 James Buchanan wrote Franklin Pierce: "The host of contractors, speculators, stockjobbers, and lobby members which haunt the halls of Congress, all desirous . . . to get their arm into the public treasure, are sufficient to alarm every friend of his country. Their progress must be arrested."

"Lobbying," or more properly, corruption and vote-buying, continued unchecked until the early twentieth century, when President Theodore Roosevelt, supported by various reform groups, began the struggle against the trusts and other scandalous situations. He had limited success for he was opposed by the lobbyists for the vested interests he was attacking; they had lost none of their power and had refined their techniques. Roosevelt's successor, Woodrow Wilson, declared war on the lobbyists and vested interests as he had promised in his first campaign for the presidency. He summed up the situation succinctly when he said:

The masters of the government of the United States are the combined capitalists and manufacturers of the United States. It is written over every intimate page of the records of Congress; it is written all through the history of conferences at the White House: that the suggestions of economic policy have come from one source, not many sources. Suppose you go to Washington. You will always find that while you are politely listened to, the men really consulted are the big men who have the biggest stake—the big bankers, the big manufacturers, the big masters of commerce, the heads of railroad corporations, and of steamship corporations. . . . Every time it has come to critical question, these gentlemen have been yielded to and their demands treated as the demands that should be followed as a matter of course. The government of the United States is a foster child of the special interests. It is not allowed to have a will of its own.

Despite Wilson's efforts and attempts by both houses of Congress to investigate and legislate against the lobbyists and special interest groups, the bribery and corruption continued unchecked. Attempts to regulate lobbying were defeated until passage of the Federal Regulation of Lobbying Act in 1946. This law has been difficult to enforce since its wording is somewhat vague and only lobbyists whose "principal purpose" is to influence Congress are required to register under the Act. Sections 266 and 267 provide:

§ 266. Persons to whom chapter is applicable
The provisions of this chapter shall apply to any person (except a political committee as defined in the Federal Corrupt Practices Act, and duly organized State or local committees of a political party), who by himself, or through any agent or employee or other persons in any manner whatsoever, directly or indirectly, solicits, collects, or receives money or any other thing of value to be used principally to aid, or the principal purpose of which person is to aid, in the accomplishment of any of the following purposes:
(a) The passage or defeat of any legislation by the Congress of the United States.
(b) To influence, directly or indirectly, the passage or defeat of any legislation by the Congress of the United States. Aug. 2, 1946, c. 753, Title III, § 307, 60 Stat. 841.
§ 267. Registration of lobbyists with Secretary of the Senate and Clerk of House; compilation of information
(a) Any person who shall engage himself for pay or for any consideration for the purpose of attempting to influence the passage or defeat of any legislation by the Congress of the United States shall, before doing anything in furtherance of such object, register with the Clerk of the House of Representatives and the Secretary of the Senate and shall give to those officers in writing and under oath, his name and business address.

More stringent measures have been proposed, but none have passed in either the House or Senate. One would think that, in view of its well-documented abuse, the lobbying process would be a fertile area for reform. To date there has been none, and only two convictions for violation of the present act have occurred. However, despite its grim beginnings and what can be termed the dark ages of interaction between business and government, since World War II the practice of lobbying has undergone a remarkable change for the better.[1]

Lobbying Today

While it would be safe to say that all of the direct lobbying—the one-on-one, "personal favor" kinds of influence buying—has not been eliminated, the effective Washington lobbyist of today is a highly sophisticated and

---

[1]For a comprehensive treatment of the history of lobbying and lobbying in general, see James Deakin, *The Lobbyists* (Washington, D.C.: Public Affairs Press, 1966).

knowledgeable person, enjoying a considerable measure of respect in government circles. He or she must be thoroughly familiar with his or her own business and how it is affected by government; know the opposition or competition and their lobbyists; and most importantly, be fully informed on the status of legislation that may impact on clients and should be willing and able to entertain, grant favors when appropriate, and contribute money where it will do the most good. To accomplish all this he or she must have good sources of information and ready access to influential, decision-making people. Above all, he or she should be personable and sociable and know how to operate in the political arena.

The lobbyist's primary function is to serve the interests of the client. An effective way to do this is to perform valuable services for the public officials. To this end, he or she maintains close contact with Congress (both individual members and committees), and is able to present factual data and persuasive arguments concerning the area of interest, business, or industry. He or she possesses considerable expertise and is especially helpful in providing briefs and memoranda and in analyzing specific legislation. These services are often welcomed by friendly members of Congress whose staffs may not be completely knowledgeable in the area to be affected by proposed legislation. The lobbyist can be helpful to legislators in countless ways and comes to be relied upon.

The laws requiring registration by lobbyists are not strictly enforced. Consequently, no precise count of their presence in Washington is possible. However, the following excerpt from an annual publication is a reliable estimate of the size of the current corps.

Washington representatives number in the thousands—the exact figure varying with the definition of "representative" used. By the criteria applied in compiling this directory—that is, persons working to influence government policies and actions to advance their own or their client's interest—the total approaches 10,000. The largest element (about 4,000) are officers of the 1,600 trade and professional associations and labor unions which keep a permanent presence in the Nation's Capital. Another 1,250 are representatives of individual corporations who, as distinguished from their marketing colleagues, are responsible for government relations. A like number are advocates of special causes from ERA to environment, from handgun control to prison reform, from saving whales to saving unborn children. Lawyers and consultants who have registered as lobbyists or foreign agents or who have been identified as representing clients in regulatory matters and legal confrontations with the government currently number about 2,500.

Over the past five years the number of persons listed in this directory has grown steadily—in some measure we have found new sources of information, but in large part because there has actually been a continuing migration of association offices to Washington, an increase in the number of advocacy groups and a gradual expansion of the public affairs/government relations profession. It remains to be seen whether the trend will continue

". . . could have swore I heard something!"

Powerful lobbies may be able to override the concerns of smaller or less influential interests.
Source: Reprinted by permission: Tribune Media Services.

beyond 1981 in the face of the Reagan Administration's efforts to eliminate excess federal regulation and to reduce the size, reach and generosity of the government. The peak may, in fact, have passed. A half dozen major corporations have closed their Washington offices or shifted the public affairs function back to corporate headquarters. Some trade associations reportedly may soon capitulate to the Capital's rising costs and move elsewhere. Mass defections are unlikely, however; for most of the political and economic imperatives which prompted the need to have representation "where the action is" persist. And any reduction in company or association personnel may be balanced by growth in independent consultants on whom these organizations will then be obliged to rely.[2]

At the large organization level, the National Association of Manufacturers—established as such in 1895—and the Chamber of Commerce are recognized as veterans in the lobbying field. Representing the broadest of constituencies, each has been highly successful in influencing the passage or defeat of legislation impacting on our free enterprise economy. Of the "*Fortune* 500" corporations, a great majority maintain their own Washington offices; a large percentage of the one thousand largest companies have some representation there. In 1984 lobbyists spent $42 million trying to influence

[2] Arthur C. Close, ed., *Washington Representatives*, 6th ed. (Washington, D.C.: Columbia Books, 1982).

Congress. This was slightly less than was spent in 1983, $43.3 million, but was still more than the amount U.S. taxpayers spent on salaries for senators and representatives. According to Congressional Record data, the biggest spender in 1984 was the Natural Gas Supply Association, $2,087,586, followed by Common Cause, $2,077,931, and Gun Owners of America, $1,409,235.

Wielding considerable influence with its high-powered makeup is the Business Roundtable founded in 1972. Its members are nearly two hundred of the chief executives of the nation's largest and most powerful corporations. Its original efforts were directed toward countering the lobbying of the powerful Labor Federation. More recently it has branched out into other fields, including tax reform, environmental concerns, and consumerism. As an effective persuader this coalition has no peers. Its individual members or the various committees into which it is organized have little trouble gaining access to high-level government officials, including the secretaries of the Cabinet and the president himself.

Grass-roots Lobbying

Direct lobbying, for the most part, involves the one-on-one, face-to-face wielding of influence by expert lobbyists. *Grass-roots lobbying* involves a third party, the constituency of the lawmaker whose vote is sought on a specific measure. Estimates of the amount spent each year by business on grass-roots lobbying are in the $1 billion range. It is not inexpensive to prepare and mail the number of letters required to elicit some fourteen million responses in the form of letters to Congress—the National Rifle Association claims it can do this and has certainly enjoyed a measure of success. Congress has rejected gun-control bills on fourteen occasions during the past ten years. The National Rifle Association has learned, as have many other lobbying groups, that members of Congress are likely to respond quickly to mail from their constituents. Grass-roots lobbying is therefore an attempt by lobbyists to influence legislators by the use of bulk mailings to the voters back home. Those who receive the mailing are urged to correspond with their congressman and take a position on what may be an item of controversial legislation. The lobbyist, of course, hopes that the position taken, and stated, will be compatible with his or her own.

Other influential groups using the grass-roots approach include organized labor, the Chamber of Commerce, the League of Women Voters, and the United States Savings and Loan League. The AFL-CIO, for example, can look to its 105 unions with some fourteen million members when support is needed on an issue vital to labor. The League of Women Voters is able to rally its 160,000 members by frequent mailings explaining various issues. The United States Savings and Loan League represents about five thousand of the country's six thousand savings and loan associations. In 1962, when a proposed tax bill inimical to the interests of the savings and loan associations was being considered, the league sent a letter to five thousand savings and loan associations.

The time has come for every savings and loan executive, officer and director to write a letter to both his United States Senators covering either or both the savings and loan tax law and the proposed withholding on interest and dividends. The time also has come for associations to address letters to their savers, borrowers, and builder and realtor friends. You will recall that earlier this year we asked every association to get ready for such a mailing to savers and others by addressing envelopes, etc. This is the time when these envelopes should be used.[3]

Grass-roots lobbying through mass mailings has its disadvantages. When a legislator is deluged by thousands of letters, most saying much the same thing, he or she may view them as artificially generated and thus questionable as truly representative of the constituency. Obviously, a mass outpouring is a pressure tactic, easily recognized as such, posing a considerable problem—the legislator may now have to solicit the constituency or at least sample it to confirm or disaffirm what the voters really want. Nevertheless, a grass-roots lobbying campaign, effectively devised and carefully managed, is an accepted means by which business can influence the legislative process.

Advocacy Advertising

The right of a company to advertise its product, to extol its merits, is a marketing device long recognized as an integral part of our free enterprise system. Annual advertising budgets for large manufacturing corporations run to millions of dollars, money spent to persuade the consuming public that the advertised product is the best on the market. Since the mid-1960s, however, large corporations have found it useful, and often necessary, to use advertising as a means of countering adverse publicity or to place before the public the company's views on controversial issues. The issues usually concern the advertiser's business, with the cost of the ad in a specific case considered money well-spent in presenting to the public the company's position. Of increasing importance in the corporate boardroom is public relations whose primary function is to protect the corporate image. Publicity campaigns directed at influencing public opinion favorably toward the company position are referred to as *advocacy advertising.*

Advocacy Advertising as Protected Free Speech

The question is frequently raised as to the right of corporations to make public pronouncements. That is, does a corporation enjoy the same broad rights of freedom of speech as do individuals under the First Amendment to

[3] James Deakin, *The Lobbyists* (Washington, D.C.: Public Affairs Press, 1966). (Twenty years later the battle over withholding was waged again. While the League was unsuccessful in preventing enactment of withholding in 1982, a provision of the 1982 Tax Act, the measure was repealed in 1983.

the Constitution? In other words, since advocacy advertising in its various forms may be considered to be commercial speech for profit, must it be distinguished from individual speech and afforded less protection? The issue has been addressed by the U.S. Supreme Court, and two of its recent decisions should be noted.

In *First National Bank of Boston v. Bellotti*, 435 U.S. 765 (1978), a consortium of national banking associations and businesses wanted to advertise its opposition to a referendum proposal that would amend the Massachusetts constitution to permit enactment of a graduated income tax. A Massachusetts criminal statute prohibited certain business corporations from spending money "for the purpose of . . . influencing or affecting the vote on any question submitted to the voters, other than one materially affecting any of the property, business or assets of the corporation." The statute's validity was upheld by the state supreme court. In reversing, thus holding the statute invalid, the U.S. Supreme Court considered the type of information the First Amendment protects and the listener's right to receive the information. The free discussion of governmental affairs, said the court, is the type of speech indispensable to decision making in a democracy and this is no less true because the speech comes from a corporation rather than an individual.

The state had argued to the effect that the corporation, because of its wealth and power, would overwhelm and dominate the debate on a referendum. In rejecting the argument the Court said that there was no proof of undue influence and that, in any event, the influence which corporate advocacy might have on the outcome is not material. In a democracy, said the Court, the people are the sole arbiters of the relative merits of conflicting arguments.

The second decision follows.

Consolidated Edison Company v. Public Service Commission of New York

U.S. Supreme Court
447 U.S. 530
(1980)

Consolidated Edison had included in its customers' monthly bills an insert discussing the benefits of nuclear power. Entitled "Independence Is Still a Goal, and Nuclear Power Is Needed to Win the Battle," the bill insert offered Consolidated Edison's opinion that the benefits of nuclear power "far outweigh any potential risk" and that nuclear power plants are safe, economical, and clean. Further, contended Consolidated Edison, increased use of nuclear energy would reduce this country's dependence on foreign energy sources.

An organization with contrary views, the National Resources Defense Council, Inc., (NRDC) requested Consolidated Edison to enclose a rebuttal prepared by NRDC in its next billing envelope. When Consolidated Edison refused, NRDC asked the Public Service Commission (PSC) of New York to open Consolidated Edison's billing envelopes to contrasting views on controversial issues of public importance. The PSC denied NRDC's request but issued an order prohibiting "utilities from using bill inserts to discuss political matters, including the desirability of future development of nuclear power." Consolidated Edison challenged the order as a violation of its First Amendment rights as incorportated by the Fourteenth Amendment.

The New York Supreme Court held the order unconstitutional, but the Appellate Division reversed and the New York Court of Appeals affirmed that judgment. The Court of Appeals held that the PSC order did not violate the Constitution because it was a valid time, place, and manner regulation designed to protect the privacy of Consolidated Edison's customers. This appeal was then taken to the U.S. Supreme Court.

Powell, Justice:

. . . The restriction on bill inserts cannot be upheld on the ground that Consolidated Edison is not entitled to freedom of speech. In *First National Bank of Boston v. Bellotti*, 435 US 765 . . . we rejected the contention that a State may confine corporate speech to specified issues. That decision recognized that "(t)he inherent worth of the speech in terms of its capacity for informing the public does not depend upon the identity of its source, whether corporation, association, union, or individual.". . . Because the state action limited protected speech, we concluded that the regulation could not stand absent a showing of a compelling state interest. . . .

The First and Fourteenth Amendments guarantee that no State shall "abridg(e) the freedom of speech." See *Joseph Burstyn, Inc. v. Wilson*, 343 US 495 . . . (1952). Freedom of speech is "indispensable to the discovery and spread of political truth," *Whitney v. California, 274 US 357* . . . (1927). . . . The First and Fourteenth Amendments remove "governmental restraints from the arena of public discussion, putting the decision as to what views shall be voiced largely into the hands of each of us, in the hope that use of such freedom will ultimately produce a more capable citizenry and more perfect polity. . . ." *Cohen v. California*, 403 US 15 . . . (1971). . . .

In the mailing that triggered the regulation at issue, Consolidated Edison advocated the use of nuclear power. The Commission has limited the means by which Consolidated Edison may participate in the public debate on this question and other controversial issues of national interest and importance. Thus, the Commission's prohibition of discussion of controversial issues strikes at the heart of the freedom to speak.

The Commission's ban on bill inserts is not, of course, invalid merely because it imposes a limitation upon speech. See *First National Bank of Boston v. Bellotti*, supra, at 786. . . . We must consider whether the State can demonstrate that its regulation is constitutionally permissible. The Commission's arguments require us to consider three theories that might justify the state action. We must determine whether the prohibition is (i) a reasonable time, place, or manner restriction, (ii) a permissible subject-matter regulation, or (iii) a narrowly tailored means of serving a compelling state interest. . . .

A restriction that regulates only the time, place, or manner of speech may be imposed so long as it is reasonable. But when regulation is based on the content of speech, governmental action must be scrutinized more carefully to ensure that communication has not been prohibited "merely because public officials disapprove the speaker's views." *Niemotko v. Maryland*, 340 US 268 . . . (1951). . . .

The Commission does not pretend that its action is unrelated to the content or subject matter of bill inserts. Indeed, it has undertaken to suppress certain bill inserts precisely because they address controversial issues of public policy. The Commission allows inserts that present information to consumers on certain subjects, such as energy conservation measures, but it forbids the use of inserts that discuss public controversies. The Commission, with commendable candor, justifies its ban on the ground that consumers will benefit from receiving "useful" information, but not from the prohibited information. . . . The Commission's own rationale demonstrates that its action cannot be upheld as a content-neutral time, place, or manner regulation. . . .

The Commission next argues that its order is acceptable because it applies to all discussion of nuclear power, whether pro or con, in bill inserts. The prohibition, the Commission contends, is related to subject matter rather than to the views of a particular speaker. Because the regulation does not favor either side of a political controversy, the Commission asserts that it does not unconstitutionally suppress freedom of speech. . . .

Consolidated Edison has not asked to use the offices of the Commission as a forum from which to promulgate its views. Rather, it seeks merely to utilize its own billing envelopes to promulgate its views on controversial issues of public policy. The Commission asserts that the billing envelope, as a necessary adjunct to the operations of a public utility, is subject to the State's plenary control. To be sure, the State has a legitimate regulatory interest in controlling Consolidated Edison's activities, just as local governments always have been able to use their police powers in the public interest to regulate private behavior. . . . But the Commission's attempt to restrict the free expression of a private party cannot be upheld by reliance upon precedent that rests on the special interests of a government in overseeing the use of its property. . . .

Where a government restricts the speech of a private person, the state action may be sustained only if the government can show that the regulation is a precisely drawn means of serving a compelling state interest. . . . The Commission argues finally that its prohibition is necessary (i) to avoid forcing Consolidated Edison's views on a captive audience, (ii) to allocate limited resources in the public interest, and (iii) to ensure that ratepayers do not subsidize the cost of the bill inserts.

The State Court of Appeals largely based its approval of the prohibition upon its conclusion that the bill inserts intruded upon individual privacy. The court stated that Commission could act to protect the privacy of the utility's customers because they have no choice whether to receive the insert and the views expressed in the insert may inflame their sensibilities. . . . But the Court of Appeals erred in its assessment of the seriousness of the intrusion.

Even if a short exposure to Consolidated Edison's views may offend the sensibilities of some consumers, the ability of government "to shut off discourse solely to protect others from hearing it (is) dependent upon a showing that substantial privacy interests are being invaded in an essentially intolerable manner." *Cohen v. California*, 403 US, at 21. A less stringent analysis would permit a government to slight the First Amendment's role "in affording the public access to discussion, debate, and the dissemination of information and ideas." *First National Bank of Boston v. Bellotti*, supra. . . .

The customers of Consolidated Edison may escape exposure to objectionable material simply by transferring the bill insert from envelope to wastebasket.

Finally, the Commission urges that its prohibition would prevent ratepayers from subsidizing the costs of policy-oriented bill inserts. But the Commission did not base its order on an inability to allocate costs between the shareholders of Consolidated Edison and the ratepayers. Rather the Commission stated that "using bill inserts to proclaim a utility's viewpoint on controversial issues (*even when the stockholder pays for it in full*) is tantamount to taking advantage of a captive audience". . . [Emphasis added.] Accordingly, there is no basis on this record to assume that the Commission could not exclude the cost of these bill inserts from the utility's rate base. Mere speculation of harm does not constitute a compelling state interest. . . .

The Commission's suppression of bill inserts that discuss controversial issues of public policy directly infringes the freedom of speech protected by the First and Fourteenth Amendments. The state action is neither a valid time, place, or manner restriction, nor a permissible subject-matter regulation, nor a narrowly drawn prohibition justified by a compelling state interest. Accordingly, the regulation is invalid. . . .

The decision of the New York Court of Appeals is reversed.

★★★

Advocacy Advertising and the Judicial Process

As the *Bellotti* and *Consolidated Edison* cases indicate, there is a discernible trend toward increased First Amendment protection for corporate speech affecting a commercial transaction and public issue-related speech in a commercial context. However, business may not find the going quite so easy when the effect of its advocacy ad campaigns may be to influence the *judicial* process. In 1978, obviously disturbed by the increasing number of jury awards of $1 million or more in personal injury lawsuits, the insurance industry took the offensive. Several companies placed ads in such publications as *Time*, *Newsweek*, the *Wall Street Journal*, and *Sports Illustrated* attacking high jury awards in liability cases. The Aetna Life and Casualty and St. Paul Property & Liability ads shown here are representative. Such campaigns are costly; Aetna's ad budget alone was $5.5 million. Perhaps the expenditure would be well justified if the ads were instrumental in bringing about a reduction in the multimillion dollar judgments being awarded.

As can be expected, the ad campaigns are viewed with some dismay by trial lawyers, individually and collectively, who specialize as plaintiff's attorney in personal injury cases. Three plaintiffs in pending personal injury suits filed an action in the New York courts seeking to enjoin *Aetna* and two magazine publishers from printing the ads which, it was felt, advocated tort law reform (*Quinn v. Aetna Life & Casualty Co.*, 409 N.Y.S. 2d 473, 1979). Plaintiffs' contention was that the ads were motivated by a desire to

You really think it's the insurance company that's paying for all those large jury awards?

"Sue thy Neighbor" is fast becoming one of America's favorite pastimes. But who really foots the bill on the "big pot" some lucky claimant wins? We *all* do.

Insurance is basically a system for sharing risk among many.

All of us chip in so there'll be money available when somebody gets hit with a loss. Rates are based on expected claims.

Most claims have a reasonable basis and are settled fairly. But many people feel that an increasing number of jury awards are excessive. When awards are out of line, everyone pays more. In the form of higher insurance rates.

Frankly, unless something is done, this could go on forever. As long as you're willing to pay these higher costs, insurance companies can pay out bigger and bigger awards.

But we at The St. Paul feel the trend toward excessive jury awards has pushed insurance premiums to levels that are too high.

What can you do if you've had enough?

Send for our "Enough is Enough" consumer booklet. It's full of information on the causes and the pro's and con's of some possible cures for high insurance rates. You'll find out how to register your views where they'll count. Along with some tips on how you can hold down your own insurance costs.

Then get involved. Support the action you want taken.

Write a letter to your legislators. Be heard.

Or you can just do nothing and figure the problem will go away. Of course if it doesn't, better keep your checkbook handy.

Enough is Enough

Write The St. Paul for your Enough is Enough booklet. Or contact an Independent Agent or broker representing The St. Paul. He's in this with you and wants to help. You'll find him in the Yellow Pages.

St. Paul Fire and Marine Insurance Company, 385 Washington St., Saint Paul, MN 55102.

Serving you through Independent Agents. St. Paul Fire and Marine Insurance Company. St. Paul Mercury Insurance Company. The St. Paul Insurance Company. St. Paul Guardian Insurance Company. The St. Paul Insurance Company of Illinois. Property and Liability Affiliates of The St. Paul Companies Inc., Saint Paul, Minnesota 55102

25849 Ed. 3-77 Printed in U.S.A.

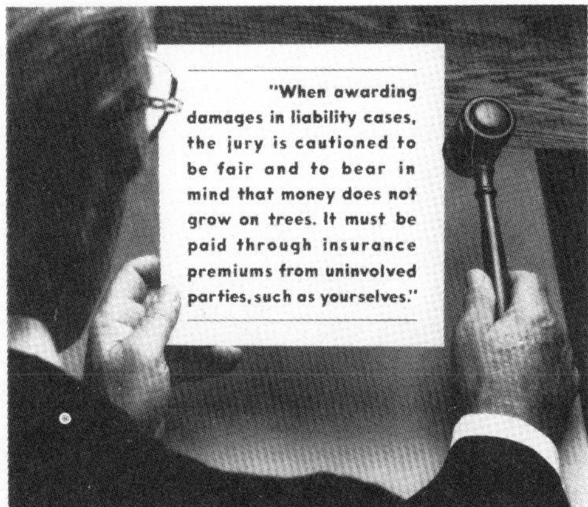

Too bad judges can't read this to a jury.

A truck without brake lights is hit from behind. For "psychic damages" to the driver, because his pride was hurt when his wife had to work, *a jury awards $480,000 above and beyond his medical bills and wage losses.*

A 67-year old factory worker loses an arm on the job. His lawyer argues that he should receive wages for all the remaining years of his life expectancy. He had been earning about $10.000 a year. The jury awards him a sum equal to almost $89.000 a year.[1]

Then there's the one...but *you* can probably provide the next example. Most of us know hair-raising stories of windfall awards won in court. Justified claims should be compensated, of course. Ætna's point is that it is time to look hard at what windfall awards are costing.[2]

What can we do? Several things:

We can stop assessing "liability" where there really *was* no fault—and express our sympathy for victims through other means.

We can ask juries to take into account a victim's *own* responsibility for his losses. And we can urge that awards realistically reflect the actual loss suffered—that they be a fair *compensation,* but not a reward.[4]

Insurers, lawyers, judges—each of us shares some blame for this mess. But it is you, the public, who can best begin to clean it up. Don't underestimate your own influence. Use it, as we are trying to use ours.

Ætna wants insurance to be affordable.

[1] The man was awarded $1.250.000, or about $89.000 a year, for the remaining 14 years of his life expectancy. The jury awarded an extra $500.000 to his wife for loss of "consortium"—the company, affection and services of her husband.

[2] A by-product of such awards has been a quantum leap in the number of personal injury and property damage suits filed. A 1977 study in California shows such suits increasing at *five times the rate of population growth.*

[3] Most awards are paid by insurance, and insurance companies spend millions more defending policyholders against lawsuits. The direct result is rising premiums for automobile and other liability coverages. The *indirect* result is higher prices for goods and services—prices which are boosted to cover the sky-rocketing insurance premiums of manufacturers, doctors, hospitals, and others who are targets for windfall awards.

[4] For example, it would help if juries were simply required to take into account payments the claimant has already received for medical bills and lost wages. Under the present system, these bills may be paid all over again.

Ætna Life & Casualty, 151 Farmington Avenue, Hartford, CT 06156

Figure 7.1 Advocacy Advertisements by Aetna Life and Casualty and The St. Paul Companies.
Source: Courtesy of Aetna Life and Casualty and The St. Paul Companies.

influence potential jurors and were misleading. That is, they failed to also inform readers that a losing defendant can move to have the verdict set aside, seek appellate review, or ask for remittitur.[4]

Defendants contended that the ads, admittedly appeals for reform of judicial process, were protected by the First Amendment and not subject to prior restraint by injunction, the only relief which plaintiffs were asking. At issue for the Supreme Court for Queens County was the need to balance protected speech of the First Amendment against the right to a fair trial afforded by the Sixth. After a discussion of the line of commercial speech cases, perhaps inappropriately since the ads were not considered for their marketing value, the court decided that the ads were misleading and were geared toward influencing jurors and prospective jurors in their decision-making process. Thus, said the court, the ad campaign threatened the impaneling of an impartial jury and could be restrained despite the First Amendment. However, since plaintiffs' case had not yet been tried, possible damage could not be proved. The court therefore refused to issue the requested injunction. After the state court decision that a cause of action did exist, the case was removed to federal court. There plaintiffs' request for injunctive relief was again denied as a constitutionally impermissible prior restraint, a clear victory for the insurance industry, if not in the entire war, at least in a major battle (*Quinn v. Aetna Life & Casualty Co.*, 482 F. Supp. 22, 1979).

In California, the Trial Lawyers Association filed complaints within the state's Department of Insurance and the Federal Trade Commission alleging that the ads are false and deceptive and arguing that corrective advertising be ordered.

More recently, the Ohio Academy of Trial Lawyers filed a complaint with the Ohio Department of Insurance alleging that certain insurance advertisements were deceptive and requesting that a hearing into the ads be held. When the commissioner of insurance refused, the academy sought judicial review of the order and the Ohio Court of Common Pleas, after an *ex parte* proceeding, ordered the Department of Insurance to issue a cease and desist order. The Ohio Court of Appeals reversed, holding that the administrative decision of the Department of Insurance was not reviewable. On May 4, 1983, the Ohio Supreme Court affirmed. *Ohio Academy of Trial Lawyers v. Dept. of Ins.*, 4 Ohio St. 3d 201. However, earlier in the proceedings the ads in question had been discontinued.

Political Action Committees (PACs)

Direct and grass-roots lobbying, as we have seen, involve the exercise of influence by special interest groups on already elected or appointed officials. Of increasing importance today, however, is the influence to be gained

[4] "Remittitur" involves the power of a trial judge to decrease the amount of money awarded by a jury to a successful plaintiff.

by playing a significant role in the election process itself. Special-interest groups are able to do so by raising large sums of money and making it available to the candidates of their choice in any given election. In 1980, approximately $30 million was given to congressional and presidential hopefuls by various business and trade associations. This seems to have been money well-placed since over 80 percent of the candidates who outspent their opponents won their individual races.

The donation of huge sums of money to assist a politician in gaining, or keeping, an elective office would seem to raise questions about the political process. Are seats in Congress being bought by the highest bidder? Are business interests using their contributions to gain overwhelming influence in Congress? The answers to those questions will vary depending upon how one views the way political campaigns are conducted. To wage a campaign for public office is an expensive undertaking when one considers the high cost of the media exposure usually necessary to success. Few aspiring politicians have the personal wealth to finance their own campaigns. Consequently, the funds must come from outside sources. The major source, since 1971, has been *political action committees (PACs)*, voluntary groups whose primary function is to raise funds to be used in support of political candidates who share the group's ideological and political beliefs.

Prior to passage of the Federal Election Campaign Act (FECA) in 1971, political campaigns were financed for the most part by private donations with little government regulation or control. As enacted, FECA limited the amount of money a candidate could spend on his or her campaign, set limits on media advertising expenditures, and imposed strict disclosure requirements. The 1971 FECA limited to $25,000 the amount any individual could contribute to a political campaign and led to the demise of the extravagant donation. However, labor unions were authorized to use union funds to establish PACs, and corporations and their shareholders, after some give-and-take in committee, were given similar privileges. Thus were born the powerful union and corporate PACs, a political phenomenon of the 1970s that continues to be a major factor in the financing of political campaigns. In the 1976 elections, for example, labor PACs contributed $17,489,000 to political candidates. Business PACs contributed somewhat less, $12,587,000. In 1980, labor union PACs contributed some $12 million to House and Senate candidates, while the corporate PACs were contributing about $35 million.

Currently, political action committees are experiencing phenomenal growth with considerable proliferation as to both numbers being formed and causes for which they are established. There are numerous PACs that exist to concentrate on one issue, such as the antiabortion, gun-control, dairy, medical, and realtors' groups. Most ambitious, however, are the conservative groups such as the National Congressional Club, founded by Senator Jesse Helms, and the National Conservative PAC—the Federal Election Commission reported that the former raised some $7.7 million and the latter more than $7.2 million for the 1982 elections.

In all, PACs raised more than $138 million for the 1982 campaigns. In the top ten were the Citizens for the Republic, originally founded by Ronald Reagan, and the fund for a Conservative Majority. Whereas the labor unions formerly dominated the field, the United Auto Workers raised a mere $1.2 million and failed to make the top ten. Much of the money is, of course, spent on candidates of the individual group's choice. However, a considerable amount is also spent in trying to defeat targeted incumbents. The controversial National Conservative Political Action Committee helped defeat five prominent Democratic senators in the 1980 elections but proved to be less effective in its 1982 war on big-name liberals.

While it may not be correct to maintain that seats in Congress are being bought by special-interest groups, it is nevertheless true that such groups, by judicious use of PAC funds, are able to exert considerable influence on the legislative process. The following are examples of sums spent by various PACs in what may be considered efforts to influence Congress as it deliberated the pros and cons of measures that would affect the constituencies of the individual PACs.[5]

PAC	Top 5 Recipients		Goal
National Automobile Dealers Association gave $40,750 to	. . . Energy and Commerce Committee members:		. . . to kill a rule requiring dealers to inform buyers of known defects of used cars. (Rule killed in Congress.)
	Phil Gramm	$5,000	
	Tom Corcoran	$4,450	
	Richard Shelby	$4,250	
	Ralph Hall	$4,250	
	Thomas Luken	$3,750	
Lockheed Aircraft Corporation gave $11,500 to	. . . Armed Services Committee members:		. . . to win government contract for Lockheed C-5B cargo plane. (Approved by Congress.)
	Howard Cannon	$3,500	
	John Tower	$2,000	
	John Warner	$2,000	
	Henry Jackson	$1,500	
	John Stennis	$1,000	
United Auto Workers gave $35,000 to	. . . Energy and Commerce Committee members:		. . . to require foreign cars sold in U.S. to use mainly American-made parts. (Bill passed by committee; 223 House sponsors; awaiting House vote.)
	Philip Sharp	$10,000	
	John Dingell	$5,706	
	Doug Walgren	$5,000	
	Richard Ottinger	$5,000	
	Edward Markey	$3,450	
National Rifle Association gave $85,000 to	. . . Judiciary Committee members:		. . . to pass McClure-Volkmer bill making it easier to buy and sell firearms. (Approved by committee; 58 Senate co-sponsors; awaiting Senate vote.)
	Charles Grassley	$8,950	
	Arlen Specter	$5,000	
	Robert Byrd	$4,950	
	Dennis DeConcini	$4,950	
	Howell Heflin	$3,500	

[5]Adapted from "Running with the PACs," *Time*, October 25, 1982.

Federal Election Campaign Reform

The Federal Election Campaign Act of 1971, as amended in 1974 and 1976 (enacting the Presidential Election Campaign Fund Act), was designed to effect political campaign reform by limiting the extent to which an influential wealthy minority may exercise its potent electoral voice. It is, in a sense, the regulation of public debate so that the average citizen's voice can be heard. It places restrictions and limitations on the role the powerful political action committees play in political campaigns. In general, federal election campaign legislation:

1. prohibits an individual from contributing more than $1,000 to any one candidate in any one primary or general election;
2. prohibits multi-candidate political committees from contributing more than $5,000 to a single candidate in one election;
3. places a ceiling on spending of candidate's personal or family funds and on the aggregate expenditures on behalf of a candidate for public office;
4. forbids a person expending more than $1,000 on one clearly identified candidate for office even if without consultation with that candidate or agent of the candidate;
5. offers federal public financing of presidential campaigns through the income tax "check-off"; and
6. prohibits any political committee not authorized by the candidate from spending more than $1,000 in support of a presidential candidate who had elected to receive federal funds.[6]

The amendments also created a new federal mechanism to enforce campaign laws—the Federal Election Commission (FEC).

Challenges to Campaign Reform Legislation

Legislation has been challenged, as a restraint on free speech, with varying degrees of success. In *Buckley v. Valeo*, 424 U.S. 1 (1976), ten plaintiffs, including a candidate for the Presidency of the United States and a United States Senator seeking reelection, filed a complaint requesting that the major provisions of the Federal Election Campaign Act (FECA) be declared unconstitutional and that the Federal Election Commission be enjoined from enforcing those provisions. It was plaintiffs' view that limiting the use of money for political purposes constitutes a restriction on communication in violation of the First Amendment. The claim was made that, in a modern setting, meaningful political communications involve the expenditure of money. Plaintiffs further alleged that the reporting and disclosure requirements of FECA unconstitutionally impinged on their right to freedom of association. The Court upheld the validity of the act's ceilings on political

[6]Numbers 5 and 6 above are provisions of the Presidential Election Campaign Fund Act.

contributions, but declared the limits on independent political expenditures by individuals and groups, and fixed ceilings on overall campaign expenditures by candidates, to be unconstitutional as impermissibly burdening the right of free expression.

Further challenges to FECA's constitutionality were denied in *Bread Political Action Committee v. The Federal Election Commission*, 635 F.2d 621 (1980), and in *California Medical Association v. Federal Election Commission*, 101 S.Ct. 2712 (1981). However, in the case that follows, the Presidential Election Campaign Fund Act's prohibition of any political committee, not authorized by a presidential candidate, from spending more than $1,000 in support of such candidate who had elected to receive federal funds was examined and found to be unconstitutional, a violation of the First Amendment.

Federal Election Commission v. National Conservative Political Action Committee,
U.S. Supreme Court
105 S.Ct. 1459 (1985)

In May 1983 the Democratic Party and the Democratic National Committee filed suit against the National Conservative Political Action Committee and the Fund for a Conservative Majority (PACs), who had announced that they would spend large sums of money to help reelect President Ronald Reagan in 1984. They specifically sought a declaration that section 9012(f) of the Presidential Election Campaign Fund Act was constitutional. If they were successful in their action the two PACs would be prohibited from expending more than $1,000 each toward reelecting President Reagan since he had elected to receive federal public financing for his campaign. [Sections 9001 *et seq.*, and 9012(f) of the Fund Act make it a criminal offense for an independent PAC to spend more than $1,000 to further the election of a candidate who had elected to receive public financing.]

In June 1983 the Federal Election Commission brought a separate action against the PACs seeking identical declaratory relief and a three-judge District Court consolidated the two cases for all purposes. (A separate important issue of the cases was "standing" of the plaintiffs to sue. That aspect of the case is not covered in this report of the opinion.)

The three-judge District Court held that the Democrats had standing but that the Democrats and the FEC were not entitled to a declaration that section 9012(f) of the Fund Act is constitutional. The court held that section 9012(f) abridges First Amendment freedoms of speech and association but did not declare it to be unconstitutional. This because the PACs had not filed a counterclaim requesting such a declaration. Cross appeals were then taken to the U.S. Supreme Court.

Rehnquist, Justice:

. . . In this case we consider provisions of the Fund Act that make it a criminal offense for political committees such as NCPAC and FCM to make independent expenditures in support of a candidate who has elected to accept public financing. Specifically, section 9012(f) provides:

(1) . . . it shall be unlawful for any political committee which is not an authorized committee with respect to the eligible candidates of a political party for President and Vice President in a presidential election knowingly and willfully to incur expenditures to further the election of such candidates, which would constitute qualified campaign expenses if incurred by an authorized committee of such candidates, in an aggregate amount exceeding $1,000.

The term "political committee" is defined to mean "any committee, association, or organization (whether or not incorporated) which accepts contributions or makes expenditures for the purpose of influencing, or attempting to influence, the nomination or election of one or more individuals to Federal, State, or local elective public office.". . . Two of the more important qualifications are that a candidate and his authorized committees not incur campaign expenses in excess of his public funding and not accept contributions to defray campaign expenses.

There is no question that NCPAC and FCM are political committees and that President Reagan was a qualified candidate, and it seems plain enough that the PACs' expenditures fall within the term "qualified campaign expense.". . . We conclude that the PACs' independent expenditures at issue in this case are squarely prohibited by section 9012(f), and we proceed to consider whether that prohibition violates the First Amendment.

The PACs in this case, of course, are not lone pamphleteers or street corner orators in the Tom Paine mold; they spend substantial amounts of money in order to communicate their political ideas through sophisticated media advertisements. And of course the criminal sanction in question is applied to the expenditure of money to propagate political views, rather than to the propagation of those views unaccompanied by the expenditure of money. But for purposes of presenting political views in connection with a nationwide Presidential election, allowing the presentation of views while forbidding the expenditure of more than $1,000 to present them is much like allowing a speaker in a public hall to express his views while denying him the use of an amplifying system. . . .

We also reject the notion that the PACs' form of organization or method of solicitation diminishes their entitlement to First Amendment protection. The First Amendment freedom of association is squarely implicated in this case. NCPAC and FCM are mechanisms by which large numbers of individuals of modest means can join together in organizations which serve to "amplify the voice of their adherents.". . . It is significant that in 1979–1980 approximately 101,000 people contributed an average of $75 each to NCPAC and in 1980 approximately 100,000 people contributed an average of $25 each to FCM.

Corruption is a subversion of the political process. Elected officials are influenced to act contrary to their obligations of office by the prospect of financial gain to themselves or infusions of money into their campaigns. The hallmark of corruption is the financial *quid pro quo:* dollars for political favors. But here the conduct proscribed is not contributions to the candidate, but independent expenditures in support of the candidate. The amounts given to the PACs are overwhelmingly small contributions, well under the $1,000 limit on contributions upheld in *Buckley*, and the contributions are by definition not coordinated with the campaign of the candidate. The Court concluded in *Buckley* that there was a fundamental constitutional difference between money spent to advertise one's views independently of the candidate's campaign and money contributed to the candidate to be spent on his campaign.

We think the same conclusion must follow here. It is contended that, because the PACs may by the breadth of their organizations spend larger amounts than the individuals in *Buckley*, the potential for corruption is greater. But precisely what the "corruption" may consist of we are never told with assurance. The fact that candidates and elected officials may alter or reaffirm their own positions on issues in response to political messages paid for by the PACs can hardly be called corruption, for one of the essential features of democracy is the presentation to the electorate of varying points of view. It is of course hypothetically possible here, as in the case of the independent expenditures forbidden in *Buckley*, that candidates may take notice of and reward those responsible for PAC expenditures by giving official favors to the latter in exchange for the supporting messages. But here, as in *Buckley*, the absence of prearrangement and coordination undermines the value of the expenditure to the candidate, and thereby alleviates the danger that expenditures will be given as a *quid pro quo* for improper commitments from the candidate. On this record, such an exchange of political favors for uncoordinated expenditures remains a hypothetical possibility and nothing more.

Finally, the FEC urges us to uphold section 9012(f) as a prophylactic measure deemed necessary by Congress, which has far more expertise than the Judiciary in campaign finance and corrupting influences. In *FEC v. National Right to Work Committee*, 459 U.S., at 210, 103 S.Ct., at 561, we stated:

While (2 U.S.C.) section 441b restricts the solicitation of corporations and labor unions without great financial resources, as well as those more fortunately situated, we accept Congress' judgment that it is the potential for such influence that demands regulation. Nor will we second-guess a legislative determination as to the need for prophylactic measures where corruption is the evil feared.

Here, however, the groups and associations in question, designed expressly to participate in political debate, are quite different from the traditional corporations organized for economic gain. In *NRWC* we rightly concluded that Congress might include, along with labor unions and corporations traditionally prohibited from making contributions to political candidates, membership corporations, though contributions by the latter might not exhibit all of the evil that contributions by traditional economically organized corporations exhibit. But this proper deference to a congressional determination of the need for a prophylactic rule where the evil of potential corruption had long been recognized does not suffice to establish the validity of section 9012(f), which indiscriminately lumps with corporations any "committee, association or organization." Indeed, the FEC in its briefs to this Court does not even make an effort to defend the statute under a construction limited in reach to corporations.

While in *NRWC* we held that the compelling governmental interest in preventing corruption supported the restriction of the influence of political war chests funneled through the corporate form, in the present case we do not believe that a similar finding is supportable: when the First Amendment is involved, our standard of review is "rigorous," *Buckley v. Valeo*, 424 U.S., at 29, 96 S.Ct., at 639, and the effort to link either corruption or the appearance of corruption to independent expenditures by PACs, whether large or small, simply does not pass this standard of review. Even assuming that Congress could fairly conclude that large-scale PACs have a sufficient tendency to corrupt, the overbreadth of section 9012(f) in this case is so great that the section may not be upheld. We are not quibbling over finetuning of prophylactic limitations, but are concerned about wholesale restriction of clearly protected conduct.

The judgment of the District Court is affirmed as to the constitutionality of section 9012(f), but is reversed on the issue of the Democrats' standing, with instructions to dismiss their complaint for lack of standing.

It is so ordered.

Questions and Problems

1. A Virginia statute declared it unprofessional conduct for a licensed pharmacist to advertise the prices of prescription drugs. Thus, a pharmacist who wished to communicate prices to the consuming public, that is, "I will sell you the X prescription drug at the Y price," would be subject to prosecution for violating the statute. The Virginia State Board of Pharmacists contended that the advertisement of prescription drugs is outside the protection of the First Amendment because it is "commercial speech." Do you agree? (*Virginia State Board of Pharmacists v. Virginia Citizens Consumer Council*, 425 U.S. 748, 1976.)

2. As the head of a cable television company you have learned that the Federal Communications Commission (FCC) proposes to make rules that will impose what you feel is an undue burden on your individual business and on the industry in general. Based on your study of Chapters 6 and 7, what steps would you take to protect your interests? Or are you powerless to make a meaningful contribution that will influence the FCC's ultimate decision? (*FCC v. Midwest Video Corp.*, 440 U.S. 689, 1979.)

3. As a registered lobbyist for a large "*Fortune* 500" company, discuss in some detail the role you would play in Washington, D.C. In what ways can you be helpful to legislators who may agree or disagree with your company's position on pending legislation?

4. As a freshman senator from a Midwestern state, concerned about lobbying abuses, rewrite sections 266 and 267 of the Federal Regulation of Lobbying Act to impose more control over lobbyists and lobbying.

5. The initial goal of the Business Roundtable in 1972 was to match or neutralize the lobbying power of the Labor Federation. In accomplishing its goal, has it become too powerful? Does management now have more influence in Washington than do the various labor organizations? Does the chief executive officer of a large corporation have more ready access to the government decision maker than does the president of a large labor union? Discuss the implications of the decline of labor's influence in Washington.

6. Bar associations, at both national and state levels, have for many years regulated the legal profession and prohibited advertising by lawyers. In 1977, two Arizona lawyers advertised their fees for certain legal services and were suspended from the Arizona bar. Is the Arizona State Bar's prohibition of advertising a permissible re-

striction on commercial speech? On what grounds might the two lawyers appeal their suspension? (*Bates v. State Bar*, 433 U.S. 350, 1977.)

7. Insurance industry advocacy ads, objected to by trial lawyers as indicated in the text, are to the effect that the increasing number of jury awards in excess of $1 million (forty-three such awards in 1976) represents an unhealthy trend. The ads further exhort the public to speak out against high awards and to let legislators know that insurance-related jury awards must be kept within reasonable boundaries. Are such ad campaigns a legitimate exercise of free speech, or are they in fact an unlawful effort to tamper with the jury system?

8. There are nearly 2,000 political action committees in existence. Candidates for Congress increasingly look to these special-interest groups for campaign financing. Does this indicate that a goal of the campaign reform law (FECA) to limit the appearance of influence of special interests in the political process is not being met? Has the law, in reality, had the opposite effect?

C·H·A·P·T·E·R 8

BUSINESS LAW—SELECTED TOPICS

Many areas of law and legal regulation are tailored exclusively to fit the business world and its problems. The remainder of this text, for the most part, is devoted to discussion and analysis of those areas of regulation. The bulk of Part II, for example, covers our antitrust laws and the broad subject of labor law. And Part III is largely devoted to the areas of consumer protection and environmental protection.

Before turning to those business-focused laws and the regulatory agencies that often implement them, however, it is essential that mention be made of a number of broader (and more traditional) fields of law that also have application to some kinds of business activities. Thus, when one considers the legal environment of business—that is, the entire "seamless web of the law" within which all businesses must operate—several of these broad fields must, at least, be surveyed. This is true not only because of their real impact upon the business world but, additionally, because many of their principles are the basis upon which the somewhat narrower, regulatory fields of law are built. For example, some acquaintanceship with elementary principles of *contract law* is necessary for a full appreciation of the antitrust laws, and the warranty provisions of *sales law* are the "jumping off" point for many of the consumer protection and product liability rules.

In this chapter and the one that follows, then, we will survey a number of traditional bodies of law which have a particularly close relationship to the business world and which collectively make up the bulk of law referred to as "business law" or "commercial law." This chapter covers the subjects of *contracts*, *sales*, *and torts*, and the next chapter surveys the subjects of *agency*, *partnerships*, and *corporations*.[1]

Contracts

A **contract** is a special kind of agreement—one that the law will enforce in the event of a breach by one of the contracting parties. Contract law is obviously important to both individuals and business firms because of its all-pervasive nature. When a person simply buys a newspaper, leaves a car at a parking lot, or purchases a ticket to an athletic event, he or she has entered into a contract of some sort. When someone borrows money, or has a painter paint a house, or insures a car, a contract has again most certainly been made—a somewhat more complex one than in the prior situations. And retailers (whether an individual running a corner store or a multimillion-dollar corporation) make contracts of an infinite variety—to buy or lease office space and equipment, to employ managers and salespersons, and to buy the goods that stock their shelves. Manufacturers, wholesalers, and financial institutions and other companies in the service industries must obviously make many of the same kinds of contracts. Even the formation of a partnership requires some kind of contract between the partners, and the formation of a corporation requires the making of a contract (using the term broadly) between the incorporators and the state.

Types of Contracts

Virtually all contracts may be classified as being either bilateral or unilateral in nature. **Bilateral contracts**, by far the most common in the business world, consist of the mutual *exchange of promises* between the parties, the actual performance of which promises is to occur at some later time. Thus when a manufacturer enters into an agreement in May with a supplier, calling for the supplier to deliver 1,000 steel wheels during September and for the manufacturer to pay upon delivery, a bilateral contract has come into existence in May. In contrast, a **unilateral contract** is formed only when one person makes an offer that is phrased in such a way as to indicate that it can be accepted only by the *performance of a specified act* (and where the specified act is subsequently performed). An example of such an offer would be the promise by a TV station to pay $5,000 to the first person who brings to its executive offices any piece of a fallen U.S. satellite. This offer can be accepted only by the actual physical production of a portion of the designated satellite; a promise by a person listening to the station that he or she will bring in the item later does not, therefore, result in the formation of a contract.

---

[1]Throughout these chapters, it must be borne in mind that space limitations permit consideration of only the basic principles of each subject.

"I'm sorry, Mr. Cheever, but there's absolutely nothing in your warranty about the Howler turning into a pumpkin."

A party to an express written contract should always read it carefully before signing.

Contracts may also be classified as being either express or implied. If the intentions of the parties are stated fully and in explicit terms (usually in writing), they constitute an **express contract**. The typical real estate lease and construction contract normally falls within this category. On the other hand, if the agreement between the parties (that is, the mutual intentions of the parties) has to be inferred in large part from their conduct and from the circumstances in which the agreement took place, the agreement is an **implied contract**. It is reasonable to infer, for example, that a person who is getting his hair cut in a barbershop actually desires the service and, by receiving the haircut, is impliedly promising to pay a reasonable price for it.[2]

[2] In exceptional circumstances the law imposes a "quasi-contractual liability" upon a person or firm even though no true contract (one based on the intentions of the parties) was ever formed. To illustrate: A quantity of lumber belonging to X is mistakenly delivered to the Y Company, a furniture manufacturer. The Y Company, unaware of the error, subsequently uses the lumber in producing a run of coffee tables. In such a case the law requires the Y Company to pay X the "reasonable value" of the lumber, because a failure to do so would result in the Y Company being unjustly enriched by receiving the lumber free.

The following case raises the twin questions of whether an express contract was formed, and, if not, whether an implied contract ever came into existence.

Rockwell & Bond, Inc., v. Flying Dutchman
Court of Appeals of Michigan
253 N.W.2d 368 (1977)

In 1972 John VanAlstyne, president of the Flying Dutchman Restaurant Corporation, defendant, decided to remodel the interior of its restaurant building. He asked Swanson Associates, an architectural firm, to draw up plans for the job, dealing at all times with Hofland, an agent of Swanson. Preliminary drawings were prepared and the project was "put out for estimates."

Rockwell & Bond, plaintiff, submitted an estimate of $55,000 to $60,000 based on these drawings and was chosen as contractor for the job. Because the drawings were tentative in nature, the estimate excluded certain items. For example, it did not include mechanical and electrical costs (although VanAlstyne thought that it did). In any event, no written contract was ever drawn up between plaintiff and defendant covering the project.

Plaintiff began work in late April, using additional drawings that were prepared on a "day-to-day and week-to-week" basis to reflect the working decisions as they were made. VanAlstyne was present almost every day, and took an active role in the project. Hofland, representing the architect, was at the job site about three times a week. Numerous changes, revisions, and decisions were made as the work progressed.

When the work was almost completed, plaintiff billed defendant for $100,156 for labor and material. Defendant paid $54,337, but refused to pay more. Plaintiff then brought this action to recover damages for breach of contract. While the record of the trial proceedings was "complicated and confusing," the gist of defendant's defense was that an *express contract* had been formed, under which its obligation was a maximum of $60,000. Plaintiff denied this, contending instead that an *implied contract* for the larger sum had come into existence.

The trial court ruled that no express contract existed, apparently on the ground that the drawings and estimate were too vague to constitute such a contract. It further ruled that an implied contract in the amount of $100,156 *did* exist, and it awarded plaintiff damages of $45,819—the balance of the contract price. Defendant appealed. (The Supreme Court of Michigan, in that part of its decision appearing below, explains why both of the rulings of the trial court were correct.)

Gillis, Judge:

. . . John Rockwell, president of plaintiff corporation, testified that it was his understanding that payments would be made on a "time and materials" basis [as distinguished from defendant's contention that a "fixed sum" contract was made]. He also stated that his company would never have given a firm estimate on drawings as incomplete as the ones initially submitted to him. . . . The types of materials and fixtures to be installed were determined on a daily basis as new drawings were prepared. . . . Defendant's own expert stated that any estimate based on the preliminary drawings would actually be a "guesstimate" because the materials used would greatly determine the cost. . . . The trial judge [thus correctly found that there was] no express agreement between the parties as to the price terms of the construction contract. . . . [The court then turned to the implied contract question.]

A contract implied in fact has been defined as one that "arises under circumstances which, according to the ordinary course of dealing and common understanding of men, show a mutual intention to contract. A contract is implied in fact where the intention as to it is not manifested by direct or explicit words between the parties, but is to be gathered by implication or proper deduction from the conduct of the parties, language used, or things done by them, or other pertinent circumstances attending the transaction. The existence of an implied contract, of necessity turning on inferences drawn from given circumstances, usually involves a question of fact, unless no essential facts are in dispute." *Erickson v. Goodell Oil Co., Inc.*, 180 N.W.2d 798 (1970). . . .

[The trial judge] analyzed the conduct of the parties, including . . . VanAlstyne's constant presence at the job site and the need to make day-to-day determinations of desired materials due to the absence of necessary specifications in the initial drawings submitted to plaintiff, [and concluded that an implied contract had been formed, obligating defendant to pay] on a "time and materials" basis. We find no mistake in his conclusion, and ample support in the evidence. . . .

[While the judgment of the trial court was thus affirmed, in essence, the case was remanded to it for the purpose of making further "factual determinations" as to the exact extent of the work that yet remained to be done.]

Elements of a Contract

Because contract law is, like torts, essentially common-law in nature, it is the courts who have spelled out, on a case-by-case basis over the years, the minimum qualities that an agreement must possess in order to constitute a contract. The elements normally required are an *agreement*, *consideration*, *competent parties*, and a *lawful objective*. Subject to exceptions we will note later, contracts need not be in writing; that is, oral contracts are generally enforceable if their terms can be proven in court.

The Agreement: An agreement requires an **offer** followed by an **acceptance.** In order for a particular proposal to constitute a legal offer, it must be reasonably definite as to what the other party is to do, and it must manifest a genuine intent to contract. Proposals that do not meet these requirements are called mere **preliminary negotiations**, the acceptance of which does not result in the formation of a contract. Suppose, for example, that X in a letter proposes to employ Y as a manager of his business for which Y would receive at the end of the first year a "fair share of the profits," and that Y sends back a letter of acceptance. In this case X's proposal is too vague to be an offer, and thus Y's "acceptance" does not result in the formation of a contract. Similarly, a statement that "I am hoping to sell my car for $2,000" fails to constitute an offer because the language does not manifest a genuine intent to contract. An expression of one's hope, or wishes, is not the legal equivalent of a letter by a car owner to a prospective buyer in which it is said "I will sell you my car for $2,000 cash." Similarly, advertisements are generally considered to be preliminary negotiations only, even if they contain a specific price for the advertised product. Thus in most instances a request by an advertiser's customer that the goods be sold to him or her at the advertised price is *not an acceptance* of an offer, but is, instead, an *offer to purchase* the goods. (While the advertiser thus normally has the right under contract law to accept or reject the offer to purchase, a rejection may constitute a violation of the state's deceptive trade practices statute, thereby subjecting the advertiser to tort liability under such act.)

Once an offer has been communicated to the offeree, it is normally terminated only by revocation, by rejection, or by "lapse of time" (the passage of an unreasonable length of time). Once any of these events has occurred, the offeree's power of acceptance has died.

A revocation is a withdrawal of the offer by the offeror. Thus if an offeree receives either a written or oral message from the offeror to the effect that the offer is no longer open, any attempted acceptance thereafter is ineffective. Normally, an offer may be revoked by the offeror at any time prior to an acceptance—even if the offeror had originally promised to keep the offer open for a stated period of time. Thus if A makes an offer to B on June 1, assuring B that he has ten days in which to accept, a revocation by telephone by A to B on June 3 terminates the offer. The major exception to this rule is where an "option contract" is entered into, which usually occurs only when the offeree pays the offeror a sum of money in return for the offeror's promise to keep the offer open. Thus, in the above example, if B had paid A $10 on June 1 in return for A's assurance that the offer would remain open, A's attempted revocation on June 3 would be ineffective.

A rejection occurs when the offeree notifies the offeror that he or she does not intend to accept the offer. A rejection has no effect until it has been legally communicated to the offeror. Thus if an offeree mails a letter of rejection but changes his mind and accepts the offer by telephone, at which time the rejection is still in the mails, the acceptance is valid. The usual rejection is a flat "no," or any words to that effect. (One form of rejection, the counteroffer, is discussed below in connection with the acceptance.)

With the exception of offers that contain fixed deadlines by which an acceptance must occur, offers remain open for a "reasonable" period of time. Once that time has passed without an acceptance, the offer lapses. In any case in which the offeror claims that the acceptance was not made within a reasonable time, the question of reasonable time is ordinarily left to the jury and thus may vary widely from case to case, depending upon the different circumstances each case presents. For example, if the offer indicates that a "quick reply" must be made, the offer may lapse after only a period of a few

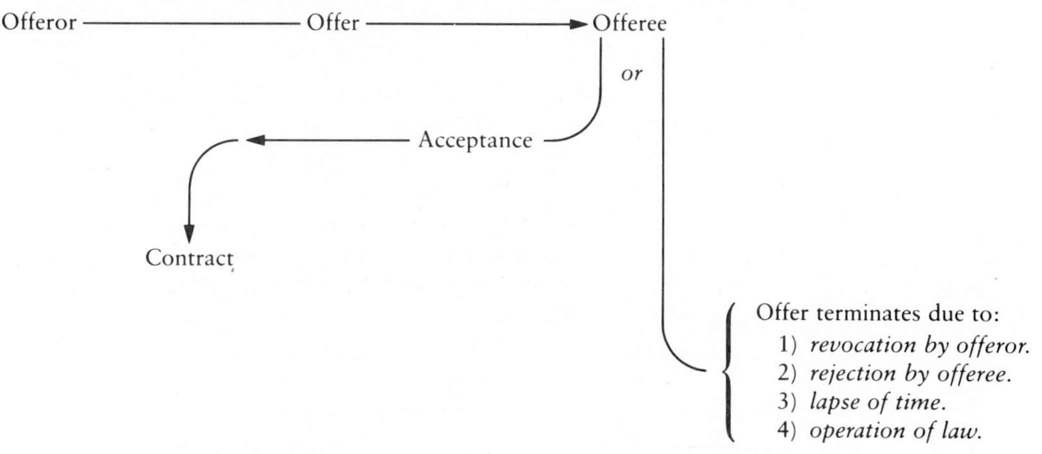

Figure 8.1 Methods of Terminating an Offer

days. In other circumstances, where the offeror or past dealings between the parties have indicated that the offeree may reasonably expect to have a substantial time to think the offer over, an offer may not lapse for weeks or even months. An offer may also be revoked by "operation of law," as when either party dies or is declared insane. In such instances the offer is revoked automatically upon the occurrence of the event. Thus if X makes an offer to Y on August 1 and X dies on August 2, a mailed acceptance by Y on August 3 is ineffective even if Y is not aware of X's death. (Figure 8.1 summarizes the ways an offer may be terminated.)

Insofar as the *acceptance* is concerned, the basic requirements are that it be both unequivocal and unconditional. Thus replies by the offeree that "your offer is the best I have received" or "I shall give your order prompt attention" do not constitute an acceptance. (And silence—a failure by the offeree to reply to the offer—is almost never construed by the courts to be an acceptance, even where the offeror states that "I will conclude we have a contract if I do not hear from you soon.")

An "acceptance" by the offeree that contains a term in conflict with a term of the offer, or which adds a new condition, is a *counteroffer* rather than an acceptance. Because a counteroffer is one form of rejection, once it is made the offeror's original offer is terminated forever. To illustrate: the X Company offers certain industrial supplies to the Y Company for $15,000, and the Y Company responds by saying it will pay only $13,000. If the X Company refuses the lower price and the Y Company then replies that it is accepting the $15,000 offer, there is no contract at this point. This concept is illustrated in Figure 8.2.

If a valid acceptance is made, and if the parties are dealing face-to-face or by telephone, the acceptance is effective immediately. If, however, the parties are negotiating by mail or by telegram, the usual rule is that the acceptance takes effect *upon dispatch* if the offeree has selected a "reasonable means of

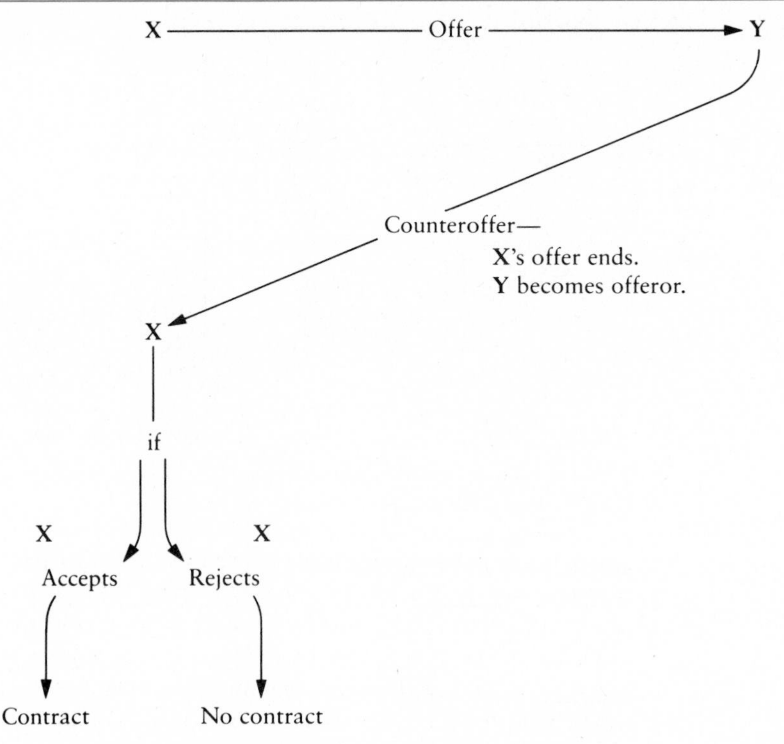

Figure 8.2 Legal Ramifications of the Counteroffer

communication" in replying. Thus if the offeree uses the same means of communication as that used by the offeror, or some other means that is commonly used in such situations, the acceptance is effective when sent. Example: A makes an offer by mail to B, who mails a letter of acceptance at noon of the day the offer is received. If A should call B later that same day to say that the offer is revoked, the attempted revocation is invalid because a contract was formed at noon.

The often-cited case below presents a typical question in the offer and acceptance area.

Richards v. Flowers et al.
District Court of Appeal, California
14 Cal. Reptr. 228 (1961)

Mrs. Richards, plaintiff, wrote defendant Flowers on January 15, 1959, as follows: "We would be interested in buying your lot on Gravatt Drive in Oakland, California, if we can deal with you directly and not run through a realtor. If you are interested, please advise us by return mail the cash price you would expect to receive."

On January 19, 1959, Flowers replied: "Thank you for your inquiry regarding my lot on Gravatt Drive. As long as your offer would be in cash I see no rea-

son why we could not deal directly on this matter. . . . Considering what I paid for the lot, and the taxes which I have paid I expect to receive $4,500 for this property. Please let me know what you decide."

On January 25, 1959, Mrs. Richards sent the following telegram to Flowers: "Have agreed to buy your lot on your terms will handle transactions through local title company who will contact you greatly appreciate your sending us a copy of the contour map you referred to in your letter as we are desirous of building at once. . . ."

On February 5, 1959, Flowers entered into an agreement to sell the property to a third party, Mr. and Mrs. Sutton. Mrs. Richards, after learning of the Sutton transaction, called upon defendant to deliver his deed to her, claiming the above correspondence constituted a contract between him and her. Flowers refused to do so, denying that his letter of January 19 constituted an offer to sell, whereupon Mr. and Mrs. Richards commenced action, asking for specific performance of the alleged contract. (The Suttons intervened in this action to protect their interest by supporting Flowers's contention that a contract was not formed between him and plaintiffs.)

The trial court ruled that defendant's letter of January 19 did constitute an offer to sell, but it further ruled that plaintiff's telegram of January 25 was not a valid acceptance under a particular California statute. Accordingly, the court entered judgment for defendant and the Richards appealed. (*Note*: the higher court agreed with the lower court that a contract had not been formed, but on a different ground: namely, that defendant's letter of January 19 was *not an offer*. The higher court's reasoning is set forth below.)

Shoemaker, Justice:

. . . Under the factual situation in the instant case, the interpretation of the series of communications between the parties is a matter of law and an appellate court is not bound by the trial court's determination. Respondent Flowers argues that the letter of January 19th merely invited an offer from appellants for the purchase of the property and that under no reasonable interpretation can this letter be construed as an offer. We agree with the respondent. Careful consideration of the letter does not convince us that the language therein used can reasonably be interpreted as a definite offer to sell the property to appellants. As pointed out in *Restatement of the Law, Contracts*, section 25, comment a.: "It is often difficult to draw an exact line between offers and negotiations preliminary thereto. It is common for one who wishes to make a bargain to try to induce the other party to the intended transaction to make the definite offer, he himself suggesting with more or less definiteness the nature of the contract he is willing to enter into. . . ." Under this approach, our letter seems rather clearly to fall within the category of mere preliminary negotiations. Particularly is this true in view of the fact that the letter was written directly in response to appellants' letter inquiring if they could deal directly with respondent and requesting him to suggest a sum at which he might be willing to sell. From the record, we do not accept the argument that respondent Flowers made a binding offer to sell the property merely because he chose to answer certain inquiries by the appellants.

Further, the letter appears to us inconsistent with any intent on his part to make an offer to sell. In response to appellants' question, respondent stated that he would be willing to deal directly with them rather than through a realtor as long as their "offer would be in cash." We take this language to indicate that respondent anticipated a *future offer* from appellants but was making no offer himself. [Emphasis added.]

Appellants refer to the phrase that he would "expect to receive" $4,500 and contend this constitutes an offer to sell to them at this price. However, respondent was only expressing an indication of the lowest price which he was presently willing to consider. Particularly is this true inasmuch as respondent wrote only in response to an inquiry in which this wording was used. We conclude that respondent by his communication confined himself to answering the inquiries raised by appellants, but did not extend himself further and did not make an express offer to sell the property. We have before us a case involving a mere quotation of price and not an offer to sell at that price. The cause, therefore, comes within the rule announced in such authorities as *Nebraska Seed Co. v. Harsh*, 1915, 152 N.W.310, wherein the seller had written the buyer, enclosing a sample of millet seed and saying, "I want $2.25 per cwt. for this seed f.o.b. Lowell." The buyer telegraphed his acceptance. The court, in reversing a judgment for plaintiff buyer, stated: "In our opinion the letter of defendant cannot be fairly construed into an offer to sell to the plaintiff. After describing the seed, the writer says, 'I want $2.25 per cwt. for this seed f.o.b. Lowell.' He does not say, 'I offer to sell to you.' The language used is general, . . . and is not an offer by which he may be bound, if accepted, by any or all of the persons addressed"; and *Owen v. Tunison*, 1932, 158 A. 926, wherein the buyer had written the seller inquiring whether he would be willing to sell certain store property for $6,000. The seller replied: "Because of improvements which have been added and an expenditure of several thousand dollars it would not be possible for me to sell it unless I was to receive $16,000.00 cash. . . ." The court, in holding that the seller's reply did not constitute an offer, stated: "Defendant's letter . . . may have been written with the intent to open negotiations that might lead to a sale. It was not a proposal to sell." It would thus seem clear that respondent's quotation of the price which he would "expect to receive" cannot be viewed as an offer capable of acceptance. . . .

Since there was never an offer, hence never a contract between respondent Flowers and appellants, the judgment must be affirmed, and it becomes unnecessary to determine whether appellant's purported acceptance complied with the statute of frauds or whether appellants failed to qualify for specific performance in any other regard.

Judgment affirmed.

★★★

Consideration: Once an offer and an acceptance occur, the second requirement of a contract—an elusive thing called **consideration**—is ordinarily present. We may initially define consideration as that element which supports a promise, thereby causing the promise to be enforceable. For example, if the A Company and the B Company enter into a contract under the terms of which the A Company is to deliver 5,000 widgets to the B Company six months later, in return for which the B Company agrees to pay $10,000 upon delivery, consideration is present on both parties' parts, and both parties are, therefore, bound by the contract. Here the promise of the A Company to deliver the goods is supported by the B Company's promise to pay, and the B Company's promise to pay is supported by the promise of the A Company to deliver.

Consideration may, however, be lacking in some situations. To illustrate: X, a longtime employee of the Y Company, decides to retire and, on his last day of work, is told by the president that the company will pay him $100 a month thereafter as long as he lives. X promptly replies, "I accept." If the Y Company stops making payments after three months, at which time X brings action to make the company continue the payments, X will lose the case. Because X, the promisee, gave nothing of value in return for the company's promise, consideration was lacking on his part and the company's promise is thus unenforceable.

A primary purpose of the consideration requirement is to prevent the exploitation of one contracting party by the other. This can be illustrated by the following example. In October, S contracts to sell a piece of land to B for $50,000, with the closing—the payment of the money by B and the delivery of a deed by S—to occur the following December 1st. In November General Motors announces that an automobile assembly plant will be built in the area, as a result of which S finds that the value of the land has increased greatly. When S complains about the price he is getting, and threatens not to go through with the deal, B—who desperately needs the property—promises to pay $75,000 for it. In such a case, B is liable to S for only $50,000. He is not liable on his promise to pay the $75,000 because that promise was unsupported by consideration on the part of S.

In any suit in which a promisor is contending that his or her promise is not enforceable because it was not supported by consideration, the traditional test applied by the courts has been to determine whether or not the promisee, under the agreement, incurred a detriment—that is, promised to perform an act, or actually performed an act, which he or she was not otherwise legally obligated to perform. (Many courts today apply a somewhat broader test, the "benefit-detriment" test, under which consideration exists if the promisor receives a benefit *or* the promisee incurs a detriment. This is little different, in most cases, from the detriment test, because the promisor rarely receives a benefit without the promisee incurring a detriment. Thus the detriment concept continues to be the dominant one, the application of which is illustrated by the following examples.)

Case 1: A contracts to buy a farm from B for $450,000. Before the closing (the date that the deed is to be delivered and the money paid), B writes to A that "because of our good business relationship over the years, I am reducing the price to $425,000." Because A has not given up a legal right (has incurred no detriment) in exchange for B's promise to reduce the price, A cannot legally hold B to the lower price.

Case 2: X contracts to build an addition to Y's home for $24,000. When the work is half completed, X complains about his high costs and threatens to quit the job. Thereupon Y promises that he will pay X $2,000 additional if X will complete the project. When X finishes the job, Y refuses to pay more than the $24,000 originally agreed upon. If X should sue Y to recover the additional $2,000, in most instances X's action will be dismissed. The usual view in such a case is that Y's promise to pay the additional money is unenforceable because X's completion of the work did not constitute consideration: X, by completing the job, *did not waive a legal right* because he already was legally bound under the initial contract to complete the project. For this reason the general rule has evolved that the mere performance of a "pre-existing obligation" by the promisee does not constitute consideration.[3] By contrast, in the case above, if Y makes the promise to pay the extra $2,000 in exchange for X's promise to put a better grade of roof on the addition than was called for under the original contract, there is now consideration on X's part and Y's promise is binding.

The case below presents a situation in which the court found both a benefit to the promisor and a detriment to the promisee.

Lampley v. Celebrity Homes, Inc.
Colorado Court of Appeals, Division II
594 P.2d 605 (1979)

Linda Lampley, plaintiff, began work at Celebrity Homes in Denver in May of 1975. On July 29 of that year Celebrity announced the initiation of a profit-sharing plan. Under that plan all employees were to receive bonuses if a certain "profit goal" was reached for the 1975 fiscal year—April 1, 1975, to March 31, 1976. (Linda was working under an at-will agreement—that is, both she and Celebrity could terminate the relationship at any time.)

Plaintiff's employment was terminated in January of 1976. At the end of March, 1976, the company announced that the profit goal had been reached, and it made its first distribution of profits in May, 1976. When plaintiff was excluded from this distribution, she brought this suit for the share allegedly due her.

In the trial court Celebrity argued that its promise to pay the bonus was a mere "gratuity" on its part, on the ground that there was no consideration on the employee's part to support its promise. The trial court rejected this contention and entered judgment for plaintiff. Celebrity appealed.

[3] These illustrations of general principles should be fleshed out by two broad observations: (a) in the "real world," *most* reputable individuals and business firms routinely live up to their promises, even those that are not supported by consideration; and (b) some states have adopted statutes that—in narrow circumstances—reject the common-law rules. For example, in some states a written "modification contract" is binding even if consideration is lacking. In such a state, if Y's promise in this case had been in writing, he would be liable despite the absence of consideration on X's part.

Kelly, Judge:

. . . In further support of its claim that the plan is not a binding contract, Celebrity contends that there was no consideration [given by plaintiff]. Benefit to the promisor or detriment to the promisee, however slight, can constitute consideration. The plan states as its objective:

Our goal is . . . to produce added employee benefits gained through a higher quality of operation. Through teamwork in our day-to-day operation, we can achieve not only higher levels of profits, but also better performance for our customers, a better quality in design of products, fair treatment of customers, subcontractors, and suppliers.

This language indicates that the plan was established as an inducement to Celebrity's employees to remain in its employ and to perform more efficient and faithful service. Such result would be of obvious benefit to Celebrity, and thus consideration was present. . . . [The court also implicitly found a detriment on the part of the promisee, as follows:]

Lampley, who was employed for an indefinite term, was not obligated to remain until 1976, and it can be inferred from the evidence in the record that she was induced to do so, in part at least, by the profit-sharing offer made to her by Celebrity. Thus, this case can be distinguished from [those] which hold that there can be no recovery where the company gets no more service as a result of such a promise than it would if no such promise had been made. The memorandum of the profit-sharing plan was an offer to add additional terms to the original employment contract, and Lampley's continued employment with Celebrity [until January 1976] was an acceptance of the offer and the consideration for the contract.

Judgment affirmed.

★★★

In exceptional circumstances a promise is binding upon the promisor even though there is no consideration on the part of the promisee. The most common example occurs in circumstances in which the doctrine *of promissory estoppel* is applied by the courts. Under that principle, a promisor is liable on his or her promise—even though there is no consideration given by the promisee—if (1) the promisor knows or should know that the promise alone is likely to induce a specific action on the part of the promisee; (2) that the promisee, after the promise is made, does take the expected action; and (3) that such action is definite and substantial in nature. For example: over a long period of time a grandfather (G) and his granddaughter (D) had planned in detail a trip she was hoping to make to Europe after her graduation from high school. In April of D's senior year in high school her family suffered a financial loss that eliminated all of their nonessential activities. In May, G—aware of the circumstances—wrote a letter to D promising to make her a gift of $7,500 by the end of the following October, and D, after graduating, spent two months in Europe. If G does not pay the $7,500 voluntarily in October, a suit by D against him would be successful because all of the promissory estoppel elements are present.

Competent Parties: The great majority of contracting parties are fully "competent." This means that, in the eyes of the law, they have the full capacity (the legal ability) to contract. When both contracting parties are competent, the contract is termed "valid" and both parties are bound by it—assuming, of course, that the other elements of a contract are also present. But some contracts are made in which one of the parties is "incompetent," meaning that he or she either possesses limited capacity to contract or is totally lacking in contractual capacity. The contract of a person possessing *partial* capacity is "voidable" (one which the incompetent party may subsequently set aside if he or she wishes), while the contract of a person with *no* capacity is "void" (one which, in the eyes of the law, never existed at all).

The most common voidable contracts are those made by **minors**, who are defined by most state statutes as natural persons under the age of eighteen. Thus, while minors may make contracts, they also generally possess the legal right to **disaffirm** (cancel) any contracts as long as they do so while still minors, or within a reasonable time after they become eighteen. The right to disaffirm is entirely one sided in nature, for the other party to the contract does not possess a similar right.

The rule, as applied to purchases of "non-necessities of life," can be illustrated as follows. M, a seventeen-year-old, purchases a used car from a dealer for $3,000 cash. A few months later, while still a minor, M returns the car and demands the return of his money. Assuming that M did not misrepresent himself as an adult at the time of contracting, M in most states is entitled to recover the full $3,000—even if the car had depreciated markedly or even been badly damaged in an accident while in his possession.[4] At an early time the minor had to show that the contract was an unfair one, or "not beneficial" to him, in order to disaffirm; today, however, such a showing is not required.

In contracts calling for the purchase of "necessities of life," such as a reasonable amount of food and clothing, the rule is that the disaffirming minor is liable to the other party for the "reasonable value" of the article furnished to him and actually used by him. Thus, in the case above, if the court ruled the car to be a necessity (as is sometimes the case where the minor is using it to support himself or herself), the car dealer is permitted to retain the reasonable value of the use of the car while it was in M's possession—e.g., $500—with only the balance of the $3,000—$2,500—being returned to the minor.

---

[4]In the case of age misrepresentation, some states flatly prohibit a disaffirmance, while others disallow disaffirmance unless the minor can show that a disaffirmance would not cause a loss to the other party.

Not all contracts can be disaffirmed on the basis of minority. For example, disaffirmance of marriage contracts and contracts of enlistment in the armed forces is not permitted on the ground of public policy, and most states have statutes prohibiting the disaffirmance of contracts made with banks and insurance companies.

Once a minor reaches the age of majority, he or she has the ability to **ratify** any disaffirmable contract made earlier. A ratification occurs when the former minor indicates to the other party, expressly or impliedly, the intent to be bound by the agreement. Thus, if a minor, after reaching the age of eighteen, promises orally or in writing that he or she will go through with the contract, an express ratification has taken place and the right to disaffirm is lost forever. Similarly, if a minor after reaching the age of eighteen continues to make monthly payments for goods purchased earlier, an implied ratification has occurred.

Another significant class of incompetent parties is intoxicated persons. In regard to contracts made by such persons, the general rule is that disaffirmance is allowed upon regaining sobriety only if the person seeking disaffirmance can show that he or she was so intoxicated as not to understand the nature of the purported agreement at the time it was made. Thus a question of fact is presented, because a lesser degree of intoxication is not grounds for disaffirmance.

Legality: The fourth element of a contract, a lawful purpose, is present only when the contract is in conformity with all applicable statutes and common-law rules. All states have statutes expressly prohibiting certain kinds of contracts, such as wagering agreements or the charging of interest above specified limits on loans. Contracts in violation of these statutes, being unlawful, are unenforceable. Similarly, contracts made by certain unlicensed persons, such as lawyers and real estate brokers who are required to be licensed by statute, are also generally illegal. In other instances a contract may also be illegal simply because it violates the "public policy" of that state, as defined by the state's supreme court on a case-by-case basis. Contracts that restrain trade unreasonably (such as an agreement by one company not to compete with another) and clauses in contracts which contain terms purporting to free a party from liability if he or she performs a service negligently (exculpatory clauses) are typical of those which are generally contrary to public policy and thus unenforceable on that ground.

While covenants (promises) not to compete are also generally disfavored by the law, they may be lawful when they are a subsidiary or auxilliary part of a larger agreement that is, itself, lawful. For example, a seller of a small retail business may, at the demand of the buyer, include in the sale agreement a promise that he or she (the seller) will not open a competing business within a specified area for a certain length of time following the sale. Such restraints are not contrary to public policy if they are not "excessive" or "unreasonable" under the circumstances; that is, if the restraints do not afford more than a reasonable protection to the buyer. Thus in the prior example, a promise by the seller not to operate a competing business within a one-mile radius of the store being sold for a period of six months following the sale is probably binding upon the seller.

Covenants not to compete are also common in employment contracts, under the terms of which the employee promises, upon termination of his or her employment, not to engage in (or work for) a competing business within a designated area for a specified period of time after such termination. Such covenants, like those in contracts under which businesses are being sold, are also lawful—i.e., binding upon the employee—if the restraints are not excessive under the circumstances. But, as the following case shows, covenants in employment contracts which cover broad geographical areas (or which extend over long periods of time) are often found to be contrary to public policy, and thus not binding upon the employee.

Slisz v. Munzenreider Corporation
Court of Appeals of Indiana, Fourth District
411 N.E.2d 709 (1980)

After graduating from Ball State University, Dan Slisz went to work at a Muncie, Indiana, store owned by the Munzenreider Corporation, a company that operated several retail furniture stores in Indiana and others throughout the U.S. After several promotions Slisz was made "managing partner" of United Freight Sales, Munzenreider's store in Bloomington, in 1975. At that time he signed an agreement with Munzenreider which contained, in addition to a compensation formula, two restrictive covenants.

Paragraph 11 provided essentially that as long as Slisz was an employee of the company he would not divulge to anyone, or use for his personal gain, any information or methods of operation acquired on the job, nor would he divulge names of past, present, or potential customers. Paragraph 12 read as follows:

The managing partner agrees that in the event of the termination of the partnership for any reason whatsoever, he will not for a period of two years from the date of such termination, then engage in or accept employment from or become affiliated with or connected with, directly or indirectly, or become interested in, directly or indirectly, in any way in any business *within the counties of Monroe, Brown, Morgan, Owen, Greene and Lawrence, Indiana,* similar or of a competive nature to *the business carried on by the partnership,* or any other city *or place wherein the partners operate a store or within thirty miles of said city where a store is maintained by the capital partners. . . . [Emphasis added.]*

Because the Bloomington store started losing money in 1978, Munzenreider moved it to a new location in that city, replaced Slisz as manager, and offered him a job with one of its stores in South Dakota. Slisz declined the offer, left his employment with Munzenreider, and opened up his own retail furniture business, Warehouse Furniture Sales, at the same location in Bloomington that was occupied by United Freight Sales prior to its move.

Munzenreider Corporation then brought this action asking for an injunction against Slisz restraining him from continued operation of his business. The trial court granted a two-year injunction, and he appealed.

Miller, Judge:

. . . In light of the broad language utilized in the instant agreement—which purported in part to prohibit involvement in *any* city where Munzenreider operated a store, in any business "*similar or of a competitive nature to*" that carried on by the partnership—combined with the fact it does not appear Slisz possessed any trade secrets, customer lists, or other special or confidential information regarding Munzenreider's operation, we conclude this restrictive language is void, and that the trial court's injunction must accordingly be reversed. [Emphasis added by the court.] . . .

Consideration of [this] appeal must begin from the general proposition that restraints on competition between an employer and his former employee, similar to that in this case involving a "managing partner," are not favored by the law, but will nevertheless be enforced where (1) the restraint is reasonably necessary to protect the employer's business; (2) it is not unreasonably restrictive of the employee; and (3) the covenant is not antagonistic to the general public interest.

[Because of the onerous effects such restraints have on employees, in applying the foregoing test] many courts have held an employer must demonstrate some "special facts" giving his former employee a unique competitive advantage or ability to harm the employer before such employer is entitled to the protection of a noncompetitive covenant. . . . Those special facts may include (but are not limited to) such things as trade secrets known by the employee, the employee's "unique" services, confidential information (such as customer lists) known to him, or the existence of a confidential relationship. At the same time, the rule is generally stated that the mere fact that an employee has acquired skill and efficiency in the performance of the work as a result of his employment does not suffice to warrant the enforcement of a covenant on his part not to compete.

[The court here noted the geographical breadth of the covenant, as follows:] The covenant encompasses not only the City of Bloomington and Monroe County and various counties adjoining it, but indeed every city and a 30-mile radius around it in which Munzenreider operates a store, and apparently without regard to whether such city is in Monroe County, the State of Indiana, or even the entire United States. It seems evident, as our courts have held, that so geographically broad a covenant may be reasonable *only in very unusual circumstances*, such as where "trade secrets" are involved. [Emphasis added.] . . .

There was no evidence to support the allegations of Munzenreider that Slisz utilized or even had access to any confidential or secret information. [Neither was there evidence that Slisz was aware of, or took with him, customer lists or information on customer requirements.] It does not appear any similar evidence involving possible harm to "good will" was presented. [The most that can be said is that a witness for Munzenreider] testified that he believed Slisz might benefit from "confused customers" responding to Munzenreider's ads by going to Slisz's store at the former Munzenreider location. . . . There was no showing that Slisz was actively soliciting Munzenreider customers by, for example, advertising his former association with the corporation's stores . . . .

Munzenreider cites *Welcome Wagon, Inc. v. Haschert*, 127 N.E.2d 103, 1955, which held there was a protectible interest in the employer (Welcome

Wagon) where its hostess, a woman . . . with a "personal following" and "extensive acquaintanceship" in her community, learned the novel and unique business methods of Welcome Wagon and then quit to establish her own similar operation in the same city, Kokomo, Indiana, using some of the same "sponsors." The special business methods included a national training program in New York . . . when she was instructed in Welcome Wagon's method of calling on brides, newlyweds and newcomers to the community. . . . We believe the situation in the instant case [does not resemble] the unusual facts of the Welcome Wagon case, since the evidence in the case at bar does not suggest Slisz possessed a particular following, unique skills, . . . or trade secrets. . . .

In short, it appears the agreement in question [merely tries to prevent Slisz from using the general skills he has acquired during his employment in the operation of any similar business in a broad geographical area. . . . We hold the covenant to be unreasonable and unenforceable. . . .

Judgment reversed.

★★★

Rescission of Contracts

In some circumstances a party to a contract may have it rescinded (set aside by a court) even if all of the basic contractual elements are present. Rescission is most commonly granted where *fraud* or *mistake of fact* is shown to exist. Essentially, fraud is the intentional misrepresentation of a fact by one person to another. If X, in selling his car to Y, tells Y that the mileage on the odometer is correct when in fact X knows that the car has been driven many miles more than the odometer shows, and if Y purchases the car believing X's statement to be true, Y is entitled to rescission if he is able to prove the above facts in court. (A statement of opinion or prediction is to be distinguished from a statement of fact, however; thus X is not guilty of fraud if he tells Y that "this is the cleanest '84 Celebrity in town," or that "used car prices absolutely won't be lower in the next six months," even if both statements prove to be false.) Once fraud is established, the innocent party usually has the choice of rescinding the contract—returning the car in the case above and recovering the purchase price—or keeping what he or she has received and recovering damages from the defrauding party.

Insofar as mistake in general is concerned, a party is not entitled to rescission simply because the contract proved to be unwise, unprofitable, or made on a mistaken assumption as to future events (for instance, that the economy was going to rebound in the coming year when in fact it does not). However, rescission *is* allowed in the case of mutual, or bilateral, *mistake of fact*—that is, when both parties are mistaken as to a material, existing fact at the time of contracting. For example: B purchases S's summer home on April 10. B later learns that, unknown to either party, the home was destroyed by fire on April 1. Since both parties entered into the contract under the mistaken assumption that the home actually existed at that time, B can have the contract set aside. A second situation where rescission is permitted arises in the case of unilateral mistake—where one party is mistaken as to a material fact, but the other party is not. In such a case, rescission is allowed only if the mistaken party can prove that the other party was or should have been aware of his or her mistake when the contract was made, and failed to correct the mistake.

Contracts in Writing

As a general rule, oral contracts are as enforceable as written ones if their terms can be established in court. However, all states have adopted a statute known as the "Statute of Frauds" which requires five major kinds of contracts to be in writing (or at least to be evidenced by a writing). The most important of these are (1) contracts calling for the sale of land or an interest therein; (2) contracts that cannot be performed within one year from the time they are made; and (3) contracts under which one party promises to pay the debt of another party. Thus oral contracts falling in any of these categories are usually unenforceable in court—although judicially-recognized exceptions in narrow circumstances have sometimes been made.

In the event that an oral contract in one of the above categories is entered into, followed by a written confirmation which is sent by one of the parties to the other, the contract is enforceable against the party sending the confirmation but not against the recipient.

Parol Evidence Rule: With limited exceptions, the parol evidence rule provides that once a written contract is entered into, neither party will thereafter be allowed to come into court and introduce parol (oral) evidence in an effort to show that there were other terms or conditions agreed upon in addition to, or different from, those of the writing. For this reason, it is extremely important that all terms and understandings be set forth whenever an agreement is reduced to writing.

Third Parties

As a general rule, contracts can be enforced only by the original contracting parties. *Beneficiaries* and *assignees*, however, are exceptions to the rule. A **beneficiary** is a person for whose benefit the contract was originally made. For example, if the A Company sells a truck to the B Company, with the B Company agreeing to pay the price of the truck to C (rather than to the A Company), C may maintain a court action to recover the price from the B Company in the event that it does not pay him voluntarily. An **assignee** is a person to whom contractual rights are assigned by one of the contracting parties after the contract has been made. To illustrate: the X Company contracts to remodel the kitchen in Y's home for $12,000, and the X Company thereafter assigns (transfers) the right to collect the $12,000 to a third

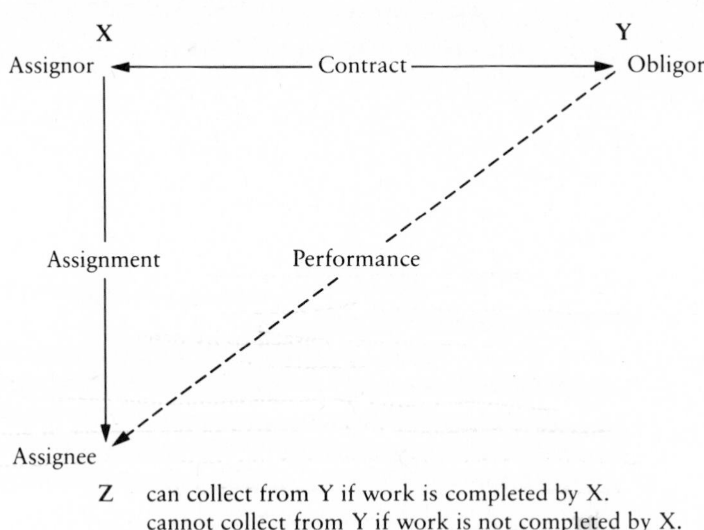

Figure 8.3 Assignment

party, Z. In this case Z, the assignee, is entitled to payment by Y, the obligor, after the X Company has completed the work. An assignee's rights are no better than the assignor's; thus in the above case if the X Company had walked off the job and never did complete it, Z could *not* recover from Y. An illustration appears in Figure 8.3

A party may assign his or her rights under a contract without the consent of the other party with two major exceptions: where the right that is attempted to be assigned is "personal" in nature, and where the terms of the contract require consent by the other party. In addition, state and federal statutes prohibit the assignment of limited types of rights in which cases, of course, assignment cannot occur even with the consent of the other party.

The following case presents an assignment problem in a modern business setting.

Schupach v. McDonald's System, Inc.
Supreme Court of Nebraska
264 N.W.2d 827 (1978)

McDonald's, defendant, is the corporation that grants all McDonald fast-food restaurant franchises. In 1959 defendant granted a franchise to a Mr. Copeland, giving him the right to own and operate McDonald's first store in the Omaha–Council Bluffs area. A few days later, in conformity with the negotiations leading up to the granting of the franchise, McDonald's sent a letter to Copeland giving him a "Right of First Refusal;" the right to be given first chance at owning any new stores that might be subsequently established in the area. In the next few years Copeland exercised this right and opened five addi-

tional stores in Omaha. In 1964 Copeland *sold and assigned all of his franchises* to Schupach, plaintiff, with McDonald's consent.

When McDonald's granted a franchise in the Omaha–Council Bluffs area in 1974 to a third party without first offering it to Schupach, he brought this action for damages resulting from establishment of the new franchise, claiming that the assignment of the franchises to him also included the right of first refusal.

A number of issues were raised in this litigation. Defendant contended, among other things, that the right it gave to Copeland was personal in nature, and thus was not transferable without its consent. Plaintiff alleged, on the other hand, that the right was not personal in nature, or, in the alternative, that its transfer was, in fact, agreed to by defendant.

On these issues the trial court ruled that the right was personal in nature. It also ruled, however, after analyzing voluminous correspondence between the parties, that defendant *had* consented to the transfer. It entered judgment for plaintiff, and defendant appealed. (Only that part of the higher court's opinion relating to these two issues appears below.)

White, Justice:

. . . McDonald's was founded in 1954 by Mr. Ray Kroc. Kroc licensed and later purchased the name McDonald's [and all other rights relating thereto] from two brothers named McDonald, who were operating a hamburger restaurant in San Bernardino, California. In 1955 Kroc embarked on a plan to create a nationwide standardized system of fast-food restaurants. . . .

At the trial, Kroc testified about the image he sought to create with McDonald's. . . . He wanted to create "an image people would have confidence in. An image of cleanliness. An image where the parents would be glad to have the children come and/or have them work there."

Kroc testified that careful selection of franchises was to be the key to success for McDonald's and the establishment of this image. . . . People were selected "who had a great deal of pride, and had an aptitude for serving the public, and had dedication."

Fred Turner, the current president of McDonald's, testified [in a similar vein]. . . . He stated that by 1957 it became apparent that McDonald's could only achieve its goal by careful selection of persons who would adhere to the company's high standards. He stated that an individual's managerial skills and abilities were a matter of prime importance in the selection process. . . .

Summarizing, the evidence is overwhelming, [and establishes the conclusion that] the Right of First Refusal was intended to be personal in nature, and was separately a grant independent of the terms of the franchise contract itself. [It also establishes the fact that] the grant depended upon the personal confidence that McDonald's placed in the grantee, and that to permit the assignability by the grantee without permission of McDonald's would serve to destroy the basic policy of control of the quality and confidence in performance in the event any new franchises were to be granted in the locality. . . .

[The court then reviewed the same correspondence which was examined by the trial court, and ruled that McDonald's had *not* given its permission to the transfer of the right. The judgment for plaintiff was therefore reversed.]

★★★

Discharge

Sooner or later all contractual obligations come to an end—that is, are "discharged." A party's obligations are most often discharged by (1) full performance on his or her part; (2) breach by the other party; or (3) the occurrence of conditions that excuse his or her performance.

The great majority of contracts are discharged by performance—both parties fully performing the acts which they have promised to do. In cases where one party claims to have performed, while the other party contends that the performance is not completely in conformity with the contract, the question arises as to the degree of performance that the law requires of the performing party. To illustrate: C, a contractor, contracts to build a home for O, owner, according to detailed plans and specifications. The contract calls for O to make partial payments as construction progresses, with the full price being $75,000. When C completes the job and requests the last payment of $7,500, O refuses to pay because of shortcomings in C's work. If C should sue O to recover the last payment, his success depends upon whether the *doctrine of substantial performance* is applicable. Under that doctrine, a promisor or performer is entitled to the contract price (minus damages, if any) if (1) his or her performance is "substantial"—very close to 100 percent, and (2) he or she acted in good faith—that is, the defects in the performance were not intentional. Thus, in the above illustration, if the breaches on C's part were merely the failure to install insulation on one part of an attic wall and the installation of 5″ drains instead of 6″ drains in the basement, C will probably recover most of the $7,500. On the other hand, if C neglected to install insulation in any of the downstairs walls, his or her breach is so significant that substantial performance has not occurred, and no recovery is allowed while the shortcoming remains uncorrected.

As might be expected, when one contracting party is guilty of a material breach of contract—one so significant that substantial performance has not occurred—the other party is freed of his or her contractual duties. Additionally, the non-breaching party is ordinarily entitled to recover damages to compensate him or her for loss that the breach has occasioned.

In some instances, contracting parties are legally excused from performing their obligations even in the absence of a breach of contract. This most often occurs where express conditions are written into the contract which either provide (1) that the parties need not perform unless and until a specified event occurs, or (2) that the parties are freed from the obligation to perform if a specified event occurs. Clauses in the first category are called "conditions precedent," and those in the second "conditions subsequent."

Thus the *failure* (non-occurrence) of a condition precedent excuses performance, and the *occurrence* of a condition subsequent has the same effect.

In limited circumstances courts will recognize implied conditions—that is, conditions recognized by the law even though they do not actually appear in the contract. Under the traditional view, for example, the courts held that, in a contract calling for the rendering of personal services, it was implied that the death or illness of the performing party would excuse performance; in a contract calling for the sale of property, it was implied that the destruction of the property (without fault on the part of the seller) prior to the time that possession was to be transferred would excuse performance; and in all contracts, a change of law making performance illegal would excuse performance. In these (and only these) situations, it was said that performance had become "impossible."

Today, the courts in an increasing number of states have substituted the "doctrine of commercial impracticability" for the traditional impossibility theory in cases where a party is contending that he or she is discharged by reason of the happening of some event subsequent to the time that the contract was made. Under this newer view, a number of subsequent events are recognized as grounds for the discharge of the parties *in addition to* the three events recognized under the impossibility doctrine. For example, a contracting party is discharged under the doctrine of commercial impracticability by the occurrence of such events as (1) an unforeseen destruction of a source of supply upon which the contracting party was depending for his or her performance; (2) a drastic increase in cost of performance caused by such unforeseen occurrences as war or local crop failure; and (3) any other contingency "the non-occurrence of which was a basic assumption upon which the contract was made."[5]

In the case below, the Supreme Court of Alaska first speaks of impossibility in the true sense. But, perhaps because of some uncertainty on this point, it reflected the tendency noted above by buttressing its decision with references to the doctrine of commercial impracticability.

Northern Corporation v. Chugach Electric Association
Supreme Court of Alaska
518 P.2d 76
(1974)

In August of 1966 the Northern Corporation, a contractor, entered into a contract with Chugach Electric Association. The contract called for Northern to install protective riprap on a dam owned by Chugach on Cooper Lake, Alaska, for $63,655. The job essentially involved the quarrying and transporting of large quantities of rock, and installing the rock on the upstream face of the dam.

The parties originally contemplated that the rock was to be drilled and shot at a designated quarry. However, when this rock was found to be unsuitable, the parties amended the contract in September so that Northern could use

[5] Section 2-615 of the Uniform Commercial Code.

alternative quarry sites, and the contract price for the job was increased by $42,000. Northern then selected a site that was at the opposite end of the lake, intending to transport the rock across the lake on the ice during the winter of 1966–1967. The contract apparently did not specify a means of transportation, but at the time of the contract amendment Chugach sent Northern a letter authorizing transportation across the lake. Work commenced in the new quarry in October, and all of the required rock was drilled and shot by the end of that month.

During the following winter Northern commenced hauling operations, but had to stop them because two of its vehicles went through the ice; a loader sank, and a tractor was recovered. Northern then told Chugach that the ice was too unsafe for the job, but Chugach and its engineering firm insisted that the job be performed. Nevertheless, in March of 1967 Northern ceased operations, apparently with Chugach's approval.

After a long period of negotiations, Chugach advised Northern in January of 1968 that it would hold Northern liable for damages for breach of contract unless all rock was hauled by April 1. In late January, when ice conditions appeared to be much more favorable than the previous year, Northern started its hauling operation again. However, in February two half-loaded trucks broke through the ice, resulting in the deaths of the drivers and loss of the trucks. Northern then advised Chugach that it considered the contract "terminated for impossibility of performance."

Northern then brought this action against Chugach, asking for (1) a ruling that the contract was impossible of performance, and (2) damages equal to the costs which it incurred in attempting to perform the contract. Chugach counterclaimed, contending that performance was not impossible, and that it was thus entitled to damages incurred between the date of completion specified in the amended contract and the date of its termination by Northern. The trial court discharged both parties on the ground of impossibility, and denied both parties' claims for damages. Both parties appealed.

In the Supreme Court of Alaska, four issues were raised. Only two of these are considered here.

Boochever, Justice:

. . . The issues on this appeal may be summarized as follows: . . .

1. Was the contract, as modified, impossible of performance?

2. If the modified contract was impossible of performance, is Northern entitled to reasonable costs in endeavoring to perform it? . . .

The focal question is whether the amended contract was impossible of performance. The September directive specified that the rock was to be transported "across Cooper Lake to the dam site when such lake is frozen to a sufficient depth to permit heavy vehicle traffic thereon," and the formal amendment specified that the hauling to the dam site would be done during the winter of 1966–1967. . . . [Despite the foregoing] Chugach contends . . . that Northern was nevertheless bound to perform [under the contract itself,] and that it could have used means other than hauling by truck across the ice to transport the rock. The answer to Chugach's contention is that, as the trial court found, the parties contemplated that the rock would be hauled by truck once the ice froze to a sufficient depth to support the weight of the vehicles. The specification of this particular method of performance presupposed the existence of ice frozen to the requisite depth. Since this expectation of the parties was never fulfilled, . . . Northern's duty to perform was discharged by reason of impossibility.

There is an additional reason for our holding that Northern's duty to perform was discharged by impossibility. It is true that in order for a defendant to prevail under the original common law doctrine of impossibility, he had to show [not only that he could not perform, but also] that no one else could have performed the contract. However, this harsh rule has gradually been eroded, and the Restatement of Contracts has departed from the early rule by recognizing the principle of "commercial impracticability." Under this doctrine, a party is discharged from his contract obligations, even if it is technically possible to perform them, *if the costs of performance would be so disproportionate to that reasonably contemplated by the parties as to make the contract totally impractical in a commercial sense*. . . . [Emphasis added.]

Removed from the strictures of the common law, "impossibility" in its modern context has become a coat of many colors, including among its hues the point argued here—namely, impossibility predicated upon commercial "impracticability." This concept—which finds expression both in case law and in other authorities—is predicated upon the assumption that in legal contemplation something is impracticable when it can only be done at an excessive and unreasonable cost. [The court here cited a California case in which the doctrine of commercial impracticability was applied, where the cost of the only alternative means of performance was ten times that of the means originally contemplated by the parties.] . . .

There is ample evidence to support [the trial court's findings that "the ice haul method of transporting riprap . . . was within the contemplation of the parties and was part of the basis of the agreement which ultimately resulted in the contract amendment,"] and that that method was not commercially feasible within the financial parameters of the contract. . . .

[The court then turned to the question of damages, and ruled that plaintiff *should* have been allowed damages to cover its costs incurred in attempting to perform the contract. It then set forth the rules that should be applied in determining this measure of damages.]

Judgment affirmed in part, reversed in part, and remanded.

★★★

Comment:

1. The court states that commercial impracticability is one form of impossibility. While this view blurs the line of demarcation that most courts have drawn between the two doctrines in the past, it is one that has had increasing acceptance in recent years.

2. In a subsequent rehearing, the Alaska Supreme Court modified its decision in this case. The modification, however, had only to do with a restating of the rules applicable to the determination of damages; the holding as to impossibility and commercial impracticability was thus unchanged.

Sales

Sales law is that branch of law applicable to a large class of contracts: contracts calling for the sale of "goods." This area of law is based to some extent upon contract law, in that sales contracts must normally possess the same elements as the ordinary contracts we have just been considering. However, it should be noted at the outset that sales law *differs from* contract law in two basic respects: (1) virtually all sales law is statutory in nature, being governed by the provisions of Article 2 of the Uniform Commercial Code (UCC),[6] and (2) sales law goes beyond contract law because most of its provisions are tailored to meet the special problems that are peculiar to sales contracts.

Introduction

Scope of Article 2: Article 2 applies only to contracts calling for the sale of *goods*—items of tangible, personal (movable) property. Thus sales law applies to contracts which call for the sale of such diverse articles as pig iron, wheat, automobiles, furniture, and designer jeans. By contrast, sales law does not apply to contracts under which rights are assigned, because rights are intangible property. Neither does sales law apply to contracts calling for the sale of a farm, home, or other building, because these types of property—not being movable in nature—are real property rather than personal property. (While the personal property and real property distinction is easy to apply in most cases, Article 2 has special rules applicable to the sale of minerals, crops, and fixtures, the latter term referring to items of personal property, such as bookcases, that have subsequently been attached to real property.)

Merchants: For the most part, Article 2 does not require the contracting parties to be merchants. That is, if the transaction is a sale of goods, it is governed by most provisions of Article 2 regardless of whether either the seller or the buyer is a merchant. However, a number of provisions do apply only to sales made by merchants, and a few provisions only to sales in which both parties are merchants.

The term "merchant" essentially means a person or firm who is in the business of selling the kind of goods that are subject to a particular contract. Thus a department store is a merchant in regard to a sale of jewelry, but is not a merchant when it sells one of its used delivery vans.

---

[6] Article 2 has been adopted in all states except Louisiana, which has its own body of sales law.

Formation of the Sales Contract

A number of provisions of Article 2 are markedly different from the basic rules of contract law that were surveyed earlier. We discuss here the most important of these variations.

Irrevocable Offers: Under contract law, we saw that an offer could normally be revoked by the offeror at any time prior to an acceptance, even though he or she had promised to keep the offer open for a stated time. The major exception to this was when an option contract was formed at the time that the offer was extended. Article 2 recognizes the option exception and, in addition, creates a second exception to the general rule by creating another type of irrevocable offer known as the *firm offer*. Under Section 2-205, an offer for the sale of goods that contains a promise that it will be held open a specified period of time *cannot* be revoked prior to that time if (1) the offeror is a merchant, and (2) the offer is in writing and signed by the offeror.[7]

Definiteness: Under contract law a contract must be reasonably definite and certain on all relevant matters. However, because the drafters of Article 2 realized that many sales contracts are somewhat fragmentary in nature (for instance, the time of delivery or the time of payment may be lacking), they drafted Section 2-204 to "save" those contracts, as far as the law is concerned, if reasonably possible to do so. That section broadly states that a sales contract is enforceable even if one or more terms are left open, so long as (1) the court feels that the parties intended to make a contract, and (2) the agreement and surrounding circumstances give the court a reasonably certain basis for granting an appropriate remedy (normally, damages) in the event of a breach. The drafters then framed additional sections that would supply missing terms in varying circumstances. The following cases illustrate the operation of Section 2-204:

Case 1: A sales contract is entered into which is complete except that it lacks a delivery date. The contract is valid, because a subsequent section of the UCC provides that in such an instance delivery must be made within a reasonable time after the making of the contract.

Case 2: A sales contract is entered into which is complete except that it lacks a price or provides that a price will be determined later. The contract is valid, because Section 2-305 contains several rules to guide the court in determining a price in either instance.

New Terms in Acceptance: In the business world one company often utilizes its own order form in making an offer to buy goods, and the offeree company "accepts" the offer by using its form (such as a "Sales Acceptance"

[7] All section numbers refer to sections of Article 2.

form) which frequently contains one or more terms *in addition to* those appearing in the offer. If one of the parties later wants out of the deal, he or she may argue that the offeree company's "acceptance" was legally a counteroffer and thus no contract was ever formed. Section 2-207 rejects this argument by providing that if the offeree's response indicates a definite intent to accept, the response *constitutes an acceptance* even if it contains terms additional to those found in the offer. This section then sets forth a number of rules to be used in determining whether the additional terms also become a part of the contract.

Contracts in Writing: Under Section 2-201, the general rule is that sales contracts must be in writing if the sales price is $500 or more. Thus if the S Co. and the B Co. make an oral agreement calling for the sale of 2,000 widgets by the S Co. to the B Co. for a price of $800, either company can subsequently refuse to go through with the deal without incurring liability to the other.

Section 2-201(3), however, contains a number of exceptions to the writing requirement, the most important of which are (1) contracts where either the seller or the buyer has fully performed prior to the attempted repudiation of the oral contract by the other party, and (2) contracts of special manufacture. These exceptions can be illustrated as follows.

1. *Performance by One Party*: If, after an oral contract has been made, the buyer pays the seller the price (and the seller accepts the payment), the contract is now binding upon the seller. That is, if the seller should subsequently refuse to deliver the goods, the buyer can recover damages from him or her even though nothing was in writing. Similarly, if after an oral contract has been made the seller delivers the goods to the buyer and the buyer accepts them, the buyer is liable for the purchase price (even though, again, the contract was entirely an oral one).

2. *Contracts of Special Manufacture*: Another part of Section 2-201(3) provides that oral contracts calling for the sale of articles of "special manufacture"—that is, goods made according to the buyer's specifications—are binding upon the buyer if two conditions exist. First, the specifications of the buyer must be such as to make the goods "not suitable for sale to others in the ordinary course of the seller's business." And, second, the seller—prior to the buyer's attempted repudiation of the contract—must have made a "substantial beginning of [the goods'] manufacture," or have made "commitments for their procurement."

Title and Risk of Loss

After a sales contract is made, some amount of time will usually pass before the goods are actually delivered to the buyer. In exceptional cases, several events may occur during this time that raise problems relative to *title* (ownership) and *risk of loss*. A creditor of the seller, for example, may bring a legal action seeking attachment (possession) of the goods while they are in the seller's hands—an action which will normally be successful only if title had not passed to the buyer prior to the attachment. Or the goods may be damaged while in the hands of a trucking company en route to the buyer, thereby requiring a court to determine which party had the risk of loss at the time the damage occurred.

The rules for determining the time of passing of title and passing of risk of loss are governed by separate sections of Article 2. However, the rules in most instances bring about the same results. Thus, in our discussion of the risk of loss rules below, it may be assumed that title passes at the same time as the risk of loss, with one exception to be noted.

Risk of Loss: Section 2-509 governs passage of risk of loss. It first provides that the parties may, by agreement, decide when risk of loss passes. In the absence of agreement, this section contains rules applicable to three basic classifications of contracts.

Classification 1: In many contracts the parties "contemplate delivery" of the goods—for example, the buyer and seller are located in different cities, and the goods will be delivered by a common carrier (such as a trucking company). In such a situation, if the contract is a "shipment contract," risk of loss normally passes to the buyer when the seller delivers the goods to the carrier. By contrast, if the contract is a "destination contract," risk of loss does not pass until the goods reach their destination—usually the buyer's place of business—and are "duly tendered" to the buyer.[8] To illustrate:

(**A**) The S Company, in Chicago, sells fifty motors to the B Company in Phoenix. The contract price is "$25,000 f.o.b. Chicago." Because of the f.o.b. term, this is a shipment contract. Thus if the goods are damaged or lost en route to Phoenix, the B Company—having the risk at that time—must still pay for them.

(**B**) Same case as above, except that the contract price is "$25,000 f.o.b. Phoenix." Because of the f.o.b. term, this is a destination contract. Thus if the goods are damaged or lost en route to Phoenix, the B Company need not pay for them (and the seller has an obligation to make a second shipment).

Classification 2: In situations where the parties do not contemplate delivery, the goods are often in the hands of a *bailee*, such as an independent warehouse, when the contract is made. At the time that the seller deposits the goods, he or she usually receives a "negotiable warehouse receipt" from the warehouseman as evidence of the transaction. The general rule in such a

[8] A due tender occurs when the buyer is given notice that the goods have arrived and are available to him or her. (The next case in the chapter presents a real-life situation in which determination of the precise time of tender was necessary in order for the court to decide whether the risk of loss had, or had not, passed to the buyer prior to the goods' theft.)

case is that risk of loss passes to the buyer when the buyer receives the warehouse receipt from the seller. Special rules apply if the warehouse receipt is nonnegotiable, or if no receipt was issued by the warehouse.

Classification 3: In contracts not falling into the first two classifications, the usual understanding is that the buyer will pick up the goods at the seller's place of business. Where the seller is a merchant, as is usually the case, *title* passes to the buyer when he or she is notified by the seller that the goods are available for pickup, but *risk of loss* does not pass until the buyer actually takes possession of the goods. Where the seller is not a merchant, title and risk both pass to the buyer when the seller notifies him or her that the goods are available.

The case below presents a typical risk of loss question.

Lumber Sales, Inc. v. Brown
Court of Appeals of Tennessee
469 S.W.2d 888
(1971)

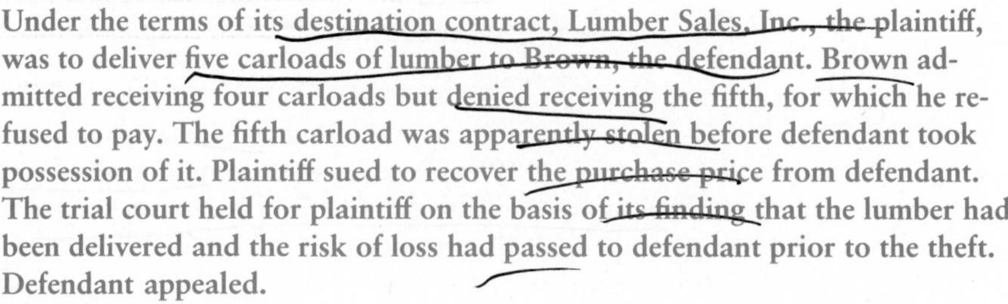

Under the terms of its destination contract, Lumber Sales, Inc., the plaintiff, was to deliver five carloads of lumber to Brown, the defendant. Brown admitted receiving four carloads but denied receiving the fifth, for which he refused to pay. The fifth carload was apparently stolen before defendant took possession of it. Plaintiff sued to recover the purchase price from defendant. The trial court held for plaintiff on the basis of its finding that the lumber had been delivered and the risk of loss had passed to defendant prior to the theft. Defendant appealed.

Puryear, Justice:

. . . The railroad siding at which the lumber was to be delivered, according to agreement of the parties, is located about one half mile from the defendant's place of business and is known as a "team track" which designation means that it is available for use by several parties, which in this case, included the defendant. Track location 609-A on this siding is a point where a loading platform is located.

The uncontroverted evidence shows that during the early morning hours of November 27, 1968, the Louisville and Nashville Railroad Company, to which we will hereinafter refer as the carrier, placed a boxcar loaded with lumber consigned to the defendant on this siding at track location 609-A.

This boxcar was designated as NW54938 and it was inspected by an employee of the carrier between 8:00 A.M. and 8:30 A.M. on November 27, 1968, at which time it was found loaded with cargo and so designated upon the carrier's records.

At 11:07 A.M. on November 27, 1968, the carrier notified one of defendant's employees that the carload of lumber had been delivered at track location 609-A.

At approximately 4:00 P.M. on that same day an employee of the carrier again inspected this boxcar at track location 609-A, found one of the seals on it to be broken and resealed it at that time. The evidence does not show whether the car was still loaded with cargo at that time or not.

The following day, November 28th, was Thanksgiving Day and the record does not disclose that the carrier inspected the boxcar on that date. But on November 29, 1968, between 8:00 A.M. and 8:30 A.M. an employee of the carrier inspected the car and found it empty.

From evidence in the record before us it is impossible to reach any logical conclusion as to what happened to the carload of lumber without indulging in speculation and conjecture, but the defendant earnestly insists that he did not unload it and there is no evidence to the contrary.

The particular Code Section applicable here is Sub-section (1) of 2-509, as follows:

Risk of loss in the absence of breach—*(1) Where the contract requires or authorizes the seller to ship the goods by carrier . . . (b) if it does require him to deliver them at a particular destination and the goods are there duly tendered while in the possession of the carrier, the risk of loss passes to the buyer when the goods are there duly so tendered as to enable the buyer to take delivery.*

The trial Court held that the risk of loss in this case did, in fact, pass to the defendant buyer.

Now let us further examine the evidence for the purpose of determining whether or not it preponderates against this conclusion of the trial Court.

There is competent evidence in the record which shows that on November 27, 1968, at 11:07 A.M. the carrier notified the defendant's employee, Mr. Caldwell, at defendant's business office, that the carload of lumber had been delivered at track location 609-A. Mr. Caldwell did not testify, so this evidence is uncontroverted.

There is no evidence in the record to the effect that the defendant declined to accept delivery at that time or asked for a postponement of such delivery until a later time.

The defendant testified that it would normally require about four or five hours for him and his employees to unload a carload of lumber and that on November 27, 1968, he and his employees were so busily engaged in other necessary work that he could not unload the lumber on that day and since the following day was Thanksgiving, he could not unload it until November 29th, at which time, of course, the carrier found the car to be empty. . . .

One Kenneth E. Crye, freight agent of the carrier, Louisville and Nashville Railroad Company, testified that on Thanksgiving Day, November 28th, he saw what he believed to be a railroad car being unloaded at track location 609-A, but he could not identify the car or the persons whom he believed to be unloading it. He qualified this testimony by saying that he was not positive that the car was being unloaded, but there was some lumber and some kind of activity on the platform, none of which appeared to be unusual.

From evidence in the record, a trier of fact could logically form one of two inferences:

(1) That the lumber was either stolen or unloaded by mistake by someone other than the defendant at some time between 8:30 A.M. and 11:07 A.M.

on November 27th; or (2) that it was stolen or unloaded at some time after 11:07 A.M. November 27th . . . .

If the first inference should be formed then the issue should be found in favor of defendant, but if the second inference should be formed, then the issue should be found in favor of plaintiff if it could also be found that the loss occurred after defendant had sufficient time to protect himself against loss after notice of delivery.

We think the second inference is the more logical of the two, especially in view of the difference between the two intervals of time and also in view of Mr. Crye's testimony to the effect that on Thanksgiving Day, November 28th, he observed some activity at track location 609-A, which he believed to be unloading of a railroad car at that location.

Of course, we recognize and adhere to the rule that the burden of proof is upon plaintiff to prove delivery of the lumber and we are not required to indulge either of the above mentioned inferences because the trial Court . . . concluded that the plaintiff had successfully carried the burden of proof . . . and the evidence does not preponderate against that Court's conclusion.

Counsel for defendant argues that the lumber in question was not duly "*so tendered as to enable the buyer to take delivery*" as required by 2-509.

However, this argument seems to be based upon the premise that it was not convenient for the defendant to unload the lumber on November 27th, the day on which it was delivered at track location 609-A and defendant was duly notified of such delivery.

This was an ordinary business day and the time of 11:07 A.M. was a reasonable business hour. If it was not convenient with the defendant to unload the lumber within a few hours after being duly notified of delivery, then he should have protected himself against risk of loss by directing someone to guard the cargo against loss by theft and other hazards.

To hold that the seller or the carrier should, under the circumstances existing in a case of this kind, continue to protect the goods until such time as the buyer may find it convenient to unload them would impose an undue burden upon the seller or the carrier and unnecessarily obstruct the channels of commerce.

The language of Sub-section (1) (b) of 2-509 does not impose such a burden upon the seller, in the absence of some material breach of the contract for delivery, and we think a reasonable construction of such language only requires the seller to place the goods at the buyer's disposal so that he has access to them and may remove them from the carrier's conveyance without lawful obstruction, with the proviso, however, that due notice of such delivery be given to the buyer. . . .

[Affirmed.]

★ ★ ★

Warranties

A warranty is an assurance or guarantee that goods will conform to certain standards. If the standards are not met, the buyer can recover damages from the seller in a breach of warranty action. Warranties can be either express or implied. An express warranty comes into existence because of the words or actions of the seller. An implied warranty is imposed upon the seller by law unless he or she takes the proper steps to disclaim it.

Express Warranties: Under Section 2-312, a seller by making a sale expressly warrants to the buyer that he or she is receiving good title, and, additionally, that no other party has a legally valid claim against the goods (such as a mortgage) of which the buyer has no knowledge.

The question of whether a particular statement made by the seller constitutes an express warranty is decided on the basis of Section 2-313. That section provides in essence that an express warranty is an *affirmation of fact or promise* made by the seller that relates to the goods. Thus a statement by the seller of a boat that "this boat is equipped with a two-year-old, one hundred horsepower engine that was overhauled last month" is an express warranty, because it contains several affirmations of fact. By contrast, a seller's statement that "this is a first-class car, the most handsome car on the road" is a mere statement of opinion, and thus not a warranty. And, a statement as to value ("this stereo is worth $700 at a minimum") is also considered to be a mere statement of opinion in most circumstances.

Implied Warranties: Under Article 2, there are two implied warranties of quality—that is, warranties of quality that may be created in the eyes of the law simply as the result of the making of a sale. These are the implied warranty of *merchantability* and the implied warranty of *fitness for a particular purpose*. If the seller is a merchant with respect to the goods being sold, the law injects into the sale contract a warranty that the goods are "merchantable"—reasonably fit for the usual purposes for which such goods are purchased. Thus if a power mower runs fitfully, or paint fails to dry after a reasonable time, the buyer of either product can recover damages from the seller in a breach of implied warranty action. This warranty can, however, be disclaimed (eliminated) under certain circumstances, the most common of which is the sale of an article "as is."

The implied warranty of fitness for a particular purpose exists, under Section 2-315, only "where the seller at the time of contracting has reason to know any particular purpose for which the goods are required, and that the buyer is relying on the seller's skill or judgment to furnish suitable goods." In such a case, there is an implied guarantee that the goods furnished shall be fit for the purpose described by the buyer.

Exclusion of Warranties: Sometimes a seller will attempt to escape warranty liability on the ground that the sales contract contained a "disclaimer" clause—such as a statement that "these goods are sold without warranties of any kind." Under Section 2-316, disclaimers are lawful in limited circumstances. In general, disclaimers are not effective against express warranties that have become a part of the contract because Section 2-316 provides that a disclaimer is of no effect if it "conflicts" with any words that create an express warranty. On the other hand, a disclaimer clause does exclude (destroy) the implied warranty of merchantability if the clause expressly so provides, or if the contract provides that the goods are being sold "as is" or "with all faults."[9]

The following case is typical of those which present the question as to the legal effectiveness of an attempted disclaimer of an express warranty.

Hauter v. Zogarts
Supreme Court of California
534 P.2d 377 (1975)

Defendants manufacture and sell the "Golfing Gizmo," a training device designed to help unskilled golfers improve their game. Defendants' catalogue states that the Gizmo is a "completely equipped backyard driving range." In 1966, Louise Hauter purchased a Gizmo from the catalogue and gave it to Fred Hauter, her thirteen-year-old son, as a Christmas present. While practicing with the Gizmo, Fred was knocked unconscious by the Gizmo's golf ball.

The Gizmo is a simple device consisting of two metal pegs, two cords—one elastic, one cotton—and a regulation golf ball. After the pegs are driven into the ground approximately twenty-five inches apart, the elastic cord is looped over them. The cotton cord, measuring twenty-one feet in length, is tied to the middle of the elastic cord. The ball is attached to the end of the cotton cord. When the cords are extended, the Gizmo resembles a large letter "T," with the ball resting at the base.

The user stands by the ball in order to hit practice shots. The instructions state that when hit correctly, the ball will fly out and spring back near the point of impact; if the ball returns to the left, it indicates a right-hander's slice; a ball returning to the right indicates a right-hander's hook. If the ball is "topped," it does not return and must be retrieved by the player. The labels on the shipping carton and on the cover of the instruction booklet urge players to "drive the ball with full power" and further state: "COMPLETELY SAFE BALL WILL NOT HIT PLAYER."

Fred Hauter testified at the trial that prior to his injury, he had practiced golf ten to twenty times at driving ranges and had played several rounds of golf. His father had instructed him in the correct use of the Gizmo. Fred had read the printed instructions accompanying the product and had used the Gizmo about a dozen times. Before the accident on July 14, 1967, he had set up the Gizmo in his front yard according to the printed instructions. The area was free of objects that might have caused the ball to ricochet, and no other

[9] Because the subject of warranties is closely connected with the larger area of products liability, it is examined further under that topic in Chapter 18.

persons were nearby. Fred then took his normal swing with a seven-iron. The last thing he remembers was extreme pain and dizziness. After a period of unconsciousness, he staggered into the house and told his mother that he had been hit on the head by the ball. He suffered brain damage and, in one doctor's opinion, is currently an epileptic.

The Hauters filed suit against the manufacturer and the seller, claiming among other allegations a breach of express and implied warranties. George Peters, a safety engineer and an expert on the analysis, reconstruction, and causes of accidents, testified for plaintiffs. In Peters's opinion, Fred Hauter had hit underneath the ball and had caught the cord with his golf club, thereby drawing the cord upwards and toward him on his follow-through. The ball had looped over the club, producing a "bolo" effect, and had struck Fred on the left temple. Peters concluded that the Gizmo was a "major hazard."

Ray Catan, a professional golfer, also testified for plaintiffs. He added that even if the club had hit the lower part of the ball, the same result probably would have occurred. He had personally tested the Gizmo, intentionally hitting low shots, and had found that his club became entangled in the cord, bringing the ball back toward him as he completed his swing. Catan described Fred Hauter as a beginner and stated that since a beginning golfer's swing usually is very erratic, the person rarely hits the ball solidly.

The jury returned a verdict for defendants, but the trial judge rendered a judgment notwithstanding the verdict (see Chapter 2) in favor of plaintiff. Defendants appealed.

Tobriner, Justice:

. . . [After holding that defendants did breach their express warranty that the Golfing Gizmo was "completely safe" and would "not hit player," as well as their implied warranty of merchantability, the court continued by discussing defendants' allegations that their warranty liability had been "impliedly" limited.]

The Gizmo is designed and marketed for a particular class of golfers—"duffers"—who desire to improve their technique. Such players rarely hit the ball solidly. When they do, testified the golf pro, "it would be sort of a mistake, really." The safety expert classed the Gizmo as a major safety hazard. Furthermore, defendants *admit* that when a person using the Gizmo hits beneath the ball as Fred Hauter apparently did, he stands a substantial chance of seriously injuring himself. . . .

Defendants nevertheless seek to avoid liability by limiting the scope of their warranties. They claim that the box containing the Gizmo and the instructions pertaining to its use clarified that the product was "completely safe" only when its user hit the ball properly. They point to no language expressing such a limitation but instead claim that a drawing in the instructions depicting a golfer "correctly" using their product *implies* the limitation. . . .

[D]efendants' argument is wholly without merit. Furthermore, they fail to meet the stern requirements of [UCC § 2-316] which governs disclaimer and modification of warranties. Although § 2-316 has drawn criticism for its vagueness, its purpose is clear. No warranty, express or implied, can be modified or disclaimed unless a seller *clearly* limits his liability. This section is designed principally to deal with those frequent clauses in sales contracts which seek to exclude "all warranties, express or implied." It seeks to protect a buyer from unexpected and unbargained language of disclaimer by denying effect to such language when inconsistent with language of express warranty and permitting the exclusion of implied warranties only by conspicuous language or other circumstances which protect the buyer from surprise.

Because a disclaimer or modification is inconsistent with an express warranty, words of disclaimer or modification give way to words of warranty unless some clear agreement between the parties dictates the contrary relationship. . . .

Moreover, any disclaimer or modification must be strictly construed against the seller. Although the parties are free to write their own contract, the consumer must be placed on fair notice of any disclaimer or modification of a warranty and must freely agree to the seller's terms. A unilateral nonwarranty cannot be tacked onto a contract containing a warranty.

In the instant case, defendants do not point to any language or conduct on their part negating their warranties. They refer only to a drawing on the box and to the notion that golf is a dangerous game; based on that meager foundation, they attempt to limit their explicit promise of safety. Such a showing does not pass muster under the code, which requires clear language from anyone seeking to avoid warranty liability. We conclude, therefore, that the trial court properly granted plaintiffs judgment notwithstanding the verdict. . . .

Affirmed.

★★★

Performance and Remedies

Article 2 contains numerous sections applicable to the related subjects of performance and remedies. Because of space limitations, we will note only the most important of these.

Performance: The basic obligation of the seller is to deliver conforming goods, and the basic obligation of the buyer is to accept the goods and pay for them, at the times and places specified in the sales contract. As to any matters on which the contract is silent, several sections "fill the gaps." For example, if the contract is not clear as to what constitutes a "delivery," Section 2-503 provides that the seller need only "tender delivery"—that is, "put and hold conforming goods at the buyer's disposition and give the buyer any notification reasonably necessary to enable him to take delivery." Further sections define tender more clearly, depending upon such matters as whether the parties contemplate delivery by a common carrier, or contemplate delivery at a warehouse, and so forth.

Article 2 goes on to provide, in general, that where a seller makes an improper tender, he or she is allowed to "cure" the defective performance by making a subsequent tender as long as the time for performance has not expired. Additionally, Section 2-615 excuses performance by the seller if events subsequent to the making of the contract render performance "commercially impracticable" (a doctrine discussed earlier under the Contracts part of this chapter).

Remedies: Where the buyer breaches the contract, the seller has a number of remedies available. These remedies under Section 2-703 are the rights (1) to cancel the contract, (2) to withhold delivery, (3) to stop delivery when the goods are in the hands of a carrier, (4) to resell the goods and recover damages, and (5) to retain the goods and recover damages for non-acceptance. Each of these remedies is available only under certain circumstances—for example, a seller obviously cannot withhold delivery if the buyer's breach occurs after delivery. Thus, when any breach occurs by the buyer, the seller must examine Sections 2-704 through 2-710 in order to determine which precise remedy or remedies are available.

When the seller breaches the contract, the buyer's remedies under Section 2-711 are the rights (1) to cancel, (2) to "cover" (by buying the goods elsewhere) and to recover damages, (3) to recover damages for non-delivery, and (4) to obtain the actual goods from the seller, in exceptional circumstances. Again, certain conditions must be met before any of these remedies is available.

Torts

While the subject of tort law is not essentially commercially oriented, it does have sufficient connection to the business world to warrant examination of its basic principles. One of the bases for this connection, but not the only one, arises from a principle of agency law that often results in an employer being held liable for the torts committed by his or her employees—a rule that is examined in detail in the Agency portion of the next chapter.

The term **tort** is usually defined as a "civil wrong." What this means is that a tort is that type of wrong which permits the injured party to bring a civil action against the wrongdoer, the "tortfeasor," for damages to recompense him or her for the injury sustained. While the term *civil wrong* is a perfectly acceptable one, two reservations must be made in the interest of accuracy: (1) the term does not include breaches of contract, which also permit the innocent parties to recover damages, and (2) the commission of some torts are also crimes—the tortfeasor may be liable for damages to the injured party, and additionally may be fined or imprisoned in a criminal action.

With these general observations in mind, we will examine the most common tort actions.

Negligence

The principles of negligence law are designed to protect persons from the *unintentional* harm resulting from the carelessness of others. Thus every person who engages in any kind of endeavor owes others the duty to use *due care* while carrying on his or her activities. A failure to use such care—often defined as "the failure to use the care of the reasonable, prudent man under the circumstances"—constitutes an act of negligence. Whether the defendant did or did not exercise due care in a particular situation is ordinarily a question of fact to be decided by the jury (or by the judge, in the absence of a jury).

Two cases presenting acts of negligence have already been encountered: the failure of International Harvester to warn its dealers of the possibility of contracting valley fever in the case in Chapter 1, and the failure of Buick Motor Company to inspect wheels made by a supplier before putting their automobiles into the stream of commerce in Chapter 2. Other examples of negligence would be the leaving of a road excavation overnight without warning flashers, and the design of a product which causes it to possess an inherent danger not readily discoverable by the ordinary users of the product.[10]

Defenses: In any tort case the defendant may be able to legally justify his or her conduct. In such instances it is said that a **defense** exists, and the defendant is normally freed of all liability. The most common defense in negligence actions is "contributory negligence"—a showing by the defendant that the plaintiff was also acting negligently at the time of the accident. At one time the defense of contributory negligence completely freed the defendant of liability. Today, however, most states have adopted some form of *comparative negligence* rule, under which the plaintiff may recover *some* damages if his or her negligence is found to be less than the defendant's. For example: if the jury finds that plaintiff's damages are $10,000 and that his or her negligence was 40 percent, with 60 percent being attributed to defendant, plaintiff's recovery would be reduced by 40 percent (i.e., the recovery would be $6,000).

Many negligence cases arise where a patron in a retail store is injured by a fall occurring on the retailer's premises. The following case sets forth the general rules applicable to such an action (and also dispels the popularly held notion that the retailer is *necessarily* liable in such actions).

Moultrey v. Great A&P Tea Co.
Superior Court of Pennsylvania
Pa. Super., 422 A.2d 593 (1981)

Phyllis Moultrey, plaintiff, entered defendant's A&P retail store in York, Pennsylvania, accompanied by her two teenage children. As she entered the store she secured a shopping cart and proceeded to the produce counter. While moving into an aisle between a vegetable counter and a fruit counter she noticed some water and some leaves of lettuce and cabbage on the floor. She maneuvered her cart to avoid the water in order to get to the banana stand, intending to buy some bananas. She pushed the cart to the side of the aisle close to the

[10] In some instances a defendant is "strictly liable in tort"—legally liable even though not guilty of negligence. The strict liability theory is discussed in Chapter 18 in conjunction with the subject of products liability.

banana stand, and circled the cart to obtain the bananas. After selecting them she ventured back toward her cart, slipped and fell to the floor. While on the floor she looked back and saw one squashed cherry, the seed of which was on her shoe. The cherry was not in the water, but rather was in a dry area closer to the cart.

Ms. Moultrey shortly thereafter brought this action to recover for the injuries she sustained. At the close of plaintiff's testimony, the trial court dismissed the action (for reasons appearing below), and plaintiff appealed.

Cercone, Presiding Judge:

. . . This is a "slip and fall" case in which the question presented is, whether in order [to have her case considered by the jury], . . . appellant-invitee must prove that appellee-proprietor [A&P] had either actual or constructive notice [of the floor's condition] which allegedly caused appellant's harm. The lower court held that appellant-invitee, Ms. Moultrey, had such a burden and failed to discharge it. . . . We affirm the lower court's order. . . .

[The court here reviewed the evidence presented above, and continued]: At trial before a jury, Ms. Moultrey and her children testified they did not know how long the cherry had been on the floor or how it got there. Further, she was unable to offer any evidence as to when the area in which she fell had last been cleaned. At the close of Ms. Moultrey's case, appellee-proprietor moved for and was granted a compulsory non-suit by the trial judge [i.e., the trial did not permit the case to go to the jury]. . . .

The parties generally agree that the existence and extent of the duty which an owner of property owes to his invitees is set forth in the *Restatement (Second) of Torts* § 343 (1965).[a] *The principle of law from which this rule of the Restatement was derived is that a possessor of land is not an insurer of the safety of those on his property*. [Emphasis added.] [Thus] the mere existence of a harmful condition in a public place of business, or the mere happening of an accident due to such a condition is neither, in and of itself, evidence of a breach of the [possessor's] duty to use reasonable care, nor raises a presumption of negligence. [The court here summarized a number of cases, and continued]:

In construing this section of the Restatement, the Pennsylvania courts have uniformly held that if the harmful transitory condition is *traceable to the [possessor of the premises or to his employees]*, then the plaintiff need not prove any notice in order to hold the possessor accountable for the resulting harm. In a related context, where the condition is one *which the possessor knows has frequently recurred*, the jury may properly find that he had actual notice of the

---

[a]Section 343 provides:

A possessor of land is subject to liability for physical harm caused to his invitees by a condition on the land if, but only if, he

(a) knows or by the exercise of reasonable care would discover the condition, and should realize that it involves an unreasonable risk of harm to such invitees, and

(b) should expect that they will not discover or realize the danger, or will fail to protect themselves against it, and

(c) fails to exercise reasonable care to protect them against the danger.

condition, [in which case the possessor is liable even if the condition is not traceable to the possessor or his employees]. Where, however, the evidence indicates that the transitory condition is traceable to persons other than [the possessor or his employees], the jury may not [find the possessor liable unless there is] other evidence which tends to prove that the possessor had actual notice of the condition, or that the condition existed for such a length of time that in the exercise of reasonable care the possessor should have known of it. . . .

Ms. Moultrey failed to adduce [produce] any evidence from which the jury could infer either that the presence of fruit matter on the floor was due to act or acts by customers which had occurred in the past and remained uncorrected, or that the harm causing act or acts likely occurred because of the manner in which fruits were packaged, displayed, and sold [by defendant-possessor]. Accordingly the trial court acted properly [in dismissing the suit].

Order affirmed.

★★★

Comment: The rule applied by the court here is, in essence, that in a slip and fall case the plaintiff must either prove that the dangerous condition (1) was caused by the defendant or its agents, or (2) that the defendant had notice of the condition—that is, that defendant actually knew of the condition or, under the circumstances, should have known of it. Because plaintiff failed to meet either test 1 or 2, her action failed.

In such cases, however, the courts of a number of states have adopted a view applicable to "unassisted customer selection stores" (such as most supermarkets and discount stores) that is more favorable to the plaintiff. This passage from *Cobb v. Skaggs Companies*, 661 P.2d 73 (1982) illustrates this view: "Merchandising methods that involve unassisted customer selection create problems with dropped or spilled merchandise. The courts have come to recognize that self-service marketing methods necessarily create the dangerous condition. Therefore the owner or proprietor is deemed to have actual notice [of the condition.]" Under this view, in actions arising out of dropped or spilled merchandise in self-service stores, once the dangerous condition is proved to exist and be the proximate cause of the injury, the defendant has notice of the condition as a matter of law.

Assault and Battery

One of the inherent rights of every member of society is that of personal security—the right to be free of physical attacks upon one's person. The violation of this right constitutes an **assault and battery**, which may be essentially defined as the "intentional, unlawful physical touching of one person by another." Thus, if X strikes Y without provocation, or pushes him to the ground, or hits him with a thrown rock, X is guilty of this tort. We are using the term *assault and battery* here in the broad sense, which includes batteries. In a strictly technical sense, however, the terms *assault* and *battery* should be distinguished. In this sense, assault is the making of a *threat* to inflict immediate bodily injury, which creates a fear of wrongful contact in the threatened party, while battery refers to the actual physical contact that usually—but not always—follows the assault. Thus if A unjustifiably fires a shot at B which misses him, A is guilty of an assault only.[11]

Defenses: The most common defenses to assault and battery actions are "privilege" and "consent." Privilege is based on recognition of the fact that under certain circumstances the use of force is entirely justified, as in self defense or in the capture or removal of a burglar from one's home. Consent, as the name implies, refers to the granting of permission for a certain amount of bodily contact. Obviously a boxer who engages in a prize fight consents to the normal physical buffeting that occurs in the ring; the same is true of anyone who engages in the sports of football and basketball.

Defamation

One of the most important rights possessed by the individual is the "right to a good reputation." Accordingly, the law has imposed the general duty on all persons to refrain from making false and defamatory statements about others. A breach of this duty constitutes the general tort of *defamation*. (If the false statement is made orally, the specific name of the tort is **slander**, and if in writing, **libel**). The tort of defamation has three elements. First, the statement must be false; second, it must be defamatory (one which subjects the victim to ridicule, loss of respect, or hatred); and, third, the statement must be "published"—that is, communicated to a third party. Thus if X tells Y that Z was once convicted of the crime of embezzlement, a statement that is untrue, X is, in most circumstances, guilty of slander. (And, as a general rule, this is so even if X honestly believed that the statement was true—subject, however, to the exceptions noted subsequently.)

Defenses: The two most common defenses to defamation actions are *truth* and *privilege*. Thus a plaintiff's slander or libel action will fail if the statement complained of is, in fact, true, or if the statement—although false—is made under circumstances in which the defense of privilege is recognized.

Absolute privilege exists in limited circumstances. This defense is based on the recognition that, in some circumstances the usual protection afforded an individual's right to a good name must give way to even more compelling matters of public policy. For this reason, statements made by federal and state legislators during legislative debates and committee hearings are absolutely privileged. This is also generally true for statements made by judges, attorneys, and witnesses during court trials (although a witness who testifies falsely under oath might subsequently be charged with the crime of perjury).

---

[11] Assault and battery is one of the most common wrongs that can be both a tort and a crime. If, for example, A wounds B by unlawfully shooting him, A's act is a tort and almost certainly a felony under the state's criminal law.

In some other circumstances the defense of *qualified privilege* is recognized. This generally occurs where (1) the statement is made in regard to a matter in which the declarant (the person making the statement) has a legitimate interest, and (2) the declarant honestly believes the statement to be true. Thus if X, in response to a request from the Y Company, writes a letter of reference regarding the qualifications of Z for a particular position, X is not liable to Z for any false statements in the letter unless Z can prove that they were made maliciously—i.e., that X knew, or should have known, that they were false.

A third kind of privilege, often called *constitutional privilege*, is recognized in defamation cases if the plaintiff is a "public figure"—such as a former U.S. Secretary of Defense or a nationally known television personality.[12] In such actions, where the defendant is typically a newspaper publisher or a broadcasting company, the U.S. Supreme Court has balanced the defendants' constitutional free speech and press rights with the plaintiffs' reputation rights. The court has done this by holding that the defendants are not liable if their statements, though false and defamatory, are made without "actual malice." (Again, actual malice exists only where the defendant actually knows the statement is false, or makes the statement with a reckless disregard of the truth—that is, having no reason to believe the statement is true.) Thus in the public figure case—unlike one brought by a private citizen—a showing by the defendant that he or she had reasonable grounds for believing the statement to be true defeats the action.

False Imprisonment

If one person unjustifiably interferes with another's right to move about—the right "to come and go"—that person has committed the tort of **false imprisonment**. Thus if X locks Y in his office, or prevents Y from leaving his office by the use of force or "by verbal compulsion and the display of available force," X has committed this tort. The same is true if X simply prevents Y, by the same means, from going onto property which Y is legally entitled to enter.

Defenses: Obviously, the tort of false imprisonment does not arise in any situation in which the detention is proven to be lawful, as, for example, where a police officer apprehends a person charged with the commission of a crime. Another situation in which a detention may be lawful arises under the

[12] In *Gertz v. Robert Welch, Inc.*, 418 U.S. 323 (1974), the U.S. Supreme Court described public figures in these words: "For the most part those who attain this status have assumed roles of especial prominence in the affairs of society. Some occupy positions of such persuasive power and influence that they are deemed public figures for all purposes. More commonly, those classed as public figures have thrust themselves to the forefront of particular public controversies in order to influence the resolution of the issues involved. In either event, they invite attention and comment."

antishoplifting statutes that most states have adopted. Under the typical statute, the owner, employees, and agents of a "retail mercantile establishment" are legally permitted to detain a suspected shoplifter for a reasonable time if they "had reasonable grounds to believe that the person so detained was committing or attempting to commit larceny on the premises." Thus, even if it turns out that the detained person was entirely innocent of the charge, he or she usually is not able to maintain a false imprisonment action against the persons making the detention.

Infliction of Emotional Distress

A person whose conduct inflicts severe mental or emotional distress upon another is guilty of a tort if his or her actions were carried on intentionally, recklessly, or outrageously. Thus, in *Turman v. Central Billing, Inc.*, 568 P.2d 1382 (1977), a collection agency was held liable to Mrs. Turman, who was blind, when it badgered her in trying to collect a small debt assigned to it for collection, even after it knew that she and the creditor had come to a satisfactory settlement. This harassment, which resulted in plaintiff's hospitalization for anxiety and severe stress, was carried out by repeated phone calls—sometimes twice a day—in which defendant's agent "shouted" at her, used profanity, told her several times that her husband would lose his job and house if she didn't pay, and called her "scum" and a "deadbeat."

Selected Business Torts

Some torts are almost entirely business related in nature. Examples of such torts are (1) the disparagement of competitors' products or services by the making of false statements of fact in regard to such products or services; (2) the selling of products under circumstances that cause customers to be misled as to the products' true manufacturer or source; and (3) the misrepresenting of used or secondhand goods as being "new."[13]

While these kinds of conduct were first recognized as torts under common-law principles, most of our business torts today are governed by comprehensive *state statutes* (often bearing the name of "deceptive trade practices acts," as noted in Chapter 4) that expressly prohibit such kinds of conduct. In addition to the three torts listed above, other kinds of business practices that are usually prohibited by such statutes are the advertising of goods or services with the intent not to sell them as advertised, and the advertising of goods or services with the intent not to supply a "reasonably expectable public demand" for them.

[13] Each of these torts will be recognized as comprising a special type of fraud, a subject discussed earlier under the Contracts portion of this chapter.

Questions and Problems

1. Charles Weber (a minor), his parents, and six uncles and aunts jointly owned a parcel of lake property in Minnesota which they used for recreational purposes. After deciding to sell one part of the land, all of the family members spent a day in cleaning up that particular area. During the cleanup one of Charles's uncles, Raymond Goetzke, threw a paint can in a fire pit, which exploded and resulted in Charles being badly burned. Charles then brought suit to recover damages from Goetzke and, additionally, all of his other aunts and uncles on the theory that the cleaning up of the land was a "joint enterprise" which made all of the participants liable for the negligent act of Goetzke. (One of the necessary elements of a joint enterprise is an agreement—that is, an express or implied contract among the participants—to achieve a common purpose.) The trial court ruled that the defendants, by jointly taking part in the cleanup, did thereby enter into an implied contract, and that consequently they all were liable under the joint enterprise theory. The defendants appealed this ruling to the Minnesota Court of Appeals. Do you think the appellate court should agree with the trial court that the defendants' conduct was sufficient to warrant a finding that an implied contract existed? Why or why not? (*Weber v. Goetzke*, 371 N.W.2d 611, 1985.)

2. A corporation employed a contractor to build a barn. Later the contractor quit the job, leaving the subcontractor unpaid. A corporation officer then told the subcontractor to finish the job, and promised that the corporation would pay him for his time and materials. Later the subcontractor finished the job, but the corporation refused to pay the amount that the subcontractor demanded. (It was, however, willing to pay a lesser sum.) In the ensuing lawsuit the corporation contended that no contract had ever been entered into here; the subcontractor, on the other hand, argued that the corporation had made a unilateral offer which he, the subcontractor, had accepted by the act of completing the barn. Do you agree with the corporation that no contract of any kind was entered into here? Why or why not? (*Redd v. Woodford County Swine Breeders, Inc.*, 370 N.E.2d 152, 1977.)

3. Blakeslee, who wished to buy some land owned by the Nelsons, wrote a letter to them asking if they would accept "$49,000 net" for the property. The Nelsons replied that they would "not sell for less than $56,000," whereupon Blakeslee wired back, "Accept your offer of $56,000 net." (*Blakeslee v. Nelson*, 207 N.Y.S. 676, 1925.) Does a contract now exist between the parties? Explain.

4. Dr. Browning made a contract with Dr. Johnson, under which he was to sell his practice and equipment to Johnson for a specified price. Before the time for performance, Browning changed his mind and asked Johnson to relieve him of his obligation to sell. Thereafter a new contract was made, under the terms of which Browning promised to pay Johnson $40,000 in return for Johnson's *cancellation of the first contract*. Later Browning refused to pay the $40,000, contending that this promise of his was not supported by consideration on Johnson's part. Is Browning correct? If not, where is the consideration on Johnson's part? (*Browning v. Johnson*, 422 P.2d 319, 1967.)

5. Dorton ordered substantial quantities of carpets from Collins & Aikman Corp. Collins & Aikman responded by sending a sales acknowledgment form. The language of the form purported to accept Dorton's offer to buy, but it also stated: "Acceptance of your order is subject to all of the terms and conditions on the face and reverse sides hereof." The acknowledgment listed several terms that were not in Dorton's offer, including the provision that disputes arising out of the contract must be submitted to arbitration. (*Dorton v. Collins & Aikman Corp.*, 453 F.2d 1161, 1972.) Was Collins & Aikman's acknowledgment an acceptance of Dorton's offer? Discuss.

6. Walcott & Steele, Inc., sold seed to Carpenter. State law required the package label to give the percentage of germination. The label on the seed bought by Car-

penter carried the required statement, but the seed did not perform at the listed percentage. Carpenter sued for breach of an express warranty, which he claimed was created by the statement regarding percentage of germination. (*Walcott & Steele, Inc. v. Carpenter*, 436 S.W.2d 820, 1969.) Did Carpenter prevail? Discuss.

7. Kassab, a cattle breeder, purchased feed which had been manufactured by Central Soya. The feed was intended for breeding cattle, but Central had accidentally included an ingredient that should be used only for beef cattle. After eating the feed, Kassab's cattle grew and prospered. Kassab was upset, however, when he discovered that the mistakenly included ingredient had caused his entire herd of prize breeding cattle to be sterile. He sued Central for breach of the implied warranty of merchantability. Central claimed that there was no such breach because the feed had made the cattle gain weight exactly as it was supposed to do. (*Kassab v. Central Soya*, 246 A.2d 848, 1968.) Is Central's contention correct? Explain.

8. A woman slipped on a piece of wax paper that was on the floor of a Denver Woolworth store, and was injured by the fall. Testimony showed that a few pieces of such paper were on the floor in the area most of the time, and came from a pizza counter in the store where there were no seating facilities; customers thus had to eat standing at nearby tables. The manager of the store claimed there was no negligence, testifying that he had an employee "constantly" sweeping in the area. In the woman's negligence action against Woolworth, do you think the company has established the fact that it was exercising "due care," and thus not negligent? Discuss. (*Jasko v. F. W. Woolworth Co.*, 494 P.2d 839, 1972.)

9. A member of the Philadelphia Eagles football team was injured, and when the team refused to pay him for the remaining two years of his contract he asked for examination by a private physician to determine the exact extent of his injuries. The doctor found he was suffering from "stress polycythemia," a nonfatal disease. Later the Eagles' team physician falsely and knowingly told reporters that the player had "polycythemia vera," which is fatal. When the player read newspaper accounts based on this false report he "broke down emotionally," could not cope with daily activities, and experienced marital difficulties. The player, after additional tests proved he had no fatal disease, sued both the team physician and the Eagles for damages for "intentional infliction of mental and emotional distress." The basic defense of both defendants was that the team physician's statement was, at most, reckless, and therefore not made intentionally to inflict distress. Discuss the validity of this defense. (*Chuy v. Philadelphia Eagles Football Club*, 595 F.2d 1265, 1979.)

C·H·A·P·T·E·R 9

AGENCY AND BUSINESS ORGANIZATIONS

In this chapter we first examine the general principles of law that are applicable to a special relationship that pervades many activities in the business world, the *agency* relationship. We then discuss the basic rules of law applicable to *partnerships* and *corporations*, the two forms of business organization through which most of the nation's business is carried on.

Agency

In a legal context the term **agency** ordinarily describes a relationship in which two parties—the principal and the agent—agree that one will act as representative of the other. The **principal** is the person who wishes to accomplish something, and the **agent** is the one employed to act in the principal's behalf to achieve it.

At one time or another, almost everyone has come into contact with the agency relationship. Anyone who has purchased merchandise at a retail store almost certainly has dealt with an agent—the salesclerk. Similarly, anyone who has ever held a job probably has served in some type of representative capacity for the employer.

The usefulness of the agency relationship in the business world is obvious. With few exceptions, no single individual—even the sole proprietor who owns and operates a business himself or herself alone—is capable of performing every act required to run a business enterprise. Similarly, even the smallest partnership must usually employ one or more persons in addition to the partners to carry on the necessary business activities. (And, as will be seen later, each partner is generally considered to be an agent of the partnership when carrying on routine partnership business.) Additionally, the one form of business organization through which most of the nation's large-scale business activities are carried on, the corporation, can, by definition, act *only* through agents. Thus most business transactions in this country are, in fact, handled by agents of one kind or another.

The term *agency* is often used loosely to describe many different types of relationships in which one party acts in a representative capacity for another. *Principal* and *agent* are also sometimes used loosely to denote the parties to various types of arrangements. However, throughout our discussion these terms are used narrowly to describe a particular type of relationship. The *principal-agent relationship*, as we use it, means a relationship in which the parties have agreed that the agent is to represent the principal in negotiating and transacting business: that is, *the agent is employed to make contracts or enter similar business transactions in behalf of the principal.*

Two other closely related relationships are those of *master-servant* and *employer–independent contractor*. In these arrangements the subordinate usually has been employed to perform *physical work* for his or her superior, and the matter in dispute usually concerns *tort liability*. Of course, a person may be hired to represent the employer in commercial dealings and also to perform physical tasks. In such a case he or she is an agent with respect to the authority to transact business and either a servant or an independent contractor with respect to the performance of physical tasks. Although courts sometimes loosely use the term *agent* to describe someone who performs physical duties, we will avoid confusion by continuing to use the term in its narrow sense—i.e., a person authorized to make contracts on behalf of the principal.

Creation of the Agency Relationship

The agency relationship is *consensual*—that is, based on the agreement of the parties. Many times it is created by a legally enforceable employment contract between the principal and the agent. A legally binding contract is not essential, however. Any words or actions on the parts of the principal and the agent which indicate that the agent is authorized to contract on behalf of the principal, and that the agent consents to the arrangement, are generally sufficient to create an agency relationship.

In fact, no formalities are required for the creation of an agency relationship in most circumstances. For example, it is not usually necessary to spell out the agent's authority in writing; oral authority is ordinarily sufficient. Exceptions do exist, however. The most common one occurs when an agent is granted authority to sell *real estate*. In a majority of states an agent can make a contract for the sale of real estate that will bind the principal only if the agent's authority is stated in writing.

Duties of Principal and Agent

Duties Owed by Principal to Agent: The primary duty owed by the principal to the agent is simply that of complying with the terms of the employment contract, if one exists. Failure of the principal to do so will render him or her liable to the agent for damages; if the breach is material, it will also justify the agent in refusing to act for the principal any further. In addition to the duty of compliance, the principal is under a duty to reimburse the agent for any expenditures reasonably incurred by the agent in furthering the interests of the principal.

Duties Owed by Agent to Principal: The primary obligations of the agent are the duty of obedience, the duty to use reasonable care, and the duty of loyalty. The duty of obedience requires the agent to obey instructions of the principal (as long as they are legal). The major exception to this obligation is where an *emergency* occurs. In such a situation, if the principal's instructions are not in his or her own best interests, the agent is justified in taking reasonable steps to protect the principal even if it means deviating from the prior instructions—again, subject only to the limitation that the deviations are lawful.

The "reasonable care" requirement, as the name implies, obligates the agent to act in a non-negligent manner at all times while representing the principal. The duty of loyalty, perhaps the most important obligation of the agent, prohibits the agent from competing with the principal in the type of business he or she is conducting for the principal. Loyalty also requires that the agent avoid any existing or potential conflicts of interest. For example, if B is hired to sell goods for R, B may not sell them to himself unless R's consent is obtained. In similar fashion, the agent may not further the interests of any third party in his or her dealings for the principal. The agent also should not work for two parties on opposite sides in a transaction unless both parties agree to it. Lastly, the duty of loyalty prohibits the agent who may have acquired *confidential information* about the principal's business during the course of the agency from disclosing such information to any third party without the principal's consent. The duties of the principal and agent are illustrated in Figure 9.1.

Liability of the Principal to Third Parties

Contractual Liability: The principal is liable on contracts negotiated by the agent only if the agent possesses some kind of *authority* to make them. Authority is classified as either "actual" or "apparent" in nature.

Actual authority is the authority that the agent has, in fact, been given by the principal. This authority is of two types: express and implied. Express

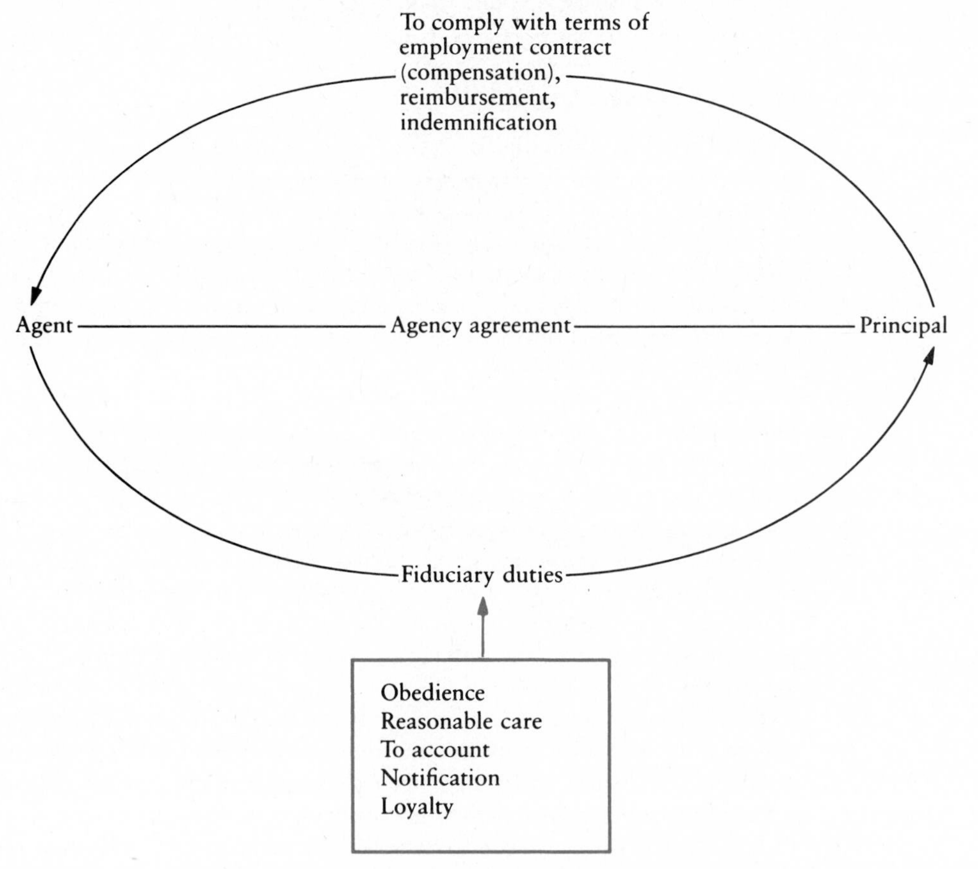

Figure 9.1 The Duties of Agents and Principals to Each Other

authority is that which is directly granted by the principal in his or her instructions to the agent. Implied authority is that authority which an agent possesses in addition to his or her express authority, and essentially refers to the authority of an agent to do any act reasonably necessary to carry out the main job that was granted to the agent. To illustrate: O, the owner of a retail store, hires M to act as manager of the store and gives M express authority to act in certain ways, for example, to purchase inventory and to make sales. In addition, M will have implied authority to handle matters that are incidental to the main purpose of the agency, such as authority to employ a plumber to repair leaks and to employ a reasonable number of salesclerks.

The term "apparent authority" is a contradiction in terms, because it refers to authority which third parties may *assume* the agent possesses, even though, in fact, actual authority is lacking. Apparent authority normally exists only where the principal, *by his or her own conduct*, has led third

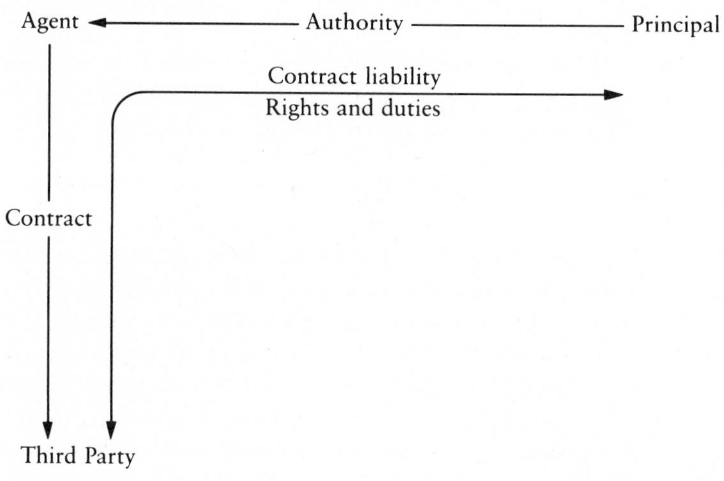

Figure 9.2 The Relationship of Principals, Agents, and Third Parties in a Typical Contract Situation

parties to believe that the agent has authority to engage in a particular transaction. To illustrate: S is a salesman for X, and over a long period of time X has given possession of goods to S which X has wanted S to sell and which S had, in fact, customarily sold. S, while making his rounds, receives a call from X who tells S not to sell the remaining goods he has in his possession. Contrary to instructions, S sells the goods to T, a third party who had purchased such goods from S before, and who had no knowledge of X's withdrawal of authority. In such a case, X is bound by the sale to T.

If a contract is made which the agent has absolutely no authority to make, the principal is not liable on such contract unless he or she subsequently *ratifies* it. A ratification occurs where the principal, with full knowledge of the terms of the contract, indicates to the third party, expressly or impliedly, that he or she will fulfill the contract even though there was no initial obligation to do so. Figure 9.2 illustrates the rule that a principal is bound by the authorized contracts made by the agent.

Tort Liability: Except for the case where the principal authorizes the commission of a tort, or furnishes the employee equipment which he or she knows the employee is unqualified to operate, the principal is liable to third parties for torts committed by the agent only where the agent is "acting within the scope of his or her employment" at the time that the tort occurred. In most instances this rule—the rule of **respondeat superior**—is easy to apply. For example, if an agent who is driving across town to negotiate a contract on behalf of his principal negligently runs into another motorist's car, the agent is clearly within the scope of his employment and the principal

is, therefore, liable to the injured motorist. On the other hand, an off-duty agent who assaults a third party during the course of a purely personal dispute is obviously outside the scope of his employment.[1]

Many real-life cases fall between these extremes, presenting situations in which the scope of employment rule is considerably more difficult to apply. The case below is typical of those in this category.

Rappaport v. International Playtex Corp.
Supreme Court, Appellate Division, New York
352 N.Y.S.2d 241 (1974)

During October 1971 Davis was employed as a salaried outside salesman by Playtex in a sixteen-county area surrounding Syracuse, New York. He had been so employed for twenty-one years. His duties included selling the employer's products directly to retail stores and preparing reports and orders relating to such sales. He did not have an office but worked out of his home at Cazenovia, New York. He was required to own and operate a motor vehicle as a condition of employment (for which he received a flat monthly reimbursement), most of his work travel being by car. He had no set hours of employment but worked whenever it was necessary, including weekends; he was, in fact, urged by his district manager to work evenings and weekends.

On October 10, a Sunday, Davis worked part of the morning at his home. He left for his then separated wife's home at Cazenovia, arriving about 1:30 p.m. and departing two hours later with the unfinished paperwork of the morning still in his car. His destination was the Canastota home of Madeline Reynolds, whom he later married. According to Davis, the purpose of the trip to the Reynolds home was "to do paper work and visit at my friend's house, and have dinner at my friend's house. . . . I do my weekly call reports for two days over there on Sunday, and I have that with me and also I have some other records and orders that I have to make out, [and] so on, key accounts and books to close." The evidence indicated that it was normal for Davis to do paperwork wherever he happened to be.

While traveling to the Reynolds home, Davis was involved in a collision with Barnum. Barnum died from his injuries; Rappaport, the executor of Barnum's estate, brought suit against Playtex, the defendant. The trial court denied defendant's motion to dismiss, and defendant appealed that action.

Cooke, Justice:

. . . Under the doctrine of *respondeat superior*, an employer will be liable for the negligence of an employee while the latter is acting in the scope of his employment and "[a]n employee acts in the scope of his employment when he is doing

[1]The rule of respondeat superior applies to the master-servant (employer-employee) relationship as well as to the principal-agent relationship; thus the employer of a truck driver who negligently strikes a pedestrian while the driver is delivering his employer's goods is liable, under the rule, to the pedestrian. (The rule does not, however, apply to the employer–independent contractor relationship.)

something in furtherance of the duties he owes to his employer and where the employer is, or could be, exercising some control, directly or indirectly, over the employee's activities." As a general rule, an employee driving to and from work is not acting in the scope of his employment, but an exception to this rule would exist in the case of an employee who uses his car in furtherance of his work and while he is driving to a business appointment, since such a person is working and under his employer's control from the time he leaves the house in the morning until he returns at night.

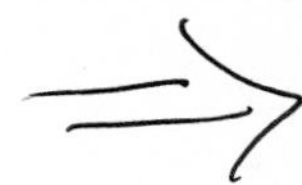

Davis testified at the examination before trial that he was enroute to Canastota to visit Madeline Reynolds and to do more paper work, the further work to be done after dinner. With relation to a trip, involving both business of the employer and a private purpose of the employee, it was said in *Matter of Marks v. Gray*, 167 N.E. 181 at page 183:

To establish liability, the inference must be permissible that the trip would have been made though the private errand had been canceled. . . . The test in brief is this: If the work of the employee creates the necessity for travel, he is in the course of his employment, though he is serving at the same time some purpose of his own. Clawsen v. Pierce-Arrow Motor Car Co., *131 N.E. 914. If, however, the work has had no part in creating the necessity for travel, if the journey would have gone forward though the business errand had been dropped, and would have been canceled upon failure of the private purpose, though the business errand was undone, the travel is then personal, and personal the risk.*

. . . While the [evidence] indicate[s] that Davis intended to perform employment related paper work at his girl friend's house following dinner and that he customarily did such work there on Sundays, he also stated that he normally did his paper work wherever he happened to be. The only reasonable inference that can be drawn is that the business purpose alone would not have launched the subject journey, and that, had Davis not known Madeline Reynolds socially or had the dinner engagement been canceled, the trip to her home at Canastota would not have been undertaken. Accordingly, it cannot be said that the employer's business was even a "concurrent cause" of the fateful trip . . . and, therefore, Davis was not in the scope of defendant's business at the time and *respondeat superior* does not apply.

Reversed. Case dismissed.

★★★

Liability of the Agent to Third Parties

There are a number of situations in which the agent may incur personal liability to the third party. We will note the most important of these here.

Liability Arising out of Contracts: By making a contract, the agent impliedly warrants (guarantees) that he or she has the principal's authority to make the contract. If it turns out that such authority is totally lacking, the

"How long do you think they'd stay there if we vented a little radioactive steam?"

By the law of agency, employees can expose the employer to tort actions if third parties are injured.
Source: Reprinted by permission: Tribune Media Services.

third party may sue the agent for damages for breach of the implied warranty of authority.

In some instances an agent acts for an undisclosed principal—that is, the agent contracts in his or her own name with the third party, the latter having no idea of a principal's existence. If the principal in such a case subsequently refuses to go through with the contract, the third party may enforce the contract against the agent personally.

An agent also incurs personal liability in the case where the purported principal is nonexistent. To illustrate: X, a member of an unincorporated church, makes a contract in the name of the church with Y. Because the unincorporated church (the purported principal) is not a legally recognized person capable of making a contract, X is personally liable on the contract in case the church refuses to live up to its terms voluntarily.

Tort Liability: The agent always has personal liability for torts committed against third parties. If the agent is completely outside the scope of his or her employment at the time of the tort, the agent is solely liable. On the other hand, if the agent *is* acting within the scope of the employment at the time of the tort (in which case the third party normally sues both the agent and principal), the third party recovers a "joint and several" judgment. To illustrate: if the third party's damages are $5,000, he or she recovers a judgment in that amount against the agent personally, a judgment in that amount against the principal personally, and a similar judgment against the agent and principal jointly. If neither the principal nor the agent subsequently pays the judgment voluntarily, the third party, armed with such a judgment, may have the court attach any of the assets of the principal, the agent, or both that are within the jurisdiction of the court and have these sold by court order in order to recover the $5,000 due. If the principal ends up paying the $5,000, he or she has a right to recover such sum from the agent, but, in practice, attempts to recover are often abandoned because of the agent's financial inability to make reimbursement.

Termination of the Agency

The various ways in which an agency may be terminated fall into two general categories: by act of the parties, and by operation of law. We will note only the most important of these here.

Termination by Act of the Parties: If an agent is employed to accomplish a particular object, such as the sale of a tract of land owned by the principal, the agency is terminated when the sale and all incidental formalities have been completed. Similarly, if the principal and agent originally agreed that the arrangement will end at a certain time, the arrival of that time obviously terminates their relationship. If nothing has been said as to the duration of the agency, and if nothing occurs to terminate it, the relationship is deemed to last for a period of time that is reasonable under the circumstances.

Another common termination is by mutual agreement. It is a basic rule of agency law that the parties can mutually cancel their contract at any time, regardless of what they may have agreed to originally. And, because the agency relationship is consensual in nature, the relationship can also be terminated (with rare exception) unilaterally—by the principal alone or by the agent alone. If no binding employment contract had existed between the two of them, the party terminating the agency usually does not incur any liability to the other by this action. On the other hand, if a binding employment contract had existed, the party terminating the relationship is liable for damages on the breach of contract theory, unless his or her termination was legally justified.

Termination by Operation of Law: The death or insanity of either principal or agent terminates most agencies immediately. Additionally, the bankruptcy of the principal will terminate the agency in most circumstances, though the bankruptcy of the agent does not terminate it *unless* the nature of the agency is such that the bankruptcy impairs the agent's ability to act for the principal.

If a change of law makes the agency or performance of the authorized act illegal, the general rule is that the agent's authority to act is extinguished when he or she learns of the change. Similarly, if the subject matter of an agency is destroyed, the agency is terminated. To illustrate: X employs Y to sell grain belonging to X that is being stored in a particular storage elevator;

the destruction by fire of the elevator and the grain will normally extinguish Y's authority.

Partnerships

While partnership law was a common-law subject at one time, the basic source of partnership law today in almost all states is the Uniform Partnership Act (UPA). Accordingly, all partnership principles discussed below are based on that act. Our discussion throughout focuses on general partnerships (those in which all partners have unlimited liability for partnership obligations), as distinguished from limited partnerships.

Nature and Formation

Section 6 of the UPA defines a **partnership** as "an association of two or more persons to carry on as co-owners a business for profit." Under this definition, "person" includes not only individuals but also corporations and other partnerships. The "co-owner" requirement distinguishes partners from those persons who are merely agents or servants of a business enterprise. Lastly, the "profit" requirement excludes nonprofit associations, such as churches and fraternal lodges.

Insofar as the legal nature of the partnership is concerned, the UPA partially rejects the common-law view that a partnership is not a separate legal enterprise apart from the partners themselves by allowing a partnership to own property in its own name. Additionally, most states permit partnerships to sue and be sued in their own names.

Any "association" to carry on a business requires either an express or implied *agreement* between the parties. Usually there is a formal, written agreement setting forth all important aspects of the relationship. However, an implied partnership agreement is sufficient; thus, if two persons manage a business jointly and share profits and losses, a partnership exists in the eyes of the law, even though such persons may not have intended to become partners and do not consider themselves to be partners.

The following case illustrates the kind of evidence considered by courts in determining whether an implied partnership agreement exists.

Grissum v. Reesman
Supreme Court of Missouri
505 S.W.2d 81 (1974)

Nora E. Grissum, plaintiff, filed this suit against Dale Reesman, defendant, who was administrator of the estate of plaintiff's deceased brother, Elwood Grissum. Plaintiff was the sole beneficiary under her brother's will. She was to receive a considerable amount of property under the will and, as a result, state inheritance taxes and federal estate taxes in rather large sums would be due. She asked the court to declare that she and her brother had been partners in a

farming operation and that the property in question belonged to the partnership. If the court ruled in her favor, the interest that she had owned in the partnership would not pass to her by her brother's will because it was already hers. Such a holding would save her approximately $57,000 in taxes. The trial court did hold for plaintiff. The State of Missouri (which was also a defendant because of the matter of state taxes) appealed. The primary question on appeal was whether a partnership had existed.

Eager, Justice:

. . . The theory of plaintiff's case was and is that a partnership was created orally between her brother and herself, back in the 1930s, to operate the farmland then owned or to be acquired, to accumulate property, and to share the benefits 50-50. . . . These two continued to farm the land together until Elwood's death in 1970. There was ample evidence that Nora did the cooking, housework and all related chores, kept the books for the operation, did most of the banking, wrote all checks and paid all the bills, fed the livestock, sorted cattle and hogs and, at times, did actual, hard farm labor. This continued through all the years. She was regularly consulted about the purchase of livestock and land; she frequently (or usually) accompanied her brother on trips for the purchase or sale of livestock, and such deals were made by agreement. The farm truck bore the legend: "Elwood & Nora Grissum Farms—Boonville Mo." Elwood had this placed on the truck. A sign was placed by Elwood over the harness shed bearing the [same] legend. . . . This was visible to anyone approaching the house from the highway. . . . Elwood Grissum told sundry people, over the years, both in the presence of Nora and out of her presence, that they were partners on a 50-50 basis. A nephew of Elwood . . . who worked with him a great deal over a period of many years, asked Elwood why they could not "go partners"; the reply was that Elwood could not do so because he already had a partner, his sister. This nephew was told at sundry times that the arrangement was a partnership; on more than one occasion he heard Nora ask Elwood when he was going to fix up the business so that she would be protected, and his answer was that they would go in and fix it up if they ever got time. In other conversations, Elwood stated on many occasions to other farmers, his doctor, and perhaps others that (in substance) he and his sister were partners in their farm enterprise "50-50," or "all the way through," or that they "owned the whole thing together," or were partners in everything. Some of these statements were made on various occasions to the same individuals. One was made so as to include the real estate. Nora, at times, made similar statements in her brother's presence. On one occasion Elwood told his nephew that he thought Nora should "come up" with her partnership half of the work (apparently meaning farm labor), and the nephew replied that she was doing more than her half. Elwood and Nora discussed and decided together on livestock deals and the general operation of the farm. The statements relating to the partnership extended back at least as far as the 1940s and they continued to within a very few weeks of Elwood's death. Nora and Elwood told their banker that everything they had was a "joint venture." All entries into the safety deposit box, except one in 1949, were made by Nora. On one occasion Elwood stated that he would have to consult Nora before buying some cattle because she was his partner; he later bought them.

A joint bank account was opened in the names of Elwood and Nora Grissum in June, 1967, with a deposit of $13,128.68, proceeds of the farm operations. Prior to that time the account had been kept in the name of Elwood Grissum. The joint account was continued until Elwood's death with all farm money deposited in it. When money was borrowed Elwood signed the notes alone. The farm insurance was applied for and issued in both names . . . from at least as early as 1957 and presumably before. It was stipulated that Elwood filed individual federal income tax returns . . . from "about" 1966 through 1969. . . . We are not advised what was done before that. For the year 1970, four returns were filed: an individual return for Elwood to the time of his death, a partnership return, a fiduciary return, and an individual return for Nora. The point of all this is that Elwood did, for some years prior to his death, report farm income on individual returns. We shall discuss this later. . . . [L]and was acquired in the name of Elwood in 1937 (presumably from his father and mother), in 1942, 1946, 1947, 1948, 1949 and 1952. . . . It is obvious that most of these tracts were purchases made to increase the farming operation. The occupancy and operation of the farm or farms started in the depression in the 1930s, with one eighty-acre tract; at Elwood's death the [property value] had increased to approximately $286,000. During all this period Nora had lived and worked on the farm. It is certainly true that both Elwood and Nora derived all their living expenses from the operation of the farm, for no other source of income is indicated. It also seems obvious that neither drew down any profits, as such, but that all excess went into the expansion of the farm operation and (some) beginning in January, 1969, into joint certificates of deposit. . . .

[A] partnership agreement may be implied from conduct and circumstances; . . . evidence of a sharing of profits constitutes prima facie evidence of the existence of a partnership and in the absence of other evidence becomes conclusive; . . . the parties are not required to know all of the legal incidents of a partnership . . . ; a partnership consists of a factual relationship between two or more persons who conduct a business enterprise together. We note further that when the essentials of such an agreement have been established, expressly or by implication, it is not to be avoided because of uncertainty or indefiniteness as to minor details and, in the absence of express agreement, it will be presumed that profits are to be shared equally. . . .

The element of profits and a sharing of profits is essential. It is important to note here that although the operation was prosperous, neither party ever drew down any profits, but put all money over and above farm expenses and living expenses into additional equipment and land, until in 1967 and 1969 when they established the joint account and bought the joint certificates of deposit. The joint account recognized Nora's interest in the farm operating funds, and the joint certificates recognized her interest and ownership in the accumulated funds. It would appear, therefore, that Nora shared in any and all profits just as much as Elwood did, but that neither saw fit to make use of them individually. It is a fair inference that either had the *right* to take profits at any reasonable time. It is probable that minor losses may have occurred over the years; if so, they were taken care of out of the general funds.

We recognize that three things speak to some extent in opposition to a partnership, namely: (1) the individual income tax returns filed by Elwood; (2) the fact that title to the real estate stood in his name; and (3) that an individual bank account in Elwood's name was maintained until 1967, although Nora drew checks upon it regularly in Elwood's name by herself. It is generally recognized that partnership property may be held in an individual name. That element is of no great materiality. When we consider the background of these individuals, the fact that they cannot be held to have known the usual or legal requirements or incidents of a partnership, and the fact that it was probably a matter of convenience to transact those certain phases of the partnership business in an individual name, we find that these things are not sufficient to prevent a conclusion that a partnership in fact existed. Certainly Nora was not an employee, for she received no wages; she was not a wife, and it was not her duty as such to perform all such services and labor. We are *clearly convinced*, and hold, that a partnership existed with the ownership of the property and the profits to be shared on an equal basis. . . .

The judgment is affirmed.

★★★

Partnership Property

Under the UPA, partnerships may own property in their own names, as we have noted. This is not only a recommended practice but also, in fact, a very common one. However, property held in the names of the individual partners may also be partnership property in the eyes of the law. For example, if X and Y are partners, and the title to an acre of land is in X's name, that land may legally be partnership property and thus subject to claims of partnership creditors if the property was purchased with partnership assets. And, while mere use of a partner's property for partnership purposes does not alone cause it to become partnership property, such use coupled with such factors as (1) the payment of taxes by the partnership, or (2) the carrying of the property on partnership books as an asset will cause a court to rule that the property is partnership property.

Operating the Business

Relations between the Partners: Partnership agreements often provide that a particular partner will be the "managing partner," exercising control over the daily operations of the business. In the absence of such agreement, all partners have equal rights in the conduct and management of the business.

Partners have certain rights in partnership property, but these are subject to several limitations. First, the partnership agreement may provide that only one partner may use or control a particular piece of partnership property. Second, in the absence of such agreement, all partners have equal rights to use partnership property, but only for partnership purposes; thus one partner is not entitled to exclusive use or possession without consent of all other partners. And last, a partner's right to possess and control partnership property cannot be transferred to a third party without the consent of all partners.

Individual partner's rights to profits of the enterprise are usually specified in the partnership agreement. If not, profits are divided equally. The same rules are applicable to division of losses.

Each partner maintains a **fiduciary relationship** with the partnership and with every other partner in matters pertaining to the partnership. This relationship is much the same as the one existing between principal and agent. (The analogy is particularly appropriate because each partner is an agent of the partnership.) Since such a relationship requires the highest standards of loyalty, good faith, and integrity, a partner who acts in his or her own self-interest and to the detriment of the partnership is accountable to it for any profits made from the endeavor.

In addition to the broad right to have other partners act with loyalty and in good faith, each partner has the right to inspect and copy partnership books. Each partner also has the right to institute a legal proceeding, called an "accounting," under certain circumstances—for example, if he or she has been wrongfully excluded from partnership business or property, or if one of the other partners has derived a personal benefit from a partnership transaction without his or her consent.

Relations with Third Parties, Generally: In partnership transactions with third parties, the law of agency governs the liabilities of the partnership, the partners, and the third party. Technically, the partnership is the principal and each partner an agent with respect to partnership affairs. Thus the partnership is liable to third parties for a partner's transactions that are contractual in nature if the partner had express, implied or apparent authority to make such transactions.

Under the UPA, a partner possesses the implied authority to engage in transactions that are for the "carrying on of the partnership business in the usual way"—i.e., transactions that are customarily carried on by partners in similar firms. Under this rule, partners usually have the implied power to borrow money on behalf of the partnership, to hire needed employees, and to purchase items reasonably necessary to the operation of the business. Additionally, partners have implied authority to sell goods and real estate belonging to the partnership if sales of such items are within the ordinary course of the business. (For example, a partner in a firm that buys and sells land has implied authority to sell a parcel of real estate owned by the partnership, while a partner in a grocery business would *not* have the implied authority to do so.)

As in agency law generally, the partnership is liable to third parties harmed by the tort or other wrongful act of a partner only if the tort was committed while the partner was acting in the ordinary course or scope of the partnership business. However, even if a partner's tort did not involve partnership business, any other partner participating in, directing, or authorizing the wrongful act is personally liable along with the one actually committing it.

In the following case, the court applies basic agency concepts contained in the UPA to plaintiff's claim against a partnership on a promissory note executed by a single partner.

Burns v. Gonzalez
Court of Civil Appeals of Texas
439 S.W.2d 128
(1969)

Gonzalez and Bosquez were partners in Inter-American Advertising Agency (hereafter called "the partnership"). The sole business of the partnership was the sale of broadcast time on XERF, a radio station located in Ciudad Acuna, Mexico. The radio station was owned and operated by a Mexican corporation, Compania Radiodifusora de Cahuila, S.A. (hereafter called "the corporation"). The corporation, in turn, was entirely owned by Gonzalez and Bosquez.

In 1957 a contract was made between the corporation and partnership, on the one hand, and Roloff and Burns, on the other. Under this contract Roloff and Burns were to pay $100,000 in return for two fifteen-minute segments of broadcast time daily over XERF for so long as the franchise of the radio station remained in force. Roloff and Burns paid the $100,000 during 1957 and 1958. In June 1962 Roloff assigned all of his rights under the contract to Burns, who apparently intended to sell the broadcast time to others.

Because of labor disputes and other problems, the radio station was shut down at various times. With some exceptions, the broadcast periods described in the 1957 contract were not made available to Burns or to the persons to whom he sold them. In November 1962 the radio station was in receivership, and it became unlikely that the broadcast periods in question would be available for at least two years. On November 28, 1962, Bosquez, purporting to act in his own behalf and in behalf of the partnership, executed a promissory note for $40,000 payable to Burns on November 28, 1964. This note was given to Burns to compensate him for the income he would have derived from selling the broadcast time during the two-year period ending November 28, 1964. Another purpose of the note was to settle any claim for breach of contract that Burns might have against the corporation.

The note was not paid when due, and Burns sued both the partnership and Bosquez and Gonzalez as individuals. The trial court rendered judgment for Burns against Bosquez, who made the note, but it held that neither the partnership nor Gonzalez was liable, for the reason that Bosquez did not possess the implied authority to sign the note. Burns appealed.

Cadena, Justice:

. . . Under Sec. 9(1), U.P.A. "Every partner is an agent of the partnership for the purpose of its business, and the act of every partner, including the execution in the partnership name of any instrument, *for apparently carrying on in the usual way the business of the partnership* of which he is a member binds the partnership, unless the partner so acting has in fact no authority to act for the partnership in the particular matter, and the person with whom he is dealing has knowledge of the fact that he has no such authority." (Emphasis added [by the court.]) In this case, in fact, Bosquez had no authority to bind the partnership by executing a negotiable instrument. [Evidently, Gonzalez and Bosquez had agreed that Bosquez could not take such action alone.] But, since this express limitation on the authority of Bosquez was unknown to Burns, then, under the language of Sec. 9(1), his act in executing the note would bind the partnership if such act can be classified as an act "for apparently carrying on in the usual way the business of the partnership."

As we interpret Sec. 9(1), the act of a partner binds the firm, absent an express limitation of authority known to the party dealing with such partner, if such act is for the purpose of "apparently carrying on" the business of the partnership in the way in which other firms engaged in the same business in the locality usually transact business, or in the way in which the particular partnership usually transacts its business. In this case, there is no evidence relating to the manner in which firms engaged in the sale of advertising time on radio stations usually transact business. Specifically, there is no evidence as to whether or not the borrowing of money, or the execution of negotiable instruments, was incidental to the transaction of business, "in the usual way," by other advertising agencies or by this partnership. . . . It becomes important, therefore, to determine the location of the burden of proof concerning the "usual way" of transacting business by advertising agencies. . . .

[The court then concluded that the burden of proof fell on the third party rather than on the nonparticipating partner. Thus Burns had the burden of proving that execution of the note by Bosquez was for the purpose of "apparently carrying on in the usual way the business of the partnership."]

The language relating to carrying on in the usual way the business of the partnership is no more than a statement of the rule concerning vicarious liability based on "apparent" authority. . . .

Our conclusion is supported by the fact that the liability of partners with respect to third persons is largely determined by reference to the principles of the law of agency. One who asserts that the particular act of an agent is within the scope of the agent's authority has the burden of proving the extent of such authority. . . . The principle for imposing liability on the nonacting party, be he partner or ordinary principal, is that he has "held out" the actor as being empowered to perform acts of the nature of the act in question. . . .

[The court noted here that, at one time, partners in trading partnerships (those engaged in the buying and selling of products or land, as distinguished from those engaged in the supplying of services) possessed the implied authority to sign partnership notes, while those in the nontrading partnerships did not possess such authority. The court, however, said that today this rule was of little importance, observing that "the UPA makes no mention of the distinction between trading and non-trading firms." The court continued]:

The power of a partner to issue commercial paper arises not from the existence of the partnership, but from the nature of the partnership business and the manner in which such business is usually conducted. This is the plain meaning of Sec. 9(1).

The only thing we know of the nature of the partnership here is that it was restricted to the sale of broadcast time over XERF on a commission basis. There is nothing to show that the transaction of such business required "periodical or continuous or frequent purchasing" or made "frequent resort to borrowing a necessity, not existing by reason of embarrassments, or on account of some fortuitous event, but for the advantageous prosecution of even a prosperous business." The assets of the partnership consisted of a few desks, chairs, typewriters and office supplies.

We disagree with the contention put forward by Burns to the effect that Bosquez was the managing partner. At best, the record reflects that both Bosquez and Gonzalez were active in the management of the business. As a matter of fact, with the exception of the . . . 1962 note. . . , the record discloses that all instruments significantly affecting the relations between the partners and Burns were signed by both Bosquez and Gonzalez.

Since the evidence does not disclose that Bosquez, in executing the 1962 note, was performing an act "for apparently carrying on in the usual way the business of the partnership," there is no basis for holding that the note sued on was a partnership obligation. . . .

The judgment of the trial court is affirmed.

Partners' Liability to Third-Party Creditors: One of the cardinal characteristics of the partnership form of business is that the individual partners are *personally liable* for the obligations of the partnership. But this liability is of a secondary nature, because a creditor having a claim against a partnership must first look to partnership property for satisfaction of the claim. The creditor can reach the assets of individual partners only after partnership assets are exhausted. Moreover, the assets of an individual partner must first be used to satisfy claims of his or her personal creditors before partnership creditors can assert their claims against such assets.

Termination

Complete termination of the partnership as a business organization is comprised of two elements: dissolution and winding up. *Dissolution* does not of itself bring the partnership business to a close; it is, rather, the "beginning of the end." Essentially, the word *dissolution* designates that point in time when the object of the partners changes from that of continuing the organization in its present form to discontinuing it. The partnership is not terminated at that time, but its object has become termination.

The second element of termination, commonly referred to as *winding up*, involves the actual process of settling partnership affairs after dissolution. After both dissolution and winding up have occurred, the partnership as an organization will have terminated.

Dissolution: The events that cause dissolution can be divided into four categories: (1) act of the parties not in violation of their agreement, (2) act of the parties in violation of their agreement, (3) operation of law, and (4) court decree. In many circumstances dissolution of a partnership can be brought about by the partners themselves without violating their partnership agreement and without the necessity of any formal legal proceedings. For example, the agreement may provide that the partnership will exist for only a specified period of time; upon expiration of this period, the partnership will obviously dissolve. Similarly, the articles of partnership may provide that the arrangement is for some expressly indicated purpose or undertaking; once that purpose is achieved, dissolution occurs. Additionally, any partnership, regardless of the terms of the original agreement, can be dissolved at any time by agreement of all the parties.

Irrespective of the terms of the partnership agreement, any partner can at any time withdraw from the partnership and cause its dissolution. If this withdrawal violates the partnership agreement, however, the withdrawing partner is liable to his or her co-partners for any damages resulting from the wrongful dissolution. Dissolution by operation occurs where the business becomes illegal or upon the death or bankruptcy of any partner. A number of situations are set forth in Section 32 of the UPA in which dissolution of a partnership can be accomplished by the issuance of a formal court decree. They can be divided into two broad categories: (1) situations in which a partner can obtain a dissolution, and (2) situations in which a third party can obtain such a decree.

Once a dissolution has occurred, the authority of individual partners to act on behalf of the partnership usually ceases, except for acts necessary to complete unfinished transactions or those appropriate for winding up partnership affairs.

Winding Up: Winding up is the second and final step after dissolution in the termination of a partnership. When dissolution has occurred and the business is to be terminated, the winding up process entails such activities as liquidating partnership property (turning it into cash), collecting outstanding accounts, paying outstanding debts, and any other actions required to bring partnership accounts to a close. After all partnership assets have been liquidated, they are distributed to those having claims against the partnership. The order in which they are distributed is of little importance if the partnership assets are sufficient to pay all claims in full. But if the assets are insufficient to completely satisfy all claims, claims are paid in the following order: (1) claims of outside creditors of the partnership; (2) claims of individual partners for repayment of loans they have made to the partnership; and (3) claims of individual partners for return of contributions they have made to the partnership's working capital. If any assets remain after satisfying these claims, they are distributed as profits to the partners in the proportion in which profits were to be shared.

Corporations

As was noted in the discussion of statutory law in Chapter 4, all states have general corporation laws that govern all aspects of corporate life. About half the states have patterned their statutes on the Model Business Corporation Act, and the laws of the remaining states are sufficiently similar that they can be discussed with some degree of generalization.

Nature

The most important characteristic of the **corporation** is its recognition as a **legal entity**—an artificial being or person separate from its stockholders and managers. As a result of this concept, the corporation can own property, make contracts, and sue and be sued in court in its own name. And an especially important consequence of the separate entity concept is the fact that the corporation alone is responsible for its debts. In other words, the stockholders (unlike the partners in a partnership) are generally *not personally liable* for corporate debts. Thus if a corporation fails, the most that the stockholders will ordinarily lose is the amount they have invested in it.

Formation

The first step in the formative process is preparation of **articles of incorporation** by the promoters—the persons forming the corporation. The articles normally must include the name of the corporation, its duration, the purposes for which it is formed, the financial structure, and provisions for regulating the internal affairs of the corporation. The basic steps in forming a corporation are illustrated in Figure 9.3.

If all requirements for incorporation specified in Figure 9.3 have been followed to the letter, it is said that a ***de jure*** corporation exists. The existence of such a corporation cannot be challenged by either the state or any other party so long as the corporation acts lawfully in the conduct of its business. Occasionally, however, there occurs some deviation from the procedures required for incorporation. If the deviation is relatively insignificant and no harm is caused to the public interest, the corporation still has de jure status. On the other hand, if the deviation is so important that there is not a substantial compliance with the mandatory incorporation procedures, there

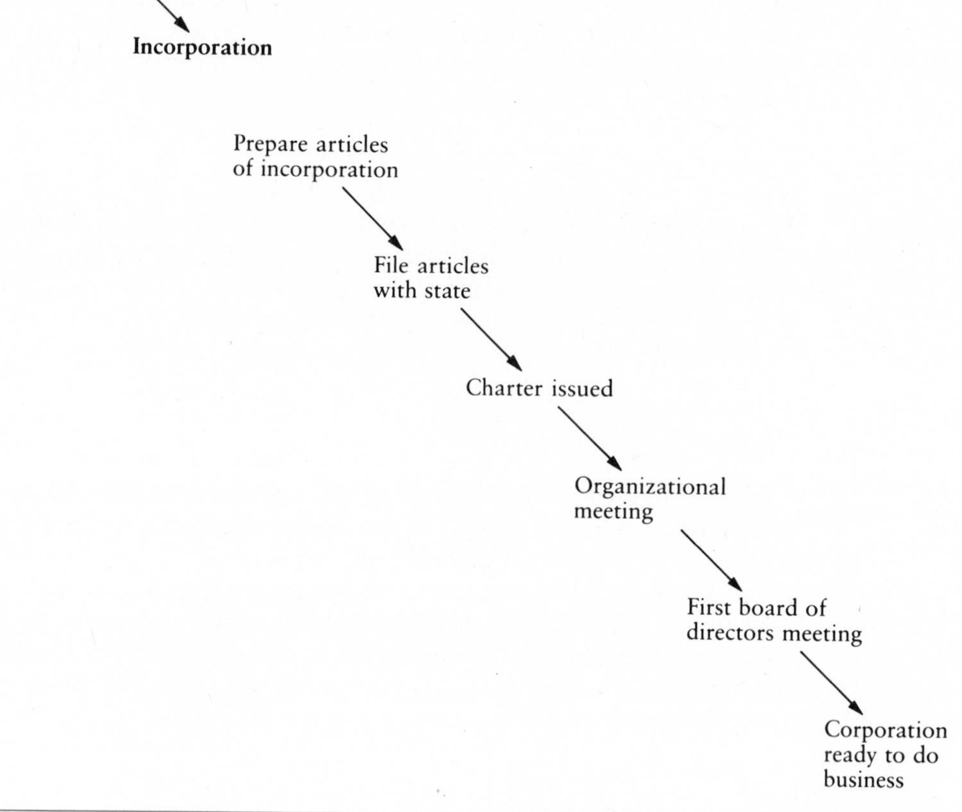

Figure 9.3 The Basic Steps in Corporate Formation

will not be a de jure corporation. There might, however, be what is commonly called a ***de facto*** corporation, a corporation in fact. The status and powers of a de facto corporation are the same as a de jure corporation, with one limited exception: the state can challenge its validity, but no other party can do so. If a corporation has neither de jure nor de facto status, the validity of its existence can be challenged by the state or by any other interested party, such as a creditor seeking to hold a shareholder *personally liable* for a corporate debt.

Financing the Corporation

The principal method of initially financing a corporation is by the issuance of **securities**, which are sold to investors. Shares of capital stock sold to investors (**shareholders**) are called *equity securities*, and bonds sold to investors are called *debt securities*. Shareholders are owners of the corporation, and bondholders are corporation creditors. Whatever kinds of shares or bonds are issued, the corporation must comply with registration laws of the state applicable to such issues, and often with all regulations of the Securities and Exchange Commission—a federal agency regulating securities sold in interstate commerce or through the mails.

Corporate Powers

As an artificial person, a corporation possesses the power to do most of the things an individual can do in the operation of a business enterprise. Corporate powers derive from several sources, classified as follows: (1) statutory powers, (2) express powers, and (3) implied powers. Statutory powers are those specifically granted by the general corporation law, and express powers are those set forth in the articles of incorporation. Implied powers are those powers of a corporation to do any other things reasonably necessary for the carrying on of its business.

A corporation is empowered to act only insofar as is necessary to further the purposes for which it was formed. Any act that is beyond the scope of its business as defined in the articles of incorporation is said to be an ***ultra vires*** act. At one time, ultra vires acts were frequently held to be void by the courts. Under this view, corporations sued on unauthorized contracts could use ultra vires as a defense to such actions. Today, however, most state statutes abolish the defense of ultra vires insofar as the parties to a contract are concerned. Thus corporations are generally liable on such contracts, and generally can enforce such contracts against the other party.

Corporate Management

The structure of corporate control can be viewed as pyramidal in nature, with the shareholders forming the broad base of the pyramid. The shareholders exercise their control, for the most part, by selecting the individuals who serve on the board of directors. The board, in turn, usually selects corporate officers and other managerial employees at the top of the pyramid; these people oversee the day-to-day operations of the firm. The relationships within this structure are illustrated in Figure 9.4.

The most important shareholder functions are (1) election and removal of directors, (2) amendment of articles and bylaws, and (3) approval of certain extraordinary corporate matters. Of these functions, the election of directors is probably the most important.

Shareholders as such are not agents of the corporation and therefore cannot bind the corporation by acting individually; their powers must be exercised collectively, such as at shareholders' meetings. Action at a shareholders' meeting is, of course, taken by voting; the number of votes a shareholder has is determined by the number of shares he or she owns.

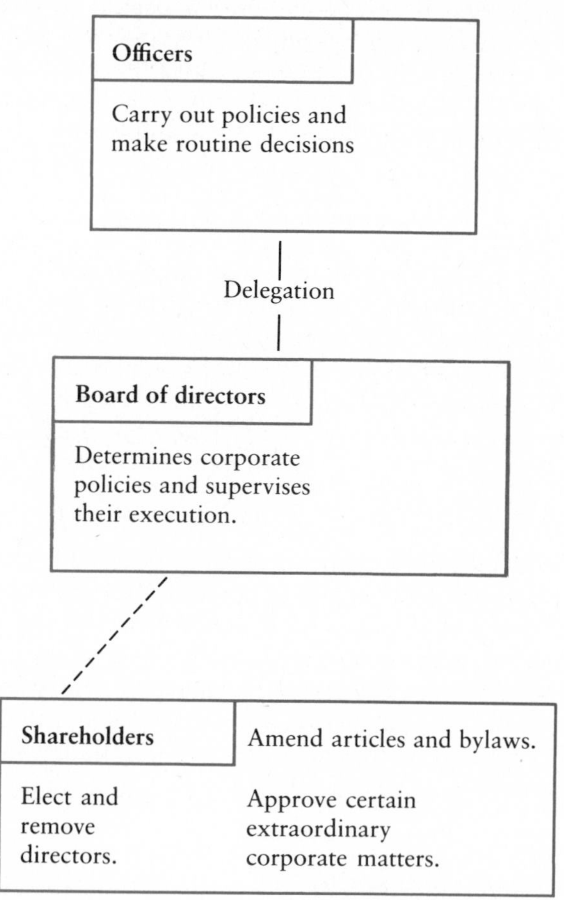

Figure 9.4 The Relationship of Shareholders, Directors, and Officers in Running the Corporation

Several methods exist by which a shareholder who owns a relatively small portion of the corporation's share can increase his or her voting power. These are (1) cumulative voting, (2) shareholder agreements, (3) proxies, and (4) voting trusts. Of these, cumulative voting merits special mention. This is the procedure by which a shareholder is entitled to take his or her total number of shares, multiply that total by the number of directors to be elected, and cast the multiplied total for any director or directors to be elected. To illustrate: O is the owner of a hundred shares of stock, and at the annual shareholders' meeting three directors are to be elected. The slate of candidates includes A, B, C, D, and E. If cumulative voting is allowed (as it usually is), O can take the total three hundred votes that he is entitled to cast and cast them all in favor of A, or divide them in any other manner he wishes, instead of casting one hundred votes each for A, B, and C.

Insofar as directors are concerned, the methods of choosing them—and their functions—are dictated by state statute and the corporate articles of incorporation. Even though the corporation is generally bound by the actions of the board, the directors are not agents of the corporation. The primary reason for this is the fact that they do not have *individual* power to bind the corporation; instead, they can only act as a body. The management powers of the board of directors usually include the following:

1. Setting of basic corporation policy in such areas as product lines, services, prices, wages, and labor-management relations.
2. Decisions relating to financing the corporation, such as the issuance of shares or bonds.
3. Determination of whether (and how large) a dividend is to be paid to shareholders at a particular time.
4. Selection, supervision, and removal of corporate officers and other managerial employees.
5. Decisions relating to compensation of managerial employees, pension plans, and similar matters.

In the next case the court discusses the rationale behind the concept that directors must act *as a board* rather than as individuals. The case also illustrates the requirement that directors be given proper notification of board meetings.

Stone v. American Lacquer Solvents Co.
Supreme Court of Pennsylvania
345 A.2d 174 (1975)

Harold E. Stone became chairman of the board of directors of American Lacquer Solvents Co. (hereafter referred to as American) on December 7, 1967. On that date, American's board of directors adopted a resolution that upon Stone's death, his wife, Rachel, would be paid an $8,000 annual pension by American until her death or remarriage. The resolution was adopted in consideration for services to be rendered to American by Stone, and it further provided that it could not be revoked without his consent.

In March 1968 Stone and his wife encountered marital difficulties. Stone contacted Shaw, the president and general manager of American, and told him that he wanted the pension resolution cancelled. Shaw contacted the company's legal counsel and, acting in accordance with his advice as to the procedure to be followed, prepared a letter from Stone to the board of directors of American, saying, "It is my wish that the Resolution dated December 7, 1967 concerning a pension for my wife Rachel be rescinded." Stone signed and personally delivered the letter to Shaw on March 3.

On March 11, 1968, Shaw convened a special meeting of the board of directors of American. Five of the seven members of the board attended the meeting; and when Stone's letter was brought to their attention, they voted unanimously to rescind the resolution of December 7, 1967. Stone was not notified of the meeting and did not attend.

Stone died on November 1, 1968; and when American refused to pay his widow, Rachel, the pension provided for in the resolution, she sued for specific performance. The trial court ruled that the resolution had been validly rescinded by the board at the meeting of March 11, 1968, and hence the plaintiff had no claim. She appealed the decision.

Eagen, Justice:

. . . As a general rule the directors of a corporation may bind a corporation only when they act at a legal meeting of the board. If they purport to act at a meeting which is not a legal meeting, their action is not that of the corporation, and the corporation, absent ratification or acquiescence, is not bound.

As to special meetings of the board of directors of a corporation, the general rule in Pennsylvania is that such a meeting held without notice to some or any of the directors and in their absence is illegal, and action taken at such a meeting, although by a majority of the directors, is invalid absent ratification or estoppel. However, this notice requirement may be waived by a director either prior or subsequent to the special meeting, provided such waiver is in writing. Additionally, any action which may properly be taken at a meeting of a board of directors of a corporation may be affected and is binding without a meeting, if a consent in writing setting forth the action so taken is signed by each and every member of the board and filed with the secretary of the corporation.

A reading of the trial court's opinion filed in support of its decree upholding the legality of the Board's action of March 11, 1968, rescinding the Board's prior Resolution providing for the payment of the pension to the plaintiff was based on three grounds, any one of which, if correct, would warrant its ruling.

First, the court concluded that Stone's letter of March 3, 1968, constituted a consent to the Board's subsequent action rescinding the pension Resolution. The difficulty with this position is that the applicable statute requires that such a consent be executed *after* the meeting and that it specifically set forth the action taken, and that it be filed with the secretary of the corporation. Stone's letter does not meet these requirements.

Secondly, the court concluded [that] Stone's letter of March 3, 1968, constituted a waiver of receipt of notice of the meeting of March 11, 1968. The difficulty with this position is that the letter does not refer to the meeting or indicate in any way that notice thereof is waived. The letter amounts to no more than an expression of desire or consent to rescind the pension Resolution.

In connection with its conclusion that Stone's letter constituted a waiver of notice of the meeting, the court reasoned that no purpose would be served by Stone's presence at the meeting since the other Directors were merely acceding to Stone's wishes and request. This analysis overlooks the rationale for the salutary rule that all directors receive notice of special meetings. That rationale is that "each member of a corporate body has the right of consultation with the others, and has the right to be heard upon all questions considered, and it is presumed that if the absent members had been present they might have dissented, and their arguments might have convinced the majority of the unwisdom of their proposed action and thus have produced a different result." We agree with this rationale and, in view of the presumption embodied therein, we cannot concur in the trial court's premise that Stone and other Directors were of one mind as regards the pension rescission. In relation to this, we specifically note that another member of the Board of Directors failed to attend the meeting of March 11, 1968, and there is nothing in the record to show if he received notice of the meeting, or ever consented to the action taken at the meeting.

Finally, the court concluded that the rescinding resolution of the Board was voidable only and that Stone's silence and failure to object thereto prior to his death amounted to a ratification. The difficulty with this position is that there is nothing in the record to show that Stone was ever made aware that the meeting of March 11, 1968, had been held or knew the rescinding resolution had been adopted by the Board. Under the circumstances, it cannot be said a ratification was effected. . . .

[R]eversed and . . . remanded for further proceedings. . . .

Rights and Liabilities of Shareholders

Rights: The primary rights of shareholders are (1) the right to vote (except for special shares without voting rights), (2) the right to dividends, (3) the preemptive right, and (4) the right to inspect corporate records. The rules applicable to dividends and the preemptive right are so numerous that they can be sketched but briefly here.

The laws of the states differ substantially with respect to the circumstances in which dividends can legally be paid. Generally, however, the following limitations are imposed:

1. Dividends cannot be paid if the corporation is insolvent, or if the payment itself will cause the corporation to become insolvent. **Insolvency** is defined either as (a) the inability of the corporation to pay its debts as they become due, or (b) the possession of insufficient assets to meet all outstanding liabilities.

2. Dividends can ordinarily be paid only from a particular source. Some states allow dividends to be paid only from "current net earnings," for example, while many states permit dividends to be paid from any existing "surplus." In effect, this latter view means that the payment of a dividend in a particular year cannot be made if it is to come out of the original capital investment in the corporation (even if "net earnings" for that year are, in fact, equal to or greater than the amount of the contemplated dividend).

Shareholders do not have an absolute right to receive dividends. Whether a dividend is to be paid ("declared") in a given situation, and how large it is to be, are largely left to the discretion of the board of directors.

In order to protect existing shareholders' proportionate interests in the corporation, the courts have traditionally recognized the preemptive right concept. When a corporation issues new stock, the common-law preemptive right gives each shareholder an opportunity to purchase the number of new shares that will maintain his or her proportionate interest in the corporation. In general, the courts have not recognized preemptive rights in the sale of "treasury stock" (stock that was originally issued by the corporation and subsequently reacquired by it), and in shares of stock issued for consideration other than money.

Liabilities: As has been seen, shareholders are usually not personally liable for the debts of the corporation; they may lose their investment in the corporation if it is a failure, but usually their liability ends there. However, personal liability questions sometimes arise in the case of *stock subscriptions*—offers made by prospective investors to buy shares of stock in a corporation after it is formed. In general, stock subscriptions of promoters cannot be revoked prior to acceptance if the promoters agree initially not to revoke, or where state statutes prohibit revocation within prescribed periods

of time. Additionally, shareholders sometimes have liability for **watered stock**—stock shares that are issued for less than par or stated value.

Corporate Managers

Rights: Corporate managers—directors and officers—possess several well-defined rights. Directors have the right to receive notice of board meetings and to attend and participate in them. They also have the right to inspect all corporate records (a right that is absolute, in most states), and the right to be indemnified (reimbursed) by the corporation for personal expenses or losses which they have incurred while acting on behalf of the corporation in good faith and in a reasonable manner. The rights of officers and other employees are essentially spelled out in their employment contracts.

Liabilities: Those who manage the corporate enterprise owe to the corporation and its shareholders a number of basic duties that can be classified under the headings of *obedience*, *diligence*, *and loyalty*. A corporate manager incurs personal liability for the failure to fulfill any of these duties. In addition to these fundamental duties, certain special liabilities are imposed by federal security laws. Unlike the previous section on the *rights* of corporate managers, where some distinctions were made between rights of directors and other managers, the *duties* and *liabilities* of all who manage the corporation are essentially the same.

"Obedience" refers to the general duty of all managers to see that the corporation obeys the law and confines its operations to those activities that are within the limits of its corporate powers. "Diligence," as the name implies, refers to the duty of managers to exercise due care—the duty not to be negligent—at all times in carrying on the corporation's business. And, as in agency law, the duty of "loyalty" springs from the fiduciary relationship which exists between the managers and the corporation. In general, loyalty demands that the managers act in good faith and with the highest regard for the corporation's interests as opposed to their personal interests. More specifically, a director or other manager must not use corporate funds for his or her own purposes, must not use confidential information for personal gain, and must not withhold information from the corporation that would be relevant to it in making business decisions.

The following case involves a claim that the corporate directors had been negligent in their management of the business.

Shlensky v. Wrigley
Appellate Court of Illinois
237 N.E.2d 776 (1968)

Shlensky, the plaintiff, is a minority shareholder in Chicago National League Ball Club, Inc. The corporation owns and operates the major league professional baseball team known as the Chicago Cubs. The individual defendants are directors of the Cubs. Defendant Philip K. Wrigley is also president of the corporation and owner of approximately 80 percent of the corporation's shares.

Shlensky filed suit in behalf of the corporation (a derivative suit), claiming that it had been damaged by the failure of the directors to have lights installed in Wrigley Field, the Cubs' home park. No trial was held, however, because the trial court dismissed his complaint on the ground that it did not set forth a claim that the law would recognize even if his version of the facts were correct. Shlensky appealed.

Sullivan, Justice:

. . . Plaintiff alleges that since night baseball was first played in 1935 nineteen of the twenty major league teams have scheduled night games. In 1966, out of a total of 1,620 games in the major leagues, 932 were played at night. Plaintiff alleges that every member of the major leagues, other than the Cubs, scheduled substantially all of its home games in 1966 at night, exclusive of opening days, Saturdays, Sundays, holidays and days prohibited by league rules. Allegedly this has been done for the specific purpose of maximizing attendance and thereby maximizing revenue and income.

The Cubs, in the years 1961–65, sustained operating losses from its direct baseball operations. Plaintiff attributes those losses to inadequate attendance at Cubs' home games. He concludes that if the directors continue to refuse to install lights at Wrigley Field and schedule night baseball games, the Cubs will continue to sustain comparable losses and its financial condition will continue to deteriorate.

Plaintiff alleges that, except for the year 1963, attendance at Cubs' home games has been substantially below that at their road games, many of which were played at night.

Plaintiff compares attendance at Cubs' games with that of the Chicago White Sox, an American League club, whose weekday games were generally played at night. The weekend attendance figures for the two teams was similar; however, the White Sox week-night games drew many more patrons than did the Cubs' weekday games. . . .

Plaintiff further alleges that defendant Wrigley has refused to install lights, not because of interest in the welfare of the corporation but because of his personal opinions "that baseball is a 'daytime sport' and that the installation of lights and night baseball games will have a deteriorating effect upon the surrounding neighborhood." It is alleged that he has admitted that he is not interested in whether the Cubs would benefit financially from such action because of his concern for the neighborhood, and that he would be willing for the team to play night games if a new stadium were built in Chicago. . . .

Plaintiff . . . argues that the directors are acting for reasons unrelated to the financial interest and welfare of the Cubs. However, we are not satisfied that the motives assigned to Philip K. Wrigley, and through him to the other directors, are contrary to the best interests of the corporation and the stockholders. For example, it appears to us that the effect on the surrounding neighborhood might well be considered by a director who was considering the patrons who would or would not attend the games if the park were in a poor neighborhood. Furthermore, the long run interest of the corporation in its property value at Wrigley Field might demand all efforts to keep the neighborhood from deteriorating. By these thoughts we do not mean to say that we have decided that the decision of the directors was a correct one. That is beyond our jurisdiction and ability. We are merely saying that the decision is one [for the] directors [to make]. . . .

Finally, we do not agree with plaintiff's contention that failure to follow the example of the other major league clubs in scheduling night games constituted negligence. Plaintiff made no allegation that these teams' night schedules were profitable or that the purpose for which night baseball had been undertaken was fulfilled. Furthermore, it cannot be said that directors, even those of corporations that are losing money, must follow the lead of the other corporations in the field. Directors are elected for their business capabilities and judgment and the courts cannot require them to forego their judgment because of the decisions of directors of other companies. Courts may not decide these questions in the absence of a clear showing of dereliction of duty on the part of the specific directors, and mere failure to "follow the crowd" is not such a dereliction.

For the foregoing reasons, the order of dismissal entered by the trial court is affirmed.

★★★

Termination

A primary characteristic of the corporation is that it can have a perpetual existence. (While a few states do place time limits on the duration of the certificate of incorporation, this is of no real consequence because renewal is usually only a formality.) This is not to say, however, that a corporation *must* exist forever. A number of different circumstances can bring about an end to its existence.

In discussing the termination of a corporation, a distinction must be made between "liquidation" and "dissolution." *Liquidation* is the conversion of the corporation's assets to cash and the distribution of these funds to creditors and shareholders. *Dissolution* is the actual termination of the corporation's existence as an artificial person—its "legal death." A liquidation can occur without an actual dissolution, as where the corporation sells its assets to another company. While the shareholders might then choose to dissolve the corporation, it would not be required that they do so. The remainder of our discussion will be devoted primarily to the various circumstances that bring about dissolution, with a final mention of the process of winding up corporate affairs after dissolution.

Voluntary Dissolution: A corporation can voluntarily terminate its own existence. Dissolution can be accomplished by the incorporators in some unusual circumstances, but the shareholders are ordinarily the only ones with such power. The board of directors does *not* have the power to dissolve the corporation.

If the corporation has never gotten off the ground, it can be voluntarily dissolved by the *incorporators*. This can occur where the corporation has not done any business and no shares have been issued. In such a situation, the incorporators dissolve the corporation by filing "articles of dissolution" with the appropriate state official, who then issues a "certificate of dissolution."

Shareholders may discontinue the corporation's existence for any reason, at any time. The most common reason for voluntary dissolution is that the enterprise has proved unprofitable.

The procedures for voluntary dissolution vary somewhat from state to state, but their general outline is basically the same. The process is usually initiated by resolution of the board of directors. A meeting of the shareholders is then called, at which time the matter is voted on. The vote required for approval varies among the states in the same manner as for mergers and consolidations, from a simple majority to four-fifths, with a *two-thirds* vote being the most common requirement. After shareholder approval, articles of dissolution are filed and the certificate of dissolution is issued.

Dissenting shareholders can challenge the dissolution in court. However, a court will issue an injunction prohibiting dissolution only if these shareholders are able to prove that the controlling shareholders dissolved the corporation in *bad faith*, with the intent of defrauding the minority.

Involuntary Dissolution: In some circumstances, a *court action* can be instituted for the purpose of dissolving the corporation. A legal proceeding of this nature can be brought by a shareholder or by the state. Dissolution ordered by a court in such a proceeding is often referred to as an "involuntary" dissolution. The laws of the various states generally provide that one or more shareholders can file a lawsuit requesting that the court dissolve the corporation. Those situations in which a *shareholder* can obtain dissolution by court order are:

Oppression of minority shareholders. In most states, oppression of minority shareholders by those in control is a ground for judicial dissolution. Oppressive conduct generally includes any act by which controlling shareholders seek to take unfair advantage of the minority. One example is the purchase of corporate assets by controlling shareholders, who then lease them back to the corporation for exorbitant rental fees.

Deadlock. Most states authorize dissolution by the court if it is proved that the corporation is unable to function because of a management deadlock. This is not a common occurrence and ordinarily could only happen in a closely held corporation. In order for there to be an unbreakable management deadlock, of course, there would have to be equal ownership interests by two separate factions and a board of directors with an even number of members split into equal, opposing groups.

Mismanagement. Courts are generally reluctant to interfere with decisions made by corporate managers. However, a court may order dissolution of the corporation if it is being so grossly mismanaged that its assets are actually being wasted.

Since a corporation derives its right to exist from the state where it is incorporated, it seems natural that the *state* should also be able to take away that right. This power can be exercised, however, only in certain circumstances. The grounds for dissolution by the state (which are remarkably similar in the various jurisdictions) are discussed below.

Failure to comply with administrative requirements. All states insist that corporations comply with various administrative requirements. With respect to some of these duties, noncompliance may be cause for dissolution at the instance of the state. The most common examples are (1) failure to file required annual reports with the secretary of state, (2) failure to pay franchise fees or other state taxes, and (3) failure to appoint or maintain a registered agent. Many states acknowledge the relative insignificance of such omissions by providing for easy reinstatement upon compliance and payment of any penalties owed.

Ultra vires acts. The performance of acts that are beyond the corporation's powers constitutes a reason for dissolution. This principle is of little practical importance today, however, because most articles of incorporation now grant such broad powers that *ultra vires* acts occur infrequently.

Dormancy. If a corporation never commences business after it is formed, or if it becomes dormant by abandoning its operations, the state can seek its dissolution in court. But the absence of corporate activity does not automatically bring about dissolution; it simply gives the state a basis for obtaining court-ordered dissolution.

Antitrust violations. In many jurisdictions, a corporation's violation of the state (not federal) antitrust laws is a cause for dissolution.

Fraudulent formation. Several states provide for dissolution where the corporation obtained its certificate of incorporation by misrepresenting material facts.

Winding Up: When voluntary dissolution occurs, the corporation's directors become **trustees** who hold corporate assets for the benefit of creditors and shareholders. They usually are allowed to wind up corporate affairs without court supervision. The directors in this situation do, however, have four basic duties:

1. They must not undertake any new business. Their authority is limited to the fulfillment of existing corporate obligations.

2. They must make a reasonable attempt to collect debts owed to the corporation.

3. After liquidation of corporate assets, they must pay creditors insofar as these assets are sufficient to do so.

4. When the claims of corporate creditors have been satisfied, they must distribute any remaining funds to shareholders. This distribution is required to be in the proportion of shareholders' respective interests and in accordance with any special rights enjoyed by preferred shareholders.

The directors can be held personally responsible for the breach of any of these winding up duties. However, if they are unwilling to serve as trustees in liquidating the corporation, a "receiver" will be appointed and supervised by a court for the purpose of winding up corporate affairs. The court can also take such action if a creditor or shareholder shows cause why the directors should not be allowed to perform this function.

In any case where dissolution is involuntary, the liquidation of corporate assets and other winding up activities are always performed by a court-appointed receiver.

Questions and Problems

1. A patron in a gambling casino in the Aladdin Hotel had several drinks and, after losing his money, called the dealer a "hateful and degrading" name. The dealer reacted by punching the gambler in the nose. When the patron sued the Aladdin Hotel for damages resulting from the assault, the hotel contended that its employee, the dealer, was not acting within the scope of his employment at the time of the incident, and that it was therefore not liable for the injury. (In other words, the hotel claimed that this was essentially a personal dispute, and not one closely connected to the carrying on of its business.) Do you agree with this? Why or why not? (*Prell Hotel Corporation v. Antonacci*, 469 P.2d 399, 1970.)

2. Bruton lent a D-8 Caterpillar rent-free to David Eckvall, who wanted to clear some land owned by Eckvall. It was agreed that Eckvall would provide an operator and pay for fuel and routine maintenance. Nothing was said about major repairs. While Eckvall was using the Cat, it broke down. Without contacting Bruton, he took it to Automatic Welding & Supply (AWS), where extensive repairs were made at a cost of $2,340. When the repairs were almost completed, Bruton happened to come into the AWS shop on other business and saw his Cat. He spoke to an AWS mechanic and learned of the scope of the repairs, but nothing was said about cost. After the repairs were completed, the Cat was returned to Eckvall's property where he used it for some time thereafter. AWS billed Bruton for the repairs. Bruton denied liability, and AWS sued. (*Bruton v. Automatic Welding & Supply*, 513 P.2d 1122, 1973.) Is Bruton responsible for the $2,340 under any principles of agency law? Discuss.

3. In 1959, Bert Bell, Commissioner of the National Football League (NFL), entered into an agreement with representatives of the NFL Players Association, which

provided for certain pension benefits for players who had retired from the NFL prior to 1959. The bylaws of the NFL required any such agreement to be approved by the owners of at least ten of the twelve NFL teams. During negotiations leading to the agreement, Bell stated that he would resign if the agreement were not approved. The agreement was not approved and the pension benefits were not paid. Those players who would have received benefits under the agreement sued both the NFL and the players association, claiming that the NFL was bound by the agreement because Bell had acted with apparent authority. (*Soar v. National Football League Players Ass'n*, 438 F.Supp. 337, 1975.) Under basic agency law principles, do you think the players should have won their lawsuit? Discuss.

4. Anderson, Richards, and Williams formed a partnership for the purpose of producing rock music concerts. The three partners initially contributed $2,000, $4,000, and $3,000, respectively, to the partnership for use as working capital. The partnership agreement made no provision for the division of profits. At the end of the first year, the partnership had made a profit of $4,500. What is each partner's share of the profits? Explain.

5. X, Y, and Z were partners in an automobile dealership. Their partnership agreement provided for continuation of the business in the event of the death of any partner. X died, and Y and Z agreed with X's widow that she would receive a lump sum payment of $50,000 and a 25 percent share of the business's profits as compensation for X's share in the partnership. It was agreed, however, that she would not be required to perform any duties for the business and would take no part in management. Is X's widow a partner of Y and Z? Explain.

6. Hanrahan, a shareholder of Puget Sound Corp., demanded the right to inspect corporate records prior to a shareholders' meeting. His purpose was to obtain the names and addresses of other shareholders so that he could urge them to elect directors who would seek a merger of Puget Sound with another corporation. Puget Sound refused the demand, and Hanrahan sued to enforce his right of inspection. (*Hanrahan v. Puget Sound Power & Light Co.*, 126 N.E.2d 499, 1955.) Will Hanrahan win? Explain.

7. Johnson, the president of Continental Co., badly mismanaged its affairs and caused the company to sustain heavy losses. The board of directors had allowed Johnson a free hand in running the company. A shareholder filed a derivative suit against Johnson and all the directors for negligence. One of the directors, Wembley, claimed that he should not be held responsible. His defense was that, because of the great distance between his home and Continental's headquarters (2,500 miles), he had not attended a board meeting in almost a year. Should Wembley's defense shield him from liability? Discuss.

8. The president of Hessler, Inc., made a contract with an employee, Farrell, in which retirement benefits were promised to him. In the past, the president had been allowed to manage the company's affairs more or less independently of the board; he also owned approximately 80 percent of the corporation's stock. When Farrell retired, the corporation refused to pay the benefits, and Farrell sued. The corporation claimed that the agreement made with Farrell by the president was invalid because it had not been approved by the board of directors. (*Hessler, Inc. v. Farrell*, 226 A.2d 708, 1967.) Is the corporation correct? Discuss.

Business and the Regulatory Environment

PART II

TRANSITIONAL NOTE
INTRODUCTION TO GOVERNMENT REGULATION OF BUSINESS

The remainder of this text is devoted primarily to government regulation of business. Before we explore specific areas of law dealing with government regulation, however, we review some of the underlying rationales for this regulatory activity.

The Market Economy

The U.S. economy is essentially capitalistic. In other words, it is based primarily on the concept of free enterprise and private ownership of the means of production. Under this system, the purchasing decisions of consumers ultimately provide the fuel on which the market operates. The interplay of supply and demand causes the market itself to regulate economic behavior. The market determines price and output, as well as the optimal level of innovation, quality, service, and so on. In ordinary circumstances, the market achieves an efficient allocation of resources. Even if the market-based economy does not always allocate resources with maximum efficiency, in this country it is preferred over a government-administered economy for another reason: it obviously harmonizes more closely with fundamental notions of free choice.

Reasons for Government Intervention in the Marketplace

Although the American economy continues to be predominantly market-based, today there is a significant degree of government involvement. Most economists who believe strongly in the validity of a market-based economy also believe that some government interference in the functioning of markets is necessary. They often disagree, however, as to *when* government involvement is needed, *what form* it should take, and *to what degree* it is required.

Some resource allocations do not fit within the market system and consequently are not viewed as business activities. Such services as national defense, police and fire protection, and public streets and highways are so-called **public goods**, which are provided by the government and paid for with tax revenues. It is impossible, or at least impractical, to charge consumers according to their use of these types of items.

In most situations, however, the market is capable of allocating resources. But there are sometimes imperfections in the way the market functions. Such imperfections, often called market failure, provide one of the most commonly asserted justifications for government involvement. In addition, even when the market works well it cannot accomplish all of society's goals.

We now examine several of the most important reasons for government regulation of business activities in the marketplace, some of which are interrelated and sometimes overlapping.

Externalities

In a few situations, **externalities** prevent the market from functioning properly. Some types of costs associated with producing a product may be involuntarily borne by persons other than the producer or customer. Since these costs, or externalities, are not accounted for in the price of the product, the market cannot properly regulate them and government must do so.

A prime example of externalities is found in the harm done by air and water pollution. If a manufacturer pollutes while producing a product, this pollution imposes costs upon society in the form of health problems, diminished property values, decreased recreational opportunities, and esthetic sacrifices. Although these are part of the costs of producing the product, they are paid for by many people who may not buy the product. Since the costs of pollution are not passed on to consumers of the product, they do not affect the demand for that product and the producer is not likely to take the initiative to control them. The market provides insufficient incentives for the producer to stop polluting, and *environmental protection laws* are necessary. The cost of complying with these laws is then borne by the producer, who passes them on to the customers who benefit from the product.

The costs of on-the-job injuries and occupational diseases provide another example of externalities. At least part of the costs to workers and their families resulting from these injuries and diseases will not find their way into the cost of the employer's product without government action. *Workers' compensation laws* requiring the payment of benefits to injured employees place some of these costs on the employer (producer) and thus put them into the cost of the product. *Occupational safety and health laws* requiring safe working conditions aim both to prevent injuries and also to put a significant portion of the costs of improving workplace safety back under the control of the market by imposing them on the employer.

Inadequate Information

A market can function correctly only when sellers and buyers have adequate information about the economic decisions they make. This information is never perfect in real-life markets, of course, but it usually is sufficient to enable the market to work.

In several situations, the purpose of government regulation may be to improve the quantity or quality of information that is made available to buyers. For example, in capital markets, most of the information relating to the value of securities is solely in the hands of the company issuing the stocks or bonds and may not be readily accessible to many investors. In addition, such information may be too voluminous and complex to be assimilated by all but the most sophisticated investors. Without government regulation, these investors must rely on the company issuing the securities to select, interpret, and divulge information. One of the main purposes of our *securities regulation laws* is to require companies that issue securities to publicly disclose particular types of information in particular ways, thus improving the investor's ability to make knowledgeable decisions.

Two other examples of government regulation intended to improve the quantity or quality of information in the marketplace are the laws (1) prohibiting deceptive advertising, and (2) requiring lenders to disclose all credit charges and rates in a uniform way.

Market Power

A market certainly is capable of functioning when one or more firms possess substantial economic power, but it often will not work as well as it otherwise might—a market ordinarily can perform at something close to an optimal level of efficiency only if economic power is relatively dispersed among a number of firms. In addition, market functioning sometimes can be impaired when there are great differences between the power possessed by sellers and that possessed by buyers.

The primary objective of *antitrust laws* is to prevent a firm, or several firms acting together, from using economic power to impede the functioning of the market.

In labor markets (markets for the sale of workers' labor to employers) there is a natural disparity between the economic power of the average employer and that of the average employee. *Labor relations laws* were enacted to equalize the economic power of employers and employees and thereby to promote industrial peace and stability by requiring employers to recognize and bargain with organized groups of employees (labor unions).

Natural Monopolies

In unusual circumstances, the production of a good or provision of a service may be a **natural monopoly**. There are at least two reasons which can work either together or separately to produce a natural monopoly: (1) the capital investment required for production may be so great that only one firm in a particular geographic area can earn a sufficient rate of return, or (2) production of the good or service may be subject to certain inherent physical limitations that make competition among two or more firms either impossible or impractical.

Public utilities, involved in activities such as electrical generation or natural gas delivery, are generally viewed as natural monopolies. In the case of a public utility, both of the above reasons are applicable. Capital costs are prohibitive, and the physical limitations of cables, pipelines, etc., make competition in a given area impractical.

If a firm operates as a natural monopoly, it has a degree of market power approaching the maximum. Market principles do not work, so government must provide a substitute for the discipline of the market. Government can either (1) treat the item as something akin to a public good and take over the production process itself, or (2) leave production in private hands but closely regulate pricing and output decisions. The second alternative is the most common response, as evidenced by the rate-setting activities of state public utility commissions.

Achieving Other Societal Goals

Some forms of government regulation may be prompted by a desire to achieve societal goals not directly related to market efficiency. In the case of some of the regulatory laws already mentioned, certain noneconomic objectives may have worked alongside the economic ones.

The operation of a market, whether efficient or inefficient, can lead to temporary individual hardships. Particular government activities affecting business may have the purpose of relieving some of these hardships. When natural market forces drive a firm out of business, laws such as those relating to *bankruptcy*, *unemployment compensation*, and *insurance for bank deposits* can soften the blow to individuals.

Finally, there are perhaps a few cases in which government regulation in a given industry may be based in part on the desires and lobbying efforts of firms in the industry to be relieved from some of the rigors of competition. A highly competitive market presents a challenge to its participants, and operating under the close supervision of a government agency may be less demanding than operating in an open market. Some authorities feel that this was true in the transportation industry. Rates charged by interstate trucking firms were regulated for years by the Interstate Commerce Commission rather than by market forces. When Congress acted to deregulate rate-setting in interstate trucking and return this function to the market itself, many trucking firms strongly opposed the deregulation.

The chapters that follow examine several of the most important areas of the law concerned with government regulation of business activities. In Part II of the text, Chapters 10, 11, and 12 deal with antitrust law; Chapter 13 with securities regulation; and Chapters 14, 15, and 16 with laws regulating the employment relationship. Part III then focuses more broadly on some of business's duties toward larger segments of society. Some of the pertinent laws obviously are regulatory in nature. Chapters 17 and 18 examine consumer protection, and Chapter 19 discusses environmental protection. Chapter 20 deals with the increasingly important area of international business, and, as a capstone, Chapter 21 explores the general topic of corporate social responsibility.

C · H · A · P · T · E · R 10

ANTITRUST LAW
INTRODUCTION AND REGULATION OF INDUSTRY STRUCTURE

Introduction to Antitrust Law

An economy such as that of the United States, which depends primarily on the interplay of market forces, cannot function properly without competition. Although the word "competition" is subject to various shades of meaning, it most often refers to a condition of economic rivalry among firms. That is, firms should be engaged in a contest for customers, the outcome of that contest ideally depending on each firm's efficiency and resulting performance.

The primary purpose of antitrust law is to preserve and encourage competition.[1] In the various types of markets, competition can take somewhat different forms. In addition, for several reasons competition cannot be as intense in some markets as in others. But the job of antitrust law is to en-

[1] The term "antitrust" derives from the fact that the so-called "business trust" was a commonly used device for suppressing competition in the 19th century. Under such an arrangement, the owners of several competing firms would transfer ownership and control of their businesses to a group of trustees, which often consisted largely of those who had owned and managed the individual companies. Each person who previously had owned an interest in a single firm would then receive a "trust certificate" evidencing an interest in the resulting aggregation. It was just one of many ways to combine firms under common control. This particular method is not ordinarily used for anticompetitive purposes today, but the term "antitrust" has stayed with us.

courage competition in its various forms and to preserve it to the extent feasible in a given market.

As pointed out in the general introduction to government regulation, most economists feel that a competitive, market-based economy produces a number of beneficial results such as efficient resource allocation and economic freedom. In the view of some authorities, there is another reason for having a strong antitrust policy in the United States—more competition in an economic sense may diminish the amount of power that large firms have over the political process and over the lives of large numbers of people.

Has antitrust law achieved its goals? This question cannot be answered with certainty because it is difficult to measure the effects of antitrust law on the American economy. There are many markets in which most of the sales are made by a few large companies. Many of these firms are quite efficient; some are not. Many do not unfairly abuse their power, but some do. In some of these markets (called **oligopolies**), competitive rivalry appears to be quite vigorous, but in a substantial number it is rather stagnant. Moreover, in some of these markets, concentration of power in a few firms is an inevitable result of extremely large capital requirements and economies of scale. On the other hand, the degree of economic concentration we find is clearly not always inevitable.

Thus, it is not surprising to find substantial disagreement among authorities concerning the wisdom and effect of antitrust law. Some say the law hasn't been enforced aggressively enough, while a few say that it has been applied too aggressively to the wrong things. However, the majority of economic and legal scholars seem to think that antitrust law has at least partially achieved its objectives, and that the American economy is better off than it would have been without antitrust. In the end, only two conclusions are certain: (1) although the *interpretation* of a few of the antitrust rules may change a bit over time, the fundamental principles will remain with us, and (2) antitrust law will continue to be controversial. With that, we now examine the law itself.

The Federal Antitrust Statutes

The first, and still the most important, of the federal antitrust laws was the Sherman Act, passed by Congress in 1890. Section 1 of this act prohibits "contracts, combinations, and conspiracies in restraint of trade." Section 2 prohibits "monopolization, attempts to monopolize, and conspiracies to monopolize."

In 1914, Congress enacted the Clayton Act with two main purposes in mind: (1) to make the prohibitions against certain anticompetitive practices more specific, and (2) to make it easier to challenge certain practices, such as mergers, when the evidence showed only probable future anticompetitive effects and not actual present effects. Section 2 of the act prohibits price discrimination, Section 3 prohibits tying and exclusive dealing agreements, and Section 7 prohibits mergers. In any of these cases, of course, the law is violated only if there is evidence of an actual or probable anticompetitive effect. In addition, Section 8 of the Clayton Act prohibits *interlocking directorates* between certain large corporations that are in direct competition with each other. An interlocking directorate occurs when the same individual serves on the boards of directors of two corporations.

Also in 1914, Congress passed the Federal Trade Commission Act (FTC Act). In addition to creating the Federal Trade Commission (FTC) as an enforcement agency, the act also prohibited "unfair methods of competition" in Section 5.[2]

In 1936 Congress enacted the Robinson-Patman Act. This act amended Section 2 of the Clayton Act to make the law against price discrimination more effective.

Several amendments to the various antitrust statutes have been passed in the years since their enactment. Some of these amendments are discussed later. Also, even though antitrust law is based on statutory enactments, much of the language in the statutes, especially the Sherman Act, is so broad that court interpretations account for most of the lawmaking process. Finally, our attention is focused strictly on *federal* antitrust law. Most states have their own antitrust laws, which usually apply to the same basic practices that are forbidden by federal law. A firm whose activities violate federal antitrust law may find itself in trouble under both the federal law and the law of those states affected by the activities.

Coverage and Exemptions

Interstate Commerce: In general, the federal antitrust laws apply whenever the particular activity being challenged, or the business of a participating firm, has a sufficient involvement with *interstate commerce*. This involvement can occur in either of two ways. First, the interstate commerce requirement is met if the challenged activity actually involves commerce in more than one state. Second, the requirement is fulfilled even though the particular activity occurs solely within one state if that activity or the general activities of an involved firm have a *substantial effect* on interstate commerce. Suppose, for example, that a bid-rigging (price-fixing) conspiracy among a group of Texas electrical contractors directly affects building construction only in Texas. If any of the affected customers do substantial interstate business, or if any of the conspiring contractors make substantial out-of-state purchases of materials or equipment, federal law applies.[3]

---

[2]This phrase in Section 5 gives the FTC its authority in the antitrust area. Another part of Section 5 prohibits "unfair or deceptive acts or practices." This phrase gives the FTC authority to engage in its other major activity—the regulation of false or misleading advertising and similar deceptive practices.

[3]The interstate commerce requirement under one statute, the Robinson-Patman Act, is less inclusive. This is explained in Chapter 12 when we discuss discriminatory pricing.

Foreign Commerce: Anticompetitive activities occurring in foreign commerce also are covered by U.S. antitrust law if there is a substantial effect on an American market. Thus U.S. imports and exports are covered as well as any other commercial activity substantially affecting our domestic economy. Sometimes, of course, the applicability of U.S. antitrust law to foreign commerce is more theoretical than real because of problems in obtaining personal jurisdiction over a foreign company, securing evidence from overseas, enforcing an American court's judgment against a company in a foreign country, and upsetting sensitive diplomatic relations.

Exemptions: Some business activities have been exempted from the antitrust laws by express congressional action or judicial decision. Several of the most important exemptions are noted below.

1. In certain instances, firms in regulated industries have limited exemptions from antitrust. The basic idea is that the activities of firms in industries that are closely regulated by specific federal agencies should be scrutinized primarily by those agencies. The nature and extent of the exemptions vary among the different regulated industries, but generally are very narrow in scope. As an example, a merger between banks which are members of the Federal Reserve System is first studied by the Federal Reserve Board. This agency is required to consider the merger's probable impact on competition. If any adverse impact is found, the Board weighs this against the public's need for a larger bank in the area. If the agency finds no significant negative effects on competition, or if it feels that such effects are outweighed by public need, the merger will be approved. An approved bank merger can still be challenged by the Justice Department on antitrust grounds, although the standards applied are somewhat more lenient than with other mergers.

2. The formation and ordinary activities (collective bargaining and striking, for example) of labor unions are exempt. Without such an exemption, unions and many of their activities could be challenged as combinations in restraint of trade.[4]

3. Agriculture and livestock producers are permitted to form selling cooperatives. Without the exemption, the joint price-setting function of such organizations would constitute illegal price fixing.

4. The Webb-Pomerene Act of 1918 was passed to permit the formation of selling cooperatives by U.S. exporters of goods. This exemption was not especially important or widely used, in large part because of great uncertainty as to just what was permitted. The Export Trading Company Act of 1982, which was intended to improve the position of U.S. exporters in world mar-

---

[4]There is more discussion on this subject in Chapter 16, Employment Law/Labor-Management Relations.

kets, included provisions making this exemption more definite and expanding it to include exports of services as well as goods.

5. Actions by state governmental bodies are exempt if done pursuant to a legitimate state interest. Thus, a state can lawfully require competency examinations for doctors, lawyers, and electricians, for instance, even though the action restricts entry into these fields and lessens the number of competitors.

6. The actions of foreign governments are exempt.

Enforcement

Justice Department: Enforcement of the federal antitrust laws can take one or more of several different forms. The U.S. Department of Justice, which operates in the executive branch under the attorney general, is the primary enforcer of federal law. The Antitrust Division of this department has authority to file lawsuits in federal district court for the enforcement of the Sherman, Clayton, and Robinson-Patman Acts.

Most of these suits are *civil* in nature. If the Justice Department proves a violation in a civil suit, the remedy granted by the court will be an *injunction*. An antitrust injunction will order the cessation of the particular illegal action and in some cases will also require substantial modification of a firm's everyday business practices so as to lessen the likelihood of future violations. When appropriate, divestiture (sale) of assets can be ordered. Many times the terms of an injunction are the result of an agreed settlement between the Justice Department and the defendant. In such cases, the injunction issued by the court (which must approve the terms of the settlement) is called a **consent decree.**

If the case falls under the Sherman Act and involves a flagrant violation (such as blatant price fixing among competitors), the Justice Department may institute a criminal prosecution in federal court. Until 1974, violation of the Sherman Act was a misdemeanor, but in that year it was changed to a felony. Upon conviction, the maximum penalty in a criminal case is a $1 million fine for corporations and a $250,000 fine or three years' imprisonment or both for individuals. Many criminal cases are also settled, the Justice Department agreeing to recommend a particular sentence to the court in return for the defendant's plea of **nolo contendere**. This plea results in a conviction but is not an admission of guilt. These settlements, like those in civil cases, are subject to court approval.

Federal Trade Commission: The FTC has authority to enforce the Clayton, Robinson-Patman, and FTC Acts. Even though it technically has no power to enforce the Sherman Act, any conduct that would violate the Sherman Act will also constitute an "unfair method of competition" under Section 5 of the FTC Act.

FTC enforcement, which is civil in nature, involves a hearing before one of the agency's administrative law judges (ALJ). The ALJ's findings of fact, conclusions of law, and recommended order will be reviewed by the five-member FTC. The FTC then issues a final order, often accompanied by a formal written opinion. This order, often referred to as a "cease and desist order," is very much like a court injunction—sometimes consisting of simple prohibitions and sometimes involving detailed regulation of business activities or even divestiture. A substantial number of FTC orders are reached by agreement between the agency and the respondent (the charged party).

An FTC order is reviewed by a U.S. Court of Appeals if the respondent appeals the agency's action or if the FTC seeks court-ordered enforcement of its decree. Violation of a final FTC order is punishable by a civil monetary penalty of up to $10,000 for each day of noncompliance.

Private Treble Damage Actions: Section 4 of the Clayton Act gives any person (individual, corporation, or state or local government agency) injured by a violation of the Sherman, Clayton, or Robinson-Patman Acts the right to sue the violator within four years after the illegal action. If the plaintiff proves the violation and the amount of damages, these damages are automatically *trebled*—multiplied by three. Treble damages serve both to punish wrongdoers and to provide a monetary incentive for private enforcement of the antitrust laws. Approximately 95 percent of all federal antitrust cases are private treble damage actions. (In some of these private lawsuits, the plaintiff may also obtain a court injunction against the violator.)

If the defendant has previously been found guilty of violating the antitrust laws in a Justice Department criminal or civil suit, a private party injured by the illegal conduct can use this previous judgment to establish a ***prima facie*** case in a subsequent treble damage suit. This means, in essence, that the plaintiff only has to prove the amount of damages. However, if the previous suit by the Justice Department had ended with a consent decree or plea of nolo contendere, a private party cannot make use of the earlier judgment.

When a large number of parties have suffered the same basic harm from an antitrust violation, one or a small group of them may institute a **class action** suit for treble damages in behalf of the group. This procedure is particularly important when a large number of relatively small claims is involved.

Very similar to the class action is a ***parens patriae*** suit by a state attorney general in behalf of the citizens of that state who have been harmed by a particular antitrust violation.

An important limitation on the private treble damage suit was imposed by the Supreme Court in *Illinois Brick Co. v. Illinois*, 431 U.S. 720 (1977). There the Court ruled that, in most instances, such a suit cannot be maintained by an *indirect purchaser*. In other words a retailer who bought through a wholesaler cannot sue a group of manufacturers for overcharges caused by a price-fixing conspiracy at the manufacturing level.

Our Plan of Study

Our approach to antitrust law is to first examine that portion of the law which focuses primarily on *industry structure*. Thus, the remainder of this chapter is devoted to the law of **monopolization** and **mergers**. The next two chapters turn to that part of antitrust which is concerned primarily with specific types of business *behavior*. Chapter 11 discusses *horizontal restraints of trade*, and Chapter 12, *vertical restraints of trade* and *price discrimination*.

Monopolization

Section 2 of the Sherman Act prohibits monopolization, attempts to monopolize, and conspiracies to monopolize. Most of the discussion in this part of the chapter relates to monopolization, although the separate offense of attempted monopolization is briefly examined. Conspiracies to monopolize are not discussed separately, because this portion of Section 2 is essentially duplicative of Section 1 of the Sherman Act.

The statute itself does not define "monopoly" or "monopolization," so the task of definition has been left to the courts. In formulating a definition, it would have been impractical for the courts to adopt the economic model of monopoly. That model pictures a market with only one seller, very high entry barriers,[5] and no close substitutes for the product being sold. A market fitting this description is extremely rare. On the other hand, a real-life market may be almost completely dominated by one firm and show most of the characteristics of a monopoly even though a few other small firms also sell in that market. Consequently, the courts have developed a somewhat more pragmatic definition: a monopoly is a firm having such an overwhelming degree of market power that it is able to control prices or exclude competition.

The Concept of Market Power

The center of this definition of monopoly is **market power**. Market power can be defined as the "ability of a firm to behave in some way other than it could in a perfectly competitive market." Elementary microeconomics teaches that a perfectly competitive market possesses the following characteristics: (1) there are large numbers of sellers and buyers; (2) there are no entry barriers; (3) the products sold by the various sellers are homogeneous—they are all the same and are viewed as such by buyers; (4) all sellers and buyers have perfect information about everything that happens in the market; and (5) every seller is so small in relation to the total market that it can do nothing that will affect the market—it has no control over the price it charges but must charge the price set by the market.

[5] An entry barrier is any condition that makes it difficult for a new firm to come into a market as a competitor. Two examples of the great variety of entry barriers are large initial capital requirements and patents.

Such a market, of course, is merely an economic model and does not actually exist. But it does give us a frame of reference. In reality, markets fall at various points between the economic model of perfect competition at one extreme and the model of monopoly at the other extreme. In virtually every real-life market, there will be firms with some degree of market power. Real-life firms generally do have *some* control over the price they charge, although the degree of control varies greatly from case to case.

Market power is critical to any examination of competition under the antitrust laws, because competition cannot be harmed without some degree of market power being in the hands of one firm or a group of firms acting together.

Thus, market power is the power to have something to say about the price of a product, the power to have some effect on the way the market operates. With respect to other issues in antitrust law, degrees of market power that are less than monopolistic can be relevant. However, in deciding whether there is a monopoly under Section 2 of the Sherman Act, courts look for an *overwhelming* degree of market power. In other words, the court must determine whether a particular market is so completely dominated by a single firm that the firm does not have to worry much about the response of competitors. For all practical purposes, the price and output of such a firm determine the market's price and output.

Measuring Market Power

Market Share: Deciding whether a company has overwhelming market power in a particular market is not an easy task. Although a number of different factors can be relevant to the question, usually the most important is the firm's *market share*. In other words, what percentage share of the relevant market does it have?

The courts have not developed hard-and-fast rules as to what market share definitely does or does not demonstrate overwhelming market power. However, a market share of less than 50 percent will almost certainly not be viewed as showing overwhelming power. On the other hand, a market share of 75 percent or more will almost always be proof of overwhelming power.

Other Factors: Factors other than market share are considered by the courts, but generally are of secondary importance when the market share is below or above the 50 to 75 percent range. These other factors obviously take on much greater importance when the share is within that range. In addition, factors other than market share may be more important when a court has had to make very rough approximations in defining the relevant market, because in such a case the court is not likely to have great confidence in the preciseness of the market share figure. (The process of market definition is discussed in the next section.)

The other factors that may be relevant to the issue of overwhelming market power can be summarized as follows.

1. The *relative size of other firms* in the market can have an effect on the alleged monopolist's power. For example, suppose that X Corporation has a 64 percent market share and is charged with monopolization under Section 2 of the Sherman Act. Also suppose that the market has another firm with about 30 to 35 percent, or perhaps two others with 17 or 18 percent each. The other firm or firms are much more likely to be serious competitors, possibly with substantial economies of scale and costs similar to X, than if the remainder of the market consisted of two dozen small firms.[6]

2. The *size and power of customers* may also be relevant. The existence of large, powerful buyers can put a damper on the market power of a potentially monopolistic seller.

3. The market's *entry barriers* have a direct relation to X Corporation's power. As previously mentioned, entry barriers can take many different forms, including large initial capital requirements, patents, well-established trademarks, trade secret technology, and difficult and specialized distribution channels. There certainly is nothing wrong or illegal about such conditions—they are simply factors that are relevant to the question of whether a monopoly exists. Regardless of the form these barriers take, the following proposition holds true: the more difficult and costly it is for new firms to enter the market, the more protected is the position of firms presently in the market. Thus, if X Corporation is in a market with high entry barriers, it can more fully exploit the power it has without attracting new competitors into the market. However, if entry barriers are relatively low, X must concern itself with potential competitors. If it fully exploits its power in the short term by charging the highest prices it can get away with, in the long term the higher profits will act like a magnet and draw new firms into the market.

4. The *direction* of the market can also be important. If the market is characterized by rapidly developing technology, or if total industry demand is expanding significantly, it will be more difficult for X to hold on to its dominant position. In such a market, a court is less likely to view a borderline market share as being evidence of overwhelming power. In addition, if X's market share has been declining significantly in recent times, this is probably due either to developing technology, expanding demand, or low entry barriers, and will be evidence tending to show that X is not a monopolist.

5. The *performance* of the alleged monopolist may sometimes shed light on the question of power. This type of evidence does not mean much by itself, but it can tip the scales when the question is close, as when the market share is 60 or 65 percent. Thus, if X Corporation has consistently earned a rate of return on its capital investment that is abnormally high, this tends to support a conclusion that the firm has a great deal of market power unless the situation is explainable for other reasons. The expansion of de-

---

[6] Thus, oligopoly may not be the most desirable market structure, but it is better than monopoly.

mand during the same time period, for instance, might explain a high rate of return.

Defining the Market

Market share is critically important to the question of whether a monopoly exists. Before market share can be computed, however, the relevant market must be defined. Market share data is a good reflection of market power only if the market has been accurately defined.

Drawing boundaries around the market usually is the first step in monopolization cases, and also is important to many other types of antitrust questions. In antitrust we seek to determine effects on competition. These effects, of course, do not occur in a vacuum. They occur in a market—a market essentially is the arena within which competitive forces are measured. Any market must be defined in terms of two elements: (1) a particular product or service, or some grouping of products or services, and (2) a geographic area. In some cases the appropriate market definition is obvious. In others the issue can be quite difficult. Often there are several choices, each of which is plausible and supported by some evidence—in such a case, the task is to choose the most supportable market definition from the range of rational alternatives.

Product Market: The importance of properly delineating the product element of the market is illustrated by the following hypothetical example. Suppose that M Company is charged with monopolizing the market for the sale of zippers in the United States. Most of M's zippers are sold to clothing manufacturers, but some are sold to fabric stores and other retail outlets for resale to consumers. M produces and sells 90 percent of the zippers sold in the U.S. If "zippers" is the proper market definition, M's market share conclusively demonstrates overwhelming market power. M argues, however, that zippers actually face stiff competition from buttons and snaps, and that the 90 percent figure does not accurately portray M's power. If buttons and snaps are included in the market definition, M's share of this larger "clothing fastener" market will be only 31 percent.

How should a court respond to M's argument? The following case, which is the leading one on the problem of product market definition, shows the type of analysis normally employed in responding to such an argument.

United States v. E.I. du Pont de Nemours & Co.
U.S. Supreme Court
351 U.S. 377
(1956)

In behalf of the U.S. government, the Department of Justice filed a civil suit charging du Pont with illegally monopolizing the market for cellophane in the United States. The government introduced evidence tending to show that the characteristics of cellophane were so different from other packaging materials that the relevant market should be defined as consisting of cellophane alone. Du Pont introduced substantial evidence showing that cellophane did, in fact, receive heavy competition from other flexible packaging materials such as

pliofilm, glassine, foil, and treated paper. The federal district court agreed with du Pont's position and ruled that the relevant product market consisted of all flexible packaging materials. On this basis, the court ruled that du Pont's share of this larger market fell far short of demonstrating monopoly power and dismissed the case. At this time, civil antitrust cases brought by the Justice Department were appealable directly from the federal district court to the U.S. Supreme Court, so the government's appeal went to the high court.

Reed, Justice:

. . . During the period that is relevant to this action, du Pont produced almost 75% of the cellophane sold in the United States, and cellophane constituted less than 20% of all "flexible packaging material" sales. . . .

Every manufacturer is the sole producer of the particular commodity it makes but its control in the above sense of the relevant market depends upon the availability of alternative commodities for buyers: i.e., whether there is a cross-elasticity of demand between cellophane and the other wrappings. This interchangeability is largely gauged by the purchases of competing products for similar uses considering the price, characteristics and adaptability of the competing commodities. . . .

If cellophane is the "market" that du Pont is found to dominate, it may be assumed it does have monopoly power over that "market." Monopoly power is the power to control prices or exclude competition. It seems apparent that du Pont's power to set the price of cellophane has been limited only by the competition afforded by other flexible packaging materials. Moreover, it may be practically impossible for anyone to commence manufacturing cellophane without full access to du Pont's technique. However, du Pont has no power to prevent competition from other wrapping materials. . . .

Cellophane differs from other flexible packaging materials. From some it differs more than from others. The basic materials from which the wrappings are made . . . are aluminum, cellulose acetate, chlorides, wood pulp, rubber hydrochloride, and ethylene gas. . . .

It may be admitted that cellophane combines the desirable elements of transparency, strength and cheapness more definitely than any of the others. Comparative characteristics have been noted thus: "Moistureproof cellophane is highly transparent, tears readily but has high bursting strength, is highly impervious to moisture and gases, and is resistant to grease and oils. Heat sealable, printable, and adapted to use on wrapping machines, it makes an excellent packaging material for both display and protection of commodities."

"Other flexible wrapping materials fall into four major categories: (1) opaque nonmoistureproof wrapping *paper* designed primarily for convenience and protection in handling packages; (2) moistureproof *films* of varying degrees of transparency designed primarily either to protect, or to display and protect, the products they encompass; (3) nonmoistureproof transparent *films* designed primarily to display and to some extent protect, but which obviously do a poor protecting job where exclusion or retention of moisture is important; and

(4) moistureproof *materials* other than films of varying degrees of transparency (foils and paper products) designed to protect and display."

But, despite cellophane's advantages it has to meet competition from other materials in every one of its uses. Food products are the chief outlet, with cigarettes next. The Government makes no challenge to Finding 283 that cellophane furnishes less than 7% of wrappings for bakery products, 25% for candy, 32% for snacks, 35% for meats and poultry, 27% for crackers and biscuits, 47% for fresh produce, and 34% for frozen foods. Seventy-five to eighty per cent of cigarettes are wrapped in cellophane. Thus, cellophane shares the packaging market with others. The over-all result is that cellophane accounts for 17.9% of flexible wrapping materials, measured by the wrapping surface.

Moreover a very considerable degree of functional interchangeability exists between these products. It will be noted that except as to permeability to gases, cellophane has no qualities that are not possessed by a number of other materials. Meat will do as an example of interchangeability. Although du Pont's sales to the meat industry have reached 19,000,000 pounds annually, nearly 35%, this volume is attributed "to the rise of self-service retailing of fresh meat." In fact, since the popularity of self-service meats, du Pont has lost "a considerable proportion" of this packaging business to Pliofilm. Pliofilm is more expensive than cellophane but its superior physical characteristics apparently offset cellophane's price advantage. While retailers shift continually between the two, the trial court found that Pliofilm is increasing its share of the business. One further example is worth noting. Before World War II, du Pont cellophane wrapped between 5 and 10% of baked and smoked meats. The peak year was 1933. Thereafter du Pont was unable to meet the competition of Sylvania and of greaseproof paper. Its sales declined and the 1933 volume was not reached again until 1947. It will be noted that greaseproof paper, glassine, waxed paper, foil and Pliofilm are used as well as cellophane.

An element for consideration as to cross-elasticity of demand between products is the responsiveness of the sales of one product to price changes of the other. If a slight decrease in the price of cellophane causes a considerable number of customers of other flexible wrappings to switch to cellophane, it would be an indication that a high cross-elasticity of demand exists between them; that the products compete in the same market. The court below held that the "[g]reat sensitivity of customers in the flexible packaging markets to price or quality changes" prevented du Pont from possessing monopoly control over price. The record sustains these findings.

We conclude that cellophane's interchangeability with the other materials mentioned suffices to make it a part of this flexible packaging material market. . . .

It seems to us that du Pont should not be found to monopolize cellophane when that product has the competition and interchangeability with other wrappings that this record shows.

The judgment of the district court in favor of du Pont is affirmed.

★★★

Comment: In the "Cellophane" case, the Supreme Court observed that customer responses to relative price changes among products is a key factor in deciding whether cross-elasticity of demand exists. What the Court did not point out, however, is that such responses are meaningful only if the prices in question are really *competitive* prices. Thus, if the evidence had shown that du Pont's price was producing a rate of return far higher than should exist in a competitive market, a relatively small increase in the price of cellophane might cause many buyers to shift to alternatives. Under such circumstances, the customer response would not necessarily show a high degree of cross-elasticity but possibly that du Pont had already exhausted its monopoly power. There are limits even to the power of a monopolist.

The basic principle of antitrust law established by the Cellophane case is that two or more products are to be included in the same market if there is substantial **cross-elasticity of demand** between the products. Although not mentioned in the case, **cross-elasticity of supply** also can be relevant to the market definition problem. This factor can arise in either of two ways.

1. Suppose the evidence demonstrates that there is in fact a substantial degree of cross-elasticity of demand among zippers, buttons, and snaps for many types of clothing. Suppose also, however, that the button and snap industries are operating at close to full capacity, and that large capital expenditures and substantial time would be required for button or snap companies to increase their production capacity. In such a case there would not be a high level of substitutability among the products and a court would be justified in treating zippers as a separate market.

2. The other situation in which cross-elasticity of supply can be important is really just the converse of the above example. An illustration is found in *Telex Corp. v. IBM Corp.*, 510 F.2d 894 (10th Cir. 1975), in which IBM was charged with monopolizing the market for computer "peripheral" equipment such as computer drives, discs, printers, and memory devices. The evidence showed that many customers already owned expensive central data processing units. When these customers sought peripheral equipment to be used with the central unit, they usually would consider only those items which were already compatible with the central unit they owned—they normally would not consider peripherals that required significant modification in order to be used with their central unit. Consequently, Telex argued that the relevant product market should be defined as including only peripheral equipment that was compatible with IBM central units. Telex's reasoning was that there was a low level of cross-elasticity of demand between peripheral equipment compatible with IBM central units and equipment compatible with other manufacturers' central units. Although this proposition was basically true, the court ruled that the market should also include peripherals compatible with non-IBM systems. The reason for this decision was that suppliers could make modifications more easily than customers could and were much more likely to do so. In other words, it appeared that suppliers of peripheral equipment not compatible with IBM

central units could switch with relative ease to producing IBM-compatible peripherals. Thus, the high level of supply cross-elasticity overcame the low level of demand cross-elasticity.

Geographic Market: In different factual settings, the geographic element of a market definition can be local, regional, national, or international. In essence, the relevant geographic market represents the area within which buyers can reasonably be expected to seek alternative sources of supply. Suppose that Q Company, located in Chicago, produces and sells a chemical used in certain manufacturing processes. If a substantial portion of Q's customers could obtain sufficient quantities of the chemical at a comparable price from another producer in St. Louis, the geographic market should include both Chicago and St. Louis. A geographic market can never be defined with absolute precision, however. Thus, suppose that one potential customer is located in northern Minnesota. For this customer, buying from St. Louis may be significantly more expensive than buying from Chicago. A court may very well ignore this one customer when defining the geographic market. Rough approximations are inevitable.

Many factors influence the geographic interplay of competition, and thus the geographic market definition. Transportation costs are perhaps the most important factor. Some products are more expensive to ship than others, and the higher the transportation costs are, the more circumscribed the geographic market is likely to be. The nature of the product and customer buying habits also play a part. For example, retail markets are more likely to be local than manufacturing markets. On the other hand, the average retail customer will probably consider suppliers within a wider area when buying big-ticket items like cars and boats than when buying bread or soft drinks. Other pertinent factors may include the reach of relevant advertising media, the scope of the available distribution network, and legal restrictions such as city or state licensing requirements. Internationally, factors such as diplomatic relations and restrictions on exports, imports, and investment may play a part.

The Requirement of Intent

If a firm has overwhelming market power, and thus a monopoly, is there automatically a violation of Section 2 of the Sherman Act? Or must something else be proved?

Courts traditionally have required additional proof that the monopolist had exhibited an *intent* to obtain or preserve a monopoly position. There are two different types of intent, *specific* and *general*, either of which is sufficient for a monopoly to be illegal. Before examining these two types of intent, it should be noted that prior to 1945 courts usually required proof of specific intent before holding a monopoly to be illegal. Beginning with *U.S. v. Aluminum Company of America*, 148 F.2d 416 (2d Cir. 1945), however, the law changed. Since then, the courts have held that proof of general intent is all that is required. If the evidence demonstrates specific intent, the monopoly certainly will be illegal, but it is not necessary for the plaintiff to go this far.

Specific Intent: Specific intent is the intent to actually achieve a prohibited objective, in this case monopolization. Specific intent can be proved by evidence that a firm has engaged in *predatory* actions. A predatory action is conduct aimed at injuring a particular competitor or potential competitor in some way that is unrelated to efficiency. Injuring another firm by being more efficient is hard-nosed, legal competition. But inflicting economic injury on another firm by stealing trade secrets, infringing upon a trademark, destroying property, inducing suppliers to cut off the competitor, and similar actions are deemed to be predatory. Such actions may also violate some other specific statute.

Another type of predatory conduct is *below-cost pricing*. A firm can price below its average total costs (including fixed and variable costs) and still increase its revenue with each sale. However, if the firm sells below **marginal cost**, it loses money on each sale. The marginal cost of a unit of goods is the cost of producing and selling just one more unit, without regard to fixed costs (overhead) or the higher unit cost of earlier production. Thus, according to many economists and a majority of the federal courts, a firm is viewed as engaging in legitimate price competition so long as it charges a price at or above marginal cost. If it charges below marginal cost for any substantial period of time, it incurs losses that can only be offset by too high profits in the future after competitors have been driven away from the market. This is not a legitimate competitive activity, and proves specific intent. It should be noted, however, that conventional accounting methods usually do not provide data on marginal costs. Consequently, courts will accept *average variable cost* as a substitute for marginal cost (variable costs are those costs that vary with production levels in the short run).

General Intent: General intent consists of intentional conduct which ultimately contributes to the acquisition or continuation of a monopoly. There does not have to be evidence that the monopolist specifically intended to monopolize the market. Evidence of general intent usually is easier to find than evidence of specific intent.

One example of conduct that can be sufficient to show general intent is an intentional course of action by a monopolist that raises entry barriers substantially and that is not justified by increased efficiency. Such conduct would have the tendency to exclude potential competitors and to prevent expansion by existing competitors. The next case illustrates this type of conduct and also shows that business behavior which is perfectly lawful by itself can nevertheless be sufficient to prove general intent when done by a monopolist. Although the opinion is that of a federal district court, this court's opinion was affirmed by the U.S. Supreme Court. The district court's opinion is presented because of its excellent discussion of the applicable legal principles. The second case, a recent decision by the U.S. Supreme Court, illustrates the circumstances in which a monopolist's refusal to deal with a smaller rival can support a finding of general intent.

United States v. United Shoe Machinery Co.
U.S. District Court for the District of Massachusetts
110 F. Supp. 295 (1953)

United Shoe Machinery made the machinery and equipment used to manufacture shoes. It supplied 75 to 85 percent of the total U.S. demand for shoe machinery. Only one other firm, Compco, could be called a significant competitor, and it was strong only in connection with machines used in one type of shoemaking process. United produced machines for all shoemaking processes and was the only company offering a full line. The government initiated a civil action in federal district court, contending that United had monopolized the national market for shoe machinery in violation of Section 2 of the Sherman Act. The district court concluded that United did possess an overwhelming degree of market power, and then turned to the question of whether the firm's conduct had demonstrated a general intent to monopolize.

Wyzanski, Judge:

. . . In supplying its complicated machines to shoe manufacturers, United, like its more important American competitors, has followed the practice of never selling, but only leasing. . . . United has, without separate charge, promptly and efficiently supplied repair service and many kinds of other service useful to shoe manufacturers. . . .

United's leases, in the context of the present shoe machinery market, have created barriers to the entry by competitors into the shoe machinery field.

First, the complex of obligations and rights accruing under United's leasing system in operation deter a shoe manufacturer from disposing of a United machine and acquiring a competitor's machine. He is deterred more than if he owned that same United machine, or if he held it on a short lease carrying simple rental provisions and a reasonable charge for cancellation before the end of the term. The lessee is now held closely to United by the combined effect of the 10-year term, the requirement that if he has work available he must use the machine to full capacity, and by the return charge which can in practice, through the right of deduction fund, be reduced to insignificance if he keeps this and other United machines to the end of the periods for which he leased them.

Second, when a lessee desires to replace a United machine, United gives him more favorable terms if the replacement is by another United machine than if it is by a competitive machine.

Third, United's practice of offering to repair, without separate charges, its leased machines, has had the effect that there are no independent service organizations to repair complicated machines. In turn, this has had the effect that the manufacturer of a complicated machine must either offer repair service with his machine, or must face the obstacle of marketing his machine to customers who know that repair service will be difficult to provide. . . .

And finally, there is no substantial substitute competition from a vigorous secondhand market in shoe machinery.

Beyond criticism is the high quality of United's products, its understanding of the techniques of shoemaking and the needs of shoe manufacturers, its efficient design and improvement of machines, and its prompt and knowledgeable service. . . . But United's control does not rest solely on its ability, its research, or its economies of scale. There are other barriers to competition, and these barriers were erected by United's own business policies. Much of United's market power is traceable to the magnetic ties inherent in its system of leasing, and not selling, its more important machines. The lease-only system of distributing complicated machines has many "partnership" aspects, and it has exclusionary features such as the 10-year term, the full capacity clause, the return charges, and the failure to segregate service charges from machine charges. . . .

In one sense, the leasing system and the miscellaneous activities just referred to were natural and normal. They are the sort of activities which would be engaged in by other honorable firms. And, to a large extent, the leasing practices conform to long-standing traditions in the shoe machinery business. Yet, they are not practices which can be properly described as the inevitable consequences of ability, natural forces, or law. They represent something more than the use of accessible resources, the process of invention and innovation, and the employment of those techniques of employment, financing, production, and distribution, which a competitive society must foster. They are contracts, arrangements, and policies which, instead of encouraging competition based on pure merit, further the dominance of a particular firm. In this sense, they are unnatural barriers; they unnecessarily exclude actual and potential competition; they restrict a free market. While the law allows many enterprises to use such practices, the Sherman Act is now construed to forbid the continuance of effective market control based in part upon such practices. Those courts hold that market control is inherently evil and constitutes a violation of §2 unless economically inevitable, or specifically authorized and regulated by law.

It is only fair to add that the more than 14,000 page record, and the more than 5,000 exhibits, representing the diligent seven year search made by Government counsel aided by this Court's orders giving them full access to United's files during the last 40 years, show that United's power does not rest on predatory practices. Probably few monopolies could produce a record so free from any taint of that kind of wrongdoing. The violation with which United is now charged depends not on moral considerations, but on solely economic considerations. United is denied the right to exercise effective control of the market by business policies that are not the inevitable consequences of its capacities or its natural advantages. That those policies are not immoral is irrelevant.

[After finding that United had violated Section 2 of the Sherman Act, the court considered what would be the most appropriate remedy. The government sought divestiture—requiring assets to be sold so that United would be split into three separate companies. The court viewed this proposal as unrealistic, primarily because United was completely unitary—it had one plant, one foundry, one set of machine-making tools, one laboratory, one managerial staff, and one labor force. Instead, the court ordered United to (1) offer all machines for sale in addition to offering them for lease, (2) eliminate the restrictive provisions in the leases, and (3) bill separately for repair service so that customers could accurately assess repair costs and examine alternatives.]

★★★

Aspen Skiing Co. v. Aspen Highlands Skiing Corp.
U.S. Supreme Court
105 S. Ct. 2847 (1985)

The plaintiff, Aspen Highlands Skiing Corp. (Highlands), and the defendant, Aspen Skiing Co. (Ski Co.), were involved in the business of operating downhill skiing facilities in the Aspen, Colorado, area. There are four major mountain facilities in the area, and most customers prefer a ticket that permits them to use all four facilities. Because of this customer preference, the companies operating the facilities at the four mountains had for several years cooperated in offering an "all-Aspen" ticket that would permit customers to use any of the four facilities. Although the four facilities were originally developed by separate firms, over a period of years Ski Co. acquired ownership of three of these facilities. The fourth was owned and operated by Highlands. After several years of cooperating to the extent necessary to offer an all-Aspen ticket because of strong customer demand for such a ticket, Ski Co. stopped the practice and began offering only a ticket that permitted access to its three facilities. Highlands suffered substantial economic damage as a result, because there was not a great demand for a ticket to just its one mountain. The skiing school operated by Highlands, which was generally recognized as the best in the area, also lost a great deal of business because of the termination of the all-Aspen ticket program.

Highlands sued Ski Co., alleging illegal monopolization in violation of Section 2 of the Sherman Act. Based upon a jury verdict, the trial court found that Aspen Ski Co. had a monopoly in the market for downhill skiing facilities in the Aspen area, and that its refusal to deal with Highlands demonstrated the requisite intent to monopolize. Highlands was awarded a judgment of $7.5 million (after trebling). The court of appeals affirmed. The only issue presented to the Supreme Court was whether the evidence was sufficient for an inference of intent to monopolize.

Stevens, Justice:

Ski Co. contends that even a firm with monopoly power has no duty to engage in joint marketing with a competitor, that a violation of §2 cannot be established without evidence of substantial exclusionary conduct, and that none of its activities can be characterized as exclusionary. . . . Ski Co. is surely correct in [stating] that even a firm with monopoly power has no general duty to engage in a joint marketing program with a competitor. . . . [In general, a firm is free to choose those with whom it wishes to deal, and this proposition also applies in most situations to a monopolist. In the case of a monopolist, however, this freedom is qualified somewhat, because a monopolist's refusal to deal may constitute evidence of unlawful exclusionary intent when it apparently was not motivated by efficiency concerns or other legitimate business justifications.]

In the actual case that we must decide, the monopolist did not merely reject a novel offer to participate in a cooperative venture that had been proposed by a competitor. Rather, the monopolist elected to make an important change in a pattern of distribution that had originated in a competitive market and had persisted for several years. The all-Aspen, 6-day ticket with revenues allocated on the basis of usage was first developed when three independent companies operated three different ski mountains in the Aspen area. It continued to provide a desirable option for skiers when the market was enlarged to include four mountains, and when the character of the market was changed by Ski Co.'s acquisition of monopoly power. Moreover, since the record discloses that interchangeable tickets are used in other multi-mountain areas which apparently are competitive, it seems appropriate to infer that such tickets satisfy consumer demand in free competitive markets. . . .

Perhaps most significantly, however, Ski Co. did not persuade the jury that its conduct was justified by any normal business purpose. Ski Co. was apparently willing to forgo daily ticket sales . . . . [The evidence supports the jury's conclusion] that Ski Co. elected to forgo these short-run benefits because it was more interested in reducing competition in the Aspen market over the long run by harming its smaller competitor. . . . That conclusion is strongly supported by Ski Co.'s failure to offer any efficiency justification whatever for its pattern of conduct. . . . Ski Co. claimed that usage could not be properly monitored. The evidence, however, established that Ski Co. itself monitored the use of the 3-area passes based on a count taken by lift operators, and distributed the revenues among its own mountains on that basis. Ski Co. contended that coupons were administratively cumbersome, and that the survey takers had been disruptive and their work inaccurate. Coupons, however, were no more burdensome than the credit cards accepted at Ski Co. ticket windows. Moreover, in other markets Ski Co. itself participated in interchangeable lift tickets using coupons. As for the survey, its own manager testified that the problems were much overemphasized by Ski Co. officials, and were mostly resolved as they arose. Ski Co.'s explanation for its rejection of Highlands' offer to hire—at Highlands' own expense—a reputable national accounting firm to audit usage of the 4-area tickets at Highlands' mountain, was that there was no way to "control" the audit. . . .

Thus the evidence supports an inference that Ski Co. was not motivated by efficiency concerns and that it was willing to sacrifice short-run benefits and customer good will in exchange for a perceived long-run impact on its smaller rival. . . . Affirmed.

★★★

Comment: Although the all-Aspen 4-mountain ticket program had been a legitimate joint venture because it resulted in a product for which there was strong demand and which could not have been offered by a single firm, the participants in such an arrangement would have to maintain independent control of their own pricing and be careful not to let the joint venture limit competition any more than necessary to achieve its legitimate goals. (See the discussion of price fixing, joint ventures, and related topics in the next chapter.)

The Problem of Limit Pricing: A firm or group of firms with substantial market power may sometimes discourage new competitors from entering the market by pricing lower than they could get away with in the short run but still higher than would be possible in a truly competitive market. Such conduct, which is called **limit pricing**, presents a dilemma. It actually just represents the positive effect that potential competitors can have on a market in the short run. On the other hand, in the long run it tends to further raise entry barriers, thwart new firms' plans to enter the market, and thereby keep the market in its present condition.

Limit pricing by a monopolist clearly does not prove specific intent, but does it prove general intent? The Supreme Court has not ruled on the point yet, but in the few lower federal court cases dealing with the question the answer has been no. Even though limit pricing does raise entry barriers, courts have been understandably unwilling to condemn the lowering of prices, even by a monopolist. (It should be noted that if two or more firms *agree* to engage in limit pricing, the agreement would constitute illegal price fixing, as discussed in the next chapter.)

Legal Monopolies: One can see from the preceding discussion of intent that it is possible for a monopoly to exist without violating Section 2 of the Sherman Act. In *U.S. v. Grinnell Corp.*, 384 U.S. 563 (1966), the Supreme Court stated that a monopoly is not illegal if it results merely from "growth or development as a consequence of a superior product, business acumen, or historic accident."

A so-called "natural monopoly," although not a common occurrence, would be an example of such a situation. If the capital investment required to start producing a product is extremely high, economies of scale are very large, and demand is relatively low and nonexpanding, one efficient plant may satisfy the entire demand. This would be a legal monopoly. Such a monopoly could also exist as a result of the lawful ownership of a scarce natural resource essential for the manufacture of a product.

A *patent*, which is granted by the federal government for a period of seventeen years, is the exclusive right to an invention, process, or formula. To obtain patent protection, the invention, process, or formula must be "new, useful, and nonobvious." The purpose of our patent system is to encourage innovation by giving the innovator the opportunity to reap higher-than-normal rewards during the prescribed time period. If possession of one or more lawful patents is the *sole* reason for a monopoly, that monopoly is legal. In practice, a monopolist frequently will own (or did so in the past) one or more patents, but there usually are additional reasons for the existence of a monopoly. Moreover, a monopoly which is attributable to patent rights becomes illegal if the patent owner seeks to expand its monopoly beyond the scope of its patents.

Attempt to Monopolize

Section 2 of the Sherman Act also prohibits the separate offense of attempted monopolization. This antitrust violation consists of two elements:

1. The charged firm must have engaged in predatory practices sufficient to prove a *specific intent* to monopolize.

2. Although the firm does not yet have a monopoly, it must be sufficiently powerful that its combination of size and predatory conduct presents a *dangerous probability* that it could become a monopolist if unchecked. Thus, predatory conduct by a firm with a 40 or 50 percent market share probably would constitute attempted monopolization.

Mergers

A merger between two companies clearly is a "combination," and if the merger has a substantial anticompetitive effect it could be invalidated under Section 1 of the Sherman Act. Early judicial interpretation of this statute, however, made it a relatively ineffective weapon against mergers. The courts held that it could only be applied to mergers between competitors, and not to other types of mergers. Moreover, the language of the statute itself permitted its use only against mergers that had actually caused a substantial restraint of trade and not to those having a probable future anticompetitive effect.[7]

As a result, Section 7 of the Clayton Act was passed in 1914. Even though this statute prohibited mergers that were demonstrated to have probable future anticompetitive effects, it nevertheless was not very effective for two reasons. First, it applied only to those mergers accomplished through stock acquisitions, and many firms circumvented the law by using asset acquisitions. Second, like Section 1 of the Sherman Act, it was interpreted as applying only to mergers between competitors.

In 1950, Congress passed the Celler-Kefauver Act, which amended Section 7 so as to close these two loopholes. In essence, modern antimerger law was born in 1950. Today, Section 7 essentially prohibits a firm from acquiring all or part of the stock or assets of another firm "where in any line of commerce in any section of the country, the effect of such acquisition may be substantially to lessen competition. . . ."

---

[7]It should be noted that in later years, in nonmerger cases, the courts frequently did interpret Section 1 of the Sherman Act in such a way as to prohibit contracts, combinations, and conspiracies having only *probable* anticompetitive effects.

"High fives! Something big must be happening over in Corporate Acquisitions."

Mergers are an important part of corporate strategy, though they often raise antitrust questions.

Source: Drawing by Lorenz; © 1981 *The New Yorker* Magazine, Inc.

What Is a Merger?

Combinations between firms can take many forms. There may be a formal corporate merger or consolidation under state corporation statutes. In many cases there is merely an acquisition of all or a substantial part of the stock or assets of another company without a formal merger. Sometimes the shareholders of the acquired company may exchange their shares of stock for shares of the acquiring company. A merger may involve a single transaction negotiated between the two firms' managers and approved by the acquired company's shareholders. On the other hand, the acquiring company's managers may go directly to the target company's shareholders through a publicly advertised *tender offer* because of opposition by the target company's managers. After the merger, there may be a total or partial integration of the two firms, or they may operate separately.

The term "merger" is used to describe a variety of combinations. Under Section 7 of the Clayton Act the form of the transaction is relatively unimportant—in fact, the statute itself does not even use the word "merger." Regardless of the form, a combination that involves a stock or asset acquisition is covered by Section 7.

Market Definition

One of the initial steps in most merger cases is definition of the relevant market. There are two reasons for the necessity of market definition. First, Section 7 clearly mandates it when referring to acquisitions which may have the effect of substantially lessening competition *in any line of commerce in any section of the country*. Second, even without the clear requirement in

Section 7, market definition would still be required because anticompetitive effects do not exist in the abstract—they must occur *somewhere*.

The methods employed by courts to define markets in merger cases are essentially the same as in monopoly cases. A good illustration of this methodology at work in merger analysis is found in *U.S. v. Philadelphia National Bank*, 374 U.S. 321 (1963). In that case, the Supreme Court struck down a merger between Philadelphia National Bank and Girard Bank, the second and third largest banks with head offices in the Philadelphia metropolitan area. The Court held that the relevant product market was commercial banking, and did not include services offered by the various other types of nonbank financial institutions. The justices recognized that some types of credit and other services offered by savings and loan companies, credit unions, and other institutions competed with certain bank services. However, they ruled that commercial banking was unique and there was not substantial cross-elasticity between it and the services of other institutions because (1) no other type of institution could legally offer checking accounts, and (2) no other type of institution actually offered the same "package" or "cluster" of services as banks did. The market share affected by the merger obviously was much larger than if other institutions had been included in the market definition. (Today, savings and loan companies, credit unions, and other financial institutions may offer checking accounts, and the total package of services offered by banks is not as unique as it once was. Thus, "commercial banking" may no longer be a separate product market but part of a larger financial services market. Regardless of this fact, the Court's *methodology* continues to be completely valid.)

The Court defined the relevant geographic market as the four-county Philadelphia metropolitan area. In the Court's analysis, it acknowledged that the large Philadelphia banks, such as the merging ones, had some customers outside this area. Also, a few banks outside the area, such as the large New York banks, did some business in Philadelphia. On the other end of the spectrum, some very small customers would not even consider searching for a bank over an area as large as four counties. However, the four-county region was chosen because this was the area in which (1) most of the customers, who were neither extremely large nor extremely small, found it practical to do their banking business, and (2) state law permitted the operation of branches by Philadelphia banks.

Trends toward Concentration

The Court in the *Philadelphia National Bank* case also took note of the historical trend toward concentration in the Philadelphia banking market. The importance of such a trend results from the underlying purpose of Section 7 of the Clayton Act. Section 7, particularly as amended in 1950, was intended to be a *preventive measure*. Congress was concerned with what it perceived as a disturbing trend toward concentration of economic power into fewer and fewer firms, and sought to discourage the movement toward oligopolistic markets.[8]

As a result, when a merger is challenged and the evidence shows a definite historical trend toward concentration in the relevant market, courts generally are more likely to invalidate the merger. Evidence of such a trend does not automatically make the merger illegal, but may tip the scales in favor of illegality when the question is a close one. Of course, a historical trend toward concentration in a given market will not weigh heavily against the challenged merger if the trend apparently was the result of natural market forces driving out less efficient firms.

Types of Mergers

Mergers traditionally have been classified as horizontal, vertical, or conglomerate. A merger is **horizontal** if the two firms are competitors and **vertical** if one of the firms sells something that the other firm buys. Any other merger is **conglomerate**. A merger may sometimes fit more than one category. For instance, in *Brown Shoe Co. v. U.S.*, 370 U.S. 294 (1962), the challenged merger involved both horizontal and vertical aspects. The reason was that each of the merging firms, Brown Shoe Co. and Kinney Shoe Co., was both a manufacturer *and* a retailer of shoes.

These classifications are important to very broadly describe the different types of fact situations, but two cautionary statements are in order.

1. How a merger is labeled does not determine whether it is legal or illegal.

2. The same basic test, whether substantial anticompetitive effects have resulted or are likely to result in the foreseeable future, is applied to all types of mergers.

Horizontal Mergers: A merger between competitors poses the greatest danger to competition: after the merger, the firms are not likely to compete. This does not mean, however, that every horizontal merger will be illegal. The following factors usually are the most important in a case involving such a merger.

1. The relative size of the firms usually is the most significant factor. At opposite ends of the spectrum, for example, a merger between two firms each having one to three percent of the market would almost never be illegal, while a merger between two firms each having 20 percent would almost always be illegal. More will be said about this factor.

2. The overall level of concentration in the market also is extremely important. As a general rule, the more concentrated a market is at the time of the merger, the more likely it is that a questionable merger will be ruled illegal.

---

[8]There is debate as to whether Congress was correct in its assessment that the American economy was coming under the control of fewer and fewer companies. Evidence can be found to support both sides of the issue.

3. As we have seen, a definite historical trend toward concentration in the market in recent years can affect the court's decision even if the market has not yet become highly concentrated.

4. If the market is characterized by high entry barriers, a questionable merger is more likely to be ruled illegal.

5. A variety of other factors can be important. For example, a firm with 15 or 20 percent of a market ordinarily could legally acquire a company with a two or three percent share. Suppose, however, that the smaller firm traditionally had been an innovator or had recently obtained a patent of major significance. Or suppose that the smaller firm traditionally had been a "maverick" and frequently had led the way in vigorous price competition. In these scenarios, the merger might very well be found to violate Section 7.

As noted above, the relative size of the merging firms themselves usually is the most important factor. In the *Philadelphia National Bank* case, the Supreme Court ruled that a horizontal merger should be *presumed* illegal when the merger causes or threatens to cause "undue" concentration of the market. In that case, the Court said that a horizontal merger between firms having a combined market share of 30 percent or more certainly is one that threatens to cause "undue" concentration. In other cases, a combined market share as low as 20 percent has led courts to engage in a presumption of illegality.

This concept of "presumptive illegality" does not mean that a merger producing a lower level of concentration is automatically legal or that one producing a higher level is automatically illegal. What it means is that, wherever the line is to be drawn, a merger above this line is illegal unless the defendants come forward with evidence showing that the merger is not likely to harm competition. In essence, the presumption shifts the burden of persuading the court from plaintiff to defendants. The *General Dynamics* case which follows provides a good example of the type of evidence that defendants might use to successfully rebut this presumption. (This case is extremely important for another reason. During the 1950s and 1960s the Supreme Court usually decided merger cases solely on the basis of market share statistics and data showing whether the number of firms in the market had been decreasing. The *General Dynamics* case marked a turning point. Beginning with this decision, and continuing since that time, the Court has engaged in a more in-depth economic analysis of challenged mergers and has considered a wider variety of factors.)

United States v. General Dynamics Corp.
U.S. Supreme Court
415 U.S. 486 (1974)

Material Service Corp. owned Freeman Coal Mining Co. In 1954 Material Service began purchasing the stock of United Electric Coal Co., and by 1959 had acquired effective control of United. General Dynamics Corp. then acquired Material Service Corp. Subsequently, the government sued General Dynamics, claiming that the merger of Freeman and United violated Section 7 of the Clayton Act.

Freeman and United together accounted for about 23 percent of total coal production in the state of Illinois. If the geographic market was defined more broadly as the Eastern Interior Coal Province, one of the country's four major coal distribution areas, the combined share would have been about 12 percent. The district court found that the merger did not violate Section 7, and the government appealed to the Supreme Court. The Supreme Court pointed out that such market share figures likely would lead to a ruling of illegality except for the existence of other important factors. These other economic factors caused the court to approve the merger regardless of the market shares.

Stewart, Justice:

. . . Much of the District Court's opinion was devoted to a description of the changes that have affected the coal industry since World War II. . . . To a growing extent since 1954, the electric utility industry has become the mainstay of coal consumption. While electric utilities consumed only 15.76% of the coal produced nationally in 1947, their share of total consumption increased every year thereafter, and in 1968 amounted to more than 59% of all the coal consumed throughout the Nation.

To an increasing degree, nearly all coal sold to utilities is transferred under long-term requirements contracts, under which coal producers promise to meet utilities' coal consumption requirements for a fixed period of time, and at predetermined prices. . . .

Because of these fundamental changes in the structure of the market for coal, the District Court was justified in viewing the statistics relied on by the Government as insufficient to sustain its case. Evidence of past production does not, as a matter of logic, necessarily give a proper picture of a company's future ability to compete. In most situations, of course, the unstated assumption is that a company that has maintained a certain share of a market in the recent past will be in a position to do so in the immediate future. . . .

In the coal market, however, statistical evidence of coal *production* was of considerably less significance. The bulk of the coal produced is delivered under long-term requirements contracts, and such sales thus do not represent the exercise of competitive power but rather the obligation to fulfill previously negotiated contracts at a previously fixed price. The focus of competition in a given time-frame is not on the disposition of coal already produced but on the procurement of new long-term supply contracts. In this situation, a company's past ability to produce is of limited significance, since it is in a position to offer for sale neither its past production nor the bulk of the coal it is presently capable of producing, which is typically already committed under a long-term supply contract. A more significant indicator of a company's power effectively to compete with other companies lies in the state of a company's uncommitted reserves of recoverable coal. . . .

The testimony and exhibits in the District Court revealed that United Electric's coal reserve prospects were "unpromising." United's relative position of strength in reserves was considerably weaker than its past and current ability to produce. While United ranked fifth among Illinois coal producers in terms of annual production, it was 10th in reserve holdings, and controlled less than 1% of the reserves held by coal producers in Illinois, Indiana, and western Kentucky. Many of the reserves held by United had already been depleted, at the time of trial, forcing the closing of some of United's midwest mines. Even more significantly, the District Court found that of the 52,033,304 tons of currently mineable reserves in Illinois, Indiana, and Kentucky controlled by United, only four million tons had not already been committed under long-term contracts. United was found to be facing the future with relatively depleted resources at its disposal, and with the vast majority of those resources already committed under contracts allowing no further adjustment in price. In addition, the District Court found that "United Electric has neither the possibility of acquiring more [reserves] nor the ability to develop deep coal reserves," and thus was not in a position to increase its reserves to replace those already depleted or committed.

Viewed in terms of present and future reserve prospects—and thus in terms of probable future ability to compete—rather than in terms of past production, the District Court held that United Electric was a far less significant factor in the coal market than the Government contended or the production statistics seemed to indicate. While the company had been and remained a "highly profitable" and efficient producer of relatively large amounts of coal, its current and future power to compete for subsequent long-term contracts was severely limited by its scarce uncommitted resources. Irrespective of the company's size when viewed as a producer, its weakness as a competitor was properly analyzed by the District Court and fully substantiated that court's conclusion that [the merger] would not "substantially . . . lessen competition. . . ."

Affirmed.

★★★

Vertical Mergers: Although less likely to harm competition than a horizontal merger, a vertical merger in some circumstances can create dangers to the competitive process. These dangers can be summarized as follows.

Supply Foreclosure: Such a merger has the potential for creating a *foreclosure of supply*. Suppose, for example, that S Company acquires B Corporation. S is a leading producer of a key component or ingredient used by B in manufacturing an end product. S probably will prefer B as a customer over B's competitors. This may or may not cause problems, depending on the circumstances. If S accounts for a large portion of the supply and if this item periodically is in short supply, B's competitors can be hurt by the merger regardless of their level of efficiency. A violation of Section 7 can exist when the evidence shows that a substantial degree of supply foreclosure is very likely.

Market Foreclosure: A vertical merger also can sometimes cause *foreclosure of a portion of the market*. If the portion foreclosed is viewed as substantial, the merger violates Section 7. This is just the other side of the coin from supply foreclosure. In the case of supply foreclosure above we were concerned with injuring competition at B's level. In the case of market foreclosure we are concerned with injuring competition at S's level. B probably will prefer S as a supplier, and if B is a major purchaser of the item in question, S's competitors could be blocked from a substantial part of the market. The competitive advantage acquired by S is not attributable to its own improved production efficiency.

In two important vertical merger cases, market foreclosure was the Supreme Court's primary concern. *U.S. v. du Pont*, 353 U.S. 586 (1957), a completely different case from the *du Pont* case involving cellophane, concerned du Pont's acquisition of a 23 percent stock interest in General Motors Corp. (GM). At that time, GM accounted for 40 to 50 percent of U.S. automobile sales. Du Pont supplied about two-thirds of GM's requirements of "automotive finishes" (paint and lacquer, for instance) and about one-half of GM's requirements of "automotive fabrics" (upholstery, for example). The Court invalidated the acquisition mainly because of its fear that du Pont's competitors were being foreclosed from almost half of the total market for auto finishes and fabrics. In *Brown Shoe Co. v. U.S.*, 370 U.S. 294 (1962), one of the Court's major reasons for striking down the Brown-Kinney merger was the concern that Brown's competitors in shoe manufacturing would be at least partly blocked from selling their shoes through Kinney's retail outlets. Kinney was the largest family-oriented shoe store chain in America.

At the present time it is difficult to determine the amount of supply or market foreclosure that will be viewed by the courts as "substantial." The evidence probably will have to demonstrate supply or market foreclosure of at least 20 percent.

Raising Entry Barriers: A vertical merger may contribute to increased *entry barriers* resulting from vertical integration. Vertical integration occurs when a firm operates at more than one level in the chain of production and distribution. Vertical integration resulting from independent expansion into another level does not raise any questions under Section 7 of the Clayton Act. If it occurs through a vertical merger, however, Section 7 does apply. Sometimes vertical integration can actually reduce costs by making distribution from seller to buyer more efficient. For instance, when seller and buyer (S and B) are owned by the same firm, selling expenses can be less, paperwork can be reduced, and supplies and requirements can be better coordinated and planned. Distribution efficiencies clearly are to be encouraged, but these cost savings can have other effects. If a substantial part of the relevant market is controlled by vertically integrated firms, a new entrant into the market will also have to enter as a vertically integrated firm in order to compete effectively. Entering a market at two levels simultaneously requires much greater capital outlays and thus makes new market entry less likely.

In the end, there are two opposing considerations. Distribution efficiencies are a positive effect in the short run; increased entry barriers are a negative effect in the long run. If competition at the lower level (B's level) is vigorous, these cost savings will be substantially passed on to ultimate consumers, and the increased entry barriers alone should not cause the merger to be illegal. On the other hand, if competition at B's level is rather stagnant, the cost savings probably will not be passed on to consumers, and the potential for increased entry barriers may lead a court to strike down the merger.

Conglomerate Mergers: Conglomerate mergers usually are not illegal. The courts have identified certain situations, however, in which Section 7 may be violated.

Perceived Potential Entrant: Suppose that X Company enters the widget market by acquiring Y Company, a producer of widgets. The merger can be illegal under the "perceived potential entrant" theory if the following factors are present.

1. For a significant period of time before the merger, X was a uniquely situated potential entrant into the widget market. In other words, the evidence shows that X had a special incentive to enter the market and the ability to do so. Entry barriers in the widget market were high, so that there were not many firms like X who were willing and able to enter. But the entry barriers were not insurmountable for a firm like X with a special incentive and substantial resources. The circumstances creating this "special incentive" vary, but often involve "product extension" or "market extension" acquisitions. A product extension merger is one in which X buys into a market that involves a product closely related to one or more of X's present products and thus represents a logical extension of X's product line. A market extension merger is one in which X buys into a market involving a product that X already sells, but in a different geographic area.[9]

2. The market for widgets was already quite concentrated, with only a handful of firms dominating. Thus, the market probably was not as competitive as it should have been.

3. The evidence shows that, prior to the merger, the major firms in the widget market perceived the existence of X as a likely future entrant into the market.

Under these circumstances, X's position "on the edge" of the widget market was probably having a beneficial effect on that market prior to the merger by causing widget makers to keep prices lower in the hope of discouraging X from actually entering. When X acquired Y, this beneficial "edge effect" disappeared. If X had entered the market on its own by build-

[9]Labels like "vertical" and "conglomerate" can be deceiving if not fully understood. The supplier-customer relationship may sometimes create this "special incentive." Thus a vertical merger in some cases may also be challenged under the potential entrant theory.

ing a widget plant (**de novo** entry), this in itself would have been beneficial. Or if X had entered the market by acquiring a very small, inconsequential firm (a "toehold" acquisition) the beneficial effect of the merger would counteract the removal of the edge effect. But if X entered by acquiring a firm that was a significant competitor in the widget market, there is nothing beneficial to counteract the removal of the edge effect. In this case the merger usually will violate Section 7.

Entrenchment: Suppose that Magnum Co. is already dominant in the market for electric motors. Giant Corp., which operates in other markets, has great financial resources and is much larger than Magnum or any other firm in the electric motor market. Giant acquires Magnum. In this situation, because of access to Giant's resources, there is a very real danger that Magnum will become even more firmly entrenched in its position of dominance in the electric motor market. In addition, other firms in that market are likely to be more timid about competing vigorously against Giant-Magnum than against Magnum alone. A third danger is that entry barriers will be raised—new firms are less likely to want to face Giant-Magnum than Magnum alone. Thus, under the so-called "entrenchment" theory (or "deep pockets" theory, so named because of the acquiring firm's formidable resources), the merger may be illegal.

Tending to Cause Reciprocity: Reciprocity essentially is "I'll buy from you if you'll buy from me." Systematic reciprocity on a fairly large scale can distort markets by foreclosing other firms without regard to their efficiency. The Supreme Court held, in *FTC v. Consolidated Foods Corp.*, 380 U.S. 598 (1965), that a merger violates Section 7 when it creates a high likelihood of reciprocity. In that case, Consolidated was a large customer of food processing firms. Consolidated acquired Gentry, which produced dehydrated onion and garlic used in food processing. The Court invalidated the merger. Despite this case, indications are that this theory will not be used against mergers to any appreciable extent in the foreseeable future.

Failing Company Defense

Suppose that M Company and P Company undertake a merger that probably would be illegal under ordinary circumstances. However, suppose further that P was in danger of failure prior to the merger. The so-called "failing company defense" can be used, and the merger will be legal, if the following facts are proved: (1) P probably will not be able to meet its financial obligations in the near future; (2) P will not be able to reorganize successfully and continue in business under the protection of Chapter 11 of the Bankruptcy Act; and (3) P has made a good faith, but unsuccessful, effort to obtain a reasonable merger offer from another firm that would pose less danger to competition than does the merger between M and P.

Merger Guidelines

The Justice Department's Antitrust Division first issued Merger Guidelines in 1968. These guidelines, which also were followed by the FTC, indicated the circumstances in which one of these agencies could ordinarily be expected to challenge a merger. The guidelines were not law, but did provide business with a valuable planning tool.

New, substantially revised guidelines were issued by the Justice Department in 1982 and revised slightly in 1984. The FTC concurred with most, but not all, of the statements in the new guidelines. Two reasons brought about the revision: (1) developing case law during the 1970s resulted in the original guidelines being somewhat stricter than the law actually being applied by the courts; and (2) political conservatives made tremendous gains in the 1980 elections, ultimately resulting in the appointment of Justice Department officials who favored more lenient treatment of mergers.

The fundamental principles of merger law discussed in this chapter continue to be the law, and basically are still reflected in the new guidelines. The guidelines indicate, however, that the Justice Department and the FTC will be more reluctant than in past years to challenge vertical and conglomerate mergers. Another switch in the political climate, however, could cause this reluctance to disappear.

One of the key innovations of the new guidelines is the use of the Herfindahl-Hirschman Index (HHI) for deciding whether to challenge horizontal mergers. This index involves the squaring of the market share of each firm in the market and then adding the squares. If, after the merger in question, the HHI is under 1,000, the merger will almost never be challenged. If the postmerger HHI is between 1,000 and 1,800, whether the merger is challenged will depend on other factors such as those discussed earlier in this chapter. In this 1,000 to 1,800 range, the Justice Department usually will take legal action only if the merging firms are large enough so that the merger adds at least 100 points to the HHI. When the postmerger HHI is above 1,800, the Justice Department usually will take legal action if the merger adds as much as 50 points. Thus, the merging firms must be very small for the merger to go unchallenged when the HHI is this high.

Premerger Notification

In 1976 Congress amended Section 7 of the Clayton Act by adding a requirement that certain large firms give advance notice and detailed information to the Justice Department and FTC of proposed mergers. The purpose of this provision is to enable these agencies to have adequate information about the transaction in advance so they can assess its probable effects and, if necessary, challenge it *before* the merger is actually consummated. This is much easier than trying to "unscramble the eggs" after the merger has already been completed.

In situations where notification is required, the firms cannot complete the merger for at least thirty days after the agencies receive notice. The waiting period is only fifteen days in the case of a merger to be accomplished through a public tender offer. If either agency requests additional information, the waiting period is extended twenty days (ten days for tender offers) from receipt of the additional information.

Premerger notification is required when (1) either firm engages in or affects interstate commerce; *and* (2) one firm has sales or assets of at least $100 million and the other firm has sales or assets of at least $10 million; *and* (3) after the proposed acquisition the acquiring firm will own at least 15 percent or $15 million worth of the stock or assets of the acquired firm.

Questions and Problems

1. McLain sued a group of real estate brokers, claiming that they had violated Section 1 of the Sherman Act by conspiring to fix brokerage commission rates in the city of New Orleans and the surrounding vicinity. The brokers contended that the Sherman Act did not apply to such an activity because of its local nature. They pointed out that all of the land they dealt with was located in the New Orleans vicinity and that their activities did not involve the purchase of anything from out of state or the sale of anything that ultimately went outside the state. McLain showed, however, that the amount of brokerage fees could have an effect on the volume of real estate transactions and that the volume of these transactions affected the demand for financing and title insurance. A significant portion of the financing and title insurance was provided by out-of-state companies. Does the Sherman Act apply to the alleged conspiracy? (*McLain v. Real Estate Board*, 444 U.S. 232, 1980.)

2. Alcoa was charged with monopolizing the U.S. market for aluminum ingot. Aluminum ingot is sold in blocks or bars to fabricators, who use it to make aluminum sheets, conduit, wiring, and other end products. Alcoa produced 90 percent of the "virgin" aluminum ingot sold in the U.S. Some of its ingot production, however, was actually fabricated by Alcoa into end products before selling it. Another factor in the market was "secondary" ingot, or aluminum ingot made from recycled aluminum. Secondary ingot was acceptable for many of the same uses as virgin ingot, but not for all of them. If the product market was defined to include all of Alcoa's virgin ingot production, including that part which Alcoa itself fabricated before selling, but not to include secondary ingot, Alcoa's market share would be about 90 percent. If the market definition also included secondary ingot, Alcoa's share would be 64 percent. If the market definition included secondary ingot, but did not include that part of Alcoa's ingot which it fabricated before selling, Alcoa's share would be 33 percent. Discuss how the product market should be defined. (*U.S. v. Aluminum Co. of America*, 148 F.2d 416, 2d Cir. 1945.)

3. Suppose that in a particular three-state region there are only two granite quarries from which granite suitable for cemetery monuments can be obtained. This type of granite is not available anywhere else in this region, and transportation costs are too high for granite to be shipped in from outside the region. Ace owns one quarry and Beta owns the other. Ace produces 60 percent of the region's total granite production from its quarry, and Beta produces the other 40 percent. Ace does not fabricate any of its granite but sells it in large blocks to firms who make cemetery monuments. Beta is also a cemetery monument maker and uses all of its granite production to manufacture monuments. It sells none to other monument manufacturers. Ace is charged by the Justice Department with monopolizing the sale of granite in this three-state region. Discuss how the product and geographic market should be defined and whether Ace is likely to be found in violation of Section 2 of the Sherman Act.

4. Spelding Co. is a manufacturer of sporting goods. In addition to producing various sport and recreational items for general use, Spelding also makes a line of higher quality and price items for use by sports professionals. Spelding is a major competitor in all the lines and categories of sporting goods it produces. It could be considered dominant, however, in only one product line: "professional grade" baseballs suitable for use in the major and minor professional baseball leagues. During the previous ten years it sold 67 percent of all the professional grade baseballs that were sold in the country. This percentage remained reasonably constant during each of these years.

The Justice Department filed suit against Spelding, claiming that the company had violated Section 2 of the Sherman Act by monopolizing the U.S. market for professional grade baseballs. Spelding contended that its 67 percent share of this line did not accurately reflect the degree of market power it possessed, because "professional grade baseballs" constituted only a small portion of several larger markets. Spelding pointed out that the dollar volume of its sales of professional grade baseballs amounted to only 5 percent of all sales of "professional grade sporting goods," 3 percent of sales of "all baseballs," and a tiny fraction of 1 percent of sales of "all sporting goods." What other types of information would be important in trying to determine whether Spelding had violated Section 2 of the Sherman Act?

5. Martex Co. produces a special type of scalpel used by surgeons. The scalpel effectively cauterizes the incision as the surgeon operates, thus eliminating much of the bleeding problem in surgery. Although Martex was not able to obtain a patent on the scalpel when it was developed several years ago, there still is only one other manufacturer of this type of scalpel. Of the total sales of the cauterizing scalpel, Martex accounts for 85 percent. The scalpel is used by most surgeons for major surgical procedures, and Martex sales represent 70 percent of the total sales of all types of scalpels. Whenever Martex sells these scalpels to surgeons or hospitals, it does so under a contract requiring the buyer to return the scalpel to Martex when it is worn out. Martex uses the worn-out scalpels in its research lab for experimentation, with the objective of improving the product.

Discuss whether Martex may have violated Section 2 of the Sherman Act.

6. The nation's second largest can producer acquired the nation's third largest producer of glass containers. Cans and bottles did not compete for all end uses, but for some uses they did compete. For example, there was clear rivalry between cans and bottles for the business of soft drink and beer producers. Both industries were relatively concentrated: the top two can manufacturers had 70 percent of can sales; the top three bottle manufacturers had 55 percent of bottle sales. If cans and bottles were viewed as a single market, the two firms would have, respectively, 22 percent and 3 percent of that market. Discuss whether this merger would violate Section 7 of the Clayton Act. (*U.S. v. Continental Can Co.*, 378 U.S. 441, 1964.)

7. Von's Grocery Co. acquired Shopping Bag Food Stores. Von's was the third largest retail grocery in the Los Angeles area, Shopping Bag was the sixth largest. Together, they accounted for 7.5 percent of retail grocery sales in the Los Angeles area. After the merger, the Von's–Shopping Bag combination was the second largest grocery chain in the area. Each firm had been very successful and had grown very rapidly during the ten years prior to the merger. The evidence also showed that, during the previous thirteen years, the number of grocery store owners operating a single store in the area dropped from 5,365 to 3,590. During the same period, the number of chains with two or more stores increased from 96 to 150. During approximately the same period, nine of the top twenty chains had acquired 126 of their smaller competitors. Discuss whether this merger would violate Section 7 of the Clayton Act. (*U.S. v. Von's Grocery Co.*, 384 U.S. 270, 1966.)

8. Lex Leather Co. was the fourth largest producer of finished leather in the United States. It purchased unfinished cowhides from slaughterhouses, and produced fin-

ished leather which it sold to manufacturers of leather products. About 80 percent of its sales were to shoe manufacturers, the remaining 20 percent going to manufacturers of other leather goods such as belts, purses, and jackets. The top six companies in the leather-selling business accounted for 78 percent of the nationwide market. Lex, the fourth largest, accounted for 10 percent of the market. Although different "grades" of leather are of different quality, there is virtually no difference within a particular grade among the different leather produced by any of the significant leather producers.

Most leather producers do not maintain direct contact with customers, because manufacturers who use leather (such as shoe manufacturers) buy leather through brokers, independent intermediaries who shop around in behalf of purchasers to find the best available price for a particular grade and quantity of leather.

Keeny Co. was a manufacturer and retailer of shoes. About 90 percent of the shoes it made and retailed were made of leather. Keeny was the fifteenth ranking manufacturer of shoes, accounting for 4 percent of the nationwide production of shoes. In retailing, Keeny was the fifth largest seller, with 8 percent of the nationwide market. Keeny's retail stores sold various brands of shoes; about 15 percent of the shoes it sold at retail were manufactured by Keeny.

Keeny acquired Lex by purchasing 100 percent of its outstanding shares of stock. The acquisition was challenged by the Justice Department under Section 7 of the Clayton Act. Discuss whether the merger would be legal or illegal under Section 7. Assume that the relevant product markets are "finished leather" and "shoes," and that the geographic markets are nationwide.

9. General Motors, Ford, and Chrysler, in that order, were the largest automobile producers in America. Together they accounted for 90 percent of domestic production. The domestic spark plug market was dominated by Champion (40 percent), AC (30 percent—wholly owned by General Motors), and Autolite (15 percent). The remainder of the spark plug market was accounted for by very small producers.

The independent spark plug makers (primarily Champion and Autolite) sold spark plugs to the automakers (primarily Ford and Chrysler) at cost or below. These original equipment (OE) plugs were sold so cheaply because auto mechanics almost always replace worn out plugs with the same brand that had been original equipment (called the OE tie). Thus, it was essential to get into the OE market in order to get into the market for replacement plugs—the aftermarket. Large profits were made in this aftermarket.

Ford, whose purchases of OE plugs from the independent spark plug makers amounted to 10 percent of all the spark plugs produced domestically, wanted to gain entry into the profitable spark plug aftermarket. It did so by purchasing Autolite's only spark plug factory, as well as its trademark and distribution facilities. Discuss whether this merger might violate Section 7 of the Clayton Act. (*Ford Motor Co. v. U.S.*, 405 U.S. 562, 1972.)

10. National Industries, Inc. (NI) is an extremely large, widely diversified firm. It is fifteenth on Fortune's list of America's 500 largest companies, has annual sales of $30 billion, and does business in many diverse markets. In one of its markets, chemical fertilizer, NI is the largest firm with annual fertilizer sales of over $4 billion. NI recently acquired Florida Phosphate Co., the nation's largest producer of phosphoric acid, with annual sales of over $750 million. Phosphoric acid is an important ingredient in many fertilizers. The four other major producers of phosphoric acid are independent firms (not part of a larger enterprise) just as Florida Phosphate was before its acquisition by NI. Because of the desire for an assured source of supply of phosphoric acid, and because of the profitability of the phosphoric acid business, NI had contemplated an entry into the business for almost five years. The possibility of NI's entry had been known to phosphoric acid producers for several years. Discuss whether the merger would violate Section 7 of the Clayton Act.

C·H·A·P·T·E·R 11

ANTITRUST LAW HORIZONTAL RESTRAINTS OF TRADE

In studying the law pertaining to monopolies and mergers, we were concerned primarily with market structure and only secondarily with specific instances of conduct. We now turn our attention to particular types of business behavior. Market structure is not irrelevant here, but its role is a secondary one. The subject of this chapter is horizontal restraints of trade—arrangements which suppress or limit competition between two or more competitors. The applicable statute is Section 1 of the Sherman Act, which prohibits "contracts, combinations, and conspiracies in restraint of trade."

The Requirement of Collusion

Suppose that four corporations, W, X, Y, and Z, have been charged with violating Section 1 of the Sherman Act by acting together to set prices or otherwise suppress competition. Each company claims, however, that its own action was *independent* of the actions of the others. One of the most fundamental principles of antitrust law is that a single firm acting entirely alone cannot violate Section 1 of the Sherman Act. Assuming that particular conduct is anticompetitive, there can be a violation of Section 1 only if two or more firms have acted together. In this regard, the key words from Section 1 are "contract, combination, and conspiracy." Outside of antitrust law these three terms have substantially different meanings. In antitrust, however, all three mean basically the same thing: there must be some type of agreement or collusion between two or more firms. (We use several terms interchangeably in this chapter: contract, combination, conspiracy, collusion, agreement, and concerted action, among others.)

Sometimes collusion is obvious. For instance, in *Chicago Board of Trade v. U.S.*, 246 U.S. 231 (1918), the challenged practice was a trading rule formally adopted by the 1,600 members of the Board of Trade. The rule required members, when engaging in one particular type of transaction after formal trading hours, to abide by the price set earlier in the day's trading session. In *National Society of Professional Engineers v. U.S.*, 435 U.S. 679 (1978), the issue was the legality of an ethical canon of the society which prohibited competitive bidding by its 69,000 members. The outcomes of both cases are discussed later in the chapter. In addition to cases like these where a group has adopted a formal rule or procedure of some kind, collusion also is obvious when the parties' anticompetitive arrangement is evidenced by a written contract, or when there is uncontroverted evidence of an express oral agreement.

If this type of direct evidence was an absolute requirement, however, Section 1 of the Sherman Act would be too easy to circumvent. Clear evidence of express agreement often is not available for either of two reasons: (1) the agreement itself may have been based solely on an implicit understanding among the parties; or (2) although there may actually have been an express agreement, the parties may have done a good job of covering their tracks because they knew their conduct was illegal or at least questionable. Consequently, courts permit the collusion requirement to be proved by circumstantial evidence.

Circumstantial Evidence

When there is no direct evidence of agreement in a Section 1 case, the court will consider all evidence that might shed light on the question. Regardless of the particular circumstances, the ultimate question for the court is the same: after examining all the evidence, is it logical to conclude that the actions of the accused companies could have resulted from independent behavior on the part of each firm? Or is it all just too much to have been coincidence—does the evidence convince the court that these events almost certainly must have resulted from agreement?

Factors such as those listed below usually are the most important when a court is answering this type of question.

1. The existence of business conditions that could have created a *motive* for conspiracy can be significant. Suppose that several firms are charged with conspiring to fix prices, and the evidence shows that just prior to the

"I don't think you'll actually find me on the list. I was an unidentified co-conspirator."

Section 1 of the Sherman Act can be violated only if there is a contract, combination, or conspiracy between two or more parties.

Source: Drawing by Whitney Darrow, Jr.; © 1980 *The New Yorker* Magazine, Inc.

alleged agreement the firms had been engaged in a vigorous price war which caused their profit margins to drop substantially. The price war then stopped abruptly and completely. Proof of motive alone does not prove collusion, but it is quite important when coupled with other evidence.

2. If available, evidence of an *opportunity* to conspire is also relevant. Thus, it would be quite revealing to find that officers from the firms in the above example had, without adequate explanation, all stayed at a nearby resort hotel the week before the alleged conspiracy.

3. Evidence of any pertinent *communications* (phone calls and memos, for example) hinting at agreement can add further weight to the contention that the defendants took concerted, not independent, action.

4. It also is very important to determine whether the firms' actions would have made *good economic sense* if done independently. If so, the case for conspiracy is weakened. If, however, their actions made economic sense only if each of them could expect the others to go along, the case for conspiracy is strengthened. For example, if total demand for a product has declined or remained static, it would not make sense for a single firm to increase prices except perhaps to cover a recent cost increase. The firm would probably lose a lot of customers. On the other hand, in these circumstances a firm might behave in such a fashion if it knew that its competitors would do the same thing at about the same time. Thus, price increases by a group of competitors under such conditions would be quite suspicious.

5. *Uniformity of action* is perhaps the most critical factor. Indeed, without proof of uniformity a Section 1 case based on circumstantial evidence will fail. Because of its importance, this topic is discussed separately in the next section.

Conscious Parallelism

Uniformity of action frequently is referred to as "parallelism" or "parallel behavior." In other words, several firms have engaged in the same or very similar behavior, either simultaneously or within a very short period of time. As pointed out, parallelism is always relevant to the collusion issue and is essential when the case depends on circumstantial evidence.

The concept of parallelism raises an issue that has caused courts difficulty for years. Suppose that there is no direct evidence of agreement, but there is evidence of parallel behavior. Assume further that there really is not any other relevant evidence. That is, there is parallelism and nothing more. Does this prove agreement? The answer is no. Let us then add an additional factor: the evidence establishes that each firm apparently *knew* at the time that the other firms were going to do (or were doing) the same thing. In the words of the courts, there was *conscious parallelism* by these firms. Does this prove agreement?

The answer here is a qualified no. The courts have said that evidence of conscious parallelism, without more, does not prove conspiracy. Moreover, it does not even create a fact issue for the jury to consider—the judge will grant a directed verdict for defendants in such a case. There must be something more than mere conscious parallelism, but there does not have to be *much* more. For example, the addition of one of the other factors discussed in the previous section—motive, opportunity, suspicious communications, or lack of economic logicality unless there was agreement—will create a fact issue regarding collusion. If the jury (or trial judge, if there is no jury) then renders a verdict against the defendants on the conspiracy issue, that verdict will be sufficiently supported by the evidence.

Many courts have gone even further by ruling that evidence of conscious parallelism, without more, effectively *shifts the burden* to the defendants to explain how the events could have transpired without any agreement. If they fail to produce a plausible explanation, there is a fact issue and sufficient evidence to support a verdict of conspiracy.

There are situations, of course, where conscious parallelism is easily explainable. For example, if all of the defendants deal with a particular labor union, and a new union contract has just caused an identical increase in their labor costs, consciously parallel pricing which reflects this common cost increase would be explainable.

In a tightly concentrated oligopoly, dominated by a very small number of large firms, conscious parallelism often is easily explainable as a natural outgrowth of the market structure. Because each firm is large and there are so few of them, they all usually know what the others are going to do and when, and respond to the other firms' actions rather quickly.[1] In this type of market pure conscious parallelism clearly would not be sufficient evidence of collusion. Thus, in some oligopolistic markets, there is the same lack of vigorous price competition that could be accomplished in other markets only only by agreement. (A real paradox is that many price-fixing agreements do, in fact, occur in oligopolies where there may not be as much to be gained by agreeing as there is in other markets. The apparent reason for this phenomenon is that the presence of only a few competitors makes it much easier, and thus more tempting, to organize and administer an anticompetitive agreement.)

Intra-Enterprise Conspiracy

For Section 1 to be violated there must be collusion between two or more *separate economic entities*. Difficult questions may exist when the alleged conspirators are part of the same overall enterprise or are otherwise affiliated in some way. Although there is some uncertainty surrounding the law relating to so-called "intra-enterprise" conspiracies, the general principles may be outlined as follows:

1. When corporate directors, officers, or employees are acting in behalf of the corporation, there *cannot* be a Section 1 "conspiracy" between these individuals or between the corporation itself and one or more of the individuals. There is only one entity involved—the corporation.

2. If a corporation has one or more divisions which are not separate corporations themselves, there *cannot* be a conspiracy between these divisions or between the corporation and one or more divisions. Again, only a single entity is involved.

3. In *Copperweld Corp. v. Independence Tube Corp.*, 104 S. Ct. 2731 (1984), the U.S. Supreme Court held that a corporation and its *wholly-owned* subsidiary are a single economic entity under Section 1 of the Sher-

---

[1]The presence of certain other factors, however, can make uniformity less inevitable, and therefore more difficult to explain when it does occur. Such factors may include (1) rapidly developing technology in the market, (2) a relatively complex product, or (3) a number of product variations offered by different firms.

man Act. In other words, even though the parent company and its subsidiary are organized as separate corporations, they constitute only one entity and are incapable of conspiring with each other when the parent owns 100 percent of the subsidiary's stock. Presumably, two wholly-owned subsidiaries of the same parent corporation also would be a single entity and thus not capable of forming a conspiracy under Section 1.

4. In the *Copperweld* case, the Court did not deal with a situation in which a parent corporation owns a controlling, but less than 100 percent, interest in another corporation. It is very likely, however, that the same rule will be applied to this type of case as to the case of a wholly-owned subsidiary. Thus, a parent and its controlled subsidiary probably are a single entity and are not capable of forming a conspiracy. Also, two controlled subsidiaries of the same parent probably are not capable of forming a conspiracy.

5. When a corporation owns an interest in another corporation that is insufficient for control, the two corporations almost certainly will be viewed by the courts as two distinct entities that are capable of forming a conspiracy under Section 1. Similarly, two corporations will be viewed as distinct entities when a third company owns a noncontrolling interest in each of the two.

Unreasonable

Restraint of Trade

The Rule of Reason

Origin: Concerted action by two or more firms violates Section 1 of the Sherman Act only if it "restrains trade." Congress neither defined the term nor gave any guidance which would assist the courts in formulating a definition. The statute speaks of "every" contract, combination, or conspiracy in restraint of trade, and thus would seem to be all-inclusive. The Supreme Court did, in fact, adopt a literal interpretation of Section 1 during the first few years after its enactment.[2]

The Court soon came to realize, however, that a literal reading of the statute could sometimes lead to ridiculous decisions, such as the invalidation of all partnership agreements. In addition, the state common-law rule that contracts in restraint of trade are void and unenforceable had for many years been applied only to those contracts that "unreasonably" restrained trade. Feeling that Congress probably had this common-law approach in mind when it passed the Sherman Act, the Supreme Court ultimately took a similar view. In *Standard Oil Co. v. U.S.*, 221 U.S. 1, and *U.S. v. American Tobacco Co.*, 221 U.S. 106, both decided in 1911, the Court adopted the so-called **rule of reason**. According to this rule, which is still the basic standard under Section 1, a business agreement is illegal if it unreasonably restricts competition.

[2] However, the cases in which this was done involved blatant violations which would have been illegal regardless of how the statute was interpreted.

Method of Analysis: The next question, of course, is how do the courts decide whether a particular arrangement is reasonable or unreasonable? In essence, the rule of reason involves an examination of the *purpose* and the *effect* of the conduct being challenged. If either its purpose *or* effect is found to be substantially anticompetitive, there is an unreasonable restraint of trade.

The defendants will always claim that their purpose was legitimate—in other words, not anticompetitive. They may insist, for example, that their motive was to promote ethical conduct in their industry, prevent fraudulent practices by their suppliers or customers, encourage product standardization or safety, or any one of many other lawful purposes. The court will examine all pertinent evidence before deciding whether the defendants are to be believed, or whether their true purpose was to limit competitive rivalry in some way. If the court concludes that, in fact, defendants' predominant purpose was to restrict competition, Section 1 is violated.

If the court rules that defendants' main purpose was legitimate, it must then examine all evidence relating to the effect of the challenged activity. A conclusion that there has been a significant suppression of competition, or that there probably will be such an effect in the future, means that Section 1 has been violated. Many times a court will study and rule on the evidence relating to competitive effect even though it has already concluded that defendants' purpose was illegal. There are two reasons for this fact: (1) the evidence relating to the purpose and effect issues frequently is intertwined and difficult to separate; and (2) the court is likely to be more comfortable with its decision if it finds an anticompetitive effect in addition to an anticompetitive purpose. To reiterate, however, a Section 1 violation can be found on the basis of an anticompetitive purpose *or* a substantial anticompetitive effect.[3]

Market Power: One factor that is important to a court's analysis of purpose and effect is the combined market power of the defendants. Substantial anticompetitive effects usually cannot take place without substantial market power. Therefore, evidence relating to whether defendants as a group had the *ability* to limit competition is relevant to the analysis of both purpose and effect. Of course, if the evidence establishes an anticompetitive purpose beyond a doubt, Section 1 is violated regardless of whether the defendants had the power to ultimately accomplish their illegal goal.[4]

---

[3] This statement is subject to one exception. If the case is a *criminal* one (most are not), the prosecution must prove that defendants *intended* to restrict competition. However, if the evidence has established the existence of actual (not just probable) anticompetitive effects, a jury is permitted to infer the existence of anticompetitive intent. Because the jury has latitude to draw such an inference, this intent requirement is not quite as important as it first appears to be.

[4] In many cases where the purpose is obviously anticompetitive, defendants' activity will constitute one of the per se offenses, but this certainly is not always true. The per se rule is discussed shortly.

Alternatives: Another factor which often plays an important part in the court's analysis of purpose and effect under the rule of reason is the existence of a *less restrictive alternative*. Suppose that the evidence indicates a possibility of harm to competitive rivalry. Assume, though, that the court is not yet convinced that there is sufficient evidence of anticompetitive purpose or substantial anticompetitive effect. Now suppose that further evidence is presented which demonstrates that the defendants could have achieved their allegedly legitimate objective by some other arrangement which would have posed less danger to competition. Evidence of such a less restrictive alternative makes it much more likely that the court will rule defendants' conduct to be a violation of Section 1. For one thing, the court will be more prone to disbelieve the defendants' assertions about the legitimacy of their purpose. For another, it now becomes clear to the court that the danger of an anticompetitive effect is greater than it should have been.

Offsetting Procompetitive Effects: A third factor that can be important under the rule of reason is the existence of *procompetitive effects* (i.e., positive effects on competition). Such a factor will not be considered by the court in its assessment of defendant's purpose. However, assuming that this purpose has been found to be legitimate, the court will consider any evidence of procompetitive effects as part of its overall assessment of competitive impact. The *Chicago Board of Trade* case, presented below, and the *BMI* case later in the chapter provide examples. In each case, the Court found the defendants' purposes to be legitimate and then weighed the competitive effects of the questioned business practice. Also in each case, there was the possibility of an anticompetitive "stabilizing" effect on market price, plus additional evidence that the defendants' conduct would have some positive effects on competition. These procompetitive effects were balanced against the possible anticompetitive effects and, in both cases, the positive effects were found to outweigh the negative effects.

We now will see the rule of reason at work in two landmark Supreme Court cases which were referred to earlier. The same basic type of analysis also is evident in some of the cases presented later in the chapter.

Chicago Board of Trade v. United States

U.S. Supreme Court
246 U.S. 231
(1918)

In the late 1800s and early 1900s Chicago was the leading grain market in the world, and the Board of Trade was the commercial center through which most of the trading in grain was done. Its 1,600 members included brokers, commission merchants, dealers, millers, manufacturers of corn products, and grain elevator owners. Grain transactions usually took one of three forms: (1) spot sales—sales of grain already in Chicago in railroad cars or elevators ready for immediate delivery; (2) future sales—agreements for delivery of grain at a later time; (3) sales "to arrive"—agreements for delivery of grain which was already in transit to Chicago or which was to be shipped almost immediately from other parts of the Midwest.

On each business day, sessions of the Board of Trade were held at which all bids and sales were publicly made. Spot sales and future sales were made during the regular session between 9:30 a.m. and 1:15 p.m. Special sessions, referred to as the "Call," were held immediately after the close of the regular session. During the Call, which usually lasted about thirty minutes, members of the Board of Trade engaged only in "to arrive" transactions. These transactions usually involved purchases from farmers or small dealers in one of the Midwestern states. Participation in the Call session was limited to members, but they could trade on behalf of nonmembers if they wished. Members also could make any of the three types of transaction privately with each other at any place, either during or after board sessions. Members could engage privately in any type of transaction at any time with nonmembers, but not on the board's premises.

With respect to "to arrive" transactions, a particular market price would be established by the public trading during the short Call session. Until 1906, however, members were not bound by that price during the remainder of the day. In that year the Board of Trade adopted what was known as the "Call rule." The rule, which applied only to "to arrive" transactions, required members to use the market price established at the public Call session when they bought grain in private transactions between the end of that session and 9:30 the next morning.

The government filed suit in federal district court, claiming that the Call rule violated Section 1 of the Sherman Act. The Board contended that the purpose and effect of the rule was to bring more of the "to arrive" transactions into the public market at the Call session. By bringing more of these transactions into the public market, the Board felt that four or five large grain warehouse owners in Chicago would no longer have such a controlling grip over "to arrive" transactions. The district court, however, ruled that evidence relating to the history and purpose of the rule was irrelevant and issued an injunction against the operation of the rule. The Board of Trade then appealed to the U.S. Supreme Court.

Brandeis, Justice:

. . . Every agreement concerning trade, every regulation of trade, restrains. To bind, to restrain, is of their very essence. The true test of legality is whether the restraint imposed is such as merely regulates and perhaps thereby promotes competition or whether it is such as may suppress or even destroy competition. To determine that question the court must ordinarily consider the facts peculiar to the business to which the restraint is applied; its condition before and after the restraint was imposed; the nature of the restraint and its effect, actual or probable. The history of the restraint, the evil believed to exist, the reason for adopting the particular remedy, the purpose or end sought to be attained, are all relevant facts. This is not because a good intention will save an otherwise objectionable regulation or the reverse; but because knowledge of intent may help the court to interpret facts and to predict consequences. The District Court erred, therefore, in striking from the [Board's] answer allegations concerning evidence on that subject. But the evidence admitted makes it clear that the rule was a reasonable regulation of business consistent with the provisions of the Anti-Trust Law.

First: The nature of the rule: The restriction was upon the period of price-making. It required members to desist from further price-making after the close of the Call until 9:30 a.m. the next business day: but there was no restriction upon the sending out of bids after close of the Call. Thus it required members who desired to buy grain "to arrive" to make up their minds before the close of the Call how much they were willing to pay during the interval before the next session of the Board. The rule made it to their interest to attend the Call; and if they did not fill their wants by purchases there, to make the final bid high enough to enable them to purchase from country dealers.

Second: The scope of the rule: It is restricted in operation to grain "to arrive." It applies only to a small part of the grain shipped from day to day to Chicago, and to an even smaller part of the day's sales: members were left free to purchase grain already in Chicago from anyone at any price throughout the day. It applies only during a small part of the business day; members were left free to purchase during the sessions of the Board grain "to arrive," at any price, from members anywhere and from nonmembers anywhere except on the premises of the Board. It applied only to grain shipped to Chicago: members were left free to purchase at any price throughout the day from either members or nonmembers, grain "to arrive" at any other market. Country dealers and farmers had available in practically every part of the territory called tributary to Chicago some other market for grain "to arrive." Thus Missouri, Kansas, Nebraska, and parts of Illinois are also tributary to St. Louis; Nebraska and Iowa, to Omaha; Minnesota, Iowa, South and North Dakota, to Minneapolis or Duluth; Wisconsin and parts of Iowa and of Illinois, to Milwaukee; Ohio, Indiana and parts of Illinois, to Cincinnati; Indiana and parts of Illinois, to Louisville.

Third: The effects of the rule: As it applies to only a small part of the grain shipped to Chicago and to that only during a part of the business day and does not apply at all to grain shipped to other markets, the rule had no appreciable effect on general market prices; nor did it materially affect the total volume of grain coming to Chicago. But within the narrow limits of its operation the rule helped to improve market conditions thus:

(a) It created a public market for grain "to arrive." Before its adoption, bids were made privately. Men had to buy and sell without adequate knowledge of actual market conditions. This was disadvantageous to all concerned, but particularly so to country dealers and farmers.

(b) It brought into the regular market hours of the Board sessions more of the trading in grain "to arrive."

(c) It brought buyers and sellers into more direct relations; because on the Call they gathered together for a free and open interchange of bids and offers.

(d) It distributed the business in grain "to arrive" among a far larger number of Chicago receivers and commission merchants than had been the case there before.

(e) It increased the number of country dealers engaging in this branch of the business; supplied them more regularly with bids from Chicago; and also increased the number of bids received by them from competing markets.

(f) It eliminated risks necessarily incident to a private market, and thus enabled country dealers to do business on a smaller margin. In that way the rule made it possible for them to pay more to farmers without raising the price to consumers.

(g) It enabled country dealers to sell some grain "to arrive" which they would otherwise have been obliged either to ship to Chicago commission merchants or to sell for "future delivery."

(h) It enabled those grain merchants of Chicago who sell to millers and exporters to trade on a smaller margin and, by paying more for grain or selling it for less, to make the Chicago market more attractive for both shippers and buyers of grain. . . .

The decree of the District Court is reversed with directions to dismiss the [government's complaint].

★★★

National Society of Professional Engineers v. United States
U.S. Supreme Court
435 U.S. 679 (1978)

The National Society of Professional Engineers was organized in 1935 to deal with the nontechnical aspects of engineering practice, including the promotion of the professional, social, and economic interests of its members. When this lawsuit was filed, the society had about 69,000 members, approximately 12,000 of which were consulting engineers who offered their services to governmental, industrial, and private clients in connection with various types of construction projects. In 1964 the Society adopted Section 11(c) of its Code of Ethics, which prohibited members from engaging in competitive bidding. The rule had nothing to do with specific fees to be charged by members for their services, but merely provided that they should not negotiate or even discuss fees until after a prospective client had selected an engineer for a particular project. The result of the rule was that selection of an engineer was based on background and reputation, not price.

The government filed suit in federal district court, claiming that the rule violated Section 1 of the Sherman Act. The Society contended that the rule was justified because it minimized the risk that competitive bidding might produce inferior, and dangerous, engineering work. The district court rejected this justification and held that the rule violated Section 1 of the Sherman Act. The court of appeals affirmed, and the Society ("petitioner") appealed to the U.S. Supreme Court.

Stevens, Justice:

. . . In *Goldfarb v. Virginia State Bar*, 421 U.S. 773, the Court held that a bar association's rule prescribing minimum fees for legal services violated § 1 of the Sherman Act. In that opinion the Court noted that certain practices by members of a learned profession might survive scrutiny under the Rule of Reason even though they would be viewed as a violation of the Sherman Act in another context. The Court said:

The fact that a restraint operates upon a profession as distinguished from a business is, of course, relevant in determining whether that particular restraint violates the Sherman Act. It would be unrealistic to view the practice of professions as interchangeable with other business activities, and automatically to apply to the professions antitrust concepts which originated in other areas. The public service aspect, and other features of the profession, may require that a particular practice, which could properly be viewed as a violation of the Sherman Act in another context, be treated differently. We intimate no view on any other situation than the one with which we are confronted today.

Relying heavily on this statement, and on some of the major cases applying the Rule of Reason, petitioner argues that its attempt to preserve the profession's traditional method of setting fees for engineering services is a reasonable method of forestalling the public harm which might be produced by unrestrained competitive bidding. To evaluate this argument it is necessary to identify the contours of the Rule of Reason and to discuss its application to the kind of justification asserted by petitioner. . . .

The Rule of Reason . . . has been used to give the Act both flexibility and definition, and its central principle of antitrust analysis has remained constant. Contrary to its name, the Rule does not open the field of antitrust inquiry to any argument in favor of a challenged restraint that may fall within the realm of reason. Instead, it focuses directly on the challenged restraint's impact on competitive conditions. . . .

The early cases foreclose the argument that because of the special characteristics of a particular industry, monopolistic arrangements will better promote trade and commerce than competition. That kind of argument is properly addressed to Congress and may justify an exemption from the statute for specific industries, but it is not permitted by the Rule of Reason.

In this case we are presented with an agreement among competitors to refuse to discuss prices with potential customers until after negotiations have resulted in the initial selection of an engineer. While this is not price fixing as such, no elaborate industry analysis is required to demonstrate the anticompetitive character of such an agreement. It operates as an absolute ban on competitive bidding, applying with equal force to both complicated and simple projects and to both inexperienced and sophisticated customers. . . .

The Society argues that the restraint is justified because bidding on engineering services is inherently imprecise, would lead to deceptively low bids, and would thereby tempt individual engineers to do inferior work with consequent risk to public safety and health. . . .

It may be, as petitioner argues, that competition tends to force prices down and that an inexpensive item may be inferior to one that is more costly. There is some risk, therefore, that competition will cause some suppliers to market a defective product. Similarly, competitive bidding for engineering projects may be inherently imprecise and incapable of taking into account all the variables which will be involved in the actual performance of the project. Based on these considerations, a purchaser might conclude that his interest in quality—which may embrace the safety of the end product—outweighs the advantages of achieving cost savings by pitting one competitor against another. Or an individual engineer might independently refrain from price negotiation until he has satisfied himself that he fully understands the scope of his customers' needs. These decisions might be reasonable; indeed, petitioner has provided ample documentation for that thesis. But these are not reasons that satisfy the Rule of Reason; nor are such individual decisions subject to antitrust attack. . . .

Petitioner's ban on competitive bidding prevents all customers from making price comparisons in the initial selection of an engineer, and imposes the Society's views of the costs and benefits of competition on the entire market place. It is this restraint that must be justified under the Rule of Reason, and petitioner's attempt to do so on the basis of the potential threat that competition poses to the public safety and the ethics of its profession is nothing less than a frontal assault on the basic policy of the Sherman Act.

The Sherman Act reflects a legislative judgment that ultimately competition will not only produce lower prices, but also better goods and services. The heart of our national economic policy long has been faith in the value of competition. The assumption that competition is the best method of allocating resources in a free market recognizes that all elements of a bargain—quality, service, safety, and durability—and not just immediate cost, are favorably affected by the free opportunity to select among alternative offers. Even assuming occasional exceptions to the presumed consequences of competition, the statutory policy precludes inquiry into the question whether competition is good or bad.

The fact that engineers are often involved in large-scale projects significantly affecting the public safety does not alter our analysis. Exceptions to the Sherman Act for potentially dangerous goods and services would be tantamount to a repeal of the statute. In our complex economy the number of items that may cause serious harm is almost endless—automobiles, drugs, foods, aircraft components, heavy equipment, and countless others, cause serious harm to individuals or to the public at large if defectively made. The judiciary cannot indirectly protect the public against this harm by conferring monopoly privileges on the manufacturers.

By the same token, [the statement in *Goldfarb v. Virginia State Bar*, quoted earlier,] cannot be read as fashioning a broad exemption under the Rule of Reason for learned professions. We adhere to the view expressed in *Goldfarb* that, by their nature, professional services may differ significantly from other business services, and, accordingly, the nature of the competition in such services may vary. Ethical norms may serve to regulate and promote this competition, and thus fall within the Rule of Reason. But the Society's argument in this case is a far cry from such a position. We are faced with a contention that a total ban on competitive bidding is necessary because otherwise engineers will be tempted to submit deceptively low bids. Certainly, the problem of professional deception is a proper subject of an ethical canon. But once again, the equation of competition with deception, like the similar equation with safety hazards, is simply too broad; we may assume that competition is not entirely conducive to ethical behavior, but that is not a reason, cognizable under the Sherman Act, for doing away with competition.

In sum, the Rule of Reason does not support a defense based on the assumption that competition itself is unreasonable. [The decision of the Court of Appeals that the Society's rule against competitive bidding violates Section 1 of the Sherman Act is affirmed.]

★★★

The Per Se Rule

As the rule of reason was being developed and applied, the federal courts recognized that certain types of group business behavior are so obviously anticompetitive that no in-depth analysis should be necessary. This idea was present in several very early cases, and was more or less formally recognized by the Supreme Court in 1927 in *U.S. v. Trenton Potteries Co.*, 273 U.S. 392. In that case the Court declared that when a group of competing firms were proved to have agreed on prices (horizontal price fixing), they could not defend their actions by arguing that the resulting prices were reasonable.

In a 1940 case, *U.S. v. Socony-Vacuum Oil Co.*, 310 U.S. 150, the Supreme Court first used the term **per se** to describe automatically illegal conduct under Section 1 of the Sherman Act. There, the Court stated that horizontal price fixing is per se illegal—in other words, there is no justification for it, no defense, and no need to prove that it had any actual anticompetitive effect. This, in essence, is what the per se rule amounts to. The Court has really just acknowledged the obvious fact that some types of conduct do not require much analysis. Some agreements are necessarily anticompetitive, for either of two reasons: (1) the inherent nature of a few types of activities, such as horizontal price fixing, makes this conclusion self-evident; (2) even if this conclusion was not self-evident originally, the courts have had sufficient experience with some kinds of group behavior to have learned that anticompetitive consequences almost invariably result.

In addition to horizontal price fixing, horizontal market divisions have also been ruled per se illegal. Boycotts, which may sometimes involve both horizontal and vertical aspects, similarly have been declared per se illegal. In the next chapter we see that some vertical arrangements, namely vertical price fixing and tying agreements, have been given per se treatment.

Two Separate Rules?

To adequately understand antitrust law, one must comprehend that the rule of reason and per se rule are not as different as may first appear. They actually are more like two varieties of the same species, the per se rule essentially being a shortened form of the rule of reason.

In the case of conduct to which the per se rule applies, the courts are dealing with actions having purposes and effects that are usually rather transparent. Regardless of the defendants' arguments about justification, fulfillment of other social goals, and so on, very little analysis is needed to discover the restriction of competition. If the rule of reason were applied to such conduct the same result would be reached in virtually every instance.

Despite these observations, the per se rule does serve two useful purposes. First, when advising a client concerning activity that clearly would constitute price fixing (or some other per se illegal conduct) an attorney is able to speak with much greater certainty than would be possible without the per se rule. Thus, the attorney's "No!" can be much more forceful. Second, in a case covered by the per se rule the court is permitted to simply exclude evidence relating to justification, alleged defenses, actual effects, and so on, and the trial process is greatly expedited.

The per se rule is really useful, however, only where the challenged conduct is relatively easy to label. Whenever there is difficulty in deciding whether particular conduct is something that can be appropriately called price fixing, market division, and so forth, the utility of the per se rule diminishes. The reason is that there must be preliminary analysis before determining whether the activity is within a per se category. This analysis involves an examination of purpose and effect and, for all practical purposes, is the same as the rule of reason.

We now turn to a discussion of particular types of conduct and their status under Section 1 of the Sherman Act.

Price Fixing

The Supreme Court has stated that any agreement which *tampers with the free market pricing mechanism* should be considered **price fixing** and thus is illegal. Such a definition clearly includes a wide variety of conduct.

Agreements Directly Setting Prices

Virtually any agreement among competitors which relates directly to price will be viewed as price fixing. An agreement between competitors X, Y, and Z that they will charge $10 per unit for the gizmos they sell is the clearest form of price fixing. Suppose that X, Y, and Z had not pegged a specific price, but had agreed on a formula to be used in computing price. This, too, would be price fixing. Similarly illegal would be an agreement setting a price floor, a range, or the amount of a discount to be given to distributors.

A question which has generated much controversy through the years is whether the agreed-upon setting of a price *ceiling*—maximum price fixing—should be treated the same as other forms of price fixing. While this form of collusive pricing behavior is far less common than other types, it does sometimes occur. The Supreme Court ruled in a 1951 case, *Kiefer-Stewart Co. v. Joseph E. Seagram & Sons*, 340 U.S. 211, that maximum price fixing is indeed per se illegal. The controversy continued, however, with a significant number of observers (though probably a minority) arguing that the law should be otherwise.

In 1982 the Court had an opportunity to reconsider the issue in *Arizona v. Maricopa County Medical Society*, 102 S. Ct. 2466. In that case, the Medical Society formed the Maricopa Foundation for Medical Care for the purpose of providing an alternative to existing health insurance plans. Both the society and the foundation consisted of most of the physicians in the area. In essence, the foundation was a nonprofit health insurance company formed and owned by its member physicians. As part of its operations, the foundation established a schedule of maximum fees for which participating doctors could receive reimbursement when performing services for patients insured by the foundation. In effect, then, there was an agreement by these doctors on the maximum fees to be charged those patients having an insurance policy with the foundation. In behalf of its citizens, the State of Arizona filed suit seeking an injunction against the practice as a violation of Section 1 of the Sherman Act. The Court reaffirmed the rule that maximum price fixing is per se illegal because it tampers with pricing decisions that should be left to individual competitors. The Court noted that this type of pricing agreement (1) tends to provide the same economic rewards to all practitioners regardless of their skill, experience, training, or willingness to employ innovative and difficult procedures in individual cases; (2) may discourage entry into the market; (3) may deter experimentation and new developments by individual doctors; and (4) may actually be a masquerade for an agreement to fix uniform prices, or may become such in the future.

Professional Fee Schedules and Guides

In the past it was common for various professional groups, such as physicians, attorneys, and engineers, to formulate and distribute fee schedules or guides. These schedules usually stated the "ordinary" or "suggested" fees for particular services or procedures. In *Goldfarb v. Virginia State Bar*, 421 U.S. 773 (1975), which was referred to in the *National Society of Professional Engineers* case, the Supreme Court held that an agreement by a professional group to follow a fee schedule is price fixing. Even if there is not an express agreement to abide by the schedule, price fixing still exists if the professional association imposes or even threatens to impose any penalties on members who do not follow the schedule.

Where a fee schedule is truly a suggested one, with no agreement to follow it and no hint of any penalty for failure to abide by it, the question of legality under Section 1 is more difficult. In such cases an individual examination must be made to determine whether there exists any evidence of a purpose to tamper with the market pricing mechanism or an effect on prices. These schedules pose inherent dangers to competition and usually should be illegal. Most professional groups have ceased all fee schedule activity.

Exchanges of Price Information

There have been many cases involving the exchange of various types of price information among groups of competitors. Although the legality of these exchanges depends on the facts of each case, they are dangerous and are frequently found to be illegal. For example, in *U.S. v. Container Corporation of America*, 393 U.S. 333 (1969), most of the manufacturers of corrugated cardboard containers in the southeastern United States regularly exchanged information concerning specific sales to identified customers, including prices and other terms of the transactions. There was no evidence of any agreement as to what a firm was to do with this information after receiving it. Most of the time the recipient would match its competitor's price, but this did not always happen. The Supreme Court made no attempt to determine the purpose of the practice, but held that it violated Section 1 because it almost certainly would have the effect of stabilizing prices. In reaching this conclusion, the Court emphasized that (1) the industry was dominated by relatively few sellers; (2) the product itself was homogeneous and simple, making price the most important factor in competition; and (3) there were no close substitutes for the product and demand was inelastic, thus giving the industry as a whole a greater degree of short-term control over price.

In another case, *Plymouth Dealers' Association of Northern California v. U.S.*, 279 F.2d 128 (9th Cir. 1960), a group of competing auto dealers exchanged a price list providing for a higher markup than previously had been used. Car sales usually were individually negotiated and the list price generally was not the actual selling price. However, the higher list price meant that bargaining with customers started at a higher level. Because this would tend to put upward pressure on prices, the federal court of appeals held the practice to be illegal price fixing.

A much older case, *Maple Flooring Manufacturers' Association v. U.S.*, 268 U.S. 563 (1925), demonstrates the circumstances in which information exchanges may be legitimate. There, competing wood flooring producers regularly submitted information to the central office of their trade association. This information related to various types of production costs, the amount of stock on hand, and the quantity, type of flooring, and prices received in actual transactions. This data was then aggregated and averaged by employees of the association before being distributed to members. In ruling that there was no proof of a purpose to limit price competition or an effect on pricing behavior, the Supreme Court emphasized several factors: (1) there was no direct communication between competitors; (2) the data received by members reflected only industry-wide averages, and identities of individual sellers and buyers could not be matched with particular figures; (3) the data was *historical*—it related only to past transactions and did not attempt to reflect current prices or future trends; and (4) all of the averaged data was available to customers, government agencies, and anyone else upon request.

Agreements Relating to Credit and Other Terms of Dealing

The various terms of sales transactions provide opportunities for competition. Terms relating to credit, delivery, and responsibility for shipping charges, for instance, usually can be negotiated, with buyers seeking the best terms available from competing sellers. Agreements diminishing these opportunities for competition are likely to violate Section 1 of the Sherman Act. Moreover, an agreement between competitors relating to a term which is actually a *component* of the pricing structure is likely to be called price fixing and stricken down rather summarily.

An example is found in *Catalano, Inc. v. Target Sales, Inc.*, 446 U.S. 643 (1980). There, a group of beer wholesalers in the Fresno, California, area agreed to eliminate the interest-free short-term credit that they customarily had granted to retailers. With very little difficulty, the Supreme Court found the agreement to be price fixing.

Agreements Relating to Supply and Demand

Effective tampering with supply or demand can affect price. Therefore, an agreement among firms having the purpose or effect of manipulating supply or demand, and thus price, violates Section 1.

In *U.S. v. Socony-Vacuum Oil Co.*, 310 U.S. 150 (1940), a number of oil refiners were charged with violating Section 1 through an arrangement to absorb excess gasoline supplies. Crude oil was being produced in great excess during the 1930s, because the Depression had lowered demand and huge new oil fields had been discovered. Excess crude oil led to excess gasoline. A substantial portion of this gasoline was produced by independent (not vertically integrated) refiners who had neither the storage capacity nor the distribution systems to absorb their production. Consequently, they dumped it on the market at whatever price it would bring, and prices plummeted. An arrangement then was made between the major vertically integrated oil companies and the independents. Under the arrangement, a major and an independent would pair off (they were called "dancing partners"), the major periodically purchasing the independent's excess supply. The major companies had the ability to hold the gasoline and strategically release it into the market at later times. The Supreme Court ruled that the purpose and effect of this supply manipulation plan was to stabilize prices, and that it therefore violated Section 1.

An agreement tampering with demand was ruled illegal in *National Macaroni Manufacturers' Association v. FTC*, 345 F.2d 421 (7th Cir. 1965). The highest quality macaroni, spaghetti, and other pasta products are made from pure durum wheat. Other hard wheats, usually called farina, are usable and less expensive but for several reasons do not work quite as well in the production of pasta. During the 1950s and early 1960s, poor crop conditions on several occasions plus increased purchases by exporters caused severe shortages of durum wheat. The prices offered by these exporters were generally higher than domestic pasta manufacturers had been paying. Prices were thus pushed up, and the members of the Macaroni Association agreed to start using a fifty-fifty mix of durum and farina. This action by 70 percent of the industry reduced demand so much that there actually was a surplus of durum. Prices then dropped. The court of appeals treated the agreement as tantamount to price fixing because it interfered with market forces in the setting of price.

Miscellaneous Agreements Affecting Price

Many other types of arrangements can interfere with the free market pricing mechanism. If this is found to be their purpose or effect, a violation of Section 1 usually occurs. Some examples of other activities found to be illegal include: (1) an agreement by hearing aid dealers not to quote prices over the telephone; (2) an agreement among retail gasoline dealers not to display any price signs except for the price computing device on the pump; and (3) the use by competing excelsior manufacturers of a common sales agency, the agency having the power to set prices.

Market Division

Market division arrangements among actual or potential competitors can take at least three forms: (1) in a *territorial* market division, the firms agree to divide geographic markets among themselves and refrain from competing in those markets; (2) in a *customer allocation* arrangement, the firms assign particular customers or classes of customers to each seller and agree not to solicit customers of another seller; (3) in a *product line* division, the firms agree to limit their activities to particular types of products or services so as to avoid competing with each other.

When a market division arrangement takes place among firms having sufficient combined power to really make it work, competition can be harmed even more than by price fixing. The reason is that a successful market division eliminates *all* forms of competition among the participants. Price fixing, on the other hand, limits or eliminates only one method of competing. Price competition certainly is the most important type, but competition in quality, service, and so on, can also be important.

Market divisions are treated as per se illegal. The seriousness with which courts view this type of restraint is well illustrated by the next case.

United States v. Topco Associates, Inc.
U.S. Supreme Court
405 U.S. 596 (1972)

Topco was a cooperative association of approximately twenty-five small and medium-sized regional supermarket chains which operated stores in thirty-three states. Each of the member chains was owned and operated independently of the others. None of the stores actually did business under the Topco name. In most areas where Topco members operated, they were healthy, vigorous companies and were in as strong a competitive position as any other chain.

The association had two major functions: (1) it served as a purchasing agent for its members, enabling them to buy in greater quantities and obtain the cost advantages enjoyed by larger supermarket chains, and (2) it enabled members to package and sell under "private labels"—brand names owned by Topco. Individual members generally were not large enough to afford a private brand system, and having private brands was important in competing with the big chains.

A chain's application for membership in Topco had to be approved first by the association's Board of Directors (made up of executives from member chains), and then by an affirmative vote of 75 percent of the members. However, if the member whose operations were closest to those of the applicant, or any member whose operations were located within 100 miles of the applicant, voted against approval, an affirmative vote of 85 percent of the members was required. Because members always accommodated each other's wishes, the approval procedure effectively gave members a veto over actual or potential competition in their territories.

After approval, each new member signed an agreement with Topco designating the territory in which that member could sell Topco brand products. No member could sell outside the specified territory, and members were thus insulated from competition in Topco's brands. A member caught selling outside its territory could have its membership terminated. In addition to the system of territorial exclusives at the retail level, Topco members also were effectively prohibited from selling at wholesale because of the competition this could indirectly create for other members.

The government filed suit in federal district court, claiming that Topco's practice of dividing markets violated Section 1 of the Sherman Act. The district court refused to apply the per se rule to this practice, and ultimately found that it did not violate Section 1. The government appealed to the U.S. Supreme Court.

Marshall, Justice:

. . . Topco essentially maintains that it needs territorial divisions to compete with larger chains; that the association could not exist if the territorial divisions were anything but exclusive; and that by restricting competition in the sale of Topco brand goods, the association actually increases competition by enabling its members to compete successfully with larger regional and national chains.

The District Court, considering all these things relevant to its decision, agreed with Topco. . . . The court held that Topco's practices were pro-competitive and, therefore, consistent with the purposes of the antitrust laws. But we conclude that the District Court used an improper analysis in reaching its result.

One of the classic examples of a *per se* violation of § 1 is an agreement between competitors at the same level of the market structure to allocate territories in order to minimize competition. Such concerted action is usually termed a "horizontal" restraint, in contradistinction to combinations of persons at different levels of the market structure, e.g., manufacturers and distributors, which are termed "vertical" restraints. This Court has reiterated time and time again that "[h]orizontal territorial limitations . . . are naked restraints of trade with no purpose except stifling of competition." . . . Such limitations are *per se* violations of the Sherman Act. . . . We think that it is clear that the restraint in this case is a horizontal one, and, therefore, a *per se* violation of § 1. . . .

Antitrust laws in general, and the Sherman Act in particular, are the Magna Charta of free enterprise. They are as important to the preservation of economic freedom and our free enterprise system as the Bill of Rights is to the protection of our fundamental personal freedoms. And the freedom guaranteed each and every business, no matter how small, is the freedom to compete—to assert with vigor, imagination, devotion, and ingenuity whatever economic muscle it can muster. Implicit in such freedom is the notion that it cannot be foreclosed with respect to one sector of the economy because certain private citizens or groups believe that such foreclosure might promote greater competition in a more important sector of the economy.

The District Court determined that by limiting the freedom of its individual members to compete with each other, Topco was doing a greater good by fostering competition between members and other large supermarket chains. But, the fallacy in this is that Topco has no authority under the Sherman Act to determine the respective values of competition in various sectors of the economy. On the contrary, the Sherman Act gives to each Topco member and to each prospective member the right to ascertain for itself whether or not competition with other supermarket chains is more desirable than competition in the sale of Topco brand products. Without territorial restrictions, Topco members may indeed "[c]ut each other's throat." But we have never found this possibility sufficient to warrant condoning horizontal restraints of trade. . . .

If a decision is to be made to sacrifice competition in one portion of the economy for greater competition in another portion this too is a decision which must be made by Congress and not by private forces or by the courts. Private forces are too keenly aware of their own interests in making such decisions and courts are ill-equipped and ill-situated for such decision-making. To analyze, interpret, and evaluate the myriad of competing interests and the endless data which would surely be brought to bear on such decisions, and to make the delicate judgment on the relative values to society of competitive areas of the economy, the judgment of the elected representatives of the people is required. . . .

We also strike down Topco's other restrictions on the right of its members to wholesale goods. These restrictions amount to regulation of the customers to whom members of Topco may sell Topco brand goods. Like territorial restrictions, limitations on customers are intended to limit intra-brand competition and to promote inter-brand competition. For the reasons previously discussed, the arena in which Topco members compete must be left to their unfettered choice absent a contrary congressional determination. . . .

Reversed.

★★★

Comment: All of the discussion in the *Topco* case seemed to assume that Topco's members refrained from competing with each other only in the sale of Topco brands. It is apparent, however, that competition among members was effectively suppressed with regard to *all* of their sales, not just sales of Topco brands.

Boycotts and Other Refusals to Deal

A firm ordinarily has complete freedom to choose those with whom it will transact business.[5] However, when two or more parties agree not to deal with some other party, antitrust problems arise. Such a group refusal to deal, usually called a boycott, has been declared per se illegal by the Supreme Court.

Refusals to deal present at least as many problems of identification and labeling as any other activity. Indeed, labeling difficulties probably occur here even more often than in the price fixing area. There are many types of group arrangements with clearly or arguably legitimate purposes which have the effect of excluding others. The question, of course, is whether the activity is something that appropriately can be called a boycott. In these situations courts make a close analysis of purpose and effect, but the analysis frequently is quite difficult to accomplish.

We first examine the law's treatment of "classic boycotts"—boycotts with relatively clear anticompetitive purposes and effects. We then take a look at a few of the other types of cases where exclusionary tendencies raise Section 1 issues.

Classic Boycotts

The classic anticompetitive boycott normally is used by a group for the purpose of either (1) *eliminating* another firm as a competitive force, or (2) *disciplining* the other firm in an effort to keep it from competing as vigorously.

The strength of the per se rule against boycotts is illustrated by several cases. In *Klor's, Inc. v. Broadway-Hale Stores, Inc.*, 359 U.S. 207 (1959), the facts showed that Klor's, a retail appliance store, had been providing stiff competition for the appliance department of Broadway-Hale, a large department store. Since the Broadway-Hale store was only one of many stores of a chain, it had substantial buying power. It used this power to get a number of important appliance manufacturers to stop selling to Klor's. The Supreme Court ruled that the agreement among the manufacturers and Broadway-Hale was illegal even though Klor's represented an immeasurably small portion of the relevant appliance market, and the market probably would not be affected by Klor's absence. The obvious concern is that such conduct, if tolerated, could eventually have a substantial impact on the market by eliminating many small competitive firms like Klor's.

---

[5] An unjustified refusal to deal by a *monopolist*, however, may sometimes be evidence of intent to monopolize, as illustrated by the *Aspen Ski* case in the previous chapter.

Another case, *Fashion Originators' Guild of America v. FTC*, 312 U.S. 457 (1941), also provides an excellent example. The guild consisted of a large number of designers and manufacturers of medium to high-priced women's fashions. Several other firms had been copying the original designs of guild members and selling the manufactured copies at relatively low prices. The guild membership agreed to stop selling to retail stores who bought from the so-called "style pirates." An elaborate system of private investigation and enforcement was implemented to effectuate the plan. The Supreme Court had little difficulty calling the arrangement a boycott and ruling it per se illegal. The "style pirates" were clearly engaged in an activity that many would brand as unfair and perhaps unethical. But it *was* competition. Competition is the basic economic policy of our nation, and if particular types of competition are to be treated as exceptions to the general policy, the decision should be made by Congress. The dress designs in question were not patented or copyrighted.[6] And even though the style piracy may have been a tort under state law, the designers should have used proper legal channels. In the Court's view, our competitive system is too sensitive to allow private, self-interested parties to determine what types of competition ought to be permitted.

Other Group Refusals to Deal

There are a number of situations in which difficult refusal-to-deal issues may arise. Three of the most common situations are presented, and then the legal standards that apply to them are discussed.

Membership in Business Groups: Whenever business firms form some type of organization for the furtherance of their mutual commercial interests, there is the opportunity for refusal-to-deal questions to arise. Suppose, for example, that many of the automotive repair businesses in Missouri, Kansas, and Oklahoma form an organization called the Midwest Auto Repair Association (MARA). The stated purposes of the group are to promote the auto repair business in various ways and encourage high ethical standards in the industry. Like any organization, MARA establishes rules for membership. One of these rules provides that only those engaged in the auto repair business full time can be members. Another rule states that any firm which has had more than three verified complaints filed against it with the local Better Business Bureau during a one-year period cannot be a member for one year after the last complaint. As a result of one of these rules, or perhaps some other membership rule, Jones is excluded from MARA. Is there an illegal refusal to deal under Section 1 of the Sherman Act?

---

[6] The designs could not have been so protected at that time. Today, however, clothing designs can be copyrighted.

Product Standards: Suppose that the Gas Burner Association (GBA) is an organization of manufacturers and dealers of gas burners. These burners, which vary in size and type, are components of heating units (residential, commercial, and industrial) which use natural, propane, or butane gas for fuel. Among other activities, GBA operates testing laboratories in which it attempts to determine the safety, utility, and durability of gas burners. It has adopted a "seal of approval" which it grants to burners that pass its tests. X Company makes a particular type of gas burner, and has applied to GBA for a seal of approval. GBA determined that the burner did not meet its standards, and refused to grant the seal. Has there been an illegal refusal to deal under Section 1?

Access to Facilities: Assume that a group of chemical manufacturing companies pool their resources and form a joint research laboratory (JRL). One of the products of their research is a new chemical compound for use in the process of removing impurities from recycled aluminum. The new compound can save recycling firms substantial time and money. JRL obtains a patent on the compound. Another chemical company, Acme, subsequently wants to participate in JRL, but the group decides it has enough members and refuses. Once again, has there been a refusal to deal which might violate Section 1?

The Legal Standards: In the case of membership rules, standard-setting and testing activities, access to group facilities, and other situations in which there is an exclusionary effect, the courts apply the same basic legal standards. Assuming that there is not a per se violation at the heart of the activity (obviously anticompetitive boycott, price fixing, or market division), the rule of reason is applied. In this type of context, the purpose-and-effect analysis of the rule of reason usually takes the following form.

1. As in any other rule of reason case, the court will examine all evidence tending to show the true purpose of the activity. Such evidence will include the history and background of the particular industry or group, the problems they claim to have been trying to solve, their combined market power, and the existence of less restrictive alternatives.

2. Assuming that the purpose of the activity is found to be legitimate, the next point of inquiry is whether the membership, certification, or access *confers a significant competitive advantage*. In other words, do firms who are included enjoy a significant advantage in competing with those excluded? If not, there generally cannot be an anticompetitive effect resulting from the exclusion. For example, if most customers pay very little attention to the Gas Burner Association's seal of approval, the seal does not give GBA much market power and denial of the seal is not likely to have any effect.

3. The rule, standard, or other action must be reasonable. The reasonableness requirement in this situation has two elements: (a) First, the action must be reasonably and logically related to the group's legitimate objectives.

Suspension of a professional basketball player for gambling was found to be reasonably related to the National Basketball Association's critical need for an appearance of integrity in *Molinas v. National Basketball Ass'n*, 190 F. Supp. 241 (S.D.N.Y. 1961). (b) Second, the rule or action must not be overly broad. In other words, it must not be more restrictive or exclusionary than is reasonably necessary to achieve the group's legitimate purposes. This is simply another application of the "least restrictive alternative" type of analysis.

The next case provides an excellent and topical illustration of how Section 1 is applied in these situations.

United States v. Realty Multi-List, Inc.
U.S. Court of Appeals, Fifth Circuit
629 F.2d 1351 (1980)

Realty Multi-List (RML) was formed in 1967 by eight real estate brokers in Muscogee County, Georgia. By 1976 a majority of the brokers in the county were members of RML. The primary function of RML was to provide a "multiple listing service" for its members. When an owner of real estate employs a broker to aid in selling the property, the owner "lists" the property with the broker. In a multiple listing service, a number of brokers pool their individual listings to increase the total inventory and improve the chances of bringing sellers and buyers together. When property is listed with an RML member and then becomes part of the pool, all members have knowledge of and access to the listing. If another member finds a buyer, he or she splits the brokerage fee with the member who originally obtained the listing.

Only RML members had access to its multiple listing service, and members were not permitted to disclose these listings to nonmembers. RML adopted a number of membership criteria. The most important of these criteria required applicants for membership to (1) "have a favorable credit report and business reputation," (2) have an office "open during customary business hours," and (3) purchase one share of stock at "a price set by the Board of Directors." (The price of a share of stock was set as high as $3,000, but was reduced to $1,000 after RML learned of the government's antitrust investigation.)

The government filed suit against RML in federal district court, claiming that these membership rules violated Section 1 of the Sherman Act. The government did not seek dissolution of RML, but only the abandonment or modification of these rules. The district court granted RML's motion for summary judgment, holding that the rules were valid as a matter of law and that a trial was unnecessary. The government appealed to the court of appeals.

Goldberg, Circuit Judge:

. . . [The court first noted that a multiple listing service like RML is basically a response to certain imperfections in real estate markets. Real estate is immovable, and this built-in geographic limitation makes it even more important that useful sales data be circulated. Without the general dissemination of such information, the market cannot function. Most sellers and buyers do not have the time or expertise to accomplish the proper dissemination of this information, so the broker serves a vital role as a go-between. The individual broker, however, is still quite limited in the attempt to overcome market imperfections. A multiple listing service greatly aids in further diminishing these imperfections.

[By serving as a central processing and distributing point for real estate listings, RML "helps reduce information and communication barriers and ease the built-in geographic barrier confronting buyer and seller." The court also observed that, by bringing information about more listings into a central market, the price-setting function of the market is improved. All parties benefit from the multiple listing service: (1) the seller can choose a broker he or she trusts and deal just with that broker, but still get much wider circulation of the listing than one broker could provide; (2) the buyer can have access to a much wider selection of properties in a shorter time period than if only one broker was involved; and (3) the broker gains access to a larger inventory of listings and obtains more exposure for his or her own listings.

[Thus, the multiple listing service itself was viewed by the court as legitimate. The court held that the membership rules should not be judged as per se illegal even though they excluded some brokers. Because of the benefits and positive competitive effects of RML, the exclusionary (and potentially anticompetitive) effect of the rules must be carefully balanced against these positive effects under the rule of reason.]

While, as we have shown, a trade group like a multiple listing service may create significant competitive advantages both for its members and for the general public, there exists the potential for significant competitive harms when the group, having assumed significant power in the market, also assumes the power to exclude other competitors from access to its pooled resources. . . . [An excluded broker is obviously harmed, but] buyers and sellers are also harmed by unjustified exclusions. Even though member brokers still compete with each other to procure listings and to sell any listing in the pool, the public is denied the incentive to competition that new entry may bring. A new entrant into the market might, for example, be more aggressive and willing to accept a lower commission rate. Exclusion of such a broker would tend to reduce the amount of price competition in the market. . . .

[To determine whether the exclusionary effect of RML's membership rules violated Section 1 of the Sherman Act, the court first examined the market power of RML. The relevant market was found to be residential housing in Muscogee County. The court noted that the question was not whether RML had a monopoly, but whether RML was of "sufficient economic importance that exclusion results in the denial of the opportunity to compete *effectively* on equal terms." The court concluded that RML appeared to have such power and that membership in it was a significant competitive advantage for brokers.]

Proceeding from the premise, then, that RML has the requisite power in the market, we turn to the standards for the evaluation of its membership criteria. First, the rules must be shown to be justified by the legitimate competitive needs of the association. . . . Second, the requirements of the rules themselves must be reasonably necessary to the accomplishment of the legitimate goals and narrowly tailored to that end. . . .

a. . . . We examine first the possible justifications for the "favorable credit report and business reputation" standards. To begin, there are no finite limitations on the size of a multiple listing service like the size limitations necessary to the operation of some sports leagues, or inherent in the allocation of space in a market building; indeed, a multiple listing service succeeds in its goals of creating a public market and reducing market imperfections only insofar as it brings all brokers and listings into its operations. Thus, any claimed rationale for exclusion from a multiple listing service must be closely scrutinized in terms of the operational needs of the service.

[The court then pointed out that, because the real estate brokerage business is closely regulated by the State of Georgia, there is not as much justification for self-regulation regarding matters like credit standing and reputation. Brokers should not be completely prevented from establishing their own ethical standards in addition to the state's regulation, but they must be very careful. The court continued:]

The problem with the requirement of a "favorable credit report and business reputation" as a condition of membership is that RML does not define these terms or the type of proof required. The inherent subjectivity of these standards is thus in no way limited. Under these standards, RML could conceivably exclude a broker whose business reputation was unfavorable because he was not sufficiently aggressive or because he was thought of as inefficient, even though he had never violated any relevant law or committed a serious breach of any duty. Similarly, a broker with a reputation as a "slow pay" but who had never actually defaulted on any financial obligation, might be excluded because he did not have a favorable credit report. Moreover, under RML's rules, these determinations might be based upon hearsay allegations or subjective impressions of an applicant's reputation or creditworthiness. In sum, RML's criteria allow it to exclude a licensed broker whom, according to RML's subjective evaluation, it determines to be generally unfit to be a member of the service. . . .

Subjective membership criteria are generally not narrowly tailored to accomplish any legitimate goal of an association. . . . Because RML's "favorable credit report and business reputation" criteria give it the power to exclude brokers from membership on grounds not justified by its competitive needs, the district court erred in upholding them. Assuming, as we must, that RML possesses the requisite market power, we conclude that the district court should have held them [to be] unreasonable.

b. The Government also argues that the district court erred in holding valid RML's requirement that an applicant must have an office "open during customary hours of business." This requirement, the Government points out, gives RML the power to exclude from membership (1) part-time brokers who are engaged in additional lines of endeavor or who otherwise do not choose to maintain full-time real estate offices and (2) brokers who do not choose or cannot afford to hire a full-time staff to keep an office open during customary business hours. The Government contends that there is no legitimate justification for a rule which has these effects and that the rule is overly broad to further any other legitimate objectives of the association.

RML . . . argues that its "customary hours" rule serves to insure that the applicant will be in a likely position to contribute listings to RML and, since the sharing of listings is the essence of RML's operation, the requirement is justified by its operational needs. Second, RML argues that its "customary hours" rule insures that members will be available to conduct negotiations and to service the listings they do furnish and hence is justified.

It may well be justified for RML to require that a prospective member be actively engaged in the business of being a real estate broker in order that he may contribute to RML's functioning. But a rule requiring that a broker be actively engaged in the business of brokering is a far cry from one requiring that he maintain an office open during customary hours of business. If, for example, a broker holds another job during regular working hours and works in his brokering business on nights and weekends, he may still be very actively engaged as a broker. Indeed, he may find that his hours as a broker mesh well with those of many clients who also hold down jobs during normal working hours and transact their real estate business in their off hours. In this manner, the off hours broker may fulfill a genuine market demand. To exclude all brokers who function primarily in this off hours market on the ground that some may not be "actively engaged" as brokers is clearly a response in excess of need. In such a case as this one, it is incumbent on RML to regulate those *practices* of its members which are necessary to its functioning, instead of needlessly excluding an entire class of brokers from membership.

Similarly, the "customary hours" rule is drawn too broadly to be justified by RML's need to insure that its members be available to service listings and conduct negotiations. As RML asserts, the concept of shared listings, which forms the basis of a multiple listing service, requires that the listing broker be available for negotiations and to close the deal since the listing broker retains the primary responsibility to the seller of the property. This need, however, will not support the total exclusion from membership of all brokers who do not maintain customary office hours. Considering again the example of the broker who conducts his real estate business during his "off hours," one cannot conclude that such a broker will not be reasonably available to carry out the duties relevant to his listings. He may, for example, be able to conduct many of his servicing and negotiating duties during his off hours and may be able to absent himself from his other job for those duties which cannot be postponed. In fact, it is in the self interest of a listing broker to make sure that he is available to supply essential services for his listings. One cannot lightly presume that a broker who supplies a listing will forfeit the commission to which he is entitled by failing to service it. Again, to the extent that there exists a danger that brokers will not be reasonably available to service their listings, it is incumbent upon RML to establish rules governing the troublesome practices of its members and not to exclude from membership an entire class of brokers on the basis of an overly broad generalization.

We thus find RML's "customary hours" rule to be overly broad to accomplish any legitimate goals of the association. . . .

c. The Government's next contention is that the district court erred in upholding RML's stock purchase requirement. As noted, RML requires new members to purchase one share of stock "at a price to be determined by the Board of Directors." Noting that RML has established no objective criteria for determining a reasonable purchase price, the Government argues that this rule is invalid on the theory that, in cases such as this one, the unrestricted power to set an entrance fee which is unrelated to either the cost of the service provided or the cost of maintaining the service as a going concern is the power to exclude, and hence to destroy competition. We agree.

Doubtlessly, RML must be allowed to establish fee schedules which allow it to recoup its costs of operation and to maintain its viability as a going concern. Among those costs which it must be allowed to recover are the start up costs involved in serving a new member. In addition, it is reasonable to assess a new member a *pro rata* contribution toward the maintenance and development of RML, including the accumulation of reasonable reserves. To require more than this, however, is to create problems. A sizeable membership fee which bears no relation to the cost factors outlined above may not only create a significant barrier to new entry into the association, but may create "a strong inference that the amount has been set up as a barrier against" new applications.

[Thus, the court held that all three membership rules appeared to be broader, and more exclusionary, than is reasonably necessary to accomplish RML's legitimate goals. It reversed the district court's summary judgment for RML and remanded the case so that a trial could be held. At this trial, the primary questions would involve how RML's rules would have to be revised in order to be reasonable.]

Noncommercial Refusals to Deal

Suppose that a group of individuals or firms engages in a group refusal to deal, or boycott, with a clearly *noncommercial* motive. Their objective may be the furtherance of some political, social, or religious purpose. Does this type of action raise antitrust questions? The answer is not an easy one, and the various court decisions in these types of cases are not always in agreement. Several generalizations can be made, however.

First, there is *not* a blanket exemption from the antitrust laws for activities with noncommercial purposes. Second, if we assume the alleged noncommercial purpose to be the group's *true* purpose, the per se rule against boycotts will not be applied. Third, the rule of reason and its analysis of purpose and effect will be applied to the particular facts of each case. Fourth, although there are a few cases in which noncommercial boycotts have been held illegal under the Sherman Act, most of the time courts find no significant anticompetitive effects and thus no violation. An example is found in *America's Best Cinema Corp. v. Fort Wayne Newspapers, Inc.*, 347 F. Supp.

328 (N.D. Ind. 1972), in which an agreement between newspapers not to advertise "X-rated" movies was challenged. There clearly was no anti-competitive purpose behind the refusal. Although the question of anti-competitive effect was much more difficult, the federal district court ultimately ruled that the evidence did not prove significant harm to competition and that Section 1 had not been violated.

Miscellaneous Group Activities

The discussion in this chapter has not exhausted the variety of group activities that may raise antitrust questions. Several other types of conduct (although not a complete compilation) are mentioned briefly below.

Joint advertising arrangements have been challenged on several occasions. If the arrangement affects the independence of any firm's price-setting discretion, there obviously is a high risk of illegality. Otherwise, the plan usually will be valid.

An agreement among competitors relating to *hours of operation* may also pose antitrust difficulties. In the case of a shopping mall, where stores share common entrances which must be locked after hours, and where customers expect most of the stores to be open at the same time, an agreement fixing uniform hours ordinarily would be valid. In situations where there is not a similar justification, however, a court will take a much closer look. An operating hours agreement is capable of being used, for instance, as a means of allocating business in much the same fashion as market division. If so used, the arrangement is illegal.

Exchanges of information on the *credit history of customers* generally are legal if there is no agreement on actual credit terms and no group decision to deny credit to a particular customer. Other exchanges of *nonprice information* also are usually valid if they have truly legitimate purposes and no significant anticompetitive effects.

It has become increasingly common in modern times for various types of organizations to engage in *group lobbying*. The effort to influence federal or state government action might be aimed at any of the governmental branches or regulatory agencies. In almost all cases, even where the participants are in the same industry, there is no antitrust issue at all. But what if a group of competitors attempts to bring about government action which will harm competition? Suppose, for instance, that a group of railroads attempts to influence passage of legislation that would make it much more difficult for trucking companies to compete against the railroads in a particular market. The Supreme Court has ruled that such action, even if clearly anticompetitive, is exempt from the antitrust laws. The reason for this exemption is that the Constitution grants a right to petition the government. If the attempt to influence government action is a "sham," however, it is not exempt. Thus, if a group is not really trying to obtain government action, but is merely attempting to suppress competition and make it look like a lobbying effort, its actions will be subject to the antitrust laws. In addition, even if governmental action is really being sought there is no antitrust exemption when the parties subvert governmental processes in their attempt to restrict competition. Examples of such subversion are bribery and perjury.

Trade Associations and Joint Ventures

Trade Associations

Earlier in the chapter brief reference was made to the activities of trade associations. Essentially, a trade association is a loosely knit organization of firms with mutual interests. Its membership usually includes firms within the same industry, but sometimes will also include suppliers or customers of these firms. The mere existence of a trade association presents no antitrust problems—most industries have some type of trade association. Moreover, the activities of these associations usually are legitimate and socially useful. Associations in some industries have been instrumental, for example, in setting product safety standards. Maintenance of ethical standards, providing arbitration procedures for settlement of disputes between members, and formation of group self-insurance pools are a few of the legitimate functions performed by associations.

On the negative side, trade associations present tremendous temptations for anticompetitive conduct. As Adam Smith observed in *The Wealth of Nations* in 1776: "People of the same trade seldom meet together, even for merriment and diversion, but the conversation ends in a conspiracy against the public, or in some contrivance to raise prices." Several of the cases and illustrations used in this chapter have involved trade associations. Thus, caution should be the watchword when a firm participates in such a group. Specialized antitrust counsel should be employed to monitor all association activities and meetings. If the organization proposes a course of action which appears likely to create antitrust problems, a prudent firm will *withdraw*—and do it in such a way that others take notice.

Joint Ventures

Although the term **joint venture** is one without a precise meaning, it has been likened to a partnership for a limited purpose. The joint research lab used as an illustration earlier in the chapter is a type of joint venture. When two or more firms collaborate for some reason, their joint undertaking may or may not be a true joint venture. The basic characteristics of a legitimate joint venture are (1) a partial pooling of resources by two or more firms, (2) a limited degree of integration of some aspect of the firms' operations, and (3) an intent to accomplish a defined business objective that could not be accomplished as efficiently (or at all) by a single firm. Situations in which joint ventures are commonly accepted as legitimate include those in which extremely large economies of scale, very high risks, or unusually extended long-term payoffs are involved in a particular business endeavor, or where the very nature of the product is such that it cannot be produced or marketed efficiently without collaboration between two or more firms.

Joint ventures usually do not violate the antitrust laws, but they can do so on occasion. Section 1 of the Sherman Act is the primarily applicable statute, and joint ventures normally are judged under the rule of reason. If formation of the joint venture involves an asset or stock acquisition, Section 7 of the Clayton Act also can be applied, although the legal standards for joint ventures basically are the same under both statutes. The risk of illegality, and the need for careful antitrust planning by the participants, obviously is greater when actual or potential competitors are involved.

Joint ventures can give rise to two types of antitrust questions. First, has the venture unreasonably suppressed competition among the participants themselves? Second, has the venture had an illegal exclusionary effect on other firms? The second question was examined in the discussion of refusals to deal. It should be recalled that the multiple listing service case presented earlier in connection with refusals to deal involved a legitimate joint venture coupled with several additional restrictions that were illegal because they were more exclusionary than necessary. With regard to the first question, a joint venture may be illegal by unreasonably restraining competition among its members in several situations, such as those discussed below. (We are assuming, of course, that the arrangement was not motivated by an anticompetitive purpose to begin with; if it was so motivated, it obviously is illegal and should not even be called a joint venture.)

1. Although formed for a legitimate purpose, a joint venture may be illegal if its formation creates substantial dangers to competition that are not likely to be offset sufficiently by increased efficiency, creation or stimulation of a market, or other procompetitive factors. This might occur, for example, if a joint venture among competitors clearly is larger than necessary to achieve its efficiency, market creation, or other legitimate goals. For example, if the venture includes competitors representing a substantial portion of the market (probably 25 percent or more), and the evidence indicates that the venture's legitimate objectives could be accomplished by a group accounting for a much smaller segment of the market, there probably is a violation of the antitrust laws because competition is endangered more than is necessary.

2. Even though a joint venture is otherwise legal, it may violate the antitrust laws if it includes an *ancillary restriction* (i.e., a specific additional restriction) that unreasonably restrains competition in a way that is not necessary for the accomplishment of the venture's legitimate objectives. The *Topco* case, presented earlier, provides an example of such a situation. Topco basically was a joint venture for the lawful purposes of cooperative buying and creating a private label system. But its market division was illegal.

Another illustration of illegal ancillary restrictions is found in the Supreme Court's recent decision in *NCAA v. Board of Regents of the Univer-*

sity of Oklahoma, 104 S. Ct. 2948 (1984). The National Collegiate Athletic Association (NCAA) is an organization with 850 colleges and universities as members. To offer a product, competitive intercollegiate athletics, the individual schools must cooperate to a substantial degree. The NCAA is a legitimate joint venture for adopting and supervising playing rules, standards of amateurism, standards for academic eligibility, regulations concerning recruitment of athletes, rules governing the size of athletic teams and coaching staffs, and championship tournaments. The NCAA did not regulate the televising of athletic events except for football. Since 1951, the organization has used various plans for regulating the sale of television broadcast rights for football games between member schools. The most recent plan set a minimum combined price to be received from the national television networks for broadcast rights to all games between member schools over a four-year period. The plan also placed strict limits on the number of times a particular school's football team could appear on television. When this plan was challenged, the Supreme Court found that it violated Section 1 of the Sherman Act because its obvious limitations on price competition and product output in the sale of television broadcast rights were not vital to the achievement of the NCAA's legitimate goals.

The following case involves a claim by a customer of a joint venture that the venture illegally limited price competition among its members.

Broadcast Music, Inc. v. Columbia Broadcasting System, Inc.
U.S. Supreme Court
441 U.S. 1 (1979)

Broadcast Music, Inc. (BMI) and the American Society of Composers, Authors, and Publishers (ASCAP) are organizations which operate essentially as clearinghouses or central markets for the licensing of performance rights to musical compositions. The 22,000 members of ASCAP, which consists of music publishing companies, composers, and lyricists, grant to it the nonexclusive rights to license performances of their copyrighted works, collect royalties, and distribute royalties to members in accordance with a formula. BMI, which operates in the same manner, has 30,000 members. Together, BMI and ASCAP hold rights to almost every musical composition copyrighted in the United States (about four million compositions). Both organizations were formed to make it possible for copyright owners to license and receive royalties for performances of their works, rights that are guaranteed by the copyright laws but which are virtually impossible for individual composers, lyricists, or publishing companies to actually enforce effectively.

ASCAP and BMI followed the practice of granting only "blanket licenses." A blanket license permits the licensee to use any music in the repertory of the licensor (BMI or ASCAP), as often as desired, for a single license fee charged for the duration of the license. Payment is set at either a flat sum or a percentage of the user's revenue. Although ASCAP and BMI grant only blanket licenses, individual copyright owners are free to negotiate licenses for their particular compositions with individual users. Such individual licensing usually is not practical, however, for most owners or users.

Columbia Broadcasting System, Inc. (CBS), one of the three national television networks, brought suit against both organizations in federal district court, claiming that blanket licensing constituted price fixing in violation of Section 1 of the Sherman Act. CBS sought an injunction that would require ASCAP and BMI to offer licenses for individual compositions at negotiated prices, so that CBS could pay only for the music it actually used but could continue dealing with the organizations rather than with individual copyright owners. The trial court held that, under the particular circumstances of the case, blanket licensing was not price fixing. It also held that the practice was not illegal under the rule of reason. The court of appeals reversed, holding that the blanket license constituted a form of price fixing and was illegal per se. BMI and ASCAP appealed to the U.S. Supreme Court.

White, Justice:

. . . The blanket license, as we see it, is not a "naked restraint of trade with no purpose except stifling of competition," but rather accompanies the integration of sales, monitoring, and enforcement against unauthorized copyright use. ASCAP and the blanket license developed together out of the practical situation in the market place: thousands of users, thousands of copyright owners, and millions of compositions. Most users want unplanned, rapid and indemnified access to any and all of the repertory of compositions, and the owners want a reliable method of collecting for the use of their copyrights. Individual sales transactions in this industry are quite expensive, as would be individual monitoring and enforcement, especially in light of the resources of single composers. Indeed, as [even] CBS recognizes, the costs are prohibitive for licenses with individual radio stations, night clubs, and restaurants, and it was in that milieu that the blanket license arose.

A middleman with a blanket license was an obvious necessity if the thousands of individual negotiations, a virtual impossibility, were to be avoided. Also, individual fees for the use of individual compositions would presuppose an intricate schedule of fees and uses, as well as a difficult and expensive reporting problem for the user and policing task for the copyright owner. Historically, the market for public performance rights organized itself largely around the single-fee blanket license, which gave unlimited access to the repertory and reliable protection against infringement. When ASCAP's major and user-created competitor, BMI, came on the scene, it also turned to the blanket license.

With the advent of radio and television networks, market conditions changed, and the necessity for and advantages of a blanket license for those users may be far less obvious than is the case when the potential users are individual television or radio stations, or the thousands of other individuals and organizations performing copyrighted compositions in public. But even for television network licenses, ASCAP reduces costs absolutely by creating a blanket license that is sold only a few, instead of thousands, of times, and that obviates the need for closely monitoring the networks to see that they do not use more than they pay for. ASCAP also provides the necessary resources for blanket sales and enforcement, resources unavailable to the vast majority of composers and publishing houses. Moreover, a bulk license of some type is a necessary consequence of the integration necessary to achieve these efficiencies, and a necessary consequence of an aggregate license is that its price must be established.

This substantial lowering of costs, which is of course potentially beneficial to both sellers and buyers, differentiates the blanket license from individual use licenses. The blanket license is composed of the individual compositions plus the aggregating service. Here, the whole is truly greater than the sum of its parts; it is, to some extent, a different product. The blanket license has certain unique characteristics: It allows the licensee immediate use of covered compositions, without the delay of prior individual negotiations, and great flexibility in the choice of musical material. Many consumers clearly prefer the characteristics and cost advantages of this marketable package, and even small performing rights societies that have occasionally arisen to compete with ASCAP and BMI have offered blanket licenses. Thus, to the extent the blanket license is a different product, ASCAP is not really a joint sales agency offering the individual goods of many sellers, but is a separate seller offering its blanket license, of which the individual compositions are raw material. ASCAP, in short, made a market in which individual composers are inherently unable to fully effectively compete.

Finally, we have some doubt . . . about the extent to which this practice threatens . . . competitive pricing as the free market's means of allocating resources. Not all arrangements among actual or potential competitors that have an impact on price are per se violations of the Sherman Act or even unreasonable restraints. Mergers among competitors eliminate competition, including price competition, but they are not per se illegal and many of them withstand attack under any existing antitrust standard. Joint ventures and other cooperative arrangements are also not usually unlawful, at least not as price-fixing schemes, where the agreement on price is necessary to market the product at all.

[T]he blanket license cannot be wholly equated with a simple horizontal arrangement among competitors. ASCAP does set the price for its blanket license, but that license is quite different from anything any individual owner could issue. . . . Moreover, the . . . District Court found that there was no legal, practical, or conspiratorial impediment to CBS obtaining individual licenses; CBS, in short, had a real choice.

With this background in mind, which plainly enough indicates that over the years, and in the face of available alternatives, the blanket license has provided an acceptable mechanism for at least a large part of the market for the performing rights to copyrighted musical compositions, we cannot agree that it should automatically be declared illegal. . . . Rather, when attacked, it should be subjected to a more discriminating examination under the rule of reason. It may not ultimately survive that attack, but that is not the issue before us today. . . .

The judgment of the Court of Appeals is reversed and the case is remanded to that court for further proceedings consistent with this opinion.

★★★

Comment: After the case was remanded, the court of appeals applied the rule of reason and agreed with the district court's original conclusion that the blanket license was legal. This decision was based essentially on the same factors that had led the Supreme Court to conclude that blanket licensing was not price fixing and had to be looked at more closely: the blanket license was a different product than the individual compositions and obviously could not be offered by individual copyright owners; the blanket license created substantial efficiencies in the market for music performance rights and constituted the only feasible way for most small copyright owners and music users to deal in this market; and the blanket license could not be offered without setting a price. Also, the court of appeals held that, for a very large user like CBS, direct negotiation of licenses with individual copyright owners was a realistic alternative. Therefore, ASCAP and BMI should not be required to offer licenses covering individual compositions.

Research and Development Joint Ventures: Joint ventures play an important role in research and development because research is often characterized by large capital requirements and economies of scale, high risks, and extended long-term payoffs. These characteristics create disincentives for the conduct of some large research projects by private companies, especially those projects that involve "basic research" (research that is not tied to a specific commercial product). Research is vital to the health of the economy, and private companies should be encouraged to engage in research and development projects to the greatest extent possible. On the other hand, antitrust law should apply to the research activities of private firms because research itself can be an important part of competition, and also because cooperative research between two or more firms can provide opportunities for other forms of cooperation that are not legitimate.

In an effort to balance these factors, Congress passed the National Cooperative Research Act of 1984. This law permits, but does not require, the participants in a research joint venture to file a notice with the Justice Department and the Federal Trade Commission (FTC) that identifies the participants and states the nature and objectives of the venture. If this notice is filed within ninety days after formation of the venture, the participants are given two types of limited protection from future antitrust suits. First, in any later antitrust suit related to the research venture, the rule of reason must be applied rather than the per se rule. This provision is more symbolic than real because a truly legitimate joint venture will almost always be examined under the rule of reason. Second, a plaintiff in a private antitrust suit against the venture can recover only single (rather than treble) damages if the plaintiff's claim is based on conduct that is within the scope of the notice that the venture had filed with the Justice Department and the FTC.

Questions and Problems

1. Five competitors meet on several occasions, discuss their problems, and one finally states: "I won't fix prices with any of you, but here is what I am going to do—put the price of my gidget at X dollars; now you all do what you want." He then leaves the meeting. Competitor number two says: "I don't care whether number one does what he says he's going to do or not, nor do I care what the rest of you do, but I

am going to price my gidget at X dollars." Number three makes a similar statement: "My price is X dollars." Numbers four and five say nothing. All leave and set their prices at X dollars. Have the five competitors violated Section 1 of the Sherman Act? Discuss.

2. Theatre Enterprises, Inc., owned and operated the Crest Theatre in a suburban shopping center located about six miles from downtown Baltimore. At that time, the downtown area was still the most important shopping district. As a result, a downtown movie theatre generally had about ten times the drawing power of a suburban theatre like the Crest. Before and after the opening of the Crest, Theatre Enterprises sought to obtain first-run films from several major film distributors. It approached each distributor individually, and was turned down on every occasion. As a result, the Crest was able to show first-run films only after the downtown theatres had shown them. Other than these delayed first-runs, Crest was left with "subsequent runs" (films that had been re-released). Theatre Enterprises sued the distributors, claiming that they had violated Section 1 of the Sherman Act by engaging in a group refusal to deal. There was no direct evidence of agreement among the distributors. Discuss whether and under what circumstances Theatre Enterprises could prevail. (*Theatre Enterprises, Inc. v. Paramount Film Distributing Corp.*, 346 U.S. 537, 1954.)

3. Assume that many clothing manufacturers provide allowances to retailers to pay for a portion of the retailers' local advertising costs. Assume also that a group of relatively small clothing retailers in Texas, Oklahoma, and Arkansas agreed to combine their allowances in a common fund. This fund would be used to pay for joint advertising. For example, the fund could be used to pay for an advertising insert in several newspapers in a particular geographic area (such as the Dallas–Fort Worth area or the Northeast Texas–Southwest Arkansas area). Such an advertisement would feature the products of several clothing retailers in that particular area. By pooling their advertising resources, these retailers hoped to achieve a greater degree of advertising efficiency—to obtain more advertising per dollar for each store. They feel that such joint advertising will enable them to more effectively compete against national department store chains. The retailers have not yet implemented the plan, and are still trying to decide how to advertise sale prices in the joint advertisements.

Fully discuss the antitrust implications of this plan if it is implemented. Will the antitrust implications depend in any way on how they decide to display sale prices in the joint ads? Discuss.

4. During a period of time in which demand for refined sugar was falling because of increasing consumer preferences for artificial sweeteners, several sugar refiners began offering price discounts to some of their larger customers in an effort to stimulate sales and decrease inventories. These discounts were generally in the form of secret rebates. Before long, most other sugar refiners and their customers learned about these rebates. Claiming that these discriminatory rebates were "demoralizing the industry at a time when market conditions were already bad" and that customers were "losing faith in the integrity of the sugar industry," these other refiners urged those granting rebates to stop the practice. The rebating refiners argued, however, that their practices were completely legitimate because "everybody knows it's cheaper to sell to large customers." The nonrebating refiners then put pressure on sugar cane and sugar beet growers and within a short time the rebating refiners were unable to buy cane and beets for making sugar. Within a month the rebating refiners all stopped the practice of favoring certain customers. The Justice Department filed suit in federal district court, claiming that the "nonrebating" sugar refiners and the growers had violated Section 1 of the Sherman Act. Discuss whether Section 1 has been violated.

5. Bunker Hill Co. was the nation's second largest miner of lead, producing 25 percent of the total. It had its own sales force in the western part of the United States but

had none in the eastern part. St. Joseph Lead Co. (St. Joe) was the largest lead miner in the country, producing 40 percent of the total, and had a nationwide sales organization. Lead is a homogeneous product; that is, even though there are different grades of lead, within each grade every producer's lead is the same. However, Bunker Hill's production costs were lower because the raw ore it mined was purer and required less refining. Bunker Hill and St. Joe entered into an agreement in which Bunker Hill made St. Joe its sales agent in the eastern United States. In other words, St. Joe was to act as the retail marketer of Bunker Hill's lead. The Justice Department charged the two companies with violating Section 1 of the Sherman Act. Suppose the evidence in the case showed that there were no independent lead dealers in the eastern United States—that is, there were no retail marketers in the East who were not part of a lead producing company. Suppose also that it had taken St. Joe many years and a large investment to develop its own sales organization. In this situation, discuss whether the arrangement between Bunker Hill and St. Joe would violate Section 1.

6. Assume that the facts in the Bunker Hill–St. Joe case are the same except for the following changes. Suppose that there *are* independent lead dealers in the eastern United States and that prior to the Bunker Hill–St. Joe arrangement Bunker Hill had sold lead in the East through such a dealer. Suppose also that in the past this independent dealer had periodically built up large inventories of lead through poor planning. Then, needing cash, the dealer had periodically sold large amounts of lead at whatever price it would bring. After this had happened several times, Bunker Hill stopped using the independent dealer and started selling through St. Joe. In this situation, discuss whether the Bunker Hill–St. Joe arrangement would violate Section 1 of the Sherman Act.

7. Holiday Inns, Inc., operated a hotel and motel franchising system. It granted licenses which permitted independent franchisees to operate lodging facilities under the Holiday Inn trademark subject to various requirements. In addition to the franchising system, Holiday Inns itself owned lodging facilities in 152 cities. Holiday Inns' franchise system included several restrictions, one of which was a "company-town policy" that generally did not permit the granting of a franchise in any of the 152 cities in which the franchisor itself owned a hotel or motel. In addition, whenever a new franchise location was proposed, Holiday Inns considered any objections from the three franchisees located closest to the proposed facility. These objections sometimes led to a decision not to grant the proposed franchise. Another restriction prohibited franchisees from operating any hotel or motel other than a Holiday Inn during the existence of their Holiday Inn franchise. American Motor Inns, Inc., which already operated forty-eight Holiday Inn franchises, applied for an additional one and was refused. It sued, claiming that these restrictions amounted to a horizontal market division in violation of Section 1 of the Sherman Act. Holiday Inns first defended against the charge by claiming that these restrictions were not horizontal, but were purely vertical, and should not be viewed as per se illegal. How should the court rule on these contentions? Discuss. (*American Motor Inns, Inc. v. Holiday Inns, Inc.*, 521 F.2d 1230, 3d Cir. 1975.)

8. Many retail department stores provide delivery service for large items purchased by their customers. In the New York City area, the presidents of three stores were talking privately about delivery problems at a Chamber of Commerce luncheon. One of them mentioned that the costs involved in maintaining delivery trucks, forklifts, and other equipment and employees were becoming too great to justify the service. The other two agreed, but all of them were concerned about the business they might lose if they discontinued delivery service. They decided to contact other department stores in the metropolitan area to find out what their feelings were. After a series of discussions among the presidents of eighteen of the twenty largest department stores in the area, they came up with the following alternative proposals.

a. They could all simultaneously stop providing delivery service.
b. They could jointly select and deal with an existing independent delivery ser-

vice. The group would investigate existing services, invite them to submit bids, and ultimately select one and jointly contract with it.

Upon hearing of these proposals, the U.S. Department of Justice initiated an investigation. The department was interested in whether any of these proposals might violate Section 1 of the Sherman Act. Discuss the legality of proposals a and b.

9. Suppose that the department stores in question 8 did not adopt proposals a or b but instead decided to consolidate their delivery services into one jointly owned and operated service. The service would have its own trucks, equipment, and employees and would operate out of a central dispatching station. The trucks and equipment initially used by the service would be contributed by individual stores. Periodically, each store would pay a particular amount to the service based on how much delivery service they used. The stores estimate that they can save at least 20 percent of their delivery costs by using the joint service and making more efficient use of their trucks, equipment, and employees.

The participating stores also recognized that other retail stores might later want to join the consolidated service. They decided that they had two options: (1) To permit no other stores to participate because the present group was of an optimal size and no further cost savings were likely to be achieved by greater participation. (2) To permit any other store to participate if it could demonstrate that (a) it had a volume of deliveries comparable to that of currently participating stores, (b) it was a member in good standing of the New York City Chamber of Commerce, (c) it would be willing to pay an initial $100,000 entry fee and contribute monthly its proportional share of the service's operating costs, and (d) it had no history of significant difficulties with labor unions.

Discuss whether the formation and operation of the joint delivery service might violate Section 1 of the Sherman Act.

10. The National Basketball Association (NBA), consisting of independently owned and operated professional basketball teams, had a rule which effectively prevented a person from playing for an NBA team until four years after his high school class had graduated. Spencer Haywood graduated from high school in 1967 and was an all-American college basketball player for two years. In 1969 he left college and began playing professional basketball, eventually signing a contract with the Seattle Supersonics in the NBA. However, the Commissioner of the NBA disapproved Haywood's contract with the Seattle team because Haywood was not yet eligible under the four-year rule. Haywood filed suit against the NBA seeking an injunction which would forbid the NBA from enforcing the four-year rule. He claimed that the agreement of the NBA teams to abide by the four-year rule amounted to a group boycott in violation of Section 1 of the Sherman Act. Discuss how the court should have analyzed and ruled on Haywood's claim. (*Haywood v. National Basketball Ass'n*, 401 U.S. 1204, 1971.)

C·H·A·P·T·E·R 12

ANTITRUST LAW
VERTICAL RESTRAINTS OF TRADE AND PRICE DISCRIMINATION

When firms operating at different levels of the distribution chain (such as seller and buyer) act together in a way that harms competition, there is a vertical restraint of trade. In this chapter several such activities are examined, including vertical price fixing, vertical nonprice restrictions, tying and exclusive dealing agreements, and reciprocity. In addition, some of the antitrust issues and related problems in the franchise arrangement are discussed. The antitrust statute that usually applies to these vertical restraints is Section 1 of the Sherman Act, which was explored in the previous chapter. Tying and exclusive dealing, however, can be challenged under Section 3 of the Clayton Act in addition to Section 1 of the Sherman Act. After completing the discussion of vertical restraints, the Robinson-Patman Act's prohibition of price discrimination is examined.

Vertical Price Fixing

Legal Status of Vertical Price Fixing

Suppose that a manufacturer sells television sets to a wholesale distributor or retail dealer under an agreement specifying that the distributor or dealer will resell the sets to its customers at or above a particular price. This is a clear example of vertical price fixing, sometimes referred to as resale price maintenance. Vertical price fixing is a per se violation of Section 1 of the Sherman Act, and has been such for many years.[1] Thus, regardless of the motives or objectives underlying the practice and regardless of its actual effect on competition, vertical price fixing is illegal.

Vertical price fixing can take different forms, but it does not involve difficulties of identification and labeling as frequently as the horizontal variety. The most common form of vertical price fixing involves an agreement setting an exact price or a minimum price for resale. However, an agreement establishing a maximum price also violates Section 1. In essence, any agreement which interferes with the independence of the buyer's resale pricing decision constitutes vertical price fixing.

Proving a Vertical Agreement

As is always true when Section 1 of the Sherman Act is applied, an *agreement* of some sort must be proved in a vertical price-fixing case. (Although an agreement is a required element of all vertical restraints challenged under Section 1, it is discussed in the context of vertical price fixing because this is where the issue arises most frequently.) Sometimes an agreement obviously exists, but the question often is an extremely difficult one. Following is an examination of some of the situations presenting these difficulties.

Coerced Agreements: The parties to vertical price fixing may be voluntary participants. In many cases, though, one party's participation is involuntary. A manufacturer, for example, may have used its power over dealers to coerce them into the arrangement. On the other hand, a single powerful dealer or a group of dealers may have pressured the manufacturer into the scheme. The "contract, combination, or conspiracy" requirement is met regardless of whether the agreement was voluntary or coerced. This rule fortunately relieves the courts of having to distinguish the many degrees of persuasion which may exist.

Suggested Resale Prices: A seller frequently suggests a price at which its buyers should resell certain items. This suggestion may take the form of a price list distributed to dealers, or a price marked on the package for each item. Although the seller clearly is attempting to influence the buyer's resale pricing decision, this practice is legal so long as the prices are really just *suggested*. Even if one or more buyers consistently follows the suggested re-

[1]From 1937 to 1975, however, Congress permitted state legislatures to exempt most vertical price fixing from the Sherman Act within their own states. The great majority of states did exercise this option by passing so-called "fair trade laws." A number of states later repealed their fair trade laws, and in 1975 Congress revoked the states' authority to permit vertical price fixing. Today, a state can legalize the practice of vertical price fixing only with respect to transactions having no effect on interstate commerce.

sale price, there still is no violation without some evidence of voluntary or coerced agreement.

Thus, if manufacturer M "suggests" a price at which retailers should sell to consumers, but couples the suggestion with surveillance, threats, or other activities aimed at securing compliance, there is sufficient evidence of agreement whenever a retailer actually does comply with the suggestion. In such a case there obviously is more than a mere price suggestion. In the end, the test is whether the resale pricing decision was really an independent one by the buyer or was apparently the result of some form of collusion or understanding between seller and buyer.

Refusal to Deal: One of the most difficult (and often confusing) issues in antitrust law involves the extent to which a seller lawfully may use a *refusal to deal* in an attempt to control buyers' resale prices. In *U.S. v. Colgate & Co.*, 250 U.S. 300 (1919), the Supreme Court stated that a "unilateral refusal to deal" cannot violate Section 1 of the Sherman Act even if controlling resale prices is the seller's ultimate goal. In other words, so long as a seller acts entirely on its own ("unilaterally"), it lawfully can refuse to sell to anyone it chooses, regardless of the motive. The problem, of course, is distinguishing between unilateral action by the seller and action that is part of a vertical price-fixing agreement between the seller and others.

Suppose that M, a manufacturer, either initially refuses to sell to R, a retailer, or later terminates an existing supplier-customer relationship with R. R then files suit against M and claims that the refusal to deal was part of a vertical price-fixing conspiracy. To create a genuine fact issue for the jury, R must present evidence indicating that (1) there was an agreement to limit price competition at R's level, and (2) M refused to deal with R because R was a price-cutter, and not for a legitimate business reason. The agreement to limit price competition at R's level could be between M and wholesalers who act as intermediaries between M and R, between M and other retailers who compete with R, or even between M and R if the evidence shows that R previously had been part of a vertical price-fixing arrangement with M and then tried to get out of it. The agreement could be an express one proved by direct evidence, or it might be inferred from a pattern of actions and communications among M and others. As mentioned in the discussion of suggested resale prices, evidence of surveillance, threats, communications indicating the existence of understandings about resale prices, and many other types of evidence will be relevant. Again, the ultimate issue under Section 1 of the Sherman Act is whether the evidence as a whole indicates that the action being challenged was independent or whether it was the product of some type of collusion.

A particular type of refusal-to-deal case that arises frequently involves a so-called "dealer noise conspiracy." In this situation, R tries to prove an agreement between M and other dealers at R's level by presenting evidence that, prior to R's termination, these other dealers had complained to M about R's price-cutting. If one or more dealers complain to their supplier

"The courts have ruled, sir, that we must divest ourselves of the Watson Company and Copper Fittings, Inc., sell off thirty percent of our mining interests, and get you a smaller desk."

Remedies in antitrust cases can be harsh.
Source: Drawing by Dana Fradon; © 1982 *The New Yorker* Magazine, Inc.

about another dealer's price-cutting and the supplier then stops selling to the price-cutting dealer, is this evidence sufficient to prove a conspiracy among the supplier and complaining dealers? In the next case, the U.S. Supreme Court deals with this question.

Monsanto Co. v. Spray-Rite Service Corp.
U.S. Supreme Court
104 S. Ct. 1464 (1984)

Spray-Rite was engaged in the wholesale agricultural chemical distribution business from 1957 to 1972. It bought insecticides and herbicides from manufacturers and resold them to farmers and retail dealers. Monsanto was one of Spray-Rite's most important suppliers. Of Monsanto's approximately one hundred distributors, Spray-Rite was its tenth largest. In 1968 Monsanto notified Spray-Rite's owner and president, Donald Yapp, that it was terminating Spray-Rite's distributorship. Spray-Rite tried to obtain Monsanto's herbicides from other distributors but was unable to buy sufficient amounts. Spray-Rite's inability to obtain Monsanto products apparently was a major contributing factor in Yapp's decision to cease business in 1972.

Spray-Rite later filed a treble damage suit against Monsanto in federal district court, claiming that Spray-Rite's termination resulted from Monsanto's enforcement of a vertical price-fixing system in violation of Section 1 of the Sherman Act. The primary basis for this contention was that the termination

of Spray-Rite was brought about by a conspiracy between Monsanto and other distributors who had complained to Monsanto about Spray-Rite's price-cutting. The jury rendered a verdict in favor of Spray-Rite for $3.5 million, which the trial court automatically tripled to $10.5 million. Monsanto appealed to the U.S. Court of Appeals for the Seventh Circuit, which affirmed the trial court's decision. Monsanto then appealed to the U.S. Supreme Court.

Powell, Justice:

The Court of Appeals . . . stated that "proof of termination following competitor complaints is sufficient to support an inference of concerted action." Canvassing the testimony and exhibits that were before the jury, the Court of Appeals found evidence of numerous complaints from competing Monsanto distributors about Spray-Rite's price-cutting practices. It also noted that there was testimony that a Monsanto official had said that Spray-Rite was terminated because of the price complaints. In substance, the Court of Appeals held that an antitrust plaintiff can survive a motion for a directed verdict if it shows that a manufacturer terminated a price-cutting distributor in response to or following complaints by other distributors.

We reject the statement by the Court of Appeals of the standard of proof required to submit a case to the jury in distributor-termination litigation, but affirm the judgment under the standard we announce today. . . .

The flaw in the evidentiary standard adopted by the Court of Appeals in this case is that it [does not sufficiently distinguish between independent action and conspiracy]. Permitting an agreement to be inferred merely from the existence of complaints, or even from the fact that termination came about "in response to" complaints, could deter or penalize perfectly legitimate conduct. As Monsanto points out, complaints about price-cutters "are natural—and from the manufacturer's perspective, unavoidable reactions by distributors to the activities of their rivals." Such complaints, particularly where the manufacturer has imposed a costly set of nonprice restrictions, "arise in the normal course of business and do not indicate illegal concerted action." Moreover, distributors are an important source of information for manufacturers. In order to assure an efficient distribution system, manufacturers and distributors constantly must coordinate their activities to assure that their product will reach the consumer persuasively and efficiently. To bar a manufacturer from acting solely because the information upon which it acts originated as a price complaint would create an irrational dislocation in the market. In sum, to permit the inference of [conspiracy solely on the basis of price-related complaints and subsequent termination, thus exposing the manufacturer to treble damage liability, would seriously] inhibit management's exercise of independent business judgment . . . .

Thus, something more than evidence of complaints is needed. There must be evidence that tends to exclude the possibility that the manufacturer and nonterminated distributors were acting independently. The plaintiff should present direct or circumstantial evidence that reasonably tends to prove that the manufacturer and others had a conscious commitment to a common scheme designed to achieve an unlawful objective. . . .

Applying this standard to the facts of this case, we believe there was sufficient evidence for the jury reasonably to have concluded that Monsanto and some of its distributors were parties to an "agreement" or "conspiracy" to maintain resale prices and terminate price-cutters. In fact, there was substantial direct evidence of agreements to maintain prices. There was testimony from a Monsanto manager, for example, that Monsanto on at least two occasions in early 1969, about five months after Spray-Rite was terminated, approached price-cutting distributors and advised that if they did not maintain the suggested resale price, they would not receive adequate supplies of Monsanto's new corn herbicide. When one of the distributors did not assent, this information was referred to the Monsanto regional office, and it complained to the distributor's parent company. There was evidence that the parent instructed its subsidiary to comply, and the distributor informed Monsanto that it would charge the suggested price. Evidence of this kind plainly is relevant and persuasive as to a meeting of minds. [In a footnote, the Court also pointed out that the threat to cut off this distributor's supply came during Monsanto's "shipping season" when herbicide was in short supply. Thus, the jury reasonably could have concluded that Monsanto sought this agreement at a time when it was able to use supply as a lever to force compliance.]

An arguably more ambiguous example is a newsletter from one of the distributors to his dealer-customers . . . just four weeks before Spray-Rite was terminated. It was written after a meeting between the author and several Monsanto officials, and discusses Monsanto's efforts to "get . . . the 'market place in order.'" The newsletter reviews some of Monsanto's incentive and shipping policies, and then states that in addition "every effort will be made to maintain a minimum market price level." The newsletter relates these efforts as follows:

In other words, we are assured that Monsanto's company-owned outlets will not retail at less than their suggested retail price to the trade as a whole. Furthermore, those of us on the distributor level are not likely to deviate downward on price to anyone as the idea is implied that doing this possibly could discolor the outlook for continuity as one of the approved distributors during future upcoming seasons. So, none interested in the retention of this arrangement is likely to risk being deleted from this customer service opportunity. Also, so far as the national accounts are concerned, they are sure to recognize the desirability of retaining Monsanto's favor on a continuing basis by respecting the wisdom of participating in the suggested program in a manner assuring order on the retail level "playground" throughout the entire country. It is elementary that harmony can only come from following the rules of the game and that in the case of dispute, the decision of the umpire is final.

It is reasonable to interpret this newsletter as referring to an agreement or understanding that distributors and retailers would maintain their prices, and Monsanto [in its company-owned stores] would not undercut those prices on the retail level and would terminate competitors who sold at prices below those of complying distributors; these were the "rules of the game."

If, as the courts below reasonably could have found, there was evidence of an agreement with one or more distributors to maintain their prices, the remaining question is whether the termination of Spray-Rite was part of or pursuant to that agreement. It would be reasonable to find that it was, since it is necessary for competing distributors contemplating compliance with suggested prices to know that those who do not comply will be terminated. Moreover, there is some circumstantial evidence of such a link. Following the termination, there was a meeting between Spray-Rite's president and a Monsanto official. There was testimony that the first thing the official mentioned was the many complaints Monsanto had received about Spray-Rite's prices. In addition, [although Monsanto claimed that it terminated Spray-Rite for not having technically trained employees capable of promoting Monsanto products, there was no evidence to substantiate this claim. Moreover, the evidence showed that Monsanto officials had neither discussed these criteria with Spray-Rite's president nor informed him that any of the criteria were not being met]. By contrast, a former Monsanto salesman for Spray-Rite's area testified that Monsanto representatives on several occasions in 1965–66 approached Spray-Rite, including one major and influential one, . . . and requested that prices be maintained. Later that same year, Spray-Rite's president testified, Monsanto officials made explicit threats to terminate Spray-Rite unless it raised its prices.

We conclude that the Court of Appeals applied an incorrect standard to the evidence in this case. The correct standard is that there must be evidence that tends to exclude the possibility of independent action by the manufacturer and distributor. That is, there must be direct or circumstantial evidence that reasonably tends to prove that the manufacturer and others had a conscious commitment to a common scheme designed to achieve an unlawful objective. Under this standard, the evidence in this case created a jury issue as to whether Spray-Rite was terminated pursuant to a price-fixing conspiracy between Monsanto and its distributors. The judgment of the court below is affirmed.

★★★

Vertical Price Restrictions in Non-Sale Transactions

Thus far we have assumed that the vertical price restrictions occurred between independent firms in a traditional sale-and-purchase transaction. When this is not the case, the rule against vertical price restraints is not as clearly applicable.

The Vertically Integrated Firm: Suppose that a manufacturer and its retail outlets are part of the same vertically integrated company. In this situation there really is no *sale* from the manufacturer to the retailer. Instead, the first sale takes place at the retail level. Since there is only one entity involved, the price setting at the retail level is not vertical price fixing.[2]

---

[2]For convenience we use the example of a company operating at both the manufacturing and retailing levels. However, the same principles apply if one company operates at both the manufacturing and wholesaling levels, or at the wholesaling and retailing levels.

Non-Sale Transactions between Independent Firms: Assume that manufacturer M and retailer R are independent firms, but that the transaction between them is something other than a sale. The most common type of non-sale transaction in such a situation is the *consignment*. In a consignment, the owner of the items transfers possession, but not title, to the other party who then sells in behalf of the owner. In the example of M and R, R is M's agent for the purpose of selling M's goods.

In a consignment, since M still owns the goods when R makes a sale, can M lawfully specify the price at which R sells? In most circumstances the answer is yes. If M is a relatively small firm, there is little likelihood of a Section 1 violation. If M is one of the leading firms in its market, there still is very little chance of illegality if the consignment method is used only occasionally. However, if M is a leading firm and makes widespread use of the consignment device as its basic method of distribution, it should be prepared to document a legitimate business justification for its actions.

For instance, the consignment could be justified in cases where the product in question is subject to (1) rapid obsolescence or deterioration, (2) highly seasonal demand, or (3) high risk of market failure because of its untested nature. In such cases, M may use consignments because retailers are not willing to accept the risk that accompanies a purchase. And if the consignment arrangement is a justifiable distribution method, it will be permissible for M to set the price at R's level. On the other hand, where M is a leading company, uses a consignment system of distribution, and is unable to demonstrate a justification for it, a court is likely to conclude that M was merely attempting to evade the rule against vertical price fixing and that M has violated Section 1.[3]

The Controversy Surrounding Vertical Price Fixing

Although vertical price fixing is per se illegal, there has been a longstanding debate as to whether the practice actually should be so condemned. The intensity of this debate has increased in recent years. Some economists and legal scholars feel that vertical price fixing should not be illegal at all, while others feel that its legal status should be determined on a case-by-case basis under the rule of reason. On the other hand, many still think that the rule of per se illegality for vertical price fixing is correct.

Arguments in Favor of Vertical Price Fixing: Those who contend that vertical price fixing should not be per se illegal ordinarily focus on the following points.

---

[3]Even if M could have justified the consignment system, it would be safer from an antitrust perspective, and probably better overall, for M simply to sell to retailers and calm their fears with a liberal buy-back policy. In this way, M could stay away from the pricing decision at R's level.

Free-Rider Problem: It is sometimes contended that vertical price fixing can serve the desirable objective of resolving the so-called "free-rider" problem. Let us suppose that M manufactures stereo equipment. To adequately market the product it is necessary for retailers to engage in local advertising, provide pre-sale demonstration and consultation to prospective customers, and offer after-sale service. Providing these services entails significant expense. In addition, maintaining a high quality repair service requires capital investment. If retailer X provides these services, its costs and usually its prices will be higher than the costs and prices of retailer Y who does not provide the services. There certainly is a possibility that customers may be attracted and informed by X's advertising and educated by X's pre-sale demonstration and consultation, but then go to Y for the actual purchase at a lower price. When this happens, Y takes a "free ride" on X's expenditures. To prevent free-riding and thus encourage retailers to make the investment necessary to adequately market M's goods, M may decide to set a minimum price for the resale of its goods.

Intrabrand vs. Interbrand Competition: A closely related argument is that vertical price fixing suppresses only *intrabrand competition*. In other words, there is an effect on price competition only among those dealing in M's brand. If vigorous competition exists between M's brand and similar goods produced by others—*interbrand competition*—restrictions on intrabrand competition supposedly will cause little harm. Proponents of this view also contend that limitations on intrabrand competition may actually improve interbrand competition. The rationale for this argument is that M's dealers can focus their competitive efforts more clearly on sellers of other brands if these dealers are freed from having to compete against each other. In addition, it is argued that M's dealers can more effectively engage in interbrand competition if vertical price fixing encourages them to invest the capital and offer the services required to provide a maximum marketing effort.

Brand Image: The contention has sometimes been made, although less frequently in recent years, that protection of a producer's brand image is a legitimate objective for vertical price fixing. If M markets and advertises a brand-name item as a "premium" product, this image may be tarnished if dealers engage in price cutting when reselling M's product to their customers.

Arguments Against Vertical Price Fixing: Those contending that the present rule making vertical price fixing per se illegal is correct usually employ the following lines of reasoning, some of which are obviously interrelated.

Benefit for Firms, Not Market: The elimination of the free-rider problem, encouragement of capital investment by dealers, protection of brand image, and other alleged benefits of vertical price fixing may actually prove beneficial only to the particular firms involved, and not to the market as a whole.

Importance of Intrabrand Competition: Many experts point out that, in a number of markets, intrabrand competition is vigorous and is quite important to the health of the market. The relative strength and importance of intrabrand competition can, of course, be examined under the rule of reason in each case. However, proponents of the per se rule for vertical price fixing seem to feel that intrabrand competition is never completely unimportant and that its elimination should always be cause for concern.

Intrabrand Affects Interbrand: The argument also is made that the dividing line between intrabrand and interbrand competition is not clearcut. Often there can be a significant interrelationship between the two, and there are frequent "spillover" effects from intrabrand to interbrand competition. Competition is competition, the argument goes, and competition between dealers in one brand is an integral part of total competition in the market.

Coverup for Horizontal Price Fixing: Vertical price fixing sometimes can be used as a guise for horizontal price fixing. Suppose that several manufacturers agree to fix prices among themselves. They also may agree to individually impose restrictions on the resale prices of their dealers. The reason for the vertical restriction is to make it easier for the manufacturers to detect any "cheating" (price cutting) by one of their group. In another situation, suppose that a group of retail dealers conspire to fix prices among themselves. They may decide to approach their supplier and demand that vertical price fixing be implemented. In this case vertical price fixing is just a method for carrying out a horizontal price fixing conspiracy. Those contending that vertical price fixing should not be per se illegal agree that it should be unlawful in these types of circumstances, but contend that a case-by-case examination is necessary to see if horizontal price fixing is really present. Those supporting the per se approach argue, however, that it frequently is far more difficult to actually *prove* the horizontal arrangement than the vertical one in these cases.

Transfer of Oligopoly: If the market for product X is very concentrated, perhaps oligopolistic, at the manufacturing level, the widespread use of vertical price fixing in the industry can transfer this generally undesirable structure to another level, such as the retail level.

Less Restrictive Alternatives: Proponents of the view that vertical price fixing should not be per se illegal generally feel that all of the above dangers can be identified if an individualized, rule of reason analysis is applied. If in a particular case the probable danger to competition outweighs the potential benefits, they say, then and only then should the practice be illegal. Perhaps the strongest argument in favor of per se treatment, however, is that there are *less restrictive alternatives* available for the accomplishment of all of the alleged benefits of vertical price fixing. In other words, there are indeed some possible benefits, but there also are some clear dangers, *and the bene-*

fits usually can be achieved without exposing the market to the dangers of vertical price fixing. For example, there are many methods by which a manufacturer can solve a free-rider problem, such as spelling out and actively enforcing dealers' contractual obligations to provide certain levels of advertising and service, providing monetary allowances to dealers for their advertising and service efforts, or even using some of the vertical nonprice restrictions discussed in the next section. Implementing and monitoring such methods for solving the free-rider problem will require some time, effort, and expense on the part of the manufacturer. On the other hand, implementing and monitoring a system of vertical price fixing also requires significant time, effort, and expense.

Vertical Nonprice Restrictions

Vertical restrictions may relate to matters other than price. The vertical nonprice restrictions that cause concern under Section 1 of the Sherman Act generally are those involving some type of market division. Following is a discussion of the relevant legal principles and an examination of the most common forms of vertical nonprice restrictions.

Legal Status of Vertical Nonprice Restrictions

All forms of vertical nonprice restriction have the common characteristic of limiting *intraband* competition. In other words, they restrict competition among dealers or distributors in the resale of a particular manufacturer's brand. For several years, from 1967 to 1977, some vertical nonprice restrictions were per se illegal. In 1977, however, in *Continental T.V., Inc. v. G.T.E. Sylvania*, 433 U.S. 36, the Supreme Court ruled that all vertical nonprice restrictions should be judged under the rule of reason. In that case, which is presented at the end of this section, the Court expressed the view that vertical nonprice restrictions should not be per se illegal because they often are used for positive competitive reasons and many times do not unreasonably suppress competition.

The type of analysis employed under the rule of reason is basically the same in this situation as in others. The courts consider evidence relating to the purpose and effect of the particular arrangement.

Purpose: Vertical nonprice restrictions may be used by a manufacturer to solve a free-rider problem by limiting intraband competition and thereby eliminating the incentive for one dealer to take a free ride on the service and promotion efforts of other dealers. In this way, the manufacturer can more easily attract aggressive, well-capitalized dealers who are willing and able to make the investment necessary to engage in the service and promotion activities necessary to market the manufacturer's product. Such limitations on intraband competition also can be used by a manufacturer in some situations to help introduce a new product or otherwise enter a new market, because dealers may demand protection from intraband competition before they are willing to take the risk involved in a new venture. Under the rule of reason, objectives such as those just discussed are viewed as legitimate, so long as the evidence supports the manufacturer's claimed justification. Because limitation of intraband competition is the means normally used to achieve these goals, such a limitation is not treated by the courts as an illegal purpose. In other words, if the evidence indicates that there were legitimate business justifications for the restrictions, the fact that the manufacturer purposely tried to accomplish its objectives by limiting intraband competition does not make the restrictions illegal.

Effect: If the restrictions were imposed for legitimate business reasons, they will be illegal under the rule of reason only if the evidence indicates that substantial anticompetitive effects are likely to result in the market as a whole. The most important factor that courts will consider is the manufacturer's market share. The higher this market share is, the greater is the likelihood that a vertical nonprice restriction will be illegal. If it is below approximately 10 percent, the restrictions usually will be found legal without further inquiry. If the manufacturer's market share is at or above this level, courts usually will look at other factors. Other factors that could increase the chances of illegality in a close case include (1) evidence that *interbrand* competition in this particular market is not very strong, and that *intrabrand* competition is unusually important; (2) evidence that most other manufacturers in this market also use such restrictions to limit intrabrand competition among their dealers; and (3) evidence that the manufacturer selected a form of nonprice restriction that limited intrabrand competition much more than was really necessary under the circumstances.

Types of Vertical Nonprice Restrictions

Exclusive Territories: Suppose that M, a manufacturer, guarantees several retail dealers that they will have the exclusive right to market M's product in their respective geographic areas. Such a restriction is usually referred to as a "territorial exclusive" or "sole outlet" arrangement. Because this type of restriction places a contractual obligation on M, and not on the dealers, M probably will not guarantee territorial exclusives unless necessary to persuade dealers to carry M's product. In other words, the particular type of restriction that is used depends partly on whether M or the dealers have more bargaining power.

If M has granted a territorial exclusive to a dealer, R, what happens if another dealer in R's territory seeks to handle M's product? In order to honor the commitment to R, M must deny the other dealer's request. If the territorial exclusive itself is legal under the rule of reason, M's denial also is legal—it is not an illegal boycott even if M and R consulted about the denial. Similarly, suppose that M terminates R and replaces that dealer with another one. Again, even though M and the substitute dealer obviously will have acted together concerning R's termination, the action does not amount to an illegal boycott. It simply is an integral part of maintaining exclusive territories, and if the particular system of territorial exclusives is legal under the rule of reason, activities necessary to implement the system also are legal.

Territorial and Customer Restrictions on Resale: Although a manufacturer sometimes will use territorial exclusives without other restrictions, it is more common to couple such an arrangement with restrictions on the dealers' resale of the product. For instance, M might require its dealers to resell only within a certain geographic area or only to certain types of customers (such as retailers, wholesalers, institutional buyers, and so forth). Restrictions on resale are actually needed in many cases for M to really honor its promises to dealers regarding exclusive territories.

If M has sufficient bargaining power when setting up its distribution system, as is often the case, M may choose to use restrictions on resale without promising territorial exclusives to dealers. In such a situation, if the need arises in the future M retains the ability to start selling through an additional dealer in an area already served by one of its existing dealers. Any business objective that can be achieved by territorial exclusives usually can be achieved by restrictions on resale without exclusives. The reason is that restrictions on the geographic areas within which a dealer may resell, or other restrictions on resale, limit intrabrand competition in essentially the same way as territorial exclusives. As we have seen, vertical nonprice restrictions use limitations on intrabrand competition to achieve their purposes.

Other Restrictions on Resale: M sometimes may place limitations on dealers' resale of the product that are less restrictive than airtight territorial or customer restrictions. One fairly common provision is the *location requirement*, which requires the dealer to sell only from a specified location. This was, in fact, the type of restriction involved in *Continental T.V. v. G.T.E. Sylvania*. Both the feasibility of such a restriction and the extent to which it limits intraband competition depend on the nature of the product and how it is marketed.

Another type of provision is one assigning each dealer an *area of primary responsibility*. It does not strictly limit a dealer to resale within its designated territory, but requires only that the territory be thoroughly served before sales can be made outside the area. This type of restriction clearly does not limit a dealer's freedom or intrabrand competition as much as an absolute territorial restriction.

A third form of vertical nonprice restriction on resale is the *profit pass-over requirement*. This type of arrangement usually is used in connection with an area of primary responsibility. It requires a dealer who makes sales outside its designated area to provide compensation to the dealer in whose area the customer is located. The purpose of the payment is to reimburse the "invaded" dealer for the effort and expense of developing customer demand in its territory. A profit pass-over requirement also is less restrictive than an absolute territorial limitation unless the required compensation is unreasonably high.

If a manufacturer or other supplier decides that some type of nonprice restriction is necessary, it is important to study the various alternatives carefully, for several reasons: (1) choosing an alternative that restricts intrabrand competition as little as possible under the circumstances greatly increases the chances that the restriction will be legal under the rule of reason; (2) it usually is in the best interest of the manufacturer to maintain as much intrabrand competition as possible among its dealers while still achieving its legitimate business objectives; and (3) the type of restriction that will work best varies substantially from one situation to another.

Comparison of Vertical Price Fixing with Vertical Nonprice Restrictions

Many of the motives for, and alleged benefits of, vertical nonprice restrictions are the same as for vertical price fixing. Arguments relating to the intrabrand-interbrand competition distinction and the free-rider problem are frequently made in behalf of these restrictions. In addition, some observers contend that such practices can assist a firm in entering a new market, maximizing its penetration of a new or existing market, and strengthening its competitive position against larger rivals. Today arguments such as these, and evidence supporting them, actually are taken into account by courts because the rule of reason is the governing principle. When vertical price fixing is involved, of course, any asserted justifications or benefits are ignored under the per se rule.

Because of the similarities between vertical price fixing and vertical nonprice restrictions, some observers see a lack of consistency in applying the per se rule to one and the rule of reason to another. Such comments usually are made to support the argument that vertical price fixing should be analyzed according to the rule of reason, and not the per se rule.

Upon closer examination, one can find some significant distinctions between vertical price fixing and vertical nonprice restrictions. First, courts are justifiably more sensitive to any arrangement aimed directly at the pricing mechanism—price is indeed the "central nervous system" of our economy. Second, vertical nonprice restrictions are not nearly so likely to be coverups for horizontal price-fixing conspiracies. Third, vertical nonprice restrictions are more likely than price fixing to actually help a firm enter a new market by inducing dealers to take the sizable risk involved. A market entry is always a positive economic factor in antitrust analysis.

We now will examine the Supreme Court's landmark decision in the *Sylvania* case.

Continental T.V., Inc. v. G.T.E. Sylvania, Inc.
U.S. Supreme Court
433 U.S. 36
(1977)

Sylvania manufactured and sold television sets through its Home Entertainment Products Division. Prior to 1962, like most other television manufacturers, Sylvania sold televisions to independent or company-owned wholesale distributors who then resold them to a large and diverse group of retailers. Prompted by a decline in its market share to a relatively insignificant 1 to 2 percent of national television sales, Sylvania conducted an intensive reassessment of its marketing strategy and in 1962 adopted the franchise plan challenged here. Sylvania phased out its wholesale distributors and began to sell its televisions directly to a smaller and more select group of franchised retailers. The main purpose of the change was to decrease the number of competing Sylvania retailers in the hope of attracting the more aggressive and competent retailers, which Sylvania felt was necessary to improve its market position.

Thus, Sylvania limited the number of franchises granted for any given area and required each retail dealer to sell Sylvania products only from the location or locations specified in the franchise agreement. These retailers were not prohibited from selling the products of competing manufacturers. A franchise did not constitute an exclusive territory, and Sylvania retained sole discretion to increase the number of retailers in an area in light of the success or failure of existing retailers in developing their market. The revised marketing strategy apparently was successful, and by 1965 Sylvania's share of national television sales increased to 5 percent, making it the eighth largest manufacturer of televisions.

In 1965 Sylvania proposed to franchise an additional retailer in San Francisco. This proposal upset Continental T.V., an existing Sylvania dealer in the city. Continental then proposed to open a new store in Sacramento. Sylvania denied Continental's request because it felt that Sacramento presently was being adequately served. Continental then began selling Sylvania televisions in Sacramento in defiance of Sylvania, and the manufacturer stopped selling to Continental.

Continental filed a treble damage suit against Sylvania, claiming that the restrictions on dealer location violated Section 1 of the Sherman Act. In federal district court Continental received a jury verdict against Sylvania for approximately $600,000 and a judgment for $1.8 million. In ruling for Continental, the district court applied the Supreme Court's 1967 decision in *U.S. v. Arnold, Schwinn & Co.*, which had held vertical nonprice restrictions to be per se illegal. When Sylvania appealed to the Court of Appeals, that court reversed and ordered a retrial because it thought that the *Schwinn* case was inapplicable to the present situation. Continental then appealed to the U.S. Supreme Court. The Supreme Court felt that the *Schwinn* case was indeed applicable to the facts of the present case, but wished to decide whether *Schwinn*

should still be the law. Thus, the issue for the Supreme Court was whether to follow its earlier decision in the *Schwinn* case and apply the per se rule, or to overrule that case and apply the rule of reason to vertical nonprice restrictions.

Powell, Justice:

. . . Since its announcement, *Schwinn* has been the subject of continuing controversy and confusion, both in the scholarly journals and in the federal courts. The great weight of scholarly opinion has been critical of the decision, and a number of the federal courts confronted with analogous vertical restrictions have sought to limit its reach. In our view, the experience of the past 10 years should be brought to bear on this subject of considerable commercial importance. . . .

Per se rules of illegality are appropriate only when they relate to conduct that is manifestly anti-competitive. As the Court explained in *Northern Pac. R. Co. v. United States*, 356 U.S. 1, 5, 78 S.Ct. 514, 518, 2 L.Ed.2d 545 (1958), "there are certain agreements or practices which because of their pernicious effect on competition and lack of any redeeming virtue are conclusively presumed to be unreasonable and therefore illegal without elaborate inquiry as to the precise harm they have caused or the business excuse for their use."

In essence, the issue before us is whether *Schwinn's per se* rule can be justified under the demanding standards of *Northern Pac. R. Co.* . . .

The market impact of vertical restrictions is complex because of their potential for a simultaneous reduction of intrabrand competition and stimulation of interbrand competition. . . .

Vertical restrictions reduce intrabrand competition by limiting the number of sellers of a particular product competing for the business of a given group of buyers. Location restrictions have this effect because of practical constraints on the effective marketing area of retail outlets. Although intrabrand competition may be reduced, the ability of retailers to exploit the resulting market may be limited both by the ability of consumers to travel to other franchised locations and, perhaps more importantly, to purchase the competing products of other manufacturers. . . .

Vertical restrictions promote interbrand competition by allowing the manufacturer to achieve certain efficiencies in the distribution of his products. These "redeeming virtues" are implicit in every decision sustaining vertical restrictions under the rule of reason. Economists have identified a number of ways in which manufacturers can use such restrictions to compete more effectively against other manufacturers. For example, new manufacturers and manufacturers entering new markets can use the restrictions in order to induce competent and aggressive retailers to make the kind of investment of capital and labor that is often required in the distribution of products unknown to the consumer. Established manufacturers can use them to induce retailers to engage in promotional activities or to provide service and repair facilities necessary to the efficient marketing of their products. Service and repair are vital for many products, such as automobiles and major household appliances. The availability and quality of such services affect a manufacturer's good will and the competitiveness of his product. Because of market imperfections such as the so-called "free rider" effect, these services might not be provided by retailers in a purely competitive situation, despite the fact that each retailer's benefit would be greater if all provided the services than if none did. . . .

Certainly, there has been no showing in this case, either generally or with respect to Sylvania's agreements, that vertical restrictions have or are likely to have a "pernicious effect on competition" or that they "lack . . . any redeeming virtue." Accordingly, we conclude that the *per se* rule stated in *Schwinn* must be overruled. In so holding we do not foreclose the possibility that particular applications of vertical restrictions might justify *per se* prohibition under *Northern Pac. R. Co.* But we do make clear that departure from the rule of reason standard must be based upon demonstrable economic effect. . . .

In sum, we conclude that the appropriate decision is to return to the rule of reason that governed vertical restrictions prior to *Schwinn*. When anticompetitive effects are shown to result from particular vertical restrictions they can be adequately policed under the rule of reason, the standard traditionally applied for the majority of anticompetitive practices challenged under § 1 of the Act. Accordingly, the decision of the Court of Appeals is affirmed.

★★★

Comment: On retrial, the district court found that Sylvania's vertical restrictions were valid under the rule of reason. This holding was based primarily on (1) Sylvania's legitimate business justification, (2) Sylvania's small market share, and (3) the court's feeling that Sylvania had chosen the "least restrictive alternative"—in other words, that the location clause was less restrictive of competition than other methods Sylvania might have used to accomplish its objectives.

Tying, Exclusive Dealing, and Reciprocity

Tying Agreements

When one party agrees to supply (sell, lease, etc.) a product only on the condition that the customer also take another product a **tying agreement** has been made. The desired item is the *tying* product, and the item the customer is required to take is the *tied* product. Tying agreements are scrutinized under both Section 1 of the Sherman Act and Section 3 of the Clayton Act. Section 3 of the Clayton Act applies only to the tying of two tangible commodities. Section 1 of the Sherman Act applies to all tying arrangements, including those in which either or both products is not a tangible commodity (such as a service or land). Today tying agreements are judged in essentially the same way under the two different statutes, so Section 3 of the Clayton Act is largely redundant.

An early landmark case provides a clear example of tying. In *International Business Machines Corp. (IBM) v. U.S.*, 298 U.S. 131 (1936), IBM was found guilty of violating Section 3 of the Clayton Act by requiring all customers leasing its tabulating machines to also purchase their tabulating cards from IBM.

Motives for Tying: Several different motivations may lead a supplier to impose tying arrangements on its customers.

Leveraging: In some cases the supplier may be trying to use the power it has in one market (the tying market) to obtain more business in another market (the tied market) where it does not possess such power. Such a practice is often referred to as "leveraging" market power from one market to another.

Discriminating among Customers: Sometimes a supplier may use tying in an effort to differentiate among customers based on the intensity with which they use the tying product. Suppose, for example, that some of IBM's tabulating machine customers had used the machines more than other customers. If IBM felt that the higher intensity users should pay more, one way to accomplish this would be to require the purchase of tabulating cards. These cards were required in direct proportion to the intensity of machine use, and would give the supplier a way of measuring and charging for degree of use.

Quality Control: A supplier may argue that tying enables it to maintain quality control standards. This, in fact, was the argument made by IBM in the tabulating machine case. The company contended that defective cards would produce inaccurate results and harm the reputation of its machines. The court did not accept IBM's quality control argument, but in certain circumstances this can be a valid defense. More will be said about this defense later.

Hiding Revenues: Occasionally a supplier may wish to disguise some of its revenues. For example, suppose that Acme Salt Co. manufactures a machine used by food canning companies to inject salt into the food during the canning process. Suppose further that Acme produces this machine under permission it received in a patent license from Jones, the machine's inventor and patent owner. As is often the case in patent licenses, Jones's compensation is a percentage of Acme's revenues from selling or leasing the machines. If Acme sells or leases machines at relatively low rates and makes its real profits by requiring customers to buy their salt requirements from Acme, the company will pay less to Jones for the patent license. In such a case, tying clearly has ethical implications as well as legal ones.

Dangers of Tying: There are several potentially harmful effects of tying agreements.

Foreclosure: Perhaps the most commonly stated danger of tying is the foreclosure of competitors in the tied market. In other words, by using its power in the tying market as a wedge in the tied market, the supplier forecloses or shuts off some part of the tied market from other firms. The disadvantage suffered by other firms does not result from their inefficiency in the tied market, but from their lack of power in the tying market—customers' buying decisions in the tied market are not based solely on legitimate factors such as price, quality, or service.

Entry barriers: When a supplier has been extremely successful in implementing tying agreements, high entry barriers may be erected around the tied market. This effect actually is an extension of the foreclosure concept. For example, before it was prohibited from doing so in the early 1950s, Eastman Kodak Co. included a fee for processing in the price of its film. Kodak enjoyed a virtual monopoly in the market for amateur photographic film. Since customers had already paid for the processing service, they almost always sent their exposed film to a Kodak lab for processing. There was virtually no competition in the processing business because new firms could not obtain a foothold in the market. Within a few years after Kodak was ordered to stop the practice, approximately 600 firms competed in the photo processing industry.

Transferred Power: The leveraging of power, in itself, is often thought to be undesirable. Even if the supplier's power in the tying market was legal, there is a strong policy against the transfer of this power to another market. The supplier's power in the tying market may well have been gained through greater efficiency or a lawful patent or copyright, but the transfer of this power to another market is not likely to be caused by such legitimate factors.

Freedom: Regardless of the effects on competition, tying limits the freedom of customers to make purchasing decisions as they see fit.

The Legal Standards: The Supreme Court has ruled that tying agreements are illegal when the following elements are proved.

1. There must be *two separate products or services*. This requirement often is obvious, but occasionally creates substantial difficulty. Most products consist of several different parts, and the supplier should not be forced to break the product down into its smallest elements. But how far can the supplier go in adding elements? A car and its tires would be viewed as a single product, but what about a car and a radio? Would it matter what type of car is being bought, or what type of radio is included? What about a car and a built-in television set? One can readily see the potentially troublesome questions that can arise. The courts and other authorities have found the following factors to be important: (a) Is it more efficient and cost effective to market the items together, and if so, does this benefit outweigh the limitation on the buyer's freedom? (b) Do sellers and buyers in the relevant markets commonly recognize the items as being a single product or two separate ones? (c) Are the items functionally dependent on each other in fixed proportions, or can they function separately and in varying proportions?

2. It must be shown that the supplier has sufficient *market power in the tying market* to enable it to significantly restrict competition in the tied market. Market power in the tying market may be caused by substantial production cost advantages, a large market share, patent or copyright protection, the uniqueness or short supply of the tying product, or other factors. In a recent case, *Jefferson Parish Hospital District v. Hyde*, 104 S. Ct. 1551 (1984), the Supreme Court held that if market share is the *only* available evidence of market power, the supplier's share must be at least 30 percent before it can support a conclusion that the supplier has substantial market power in the tying market.

3. The supplier's tying activities must have affected a *substantial amount of commerce in the market for the tied product.* In this context, substantiality is determined by the supplier's total dollar volume of business in the tied market received from all customers under the tying program. The Supreme Court held in one case that $500,000 is enough, and indicated in another case that as little as $190,000 may be enough.

The courts have stated that if all three elements are proved, tying is per se illegal. If the first element and either the second or the third are proven, tying supposedly is judged under the rule of reason. As a practical matter, however, a tying agreement is almost never found to be illegal unless all three elements are proved.

In most tying cases, the critical issue is whether the supplier has sufficient power in the tying market. The next two cases deal with this question.

United States v. Loew's, Inc.

U.S. Supreme Court
371 U.S. 38
(1962)

A number of motion picture film distributors engaged in the practice of "block booking" when granting licenses of films to television stations. In the case of copyrighted motion picture films, a license is the contractual permission to show a film in return for a fee. Under the block booking practice, a distributor would license films to stations only in packages. For example, one television station paid $118,800 for the license of ninety-nine films: to get "Treasure of the Sierra Madre," "Casablanca," "Johnny Belinda," "Sergeant York," and "The Man Who Came to Dinner," the station also had to take such films as "Nancy Drew Troubleshooter," "Tugboat Annie Sails Again," "Kid Nightingale," "Gorilla Man," and "Tear Gas Squad." In another situation, to get "Gone With the Wind," a station had to take films such as "Getting Gertie's Garter."

The government filed a civil suit against six major distributors, claiming that block booking amounted to tying in violation of Section 1 of the Sherman Act. The district court ruled in favor of the government and issued an injunction prohibiting the practice. The distributors appealed to the Supreme Court. The Court refers to them as appellants throughout its opinion.

Goldberg, Justice:

. . . This Court has recognized that "[t]ying agreements serve hardly any purpose beyond the suppression of competition. . . ." They are an object of antitrust concern for two reasons—they may force buyers into giving up the purchase of substitutes for the tied product, and they may destroy the free access of competing suppliers of the tied product to the consuming market. A tie-in contract may have one or both of these undesirable effects when the seller, by virtue of his position in the market for the tying product, has economic leverage sufficient to induce his customers to take the tied product along with the tying item. The standard of illegality is that the seller must have "sufficient economic power with respect to the tying product to appreciably restrain free competition in the market for the tied product." Market dominance—some power to control price and to exclude competition—is by no means the only test of whether the seller has the requisite economic power. Even absent a showing of market dominance, the crucial economic power may be inferred from the tying product's desirability to consumers or from uniqueness in its attributes.

The requisite economic power is presumed when the tying product is patented or copyrighted. . . . Since one of the objectives of the patent laws is to reward uniqueness, the . . . existence of a valid patent on the tying product, without more, establishes a distinctiveness sufficient to conclude that any tying arrangement involving the patented product would have anticompetitive consequences. . . . In *United States v. Paramount Pictures, Inc.*, 334 U.S. 131, the principle of the patent cases was applied to copyrighted feature films which had been block booked into movie theaters. . . . It is said that reward to the author or artist serves to induce release to the public of the products of his creative genius. But the reward does not serve its public purpose if it is not related to the quality of the copyright. Where a high quality film greatly desired is licensed only if an inferior one is taken, the latter borrows quality from the former and strengthens its monopoly by drawing on the other. The practice tends to equalize rather than differentiate the reward for the individual copyrights. Even where all the films included in the package are of equal quality, the requirement that all be taken if one is desired increases the market for some. Each stands not on its own footing but in whole or in part on the appeal which another film may have. . . .

Appellants attempt to distinguish the *Paramount* decision in its relation to the present facts: the block booked sale of copyrighted feature films to exhibitors in a new medium—television. Not challenging the District Court's finding that they did engage in block booking, they contend that the uniqueness attributable to a copyrighted feature film, though relevant in the movie-theater context, is lost when the film is being sold for television use. Feature films, they point out, constitute less than 8% of television programming, and they assert that films are "reasonably interchangeable" with other types of programming material and with other feature films as well. . . . They say that the Government's proof did not establish their "sufficient economic power" in the sense contemplated for nonpatented products.

Appellants cannot escape the applicability of *Paramount Pictures*. A copyrighted feature film does not lose its legal or economic uniqueness because it is shown on a television rather than a movie screen.

The district judge found that each copyrighted film block booked by appellants for television use "was in itself a unique product"; that feature films "varied in theme, in artistic performance, in stars, in audience appeal, etc.," and were not fungible; and that since each defendant by reason of its copyright had a "monopolistic" position as to each tying product, "sufficient economic power" to impose an appreciable restraint on free competition in the tied product was present.

Moreover, there can be no question in this case of the adverse effects on free competition resulting from appellant's illegal block booking contracts. Television stations forced by appellants to take unwanted films were denied access to films marketed by other distributors who, in turn, were foreclosed from selling to the stations. . . . There may be rare circumstances in which the doctrine we have enunciated under § 1 of the Sherman Act prohibiting tying agreements involving patented or copyrighted tying products is inapplicable. However, we find it difficult to conceive of such a case, and the present case is clearly not one. . . .

We do not suggest that films may not be sold in blocks or groups, when there is no requirement, express or implied, for the purchase of more than one film. All we hold to be illegal is a refusal to license one or more copyrights unless another copyright is accepted.

Affirmed.

★★★

United States Steel Corp. v. Fortner Enterprises, Inc.
U.S. Supreme Court
429 U.S. 610
(1977)

Fortner, a real estate developer, wished to finance the purchase and subdivision of land near Louisville, Kentucky. U.S. Steel Homes Credit Corp. ("Credit Corporation"), a wholly owned financing subsidiary of U.S. Steel Corp., offered Fortner approximately $2 million worth of financing on the condition that Fortner would purchase prefabricated houses for each residential lot in the subdivision from U.S. Steel's "Home Division." To obtain the financing, Fortner bought 210 homes from U.S. Steel for $689,000.

Fortner later claimed that the houses were defective as well as overpriced, and filed a treble damage suit against U.S. Steel. In this suit, Fortner claimed that U.S. Steel had used tying agreements in violation of Section 1 of the Sherman Act. Credit on extremely attractive terms was alleged to be the tying product, and prefab houses the tied product. The federal district court originally granted summary judgment for U.S. Steel, but the Supreme Court reversed. In that decision, the Supreme Court ruled that there clearly was a substantial amount of commerce in the tied product, several million dollars worth of prefab homes having been sold by U.S. Steel under such arrangements. The Court sent the case back, however, for a trial on the question of

whether U.S. Steel had "appreciable economic power" in the tying market (credit).

Subsequently, Fortner won the case in the district court, and the court of appeals affirmed. The judgment in Fortner's favor was for damages (after trebling) of $270,000. U.S. Steel appealed to the Supreme Court, where the sole issue was U.S. Steel's power in the credit market. In the Court's opinion, U.S. Steel's Home Division and the Credit Corporation are referred to as petitioners.

Stevens, Justice:

. . . The evidence supporting the conclusion that the Credit Corporation had appreciable economic power in the credit market relates [essentially to the fact that] the financing provided to Fortner was "unique," primarily because it covered 100% of Fortner's acquisition and development costs. . . .

The finding that the credit extended to Fortner was unique was based on factors emphasized in the testimony of Fortner's expert witness, Dr. Masten, a professor with special knowledge of lending practices in the Kentucky area. Dr. Masten testified that mortgage loans equal to 100% of the acquisition and development cost of real estate were not otherwise available in the Kentucky area; that even though Fortner had a deficit of $16,000, its loan was not guaranteed by a shareholder, officer, or other person interested in its business; and that the interest rate of 6% represented a low rate under prevailing economic conditions. Moreover, he explained that the stable price levels at the time made the risk to the lender somewhat higher than would have been the case in a period of rising prices. Dr. Masten concluded that the terms granted to respondent by the Credit Corporation were so distinctly unique that it was almost inconceivable that the funds could have been acquired from any other source. It is a fair summary of his testimony, and of the District Court's findings, to say that the loan was unique because the lender accepted such a high risk and the borrower assumed such a low cost. . . .

[The District Court's finding of uniqueness] is particularly important because the unique character of the tying product has provided critical support for the finding of illegality in prior cases. . . . These decisions do not require that the defendant have a monopoly or even a dominant position throughout the market for a tying product. . . . They do, however, focus attention on the question whether the seller has the power within the market for the tying product, to raise prices or to require purchasers to accept burdensome terms that could not be exacted in a completely competitive market. In short, the question is whether the seller has some advantage not shared by his competitors in the market for the tying product.

Without any such advantage differentiating his product from that of his competitors, the seller's product does not have the kind of uniqueness considered relevant in prior tying cases. [We made this point explicitly when we issued our earlier ruling in this case and sent it back to the District Court for trial:] "We do not mean to accept petitioner's apparent argument that market power can be inferred simply because the kind of financing terms offered by a lending company are 'unique and unusual.' We do mean, however, that uniquely and unusually advantageous terms can reflect a creditor's unique economic advantages over his competitors."

[At that time, we also said:] "Uniqueness confers economic power only when other competitors are in some way prevented from offering the distinctive product themselves. Such barriers may be legal, as in the case of patented and copyrighted products, or physical, as when the product is land. It is true that the barriers may also be economic, as when competitors are simply unable to produce the distinctive product profitably, but the uniqueness test in such situations is somewhat confusing since the real source of economic power is not the product itself but rather the seller's cost advantage in producing it."

Quite clearly, if the evidence merely shows that credit terms are unique because the seller is willing to accept a lesser profit—or to incur greater risks—than its competitors, that kind of uniqueness will not give rise to any inference of economic power in the credit market. Yet this is, in substance, all that the record in this case indicates. . . .

Although the Credit Corporation is owned by one of the Nation's largest manufacturing corporations, there is nothing in the record to indicate that this enabled it to borrow funds on terms more favorable than those available to competing lenders, or that it was able to operate more efficiently than other lending institutions. In short, the affiliation between the petitioners does not appear to have given the Credit Corporation any cost advantage over its competitors in the credit market. Instead, the affiliation was significant only because the Credit Corporation provided a source of funds to customers of the Home Division. That fact tells us nothing about the extent of petitioners' power in the credit market. . . .

The unusual credit bargain offered to Fortner proves nothing more than a willingness to provide cheap financing in order to sell expensive houses. Without any evidence that the Credit Corporation had some cost advantage over its competitors—or could offer a form of financing that was significantly differentiated from that which other lenders could offer if they so elected—the unique character of its financing does not support the conclusion that petitioners had the kind of economic power which Fortner had the burden of proving in order to prevail in this litigation.

The judgment of the Court of Appeals is reversed.

★★★

The Quality Control Defense: When the three elements of illegality have been established, tying is almost invariably illegal. Despite the courts' use of the "per se" label, however, they have recognized a defense to tying in certain limited circumstances. This defense is sometimes called the "quality control" or "goodwill" defense.

As mentioned earlier, a supplier sometimes may contend that its own version of the tied product must be used to prevent malfunctioning of the tying product, customer confusion, or other consequences which may harm the supplier's reputation and goodwill. This argument usually is not accepted by courts because the quality control objective generally can be accomplished in ways that are less restrictive than tying. In most circumstances the supplier can achieve the necessary control and protection by providing detailed specifications concerning the auxiliary product. When the product is *leased*, the supplier can require the customer to follow the specifications as a condition of the lease. Exercising such control is somewhat more difficult when the product is *sold*, but in such a case the supplier frequently can condition the product's warranty on the customer's compliance with specifications. After expiration of the warranty, control obviously is more difficult. In situations where the auxiliary product is truly necessary and there is a legitimate quality control problem, tying usually will be legal if specifications are either impossible or infeasible.

For example, in *Dehydrating Process Co. v. A.O. Smith Corp.*, 292 F.2d 653 (1st Cir. 1961), the manufacturer of a patented device for unloading grain silos had tried for several years to sell the item separately. Despite providing specifications to customers and regularly consulting with them, the manufacturer found that customers frequently installed the unloaders in silos that did not have correct mechanical tolerances or that were not slippery enough on their inside surfaces. The manufacturer took back many unloaders for refunds, and suffered some damage to its reputation. As a result of this experience, the manufacturer instituted a policy of only selling the unloader along with its patented glass-lined silo. When this practice was challenged as a tying arrangement, the court held it to be legal.

Even if the manufacturer has not had experiences such as those in the *A.O. Smith* case, the "quality control" (or "goodwill") defense sometimes may exist because the product involves *new technology*. The best example of this situation is found in *U.S. v. Jerrold Electronics Corp.*, 187 F. Supp. 545 (E.D. Pa. 1960), a federal district court decision which was unanimously affirmed by the Supreme Court. In that case the court ruled that Jerrold, in attempting to inaugurate a cable television system, had engaged in tying by requiring purchasers to buy all of the various components of the system as well as installation and subsequent maintenance service. The court held, however, that the tying was initially legal because (1) cable television was a new industry with an uncertain future, thus making its initial performance crucial, and (2) the equipment was quite sensitive and its installation or repair by untrained personnel would produce unsatisfactory results. After the industry had matured, the court said, the tying was no longer justifiable.

Full-Line Forcing: A final comment is warranted concerning a practice frequently referred to as *full-line forcing*. Suppose that M, a manufacturer of washing machines, dryers, and other large household appliances, requires retail dealers to stock a full line of M's products or none at all. Is this an illegal tying agreement? Should dealers be permitted to select only some items from M's total product line? The court decisions dealing with this question have not been consistent. In general, the courts have indicated that full-line forcing is legal if dealers are not forced to overstock and not prevented from handling competing brands.

Exclusive Dealing

An exclusive dealing agreement involves the buyer's commitment that it will purchase a particular product only from the seller (and, implicitly or explicitly, *not* from the seller's competitors). Many times these arrangements are called "requirements contracts" because the parties often speak in terms of the buyer's commitment to purchase its "requirements" of a product from the seller.[4] The primary danger of exclusive dealing is that the seller's competitors may be *foreclosed* from that portion of the market represented by the buyer's purchases.

Legal Status: The statutes which apply to exclusive dealing agreements are Section 1 of the Sherman Act and Section 3 of the Clayton Act. Courts traditionally have recognized that exclusive dealing can have legitimate business purposes. For example, a long-term requirements contract between an electrical utility and a coal supplier may serve several beneficial ends. It will give the utility reasonable assurance of an adequate fuel supply, which is critical to the utility's ability to provide electricity to its customers. Because the supplier has an assured market for an estimated portion of its production, it can better plan production needs and frequently offer the utility a lower price than otherwise would be available. Utilities normally receive much lower prices under long-term requirements contracts than they can obtain in individual transactions on the "spot market."

Because of factors such as these, courts have not treated exclusive dealing as harshly as tying. Exclusive dealing is judged according to the rule of reason, and is illegal only if it results in *foreclosure of a substantial portion of the relevant market*. Thus, exclusive dealing is likely to violate the law only when a relatively large company makes widespread use of the practice to distribute its product.

An example of a situation in which exclusive dealing has been ruled illegal is found in *Standard Oil of California v. U.S.*, 337 U.S. 293 (1949). Standard sold petroleum products through its own retail service stations, to the operators of independent retail service stations, and to industrial users. Its sales of gasoline to independent stations were made under exclusive dealing agreements which obligated them to buy all their requirements from Standard. The seven western states in which Standard sold were viewed by

---

[4]The reverse of a requirements contract is an "output contract," in which the seller obligates itself to sell its output of an item to the buyer (and, thus, not to sell it to the buyer's competitors). Although it is conceivable that an output contract, or a series of such contracts, might violate Section 1 of the Sherman Act, the possibility is extremely unlikely. Section 3 of the Clayton Act does not cover output contracts.

the Court as a distinct geographic market. Standard's sales to independent stations under exclusive dealing agreements amounted to approximately seven percent of total gasoline sales in that market. The Court ruled that this represented a substantial share of the relevant market that had been foreclosed—made unavailable—to Standard's competitors.

Today, however, the Supreme Court probably would require evidence of a larger percentage foreclosure than it required in the *Standard Oil of California* case. The portion of the market foreclosed most likely would have to exceed 10 percent before the Court would view it as substantial.

Reciprocity

An arrangement whereby a buyer says, essentially, "I'll buy from you only if you'll buy from me," is called **reciprocity** (or reciprocal dealing). Suppose, for example, that an office machines manufacturer buys property, casualty, and liability insurance only from those insurance companies who agree to buy their office machines from the manufacturer. This is reciprocity.

Reciprocity is very similar to tying. In tying, a firm uses market power as a *seller* in one market to obtain business in another market; in reciprocity, a firm uses market power as a *buyer* in one market to obtain business in another market. Reciprocity thus involves the leveraging of buying power.

The practice of reciprocity poses the same dangers to competition as tying. Moreover, there appear to be no legitimate business purposes for reciprocity, whereas such justifications can occasionally be made for tying. Although there is not a great deal of formal case law on reciprocity,[5] the applicable legal standards under Section 1 of the Sherman Act (Section 3 of the Clayton Act does not apply) apparently are the same as for tying. Therefore, reciprocity is illegal when the practicing firm (1) has substantial power in the market in which it buys, and (2) does a substantial dollar volume of business in the market in which it sells under reciprocity arrangements. In addition, some of the relatively few court decisions on the subject have indicated that reciprocity is illegal regardless of the volume of business affected if a company uses its buying power to *coerce* one or more other firms into reciprocity arrangements.

Special Problems in Franchising

In the *Sylvania* case and also in one of the illustrations of tying, firms were engaged in a **franchising** operation. Because franchising has become a common method of doing business, and sometimes involves unique problems

---

[5] Many government actions have been instituted against the practice, but most of these were won by the government through settlements, thus producing no precedent-setting court opinions.

under antitrust and related laws, the subject will be examined a bit more closely.

The Nature of Franchising

In a franchise arrangement, the "franchisor" owns and promotes a trademark. Agreements are made with "franchisees," independent entrepreneurs who own and operate local outlets (such as fast-food restaurants, motels, or auto muffler shops). The typical franchising agreement gives the franchisee the right to use the franchisor's trademark (a trademark license) and places various restrictions on the way the local outlet is operated. These restrictions apply to matters such as building design and appearance, quality and appearance of the product being sold, standards of cleanliness, and so on. Their purpose is to insure uniformity of franchisee quality and appearance so that the entire franchising system can be promoted over a wide geographic area. The franchisee is required to pay a royalty for use of the trademark, which usually is a percentage of the franchisee's gross sales, and the franchisor usually provides national advertising and various kinds of assistance in return, such as computer programs for inventory control and payroll records.

Franchising and the Antitrust Laws

In essence, the antitrust laws apply to franchising in the same way as to other vertical relationships. In some circumstances, however, franchising poses special problems. For example, courts have had some difficulty applying the rules regarding tying agreements in the franchising context.

One of the most perplexing problems is whether the trademark license itself is a separate product. Many courts have held that it is. Thus, when a franchisee is required to purchase something as a condition to receiving the license, tying occurs. Some observers have argued, though, that the trademark license is but one element of a single product—the franchise system. In recent years some courts have agreed with this argument in two situations: (1) There is only one product, and no tying exists, where the trademark and the required items (such as store premises, equipment, fixtures, signs, accounting services) are part of the franchise system's method of doing business, and where each item is an ingredient in the system's "formula for success." (2) A trademark license and a product should be considered as a unit where consumers view the trademark as identifying the source of the goods. In this latter situation, for instance, Shell Oil Co. could lawfully require a gasoline wholesaler to use the Shell trademark only in connection with the sale of Shell-supplied gasoline.

In other situations, however, a franchisor may violate antitrust laws by requiring that franchisees purchase certain items. Such a requirement is illegal when applied to items that can be obtained elsewhere without affecting the image or basic business methods of the franchising system.

Related Laws Applying to Franchising

Automobile Dealer Franchise Act of 1956: This law gives an automobile dealer (franchisee) the right to sue the automobile manufacturer (franchisor) for damages resulting from the failure of the manufacturer "to act in good faith" in complying with the terms of the franchise agreement and in terminating the franchise. Most courts have found violations of the act only where the manufacturer has engaged in coercion or intimidation. For example, a manufacturer was held to have violated the act by terminating a dealer supposedly for not meeting its sales quota, when the manufacturer's true motive apparently was to replace the dealer with a company-owned dealership.

Petroleum Marketing Practices Act of 1978: This act specifies reasons which constitute good cause for an oil company's termination or nonrenewal of a gasoline dealer's franchise. These reasons include various types of dealer misconduct, such as fraud, nonpayment of sums owed to the franchisor, and misbranding or adulteration of fuel. The oil company must notify the dealer within a certain time period after discovering the misconduct, and then must give the dealer at least ninety days before termination or nonrenewal takes effect. The oil company is liable to the dealer for damages if the company does not comply with notice requirements or if the termination or nonrenewal is for an improper reason. The dealer also may receive punitive damages when evidence shows that the company's violation was willful.

FTC Franchise Rule: In 1979, the Federal Trade Commission promulgated an administrative rule covering all franchising arrangements except for gasoline or automobile franchises. The FTC rule is a comprehensive disclosure statute. When offering a franchise to a prospective franchisee, the franchisor must make available a wide variety of detailed information. Required disclosures include (1) amounts and schedules of payments to be made by the franchisee, (2) restrictions to be placed on the franchisee's operations, (3) detailed information relating to the experience and background of the franchisor's officers and directors, (4) financial statements of the franchisor for the last three years, (5) grounds for franchise termination, (6) the number of franchisees terminated in the previous year, and other relevant information. In addition, if the franchisor makes any earnings prediction to a prospective franchisee, this prediction must have a reasonable basis, and supporting documentation must be made available. The FTC has power to enforce this rule by levying penalties of up to $10,000 and instituting lawsuits for damages in behalf of franchisees.

Price Discrimination

Although the original version of Section 2 of the Clayton Act contained a prohibition of **price discrimination**, it proved ineffective because of certain major loopholes. In 1936 Congress enacted the Robinson-Patman Act in an effort to make the law against price discrimination more effective. The main purpose of Congress in passing this law was to protect small businesses from having to pay higher prices for their goods than larger companies.

Elements of a Robinson-Patman Act Violation

Section 2(a) of the Robinson-Patman Act prohibits a seller in interstate commerce from charging different prices to different purchasers for goods of like grade and quality, where the effect of the price differential may be to substantially lessen competition. Each element of this provision will be examined more closely.

Interstate Commerce: The interstate commerce requirement in the Robinson-Patman Act is the strictest of all the antitrust laws. It is not enough that the seller or buyer is an interstate company or that the transaction affects interstate commerce—at least one of the relevant sales must actually cross state lines. (Exports to foreign countries are not covered by the Act, although the other nation may have an applicable law.)

Different Prices: To the economist, price discrimination means the use of different cost-price ratios for different customers. Thus, a seller engages in *economic* price discrimination by charging the same price to customers X and Y if the cost of selling to them differs. Under the Robinson-Patman Act, however, price discrimination exists only where the seller actually charges different prices to different customers.

Different Purchasers: There obviously is no violation of the Robinson-Patman Act when a seller charges different prices at different times to the same purchaser. More importantly, however, the word "purchaser" makes it clear that the law applies only to *sales* transactions, and not to leases, licenses, consignments, or other types of transaction.

Goods: The Robinson-Patman Act applies only to discriminatory sales of *goods*—tangible commodities. Thus, sales of services, land, or intangible property rights are not covered.

Like Grade and Quality: This language means that the Act covers only sales of the *same* product to different purchasers. Thus, it clearly is not a violation for a seller to sell a unit of the regular grade of a product to X at $5 and the premium grade to Y at $7. To avoid the law's applicability, however, the difference must be more than trivial. Putting an extra, nonfunctional bolt into a washing machine, for instance, would not cause it to be a different product under the Robinson-Patman Act.

In *FTC v. Borden Co.*, 383 U.S. 637 (1966), Borden sold "private label" evaporated milk (milk packaged by Borden with a store's own label) to grocery store chains at lower prices than it sold Borden brand evaporated milk, even though the milk was identical. When a non-chain store bought Borden brand milk, the FTC contended, price discrimination occurred. The Supreme Court agreed with the FTC and held that the Borden brand and private label milk were of like grade and quality. Thus, different labels and consumer preferences do not make products different if they are physically identical.

Competitive Injury: A violation of the Robinson-Patman Act occurs only if there is evidence showing a likelihood of substantial harm to competition. Of course, if the lawsuit is filed by a private party seeking treble damages, the plaintiff must present evidence showing actual harm to its business. Generally speaking, isolated or sporadic instances of price discrimination will not violate the Robinson-Patman Act because it usually will be impossible to prove competitive injury. Competitive injury usually can be established only where the discrimination was recurring and systematic.

Injury to competition may occur in two different contexts, referred to as *primary level* and *secondary level* injuries. A seller's price discrimination may cause both types of injury simultaneously, but in most cases causes only one or the other.

Primary Level: This is a competitive injury at the seller's level. It may be illustrated thusly.

S_1 – – – – – – – – S_2
(competitors)
C_1 C_2

S_1 and S_2 are competitors. S_1 charges C_1 a price of \$10 per unit and C_2 \$9 per unit. If this discrimination by S_1 causes economic harm to S_2, such as by taking customer C_2 away from S_2, a primary level injury has occurred. S_2 may prove this injury in either of two ways: (1) S_2 may show that it has lost a significant *market share* as a result of S_1's discriminatory pricing, or (2) S_2 may show that S_1's \$9 price to C_2 was *predatory* (below cost) in addition to being discriminatory. The court will infer competitive harm from predatory intent.

Secondary Level: This is a competitive injury at the buyer's level. It may be illustrated thusly.

S_1
C_1 – – – – – – – – C_2
(competitors)

C_1 and C_2 are competitors. If the discriminatory pricing of S_1 hurts C_1 in competing with C_2, a secondary level injury has occurred.

Defenses to a Charge of Price Discrimination

Upon proof of the basic elements of a Robinson-Patman Act violation, the plaintiff has established a prima facie case. In other words, the plaintiff wins unless the defendant comes forward with proof of a defense. There are three defenses to a charge of price discrimination.

Cost Justification: Section 2(a) states that the prohibition of price discrimination does not prevent differential prices "which make only due allowance for differences in the cost of manufacture, sale, or delivery." Most cases in which the cost justification defense is raised involve so-called "quantity discounts." A seller can lawfully grant a price discount to purchasers of large quantities only if this discount merely represents a passing on of cost savings. Suppose, for instance, that X and Y are customers of S. X buys in much larger quantities than Y does, so that S's transportation costs per unit of goods are lower for sales to X than for sales to Y. If it desired, S could lawfully pass this per unit cost savings to X.

A seller must exercise caution in granting quantity discounts. The cost justification defense cannot be used where the seller simply assumes that it is cheaper to sell in larger quantities and grants price concessions based on this assumption. In one case, the court refused to accept generalized data showing that it usually is cheaper to sell to grocery store chains than to independent grocers. To establish this defense, the seller must present evidence which actually *demonstrates* that unit costs were lower for large volume sales to certain customers than for smaller volume sales to other customers, and that the price discounts did no more than pass on all or part of the lower costs.

The following case illustrates the applicability of the Robinson-Patman Act to a system of quantity discounts that were not sufficiently justified by cost differences. In this case there also is an example of secondary level injury.

Federal Trade Commission v. Morton Salt Co.
U.S. Supreme Court
334 U.S. 37
(1948)

The Morton Salt Company manufactured and sold different brands of table salt to wholesalers (jobbers) and to large retail grocery chains. Morton sold its finest brand of salt, Blue Label, on a "standard quantity discount system" which was purportedly available to all of its customers.

The Federal Trade Commission, after a hearing, concluded that Morton's sales of salt under the system resulted in price discrimination in violation of Section 2 of the Robinson-Patman Act. Accordingly, the FTC issued a cease and desist order prohibiting further sales of salt under this system. A U.S.

Court of Appeals set aside this order, finding no violation of the Act. The FTC appealed this judgment to the U.S. Supreme Court.

In this appeal, there were two primary issues: (1) whether the discount system resulted in price discrimination within the meaning of the Robinson-Patman Act, and (2) if so, whether the discrimination caused an injury to competition. (In the decision of the U.S. Supreme Court, Morton is referred to as "the respondent" throughout.)

Black, Justice:

. . . Under [respondent's] system the purchasers pay a delivered price, and the cost to both wholesale and retail purchasers of this brand differs according to the quantities bought. These prices are as follows, after making allowances for rebates and discounts:

	Per Case
Less-than-carload purchases	*$1.60*
Carload purchases	*1.50*
5,000-case purchases in any consecutive 12 months	*1.40*
50,000-case purchases in any consecutive 12 months	*1.35*

Only five companies have ever bought sufficient quantities of respondent's salt to obtain the $1.35 per case price. These companies could buy in such quantities because they operate large chains of retail stores in various parts of the country. As a result of this low price these five companies have been able to sell Blue Label salt at retail cheaper than wholesale purchasers from respondent could reasonably sell the same brand of salt to independently operated retail stores, many of whom competed with the local outlets of the five chain stores. . . .

In addition to these standard quantity discounts, special allowances were granted certain favored customers who competed with other customers to whom [the allowances] were denied.

Respondent's basic contention, which it argues this case hinges upon, is that its "standard quantity discounts, available to all on equal terms, as contrasted, for example, to hidden or special rebates, allowances, prices or discounts, are not discriminatory, within the meaning of the Robinson-Patman Act." Theoretically, these discounts are equally available to all, but functionally they are not. For as the record indicates (if reference to it on this point were necessary), no single independent retail grocery store, and probably no single wholesaler, bought as many as 50,000 cases or as much as $50,000 worth of table salt in one year. Furthermore, the record shows that, while certain purchasers were enjoying one or more of respondent's standard quantity discounts, some of their competitors made purchases in such small quantities that they could not qualify for any of respondent's discounts, even those based on carload shipments. The legislative history of the Robinson-Patman Act makes it abundantly clear that Congress considered it to be an evil that a large buyer could secure a competitive advantage over a small buyer solely because of the large buyer's quantity purchasing ability. The Robinson-Patman Act was passed to deprive a large buyer of such advantages except to the extent that a lower price could be justified by reason of a seller's diminished costs due to quantity manufacture, delivery, or sale, or by reason of the seller's good faith effort to meet a competitor's equally low price. . . .

[The Court then agreed with the FTC that Morton's evidence failed to justify its price differential—that Morton was unable to show that the discounts that it gave its very large customers were based on actual cost savings alone. The Court then turned to the second question, the magnitude of the effect of the discrimination.]

It is argued [by respondent] that the findings fail to show that [its] discriminatory discounts had in fact caused injury to competition. There are specific findings that such injuries had resulted from respondent's discounts, although the statute does not require the Commission to find that injury has actually resulted. The statute requires no more than that the effect of the prohibited price discriminations "may be substantially to lessen competition . . . or to injure, destroy or prevent competition." After a careful consideration of this provision of the Robinson-Patman Act, we have said that "the statute does not require that the discriminations must in fact have harmed competition, but only that there is a reasonable possibility that they 'may' have such an effect." *Corn Products Co. v. Federal Trade Comm'n*, 324 U.S. 726. Here the Commission found what would appear to be obvious, that the competitive opportunities of certain merchants were injured when they had to pay respondent substantially more for their goods than their competitors had to pay. The findings are adequate. . . . Judgment [of the Court of Appeals] reversed, [and order of the FTC reinstated.]

★ ★ ★

Comment: The Court indicated that the FTC did not have to prove that Morton's price discrimination had actually harmed competition, but only that there was a reasonable possibility of such an effect. This is the rule when price discrimination is challenged by the FTC or the Justice Department. As mentioned earlier, however, if a private party (such as one of Morton's customers who did not receive the discount) sues for treble damages, it must demonstrate actual harm. The plaintiff might do this, for instance, by showing that it had actually lost business because of the cost disadvantage.

Meeting Competition: Section 2(b) states that a seller does not violate the Act if a lower price to one buyer "was made in good faith to meet an equally low price of a competitor." Assume that S generally charges $10 per unit for its widgets, but receives information that Q, a competitor of S, has been offering comparable widgets at $9 per unit. S can lawfully meet Q's competition by charging $9 per unit in those markets where S and Q are rivals even though S continues to charge $10 per unit in other markets. Or, if Q offers the $9 price to one customer, S can match the offer to this customer while continuing to charge $10 to other customers.

There are two noteworthy limitations on S's use of the meeting competition defense: (1) S cannot knowingly *beat* Q's price, but can only meet it, and (2) S cannot even meet Q's price if S knows that Q's price is itself an illegally discriminatory one.

The Problem of the Lying Buyer: In addition to these limitations, S also must take precautions against the possibility of a "lying buyer." Suppose that S is told by a customer, C, that Q is offering a lower price than S. If C states that Q's price is $9, can S simply lower its price to C to $9? What if C was lying, and Q's price was really $9.75, so that S's $9 price to C actually beat Q's price? Or, what if C had told S that Q was offering a lower price, but C did not tell S exactly what Q's price was? Can S simply "guess" at Q's price and lower its own price to C in accordance with the guess? What if C's statement that Q was selling cheaper was untrue? Even if it was true, what if S "guesses wrong" and beats Q's actual price? The answer to all these questions is found in the requirement that S must act "in good faith." If Q's price really was not as low as C had said, or if S unintentionally beats Q's price, S can still use the defense if S merely made a good faith attempt to meet competition. However, in order to act in good faith, S ordinarily cannot just take C's word for the matter if there are other reasonable avenues for verifying what C has said. For example, S can check with other customers for possible verification. Even if S obtains no information from such sources, S must show that it made the effort. In attempting to verify C's story, S should never go so far as to contact Q directly. Such contact with a competitor regarding price may constitute horizontal price fixing.

Geographic Price Differences: Until recently, the meeting competition defense could be used by a seller only when responding to the lower price offered by a specific competitor. In 1983, however, the Supreme Court expanded the defense by ruling that a seller lawfully may charge different prices in different geographic markets if the prices are in line with generally prevailing prices in those markets. Thus, a seller may now respond to different price levels in different geographic markets even if the seller does not pinpoint a specific competitor whose price is being matched.

Changing Conditions: Section 2(a) expressly permits a seller to change prices in response to changing conditions which affect the marketability of the goods, such as imminent deterioration of perishable commodities or obsolescence of seasonal goods. Thus, a customer who recently paid $10 per unit for an item cannot successfully allege price discrimination when the seller subsequently charges $7 per unit to another customer because of changed conditions such as those indicated.

Other Provisions of the Robinson-Patman Act

Several other important provisions are found in the Robinson-Patman Act. Although the Act focuses primarily on the *seller's* discriminatory pricing, Section 2(f) states that a *buyer* is in violation if it "knowingly induces or receives an illegally discriminatory price." This section has not been very effective, because it applies only if the evidence demonstrates that the buyer knew the price was discriminatory *and* knew that the seller had no defense.

Section 2(c) makes it illegal to pay a commission or fee to a broker or other intermediary where the broker actually works for or is controlled by the buyer. This type of "phony brokerage" actually is a form of secret price discount to the buyer. If the practice occurs, however, it is illegal regardless of any effect on competition, and there are no defenses.

Sections 2(d) and (e) apply to a seller of goods who provides customers with funds, services, or materials to assist them in displaying, advertising, or otherwise handling the goods bought from the seller. The funds, services, or materials must be provided on a *proportionally equal basis* to all customers who compete with one another. Proof of a violation of Sections 2(d) and (e) does not require evidence of competitive injury. The only applicable defense is meeting competition.

The Robinson-Patman Controversy

The Robinson-Patman Act has been controversial almost since its inception. Criticism of the Act has taken many forms. The criticism most often voiced is that price discrimination frequently constitutes healthy *price competition*, and that the practice ultimately lowers prices for consumers. Those holding this view argue that economic efficiency is sacrificed by the law's attempt to protect small business. On the other hand, proponents of the Robinson-Patman Act contend that price discrimination can only produce lower prices in the short run. They argue that, in the long run, price discrimination can drive small firms out of business, thus leading to more concentrated markets and eventually to higher prices.

Primarily because of this controversy, the Justice Department traditionally has done almost nothing to enforce the Robinson-Patman Act. The FTC enforced the Act rather aggressively until the 1970s, when it began to relax its enforcement effort. Private treble damage suits, however, continue to be an important and frequently used tool for enforcing the Robinson-Patman Act.

Questions and Problems

1. Chemco is a manufacturer of various agricultural chemicals such as herbicides and insecticides. Most of these products were sold to wholesale distributors who then resold either to retail dealers or directly to farmers. During a twenty-day period in late 1980, Chemco received individual complaints from five of its distributors in the Pacific Coast region of the country. These distributors complained that a sixth distributor, Ace, had been significantly undercutting their prices and hurting their sales. Chemco made no promises to them, but a month later it announced to all of its distributors across the nation that it was implementing a new policy. Chemco's new policy was that, in the future, it would sell only to those distributors who would indicate in advance their intent to abide by Chemco's schedule of suggested resale

prices. Most distributors responded affirmatively to Chemco's new policy. Those few who did not respond affirmatively were discontinued as Chemco distributors. One of those who did not respond affirmatively and who was discontinued was Ace. Discuss whether Chemco and its distributors may have violated Section 1 of the Sherman Act.

2. Firms A, B, C, D, and E were wholesale distributors of the Specific Electric brand of home appliances (including large appliances such as washing machines, dryers, and kitchen ranges, and small ones such as toasters, portable hair dryers, and radios) to various types of retail stores. For almost a year these distributors had lost a significant number of sales to X, another wholesaler who sold the Specific Electric brand. The recent success of X had been due primarily to his practice of reimbursing retailers 25 percent of the costs they incurred in providing warranty service on Specific brand appliances. The manufacturer of the Specific brand had traditionally reimbursed retailers for 50 percent of their warranty service costs; thus, when X reimbursed them another 25 percent, the retailers only had to bear 25 percent of total warranty service costs. Wholesalers A, B, C, D, and E individually complained to Specific, the manufacturer, about the practices of X. After receiving these complaints over a period of eighteen months, Specific contacted each of the wholesalers individually and told them it would rectify the situation by reimbursing all warranty costs. Shortly thereafter, Specific began reimbursing retailers for 100 percent of the cost of providing warranty service on Specific brand appliances. Thereafter, X was not as much of a problem for A, B, C, D, and E. X then sued Specific and the other wholesalers, claiming a violation of Section 1 of the Sherman Act. Discuss whether X will prevail.

3. Manufacturer M required all of its wholesalers to provide M with written justification for any sale by a wholesaler to a retailer in which the wholesaler added less than a 20 percent markup over what it had paid for the goods. M closely monitored its wholesalers to make sure that they complied with the requirement. Before the policy was begun, M's wholesalers had frequently competed by granting discounts to retailers. After M's policy was implemented, however, the wholesalers very rarely cut prices and almost never sold to retailers at less than a 20 percent markup. The Justice Department filed suit against M, claiming a violation of Section 1 of the Sherman Act. Discuss.

4. Sarco, Inc., a manufacturer of various types of electronic equipment and devices used for industrial and medical purposes, sold its products to franchised dealers who then resold to their customers. Many of the products were complicated and relatively expensive. As a result, dealers needed to be carefully selected and trained so that they would be knowledgeable about the products and could offer essential consultation and demonstration services to potential customers. In addition, it was necessary that dealers be able to expertly perform repairs on the products. Sarco, which accounted for between 10 and 18 percent of national sales in its various product lines, granted each dealer an exclusive territory and required each to sell only in that territory. Sarco's distribution system was challenged under Section 1 of the Sherman Act. Discuss whether the system is likely to be legal or illegal under Section 1 of the Sherman Act.

5. Epitome Corp. manufactures stereo equipment, which it sells to franchised wholesale distributors. It assigns each distributor a territory. In its own territory, there are no restrictions on the distributor's resale price. If it sells outside its designated territory, however, the distributor must sell at or above a price set by Epitome. A distributor filed suit against Epitome, claiming that this distribution system was per se illegal under Section 1 of the Sherman Act. Epitome contended that the rule of reason should be applied in analyzing this system. Who is correct? Discuss.

6. In the 1800s Congress had granted the Northern Pacific Railway Co. approximately 40 million acres of land in several northwestern states and territories to facili-

tate the company's construction of a railroad line. Much of the land contained valuable stands of timber and mineral resources. Also adding to its value was its strategic location in checkerboard fashion amid private landholdings and within relatively short distances from important transportation facilities. The company received much more land than it needed for track construction, and in later years it sold or leased several million acres to others. These sales or leases usually contained preferential routing clauses, which required the other party to use Northern Pacific for shipping all commodities produced or manufactured on the land. These clauses required the use of Northern Pacific, however, only if its rates were comparable to those of competing railroads. The government filed suit against Northern Pacific, claiming that these preferential routing clauses violated Section 1 of the Sherman Act. Discuss whether these clauses were illegal. (*Northern Pacific Railway Co. v. U.S.*, 356 U.S. 1, 1958.)

7. Trailer Mart, Inc., sold mobile homes. It also owned several mobile home parks in very desirable locations. Trailer Mart had for several years leased lots in its mobile home parks on the condition that the lessee purchase one of Trailer Mart's mobile homes. A competing mobile home seller sued Trailer Mart, claiming that the defendant's practice constituted illegal tying. Trailer Mart contended that only one product was involved, and even if there were two separate products, it had no economic power in the tying market. Discuss whether there is likely to be a violation of Section 1 of the Sherman Act.

8. Combustion Engineering Co. (CEC) developed and marketed a device which, when attached to an automobile engine, would enable the engine to use a wide variety of fuels such as methanol and kerosene. The device required considerable care and expertise in its installation and servicing in order to function properly. When the device was introduced, CEC's personnel were the only ones capable of reliably performing such services. CEC sold the devices only on the condition that its personnel perform the installation and future maintenance. During the six years after the device was introduced, its sales totalled $25 million. Revenues from installation and maintenance services during this period totalled $3 million. At this time, the Justice Department's Antitrust Division began investigating CEC's marketing practices. Discuss whether any antitrust violations have occurred.

9. Your company produces and sells various types of industrial chemicals. One of your customers has told you that one of your competitors has offered him a lower price on a particular chemical than you are offering him. You want very much to sell to this customer but you know that your company cannot afford to sell to everyone at this lower price. What's the problem in selling to this customer at a selectively lower price? Can you legally make such a sale? Explain. What should you do and what should you not do in your effort to lawfully sell to this customer at a selectively lower price? Explain.

10. Universal-Rundle Corp. made plumbing fixtures which it sold to hardware and plumbing supply stores, home builders, and other purchasers. It also manufactured a line of plumbing fixtures for Sears, Roebuck and Co., a large retail department store chain. Sears sold these fixtures under its own private brand and competed with some of the hardware and plumbing stores that also bought from Universal. The fixtures made for Sears were slightly different in dimensions and design than those made for the other stores because Sears aimed more specifically at the do-it-yourself customer. Although the unit cost of the fixtures made for Sears differed very little from the cost of those made for other stores, Universal sold to Sears for 10 percent less. The FTC charged Universal with violating the Robinson-Patman Act. Discuss what the result should be. (*In re Universal-Rundle Corp.*, CCH Trade Reg. Rep. § 16,948, FTC Dkt. 8070, 1964.)

C·H·A·P·T·E·R 13

SECURITIES REGULATION

The great stock market crash of 1929 was one of the most dramatic turning points in American economic history. That event not only ushered in the Great Depression but also heralded the creation of modern securities regulation. Securities regulation is one of the most complicated areas of the law; attorneys who practice in the securities field are among the most specialized and well-paid of all lawyers. Although this vast, everchanging subject may be intimidating to the novice, few persons in business can remain ignorant of its effects on the way business is done in this country.

Many aspects of securities regulation are highly visible. Most Americans are familiar with the hustle and bustle of the New York Stock Exchange. Over thirty million Americans own stock, many in major corporations such as General Motors and IBM. Through securities regulation the federal government, and to a lesser degree the states, regulate trading on the stock exchanges, protect the interests of shareholders, and attempt to ensure that the collapse of 1929 is never repeated.

In this chapter, some of the more important aspects of the law of securities regulation are surveyed.

Introduction to Securities Regulation

As explained in Chapter 9, there are various forms of business organizations including partnerships and corporations. There are sufficient advantages to incorporation, especially for very large businesses, that almost three million corporations exist in the United States. The corporate form allows for accumulation of capital from investment from many shareholders. These investors do not directly own the assets of the business; rather, they own part of the corporate entity, as evidenced by shares of stock. Shares of stock constitute the most familiar type of security regulated by federal and state governments.

A security such as a stock or a bond has no intrinsic value—its value lies in the ownership interest which it represents. The value of that ownership interest may be difficult to discover and easy to misrepresent. Securities may be produced in nearly limitless supply at virtually no cost by anyone with access to a printing press. For all these reasons, fraud, manipulation, and deceit have been frequent companions of the security. Government regulation of securities dates back to at least 1285, when King Edward I of England attempted to gain some control over the capital markets by licensing brokers located in London.

Securities regulation in the United States was almost nonexistent until 1911, when Kansas enacted securities laws. Other states soon followed suit, but without federal laws, companies could evade regulation by operating across state lines.

The 1920s were an especially active time for the issuance and trading of securities. The securities business was then characterized by price manipulation, deceitful practices, selling on excessive credit, and the abuse of secret information by corporate insiders. Of the $50 billion of new securities offered for sale in the United States in the 1920s, about one-half were worthless. The public and the national economy were devastated when stock market prices fell 89 percent between 1929 and 1933, finally producing federal action.

Federal legislation

The first federal securities law was the **Securities Act of 1933** (the 1933 Act) which regulated the initial issuance of securities by companies. Fraudulent and deceptive practices were outlawed, and registration was required before a new security may be offered or sold, unless that security is entitled to an exemption from registration.

A year later, Congress passed the **Securities Exchange Act of 1934** (the 1934 Act), which extended federal regulation to trading in securities already issued and outstanding, required registration of securities brokers and dealers, and created the Securities Exchange Commission (SEC), the federal agency which enforces the federal securities laws through its extensive powers.

In 1935, Congress passed the *Public Utility Holding Company Act* in response to manipulative and monopolistic practices in the public utilities industry. The SEC in its early years was largely concerned with correcting abuses in the financing and operating of large public utilities. Because the commission has been very successful in this area, separate enforcement of the Public Utility Holding Company Act is no longer a major SEC priority, and some SEC officials have urged repeal of the Act.

The next securities law passed by Congress was the *Trust Indenture Act of 1939*, which helped protect persons investing in bonds, debentures, notes, and other debt securities by imposing qualification requirements on trustees of such instruments. A year later, the *Investment Company Act of 1940* imposed additional requirements on companies engaged primarily in the business of investing, reinvesting, and trading securities. For example, that Act prohibits anyone found guilty of securities fraud from being associated with investment companies and bans transactions between such companies and their officers without prior SEC approval. The *Investment Advisers Act of 1940* required persons or firms who engage in the business of advising others about investments for compensation to register with the SEC, as brokers and dealers are required to register under the 1934 Act.

The *Securities Investor Protection Act of 1970* amended the 1934 Act in response to a rash of failures in the late 1960s in the broker-dealer business. The Act creates the Securities Investor Protection Corporation (SIPC), which manages a fund to protect investors from the failure of broker-dealers in the same manner as the Federal Deposit Insurance Corporation protects the customers of banks.

In 1977 Congress passed the *Foreign Corrupt Practices Act* (FCPA) in response to questionable foreign political payments by U.S. companies, disclosed in the wake of the Watergate scandal. This act bans bribery of high foreign political officials and establishes certain accounting requirements for corporations so that such illegal activities cannot be easily concealed. Substantial criminal penalties are provided for violation.

The Racketeering Influenced and Corrupt Organizations Act of 1970, though not a securities act in any strict sense, must also be noted. Congress passed RICO to attack organized crime, especially its infiltration into legitimate business. However, RICO neither includes a definition of organized crime nor expressly requires a link between a defendant's activities and organized crime. Therefore, about nine-tenths of the suits brought under RICO have had no connection with professional criminals. A RICO plaintiff need prove only: (1) a pattern of racketeering activity by defendant; (2) the existence of an enterprise affecting interstate commerce; (3) a nexus between the pattern of racketeering activity and the enterprise; and (4) an injury to plaintiff's business or property by reason of the racketeering activity. Because racketeering activity is defined by a long "laundry list" of offenses, including mail fraud, wire fraud, and securities fraud, and a pattern is proved by showing defendant has committed two or more such acts within a ten-year period, securities claims can easily be turned into RICO claims. The main reason for wanting to do this is that RICO's civil remedies include treble damages, and the securities laws do not.

Of these acts, the 1933 Act and the 1934 Act remain the most important.

What Is a Security?

Securities are commonly thought of as the stock issued by corporations. The shares of common and preferred stock issued by corporations constitute a major type of security. These are *equity securities* which evidence an ownership interest in the corporation. Holders of equity securities are normally entitled to vote as to important corporate matters and to receive dividends as their share of the corporate profits. The other major type of security is the *debt security*, such as the bond, note, or debenture. Holders of debt securities are creditors rather than owners. They have no voice in corporate affairs but are entitled to receive regular interest payments according to the terms of the bond or note.

Because the inventive mind of man has devised an inordinate variety of investment interests, securities regulation goes beyond items that are clearly labeled "stocks" or "bonds." Section 2(1) of the 1933 Act broadly defines security to include

any note, stock, treasury stock, bond, debenture, evidence of indebtedness, certificate of interest or participation in any profit-sharing agreement, . . . investment contract, voting-trust certificate, fractional undivided interest in oil, gas or other mineral rights, or, in general, any interest or instrument commonly known as a 'security'. . . .

This broad definition has, of necessity, been liberally construed by the courts. Interests in limited partnerships, condominiums, farm animals with accompanying agreements for their care, franchises, whiskey warehouse receipts, and many other varied items have been deemed to be securities.

The inclusion of the term "investment contract" in the 1933 Act's definition of security has produced much litigation. Some very interesting investment opportunities have been held to constitute investment contracts, as the following case illustrates.

Smith v. Gross
United States
Court of Appeals
604 F.2d 292
(9th Cir. 1979)

Gross used a promotional newsletter to solicit buyer-investors to raise earthworms in order to help him reach his quota of selling earthworms to fishermen. Buyers were promised that the seller's instructions would enable them to have a profitable worm farm, that the time required was similar to that of a garden, that the worms doubled in quantity every sixty days, and that Gross would buy back all bait-size worms produced by buyers at $2.25 per pound.

The Smiths invested, but later sued claiming that contrary to Gross' representations, the worms multiplied at a maximum of eight rather than sixty-four times per year, and that the promised profits could be achieved only if the multiplication rate were as fast as represented and Gross repurchased the Smith's production at $2.25 per pound, which was much higher than the true market value. Gross could pay that amount only by selling the worms to new worm farmers at inflated prices.

The Smiths claimed that Gross made false representations which violated the federal securities laws. The federal district court dismissed the action for want of subject matter jurisdiction after concluding that no "security" was involved in the case. The Smiths appealed.

Per Curiam:

. . . The Smiths contend that the transactions between the parties involved an investment contract type of security. In *SEC v. W.J. Howey Co.*, 328 U.S. 293, 301 (1946), the Supreme Court set out the conditions for an investment contract: "[t]he test is whether the scheme involves [1] an investment of money [2] in a common enterprise [3] with profits to come solely from the efforts of others." This court in *SEC v. Glenn W. Turner Enterprises, Inc.*, 474 F.2d 476, 482 (9th Cir.), *cert. denied*, 414 U.S. 821 (1973), held that, despite the Supreme Court's use of the word "solely," the third element of the *Howey* test is "whether the efforts made by those other than the investor are the undeniably significant ones, those essential managerial efforts which affect the failure or success of the enterprise." The *Turner* court defined a common enterprise as "one in which the fortunes of the investor are interwoven with and dependent upon the efforts and success of those seeking the investment or of third parties."

We find this case virtually identical with *Miller v. Central Chinchilla Group, Inc.*, 494 F.2d 414 (8th Cir. 1974). In *Miller* the defendants entered into contracts under which they sold chinchillas to the plaintiffs with the promise to repurchase the offspring. The plaintiffs were told that it was simple to breed chinchillas according to the defendants' instructions and that the venture would be highly profitable. The plaintiffs alleged that the chinchillas were difficult to raise and had a high mortality rate, and that the defendants could return the promised profits only if they repurchased the offspring and sold them to other prospective chinchilla raisers at an inflated price.

The *Miller* court focused on two features in holding there was an investment contract: (1) the defendants persuaded the plaintiffs to invest by representing that the efforts required of them would be very minimal; and (2) that if the plaintiffs diligently exerted themselves, they still would not gain the promised profits because those profits could be achieved only if the defendants secured additional investors at the inflated prices. Both of these features are present in the instant case. We find *Miller* to be persuasive and consistent with *Turner*. . . .

There was a common enterprise as required by *Turner*. The Smiths alleged that, although they were free under the terms of the contract to sell their production anywhere they wished, they could have received the promised profits only if the defendants repurchased above the market price, and that the defendants could have repurchased above the market price only if the defendants secured additional investors at inflated prices. Thus, the fortune of the Smiths was interwoven with and dependent upon the efforts and success of the defendants.

We also find that here, as in *Miller*, the third element of an investment contract set forth in *Turner*—that the efforts of those other than the investor are the undeniably significant ones—was present here. The *Miller* court noted that the plaintiffs there had been assured by the sellers that the effort needed to raise chinchillas was minimal. The significant effort necessary for success in the endeavor was that of the seller in procuring new investors who would purchase the chinchillas at inflated prices. Here, the Smiths alleged that they were promised that the effort necessary to raise worms was minimal and they alleged that they could not receive the promised income unless the defendants purchased their harvest.

We find the analysis in *Miller* persuasive and hold that the Smiths alleged facts that, if true, were sufficient to establish an investment contract. . . .

The judgment of the district court is reversed.

★★★

1933 Act: Regulating the Issuance of Securities

A major portion of federal securities regulation concerns the issuance of securities by companies. Congressional investigations following the 1929 stock market crash disclosed that enthusiasm for investment opportunities in the 1920s was often so great that large offerings of stock would be gobbled up by an investing public which knew virtually nothing about the selling company.

The goal of the 1933 Act is to protect the investing public. The 1933 Act is a disclosure statute which is frequently called the "Truth in Securities" law. The act requires full disclosure by companies wishing to issue and sell stock to the public. By requiring such companies to file a registration statement with the SEC and to use an offering circular called a prospectus when attempting to sell securities, the law attempts to enable the investor to make an informed decision. The SEC, which is charged with enforcement of the law, does not attempt to pass on the value of the securities offered nor to advise investors to purchase or not purchase the securities of particular companies.

The 1933 Act also protects investors by prohibiting fraud and deceit in the distribution of shares, even those which the law does not require to be registered.

The Registration Process

Elements of the Process: Securities are distributed much like any product. The corporation selling securities to raise capital, the *issuer*, is analogous to the manufacturer of goods. *Underwriters* act as wholesalers, *dealers* act as retailers, and the *investor* is a consumer. By regulating the activities of the issuer, underwriter, and dealer, the 1933 Act seeks to ensure that the investor has access to adequate information before purchasing a particular security.

The keystones to the disclosure process are the registration statement and the prospectus, the contents of which are discussed presently. Section 5(a) of the 1933 Act makes it unlawful to sell or deliver any security without first filing with the SEC a registration statement which has become effective. Section 5(b) (1) makes it unlawful to sell a security by means of a prospectus which does not meet statutory standards. Section 5(b) (2) makes it unlawful to sell securities which are not accompanied or preceded by a prospectus.

SEC Approval: The registration statement filed with the SEC is not automatically effective. Rather, the staff of the SEC reviews the statement for omissions and inaccuracies. Some reviews may be more thorough than others. Because of budgetary cutbacks and staff reductions, the SEC in recent years has had to give cursory reviews to many registration statements, reserving the full review process primarily for statements filed by new issuers selling to the public for the first time.

Section 8(a) of the 1933 Act provides that if the SEC is silent, the registration statement automatically becomes effective on the twentieth day after its filing. Whenever the SEC requires changes in the statement because insufficient or inaccurate information has been disclosed, each amendment that must be filed restarts the twenty-day period. Because the SEC has substantial powers to delay or even to block issuance of shares pursuant to a defec-

"Well, we could release it as provisional data, leak it as projected figures, or just shove it all under the rug."

Securities laws seek to require corporations to disclose all information that is important to investors.

Source: Drawing by Stevenson; © 1976 *The New Yorker* Magazine, Inc.

tive registration statement, most issuers strive to satisfy quickly any SEC objections to the form or content of the registration statement. The review process is aimed at ensuring that full information in the proper form is contained in the registration statement.

When a prospective issuer has satisfied any SEC objections to the registration statement, the issuer must usually file a final amendment to set the price of the shares to reflect market conditions which have changed since the statement was first filed. If certain conditions pertaining to distribution of the prospectus are met, the SEC has the power (under SEC Rule 460) to accelerate the effective date by allowing the registration statement to become effective immediately after the price amendment, without the twenty-day waiting period.

The registration process may be analyzed in terms of its three major time periods. The first stage of the process is the period before the registration statement is filed (the "pre-filing" period). The second stage lasts from the filing of the statement until it becomes effective (the "waiting" period). The final stage is, of course, after the statement becomes effective (the "post-effective" period).

The Pre-Filing Period: To prevent circumvention of the provisions of Section 5, an issuer is strictly limited during the pre-filing period. The issuer may not sell or even offer to sell a security before the registration statement is filed. The term "offer" is broadly construed and encompasses not only formal sales campaigns, but any type of activity meant to "precondition" the market. A simple speech by a corporate executive or a press release about how well the company is doing may be improper if it "just happens" to be soon followed by the filing of a registration statement.

The only activities permitted during the pre-filing period, other than normal advertising and communications with shareholders by an issuer, are preliminary negotiations between the issuer and underwriters. This is necessary because a large distribution of securities may require that an entire syndicate of underwriters be assembled.

The Waiting Period: The purpose of the waiting period is to slow the distribution process so that the dealers and the public have time to familiarize themselves with the information disclosed in the registration process. Though no sales may be consummated during this period, certain types of offers are allowed, and underwriters may now make arrangements with dealers for their assistance in distribution.

In addition to oral offers, certain types of written offers are permissible during the waiting period. For example, an issuer may place in *The Wall Street Journal* a short announcement known as a tombstone ad because it is usually surrounded by a black border. Under SEC Rule 134, the announcement may state only a few limited items, such as (1) the kind of security, (2) the amount, (3) by whom purchase orders will be executed, and (4) the location at which a prospectus may be obtained. The announcement must state that no offer to purchase can actually be accepted during the waiting period, and that an indication of interest is not binding on a prospective investor.

Offers may also be made by use of a preliminary prospectus, which contains information from the registration statement then under review. These are called "red herring" prospectuses, because SEC Rule 430 requires that a special legend be printed in red ink on each one labeling it a preliminary prospectus, stating that a registration statement has been filed but is not yet effective, that no final sale can be made during the waiting period, and that it does not constitute an offer to sell.

Allowing offers to be made by use of the preliminary prospectus encourages the dissemination of information about the issuer. So does the SEC practice under Rule 460 of conditioning acceleration upon a prior distribution of "red herring" prospectuses to all underwriters and dealers who might participate in the distribution. Furthermore, Rule 15c2-8 of the 1934 Act makes it an illegally deceptive practice for a managing underwriter to fail to take reasonable steps to ensure that dealers receive sufficient copies of the preliminary prospectus, for dealers to fail to provide sufficient copies to their salesforce, and for dealers to fail to provide copies to investors desiring them.

Post-Effective Period: Once the registration statement becomes effective, sales of securities may be completed. However, the law still imposes requirements aimed at encouraging dissemination of information. With some exceptions, the issuer, underwriter, and dealer must provide a copy of the final prospectus with every written offer, supplemental sales literature, written confirmation of sale, or delivery of securities. The prospectus must be used as long as the distribution is taking place; if this period extends beyond nine months, Section 10(a) (3) requires that the prospectus be updated to reflect more recent information on the status of the issuer. In addition, the issuer must update the prospectus whenever important new developments occur; otherwise the information can become stale and misleading, resulting in liability for fraud under Section 17(a) of the 1933 Act.

Shelf Registration: Traditionally, an issuer has been required to file a new registration statement every time it sought to initiate a new distribution of stock. Recently, however, through Rule 415 the SEC established a system known as *shelf registration* for the 1,400 or so largest corporations. Under this system a company is allowed to file one registration statement announcing its long-term plans for sales of securities. Then, whenever the company thinks market conditions and its own financial needs require the sale of securities, it can issue the additional securities without going through the registration process described above to achieve SEC approval because it already has a registration statement and a prospectus "on the shelf." If periodically updated, the registration statement will remain continuously effective. Rule 415 enhances the ability of corporations to raise capital on short notice, but thus far its use has been restricted primarily to the larger, more reliable corporations.

Disclosure Requirements

The information disclosure requirements of the 1933 Act and the 1934 Act were for a long time separate, often overlapping, and sometimes conflicting. In recent years, the SEC has made an effort to coordinate the requirements for information disclosure contained in the two acts. The filing requirements of the 1934 Act must be mentioned here because they now bear significantly on the disclosure requirements of the 1933 Act regarding the registration statement and prospectus.

Registration and Reporting: Section 12 of the 1934 Act requires all companies whose securities are traded on the national stock exchanges (such as the New York Stock Exchange) and any other companies with more than three million dollars in assets and more than five hundred shareholders to register their securities with the SEC. These companies are referred to as registered or reporting companies. There are about ten thousand such companies. The required registration statement must contain extensive information about such areas as the organization, financial structure and nature of the business, the structure of present classes of stock, the directors and officers and their remuneration, important contracts, balance sheets, and profit-and-loss statements for the three preceding fiscal years.

Section 13 requires that the registration statement be continually updated with annual reports (called 10-Ks) and quarterly reports (10-Qs). In addition, if important facts change between quarterly reports, the company should amend the registration statement by use of an 8-K report.

Integration of Registration Requirements: Despite all the information made public under the 1934 Act, even reporting companies have traditionally had to go through the expensive registration process under the 1933 Act, which required disclosure of information already made public in the 1934 Act reports. Complaints about the expense of filing a full 1933 Act registration statement—estimated at $100,000 to $200,000 per statement—prompted the SEC to attempt to streamline the requirements. The shelf registration procedure is one such attempt. Another step to integrate the disclosure requirements of the two Acts was taken in early 1982 when the SEC reduced the disclosure requirements under the 1933 Act for some companies.

Until the 1982 changes, there were approximately fourteen different forms for registration under the 1933 Act, each tailored to a different type of offering. The main form applicable to most full-blown registration statements, Form S-1, required extensive disclosures regarding such matters as the plan of distribution; the intended use of proceeds; the company's capital structure; a summary of earnings; description of the registrant's organization, business, and property; a listing of directors and executive officers; and financial statements.

The new amendments sought to make disclosure requirements uniform under the 1933 and 1934 Acts and to utilize the periodic reports of the 1934 Act to satisfy many of the disclosure requirements of the 1933 Act registration statements by a process of incorporation by reference. The core of the new procedure is a three-tiered registration structure which creates three distinct categories of registration statement, depending upon the issuer's financial size and prior reporting history. Form S-3, applicable to the larger and more reliable corporations, maximizes incorporation by reference of 1934 Act disclosures, and has minimal prospectus disclosure requirements. Form S-2 is used by other reporting companies which have been filing 1934 Act reports for at least three years. Some incorporation by reference is allowed. Form S-1, designed primarily for companies going public for the first time, resembles the former Form S-1 by requiring full disclosure in the prospectus and registration statement and allowing no incorporation by reference to the 1934 Act reports.

Section 10 of the 1933 Act, as supplemented by various rules issued by the SEC, controls the content of the prospectus. The most important information in the registration statement regarding the financial structure, organization, operations, and officers and directors of the issuer must be summarized in the prospectus (unless incorporation by reference is allowed under the new system).

Materiality: Exactly which details must be included in the registration statement and prospectus is a matter governed not only by statutes and rules, but also by the concept of materiality. The most important element in the disclosure provisions of both the 1933 and 1934 Acts is that all matters that are important or material to an investor's decision should be disclosed. Materiality is an elusive concept, but the Supreme Court has described information as material "if there is a substantial likelihood that a reasonable shareholder would consider it important" in making an investment decision.[1] This is usually limited to matters having a significant bearing on the economic and financial performance of the company.

Examples of material facts include an erratic pattern of earnings, an intention to enter into a new line of business, adverse competitive conditions, litigation with the government which might lead to imposition of a financially damaging fine, and a substantial disparity between the price at which the shares are being offered to the public and the cost of the shares owned by officers, directors, and promoters. Recently, the SEC even decided that large public companies should be required to disclose the impact of inflation on their operations. The following case illustrates one application of the concept of materiality in the 1933 Act disclosure context.

---

[1] *TSC Industries, Inc. v. Northway, Inc.*, 426 U.S. 438, 449 (1976).

In the Matter of Doman Helicopters, Inc.
Securities Exchange Commission
41 S.E.C. 431 (1963)

Doman Helicopters, Inc. was formed in 1945, but never was able to do business on a profitable basis. Except for one experimental model sold in 1950, two prototypes delivered to the Army in 1956 and 1957 (both subsequently repurchased by Doman), and one helicopter on loan to its Italian licensee, by 1962 Doman had never manufactured or sold any helicopters. Instead, it had continually flirted with bankruptcy. By September 30, 1961, its accumulated losses totalled over $5.7 million. On January 31, 1962, Doman's current liabilities were $292,446 while its assets were only $13,178.

On April 19, 1962, Doman filed a Form S-1 registration statement proposing to publicly offer 681,971 shares, some to current shareholders, some to creditors, and some to the public. The contemplated price was $1.50 per share. Doman's future plans were predicated on development of a proposed helicopter, the D-10B.

The SEC commenced a proceeding under Section 8(d) of the 1933 Act to determine whether a stop order should issue suspending the effectiveness of Doman's registration statement. The focus of the investigation was on deficiencies in the prospectus.

By the Commission:

. . . 1. Status and Prospects of the Model D-10B. The prospectus describes the D-10B as though it were an existing and operational helicopter possessing superiority in specified respects [economy of operation, range, payload per dollar invested] over other helicopters offered on the market. . . . There is no adequate factual foundation for the[se] statements, and they were false and misleading.

The D-10B has never been flown or tested or even assembled in prototype form, crucial facts which are nowhere disclosed in the registration statement.

2. The Doman Hingeless Rotor System. The prospectus makes the following claims for the so-called "Doman Hingeless Rotor System": "In comparison with other devices, this system provides greater inherent stability in forward flight, less vibration in any flight attitude or maneuver, long life for the rotor and blade assembly, relatively low initial and maintenance costs and exceptional permissible range of the center of gravity of the fuselage and its cargo.". . .

These representations present in their totality a misleading picture of uniqueness and substantiated superiority of the Doman rotor system. That system has been used only on a few converted or prototype models. No production model using the Doman rotor system has ever been subjected to normal day to day usage by a user or customer. In such circumstances the unqualified claims as to superior durability and lower maintenance costs were not warranted, and it was deceptive to describe the system as "fully developed and proven.". . .

3. Efforts to Secure Defense Contracts. The prospectus makes only a passing reference to the fact that registrant unsuccessfully attempted to secure a military market for its helicopters. It does not disclose the nature of those attempts or of the action of the Department of Defense with respect to them. Registrant had from 1951 to 1962 made strenuous and persistent efforts to interest that Department in its proposals and devices. The Department made a number of tests

with the two prototype helicopters that it purchased from the registrant and made an extensive study of the Doman rotor system. It found "no significant advantages in the Doman rotor system over other types," and those findings were reaffirmed upon successive reviews following objections raised by registrant. . . . Irrespective of the correctness of the Department's conclusions, they constitute a determination by the technical staff and responsible authorities of the largest single purchaser of helicopters that for their purposes registrant's rotor system had no special merit. Such determination was a significant adverse factor, and the failure to disclose it rendered the prospectus misleading.

4. Application of Proceeds. The prospectus stated that the proceeds of the offering would be used to develop the D-10B, but failed to state the order of priority in which the proceeds would be applied as required by Instruction 2 to Item 3 of Form S-1. The prospectus did not adequately disclose that except to the extent that the creditors to whom part of the offering is to be made elected to take stock in exchange for their debt claims, $292,466 of the proceeds from the public offering would first have to be applied to the liquidation of registrant's outstanding indebtedness, thereby reducing and perhaps exhausting the funds that the prospectus stated would be allocated to the D-10B. It also failed to disclose that approximately $13,000 of the estimated proceeds would have to be used to pay the accrued salaries of certain officers and directors, and that a large portion of the proceeds would have to be used to meet current expenses, which were being incurred at the rate of $11,000 per month, and would be used for that purpose even if the proceeds of the offering were insufficient to permit registrant to go forward with its D-10B program.

5. Dilution Aspects of Offering. The prospectus fails to disclose the dilution aspects of the offering. As of January 31, 1962, registrant's shares had a book value of minus 30 cents per share. If all the shares that the registrant proposes to offer to its existing stockholders and to its creditors were in fact sold at the proposed offering prices, that book value would increase to 55 cents per share. Purchasers paying $1.50 per share would therefore suffer an immediate dilution of 95 cents per share, the benefit of which will inure entirely to the present stockholders. It was pertinent to an informed appraisal by the persons to whom the securities being offered may be sold that this dilution be described in the prospectus. . . .

A stop order will issue.

★★★

Exemptions

In certain situations where there is less need for regulation, Sections 3 and 4 of the 1933 Act provide exemptions from Section 5's registration requirements (though not from the anti-fraud provisions of the 1933 and 1934 Acts).

Perhaps the most important exemption is that for "transactions by any person other than an issuer, underwriter, or dealer" provided by Section 4(1).

This simply means that once the issue is sold to the investing public, the public may trade, and the dealers may handle most transactions, without any worry about registration or prospectus delivery requirements. Thus, the 1933 Act does not apply to so-called "secondary trading," which is regulated by the 1934 Act.

Section 3(a) exempts from registration the securities of governments (state and federal), charitable organizations, banks, savings and loans, and common carriers, which are regulated under other federal laws.

Small Issues: There are also exemptions for small issues and small issuers. Section 4(2) exempts "transactions by an issuer not involving any public offering," an exemption used primarily in connection with (1) bank loans, (2) privately negotiated sales of securities to large institutional investors (private placements), and (3) the promotion of business ventures by a few closely related persons. Section 3(b) authorizes the SEC to exempt securities if it finds that registration "is not necessary in the public interest and for the protection of investors by reason of the small amount involved [a five-million-dollar ceiling] or the limited character of the public offering."

Regulation D: Specific SEC rules flesh out the 4(2) and 3(b) exemptions, and all were renumbered and revamped in early 1982 with the promulgation of Regulation D. A key concept in Regulation D is that of the "accredited investor" which, by its nature, is not likely to need government protection in its investment decisions. "Accredited investors" include (1) institutional investors, such as pension funds and banks, (2) the seller's "insiders" such as directors and officers, (3) an individual with a net worth of over $1 million, (4) an individual with an annual income of over $200,000 for three consecutive years, and (5) a person who buys $150,000 of securities at one time (so long as the total purchase does not exceed 20 percent of the investor's net worth).

Regulation D's Rule 504 exempts from registration any issuance in a twelve-month period totalling less than $500,000 (reduced by amounts sold in reliance on other exemptions). This exemption is aimed at smaller businesses and is not available to 1934 Act reporting companies.

Rule 505 allows a company, including reporting companies, to sell up to five million dollars (reduced by amounts sold in reliance on other exemptions) in securities in any twelve-month period without registering, provided the sales are to no more than thirty-five unaccredited investors. The number of sales to accredited investors is not limited. However, no general advertising or soliciting is allowed.

Rule 506 clarifies Section 4(2)'s exemption by allowing companies, including reporting companies, to sell an unlimited amount of securities in an issuance if sales are limited to thirty-five unaccredited investors and an unlimited number of accredited investors. There is an obligation on the part of the issuer to make a determination that all purchasers are "sophisticated" and therefore capable of protecting themselves without the assistance of a registration statement and prospectus. Accredited investors are assumed to be sophisticated, and an unsophisticated purchaser may act through a sophisticated purchaser representative. No general advertising or soliciting is allowed, or the distribution would lose its nonpublic nature.

Rule 502 provides that if any sales are made to unaccredited investors pursuant to Rules 505 and 506, all purchasers must be given certain specified information about the issuer. The required information is less comprehensive than the normal prospectus.

A small issues partial exemption of decreasing importance is Regulation A, under which the SEC allows an issuer to sell up to $1.5 million of securities in a twelve-month period with minimal disclosure requirements. An unaudited circular is permitted in place of the more detailed prospectus.

Local Offerings: A final important exemption is Section 3(a) (11)'s exemption for intrastate offerings, which applies where a selling company doing business in a state offers and sells securities only to residents of the same state and intends to use the proceeds there. An issuer, according to Rule 147, is doing business within a state if (1) it derives 80 percent or more of its revenue from operations within the state, (2) at least 80 percent of its assets are located within the state, (3) at least 80 percent of the net proceeds of the issuance will be used within the state, and (4) the issuer's principal office is located there. Offer of the shares for sale to a single nonresident will void the exemption. Federal regulation is deemed unnecessary because of the availability of state regulation and the close proximity of purchaser to seller.

Enforcement and Civil Liabilities

Government Action: The SEC has numerous powers to enforce compliance with the provisions of the 1933 Act. For example, if the SEC believes that a registration statement is incomplete or inaccurate, Section 8(b) authorizes issuance of a "refusal order" which prevents the statement from becoming effective until SEC objections are satisfied. If inaccuracies are discovered after the effective date, the SEC may issue a "stop order" pursuant to Section 8(d), as was done in the Doman Helicopters case, to suspend the effectiveness of the statement. Section 8(e) authorizes the SEC to conduct an "examination" to fully investigate whether a stop order should issue.

More generally, Section 19(b) gives the SEC power of subpoena to aid investigations of any potential violation of the 1933 Act. Section 20(b) allows the SEC to go into federal district court to seek an injunction whenever it appears that any person is violating the 1933 Act.

The 1933 Act even contains criminal provisions. Section 24 provides that any person who willfully violates any provision of the Act or any SEC rule, or any person who willfully makes an untrue statement or omits a material fact in a registration statement is subject to a fine of not more than $10,000, imprisonment of not more than five years, or both.

Private Suit:

Section 11: An investor who is injured after buying securities with reliance on a rosy picture falsely painted in a prospectus will probably not be satisfied with the SEC's injunction remedy or even criminal prosecution. The investor will desire to recoup losses through a civil action for damages, and the 1933 Act has express provision for such lawsuits. Section 11 states that if "any part of the registration statement, when such part became effective, contained an untrue statement of a material fact or omitted to state a material fact required to be stated therein or necessary to make the statements therein not misleading, any person acquiring such security" may file a civil action. Potential defendants in such an action include every person who signed the registration statement (which includes the issuer, its principal executive officers, chief financial officer, principal accounting officers, and a majority of the board of directors), every person who was a director or identified as about to become a director, every accountant, every appraiser or other expert who is named as having helped prepare it, and every underwriter.

The Section 11 cause of action is loosely patterned after a common-law fraud action, but is modified so as to greatly ease a plaintiff's burdens in seeking recovery. For example, the common-law fraud elements of privity of contract and reliance are not necessary in a Section 11 claim so long as plaintiff can trace the purchased shares back to the defective offering and show they were not previously issued shares of the same company being publicly traded at the same time.

If plaintiff proves the registration statement contained misstatements or omissions of material facts, the law presumes that these caused plaintiff's damages, and the burden of proof shifts to defendants to prove that other factors were the true cause of plaintiff's losses.

Furthermore, Section 11 does not require proof of fraudulent intent. Proof of misstatement or omission shifts the burden of proof to defendants to establish that they were guilty of neither fraudulent intent nor negligence in preparing the registration statement. Individual defendants must establish that they used "due diligence" in preparing the registration statement. The amount of diligence that is due from a defendant depends on his or her position as an "insider" (with full access to key information) or an "outsider," and a defendant is generally allowed to rely on "expertised" portions of the statement—those portions prepared by experts such as independent auditors. The due diligence defense is not available to the issuing company, which is strictly liable for inaccuracies in the registration statement.

Section 12: Section 12(1) allows an investor to recover when offers or sales are made in violation of Section 5—that is, without the filing of a registration statement, by use of a defective prospectus, or where securities are delivered without an accompanying prospectus. The elements of a Section 12(1) claim are very similar to those of a Section 11 claim, except that lack of privity of contract is a valid defense under Section 12(1). Thus, if an issuer sold to an underwriter, who sold to a dealer, who sold to plaintiff, plaintiff could recover only from the dealer, even though the issuer and underwriter violated Section 5.

Section 12(2) renders civilly liable any person who sells securities by use of a misstatement or omission of material fact who "shall not sustain the burden of proof that he did not know, and in the exercise of reasonable care could not have known, of such untruth or omission." This section applies even to sales of securities which were exempt from registration. Due diligence is an affirmative defense. Lack of privity is also a defense, although many courts have limited its usefulness by rendering liable not only the person who actually conveyed the title to the buyer, but also any person, such as a stockbroker, who substantially facilitated or participated in the sale.

1934 Act: Regulating the Trading of Securities

While the 1933 Act regulates primarily the initial issuance of securities, the 1934 Act regulates the subsequent trading of those securities. An array of complex problems comes within the purview of the 1934 Act. The general registration and reporting requirements of the 1934 Act have already been discussed. Attention is now turned to several other major concerns of the Act.

Insider Trading

Knowledge of the inner workings of a corporation would be very valuable in making investment decisions. For example, if a corporate vice-president learned that his company's scientists had just been granted an important patent which will open up a new sales field, he would have a distinct trading advantage over the general investing public.

Insider trading was a widespread phenomenon in the 1920s, yet the common law provided little protection from such abusive practices. In one 1933 case, for example, plaintiff stockholder sold his stock in a mining company after reading in the newspaper that the mining company had discontinued copper exploration in a certain field. Defendants, directors of the corporation, purchased the shares on the stock exchange because they knew something plaintiff did not—that the company planned a new test of the field based on a new geological theory. The value of the stock rose when the inside information became public knowledge. Plaintiff was denied recovery when the court held that the directors had not breached their fiduciary duty to the corporation's shareholders by failing to disclose the information about the exploration. The court stressed the impersonal nature of the sales through a stock exchange.[2]

---

[2] *Goodwin v. Agassiz*, 283 Mass. 358, 186 N.E. 659 (1933).

Section 16(b): One response to the insider trading problem is Section 16 of the 1934 Act. Subsection (a) is a reporting requirement which applies to three categories of persons: officers, directors, and owners of more than 10 percent of the shares of any one class of stock of a 1934 Act reporting company. These three categories of persons are deemed the corporation's "insiders." Section 16(a) requires that they file two types of reports with the stock exchanges and the SEC: an initial report revealing the holdings when a director or officer takes office or when a stockholder first obtains a 10 percent holding, and an additional report each month thereafter in which a change in holdings occurs.

Subsection (b) of Section 16 provides that any profits realized by such an insider in connection with a purchase and sale or sale and purchase within a six-month period is an illegal "short-swing" profit. Any such profit may be recaptured by the issuer.

The striking aspect of Section 16(b) liability is its near absolute nature. Because of the difficulty of proving that someone has improperly used inside information for personal gain, Congress elected to omit such actual use as a requirement for Section 16(b) liability. Instead, if someone fitting the definition of an insider does have a purchase and sale or sale and purchase within a six-month period which result in a profit, liability is automatic. There are no defenses. Even proof that inside information was not used is no defense in a standard transaction.

Calculation of Profit: Another extraordinary feature of Section 16(b) is the manner in which the profit realized is calculated. A first-in, first-out matching of shares might seem a sensible approach to calculating profits. However, in order to discourage insider trading, the courts have held that all purchases and sales or sales and purchases within a six-month period should be matched on a lowest-in, highest-out basis in order to maximize the profits that may be recaptured. Furthermore, transactions which resulted in a loss will not be deducted from those which were profitable. For example, assume that an insider engaged in the following transactions involving a company's securities:

January 1, bought 1,000 shares at $5 per share

February 1, bought 1,000 shares at $8 per share

March 1, sold 1,000 shares at $4 per share

April 1, sold 1,000 shares at $7 per share.

All transactions occurred within a six-month period, so all could be matched for Section 16(b) purposes. It seems apparent the insider spent $13,000 in buying the shares, but received only $11,000 when they were sold, resulting in an actual loss of $2,000. But for Section 16(b) purposes, the January 1 purchase (lowest-in) will be matched with the April 1 sale (highest-out), to show a $2,000 profit. When the remaining February 1 purchase is matched with the remaining March 1 sale, a $4,000 loss is produced, but such losses are disregarded in Section 16(b) calculations. Therefore, although the insider has sustained an actual loss of $2,000, according to Section 16(b) an illegal profit of $2,000 is calculated, which may not be kept.

Incentive to Sue: The SEC has no enforcement powers for Section 16(b) violations. Nor does the person who bought from or sold to the insider have a right to sue. Rather, the right to recoup the insider's profit belongs to the corporation itself. Because the corporation's decision to sue must be made by some of the very people at which the statute is aimed—the officers and directors, Section 16(b) provides that if the corporation refuses a request to file suit, any shareholder may file a derivative action on the corporation's behalf.

In order to encourage enforcement of Section 16(b), the courts have liberally construed its enforcement provisions, holding that a plaintiff need be a shareholder only at the time suit is brought, not necessarily at the time of the violation. Because the recovery goes into the corporate till and any shareholder would profit only indirectly and usually in a miniscule amount, it would seem that there is little incentive to bring such an action. The courts have added incentive by liberally granting attorney's fees to prevailing plaintiffs. Because of the near absolute liability under Section 16(b), some attorneys have found it lucrative to search the Section 16(a) reports on insider holdings for transactions resulting in a profit, to purchase a single share of the subject corporation's stock, and then to sue when the corporation refuses to do so. Attorney's fee awards well into six figures are unusual but not unknown in Section 16(b) litigation.

Unorthodox Transactions: The Supreme Court has fashioned one exception to the general strict liability approach to Section 16(b)'s proscription against insider trading. For certain "unorthodox transactions," such as involuntary mergers where the trading insider had no realistic opportunity to attain or abuse inside information, the Court has refused to find liability. The main Supreme Court case outlining this pragmatic approach is *Kern County Land Co. v. Occidental Petroleum Corp.*, 411 U.S. 582 (1973), which arose out of Occidental's unsuccessful attempt to acquire Kern by means of a public tender offer. Seeking to buy a controlling interest in Kern, Occidental offered to buy Kern shares at $83.50 per share. Kern's management vigorously opposed the Occidental offer, advising Kern shareholders not to sell. Kern's management negotiated a defensive merger with Tenneco Corporation under terms which would allow Kern's shareholders to receive $105 per share from Tenneco. Although Occidental had acquired over 10 percent of Kern's shares before the Tenneco deal, thus becoming an insider of Kern, it ultimately lost out to the higher Tenneco offer. Not wishing to remain a minority shareholder in a company controlled by Tenneco, within six months of the tender offer Occidental sold its shares of Kern to Tenneco, receiving a total profit of over $19 million. The Tenneco subsidiary into which Kern's assets were placed following the merger then brought a Section 16(b) action to recover Occidental's profits.

The Supreme Court denied recovery, stressing that the possibility that Occidental had any confidential information about Kern was "extremely remote" in light of its adversary relationship with Kern's management. Also, the Court characterized the sale of Kern stock to Tenneco as "involuntary," the result of Occidental's loss in the tender offer battle. The Court concluded that Congress did not intend Section 16(b) to apply to such an extraordinary transaction where there was no opportunity for access to inside information.

Section 10(b): Another provision of the 1934 Act which regulates insider trading, as well as many other facets of securities trading, is Section 10(b). This provision makes it unlawful to "use or employ, in connection with the purchase or sale of any security, . . . any manipulative or deceptive device or contrivance in contravention of such rules and regulations as the Commission may prescribe. . . ."

Pursuant to Section 10(b), the SEC has issued the most important of all its rules, Rule 10b-5, quoted in full:

It shall be unlawful for any person, directly or indirectly, by the use of any means or instrumentality of interstate commerce, or of the mails, or of any facility of any national securities exchange,

(1) to employ any device, scheme or artifice to defraud,

(2) to make any untrue statement of a material fact or to omit to state a material fact necessary in order to make the statements made, in the light of the circumstances under which they were made, not misleading, or

(3) to engage in any act, practice, or course of business which operates or would operate as a fraud or deceit upon any person, in connection with the purchase or sale of any security.

General Provisions: One important category of Rule 10b-5 cases involves insider trading. Although a Section 10(b) case is more difficult to prove, its coverage is broader than Section 16(b)'s. The broad purpose of Section 10(b) and Rule 10b-5 is to protect the investing public by preventing fraud and equalizing access to material information. Section 10(b) applies to any purchase or sale by any person of any security—there are no exceptions. Thus, small close corporations (the shares of which are not offered to the public for sale but are typically held by just a few, perhaps members of a single family) are covered as well as the largest public corporations. Transactions covered include those occurring on the stock exchanges, in over-the-counter sales through stock brokers, or even in privately negotiated sales. Any person connected with the transaction is regulated, not only insiders as in Section 16(b).

Unlike Section 16(b), Section 10(b) requires proof of actual use of inside information to establish a violation. There is no automatic presumption. However, if such an abuse of nonpublic information is proved, there is a variety of remedies available. The SEC can hold disciplinary proceedings if a regulated broker, dealer, or underwriter is involved. It can also go to court to obtain an injunction halting the illegal practices and perhaps an order rescinding the fraudulent sale. A willful violation of Section 10(b), or of any provision of the 1934 Act, subjects the violator to the criminal provisions of Section 32, which carry penalties of imprisonment up to five years, a fine or both. To discourage insider trading, Congress passed the Insider Trading Sanctions Act of 1984 (ITSA), which increased the maximum fine for a criminal violation of any 1934 Act provision from $10,000 to $100,000, and authorized the SEC in insider trading cases to seek relief in the form of disgorgement of illicit profits and assessment of a civil money penalty of up to three times the profit gained or loss avoided.

Private Suits: Perhaps the most important remedy for a Section 10(b) violation is the private civil lawsuit which may be brought by victims of fraud against the perpetrators. Although the 1934 Act does not explicitly provide for such a private right of action, the courts have implied one since 1946.[3] Private lawsuits brought under Section 10(b) and Rule 10b-5 in the 1960s and 1970s dramatically altered the law of securities regulation in the United States.

Potential defendants in an insider-trading case brought under Section 10(b) include corporate insiders [defined more broadly than in Section 16(a)], persons who receive nonpublic information from such insiders ("tippees"), and persons in a "special relationship" with the issuer, such as brokers and investment bankers.

A leading case, *SEC v. Texas Gulf Sulphur Co.*, 401 F.2d 833 (2d Cir. 1968), which involved the purchase of securities of the Texas Gulf Sulphur Company by its employees and their tippees who possessed nonpublic information about a massive ore strike by the company in Canada, laid down the basic "abstain or disclose" rule in these words: "Anyone in possession of material inside information must either disclose it to the investing public, or, if he is disabled from disclosing it in order to protect a corporate confidence, or he chooses not to do so, must abstain from trading in or recommending the securities concerned while such inside information remains undisclosed."

The "abstain or disclose" rule promotes fairness in securities transactions by equalizing access to important information affecting the value of traded securities. An illustrative violation is discussed in the following SEC proceeding.

[3] *Kardon v. National Gypsum Co.*, 69 F.Supp. 512 (E.D.Pa. 1946).

Investors Management Co., Inc.
Securities Exchange Commission
44 S.E.C. 633 (1971)

In 1966 Douglas Aircraft was planning to issue debentures for public sale through its underwriter, Merrill Lynch. Douglas had publicly estimated that its per share earnings would be $4 to $4.50 for 1966 and $8 to $12 for 1967. On June 20, 1966, Douglas informed the Merrill Lynch vice-president in charge of the underwriting that Douglas had sustained a loss in May, and now expected to only break even in 1966, with 1967 earnings projected at only $5 to $6 per share. On June 21, this information was relayed to Merrill Lynch investment advisers, who in turn contacted a few large customers, who quickly sold their Douglas stock. The stock, which was trading at 90 on June 21, fell to 76 on June 24 when the information about the reduced earnings projections became public, and to 69 the next day.

The SEC initiated administrative proceedings against Merrill Lynch and several of the selling tippees. Merrill Lynch settled with the SEC, accepting certain sanctions. The hearing examiner found the remaining respondents willfully violated Section 10(b) and Rule 10b-5. The Commission itself then reviewed those findings.

By the Commission:

. . . It is clear that . . . the conduct of respondents in this case came within the ambit and were violative of the antifraud provisions of the securities laws. All the requisite elements for the imposition of responsibility were present on the facts found by the examiner. We consider those elements to be [1] that the information in question be material and non-public; [2] that the tippee, whether he receives the information directly or indirectly, know or have reason to know that it was non-public and had been obtained improperly by selective revelation or otherwise, and [3] that the information be a factor in his decision to effect the transaction. We shall discuss these elements in turn in light of the contentions that have been presented by the parties and pertinent considerations under the securities laws.

With respect to materiality, we held in our findings with regard to Merrill Lynch in these proceedings that the information as to Douglas' earnings that it divulged was material because it "was of such importance that it could be expected to affect the judgment of investors whether to buy, sell or hold Douglas stock and, if generally known, . . . to affect materially the market price of the stock." Among the factors to be considered in determining whether information is material under this test are the degree of its specificity, the extent to which it differs from information previously publicly disseminated, and its reliability in light of its nature and source and the circumstances under which it was received. While the test would not embrace information as to minor aspects or routine details of a company's operations, the information received by the respondents from Merrill Lynch was highly significant since it described a sharp reversal of Douglas' earnings realization and expectations. Although all respondents did not receive identical information, in each instance the information received was specific and revealed the existence and significant extent of the adverse earnings developments. Such extraordinary information could hardly help but be important to a reasonable investor in deciding whether he should buy, sell or hold Douglas stock. The information's significance was immediately clear; it was not merely one link in a chain of analytical information. . . .

The requirement that the information divulged be non-public was also satisfied here. Information is non-public when it has not been disseminated in a manner making it available to investors generally. Although during the first half of 1966 some aerospace analysts had indicated pessimism concerning Douglas' earnings prospects, and there were adverse rumors circulating in the financial community on June 21, 22 and 23 regarding Douglas' earnings, the information conveyed to respondents by Merrill Lynch personnel was much more specific and trustworthy than what may have previously been known to those analysts or could be said to have been general knowledge. . . .

We consider that one who obtains possession of material, non-public corporate information, which he has reason to know emanates from a corporate source, and which by itself places him in a position superior to other investors, thereby acquires a relationship with respect to that information within the purview and restraints of the antifraud provisions. . . . When a recipient of such corporate information, knowing or having reason to know that the corporate information is non-public, nevertheless uses it to effect a transaction in the corporation's securities for his own benefit, we think his conduct cannot be viewed as free of culpability under any sound interpretation or application of the antifraud provisions. . . .

In this case, it is clear that respondents had the knowledge requisite to a finding of violation of Rule 10b-5. They knew Merrill Lynch, from whom they obtained the Douglas information, was the prospective underwriter of the company's securities. As professionals in the securities industry, they knew that underwriters customarily receive non-public information from issuers in order to make business judgments about the proposed public offering. Although such information is not publicly disclosed, it may be conveyed to the prospective underwriter by the issuer for a valid corporate purpose; however, the prospective underwriter, as we have previously held, may not properly disclose or use the information for other than that purpose. Under the circumstances there can be no doubt that respondents, all of whom were sizeable existing or potential customers of Merrill Lynch, knew or had reason to know that they were selectively receiving non-public information respecting Douglas from Merrill Lynch. . . .

Accordingly, it is ordered that the imposition by the hearing examiner of the sanction of censure upon the above-mentioned respondents be and it hereby is, affirmed.

★★★

Potential Plaintiffs: The preceding case was an SEC administrative action. Investors who bought Douglas shares while Merrill Lynch's tippees were selling on the basis of inside information brought a private civil action, *Shapiro v. Merrill Lynch*, 495 F.2d 228 (2d Cir. 1974). In this class action, the Second Circuit Court held that defendant tippers and tippees could be liable for damages "not only to the purchasers of the actual shares sold by defendants (in the unlikely event they can be identified) but to all persons who during the same period purchased Douglas stock in the open market without knowledge of the material inside information which was in the possession of defendants." Thus, although defendants sold only about one-half of the total Douglas shares sold during the relevant period, they were held liable to all the purchasers of stock who bought Douglas shares during that time period only to see their value tumble upon public disclosure of the inside information.

Measure of Damages: The *Shapiro* case's method of measuring liability can be draconian. Therefore, the trend is to limit recovery to disgorgement of the amount of illicit profits gained by the traders.[4] If plaintiffs' losses exceed the disgorged profits, they share recovery on a *pro rata* basis. The "disgorgement" measure of damages has been analogized to punishing bank robbers merely by making them give back the loot. It leaves the civil fines and treble damages which the SEC can secure under ITSA as the major deterrents to insider trading.

"Outsider" Trading: The most controversial issue in this area today concerns which types of persons outside the normal categories of corporate insiders and their tippees should be liable for trading on inside information. The Supreme Court made it clear in *Chiarella v. United States*, 445 U.S. 222 (1980), that, contrary to some inferences that can be drawn from the *Investors Management Co.* opinion, a duty to disclose or abstain does not arise solely from possession of confidential inside information. A duty must arise from some fiduciary-like relationship.

The lower courts have not been especially restrictive in their application of the *Chiarella* holding. For example, in *SEC v. Materia*, 745 F.2d 197 (2d Cir. 1984), Materia, a proofreader for a printing firm that handled tender offer documents, deciphered tender offer targets and traded in their shares or passed the information to others before the tender offers were publicly announced. Materia owed no duty to the shareholders of the corporations in whose shares he traded—the tender offer targets. However, he was held liable because he had breached a duty of confidentiality owed his employer and his employer's client, the tender offeror.

False or Inadequate Corporate Disclosures

A second major category of Section 10(b) cases relates to disclosures of information about corporations. We have already noted the registration and reporting requirements of the 1934 Act. The registration forms—the 10-Ks,

[4] *Elkind v. Liggett & Myers, Inc.*, 635 F.2d 156 (2d Cir. 1980).

10-Qs, and 8-Ks—are all designed to promote full disclosure of information important to the investing public. When a corporation or some person fraudulently misstates or fails to disclose material information, a Section 10(b) violation may occur.[5]

An investor who is injured because he or she bought or sold shares on the basis of inaccurate or incomplete corporate information may bring a private cause of action under the antifraud provisions of Section 10(b). The requirements of a valid claim in such a lawsuit are patterned after those of common-law fraud: (1) a misrepresentation of material fact, (2) made by defendant with knowledge of the falsity, (3) an intent to induce plaintiff to rely, (4) actual reliance by the plaintiff, (5) privity of contract between plaintiff and defendant, and (6) damage sustained. Modification of some of these common-law elements has been a source of controversy in this type of Section 10(b) case.

Privity: Privity of contract has been largely eliminated as a requirement of a Section 10(b) cause of action in the corporate disclosure setting. An injured shareholder is normally allowed to sue those persons responsible for false statements whether or not the stockholder purchased shares from or sold shares to the defendants.

Intent: Actual intent to defraud arising from knowledge of the falsity of a statement is a traditional element of common-law fraud. In order to advance the remedial purposes of the 1934 Act, many lower courts formerly interpreted Section 10(b) so as to virtually eliminate the requirement of intent by holding defendants liable though they were guilty of nothing more than simple negligence.

The Supreme Court settled the matter in a more traditional fashion in *Ernst & Ernst v. Hochfelder*, 425 U.S. 185 (1976). The case involved a small brokerage firm named First Securities, owned and controlled by its president, Nay. When Nay committed suicide, an investigation disclosed that for many years he had been converting customers' funds to his personal use. Plaintiffs, investors victimized by Nay's fraudulent scheme, sued First Securities's accounting firm, Ernst & Ernst, claiming that it negligently performed periodic audits in that it failed to discover Nay's scheme. There was no claim that Ernst & Ernst knew of Nay's fraud. The Supreme Court held that even if Ernst & Ernst's auditors had been negligent, the firm was not liable for a Section 10(b) violation "in the absence of any allegation of 'scienter'—intent to deceive, manipulate, or defraud."

The question has subsequently arisen as to whether a defendant should be liable if guilty of "recklessness," which means being highly negligent or so careless as to exhibit a complete disregard for possible damage to oth-

---

[5] False or misleading statements in documents filed with the SEC may also lead to liability under Section 18(a) of the 1934 Act.

ers. Most lower courts have concluded that reckless conduct is sufficient for imposition of liability, although the Supreme Court has not spoken on the issue.

Reliance: In a common-law fraud case, plaintiff must normally prove that the defendant's fraudulent statement was relied on in making the sale or purchase. In order to advance the broadly remedial purposes of the 1934 Act, some adjustments have been made to the traditional reliance requirement.

A misleading corporate disclosure can occur either when a material fact is concealed or when it is misrepresented. Because it is impractical to require an investor to prove reliance on a fact that was concealed from him, the Supreme Court has eliminated the reliance requirement in concealment cases. In *Affiliated Ute Citizens v. United States*, 406 U.S. 128 (1972), plaintiffs, mixed-blood Ute Indians, sold shares in the Ute Development Corporation through defendants, banks officials. Defendants failed to disclose to plaintiffs their own interest in the transactions or the fact that shares were trading at higher prices among whites. The Court held:

> *Under the circumstances of this case, involving primarily a failure to disclose, positive proof of reliance is not a prerequisite to recovery. All that is necessary is that the facts withheld be material in the sense that a reasonable investor might have considered them important in the making of this decision. This obligation to disclose and this withholding of a material fact establish the requisite element of causation in fact.*

In cases of active misrepresentation, proof of reliance is practicable; nonetheless, there have been some important modifications of the reliance requirements even in misrepresentation cases, due partly to the impersonal nature of transactions which occur through the stock exchanges. For example, in *Panzirer v. Wolf*, 663 F.2d 365 (2d Cir. 1981), plaintiff read an article in *The Wall Street Journal* which favorably mentioned a particular company. After reading the article, plaintiff purchased stock in the company. Soon thereafter the company went bankrupt. Plaintiff sued the company's officers and accountants under Rule 10b-5, alleging that the company's annual report was filled with false information which became the basis of the newspaper article. Though plaintiff never read the annual report, she was held to have satisfied the reliance requirement. In short, she was allowed to rely on the "integrity of the marketplace." Another example follows.

Blackie v. Barrack
U.S. Court of Appeals
524 F.2d 892 (9th Cir. 1975)

In fiscal 1970, Ampex Corporation reported a $12 million profit. Soon losses began to occur, but their full extent was not revealed until over two years later, when Ampex reported a $90 million loss for fiscal 1972. The company's independent auditors withdrew certification of 1971 financial statements and refused to certify those of 1972 because of suspicions that much of the loss had been sustained earlier but concealed. A class action was filed by Ampex

shareholders who purchased during the two-year period in which Ampex was issuing annual reports, interim reports, SEC filings, and press releases which inaccurately stated the company's financial condition. Defendants included Ampex, its officers, and its independent auditors.

The trial judge certified a class action, rejecting the contention of defendants that a class action was inappropriate because each and every class member (purchasers of twenty-one million shares in 120,000 transactions) would have to separately prove reliance on a particular misstatement. Defendants appealed the class certification on this and other grounds.

Koelsch, Judge:

. . . Individual questions of reliance are . . . not an impediment [to class certification]—subjective reliance is not a distinct element of proof of 10b-5 claims of the type involved in this case.

The class members' substantive claims either are, or can be, cast in omission or non-disclosure terms—the company's financial reporting failed to disclose the need for reserves, conditions reflecting on the value of the inventory, or other facts necessary to make the reported figures not misleading. [The court then quoted the above passage from the Affiliated Ute case holding that reliance is not an element of proof in a concealment case.]

Moreover, proof of subjective reliance on particular misrepresentations is unnecessary to establish a 10b-5 claim for a deception inflating the price of stock traded in the open market. Proof of reliance is adduced to demonstrate the causal connection between the defendant's wrongdoing and the plaintiff's loss. We think causation is adequately established in the impersonal stock exchange context by proof of reliance. Materiality circumstantially establishes the reliance of some market traders and hence the inflation in the stock price—when the purchase is made the causal chain between defendant's conduct and plaintiff's loss is sufficiently established to make out a prima facie case. . . .

That the prima facie case each class member must establish differs from the traditional fraud action, and may, unlike the fraud action, be established by common proof, is irrelevant; although derived from it, the 10b-5 action is not coterminous with a common law fraud action.

Here, we eliminate the requirement that plaintiffs prove reliance directly in this context because the requirement imposes an unreasonable and irrelevant evidentiary burden. A purchaser on the stock exchanges may be either unaware of a specific fact representation, or may not directly rely on it; he may purchase because of a favorable price trend, price earnings ratio, or some other factor. Nevertheless, he relies generally on the supposition that the market price is validly set and that no unsuspected manipulation has artificially inflated the price, and thus indirectly on the truth of the representations underlying the stock price—whether he is aware of it or not, the price he pays reflects material representations. Requiring direct proof from each purchaser that he relied on a particular representation when purchasing would defeat recovery by those whose reliance was indirect, despite the fact that the causational chain is broken only if the purchaser would have purchased the stock even had he known of the misrepresentation. We decline to leave such open market purchasers unprotected. The statute and rule are designed to foster an expectation that securities markets are free from fraud—an expectation on which purchasers should be able to rely. . . .

Affirmed.

★★★

Although the outer limit of permissible 10b-5 actions is not completely settled, the Supreme Court has attempted to confine the actions to situations involving deceit and manipulation. Simple corporate mismanagement or breaches of fiduciary duty by corporate officials, not involving deceit, are not actionable under Rule 10b-5.[6]

Proxy Regulation

Although most corporate decisions are made by the officers and directors, shareholders do occasionally vote on matters of importance. At the annual shareholders meeting, which state incorporation laws require be held, the shareholders elect directors to the board of directors. Their approval may also be required for certain extraordinary matters, such as amendments to corporate bylaws or articles of incorporation, mergers, or sales of major assets.

Valid shareholder approval requires at least a majority vote (and sometimes a ⅔ or ¾ approval) of a quorum of shares eligible to vote. However, in a large corporation with thousands of shareholders, it is very unusual for more than a small percentage of shareholders to appear at the annual meeting. In order to obtain a quorum, corporate management is usually required to solicit **proxies** from the shareholders. A proxy is an authorization to vote shares owned by someone else. At a typical corporation's annual meeting, incumbent management will solicit and receive proxies from a sufficient number of shareholders to vote itself into control for another year.

Section 14(a) of the 1934 Act prohibits solicitation of proxies for any shares registered under the Act in contravention of rules promulgated by the SEC. The rules which the SEC has issued have three broad goals: full disclosure, fraud prevention, and increased shareholder participation.

Full Disclosure: State laws have not always required corporate management to be responsive to the informational needs and desires of shareholders. The SEC, knowing that most major corporations solicit proxies at least annually, requires in Rule 14a-3 that no soliciting occur unless each person solicited is furnished with a written proxy statement containing the information specified in Schedule 14A.

---

[6] *Santa Fe Industries v. Green*, 430 U.S. 462 (1977).

Schedule 14A contains over twenty items, some of which are applicable only if specified matters, such as merger approval, are involved. In the typical solicitation by management relating to election of directors, the proxy statement must be accompanied by an annual report to contain, *inter alia*, comparative financial statements for the last two fiscal years, a summary of operations, a brief description of the business done by the issuer and its subsidiaries, and identification of the issuer's directors and executive officers and their principal occupations. This information must be clearly presented.

Rule 14a-6 requires that preliminary proxy soliciting material be submitted to the SEC for review at least ten days before actual solicitation. The SEC can require changes before the material is mailed. Copies of the final statement are to be provided the SEC and any exchange where the issuer's shares are registered.

In order to advance the informational needs of the shareholders of registered corporations which do not engage in proxy solicitation in a particular year, Section 14(c) requires that such corporations still file with the SEC and transmit to all shareholders information substantially equivalent to that required by Schedule 14A. This must be done prior to any annual shareholder meeting.

Proxy Contests: Normally, incumbent management will face no organized opposition in the election of directors at the annual meeting. But if the corporation is floundering financially, perhaps a group of "insurgent" shareholders will attempt to elect its own slate of candidates to the board of directors. Or perhaps the insurgents have lined up a merger with or tendered their shares to another corporation, which intends to fire incumbent management, and incumbent management has negotiated a proposed defensive merger with yet another company, which would be willing to retain the incumbents in their present positions. In these and other situations, proxy contests arise over the control of the corporation. Incumbent management and insurgent shareholders vie for sufficient proxies to prevail in the shareholders' vote. Federal regulations specify the procedure for such contests and punish any fraud which may occur.

Prior to solicitation, Rule 14a-11 requires insurgents to file an informational statement with the SEC and exchanges disclosing the participants in the insurgent group—those persons soliciting the proxies, financing the effort, or serving as attorneys and accountants for the group. Schedule 14B sets out the information which must be disclosed about the participants, including their employment history, past criminal violations, and stock holdings. At the time of solicitation, the insurgents must provide the shareholders with their own proxy statement similar to that management is required to provide.

Insurgents' Rights: One of the most important tools in a proxy fight is the shareholder list. It is essential for the proxy solicitor to know who the corporation's shareholders are, where they can be contacted, and the extent of their holdings. Incumbent management will have such a list, but it is not readily available to insurgents under most states' laws.

In order to even the odds, Rule 14a-7 provides that upon the insurgents' request, incumbent management must either mail the insurgents' proxy solicitation materials for them (at the insurgents' expense), or provide the insurgents with a shareholder list. If the former option is chosen, incumbent management is under no obligation to mail the insurgents' materials until the earlier of either the date incumbent management sends out its own materials, or the date incumbent management began to solicit proxies the preceding year.

Antifraud: Proxy contests sometimes become quite heated. To prevent fraud, Rule 14a-9 prohibits the use of false or misleading statements to solicit proxies. The term "solicitation" is broadly defined to cover both statements seeking proxies and communications urging shareholders to refuse to give proxies. Thus, if incumbent management falsely states or omits to state a material fact in urging shareholders not to grant proxies to an insurgent group, a violation of Rule 14a-9 and Section 14(a) occurs. A private cause of action is available to remedy such a violation.

Shareholder Proposals: The shareholder proposal is a method by which the shareholders can attempt to influence the course set by the officers and directors of a corporation. In a shareholder proposal, a shareholder suggests a matter to be placed on the agenda of the annual meeting (or a special shareholder meeting) for a vote by shareholders.

Procedures: Rule 14a-8 regulates such proposals. Subsection (a) lists the requirements for such a proposal. These requirements were recently tightened to make it a little more difficult for a shareholder to properly submit a proposal. The proponent, who must have owned for one year prior to the meeting date the lesser of $1,000 worth of shares or one percent of the outstanding shares of a class, may submit one proposal each year. The proposal, plus a supporting statement, may not cumulatively exceed 500 words. It must be delivered to management at least 120 days prior to the date of the previous year's annual meeting. A proper shareholder proposal must be printed by management in its proxy solicitation materials and placed on the agenda of the annual meeting.

To protect management from burdens caused by "crackpots," subsection (c) of Rule 14a-8 provides several grounds upon which management can refuse to include a proposal in its proxy materials. For example, a proposal may be omitted if it would require violation of state or federal law, relates to a personal claim or grievance, is not a proper subject for shareholder concern under state law, is not significantly related to the issuer's business, or relates to the ordinary business operations of the corporation (the day-to-day matters delegated to corporate officers). Management may also omit proposals which have been submitted recently but which received virtually no shareholder support.

Should management decide to omit the proposal, under Subsection (d) it must so inform the proponent and submit all relevant materials to the SEC for possible review. Management should express the reasons for its decision, supported by an opinion of legal counsel.

Proper Proposals: Matters which are clearly of proper shareholder concern include proposals for selection of an independent auditing firm by shareholder vote, proposals to amend the bylaws, and proposals to adopt cumulative voting (a method of voting which increases the voice of minority shareholders). In recent years, many shareholder proposals have dealt with social and political issues. Proposals have called for corporations to stop manufacturing napalm, to cease doing business in South Africa, to cease trading with the Soviet Union and other communist nations, and to invest in solar rather than nuclear energy. So long as the proposal has some connection with a shareholder's economic interests as an owner and is not a purely social or political statement, it usually is a proper matter for shareholder consideration.

Shareholder proposals seldom receive more than 2 to 3 percent of the vote at a major corporation's shareholder meeting when opposed by management. Some question exists whether the shareholder proposal mechanism is worth the burden. Proponents note that such proposals attract publicity and indirectly place pressure on management. Supporters also point to several instances where corporations appear to have been influenced by the proposals to stop doing business in South Africa, to publish equal employment opportunity statistics, to place minorities and women on the board of directors, to cease illegal campaign contributions abroad, and the like.

Tender Offers

A final important area of federal securities law regulates a method of taking control of a corporation, called a "tender offer." In a typical tender offer, one corporation (the "offeror") will publicly offer to purchase a controlling interest (over 50 percent of the shares) in another corporation (the "target"). The target's shareholders are invited to tender their shares to the offeror in return for cash or the offeror's equity or debt securities (or a combination) in an amount usually well above the prior market price of the target's stock. Two examples of large tender offers occurred in 1981—the du Pont takeover of Conoco and the U.S. Steel Corporation's purchase of Marathon Oil Company. Both purchases involved sums exceeding $6 billion.

Because of the easy availability of credit then and lack of government regulation, the tender offer gained widespread usage in the 1960s. One variety, termed the "Saturday Night Special," featured a "take-it-or-leave-it" offer to the target's shareholders with a very short time for them to make up their minds. Afraid of losing an opportunity to sell their shares at above the market price, shareholders frequently would tender their shares without time to learn anything about the offeror or to evaluate the possibility of a higher offer from a different source.

Federal Legislation: Comprehensive federal regulation of tender offers began with the passage of the Williams Act in 1968. That act amended Sections 13 and 14 of the 1934 Act with the basic purpose of increasing both the amount of information flowing to target shareholders and the time available to utilize that information.

Filing Requirements: Section 13(d) of the 1934 Act requires that any person or group acquiring more than 5 percent of the shares of any corporation must file a Schedule 13D within ten days with the SEC. That schedule requires disclosure of the background of the person or group, their source of funds, their purpose, the number of shares owned, relevant contracts or other arrangements with the target, and any plans for change of the target's affairs.

Procedural Rules: Section 14(d) and Rule 14d-2 provide that a tender offer is commenced on the date of public announcement of the offer. On that date, Rule 14d-3 requires the offeror to file with the SEC a Schedule 14D-1, which requires informational disclosures similar to those of Schedule 13D.

The target's management may support a tender offer; perhaps the management even negotiated it. But tender offers frequently are "hostile," and the offeror intends to replace the target's management with its own people. Even if the target's management opposes the offer, Section 14(d) and Rule 14d-5 require the target's management to mail the tender offer to the target's shareholders or to promptly provide the offeror with a shareholder list so it can do the mailing itself.

Formerly, target management would sometimes "stonewall" when a tender offer was made that management could not in good faith tell the shareholders was not a good offer. The hope was that silence might confuse the shareholders. Today, target management is required by Rule 14e-2, within ten days of the offer's effective date, to state whether it supports the tender offer, opposes it, or has inadequate information to make a judgment. Also, target management must, if it takes a position, file with the SEC a Schedule 14D-9. This document (a) discloses whether the officers and directors intend to hold their shares or to tender, (b) describes any contractual arrangements management may have with the offeror (for instance, the offeror sometimes can obtain management's support through monetary incentives), and (c) discloses any concrete negotiations with a "white knight"—a company willing to make a competing tender offer that is more advantageous to incumbent management.

Substantive Rules: Substantively, Section 14(d) and Rule 14e-1 provide that a tender offer must be held open for a minimum of twenty days, so the target's shareholders will have an opportunity to fully evaluate the offer. No more Saturday Night Specials will occur. If more shares are tendered than the offeror wishes to purchase, the offeror must purchase from each shareholder on a *pro rata* basis. This requirement promotes equal treatment of shareholders.

Additionally, shareholders are granted certain withdrawal rights by Rule 14d-7. If shareholders tender their shares, but change their minds before the offeror accepts, they have the right to withdraw the tendered shares within the first fifteen days after the effective date, after sixty days have passed, or during the ten days following any competing tender offer.

What if an offeror initiates the tender offer at $40 per share, seeking to purchase 51 percent of the target's shares, but only 25 percent are tendered? The offeror may choose to extend the offering period and amend the offer to $50 per share. This higher price must be given to all tendering shareholders, including those who were willing to sell at the lower price.

The final important provision of the Williams Act is Section 14(e), the prohibition of fraud or manipulation in either supporting or opposing a tender offer.

Remedies: Violations of Sections 13(d), 14(d), and 14(e) may be remedied by civil actions for injunctive relief. Injured shareholders who, relying on fraudulent statements, either tendered when they would not have done so had they known the truth, or failed to tender when they would have had they not been defrauded, also can sue for damages under Section 14(e). Defeated tender offerors and target companies probably cannot sue for such damages, because the Williams Act was not meant to protect them. However, they can seek injunctive relief, because an injunction blocking illegal activity will inure to the benefit of the shareholders.

Defensive Tactics: A recent controversy has focused on the latitude that should be accorded target management in opposing hostile tender offers. Normally, a court is hesitant to review the business judgments of a corporation's management. However, in recent years target managements have often taken extreme measures to fend off tender offers. For example, they have taken out large loans which are payable in full immediately upon a change in control of the corporation. They have moved the corporation to states with laws which tend to make tender offers more difficult to successfully consummate. They have acquired competitors of the offeror to create an antitrust impediment to the tender offer. They have even sold the corporation's "crown jewel" (the subsidiary which attracted the offer in the first place) and threatened "corporate suicide" (liquidation and dissolution).

There have been several legal challenges to defensive tactics utilized by target managements to fend off tender offers. One basis for attack is the argument that target managements are breaching their fiduciary duties to shareholders by using defensive tactics to save their jobs at the expense of the shareholders' opportunity to sell at a profit. As an example, a few years ago a corporation was contemplating a tender offer for the shares of Marshall Field & Co. at $42 each at a time when Marshall Field shares were trading on the open market at $20 per share. The offer was called off after Marshall Field's management created antitrust problems for the potential acquirer, and soon thereafter Marshall Field stock traded at under $15 per share. Naturally some shareholders were quite upset at having lost the opportunity to profit. Nonetheless, in *Panter v. Marshall Field & Co.*, 646 F.2d 271 (7th Cir. 1981), no breach of fiduciary duty was found. The business judgment rule was applied, cloaking target management's actions with a presumption of propriety. Only occasionally in recent years have courts found that management went too far in defending against hostile takeovers.

A few defensive tactics have been invalidated as violative of state corporate codes. For example, some corporations have tried to prevent takeovers by putting into effect provisions that, upon some entity's gaining control of 20 percent of a corporation, give multiple votes to all other shares but not to those of the 20 percent holder. This can make it impossible for a tender offeror to gain voting control of the corporation, but some courts have invalidated the tactic because of state corporate laws requiring that all shares of a class have equal voting rights.

A third basis for attacking defensive tactics is that they are "manipulative" in violation of § 14(e) of the Williams Act. The Supreme Court dealt a serious blow to this argument in the following case.

Schreiber v. Burlington Northern, Inc.
105 S.Ct. 2458 (1985)

On December 21, 1982, Burlington Northern, Inc. made a hostile tender offer for 25 million shares of El Paso Gas Co. at $24 per share. Though El Paso's management initially opposed the offer, its shareholders fully subscribed it. Burlington did not accept the tendered shares, however. Instead, after negotiations with El Paso's management, Burlington rescinded the December tender offer, purchased 4 million shares from El Paso, substituted a new tender offer for only 21 million shares at $24 each, and recognized certain contractual arrangements between El Paso and its management which guaranteed the managers substantial compensation upon a change of control ("golden parachutes"). Over 40 million shares were tendered in response to the second tender offer.

Rescission of the first offer diminished payment to those shareholders who had tendered during the first offer. Not only were fewer shares purchased, but the shareholders who retendered were subjected to substantial proration. Petitioner Schreiber sued on behalf of similarly situated shareholders, alleging that Burlington, El Paso, and members of El Paso's board violated § 14(e). She claimed that withdrawal of the first tender offer coupled with substitution of the second was a "manipulative" distortion of the market for El Paso stock.

The trial court dismissed the suit for failure to state a claim. The Third Circuit Court of Appeals affirmed. Schreiber petitioned to the Supreme Court.

Burger, Chief Justice:

We are asked in this case to interpret § 14(e) of the Securities Exchange Act. The starting point is the language of the statute. Section 14(e) provides:

It shall be unlawful for any person to make any untrue statement of a material fact or omit to state any material fact necessary in order to make the statements made, in the light of the circumstances under which they are made, not misleading, or to engage in any fraudulent, deceptive or manipulative acts or practices, in connection with any tender offer or request or invitation for tenders, or any solicitation of security holders in opposition to or in favor of any such offer, request, or invitation. The Commission shall, for the purposes of this subsection, by rules and regulations define, and prescribe means reasonably designed to prevent, such acts and practices as are fraudulent, deceptive, or manipulative.

Petitioner reads the phrase "fraudulent, deceptive or manipulative acts or practices" to include acts which, although fully disclosed, "artificially" affect the price of the takeover target's stock. Petitioner's interpretation relies on the belief that § 14(e) is directed at purposes broader than providing full and true information to investors.

Petitioner's reading of the term "manipulative" conflicts with the normal meaning of the term. We have held in the context of an alleged violation of § 10(b) of the Securities Exchange Act:

Use of the word "manipulative" is especially significant. It is and was virtually a term of art when used in connection with the securities markets. It connotes intentional or willful conduct designed to deceive or defraud *investors by controlling or artificially affecting the price of securities.* Ernst & Ernst *v.* Hochfelder, *425 U.S. 185, 199 (1976) (emphasis added).*

The meaning the Court has given the term "manipulative" is consistent with the use of the term at common law, and with its traditional dictionary definition.

Our conclusion that "manipulative" acts under § 14(e) require misrepresentation or nondisclosure is buttressed by the purpose and legislative history of the provision. "The purpose of the Williams Act is to insure that public shareholders who are confronted by a cash tender offer for their stock will not be required to respond without adequate information." *Rondeau v. Mosinee Paper Corp.*, 422 U.S. 49, 58 (1975).

The expressed legislative intent was to preserve a neutral setting in which the contenders could fully present their arguments. The Senate sponsor [said]:

We have taken extreme care to avoid tipping the scales either in favor of management or in favor of the person making the takeover bids. S. 510 is designed solely to require full and fair disclosure for the benefit of investors. The bill will at the same time provide the offeror and management equal opportunity to present their case.

To implement this objective, the Williams Act added §§ 13(d), 13(e), 14(d), 14(e), and 14(f) to the Securities Exchange Act. Some relate to disclosure; §§ 13(d), 14(d) and 14(f) all add specific registration and disclosure provisions. Others—§§ 13(e) and 14(d)—require or prohibit certain acts so that investors will possess additional time within which to take advantage of the disclosed information.

Section 14(e) adds a "broad antifraud prohibition," *Piper* v. *Chris Craft Industries*, 430 U.S. 1, 24 (1977), modeled on the antifraud provisions of § 10(b) of the Act and Rule 10b-5. Nowhere in the legislative history is there the slightest suggestion that § 14(e) serves any purpose other than disclosure, or that the term "manipulative" should be read as an invitation to the courts to oversee the substantive fairness of tender offers; the quality of any offer is a matter for the marketplace.

To adopt the reading of the term "manipulative" urged by petitioner would not only be unwarranted in light of the legislative purpose but would be at odds with it. Inviting judges to read the term "manipulative" with their own sense of what constitutes "unfair" or "artificial" conduct would inject uncertainty into the tender offer process. An essential piece of information—whether the court would deem the fully disclosed actions of one side or the other to be "manipulative"—would not be available until after the tender offer had closed. This uncertainty would directly contradict the expressed Congressional desire to give investors full information.

Congress' consistent emphasis on disclosure persuades us that it intended takeover contests to be addressed to shareholders. In pursuit of this goal, Congress, consistent with the core mechanism of the Securities Exchange Act, created sweeping disclosure requirements and narrow substantive safeguards. The same Congress that placed such emphasis on shareholder choice would not at the same time have required judges to oversee tender offers for substantive fairness. It is even less likely that a Congress implementing that intention would express it only through the use of a single word placed in the middle of a provision otherwise devoted to disclosure.

We hold that the term "manipulative" as used in § 14(e) requires misrepresentation or nondisclosure. Without misrepresentation or nondisclosure, § 14(e) has not been violated.

Applying that definition to this case, we hold that the actions of respondents were not manipulative. The amended complaint fails to allege that the cancellation of the first tender offer was accompanied by any misrepresentation, nondisclosure or deception. The District Court correctly found, "All activity of the defendants that could have conceivably affected the price of El Paso shares was done openly."

Petitioner also alleges that El Paso management and Burlington entered into certain undisclosed and deceptive agreements during the making of the second tender offer. The substance of the allegations is that, in return for certain undisclosed benefits, El Paso managers agreed to support the second tender offer. But both courts noted that petitioner's complaint seeks redress only for injuries related to the cancellation of the first tender offer. Since the deceptive and misleading acts alleged by the petitioner all occurred with reference to the making of the second tender offer—when the injuries suffered by petitioner had already been sustained—these acts bear no possible causal relationship to petitioner's alleged injuries.

Affirmed.

★★★

State Regulation

Because every state has its own system of securities regulation, corporations must always be cognizant of these rules also. The Commissioners on Uniform State Laws have produced the Uniform Securities Act, which has been used as a pattern for many states' laws. Still, because many large states have not followed this act and many have amended it to varying degrees, there is a lack of uniformity which complicates the marketing of securities. Perhaps the Revised Uniform Securities Act, promulgated in late 1985, will lead to more uniformity. It will likely change some of the present state practices described below.

Registration

Most states have laws which, like the 1933 Securities Act, regulate the original distribution of securities. A corporation which intends to market its shares nationwide must comply with not only the 1933 Act but also approximately forty separate state registration laws. There are three basic systems of state registration. Some states use *registration by notification*, which requires the filing of certain material and then a waiting period before the securities may be sold, similar to the procedure under the 1933 Act.

Registration by qualification is used by some states. This process goes beyond the simple disclosure philosophy of the 1933 Act and actually involves merit review of the securities by state officials. Typically, states using merit review refuse to allow sales of securities which do not meet a "fair, just and equitable" standard. The standard may not be met, for example, if the organizers and promoters of the corporation intend to sell to the public at per share prices much greater than they themselves paid.

The third type is *registration by coordination*, which results in automatic state approval whenever a security's registration has become effective under the 1933 Act at the federal level.

Some states allow registration by more than one method.

Exemptions

States' registration laws contain exemptions, as does the 1933 Act. There is an ongoing effort to coordinate state and federal exemptions to produce uniformity. A uniform system of exemptions would greatly simplify matters for a corporation planning a widespread distribution of securities, but the chances of achieving complete uniformity appear slim.

Other Provisions

Many states' securities laws also contain antifraud provisions similar to those in the 1933 and 1934 federal laws. In states without such laws, the courts have extended the common law of fraud to prohibit deceitful securities practices.

Some states also have qualification and registration provisions governing the activities of securities brokers and dealers. Again, the state provisions are usually similar to federal registration provisions in the 1934 Act.

Finally, about thirty-five states have passed rules governing tender offers. The Williams Act adopts a neutral approach, seeking to favor neither the offeror nor the target management, but to serve only the informational needs of the target's shareholders. Many state tender offer laws favor target management by placing significant procedural roadblocks in the offeror's way. A recent Supreme Court decision indicates that state laws which directly contradict the Williams Act in some specific manner are invalid.[7]

Questions and Problems

1. Co-op City was a massive, government-subsidized housing complex, operated as a nonprofit corporation. To acquire an apartment, eligible prospective tenants had to buy eighteen shares of Co-op stock for each room at $25 per share. The purchase was in effect a recoverable deposit. The shares could not be transferred to a non-tenant, did not carry votes as to management of the co-op, and had to be offered to the co-op for sale at the initial selling price whenever the tenant moved out. When rental rates went up, some tenants sued claiming inadequate disclosure under the federal securities law. Discuss whether these "shares of stock," as they were labeled, constituted securities under federal law. (*United States Housing Foundation, Inc. v. Forman*, 421 U.S. 837, 1975.)

2. Holiday Inns' profits for the first quarter of 1975 were 20 cents per share. In the spring of 1976, Holiday Inns made a public offering. Straus purchased Holiday Inns stock on March 23, 1976, but its value declined soon thereafter when it was disclosed that Holiday Inns' profits for the first quarter of 1976 were only 7 cents per share. Plaintiff sued under Section 11 of the 1933 Act because the prospectus had not disclosed the drop in profits. Holiday Inns claimed that of the 13 cent decline, 12 cents occurred in March, and that could not have been known at the time Straus purchased. Discuss Holiday Inns' disclosure responsibilities in light of the concept of materiality. (*Straus v. Holiday Inns, Inc., 460 F.Supp. 729, S.D.N.Y. 1978.)*

3. The SEC sued seeking to enjoin Schlitz Brewing Co. from further violations of the antifraud provisions of the 1933 and 1934 Acts. The suit was predicated on Schlitz's failure to disclose in its registration statements, prospectuses, and periodic

---

[7] *Edgar v. MITE Corp.*, 102 S.Ct. 2629 (1982).

reports that (1) it was involved in a nationwide scheme to induce retailers to purchase Schlitz's products by making kickback payments, and (2) it had violated Spanish tax and exchange laws. Schlitz claimed the omissions were nonmaterial, especially considering that the alleged kickbacks amounted to $3 million compared to Schlitz's annual sales of $1 billion. The SEC claimed they were material because they reflected on the integrity of management. Discuss. (*SEC v. Jos. Schlitz Brewing Co.*, 452 F.Supp. 824, E.D.Wis. 1978.)

4. Plaintiffs were worried about tax liability, so they consulted defendant, a tax adviser. Defendant recommended that plaintiffs look into a particular real estate deal which he described as the "best investment so far as tax shelter is concerned" he had ever seen. Plaintiffs invested in the deal, but did not get the tax break they wanted. Plaintiffs sued defendant under Section 12(2) of the 1933 Act because of alleged misrepresentations the sellers made regarding the property's taxable basis. Defendant was not a seller, so he raised the defense of lack of privity. Discuss. (*Croy v. Campbell*, 624 F.2d 709, 5th Cir. 1980.)

5. Claiming the intrastate exemption of Section 3(a) (11) of the 1933 Act, McDonald Investment Company did not register its offering of shares with the SEC. McDonald is a Minnesota corporation with its only offices in that state. It sold shares to only Minnesota residents. However, the funds were raised to lend to real estate developers in Arizona. Discuss the availability of the exemption. (*SEC v. McDonald Investment Co.*, 343 F. Supp. 343, D.Minn. 1972.)

6. Texas International Airlines (TI) purchased 121,000 shares of National Airlines (National) after it had become a 10 percent owner of National during a takeover attempt. But National negotiated a defensive merger with Pan American, which made its own tender offer which was to be consummated on September 6, 1978. However, TI chose not to wait until that date to sell its shares. Instead, on July 28, 1978, TI sold all its National shares to Pan Am at the tender offer price. TI claimed it had no § 16(b) liability on the 121,000 shares. Correct? (*Texas International Airlines v. National Airlines, Inc.*, 714 F.2d 533, 5th Cir. 1983.)

7. A registered broker-dealer's salesforce repeatedly made false and misleading statements in an effort to sell Lawn-A-Mat common stock. After several complaints were ignored, the SEC sought an injunction to halt the illicit practices. One respondent was the sales supervisor, who was informed of the misdeeds but did not take affirmative steps to prevent a recurrence of the deceit. One issue which arose was whether the SEC would have to prove scienter in order to obtain an injunction against practices which allegedly violated Rule 10b-5. Discuss. (*Aaron v. SEC*, 446 U.S. 680, 1980.)

8. Plaintiff purchased some industrial revenue bonds which turned out to be largely worthless. Later he sued under Rule 10b-5, claiming that the bonds' offering circular contained such fraudulent statements that the bonds could never have been placed on the market without the misrepresentations. However, plaintiff admitted that he had not read the circular before purchasing. Should this admission bar recovery? Discuss. (*Shores v. Sklar*, 647 F.2d 462, 5th Cir. 1981.)

9. The management of IBM decided to omit from its proxy solicitation materials a shareholder proposal calling for an end to all the company's business dealings with Communist countries. This decision was submitted to the SEC for review in accordance with Rule 14a-8. Discuss. (*International Business Machines Corp.*, 1979 *Federal Securities Law Reporter* (CCH) §82,009, 1979.)

10. Pantry Pride made a hostile tender offer for Revlon at $47.50. Revlon engaged in certain defensive tactics, leading Pantry Pride to raise its bid to $53 per share. Revlon's board then approved a deal to sell to Forstmann at $56. Pantry Pride raised its offer to $56.25. Forstmann responded by raising its bid to $57.25, contingent upon Revlon (a) giving it an option to buy two Revlon divisions for $100–175 million below value if another acquiror such as Pantry Pride bought 40% of Revlon, (b) agreeing not to seek out a competing bidder, and (c) paying a $25 million cancellation fee if another acquiror got more than 19.9% of Revlon's stock. Revlon's board consented. Pantry Pride raised its offer to $58, conditioned on cancellation of the favorable provisions to Forstmann. Pantry Pride then went to court challenging the legality of the arrangements with Forstmann as a breach of the Revlon board's fiduciary duty to its shareholders. Discuss. *Revlon, Inc. v. McAndrews & Forbes Holdings, Inc.*, _____ A.2d _____ (Del. 1986).

C · H · A · P · T · E · R 14

EMPLOYMENT LAW
PROTECTION OF THE WORKER'S SAFETY AND WELFARE

As in many other areas of law, the legal principles governing the employer-employee relationship were primarily the product of the courts until this century. In other words, employment law was essentially a part of the body of common law. During the twentieth century, however, actions by Congress, state legislatures, and federal and state administrative agencies have had a far-reaching impact on the law of employment. Many new rights and responsibilities have been incorporated into the employment relationship. For example, laws have been passed to deal with workplace safety, the economic security of disabled and retired workers, employment discrimination, labor-management relations, and a host of other problems.

One very important area of employment law—the law of *agency*—is still governed primarily by common-law principles. These principles give us answers to questions concerning the duties of care, obedience, and loyalty owed by an employee to the employer. The law of agency also is concerned with the liability of an employer for the torts and contracts of employees. These matters were discussed in more detail in Chapter 9. Moreover, the law of **contracts**, which is predominantly common law, continues to have a significant effect on the employment relationship. Many of the rights and responsibilities of this relationship can be, and often are, determined by a contract between the parties. Contract law was discussed in Chapter 8.

This chapter surveys several of the most important statutory laws concerning employment—those dealing with compensation for job-related accidents and diseases, improvement of workplace safety, wage and hour standards, pension plan protection, Social Security, and unemployment compensation. The next two chapters deal with the complex areas of employment discrimination and labor-management relations.

The Employee-Independent Contractor Distinction

In general, the various laws discussed in this and the next two chapters apply to employees, not to independent contractors. A person is an employee when an employer has the right to control the method and manner of doing a particular job. An independent contractor is hired to accomplish a result and is not subject to the employer's control as to the details of performing the work. In most situations the distinction is obvious: for example, a stenographer or factory worker almost always is an employee; a construction contractor hired to erect a building is clearly an independent contractor. When the distinction is not so clear, various factors are taken into account. Some facts which would increase the likelihood of a person being an independent contractor are: (1) the person has his or her own independent business or profession; (2) the person uses his or her own tools, equipment, or workplace to perform the task; (3) the person is paid by the job, not by the hour, week, or month; (4) the person has irregular hours of work; and (5) the person is performing a task that is not part of the employer's regular business. None of these factors automatically makes someone an independent contractor; each must be weighed along with all the other evidence relating to the question of control.

Compensation for Job-Related Injuries and Diseases

On-the-job injuries and work-related diseases have always been with us. These problems, with their enormous social costs and individual tragedies, became much more acute in the latter nineteenth and early twentieth centuries, in part because of rapid industrialization. In addition, there was a growing recognition that society must deal more adequately with a variety of problems facing the workforce.

By this time the principle was already well established in common law that an employer was legally responsible for the injury or death of employees resulting from the employer's negligence (for example, knowingly permitting an unsafe condition in the workplace). An employee seeking compensation for injuries was faced with bringing a lawsuit against an employer who usually had far greater resources. Moreover, the employee was required to prove that the employer had actually been negligent in some particular way, often a difficult task.

The common law also recognized three defenses of the employer that might defeat the employee's claim even if it was proved that the employer had been negligent. The first two, contributory negligence and assumption of risk, were recognized as defenses to a charge of negligence in any setting, including the workplace. The defense of *contributory negligence* completely barred the employee from recovering any compensation for injuries if the employer proved that the employee's own negligence, however slight, had contributed to the injury. The *assumption of risk* defense prevented the employee from prevailing on the claim if it was shown that he or she had known and understood before the injury that danger was present and had voluntarily assumed the risk. The third defense, the *fellow-servant rule*, applied only to a claim of negligence in the employment setting. It excused the employer from responsibility for an employee's on-the-job injury if it was caused by another employee (a "fellow servant"). Thus, the injured employee was denied recovery even if the other employee had been negligent and even if the employer would have been liable had the injury occurred to a nonemployee.

The harshness with which the law treated the disabled employee led to demands for change. Between 1900 and 1910 many states passed statutes modifying the employer's defenses against a claim of negligence. Nonetheless, the employee was still faced with the burden of a lawsuit in which the employer's negligence must be proved. Other legal remedies were urged, and in 1911 the first significant workers' compensation statute was enacted in the United States. Today, all states have enacted such legislation. Similar workers' compensation laws are found in England and the Canadian provinces.

The basic thrust of modern workers' compensation legislation is to provide payments to injured employees for medical expenses and lost income regardless of whether the employer or anyone else was at fault. The costs of paying these benefits, or the premiums for insurance to pay them, are borne by the employer. The payments or premiums are viewed as costs of production and, to the extent permitted by the marketplace, are passed on to the employer's customers in the price of the goods or services sold. Thus, the financial risk of on-the-job injury or work-related disease is at least partly spread across the society that benefited from the injured employee's labor.

The objectives of workers' compensation laws have been achieved only in part during the first seventy years of their existence. In many states the benefits payable to an injured employee traditionally have been set unrealistically low. In addition, certain classes of employers and employees usually were excluded from coverage. As a result, the federal government in 1970 created the National Commission on State Workmen's Compensation Laws to study the problem and make recommendations. In 1972 the Commission issued its report, in which it concluded that state workers' compensation legislation is theoretically sound in its "no-fault" approach to work-related injuries and diseases, but that in most states a number of changes were necessary for the system to achieve its goals. The Commission was particularly concerned about incomplete coverage and inadequate compensation. In 1976 a task force of representatives from several federal government agencies was similarly critical of existing state laws.

Although these groups recommended change, they both felt that a unified federal system of workers' compensation was *not* the answer. Legislation has been introduced in Congress on several occasions that would involve the federal government in setting minimum standards for state workers' compensation laws, but these bills have never received sufficient support to come even close to passage. In the past several years, many state legislatures obviously have noticed the criticisms directed at workers' compensation laws, and have significantly liberalized their provisions in favor of the injured employee.

The remainder of this section examines the basic provisions of state workers' compensation statutes and then briefly discusses several federal statutes which have been enacted by Congress to deal with particular groups of employees.

State Workers' Compensation Laws

General Coverage: Practically all industrial employment is covered by workers' compensation. In about two-thirds of the states, the workers' compensation laws apply regardless of the number of employees a firm has. In the other states, employers with fewer than a specified number of employees (usually three to five) are exempt. Most states exclude farm laborers, domestic servants, and casual employees because their work is often of a sporadic or multi-employer nature. In most states, however, employees who are excluded from required coverage can be covered by workers' compensation if the employer voluntarily chooses to participate.

In addition to covering most private employment, the workers' compensation statutes of almost all states cover state and local government employees. Federal government employees, as well as maritime, railroad, and airline employees, are protected by federal legislation which will be discussed later.

At one time, a substantial number of states had workers' compensation laws which were "elective" rather than "compulsory." Today, however, only three states have elective systems.[1] In these states, an employer may choose not to be governed by the workers' compensation law. In such a case, an injured employee must bring suit against the employer and prove the employer's negligence, but the employer is not permitted to assert the three common-law defenses.

The nationwide trend during the 1970s and 1980s has been to bring more and more employees into state workers' compensation systems, primarily by reducing the number of exemptions from coverage and by changing from elective to compulsory systems. By the mid-1980s approximately

---

[1] As of January 1, 1985, South Carolina, New Jersey, and Texas had elective systems.

90 percent of all civilian employees paid on a wage or salary basis were covered by workers' compensation.

How Workers' Compensation Laws Operate: Assume that Roger, an employee in an aluminum fabricating plant, injures his hand while working. If Roger is covered by workers' compensation he usually cannot sue his employer for damages resulting from the injury.[2] Instead, he notifies his employer of his claim within a prescribed period of time. In many cases, the employer (or the employer's insurance carrier) will simply pay the employee the amount prescribed by state law, and the claim will be settled. On the other hand, if the employer or insurance company feels there is a question about the nature or severity of the injury, or perhaps whether it was job-related at all, a settlement may not be forthcoming. In such a case, the employee must file a formal claim with the designated state agency. In a few states, such claims are filed directly in a court, but in most states they are filed with an administrative agency.[3] These agencies are given various names, such as Industrial Accident Board or Workers' Compensation Commission.

A No-Fault System: As mentioned previously, workers' compensation is a no-fault system. If the agency (or the court) decides that the injury was job-related, compensation is awarded regardless of whether the employer, employee, or anyone else was at fault. The employee does not have to prove that the employer was negligent, and there are virtually no defenses. The major exception is that workers' compensation does not cover intentionally self-inflicted injuries. There may, of course, be a controversy as to the nature or extent of the injury, but such a controversy is resolved by the agency or court as are other factual disputes—on the basis of the evidence.

Appeal: Either party can appeal if dissatisfied with the initial ruling. In most states the appeal is from the agency to a court. In those few states in which a court makes the initial ruling, the appeal is to a higher court.

Outsiders: Even though workers' compensation laws ordinarily do not permit an injured employee to sue the employer or another employee for negligence, such a suit can be brought against an outsider who caused the injury. For example, if the employee's injury is caused by a defectively made machine that the employer had purchased, the employee will be able to sue the machine's manufacturer on the basis of negligence or strict tort liability.[4] Similarly, suppose that the employer had hired an independent contractor to renovate its business premises, and the job had been done negligently. If, be-

---

[2] In the rare case in which the employee can prove that the employer *intentionally* caused the injury or was guilty of *gross negligence*, the employee is permitted to sue the employer.

[3] Even if a claim is settled, the employer must report the injury to the agency or court.

[4] See Chapter 18 for a detailed discussion of products liability.

cause of this negligence, a newly installed light fixture falls on an employee, he or she usually can sue the independent contractor.[5]

Course of Employment: The typical workers' compensation statute provides coverage for "personal injury caused by accidents arising out of and in the course of employment." Under such a standard, many injuries are clearly job related and thus covered without question. An employee working in a factory who suffers a back injury while carrying a heavy load as part of his job duties is obviously covered by workers' compensation. Employees usually are also covered while engaging in actions that are reasonably incidental to job duties. For example, an employee on a lunch break who slips and falls in the employer's cafeteria would be covered. Similarly, an employee who uses shower facilities provided by the employer at the workplace will be covered for an injury from a fall while showering.

Sometimes, however, a difficult course-of-employment question can be presented. Suppose that an employee is injured while attending an employer-sponsored activity such as a company picnic. If attendance was required explicitly, or if the evidence indicates that attendance was implicitly required because failure to attend such functions could adversely affect an employee's career, an injury suffered at the picnic would be covered. The question whether the activity was implicitly required is often a very close one.

An employee whose job requires travel will normally be able to receive workers' compensation benefits for almost any injury related to the various risks involved in traveling. Automobile accidents while traveling for the employer clearly would be included. In addition, injuries sustained while stopping to help a stranded motorist or to direct traffic at the scene of an accident, for example, would be covered. An employee is usually not covered, however, while merely commuting between home and work.

When an employee's job responsibilities require him or her to be away from home on a 24-hour basis, the course of employment is expanded to include virtually all reasonable activities. For example, if Jones's employer sends her to another city on business for two weeks, Jones obviously would be covered by workers' compensation while traveling and also while actually doing the employer's business in the other city. In addition, Jones would be within the course of employment while staying in the hotel, going out to dinner, or attending a concert during the evening in the other city. Any such voluntary activity that is reasonable and does not greatly increase the employee's risk of injury is normally covered by workers' compensation in the away-from-home situation. On the other hand, if Jones went skydiving or

[5] In cases where an outsider is responsible, damages collected from the outsider generally are deducted from the amount for which the employer or its insurance carrier are responsible under workers' compensation law. Or, the employer or insurance carrier may initially pay the employee's workers' compensation claim and then sue the outsider. Any money recovered from the outsider above the amount of the workers' compensation claim would have to be paid over to the employee.

drove a car in a demolition derby during her off hours in the other city, any resulting injury probably would not be covered by workers' compensation because the activity greatly increased her risk of injury.

In the common situation in which an employee's injury occurs while he or she is on the employer's premises, the agencies and courts generally have shown a tendency in recent years to rule in the employee's favor when the course of employment question is a close one. On the other hand, an agency or court will only go so far—the injury must have at least some reasonable relation to the employee's work. For instance, an injury incurred by an employee while fighting, playing a practical joke, or otherwise clearly departing from job duties will not be covered unless the evidence demonstrates that the employer or a supervisor knew that such activities were customary and did not take adequate steps to stop them. The following case illustrates the usual approach of courts when they have to decide whether (and under what circumstances) an employee's departure from duties should cause a denial of workers' compensation benefits.

Segler v. The Industrial Commission,
Supreme Court of Illinois
406 N.E.2d 542 (1980)

Gary Segler was employed by Caterpillar Tractor Co. as a "punch-out monitor" in one of its factories. Approximately twenty to twenty-five feet from his work station, there was a large industrial oven, through which passed a conveyor-roller system. Block-like thirty-inch-high flasks, which contained molds, were fixed at regular intervals on the conveyor. They were transported on the conveyor into the oven. Segler testified that, in order to reach his work area, he was regularly required to pass through the spaces between the flasks.

One morning, the conveyor system was not operating, but the oven was warm. Segler, having previously observed one employee put food into the oven, placed a frozen pot pie on a shelf inside the oven. Approximately thirty minutes later, as he reached into the oven to retrieve the pie, the conveyor system was started. The flask nearest the oven struck and moved Segler's right foot, placing him in a position between one flask and the oven. A vertically protruding pin, approximately 1½ inches in diameter and 3½ inches high, affixed to the advancing flask, struck Segler's left hip, forcing him against the oven. Thus wedged, Segler was injured as the flask pin tore through his left, then his right, hip and buttocks.

Segler (claimant) filed a claim for workers' compensation benefits with the Illinois Industrial Commission. The Commission denied Segler's claim, ruling that his injury had not arisen out of and in the course of his employment. Segler appealed to the Circuit Court of Peoria County, which affirmed the Commission's decision. Segler then appealed to the Illinois Supreme Court.

Moran, Justice:

. . . An injury is compensable under workmen's compensation only if it arose out of and in the course of employment. To "arise out of" employment, an injury must have its origin in some risk connected or incidental to the employee's duties so that there is a causal connection between the injury and the employment. An injury is "in the course of" employment when it occurs within the period of employment, at a place where the employee can reasonably be expected to be in the performance of his duties, and while he is performing those duties or doing something incidental thereto. Acts of personal comfort are generally held to be incidental to employment duties and, thus, are in the course of employment. However, if the employee voluntarily and in an unexpected manner exposes himself to a risk outside any reasonable exercise of his duties, any injury incurred as a result will not be within the course of employment.

In the present case, the claimant was not in the reasonable exercise of his duties at the time the injury occurred. He was performing no job task in that area, and his actions cannot be thought of as beneficial to the employer. Instead, the claimant voluntarily undertook a course of action solely for his own benefit, thereby exposing himself to a risk greater than that to which he would have been exposed had he been pursuing his assigned duties at his designated work area 25 feet away. His actions were, in fact, unnecessary, inherently dangerous and unreasonable.

Despite the fact that an employee chooses an unreasonable and unnecessary risk, the employer may, nonetheless, be held liable if he has knowledge of or has acquiesced in such a practice or custom. In the present case, however, there is no basis for finding that the employer had knowledge of or acquiesced in such an act. The claimant himself testified that, during the 1½ years he had worked in this area, he had seen only one person place food in the oven.

The claimant argues that his injuries are compensable since he was regularly required to pass over the conveyor in order to get to and from his work area and since his act of placing a pot pie in the oven exposed him to no greater risk than that to which he was daily exposed. At the time of injury, however, claimant was not going to and from his work station and was, in fact, between the oven and a flask, not between two fixed flasks, his customary point of crossing the conveyor.

We have often stated the rule that it is within the unique province of the Commission to draw inferences from facts presented and to determine whether the injury was the result of unreasonable, unexpected and unnecessary risks to which an employee voluntarily exposed himself. We find that, under the instant circumstances, the Commission could find that the claimant's conduct constituted an unreasonable risk and, consequently, that the injury did not arise out of or in the course of employment. Such a conclusion is not against the manifest weight of the evidence.

Judgment affirmed.

★ ★ ★

Occupational Diseases: Workers' compensation laws originally made no provision for job-related diseases. Today, however, all states provide coverage for them. Thus, an employee who has incurred a disease "arising out of and in the course of employment" may recover essentially the same benefits as one who has suffered an on-the-job injury. Most such diseases result from prolonged exposure to certain substances in the workplace. Examples include silicosis from silicon, asbestosis from asbestos, and radiation disability from radioactive materials.[6] Loss of hearing from prolonged noise exposure is another example.

In recent years the issue of job-related *stress* has been especially troublesome for courts and workers' compensation commissions. Sometimes the continual physical or psychological stress of an occupation actually disables a worker by causing an emotional breakdown or physical illness such as a heart attack or an ulcer. When there is clear proof that job stress was the primary cause of the disabling condition, should the condition be treated as a compensable injury or disease? The commissions and courts have said yes when stress is proved to have caused an identifiable *physical* ailment. When the stress has caused a purely psychological or emotional disability, commissions and courts in a majority of states have held that the disability is covered by workers' compensation, but in a number of states they have held that it is not covered.

Insurance Requirements: In all states, an employer who is subject to the workers' compensation law is required to insure against employees' claims for benefits. Ordinarily the employer meets this requirement by purchasing insurance from a private insurance carrier. In six states, however, employers must pay premiums to a state-administered insurance fund rather than to a private carrier.

In forty-seven states employers are permitted the option of self-insuring. In other words, under state supervision an employer can set up a reserve fund to cover claims and regularly contribute to it instead of paying insurance premiums. Generally, only a large company with many employees is capable of self-insuring. However, twenty-six states do permit smaller employers to join together in a group self-insurance pool.

Benefits: The benefits payable as the result of a job-related injury or disease are of four types: *medical*, *income replacement*, *death*, and *rehabilitation*.

Medical Benefits: Perhaps the most important workers' compensation benefit received by an injured employee is the payment of all medical expenses. This payment is usually provided without any dollar or time limits.

Income Replacement: An injured employee who misses work and consequently loses income is entitled to cash benefits to partially replace the lost income. In all states a waiting period must elapse before income replacement benefits are payable. In other words, the employee must be out of work for a certain period of time before there is a right to this type of compensation.

[6] Coal miners suffering from black lung disease as a result of prolonged exposure to coal dust are covered by separate federal legislation, the Black Lung Act.

The typical waiting period ranges from three to seven days. However, if the disability continues for more than a specified time (from one to six weeks in various states), benefits are made retroactive to the actual date of injury.

The benefits payable, and the method of calculation, depend on the extent (total or partial) and the duration (permanent or temporary) of the disability. Most of the benefits paid are for either temporary total or permanent partial disability. For example, an employee who breaks a leg and cannot work for three months has a temporary total disability. Income replacement benefits in such a case will be a certain percentage (usually 66⅔, but ranging from 60 to 90) of the employee's current average weekly wages. In many states, the amount of the payment is subject to minimum and maximum limits. This weekly amount is paid for the duration of the disability. Of course, total disability sometimes is permanent, such as a paralyzing or brain-damaging injury. In such cases, most state laws provide for permanent payment of the specified weekly amount.[7] In a few states, however, a time limit is placed on payments for permanent total disability (such as five hundred weeks in Indiana).

An injury that causes only a partial inability to continue at one's job may also be of either a temporary or permanent nature. The loss, or loss of use, of a member of the body is one type of injury resulting in permanent partial disability. Most states provide specified lump-sum compensation for so-called *scheduled injuries*. In other words, the law includes a schedule, or list, of body members and a set amount of compensation for the loss of that particular member. For example, an employee losing the sight in one eye as a result of an on-the-job accident would receive an amount ranging from $9,000 in North Dakota to $76,610 in Connecticut. In addition to the scheduled amount, most state laws also would provide this employee with benefits for temporary total disability during recovery.

Death Benefits: When an industrial accident or occupational disease causes death, the laws of all states provide for benefits to be paid to the worker's spouse and children. The amount usually varies with the number of dependents and is a stated percentage of the employee's average weekly wages. In most states these payments are subject to minimum and maximum limitations. Death benefits to a spouse ordinarily terminate upon remarriage, and benefits for children cease when they reach a certain age. Several states also impose a maximum time limit (such as 450 weeks in Mississippi) on the payment of death benefits regardless of a spouse's remarriage or the age of children.

Rehabilitation Benefits: In addition to helping ease the financial burden of job-related injuries and diseases, workers' compensation also should attempt to return the worker to productivity as soon as possible. In fur-

---

[7] Most state laws now provide for annual increases to compensate for inflation.

therance of this objective, almost all states require that at least some financial assistance be provided for rehabilitative therapy and training.

Federal Workers' Compensation Laws

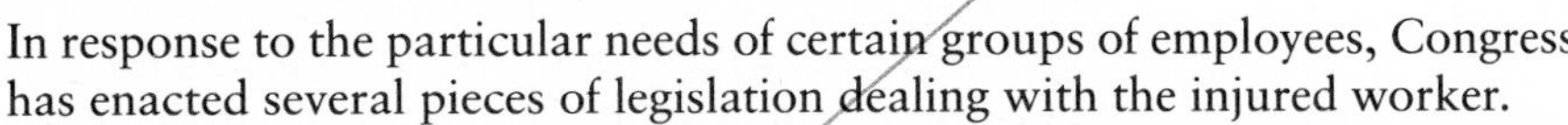

In response to the particular needs of certain groups of employees, Congress has enacted several pieces of legislation dealing with the injured worker.

The Federal Employees' Compensation Act (FECA) provides a comprehensive workers' compensation system for civilian employees of the federal government. The provisions of FECA are very much like those of the typical state workers' compensation statute, except that its benefits are significantly higher.

The Longshoremen's and Harbor Workers' Compensation Act (Longshore Act) provides a compensation system for dock workers. It, too, is similar to most state workers' compensation laws, but with generally higher benefits.

The job-injury law for employees of interstate railroads and airlines is the Federal Employers' Liability Act (FELA). FELA is quite different from other workers' compensation laws in that it does not provide for a no-fault system. Instead, the employer is liable for an employee's injury only if the employer was negligent. The employer's common-law defenses against a claim of negligence, however, have been almost completely abrogated. The only substantive defense remaining under the FELA is *comparative negligence*. In other words, if a jury concludes that the employee's own negligence contributed a certain percentage to the injury, the amount of damages is reduced by that percentage. Another federal law, the Jones Act, applies the rules of FELA to workers on seagoing vessels.

Promoting Job Safety and Health

With regard to job-related accidents and diseases, the goal of society should be *prevention*, not just compensation. Workers' compensation laws have had little effect on the accident and disease rate. By the late 1960s, when workers' compensation laws had been on the books for fifty years or more, about 14,500 persons were killed annually as a result of industrial accidents. Approximately 2.2 million workers were disabled on the job each year, causing an annual loss of 250 million employee work days. An estimated 390,000 workers each year developed occupational diseases. Moreover, the rate of industrial accidents and diseases continued to increase at an alarming rate. If workers' compensation laws had provided more liberal employee benefits and thus placed more financial responsibility on employers, perhaps there would have been a greater incentive to make the workplace safer.

Most states had industrial safety laws as early as 1920. These laws obviously were ineffective. Congress had enacted specialized safety legislation before 1970. For example, the Coal Mine Safety Act was passed in 1952 and was superseded in 1969 by the Coal Mine Health and Safety Act. The Maritime Safety Act was made law in 1958 to improve working conditions of maritime employees. In 1966, Congress passed the Metal and Nonmetallic Mine Safety Act. In 1969 legislation was adopted to establish safety standards on federally funded construction projects. The Federal Railway Act of 1970 contained several provisions aimed at employee safety.

These specialized statutes paved the way for a more comprehensive response to the job safety problem—the Occupational Safety and Health Act of 1970, in which Congress attempted to promote health and safety across all segments of American industry.

The Occupational Safety and Health Act of 1970

General Coverage: The Occupational Safety and Health Act, usually referred to as OSHA, covers almost all private employers. It also applies to the federal government as an employer, but not to state and local governments. Small farms, employing ten or fewer workers, are exempt unless they use migrant labor camps. In addition, employers already regulated by specialized federal safety legislation, such as the Coal Mine Health and Safety Act, are exempt from OSHA.

Standards: OSHA places the responsibility for developing detailed occupational safety and health standards on the Secretary of Labor. The Secretary carries out this responsibility through the Occupational Safety and Health Administration (also called OSHA, or sometimes the OSH Administration), which is part of the U.S. Department of Labor.[8] These standards usually are *affirmative* rather than *prohibitive*. In other words, OSHA standards ordinarily do not prohibit particular actions. Instead, they affirmatively require the maintenance of safe conditions, or the adoption and use of one or more practices, methods, or operations necessary to make the workplace safer.

When OSHA was passed, many safety standards had already been developed by private standard-setting organizations, industry trade associations, and other government agencies. The Labor Department adopted many of these preexisting standards as its own in order to bring them under the uniform interpretative and enforcement procedures of OSHA. For example, a number of OSHA standards have come from the American National Standards Institute and the American Society for Testing and Materials. One of OSHA's most important standards, dealing with electrical wiring in the workplace, was taken primarily from the National Electrical Code. This code had been developed previously by the National Fire Protection Association. An example of standards developed under prior federal legislation

[8] In referring to the Labor Department in this discussion of OSHA, we usually are referring to the Labor Department's Occupational Safety and Health Administration.

and subsequently adopted by the Labor Department are the safety rules for federally financed construction projects.

The Labor Department also has developed, and continues to develop, many new standards. In doing so, it relies heavily on the recommendations of the National Institute for Occupational Safety and Health (NIOSH). This agency, which operates as part of the Department of Health and Human Services, was created by Congress to conduct studies and research for the development of recommended safety and health standards. Prior to considering a new standard, the Labor Department also will consult frequently with one or more advisory committees. These committees consist of representatives from management, labor, the public, and the occupational safety and health professions, appointed by the Secretary of Labor and the Secretary of Health and Human Services. It also must be kept in mind that the adoption of standards under OSHA is a type of government agency rulemaking. As a result, such adoption normally must be preceded by notice to affected parties, a public hearing, and opportunity for public comment.

A few examples of standards developed under OSHA include rules mandating eye goggles for employees operating saws, sanders, and similar equipment; maximum noise levels; protective guards on various kinds of factory machines; maximum levels of exposure to toxic substances such as lead and asbestos; and safety nets, scaffolds, temporary floors, or other safety devices for employees working more than twenty-five feet above the ground.

The General Duty Clause: OSHA contains a provision, often referred to as the "general duty clause," which defines an employer's basic obligation to its employees where no specific standards are applicable. Under the general duty clause, an employer is required to provide every employee with a workplace that is free from recognized hazards which are actually causing or are likely to cause death or serious physical harm. In speaking of "recognized" hazards, OSHA is referring to conditions that generally would be considered hazardous in the industry involved, or that an employer knew or should have known were hazardous.

In *REA Express, Inc. v. Brennan*,[9] an employer was ruled to have violated the clause by permitting untrained employees to attempt electrical repairs on a wet concrete floor without protective equipment. In other cases, violations have been found where an employer failed to brace a free-standing wall on a construction site, operated a freight elevator with its rear shaftway doors open, and transported farmworkers in a standing position amid unsecured cargo in the back of a truck.

Rights and Responsibilities of Employees: The law not only imposes a duty on the employer to keep the workplace safe and follow OSHA standards,

---

[9] 495 F.2d 822 (2d Cir. 1974).

but it also requires the *employee* to comply with prescribed safety and health rules. An employee's willful failure to comply is grounds for dismissal.

In addition to this duty of compliance, an employee also has the right to avoid unreasonably dangerous situations. When the employee (1) acts in good faith, (2) has a reasonable basis for believing that an assigned task poses a substantial risk of serious injury or death, and (3) has a reasonable belief that disobeying the employer is the only available alternative, the employee may refuse to perform the task. Under these conditions, the employee is protected by OSHA from being dismissed or otherwise penalized by the employer.

Recordkeeping and Notice Requirements: Employers with more than ten employees are required to keep detailed records of most types of job-related injuries and illnesses. In a special log supplied by the Labor Department, an *injury* must be recorded within six days after the employer learns of it if the injury resulted in (1) death, (2) one or more lost workdays, (3) restriction of work or motion, (4) loss of consciousness, (5) transfer to another job, or (6) medical treatment other than first aid. A job-related *illness* must be recorded regardless of its severity. Records relating to a particular injury or illness must be retained for at least five years after the date of the occurrence, and must be made available for inspection by the Labor Department or the relevant state agency. Annual summaries of this data must be posted where notices to employees are customarily posted. This has to be done no later than February 1 and kept there until March 1. In addition, some employers are selected each year for required participation in a statistical survey of occupational injuries and illnesses.

If an on-the-job accident occurs which results in the death of an employee or the hospitalization of five or more employees, all employers (regardless of size) must immediately report the accident in detail to the nearest office of the Labor Department's Occupational Safety and Health Administration.

Inspections: In addition to developing standards, the Labor Department's Occupational Safety and Health Administration also has responsibility for enforcing OSHA. Unannounced inspections of workplaces are conducted by the agency's compliance officers.[10] In *Marshall v. Barlow's, Inc.*,[11] the Supreme Court dealt with the question whether such an inspection requires a search warrant under the Fourth Amendment to the Constitution. The Court held that a warrant is required if the employer demands it. This requirement has had little effect on OSHA enforcement for two reasons. First, only about 2.5 percent of employers have been demanding a search warrant. Second, the warrant is much easier to obtain than it is in a criminal inves-

[10] Any person giving unauthorized advance notice of an OSHA inspection may be punished by a fine of up to $1,000, imprisonment for up to six months, or both.

[11] 436 U.S. 307 (1978).

tigation. A federal court or magistrate will issue a warrant for OSHA purposes if it appears either (1) that there was a reasonable, *uniformly applied* basis for selecting that particular workplace for inspection or (2) that the Labor Department is acting pursuant to an employee complaint. The reasonable basis could include a history of violations by the employer, or a high accident or disease rate in the particular industry. In the case of employee complaints, the Labor Department must have reasonable grounds to believe that a violation of the law or a danger to health and safety exists.

The compliance officer must present proper credentials before conducting the inspection. The employer or its representative, plus a representative of the employees, are entitled to accompany the compliance officer during an inspection. Employees also may be interviewed privately. They may not be discriminated against in any way for having originally filed a complaint or for subsequently cooperating with a compliance officer. After the inspection a closing conference is held, in which the compliance officer and employer discuss workplace conditions and any possible violations.

Citations: If the inspection discloses violations of OSHA, the Labor Department will usually issue and mail a written citation to the employer. This must be done as soon as possible, but never later than six months after the alleged violation. A copy of the citation must be posted at the workplace near the site of the violation. The citation describes the nature of the alleged violation and fixes a reasonable time for correction ("abatement") of the condition. If a penalty is assessed, it must be stated in the citation. Penalties may be as much as $1,000 for each violation. Whether a penalty is assessed, and its amount, are determined by the seriousness of the violation as well as the employer's size, good faith, and past history of compliance. Repeated or willful violations can result in penalties of as much as $10,000 each. In addition, the employer can be criminally prosecuted for a willful violation that caused death.

The employer, an employee, or an authorized employee representative (such as a union) may contest the alleged violation, abatement date, or proposed penalty. A notice of contest must be filed with the Occupational Safety and Health Administration within fifteen working days after receipt of the citation, or it becomes final. If the citation is contested, it will be reviewed by the Occupational Safety and Health Review Commission, an independent quasi-judicial administrative agency created solely for this purpose. The decision of the Review Commission may be appealed to a federal court of appeals.

State Enforcement Plans

One of the primary reasons for OSHA's enactment was that the states had not taken adequate steps to promote job safety and health. In addition to providing for a uniform federal safety and health program, OSHA also encourages individual states to develop new measures. Under Section 18 of OSHA, a state may submit a safety and health regulatory plan to the Labor Department. If the Department concludes that the state plan contains standards and enforcement procedures which are at least as effective as OSHA's, it will approve the plan. In a state with an approved plan, the Labor Department relinquishes jurisdiction to state authorities. However, the Department will continue to monitor the state's activities and will revoke its approval if enforcement procedures prove to be inadequate. As of this writing, twenty-three states and two territories had approved plans, although seven of these states withdrew their plans after federal approval.

An Appraisal of OSHA

During the first few years after OSHA's passage, its implementation and enforcement by the Labor Department were severely criticized. A number of OSHA standards, often consisting of dozens of pages each, concerned matters that were quite trivial. OSHA seemed more concerned with things such as bathroom locations, design of toilet seats, and the details of how ladders should be built than with major workplace hazards.

In the late 1970s and early 1980s, the Labor Department began to focus its enforcement efforts on more important hazards and on particular high-risk industries. In late 1981, the Department announced that it would no longer conduct routine inspections of workplaces in industries with relatively low accident rates. In such industries, of course, the Department will still respond to employee complaints about specific hazards. In addition, an intensified effort has been made in recent years to reduce worker exposure to carcinogens and other toxic substances.

The Department has simplified many of its standards and repealed a number of others. In some cases, performance-oriented standards have replaced earlier, more complex ones. In other words, simple standards stating broad goals but leaving the method of achieving those goals to individual employers have been substituted for some of the detailed procedures for achieving worker protection.

Paperwork requirements have been reduced somewhat, particularly for small businesses. In addition, recent amendments have provided that no penalties may be assessed for first-time nonserious violations unless ten or more violations are discovered during an inspection. These same amendments state that no penalties may be assessed against small employers who have requested on-site consultation and make good faith efforts to correct the violations.

OSHA and its enforcement have become more sensible and realistic as a result of these changes. The most important question, however, is whether OSHA and its enforcement have improved workplace safety. After a noticeable decline in the job accident and disease rate during the mid-1970s, the rate began to climb late in the decade and was almost as high at the end of the decade as it had been at the beginning. From 1980 to 1983 the rate again declined substantially, and despite another rise in 1984 the rate was significantly lower in the mid-1980s than it had been in 1970. It is impossible to know how much OSHA contributed to this overall decline, but a reasonable assumption is that the federal regulatory action has played some part.

The following case provides a concluding overview of OSHA by showing how an OSHA standard dealing with a major employee health problem, brown lung disease, was developed, put into effect, and challenged by a group of employers.

American Textile Manufacturers v. Donovan
U.S. Supreme Court
452 U.S. 490
(1981)

The air in cotton mills ordinarily contains substantial amounts of cotton dust. Cotton dust has been defined as "dust present in the air during the handling or processing of cotton, which may contain a mixture of many substances including ground up plant matter, fiber, bacteria, fungi, soil, pesticides, non-cotton plant matter and other contaminants which may have accumulated with the cotton during the growing, harvesting, and subsequent processing or storage periods."

The inhaling of cotton dust for a prolonged period of time can cause byssinosis, often called "brown lung" disease. In its mildest form, byssinosis produces chest tightness, shortness of breath, coughing, and wheezing. In its most serious form, it is a chronic, irreversible, and completely disabling lung disease. The advanced stage of byssinosis is clinically similar to severe emphysema or asthma and can cause sudden death from heart failure as a result of strain on the cardiovascular system. The disease sometimes advances through different stages, but in many cases the advanced stage will suddenly appear. Studies showed that at least 25 percent of cotton mill workers suffered some form of byssinosis.

In 1968, two years before OSHA's enactment, the Labor Department had limited cotton dust at mills doing government contract work to 1.0 milligrams per cubic meter of air (1.0 mg/m^3) averaged over an eight-hour day. Shortly after the enactment of OSHA, the Department, acting through its Occupational Safety and Health Administration, adopted this exposure limit as a temporary OSHA standard for all cotton mills. After extensive research and study, the National Institute for Occupational Safety and Health (NIOSH) in 1974 adopted a new measurement unit of "respirable" (particles small enough to enter the lungs) rather than total dust, and recommended that worker exposure be limited to 0.2 mg/m^3 of respirable dust.

In late 1976 the Labor Department formally proposed the 0.2 mg/m^3 limit as a permanent OSHA standard for all segments of the cotton industry. Interested parties were invited to submit written comments, and public hearings were held at several locations across the nation in 1977. Public participation was widespread, involving representatives from industry and the workforce, scientists, economists, industrial hygienists, and many others. The comments

and the transcript of the written and oral testimony given at these hearings filled 105,000 pages.

In 1978, the department promulgated a final cotton dust standard. The standard limited worker exposure to respirable cotton dust, averaged over an eight-hour period, to 0.2 mg/m^3 in yarn manufacturing, 0.75 mg/m^3 in slashing and weaving operations, and 0.5 mg/m^3 in all other cotton industry processes. The Department chose an implementation strategy for the standard that depended primarily on a mix of engineering controls, such as installation of ventilation systems, and work practice controls, such as special floor sweeping procedures. Full compliance was required within four years, except to the extent that employers could establish that the engineering and work practice controls were infeasible. During this compliance period, and at certain other times, the standard required employers to provide respirators to employees. Other requirements included monitoring cotton dust exposure, medical surveillance of all employees, annual medical examinations, employee education and training programs, and posting of warning signs. Another provision required employers to transfer employees unable to wear respirators to another position, if available, having a dust level at or below the required limits, with "no loss of earnings or other employment rights or benefits as a result of the transfer."

The American Textile Manufacturers Institute and others representing the cotton industry challenged the validity of the standard in a U.S. Court of Appeals. The basis for this challenge was that the Labor Department's Occupational Safety and Health Administration (officially acting under the name of Donovan, the Secretary of Labor) had not engaged in "cost-benefit analysis" prior to adopting the standard. A U.S. Court of Appeals upheld the standard, and the textile manufacturers appealed to the U.S. Supreme Court.

Brennan, Justice:

. . . The principal question presented in this case is whether the Occupational Safety and Health Act requires the [Labor Department], in promulgating a standard pursuant to § 6(b) (5) of the Act, to determine that the costs of the standard bear a reasonable relationship to its benefits. [The manufacturers] urge not only that [the Department] must show that a standard addresses a significant risk of material health impairment, but also that [it] must demonstrate that the reduction in risk of material health impairment is significant in light of the costs of attaining that reduction. [The Department contends] on the other hand that the Act requires [it] to promulgate standards that eliminate or reduce such risks "to the extent such protection is technologically and economically feasible."

The starting point of our analysis is the language of the statute itself. Section 6(b) (5) of the Act provides:

The Secretary, in promulgating standards dealing with toxic materials or harmful physical agents under this subsection, shall set the standard which most adequately assures, to the extent feasible, *on the basis of the best available evidence, that no employee will suffer material impairment of health or functional capacity even if such employee has regular exposure to the hazard dealt with by such standard for the period of his working life.* [Emphasis added.]

Although their interpretations differ, all parties agree that the phrase "to the extent feasible" contains the critical language in § 6(b) (5) for purposes of this case.

The plain meaning of the word "feasible" supports [the Department's] interpretation of the statute. According to Webster's Third New International Dictionary of the English Language, "feasible" means "capable of being done, executed, or effected." Thus, § 6(b) (5) directs the [Labor Department] to issue the standard that "most adequately assures . . . that no employee will suffer material impairment of health," limited only by the extent to which this is "capable of being done." In effect then, as the Court of Appeals held, Congress itself defined the basic relationship between costs and benefits, by placing the "benefit" of worker health above all other considerations [except] those making attainment of this "benefit" unachievable. Any standard based on a balancing of costs and benefits by the [Labor Department] that strikes a different balance than that struck by Congress would be inconsistent with the command set forth in § 6(b)(5). Thus, cost-benefit analysis by OSHA is not required by the statute because feasibility analysis is.

When Congress has intended that an agency engage in cost-benefit analysis, it has clearly indicated such intent on the face of the statute. . . . A recent example is the Outer Continental Shelf Lands Act Amendments of 1978, providing that offshore drilling operations shall use:

the best available and safest technologies which the Secretary [of the Interior] determines to be economically feasible, *wherever failure of equipment would have a significant effect on safety, health, or the environment, except where the Secretary determines that the* incremental benefits are clearly insufficient to justify the incremental costs of using such technologies.

This and other statutes demonstrate that Congress uses specific language when intending that an agency engage in cost-benefit analysis. . . .

The legislative history of the [Occupational Safety and Health] Act, while concededly not crystal clear, provides general support for [the Labor Department's] interpretation of the Act. The congressional reports and debates certainly confirm that Congress meant "feasible" and nothing else in using that term. Congress was concerned that the Act might be thought to require achievement of absolute safety, an impossible standard, and therefore insisted that health and safety goals be capable of economic and technological accomplishment. . . .

Not only does the legislative history confirm that Congress meant "feasible" rather than "cost-benefit" when it used the former term, but it also shows that Congress understood that the Act would create substantial costs for employers, yet intended to impose such costs when necessary to create a safe and healthful working environment. Congress viewed the costs of health and safety as a cost of doing business. Senator Yarborough, a cosponsor of the bill, stated: "We know the costs would be put into consumer goods but that is the price we should pay for the 80 million workers in America." He asked:

> *One may well ask too expensive for whom? Is it too expensive for the company who for lack of proper safety equipment loses the services of its skilled employees? Is it too expensive for the employee who loses his hand or leg or eyesight? Is it too expensive for the widow trying to raise her children on meager allowance under workmen's compensation and social security? And what about the man—a good hardworking man—tied to a wheel chair or hospital bed for the rest of his life? That is what we are dealing with when we talk about industrial safety. . . . We are talking about people's lives, not the indifference of some cost accountants.*

Senator Eagleton commented that "the costs that will be incurred by employers in meeting the standards of health and safety to be established under this bill are, in my view, *reasonable and necessary costs of doing business.*"

Other Members of Congress voiced similar views. Nowhere is there any indication that Congress contemplated a different balancing by OSHA of the benefits of worker health and safety against the costs of achieving them. Indeed Congress thought that the *financial costs* of health and safety problems in the workplace were as large or larger than the *financial costs* of eliminating these problems. In its statement of findings and declaration of purpose encompassed in the Act itself, Congress announced that "personal injuries and illnesses arising out of work situations impose a substantial burden upon, and are a hindrance to, interstate commerce in terms of lost production, wage loss, medical expenses, and disability compensation payment."

[The judgment of the Court of Appeals is affirmed. The Labor Department did not have to use cost-benefit analysis in promulgating the cotton-dust standard. The standard is valid.]

★★★

Regulating Labor Standards

Prior to the Great Depression of the 1930s, the federal government had not been significantly involved in the regulation of basic labor standards. As a safety measure Congress in 1907 had set a maximum sixteen-hour day for certain interstate railroad workers, but wage and hour legislation had otherwise been left to the states. During the late 1800s and early 1900s, a substantial number of states enacted legislation setting minimum wages and maximum hours for women and children because they were viewed as having insufficient bargaining power for self-protection. Several states also had maximum hour statutes for workers in certain hazardous occupations.

In 1933, with national unemployment at 25 percent, Congress attempted to limit hours of work so as to spread available employment over a larger segment of the population. This legislation, the National Industrial Recovery Act (NIRA), also contained other provisions aimed at relieving the depressed state of the economy. In 1935, however, the statute was declared unconstitutional by the Supreme Court, partly because it delegated too much legislative power to the executive branch without sufficient guidelines.[12]

In 1938 Congress passed our present federal wage and hour law, the Fair Labor Standards Act (FLSA). It is a law which, in essence, establishes a floor for wage rates and requires that employees be paid a premium for overtime work. FLSA also contains protective child labor provisions.[13] The ultimate goal of the law was to upgrade labor standards and create a somewhat more realistic relationship between workers' earnings and the cost of living, and thereby reduce poverty.

The Fair Labor Standards Act

Basic Coverage: The coverage of the Fair Labor Standards Act (FLSA) is extremely broad. In the case of a private employer, an employee ordinarily will be covered by the Act if any aspect of the employer's business enterprise has any involvement with interstate commerce. Moreover, all civilian employees of the federal government and all state and local government workers are covered by FLSA. As we will see in the next section, however, FLSA rules on "overtime" are somewhat different for state and local government workers than for other types of employees.

The Act specifically exempts some employees from its minimum wage and overtime provisions. Employees with substantial managerial or supervisory responsibilities are excluded from FLSA. In addition, outside salespeople and professional employees such as lawyers and accountants are not covered by the Act. These types of employees would rarely benefit from the minimum wage provisions, and the nature of their work is often such that it cannot fit a normal workweek schedule for overtime purposes. Moreover, they normally have more opportunities to protect themselves economically than many other types of employees.

Employees who are members of a union having a collective bargaining agreement with the employer are not covered by FLSA's overtime provisions if the agreement provides for certain maximum hours over a six-month or one-year period. In this latter situation, Congress viewed the overtime provisions of FLSA as unnecessary.

FLSA also exempts the employees of certain small retail stores and small farms, many of which could not bear the cost of compliance. To encourage

---

[12] *Schechter Poultry Corp. v. United States*, 295 U.S. 495 (1935). The Court also took a much more restrictive view of congressional power over interstate commerce than it does today, and held that Congress had exceeded its constitutional authority by regulating an essentially local activity.

[13] In 1963 Congress added the Equal Pay Act to FLSA. Since it focuses on sex discrimination rather than minimum employment standards, it is discussed in the next chapter.

"But you already get the tops in job benefits now . . . which is, I let you work here!"

Federal laws such as FLSA do not require an employer to grant fringe benefits.
Source: Reprinted by permission: Tribune Media Services.

their employment in specially designed programs, learners, apprentices, and handicapped workers may sometimes be paid less than the minimum wage if specific government approval has been obtained. Also to encourage their employment, full-time students working in retail or service establishments, agriculture, or institutions of higher education may be paid subminimum wages with special government permission.

Many states also have minimum wage and overtime laws. The primary function of these laws is to provide some degree of protection for those employees not covered by FLSA, such as workers in small retail stores.

Minimum Wage and Overtime: The first minimum wage was set at 25 cents per hour in 1938. Since January 1, 1981, the minimum wage has been \$3.35 an hour. Covered employees must be paid at least this amount for the first forty hours worked in a week. If more than forty hours are worked in a given week, the employee must be paid at least one and one-half times his or her regular wage rate for each hour over forty. Thus, an employee who regularly makes \$6.00 an hour is entitled to \$9.00 an hour for time worked past forty hours.[14] In the case of state and local government workers, however,

[14] If a covered employee makes less than the minimum wage, the overtime to which he or she is entitled is one and one-half times the minimum wage.

FLSA permits their employers to grant future time-off ("comp time") at a time-and-a-half rate instead of overtime pay.

Some employees are not paid on an hourly basis. For instance, a worker's pay might be based on a piecework rate, a weekly, biweekly, or monthly salary, or a salary plus commission. Regardless of the basis, a covered employee must receive at least the minimum wage for each hour worked in a week. Thus, at the present minimum of $3.35 an hour, a salaried employee or pieceworker must receive at least $134 for a forty-hour week. Overtime for such workers is computed as one and one-half times the average hourly pay during a given week. In the case of pieceworkers, however, the law provides a second method for figuring overtime if the employee and employer agree to it beforehand. This method involves payment of one and one-half times the piece rate during overtime hours.

To give needed flexibility to employers, the standard forty-hour workweek does not have to begin on Monday—an employer might, for example, choose to keep the payroll records on a Wednesday through Tuesday basis. For minimum wage and overtime purposes the workweek must, however, consist of seven consecutive twenty-four-hour periods. With certain very narrow exceptions, there can be no averaging of two or more workweeks.

Except for its minimum wage and overtime provisions, FLSA does not attempt to regulate the terms of employment relationships. For example, it does not require an employer to give vacations or holidays, whether paid or unpaid. It has no provisions concerning rest periods during the day, premium pay rates for holidays or weekends, pay raises, or fringe benefits. In addition, there is no prohibition against compulsory overtime. No limit is placed on the hours an employee may work, unless the employee is under sixteen years of age. All of these matters are left to be determined by agreement between employer and employee or employer and labor union.

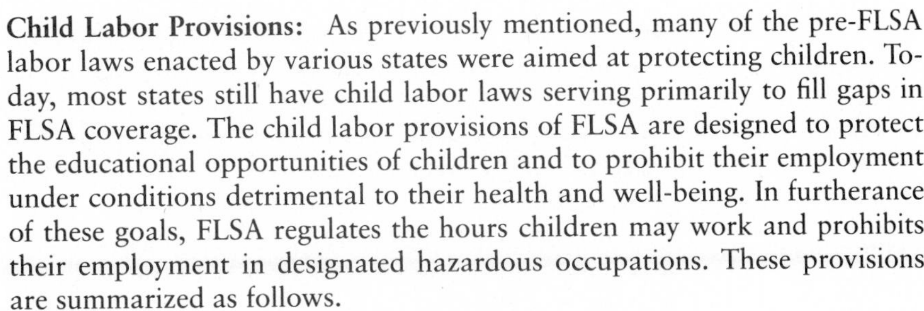

Child Labor Provisions: As previously mentioned, many of the pre-FLSA labor laws enacted by various states were aimed at protecting children. Today, most states still have child labor laws serving primarily to fill gaps in FLSA coverage. The child labor provisions of FLSA are designed to protect the educational opportunities of children and to prohibit their employment under conditions detrimental to their health and well-being. In furtherance of these goals, FLSA regulates the hours children may work and prohibits their employment in designated hazardous occupations. These provisions are summarized as follows.

1. A person eighteen years of age or older may work at any job without restrictions on hours.

2. A person sixteen or seventeen years of age may work without restrictions on hours, but not in occupations defined as hazardous. Examples of hazardous occupations include mining, logging, roofing, excavation, operat-

ing many types of power-driven machines or saws, and work involving exposure to radioactive substances.

3. A person fourteen or fifteen years of age may work only certain hours, and may not work in a hazardous occupation. Someone of this age may not work during school hours and may work no more than three hours on a school day, eighteen hours in a school week, eight hours on a nonschool day, or forty hours in a nonschool week. Work may not begin before 7 a.m. or end after 7 p.m., except that evening hours are extended to 9 p.m. in the summer. These restrictions are relaxed slightly for fourteen- and fifteen-year-olds in an approved Work Experience and Career Exploration Program.

4. Although fourteen is the minimum age for most work, children under this age may deliver newspapers, work in entertainment, work for their parents, and with some restrictions work in agriculture.

Administration and Enforcement: FLSA is administered and enforced by the Labor Department's Wage and Hour Division. The Division requires complete employment and payroll records to be maintained, although these required records usually are no more extensive than good personnel practices would dictate. On an informal basis, the Division often advises employers as to changes in their business practices which would bring them into compliance with the law.

Willful violations of FLSA may be prosecuted criminally, resulting in large fines and, for a second offense, imprisonment. Those violating the law's child labor provisions, whether willfully or not, can be forced to pay a penalty of $1,000 per violation. The Division may supervise the payment of back wages under a settlement between the parties. In addition, the Division may bring suit in federal district court for an injunction restraining an employer from violating the law. A lawsuit against the employer for back wages may be brought by either the employee[15] or the Division. If the court finds a violation and orders back wages to be paid, it may also order the employer to pay an additional amount equal to the back wages. This additional amount is referred to in FLSA as "liquidated damages." Actually, however, these damages are more in the nature of punishment because the court may reduce or refuse to award this amount if it concludes that the employer attempted in good faith to comply with the law.

The following case illustrates some of the problems an employer can have in attempting to comply with FLSA—particularly when lower level managers fail to follow top management's orders.

---

[15] If a successful back-wage suit is brought by the employee, he or she can recover court costs and reasonable attorney fees from the employer.

Brennan v. General Motors Acceptance Corp.
U.S. Court of Appeals
Fifth Circuit
482 F.2d 825
(1973)

General Motors Acceptance Corp. (GMAC) is in the business of providing financing for buyers of General Motors automobiles. It has numerous offices across the country. In each area of operation GMAC has employees whose basic job is collecting overdue accounts and repossessing automobiles. Their jobs naturally demand long and irregular hours in the field. Because they work on their own and without direct supervision, GMAC computes their hours worked (and thus their wages) by relying on time sheets completed by the employees in the field.

Despite efforts of upper management to encourage accurate overtime reporting, collection employees in some areas consistently understated their overtime because of pressure from their immediate supervisors. After an investigation by the Labor Department's Wage and Hour Division, Brennan, the Secretary of Labor, filed suit in a federal district court in Florida charging that GMAC had illegally failed to pay overtime to twenty-six collection employees in that area. The district court ruled that GMAC had violated the Fair Labor Standards Act. The court then issued an injunction prohibiting GMAC from violating FLSA's overtime and record-keeping provisions and requiring that the company pay these employees $92,000 for overtime they should have received during the three years prior to the lawsuit. GMAC appealed to the U.S. Court of Appeals.

Thornberry, Circuit Judge:

. . . GMAC's principal argument is that it cannot have violated the FLSA because it had no knowledge of the unreported overtime. The company relied on its employees to report fully all the hours worked. In fact the record contains a series of memoranda and instructions promulgated by upper management to encourage full reporting of all hours worked by employees. If the employees are not paid for all overtime hours worked it is because they have voluntarily failed to report those hours to the company. While it may be true that the company has had no actual knowledge of the unreported overtime hours, we believe the company had constructive knowledge. . . .

[T]he trial court found that during the three years preceding this lawsuit twenty-six employees had been working an average of thirteen hours of overtime each week. It would seem that an employer exercising reasonable diligence would acquire knowledge of this fact. Indeed, GMAC's upper management regularly encouraged the full reporting of overtime and sought to learn of all overtime worked, but the trial court found that the employees' immediate supervisors insisted that all work be completed within certain defined time limits and that "the pervasive effect of such instructions from defendant's supervisors to its employees was that an employee was limited in the number of hours he could turn in for payroll purposes irrespective of the number of hours actually worked. The defendant's district representatives, field representatives and certain of the outside telephone collection men regularly worked in excess of forty hours per week but with rare exception, were only allowed to turn in, record, and be paid for forty to forty-two hours." Because the immediate supervisors were primarily responsible for the employees' failing to report all overtime, we believe they may have had actual knowledge of the unreported overtime. At the very least they had constructive knowledge, for they had the opportunity to get truthful overtime reports but opted to encourage artificially low reporting instead. The company cannot disclaim knowledge when certain segments of its management squelched truthful responses.

GMAC appeals also from the trial court's finding that its violation of the FLSA was *willful*. The law provides a two-year limitation on actions to recover unpaid compensation, "except that a cause of action arising out of a willful violation may be commenced within three years after the cause of action accrued." Thus a finding of willfulness increases defendants' exposure to liability by fifty percent. GMAC advances two reasons why its actions in any violation of the FLSA cannot be characterized as willful. First, the upper levels of GMAC management frequently instructed branch managers and employees in the importance of accurate, honest overtime reporting and made every effort to encourage employees to report all hours worked. Second, some employees falsified their activities report and prevented GMAC management from knowing how many hours they were working. Thus, if GMAC gave its employees every opportunity to report all overtime hours worked and encouraged the employees to do so, and some employees responded by falsifying their overtime reports, any violation of the FLSA by defendant was purely inadvertent and not willful. We disagree with this view. . . .

Stated most simply, we think the test [for willfulness] should be: Did the employer know the FLSA was in the picture? . . . The record indicates that GMAC was apprised of the meaning and scope of the FLSA by virtue of previous wage-hour investigations which disclosed a number of violations. These investigations ended in stipulated settlements. GMAC's awareness is also indicated in memoranda issued by its corporate headquarters. One such memorandum, dated January 27, 1969, recognizes that the long and irregular hours worked by the field personnel of the branch offices, coupled with the responsibility of management to maximize efficiency and effectively utilize employees' time, could result in the underreporting of hours of work and that such underreporting might "subject GMAC to possible unanticipated legal liability." The memo added that "field employees constitute the major potential problem for GMAC in Wage and Hour Law compliance." Other memoranda and instructions in the record also indicate a keen GMAC awareness of the wage and hour problem presented by their district and field representatives and telephone collection men. These memoranda and instructions communicated FLSA awareness from upper management to lower management and to employees.

Despite these instructions and memoranda the employees' immediate supervisors persistently reminded the employees that their jobs were to be performed in forty to forty-two hours. Once again we must note the lower court's finding that "the pervasive effect of such instructions from defendant's supervisors to its employees was that an employee was limited in the number of hours he could turn in for payroll purposes irrespective of the number of hours actually worked." Thus while one level of management had a keen awareness of possible FLSA violations in the area of overtime compensation, a lower level of management intentionally proceeded with a course of action that has now been characterized as a FLSA violation. . . . [S]uch a violation must be termed willful. The trial court was correct in allowing a three-year statute of limitations. [Thus, the employer's liability for unpaid overtime extends to a three-year period prior to this lawsuit.] . . .

The judgment of the district court is affirmed.

★★★

Comment: In *Trans World Airlines v. Thurston*, 105 S. Ct. 613 (1985), the United States Supreme Court dealt with a question of "willfulness" under another statute, the Age Discrimination in Employment Act (see Chapter 15 for a discussion of that statute). In the *TWA v. Thurston* case, the Supreme Court stated that a violation is "willful" only if the evidence shows that the defendant either (1) knew that its conduct was illegal or (2) acted with "reckless disregard" for the legality or illegality of its conduct. The Court expressly stated that willfulness is not proved by merely showing that the particular law in question was "in the picture" (as the court in *Brennan v. GMAC* had stated). Although we do not know with certainty, it is probable that the Supreme Court's requirements for proving willfulness in an Age Discrimination case will also be adopted for FLSA. If this happens, the three-year statute of limitations and resulting 50 percent increase in liability for an FLSA violation will be applied only if the employer either knew it was violating FLSA or acted with reckless disregard for whether it was violating FLSA. In the *Brennan v. GMAC* case, the result probably would be the same under this new standard. GMAC's lower level supervisors very likely would be found to have acted with reckless disregard for the legality of their conduct. The company would be responsible for this reckless disregard by its supervisory employees.

Other Federal Labor Standards Laws

Several other federal laws focus on minimum labor standards for employers who contract with the federal government. The Davis-Bacon Act, passed in 1931, determines wage rates for federally financed or assisted construction. It does not set a minimum wage, but requires employers involved in such construction to pay its employees at least the prevailing rate for similar work in that locality. The prevailing rate is determined by the Labor Department, and will never be set below FLSA's minimum wage. Overtime under Davis-Bacon is required for hours over forty per week *or* eight per day. A noncomplying employer can have its federal construction contract terminated, and will be liable for any of the government's additional costs in getting someone else to complete the project.

Two other enactments containing almost identical provisions apply to employers making other types of contracts with the federal government. The Walsh-Healey Act of 1936 applies to employers contracting to furnish goods and supplies to the government. The Service Contract Act of 1965 applies to employers contracting to provide services for the government. The "prevailing rate" under the Service Contract Act is determined by the Labor Department for the particular locality, as it is under the Davis-Bacon Act. Under Walsh-Healey, however, the prevailing rate is set by the Labor Department for entire industries. Overtime under the Walsh-Healey and Service Contract Acts is required for hours over forty per week *or* eight per day, as it is under the Davis-Bacon Act.[16]

Private Employee Benefit Plans

Today many employers make various benefit plans available to their employees. Many of these are *pension plans* which provide retirement income. Others are *welfare plans* which may provide benefits for sickness, accidents, unemployment, and other contingencies. Both types of plans may sometimes be offered simultaneously. Such plans are financed by the contributions of employers, employees, or both.

In past years, benefit plans were much less common and were usually viewed by employers as rewards to selected employees for long service or special achievement. With the rise of the union movement and the resulting increase in employee bargaining power, benefit plans came to be viewed by employees as something to which they were entitled. In addition, many employers began to see these plans as a means to attract and keep good employees. The increased popularity of private benefit plans during the past several years has also been due partly to federal tax incentives. In the case of many pension plans, for example, employer contributions are tax-exempt, and income taxes on employee contributions may be deferred until retirement when the individual's tax bracket will presumably be lower.

Although many pension plans have been created by a single employer for its employees, some plans have resulted from collective bargaining agreements between a union and a *group* of employers. Such plans ("Negotiated Multi-Employer Plans") cover all the union's members, even though several different employers are involved.

Many pension plans were operated properly, but many were not. Some plans were not adequately funded, or were mismanaged so badly that little money remained to ultimately pay employee benefits. Plans were sometimes drafted with unfairly technical coverage requirements, or were manipulated

[16] Exemptions are provided from the Davis-Bacon Act for any contract in an amount less than $2,000; from the Walsh-Healey Act for any contract of less than $10,000; and from the Service Contract Act for any contract of less than $2,500. Even if these laws are inapplicable, however, FLSA may still apply.

so that executive personnel received most of the benefits. During congressional hearings on pension plan abuses, one official of the Labor Department testified that "if you remain in good health and stay with the same company until you are sixty-five years old, and if you haven't been laid off for too long a period, and if there is enough money in the fund, and if that money has been prudently managed, you will get a pension." To correct these and other problems, Congress in 1974 passed the Employee Retirement Income Security Act, usually called ERISA or the Pension Reform Act.

Coverage and Participation

Although ERISA covers both pension and welfare plans, its primary focus is on pension plans. Most of the law's requirements for disclosing information to employees and making periodic reports to the government are applicable to both types. Other protective provisions generally apply only to pension plans, however, because they historically have been the object of more serious abuses than welfare plans. Although ERISA does *not* require an employer to have a pension plan, one who chooses to offer such a plan is subject to numerous rules aimed at assuring fulfillment of the plan's promises and the employees' reasonable expectations.[17]

Many pension plans require employees to meet age and service requirements before they are permitted to participate. In the past, many employees were excluded by unreasonable participation rules. Since the enactment of ERISA, however, participation generally cannot be denied or postponed because of age or length of service beyond the time an employee reaches age twenty-one and completes one year of service.[18] In order to protect part-time and seasonal employees, ERISA in most situations defines a "year of service" as at least 1,000 hours of service during a twelve-month period.

Employees who begin working for a particular employer late in life also are protected. An employer making a pension plan available to employees generally cannot exclude such workers from participation. This prohibition against exclusion is absolute in the case of so-called **defined contribution plans**. These are plans which specifically set forth either the amount of or the method for computing contributions. In the case of **defined benefit plans**, the amount of benefits or method of computing benefits (but not contributions) is specified. An employer offering a defined benefit plan may exclude from participation any employee who begins employment within five years of the plan's normal retirement age. In either case, of course, the employee's length of service can (and usually will) affect the amount of retirement benefits.

---

[17] ERISA covers only *private* pension plans, not governmental ones.

[18] Three years' service can be required if the plan provides for full and immediate vesting. In the case of special pension plans for the self-employed and their employees (called Keogh plans), three years' service may be required for participation, but there can be no age requirement.

Protection of Employee Benefits

The Vesting Right: Pension benefits are said to **vest** whenever a participating employee acquires a legally enforceable right to them, even if there is no right to actually *collect* the benefits until a later time. Before ERISA it was common for a plan to contain no provision for vesting prior to a specified retirement age. Thus an employee could work for the same employer and participate in a plan for many years, quit or be fired before retirement, and then later find that he or she had no right to pension benefits at retirement. In such a situation, the most the employee could hope for would be to get back any personal contributions to the plan.

Under ERISA, pension benefits based on the employee's own contributions must vest immediately and completely. With regard to benefits based on the employer's contributions, ERISA requires every pension plan to contain a vesting provision, but permits the employer to choose one of three alternatives. The most frequently chosen standard provides for complete vesting after ten years of service. An employee participating in such a plan could quit after ten years and still be assured of later receiving benefits at retirement. These benefits would, of course, be less than if the employee had worked longer, but whatever benefits had already accrued when he or she quit would be payable at retirement. The other two standards both permit partial vesting to begin after five years' service, gradually increasing to complete vesting. (These two use different formulas for reaching complete vesting, but under either formula it must occur at fifteen years' service or less.)[19]

Breaks in Service: A *break in service*, such as an interruption of employment because of layoff or sickness, can have a significant effect on vesting and on the amount of benefits accrued. Before ERISA there were no minimum standards for the treatment of breaks in service. A participating employee could, for example, retire after thirty years' service and receive no pension because the plan required twenty years' *continuous* service for vesting and he or she had been laid off for two months in the middle of the thirty years. ERISA provides certain minimum standards for dealing with breaks in service. These rules are extremely complex, but essentially they prevent short breaks in service from having any substantial effect on vesting or accrual of benefits.

Protection from Inadequate Financing: To insure that money will be available to pay promised pension benefits, ERISA requires employers to set aside sufficient funds each year to cover the benefit liabilities which have accrued

---

[19] Even if a plan complies with one of the required vesting standards, earlier vesting may sometimes be required. Most plans are *qualified*, which means that they have met Internal Revenue Service (IRS) requirements for tax-exempt status. If the IRS finds that a particular plan discriminates in favor of certain employees, such as executives, or that employees are frequently fired just before vesting, the IRS can order the employer to implement a faster vesting procedure.

during that year. If earned benefits had been unfunded prior to ERISA, these liabilities must be amortized and gradually funded along with current pension liabilities. The funding process is monitored by actuaries and adjusted every three years to assure the financial soundness of the plan. Whenever inadequate funding is found, the employer must pay an excise tax on the amount of the inadequacy in addition to making up the deficit.

Protection from Mismanagement: The continual funding of a pension plan means that there will be a body of assets. These assets, often called the *pension fund*, must be placed in either a trust or an insurance contract. ERISA establishes rules for the management and use of the pension fund. Those persons having responsibility for investing and otherwise supervising the fund are regarded as *fiduciaries*. These individuals, who must be bonded (insured) against fraud or other dishonesty, are prohibited from using pension fund assets for certain kinds of transactions. A pension fund manager cannot act with self-interest, and cannot engage in any transaction creating an actual or potential conflict of interest. All actions are to be solely in the best interests of the pension plan's beneficiaries. Thus, the pension manager cannot sell or buy pension assets for his or her own account, and cannot receive any personal consideration from the other party to a transaction involving pension assets. The manager's compensation is paid by the employer or union setting up the plan, or by the plan itself. Moreover, pension assets usually cannot be used for transactions with other parties who have any connection with the employer, the employee's union, or the plan itself. As exceptions to this rule, however, the pension plan can invest up to ten percent of its assets in the employer's securities (stocks and bonds, for instance), and can in some circumstances make loans to participating employees.

Managers of pension assets are required to exercise a high degree of care and prudence in investing those assets. In essence, a person must exercise the same care and skill that would be exercised in similar circumstances by a prudent, experienced pension plan manager. This standard will be violated if the assets are either left idle or placed in investments that reasonably cannot be expected to produce a fair return. On the other hand, the standard of "experienced prudence" will also be violated if assets are placed in investments that are too risky or speculative, even though they have some potential for high returns. The manager must follow a moderate, well-balanced investment strategy. The advice of lawyers, actuaries, and other professionals may be relied upon if prudent to do so under the circumstances. Anyone who has mismanaged or misused pension assets is responsible to the plan's beneficiaries for any resulting loss.

Fair Allocation of Benefits: In the past, some pension plans were unfairly weighted in favor of a few influential employees who exercised a degree of control over the plan. ERISA prohibits such discrimination, and a plan that gives unfair advantage to a few key people cannot receive tax-exempt status. A pension plan can legally pay different benefits to different individuals, but these differences must result from a fair and uniformly applied method of computation that is based on legitimate factors, such as length of service and salary level.

Termination of a Plan: ERISA does not prohibit termination of any existing pension plan. It does, however, contain provisions aimed at protecting and insuring payment of those employee benefits that had vested before termination. Similar protections are provided for the merger of one pension plan with another. ERISA created a government agency, the Pension Benefit Guaranty Corporation (PBGC) to administer a federally chartered pension insurance program. It operates in a fashion somewhat similar to the Federal Deposit Insurance Corporation, which insures bank deposits. Each pension plan pays premiums to PBGC, which uses these premiums to establish a reserve. If a plan terminates or merges and insufficient assets are available to cover vested benefits, PBGC pays the beneficiaries within certain limits. The employer whose employees are covered by the plan is then liable to PBGC for the deficiency, up to an amount equal to 30 percent of the employer's net worth.

Portability: ERISA does not require pension plans to be *portable*—an employee who changes jobs usually cannot transfer a pension plan from one employer to another. The employee is entitled to receive his or her own contributions to the former employer's plan, as well as any other vested benefits, but if the subsequent employer offers a pension plan, the employee essentially will have to start over with the new plan.

There are two exceptions to this nonportability characteristic. The first applies to "Negotiated Multi-Employer Plans," which were mentioned earlier. Where a pension plan has resulted from an agreement between a labor union and a group of employers, ERISA permits a participating employee to transfer his or her plan from one employer to another employer within that multi-employer group.

The second exception applies to so-called "Simplified Employee Pension Plans," which were created by the Revenue Act of 1978. Under such a plan, an employer may contribute as much as 15 percent of the employee's income or $30,000, whichever is less, to an individual retirement account (IRA) for each employee. These funds are deposited with a financial institution approved by the Internal Revenue Service, such as a bank, insurance company, mutual fund, or savings and loan association. The employee may select the institution, so long as it is on the approved list. From the employee's viewpoint, one of the primary advantages of a Simplified Plan is that it is not tied to a particular employer. The plan belongs to the employee and may be continued with another employer. If a subsequent employer does not offer a plan, the employee may keep the previously contributed funds in the IRA and continue the account as a regular IRA.

In addition to portability, Simplified Plans offer other advantages. The employer has an income tax deduction for amounts contributed, but the employee does not pay tax on the income placed in an IRA until it is actually received in the form of retirement benefits. However, if an employee withdraws funds from an IRA before age 59½, a penalty is assessed in addition to income tax on the amount withdrawn. On the employer's side, such plans are particularly attractive to small companies which do not have the resources to implement and manage a full-scale pension plan. Many of ERISA's requirements for participation, fair allocation, and so forth are also applicable to Simplified Plans. Some of ERISA's other rules, however, such as those relating to employer liability for managing pension fund assets, do not apply to Simplified Plans because the employer has no control over the assets.

Administration and Enforcement

Administration and enforcement of ERISA is shared by the Labor Department and the Internal Revenue Service (part of the Treasury Department). Business has severely criticized what it views as overlap and inconsistency in the administration of ERISA by two different agencies. In 1978 legislation was passed to reduce the duplication of paperwork required by the two agencies and to more clearly outline their respective areas of authority.

In addition to government enforcement, a participating employee who is damaged by a violation of ERISA also has the right to sue in federal court.

Some Unintended Effects

Since the enactment of ERISA, business people have voiced concern about the burden and uncertainty created by the statute. They have contended that the burden of compliance, including paperwork, is too high. They also have expressed a feeling of uncertainty about the meaning of ERISA's standards for managing and using pension plan assets. Which investments are considered prudent? As a result, since 1974 the number of new private pension plans has decreased dramatically, and the termination of existing plans has increased substantially. In addition, some observers have contended that uncertainty as to where pension assets can be invested under ERISA's standards has diverted huge amounts of capital from socially desirable investments to those that are preeminently safe. Thus ERISA may need modification before it can achieve its goals.

Other Laws Affecting Employment

Social Security

The Social Security Act was passed by Congress in 1935 to relieve some of the economic insecurity of older workers. It is essentially a compulsory, government-administered annuity and insurance program. The Act originally provided only for monthly payments to retired workers sixty-five years of age and over, plus a small lump-sum payment to surviving dependents upon the death of a covered worker. Through the years, however, many other benefits have been incorporated into the Social Security system. In addition to the basic retirement and lump-sum death benefits, Social Security now provides monthly payments for disabled workers, the spouse and minor children[20] of retired or disabled workers, and dependent parents of a deceased worker. The age at which a retired worker or spouse can receive monthly benefits has been lowered from 65 to 62, but smaller payments are received if the lower age is elected. In addition, the Medicare program was incorporated into Social Security in 1966. Under this plan, individuals who are entitled to Social Security benefits and who are at least 65 or disabled may also receive payments for medical expenses.

Since the program's inception, exemptions from coverage have been greatly reduced, so that today over 90 percent of all employees are included in the Social Security system.

From the beginning Social Security has been funded by a tax collected from both employers and employees. In 1935 the employer and employee each paid a tax of 1 percent of the employee's wages or salary; in 1986 the employer and employee each paid 7.15 percent. The tax for self-employed persons traditionally has been about three-fourths of the combined employer-employee tax. However, this difference will gradually disappear and by 1990 the combined employer-employee rate and the self-employment rate will be the same (15.3 percent). The maximum employee income on which this tax is collected rose from $3,000 in 1935 to $42,000 in 1986 and will increase automatically in the future.

Despite dramatic increases in the amount being collected to finance Social Security, the program has not been financially sound in recent years. There are several reasons for this situation. Social Security has expanded through the years to provide benefits for many more people. The size of monthly payments has been increased substantially over the years (although these payments do not, and never have, provided enough money for most people to live on). The Social Security system was never able to accumulate the large reserve that Congress originally contemplated. Instead, it continually has had to rely almost completely on current revenues. And finally, increasing life expectancies during the past fifty years have put a greater financial strain on the system by lengthening the average time that benefits must be paid to retirees.

In the years to come, the Social Security system will remain viable only if revenues are increased, benefits are reduced, or both.

---

[20] The phrase "minor children" is a simplification. Children to whom payments are made are those who are unmarried and under age eighteen (twenty-two if full-time students). Older children can receive monthly payments if they are unmarried and were severely disabled before age twenty-two.

Unemployment Compensation

The extremely high unemployment levels of the Depression era spawned a federal attempt to provide partial income replacement for unemployed workers. The Social Security Act of 1935 included provisions imposing a three-percent tax on the payroll of most employers to finance the payment of unemployment compensation.

Since 1935, operation of the unemployment compensation system has been taken over almost completely by the individual states. In the original enactment, Congress stated that employers would be excused from 90 percent of the tax (2.7 of the 3 percent) in any state which adopted a federally approved compensation plan. All states have done so. Each state must levy a tax to finance its own system, and most states adopted taxes equal to the amount that could be credited against the federal tax. Today, an employer's basic unemployment tax liability is 0.8 percent to the federal government and 5.4 percent to the state. This tax is payable, however, only on the first $7,000 of each employee's wages. In addition, a particular employer's actual tax may be somewhat lower or higher than this basic rate because the "experience rating" of the employer will cause an adjustment of its tax rate. In other words, an employer with a record of maintaining a relatively stable workforce will pay a smaller unemployment tax than one with a poorer record. Such a system encourages employers to strive for less turnover among their employees. On the other hand, it also tends to worsen fluctuations in the business cycle, because unemployment taxes are generally higher when the overall economy is doing poorly and lower when it is doing well.

Each state has its own rules for determining when an employee is entitled to benefits. For instance, there are statutory formulas to insure that an employee has been employed on a reasonably regular basis for a period of time prior to the present unemployment. In addition, most states permit an individual to file a claim for unemployment compensation only after he or she has been unemployed for a certain period of time, usually one week. To be eligible for benefits, a person also must register with the state employment agency, which will assist in finding new employment. A person who refuses to accept reasonably suitable work is disqualified from receiving unemployment benefits. In addition, benefits usually will not be paid to someone who has been fired for good cause or who quit work without good cause. For example, courts have held that an employee has good cause for quitting, and is therefore entitled to benefits, when he or she quits to take care of a seriously ill or injured family member or quits because of extreme heat and dust in the workplace. On the other hand, courts have held that an employee does not have good cause for quitting, and is therefore not entitled to benefits, when he or she quits because of dissatisfaction with pay or because of a reasonable request by the employer to change working hours. In most states, a striking employee is not permitted to collect unemployment compensation. Those who are *unable* to work are not eligible for these payments, because other more appropriate benefits are available. Unemployment compensation is intended essentially for workers who have been "laid off" or have had to quit through no fault of their own.

Benefits are computed in various ways in different states. They usually are based on some stated fraction of average wages during a recent period, subject to minimum and maximum amounts. In most states benefits can be received for a maximum of twenty-six weeks. If the general level of unemployment reaches a prescribed level, however, benefits ordinarily are available for an additional period, usually thirteen weeks. One-half of the benefits paid during this extended period are financed by the federal government.

Although most types of employment are covered by state unemployment compensation statutes, there are some exemptions. Many states, for example, exempt employees of small farms, the federal government, and churches. The employment of immediate family members and full-time students also is usually exempted.

Questions and Problems

1. Chennault worked as a mechanic for Chicago Extruded Metals. One day after work, Chennault was taking a shower in the washroom provided by the employer for this purpose. As he dried himself he saw a cockroach going up the wall nearby. He climbed on a bench and attempted to swat the roach with his towel. As he did so, Chennault slipped off the bench and fell, causing substantial injury to his leg. (a) Assume that you are Chennault's supervisor. After getting medical aid for Chennault, what is the next thing you should do regarding his injury? (b) If Chennault files a claim for workers' compensation benefits, is he legally entitled to receive payment? Discuss. (*Chicago Extruded Metals v. Industrial Commission*, 395 N.E.2d 569, Ill. 1979.)

2. Shearer worked as a carpenter for seventeen years for Republic Steel Co. During that time he was almost continually exposed to steel, cement, and blast furnace dust, as well as various types of noxious fumes. Shearer developed chronic bronchitis and emphysema, finally becoming totally disabled. He filed a claim for workers' compensation benefits, and his employer contended that benefits were not payable because (a) he had not suffered an "injury," and (b) there was no way to pinpoint which substance irritated his lungs. Would Shearer receive payment? Discuss. (*Republic Steel v. Industrial Commission*, 399 N.E.2d 1268, Ohio 1980.)

3. McKeever worked as an attorney for the legal department of New Jersey Bell Telephone Co. While driving home from work one day he was killed in an automobile accident. His family filed a claim for workers' compensation death benefits. During the legal proceedings involving the claim, it was shown that (a) the workload of a corporate attorney like McKeever was so heavy that at-home work was essential to get the job done; (b) McKeever had work in his briefcase with him at the time of his death; (c) the employer encouraged employees like McKeever to take work home, and knew that they often did so; and (d) the employer benefited from McKeever's "off-duty" legal work. Is this workers' compensation claim a valid one? Discuss. (*McKeever v. New Jersey Bell Telephone Co.*, Workmen's Comp. Law Rep. (CCH) §2,566, N.J. Super. Ct. App. Div. 1981.)

4. Greencastle Manufacturing Co. operated several mechanical power presses. An earlier OSHA citation had notified Greencastle that its presses must be equipped with guards on every operation. After that citation, an OSHA compliance officer observed a company press being operated without a guard. Under OSHA, the penalty is greater for a "repeated" violation. Greencastle argued that the second violation was not a repeated one for several reasons. First, the previous citation had been issued for another press, which used different dies and presented different problems in designing guard devices. Second, Greencastle had sought the Labor Department's assistance without success when it had difficulty in designing a guard for the press. Third, employees who had complained about the risk involved in removing scrap from a moving press without a guard had been instructed by Greencastle to stop the presses when necessary to remove scrap. Should Greencastle be held liable for a repeated violation? Discuss. (*Greencastle Mfg. Co.*, 1980 O.S.H.D. ¶ 24,301.)

5. An employee of Davey Tree Expert Co. was electrocuted when the limb of a tree which he was trimming fell against a high-voltage power line. Electrocution caused by limbs touching high-voltage lines is a recognized hazard in the industry. The method used by the employee to trim the tree—notching the limb and pulling it to make it fall parallel to the wires—is an accepted practice in the tree trimming business. (a) Identify the hazard in this case. (b) Should Davey Tree Expert Co. be found guilty of violating OSHA's general duty clause? (c) Should the infeasibility of either insulating or de-energizing the power lines be taken into account in determining whether Davey violated the general duty clause? Discuss. (*Davey Tree Expert Co.*, 11 O.S.H.C. 1898, 1984.)

6. Adcock worked forty-seven and one-half hours per week on a fixed salary for Hendersonville Bowling Center. About 15 percent of his time was spent doing routine maintenance work. The remainder of his time was devoted to general managerial duties, including hiring, firing, promoting, and supervising other employees. He was subject to call at irregular hours for emergencies, and was allowed flexibility in taking time off for personal needs. All of his work was subject only to very general supervision by the owner. A suit was brought in Adcock's behalf by the Labor Department, claiming that Adcock was covered by FLSA and should be paid overtime. The employer contended that Adcock was an executive, or managerial, employee and thus was not covered by FLSA. Is Adcock covered by FLSA? Discuss. (*Marshall v. Hendersonville Bowling Center*, 483 F. Supp. 510, M.D. Tenn. 1980.)

7. Pascal had a contract with the Singapore Hotel to park cars and carry luggage for guests and to keep the hotel front clean. The hotel paid him a percentage of the gratuities received. Pascal hired Weisel to park the cars, and paid him part of what Pascal got from the hotel. The hotel required Weisel to wear a Singapore Hotel uniform and to follow the hotel manager's instructions. The hotel gave Weisel various benefits such as a Christmas bonus and meal discounts. On one occasion Weisel struck a guest with a car Weisel was parking, and the hotel's insurance company paid the claim. Was Weisel an employee of the hotel so as to require the hotel to comply with FLSA's minimum wage provision, or was he an independent contractor and not covered by FLSA, as the hotel claimed? Discuss. (*Weisel v. Singapore Joint Venture*, 602 F.2d 1185, 5th Cir. 1979.)

8. Century Manufacturing Co. had both a cash profit-sharing plan and a retirement plan. The employer contributed a percentage of each employee's annual compensation to that employee's retirement plan. In determining an employee's annual compensation for retirement plan purposes, the amount received as cash profit-sharing was added to the employee's annual salary. Century consistently represented to its employees that it was paying nearly 50 percent of its profits before taxes into the profit-sharing plan and the plan actually did require corporate contributions in that amount. Corporate profit was defined in the profit-sharing plan as net income reportable for federal income tax purposes, after deducting all costs and expenses, including bonuses. Century did not tell its employees, however, that executive "bonuses" equal to one-third of pretax profits were being deducted each year prior to splitting the profits with the employees. These bonuses were neither paid nor ac-

crued. Did Century violate its fiduciary duty under ERISA relative to the retirement plan when it misrepresented the amounts being paid to employees under the profit-sharing plan? Discuss. Can Century defend on the grounds that generally accepted accounting principles permit a company to deduct an unpaid bonus as an expense? Discuss. (*Monson v. Century Mfg. Co.*, 739 F.2d 1293, 8th Cir. 1984.)

9. The trustees for the Teamster's Local 282 Pension Trust Fund proposed to lend $20 million from pension fund assets to Green for partially financing construction of a large hotel and gambling casino in Las Vegas. The loan was to be secured by a mortgage on the hotel and casino. There was evidence that Green might have difficulty obtaining the remainder of the financing for the project and that there was a reasonable chance that such a project would not be financially successful if completed. The pension fund's total assets were $55 million. The Labor Department sued to prevent the trustees from making the loan, claiming that it was not a prudent investment and committed too large a portion of the fund's assets to a single venture. Should the Labor Department prevail? Discuss. (*Marshall v. Teamsters Local 282 Pension Trust Fund*, 458 F. Supp. 986, E.D. Wis. 1978.)

10. Trussel worked as a stenographer, receptionist, and bookkeeper for a law firm. While much of her work was acceptable and she tried hard, some of her work contained misspellings, visible erasures, and mathematical errors. She was discharged. Was she terminated for good cause, thus disqualifying her for unemployment compensation? Discuss. (*Seavy and Jensen v. Industrial Commission*, 523 P.2d 157, Colo. App. 1974.)

C·H·A·P·T·E·R 15

EMPLOYMENT LAW PROTECTION AGAINST DISCRIMINATION

The Concept of Equal Opportunity

The law of employment discrimination is but one part of a larger body of law often referred to as **civil rights law**. The objective of civil rights law is to guarantee equal treatment for all of the nation's residents. This goal of equal opportunity extends to housing, education, public accommodations (such as restaurants, hotels, theaters, and transportation), and credit as well as to employment.

The fundamental premise of employment discrimination law is that there cannot be true equality among this country's residents unless there is equal *economic* opportunity. It does very little good to have equal access to quality housing and public accommodations, for example, if one has little chance of ever being able to afford them.

Economic opportunity in the United States traditionally has not been equal—the evidence of this fact is simply too strong to deny. Even after employment discrimination of various types has been declared illegal by Congress and many state legislatures, striking imbalances still remain in our nation's workforce. For example, the unemployment rate for blacks generally is about twice the rate for whites. The average black family's income is about

"Just guess which one's salary we're getting 60% of?"

Despite laws prohibiting employment discrimination, real equality can be slow in coming.
Source: Reprinted by permission: Tribune Media Services.

70 percent of the average white family's. Average Hispanic family income is about 75 percent of average white family income. Approximately 55 percent of American Indians live below the poverty level, and their rate of unemployment is about 50 percent. There also is ample evidence of economic imbalance with respect to older workers, women, and the handicapped.

There are many different causes for the economic disadvantages borne by certain groups within our society. Some of the disparities can be attributed to different pressures, goals, and expectations within different groups. Such cultural differences sometimes have historical origins with little or no relation to actual discrimination. In some cases disadvantages are traceable to differences in language, education, training, and even geographic location. However, these are not the only reasons. We know from experience that there has been and still is discrimination. Some of it has been conscious, and some has been the unconscious result of stereotypes, unrecognized bias, and sheer habit. Although there is no way to tell exactly how much of the traditional imbalance in employment opportunity has resulted from conscious and unconscious discrimination, logic dictates the conclusion that discrimination has played a part.

Before the advent of modern civil rights legislation, common-law principles controlled the employment relationship. The relevant bodies of law—torts, contracts, and agency (discussed in Chapters 8 and 9)—did not provide any meaningful legal protection against employment discrimination. These areas of law continue to be extremely important in general, but today their specific application to the employment relationship has been significantly modified by statutory enactments.

Of the various laws dealing specifically with employment discrimination, the most important is Title VII of the 1964 Civil Rights Act. This chapter focuses on Title VII and then concludes by briefly surveying several other employment discrimination laws.

Title VII of the 1964 Civil Rights Act

The Civil Rights Act of 1964 is a comprehensive federal enactment prohibiting discrimination in various settings, including housing, public accommodations, and education. Title VII of the Act deals specifically with discrimination in employment.[1] Title VII essentially prohibits employment discrimination against individuals because of their *race*, *color*, *religion*, *sex*, or *national origin*. Before examining some of the many substantive issues raised by this basic prohibition, we take a brief look at the coverage and administration of Title VII.

Coverage

The provisions of Title VII apply to employers, employment agencies, and labor organizations.

Employers: Under Title VII, an employer is a person who has employees. The definition of "person" is very broad, including individuals, corporations, partnerships, and virtually all other entities. An employer is subject to Title VII if it (1) has fifteen or more employees, *and* (2) is engaged in an activity that affects interstate or foreign commerce. The commerce requirement of Title VII is satisfied by activities having an exceedingly slight and indirect impact on interstate or foreign commerce. It is a requirement that usually is present.

State and local governments are also within the definition of employer, and their employment practices are covered by Title VII. In most instances, the federal government's employment practices are also covered. The procedures for enforcing Title VII are substantially different, however, when the federal government is the employer.

Employment Agencies: An employment agency is "any person regularly undertaking to procure employees for an employer." The job placement and referral activities of such an agency are covered by Title VII if the agency procures employees for any employer who is covered.[2] Regardless of whether

[1] When referring to Title VII of the 1964 Civil Rights Act, we are including the amendments to Title VII which Congress passed in 1972 and 1978.

[2] If an employment agency itself meets the Title VII definition of employer, its own employment practices are subject to Title VII.

there is any illegal discrimination by the employers it serves, an agency violates Title VII if it discriminates in publicizing job openings, interviewing applicants, or referring prospects to employers.

Even though the help-wanted ads of a newspaper would technically bring it within the definition of an employment agency, the courts have ruled that it is not such an agency because that is not its primary business.[3] It is illegal to publish employment advertisements indicating a discriminatory intent, but it is the employer that is liable for publishing such an ad, not the newspaper or other medium.

Labor Organizations: Title VII's definition of labor organization includes almost any organization—such as a labor union—which represents employees in dealing with employers. If a labor union deals with an employer that is subject to Title VII, the union is also subject to that law if it has at least fifteen members *or* if it operates a "hiring hall."[4] Thus, most labor unions are covered, and their membership rules as well as all their activities in representing employees must meet the standards of Title VII.

Administration

Title VII is administered by the Equal Employment Opportunity Commission (EEOC), an independent federal administrative agency with five presidentially appointed members.[5] As part of its job in overseeing compliance with Title VII, EEOC has authority to issue legally binding *regulations* concerning the details of compliance with Title VII. Additionally, the agency may issue nonbinding *guidelines* which are intended merely to advise firms concerning their employment policies.

When EEOC receives a discrimination complaint or otherwise has reason to believe that Title VII may have been violated, it conducts an investigation to determine whether there really is evidence of a violation. If EEOC determines that enough evidence exists to indicate that Title VII probably has been violated, the agency is required to attempt conciliation—it cannot immediately file charges. Instead, the law requires that EEOC first attempt to deal with the questionable employment practices by obtaining the employer's agreement to eliminate them.

Whenever its conciliation efforts have failed, EEOC is empowered to enforce Title VII by filing suit in federal district court. About three-fourths of

---

[3] Although the job placement and referral activities of newspapers may not be covered, their own employment activities are covered if they meet Title VII's definition of employer, which is almost always the case.

[4] A hiring hall is an employment referral or placement service operated by a union. It is most commonly used in industries where employment is seasonal or otherwise noncontinuous, such as construction and shipping.

[5] If the alleged violator of Title VII is a state or local government employer, the U.S. Attorney General serves as the enforcing agency.

the states have their own employment discrimination laws, many of them bearing a close resemblance to Title VII. Many of these states also have agencies which perform the same types of enforcement functions at the state level that EEOC performs at the federal level. In such states, EEOC will not take action on a complaint until the state agency has been notified of the complaint and has had at least sixty days to handle it. Even after the expiration of this sixty-day period, EEOC will not become involved if the state agency has successfully resolved the matter or is still actively pursuing it.

In general, individuals claiming to have been victims of illegal discrimination are required to file a complaint with the state discrimination agency or EEOC within 180 days after the alleged discriminatory act occurred. The individual is permitted to file suit personally in federal court, but *only* after the state agency and EEOC have had an opportunity to take action.

Although enforcement of Title VII by an individual, a state agency, or EEOC usually is based on an individual complaint relating to a specific instance of discrimination, lawsuits under Title VII sometimes are based on charges that the employer engaged in a general "pattern or practice" of discrimination over an extended period of time. A pattern or practice of discrimination may be alleged in a "class action," in which one or a small number of persons file suit in behalf of themselves and a much larger group of persons who may have been affected by the same overall pattern or practice. A pattern or practice case also can be filed by EEOC on its own initiative, without there having been any complaint by an individual or a group. In either a class action or an EEOC case, if the court concludes that there was an illegal pattern or practice of discrimination there is then a presumption that all persons within the affected group were subjected to discrimination. Any such person can subsequently assert a claim, the burden resting upon the employer to prove that this particular employee was *not* harmed by the discriminatory pattern or practice.

When a court determines that Title VII has been violated, it is empowered to grant an injunction prohibiting further violations and ordering specific types of action. For example, an injunction may require the defendant to hire (or rehire) individuals who have been discriminated against. The defendant can even be ordered to pay retroactive wages ("back pay") or to grant retroactive seniority when the court feels that such remedies are appropriate. If a firm has a significant imbalance in its workforce because of past discrimination, the court may require that firm to implement an "affirmative action" program aimed specifically at recruiting minority employees.[6]

Who Is Protected?

Although the meaning and scope of the terms race, color, national origin, sex, and religion frequently are clear, this is not always the case. Difficult questions can sometimes arise as to *whom* Congress intended to protect.

---

[6] More is said later in this chapter about the concept of affirmative action.

Race, Color, and National Origin: Although the civil rights movement which culminated in the 1964 Civil Rights Act focused primarily on the treatment of blacks, Title VII's prohibition of racial discrimination in employment is very broad. Title VII obviously protects blacks, but it also protects many other classes from unequal treatment. For example, Hispanics, American Indians, and Asian-Americans clearly are within the scope of Title VII.

The Supreme Court has ruled that Title VII's prohibition of discrimination based on "national origin" does not prohibit employment discrimination based solely on the lack of United States citizenship. In other words, an employer may follow a policy of hiring only U.S. citizens without violating Title VII. The employer cannot, however, give unequal treatment to different noncitizens based on their country of origin. Furthermore, discrimination based on the lack of U.S. citizenship cannot be used as a mere cloak to disguise discrimination that in reality is based on race or national origin.[7]

The question of whether Title VII protects whites against racial discrimination has been a troublesome one. In *McDonald v. Santa Fe Trail Transportation Co.*, 427 U.S. 273 (1976), the Supreme Court ruled that whites are within the scope of Title VII's protection. In that case three employees, one black and two white, were caught stealing from the employer. Although there was absolutely no basis other than race for distinguishing between the employees, the employer fired only the two white employees. The Court held that the employer's action against the white employees violated Title VII. This was true despite the fact that there was an obvious justification for the firing, and that there would not have been a Title VII violation if the employer had fired all three employees.

The fact that whites are also protected against racial discrimination has obvious implications for affirmative action programs granting various employment preferences to minorities, discussed later in this chapter.

In addition to protecting the employee or job applicant from discrimination based on his or her race, color, or national origin, Title VII also protects that individual from employment discrimination based on the race, color, or national origin of his or her family members or friends.

Sex: Title VII's prohibition of sex discrimination is aimed primarily at employment discrimination against females. It also includes males, however,

---

[7]Different rules may apply if *federal, state, or local government* action results in discrimination based on lack of U.S. citizenship. The employment practices, as well as other actions, of government entities are subject to the constitutional guarantee of equal protection. This guarantee applies to both citizens and noncitizens within this country. Therefore, a government policy causing employment discrimination is valid only if it has a reasonable basis. For example, the Supreme Court has held that states have a reasonable basis for refusing to permit noncitizens to work as state police officers or public school teachers, but that they do not have a reasonable basis for refusing to grant licenses to noncitizen lawyers and engineers.

Moreover, a few lower federal courts have ruled that another statute—Section 1981, discussed later—applies to intentional, unreasonable discrimination based on lack of U.S. citizenship.

because it prohibits any type of discrimination based on a person's gender. Thus, in *Diaz v. Pan American World Airways*, 442 F.2d 385 (5th Cir. 1971), the court held that an airline's "women only" policy for hiring flight attendants violated Title VII. The definition of sex discrimination does not go any further than gender-based actions, however—it does *not* include discrimination based on sexual preferences or practices.

Religion: The term "religion," as used in Title VII, obviously includes well-recognized faiths such as Jewish, Catholic, and the various Protestant denominations. However, the courts have adopted the same definition that has been used in connection with First Amendment religious freedom and, as a result, the term is a rather broad one also including unorthodox beliefs. The Supreme Court, in *United States v. Seeger*, 380 U.S. 163 (1965), said that a particular belief qualifies as being "religious" if it is a "sincere and meaningful belief occupying in the life of its possessor a place parallel to that filled by the God of those admittedly qualified." Regarding unorthodox beliefs, there is no protection if a court is convinced that the purported belief is not sincerely and genuinely held, but is just adopted for some ulterior motive.

Proving Discrimination

Illegal discrimination can be proved in either of two ways. First, the plaintiff (EEOC, state agency, or individual claimant) may show that the defendant had engaged in *intentional* discrimination—sometimes referred to as "disparate treatment." Second, the plaintiff may show that some employment practice or policy of the defendant has had a discriminatory *effect*—sometimes referred to as "disparate impact." The two methods of proving illegal discrimination will now be considered in detail.

Intentional Discrimination

In general, any employment decision or practice which treats individuals unequally *because of* race, color, religion, sex, or national origin violates Title VII. Illegal discrimination might occur, for example, in connection with firing, refusing to hire, refusing to train or promote, granting unequal compensation or fringe benefits, or practicing any type of segregation or classification of employees or applicants that tends to deprive them of employment opportunities.

Intent to Discriminate: A violation of Title VII may be proved by showing that an employer[8] *intended* to discriminate for a prohibited reason. There

---

[8] Although Title VII covers employers, employment agencies, and labor organizations, most Title VII violations involve employers. For the sake of convenience the word "employer" is used in the remainder of the chapter to refer to all three types of entities.

obviously would be a violation, for instance, if an employer maintained an express policy of "whites only" for admission of employees to a management training program.

Prima Facie Case: Express discrimination such as this became much less common after employers became fully aware of Title VII and its requirements. Intentional discrimination still occurs, but that intent usually is not expressed so openly as before. Recognizing this fact, the courts have ruled that an **inference of discriminatory intent** may be drawn in certain circumstances. When EEOC or an individual plaintiff proves facts which make it logical to conclude that intentional discrimination probably has occurred, the courts hold that a *prima facie* case of discrimination exists.

Suppose, for example, that an individual job applicant is rejected and has reason to believe that the employer's refusal to hire was motivated by unlawful discrimination. Even though there was no explicit discriminatory motive on the employer's part, a prima facie violation of Title VII can be established by showing that (1) the applicant is within a protected class (racial or ethnic minority or female); (2) the applicant applied for a job for which the employer was seeking applicants; (3) the applicant was qualified to perform the job; (4) the applicant was not hired for the job; and (5) the employer either filled the position with a nonminority person or continued trying to fill it. If the claim of discrimination is based on a discharge rather than a refusal to hire, a prima facie case can be established by showing that (1) the plaintiff is within a protected class; (2) the plaintiff was performing the job satisfactorily; (3) the plaintiff was discharged, and (4) the plaintiff's work was then assigned to someone who was not within a protected class. In other employment decisions, the requirements of a prima facie case would similarly have to be modified to fit the circumstances.

Employer's Rebuttal: When the plaintiff in such a case introduces evidence sufficient to create a prima facie case, the burden then shifts to the employer to bring forth evidence of a *legitimate, nondiscriminatory reason* for plaintiff's rejection. To overcome plaintiff's prima facie case, the employer can introduce evidence relating to matters such as the applicant's past experience and work record, letters of recommendation, or the superior qualifications of the person actually hired. An example is found in *Peters v. Jefferson Chemical Co.*, 516 F.2d 447 (5th Cir. 1975), in which the employer successfully rebutted the female plaintiff's prima facie case by showing that she had not been hired as a laboratory chemist because she had not done laboratory work for several years. The court did not require the employer to prove that her skills were actually inadequate, but accepted the employer's assumption that laboratory skills diminish from nonuse over a substantial period of time. In another case, *Boyd v. Madison County Mutual Insurance Co.*, 653 F.2d 1173 (7th Cir. 1981), a male employee established a prima facie case of sex discrimination against the employer by showing that the employer had a policy of awarding attendance bonuses only to clerical employees, all of whom were women. The employer was able to successfully rebut the prima facie case by demonstrating that there had been a serious absenteeism problem with clerical staff and that the bonus policy was aimed at correcting that problem.

In a case based on an allegedly discriminatory discharge, the employer might overcome plaintiff's prima facie case by showing evidence of plaintiff's poor performance, absenteeism, insubordination, and so on.

The types of reasons that are sufficient to rebut plaintiff's prima facie case may vary from one kind of job to another. For instance, some jobs require skills that are quite subjective and extremely difficult to measure. Many executive and professional jobs are of such a nature, requiring traits such as creativity, initiative, ability to delegate and supervise, communicative skills, and a facility for persuasion. With regard to jobs that are inherently subjective, an employer usually will be permitted to use subjective justifications for the action taken. Thus, an attorney could be rejected because of "poor reputation," so long as the employer actually had some evidence of this fact. On the other hand, a court ordinarily will not accept an employer's purely subjective evaluation of an individual when the job in question requires little skill or responsibility or when it requires skills that can be objectively measured.

Pretext: If the plaintiff establishes a prima facie Title VII violation and the employer fails to come forth with acceptable evidence of a legitimate, nondiscriminatory reason, the plaintiff wins. If the employer does produce such evidence, the plaintiff will lose unless he or she can then convince the court that the employer's asserted reason was really just a "pretext"—that is, a cover-up for intentional discrimination. Plaintiff might be able to show, for example, that the employer's "legitimate reason" was applied discriminatorily. In *Corley v. Jackson Police Dept.*, 566 F.2d 994 (5th Cir. 1978), the employer proved that the plaintiffs, black police officers, had been fired for accepting bribes. Although this clearly was a legitimate reason for firing them, the plaintiffs proved that white officers who also had been accused of the same conduct by an informant were not investigated as thoroughly and were not fired. The court held that the employer's reason was a pretext for racial discrimination and that Title VII had been violated.

Other examples of employment practices which may constitute intentional discrimination are examined below. These are only examples, however; discriminatory treatment can take an almost endless variety of forms.

Segregation: Any type of employee segregation by an employer will violate Title VII if the segregation is proved to have been based on race, color, religion, sex, or national origin. Maintaining separate rest rooms or eating places for black and white employees has been ruled illegal, as has employer sponsorship of racially segregated social activities for employees. In *Rogers v. EEOC*, 454 F.2d 234 (5th Cir. 1971), the court held that the employer had violated Title VII by its practice of assigning Hispanic customers to Hispanic employees and white customers to white employees.

Harassment or Intimidation: Verbal or physical harassment or intimidation of employees violates Title VII if it is based on race, color, religion, sex, or national origin. It is illegal for the employer to engage in such conduct or to knowingly permit other employees to do it. Thus, if an employer knows that one or more employees of a particular ethnic group are being harassed by the repeated ethnic jokes, slurs, or offensive language of other employees, the employer is in violation of Title VII if no action is taken to stop the harassment.

"Sexual harassment" constitutes discrimination on the basis of sex. To prove that an employer is guilty of illegal sexual harassment, the following facts must be established:

1. The employer, *or* someone working for the employer in a supervisory capacity, requested sexual favors from an employee.

2. The request was a term or condition of employment, or was reasonably seen by the employee as such a term or condition. This means that the request either (a) was actually part of the employment and would have an effect on the employee's status or opportunity, or (b) the employee reasonably interpreted the request as being part of the employment and having such an effect.

Under these circumstances, the employee subjected to the request has a basis for filing a complaint under Title VII. *Other employees* may even have a basis for filing such a complaint if the employee in question has actually been rewarded for submitting to the request.

If unwelcome, on-the-job sexual advances are made by a *nonsupervisory* employee toward another employee, there is a violation of Title VII by the employer only if the employer (or someone working for the employer in a supervisory capacity) actually knows what is going on and fails to take adequate steps to stop it.*

Appearance Requirements: Discrimination can exist in unequal appearance standards. In one case, an employer was found to have violated Title VII by prohibiting black employees from having beards or mustaches, but permitting them for whites. Other types of grooming standards, such as those relating to dress or hair length, are also illegal if applied differently on the basis of race, color, religion, or national origin.

---

* This discussion of sexual harassment is based on a number of lower federal court rulings. As this text went to press, the Supreme Court agreed to review its first sexual harassment case, *PSFS Savings Bank v. Vinson*, 753 F.2d 141 (D.C. Cir. 1985). The Court will consider several issues, including whether an employer is absolutely liable for sexual harassment committed by a supervisory employee without the employer's knowledge.

On the other hand, courts have held that different grooming policies for male and female employees do not violate Title VII if these different standards are reasonable and are not more burdensome on one sex than on the other. The different standards must be enforced for both sexes and cannot significantly affect the job opportunities of either sex. Thus, an employer could require different uniforms for male and female employees if the requirement is reasonable and does not adversely affect either group.

Employment Rules Concerning Family: Discrimination against a woman because of pregnancy or childbirth is viewed as discrimination based on sex. Consequently, employer actions such as discharging women who become pregnant, or requiring them to take an involuntary leave of absence, are illegal unless it can be shown in a particular case that pregnancy significantly interferes with job performance. Similarly, it is a violation of Title VII to treat pregnancy different than other disabilities or conditions with respect to sick leave, health insurance, or other benefits provided by the employer.

In *Phillips v. Martin Marietta Corp.*, 400 U.S. 452 (1971), the Supreme Court struck down the employer's policy of refusing to hire women with preschool-aged children, but not having such a rule for men. Employers may lawfully impose rules relating to family matters, but only if these rules are applied equally to both sexes. For example, an employer could require its employees to be single, but could not legally have this rule for only its women employees.

Compensation and Benefits: It is illegal to base compensation or benefits on race, color, religion, sex, or national origin. A very difficult question is raised, however, when an employer establishes a pension plan providing for lifetime payments after retirement. Can the employer require female employees to pay more into the plan while they are working or accept smaller monthly payments after retirement because women, on the average, live longer than men? In the following case, the Supreme Court provides an answer.

Los Angeles Department of Water & Power v. Manhart
U.S. Supreme Court
435 U.S. 702 (1978)

The Los Angeles Department of Water & Power provided retirement, disability, and death benefit programs for its employees. Upon retirement each employee was eligible for a monthly benefit computed as a fraction of salary multiplied by years of service. These benefits were funded by contributions from employees and the employer, plus income generated by contributed funds.

Based on a study of mortality tables and its own experience, the employer determined that its 2,000 female employees, on the average, would live a few years longer than its 10,000 male employees. Thus, the cost of a pension for the average retired female would be greater than for the average retired male. Consequently, the employer required female employees to make monthly con-

tributions which were 14.84 percent higher than the contributions required of comparable male employees.

Manhart, a female employee, filed a class action suit in behalf of herself and other female employees of the department, claiming that this differential contribution requirement constituted sex discrimination in violation of Title VII. The federal district court and the Court of Appeals both ruled in favor of the employees, and the employer appealed to the U.S. Supreme Court.

Stevens, Justice:

. . . There are both real and fictional differences between women and men. It is true that the average man is taller than the average woman; it is not true that the average woman driver is more accident prone than the average man. Before the Civil Rights Act of 1964 was enacted, an employer could fashion his personnel policies on the basis of assumptions about the differences between men and women, whether or not the assumptions were valid.

It is now well recognized that employment decisions cannot be predicated on mere "stereotyped" impressions about the characteristics of males or females. . . . This case does not, however, involve a fictional difference between men and women. It involves a generalization that the parties accept as unquestionably true: Women, as a class, do live longer than men. The Department treated its women employees differently from its men employees because the two classes are in fact different. It is equally true, however, that all individuals in the respective classes do not share the characteristic that differentiates the average class representatives. Many women do not live as long as the average man and many men outlive the average woman. The question, therefore, is whether the existence or nonexistence of "discrimination" is to be determined by comparison of class characteristics or individual characteristics.

The statute makes it unlawful "to discriminate against any *individual* with respect to his compensation, terms, conditions, or privileges of employment, because of such *individual's* race, color, religion, sex, or national origin." [Emphasis added.] The statute's focus on the individual is unambiguous. It precludes treatment of individuals as simply components of a racial, religious, sexual, or national class. . . . Even a true generalization about the class is an insufficient reason for disqualifying an individual to whom the generalization does not apply. . . .

It is true, of course, that while contributions are being collected from the employees, the Department cannot know which individuals will predecease the average woman. Therefore, unless women as a class are assessed an extra charge, they will be subsidized, to some extent, by the class of male employees. It follows, according to the Department, that fairness to its class of male employees justifies the extra assessment against all of its female employees.

But the question of fairness to various classes affected by the statute is essentially a matter of policy for the legislature to address. Congress has decided that classifications based on sex, like those based on national origin or race, are unlawful. . . .

Finally, there is no reason to believe that Congress intended a special definition of discrimination in the context of employee group insurance coverage. It is true that insurance is concerned with events that are individually unpredictable, but that is characteristic of many employment decisions. Individual risks, like individual performance, may not be predicted by resort to classifications proscribed by Title VII. Indeed, the fact that this case involves a group insurance program highlights a basic flaw in the Department's fairness argument. For when insurance risks are grouped, the better risks always subsidize the poorer risks. Healthy persons subsidize medical benefits for the less healthy; unmarried workers subsidize the pensions of married workers; persons who eat, drink, or smoke to excess may subsidize pension benefits for persons whose habits are more temperate. Treating different classes of risks as though they were the same for purposes of group insurance is a common practice that has never been considered inherently unfair. To insure the flabby and the fit as though they were equivalent risks may be more common than treating men and women alike; but nothing more than habit makes one "subsidy" seem less fair than the other. . . .

An employment practice that requires 2,000 individuals to contribute more money into a fund than 10,000 other employees simply because each of them is a woman, rather than a man, . . . constitutes discrimination and is unlawful. . . .

[Although the Supreme Court agreed with the lower courts that Title VII had been violated, it disagreed with them on the question of whether the employer should have to repay all the excess contributions that had been paid by women in the past. The lower courts had ruled that repayment was required. The Supreme Court held that the practice must be stopped, but that the employer did not have to repay all prior excess contributions. The reason was that many pension plans had been structured like this one for many years on the assumption that using standard mortality tables was valid. To suddenly make this pension fund, and others across the country, *retroactively* liable could cause financial havoc and endanger their ability to pay benefits to innocent retirees.]

★★★

Accommodation of Religious Practices: Title VII's prohibition of employment discrimination based on religion includes both religious beliefs and religious practices. Section 701(j) provides that the term "religion" includes "all aspects of religious observance and practice." Congress recognized, however, that an employer's ability to efficiently operate its business could be hindered severely by having to accommodate every religious practice of every employee. As a result, Title VII only requires an employer to make *reasonable* accommodation for employees' religious practices.

Section 701(j) contains a provision stating that an employer may refuse to make a requested adjustment for an employee's religion if the employer "demonstrates that he is unable to reasonably accommodate to an employee's or prospective employee's religious observance or practice without undue hardship on the conduct of the employer's business." For example, a school board was held to have violated Title VII when it refused to grant a teacher a one-week leave of absence to attend a religious convocation. Attendance at the convocation was required by the teacher's religion, and a reasonably competent substitute teacher was available to handle his classroom duties. The next case is an illustration of the limits of an employer's duty to accommodate religion.

Trans World Airlines, Inc. v. Hardison
U.S. Supreme Court
432 U.S. 63
(1977)

Larry Hardison worked for Trans World Airlines (TWA) as a clerk in the stores department of TWA's maintenance and overhaul base in Kansas City, Missouri. The stores department provided parts and supplies for the airplane maintenance and overhaul operation. It was essential that this department operate twenty-four hours a day, seven days a week, and whenever an employee's job was not filled (because of sickness or vacation, for example), a supervisor or an employee from another department had to be used to cover the job.

Hardison, like other employees at the Kansas City base, was subject to a seniority system contained in a collective bargaining agreement that TWA maintained with the International Association of Machinists and Aerospace Workers (IAM). The seniority system was implemented by the union steward through a system of bidding by employees for particular shift assignments as they became available. The most senior employees had first choice for job and shift assignments, and the most junior employees were required to work when the union steward was unable to find enough people willing to work at a particular time or in a particular job to fill TWA's needs.

In the spring of 1968 Hardison began to study the religion known as the Worldwide Church of God. One of the tenets of that religion is that one must observe the Sabbath by refraining from performing any work from sunset on Friday until sunset on Saturday. Certain other religious holidays must also be observed.

When Hardison informed Everett Kussman, the manager of the Stores Department, of his religious conviction regarding observance of the Sabbath, Kussman agreed that the union steward should seek a job swap for Hardison or a change of days off. It was also agreed that Kussman would try to find Hardison another job that would be more compatible with his religious beliefs.

For a time, Hardison was able to observe his Sabbath regularly because he had sufficient seniority to keep from working Saturday most weeks. However, he then transferred from Building 1 to Building 2, apparently so that he could work the day shift instead of the night shift. The two buildings had entirely separate seniority lists, and in Building 2 Hardison was second from the bottom of the list.

In Building 2 Hardison was asked to work Saturdays when a fellow employee went on vacation. TWA agreed to permit the union to seek a change of work assignments for Hardison, but the union was not willing to violate the seniority provisions set out in the collective bargaining contract, and Hardison had insufficient seniority to bid for a shift having Saturdays off.

A proposal that Hardison work only four days a week was rejected by the company. Hardison's job was essential and on weekends he was the only avail-

able person on his shift to perform it. To leave the position empty would have impaired supply shop functions, which were critical to airline operations. To fill Hardison's position with a supervisor or an employee from another area would have understaffed another operation, and to employ someone not regularly assigned to work Saturdays would have required TWA to pay premium wages.

When an accommodation was not reached, Hardison refused to report for work on Saturdays. After a hearing, Hardison was discharged on grounds of insubordination for refusing to work during his designated shift.

Hardison filed a complaint with EEOC and later filed suit in federal district court, claiming that TWA and the union, IAM, had violated Title VII by not making reasonable accommodation for Hardison's religious beliefs. The district court ruled against Hardison, the Court of Appeals reversed and ruled in Hardison's favor, and the employer and union appealed.

White, Justice:

. . . Any employer who, like TWA, conducts an around-the-clock operation is presented with the choice of allocating work schedules either in accordance with the preferences of its employees or by involuntary assignment. Insofar as the varying shift preferences of its employees complement each other, TWA could meet its manpower needs through voluntary work scheduling. In the present case, for example, Hardison's supervisor foresaw little difficulty in giving Hardison his religious holidays off since they fell on days that most other employees preferred to work, while Hardison was willing to work on the traditional holidays that most other employees preferred to have off.

Whenever there are not enough employees who choose to work a particular shift, however, some employees must be assigned to that shift even though it is not their first choice. Such was evidently the case with regard to Saturday work; even though TWA cut back its weekend work force to a skeleton crew, not enough employees chose those days off to staff the Stores Department through voluntary scheduling. In these circumstances, TWA and IAM agreed to give first preference to employees who had worked in a particular department the longest.

Had TWA nevertheless circumvented the seniority system by relieving Hardison of Saturday work and ordering a senior employee to replace him, it would have denied the latter his shift preference so that Hardison could be given his. The senior employee would also have been deprived of his contractual rights under the collective-bargaining agreement.

It was essential to TWA's business to require Saturday and Sunday work from at least a few employees even though most employees preferred those days off. Allocating the burdens of weekend work was a matter for collective bargaining. In considering criteria to govern this allocation, TWA and the union had two alternatives: adopt a neutral system, such as seniority, a lottery, or rotating shifts; or allocate days off in accordance with the religious needs of its employees. TWA would have had to adopt the latter in order to assure Hardison and others like him of getting the days off necessary for strict observance of their religion, but it could have done so only at the expense of others who had strong, but perhaps nonreligious, reasons for not working on weekends. There were no volunteers to relieve Hardison on Saturdays, and to give Hardison Saturdays off, TWA would have had to deprive another employee of his shift preference at least in part because he did not adhere to a religion that observed the Saturday Sabbath.

Title VII does not contemplate such unequal treatment. The repeated, unequivocal emphasis of both the language and the legislative history of Title VII is on eliminating discrimination in employment, and such discrimination is proscribed when it is directed against majorities as well as minorities. Indeed, the foundation of Hardison's claim is that TWA and IAM engaged in religious *discrimination* when they failed to arrange for him to have Saturdays off. It would be anomalous to conclude that by "reasonable accommodation" Congress meant that an employer must deny the shift and job preference of some employees, as well as deprive them of their contractual rights, in order to accommodate or prefer the religious needs of others, and we conclude that Title VII does not require an employer to go that far. . . .

The Court of Appeals also suggested that TWA could have permitted Hardison to work a four-day week if necessary in order to avoid working on his Sabbath. Recognizing that this might have left TWA shorthanded on the one shift each week that Hardison did not work, the court still concluded that TWA would suffer no undue hardship if it were required to replace Hardison either with supervisory personnel or with qualified personnel from other departments. Alternatively, the Court of Appeals suggested that TWA could have replaced Hardison on his Saturday shift with other available employees through the payment of premium wages. Both of these alternatives would involve costs to TWA, either in the form of lost efficiency in other jobs or higher wages.

To require TWA to bear more than a *de minimis* cost in order to give Hardison Saturdays off is an undue hardship. Like abandonment of the seniority system, to require TWA to bear additional costs when no such costs are incurred to give other employees the days off that they want would involve unequal treatment of employees on the basis of their religion. By suggesting that TWA should incur certain costs in order to give Hardison Saturdays off the Court of Appeals would in effect require TWA to finance an additional Saturday off and then to choose the employee who will enjoy it on the basis of his religious beliefs. While incurring extra costs to secure a replacement for Hardison might remove the necessity of compelling another employee to work involuntarily in Hardison's place, it would not change the fact that the privilege of having Saturdays off would be allocated according to religious beliefs.

As we have seen, the paramount concern of Congress in enacting Title VII was the elimination of discrimination in employment. In the absence of clear statutory language or legislative history to the contrary, we will not readily construe the statute to require an employer to discriminate against some employees in order to enable others to observe their Sabbath.

[Thus, the Supreme Court reversed the court of appeals and reinstated the district court's ruling that TWA and IAM had not violated Title VII. The Supreme Court also noted that reasonable accommodation *had* been made by reducing weekend shifts to minimum crews and allowing voluntary trading of shifts.]

★★★

Neutral Employment Practices with Discriminatory Effects

We have seen that a violation of Title VII can be proved by showing that the employer intended to discriminate. This proof is accomplished either by presenting direct evidence of discriminatory motive or by establishing a prima facie case from which discriminatory intent can be inferred.

Another way to prove that an employer has violated Title VII is to show that a particular employment rule or practice, although apparently neutral on its face, actually has an unequal impact on a protected group. Examples include height and weight requirements having the effect of excluding a disproportionate number of females, or a standardized test having the effect of excluding a disproportionate number of persons from a particular ethnic group. In such a case, the plaintiff is not required to show that the defendant had an intent to discriminate. The procedure for establishing a Title VII violation in this way, however, is similar to the procedure for establishing a prima facie case of discriminatory intent.

Prima Facie Case: The individual plaintiff, or EEOC acting in the individual's behalf, must initially prove that the employment practice in question has an adverse impact on the protected group of which the individual is a member. This can be accomplished by the use of several different types of evidence. It could be shown, for example, that the employment practice has caused the employer to hire 40 percent of the whites who had applied, but only 20 percent of black applicants. Or, in another situation, discriminatory impact might be proved by showing that some action of the employer had the effect of eliminating 75 percent of all women from possible consideration even though women comprise approximately one-half of the total population. Still other types of evidence might be used in other cases.

It is important to realize, however, that the method used to prove discriminatory impact must be tailored to fit the particular employment practice being challenged and the particular group allegedly being affected. Thus, a court usually would not accept a comparison of the employer's minority hiring rate with general population statistics where the job in question required special qualifications. For example, if the job required a degree in mechanical engineering, the employer's experience in filling that job would need to be compared with the available population of mechanical engineers. The geographic area in which the statistical comparison should be made will also differ from one case to another. Suppose, for instance, that a plaintiff is trying to establish discriminatory impact in the case of an employer in San Francisco. If the job in question involves unskilled or semiskilled labor, general population statistics for the San Francisco–Oakland Bay area would probably be appropriate for comparison. On the other hand, if the job requires such special training and qualifications that the employer normally would have to recruit over a wider geographic area, the appropriate base for statistical comparison would be the population of qualified individuals in that larger area, such as the United States.

If the plaintiff proves discriminatory impact, a prima facie case of illegal discrimination has been established. The burden then shifts to the employer.

Employer's Rebuttal: As we have seen, an employer may successfully overcome a prima facie case of discriminatory intent by showing that the challenged action was prompted by a legitimate, nondiscriminatory reason. When plaintiff has established a prima facie case by proving discriminatory *impact*, the employer's task of rebuttal is somewhat more difficult, however. In an impact case, the employer is required to show "business necessity" by proving that (1) the challenged employment practice is necessary to achieve some legitimate business objective, (2) the practice actually achieves this objective, and (3) there is no other reasonably available method for accomplishing the objective without discriminatory impact.

It should be noted that there is no formal inquiry into the question of pretext in an impact case, because the basic issue in the case is *effect*, not motive.

On the other hand, intent and impact are not mutually exclusive—in a given case there might be evidence sufficient to create a prima facie case of intent and also evidence of discriminatory impact. In such a case, the plaintiff can use both methods to prove discrimination. The following case illustrates a situation in which both discriminatory intent and impact were shown. This case also demonstrates that using the so-called "old boy network" method of personal contacts for hiring can often lead to Title VII problems.

Grant v. Bethlehem Steel Corp.
U.S. Court of Appeals
Second Circuit
635 F.2d 1007
(1980)

Bethlehem Steel Corporation's Fabricating Steel Construction Division was engaged in the construction of steel framework for skyscrapers, bridges, and other structures. The employees on these construction projects, who were called ironworkers, worked together in groups of three to six. Each group worked under the leadership of a foreman. No special education or training was required for the job of ironworker. To be a foreman, an ironworker needed safety consciousness, leadership qualities, and productiveness.

Prior to enactment of Title VII, there had been a long history of racial discrimination in the hiring of ironworkers in the New York City area. Several factors, including Title VII, a shortage of ironworkers, and community pressure, led to the admission of blacks into the ironworker trade by the 1960s. Black and other minority ironworkers did not, however, advance to become

foremen. On ten representative projects in the 1970s, Bethlehem employed blacks in 10 percent of its 1,018 ironworker jobs but hired only one black for 126 foreman jobs.

The method used for selection of foremen on Bethlehem's steel projects was rather haphazard. On each steel construction project Bethlehem employed a project superintendent, who chose the foreman for the project. The superintendents, all of whom were white, were given uncontrolled discretion to hire whom they pleased. These superintendents hired by word of mouth on the basis of wholly subjective criteria. No foremen's jobs were posted and no list of eligible foremen was kept. Instead, upon hearing informally of an upcoming Bethlehem project (the superintendent would learn this fact as much as eight months to a year in advance), the superintendent would communicate with persons in the trade he knew or who were recommended to him by others, and line them up as prospective foremen for the project. Others interested in the job of foreman would rarely have the chance to apply for the job on any given project, since only persons solicited by the superintendent would know of the project in advance. By the time the project became known generally and notice of it was posted in the union hiring hall, there would usually no longer be any foreman openings available.

Three individuals, Grant, Ellis, and Martinez, attempted on several occasions to obtain foreman jobs with Bethlehem but were unsuccessful. Grant and Ellis were black, and Martinez was a dark-skinned Puerto Rican. All were in their forties and fifties and had many years of wide-ranging experience in ironwork, spotless work records, and excellent reputations. In addition, Ellis had worked as a foreman for two other companies, Martinez had been a foreman on one previous project for Bethlehem, and Grant had been supervisor on several projects for other companies outside the U.S.

Their repeated efforts to become foremen for Bethlehem were frustrated primarily by two Bethlehem superintendents, Deaver and Driggers. Both had been Bethlehem superintendents in New York for many years and had never hired a black or Puerto Rican foreman. They both hired foremen by word of mouth from among friends and those recommended by other foremen, union officials, or superintendents. Neither of them ever kept any list of ironworkers qualified to become foremen. They defended their subjective hiring practices by pointing to the dangers of ironwork and asserting that no objective method of evaluation would have let them effectively determine an individual's competence to handle the heavy responsibility of the position.

Grant, Ellis, and Martinez, plaintiffs, brought a class action suit in federal district court against Bethlehem, Deaver, and Driggers, contending that the hiring practices in question were discriminatory both in treatment (intent) and impact. The district court ruled that defendants had not violated Title VII, and plaintiffs appealed.

Mansfield, Circuit Judge:

. . . [Plaintiffs] assert that friendship and nepotism rather than assessment of ability formed the basis for the superintendents' selections, and that since blacks tended to be excluded from the all-white superintendents' friendship, they were also unlawfully excluded from jobs as foremen. In support of these allegations, [plaintiffs] point out that the supervisors often went to considerable length to solicit people whom they knew for foreman positions, sometimes calling them on the phone or personally going to ask them to work. One superintendent, Driggers, hired his two sons as foremen, notwithstanding that they had less ironwork experience than the three named plaintiffs and had not served as foremen before. On another occasion, Superintendent Deaver hired a foreman whom he knew had a drinking problem. One member of the gang which this man supervised suffered a fatal accident because he was not following safety regulations. Similarly, Deaver rehired a foreman who had lost a gang member on his last project when a column for which he was responsible fell; the same foreman lost a derrick on the new project, and left work with a nervous breakdown. [Plaintiffs] urge that concern for workers' safety could not have been the primary motive behind these hirings. . . .

[W]e find insufficient the district court's grounds for holding that plaintiffs failed to make out a prima facie case of discriminatory treatment. . . .

The Supreme Court's holding in *Furnco Construction Co. v. Waters*, 438 U.S. 567 (1978), does not dictate a different result. There the Court held that employers had a responsibility only to offer blacks the same employment opportunities as whites, not to solicit blacks or otherwise devise hiring methods that would maximize black employment. Here blacks were not offered the same employment opportunities as whites. The district court stated that "if Bethlehem had taken affirmative steps to find qualified blacks, one or more additional black foremen would have been appointed," but concluded that Bethlehem's failure to take such steps could not be illegal, given the logic of *Furnco*. Contrary to the district court's conclusion, we believe that the failure to solicit qualified blacks as foremen constitutes a form of unacceptable discrimination in this case, since whites were here being solicited at the same time, even though the whites made no applications for the foreman's jobs for which they were hired. . . .

[Plaintiffs] made out a strong prima facie case of discriminatory treatment under Title VII. . . .

Nor can we accept the district court's conclusion that [plaintiffs] failed to make out a prima facie case of discriminatory impact under Title VII. The undisputed statistics point strongly toward discrimination. After a "long history of discrimination against blacks in the hiring of ironworkers" Bethlehem during the 1970–75 period employed 1,018 ironworkers, of whom 102 were black or Puerto Rican. During the same period it appointed 126 whites as foremen and only 1 black. . . .

Prior foreman experience is a factor properly considered in weighing the defense of business necessity. But without an inquiry into the nature and extent of the experience insofar as it may indicate superior competence on the part of the ironworkers, it cannot be categorized as [absolutely necessary] for appointment as foremen. An incompetent foreman should not be repeatedly hired over a qualified ironworker without foreman experience merely because the former had the good fortune to have been hired once as a foreman. Here, [plaintiffs] produced creditable evidence that the superintendents selected some foremen on the basis of friendship without knowledge of or inquiry into their prior safety history. Some of these foremen, as noted above, possessed bad safety records that would have excluded them from rehiring in a strictly merit-based hiring system. No business necessity dictated that these men be rehired without superintendents assuming any responsibility to consider qualified blacks for the job.

The record, moreover, shows that fully 50% of the foremen hired on the 10 sample projects had worked for Bethlehem less than a year before being made foremen. Each of the named plaintiffs, who were qualified to be foremen, had longer Bethlehem tenure. Many of these other foremen did not have the extensive experience gained by [plaintiffs] as ironworkers and foremen in outstanding companies other than Bethlehem. [Plaintiffs] adduced evidence that Bethlehem supervisors hired their sons, friends, and persons whom they trusted, often despite these men's relatively slight experience as Bethlehem ironworkers, even though persons with Bethlehem foreman experience (including [plaintiff] Martinez) were available for the job. . . .

[On the question of discriminatory impact, defendants also argue] that it was incorrect to view the entire Bethlehem ironworker force as the pool of qualified candidates for foreman positions. The presence of 10% blacks in the ironworkers' labor force, the argument goes, does not suggest that 10% participation in the foreman ranks should follow. Before 1972 there were few minority workers in the union, and most blacks who belonged to the union in 1975 had been members a relatively short time. Those blacks who belonged to the workforce during the early 1970s took up a comparatively larger segment of the apprentice and trainee pools. The legacy of admitted past discrimination gave blacks less average experience per man than whites. The ratio of qualified blacks to qualified whites in the workforce, [defendants] concluded, was therefore substantially smaller than the overall percentage of blacks in the workforce.

This background, though partially true, does not justify the assumption that there were *no* appreciable blacks in the workforce with the ability to be good foremen. Though the union had few black members in the early 1970s, many black "permit" workers were working on iron work projects during that period, and some even earlier. Some black workers, including the three named plaintiffs, had more experience at Bethlehem and elsewhere than at least several of the whites hired as foremen. Moreover, as all parties have recognized, experience is only one of several factors to be considered when selecting foremen. It defies common sense to suggest that only one black was sufficiently experienced and competent to merit selection as a foreman during this period when 126 foreman jobs were filled. It would not have created any substantial difficulty for supervisors to maintain a pool of "eligibles" to be notified of foreman openings, from whom they would choose the foremen for new projects. Such a pool would undoubtedly have contained some qualified blacks. . . .

For all of these reasons we hold that [plaintiffs] have made out a prima facie case of not only discriminatory treatment but discriminatory impact as well. We remand the case to permit [defendants] to introduce additional evidence that their discriminatory conduct may have been justified by business necessity, and for any rebuttal testimony by the plaintiffs. As the evidence thus far introduced is insufficient to meet the burden on the defendants, if no additional defensive evidence is offered the sole remaining issue would be backpay damages.

[Reversed and remanded.]

★★★

Comment: Defendants were required to prove **business necessity**, rather than just having to show a nondiscriminatory reason for their conduct, because the plaintiffs had proved discriminatory impact. Because of the way the Court of Appeals viewed the evidence that defendants had already presented on the question of business necessity, it is doubtful that the defendants would be able to win after the case was sent back to the lower court.

We now examine several specific types of employment practices which have given rise to claims of discriminatory impact.

Physical Requirements: Many jobs do, in fact, require certain physical characteristics such as strength or agility. In setting minimum qualifications for such a job, the employer must be very careful to design the standard as narrowly as possible. If substantial strength is required for a particular factory job, for instance, it may be convenient (and tempting) for the employer simply to require all applicants for the job to be at least six feet tall and 180 pounds. Such a requirement would, however, have a disproportionate impact on certain groups, such as women, Hispanics, and Asian-Americans.

In *Dothard v. Rawlinson*, 433 U.S. 321 (1977), the Supreme Court held that Title VII had been violated by a requirement that state prison guards in Alabama be at least five feet, two inches and weigh 120 pounds. Statistics showed that the requirement would exclude over 40 percent of the female population but less than 1 percent of males. The Court permitted the use of generalized national statistics for purposes of comparison because there was no reason to suppose that physical height and weight characteristics of Alabama men and women differed significantly from those of the national population. The Court observed that general population statistics were appropriate for the additional reason that, in this case, data concerning actual applicants might not be very valuable. The reason, in the words of the Court, was that "the application process might itself not adequately reflect the actual potential applicant pool, since otherwise qualified people might be discouraged from applying because of a self-recognized inability to meet the very standards being challenged as discriminatory." The Court then observed that strength might indeed be a legitimate qualification for the job, but that the employer could not rebut plaintiff's prima facie case because there was no evidence showing a correlation between the size requirement and the amount of strength actually required for the job. In other words, the employer needed to determine how much strength is needed for the particular job and design a test to measure whether individual applicants actually possessed it.

In other cases, courts have recognized that various jobs require certain physical attributes or skills. Even if an employment rule requiring a particular attribute or skill has a discriminatory impact, the employer can prevail by showing that the attribute or skill is necessary for the job and that a valid, objective method was used to test applicants for the requirement.

Educational Requirements and Nonphysical Skills: Minimum educational requirements, such as a high school diploma, college degree, and so forth, frequently have a disproportionately adverse impact on racial minorities. Such requirements ordinarily violate Title VII in the case of unskilled or semiskilled jobs. The reason is that employers usually are unable to show that general educational achievement is necessary for the performance of these types of jobs.

In *Griggs v. Duke Power Co.*, 401 U.S. 424 (1971), the Supreme Court struck down the employer's practice of requiring a high school diploma as a prerequisite for all of its jobs. Evidence showed that in North Carolina, where the employer was located and from which almost all of its employees came, high school diplomas were possessed by about three times as many whites as blacks. The employer was unable to show that the diploma was really necessary for most of its jobs—it had adopted the requirement because of the feeling that the overall quality of its workforce would be improved as a result.

In contrast, courts usually have approved minimum educational requirements for jobs involving substantial responsibility, skill, or independent judgment. Such requirements have been upheld in cases involving police officers, teachers, airline flight engineers, and laboratory technicians, even without any actual demonstration by the employer that the particular educational achievement was essential to that job.

Specific nonphysical skills, like specific physical skills, legally can be required for a job despite discriminatory impact if the employer can show that the particular skill is essential for the job. For example, proficiency in English or some other language can be required if the job demands it.

Testing: Employers frequently require job applicants to perform satisfactorily on standardized tests designed to measure intelligence, aptitude, personality, achievement, or specific skills. Such tests are recognized as being valuable aids in the process of selecting the best qualified people for a variety of jobs. One of the main advantages of these tests is their relative objectivity. Section 703(h) of Title VII states that it is permissible "for an employer to give and to act upon the results of any professionally developed ability test provided that such test, its administration or action upon the results is not designed, intended, or used to discriminate because of race, color, religion, sex, or national origin."

However, the courts have interpreted this provision in such a way that standardized tests are treated essentially like other employment practices. That is, even if there is no evidence of discriminatory motive surrounding the test, it nevertheless can violate Title VII by having a discriminatory impact. If the test is shown to have a discriminatory impact, the employer must be prepared to rebut the prima facie case by proving that the test is legitimately job related.

In *Griggs v. Duke Power Co.*, the employer, in addition to requiring a high school diploma, also required job applicants to pass two standardized tests. One was the Wonderlic Personnel Test, which purported to measure general intelligence, and the other was the Bennett Mechanical Comprehension Test. Use of these tests was shown to have had a discriminatory impact on blacks, and the employer was unable to establish any correlation between success on the tests and job performance. As a result, the Supreme Court ruled that the employer's testing violated Title VII. The Court stated: "Nothing in the Act precludes the use of testing or measuring procedures; obviously they are useful. What Congress has forbidden is giving these devices and mechanisms controlling force unless they are demonstrably a reasonable measure of job performance. Congress has not commanded that the less qualified be preferred over the better qualified simply because of minority origins. Far from disparaging job qualifications as such, Congress has made such qualifications the controlling factor, so that race, religion, nationality, and sex become irrelevant. *What Congress has commanded is that any tests used must measure the person for the job and not the person in the abstract*." [Emphasis added.]

The Four-Fifths Rule: EEOC has adopted Uniform Guidelines on Employment Selection Procedures, which provide a specific formula for determining when a standardized test has a discriminatory impact. These Guidelines state that a test is considered to have a discriminatory impact if it results in a selection rate for any race, sex, or ethnic group that is less than four-fifths of the selection rate for the group with the highest rate. For example, suppose that one hundred white males apply for a job and take a required test. If fifty of them pass it and are hired, the selection rate for that group is 50 percent. If sixty males of a particular ethnic minority apply and take the same test and twelve of them pass it and are hired, the selection rate for that group is 20 percent. Since 20 percent is less than four-fifths of 50 percent, the test would be viewed as having a discriminatory impact. If twenty-four out of the sixty minority males had passed the test, the selection rate for that group would be 40 percent. Since 40 percent is four-fifths of 50 percent, the test then would not be viewed as having a discriminatory impact. Although the courts are not required to follow this four-fifths rule when considering standardized tests, they probably will in most cases. The Supreme Court has said that courts should give "great deference" to EEOC's Guidelines.

The Validation Requirement: When a test is shown to have a discriminatory impact, EEOC's Guidelines require the employer to "validate" the test. In other words, the employer has the burden of showing, through the use of professional validation studies, that the test is "predictive of or significantly correlated with important elements of work behavior which comprise or are relevant to the job or jobs for which candidates are being evaluated."

In specifying the methods by which tests can be validated, the Guidelines rely upon the validation standards established by the American Psychological Association. Validation can be accomplished by one of three methods. (1) *Criterion related validity* is the statistical relationship between test scores and actual job performance. The employer must thoroughly analyze the job and develop objective standards for measuring job performance. For example, a weighted combination of production rate, error rate, and absenteeism might be appropriate for a particular job. For criterion validity, it has been held that a correlation between test scores and job performance of +0.3 is sufficient (+1.0 is perfect). (2) *Content validity* establishes that the test actually measures the ability to perform specific job functions. Thus a typing test would be content valid for a secretary. (3) *Construct validity* indicates that the test identifies one or more psychological traits required for successful job performance. A test that measures patience would be construct valid for a kindergarten teacher. This method is the least often used because of its difficulty.

Seniority Systems: Seniority is the length of service of an employee. Many employers use seniority as the basis for determining matters such as which employees are laid off first when jobs are reduced and which ones have the first opportunity to transfer to vacant jobs (as in *TWA v. Hardison*). Some seniority systems are implemented unilaterally by employers, but most are found in collective bargaining agreements negotiated between employers and labor unions.

Seniority systems are almost universally recognized as providing a logical, objective method for making certain types of personnel decisions. The operation of such a system, however, may sometimes have an adverse impact on minorities and women. The reason for this is that equal employment opportunity is still a relatively new concept and, as a result, minority and women employees on the average have substantially less seniority than white male employees. When a lay-off occurs, it usually has a disproportionately greater impact on minorities and women when those with less seniority are laid off first.

However, because of the feeling that seniority is a legitimate, and even essential, employment practice, Congress gave it special treatment in Title VII. Section 703(h), which dealt with testing, also contains a provision stating that operation of a seniority system does not violate Title VII unless the employer *intended* to discriminate. In other words, discriminatory impact by itself is not enough to make a seniority system illegal; there must be proof of an intent to discriminate.

A question left unanswered by the statutory language was whether a seniority system would violate Title VII by causing the effects of past discrimination to be perpetuated. The Supreme Court, in *International Brotherhood of Teamsters v. United States*, 431 U.S. 324 (1977), ruled that a genuine seniority system, implemented and operated without any discriminatory intent, does not violate Title VII merely by continuing the effects of discriminatory practices which had occurred *before* enactment of Title VII. On the other hand, the Court said that such a seniority system is illegal insofar as it continues the effects of previous discriminatory practices which had occurred *after* enactment of Title VII. Thus, employees showing that they had been illegally discriminated against after the effective date of Title VII could be granted retroactive seniority.

Other Practices: Various other employment practices have created issues of discriminatory impact under Title VII. For example, the practice of refusing to hire individuals with criminal records has been challenged because it affects a disproportionately high percentage of minority applicants. The courts have held that such a practice violates Title VII if it is general in nature and does not take into account the type of job or type of criminal offense. On the other hand, a rule excluding those with serious criminal records does not violate Title VII with respect to jobs involving trust (such as a bank teller) or significant responsibility.

In another case, an employer's policy against beards was found to have a discriminatory impact on black males, because they are more prone than white males to suffer skin irritation from shaving. The court ruled, however, that the employer had rebutted the prima facie case of discrimination by showing business necessity. The basis for this conclusion was that the employer, a supermarket chain, had a real need to present an image of neatness to the public.

Hiring preferences for military veterans have a discriminatory impact on women since the majority of veterans are men. With respect to federal, state, and local government employers, however, Title VII expressly exempts such preferences.[9]

Employment rules relating to the language one speaks have been challenged on several occasions as having a discriminatory impact on a particular group because of race or national origin. In addition, language rules have sometimes been used as a guise for intentional discrimination. The following case shows that language rules can be legitimate in certain circumstances, however.

Garcia v. Gloor

U.S. Court of Appeals Fifth Circuit 618 F.2d 264 (1980)

Hector Garcia, twenty-four, whose grandparents immigrated from Mexico, could speak both English and Spanish. He was born in America, but he always spoke Spanish in his own household. Garcia was employed as a salesman by Gloor Lumber and Supply, Inc., in Brownsville, Texas. His duties included stocking his department and keeping it in order, assisting other department salespersons, and selling lumber, hardware, and supplies.

---

[9] The Supreme Court has ruled, in *Personnel Administrator of Massachusetts v. Feeney*, 442 U.S. 256 (1979), that veterans' hiring preferences by government employers also do not violate the Equal Protection clause of the Constitution because such preferences achieve the legitimate goal of providing an incentive for military service.

Gloor had a rule prohibiting employees from speaking Spanish on the job unless they were communicating with Spanish-speaking customers. Most of Gloor's employees were bilingual, but some who worked outside in the lumber yard did not speak English. The rule did not apply to those employees. It also did not apply to conversation during work breaks. On one occasion, Garcia was asked a question by another Mexican American employee about an item requested by a customer and he responded in Spanish that the article was not available. Alton Gloor, an officer and stockholder of Gloor, overheard the conversation. Thereafter Garcia was discharged.

Garcia sued Gloor, claiming that the employer had violated Title VII by discriminating on the basis of national origin. The federal district court ruled in favor of the employer, and Garcia appealed.

Rubin, Circuit Judge:

. . . [The lower court concluded] that Mr. Garcia's discharge was for a combination of deficiencies—failure to keep his inventory current, failure to replenish the stock on display from stored merchandise, failure to keep his area clean and failure to respond to numerous reprimands—as well as for violation of the English-only rule. The court also found that the English-only policy was not strictly enforced but that Mr. Garcia had violated it "at every opportunity since the time of his hiring. . . ."

In addition to offering this evidence to justify firing Mr. Garcia, Mr. Gloor testified that there were business reasons for the language policy: English-speaking customers objected to communications between employees that they could not understand; pamphlets and trade literature were in English and were not available in Spanish, so it was important for employees to be fluent in English apart from conversations with English-speaking customers; if employees who normally spoke Spanish off the job were required to speak English on the job at all times and not only when waiting on English-speaking customers, they would improve their English; and the rule would permit supervisors, who did not speak Spanish, better to oversee the work of subordinates. The district court found that these were valid business reasons and that they, rather than discrimination, were the motive for the rule.

An expert witness called by the plaintiff testified that the Spanish language is the most important aspect of ethnic identification for Mexican-Americans, and it is to them what skin color is to others. Consequently, Mr. Garcia contends, with support from the Equal Employment Opportunity Commission (EEOC), that the rule violates [Title VII]. . . .

Of the eight salesmen employed by Gloor in 1975, seven were Hispanic, a matter perhaps of business necessity, because 75% of the population in its business area is of Hispanic background and many of Gloor's customers wish to be waited on by a salesman who speaks Spanish. Of its 39 employees, 31 were Hispanic, and a Hispanic sat on the Board of Directors. There is no contention that Gloor discriminated against Hispanic-Americans in any other way.

The narrow issue is whether the English-only rule as applied to Mr. Garcia imposed a discriminatory condition of employment. . . .

The refusal to hire applicants who cannot speak English might be discriminatory if the jobs they seek can be performed without knowledge of that language, but the obverse is not correct: if the employer engages a bilingual person, that person is granted neither right nor privilege by the statute to use the language of his personal preference. Mr. Garcia was bilingual. Off the job, when he spoke one language or another, he exercised a preference. He was hired by Gloor precisely because he was bilingual, and, apart from the contested rule, his preference in language was restricted to some extent by the nature of his employment. On the job, in addressing English-speaking customers, he was obliged to use English; in serving Spanish-speaking patrons, he was required to speak Spanish. The English-only rule went a step further and restricted his preference while he was on the job and not serving a customer.

Let us assume that, as contended by Mr. Garcia, there was no genuine business need for the rule and that its adoption by Gloor was arbitrary. [Title VII] does not prohibit all arbitrary employment practices. It does not forbid employers to hire only persons born under a certain sign of the zodiac or persons having long hair or short hair or no hair at all. It is directed only at specific impermissible bases of discrimination—race, color, religion, sex, or national origin. National origin must not be confused with ethnic or sociocultural traits or an unrelated status, such as citizenship or alienage. . . .

The argument is made that the rule is discriminatory in impact, even if that result was not intentional, because it was likely to be violated only by Hispanic-Americans and that, therefore, they have a higher risk of incurring penalties. . . . However, there is no disparate impact if the rule is one that the affected employee can readily observe and nonobservance is a matter of individual preference. Mr. Garcia could readily comply with the speak-English-only rule; as to him nonobservance was a matter of choice. In similar fashion, an employer might, without business necessity, adopt a rule forbidding smoking on the job. The Act would not condemn that rule merely because it is shown that most of the employees of one race smoke, most of the employees of another do not and it is more likely that a member of the race more addicted to tobacco would be disciplined.

We do not denigrate the importance of a person's language of preference or other aspects of his national, ethnic or racial self-identification. Differences in language and other cultural attributes may not be used as a fulcrum for discrimination. However, the English-only rule, as applied by Gloor to Mr. Garcia, did not forbid cultural expression to persons for whom compliance with it might impose hardship. While Title VII forbids the imposition of burdensome terms and conditions of employment as well as those that produce an atmosphere of racial and ethnic oppression, the evidence does not support a finding that the English-only rule had this effect on Mr. Garcia. . . .

In some circumstances, the ability to speak or the speaking of a language other than English might be equated with national origin, but this case concerns only a requirement that persons capable of speaking English do so while on duty. . . .

Our opinion does not impress a judicial imprimatur on all employment rules that require an employee to use or forbid him from using a language spoken by him at home or by his forebears. We hold only that an employer's rule forbidding a bilingual employee to speak anything but English in public areas while on the job is not discrimination based on national origin as applied to a person who is fully capable of speaking English and chooses not to do so in deliberate disregard of his employer's rule.

Affirmed.

★★★

Bona Fide Occupational Qualification

Section 703(e) of Title VII provides that it is not illegal to discriminate on the basis of religion, sex, or national origin in situations where religion, sex, or national origin is a "bona fide occupational qualification" (BFOQ). Race or color cannot be a BFOQ. Congress intended the BFOQ provision to be a very limited exception that would apply only to rare situations. EEOC and the courts have followed this intent by recognizing the exception very infrequently.

Most of the situations in which BFOQ has been an issue have involved sex discrimination. Stereotypes or traditional assumptions about which jobs are appropriate for males or females do not establish the BFOQ exception. A basic principle of Title VII is that the individual should decide whether the job is appropriate, assuming that person is qualified to perform it. Thus, males cannot automatically be barred from jobs such as airline flight attendants or secretaries, and females cannot be barred from mining, construction, or other jobs requiring lifting, night work, and so forth. Even the fact that the employer's customers strongly prefer employees to be of one sex or the other does not create the BFOQ exception.

In a few circumstances, however, gender is an essential element of the job. For example, the BFOQ defense has been permitted where one sex or the other is necessary for authenticity, as in the case of models or actors. In addition, being a woman has been held to be a BFOQ for employment as a salesperson in the ladies' undergarments department of a department store, and as a nurse in the labor and delivery section of an obstetrical hospital. Being a man has been held to be a BFOQ for employment as a security guard, where the job involved searching male employees, and also as an attendant in a men's restroom.

Affirmative Action and Reverse Discrimination

The primary strategy in the legal battle against employment discrimination has been simply to prohibit discriminatory practices and to strike them down when they are discovered. Another important weapon, however, has been **affirmative action**—actually giving preferences to minorities and women in the hiring process. In many cases, affirmative action programs include goals and timetables for increasing the percentage of minorities and women in the employer's workforce. The basic purpose of affirmative action is to rectify previous discrimination.

Affirmative action has been used by some courts as a remedy in specific cases of discrimination. In other words, after concluding that an employer had practiced discrimination, some courts have both ordered the cessation of the practice and required the employer to implement an affirmative action program. In addition, some employers, either on their own or in connection with union collective bargaining agreements, have instituted voluntary affirmative action programs.

Since their inception, affirmative action programs have raised difficult legal questions. By granting preferences to minorities and women, these programs discriminate in some degree against white males. White males are protected against race and sex discrimination by Title VII; does so-called **reverse discrimination**, brought about by affirmative action programs, violate Title VII or other discrimination laws?

In *United Steelworkers of America v. Weber*, 443 U.S. 193 (1979), the Supreme Court ruled that *voluntary* affirmative action programs are permissible under Title VII in certain circumstances. In several other cases, lower courts have upheld *mandatory* affirmative action programs in similar circumstances. As a limited exception to the basic prohibition against discrimination, reverse discrimination brought about by affirmative action programs is legal under the following conditions.

1. There must be a formal, systematic program—the employer cannot discriminate against nonminorities on an isolated, ad hoc basis.

2. Any such program must be temporary—it must operate only until its reasonable minority hiring goals are reached.

3. The program cannot completely bar the hiring or promotion of nonminority workers.

4. The program cannot result in the actual firing of nonminority workers.

5. The program cannot force the employer to hire or promote unqualified workers.

6. If the program is court-ordered, it must be based on evidence that there actually had been discrimination by the employer in the past. If the program is voluntary, it can be based either on evidence of past discrimination or merely on evidence that in the past there had been an underutilization of minorities or women by the employer.*

The Doctrine of Comparable Worth

As we will see shortly, a separate federal statute, the Equal Pay Act of 1963, prohibits sex-based discrimination in rates of pay. This law applies only when a male and a female are doing jobs that are substantially the same.

---

* As this text went to press, the Supreme Court agreed to review an important affirmative action case, *Local 638 v. EEOC*, 753 F.2d 1172 (2d Cir. 1985). The Supreme Court's decision in this case should provide further guidance for implementation of affirmative action programs.

Therefore, the Equal Pay Act does not apply to a situation in which a male and a female receive different pay for jobs that are different, even if the evidence indicates that the two jobs are of equal economic value to the employer. Although the doctrine of "comparable worth" does not provide a basis for a claim under the Equal Pay Act, the fact that men and women receive different pay for jobs that are of comparable worth to the employer might be relevant in a Title VII case in some circumstances. Suppose, for example, that a female employee claims that her employer violated Title VII by intentionally placing males and females in different categories of job because of their sex, or by setting different rates of pay for different jobs because one category of job was held primarily by men and the other primarily by women. In such a situation, evidence that the two categories of job were of comparable economic value to the employer would be a relevant factor to be considered by a court when it decides whether an inference of discriminatory intent is warranted.

Although evidence of different pay for jobs of comparable worth may in some circumstances be relevant to a possible inference of discriminatory intent, the courts thus far have held that evidence of comparable worth, by itself, does not establish a violation of Title VII. In other words, the fact that an employer has different pay rates for two different jobs of comparable worth, one type of job being held primarily by males and the other primarily by females, does not establish a violation of Title VII. Other evidence of gender-based discrimination would have to be present.

It is quite common for employers to base pay rates for different jobs on prevailing market rates for such jobs in the area. If such dependence on the market creates a situation in which women and men are paid differently for jobs of comparable worth, has the employer violated Title VII? In the following case, the court attempts to answer this difficult question.

American Federation of State, County, and Municipal Workers v. State of Washington

U.S. Court of Appeals Ninth Circuit
770 F.2d 1401 (1985)

Legislation in the State of Washington required the salaries of state employees to reflect prevailing market rates. Every two years the state conducted an extensive survey to determine market rates for various jobs. This data was then used, along with other factors, to set salaries for the next two years.

The American Federation of State, County, and Municipal Employees (AFSCME) filed suit in federal district court in behalf of a class of 15,000 state employees who worked, or had previously worked, in job categories that were at least 70 percent female. AFSCME charged that the market-based salary system violated Title VII because it amounted to sex discrimination. A study of comparable worth evaluated state jobs on the basis of knowledge and skill, mental demands, accountability, and working conditions. This study (the "Willis study") found a wage differential of about 20 percent, to the disadvantage of employees in jobs held mostly by women, for jobs determined to be of comparable worth. This study had actually been commissioned by the State of Washington itself. The trial court held that the market-based system violated Title VII on the basis of both discriminatory intent (disparate treatment) and

effect (disparate impact), and ordered the state immediately to implement a compensation system based on comparable worth and to award back pay to those affected by the market system. The state appealed to a U.S. Court of Appeals.

Kennedy, Circuit Judge:

The trial court erred in ruling that liability was established under a disparate impact analysis. . . . AFSCME's disparate impact argument is based on the contention that the State of Washington's practice of taking prevailing market rates into account in setting wages has an adverse impact on women, who, historically, have received lower wages than men in the labor market. Disparate impact analysis is confined to cases that challenge a specific, clearly delineated employment practice applied at a single point in the job selection process. . . . [T]he decision to base compensation on the competitive market, rather than on a theory of comparable worth, involves the assessment of a number of complex factors not easily ascertainable, an assessment too multifaceted to be appropriate for disparate impact analysis. . . . [T]he compensation system in question resulted from surveys, agency hearings, administrative recommendations, budget proposals, executive actions, and legislative enactments. A compensation system that is responsive to supply and demand and other market forces is not the type of specific, clearly delineated employment policy [that can] support a claim under disparate impact theory. . . .

We consider next the allegations of disparate treatment. . . . AFSCME contends discriminatory motive may be inferred from the Willis study, which finds the State's practice of setting salaries in reliance on market rates creates a sex-based wage disparity for jobs deemed of comparable worth. AFSCME argues from the study that the market reflects a historical pattern of lower wages to employees in positions staffed predominantly by women; and it contends the State of Washington perpetuates that disparity, in violation of Title VII, by using market rates in the compensation system. The inference of discriminatory motive which AFSCME seeks to draw from the State's participation in the market system fails, as the State did not create the market disparity and has not been shown to have been motivated by impermissible sex-based considerations in setting salaries. . . .

Neither law nor logic deems the free market system a suspect enterprise. Economic reality is that the value of a particular job to an employer is but one factor influencing the rate of compensation for that job. Other considerations may include the availability of workers willing to do the job and the effectiveness of collective bargaining in a particular industry. . . . We find nothing in the language of Title VII or its legislative history to indicate Congress intended to abrogate fundamental economic principles such as the laws of supply and demand or to prevent employers from competing in the labor market. . . .

While the Washington legislature may have the discretion to enact a comparable worth plan if it chooses to do so, Title VII does not obligate it to eliminate an economic inequality that it did not create. . . . Title VII was enacted to ensure equal opportunity in employment to covered individuals, and the State of Washington is not charged here with barring access to particular job classifications on the basis of sex.

We have recognized that in certain cases an inference of intent may be drawn from statistical evidence. We have admonished, however, that statistics must be relied on with caution. Though the comparability of wage rates in dissimilar jobs may be relevant to a determination of discriminatory animus, job evaluation studies and comparable worth statistics alone are insufficient to establish the requisite inference of discriminatory motive critical to the disparate treatment theory. The weight to be accorded such statistics is determined by the existence of independent corroborative evidence of discrimination. . . .

We also reject AFSCME's contention that, having commissioned the Willis study, the State of Washington was committed to implement a new system of compensation based on comparable worth as defined by the study. Whether comparable worth is a feasible approach to employee compensation is a matter of debate. . . . Assuming, however, that like other job evaluation studies it may be useful as a diagnostic tool, we reject a rule that would penalize rather than commend employers for their effort and innovation in undertaking such a study. . . . The results of comparable worth studies will vary depending on the number and types of factors measured and the maximum number of points allotted to each factor. A study that indicates a particular wage structure might be more equitable should not categorically bind the employer who commissioned it. The employer should also be able to take into account market conditions, bargaining demands, and the possibility that another study will yield different results. . . .

The State of Washington's initial reliance on a free market system in which employees in male-dominated jobs are compensated at a higher rate than employees in dissimilar female-dominated jobs is not in and of itself a violation of Title VII, notwithstanding that the Willis study deemed the positions of comparable worth. . . . Reversed.

★★★

Comment: It should be noted that the Washington state legislature had decided in 1983 to gradually phase in a compensation system based on comparable worth over a ten-year period. As noted, however, the trial court's decision had required immediate implementation, and that court's back pay order would have cost the state many millions of dollars.

Other Sources of Employment Discrimination Law

Although Title VII of the 1964 Civil Rights Act is the most important source of law prohibiting employment discrimination, there are several other significant laws in this area which merit discussion.

Executive Orders: Even prior to the 1964 Civil Rights Act, the President had issued several "executive orders" which prohibited employment discrimination by employers doing work under federal government contracts. The President's authority to issue these orders derives from inherent constitutional power to specify the terms of contracts made by the federal government.

Executive Order 11246, currently in force, was issued in 1965. It applies to all employers who have a contract with the federal government (or a subcontract thereunder) which is to be performed within the United States and exceeds $10,000 in amount. The order prohibits these employers from discriminating on the basis of race, color, religion, sex, or national origin, and requires them to take affirmative action to insure that employees and job applicants are treated in a nondiscriminatory manner. A covered employer is also required to include a statement of its nondiscrimination policy in employment advertisements, and to notify any union it deals with that the employer is operating under Executive Order 11246. In addition, the employer is required to include a provision in any agreement with a subcontractor that commits the subcontractor to observe the executive order.

If an employer has a federal government contract or subcontract of $50,000 or more, and at least fifty employees, the employer is also required to prepare a formal, written affirmative action plan. Preparation of such a plan involves a thorough analysis of the employer's present workforce and the available pool of qualified minorities and women in the appropriate area. If this analysis and comparison shows that minorities and women are underrepresented in the workforce, the employer must set specific goals and timetables for correcting the imbalance. The employer is then required to pursue these goals in good faith. Failure to meet a goal is not a violation of the executive order so long as there is evidence that the employer has made a good faith effort to achieve it.

The Office of Federal Contract Compliance Programs (OFCCP) in the Labor Department supervises compliance with Executive Order 11246. The penalty for noncompliance is total or partial cancellation of the employer's government contract and ineligibility for further government contracts until compliance is achieved.

The Equal Pay Act: In 1963, one year before passage of Title VII, Congress enacted the Equal Pay Act as an amendment to the Fair Labor Standards Act. The Equal Pay Act prohibits an employer from paying an employee of one sex less than an employee of the opposite sex when the two employees are performing jobs that require "equal skill, effort, and responsibility," and are doing the jobs "under similar working conditions." Thus, the Equal Pay Act is very narrowly drafted, applying only to discrimination between the sexes, and only to discrimination in pay rates. Trivial differences between two jobs do not prevent them from being considered equal—what is required is that the jobs be *substantially* the same in terms of skill, effort, and responsibility. On the other hand, if the two jobs are really different, an employee being paid less cannot successfully claim a violation of the Equal Pay Act by contending that the jobs are of "comparable worth"—that is, of equivalent value to the employer. As we have already seen, however, there is a violation of Title VII if the evidence shows that men and women were intentionally placed in different jobs because of their gender.

Claims under the Equal Pay Act usually arise from jobs being done simultaneously by males and females. Suppose, however, that a female replaces a male in a particular job and receives less pay despite doing exactly the same job. In such a case, the female employee has a claim under the Act.

If an employee proves the basic elements of an Equal Pay Act violation, the employer is guilty unless it can prove one of four defenses. Employees of different sexes can be paid differently if the payment is based on (1) a seniority system; (2) a formal, consistently followed merit system that is used by the employer in good faith; (3) a system which measures earnings by quantity or quality of production (such as payment on a piecework basis); or (4) a factor other than sex. An example of a "factor other than sex" would be a night-shift differential—thus, there is no violation of the Act if a male employee working on the night shift receives more pay than a female on the day shift, assuming that the night shift has been available to women who want it.

The Equal Pay Act is interpreted and enforced by EEOC. In addition, an individual claiming a violation can file suit in federal court. In many cases, a violation of this Act will also be a violation of Title VII. If an individual has a claim under the Equal Pay Act, however, there are several reasons why he or she might prefer to sue under that statute rather than under Title VII. First, the individual does not have to initially file a complaint with EEOC or a state agency and await the outcome of their action—he or she can simply go to court. Second, the time period during which an Equal Pay Act claim can be asserted (two or three years, depending on the circumstances) is much longer than the time period for filing a claim under Title VII. Third, the Equal Pay Act permits a claimant to recover back wages *plus* an additional amount equal to the back wages. Fourth, an individual plaintiff can receive a jury trial under the Equal Pay Act, whereas there is no jury in Title VII cases.

Age Discrimination in Employment Act: Although Title VII of the 1964 Civil Rights Act does not prohibit age discrimination, Congress passed separate legislation dealing with this problem in 1967 and broadened its coverage in 1974 and again in 1978. The Age Discrimination in Employment Act (ADEA) prohibits all forms of employment discrimination based on age if the victim of the discrimination is between the ages of 40 and 70. The law does not apply unless the complaining party is within the 40-to-70 age bracket. If a person within this age group proves that he or she is a victim of age discrimination, the age of another person favored at the victim's expense does not matter. On the other hand, in a case in which there is a close factual question relating to the employer's discriminatory intent, the age of another person who was allegedly favored at the victim's expense is a relevant part of the process of drawing an inference. Thus, when a close question of discriminatory intent is presented, a 50-year-old complaining party usually will have much greater difficulty convincing a court of the employer's discriminatory intent if the person supposedly favored because of age is 55.

Like Title VII, ADEA applies to discrimination by employers, employment agencies, and labor organizations, as well as federal, state, and local government agencies. The types of employment actions that constitute discrimination, and the methods for proving discrimination under ADEA, are similar to the standards applied under Title VII. Although a violation of ADEA can be proved by showing either discriminatory intent or effect, almost all ADEA cases involve allegations of discriminatory intent. It is much more difficult to establish a prima facie case of discriminatory effect under ADEA than it is under Title VII. Consequently, the plaintiff alleging age discrimination normally must show explicit discriminatory intent or introduce evidence which is sufficient to support a logical inference that the employer's action was based on the plaintiff's age. The burden is then on the employer to show that there was some other reason for the action and that age was not really a determining factor.

ADEA contains a bona fide occupational qualification defense that is practically identical to Title VII's BFOQ defense. It is interpreted narrowly and applied only in unusual cases. In *Western Airlines, Inc. v. Criswell*, 53 U.S.L.W. 4766 (1985), the Supreme Court affirmed the lower court's decision that Western Airlines' policy of mandatory retirement for flight engineers at age 60 violated ADEA. Because a flight engineer is a member of the cockpit crew, Western argued that being less than 60 is a bona fide occupational qualification. The Supreme Court held that an employer must meet two requirements in order to establish the BFOQ defense under ADEA. First, the employer must prove that the age requirement is reasonably necessary to the essence of the employer's business (such as the safe transportation of passengers). Second, the employer must have a factual basis for believing either (1) that all or substantially all of the employees over a particular age are unable to safely and efficiently perform the necessary task, or (2) that it would be impractical to make such a determination on an individual basis. Western's evidence did not fulfill either alternative of the second requirement.

Also like Title VII, ADEA permits employers to use bona fide seniority systems even if age discrimination results. Another exception permits a company to require an executive to retire at age 65 if he or she will receive at least $44,000 a year in retirement income.

ADEA can be enforced by either EEOC, a state agency, or an individual victim of age discrimination. Like Title VII, ADEA requires an individual first to file a complaint with EEOC or the appropriate state agency within 180 days after the alleged discrimination occurred, and to await agency action for a stated period of time before filing a lawsuit in federal court. A jury trial is permitted under ADEA, unlike Title VII. Also, a plaintiff generally is able to recover greater monetary damages under ADEA than is possible for a plaintiff in a Title VII case.

The Rehabilitation Act: The Rehabilitation Act of 1973 provides limited protection for handicapped individuals against employment discrimination. The Act defines "handicapped individual" as "any person who (a) has a physical or mental impairment, which substantially limits one or more of such person's major life activities, (b) has a record of such an impairment, or (c) is regarded as having such an impairment."

The definition of handicapped is quite broad. It includes mental retardation, emotional disorders, and learning disabilities, as well as various physical disabilities such as paralysis, blindness, deafness, and amputation. Those having severe conditions such as epilepsy, heart disease, kidney disease, and so forth also are within the definition. Although narcotics addiction or alcholism can be included in the definition of handicapped, the Act specifically provides that it does not cover a *current user* of alcohol or drugs if such use prevents that person from performing the duties of the job or if employing that person would cause risk to the property or safety of others.

The Rehabilitation Act does not have the type of broad focus that Title VII has. Instead, its provisions apply only to (1) federal agencies, (2) employers having contracts with the federal government exceeding $2,500, and (3) any program receiving federal financial assistance. All of these are prohibited from discriminating against the handicapped. In addition, (1) and (2) are required to take affirmative action regarding the hiring and promotion of handicapped individuals. If an employer has federal contracts of at least $50,000 and fifty or more employees, its affirmative action plan must be a formal, written one.

The Act is enforced against federal agencies by EEOC or private lawsuit, against federal contractors by the Office of Federal Contract Compliance Programs, and against government-assisted programs by a variety of federal departments and agencies under the coordination of the Department of Justice.

Only those handicapped individuals who are qualified for the particular job in question are protected by the Rehabilitation Act. Agencies, contractors, and programs are required to make "reasonable accommodation" (slight adjustments, such as letting a diabetic eat midmorning and midafternoon snacks), but the handicapped person must be able to do the job.

The Constitution: Under the Fifth and Fourteenth Amendments to the U.S. Constitution, federal, state, and local government action must have a reasonable, rational basis. This constitutional protection against arbitrariness applies to all types of government action, including government employment practices. Discrimination by a government employer against a racial minority will always be unconstitutional. Discrimination based on religion, sex, national origin, age, or handicap is unconstitutional unless it can be shown that the discrimination was necessary for the furtherance of some legitimate public interest. For example, a mandatory retirement age of fifty for state police was held to be valid under the Constitution because it furthered the legitimate public interest in maintaining a physically prepared police force. On the other hand, a rule permitting only males to be hired as pages in a state legislature was held to be unconstitutional.

There is a great deal of overlap between this constitutional protection and the protection granted by Title VII. Thus, employment discrimination by a government employer sometimes will violate both the Constitution and Title VII. As a general proposition, however, it is substantially more difficult to prove that government employment discrimination violates the Constitution than it is to prove that it violates Title VII. The Constitution usually can be applied only to obvious, intentional discrimination.

Civil Rights Act of 1866: Shortly after the Civil War, Congress enacted several pieces of civil rights legislation. One of the most important is commonly referred to as Section 1981.[10] This provision, which was part of the Civil Rights Act of 1866, states that "all persons . . . shall have the same right to make and enforce contracts . . . as enjoyed by white citizens."

For over one hundred years it was assumed that Congress had enacted this statute pursuant to the Fourteenth Amendment's Equal Protection Clause, which only applies to government action. In 1968, however, the Supreme Court ruled that the statute actually had been enacted pursuant to the Thirteenth Amendment (abolition of slavery), which applied to both government and private action. Since employment relationships are included within the phrase "to make and enforce contracts," discrimination by private employers violates Section 1981. This law applies primarily only to *racial* discrimination, although some lower courts have also applied it to discrimination based on national origin or citizenship. Section 1981 does not prohibit discrimination based on sex, religion, age, handicap, or other reason.

The Supreme Court has held that Section 1981 prohibits only *intentional* discrimination. Thus, a violation of this statute cannot be established merely by showing discriminatory effects. With respect to intentional discrimination based on race, national origin, or citizenship, Section 1981 is interpreted and applied almost identically to Title VII. From a procedural standpoint, however, it can be quite important. Section 1981 is not enforced by EEOC or any other agency, and an individual does not have to complain to the agency and await its action before filing a lawsuit. In addition, the time period during which a complaint can be filed is much longer under Section 1981 than under Title VII, and the potential monetary recovery is much greater under Section 1981.

Protection Against Retaliation

Occasionally an employer may become displeased with something an employee does, even though the employee is satisfactorily performing the job and his or her conduct has been lawful and proper. If the employer retaliates

[10] It is so called because it is found in Section 1981 of Title 42 of the United States Code.

by firing, demoting, or otherwise punishing the employee, the question arises whether the employee has any legal recourse against the retaliation.

At common law, of course, the employee's only protection was by contract. An employer could be sued for retaliating against proper, lawful conduct only if the employer's action constituted a breach of contract. This usually was not the case, because most employees worked without individual contracts. The rise and legal recognition of the union movement extended significant protection to unionized employees, because most employer-labor union contracts permit the employer to discharge or otherwise punish a union member (employee) only if there is "good cause" for doing so.

Many of the statutes passed in recent decades dealing with employment contain limited protection against retaliation. For example, many state workers' compensation statutes include provisions prohibiting the employer from retaliating against an employee for filing a claim for compensation or cooperating with the investigation of a claim. By statute or judicial decision, employees are protected in most states against retaliation for serving on a jury. The major federal employment laws, including the Occupational Safety and Health Act, Fair Labor Standards Act, Pension Reform Act, and Title VII of the 1964 Civil Rights Act, contain provisions protecting employees from employer retaliation resulting from the employee's assertion of any right granted by these laws or cooperation with any investigation or legal proceeding connected with them.

Very recently, a few state courts have begun to change the common law by protecting employees against retaliation when the employer's action is against public policy. For example, one court ruled that an employee had a legal claim against the employer for firing the employee because of his attempts to persuade the employer (a bank) to comply with consumer credit laws. Although most courts have not yet granted protection against retaliation on public policy grounds, recognition of the concept could very well be a future trend.

Questions and Problems

1. Five employees of Omni Georgia were fired and replaced by Orientals of Korean origin. The fired employees were all of U.S. origin; some were white and some were black. The supervisor who made the hiring and firing decisions was an Oriental of Japanese origin. The fired employees sued the employer, claiming that Title VII had been violated. No evidence was presented as to the actual motive for the firings and replacements. Has Title VII been violated? Discuss. (*Bullard v. Omni Georgia*, 640 F.2d 632, 5th Cir. 1981.)

2. An employee belonged to the Black Muslim faith. She was required by her religion to wear dresses that substantially covered her legs and arms, and that had a high neckline. Her supervisor told her that such attention-getting clothing was inappropriate and she must change her style of dress or be dismissed. Other female employees were permitted to wear miniskirts, which were fashionable at the time and which were considered by the employer to be more "business-like." EEOC con-

tended that the employer had violated Title VII. Discuss whether this contention is correct. (CCH EEOC Decisions §6,283, 1973.)

3. Young, an atheist, was employed as a teller at a branch office of Southwestern Savings & Loan. All Southwestern employees were required to attend a monthly staff meeting at the main office devoted to various business matters. These meetings were always opened with a short religious talk and a prayer, both nondenominational in nature. Young, who felt that her freedom of conscience was violated by the religious portion of the meetings, stopped attending the meetings altogether. She did not, however, register any protest with anyone at Southwestern, nor did she tell them why she had stopped attending the staff meetings. After a few months her absence was noted, and she revealed her objection to the religious portion of the meetings to her supervisor, who informed her that attendance was required and that she could simply "close her ears" during the brief opening devotionals. At the close of business that day Young checked in her cash drawer, turned in her keys, and informed her supervisor that she was leaving Southwestern. Pressed for a reason, she stated that she could not attend the "prayer meetings." She refused to submit a letter of resignation, however, and stated that she was "being fired." Does Young have a Title VII claim against Southwestern for religious discrimination? Discuss. Is the fact that Southwestern had a policy (unknown to Young and her supervisor) permitting employees who objected to miss the religious portion of the meetings relevant to a Title VII claim? (*Young v. Southwestern Savings & Loan Ass'n*, 509 F.2d 140, 5th Cir. 1975.)

4. Margaret Hasselman worked as a lobby attendant in an office building managed by Sage Realty. She was required by her employer to wear a "revealing and provocative" uniform which caused her to be subjected to repeated and abusive sexual harassment by various people. She finally refused to wear the uniform and was fired. EEOC filed suit against the employer. Did the employer's actions violate Title VII? Discuss. (*EEOC v. Sage Realty Corp.*, 507 F. Supp. 599, S.D.N.Y. 1981.)

5. The New York City Transit Authority, which operated the subway system and certain bus lines, had a rule excluding from employment any person who regularly used narcotics. The Authority interpreted this rule as also applying to users of methadone, including those receiving methadone maintenance treatment for curing heroin addiction. Most of the Transit Authority's employees worked in jobs that were highly safety-sensitive and required maximum alertness and competence. These jobs included operating buses and subway cars; maintaining the buses, subway cars, tracks, and tunnels; operating cranes; and handling high-voltage equipment. A substantial number of other jobs involved the handling of large sums of money. Several former and prospective employees, all on methadone programs, sued the Authority for allegedly violating Title VII. Plaintiffs introduced evidence showing that (a) 81 percent of the employees who were referred to the Authority's medical director for suspected drug use were black or Hispanic, and (b) 63 percent of the persons in New York City participating in publicly operated methadone maintenance programs were black or Hispanic. Discuss whether the Transit Authority violated Title VII. (*New York City Transit Authority v. Beazer*, 440 U.S. 568, 1979.)

6. To be eligible for promotion to the position of welfare eligibility supervisor in the Connecticut Department of Income Maintenance, candidates were required to pass a standardized written examination. Only those passing the test formed the eligibility pool from which individuals were selected for promotion. The passing rate of blacks was approximately 54 percent, that of whites was about 79 percent. Selection for promotion from the eligibility pool was based on past work performance, supervisors' recommendations, and seniority. In addition, in the final step of the process an affirmative action program was employed to insure substantial representation of minority candidates at the supervisory level. Several black employees who failed the

test filed suit claiming that the test had a discriminatory impact on their group. The State of Connecticut responded by arguing that the test should not be considered alone, and that plaintiffs had not established a prima facie case of discrimination, because the *total* selection process did not have a discriminatory impact. Have plaintiffs established a prima facie violation of Title VII, thus requiring the defendant to formally validate the test? Discuss. (*Connecticut v. Teal*, 457 U.S. 440, 1982.)

7. Fernandez, a female employee of Wynn Oil Co., had worked in various positions for the company over a seven-year period. She sought a promotion to the position of director of international marketing, which would have required her to work with Latin American customers and distributors. The cultural preferences and mores of these customers and distributors were such that a male would be preferable for the job. It was shown, for example, that a female in the position would "have great difficulty in conducting business in South America from a hotel room." She was not given the promotion and later sued Wynn, claiming that the employer had practiced sex discrimination in violation of Title VII. Wynn claimed that sex was a BFOQ for this job. Who is right? Discuss. (*Fernandez v. Wynn Oil Co.*, 653 F.2d 1273, 9th Cir. 1981.)

8. Weeks, a female, had worked for the telephone company in Georgia for nineteen years before asking that she be given the job of switchman. Her request was denied, and she was told that women were not eligible for the job because it was strenuous and required the employee to be on twenty-four hour call. A state statute in Georgia prohibited women from being employed in a job that would require them to lift over thirty pounds. Weeks claimed that her employer had illegally discriminated on the basis of her sex, and the employer contended that sex was a BFOQ for this job. Was there a violation of Title VII? Discuss. (*Weeks v. Southern Bell Telephone & Telegraph Co.*, 408 F.2d 228, 5th Cir. 1969.)

9. Lehman, a white male, and Tidwell, a black male, worked as temporary, part-time employees for Yellow Freight System, an interstate trucking company. Their duties primarily involved driving trucks in Indiana. Yellow Freight usually filled open positions for regular truck drivers from among those who had worked as temporary drivers. When such a position became open at the employer's Muncie, Indiana, terminal, both Lehman and Tidwell applied for the job. Lehman had the appropriate driver's license plus substantial truck driving experience, whereas Tidwell did not have the required license and his only truck driving experience was that which he received during his one month as a temporary for Yellow Freight. McDonald, manager of the Muncie terminal, hired Tidwell and rejected Lehman. The employer had to train Tidwell after hiring him. Yellow Freight had a formal affirmative action plan for its nationwide operation, but McDonald knew practically nothing about the plan and paid no attention to it. Instead, he took his own affirmative action by explicitly preferring minorities in this and several other instances. Lehman sued Yellow Freight, claiming he had been discriminated against because he was white. Did McDonald's actions violate Title VII? Discuss. (*Lehman v. Yellow Freight System, Inc.*, 651 F.2d 520, 7th Cir. 1981.)

10. Coates was a field engineer in the Danville, Virginia, office of NCR. Field engineers maintained and repaired NCR equipment under maintenance agreements with customers. During the early 1970s NCR was phasing out the manufacture of electromechanical office equipment in favor of electronic equipment. This change required the retraining of field engineers to service the electronic equipment. Younger men were generally selected for this training over the older employees. It was felt that the younger employees, who usually had lower productivity, could be more easily spared from field operations for retraining than could the older employees. Even when older employees were selected for retraining, the heavy demands made upon their time in the field often made scheduling impossible. In 1974, principally because of an economic downturn, the Danville manager was directed to recommend several field engineers for discharge. Ability to service the new electronic equipment was to be a principal criteria in deciding whom to recommend for discharge. The Danville manager therefore used training level as a criterion, and discharged two employees—Coates, who was 50 years old, and another who was 40. Neither had been trained on the new electronic equipment. Coates filed suit alleging a violation of ADEA. Discuss whether Coates should win. (*Coates v. National Cash Register Co.*, 433 F. Supp. 655, W.D. Va. 1977.)

C·H·A·P·T·E·R 16

EMPLOYMENT LAW
LABOR-MANAGEMENT RELATIONS

The Rise of Organized Labor

In most types of relationships harmony is a highly desirable goal. In the relationship between employer and employee, some degree of harmony is critical to efficient production. On the other hand, one must realize that a certain amount of tension is an inevitable part of this association. Although employer and employee share the common goal of making the business enterprise an economic success, they also have conflicting interests. The employer is a buyer of labor, the employee a seller. The employer wants to obtain labor at the lowest possible cost; the employee wants to receive the highest possible price and best possible conditions.

In the average situation, the employer has much greater bargaining power than the employee. In purely economic terms, the employer is much more important to the individual employee than the employee is to the employer. Consequently, the tendency of employees has been to unite in an attempt to increase their bargaining power. By dealing with the employer as a group, employees usually have been able to negotiate higher wages and better hours and working conditions than any single employee could have obtained. All or a substantial part of the employer's workforce usually is quite important

"... coupled with a guaranteed increase in pay corresponding to the rise in the cost of living to be reviewed every three months, higher compensation for training flights, coffee break every three houses ..."

Union-management negotiations must focus on particular needs of both sides.

Source: Reprinted from *Wright Side Up*; copyright © 1981 by Don Wright. Reprinted by permission of Simon & Schuster.

economically to the employer. This increased power has given employee groups, or unions, the ability to use various economic weapons. Strikes—work stoppages by unions—have been particularly effective. Picketing the employer's premises—walking in highly visible places with signs and placards—sometimes has been useful in obtaining public sympathy and assistance from other employee unions. Attempts by unions to persuade the public to boycott—stop buying—the employer's products usually have not been very successful, but on a few occasions these attempts have resulted in significant economic pressure on the employer.

Employers have not been without weapons in these confrontations. In some situations, employers have successfully countered union demands by "lockout"—temporarily barring employees from the workplace. Hiring replacements for striking workers has been successfully accomplished by employers in some labor disputes. The present legal status of these economic weapons is discussed later in the chapter.

During the early stages of the American labor movement, employers frequently used the courts to stifle employee organizations. Until the mid-1800s, the **criminal conspiracy doctrine** was effectively used. The combination of employees was viewed as being a criminal offense in and of itself, without regard to any particular actions taken by the union. After courts began to view unions as legal organizations in the mid-1800s, employers pursued other routes. In many cases they were able to file civil suits and obtain *injunctions* against particular union activities, such as strikes and pickets. If union members violated the court's injunction, they could be fined and jailed for contempt of court. In 1890 employers obtained a new weapon when Congress passed the Sherman Act. Although the Sherman Act was aimed primarily at anticompetitive activities by *business firms*, employers were able to use the Sherman Act against unions by convincing many courts that union activities were "combinations in restraint of trade" and thus in violation of the Act.

Many of the labor disputes of the late 1800s and early 1900s caused significant disruptions of commercial activity. Several disputes, such as the Pullman Strike in 1893, resulted in actual violence. These incidents served to highlight the fact that the peaceful, expeditious resolution of labor disputes should be a high national priority. Public opinion regarding organized labor continued to be deeply divided; but regardless of their personal views of the issue, more people began to recognize the need for some kind of new approach to the labor problem. Moreover, with the Great Depression of the 1930s came a close reexamination of our economic system, including the place of organized labor in the system.

Thus, during the late nineteenth century and first three decades of the twentieth century, the stage was gradually set for major legislative action. During this same era, organized labor grew in number and political power, creating further pressure on government policy makers to provide solutions. The most important statutory enactments resulting from the rise of organized labor are now examined.

Federal Legislation

Legislation Prior to 1935

Clayton Act: Enacted in 1914, the Clayton Act essentially is an antitrust law dealing with mergers and several other anticompetitive business practices. In Section 6 of the Act, however, Congress provided an exemption from the antitrust laws for the organization and normal activities of labor unions.

Under this exemption, labor unions can organize, collectively bargain with an employer, and use economic weapons such as strikes and pickets without violating the Sherman Act or other antitrust law. The exemption, however, is not absolute. A labor union can violate the Sherman Act if it joins with someone outside organized labor (such as the employer) to suppress free trade in a manner that is not closely related to legitimate union objectives. For example, there is no antitrust exemption for an agreement between union and employer to the effect that the employer will not buy goods from another company that employs nonunion workers.

Railway Labor Act: Because of its obvious impact on interstate commerce, its importance to the general public, and its history of labor strife, the railroad industry was the object of the first significant piece of federal labor legislation. The Railway Labor Act, passed in 1926 and amended several times through the years, is still the basic statute governing labor-management relations in the rail industry. Its coverage was extended to airlines in 1936. Although there are major differences, in many respects this Act is similar to the National Labor Relations Act, discussed later.

Norris-La Guardia Act: In 1932 Congress passed the Norris-La Guardia Act, which clearly recognized the legitimacy of labor unions and effectively removed the power of federal courts to issue injunctions against most union activities. The Act did not actually require employers to recognize and bargain with unions, but it did free the unions to use economic weapons to bring about such recognition and bargaining. Because of the Norris-La Guardia Act, federal courts today grant injunctions in labor disputes only under unusual and compelling circumstances, such as when violence is involved.[1]

Another important section of Norris-La Guardia prohibited "yellow dog" contracts, in which the employer obtained the agreement of individual employees that they would not join a labor union. This legal prohibition of yellow dog contracts is still in effect.

The National Labor Relations Act and Its Amendments

The Original National Labor Relations Act: The first truly comprehensive federal legislation in the area of labor-management relations was the National Labor Relations Act of 1935 (NLRA or Wagner Act). This Act (1) established methods for selecting the labor union that would represent a particular group of employees, (2) required the employer to bargain with that union, (3) prescribed certain fundamental rights of employees, (4) prohibited several specified "unfair labor practices" by employers, and (5) created the National Labor Relations Board to administer and enforce the NLRA.

The Taft-Hartley Amendments: After passage of the NLRA, labor unions enjoyed tremendous gains in membership and power. Total union membership in this country increased from approximately three million to fifteen million from 1935 to 1947. During the years immediately after World War II, many people began to feel that unions had acquired too much power, and there was some evidence to support this view. A number of critical industries suffered crippling strikes during periods of high consumer demand after the war. The public became less supportive of labor unions because of these strikes and also because of practices such as "secondary boycotts" (discussed later) which many viewed as unfair. The apparent power of particular

[1] *State* courts also are generally prohibited from enjoining nonviolent union activities under the principle of *federal preemption*. This prohibition is discussed shortly.

individuals in organized labor—the so-called "labor bosses"—also contributed to the increasing public distrust of unions.

Factors such as these led Congress in 1947 to enact the Labor-Management Relations Act, usually called the Taft-Hartley Act. The Taft-Hartley Act, which amended the NLRA, attempted to place employer and union power more in balance by (1) prohibiting particular unfair labor practices by *unions*; (2) outlawing the "closed shop," an agreement between union and employer that the employer will require all employees to join the union as a condition of their employment; (3) creating the Federal Mediation and Conciliation Service for the purpose of assisting employers and unions to reach compromises; (4) giving employers and unions (and sometimes individual employees) the power to file lawsuits to enforce collective bargaining agreements; and (5) giving the President authority to intervene in industry-wide labor disputes when, in the President's opinion, the occurrence or continuance of the dispute would "imperil the national health or safety." In the last situation the President may appoint a board of inquiry to study the dispute and make a written report that identifies the positions of employer and union. After receiving this support, the President has authority to ask a federal district court for an injunction prohibiting a lockout by the employer or a strike by the union for a period of eighty days. (This injunction is sometimes called a "back to work order," and the period of time an "eighty-day cooling-off period.") If no settlement has been reached by the end of eighty days, the lockout or strike can continue unless Congress stops it by emergency legislation.

The Landrum-Griffin Amendments: During the 1950s there was increasing concern about the internal operations of many unions. The primary focus of this concern was evidence of a lack of democratic processes within a number of unions and actual corruption on the part of some union leaders. To protect rank-and-file employees from exploitation by union officials, Congress in 1959 passed the Labor-Management Reporting and Disclosure Act. Generally referred to as the Landrum-Griffin Act, this legislation amended the NLRA by (1) establishing a so-called bill of rights for union members, (2) requiring public financial disclosure by unions and union leaders, and (3) regulating the procedures for election of union officials by members.

When federal labor relations law is discussed in the remainder of this chapter, the general term of NLRA refers to the original NLRA plus the Taft-Hartley and Landrum-Griffin amendments, as well as several other minor amendments.

The Limited Role of State Law

Both the federal and state governments exercise regulatory authority over many matters, such as securities trading and anticompetitive business practices. In the case of labor-management relations, however, the Supreme

Court has ruled that there is such a great need for a truly uniform national labor policy that **federal preemption** should be the rule. In other words, labor relations law is almost exclusively the province of Congress, the federal courts, and the National Labor Relations Board. State legislatures, agencies, and courts have almost no jurisdiction over these matters.

There are, however, a few limited exceptions. For example, state courts or agencies may exercise jurisdiction over particular activities or businesses when the NLRA does not apply or when the National Labor Relations Board has refused to take jurisdiction because of an insubstantial effect on interstate commerce. Also, state courts are permitted to hear a few types of cases arising from labor disputes, such as lawsuits against those who have committed or threatened violence in these disputes.

The National Labor Relations Board

The NLRA is administered and enforced by the National Labor Relations Board. This agency is divided into two divisions, the Board itself and the General Counsel. The Board consists of five members appointed by the President for five-year terms. The General Counsel is appointed by the President for a four-year term. Most of the work of the General Counsel's division is done by thirty-one regional field offices located throughout the country, each headed by a Regional Director.

The Board and the General Counsel perform distinct but interrelated functions in carrying out the two principal activities required by the NLRA: deciding whether employer or union conduct constitutes an unfair labor practice, and determining whether a particular union is the appropriate representative for a group of employees.

Unfair labor practice cases begin when an employer, employee, or union files a charge with one of the regional offices. The charge will be investigated, and if it has merit the Regional Director will file a formal complaint. A trial-like hearing on the complaint will then be conducted before one of the Board's Administrative Law Judges (ALJ), attorneys from the regional office acting as prosecutors. The ALJ's decision on what the facts are, what the applicable law is, and what remedy should be ordered are then reviewed by the Board itself. If the Board determines that an unfair labor practice has been committed, it issues an administrative order. Depending on the nature of the case, this order may require the respondent (that is, the one charged) to (1) "cease and desist" particular illegal activities; (2) engage in genuine, good-faith bargaining with the other party to the labor dispute; (3) rehire illegally discharged employees, and in some cases pay them back wages; or (4) take any other steps deemed necessary to effectively correct the unfair labor practice.

A decision of the Board in favor of the respondent usually goes no further. A decision against the respondent, however, is frequently reviewed by a U.S. Court of Appeals. If the court upholds the Board's decision, the court will order compliance. Failure to comply with this court order can result in a fine, a jail term for contempt of court, or both. Review of the Board's decision by a U.S. Court of Appeals can take place in either of two ways: the respondent may appeal directly to the court, or the Board may initiate the review process by asking the court for an enforcement order. In either case, the Court of Appeals' decision will be reviewed by the Supreme Court only in those few instances in which the high court grants a writ of certiorari.

The other major regulatory function required by the NLRA—supervising the selection of an employee representative (union)—also begins at the regional office level. In fact, the representation decisions made at this level are usually final. In a few limited situations, however, a decision made by the Regional Director in a representation proceeding can be appealed to the Board, with subsequent appeal to a U.S. Court of Appeals.

After examining the scope of the NLRA, the NLRA's regulation of the representative selection process is examined as well, followed by particular types of conduct that may constitute unfair labor practices.

Scope of the NLRA

General Coverage

In general, the NLRA is the governing law whenever (1) there is a "labor dispute" (2) involving an employer whose business activity either *involves* or *affects* interstate commerce.

The term "labor dispute" is a very broad one, defined in Section 2(9) of the NLRA as "any controversy concerning terms, tenure or conditions of employment, or concerning the association or representation of persons in negotiating, fixing, maintaining, changing, or seeking to arrange terms or conditions of employment. . . ."

The test for interstate commerce is also very broad. By including within the NLRA's coverage any business whose activities even *affect* interstate commerce, Congress has exercised the maximum authority granted to it by the Constitution's Commerce Clause. On the other hand, when administering and enforcing the NLRA, the National Labor Relations Board does not always use its jurisdiction to the fullest extent. When a particular business has only a minimal effect on interstate commerce, the Board has the legal discretion to refuse to take jurisdiction. For a number of years, the Board has followed certain objective standards in determining whether to exercise jurisdiction over a labor dispute. For example, the Board will assert its authority over a labor dispute involving a retail business only if the total enterprise affects interstate commerce *and* has a total volume of business of at least $500,000 annually. (Other dollar amounts are used for nonretail businesses, office buildings, newspapers, public utilities, transportation firms, hotels, and other categories.)

Exemptions

The NLRA expressly exempts *federal, state, and local government employment*. Federal government employees do, however, have limited organizational and collective-bargaining rights under an executive order first issued by President Kennedy in 1962. In some states, the employees of state and local governments have been given certain organizational and collective bargaining rights by state statute.

Railroads and *airlines* are not within the NLRA because their labor relations are governed by the Railway Labor Act. *Agriculture employees* and *domestic servants* also are excluded as they are from many other federal and state employment laws. *Independent contractors* are similarly not included in the NLRA and most other employment legislation.

Supervisory employees—those who spend the bulk of their time directing the work of subordinate employees—are not covered by NLRA. *Managerial employees*—those who formulate policy and make management decisions—also are excluded. These two classes of employees obviously are closely related, and a particular employee may perform both functions. Both exemptions grow out of the idea that an employer is entitled to the undivided loyalty of its own representatives. In any event, one whose primary duties are either supervisory, managerial, or both, is not covered by NLRA. An individual also will be excluded from NLRA's coverage if he or she is a so-called "confidential employee"—one who works closely with a manager on labor relations matters. An example is the secretary to the company's vice president in charge of labor relations.

The question whether the duties of particular employees are sufficiently managerial in nature to exclude them from the NLRA often is an easy one, but not always. Perhaps nowhere is it more difficult than in the case of university faculty.

National Labor Relations Board v. Yeshiva University
U.S. Supreme Court
444 U.S. 672 (1980)

Yeshiva is a private university in New York City which conducts a broad range of arts and sciences programs in five undergraduate and eight graduate schools. Like most universities, it is governed by a central administrative hierarchy including, in descending order, the board of trustees, president, several vice presidents, and the deans or directors of individual schools.

Subject to ultimate control by the central administration, the faculty in each school effectively determined its curriculum, grading system, admission and continuance standards, academic calendars, and course schedules. The faculty also was active in nonacademic decision making, including faculty hiring, tenure, termination, and promotion. Faculty recommendations in all those areas could be vetoed by the central administration, but in practice they usually were followed.

The Yeshiva University Faculty Association ("the Union") filed a representation petition with the National Labor Relations Board ("the Board"), seeking certification as bargaining agent for the faculty. The University opposed the petition, claiming that faculty were managerial personnel and thus excluded from the NLRA ("the Act"). After conducting hearings, the Board granted the petition and ordered an election, at which the faculty selected the Union as its bargaining representative. The University refused to recognize the

Union, whereupon the Board found the University guilty of an unfair labor practice and ordered it to recognize and bargain with the Union. The University refused, and the Board sought an enforcement order in the Court of Appeals. Disagreeing with the Board, the court ruled that the faculty were managerial employees and declined to enforce the Board's order. The Board appealed to the U.S. Supreme Court.

Powell, Justice:

. . . The Act was intended to accommodate the type of management-employee relations that prevail in the pyramidal hierarchies of private industry. In contrast, authority in the typical "mature" private university is divided between a central administration and one or more collegial bodies. This system of "shared authority" evolved from the medieval model of collegial decisionmaking in which guilds of scholars were responsible only to themselves. At early universities, the faculty were the school. Although faculties have been subject to external control in the United States since colonial times, traditions of collegiality continue to play a significant role at many universities including Yeshiva. . . .

Managerial employees are defined as those who "formulate and effectuate management policies by expressing and making operative the decisions of their employer.". . . Managerial employees must exercise discretion within or even independently of established employer policy and must be aligned with management. . . .

The Board does not contend that the Yeshiva faculty's decisionmaking is too insignificant to be deemed managerial. Nor does it suggest that the role of the faculty is merely advisory and thus not managerial. Instead, it contends that the managerial exclusion cannot be applied in a straightforward fashion to professional employees because those employees often appear to be exercising managerial authority when they are merely performing routine job duties. The status of such employees, in the Board's view, must be determined by reference to the "alignment with management" criterion. The Board argues that the Yeshiva faculty are not aligned with management because they are expected to exercise "independent professional judgment" while participating in academic governance, and because they are neither "expected to conform to management policies [nor] judged according to their effectiveness in carrying out those policies." Because of this independence, the Board contends there is no danger of divided loyalty and no need for the managerial exclusion. In its view, union pressure cannot divert the faculty from adhering to the interests of the university, because the university itself expects its faculty to pursue professional values rather than institutional interests. . . .

The controlling consideration in this case is that the faculty of Yeshiva University exercise authority which in any other context unquestionably would be managerial. Their authority in academic matters is absolute. They decide what courses will be offered, when they will be scheduled, and to whom they will be taught. They debate and determine teaching methods, grading policies, and matriculation standards. They effectively decide which students will be admitted, retained, and graduated. On occasion their views have determined the size of the student body, the tuition to be charged, and the location of a school. When one considers the function of a university, it is difficult to imagine decisions more managerial than these. To the extent the industrial analogy applies, the faculty determines within each school the product to be produced, the terms upon which it will be offered, and the customers who will be served. . . .

In arguing that a faculty member exercising independent judgment acts primarily in his own interest and therefore does not represent the interest of his employer, the Board assumes that the professional interests of the faculty and the interests of the institution are distinct, separable entities with which a faculty member could not simultaneously be aligned. . . . In fact, the faculty's professional interests—as applied to governance at a university like Yeshiva—cannot be separated from those of the institution.

In such a university, the predominant policy normally is to operate a quality institution of higher learning that will accomplish broadly defined educational goals within the limits of its financial resources. The "business" of a university is education, and its vitality ultimately must depend on academic policies that largely are formulated and generally are implemented by faculty governance decisions. Faculty members enhance their own standing and fulfill their professional mission by ensuring that the university's objectives are met. But there can be no doubt that the quest for academic excellence and institutional distinction is a "policy" to which the administration expects the faculty to adhere, whether it be defined as a professional or an institutional goal. . . .

The University requires faculty participation in governance because professional expertise is indispensable to the formulation and implementation of academic policy. It may appear, as the Board contends, that the professor performing governance functions is less "accountable" for departures from institutional policy than a middle-level industrial manager whose discretion is more confined. Moreover, traditional systems of collegiality and tenure insulate the professor from some of the sanctions applied to an industrial manager who fails to adhere to company policy. But the analogy of the university to industry need not, and indeed cannot, be complete. It is clear that Yeshiva and like universities must rely on their faculties to participate in the making and implementation of their policies.

Affirmed. [The faculty cannot form a union under the protection of the NLRA.]

★★★

Selecting the Bargaining Representative

The basic thrust of the NLRA is to permit employees to combine, select a representative for the group (a labor union), and bargain with the employer. The employer, in turn, is required to recognize and bargain with the representative. With bargaining power being relatively equal on both sides (or at least not drastically unequal), peaceful relations and essential fairness are more likely to result.

Initial Organizing

The organizational effort sometimes begins with several employees who feel they could benefit from collective bargaining. If there appears to be widespread interest, the next step may be to contact an established labor union, whose agents would then proceed with the organizational effort. Or the original group of employees may have contacted the union at an earlier stage, with union agents taking the initial step of determining and generating interest. In some cases, an agent of the union may have actually originated the movement by contacting employees before the employees themselves had taken any steps toward organizing.

A group of employees do not have to become part of an established union—they can form their own labor organization. Because there are already so many labor unions in existence, the formation of a completely new one today is the exception rather than the rule. Most of the existing unions are affiliated with national or international labor organizations, such as the International Longshoremen's Association. In addition, many of the national organizations have formed a loose federation with one another (the AFL-CIO).

In any event, a group of employees may choose a union and the employer may voluntarily recognize it without any formal involvement by the National Labor Relations Board. For several reasons, however, this usually is not the case. More often than not, a union is chosen by means of a formal election supervised by one of the regional NLRB offices. An employer may want such an election because it doubts that a majority of its employees wish to join a union. Or the employer may be so opposed to the idea that it would require a formal election in any event. In some cases an employer may desire an election because two or more rival unions demand recognition. In a majority of situations, though, it is the union that requests a supervised election. This may be because the employer has refused to recognize the union, or it may be because the union wants the protection afforded by such an election. If a union is selected by employees as their official bargaining representative in a supervised election, the union becomes *certified* and is protected from challenge by a rival union for at least one year.

The Representation Election

Petition: The first step in the representation election procedure is the filing of a petition with the Board's Regional Director. The employer is permitted to petition for an election if a union has demanded recognition by the employer. However, if the demanding union is already the certified representative of employees and the employer wishes to test the union's status by election, the employer must also demonstrate that there is good reason to believe that a majority of employees no longer support the union.

A union, or a group of employees, may petition for an election only if they produce evidence of substantial employee interest in being represented by the particular union. To establish this substantial interest, the union must submit written documentation signed by at least 30 percent of the employees in the group to be represented. This documentation often takes the form of signed "authorization cards," on which each employee expresses a desire to be represented by the union. Signed applications for union membership or similar evidence can also be used. After one union has met the substantial interest requirement, another union may also have its name placed on the election ballot merely by showing that at least one employee in the group supports this rival union.

Before ordering an election, the Board will first decide whether the employer and employees are within the Board's jurisdiction under NLRA. If jurisdiction is present and the employer and union agree on all issues relating to the election, the Board may proceed to hold an election without further inquiry. On the other hand, if there is disagreement over any issue—such as the appropriateness of the bargaining unit, which employees are eligible to vote, or the time and place of the election—the Board will conduct a hearing to resolve the disputed issues.

Appropriate Bargaining Unit: An employer is required to bargain with a union only if the union represents the majority of employees in a unit that is "appropriate for the purposes of collective bargaining." Thus, if there is any question at all on this matter, the Board will not hold an election until it has been determined that the group of employees involved is an "appropriate bargaining unit."

The NLRA specifically states that professional employees cannot be included in a unit of nonprofessional employees unless a majority of the professional employees approve their inclusion in the unit. The law also prohibits security guards who protect property or safety on the employer's premises from being included in a unit with other employees.

Aside from these restrictions, the Board has wide discretion in deciding whether a particular employee group is an appropriate unit. The most important factor in this decision is *mutuality of interest*. In other words, is there substantial similarity of skills, wages, hours, and other working conditions among members of the group so that their interests are basically the same?

Even where mutuality of interest supports a conclusion that a group of employees is an appropriate bargaining unit, the Board may permit a portion of the group to be excluded and to form their own separate bargaining unit. Suppose that the employer operates a large chain of retail department stores. If the employees at one store, or at several stores in a particular area, wish to form a bargaining unit separate from the employees at other stores, the Board will often permit them to do so. Similarly, the Board might permit separate units of sales and nonsales employees if a majority of employees in one of these groups so desire. (From this discussion, it is obvious that an employer may have to deal with more than one union.)

Circumstances Precluding an Election: Even if the basic requirements for an election are met, there are certain circumstances in which the Board will not permit the election to be held.

Prior Election: If a valid representation election has been held for this bargaining unit during the preceding twelve months, the Board will not allow another election. This is true regardless of whether a union was actually chosen and certified in the previous election. For the sake of workplace stability, there obviously must be a limit to how often elections can be held. In addition, if a union was certified in the previous election, this twelve-month period provides it with a reasonable opportunity to negotiate a collective-bargaining agreement with the employer.

Existing Agreement: If a valid collective bargaining agreement already exists, the employer and union who made the contract usually cannot petition for a representation election during the term of the agreement. However, a collective-bargaining agreement operates as a bar to an election petition by a *rival union* for a maximum of three years. Thus, if the contract between employer and one union is for a term of four years, another union may petition for an election after three years.

Exceptions do exist to the so-called "contract-bar rule." An existing contract does not bar an election if the contract (1) contains no stated duration, *or* (2) is so skeletal in nature that it covers only one or two of the many subjects that are normally included in such agreements.

Pending Unfair Labor Practice Charge: The Board usually will not permit an election while an unresolved unfair labor practice charge is pending, if that charge is related in some way to the employee organizing effort. An example would be a charge that the employer had discriminated against particular employees because of their union organizing efforts. In these situations, the Board feels that the air should be cleared, so to speak, before an election is held. Of course, an employer cannot use this rule to continually prevent union certification by committing unfair labor practices. If the union clearly demonstrates majority support and the Board feels that the employer's conduct will continue to prevent a free election atmosphere, the Board will certify the union without an election.

Election Procedures: Within seven days after the Board has ordered an election to be held, the employer must submit an accurate list of employees who are eligible to vote. The Board makes this list available to any union which will be on the ballot. Under most circumstances, an employee is eligible to vote even if he or she is striking at the time. An employer's noncompliance with the eligibility list requirement can invalidate an employer victory in the election. The election normally is held about thirty days after the Board orders it, usually at the employer's premises with agents of the

Board present to supervise. Voting is by secret ballot in enclosed booths. After the election the Board will canvass the results. If one of the choices on the ballot (that is, a particular union or "no union") receives a majority and there were no significant irregularities in the proceedings, the Board certifies the results.

The Requirement of Laboratory Conditions

After the Board orders an election, a campaign usually occurs in which the union attempts to persuade employees to select it as their bargaining representative. The employer also has the right to participate in this campaign, but must be very careful in doing so. The reason is that every employee *knows* the employer has the power to terminate his or her employment. Employees may feel this power to be particularly present at this time, before they obtain the protection of unionization. And many of them may not know that it is illegal for the employer to take action against them because of their attempt to unionize. Thus the workplace environment immediately prior to a representation election is a sensitive one. Words or conduct of the employer at this time can very easily damage the employees' complete freedom of thought, word, and action necessary to a fair, accurate election. The Board and federal courts have ruled that so-called "laboratory conditions" must be maintained prior to a representation election. This phrase essentially means that the pre-election atmosphere has to be untainted by fear—employees must be given an opportunity to objectively evaluate the pros and cons of joining a union and exercise a completely free choice.

Consequences of Disturbing Laboratory Conditions: Actions by the employer before a representation election may sometimes amount to an unfair labor practice. For example, the employer commits an unfair labor practice by discriminating in some way against an employee because of the employee's support of a union. Conversely, an attempt by the employer to support or dominate the union unduly, thus destroying its effectiveness as a true representative of employees, is also an unfair labor practice. Such practices can occur in many different circumstances, including the pre-election campaign. Unfair labor practices are examined in more detail later in the chapter.

Laboratory conditions may be disturbed even without the occurrence of unfair labor practices. If laboratory conditions have been upset and the subsequent election results in a "no-union" vote, the Board will invalidate the election and order a new one. And, of course, if unfair labor practices have occurred, other remedies also can be ordered.

Examples: There are many examples of situations in which the Board has set aside elections because laboratory conditions have been disturbed. In one case, a new election was ordered because the employer had injected racial prejudice into the election campaign. In another, the Board invalidated an election because during the campaign the employer had distributed to employees an outdated and misleading government publication about the reemployment rights of striking workers. Several cases have arisen in which *third parties*, such as newspapers or other business firms, have upset laboratory conditions by threatening that employees will be blacklisted by other companies if they join a union, or by making unsubstantiated claims that plant closings will result from unionization. In a situation such as this, the employer can sometimes prevent a disruption of laboratory conditions by promptly publishing or distributing to employees a statement disclaiming any connection with the third-party threats or allegations.

Employer Free Speech Rights: During an election campaign the employer does, however, have the right to present its views to employees about the pending election. Although an employer is not permitted to make threats or other coercive statements, it can lawfully state that it will be firm in dealing with the union if one is selected. Statements by the employer that it will exercise particular legal rights usually are permissible, as well. For instance, in one case a court concluded that an employer had acted properly during a union organizing effort when it told employees that they "may be replaced" if they went on strike. (As we will see later, replacement of striking employees is indeed an employer's legal right in many circumstances.)

When making predictions about possible *economic* consequences of unionization, the employer similarly must be careful to avoid statements that would be viewed as threatening or coercive. Minor misstatements of fact about economic consequences usually will not cause a disruption of laboratory conditions. However, if the misstatement of fact involves a matter of fundamental concern to employees, it might be viewed as threatening or coercive and as grounds for setting aside the election. For example, it would be proper for the employer to predict that unionization will cause the company's labor costs to rise so much that it may have to close the plant *only* if there is some objective evidence to back up the statement. The employer's misrepresentation about something as fundamental as a plant closing would probably be viewed as threatening or coercive and, consequently, as tainting the pre-election atmosphere sufficiently to invalidate the election.

Assuming that the content of employer statements is proper, the employer is permitted to present its views to "captive audiences." In other words, the employer may legally assemble employees on company property during working hours for the purpose of presenting anti-union views. The employer is not required to give the union an equal opportunity to speak to such a captive audience. During the twenty-four hours immediately preceding an election, however, a cooling-off period is in effect, when the employer's right to present anti-union views is more limited. Captive audience speeches cannot be made in this period. The only way the employer can legally speak to a group of employees is for the speech to be made on the employees' own time and for attendance to be voluntary. This cooling-off period does not prohibit the employer or its representative, such as a supervisor, from making very brief statements urging a "no union" vote to individual employees at their work stations. It also does not prohibit the employer's distribution of anti-union literature or presentation of anti-union advertisements over the news media. (These cases assume that the content of the employer's statements is proper.)

As strange as it may seem, the employer's granting of employee benefits may even be improper if the action is taken shortly before an election, the benefits are substantial, and the overall circumstances indicate that employee freedom of choice was hindered by the action. In the following case, such conduct disrupted pre-election laboratory conditions and also constituted an unfair labor practice.

National Labor Relations Board v. Exchange Parts Co.
U.S. Supreme Court
375 U.S. 405
(1964)

Exchange Parts Co. rebuilds automobile parts at a factory in Fort Worth, Texas. On November 9, 1959, the International Brotherhood of Boilermakers, Iron Shipbuilders, Blacksmiths, Forgers and Helpers told the company that the union was conducting an organizational campaign at the factory and that a majority of the employees supported the union. On November 16 the union petitioned the Board for an election. After conducting hearings, the Board on February 19, 1960, ordered that an election be held.

On February 25 the company held a dinner for employees, at which Vice-President McDonald told them that they could decide whether a previously announced extra day of vacation in 1960 would be a "floating holiday" or would be taken on their birthdays. The employees voted for the latter. McDonald also referred to the forthcoming representation election as one in which the employees would "determine whether they wished to hand over their right to speak and act for themselves." He stated that the union had distorted some of the facts and pointed out the benefits obtained by the employees without a union.

On March 4 Exchange Parts sent its employees a letter which spoke of "the *Empty Promises* of the Union" and "the *fact* that *it is the Company that puts things in your envelope. . . .*" After mentioning a number of benefits, the letter said: "The Union can't put any of those things in your envelope—*only the Company can do that.*" Further on, the letter stated: "it didn't take a Union to get any of those things and . . . it won't take a Union to get additional improvements in the future." Accompanying the letter was a detailed statement of the benefits granted by the company since 1949 and an estimate of the monetary value of such benefits to the employees. Included in the statement of benefits for 1960 were the birthday holiday, a new system for computing overtime during holiday weeks which had the effect of increasing wages for those weeks, and a new vacation schedule which enabled employees to extend their vacations by sandwiching them between two weekends.

The election was held on March 18, and the union lost. Subsequently, the Board ruled that the company's actions were done with the specific intent to

induce employees to vote against the union, thus disrupting laboratory conditions and also amounting to an unfair labor practice. The Board sought enforcement of its ruling in the Court of Appeals. The Court of Appeals refused, and the Board appealed the decision to the U.S. Supreme Court.

Harlan, Justice:

. . . Section 8(a)(1) [of the NLRA] makes it an unfair labor practice for an employer "to interfere with, restrain, or coerce employees in the exercise of [their rights to form and participate in labor organizations]." . . . We think the Court of Appeals was mistaken in concluding that the conferral of employee benefits while a representation election is pending, for the purpose of inducing employees to vote against the union does not "interfere with" the protected right to organize. . . .

In *Medo Photo Supply Corp. v. N.L.R.B.*, 321 U.S. 678, 686, this Court said: "The action of employees with respect to the choice of their bargaining agents may be induced by favors bestowed by the employer as well as by his threats or domination." Although in that case there was already a designated bargaining agent and the offer of "favors" was in response to a suggestion of the employees that they would leave the union if favors were bestowed, the principles which dictated the result there are fully applicable here. The danger inherent in well-timed increases in benefits is the suggestion of a *fist inside the velvet glove*. [Emphasis added.] Employees are not likely to miss the inference that the source of benefits now conferred is also the course from which future benefits must flow and which may dry up if it is not obliged. . . .

We cannot agree with the Court of Appeals that enforcement of the Board's order will have the "ironic" result of "discouraging benefits for labor." The beneficence of an employer is likely to be ephemeral if prompted by a threat of unionization which is subsequently removed. Insulating the right of collective organization from calculated good will of this sort deprives employees of little that has lasting value.

Reversed. [The Board's order should be enforced.]

★★★

The Union's Campaign: Individual pro-union employees and professional union representatives will, of course, present arguments in support of unionization during the campaign. Although most of the cases involving the disruption of laboratory conditions have involved employer statements and conduct, union supporters also are prohibited from upsetting these conditions. For example, representation elections won by the union were invalidated in one case where the union provided free insurance coverage or other benefits to employees who joined the union before the election, and in another case where union supporters threatened that violence would result from a union loss.

Subject to certain limitations, union supporters are subject to the employer's rules regarding use of company time and property for pro-union campaigning. Although the employer cannot completely prohibit such campaigning, the following restrictions may be imposed.

1. An employer may restrict employees from campaigning during their actual working time. They cannot, however, be prohibited from these activities during lunch and break periods and other free times. However, an employee who works one shift can be prohibited from campaigning on company property during another shift when he or she is completely off duty because such an employee is likely to "get in the way" on another shift.

2. Employer rules may reasonably restrict the *places* where campaigning occurs so as to prevent interference with company operations. For example, distribution of handbills, union authorization cards, and other written materials can be restricted to nonworking areas such as the parking lot or company cafeteria, because the resulting litter might cause a safety problem in working areas. Other forms of campaigning, such as verbal solicitation and message buttons, can be prohibited in working areas only if there is evidence that safety or company operations would be adversely affected by solicitation. For instance, the employer can lawfully prohibit any type of campaigning in areas of a retail establishment that are open to customers. Similarly, campaigning could also be prohibited in areas where dangerous machinery was in operation or other work requiring intense concentration was being done.

3. An employer can absolutely prohibit solicitation on company property by *nonemployees*, except in the rare situation (such as a remote logging camp, a seagoing vessel, or a resort hotel) where there is no other available means for union agents to contact employees.

4. All these situations assume that the employer's rules are nondiscriminatory. A rule that otherwise would be valid is not permitted if it discriminates against pro-union solicitation. For example, a rule that prohibits worktime union campaigning by employees, but permits other types of worktime solicitation (for charities, athletic events, and the like), will be invalid.

Decertification: As we have seen, the status of a certified union cannot be challenged during the 12-month period after it was selected as bargaining representative. Its status also cannot be challenged by the employer or employees during the existence of a valid collective bargaining agreement. After expiration of the 12-month period or the collective bargaining agreement, the representative status of the union can be challenged, but there is a strong presumption that the union continues to enjoy majority employee support.

If the employer can overcome this presumption by demonstrating that it has reasonable grounds for a good faith belief that the union has lost its majority support, the employer may legally withdraw its recognition of the union and refuse to bargain with it. This is very difficult for the employer to accomplish, and such action often results in an unfair labor practice proceeding in which the employer is found guilty of violating the duty to bargain in good faith.

Employees or a rival union may overcome the presumption of continued majority support only by filing a petition with the NLRB for a *decertification election*. The NLRB will call such an election if there is a demonstration (by signed cards or similar means) that at least 30 percent of the employees in the unit wish to have an election to test the union's majority support. If called by the NLRB, the election is conducted in much the same way and according to the same rules as an initial representation election.

The Collective-Bargaining Process

After a group of employees has selected a union as its representative, the process of bargaining with the employer will begin. The objective of this bargaining is to reach an agreement with the employer covering the various aspects of the employment relationship.

The Exclusive Representative Concept

The principle of *majority rule* is a basic element of collective bargaining. When a particular group of employees is an appropriate bargaining unit under the NLRA, and when a majority of the employees in that unit has chosen a particular union as the unit's representative, that union is the *exclusive* representative for *all* employees in the unit. In other words, those employees who did not support the union are bound by the collective bargaining agreement ultimately made between employer and union. This is true even for employees who do not formally join the union. There can be no contract negotiation between the employer and any individual or splinter group within the employee unit.

Similarly, a group of employees who take action on their own, without authorization by a majority of the employee unit, is not protected from employer discipline. Thus, an employer usually can legally fire or otherwise penalize employees who engage in a so-called **wildcat strike**—a work stoppage that has not been formally approved by a majority vote.

The union's status as exclusive bargaining representative carries with it a legal duty of *fair representation*. Since each employee is bound by decisions of the majority, the union must be fair to all. The duty of fair representation obviously would be breached if the union treated employees differently on the basis of race, color, religion, sex, or national origin.[2] It also could be violated in other ways, such as the failure of a union steward[3] to properly process an employee's grievance against the employer because of personal animosity between them or because the employee had not joined the union. An affected employee may sue the union for damages for violating this duty.

---

[2] Such conduct usually would also violate Title VII of the 1964 Civil Rights Act.

[3] A union steward is an employee who also serves as the union's agent in a particular department or other section of the company.

Subjects of Collective Bargaining

The various subjects that may arise in the negotiation of a collective-bargaining agreement will be either mandatory, illegal, or permissive.

Mandatory Subjects: In Section 8(d), the NLRA *requires* employer and union to engage in collective bargaining on "wages, hours, and other terms and conditions of employment." Examples of matters that the courts have found to be mandatory subjects include (1) wage rates, (2) group insurance coverage, (3) profit-sharing and stock-purchase plans for employees, (4) retirement plans, (5) availability and prices of food sold on the employer's premises, (6) paid vacations, holidays, sick leave, and break periods, (7) job classifications and types of work to be performed by employees in each classification, (8) seniority rules governing the order of employee layoffs and other matters, (9) rules relating to hours of work, shift rotations, and overtime, (10) safety rules and practices, (11) procedures for resolving employee grievances against the employer, and (12) replacement of current employees with those of an independent contractor to do the same work.

The fact that a particular matter is a mandatory collective-bargaining subject does not mean that the employer and union are required to include it in their contract. What it means is that if any action is to be taken concerning a mandatory subject, the employer cannot make an independent decision about it, but must negotiate the question with the union. There are, however, some exceptions to this rule. First, if the employer has done something a particular way for a long period of time and the union has not objected or insisted upon bargaining about it, the employer can simply continue as before. Bargaining would be required only if a change from prior practice is proposed by employer or union. Second, in the collective-bargaining agreement the union may expressly give the employer the right to unilaterally decide particular matters.

Illegal Subjects: Although the types of provisions to be negotiated and possibly included in a collective-bargaining agreement are generally left up to the employer and union, there are a few items that are prohibited. Closed shop and hot cargo provisions, both of which are discussed later, are examples of illegal subjects that cannot be included in the collective bargaining agreement or even injected into the bargaining process.

Permissive Subjects: If a topic is neither mandatory nor illegal, it is permissive. A permissive subject is one that can be negotiated and included in the collective bargaining agreement if the parties wish. Neither party, however, has the right to insist that such a topic be a subject of bargaining.

Most permissive subjects involve either (1) matters of company policy that do not directly involve the employment relationship, or (2) internal union matters. In the first category would be decisions relating to corporate organization, plant locations or closings, financing, product design, marketing practices, and so forth. The union cannot demand that collective bargaining include management prerogatives like these. In the second category would be matters such as the amount or method of collection of employee contributions to the union strike fund, or the method of submitting a new collective bargaining agreement to employees for a ratification vote. The employer cannot demand that bargaining include such union prerogatives.

Even though an employer cannot be forced to bargain with the union about management decisions that do not directly involve labor relations, the company can be required to bargain about the *effects* of such decisions on employees. For example, decisions relating to the closing of a plant or sale of substantial assets can be (and usually are) made unilaterally by the employer. But issues concerning possible retraining and transfer of displaced employees, severance pay, and the like are mandatory subjects of collective bargaining. The case that follows illustrates this concept.

First National Maintenance Corp. v. National Labor Relations Board
U.S. Supreme Court
452 U.S. 666
(1981)

First National Maintenance Corp. (FNM) is in the business of providing cleaning, maintenance, and related services for commercial customers in the New York City area. It contracts with each customer and then hires employees to perform services at the customer's place of business. These employees work only at one customer's premises, and are not transferred between different locations. From the customer FNM receives reimbursement of its labor costs plus an agreed management fee.

In April 1976, FNM made such an agreement with Greenpark Care Center, a nursing home in Brooklyn. FNM employed approximately thirty-five workers at Greenpark. During the spring and early summer of 1977, the business relationship between FNM and Greenpark broke down because of a dispute over the amount of FNM's management fee. FNM had agreed to lower it from the original $500 per month to $250, but then found this to be insufficient and sought to have the $500 fee reinstated. Greenpark refused and on June 30 FNM gave thirty days notice (as permitted in the contract) that it was terminating the agreement.

However, during this same general period, the National Union of Hospital and Health Care Employees was conducting an organizational campaign among FNM's Greenpark employees. A representation election had been held on March 31, 1977, at which the union was selected as bargaining representative. During early July the union's vice-president wrote to FNM seeking to initiate the collective bargaining process. FNM did not respond, and on July 28 FNM notified its Greenpark employees that they would be discharged on July 31. The union tried to get FNM to negotiate with it about the matter but FNM refused.

Subsequently, the Board ruled that FNM had committed an unfair labor practice and ordered it to bargain with the union about its decision to terminate the Greenpark operation and the consequences of that decision. The Board also required FNM to pay these employees from the date of the discharge until the situation was resolved. If bargaining resulted in resumption of

the Greenpark operation, discharged employees were to be given their jobs back; otherwise, they had to be offered similar jobs at other FNM operations. The Court of Appeals ordered enforcement of the Board's ruling, and FNM appealed to the U.S. Supreme Court.

Blackmun, Justice:

. . . [The Court compared this case with two of its previous decisions. In *Textile Workers v. Darlington Mills*, 380 U.S. 263 (1965), the Court ruled that "an employer has the absolute right to terminate his entire business for any reason he pleases" without bargaining. The other case, *Fibreboard Paper Products Corp. v. NLRB*, 379 U.S. 203 (1964), involved an employer's decision to subcontract for maintenance work previously done by its own employees. The Court in that case noted that the primary motivation for the decision was a desire to reduce labor costs, a matter which is "peculiarly suitable for resolution within the collective bargaining framework." In ruling that Fibreboard's decision was a mandatory bargaining subject, the Court also said:

The Company's decision to contract out the maintenance work did not alter the Company's basic operation. The maintenance work still had to be performed in the plant. No capital investment was contemplated; the Company merely replaced existing employees with those of an independent contractor to do the same work under similar conditions of employment. Therefore, to require the employer to bargain about the matter would not significantly abridge his freedom to manage the business.

In the present case, the Court observed that FNM's decision was not one to close down its entire business as in *Darlington*, but also was different from the decision in *Fibreboard*. FNM's decision was motivated by economic concerns *other* than labor costs.] . . .

In order to illustrate the limits of our holding, we turn again to the specific facts of this case. First, we note that when petitioner decided to terminate its Greenpark contract, it had no intention to replace the discharged employees or to move that operation elsewhere. Petitioner's sole purpose was to reduce its economic loss, and the union made no claim of anti-union animus. In addition, petitioner's dispute with Greenpark was solely over the size of the management fee Greenpark was willing to pay. The union had no control or authority over that fee. The most that the union could have offered would have been advice and concessions that Greenpark, the third party upon whom rested the success or failure of the contract, had no duty even to consider. These facts in particular distinguish this case from the subcontracting issue presented in *Fibreboard*. Finally, while petitioner's business enterprise did not involve the investment of large amounts of capital in single locations, we do not believe that the absence of significant investment or withdrawal of capital is crucial. The decision to halt work at this specific location represented a significant change in petitioner's operations, a change not unlike opening a new line of business, or going out of business entirely. . . .

[Reversed. FNM cannot be required to bargain over its termination decision. It can, however, be required to negotiate with the union about possible alternatives for the employees other than discharge.]

The Duty to Bargain in Good Faith

When negotiating a collective-bargaining agreement or some modification of it, the employer and union are required to *bargain in good faith* about mandatory subjects. This duty essentially requires each party to take an active part in trying to reach agreement with the other by making honest, reasonable propositions concerning mandatory subjects of bargaining. They are not legally required to make an agreement—the fact that negotiations reach an impasse on mandatory subjects does not necessarily mean that the parties have not bargained in good faith. On the other hand, bargaining to an impasse, or breaking off negotiations because of an inability to reach an agreement on a *nonmandatory* (permissive) subject of collective bargaining is a violation of the duty to bargain in good faith and constitutes an unfair labor practice.

Good or bad faith is a question of subjective intent, but judgments about someone's intent must be based on outward indications—words and conduct. For example, bad faith would be inferred where an employer offers terms that are so unreasonable that no responsible employee representative could ever accept them. Other examples of action that would show a lack of good faith would be a persistent "take-it-or-leave-it" attitude or obvious delaying tactics.

In addition to placing the general duty of good faith bargaining on the parties, Section 8(d) of the NLRA also spells out certain procedural aspects of the duty when a collective bargaining agreement already exists. Specifically, when either the employer or union wishes to terminate or modify an existing agreement, it must proceed as follows:

1. It must give written notice of this intention to the other party at least (a) sixty days prior to the expiration date of the contract, or (b) sixty days prior to the time it proposes to terminate or modify, if the contract contains no expiration date.

2. It must offer to meet and confer with the other party for the purpose of negotiating a new contract or a contract containing the proposed modifications.

3. It must notify the Federal Mediation and Conciliation Service and any appropriate state mediation agency within thirty days after the first notice, unless an agreement has been reached by that time.

4. It must continue to comply with the terms of the existing contract, without resorting to a strike or lockout, for a period of at least sixty days after the first notice or until the expiration date of the contract, whichever occurs later.

Grievance Procedures and Arbitration

The types of terms in a collective-bargaining agreement will vary substantially from one situation to another. Most of the terms relate to the kinds of topics mentioned earlier as mandatory bargaining subjects. Of special importance to the effectiveness of the collective-bargaining process are those contractual provisions relating to the resolution of disputes.

Grievance Procedures: Two examples will illustrate the significance of dispute resolution procedures.

1. The employer begins assigning certain work to supervisors, and several employees claim that this action violates job classification provisions of the collective bargaining agreement. The primary concern of the employees and the union is the actual or potential loss of jobs for union members.

2. The employer alleges that an employee has violated a specific workrule (smoking in a no-smoking area or failure to follow a safety rule, for example) or has otherwise acted improperly (such as being insubordinate to a supervisor or absent without excuse). The employer then proposes to discharge the employee or perhaps levy some lesser penalty, such as placing a written reprimand in the employee's personnel file. The employee disputes the alleged facts, claims that he or she was not properly notified of the rule, or perhaps asserts that the proposed penalty is not permitted for the alleged offense under the terms of the collective-bargaining agreement. Regarding the last possibility, most collective-bargaining agreements provide that the employer can fire an employee only for "good cause." One of the most common factual disputes is whether particular conduct by the employee amounts to good cause for discharge.

A key feature of the average collective bargaining agreement is a set of formal procedures for the handling of "grievances." The typical grievance procedure requires an affected employee to file a formal written grievance (complaint) with the union's local office or with a designated union agent. The union then takes the grievance to the employer.[4] Procedures usually call for initial consultation between lower level representatives of the employer (such as a department supervisor) and the union (such as a union steward). If they cannot reach agreement on how the dispute should be resolved, the question will go to higher level representatives. This process sometimes in-

[4]Even if there are formal grievance procedures in the agreement, the NLRA gives each employee the right to bypass the union and take the grievance directly to the employer *if* the employer is willing to hear it.

volves several different levels within both the employer's and union's organizational structures.

Arbitration: When the last step is completed without any resolution of the dispute, grievance procedures generally require the employer and union to use binding *arbitration*. The collective-bargaining agreement may have included detailed procedures for selecting an arbitrator and conducting the arbitration proceeding. In many agreements, however, it is simply provided that arbitration will be conducted according to the rules of an established organization such as the American Arbitration Association (AAA), or a government agency like the Federal Mediation and Conciliation Service (FMCS).[5] In some cases the agreement may adopt the procedures of AAA or FMCS with particular modifications.

The employer and union may agree on an individual from an AAA or FMCS list to serve as arbitrator, or each may pick one and these two will then choose the arbitrator. In some cases the employer and union will each choose a person, these two will pick a third, and all three will form an arbitration panel. Sometimes a company and a union with a large volume of grievances will contract with a person to serve as arbitrator in all their disputes during a stated time period. Whatever the selection method, arbitrators most often are either practicing attorneys or professors of law, economics, industrial relations, or business. There are even a few fulltime professional labor arbitrators.

The arbitrator conducts a hearing which is much less formal than a trial. Testimony and other evidence are presented, but formal rules of evidence are not strictly adhered to. On the basis of this hearing, the arbitrator determines what the facts are and how the collective-bargaining agreement should apply to the dispute. A relatively short written opinion usually is prepared, giving the basic facts and the arbitrator's decision. The judgment of an arbitrator is called an award.

When the collective-bargaining agreement calls for arbitration, a grievance must be handled in this way if it is "arbitrable." *An arbitrable grievance is simply a dispute that is within the scope of the collective-bargaining agreement and involves the interpretation or application of that agreement.*

The Board and the courts usually will refuse to hear a case that properly belongs in arbitration. (This is true even if the conduct on which the grievance is based might also be an unfair labor practice.) However, if one party refuses to submit an arbitrable grievance to arbitration, the other party can file a lawsuit in state or federal court for breach of the collective-bargaining agreement. The remedy will be a court order requiring arbitration. If arbitration has been used but one party refuses to comply with the arbitrator's

---

[5]This federal government agency primarily serves the *mediation* function—attempting to bring the parties to an agreement in collective bargaining. It also has a set of arbitration rules and a roster of private individuals willing to serve as arbitrators, much the same as AAA.

award, the other party can go to court and obtain an order enforcing the award. And finally, where a grievance has been arbitrated and one party is dissatisfied with the arbitrator's decision, that party's right to appeal to a court is extremely limited. There generally can be a successful appeal only if the arbitrator has (1) acted in bad faith by not considering the evidence or by conspiring with one of the parties, (2) decided a question or made an award that was outside the scope of the power given to the arbitrator by the collective-bargaining agreement, or (3) made a decision that upholds an illegal provision in the agreement or otherwise violates the law.

We now will see an illustrative arbitration decision.

In re Great Atlantic & Pacific Tea Co. and Amalgamated Food Employees Union
71 Lab. Arb. 805 (1978)

The employee, who was identified only as M, had worked as a stocker and checker for the company's A&P supermarkets in the Pittsburgh area since 1950. After many years without any recorded problems, a series of complaints were made against him by various people. In 1973 he pushed another employee to the floor and threatened to beat him up. The company tried to fire him, but in arbitration the discharge was reduced to a suspension. In 1976 and 1977 a number of complaints were made against M, including threatening a supervisor in the presence of customers, arguing with a sales manager, insults, alteration of time records, and arguing with a customer. In 1977 the company again fired him but an arbitrator again reduced the penalty to a suspension.

In 1978, M had two altercations with customers. In one instance a customer asked for a sale coupon and M said, "All of you Kennedy Township housewives are the same." The customer responded, "Have a nice day anyhow," and M said, "I will if you don't come back!" Another time, he referred to a customer's children as "brats." During this same period, M had difficulties with another checker. He also told the company's district manager that "He would never come down to the level of the customer," and "I am my own man, and I won't come down to their level or yours!" The company again fired M, he filed a grievance with the union, and the dispute went to arbitration. The collective bargaining agreement permitted discharge only for "good and sufficient cause."

Nernberg, Arbitrator:

. . . I am not unmindful of the fact that M has served the Company for twenty-eight years, and much of this time has been spent as a satisfactory, productive, and at times, exemplary employee. On the other hand, I cannot overlook the fact that the grievant has been given one chance after another by Management and by two other Arbitrators. I cannot conceive of a place where work could be found for M where he could function without further altercations developing. Unfortunately for M, we must impose "capital punishment," that is as the term is used in labor and industry; he must be terminated. This is obviously a harsh measure and one which should not be taken lightly, but with all the evidence considered, there is no alternative.

★★★

Unfair Labor Practices

On several occasions we have referred to the fact that certain types of conduct by the employer or union are illegal under the NLRA as "unfair labor practices." Essentially, the law relating to unfair labor practices represents a further attempt to encourage industrial peace—in this case by prohibiting unreasonable abuses of the power that the parties may sometimes possess.

We have already seen that the disruption of laboratory conditions prior to a representation election may involve conduct of such a threatening or coercive nature as to also constitute an unfair labor practice. One unfair labor practice, the failure to bargain in good faith, was examined in some detail. Now we take a look at other such practices. Section 8(a) of the NLRA deals with unfair labor practices of the employer, and Section 8(b) with those of the union.

Employer Unfair Labor Practices

Coercion and Discrimination: As seen in the *Exchange Parts* case, Section 8(a)(1) makes it illegal for an employer "to interfere with, restrain, or coerce employees" in connection with their right to participate (or refuse to participate) in a labor union. Section 8(a)(3) makes it illegal to discriminate against employees for the purpose of encouraging or discouraging union membership. In a few instances particular conduct violates only one of these provisions, but in most situations conduct that violates one of them also violates the other. Generally speaking, almost any type of employer action can be either legal or illegal under these provisions depending on whether surrounding circumstances indicate legitimate business reasons or anti-union motivation. Several illustrations follow.

Lockouts: A lockout is a temporary barring of employees from the workplace in anticipation of a strike. This economic countermeasure by the employer is legal if there are special circumstances indicating that the timing of a possible strike might be especially harmful to the employer. For example, in *American Ship Building Co. v. NLRB*, 380 U.S. 300 (1965), collective bargaining for a new contract had reached a stalemate and the employer feared that the union would intentionally delay a strike until the busy season. The employer used a temporary lockout before the busy season began so as to control the timing of the work stoppage. In this way, the employer hoped to exert sufficient economic pressure to bring about further compromise on the union's part. The Supreme Court ruled that no unfair labor practice had been committed. However, if there had not been this clear evidence of special economic justification, or if the union had been on the brink of losing its majority support and the lockout effectively destroyed it, the employer's action probably would have been illegal.

Threatening Behavior: Threatening employer behavior may violate Section 8(a) in many different settings. For instance, surveillance of employees through the use of spies or informers is illegal if it relates to any aspect of employees' organizational rights (such as initial organization, election, pending strike, or picketing). Outright threats of discharge or other disciplinary measures against employees because of their union activity are blatantly illegal. More subtle threats may also violate Section 8(a). Interrogation of employees about their union membership or activities will be scrutinized very closely by the Board and the courts. Such interrogation can be used legally to obtain information in which the employer has a legitimate interest. For example, the employer can lawfully question employees to determine whether a union has majority support, whether union campaigning has been taking place on company time, or whether employees generally support a threatened strike. The employer must be careful, however, to maintain an atmosphere that is nonthreatening and noncoercive. In this regard, when questioning employees it is wise for the employer to emphasize that there is no intent to penalize anyone.

Employee Discipline: To efficiently run its business the employer must be free to discharge or otherwise discipline its employees for poor performance or improper conduct. This power cannot be used, though, to restrain union activity. There generally is no problem for the employer if the disciplined employee has not shown active support for the union. On the other hand, when discipline is exercised against a worker who has been somewhat active in union-related matters, the employer must be prepared to document legitimate reasons for the discipline. If the employer is not able to substantiate these legitimate reasons, the Board is likely to infer an anti-union motivation. Even if there is evidence of justification for the discipline (tardiness or poor performance, for example), there may still be an unfair labor practice if other employees not so active in the union have not received similar penalties for similar conduct.

Treatment of Strikers: When employees go on strike, how the employer can treat them depends on the nature of the strike. If the strike itself is an illegal one, such as a wildcat strike, striking employees can be fired with no right to reinstatement. If the strike is legal, strikers cannot be fired. The employer can, however, hire replacements to keep its business going. When the strike ends, or even when a single striker wants to come back to work, does the employer have to grant reinstatement? The answer hinges on the reason for the strike. If employees had gone on strike to protest conduct of the employer which had amounted to an unfair labor practice, the employer must grant full reinstatement even if the replacements have to be fired to make room. Failure to do so constitutes another unfair labor practice.

On the other hand, the employer's reinstatement duties are more limited where the strike was an economic one. An economic strike is one staged for any purpose other than protesting an unfair labor practice, such as supporting the union's demand for recognition or pressuring the employer to accept particular terms during collective bargaining. In this situation, strikers are entitled to reinstatement if replacements had been expressly hired only for the duration of the strike. However, if the replacements were hired as permanent employees, the employer does not have to fire them in order to reinstate strikers. Here the duty of the employer is simply to notify the striker whenever the same or a similar job becomes open and to give the striker a priority over new applicants. This duty does not exist at all if the striker has already obtained regular, comparable employment elsewhere.

As a practical matter, the union often bargains for and obtains the employer's agreement to reinstate economic strikers, and the employer is bound by such an agreement.

Domination or Assistance: To assure that the union truly represents employees and is not just an arm of the employer, Section 8(a)(2) prohibits the employer from dominating or assisting the union. Several examples illustrate the nature of this provision.

1. The employer cannot provide significant financial support, materials, facilities, or services to the union.
2. The employer cannot actively solicit members for a union. Thus, during the organizational stage an employer who favors one union over another can go no further than to generally indicate its preference.
3. The employer cannot assist in drafting the union's constitution or bylaws.

A line necessarily must be drawn between domination or assistance and minor instances of cooperation. It is not illegal, for example, to permit the union to post notices on a company bulletin board, to withhold union dues from employees' paychecks and turn them over to the union (but only with respect to employees who consent), or to permit a union official to come onto company property to speak with employees. Of course, a lengthy series of minor favors might sometimes add up to evidence of domination.

Union Unfair Labor Practices

Section 8(b) of the NLRA itemizes the types of labor union conduct which are condemned as unfair labor practices. The most important of these are examined below, as are some situations in which particular union conduct may be legal or illegal on other grounds.

Coercion: Much like the employer, the union is prohibited from engaging in restraint or coercion of employees in connection with their decision whether to participate in a union. Because unions have less inherent power over employees than does the employer, union conduct is not nearly so likely to constitute restraint or coercion. There are, however, certain situations in which a union's conduct unduly impinges on employee's rights.

It obviously is illegal for a union to threaten or commit acts of violence in order to pressure employees into cooperating. Moreover, the union cannot threaten or actually engage in economic coercion. For instance, it is an unfair labor practice for a union agent to threaten that those employees who don't join the union will ultimately lose their jobs. Also illegal is the union's waiver of dues or fees for those who join prior to a representation election.[6]

Picketing the employer's premises generally is legal if it is peaceful and for a lawful purpose. It becomes an illegal activity if it involves actual or threatened violence, or if it is used to coerce employees or the employer to do something else that is unlawful. Mass picketing ("belly-to-back" picketing) in which employees walking the picket line are so numerous and situated so closely as to practically form a wall is illegal. Similarly illegal is the blocking of any entrance by picketers.

Discrimination: It is an unfair labor practice for a union to discriminate or induce the employer to discriminate against employees because of their nonmembership or inactivity in the union. However, this prohibition obviously does not prevent a union from requiring *reasonable* membership rules, initiation fees, and dues.

In certain industries, such as construction, the building trades, and maritime shipping, it is customary for the union to operate a hiring hall—a job referral or clearinghouse service for workers. A union may lawfully operate a hiring hall, and even obtain an employer's agreement to get employees there, so long as the union does not discriminate on the basis of union membership.

Most unions attempt to obtain some type of "union security clause" in the collective-bargaining agreement. These clauses take various forms. A "closed shop" clause requires individuals to be union members before they can be hired by the employer. Closed shop provisions are unfair labor practices by both the employer and union because they discriminate on the basis of union membership and also constitute undue employer assistance of the union.

Although somewhat similar to a closed shop clause, a "union shop" or "agency shop" clause is generally permitted by the NLRA. This type of provision does not require union membership as a prerequisite to employment, but obligates the employer to require employees to begin paying union dues within thirty days after being hired and to continue paying them thereafter.[7]

---

[6] In addition to being coercive and thus constituting an unfair labor practice, this action clearly would also disturb pre-election laboratory conditions.

[7] In the construction and building trades industry, a union shop or agency shop clause can require employees to join or pay dues within *seven days* after they are hired.

ıents, Congress has specifically dele-
ɔf the NLRA expressly permits state
ıws. These laws, which have been
ınion shop or agency shop clauses.
ıcy shop agreement is legal only in

ıat picketing can be unlawful if it is
ıg generally is not viewed by the
an employer to initially recognize

ng by any union is absolutely pro-
ɛntation election during the past
een no election during that time, a
: to secure recognition if the em-
ıother union and the incumbent
ged. *Third*, even if recognitional
ıst petition the Board for a repre-
ɔicketing begins. The union's fail-
auses the recognitional picketing

ıctice for a union to engage in
ay for work that is not actually
...id meal breaks, holidays, vacations, and so forth. It also does not prohibit the union from resisting automation or even bargaining for wasteful job procedures. Only blatant instances of "make work"—creating positions and requiring pay where there is no work to be done—are illegal.

Strikes: A strike is one of the most powerful weapons of organized labor. Subject to certain limitations, it is a legitimate method of exerting economic pressure on the employer.

A strike is legal only if it consists of a complete work stoppage by the participating majority. It is an unfair labor practice for a union to engage in either a work "slowdown" or an "on-again, off-again" work stoppage.

It also is an unfair labor practice to use a strike to achieve an illegal objective, such as pressuring the employer to agree to a closed shop, featherbedding, or other illegal contract term.

Sometimes an employer may be able to obtain a "no-strike" clause in return for some concession by the employer. These promises not to strike are enforceable against the union while the agreement is in effect. A strike in violation of such a clause is not an unfair labor practice, but merely a breach of contract. Thus, the appropriate method of resolution is arbitration or a lawsuit seeking an injunction or damages, rather than a Board hearing.

We have previously seen that wildcat strikes are not permissible. Such a strike, unauthorized by the majority, does not cause the union to be liable for an unfair labor practice—the result of its illegality is that the strikers have no protection from discharge.

Even when a strike is majority-authorized, an employee who wishes not to strike is legally free to continue coming to work. Although the union may not prohibit an employee from crossing a picket line or otherwise defying a majority-authorized strike, the union may levy a reasonable fine against the employee if that employee is a member of the union and does not formally resign from membership before defying the strike.

Secondary Boycotts: A general principle in the NLRA is that labor disputes should be "kept in the family." In other words, the union should not purposely draw innocent third parties into the dispute. No kind of economic pressure should be used by a union against a *secondary party*—one with whom the union does not have a labor dispute.

Hot Cargo Agreements: A common form of secondary boycott is the so-called "hot cargo" agreement. Such an arrangement includes almost any type of union-employer agreement that the employer will not do business with a third party. For example, suppose that the Teamsters' Union represents the truck drivers of Convoy Trucking Co. The union is trying to organize and represent employees at Southern Paper Co., or perhaps merely supports the organizing effort of some other union at Southern. If the Teamsters' Union obtains Convoy's agreement not to transport Southern's products, the union and employer both have committed an unfair labor practice. If the union had used a strike, picket, or other pressure in an attempt to obtain the agreement but Convoy had refused to go along, only the union would be guilty.[8]

Other Secondary Boycotts: A similar type of secondary boycott by a union is one that directly pressures a third party in order to indirectly pressure the employer. In such a case the union ordinarily is the only party guilty of an unfair labor practice. Suppose that the Retail Clerks' Association and the Giant Food Mart grocery chain are at an impasse in their negotiation of a new collective-bargaining agreement. It is normal, and usually quite legal, for the union to strike and to picket against Giant. However, if the union pickets the factory of a vegetable canning company or uses other kinds of pressure in an attempt to persuade the canning company's employees not to handle goods to be sold to Giant, the union commits an unfair labor practice.

---

[8]The construction and clothing industries have limited exemptions from the rule against hot cargo agreements. Stated very generally, a union and an employer in either of these industries may lawfully agree that the employer cannot subcontract work to any other employer who has not signed a collective-bargaining agreement with the union.

Requests That Others Not Cross Picket Line: There are three situations which come rather close to an illegal secondary boycott, but which are in fact legal. First, when a union is lawfully picketing the employer in a primary labor dispute with that employer, it is permissible for picketing employees to ask others not to cross the picket line. These others might be fellow employees *or even employees of another employer* who have come to make pickups or deliveries, to do repair work, or for other reasons. They have the legal right to choose whether or not to cross the picket line, and if they refuse to cross it there is no secondary boycott or other unfair labor practice.

Product Picketing: It is lawful for a union to use peaceful picketing to *inform the public* that a particular product is produced by an employer with whom the union has a labor dispute. For example, a union engaged in a labor dispute with Acme Milk Company can peacefully picket in front of a supermarket with signs asking customers not to buy Acme milk because "it is produced by nonunion labor," "Acme doesn't treat its employees right," and so on. There is not an illegal secondary boycott if supermarket customers respond by refusing to buy Acme milk or even by not going into the store. (The union could also legally advertise in the media, pass out handbills, or use other publicity in an effort to obtain a consumer boycott.) However, if union requests are directed at the supermarket's employees, or if the picketing causes a work stoppage or interruption of deliveries at the supermarket, there is an illegal secondary boycott.

The Ally Doctrine: A secondary boycott is legal if the secondary employer is an "ally" of the employer with whom the union has a labor dispute. This occurs, for instance, where the secondary employer has been assisting the primary employer in the labor dispute (such as performing work that normally would be done by striking employees).

In the average case, a secondary boycott starts out with a labor dispute between the union and primary employer. Suppose that there is no basic labor dispute, however, and the union's underlying motive is political. Is a secondary boycott illegal in such a situation?

International Longshoremen's Assn. v. Allied International, Inc.
U.S. Supreme Court
102 S. Ct. 1656 (1982)

As a protest against the Russian invasion of Afghanistan, members of the International Longshoremen's Association (ILA) stopped handling cargoes arriving from or destined for the Soviet Union. The union's president ordered the boycott on January 9, 1980, in response to overwhelming demands for such action from union members.

Allied International is an American company that imports Russian wood products for resale in the United States. As a result of the boycott, Allied's shipments were disrupted completely. Ultimately it was forced to renegotiate its Russian contracts, substantially reducing its purchases and jeopardizing its

ability to supply its own customers. Allied initiated an unfair labor practice proceeding with the Board, in which Allied prevailed. Separately, Allied filed suit in federal district court for damages resulting from ILA's alleged secondary boycott. Similar suits by two other importers, Waterman and Clark, were consolidated with Allied's. The district court ruled that ILA's political motive made the secondary boycott legal under the NLRA. The Court of Appeals reversed, holding that the NLRA's prohibition of secondary boycotts did indeed apply to ILA's action. ILA appealed to the U.S. Supreme Court.

Powell, Justice:

. . . [The Court first rejected the union's argument that this case is similar to previous ones in which it had been held that the "maritime operations of foreign-flag ships employing alien seamen" are not covered by the NLRA. The Court stated that] ILA's refusal to unload Allied's shipments in no way affected the maritime operations of foreign ships. The boycott here did not aim at altering the terms of employment of foreign crews on foreign-flag vessels. It did not seek to extend the bill of rights developed for American workers and American employers to foreign seamen and foreign shipowners. . . . As the Court of Appeals explained, this drama was "played out by an all-American cast." "[A]n American union has ordered its members not to work for an American stevedore which had contracted to service an American ship carrying goods of an American importer."

[The Court then turned to the main question—whether this boycott was illegal.] The secondary boycott provisions in § 8(b)(4)(B) prohibit a union from inducing employees to refuse to handle goods with the object of forcing any person to cease doing business with any other person. By its terms the statutory prohibition applies to the undisputed facts of this case. The ILA has no dispute with Allied, Waterman, or Clark. It does not seek any labor objective from these employers. Its sole complaint is with the foreign and military policy of the Soviet Union. As understandable and even commendable as the ILA's ultimate objectives may be, the certain effect of its action is to impose a heavy burden on neutral employers. And it is just such a burden, as well as widening of industrial strife, that the secondary boycott provisions were designed to prevent. . . .

Neither is it a defense to the application of § 8(b)(4) that the reason for the ILA boycott was not a labor dispute with a primary employer but a political dispute with a foreign nation. Section 8(b)(4) contains no such limitation. In the plainest of language it prohibits "forcing . . . any person to cease . . . handling . . . the products of any other producer . . . or to cease doing business with any other person." The legislative history does not indicate that political disputes should be excluded from the scope of § 8(b)(4). The prohibition was drafted broadly to protect neutral parties, "the helpless victims of quarrels that do not concern them at all." . . .

We would create a large and undefinable exception to the statute if we accepted the argument that "political" boycotts are exempt from the secondary boycott provision. The distinction between labor and political objectives would be difficult to draw in many cases. In the absence of any limiting language in the statute or legislative history, we find no reason to conclude that Congress intended such a potentially expansive exception to a statutory provision purposefully drafted in broadest terms. . . .

The judgment of the Court of Appeals is affirmed.

★★★

Questions and Problems

1. A group of buyers for Bell Aerospace Co. sought to form a bargaining unit under the NLRA. These buyers had authority to select suppliers, negotiate purchase prices, and commit the company's credit, but did not deal with management policy regarding any aspect of labor relations. The Board granted a union's petition for a representation election among these employees, an election was held, and the union won. The company refused to recognize the union, an unfair labor practice charge was filed, and the case ultimately went to the Supreme Court. Discuss how the Court would rule on the question whether these employees could form a bargaining unit under the NLRA. (*NLRB v. Bell Aerospace Co.*, 416 U.S. 167, 1974.)

2. You are the assistant plant manager for Essex Co. The plant manager gave you instructions to prepare a rule regarding employee solicitation on company property. His concern was that some employees were "talking and passing stuff around when they should be working." After thinking about it, you have decided to post signs that say either "No solicitation during working time," or "No solicitation during working hours." You are not sure whether the wording makes any difference. Discuss which of these two choices is more likely to be legal.

3. Serv-Air, Inc. had a "no-solicitation" rule for employees which was properly restricted as to time and place. However, the company occasionally permitted solicitation on the premises for contributions to buy flowers for widows of deceased employees. During a union organizing campaign, the no-solicitation rule was applied and the union contended that the occasional exception granted by the company for flowers caused the rule to be invalid. The union thus claimed that the rule could not be applied to campaigning prior to a representation election. Is the union correct? Discuss. (*Serv-Air, Inc. v. NLRB*, 395 F.2d 557, 10th Cir. 1968.)

4. Contract negotiations between the union and Mackay Co. were not going well, and the union staged a strike in support of its demands. Mackay hired regular, full-time replacements for the strikers. When the strikers realized that their strike would not succeed, they offered to return to work. Five of the replacements wanted to continue working, so Mackay reinstated all but five of the strikers. The five who were not replaced had been among the most active in supporting the union and its strike. Did Mackay commit an unfair labor practice in its treatment of the strikers? Discuss. (*NLRB v. Mackay Radio & Telegraph Co.*, 304 U.S. 333, 1938.)

5. Truitt Manufacturing Co. and the union were negotiating for a new collective-bargaining agreement. The union demanded a wage increase of ten cents an hour, but the employer offered only two-and-one-half cents. Truitt stated that its average wage was already more than its competitors, and that an increase of more than two-and-one-half cents would break the company. The union asked to see the company's financial records to substantiate its claims. The company declined on the grounds that its financial records were confidential and not something to be bargained about. The union charged that Truitt had committed an unfair labor practice by not bargaining in good faith. Is the union correct? Discuss. (*Truitt Manufacturing Co. v. NLRB*, 351 U.S. 149, 1956.)

6. Oil Transport Co. (OTC) is a carrier engaged in transporting goods by truck. The Texas Railroad Commission had regulatory powers over the rates OTC could charge shippers within Texas. In 1979, the Commission decided that because of an increase in truck fuel costs, OTC and other carriers subject to its jurisdiction should be allowed to pass on these increased costs to shippers in the form of a "fuel adjustment charge." The Commission's order provided that the amount of increased revenues thereby authorized was "to accrue and be paid only to the purchaser of fuel, with no portion thereof to be expended for any other costs incurred by carriers." OTC's collective-bargaining agreement with the Union of Transportation Employees provided that drivers' pay would be based on a percentage of revenue from freight rates, and expressly stated that "fuel surcharges will be used in computation of pay." OTC refused to include the fuel adjustment charge in computing drivers' pay, claiming that the Commission's order prohibited OTC from doing so. One of OTC's drivers filed a grievance which ultimately was submitted to arbitration. After an arbitration proceeding, the arbitrator directed OTC to include the amount of the fuel adjustment charge authorized by the Commission. OTC refused to comply with the arbitrator's award, and the union filed suit in federal court to enforce the award. One of the legal grounds for denying enforcement of an arbitrator's award is that enforcement by a court would violate public policy, and OTC defended by contending that the award in question conflicted with established public policy as declared by the Commission. Discuss whether the court should have enforced the award. (*Union of Transportation Employees v. Oil Transport Co.*, 591 F. Supp. 439, N.D. Tex. 1984.)

7. Jefferson Standard Broadcasting Company was involved in negotiating a new contract with the union. The major issue in the dispute was whether to include an arbitration clause in the new contract as in the old one. While negotiations were going on, several employees who were still on the payroll (there was no strike) distributed handbills to the public during their off-duty hours. These handbills severely criticized the quality of programming on the employer's television station, but said nothing about a union, collective bargaining, or the disputed arbitration provision. The employer fired these employees, and the union charged that this action was an unfair labor practice. Is the union correct? Discuss. (*NLRB v. International Brotherhood of Electrical Workers, Local 1229*, 346 U.S. 464, 1953.)

8. You are assistant personnel director for Remco Metals Co. Remco and the union had reached an impasse in their bargaining for a new collective-bargaining agreement, and the employees went on strike. During negotiations the union had demanded an increase of seventy-five cents an hour, from $7.10 to $7.85. Remco would not agree to go higher than $7.25. After the strike began, you and your boss, the personnel director, discussed how to go about hiring replacements. The personnel director suggested that it might be wise to hire replacements at about $7.75 an hour to ensure that the company could attract good workers under these tension-filled circumstances. These replacements would also have all the benefits that striking employees had previously had. The personnel director supposed that "some of the strikers might even come back as replacements." This idea disturbs you, and you are trying to decide how to respond. What advice should you give your boss? Discuss.

9. A maritime shipping company was engaged in a labor dispute with the union. At this time, one of the company's ships was being serviced at a drydock owned by another firm. The union tried to picket the employer's ship, but the drydock company denied the union access to the individual berth where the particular ship was located. The union then picketed the main entrance to the drydock repair facility. The owner of this facility claimed that the union was engaging in an illegal secondary boycott of the drydock. Is the drydock owner correct? Discuss. (*Sailors' Union of the Pacific (Moore Dry Dock Co.)*, 92 N.L.R.B. 547, 1950.)

10. A building stone supplier and the union were involved in a labor dispute, and a strike was called. The company ordinarily delivered stone to construction companies on its own trucks. During the strike, however, these construction companies (the supplier's customers) made arrangements with independent trucking companies to make deliveries and deducted the delivery cost from the purchase price of the stone. Striking employees of the stone supplier picketed both the customers and the trucking companies. An unfair labor practice charge was filed against the union for allegedly engaging in a secondary boycott of these other firms. What should the ruling be in this case? Discuss. (*Laborers Local 859 v. NLRB,* 446 F.2d 1319, D.C. Cir. 1971.)

Business and Society PART III

C·H·A·P·T·E·R 17

CONSUMER PROTECTION LAW

The law of consumer protection is primarily statutory. Consumers derive their rights and incur obligations from the many state and federal statutes available for their benefit. A number of statutes protect consumers in the financial dealings associated with borrowing money or buying on credit. Others afford protection in the purchasing process and set guidelines for the degree of performance and satisfaction it is reasonable to expect from a purchase. Trade regulations issued by the Federal Trade Commission protect consumers who may be taken advantage of or misled by false and deceptive trade practices. Bankruptcy law provides relief for those who have overextended themselves and are no longer able to manage their financial affairs.

During recent years the creditor-debtor relationship has undergone a significant shift in emphasis from protection of the creditor to protection of the debtor in the consumer transaction in which someone borrows to purchase a product or purchases the product on credit. This is not to say that the creditor, or seller, is completely at the mercy of the buyer, or debtor. The bulk of consumer protection law does favor the buyer and is designed to protect the borrower from such things as usury (lending money at interest rates higher than the law allows), excessive garnishments (when the debtor's employer withholds a portion of wages to be paid to the employee's creditor), and hidden costs in credit transactions. However, the seller has also had rights defined by the numerous laws on the subject. A knowledge of the basic provisions of consumer protection statutes is essential for the businessperson of today to operate a commercially successful venture and conduct consumer transactions within the law.

The first part of this chapter addresses the rights of consumers who buy on credit or borrow the funds to make a purchase of consumer goods. Development of consumer protection law in credit transactions had been rapid and far-reaching. To a large extent, it is a direct result of the government's expanding role in the regulation of business. This increased role was, at least in part, deemed necessary to curb or eliminate sharp practices and abuses employed by business to take advantage of the less sophisticated consumer. There is nothing new in the idea that the consumer should be entitled to protection in dealing with business. Lending money has long been regulated by state usury laws, and both federal and state legislation protect the investor from unscrupulous dealers in securities. However, recent efforts to protect the consumer have been most dramatic. This is especially evident in the field of credit transactions.

This chapter also examines the work of the Federal Trade Commission (FTC) in unfair and deceptive trade practices as that agency enforces Section 5 of the Federal Trade Commission Act. The FTC has been successful in curbing many of the predatory trade practices that created concern for the consumer and brought about the enactment of the Wheeler-Lea amendment to Section 5.

Finally, since ours is largely a cashless society and easy credit can create problems for those who prove to be poor managers, provisions of what is increasingly the last resort for an overextended consumer, a petition for discharge in bankruptcy under the Bankruptcy Reform Act of 1978, are examined.

Credit Transactions

The Consumer Credit Protection Act

Today it is an easy matter for the average householder to obtain and use credit cards. Cash purchase of major appliances and automobiles is now a rare occurrence, and even supermarket purchases may be paid for by check. This proliferation of credit has resulted in legislation that defines the rights and obligations of those who deal in it.

Congress enacted the Consumer Credit Protection Act (CCPA) in 1968 in response to unscrupulous and predatory practices on the part of creditors in consumer transactions. Congress was concerned with consumer credit disclosure methods, credit advertising, garnishment methods, questionable procedures used by some credit reporting agencies, and certain debt collection practices (a problem recognized in a 1977 amendment to the act).

Truth in Lending

The purpose of the truth in lending section of the CCPA is to strengthen competition among institutions that extend consumer credit. The section requires credit terms to be disclosed so that consumers can more readily compare the credit terms available to them and avoid the uninformed use of credit. For purposes of the act, a creditor subject to its provisions is one who regularly extends credit to consumers, normally the seller. However, the term creditor also includes a seller who arranges credit for the buyer with a person or entity that does not normally extend credit. Protected under the act are natural persons, that is, individuals who purchase consumer goods for personal, family, or household use. Not covered by the act are personal loans between friends, loans to individuals for business purposes, or loans to corporations or partnerships.

The consumer credit cost disclosure portion of the truth in lending section requires creditors to disclose to the consumer both the finance charge and the annual percentage rate (APR) of the finance charge. (The act also applies, even if no finance charge is imposed, if a credit agreement requires payment in more than four installments.) The finance charge is the total of all charges for the extension of credit. It includes such items as interest, service or carrying charges, investigation or credit report fees, and premiums for any insurance the creditor requires as protection for the loan. The finance charge does not include certain items of expense to the debtor paid to parties other than the creditor. Such items include taxes and, in the case of credit secured by an interest in real estate, fees for title examination, title insurance, and preparation of a deed or other necessary documents.

When the finance charge has been determined, it must then be expressed as an annual percentage rate. The APR often is substantially higher than the annual interest rate. For example, if the finance charge, including 6 percent annual add-on interest, amounts to 1¼ percent per month, the APR is 15 percent, or 9 percent higher than the annual interest. These facts, together with information on delinquency or default charges, a description of any property used as security, and the total of the amount to be financed, must be revealed to the borrower in a disclosure statement before credit is extended. The information contained in the disclosure statement permits the borrower to compare credit from various sources and select the creditor whose terms are the most favorable.

The Truth in Lending Act does not put a ceiling on interest rates or limit finance charges. Its main requirement is that a creditor who regularly extends credit in the ordinary course of business must make a full disclosure of the cost of credit to the consumer.

Other features require that the number of payments and the amount of each be disclosed and that complete disclosure be made when credit is advertised, when the loan is made or credit extended, and when periodic billing takes place. If the transaction involves a security interest in real property, the borrower has three business days from the date of the transaction to rescind the agreement without penalty. This right to rescind must be brought to the attention of the borrower by means of a special notice to the customer on a prescribed form.

Detailed procedures of the act are contained in Regulation Z, issued by the Federal Reserve Board under the authority of the CCPA. Criminal penalties for willfully and knowingly failing to comply with the requirements of the act are a fine of up to $5,000, imprisonment for one year, or both. Civil penalties can be recovered by the debtor in an amount equal to twice the finance charge but not less than $100 or more than $1,000, plus costs and attorney's fees in appropriate cases. Under the Truth in Lending Simplification and Reform Act, effective March 31, 1982, a creditor is exempt from liability if within sixty days after an error is discovered, the buyer is notified of such error and appropriate adjustments are made to ensure that there is no overpayment.

The following case is a good analysis of the provisions of the Truth in Lending Act, particularly the requirement for disclosing the real cost of credit in computing the true finance charge in a consumer transaction.

Joseph v. Norman's Health Clubs, Inc.

U.S. Court of Appeals
Eighth Circuit
532 F.2d 86
(1976)

A number of plaintiffs brought this action against Norman's Health Club and two finance companies, alleging that the activities of all three defendants violated the federal Truth in Lending Act.

Norman Saindon, one of the defendants, owned and operated a chain of health clubs in the St. Louis, Missouri, area. "Lifetime memberships" were offered to the public for $360, payable in twenty-four equal installments of $15 each. Ninety-eight percent of club members chose to sign installment notes rather than pay cash for their memberships. The health club then discounted these notes to finance companies—the club sold the notes to the finance companies for amounts considerably less than their face amounts, with the discounts ranging from $85 to $165 on the $360 notes.

The gist of the plaintiffs' complaint was that a number of patrons who paid cash for their memberships had been granted a 10 percent price reduction from the basic price charged installment members and that the failure of the health club and the finance companies to disclose this fact and information about the discounts to the installment members violated the Truth in Lending Act (TILA) of 1969.

The trial court entered a judgment in favor of the plaintiffs against the health club but not against the two finance companies, ruling that there was no violation of TILA by the finance companies, on the ground that they had "not extended credit" to the plaintiffs and the TILA therefore did not apply to them. The plaintiffs appealed.

Lay, Circuit Judge:

. . . The fundamental purpose of the Truth in Lending Act, 15 U.S.C. § 1601 et seq., is to require creditors to disclose the "true" cost of consumer credit, so that consumers can make informed choices among available methods of payment.

See 15 U.S.C. § 1601; *Mourning v. Family Publications Service, Inc.*, 411 U.S. 356, 364-65, 93 S.Ct. 1652, 1658, 36 L.Ed.2d 318, 326 (1973). . . . The Act is remedial in nature.

The Act was intended to change the practices of the consumer credit industry, and the statute reflects Congress' view that this should be done by imposing disclosure requirements on those who "regularly" extend or offer to extend consumer credit. In interpreting the Act, the Federal Reserve Board and the majority of courts have focused on the substance, rather than the form of credit transactions, and have looked to the practices of the trade, the course of dealing of the parties, and the intention of the parties in addition to specific contractual obligations. Thus, in *Mourning v. Family Publications Service, Inc., supra*, the Supreme Court said:

> *The hearings held by Congress reflect the difficulty of the task it sought to accomplish. Whatever legislation was passed had to deal not only with the myriad forms in which credit transactions then occurred, but also with those which would be devised in the future. . . . The language employed evinces the awareness of Congress that some creditors would attempt to characterize their transactions so as to fall one step outside whatever boundary Congress attempted to establish. 411 U.S. at 365, 93 S.Ct. at 1658, 36 L.Ed.2d at 327.*

The statute requires certain information, such as total finance charges and the applicable annual percentage rate, to be disclosed "to each person to whom consumer credit is extended and upon whom a finance charge is or may be imposed." 15 U.S.C. § 1631(a). "Credit" includes "the right granted by a creditor to a customer to . . . incur debt and defer its payment." Reg Z, 12 C.F.R. § 226.2(1). The Act does not apply to loans or credit sales made "for business and commercial purposes" 15 U.S.C. § 1603(1); it covers only extensions of consumer credit, defined in the Act as credit "offered or extended (to) a natural person . . . primarily for personal, family, household, or agricultural purposes." 15 U.S.C. § 1602(h). Failure to comply renders the creditor liable to the consumer in an amount equal to twice the finance charge, but not less than $100 or more than $1,000. 15 U.S.C. § 1640(a). In the Act, Congress gave the Federal Reserve Board authority to promulgate regulations to ensure compliance. 15 U.S.C. § 1604; see *Mourning v. Family Publications Service, supra* at 365, 371-72, 93 S.Ct. at 1661, 36 L.Ed.2d at 330. Pursuant to that grant of authority, the Board promulgated Regulation Z, 12 C.F.R. § 226.1 *et seq.* . . .

In the instant case, the finance companies operated under a definite working arrangement with the Club. The evidence discloses that (1) the finance companies were alerted almost simultaneously with the customer's execution of a note; (2) an immediate credit check was then made by the finance companies; (3) if the customer's note was accepted, the finance companies paid the Club the amount of the note less the discount; (4) the finance companies accepted assignments without recourse to the Club, thus relying solely on the customer for payment; (5) the finance companies often contacted the customer the same day and upon approving him, the companies would send out their payment book describing the manner of payment and the notice of late charges (not mentioned in the note assigned); (6) the finance companies carried the note on their books as a "loan" and listed a "finance charge"; and (7) thereafter, the finance companies treated the club member in the same manner as they did their direct consumer loan customers. The situation was no different than if the finance companies had gone to the Club with the prospective member, paid the Club for the membership and then taken the customer's note just as they did take it.

We find, as have all but one of the courts faced with similar facts, that where the third-party financer becomes intimately involved in the relevant credit transactions it may become liable as an extender of credit. . . .

Finding liability, the remaining issue is whether the discount constituted a finance charge under the Act.

The district court did not discuss whether the discount on the notes assigned to the finance companies was a finance charge which should have been disclosed by the Club. The district court did note, however, that unitary price schemes, under which the seller offers goods for the same price, whether paid in cash or on the installment plan, can hide a finance charge. 386 F.Supp. at 791.

The Act defines "finance charge" as:

the sum of all *charges, payable directly or* indirectly by the person to whom the credit is extended, *and imposed directly or* indirectly *by the creditor as an incident to the extension of credit including . . . any amount payable under a discount . . . system. 15 U.S.C. § 1605(a).*

The fact that a particular charge may not be included in the definitions of interest found in state usury laws is not controlling, for "finance charge" under TILA was intended to include not only "interest" but many other charges for credit. H.R. Rep. No. 1040, 90th Cong., 2d Sess., 2 U.S.Code Cong. & Admin. News pp. 1962, 1977 (1968). The Federal Reserve Board has ruled that discounts paid by a seller (such as the Health Club) of consumer accounts receivable must be included in the stated finance charge if and to the extent that they are passed to the consumer. See 12 C.F.R. §§ 226.4(a), 226.406; FRB Letter No. 433 (Jan. 21, 1971) by Tynan Smith, CCH Consumer Credit Guide, para. 30, 627.

In the instant case, it is obvious that all of the discount originally agreed upon by the Club and the finance companies was passed along to the customers as a charge for use of credit. It may be, however, that some portion of the subsequent increases in the discount was not passed along to the customers and was rather absorbed by the Club as a reduction in its profit. On the other hand, adding more members may have permitted the seller so to reduce cost per member that it could provide the same services without increasing the face amount of the note. The district court should explore this matter on remand. See 12 C.F.R. § 226. 406.

Since the amount of the discounts charged by the finance companies varied from time to time, it is necessary to remand to the district court for computation of the penalty to be assessed under the Act in favor of the plaintiffs and against the finance companies.

The judgment in favor of the finance companies is vacated and the cause reversed and remanded for further proceedings.

★★★

Real Estate Settlement Procedures Act

TILA is applicable to loans for the purchase of real estate. Additional protection for a home buyer is afforded by the Real Estate Settlement Procedures Act (RESPA). Settlement costs include attorneys' fees; title insurance; fees for inspections, surveys, and appraisals; agents' or brokers' fees; taxes; insurance; and many other miscellaneous items. Congress found that because of the variation of items included in the settlement costs and the amount charged for each, significant reforms were needed in the real estate settlement process. The purpose of RESPA, enacted in 1974 and substantially amended in 1976, is to insure that buyers of residential property are given timely information on the nature and costs of the settlement process and that they are protected against obvious abuses. The act requires that effective advance disclosure be made to home buyers and sellers. It prohibits kickbacks or referral fees and, in general, affords considerable protection against unknown costs to the buyer.

RESPA applies to all federally related mortgage loans (most mortgage loans on residential property are federally related) and is administered and enforced by the secretary of housing and urban development. The secretary has issued a comprehensive regulation, known as Regulation X, to prescribe procedures for curbing questionable practices in real estate transactions.

Restrictions on Garnishment

Garnishment can be defined as the legal proceedings of a judgment creditor to require a third person owing money to a debtor or holding property belonging to a debtor to turn over (to the court or sheriff) the property or money for the satisfaction of the judgment. For example, a creditor who has been unable to collect a debt from a debtor could bring an action in the courts and obtain a judgment against the nonpaying debtor. After being awarded the judgment by successfully proving the existence of the debt and its nonpayment, the creditor may then obtain a writ of garnishment. This writ may then be served on the debtor's employer, directing the employer to deduct a specified amount from the employee's wages to be paid directly to the creditor until the debt is satisfied. Savings and checking accounts and other assets of the debtor held by a third party may also be garnished.

Congressional hearings leading to the enactment of the CCPA revealed that the unrestricted garnishment of wages encouraged predatory extension of credit; that employers were often quick to discharge an employee whose wages were garnished; and that the laws of the states on the subject were so different they effectively destroyed the uniformity of the bankruptcy laws and defeated their purpose. Consequently, the CCPA section on garnishment sets limits on the extent to which the wages of an individual can be garnished. In general, wages cannot be garnished in any workweek in excess of 25 percent of the individual's disposable (after-tax) earnings or the amount by which the disposable earnings for that workweek exceed thirty times the federal minimum hourly wage, whichever is less. Such restrictions do not apply in the case of a court order for the support of any person (wife or child, for example), any order of a court of bankruptcy under Chapter 13 (Adjustment of Debts of an Individual with Regular Income) of the Federal Bankruptcy Act, or any debt due for state or federal taxes.

Garnishment proceedings are also governed by state law. In fact, a state law may be given effect if its provisions provide more protection for the debtor than does the federal law. In a Montana case the United States obtained a judgment against a debtor and sought a writ of garnishment against the debtor's wages. The U.S. district court held that Montana's law of garnishment was applicable since it exempted wages of a head of family necessary for the use and support of his family. The federal law has no such broad exemption. *U.S. v. Dumont*, 416 F.Supp. 632 (1976).

Garnishment of wages may work a hardship on employers who have the administrative burden of deducting the garnishment amount and forwarding it to the judgment creditor. Further, an employee whose wages are garnished may feel that the reduced paycheck warrants a commensurate reduction in effort or production. Nevertheless, an employer may not discharge the employee solely because of garnishment for a single debt, even if the garnishment is repeated. Violations by an employer are subject to a fine of not more than $1,000, imprisonment for up to one year, or both.

The Fair Credit Reporting Act

The section of the CCPA known as the Fair Credit Reporting Act is directed at consumer reporting agencies. It is an effort by Congress to insure that the mechanism developed for investigating and evaluating the creditworthiness, credit standing, credit capacity, character, and general reputation of consumers is fair with respect to the confidentiality, accuracy, relevance, and proper utilization of the reported information. Too often in the past a consumer was denied credit because of misleading or inaccurate information supplied to a prospective creditor by a consumer reporting agency.[1] The effect could be devastating, particularly as it affected a consumer's credit standing and general reputation in the business community.

The information on individual consumers is derived from many sources, including creditors, court and other official records, neighbors, and, in many cases, from facts consumers supply themselves. Information accumulated in a *consumer report* and disseminated to users can and often does include such items as judgments, liens, bankruptcies, arrest records, and employment history. In addition, the Fair Credit Reporting Act covers the *investigative reports* made by credit reporting agencies. Often used by prospective employers or by insurance companies, investigative reports are

[1] This is not an agency of the government. Such agencies are persons or businesses that regularly assemble and evaluate credit information and provide it to others for a fee.

"Creditor harassment? I told him real polite I'd break his legs."

Certain debt-collection practices are forbidden by law.
Source: Reprinted by permission of Charles Barber.

more personal in nature than consumer reports and can contain information on the subject's personal habits, marital history, education, political affiliation, and other private matters. When an investigative report is requested on a consumer, the consumer must be notified in writing within three days of the request and has a right to be informed of the nature and scope of the investigation.

With regard to both consumer reports and investigative reports, the law provides that, upon request and proper identification, consumers are entitled to know the nature and substance of all information about them (except medical information) in the agency's file, the sources of the information, and the identity of those who have received the report from the credit reporting agency. Those entitled to receive consumer reports include businesses that may want to extend credit to the consumer, prospective employers or insurers, and government licensing agencies that may be concerned with the financial responsibility of the consumer. Access to the information can also be gained by court order. In addition, an investigative report cannot be prepared on an individual consumer unless that person is first notified and given the right to request information on the nature and scope of the pending investigation.

An important provision of the act requires that all information in consumer reports be current and that consumer reporting agencies maintain reasonable procedures designed to avoid violations of certain other provisions. This is an obvious effort to reduce the incidence of carelessly prepared reports containing inaccurate information.

Civil penalties for a negligent violation of the act include the actual damages to the consumer and, in a successful action, court costs and reasonable attorney's fees. In the case of willful noncompliance, punitive damages may also be awarded to the successful plaintiff consumer. Administrative enforcement of the act and compliance with its provisions is a function of the Federal Trade Commission because violations are considered unfair or deceptive acts or practices.

Credit Cards

The widespread use of credit cards, issued by all manner of companies, has created problems when a card has fallen into the wrong hands through loss or theft. Many companies provided their credit cards indiscriminately to any person who might want one and to many who had not requested them. It was difficult to determine who should assume the liability for unauthorized credit card purchases: the person to whom the card was issued, the unauthorized user, the merchant who made the sale, or the credit card issuer.

Congress addressed the problem in CCPA provisions that prohibit the issuance of credit cards except in response to a request or application and that place limits on the liability of a cardholder for its unauthorized use. In general, if a cardholder loses a credit card and it is used by someone without authority to do so, the cardholder is liable if: (1) the liability does not exceed $50; (2) the card is an accepted card; (3) the issuer has given notice to the cardholder as to the potential liability; (4) the issuer has provided the cardholder with a description of a means by which the card issuer may be notified of loss or theft of the card; (5) the unauthorized use occurs before the cardholder has notified the issuer that an unauthorized use of the card has occurred; and (6) the card issuer has provided a method whereby the user of the card can be identified as the authorized user.

The above provisions protect the legal cardholder. Unauthorized use of a credit card can result in severe penalties. If the unauthorized transaction involves goods or services having a retail value of $1,000 or more, the penalty can be a fine of up to $10,000, imprisonment for up to ten years, or both.

The Collection of Debts

A 1977 amendment to the CCPA, the Fair Debt Collection Practices Act, became effective March 20, 1978. It has as its purpose the elimination of abusive debt collection practices by those who collect debts for others (collection agencies) and the protection of individual debtors against debt collection abuses. The act was brought about by the unscrupulous methods used by some debt collectors in pursuing debtors. Instances of harassment in the form of threats of violence, the use of obscene or profane language, publication of lists of consumers who allegedly refused to pay their debts, and annoyance by repeated use of the telephone were commonplace before the act was passed.

The debt collector's communications with others and with the debtor in an effort to locate the debtor are governed by a provision of the Act. The debt collector is prohibited from making false representations or misleading the debtor about the nature of the collection process. While the debt collector may contact persons other than the debtor, such contacts must be restricted to efforts to determine the debtor's home address, phone number, and place of employment. If the debtor has retained an attorney and the collector has knowledge of this, subsequent communications must be with the attorney.

The debt collector cannot solicit or take from any person a check postdated by more than five days without notice of the intent to deposit the check. On occasion, debt collectors have encouraged the debtor to write a postdated check for the amount of the debt knowing that the debtor had insufficient funds to cover the check. A threat to deposit the postdated check was often enough to compel the debtor to seek the funds necessary to pay the collector and thereby avoid criminal prosecution for issuing a bad check. The act further provides that written notice of the amount of the debt and the name of the creditor be sent to the consumer together with a statement that, unless the consumer disputes the validity of the debt within thirty days, the debt collector can assume it is a valid obligation. If the consumer owes multiple debts and makes a single payment, the debt collector cannot apply the payment to any debt that is disputed by the consumer.

The Fair Debt Collection Practices Act protects the consumer debtor and places the burden on the debt collector. Compliance with the act is enforced by the Federal Trade Commission, since violations are considered to be unfair or deceptive trade practices. A debt collector who fails to comply with the provisions of the act may incur civil liability to the extent of actual damages sustained by an individual plaintiff, additional damages not to exceed $1,000, and court costs and reasonable attorney's fees. However, an action brought by a debtor in bad faith and for the purpose of harassment can result in the award of reasonable fees and costs to defendant's attorney.

The following case serves to illustrate the extent to which an overzealous debt collector will go—in this instance, to repossess an automobile.

Ford Motor Credit Company v. Frances C. Sheehan
373 So.2d 956 (Fla.App.1979)

In October 1974 Sheehan purchased a Ford automobile which was financed by Ford Motor Credit Company (Ford Credit) pursuant to the terms of a retail installment contract. He later moved to various locations and became delinquent in his payments. Unable to locate Sheehan, Ford Credit assigned the account to a central recovery office maintained by it in Michigan. On May 1, 1975, Sheehan's mother, who lived in Rhode Island, received a telephone call from a woman who identified herself as being employed by Mercy Hospital in San Francisco, California. Sheehan's mother was told by the woman that one

or both of Sheehan's children had been involved in a serious automobile accident and that the caller was attempting to locate Sheehan. Sheehan's mother supplied information concerning her son's home and business addresses and phone numbers in Jacksonville, Florida. Sheehan, upon returning a phone call from his mother and learning of the alleged accident, spent seven hours calling hospitals and the police in San Francisco. He finally was able to determine that the information given to his mother was false. The following day his automobile was repossessed by Search International, an independent contractor with Ford Credit.

Ervin, Judge:

. . . Ford Motor Credit Company appeals jury verdicts awarding Sheehan compensatory and punitive damages on one count of a complaint charging intentional infliction of mental distress and a second count alleging a violation of Section 559.72(7), Florida Statutes (1975) [which prohibits anyone while collecting consumer claims to engage willfully in conduct which can reasonably be expected to abuse or harass the debtor or any member of his family]. . . .

The jury awarded Sheehan $4,000 compensatory damages and $11,000 punitive damages. As to that count charging a violation of Section 559.72(7), we conclude the statute has no application since it cannot regulate actions of individuals in Michigan or Rhode Island. [The parties agreed that the telephone call from the unidentified person representing she was employed by a hospital in San Francisco in fact emanated from Ford Credit's office in Dearborn, Michigan.] . . .

We affirm the verdict assessing damages as to that count alleging intentional infliction of mental distress. The majority rule recognizes the tort of severe emotional distress intentionally caused by a defendant. . . . Section 46(1) of the Restatement states the rule in the following manner:

(1) One who by extreme and outrageous conduct intentionally or recklessly causes severe emotional distress to another is subject to liability for such emotional distress, and if bodily harm to the other results from it, for such bodily harm.

There is hardly any question that under the majority rule Ford Motor Credit would be liable to Sheehan for the distress it caused him. . . . While Ford Motor Credit did not directly communicate the false information to Sheehan, it was the causative force which set into motion the communication resulting in Sheehan's severe emotional distress. Whether or not Ford Motor Credit intended to inflict severe emotional distress is immaterial. Where the actor knows that such distress is certain, or substantially certain to result from his conduct, the rule applies.

Sheehan testified that following a conversation with his sister, who relayed the false information to him concerning his children, he was extremely worried, upset, and nearly out of his mind for a continuous period of seven hours while he attempted to discover the condition of his children. This testimony is sufficient proof of emotional distress which "includes all highly unpleasant mental reactions, such as fright, horror, grief, . . . worry, . . ." Comment j. While

Sheehan's testimony, considered alone, is not proof of severe emotional distress, when combined with the conduct of Ford Motor Credit, its submission to the jury was entirely appropriate. . . .

We conclude that there is in Florida no bar to an independent action for intentional infliction of severe mental distress when the conduct alleged is "so outrageous in character, and so extreme in degree, as to go beyond all bounds of decency. . . ." As stated, Ford Motor Credit's conduct falls within that description. Because of the uncertainty of what rule applies in Florida and because of the obvious conflict in cases, we certify the following question to the Florida Supreme Court as one of great public interest:

MAY ONE RECOVER DAMAGES FOR INTENTIONAL INFLICTION OF SEVERE MENTAL DISTRESS WHICH IS NOT INCIDENTAL TO OR CONSEQUENT UPON ANY SEPARATE TORT OR OTHER ACTIONABLE WRONG?

The verdict entered on the count finding violation of Section 559.72(7) is reversed, and the judgment entered upon the common law count is affirmed. The case need not be remanded for new trial. While we reverse the verdict entered on one of the two counts, we consider the verdicts sufficiently severable to sustain the total damages awarded.

★★★

Fair Credit Billing

Debtor disputes with merchants or other creditors over a periodic statement of account are common occurrences. Prior to the Fair Credit Billing Act, the burden rested mainly on the customer—the debtor—to get things straightened out. This is no longer true. The Act requires that creditors maintain procedures whereby consumers can complain about billing errors and obtain satisfaction within a specified period, not later than two billing cycles or ninety days. The consumer must give the creditor notice of the billing error with a statement explaining the reasons for questioning the item or items felt to be in error. The creditor must then either make appropriate corrections in the consumer's account or conduct an investigation into the matter. If, after the investigation, the creditor feels that the statement is accurate, the debtor must be notified and told why the creditor believes the original statement of account to be correct. The Act requires that payments be credited promptly and that any overpayment be refunded (on request by the debtor) or credited to the debtor's account.

Equal Credit Opportunity

The Equal Credit Opportunity Act prohibits discrimination based on race, color, religion, national origin, sex, marital status, or age in connection with extensions of credit. In addition, a credit applicant may not be discriminated against because all or some of his or her income is derived from a public assistance program. The applicant must, however, have contractual capacity; minors, for example, cannot insist on credit under the Act. The enactment was the result of complaints by married persons that credit frequently had been denied unless both parties to the marriage obligated themselves. Each party may now separately and voluntarily apply for and obtain a credit account, and state laws prohibiting separate credit no longer apply. A credit applicant who is denied credit is entitled to know the reasons for such denial. Wrongful denial of credit can result in an award of actual damages suffered plus punitive damages of $10,000. If a group or class has been discriminated against, the Equal Credit Opportunity Act provides for class actions and, in successful cases, $500,000 or 1 percent of the net worth of the guilty party, whichever is less, as damages.

Role of the Federal Trade Commission

Originally enacted in 1914 to strengthen the enforcement of statutes prohibiting business practices that were found to be anticompetitive, the Federal Trade Commission Act, as amended, now plays a substantial role in protecting consumers from unfair and deceptive trade practices. (The FTC, as an enforcer of the antitrust laws is briefly discussed in Chapter 10.) The Wheeler-Lea Act of 1938 amended Section 5 of the Federal Trade Commission Act so as to make unfair methods of competition in commerce and unfair or deceptive acts or practices illegal. Included was a grant of power to the FTC to deal with certain deceptive advertising practices. As the House committee stated in reporting out the Wheeler-Lea Act, "This amendment makes the consumer, who may be injured by an unfair trade practice, of equal concern before the law, with the merchant or manufacturer injured by the unfair methods of a dishonest competitor." Thus the FTC began its guardianship over the consumer who was increasingly being bombarded with false or deceptive claims by merchants eager to have their shares of a highly competitive and burgeoning market. Especially targeted by the FTC for oversight and remedial action are such practices as deceptive or false advertising and other unfair procedures that mislead the consumer. In upholding FTC enforcement action the courts have considered a trade practice to be "unfair" when it offends established public policy and when the practice is immoral, unethical, oppressive, unscrupulous, or substantially injurious to consumers. A trade practice is deceptive when it has a tendency and capacity to deceive the consumer. Actual deception need not be proved or found.

The FTC is a powerful agency. In performing its enforcement functions it may use its subpoena power to compel a business being investigated to produce business records and documents and can order individuals to appear and testify at its proceedings. Investigations by the FTC are normally initiated when a consumer, or a competitor of the company to be investigated, or a special interest consumer group files a complaint. The investigation may be informal at first and may terminate if the company being investigated voluntarily agrees to stop the activity that brought about the complaint. Or, the company, upon being advised that a formal complaint is to be filed, may agree to a *consent order*. If the company wishes to adjudicate the matter, a hearing is held before an administrative law judge, whose finding of facts and opinion are then reviewed by the full five-member commission. Based upon the facts as found by the administrative law judge, the commission may dismiss the complaint or issue a *cease and desist order*. Judicial review of the FTC's orders may be made in the U.S. courts of appeal if a company wishes to contest the decision.

While it is difficult to fault a merchant for trying to increase the volume of business, the methods used to accomplish this may be unethical and involve deception. A seller may, for example, offer an item free of charge with a purchase of one of the items at the "regular" price. However, the regular price may be considerably higher than is normally charged for the item. Or, a merchant may advertise a particular item at a very attractive price to get shoppers into the store, but a prospective buyer is told by the salesperson that the advertised item is no longer available or that the customer would be better off to purchase a more expensive product. (This tactic is known as *bait and switch*.) These kinds of promotional schemes and others are unfair and deceptive and are the target of the FTC's Bureau of Consumer Protection.

False and Misleading Advertising

In 1976 the FTC entered a consent order requiring the STP Corporation and its Chicago advertising agency to cease and desist making false and misleading effectiveness claims and representations for its products. (87 F.T.C. 56) Three of STP's products were involved. Of the many ads cited by the FTC, the following are typical.

STP Oil Treatment: "I'm a retired banker who likes to tinker with his car. I use STP Oil Treatment and value it very highly. I asked the dealer if it would be alright to use STP. He says, 'If all our customers used it, we might just as well close down our repair shop.'"

STP Gas Treatment: STP . . . cleans and tunes your engine as you drive . . . You'll feel the difference with the very first can.

STP Dual Oil Filter: STP Corporation unconditionally guarantees this filter. It meets or exceeds all listed American automobile manufacturers' original equipment and/or warranty specifications.

With regard to these ads, the FTC found that the use of STP Oil Treatment will not prevent every car which uses it from breaking down or requiring engine repairs; that STP Gas Treatment will not provide a complete tune-up or the equivalent of a complete tune-up as the car is driven; and that the STP Dual Oil Filter does not meet or exceed all automobile manufacturers' original equipment specifications for oil filters.

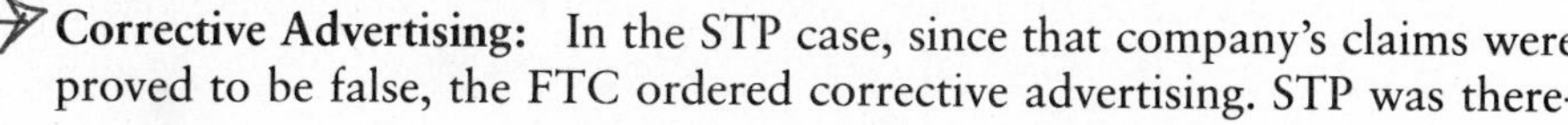

Corrective Advertising: In the STP case, since that company's claims were proved to be false, the FTC ordered corrective advertising. STP was therefore required to expend a substantial portion of its advertising budget to advise consumers that its previous ads were less than completely truthful. A finding by the FTC that a particular product does not perform as advertised is a blow to the manufacturer; imposition of the corrective advertising sanction can adversely affect both reputation and profits.

Use of Deceptive Techniques

With the advent of television as an advertising medium, big business was quick to use it to extol the virtues of its products in graphic detail. Advertising budgets of large companies are in millions of dollars. (In the Warner-Lambert case, discussed in Chapter 1, the corrective advertising was limited to the first $4 million to be spent by the company.) Advertising agencies were called upon to devise attractive commercials for their clients' products. It was inevitable that some of these ads would use techniques that might be considered deceptive. For example, in ads for its vegetable-type soups, the Campbell Soup Company in 1970 showed pictures of a bowl of its soup with an apparently ample supply of the solid ingredients on the top or at the surface of the bowl. However, this appearance was created by putting glass marbles in the bowl, thus forcing the solid ingredients to the top for the pictures. The company was ordered to cease and desist this deceptive practice. (77 F.T.C. 664 [1970])

In an earlier case, the ad agency for Colgate-Palmolive Company had developed a television commercial purporting to demonstrate that Colgate's Rapid Shave could soften sandpaper and would therefore effectively soften the toughest beard. In its ad, what was claimed to be sandpaper was actually plexiglass to which sand had been applied. The Supreme Court upheld the FTC's cease and desist order with respect to the misleading commercial. (*Federal Trade Commission v. Colgate-Palmolive Co.*, 380 U.S. 374 [1965])

It should be noted that the advertising agency involved is usually held to be equally liable with its client when deceptive advertising is proved and refunds or other restitution are ordered as a part of the remedy.

The following case is another example of the kinds of advertising techniques the FTC finds to be deceptive trade practices.

Libby-Owens-Ford Glass Company v. F.T.C.
U.S. Court of Appeals, Sixth Cir., 352 F.2d 415 (1965)

Petitioners Libby-Owens-Ford (LOF) and General Motors (GM) were charged by the FTC with unfair and deceptive acts and practices and unfair methods of competition in violation of Section 5 of the Federal Trade Commission Act. The FTC issued a cease and desist order and petitioners sought and were granted judicial review.

Per Curiam:

. . . Specifically, the facts as to LOF involved twenty-two television commercials purporting to show the superiority of safety plate glass used in all of the windows of GM cars over safety sheet glass used in the side and rear windows of non-GM cars. The facts as to GM involved the televising of one commercial on two separate occasions purporting to show the same superiority.

The Commission found in both cases that the commercials contained false representations that the plate glass used in the side and rear windows of GM cars was the same grade and quality as the plate glass used in the windshields of GM cars, and that the sheet glass used in the side and rear windows of non-GM cars was the same grade and quality as sheet glass used in home windows. The Commission also found that the commercials in both cases contained false demonstrations achieved through the use of undisclosed "mock-ups" or "props." In respect to LOF it was found that the commercials exaggerated the distortion in sheet glass by using different camera lens in filming, more acute angles, and other techniques, including taking a photograph through an open window instead of through the plate glass window as the viewer was led to believe. As to GM the same exaggeration was achieved by the use of streaks of vaseline applied to the glass being photographed and panning the camera from side to side as though the viewer were walking past a home window. Based on these findings the Commission ordered LOF and GM to cease and desist from such practices. . . .

The decision of the Supreme Court in *Federal Trade Comm's v. Colgate-Palmolive Co.*, 380 U.S. 374 . . . disposed of the "mock-up" issue here. There, the Court held that the undisclosed use of mock-ups was a deceptive practice even though the test, experiment or demonstration actually proved the product claim.

On the authority of Colgate we sustain the Commission's order barring LOF and GM from using undisclosed mock-ups in advertising automotive glass products. We find no merit in LOF's contention that it should not be held liable for the use of props by the film producer who, it claims, was an independent contractor. It asserted that in good faith it directed the advertising agency to present a fair commercial and it was unaware of the use of the open window. In our opinion LOF may not delegate its advertising to an independent contractor and escape liability for the acts of its advertising agency and film producer in advertising LOF products.

GM claimed that the order was improper as to it because it abandoned its single commercial eighteen months prior to the Commission's complaint and, as found by the Commission, had no intention of using the commercial again. It also argued on the same grounds that there is no public interest. It was within the Commission's discretion to determine if the public interest was affected, and to frame an order to protect against related and similar practices in the future, some of which were not embraced in GM's assurances. . . .

The only remaining questions go to the scope of the orders which both petitioners claimed were too broad. We think the order entered against LOF was not too broad and was authorized by Colgate. The Commission had authority to stop misrepresentations as to other glass products in other advertisements. The order against GM was also authorized except the following language contained in paragraph 1(a) therein: "or otherwise misrepresenting the grade or quality of glass used in any window." We believe this portion of the order was too vague and indefinite to warrant enforcement. It is therefore ordered that the quoted language be stricken from the order.

The order of the Commission in No. 15,663 is affirmed and enforced.

The order of the Commission in No. 15,664 is affirmed and enforced as modified.

★★★

Endorsements by Well-known Personalities

Many celebrities derive considerable income by endorsing various products. Much of the consuming public, particularly the fans of the celebrity involved, are frequently influenced to buy and use the product because of a testimonial by the celebrity. The FTC has become increasingly watchful of such advertising and will act if the ads prove to be false or deceptive and if the personality involved does not in fact use the product being endorsed. In a case that attracted some attention in 1978, Pat Boone and his corporation, Cooga Mooga, were involved in advertising a product called *Acne-Statin*. The advertisement in question, with photographs of Pat and Debbie Boone, read, in part: "ACNE? Our girls got lasting help with ACNE-STATIN." The FTC was able to prove that not only was *Acne-Statin* ineffective as a cure for acne but the Boone girls did not in fact use the product. Consequently, the FTC issued a cease and desist order, and Boone and his corporation were ordered to pay a share of any refunds or restitution that might be made to those who purchased the product during the advertising campaign that featured the Boones' endorsement. (92 F.T.C. 310 (1978))

The FTC and Consumer Installment Sales

Prior to 1976 a consumer who purchased on credit and signed an installment note might have problems if the purchase proved to be less than satisfactory. For example, suppose that a person buys a television set from a retailer and gives the retailer an installment note in payment for it. The retailer then negotiates the instrument to a third party (usually a lending institution), who probably qualifies as a holder in due course. The *holder in due course* of a negotiable instrument enjoys protection against certain defenses that can be asserted by an obligor against an *ordinary* holder if an action is brought on the negotiable instrument.

In such a case, if the television set does not work properly (or even if it is never delivered), the buyer remains fully liable to the holder in due course of the installment note. The only recourse is to harass the retailer until a workable set is delivered or to recover damages for breach of contract—certainly an unsatisfactory solution for the buyer. Consequently, and also because of the diverse measures in effect at the state level, the FTC, in 1975, promulgated its Rule to Preserve Buyers' Claims and Defenses in Consumer Installment Sales. This rule, usually referred to as the FTC Holder in Due Course rule, took effect in May of 1976.

In general the FTC rule applies to two situations: (1) when a buyer of consumer goods executes a sales contract that includes giving a promissory note to the seller, and (2) when a seller of consumer goods arranges for a direct loan by a third party—usually a bank or other commercial lending institution—to the customer in order for the sale to be made.

In regard to the first situation, the rule provides in part:

In connection with any sale or lease of goods or services to consumers, in or affecting (interstate) commerce . . . it is an unfair or deceptive trade practice . . . for a seller, directly or indirectly to (a) Take or receive a consumer credit contract which fails to contain the following provisions in at least ten point, bold face type:

NOTICE

ANY HOLDER OF THIS CONSUMER CREDIT CONTRACT IS SUBJECT TO ALL CLAIMS AND DEFENSES WHICH THE DEBTOR COULD ASSERT AGAINST THE SELLER OF GOODS OR SERVICES OBTAINED PURSUANT HERETO OR WITH THE PROCEEDS HEREOF. RECOVERY HEREUNDER BY THE DEBTOR SHALL NOT EXCEED AMOUNTS PAID BY THE DEBTOR HEREUNDER.

If the buyer obtains a direct loan from a third party, the notice reads:

ANY HOLDER OF THIS CONSUMER CREDIT CONTRACT IS SUBJECT TO ALL CLAIMS AND DEFENSES WHICH THE DEBTOR COULD ASSERT AGAINST THE SELLER OF GOODS AND SERVICES OBTAINED WITH THE PROCEEDS HEREOF. RECOVERY HEREUNDER BY THE DEBTOR SHALL NOT EXCEED AMOUNTS PAID BY THE DEBTOR HEREUNDER.

The rule does not apply to contracts of commercial buyers (as distinguished from consumer buyers), and commercial contracts account for a great deal of commercial paper activity. Further, the rule applies only to consumer purchases on credit; purchases in which checks are given in full payment are not subject to it. Finally, the rule permits the assertion of only those personal defenses which the purchaser could assert against the seller of the goods, such as fraud or breach of contract.

The failure by a seller to include the required notice in each consumer credit contract subjects that person to a possible fine of up to $10,000 and to possible liability in a civil suit brought by the customer to recover damages incurred as a result of such failure.

Looking Ahead

The FTC is a powerful agency that has not been reluctant to use the authority given it by the 1938 Wheeler-Lea amendment to the Federal Trade Commission Act. It was only a matter of time before some of its policies, as expressed by the many trade regulation rules it promulgated, would be called into question. This happened when the American Bar Association

(ABA) issued a report in 1970 criticizing the FTC generally with some emphasis on specific approaches taken by that agency as a consumer advocate. The ABA suggested that the FTC had developed a hit-and-miss style of enforcement through use of its consent orders and its overbroad rules relating to individual complaints as they might arise. Consequently, the FTC responded by concentrating on problems that might be industry-wide in nature and by promulgating rules the impact of which was substantial on those industries affected. Such industries and activities included insurance, the funeral business, franchising, and children's advertising.

Industry is not without representation or influence in the legislative branch. In 1980, Congress enacted the Federal Trade Commission Improvements Act for the purpose of limiting the scope of FTC action in the areas mentioned above. The Act provides for a legislative veto over FTC rules. In essence the Act requires that the FTC, after promulgating a final rule, submit the rule to committees of both houses of Congress for review. Such rule becomes effective ninety days after submission unless both houses adopt a concurrent resolution disapproving the rule. While the 1980 Act may reform certain FTC practices, its long-term effects remain to be seen. It is somewhat anomalous for Congress to create an agency, give it broad, sweeping powers, and then legislate limitations on the exercise of those powers. This is, in effect, a substitution of Congressional judgment for the considerable expertise acquired by the FTC in its role as a trade regulator. (As a matter of fact, on June 23, 1983, the U.S. Supreme Court declared the legislative veto to be an unconstitutional usurpation of power by Congress. *Immigration and Naturalization Service v. Chadha*, 51 L.W. 4907.)

Bankruptcy—Relief for the Overextended Consumer

Each year thousands of consumers file petitions in the federal courts for a discharge in bankruptcy. What they are seeking is a discharge from the obligations they are unable to pay. The effect of such a discharge is to bar the bankrupt's creditors from further efforts to collect. In recent years the number of bankruptcies has by far exceeded the total number of both criminal and civil actions in the federal courts. In fact, the annual number of bankruptcies has increased by 1,000 percent over the past thirty years. For the year ending June 30, 1981, there were 360,329 cases filed. This represents a 43.8 percent increase over the previous year.

The average bankrupt is a so-called blue-collar worker, male, thirty years of age. He is married and has two or three children. He owes $30,000 and has $18,000 in assets, most of which is encumbered. The major cause of bankruptcy is poor financial management brought about by readily available installment purchasing and the use of credit cards. Other significant causes, in order of their frequency, include domestic problems, loss of employment, illness, and obligations on which the bankrupt is a cosigner. Business failures account for about 10 percent of the bankruptcies.

In England, prior to 1861, it was not unusual for a debtor to be thrown in prison until the debts were paid. Many early American colonists were debtors who had experienced debtor's prison and were not enthusiastic about that kind of treatment. Their views are reflected in the U.S. Constitution in a provision recognizing the problems of debtors. Article I, Section 8, clause 4 provides that "The Congress shall have the power . . . to establish . . . uniform laws on the subject of bankruptcies throughout the United States." This notwithstanding, the handling of insolvency matters was effectively left to the states until 1898 when Congress passed the first comprehensive bankruptcy act. This has been substantially revised in 1938 and, more recently, in 1978.[2]

The purpose of the bankruptcy law is to permit the debtor to make a fresh start free of the prior debts he or she was unable to pay, in part or entirely. A good faith creditor who, as a result of the debtor's discharge in bankruptcy, now finds that all or a portion of the debt is uncollectible, may question the fairness of the procedure. The merchant's so-called bad debts are in effect a cost of doing business, losses that must be passed on to the consumer in the form of higher prices.

Bankruptcy Proceedings Today

The 1978 Act recognizes the uniqueness of bankruptcy proceedings by creating a separate system of federal bankruptcy courts. Each federal district within the United States contains such a court. Bankruptcy judges are appointed by the president for fourteen-year terms. The bankruptcy law provides for three different proceedings: (1) liquidation; (2) reorganization; and (3) adjustment of the debts of an individual with regular income. The liquidation proceeding, often referred to as "straight bankruptcy," is the most common type. Brief mention is also made of the other two types.

Liquidation Proceedings: Stated very generally, the object of a liquidation proceeding under Chapter 7 of the Bankruptcy Act is to sell the debtor's assets, pay off creditors insofar as possible, and legally discharge the debtor from further responsibility. A liquidation proceeding will be either a voluntary case commenced by the debtor, or an involuntary case commenced by creditors. The filing of a voluntary case automatically subjects the debtor and any property to the jurisdiction and supervision of the Bankruptcy Court.

Any debtor, whether an individual, a partnership, or a corporation, may file a petition for voluntary bankruptcy, with the following exceptions: (1) banks; (2) savings and loan associations; (3) credit unions; (4) insurance companies; (5) railroads; and (6) governmental bodies. These exempted organizations are covered by special statutes, and their liquidation is supervised by particular regulatory agencies. A debtor does not have to be insolvent in order to file a petition for voluntary bankruptcy, but it is usually

[2] This act, the Bankruptcy Reform Act of 1978, became effective October 1, 1979.

insolvency that prompts such a petition. Insolvency is defined as the financial condition of a debtor whose debts exceed the fair market value of assets.

In an involuntary case, filed by creditors, if the debtor has twelve or more creditors, at least three must join in filing the case. If there are fewer than twelve creditors, the involuntary case may be filed by one or more of them. Regardless of the number of creditors, those filing the petition must have noncontingent unsecured claims against the debtor totalling at least $5,000.

The Trustee: After the debtor becomes subject to the bankruptcy proceeding, the court must appoint an *interim trustee* to take over the debtor's property or business. Within a relatively short time thereafter, a *permanent trustee* is usually elected by the creditors, but if they do not do so, the interim trustee receives permanent status.

The trustee is an individual or corporation who, under the court's supervision, administers and represents the debtor's estate. (The property that makes up the debtor's estate is discussed later.) The basic duties of the trustee are to:

1. Investigate the financial affairs of the debtor
2. Collect assets and claims owned by the debtor
3. Temporarily operate the debtor's business if necessary
4. Reduce the debtor's assets to cash
5. Receive and examine the claims of creditors, and challenge in bankruptcy court any claim which the trustee feels to be questionable
6. Oppose the debtor's discharge from obligations when the trustee feels there are legal reasons why the debtor should not be discharged
7. Render a detailed accounting to the court of all assets received and the disposition made of them
8. Make a final report to the court when administration of the debtor's estate is completed.

In the capacity of representative of the debtor's estate, the trustee has the power to sue and be sued in that capacity and to employ accountants, attorneys, appraisers, auctioneers, and other professionals. He or she may also bring actions to set aside the debtor's transfers of assets that may have been fraudulent, including property that had been transferred to a third party within one year prior to filing the bankruptcy petition. If, for example, a debtor had "sold" an automobile or boat to a brother for ten dollars in contemplation of bankruptcy, it can be presumed that he or she did so to remove the property from the estate. Such a transfer is considered an attempt to defraud creditors, and the trustee may therefore reclaim the property for inclusion in the bankrupt's estate.

Creditors' Meetings: Within a reasonable time after commencement of the case, the bankruptcy court must call a meeting of creditors. The debtor will have already supplied the court with a list of creditors, so that they may be notified of the meeting. The judge of the bankruptcy court is not permitted to attend a creditors' meeting.

At the first meeting, creditors will usually elect the trustee. At least twenty percent of the total amount of unsecured claims which have been filed and allowed must be represented at the meeting. A trustee is elected by receiving the votes of creditors holding a majority, in amount, of the unsecured claims represented at the meeting. The other major item of business at the first creditors' meeting is an examination of the debtor. The debtor, under oath, will be questioned by the creditors and the trustee concerning the debtor's assets and matters relevant to whether the debtor will be entitled to a discharge.

Duties of the Debtor: The bankruptcy law imposes the following duties on the debtor:

1. Within a reasonable time after commencement of the proceedings, file with the court a list of creditors, a schedule of assets and liabilities, and a statement of financial affairs

2. Cooperate and respond truthfully during the examination conducted at the first creditors' meeting

3. Surrender to the trustee all property to be included in the debtor's estate, as well as all documents, books, and records pertaining to this property

4. Cooperate with the trustee in whatever way necessary to enable the trustee to perform his or her duties

5. Appear at the hearing conducted by the court concerning whether the debtor should be discharged.

A debtor who fails to fulfill any of these duties may be denied a discharge from liabilities.

The Debtor's Estate: The property owned by the debtor which becomes subject to the bankruptcy proceeding, ultimately to be sold by the trustee, is the *debtor's estate*. This includes all tangible and intangible property interests of any kind, unless specifically exempted. For example, the estate could consist of consumer goods, inventory, equipment, any of the various types of interests in real estate, patent rights, trademarks, copyrights, accounts receivable, and various contract rights.

Exemptions: A debtor who is an individual (rather than a partnership or corporation) may claim certain exemptions for certain types of property not to be included in the debtor's estate. The debtor may keep such property and still receive a discharge from liabilities at the close of the proceedings. Every state has exemption statutes setting forth the types of property which are exempt from seizure under a writ of execution. Before passage of the new bankruptcy law, the debtor's exempt property in a federal bankruptcy case was determined solely by the exemption statutes of the state where he or she lived. The Bankruptcy Reform Act of 1978, however, includes for the first time a list of federal exemptions which are available to the debtor in bankruptcy regardless of the state of domicile.

The debtor may claim the following exemptions under the federal law:

1. The debtor's interest in a homestead used as a residence, up to a value of $7,500

2. The debtor's interest in a motor vehicle, up to $1,200

3. The debtor's interest, up to $200 per item, in household furnishings, appliances, wearing apparel, animals, crops, or musical instruments which are owned primarily for personal, family, or household (nonbusiness) uses

4. The debtor's interest in jewelry, up to a total of $500, which is owned primarily for personal, family, or household uses

5. The debtor's interest in any kind of property, up to a limit of $400 plus any unused portion of the $7,500 homestead exemption

6. The debtor's interest in implements, tools, or professional books used in his or her trade

7. Any unmatured life insurance policies owned by the debtor (except for credit life policies)

8. Professionally prescribed health aids

9. The debtor's right to receive various government benefits, such as unemployment compensation, social security, and veteran's benefits

10. The debtor's right to receive various private benefits, such as alimony, child support, and pension payments, to the extent reasonably necessary for support of the debtor or the debtor's dependents.

It is not likely that the new law will achieve uniformity of exemptions since it permits the debtor to choose either the federal exemptions or those of the state where the debtor lives. That is, the debtor may choose one or the other, as a whole; there cannot be a selection of some exemptions from the federal law and some from a state law. And, since some state exemption laws are more liberal than the federal, especially those placing no dollar limit on the homestead exemption, disparate state exemption laws will continue to be important in federal bankruptcy cases. This is made even more true by the fact that, for some reason, Congress also stated in the new law that any state legislature can prohibit debtors in that state from using the federal exemptions in a bankruptcy case.

Claims against the Debtor: As a general rule, any legal obligation of the debtor gives rise to a claim against the estate in the bankruptcy proceeding. Subject to certain specific limitations, any claim filed with the bankruptcy court is allowed unless it is contested by an interested party, such as the trustee, debtor, or another creditor. If challenged, the court will rule on the claim's validity after pertinent evidence is presented at a hearing held for that purpose. In this regard, claims against the debtor's estate will be subject to any defenses that the debtor could have asserted had there been no bankruptcy. The fact that a claim is allowed does not mean that the particular creditor will be paid in full.

Distribution of the Debtor's Estate: A secured creditor—that is, one having a security interest or lien in a specific item of property—can proceed directly against that property for satisfaction of the claim. This is true even though the debtor is or is about to become subject to a bankruptcy proceeding. In a sense, then, secured creditors have priority over all classes of unsecured creditors.

When the trustee has gathered all the assets of the debtor's estate and reduced them to cash, these proceeds are distributed to unsecured creditors. There are certain unsecured claims which are given priority in this distribution. These claims are paid in full in the order of their priority, assuming there are sufficient proceeds available. The following six classes of debts are listed in order of priority. Each class must be fully paid before the next is entitled to anything. If the available funds are insufficient to satisfy all creditors within a class, payment to creditors in that class is made in proportion to the amount of their claims.

1. First to be paid are all costs and expenses involved in the administration of the bankruptcy proceeding, such as the trustee's fee and accountants' and attorneys' fees.

2. If the proceeding is an involuntary one, the second priority is any expense incurred in the ordinary course of the debtor's business or financial affairs after commencement of the case but before appointment of the trustee.

3. Next is any claim for wages, salaries, or commissions earned by an individual within ninety days before the filing of the petition or the cessation of the debtor's business, whichever occurs first. This priority is limited to $2,000 per individual.

4. The fourth priority is any claim for contributions to an employee benefit plan arising from services performed within 180 days before filing or business cessation. Again the limit is $2,000 per individual. However, a particular individual cannot receive more than $2,000 under the third and fourth priorities combined.

5. Next are claims of individuals, up to $900 per person, for deposits made on consumer goods or services that were not received.

6. Claims of governmental units for various kinds of taxes, subject to time limits that differ depending on the type of tax, are the last priority.

If all priority claims are paid and funds still remain, other unsecured creditors (called *general creditors*) are paid in proportion to the amounts of their claims. Any portion of a priority claim that was beyond the limits of the priority is treated as a general claim. An example would be the amount by which an individual's wage claim exceeded $2,000.

Discharge: After the debtor's estate has been liquidated and distributed to creditors, the bankruptcy court will conduct a hearing to determine whether the debtor should be discharged from liability for remaining obligations. Under certain circumstances the court will refuse to grant the debtor a discharge. These are as follows:

1. Only an individual, not a corporation or partnership, can receive a discharge.

2. A debtor will be denied a discharge if he or she had previously received such a discharge within six years before the present bankruptcy petition was filed.

3. The debtor will be denied a discharge if he or she has committed any of the following acts: (a) intentionally concealed or transferred assets for the purpose of evading creditors, within one year before the filing of the petition or during the bankruptcy proceedings; (b) concealed, destroyed, falsified, or failed to keep business or financial records unless there was reasonable justification for such action or failure; (c) failed to adequately explain any loss of assets; (d) refused to obey a lawful court order or to answer a material court-approved question in connection with the bankruptcy case; or (e) made any fraudulent statement or claim in connection with the bankruptcy case.

4. If a discharge has been granted, the court may revoke it within one year if it is discovered that the debtor had not acted honestly in connection with the bankruptcy proceeding.

Nondischargeable Claims: Even if the debtor is granted a general discharge from obligations, there nevertheless are a few types of claims for which he or she will continue to be liable. Examples of these nondischargeable debts are taxes, liability for a willful and malicious tort, claims for alimony and child support, and obligations for student loans.

Reaffirming a Debt that Has Been Discharged: Prior to the 1978 Act, a debtor could renew his or her obligation on a debt that had been discharged in bankruptcy simply by expressing a willingness to be bound. This reaffirmation required no new consideration by the creditor, but some states did require it to be in writing. The new law, however, places significant restraints on the making of a reaffirmation. Specifically, a reaffirmation is not valid unless the bankruptcy court conducted a hearing at which the debtor was fully informed of the consequences of his or her action, and the agreement to reaffirm was made before the debtor's discharge. In addition, the debtor can rescind the reaffirmation within thirty days after it was made.

Business Reorganization: If it is felt that reorganization and continuance of a business is feasible and preferable to liquidation, a petition for reorganization may be filed under Chapter 11 of the Act. The reorganization procedure is intended for use by businesses, but it does not matter whether the owner of the business is an individual, partnership, or corporation. A reorganization case can be either voluntary or involuntary, and the requirements for filing an involuntary case are the same as for a liquidation proceeding. In general, the types of debtors exempted from reorganization proceedings are the same as those exempted from liquidation proceedings. The major difference in coverage is that a railroad can be a debtor in a reorganization proceeding.

Adjustment of Debts: Since there is some stigma attaching to a bankrupt, Chapter 13 of the Act, Adjustment of Debts of an Individual with Regular Income, provides a method by which an individual can pay his or her debts from future income over an extended period of time. It is intended for use primarily by an individual whose primary income is from salary, wages, or commissions—an employee. The debtor must be an individual; partnerships and corporations cannot file an adjustment case.

There is no such thing as an involuntary adjustment case; only the debtor can file the petition. The bankruptcy court will always appoint a trustee in such cases to receive and distribute the debtor's income on a periodic basis.

The debtor alone prepares and files an adjustment plan with the court—not the trustee, creditors, or anyone other than the debtor. The plan designates the portion of the debtor's future income that is turned over to the trustee for distribution to creditors, describes how creditors are to be paid, and indicates the period of time during which payment is accomplished. The court must confirm the plan if it is proposed in good faith and all secured creditors have accepted it.

At any time before or after confirmation of the plan, the debtor has the privilege of converting the adjustment proceeding to a liquidation case. The bankruptcy court may convert the adjustment proceeding to a liquidation case, or dismiss the case altogether, if the debtor fails to perform according to the plan. On the other hand, if the debtor does perform, he or she will ordinarily be granted a discharge upon completion of the payments provided for in the plan. There is no discharge from the types of claims that cannot be discharged in a liquidation case.

Questions and Problems

1. Long Island Trust Co. recovered a judgment for $914.38 against Cheshire. When the judgment remained unsatisfied to the extent of $607.50, Long Island Trust caused an income execution (garnishment) to be served on the U.S. Postal Service, Cheshire's employer, directing that 10 percent of Cheshire's biweekly wages be paid to the county sheriff for the benefit of Long Island Trust. U.S. Postal Service refused to comply claiming that more than 25 percent of Cheshire's disposable income was already being withheld for court-ordered support payments under New York law and that further deductions would be a violation of the Consumer Credit Protection Act. Long Island Trust argued that the Act permits simultaneous garnishments for payment of family support and payment of judgment creditors, even when the amount of the support garnishment exceeds 25 percent. Is Long Island Trust's contention correct? (*Long Island Trust Co. v. U.S. Postal Service*, 647 F.2d 336, 1981.)

2. A debt collection agency, in attempting to recover from Harvey a debt represented by four bad checks, a total of $125, she had passed, wrote her a letter stating that she ignores her mail and her bills, and lacks the common sense to manage her financial matters properly. Would such a letter violate the provisions of the Fair Debt Collection Practices Act, thus rendering the collection agency liable for damages? (*Harvey v. United Adjusters*, 509 F.Supp. 1218, 1981.)

3. Georgia law requires that promissory notes involved in consumer loans be notarized. In several such loans the notes were notarized and a one-dollar notary fee was imposed on the borrowers. Should the notary fee be included in the finance charge or the annual percentage rate? (*Buford v. American Finance Co.*, 333 F.Supp. 1243, 1971.)

4. An overzealous merchant will sometimes entice customers into a store by advertising goods at an attractively low price. However, prospective purchasers are then discouraged from buying the low-priced goods and, by various means, are convinced to buy instead similar goods at a higher price. Would the fact that an eyeglass company that advertised eyeglasses for $7.50 (including lenses, frames, and case), sold only ten pairs a year of the $7.50 glasses but during the same period sold nearly 1,400 pairs of more expensive glasses indicate an unfair or deceptive trade practice? (*Tashof v. FTC*, 437 F.2d 707, 1970.)

5. Review the holder in due course rule issued by the FTC in 1975. What kinds of consumer problems is it intended to cure? If you were a lending institution executive, how would you view future acquisitions of short-term promissory notes given to merchants by consumers?

6. Has federal law regulating the issuance and use of credit cards significantly affected the volume of credit card sales? What steps would you take if you have lost a credit card? What is your liability to the card issuer if an unknown party has made purchases in the amount of $500 using your card, and the issuer has billed you for that amount?

7. The ABC Partnership wants to take on a new product line and will need to borrow $12,000 from a local bank. Does the Truth in Lending Act apply to this lending transaction?

8. Bankruptcy is a creditor-debtor problem of major proportions. Are the procedures, as set forth in the Bankruptcy Reform Act, fair to both debtor and creditor? What changes would you consider to be advisable? For example, should a debtor who has been discharged in bankruptcy be prohibited from purchasing on credit for a certain number of years?

9. A debtor has incurred debts far in excess of ability to pay.
   a. Can the creditors file a petition to require that he or she enter into a Chapter 13 Adjustment plan?
   b. If he or she wants to avoid straight bankruptcy (liquidation), can a bankruptcy trustee file a Chapter 13 plan?
   c. If he or she files a plan, can back taxes and child support payments be discharged?

10. Martin was an American Express credit card holder. In 1975 he gave his card to a business associate to be used for purchases in connection with a venture the two of them were pursuing. Martin later claimed that he had orally instructed and authorized the associate to charge only up to $500 on the card. When Martin was billed $5,300 by American Express for charges made on his card by the associate, he refused to pay and American Express brought an action to recover the entire $5,300. In what amount is Martin likely to be liable? (*Martin v. American Express, Inc.*, 361 So.2d 597, 1978.)

C·H·A·P·T·E·R 18

PRODUCT LIABILITY

Each year millions of consumer products–related accidents occur. The cost to the victims in terms of suffering, time, and money is tremendous. The expense to manufacturers and merchants is enormous. Increased attention must be then given by manufacturers to higher standards of design, development, and production to ensure that products are as safe as possible, which adds costs to the manufacturer and to the buyer, because the increased costs of production are passed on by the producer as a cost of doing business. Of special concern to the manufacturer or distributor is the possibility that an injury or death caused by a dangerously defective product will result in a lawsuit and a substantial damages award to the injured consumer or, if there has been a death, to any survivors. An extensive survey of civil jury cases in state and federal courts in Cook County, Illinois, by the Institute of Civil Justice (an arm of the Rand Corporation) revealed that during the period 1960 to 1979 half of the judgments in product liability cases exceeded $82,000. The average product liability judgment reached $377,000 in the 1975 to 1979 period.[1] Today, nationwide, every 36 hours a plaintiff wins a lawsuit that involves an award of more than $1 million in damages.

[1]Rand News Release: The Institute for Civil Justice; March 9, 1982.

As the figures from Cook County indicate, jury awards can be in the millions of dollars. The cost to a manufacturer of paying such judgments may be so prohibitive that the item, otherwise profitable, must be discontinued. And, in an extreme case, the business itself may be forced to shut down.

Product liability lawsuits can sometimes have industry-wide implications. Even though an individual manufacturer produced the injury-causing product, the entire industry may be held accountable under certain circumstances. An example of this situation is found in a case involving the pharmaceutical industry. The plaintiff brought action against eleven drug manufacturers alleging that a product they had made and distributed, diethylstilbestrol (DES), taken by her mother, had caused serious harm during the gestation period resulting in the plaintiff's birth. The plaintiff was unable to identify the specific company that had made the drug her mother had taken, and the trial court dismissed the complaint. On appeal, the Supreme Court of California reversed. Its decision was to the effect that all eleven of the defendants could be held liable unless they, as individual manufacturers, could prove that they did not make the drug that caused the injuries. While recognizing that there would be practical problems of allocating damages among those in the industry, the court held that each manufacturer's liability would be approximately equivalent to the damages caused by the DES it manufactured. In effect, if one company could be proved to have one-half of the market in DES, that company would be held liable for a proportionate share of the judgment. *Sindall v. Abbott Laboratories*, 607 P.2d 924 (1980).

In Missouri, the Supreme Court of that state rejected California's approach and denied recovery to a plaintiff who was unable to prove who made the particular drug taken by the mother. *Zafft v. Eli Lilly & Co.*, 676 S.W.2d 241 (Mo. 1984). But in Washington, the court took the other extreme—the plaintiff need only sue one defendant and prove four elements: that the mother took DES, that DES caused the plaintiff's subsequent injury, that the defendant produced or marketed the type of DES the mother had taken, and that defendant's conduct breached a legal duty to plaintiff. *Martin v. Abbott Laboratories*, 689 P.2d 368 (Wash. 1984).

Another example is the current controversy over the cancer-producing properties of asbestos. During the late 1970s some 17,000 lawsuits were filed against asbestos manufacturers by asbestos workers and their survivors, claiming millions of dollars in damages they allege were caused by asbestos. Johns-Manville Corporation, the largest producer of asbestos, is named in most of the suits, which claim that the dangers of asbestos were known and that employees and others were not warned. Some defendants claim that in making asbestos they were merely following government specifications, known as the government contract defense, which has been allowed by the courts in other litigation. One defendant manufacturer, Unarco Industries, with only 4 percent of the market share of asbestos, filed for bankruptcy in July, 1982, prompting Johns-Manville to request stay orders (an order by the court to arrest or stop the judicial proceedings pending clarification of material questions) on all cases in which it and Unarco are co-defendants. Stay orders have been granted by the judges in several cases, delaying a substantial portion of asbestos litigation. As Johns-Manville pointed out, the lawsuits are seeking to impose industry-wide liability. Another stumbling block was presented later in 1982 when Johns-Manville Corporation itself filed a petition for bankruptcy.

In July 1985 a proposal was submitted to the Bankruptcy Judge presiding over the Manville Chapter 11 (reorganization) proceeding whereby funding would be provided for asbestos victims, both existing and future. Key features of the settlement provide that Manville put up $846.5 million, contribute another $75 million annually, and turn over 50 percent of its common stock to the fund. While a final decree may issue in late 1986, many problems remain unresolved. The effects on the industry, however, will clearly be significant.

The expansion of the law of product liability is a fairly recent phenomenon. Current law, both statutory and by court decisions, is consumer-protection oriented. In the past, a manufacturer could feel somewhat secure if he designed, developed, produced and marketed a product using reasonable care. If a company provided understandable instructions for the product's assembly and use, and if it extended an appropriate warranty to the buyer, the company was under no obligation to make the product accident-proof. Today, manufacturers are confronted with a different situation. *Caveat emptor*—let the buyer beware does not apply in the modern marketplace.

The cost to business, and ultimately to the consuming public, cannot be disregarded. The National Traffic and Motor Vehicle Safety Act of 1966 focuses on automobile design and construction and directs the secretary of transportation to establish safety standards for motor vehicles. Automobile manufacturers claim that much of the increase in the cost of automobiles comes from the added safety features required to meet those standards.

In another product line, the Consumer Product Safety Commission, about which we will have more to say, has issued a rule that now requires the installation of "deadman controls" on walk-behind mowers. This safety feature stops the mower blade within three seconds after the operator releases the mower handle. The new safety device should prevent some of the estimated 77,000 injuries caused each year by power mower blades at a cost to the consumer of $15 to $50.

This chapter examines the extent to which the manufacturer may be liable to the consumer under the concepts that permit the consumer to recover damages for a product-related injury—*negligence*, *breach of warranty*, and *strict product liability*. The law in these areas is diverse since the states are not in agreement as to which theory might apply in any given set of circumstances.

Negligence

From early case law **negligence can be defined as the failure to act as a reasonable person would.** Failure to use the ordinary care demanded by a specific set of circumstances can be negligence, as can inattention and carelessness that cause injury. Each individual has a legal duty to conduct affairs in such a manner as not to cause harm. A breach of this legal duty can be actionable negligence—that is, an injured plaintiff may sue the defendant alleging some degree of deviation from the standard of conduct imposed by the law of torts on the defendant.

Insofar as manufacturers' liability is concerned, negligence is usually predicated on negligent manufacture or negligent design. If materials are used that are not strong enough to resist stresses of normal use, or if defects in products result from the inadequate training of production line employees, a case of negligent manufacture has been made out. Similarly, if a product is designed in such a way that it creates a danger in ordinary use that is not anticipated by the consumer, the manufacturer may be subject to liability.

Under the rule adopted by most states, not only is there a duty to use reasonable care to design a product so that an accident is unlikely, there is a duty to design it so that injuries will be minimized if an accident does occur. To illustrate: X is the driver of a car that explodes after being struck in the rear by a car being negligently driven by Y. X may recover from Y, the negligent driver, for the initial injuries and may possibly recover from the auto manufacturer for the additional injuries resulting from the explosion. If, for example, the gas tank were located immediately ahead of the rear bumper, or unreasonably close to a sharp frame member that was likely to puncture it, the manufacturer may be guilty of negligence in design.

Duty to Warn: The manufacturer may also be negligent if it fails to provide the user of the product with an adequate warning of any foreseeable or latent dangers in using the product or, if assembly is required, to provide an understandable and correct set of assembly instructions. In an especially disastrous explosion case, Justice Jackson, in a well-reasoned dissent, stated:

This is a day of synthetic living, when to an ever-increasing extent our population is dependent upon mass producers for its food and drink, its cures and complexions, its apparel and gadgets. These no longer are natural or simple products but complex ones whose composition and qualities are often secret. Such a dependent society must exact greater care than in more simple days and must require from manufacturers or producers increased integrity and caution as the only protection of its safety and wellbeing. Purchasers cannot try out drugs to determine whether they kill or cure. Consumers cannot test the youngster's cowboy suit or the wife's sweater to see if they are apt to burst into fatal flames. Carriers, by land or by sea, cannot experiment with the combustibility of goods in transit. Where experiment or research is necessary to determine the presence or the degree of danger, the product must not be tried out on the public, nor must the public be expected to possess the facilities or the technical knowledge to learn for itself of inherent but

"Very nice . . . I'll take it!"

Marketing a dangerous product does not necessarily impose product liability on the manufacturer.

Source: Reprinted by permission: Tribune Media Services.

latent dangers. The claim that a hazard was not foreseen is not available to one who did not use foresight appropriate to his enterprise.[2]

In an Indiana case, a former high school football player was paralyzed by a neck injury suffered when his football helmet failed to protect him from a blow to the head (*Bedan v. Rawlings Sporting Goods, Inc.*, Johnson County, Indiana, Circuit Court, No. 27,251, November 1981). As a result of the $5.8 million judgment awarded the injured player by an Indiana jury, the defendant manufacturer is suggesting that the National Football League consider establishing a Sports Rehabilitation Foundation to provide support to high school, college, and professional players who may be permanently disabled playing football. In exchange for support, injured players would agree not to sue the manufacturer of the equipment involved. Because of earlier high awards for helmet-related injuries, several manufacturers have stopped making the helmets—the president of the defendant company has suggested that American manufacturers might stop making football helmets completely since there is general agreement that little can be done to improve the product. Pertinent to our discussion is the fact that plaintiff's law-

---

[2] *Dalehite v. United States*, 346 U.S. 15 (1953). The principal issue was whether or not the U.S. government was liable in damages for the $200 million claimed as a result of the explosion of a ship loaded with fertilizer in Texas City, Texas. While the majority held that the government was negligent, and would agree with Justice Jackson, liability was denied because of governmental immunity.

yers argued successfully that the manufacturer had failed to warn that the helmet could not provide total protection.

State of the Art Requirement: With regard to competence in its field and the quality and safety of its product line, the manufacturer must stay informed of current developments and fully utilize the technological advances which will not only improve the product but will also make it more safe for the consumer. The courts invariably attribute to the manufacturer superior skill and knowledge in a product line, and it would seem only reasonable that attention to consumer safety makes good economic sense. In fact, even though a particular manufacturer may have lagged behind in trying to keep up with the state of the art in its field, the knowledge and expertise it lacks may be imputed by the courts—that is, it will be held accountable for information it does not have. To illustrate, in a case involving what should have been a routine hair treatment, a plaintiff was awarded a $65,000 judgment when defendant's hair dye, properly applied in accordance with the instructions on the container, caused a severe and disabling reaction. The court held that defendant should have been aware of even small risks involved in use of its product, including those warned of in two articles appearing in medical journals in foreign languages, French and Finnish. The court stated: "in manufacturing and distributing hair dye, the appellant is held to the skill of an expert in that particular business, 'to an expert's knowledge of the arts, materials and processes,' and is bound to keep reasonably abreast of scientific knowledge and discoveries concerning his field and, of course, is deemed to possess whatever knowledge is thereby imparted. *Braun v. Roux Distributing Company*, 312 S.W.2d 758 (1958).

Defenses: Proof of negligence on the part of a defendant manufacturer will not necessarily assure a judgment in a plaintiff's favor. The defendant may plead and prove *contributory negligence* on the part of the plaintiff. That is, the defendant may allege that, even though it may have been guilty of negligence, the plaintiff should be denied judgment because he or she, too, was guilty of some act of carelessness that itself contributed to the injury. For example, the injured consumer may not have followed the instructions for assembly of the product or may have ignored any appropriate warning provided by the manufacturer. Or the product may have been used for a purpose not contemplated or foreseeable by the manufacturer. A finding of contributory negligence may be a complete bar to plaintiff's action.

Within the last few years a majority of states have adopted *comparative negligence* rules either by statute or by judicial decision. While these rules vary substantially, they have one common concept: in most situations a finding of contributory negligence does not totally bar the plaintiff's claim. A common form of comparative negligence law is the 50 percent statute which provides that a plaintiff can recover proportionate damages if his or her negligence is not greater than the defendant's. For example, if the jury finds that a plaintiff's total damages were $10,000 and that plaintiff's negligence amounted to 40 percent (with 60 percent attributable to the defendant), plaintiff's recovery would be reduced by 40 percent for a judgment for $6,000. On the other hand, if plaintiff's negligence were found to be greater to any degree than defendant's, no damages would be awarded.

A defendant may claim *assumption of risk* by the plaintiff in that the plaintiff had positive knowledge of a dangerous defect in a product, yet continued to use it. For example, a consumer may have purchased a power tool that occasionally gives electrical shock from a short circuit when plugged in and in use. Assumption of the risk may also be claimed by a defendant if the plaintiff had completely misused the product, that is, had put it to some use for which it was not intended, thereby rendering it dangerous. The owner of a lightweight power mower, for example, might try to pick it up and use it as a hedge trimmer, thereby assuming the risk of being seriously injured.

The negligence theory has its shortcomings. The plaintiff must allege and prove that a duty was owed by defendant; that the duty was breached; that the plaintiff was injured; and that defendant's breach was the proximate cause of plaintiff's harm. Imagine the cost in time and money to a plaintiff who, to prove negligence in design or manufacture, must gain access to defendant's development plans and assembly line to pinpoint the specific act or omission that resulted in a defective, injury-producing product. This could be such a formidable task as to discourage the most aggressive plaintiff from pursuing his case.

One hurdle that no longer needs to be overcome is the *privity of contract* (contract relationship) requirement that existed some years ago. The general view today is that there need be no privity of contract between a plaintiff and a defendant where an action brought against a manufacturer is based on the charge of negligence. This view received its most substantial impetus in this country, as shown in Chapter 3, from the rule of the MacPherson case. The only limitation upon this rule is that the product in question must be one that is likely to cause injury if negligently made.

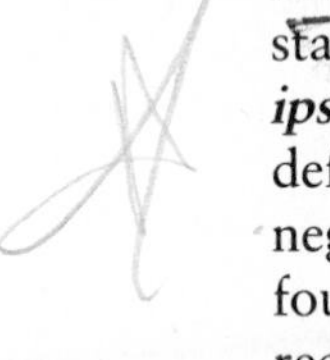

Res Ipsa Loquitur: Negligence, as other facts, may be proved by circumstantial evidence. Useful to a frustrated plaintiff may be the doctrine of ***res ipsa loquitur***, meaning "the thing speaks for itself." If a product proves to be defective it would seem a natural inference that the manufacturer has been negligent at some step or phase of the production process. Consequently, if four required conditions are proven by plaintiff to exist there may be a recovery of damages even though no specific act of negligence can be identified. First, the injury-causing event must be of the kind that does not ordinarily happen unless someone was negligent; second, the defendant must have had exclusive control of the injury-producing product; third, the plaintiff must not have contributed to the injury; and fourth, evidence of what happened (the negligent act) is best known by the defendant who usually is not willing to volunteer information.

To illustrate the use of the doctrine, suppose that a woman undergoes surgery in a hospital and in the recovery room, after surgery, is found to have a severe, permanently disfiguring burn on her right forearm. Operating room personnel and others who may have had contact with the patient disclaim any knowledge of how the injury could have been caused. It is certain that the burn had occurred at some time after the patient had been wheeled into surgery and anesthetized. While the injured plaintiff may find it difficult to prove specific negligence, the circumstances are such that an inference of negligence on the part of others is raised. This does not shift the burden of proof of reasonable care to the defendant but, should the defendant fail to go forward with evidence refuting the allegations of negligence, the jury may be unfavorably disposed.

Res ipsa loquitur is not a panacea nor can a plaintiff be any more certain of victory than if another approach were used involving conventional, real evidence. However, the doctrine is a viable avenue in most jurisdictions and has been successfully pursued in a variety of cases.

The case that follows involved the alleged negligence of the Ford Motor Company in failing to properly test and inspect a carburetor return spring before installing it on a new car during the assembly process. The circumstances of the case are similar to those of *MacPherson v. Buick Motor Co.*, the landmark decision of 1916.

Karczewski v. Ford Motor Company
U.S. Dist. Ct., N.D. Indiana, 382 F.Supp. 1346 (1974)

Plaintiff Karczewski purchased a used 1969 Mustang from a private party and was involved in an accident when, according to plaintiff's allegations, the carburetor return spring assembly broke, causing the vehicle to go out of control and into a telephone pole and tree. The case was submitted to the jury on the alternative bases of negligence, implied warranty, and strict liability. (Only the negligence theory is discussed here.)

The Indiana jury returned a verdict in favor of plaintiff and against the defendant, Ford Motor Company, in the amount of $10,000. An appeal resulted when defendant claimed that the trial court should have either directed a verdict in its favor, or granted a judgment notwithstanding the verdict of the jury for plaintiff, and made motions accordingly.

Sharp, District Judge:

. . . On September 24, 1969 in Munster, Indiana the plaintiff was operating his automobile on a public street. In the middle of a block after stopping at a stop sign and making a left turn the car went out of control and started to spin around. The plaintiff tried to straighten it out and lost control of it completely. It hit a telephone pole and a tree and then bounced up. It was leaning up against a tree with the front end off of the ground when it came to rest. He attempted to brake the car before the collision but was unable to do so.

As a result of this collision the plaintiff sustained a laceration in his face, medical expenses, damage to his car and a permanent cut on his head. A photograph was displayed to the jury showing the two black eyes, the swelling in the plaintiff's head and the scar in his hairline. The plaintiff also lost some time at work. The so-called specials, including damage to personal property, in this case were in the approximate sum of $2600.00.

The plaintiff also called as an expert witness, Mr. Vucko, a mechanic-bodyman with experience working on automobiles since 1943. . . . He examined the carburetor return spring assembly of this automobile immediately after the accident and found that it was broken. His exact testimony was as follows:

A *Well, the shaft from the spring to the hook. And it was just the steel rod that was broken.*
You have a coil, and then you have a rod, and then you have a hook, where it hooks into a hole on the bracket. And it returns the throttle valve when you release the accelerator.". . .
Q *Was there any indication that there was any metal—or that any metal would have pressed against the carburetor return spring?*
A *I didn't see any, no.*

The question was then asked as to whether or not this expert had an opinion as to whether the carburetor return spring was broken before or after this collision. The expert testified that he had repaired thousands of automobiles and could not recall one in the shop which was broken after an accident. He also testified that he had never seen a carburetor return spring break on a relatively new car, one year old, due to abuse. . . .

The only witness for the defendant was James Scott, a product quality engineer, in the employ of the Ford Motor Company. Detailed drawings and an actual carburetor assembly were placed in evidence and displayed to the jury. . . . The carburetor in question was a 4-V carburetor used in the 1969, 428, 4-V engine. It is manufactured by the Holley Corporation who provide the same to the Ford Motor Company. . . . This witness testified extensively on a so-called fail-safe system in this particular carburetor. During the course of the trial while the carburetor was being handled by the witness and plaintiff's counsel, in the presence of the jury, a spring on it apparently broke. The spring here in question is purchased by the Ford Motor Company in massive quantities but the Ford Motor Company itself engages in no testing of this particular element. Mr. Scott testified that the manufacturer engages in a testing procedure of the springs before they are delivered to the Ford Motor Company. There is no individual testing of the springs in question. He also testified that the Ford Motor Company did not make specific examinations of these springs before they were installed to detect any defects in them. Mr. Scott testified that these springs were placed in a cardboard box along the assembly line and someone on the assembly line picks up the spring and hooks it into the carburetor on each end of the bracket. On cross-examination he stated:

Q *Okay. They're just in a paper box, a carton?*
A *Cardboard box, yes.*

Q *Cardboard box. And what does he do with it?*
A *He picks up the spring and hooks it onto the carburetor on each end of the bracket.*
Q *He doesn't look at the spring to make sure it's al right (sic), does he?*
A *What do you mean by 'all right'?*
Q *I mean, he doesn't pick it up first, examine it, and then put it in?*
A *No.*

Mr. Scott also testified to a report made by the Ford Motor Company as a result of the investigation of this incident. The conclusion in said report was that it couldn't determine whether the spring broke before or after the collision. Mr. Scott also testified that there had been a change in the type of steel used in these springs and that it was possible that there could be defective steel in the springs. . . .

It is also elementary that the verdict of the jury may be sustained if there is evidence to support any one of the three bases which the plaintiff asserted for recovery in this case. This Court heard all of the evidence and concludes that it is possible for the jury to have inferred from the facts in the case a basis for recovery under any of the three asserted. . . .

In regard to negligence there is evidence from which the jury might have properly inferred that the Ford Motor Company failed to properly test and inspect the spring in question before installing the same. There is evidence from which the jury might infer that the failure of said spring was the proximate cause of the collision in question and the resulting damage. The liability based on negligence of the failure of an automobile manufacturer to test and inspect its finished product has a most respectable history which has *MacPherson v. Buick Motor Co.*, 217 N.Y. 382, 111 N.E. 1050 (1916), as its earliest benchmark. . . .

Therefore, the defendant's motions are hereby denied.

★★★

Breach of Warranty

A **warranty** with regard to consumer products is an assurance or guarantee that they will conform to certain standards. If the standards are not met, the buyer can recover damages from the seller. In such a case the buyer or a remote user need not show negligence on the part of the seller since the warranty arises out of the contract for sale. The buyer must, however, give notice of the breach of warranty to the seller or be barred from a recovery.

Warranties can be either express or implied. An *express warranty* comes into existence because of the words or actions of the seller. An *implied warranty* is imposed upon the seller by law unless he or she takes the proper steps to disclaim it. Warranties relate to either the soundness of the seller's title to the goods or the quality of the goods, the latter being the most important and the most frequently litigated. Lawsuits by buyers alleging breach of a warranty of quality are probably more common than any other type of dispute in the law of sales, Article 2 of the Uniform Commercial Code (UCC).

The immediate purchaser of the warranted goods may have damages when the warranty is breached. Additionally, since the privity requirement no longer exists, the warranty is extended to any natural person who is in the family or household of the buyer, who is a guest in the buyer's home, or who might reasonably be expected to use the goods or be affected by them. The seller's right to exclude or limit warranties, discussed later in this chapter, does not include this extension.

In a landmark case, Mr. Henningsen purchased a new Plymouth automobile for his wife. The car was originally sold by Chrysler Corporation to one of its dealers. When the steering gear failed, causing personal injury to the driver, Mrs. Henningsen, the couple filed a breach of warranty action against both Chrysler and the dealer, Bloomfield Motors, who had sold the car to Mr. Henningsen. Defendants claimed that the implied warranty of merchantability did not extend to Mrs. Henningsen since she was not a party to the contract for sale. That is, no privity of contract existed between either Chrysler or Bloomfield and Mrs. Henningsen. The court, in holding for the plaintiffs, with respect to Mrs. Henningsen said that "it would be wholly opposed to reality to say that use by such persons (Mrs. Henningsen) is not within the anticipation of parties to such a warranty of reasonable suitability of an automobile for ordinary highway operation." *Henningsen v. Bloomfield Motors, Inc.*, 161 A.2d 69 (1960).

Warranties of Title

Before a consideration of express and implied warranties of quality, brief mention should be made of *warranties of title*, in most sales automatically extended by the seller. Few buyers will want to purchase goods to which the title may be questionable. Section 2-312 of the UCC imposes two basic types of title warranties. The first is a warranty that the title conveyed shall be good and its transfer rightful. This warranty is obviously breached if the seller has stolen the goods from some third party and has no title at all. Other breaches are not so obvious. Suppose that after buying goods from S, B is approached by T, who claims that he is the rightful owner. Upon investigating, B finds that there is some basis for T's claim, although considerable doubt exists as to whether T or S was the true owner. This doubt can likely be resolved only by a lawsuit. Will B have to become involved in a lawsuit to determine if he bought a good title from S? Or has S breached his warranty of title by conveying a questionable title, thereby enabling B to return the goods to S and get his money back (leaving S and T to resolve their own problems)? The answer is that B purchased goods—not a lawsuit.

The second type of title warranty is that the goods shall be delivered free from any security interest or other lien or encumbrance of which the buyer at the time of contracting has no knowledge. This warranty will be breached, for example, if S sells mortgaged goods to B without telling B of the mortgage (security interest or lien).

Express Warranties

An express warranty is a statement of fact about the goods being sold (or a promise about performance capabilities) which results from specific statements made by the seller, orally or in writing. Thus, if S tells B that a used car has not been driven over 35,000 miles, an express warranty has been made. The same is true if S promises B that the exterior paint he is offering for sale will not chip, crack, or peel within three years after its application. In both these cases, if B purchases the goods in question and later proves that the statements were false, he can maintain a breach of warranty action against the seller, even if the seller honestly believed that the statement was true.

Express Warranties of Quality: To create an express warranty, the seller does not have to use the words warranty or guarantee, and the buyer does not have to show that the seller intended to make a warranty. Under Section 2-313 of the UCC, express warranties can be created in three different ways.

1. The seller may make an *affirmation of fact or a promise* relating to the goods, thereby creating an express warranty that the goods will conform to the affirmation or promise. For example, the seller might claim, "This boat is equipped with a two-year-old, 100 horsepower engine that was overhauled last month." The statement contains several affirmations of fact—that the boat is equipped with an engine, that the engine is two years old, that it has 100 horsepower, and that it was overhauled last month. Note that a seller's expression of opinion or commendation ("This is a first-class boat") does not constitute an express warranty. Nor does a statement that merely relates to the value of the goods ("This boat is worth $25,000 at retail").

2. A descriptive word or phrase used in a sale of goods may create an express warranty that the *goods will conform* to the description. A sale of pitted prunes or seedless grapes warrants that the fruit will have no seeds. Use of recognized trade terms may also constitute a description. For example, the term *Scotchgard*, used in connection with furniture upholstery, is descriptive of fabric that has been treated with a certain product so as to make it water and stain resistant. Goods described by a trade term are warranted to possess those characteristics generally associated with the term in the trade or business involved.

3. Where a sample or model is provided to the buyer, and the evidence indicates that the parties treated it as establishing a standard of quality for the sale, there exists a warranty that the *goods will conform* to the sample or model. A sample is taken from the mass to be sold, whereas a model represents the goods to be sold but is not taken from them. For example, one bushel of wheat drawn from a store of a thousand bushels to be sold is a sample. While the UCC makes no distinction between a sample and a model, a sample is more likely to create an express warranty than a model.

Since a sample is actually taken from the quantity to be sold, it is usually easier for the buyer to prove that a sample was intended to establish a standard of quality for the sale.

Implied Warranties

Implied warranties are those imposed by law, resulting automatically from the making of a sale in certain circumstances. Unlike the requirements for an express warranty, the merchant need not make specific statements as to performance or quality. Implied warranties are extended when the sale is made. The UCC, Sections 2-314 and 2-315, creates two types of implied warranties of quality, *merchantability* and *fitness for a particular purpose.*

Merchantability: If the seller is a merchant, defined by the UCC as one who deals in goods of the kind being sold, the law injects into the contract a warranty that the goods are "merchantable." (When Jones, a carpenter, sells his used car to a neighbor, no implied warranty of merchantability exists because Jones is not a merchant who deals in automobiles; he is a casual seller.) Merchantable means essentially that the goods must be fit for the ordinary purposes for which such goods are used. Shoes, for example, must have their heels attached well enough that they will not break off under normal use, but the warranty does not require that ordinary street shoes be fit for mountain climbing. The implied warranty of merchantability does not guarantee that goods will be of the highest quality available. They are required to be of only average or medium grade, around the middle range of quality. They must, however, be adequately packaged and labeled.

Applied to food, the implied warranty of merchantability can be equated with wholesomeness. A pork chop tainted with spoilage, for instance, is not merchantable. Many court cases have involved objects in food that caused harm to the consumer, ranging from a mouse in a bottled soft drink to a screw in a slice of bread. In such cases the courts traditionally have distinguished between foreign and natural objects, usually finding that if the object is foreign (such as the mouse or screw), the warranty of merchantability has been breached. If, on the other hand, the object is natural (such as bones in fish stew), no breach has occurred. A few courts have rejected this distinction and have instead based their decisions on the reasonable expectations of the consumer. The controlling factor in this approach is whether a consumer would reasonably expect such an object to be in the food. One might expect to find a chicken bone in a piece of fried chicken but perhaps not in a chicken sandwich.

Fitness for a Particular Purpose: The UCC, in Section 3-315, provides: "Where the seller at the time of contracting has reason to know any particular purpose for which the goods are required and that the buyer is relying on the seller's skill or judgment to furnish suitable goods, there is . . . an implied warranty that the goods shall be fit for such purpose." For this warranty to apply, the seller must have reason to know of the particular purpose for which the goods are needed by the buyer; the seller must have reason to know that the buyer is relying on the seller's skill or judgment; and the warranty of fitness for a particular purpose must arise at the time of contracting. For example, suppose that a buyer wants to paint the stucco walls of a house. Because of the chalky and powdery nature of the walls, they are somewhat difficult to paint. The buyer specifically informs the seller of the problem, requesting assistance. The seller recommends a certain brand of paint, which the buyer purchases. Despite the fact that the buyer carefully follows the seller's instructions in applying the paint, it blisters and peels within a short time. Even though the paint was probably merchantable and would have been fit for its ordinary purposes, an implied warranty of fitness for the particular purpose has been created and breached.

Excluding and Limiting Warranties

While it is difficult for a seller to completely avoid extending a warranty, the UCC does provide procedures whereby warranties may be disclaimed or limited. The warranty of merchantability can be disclaimed orally or in writing. If it is in writing, the disclaimer must be conspicuous. It must expressly use either the word *merchantability* or other explicit words. The seller can, for example, have the buyer take the goods as is or with all faults. The law of warranties and their exclusion can be a troublesome area for the seller and the buyer. (Familiarity with the UCC is essential unless a seller refuses to sell, probably the only sure way to avoid extending some kind of warranty to a consumer.)

The following case illustrates the workings of an express warranty, one which may have been expanded by advertising contained in defendant's catalog.

Community Television Services, Inc. v. Dresser Industries, Inc.
U.S. Court of Appeals 8th Circuit 586 F.2d 637 (1978)

In 1965, two television stations in South Dakota created a separate corporation, Community Television Services, Inc. (Community), for the purpose of constructing and operating a 2,000-foot tower that would broadcast signals for both stations. Community contracted with Dresser Industries, Inc. (Dresser), who designed, manufactured, and erected the tower for a price of $385,000. The tower was completed in 1969, and Community used it until 1975. During this time, Community regularly inspected and properly maintained the tower. On January 10 and 11, 1975, a severe winter blizzard occurred in the area where the tower was located. During the early morning hours of January 11, as the storm reached its height with wind speeds of up to eighty miles per hour near the top of the tower, the structure collapsed.

Dresser denied responsibility and Community sued in federal district court for breach of an express warranty. The verdict and judgment in the trial court were in favor of Community, the plaintiff, for damages of $1,274,631.60, and Dresser, the defendant, appealed.

Lay, Circuit Judge:

. . . Expert witnesses called by both sides differed in their opinions as to the cause of the collapse. Community's experts testified that they had eliminated metallurgical or mechanical failure or abnormal wind loading as the cause of collapse. They theorized that the cause was high winds setting up a phenomenon known as mechanical resonance. They concluded that because of the resonance, the tower members "were inadequate to support the load that they sustained." On the other hand, Dresser's experts testified that a combination of ice on the upper fourth of the tower enlarged the tower members to a greater load than their designed wind loading capacity. Community attempted to refute Dresser's ice theory by calling several witnesses who testified that they did not see any such ice on or near the area where the tower collapsed. In turn, Dresser countered Community's theory through expert testimony that relatively constant winds were necessary for resonance to begin, and the winds were gusty and varied in speed and direction at the time of collapse. Furthermore, Dresser argued that the warranty did not guarantee against mechanical resonance, and experts testified that its prevention was beyond the current state of the art.

The specifications incorporated in the sale contract included a specified "Design Wind Load," which set forth the tower's capacity to withstand wind velocity as measured in pounds of pressure per square foot against the flat surface of its members. The specification reads: "The tower shall be designed to resist a uniform wind load per drawing T-5172, sheet S-1, 60 psf on flats." The trial court instructed the jury that this specification constituted an express warranty that the structure would withstand wind exerting pressure of 60 pounds per square foot on the flat surfaces of the tower. Dresser's advertising materials and the testimony of experts at trial revealed that the wind velocity necessary to create 60 pounds of pressure on the flat surfaces of the tower would be approximately 120 miles per hour. The evidence showed that the wind loading specifications referred, at least in engineering parlance, to "a force caused by the wind that is introduced parallel to the ground . . . (which) would be tending to blow the structure over."

Dresser argues that the trial court erred in failing to direct a verdict on the express warranty claim or grant it judgment notwithstanding the verdict, because expert testimony that the tower met the design specification was uncontradicted. Community's own experts stated unequivocally that in their opinion the tower conformed in a mathematical or analytical sense to the 60 pounds per square foot wind loading specification. If the warranty may be restricted to the technical specification set forth in the written contract, we would find Dresser's argument convincing. However, we agree with Community that the warranty was amplified, in advertising materials Dresser gave to Community prior to purchase of the tower, to promise more than mere compliance with technical measurements. In an advertising catalog, Dresser made the following supplementary affirmation:

Wind force creates the most critical loads to which a tower is normally subjected. When ice forms on tower members thereby increasing the surface area resisting the passage of wind, the load is increased.

Properly designed towers will safely withstand the maximum wind velocities and ice loads to which they are likely to be subjected. Dresser-Ideco can make wind and ice load recommendations to you for your area based on U.S. Weather Bureau data.

In the winter, loaded with ice and hammered repeatedly with gale force winds, these towers absorb some of the roughest punishment that towers take anywhere in the country . . . yet continue to give dependable, uninterrupted service.

Although we agree with Dresser that a seller cannot be held to be the insurer of its product, Dresser nevertheless provided the catalog to Community to induce purchase of its product, and in the absence of clear affirmative proof to the contrary, the above affirmation must be considered part of the "basis of the bargain." Standing alone, the statements provide a warranty that Dresser's tower would be properly designed so as to safely withstand the maximum wind velocities and ice loads to which it would likely be subjected. Dresser did not indicate that this broad affirmation was superseded or cancelled by the technical specification in the contract. When the affirmation is read in tandem with the contract, as part of the "fabric" of the agreement of the parties, it enlarges the warranty created by the technical wind loading specification, giving evidence of its full intent and scope.

We find that the statements in the advertising catalog, which supplement the wind load specification, could reasonably have been found by the jury to be an affirmation of fact or a promise concerning the actual durability or performance of the tower during the wind and ice storms to which it was likely to be subjected.

Although Dresser's defense was that the tower collapsed by reason of excessive loading due to ice on the tower members, no disclaimer or limitation of the warranty that a properly designed tower would safely withstand the maximum wind and ice loads to which it was likely to be subjected appeared in the advertising materials or the contract. Under the *integrated* warranty given, a purchaser could reasonably assume that the tower, if properly designed for its location, would withstand maximum wind speeds to which it was likely to be subjected, even if ice accumulated on the tower members. While the blizzard was a severe one, the evidence does not support the conclusion that the wind alone, or the combination of wind and ice which Dresser claimed caused the collapse, was not within the range of storm conditions to be reasonably contemplated for the tower's location. Breach of a warranty created by statements describing the specific capacity of goods is proved when the product is shown by direct or circumstantial evidence to have failed to perform reasonably and safely the function for which it was intended by the manufacturer. In view of the affirmation made in the catalog, there was sufficient evidence for the jury to reasonably find that the tower was not as durable as it was warranted to be.

(Affirmed.)

★★★

The Magnuson-Moss Warranty Act

This statute, enacted by Congress in 1975, is consumer oriented. It applies only to purchases by ultimate consumers for personal, family, or household purposes, not to transactions in a commercial or industrial setting. The Warranty Act, which is usually enforced by the Federal Trade Commission (FTC), does not regulate the safety or quality of consumer goods. Instead it prevents deceptive warranty practices, makes consumer warranties easier to understand, and provides an effective means of enforcing warranty obligations. (While the federal Warranty Act is limited to consumer transactions, the UCC warranty rules are not. Thus, in nonconsumer transactions the UCC rules continue in effect. But in consumer goods transactions, the federal law has in some respects modified these rules.)

The Warranty Act does not require anyone to give a warranty on consumer goods. The Act applies only if the seller voluntarily chooses to make an express written warranty. The seller who does provide a written warranty must label it as either a full or a limited one. Under a full warranty the warrantor must assume certain minimum duties and obligations for products costing ten dollars or more. For instance, he or she must agree to repair or replace any malfunctioning or defective product within a reasonable time and without charge. If the warrantor makes a reasonable number of attempts to remedy the defect and fails to do so, the consumer can choose to receive either a cash refund or replacement of the product without charge. No time limitation can be placed on a full warranty, and consequential damages (such as for personal injury or property damage) can be disclaimed only if the limitation is conspicuous.[3] A written warranty that does not meet the minimum requirements must be designated conspicuously as a limited warranty. However, if a time limit (such as twenty-four months) is all that prevents the warranty from being a full one, it can be designated as a "full twenty-four month warranty."

The written warranty to which the Act applies is much more narrowly defined than is an express warranty under the UCC. Specifically it is (1) any written promise or affirmation of fact made by a supplier to a purchaser relating to the quality or performance of the product and affirming or prom-

---

[3]The UCC provides that a limitation of consequential damages for injury to the person in the case of consumer goods is "unconscionable." The courts will not generally enforce such limitations. This presents somewhat of a conflict. However, since the state law (UCC) extends more protection than the federal (Magnuson-Moss) it is likely that the UCC provision will be given effect.

ising that the product is defect-free or will meet a specified level of performance over a period of time, or (2) a written undertaking to refund, repair, replace or take other action with respect to the product if it fails to meet written specifications. Obviously, many express warranties, such as those created by description or sample, will continue to be governed only by the UCC even though a consumer transaction is involved. Other state laws may also govern in particular areas. For example, more than 30 states have enacted so-called lemon laws designed to provide relief for the buyer of a new car that is chronically defective. Basically similar, the statutes define a lemon as a car that has had a major defect, covered by warranty, unrepaired by the dealer after at least four attempts. Additionally, the car must have been out of service for at least thirty days during the four-attempt period. Replacement of the car with a new car is not automatic but is possible after neutral arbitration or mediation. The arbitration award would be binding on the manufacturer but not on the buyer, who could appeal to the courts.

Since the Warranty Act deals only with written warranties, it has no effect on the implied warranties of merchantability and fitness for a particular purpose defined by the UCC. The Act does depart from the UCC by prohibiting a disclaimer of an implied warranty (1) if an express written warranty is given, or (2) if within ninety days after the sale, a service contract is made with the consumer.[4] A supplier providing an express written warranty with a time limitation can limit the duration of an implied warranty to the duration of the express warranty. A supplier who gives neither a written warranty nor a service contract can disclaim an implied warranty under the conditions imposed by the UCC.

Strict Product Liability

As noted, a consumer who has purchased a defective product may have a remedy based on the negligence of the seller, the manufacturer, or both. The measure of damages is typically the loss suffered as a result of personal injury or property damage caused by the defective product. It is also a reasonable approach for a consumer to hold the seller accountable for warranties extended, thereby assuring that the consumer will be compensated or have an adjustment made when the product falls short of the guarantees made by the seller. However, since both of those avenues to recovery have their shortcomings and consumers are frequently thwarted in pressing legitimate claims, the courts have increasingly, since the early 1960s, imposed **strict liability** on manufacturers for injuries caused by defective products.

One of the landmark cases in the area is *Greenman v. Yuba Power Products, Inc.*, 59 Cal.2d 57 (1963). In that case, plaintiff suffered severe head injuries when a piece of wood flew out of a Shopsmith combination power saw, drill, and wood lathe he was using. Having failed to give timely notice of

[4]Under a service contract, the seller agrees to service and repair a product for a set period of time in return for a fee.

a breach of warranty as required by California law, plaintiff would no doubt have been unsuccessful in attempting to recover under that theory. However, in finding defendant, Yuba Power Products, liable for negligence, the court said:

A manufacturer is strictly liable in tort when an article he places on the market, knowing that it is to be used without inspection for defects, proves to have a defect that causes injury to a human being. Recognized first in the case of unwholesome food products, such liability has now been extended to a variety of other products that create as great or greater hazards if defective.

The respected and often cited Restatement of Torts 2d adopts the strict liability view in Section 402A:

(1) One who sells any product in a defective condition unreasonably dangerous to the user or consumer or to his property is subject to liability for physical harm thereby caused to the ultimate user or consumer, or to his property, if (a) the seller is engaged in the business of selling such a product, and (b) it is expected to and does reach the user or consumer without substantial change in the condition in which it is sold.

(2) The rule stated in Subsection (1) applies although (a) the seller has exercised all possible care in the preparation and sale of his product, and (b) the user or consumer has not bought the product from or entered into any contractual relation with the seller.

As the theory of strict product liability has evolved, it offers to the consumer most of the advantages of both warranty and negligence theories.

1. The buyer does not have to prove that a warranty existed or that the defect was caused by the seller's negligence. He or she must prove only that the goods were dangerously defective when they left the seller's hands and that this defect caused the buyer's injury.

2. As with the negligence theory, the seller's responsibility under the strict liability theory is usually not affected by a contractual disclaimer; nor is it affected by the buyer's failure to give notice to the seller within a reasonable time after discovery of the defect.

3. Contributory negligence on the part of the buyer cannot be used as a defense by the seller. Thus, a buyer's failure to inspect the goods or to discover the defect will not prevent recovery of damages. Even misuse of the goods usually will not prevent recovery if the misuse is of a type which the seller could have reasonably foreseen. Practically the only defense to a strict liability claim is assumption of risk. If the buyer knows of the defect and the possible danger but uses the goods anyway, the seller is not liable.

4. As with the negligence theory, privity of contract is not a requirement for recovery under the strict liability theory.

There are certain disadvantages of the strict liability doctrine. Like negligence, it generally has not been applied to purely economic injuries but only to physical injuries to a person or property. Further, it ordinarily can be used only against a seller who is in the business of selling goods, a merchant.

The following case arose out of the alleged failure of a manufacturer to provide an adequate warning as to a defective condition that made the product unreasonably dangerous. While the case was eventually submitted to the jury on a theory of negligence, plaintiffs had also sought recovery on strict liability and breach of warranty grounds. This is not unusual in product liability lawsuits. Here, however, the court examines the distinction between a cause of action based on negligence and one based on strict liability.

Freund v. Cellofilm Properties, Inc.
Supreme Court of New Jersey
432 A.2d 925 (1981)

Plaintiff Freund suffered extensive second and third degree burns in an industrial accident at his employer's paint factory when a commercial chemical dust, nitrocellulose, suddenly ignited. Plaintiff and his wife brought the action against several individuals and corporations but, as a result of trial motions, Hercules, Inc., the manufacturer of the nitrocellulose, was the only defendant left in the case. The major disputed issues were the exact cause of the fire and the adequacy of the warning provided by Hercules.

Plaintiff requested the trial court to instruct the jury that a manufacturer of a product is strictly liable if the product is defective by virtue of inadequate warnings and the defect proximately causes injury to a reasonably foreseeable consumer or user. Plaintiff also requested the trial court to instruct the jury that proof of the manufacturer's negligence in the making or handling of the article is not required.

The trial court refused to give plaintiff's instructions, instead charging the jury on negligence and proximate cause. The jury returned a unanimous verdict for defendant Hercules and the trial court's decision was affirmed by the Superior Court, Appellate Division. The Supreme Court of New Jersey granted certification.

Handler, Justice:

. . . On July 11, 1974 Freund and two other workers were assigned to prepare the chute on (a paint) mixer for cleaning. They opened the hatch to the mixer and one of the plaintiff's co-workers, Krowska, began sweeping nitrocellulose dust from around the mixer. The entire area suddenly erupted into flames, resulting in severe burns to both plaintiff and Krowska, who ultimately died from his injuries. . . .

Hercules experts, Doyle and Williams, testified that the sweeping was probably done in the presence of highly flammable vapors escaping from the recently opened mixer. Doyle testified that the least readily ignitable of the vapors was still ten to twenty times more flammable than dry nitrocellulose dust. In Williams' opinion, the vapors from the mixer ignited first, setting off the fire.

The drums of nitrocellulose contained a warning, *viz*:

Fire may result if container is punctured or severely damaged—Handle carefully—Do not drop or slide—Hazard increases if material is allowed to dry—Keep container tightly closed when not in use—In case of spill or fire soak with water—For further information refer to MCA Chemical Safety Data Sheet DS-96.

Below this warning, in large letters, appeared the words

"DANGER—FLAMMABLE"

Plaintiff testified that he was aware of the "warning" on the drums but had never bothered to read it. Plaintiffs' expert, Braidech, stated that while the warnings contained on the nitrocellulose drums were adequate to warn of the dangers involved in transporting nitrocellulose, they were not sufficient warnings for the job. On cross-examination, however, he admitted that no fire would have occurred had the warnings contained on the drums of nitrocellulose been heeded.

Cellofilm's plant superintendent testified that the company had a long-standing cleanup procedure for dealing with nitrocellulose spills. Employees were instructed to clean up the spills as soon as possible after they occurred and to soak all spills with water before picking them up. A poster provided by the manufacturer, Hercules, and displayed in the employee locker room warned of the dangers of dry nitrocellulose and instructed that in case of a spill, the chemical should be wet with water before cleanup. . . .

As noted, this personal injury case involves a manufactured product claimed to be defective because of a failure to provide an adequate warning as to its dangers. The primary issue is whether the trial judge committed error in presenting the case to the jury on the theory of negligence rather than principles of strict liability. . . .

Courts and leading scholars have struggled with these concepts. Some courts have examined and compared the application of strict liability and negligence theories in the inadequate warning area and concluded that there is little, if any, difference between the two theories in this context. . . . The conclusion reached by these courts has been that "(u)nder either theory, the recovery ultimately depends upon a subjective determination by the trier of the facts of what constitutes reasonable warning under all of the circumstances.". . .

A growing trend of cases and authority, however, has perceived a difference between the utilization of strict liability, as opposed to negligence, in the inadequate warning area. . . . *Phillips v. Kimwood Machine Company*, (525 P.2d 1033) a seminal case, enunciated the rationale for the distinction, *viz:* In the strict liability case we are talking about the condition (dangerousness) of an article which is sold without any warning, while in negligence we are talking about the reasonableness of the manufacturer's actions in selling the article without a warning. . . . In other words, these courts have viewed the strict liability approach as product-oriented, as opposed to the negligence approach which is conduct-oriented. . . .

Although this Court has never considered the precise question of whether there exists any true difference in the proofs necessary to establish negligence, as opposed to strict liability, in an inadequate warning products liability case, the principles illuminated above are basically consistent with our recent decisional law. The Court in *Suter v. San Angelo Foundry & Machine Company*, (406 A.2d 140), in discussing a design defect case, pointed out that in charging the jury as to the standards of liability applicable to the manufacturer, it must be "assum(ed) that the manufacturer knew of the harmful propensity of the product.". . . We further concluded in that case that where the design defect was not self-evident, "the trial court should also charge the jury on whether the manufacturer, it being deemed to have known of the harmful propensity of the product, acted as a reasonably prudent one.". . .

We agree with the weight of authority that there is a significant distinction between negligence and strict liability theory, at least in terms of imputing to the manufacturer knowledge of the dangers inherent in the product. Thus, given the importance of user protection and the need for uniformity and consistency in products liability cases, we hold generally that in inadequate warning design defect cases, a strict liability charge should be given.

The question still remains as to the significance of the trial court's insistence on charging the jury solely based upon negligence. To evaluate this issue next entails an inquiry as to the elements that must be included in an appropriate charge to a jury in a case where the alleged defect consists of an inadequate warning of product safety. . . .

Hence, a products liability charge in an inadequate warning case must focus on safety and emphasize that a manufacturer, in marketing a product with an inadequate warning as to its dangers, has not satisfied its duty to warn, even if the product is perfectly inspected, designed, and manufactured. Moreover, and importantly, the charge must make clear that knowledge of the dangerous trait of the product is imputed to the manufacturer. It must also include the notion that the warning be sufficient to adequately protect any and all foreseeable users from hidden dangers presented by the product. This duty must be said to attach without regard to prevailing industry standards. In short, it must be explained that an adequate warning is one that includes the directions, communications, and information essential to make the use of a product safe.

In this case, despite the admission by Hercules that it knew of the harmful propensities of its product, we conclude that there is a sufficient difference between the strict liability charge we have developed, and the negligence charge actually given, to justify a reversal. The terminology employed by the trial judge was riddled with references to negligence, knowledge and reasonable care on the part of a manufacturer and industry standards, as well as terms of limitation. . . .

We cannot be completely confident that the noted deficiencies in the trial court's charge did not, separately or cumulatively, affect the jury's deliberations and assessment of liability. We conclude, then, that under the facts of this case, the use of the negligence charge was not harmless error. . . .

The judgment below is reversed and the matter remanded for a new trial.

★ ★ ★

Product Liability Legislation

There can be little question that the consumer has more advantages than the manufacturer or other seller in a product-related controversy. Concern for the consumer and, on the other hand, sometimes cavalier treatment of the manufacturer, have led to uncertainty in the law as developed by the courts. There is a great variance found in the statutes of those states that attempt to deal with the problem by legislation—some twenty-eight states have different product liability laws. The impact of this aspect of legal environment on business and industry is tremendous. Many feel that the ultimate solution lies in uniform laws at the federal level.

The Model Uniform Product Liability Act

In late 1979 the Department of Commerce, after several years of study by a Federal Product Liability Task Force, devised and offered for use by the states a Model Uniform Product Liability Act (UPLA). The Act attempts to strike a balance between stability and fairness for manufacturers and the legitimate rights of those who suffer losses caused by defective products. Quite importantly, the act would obviate the necessity for the piecemeal reform now being undertaken by individual states. However, the states are not likely to rush to adopt UPLA since many, if not all of them, feel that consumer protection is best left to the individual states. If true uniformity is to become reality, federal legislation will be required and is now being proposed.

The Proposed Federal Product Liability Act

As a natural consequence of the model act referred to above, the Senate has proposed that a federal Product Liability Act (PLA) be created to preempt state legislation and establish nationwide uniformity. The draft of the proposed PLA reveals that its provisions are generally more favorable to the manufacturer than are the case law and statutes now being followed by the states. The proposed act, a product of the Senate Commerce Consumer Subcommittee, is rather lengthy, containing fourteen comprehensive sections. A few of its provisions bear mentioning although, if eventually enacted into law, considerable revision will no doubt be made.

For purposes of the act a product liability action is defined as any civil action brought against a manufacturer or product seller, for harm caused by a product, without regard to state law theories of strict liability in tort, negligence, breach of warranty, failure to warn or instruct, or misrepresentation, which previously governed such an action. State law is superseded to the extent the act addresses the issue. The act provides that a manufacturer is liable if the claimant establishes by a preponderance of the evidence that the product is unreasonably unsafe in construction, in design, because of a failure to provide adequate warnings or instructions, or because the product did not conform to an express warranty. It further provides that other product sellers (retailers, leasers, installers, packagers, or others placing a product in the stream of commerce) are liable only for their own fault.

With regard to contributory negligence and assumption of the risk, a section on comparative responsibility would not bar recovery but would reduce compensatory damages awarded to the claimant by an amount proportionate to the claimant's responsibility.

Under present law in a few jurisdictions, judgments have been awarded for injuries caused by products sold many years in the past. The proposed act would set a twenty-five-year limitation on capital goods (goods used in a trade or business costing more than $1,000). The same section establishes a two-year limitation on bringing claims, the period beginning to run from the time the claimant discovered or should have discovered the harm. With regard to punitive damages, the product seller can be subject to them if the harm was suffered as a result of the reckless disregard of the product seller for the safety of product users.

The proposed Product Liability Act is supported by the Product Liability Alliance, which includes some 150 organizations. Among these are the National Association of Manufacturers, the National Association of Wholesale Distributors, and the American Insurance Association. Opposed to the act are, among others, the American Bar Association and the Association of Trial Lawyers of America. They feel, respectively, that control of products law should be left to the states and that the burden of proof is being shifted to the victim, the injured consumer.

The Consumer Product Safety Act

Because of what it considered to be an unacceptable number of consumer products which present unreasonable risks of injury being distributed in commerce, Congress in 1972 enacted the Consumer Product Safety Act (CPSA). The stated purposes of CPSA are to protect the public against unreasonable risks of injury associated with consumer products; to assist consumers in evaluating comparative safety of products; to develop uniform safety standards, and to promote research and investigation into the causes and prevention of product-related deaths, illnesses, and injuries. The Act created another administrative agency, the independent, regulatory Consumer Product Safety Commission (CPSC). The commission is made up of five commissioners, none of whom can be removed except for neglect of duty or malfeasance in office. Initial commission members were appointed to serve for three, four, five, six, and seven years, respectively, to provide continuity, with no more than three of the members to be affiliated with the same political party.

The functions of other departments of the government in connection with administering certain consumer protection statutes were transferred by the CPSA to the CPSC. These statutes include the Child Protection and Toy

Safety Act, the Federal Hazardous Substances Act, the Poison Prevention Packaging Act, and the Flammable Fabrics Act.

For purposes of the CPSA the term *consumer product* means any article, or component part thereof, produced or distributed (1) for sale to a consumer for use in or around a permanent or temporary household or residence, a school, in recreation, or otherwise, or (2) for the personal use, consumption, or enjoyment of a consumer in or around a permanent or temporary household or residence, a school, in recreation, or otherwise. Excepted as being otherwise regulated are such items as tobacco, motor vehicles, pesticides, aircraft, boats, and certain drugs, devices, or cosmetics. The functions of the CPSC are those commensurate with all aspects of improved product safety and the elimination of hazards to consumers. For example, the CPSC may require manufacturers to provide it with notice when a new consumer product is being considered for development and production. The notice must be given prior to placing the new product on the market. This requirement will permit the CPSC to have tests conducted if there is a question as to the safety of the proposed product.

Maintenance of an Injury Information Clearing House: From time to time there is published in various media a list of the consumer products that are considered to be dangerous because of the frequency of injuries associated with their use. Much of the information regarding frequency of injury by certain products is gathered by the National Electronic Injury Surveillance System (NEISS). Established under CPSA, NEISS is a computer network connecting more than one hundred hospital emergency rooms across the country. During the latter half of 1977, to illustrate its use, there were some 3,000 toy-related injuries of varying degrees of severity recorded by NEISS. Thousands of others were no doubt treated at nonreporting hospitals, physicians' offices, or at home. Consequently, the magnitude of the problem, the potential for injury to children, brought the multibillion-dollar toy industry under the close scrutiny of the CPSC. With regard to other products, the CPSC index of injury-causing products provides a relative ranking according to frequency and severity of injuries. High on the list are bicycles, football and baseball equipment, swings and slides, and power lawn mowers.

CPSC Rulemaking: The CPSC may develop and promulgate consumer product safety standards that impose requirements on manufacturers. These standards may relate to performance, composition, contents, design, construction, finish, or packaging of a consumer product. Additionally, standards may require that consumer products be marked with or accompanied by clear and adequate warnings or instructions. The procedure for developing safety standards and promulgating them to all concerned is somewhat complex but is generally in accordance with the Administrative Procedure Act discussed in Chapter 6.

Banning Hazardous Products: If a product is found to present an unreasonable risk of injury, and no feasible safety standard would protect against such injury, the CPSC may propose and promulgate a rule imposing a ban on the product. For example, a recent CPSC Banned Products List contained more than 400 toys considered to be hazardous. The most frequently appearing objectionable features, that is, those parts of the toy which constituted a hazard, were straight pins (used in many cases to secure hats on dolls), removable squeakers in toy animals (risk of ingestion), sharp points or edges, hazardous dye, and the smallness of the object, again creating the possibility of ingestion or aspiration by a youngster. It is unlawful for any person to manufacture, offer to sell or otherwise distribute, or import into the United States any banned hazardous product.

Penalties for Violation of CPSA: Any person knowingly violating the provisions of the Act is subject to a civil penalty of $2,000 for each violation, not to exceed $500,000 for any related series of violations. A knowing and willful violation, the violator having been warned by the CPSC, can result in a criminal penalty of up to a $50,000 fine, one year imprisonment, or both. Individual officers and directors of corporations may also be subject to criminal penalties regardless of any penalty to which their company is subject.

Risk Management

This chapter has focused on the liability that may be incurred by a manufacturer or other seller of goods to consumers who, as a class, enjoy protection by the courts and statutes at both federal and state levels. It necessarily follows that industry must be vitally concerned about the risks of producing and marketing consumer products and must take advantage of whatever means are available to minimize the risk. The dollar cost to recall, and make adjustments to, defective products can be high. Other costs, such as the effect on the reputation of the manufacturer, can be catastrophic, particularly if the product involved has caused serious injury or death. The manufacturer must therefore constantly seek to minimize the risk or, where possible and affordable, shift it to an underwriter.

More and more corporations are looking to corporate risk management specialists for solutions to their product liability problems. During the period of 1975 to 1980 the membership roster of the Risk and Insurance Management Society, the leading trade association of corporate risk managers, increased 62 percent to nearly 3,000. This specialist's job is to ask, "What if . . . ?" and then to plan for the answer. Typical planning will focus on such things as product design, safety engineering, quality control, testing, and the development of adequate warnings and instructions to accompany the product. However, because no product will ever be completely accident-proof, consideration must be given to product liability insurance coverage.

Products hazard coverage can be tailored to fit the individual risk. For example, *products recall* insurance can be obtained to cover such items as media announcements, destruction or disposal of the recalled product, and wages and salaries for any additional employees hired to handle the activities required for disposition or correction of the recalled item. Although coverage can be through a comprehensive general liability policy, coverage for a specific product can also be obtained. Whether or not such coverage is affordable will depend primarily upon the hazards presented by the product. A pillow presents few hazards; a power mower (high on the list of CPSC dangerous products), presents great hazard. In the area of toys, bodily injury coverage for chemistry sets and fuel-powered toys, such as rockets and planes, is more than triple the same coverage for such items as wooden blocks and balls.

Risk management is a complex subject best left to the experts for advice and counsel and the development of comprehensive plans to minimize risks and prevent losses. Without such plans, the manufacturer may find that the risks of continuing a particular product line or even staying in business are too great to assume.

Questions and Problems

1. In 1950, while feeding onions into an onion-topping machine, the plaintiff's hands became caught in its steel rollers, and he was severely injured. In his suit against the manufacturer for negligence he alleged that the machine should have been equipped with a guard or stopping device. In denying recovery the court said: "We have not yet reached the state where a manufacturer is under the duty of making a machine accident proof or foolproof. Just as the manufacturer is under no obligation, in order to guard against injury resulting from deterioration, to furnish a machine that will not wear out, . . . so he is under no duty to guard against injury from a patent peril or from a source manifestly dangerous." Would the same set of circumstances result in the same opinion today? (*Campo v. Scofield*, 95 N.E.2d 802, 1950, and *Micallef v. Miehle Co.*, 348 N.E.2d 571, 1976.)

2. Kilmer bought a new Porsche from a Cedar Rapids dealer. Four days later the steering mechanism failed while she was negotiating a curve. In the resulting accident a passenger, Holmquist, was severely injured. When he sued the dealer on the strict liability theory, the dealer pointed out the fact that there was no evidence at the trial showing any specific defect in the steering mechanism, even though the car was examined by experts after the accident, and the dealer thus contended that the strict liability theory was inapplicable. What argument might Holmquist offer to rebut the dealer's contention? (*Holmquist v. Volkswagen of America, Inc.*, 261 N.W.2d 516, 1977.)

3. Burrus, a job printer, purchased a printing press from Itek Corp. for $7,000. Itek's representatives worked for several days installing the press and trying to get it to work satisfactorily. However, the machine never performed properly more than two hours out of an eight-hour working day. Consequently, about sixty days after the purchase, Burrus requested that Itek replace the machine and when Itek refused brought an action against it for breach of warranty. What result? (*Burrus v. Itek Corp.*, 360 N.E.2d 1168, 1977.)

4. An interior decorator selected and hired by the Stardust Hotel in Las Vegas designed a pattern for the carpet to be used in the hotel lobby and casino showroom. A sample run of the chosen pattern was taken to the hotel by the interior decorator and was approved. The Stardust then issued a detailed purchase order designating the type and length of yarn, weight per square yard, type of weave, color, and pattern. The carpet which was manufactured, delivered, and installed was consistent with the sample and precisely conformed to the detailed purchase order. Upon installation, however, the carpet did shade and, apparently, to a much greater extent than the Stardust or its representative had anticipated. It was clear from the testimony that shading is an inherent characteristic of all pile carpeting. The Stardust refused to pay, claiming that the carpet "shaded" excessively, giving it a mottled effect and the appearance of being water stained. Mohasco, the carpet manufacturer, sued Stardust to recover the price, $18,242.50. What result? (*Mohasco Industries, Inc. v. Anderson Halverson Corp.*, 520 P.2d 234, 1974.)

5. Discuss the following with a view to liability, if any, of the manufacturer or processor.

a. A small piece of china or crockery, in a can of dry-roasted peanuts, that chips one of the teeth of a consumer.
b. A piece of clamshell in a can of chowder that breaks a consumer's dentures.
c. A chicken bone from canned chicken, the can being labeled "boneless chicken," that causes a consumer to choke, necessitating the use of the Heimlich maneuver.

6. Discuss the three theories of recovery for a consumer who is injured by a defective product. Which of the three would you use if the new lawn mower you have purchased proves to have a defective carburetor, catches fire, and destroys your garage? What doctrine is available to a plaintiff who is unable to prove specific acts of negligence?

7. Based on the Consumer Product Safety Act's definition of a consumer product, may the Consumer Product Safety Commission promulgate safety standards for the following?

a. An aerial tramway that is ridden by patrons of an amusement park
b. A Honda motorcycle
c. Special sunglasses worn by professional baseball players
d. A used Piper Cub airplane
e. A baby crib to be used in the maternity ward of a hospital.

8. Plaintiff Jamieson was using a rubber rope exerciser attached to a doorknob. While stretching it with her feet, in accordance with the accompanying instructions, it slipped off the doorknob and struck her across the eyes, causing a detached retina. Has the manufacturer of the rubber rope breached a duty to the injured consumer? (*Jamieson v. Woodward & Lothrop*, 247 F.2d 23, 1957.)

9. Two Puerto Rican farm workers died from handling and exposure to parathion, a poisonous crop-dusting compound. The chemical was registered under the Federal Insecticide, Fungicide, and Rodenticide Act. Drums of the chemical contained labels on which the following appeared: "WARNING: May be fatal if swallowed, inhaled or absorbed through skin. Rapidly absorbed through skin. Do not get in eyes or on skin. Wear natural rubber gloves, protective clothing and goggles. In case of contact wash immediately with soap and water. . . . Keep all unprotected persons out of operating areas or vicinity where there may be danger of drift. . . ." In a wrongful death action, is the manufacturer likely to be liable? (*Hubbard-Hall Chemical Corp. v. Silverman*, 340 F.2d 402, 1965.)

10. The wife of the purchaser of a new automobile was injured when the steering mechanism failed, causing an accident. The contract for purchase was between the seller and the husband of the injured party. It contained a disclaimer which, under a literal interpretation, would limit buyer's remedy to replacement of defective parts, with no liability of the seller for personal injuries. Will the seller be liable in this case? Consider the concepts of privity and negligence.

C · H · A · P · T · E · R 19

ENVIRONMENTAL LAW

During the decade from 1980 to 1990, public and private expenditures for pollution control are expected to amount to $500 billion. Industry's share alone will be staggering. Nevertheless, it is a burden that must be assumed as part of the cost of doing business. This was not the case as late as the 1950s, when concern for the quality of the environment was either nonexistent or was expressed by a relatively small number of environmentalists. Today, however, there is concern, bordering on preoccupation, about the environment and the effect of its continued degradation. This general awakening occurred in the late 1960s when the seriousness of the consequences of continued pollution was realized by the public and by those in a position to do something about it. More recently, this threat to human health and general well-being has become well known as new problems arise, are aired by the media and, quite frequently, are settled in the courts. The accident at the Three Mile Island nuclear facility, the discharge of kepone into the James River of Virginia, the contamination by dioxins of Times Beach, Missouri, and other communities, and the indiscriminate dumping of hazardous wastes in Love Canal are current examples of serious ecological problems. They are of grave concern to those exposed to the particular danger and, in a less personal sense, to the industries that bear the responsibility for creating the problem.

Regulation in the environmental area is a relatively recent undertaking by government at both federal and state levels. However, once the problem was recognized, government lost no time in its efforts toward a solution. During the 1970s much of the legislation directed at eliminating or at least minimizing pollution and its effects was enacted. Most of the resulting measures impact on business and impose additional burdens on what many consider to be an already overregulated economy. The thousands of rules and regulations issued by the Environmental Protection Agency (EPA) have become a part of the legal environment of business with which industry must become familiar. Many small firms have gone out of business because they could not meet various antipollution requirements imposed by the EPA. Others, both large and small, have found that compliance has become an extremely costly budget item.

Chapter 6 discusses administrative agencies. Each of them regulates, in its own way, some sector of business or society, issuing rules and regulations which mandate participation by business in the search for solutions to the problems that have existed for years or that have been brought about by the technological progress of recent times. EPA's regulatory measures have been especially troublesome for industry. In fact, they are considered by a substantial cross-section of big business to be more burdensome than the requirements imposed by any other agency of the federal government. The Reagan administration, with a view to regulatory reform, established a Presidential Task Force on Regulatory Relief under the leadership of the vice-president. On March 25, 1981, the vice-president addressed a letter to the business community seeking comments and recommendations in the area of regulatory reform. EPA rules, regulations, and policies were the subject of four times as many comments as those of any other agency. As could be expected, industries submitting detailed comment and suggestions for relief included chemicals, petroleum, fertilizer, brewing, textiles, and paint companies. These industries are among those subject to extensive regulation as prime contributors to the pollution problem. It is upon such industries that much of the financial burden of required antipollution measures falls.

This chapter examines some of the known causes of pollution and the major remedial measures designed to prevent further deterioration of the environment. There are common-law remedies that have always been available. However, primary emphasis will be on the major statutes with which business is most concerned.

The Common Law and Pollution

Common-law remedies to stop pollution or to control it have little utility for business in dealing with environmental law because the problem is far too big to be treated on an individual case-by-case basis. The law of torts, for example, is primarily a remedial or loss-shifting device more useful to individual plaintiffs who may have suffered some environmental harm. A farmer may have had a water supply contaminated by industrial discharge of pollutants into a stream. Homeowners near a sanitary landfill may be exposed to noxious fumes from the constant trash fires used by the landfill to dispose of burnable refuse. Or homeowners may suffer property damage when caustic fumes from a chemical plant blanket their property, killing vegetation and causing housepaint to peel and crack. In each case the individual plaintiff may seek injunctions to prohibit further damage from the pollutants and, in appropriate cases, recover money damages. The common-law tort remedies available include nuisance, negligence, trespass and strict liability.

Nuisance

It has long been a legal theory that one may use his or her property in any manner so long as such use of the property does not interfere with the rights of others. When property is used in such a manner that it inflicts harm upon others there may be a cause of action in tort for nuisance. If the harm is widespread, affecting the common rights of a substantial segment of a community, the nuisance may be considered to be public in nature—if an individual's right to quiet enjoyment of land is disturbed by unreasonable and unwarranted use of property by another property owner, there may be a private nuisance. Most public nuisances are abated through action by public officials charged with controlling the facility that may be causing the harm. An action to abate a private nuisance is usually brought by the party affected against the party whose conduct gives rise to the nuisance.

In either case, public or private nuisance, the court is often called upon to balance the interests of plaintiff and defendant. It would be unthinkable to summarily close an offending industrial plant or activity that supports an entire community. So too, residents near a large airport may be expected to endure some inconvenience caused by noise and vibration. In fashioning a remedy the court may consider who was there first. A homeowner who buys near an existent airport or industrial facility may not find the courts very sympathetic when a complaint is registered, but this is not invariably the case.

In 1959 a major developer purchased some 20,000 acres of farm land near Phoenix, Arizona, for the development of a retirement village to be known as Sun City. Nearby were cattle feedlots, later purchased and expanded by Spur Industries. As the developer completed houses and Spur continued its expansion, only 500 feet separated the two operations. Prevailing winds blew flies and odors from the cattle areas over the homesites, thus making it difficult to sell the sites most affected. The developer filed a nuisance action against Spur, asking that Spur be enjoined from operating its cattle feedlots in the vicinity of the housing development. The court permanently enjoined Spur from operating the feedlots but further held that Spur should be awarded damages, a reasonable amount of the cost of moving or shutting down, because the developer had brought people to the nuisance, thus causing Spur damage. *Spur Industries, Inc. v. Del E. Webb Development Co.*, 108 Ariz. 178, 494 P.2d 700 (1972).

Enjoining a nuisance where the offending company has a substantial investment in the community may not always be in the best interests of either plaintiff or defendant. The following case is a good example of how the courts sometimes fashion a remedy that compensates damaged plaintiffs while at the same time limiting overall economic hardship.

Boomer v. Atlantic Cement Company
Court of Appeals of New York
257 N.E.2d 870 (1970)

Defendant Atlantic Cement operated a large cement plant near Albany, New York. Neighboring landowners brought an equitable action seeking damages and an injunction. Their complaint alleged that they had suffered, and would continue to suffer, property damage caused by dirt, smoke, and vibration from the cement plant. The trial court found that the cement plant was a nuisance and awarded temporary damages but refused to issue an injunction. The record disclosed that Atlantic Cement had more than $45 million invested in the plant and provided employment for some 300 employees. In awarding temporary damages to landowners the trial court further granted the right to bring later suits for future damages. The intermediate appellate court affirmed the judgment, and the landowners appealed.

Bergan, Judge:

. . . The public concern with air pollution arising from many sources in industry and in transportation is currently accorded ever wider recognition accompanied by a growing sense of responsibility in State and Federal Governments to control it. Cement plants are obvious sources of air pollution in the neighborhoods where they operate.

But there is now before the court private litigation in which individual property owners have sought specific relief from a single plant operation. The threshold question raised by the division of view on this appeal is whether the court should resolve the litigation between the parties now before it as equitably as seems possible; or whether, seeking promotion of the general public welfare, it should channel private litigation into broad public objectives. . . .

Effective control of air pollution is a problem presently far from solution even with the full public and financial powers of government. In large measure adequate technical procedures are yet to be developed and some that appear possible may be economically impracticable.

It seems apparent that the amelioration of air pollution will depend on technical research in great depth; on a carefully balanced consideration of the economic impact of close regulation; and of the actual effect on public health. It is likely to require massive public expenditure and to demand more than any local community can accomplish and to depend on regional and interstate controls.

A court should not try to do this on its own as a by-product of private litigation and it seems manifest that the judicial establishment is neither equipped in the limited nature of any judgment it can pronounce nor prepared to lay down and implement an effective policy for the elimination of air pollution. This is an area beyond the circumference of one private lawsuit. It is a direct responsibility for government and should not thus be undertaken as an incident to solving a dispute between property owners and a single cement plant—one of many—in the Hudson River valley.

The cement making operations of defendant have been found by the court at Special Term to have damaged the nearby properties of plaintiffs in these two actions. That court, as it has been noted, accordingly found defendant maintained a nuisance and this has been affirmed at the Appellate Division. The total damage to plaintiffs' properties is, however, relatively small in comparison with the value of defendant's operation and with the consequences of the injunction which plaintiffs seek. . . .

The rule in New York has been that such a nuisance will be enjoined although marked disparity be shown in economic consequence between the effect of the injunction and the effect of the nuisance. . . .

Although the court at Special Term and the Appellate Division held that injunction should be denied, it was found that plaintiffs had been damaged in various specific amounts up to the time of the trial and damages to the respective plaintiffs were awarded for those amounts. The effect of this was, injunction having been denied, plaintiffs could maintain successive actions at law for damages thereafter as further damage was incurred.

The court at Special Term also found the amount of permanent damage attributable to each plaintiff, for the guidance of the parties in the event both sides stipulated to the payment and acceptance of such permanent damage as a settlement of all the controversies among the parties. The total of permanent damages to all plaintiffs thus found was $185,000. This basis of adjustment has not resulted in any stipulation by the parties.

This result of Special Term and at the Appellate Division is a departure from a rule that has become settled; but to follow the rule literally in these cases would be to close down the plant at once. This court is fully agreed to avoid that immediate drastic remedy; the difference in view is how best to avoid it.

One alternative is to grant the injunction but postpone its effect to a specified future date to give opportunity for technical advances to permit defendant to eliminate the nuisance; another is to grant the injunction conditioned on the payment of permanent damages to plaintiffs which would compensate them for the total economic loss to their property present and future caused by defendant's operations. For reasons which will be developed the court chooses the latter alternative.

If the injunction were to be granted unless within a short period—e.g., 18 months—the nuisance be abated by improved methods, there would be no assurance that any significant technical improvement would occur.

The parties could settle this private litigation at any time if defendant paid enough money and the imminent threat of closing the plant would build up the pressure on defendant. If there were no improved techniques found, there would inevitably be applications to the court at Special Term for extensions of time to perform on showing of good faith efforts to find such techniques.

Moreover, techniques to eliminate dust and other annoying by-products of cement making are unlikely to be developed by any research the defendant can undertake within any short period, but will depend on the total resources of the cement industry nationwide and throughout the world. The problem is universal wherever cement is made.

For obvious reasons the rate of the research is beyond control of defendant. If at the end of 18 months the whole industry has not found a technical solution a court would be hard put to close down this one cement plant if due regard be given to equitable principles.

On the other hand, to grant the injunction unless defendant pays plaintiffs such permanent damages as may be fixed by the court seems to do justice between the contending parties. All of the attributions of economic loss to the properties on which plaintiffs' complaints are based will have been redressed.

The nuisance complained of by these plaintiffs may have other public or private consequences, but these particular parties are the only ones who have sought remedies and the judgment proposed will fully redress them. The limitation of relief granted is a limitation only within the four corners of these actions and does not foreclose public health or other public agencies from seeking proper relief in a proper court. . . .

Thus is seems fair to both sides to grant permanent damages to plaintiffs which will terminate this private litigation. The theory of damage is the "servitude on land" of plaintiffs imposed by defendant's nuisance. . . .

The judgment, by allowance of permanent damages imposing a servitude on land, which is the basis of the actions, would preclude future recovery by plaintiffs or their grantees. . . .

This should be placed beyond debate by a provision of the judgment that the payment by defendant and the acceptance by plaintiffs of permanent damages found by the court shall be in compensation for a servitude on the land.

★★★

Negligence, Trespass, and Strict Liability

The tort of negligence involves the breach by defendant of a duty owed to plaintiff to use reasonable care to avoid injury to plaintiff's person or property. In the *Atlantic Cement* case suitable technology for controlling or eliminating pollution was not yet available. Had such equipment been available, the company's failure to install and use it would be considered negligence, a breach of the duty to use reasonable care.

The use of trespass as a means of pollution control has limited application since it is most often claimed on an individual basis. An intentional entering onto another's land without permission is a trespass. So too, causing particles to be borne onto another's land may be trespass if the owner of the source of the particles has reason to believe that the activity would cause damaging deposits. For example, a physical and obvious trespass occurs when cement dust from a plant is deposited, layer on layer, upon the property of nearby residents.

In certain cases where the threat or damage is caused by abnormally or inherently dangerous activities, the theory of strict liability may be used to recover damages or put a stop to the activity. The spraying of crops with toxic chemicals and the storage or use of explosives or other hazardous materials are examples of activities that may result in strict liability on the defendant. In such cases, the claim by defendant that there was no negligence or that reasonable care was used is not a defense. The inherent danger of the activity and resulting damage are sufficient to permit recovery by plaintiff.

The National Environmental Policy Act (NEPA)

Recognizing that a national policy was needed, Congress enacted the National Environmental Policy Act (NEPA) in 1969 to "encourage productive and enjoyable harmony between man and his environment and biosphere and stimulate the health and welfare of man; to enrich the understanding of the ecological systems and natural resources important to the Nation; and to establish a Council on Environmental Quality." NEPA is a major step toward making each generation responsible to succeeding ones for the quality of the environment.

Environmental Impact Statements

NEPA requires that an environmental impact statement be prepared by the appropriate agency whenever proposed major federal action will significantly affect the quality of the human environment. (Private enterprise may also be required to prepare an environmental impact statement if federal funds have been committed to a particular private venture.) Responsible officials must provide a detailed statement describing the environmental impact of the proposed action, unavoidable adverse effects, acceptable alternatives to the proposed project, and any irreversible and irretrievable commitments of resources involved. To illustrate, the deployment of the proposed MX intercontinental ballistic missile system in the western states has created considerable controversy. Deployment as envisaged by the United States Air Force would be a major federal action that would significantly affect the quality of the human environment. Consequently, the Air Force prepared and submitted to the Environmental Protection Agency (EPA) a draft environmental impact statement containing its analysis of the environmental effects of deploying the missile system. The draft statement was not well received, perhaps because of the controversy the proposed project had created. EPA labeled the draft as ER-2, a designation signifying reservations about a draft that does not contain sufficient information to permit full assessment of the project's environmental effects. The EPA was concerned about air and water quality and disposal of solid waste. The Department of the Interior saw the project as impinging on designated wilderness areas, and the Forest Service was concerned that national forest lands would be adversely affected with planned construction disrupting wildlife in the area. Consequently, additional work would be needed to satisfy the concerns of various agencies and groups of environmentalists.

The preparation of environmental impact statements can be a costly and time-consuming task. Of the thousands that have been prepared since the requirement was imposed, many have run to more than 1,000 pages. Often written in the jargon peculiar to the project sponsor, a particular statement might be a largely incomprehensible document amounting to sheer guesswork. Consequently, new rules were issued in 1978 to simplify the process. Length is now limited to 150 pages (except in unusual circumstances); the statement must be clear, to the point, and in plain English; and all key points and conclusions must be set forth in a summary of no more than fifteen pages. Simplification and streamlining may be administratively helpful but do not quiet the criticism that the environmental impact statement, no matter how well it may be prepared, is merely a prediction as to future environmental consequences of a proposed federal action.

"Your honor, if counselor for the Clean Air League is through with his opening statement, I'd like to call my first witness!"

The battle for clean air.

Source: Reprinted with permission from the *ABA Journal*, the magazine of the Legal Profession.

The Environmental Protection Agency (EPA)

Until 1970 the responsibility for administering antipollution measures was divided among several government agencies. The Department of the Interior was concerned with water quality; the Department of Health, Education and Welfare (now the Department of Human Resources) administered air pollution control, solid waste, and water standards; and the Department of Agriculture was primarily responsible for pesticide registration and use. Recognizing that the environment is a single, interrelated system, President Nixon, in his Reorganization Plan No. 3, established the Environmental Protection Agency (EPA) to which the above and other functions were transferred for administration. The EPA establishes and enforces environmental protection standards, conducts research on pollution, provides assistance to state and local antipollution programs through grants and technical advice, and generally assists the Council on Environmental Quality (CEQ). The CEQ was established by executive order to facilitate implementation of NEPA by issuing guidelines for the preparation of impact statements and generally to assist and advise the president on environmental matters. In its guidelines, CEQ has required that the environmental impact statements discussed above be prepared as early in the decision-making process as possible and that other agencies and the public be given a chance to comment and criticize before any final decision is made to go ahead with major federal action.

Consolidation of diverse functions under one agency has provided a center of control for the continuing war on pollution. How it works can be illustrated by examining a few of the major areas of concern.

Water Pollution Control

The history of water pollution control provides some insight into how attention was gradually focused on a serious threat to the environment. Conservation and quality of water was the first environmental concern to be addressed by government. As early as 1790 Congress was concerned with the nation's navigable rivers and harbors, primarily to ensure that they remained navigable and free of obstructions. In that year Congress approved Rhode Island, Maryland, and Georgia statutes that imposed duties on shipping to finance improvements of waterways. As commerce expanded, so did the role of the federal government in fostering and regulating it. Early legislation was directed at keeping waterways navigable, but the pollution problem was finally addressed in 1886 when Congress enacted legislation prohibiting the dumping of refuse into New York City harbor. The Rivers and Harbors Act of 1890 made similar antidumping provisions applicable to all navigable waters. Responsibility for administration rested in the secretary of war, and considerable authority was given to the Army Corps of Engineers.

As part of an effort to remedy what had been ineffectual piecemeal legislation, the 1899 Rivers and Harbors Appropriation Act made it unlawful for ships and manufacturing establishments to discharge refuse into any navigable water of the United States or into any tributary of a navigable waterway. However, it was permissible under the act to discharge liquid wastes from streets and sewers into such waterways and tributaries. Legislation still emphasized obstructions to navigation but became increasingly useful as an antipollution device in the absence of statutes that could attack the problem more directly.

Clean Water Legislation

Efforts to clean up the nation's waterways began in earnest with the passage of the Federal Water Pollution Control Act in 1948 and continued, though piecemeal, through the amending process until the 1972 amendments provided a comprehensive plan to eliminate pollution. Since industry in this country uses a significant amount of water in its manufacturing and processing activities, the 1972 amendments set standards and guidelines on an industry-by-industry basis for controlling water pollution from industrial sources. The types of discharges with which the law is concerned are as varied as the industries to be controlled—thermal pollution from heat generating plants and particulates and toxic wastes from manufacturing activities are subject to regulation and continual monitoring to assure that prescribed standards are being met. In general, industry is expected to control and eliminate its discharge of pollutants through the "best available" technology as soon as may be feasible.

The law places primary responsibility on the states but provides for federal aid to local governments and small businesses to help them in their efforts to comply with the law's requirements. It also provides a licensing and permit system, at both state and federal levels, for discharging into waterways and a more workable enforcement program. Penalties for violations range from $25,000 per day and up to one year in prison for a first offense to a minimum of $50,000 per day and two years in prison for subsequent violations. Amendments currently proposed by EPA would permit that agency to administratively assess civil penalties not to exceed $5,000 per day for minor violations.

Compliance with EPA requirements can be costly. The following case illustrates the difficulty experienced by certain industries in meeting standards for controlling water pollution effluents.

EPA v. National Crushed Stone Ass'n.
U.S. Supreme Court
449 U.S. 64
(1980)

In order to reduce or eliminate pollution of our waterways the Federal Water Pollution Control Act directs the EPA to set limitations on the effluents that can be discharged by industrial activities. Sources of pollution are to meet certain standards by 1977 based on the use of the "Best Practicable control Technology currently available (BPT)." Nineteen eighty-seven standards are to be met by the use of the "Best Available Technology economically available (BAT)." The Act further provides for variances from the 1987 effluent limita-

tions for individual point sources if they can show that such modified requirements will represent the maximum use of technology within the economic capability of the owner or operators. However, there is no similar variance provision authorizing consideration of the economic ability of the individual operator to meet the cost of complying with the 1977 (BPT) standards.

In 1977 the EPA set pollution discharge limitations for the coal mining industry and certain sectors of the mineral mining and processing industry. Under the regulations a greater than normal cost of compliance will be considered on a request for a variance, but a variance will not be granted on the basis of the applicant's economic inability to meet the cost of implementing the uniform standard.

National Crushed Stone and others challenged the standards of EPA's 1977 "best practicable control technology currently available" and the variance clause because, if no variance was granted, cost of compliance would be so prohibitive as to necessitate going out of business. The Court of Appeals, believing that the BAT limitations are to be more stringent than the BPT limitations and that the variance provision for BPT must be at least as flexible as that for BAT with respect to affordability, set aside the variance provision as being unduly restrictive.

White, Justice:

. . . To obtain a variance from the 1977 uniform discharge limitations a discharger must demonstrate that the "factors relating to the equipment or facilities involved, the process applied, or other such factors relating to such discharger are fundamentally different from the factors considered in the establishment of the guidelines." Although a greater than normal cost of implementation will be considered in acting on a request for a variance, economic ability to meet the costs will not be considered. A variance, therefore, will not be granted on the basis of the applicant's economic inability to meet the costs of implementing the uniform standard.

The Court of Appeals for the Fourth Circuit rejected this position. It required EPA to "take into consideration, among other things, the statutory factors set out in § 301(c)," which authorizes variances from the more restrictive pollution limitations to become effective in 1987 and which specifies economic capability as a major factor to be taken into account. . . .

Section 304(b) of the Act, 33 U.S.C. § 1314(b), is again divided into two sections corresponding to the two levels of technology, BPT and BAT. Under § 304(b)(1) the Administrator is to quantify "the degree of effluent reduction attainable through the application of the best practicable control technology currently available (BPT) for classes and categories of point sources. . . ." In assessing the BPT the Administrator is to consider:

"the total cost of application of technology in relation to the effluent reduction benefits to be achieved from such application, . . . the age of equipment and facilities involved, the process employed, the engineering aspects of the application of various types of control techniques, process changes, non-water quality

environmental impact (including energy requirements), and such other factors as the Administrator deems appropriate."

Similar directions are given the Administrator for determining effluent reductions attainable from the BAT except that in assessing BAT total cost is no longer to be considered in comparison to effluent reduction benefits. . . .

No such explicit variance provisions exists with respect to BPT standards, but in *E.I. du Pont de Nemours v. Train*, 430 U.S. 112 . . . (1977), we indicated that a variance provision was a necessary aspect of BPT limitations applicable by regulations to classes and categories of point sources. . . . The issue in this case is whether the BPT variance provision must allow consideration of the economic capability of an individual discharger to afford the costs of the BPT limitation. For the reasons that follow, our answer is in the negative. . . .

To put the matter another way, under § 304, the Administrator is directed to consider the benefits of effluent reductions as compared to the costs of pollution control in determining BPT limitations. Thus, every BPT limitation represents a conclusion by the Administrator that the costs imposed on the industry are worth the benefits in pollution reduction that will be gained by meeting those limits. To grant a variance because a particular owner or operator cannot meet the normal costs of the technological requirements imposed on him, and not because there has been a recalculation of the benefits compared to the costs, would be inconsistent with this legislative scheme and would allow a level of pollution inconsistent with the judgment of the Administrator. . . .

Because the 1977 limitations were intended to reduce the total pollution produced by an industry, requiring compliance with BPT standards necessarily imposed additional costs on the segment of the industry with the least effective technology. If the statutory goal is to be achieved, these costs must be borne or the point source eliminated. In our view, requiring variances from otherwise valid regulations where dischargers cannot afford normal costs of compliance would undermine the purpose and the intended operative effect of the 1977 regulations.

The Administrator's present interpretation of the language of the statute is amply supported by the legislative history, which persuades us that Congress understood that the economic capability provision of § 301(c) was limited to BAT variances; that Congress foresaw and accepted the economic hardship, including the closing of some plants, that effluent limitations would cause; and that Congress took certain steps to alleviate this hardship, steps which did not include allowing a BPT variance based on economic capability. . . .

Instead of economic variances, Congress specifically added two other provisions to address the problem of economic hardship.

First, provision was made for low-cost loans to small businesses to help them meet the cost of technological improvements. . . .

Second, an employee protection provision was added, giving EPA authority to investigate any plant's claim that it must cut back production or close down because of pollution control regulations. . . . This provision had two purposes: to allow EPA constantly to monitor the economic effect on industry of pollution control rules and to undercut economic threats by industry that would create pressure to relax effluent limitation rules. . . .

As we see it, Congress anticipated that the 1977 regulations would cause economic hardship and plant closings: "The question . . . is not what a court thinks is generally appropriate to the regulatory process; it is what Congress intended for *these* regulations." . . .

We conclude, therefore, that the Court of Appeals erred in not accepting EPA's interpretation of the Act. EPA is not required by the Act to consider economic capability in granting variances from its uniform BPT regulations.

The judgment of the Court of Appeals is

Reversed.

★★★

In an area of special significance to coastal cities, the Clean Water Act requires that the dumping of sewage sludge into the ocean end as soon as possible. Because this could pose a considerable problem for municipalities dumping waste into the ocean from waste water treatment plants, many millions of dollars have been appropriated for research into the problem.

The Clean Water Act also takes up the threat to coastal and resort areas posed by the transport of petroleum products. All too frequently, vessels from small coastal barges to huge supertankers accidentally discharge their cargoes into the sea near the coast. The ecological effect on fish, shellfish, and waterfowl and on the public and private shorelines and beaches is immeasurable. Consequently, the Clean Water Act imposes severe sanctions on those responsible for such pollution. The owner or operator of a grounded oil-carrying vessel can be liable for up to $250,000 of the cost of cleaning up its spilled cargo; if the oil spill is the result of willful negligence or misconduct, the owner or operator of the vessel can be held liable to the United States government for the full cost of cleaning up the shore. Operators of onshore and offshore facilities are also held liable for spillage and pollution, under ordinary conditions, to the extent of $50 million and, where willful negligence and misconduct are involved, to the full extent of the cost of cleanup and removal, including the restoration or replacement of natural resources damaged or destroyed by the discharge of oil or hazardous substances.

Clean Air

The Clean Air Act of 1970 is the primary federal legislation directed at air pollution. Under the administration of the EPA, it set a three-year deadline for attaining the primary ambient (outside) air quality standards Congress had designed to protect public health. Since achieving the standards is costly, the EPA's role is to balance the economic, technological, and social factors that must be considered in attaining the clean air goals that have been set.

Several programs form the essential elements of the Clean Air Act. Foremost is the setting of primary (health) and secondary (welfare) ambient air quality standards. Having been set, the standards are proving difficult to meet, and time was lost in various attempts by federal and state agencies to balance the economic, technological, and social factors. There have been, however, significant reductions in sulfur dioxide concentrations, total suspended particulates, and carbon monoxide.

Another program of the act requires the states to draft *state implementation plans* (SIPs) for achieving ambient air quality standards. When approved by the EPA, such plans permit the states to enforce air quality standards within their borders. Operators of air pollution sources may be required to monitor, sample, and keep appropriate records, all of which are subject to on-premises inspections by the EPA.

Of particular concern to industry is the program for setting *new source performance standards* (NSPSs)—emission standards for various categories of large industrial facilities. The goal is for large industrial polluters to reduce emissions to meet primary and secondary standards in accordance with prescribed schedules. To do this, major polluters must use the best acceptable control devices, those with proven capabilities to reduce emissions and, ultimately, pollution. In order to make it easier for industry to meet federal clean air standards, the EPA is currently proposing what it calls the "bubble concept." A large plant with multiple emission points (stacks) would not have to meet standards for each one. The plant would instead be under a "bubble" with a single allowable emission level. Plant management could then choose each point source or, with the bubble concept, meet the sum total of emission limits using the most economical means available to control the problem.

Monitoring, sampling and record keeping are essential elements of the enforcement procedures used by EPA. So too is the on-site inspection of large industrial facilities. Nevertheless, the enforcement of the Clean Air Act presents problems for both regulated and regulator. In the following case, the means used by an EPA official to gather evidence of pollution was challenged, by the industrial facility being investigated, on constitutional grounds.

Dow Chemical Company, Petitioner, v. United States, ______ U.S. ______ (1986); 54 LW 4464

EPA was in the process of investigating Dow's Midland, Michigan plant to check emissions from the power houses located in Dow's facility for possible violations of federal air quality standards. In September 1977 EPA made an on-site inspection of the power houses and was later given schematic drawings of them by Dow. EPA next requested entry onto the premises for purposes of inspecting the power houses and advised Dow that it would be taking photographs of the Dow layout and facilities. Dow objected to the taking of photographs and denied EPA's request for entry.

EPA suggested to Dow that a search warrant would be sought but, instead, decided to obtain aerial photographs of Dow's facility. On February 6, 1978 EPA hired Abrams Aerial Survey Corporation to take the photographs and instructed Abrams as to altitude, location, and direction from which the photo-

graphs were to be taken. Abrams, on February 7, took approximately seventy-five color photographs of various parts of Dow's plant and turned them over to EPA. Upon learning that the aerial pictures had been taken, Dow brought an action challenging EPA's *warrantless* use of aerial photography.

The District Court was struck by the vivid detail and resolution of the pictures. "As amply demonstrated by Dow at a hearing before the Court, some of the photographs taken from directly above the plant at 1,200 feet are capable of enlargement to a scale of 1 inch equals 20 feet, or greater, without significant loss of detail or resolution. When enlarged in this manner, and viewed under magnification, it is possible to discern equipment, pipes, and power lines as small as one-half inch in diameter."

The District Court held that the EPA flyover and aerial photography of Dow's plant constituted an unreasonable search in violation of the Fourth Amendment and that EPA had exceeded its statutory authority. EPA was therefore enjoined from conducting further aerial surveillance. 536 F.Supp. 1355 (1982). From this decision an appeal was taken by the EPA.

The Circuit Court of Appeals reversed holding that Dow had no actual expectation of privacy from the air, but even if it did have such an expectation, the expectation was unreasonable. The court held Dow's Midland plant to be more like "open fields" than a home or office. Therefore, an inspection from the air which would otherwise be a search becomes a non-search for Fourth Amendment purposes. The court further held that the EPA had not exceeded its authority in conducting aerial surveillance since the language of the statute (The Clean Air Act) clearly does not foreclose this technique. 749 F.2d 307 (1984). From this decision an appeal was taken by Dow Chemical.

Burger, Chief Justice:

The photographs at issue in this case are essentially like those commonly used in mapmaking. Any person with an airplane and an aerial camera could readily duplicate them. In common with much else, the technology of photography has changed in this century. These developments have enhanced industrial processes, and indeed all areas of life; they have also enhanced law enforcement techniques. Whether they may be employed by competitors to penetrate trade secrets is not a question presented in this case. Governments do not generally seek to appropriate trade secrets of the private sector, and the right to be free of appropriation of trade secrets is protected by law.

Dow nevertheless relies heavily on its claim that trade secret laws protect it from any aerial photography of this industrial complex by its competitors, and that this protection is relevant to our analysis of such photography under the Fourth Amendment. That such photography might be barred by state law with regard to competitors, however, is irrelevant to the questions presented here. State tort law governing unfair competition does not define the limits of the Fourth Amendment. . . . The Government is seeking these photographs in order to regulate, not to compete with, Dow. If the Government were to use the photographs to compete with Dow, Dow might have a Fifth Amendment "taking" claim. Indeed, Dow alleged such a claim in its complaint, but the District Court dismissed it without prejudice. But even trade secret laws would not bar all forms of photography of this industrial complex; rather, only photography with an intent to use any trade secrets revealed by the photographs may be proscribed. Hence, there is no prohibition of photographs taken by a casual passenger on an airliner, or those taken by a company producing maps for its map-making purposes.

Dow claims first that EPA has no authority to use aerial photography to implement its statutory authority for "site inspection" under § 114(a) of the Clean Air Act, 42 U.S.C. § 7414(a); second, Dow claims EPA's use of aerial photography was a "search" of an area that, notwithstanding the large size of the plant, was within an "industrial curtilage" rather than an "open field," and that it had a reasonable expectation of privacy from such photography protected by the Fourth Amendment.

Under § 114(a)(2), the Clean Air Act provides that "upon presentation of . . . credentials," EPA has a "right of entry to, upon, or through any premises." Dow argues this limited grant of authority to enter does not authorize any aerial observation. In particular, Dow argues that unannounced aerial observation deprives Dow of its right to be informed that an inspection will be made or has occurred, and its right to claim confidentiality of the information contained in the places to be photographed, as provided in § 114(a) and (c). It is not claimed that EPA has disclosed any of the photographs outside the agency.

Section 114(a), however, appears to expand, not restrict, EPA's general powers to investigate. Nor is there any suggestion in the statute that the powers conferred by this section are intended to be exclusive. There is no claim that EPA is prohibited from taking photographs from a ground-level location accessible to the general public. The EPA, as a regulatory and enforcement agency, needs no explicit statutory provision to employ methods of observation commonly available to the public at large; we hold that the use of aerial observation and photography is within the EPA's statutory authority.

We turn now to Dow's contention that taking aerial photographs constituted a search without a warrant, thereby violating Dow's rights under the Fourth Amendment. In making this contention, however, Dow concedes that a simple flyover with naked-eye observation, or the taking of a photograph from a nearby hillside overlooking such a facility, would give rise to no Fourth Amendment problem.

In *California v. Ciraolo*, ____ U.S. ____ (1986), decided today, we hold that naked-eye aerial observation from an altitude of 1,000 feet of a backyard within the curtilage of a home does not constitute a search under the Fourth Amendment.

In the instant case, two additional Fourth Amendment claims are presented: whether the common-law "curtilage" doctrine encompasses a large industrial complex such as Dow's, and whether photography employing an aerial mapping camera is permissible in this context. Dow argues that an industrial plant, even one occupying 2,000 acres, does not fall within the "open fields" doctrine of *Oliver v. United States* but rather is an "industrial curtilage" having constitutional protection equivalent to that of the curtilage of a private home. Dow further contends that any aerial photography of this "industrial curtilage" intrudes upon its reasonable expectations of privacy. Plainly a business establishment or an industrial or commercial facility enjoys certain protections under the Fourth Amendment. See *Marshall v. Barlow's, Inc.*, 436 U.S. 307 (1978); *See v. City of Seattle*, 387 U.S. 541 (1967).

Dow plainly has a reasonable, legitimate, and objective expectation of privacy within the interior of its covered buildings, and it is equally clear that expectation is one society is prepared to observe. Moreover, it could hardly be expected that Dow would erect a huge cover over a 2,000-acre tract. In contending that its entire enclosed plant complex is an "industrial curtilage," Dow argues that its exposed manufacturing facilities are analogous to the curtilage surrounding a home because it has taken every possible step to bar access from ground level.

The Court of Appeals held that whatever the limits of an "industrial curtilage" barring *ground*-level intrusions into Dow's private areas, the open areas exposed here were more analogous to "open fields" than to a curtilage for purposes of aerial observation. . . . The intimate activities associated with family privacy and the home and its curtilage simply do not reach the outdoor areas or spaces between structures and buildings of a manufacturing plant.

We conclude that the open areas of an industrial plant complex with numerous plant structures spread over an area of 2,000 acres are not analogous to the "curtilage" of a dwelling for purposes of aerial surveillance; such an industrial complex is more comparable to an open field and as such it is open to the view and observation of persons in aircraft lawfully in the public airspace immediately above or sufficiently near the area for the reach of cameras.

We hold that the taking of aerial photographs of an industrial plant complex from navigable airspace is not a search prohibited by the Fourth Amendment.

Affirmed.

★★★

The last program of the Clean Air Act involves the automobile and the fuel it burns. In order to reduce pollution from the combustion engine, emission standards must be achieved and fuel additive regulations must be developed and followed. This has been done, and the resulting standards are of some concern to the auto and fuel industries. Meeting the challenge has resulted in development of the catalytic converter and the extensive use of unleaded gasoline. However, there are indications that the catalytic converter, while controlling carbon monoxide and hydrocarbon emissions, may actually add to pollution in the form of sulfuric acid emission. Further, due to the higher cost of unleaded fuel and mechanical problems (real or imagined) caused by the catalytic converter, motorists in increasing number have taken measures to bypass the converter and burn leaded gasoline. A federal statute now prohibits such practices. Lead, as an additive to gasoline, improves automotive performance at relatively low cost. Since 1980 the EPA has limited large refiners to 0.5 gram of lead per gallon. In the spring of 1982 it was revealed that the EPA had been advising oil companies that they could increase the lead content of regular gasoline to 0.549 gram per gallon. This action, unofficial though it may have been, caused an outcry by environmentalists and others concerned for the health hazard presented by lead. Consequently, the EPA has ordered a 90 percent reduction in the amount of lead in gasoline by the beginning of 1986 and may ban lead entirely as early as 1988. New evidence has indicated a link between lead exposure and high blood pressure and other adverse health effects.

With regard to motor vehicle emissions of carbon monoxide and nitrogen oxides, a bill has recently been introduced that would ease the present standards. The bill would require that EPA, if appropriate, develop alternatives and practicable approaches to mobile source emissions control. New approaches should stimulate economic growth, reduce costs, and improve emissions control consistent with safety, conservation, and consumer needs.

Acid Rain

A current problem that is receiving increased attention is the threat to the environment posed by acid rain. This pollutant is caused when sulfur dioxide, emitted principally by coal-burning plants in the Midwest and northeastern states, combines with oxygen in the upper air to form sulfur trioxide, which with water forms dilute solutions of nitric and sulfuric acids. The acid then comes down as rain, causing considerable harm to foliage, trees, lakes, streams, and fish and other wildlife. In New York's Adirondack region alone at least 200 of its lakes and ponds have become so acidic that fish cannot survive. In other New England areas the acid is so pervasive that water conduits have dissolved, leading to high levels of lead in drinking water. The problem has assumed international proportions since Canada is even more affected than the United States and lays much of the blame on American utility companies burning high-sulfur coal. While there is controversy over possible solutions to the problem, there is some consensus that immediate steps must be taken to reduce the amount of sulfur dioxide being injected into the upper air by the tall stacks of the energy-producing and ore-smelting industries.

Three different bills have been introduced in Congress that would abate and control acid rain by forcing major emitters to install scrubbers and resort to coal washing. Other emitters would be forced to shift to low-sulfur coal. Reduction in sulfur dioxide emissions under the bills would range from 8 to 10 million tons. However, the estimated cost to industry to comply with the proposed legislation is $2 billion to $3 billion, hitting those in the midwestern states the hardest. The Illinois Power Company estimated the capital costs of retrofitting the fifty largest emitters east of the Mississippi River at $12 billion. Further, the coal industry claims that, while employment would rise in the states which produce low-sulfur coal, some 98,000 jobs would be lost in the Midwest and in states producing high and medium-sulfur coal.

Efforts to devise a legislative solution to the acid rain problem are stalled in Congress. Meanwhile, research reveals that acidic rain is falling well outside the New England area in states from Pennsylvania to Florida and in California, Colorado, and Texas.

Solid Waste and Its Disposal

The disposal of the millions of tons of solid waste produced annually in this country presents a problem of staggering proportions. Periodic garbage pick-ups at residences or small businesses, or weekly trips to the county or municipal sanitary landfill, solve the problem for most people. However, less than 10 percent of solid waste is classified as residential, commercial, or institutional. The greater portion is classified as agricultural or mineral. Agriculture alone contributes over 50 percent. Undisposed of, the waste creates enormous health and pollution problems; inadequate disposal methods often create greater hazards. If burned, solid waste pollutes the air. If dumped into waterways, lakes, or streams, the Clean Water Act is violated. Consequently, federal statutes have been enacted to combat the problem. Chief among these is the Solid Waste Disposal Act of 1965 and the 1976 amendment known as the Resource Conservation and Recovery Act. The primary goal of these laws is more efficient management of waste and its disposal through financial and technical assistance to state and local agencies in the development and application of new methods of waste disposal. The 1976 Act establishes an Office of Solid Waste within the Environmental Protection Agency and directs special attention to the management and ultimate disposal of hazardous waste.

Hazardous Waste

The Resource Conservation and Recovery Act defines "hazardous waste" as a solid waste, or combination of solid wastes, which because of its quantity, concentration, or physical, chemical, or infectious characteristics may:

(A) cause, or significantly contribute to an increase in mortality or an increase in serious irreversible, or incapacitating reversible, illness; or
(B) pose a substantial present or potential hazard to human health or the environment when improperly treated, stored, transported, or disposed of, or otherwise managed.

About 40 to 50 million metric tons of hazardous wastes are produced in the United States every year. Chemical and associated products manufacturing plants account for more than half the total.

Serious health problems caused by hazardous waste continue to arise as the aftermath of earlier indiscriminate dumping of billions of pounds of dangerous chemical waste. In fact, developing a fail-safe system of disposing of hazardous substances is probably the most serious problem that confronts the EPA today. The main thrust of the 1976 Act is toward hazardous waste management, from generation to disposal. To accomplish this the statute provides for and requires the systematic control of collection, source separation, storage, transportation, processing, treatment, recovery, and disposal of hazardous wastes. Many of the common practices employed by industry have proven to be grossly inadequate, as the Love Canal disaster illustrates. Hooker Chemical's disposal methods there exposed the local residents to risks which have not yet been fully evaluated. There is, for example, some evidence that the frequency of miscarriages and incidence of birth defects increased in the area, and millions of dollars in lawsuits have been filed against the company. Additionally, the firm, a subsidiary of Occidental Petroleum Corporation, will be required to spend millions of dollars on cleanup operations in its three Niagara Falls area disposal sites. (On April 30, 1982, the U.S. District Court for the Western District of New York approved a settlement under which Hooker Chemical would spend about $30 million to clean up its Hyde Park landfill.)

It is often difficult to assign responsibility for dangerous dump sites that may have been abandoned for many years. Consequently, the 1976 Act institutes a manifest system by which hazardous wastes will be controlled from generation to ultimate disposal. If a generator, which produces hazardous waste, is to store such waste on its premises, a permit to do so must be obtained from EPA or the state in which the premises are located. If, however, the waste is to be transported to an off-premises disposal site, the manifest system is used to keep track of the material. The generator prepares a document on which are listed its name, the name of the transporter, the name and address of the approved disposal site, and a description of the kind and quantity of the waste. Signed copies of the manifest are provided at all stages of the process so that the generator, when it receives a copy from the owner of the disposal facility, knows that its hazardous waste has been properly disposed of.

The Hazardous and Solid Waste Amendments of 1984 strengthen enforcement of the Resource Conservation and Recovery Act. They increase penalties for violations and expand EPA's authority to conduct criminal investigations, authorize direct action against guarantors of the financial responsibility of the violating facility when the facility is insolvent, and explicitly authorize private citizens to bring suit when there is an imminent hazard and EPA is not prosecuting.

The Comprehensive Environmental Response, Compensation, and Liability Act of 1980 ("Superfund")

The EPA, as of October 23, 1981, had identified what it referred to as the 115 worst dump sites in the United States. These sites are located in forty-five states, with sixteen in Florida, twelve in New Jersey, and eight each in New York and Pennsylvania. Over twenty of the sites were considered to be more dangerous than the Love Canal site. Cleanup of the targeted sites would have been nearly impossible prior to enactment of the Comprehensive

Environmental Response, Compensation, and Liability Act of 1980, known as "Superfund." Either the authority was lacking or funds were not available for cleanup of abandoned dump sites and for remedial emergency action in case of spills of toxic substances. For example, in 1961 a barge loaded with more than 2 million pounds of liquid chlorine sank in the Mississippi River near Vidalia, Louisiana. After unsuccessfully attempting to raise the barge, the owner notified the Army Corps of Engineers that it was abandoning the wreck. Fearful that the lethal chlorine gas would be released, the United States demanded that the owner remove the barge. When this demand was refused, the government raised the barge, chlorine tanks intact, and billed the owner for the cost of the operation, $3,081,000. Finally in 1967, the U.S. Supreme Court ruled that the owner was liable for the cost of the salvage operation, thus terminating this long and costly handling of an environmental emergency. *Wyandotte Transp. Co. v. United States*, 389 U.S. 191 (1967).

Superfund establishes a $1.6 billion Hazardous Substance Response Trust Fund to cover the cost of "timely government responses to releases of hazardous substances into the environment." Funding will be through taxes levied by the Internal Revenue Service on certain designated, potentially dangerous chemicals and on petroleum products. For example, of the forty-two designated chemicals, acetylene, benzene, and butane are taxed at $4.87 per ton. Sulfuric acid is taxed at 26¢ per ton and nitric acid at 24¢. Crude oil is taxed at 79¢ per barrel, even though the Act does not cover oil spills.

The Act imposes strict liability on the owners of polluting agencies and others for the cost of removal of hazardous wastes and any remedial action deemed necessary. Further, those involved in handling hazardous wastes are required to have liability insurance coverage to help pay the damages resulting from releases of hazardous substances into the environment.

While many feel that Superfund penalizes entire industries for the isolated misdeeds of a few companies, the cleanup of toxic waste sites continues as a high-priority item. The Congressional Office of Technology Assessment predicted in 1985 that some 10,000 waste sites may require cleanup under Superfund at a cost of $100 billion and could require 50 years of concentrated effort. In late 1985 the Senate passed and sent to the House its proposed bill to expand the Superfund program and proposed an appropriation of $7.5 billion. Environmentalists urge that this amount falls far short of what is needed.

Toxic Substances Control Act

In addition to the identifiable pollutants that are controlled at the source by the EPA, a more serious threat may be posed by the thousands of chemicals and compounds that are manufactured for commercial and generally beneficial use. These include herbicides, pesticides, and fertilizers, some of which may be highly toxic as single elements or which may become toxic when combined with other elements. It has recently become apparent that toxic substances, initially applied to serve some useful purpose, are working their way into the environment by various means. Of grave concern is the long-range effect such substances have on human health. It is not presently known how humans are affected if exposed to low concentrations of chemicals over a long period of time. The current experience at Times Beach, Missouri, and other communities where deadly dioxins were deposited years ago indicates that there may be severe health problems for the residents of those communities.

In 1976 Congress enacted the Toxic Substances Control Act (TSCA). Under the Act the EPA is required to develop a comprehensive inventory of existing chemicals by calling on manufacturers to report the amount of each chemical substance they produce. TSCA imposes testing requirements on manufacturers and requires notice to the EPA when a new substance is being considered for development and production. The main purpose of the Act is to prohibit the introduction of substances that would present an uncontrollable risk. Additionally, TSCA provides for testing, warnings, and instructions leading to the safe use of toxic chemicals with minimal effects on humans and the environment. Enforcement procedures permit the EPA to issue an order to prohibit the manufacture of high risk substances. If the order is challenged by a producer or processor the EPA may seek an injunction in a federal court to stop the proposed manufacturing of the product.

Radioactive Wastes

Federal efforts to find suitable storage and disposal methods for radioactive wastes, from both nuclear weapons development and from the commercial nuclear power industry, intensified during the seventies. Radioactive wastes, which are created as uranium fissions and releases energy in nuclear reactors, are a significant potential environmental hazard which must be isolated from the biosphere for hundreds of thousands of years. The wastes contain both highly radioactive but shorter-lived wastes, with half-lives of tens to hundreds of years, and less radioactive but longer-lived species, such as plutonium, which has a half-life of about 25,000 years. (The half-life of a radioactive element is the time required for a given quantity of the element to decay or disintegrate into one-half of the original quantity. Isolated storage over many half-lives is necessary before most wastes become harmless.)

The lack of permanent, safe storage or disposal for high-level radioactive wastes from nuclear reactors has become a major concern in recent years. Radioactive wastes are now temporarily stored in tanks at commercial and government nuclear facilities. Large quantities of radioactive wastes from nuclear weapons production are stored in tanks and bins at government installations in Idaho, South Carolina, and Washington.

Concern about nuclear radiation and safe disposal of radioactive waste has increased. The nuclear industry's capacity to store its wastes in on-site facilities will soon be reached, perhaps as early as 1988. The problem therefore assumes critical proportions and must be resolved now. The federal Office of Technology Assessment, an agency that performs technical analyses for Congress, has suggested that an independent, single-purpose management agency is needed to ensure the adequate and stable management of high-level nuclear waste disposal.[1] In January 1982 the president signed a bill that specifically addresses the nuclear waste disposal problem. Under this legislation two federally run repositories would be established for the spent fuel accumulations of commercial reactors. One such site would be selected on recommendations of the Department of Energy, by 1987 and licensed by the end of 1990. The other would be chosen by 1990 and licensed by the end of 1993. Six states—Louisiana, Mississippi, Nevada, Texas, Utah, and Washington—are being considered as possible sites. The storage of civilian waste would be paid for by a fee of one mill per kilowatt hour to be charged to customers of nuclear facilities. The charge would be adjusted annually by the Energy Department and the funds would be transferred to a federal trust fund for administration. The sites would also provide storage for military waste.

Noise Control

The Noise Control Act of 1972 represents the first major federal effort to eliminate a problem created by excessive noise emanating from sources to which the public is exposed on a continual basis. It empowers the EPA to establish noise emission standards for specific products in cooperation with agencies otherwise concerned with them and to limit noise emissions from those products that can be categorized as noise producers. The act specifically lists transportation vehicles and equipment, machinery, appliances, and other commercial products. The act subjects federal facilities to state and local noise standards and expressly reserves the right to control environmental noise in the states through licensing and regulation or restriction of excessively noisy products.

Noise pollution law has not developed nearly so rapidly as water and air pollution law. Nevertheless, the problem has been identified and something is being done about it. The thrust of the Noise Control Act is toward reducing environmental noise in an effort to prevent what are recognized as long-range effects (hearing problems) on public health and welfare. Violations of the prohibitions of the act are punishable by a fine of $25,000 per day, one year in prison, or both. A second conviction can result in a fine of $50,000 per day, imprisonment for two years, or both.

The controversy over the British and French airplane, the SST Concorde, when it was put into service to this country is indicative of the concern over

---

[1] High-level wastes are by-products of the reprocessing of used fuel elements from nuclear reactors. Low-level wastes are gaseous, liquid, and solid wastes from reactors and other nuclear facilities.

excessive noise. Many considered the supersonic plane to be so loud that it should not be permitted to fly over and into the United States. Its inaugural and subsequent early flights were highly monitored by U.S. airports to determine precise noise levels for comparison with those of traditional subsonic airplanes. While state and local authorities are given the right to control environmental noise, federal authority is asserted in certain situations where, for example, uniformity is necessary or foreign policy considerations are compelling.

In 1971 the Massachusetts House of Representatives considered an act that would have prohibited the SST from landing anywhere in Massachusetts. However, having second thoughts about the constitutionality of its proposed bill, the House asked the state's high court: "Is it constitutionally competent for [this state] to enact [a bill] which in effect prohibits the landing of any commercial supersonic transport aircraft at any airport within the commonwealth notwithstanding that the operation of such aircraft in interstate and international commerce is regulated by the Congress?" The court answered in the negative reminding the House that the Federal Aviation Authority prescribes standards for the measurement of aircraft noise and sonic boom and rules and regulations for the control and abatement of aircraft noise and sonic boom. The court went on to question whether such a bill would impose an unreasonable or discriminatory burden on interstate commerce or conflict with treaty obligations of the United States Government.

Resource Management

There is a difference of opinion as to how to best utilize this country's natural resources. Unrestricted strip mining and the ongoing search for new sources of gas and oil have had what environmentalists consider to be an adverse impact on the areas affected by the need for additional energy. On the other side are the industrialists, primarily lumber and oil interests, who predict dire consequences if more lands and offshore sites are not opened for exploitation. Under the Carter administration millions of acres of federal land were set aside as wilderness areas immune from commercial ventures that would detract from their natural beauty. The Reagan administration, however, has reconsidered this policy with a view to opening up more federal land for development. In early 1983, for example, the administration decided to reevaluate how much mining, drilling, and other development it will permit on 29 million acres of federal land that includes large parcels previously designated as wilderness areas.

The administration has been criticized by environmental groups, such as the Wilderness Society and the Sierra Club, for its alleged insensitivity to the need to protect and preserve much of the natural beauty of the land for future generations. It is likely, however, that some balance will have to be struck. The need for new sources of energy and raw materials may take precedence over the preservation of wilderness areas, but measures will no doubt be adopted that will minimize the permanent damage caused by commercial development.

The EPA, Industry, and Society

The interplay between government and industry becomes ever more heated and intense as the EPA develops and promulgates myriad complex regulatory measures with which industry is hard put to comply. Society, the consuming public, bears much of the brunt of the struggle since it pays the taxes to support the regulatory agencies and the higher prices made necessary by the increased cost of production to industry. Public and private expenditures for pollution control in 1979 totaled $54 billion, 2.3 percent of the gross national product. Yet, in one area, clean air, a recent Harris poll revealed that 80 percent of the public are opposed to the easing of existing federal air pollution regulations. Consequently, the early zeal with which the pollution problem was attacked, controlling it no matter what the cost, is still present in a large segment of society. However, the goals set by the environmentalists in many areas, such as auto emissions, sulfur dioxide and acid rain, and hazardous waste disposal, may prove to be difficult to reach and maintain.

The Reagan administration has proposed and is implementing regulatory relief in several areas. The "bubble concept" for controlling air pollution provides industry with some degree of flexibility. The Office of Management and Budget, now assigned a greater role in the oversight of EPA regulations, has indicated that the EPA has not given enough attention to balancing the cost of industry compliance with the benefits to be derived from major environmental regulations, which signals a trend toward greater economic consideration by the administration. Nevertheless, while there may be some easing of regulation if the economic impact of pollution control is given more consideration, efforts to clean up the environment will quite likely withstand the challenge.

Questions and Problems

1. In 1981 explosions occurred in the Louisville, Kentucky, sewer lines. It was determined that the Ralston Purina Company had caused the explosion by discharging 18,000 gallons of hexane (a flammable and explosive industrial solvent) into the Louisville sewer system. What environmental protection laws may Ralston Purina be guilty of violating?

2. A paper recycling company in Wells River, Vermont, was found by the EPA to be polluting the Wells River and was ordered by the federal court to install pollution control equipment at the plant. Subsequent inspections by EPA revealed that the pollution control equipment had been obtained but never installed and that the president of the firm had falsified reports regarding the level of pollutants in the discharged waste material. If the company is held to be liable for its actions, to what extent, if at all, can penalties be imposed on its president?

3. Union Electric Co., an electrical utility company servicing metropolitan St. Louis and large portions of Missouri, was informed that sulfur dioxide emissions from its coal-fired generating plants violated the Missouri plant sulfur dioxide restrictions. Union claimed that it had encountered economic and technological difficulties that made compliance with the emission limitations impossible. For example, it claimed that low-sulfur coal had become too scarce and expensive; that the installation of unsatisfactory sulfur dioxide removal equipment would cost over $500 million; and that to operate and maintain such equipment would cost over $120 million a year. Should the EPA grant this company a variance, if to do so would permit the company to operate? Discuss the economic implications of this situation. (*Union Electric Co. v. EPA*, 427 U.S. 246, 1975.)

4. Why has it taken so many years to discover that hazardous wastes were being disposed of in ways that have proven to be extremely dangerous to the human environment? What steps are being taken to correct the problem?

5. There seems to be a move toward more cost analysis in the environmental regulation area. Should the relaxing of standards for controlling auto emissions, effluents into waterways, and sulfur dioxide into the atmosphere be governed by the state of the economy? If the EPA is acting on its own to ease restrictions on "big business," should legislation be enacted to strengthen present laws so that the human environment becomes more important than the economy? Could a formula be devised under which environmental regulations could be held in abeyance during periods of economic recession?

6. The Georgia State Implementation Plan for achieving compliance with the National Ambient Air Quality Standards of the Clean Air Act would reduce the ground level intensity of sulfur dioxide emissions by requiring the construction of very tall stacks. This would permit harmful pollutants to be dispersed over a wider area thus reducing ground level concentrations in the vicinity of the facility. Is Georgia's plan likely to withstand attack by environmentalists? (*Natural Resources Defense Council, Inc. v. EPA*, 489 F.2d 390, 1974.)

7. The General Services Administration proposed to build an annex to the U.S. courthouse in lower Manhattan that would include a jail and detention center known as the Metropolitan Correction Center. Residents and business people of the area objected to this project since traffic would be increased and the jail and detention center would be frequented by drug users and criminals. The District Court denied an injunction against construction, holding that the proposed major federal action would not "significantly affect the quality of the human environment." Do you agree? (*Hanly v. Kleindienst*, 471 F.2d 823, 1972.)

8. An employee of Standard Oil of Kentucky accidentally left open a shut-off valve, causing a large quantity of aviation gasoline to flow into the St. Johns River in Florida. The Rivers and Harbors Act of 1899 provides, in part, that: "It shall not be lawful to throw, discharge, or deposit . . . any refuse matter of any kind or description whatever other than that flowing from streets and sewers and passing therefrom in a liquid state, into any navigable water of the United States." Is commercially valuable gasoline considered refuse for purposes of the Act, thus making Standard Oil guilty of a violation? (*U.S. v. Standard Oil Co.*, 384 U.S. 224, 1966.)

9. Several states have enacted so-called bottle bills requiring that beer and soft drinks be sold only in returnable glass bottles. If such statutes are held to be constitutional, withstanding challenges by bottling firms as violations of the commerce, due process, and equal protection clauses, what are the environmental implications? Consider also the efforts by the aluminum industry to clean up the great outdoors. (*American Can Co. v. Oregon Liquor Control Commission*, 517 P.2d 691, 1973.)

10. Is it true that under the Superfund concept the cost of cleanup of hazardous waste dump sites will be borne by the government using funds paid into the Hazardous Substance Response Trust Fund?

C · H · A · P · T · E · R 20

THE LEGAL ENVIRONMENT OF INTERNATIONAL BUSINESS

Introduction

This chapter provides an introduction to the basic aspects of international trade as they bear most directly on persons engaged in commercial transactions across national borders. It does not pursue in any detail many related and very important fields such as public international law, which regulates legal and political relationships among sovereign states, and private international law, which comprises a system of rules used to identify the law applied in a given matter where a choice exists among several legal systems.

International trade law has a long and interesting history in Western society. It extends at least as far back as Greek and Roman practices which regulated trade among the nations encompassed within their empires. This body of law continued to evolve and flourish with increasing trade activity in the Middle Ages until there emerged a set of truly international principles cutting across national boundaries and observed by commercial people throughout Europe, identified as ***lex mercatoria***, the law merchant. The commercial codes now in force in most European nations and almost all states of the American Union are the direct descendants of these medieval legal models.

An interesting and important aspect of these codes—both early and modern—is that they are attempts to formalize existing commercial practice and give it the force of law. The early codes were not, in the main, sparked by a desire or need for external, governmental regulation through national law. They were upheld by commercial traders even where they were at odds with local law, and they were frequently enforced through special commercial courts separate and apart from the regular court system which applied "regular" law. Many aspects of this *lex mercatoria* remain today, as in the provisions of the Uniform Commercial Code which "legalize" commercial customs, and in the existence in many European countries of separate commercial courts, which apply their own separate commercial codes.

Today we classify within the term "international trade" any movement of goods, services, or capital across national boundaries. In its normal use, the term includes three major components:

1. The *export* of goods, services, or commodities from one country to another
2. The *import* of goods, services or commodities into one country from another
3. Of increasing importance since the end of the Second World War, *foreign direct investment*, such as the acquisition of interests in capital facilities in one country by investors from another.

Each of these components of international trade is distinct from the other; each raises particular legal and business issues; and each has been met with a distinct legal response intended to facilitate, harmonize, and regulate this aspect of global commercial and economic relations. With the growth in complexity of modern trade, the competition among nations as expressed in trade policy, and the growing presence of centrally planned economies in socialist bloc and Third World countries, the three main facets of international trade noted above have come to demonstrate, to varying degrees, three different sources of regulations:

1. Procedures developed by the *international trading community*, intended to ease trading relations and foster the resolution of disputes
2. Regulations developed by national governments designed to protect national trading interests and to make them more competitive in international markets
3. Laws and standards for international trade relations established by *international governmental organizations* such as the United Nations and the Organization for Economic Cooperation and Development, intended to harmonize trading community and national principles, to eliminate trade abuses, and to develop a greater participation in world trade, especially on the part of those nations which form the Third World.

This chapter will examine some of the major features of each of these components of the international trade framework.

The International Sales Contract

Although foreign direct investment has become an increasingly important factor in world trade in the last thirty years, most international business transactions still relate to the transfer of goods across national frontiers. This type of transaction—an export from the seller's perspective and an import from the buyer's point of view—is fundamentally a contract of sale, much like its domestic cousin in its essential features. However, special factors complicate the international sales transaction that are usually not present in domestic sales. Great distances will normally separate the buyer and seller and this circumstance will raise nettlesome issues of transportation costs, including **inland freight** from the seller's plant, **ocean-** or **air-freight** for the international transport of the goods, and costs for movement from the place of import to the buyer's place of business. Insurance of the goods at each point of the transaction should be addressed. Moreover, the parties to the sale each represent different legal systems; the parties should therefore consider the choice of law to apply to the transaction. Usually the law of the seller or the buyer will apply to the transaction but, in some special cases, a third legal system may be selected. An overriding factor in the formation of the international sales contract is that the parties do not, in the normal situation, know each other; this ignorance can lead to uneasiness over the creditworthiness of the buyer and the dependability of the seller, and anxiety about the enforcement of the obligations of the parties if there should later be a breach of the contract.

In response to these and other concerns, international private sector traders have, over the course of centuries, devised a series of specialized but fairly standard techniques and legal devices. These frequently take the form of supplementary or "side" contracts which support and facilitate the performance of the basic sales contract, which remains the heart of the transaction. The international sales transaction is, therefore, best understood as a complex of interrelated contracts.

Financing the Transaction: The Letter of Credit

Because of the presumed lack of knowledge on the part of the seller (who is usually the exporter of the goods) as to the creditworthiness of the buyer, typical domestic methods of payment for goods sold (such as cash or sale on open account) do not lend themselves well to the international sales transaction. For this reason, the export trade has developed a traditional reliance on the **letter of credit** financing device.[1] Basically, the letter of credit is an assurance by the bank of the buyer (the importer) in finalized form (i.e., "irrevocable") that funds in payment for the goods sold by the exporter/seller

[1] Standardization in the use and implications of the letter of credit device has been advanced by the publication of *Uniform Customs and Practice for Documentary Credits*, Publication No. 400, (Paris: The International Chamber of Commerce, 1984).

are available and beyond the control of the buyer and that these can be obtained by the seller, without the intervention of the buyer, when the seller performs certain stipulated acts and formalities. These obligations of the seller normally relate to the provision of documentary proofs that the goods have been shipped and that other contractual obligations of the seller have been fulfilled and are thus beyond the arbitrary control of the seller.

The letter of credit is essentially a means to make the seller comfortable that the goods will be paid for and to assure the buyer that the purchase money will not be released to the seller until proper, conforming goods are suitably shipped.

The letter of credit basically is a contract between the seller and the bank of the buyer/importer. It also entails contractual commitments between the buyer and the bank. Most often, the buyer does not have sufficient funds on deposit with the bank issuing the letter of credit to pay for the goods outright. Otherwise the buyer could have arranged for a simpler, more direct method of payment to the seller, such as a direct cash payment or a bank transfer. Therefore, the letter of credit procedure is, from the perspective of the buyer, much like a loan and, like a loan, it often involves subsidiary contractual arrangements to assure the bank of timely repayment. These arrangements address issues regarding time terms, rates of interest, and security or collateral to guarantee repayment to the bank. Unlike the usual bank loan transaction, however, the bank commits itself to distribute funds not to the borrower, but rather to the borrower's business partner, the seller of the goods.

This pattern can become further complicated, however, by the simple fact that the seller may have no more confidence in the buyer's bank than in the buyer itself. The buyer's bank is, after all, typically a foreign bank, located at a great distance from the seller and situated in a foreign jurisdiction. It is not unusual, then, for the seller to involve its own bank in these transactions to transmit the funds or to confirm or guarantee the performance of the buyer's bank which is issuing the letter of credit. In these circumstances, the seller's bank may undertake only to accept the transfer of funds from the buyer's bank and to credit these to the account of the seller (an "advising" bank); it may go further, however, and contract to guarantee this payment to the seller (a "standby" or "confirming" bank).[2] In either event, an additional layer of contractual obligation will appear, this time between the seller and its bank and, further, between the seller's bank and the buyer's bank.

The seller's right to payment from the bank under the letter of credit arrangement will depend upon the presentation to the bank of all required documents to prove the shipment of the goods in accordance with the contract of sale. These documents can include:

[2] American banks have traditionally been reluctant to involve themselves with "standby" letters of credit. Recent amendments to the ICC's *Uniform Customs and Practice for Documentary Credits* may encourage them to use the standby procedure which has long been a feature of European banking.

Inland and ocean **bills of lading** to establish receipt of the goods by the shipper and to serve as "documents of title" for the merchandise

Commercial invoices and packing lists to attest to the contents of bulk and packaged materials

An **export license** and shipper's export declaration to show compliance with any applicable export controls

Any **import licenses**, consular invoices, or **certificates of origin** necessary to comply with the import laws of the receiving country

All of these documents must be in strict compliance with the terms set out in the letter of credit, a principle which is illustrated by the following case.

Board of Trade of San Francisco v. Swiss Credit Bank
728 F.2d 1241 (9th Cir. 1984)

Swiss Credit Bank refused to honor a letter of credit issued in favor of the plaintiff's assignor (Antex Industries) for the sale of 92,000 microchips to Electronic Arrays for use in electronic computers. When the letter was presented to the bank, it was accompanied by an air waybill showing that the goods had been airfreighted to their destination. The letter of credit stipulated that a "full set clean on board bills of lading," evidencing ocean shipment of the microchips, was to have been presented.

Boochever, Circuit Judge:

. . . SCB dishonored the letter of credit because of Antex's failure to comply with its terms. [It is conceded] for purposes of this appeal that the letter of credit required marine shipment and that Antex's air shipment was nonconforming. [It is maintained], however, that the dishonor was improper, because the manner of shipment was not material.

This court's earlier decision in the case precludes [the] argument that Antex's noncompliance with the terms of the letter of credit was not a material defect. . . . As we noted in the prior decision, strict compliance with the letter's terms was required:

The Bank notes that strict compliance with the terms of the letter of credit is required. . . . In this case the shipment was by air, not ocean; and if the Bank's interpretation of the letter of credit is correct, the refusal to pay was not wrongful.

Even if we were not bound by the prior decision, we would reach the same result. The issuer of a letter of credit should not be placed in the position of having to determine whether an unauthorized method of shipment is material. In this instance, whether air shipment would have been considered hazardous by the parties or apt to cause damage to sensitive electronic equipment is not the type of evaluation that should be required in a transaction where promptness and certainty are of the essence. Absent a waiver, an issuer may insist on strict compliance with the terms of a letter of credit. In fact, the parties here agreed to be bound by the Uniform Customs and Practice for Documentary Credits (1974 Revision) International Chamber of Commerce (Brochure No. 290), which requires strict compliance with all terms of the letter of credit.

We conclude that SCB was justified in dishonoring the letter of credit because of Antex's failure to comply with its terms. The district court's judgment is AFFIRMED.

★ ★ ★

The complexity of these multilayered arrangements is greatly reduced by the frequency with which they are used and their corresponding familiarity in the international trading community. It may help to chart out the usual financing techniques of a typical international sales transaction in goods.

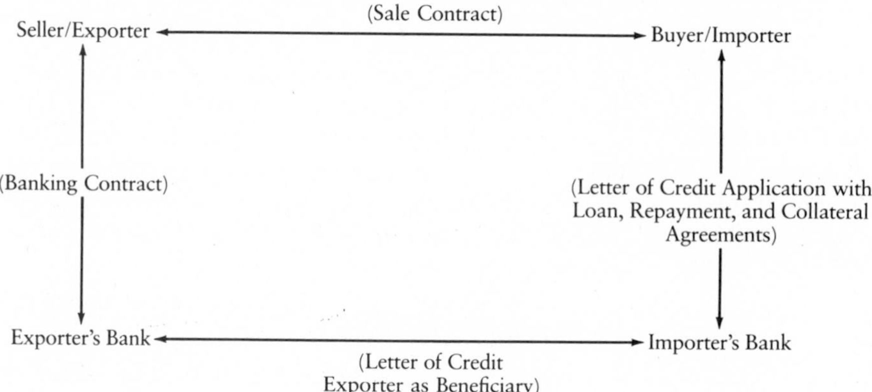

Trade Terms

Financing is, of course, only a means to an end, and a myriad of other factors—almost all of them bearing directly on the ultimate price paid for the goods—will be resolved in the terms of the international sales contract. The parties may wish to provide for a fixed rate of currency exchange or to specify the currency of payment for the contract; they may elect to identify the "official" language of the sales contract, or to provide that two or more languages each represent the agreed terms of the transaction; they may choose the applicable law and identify the court which will have jurisdiction in the event of a subsequent disagreement; or they may decide to refer any contract disputes to binding or nonbinding arbitration. Contract clauses such as these, while very important, may or may not appear in the final contract, depending upon a host of subtle factors, including the current economic and political climate, the degree of mutual trust and familiarity between the parties, the extent to which they share common linguistic, cultural, business, or legal traditions, and others. For instance, an American exporter will have, in most cases, fewer questions about the conditions of commerce with a long-time Canadian business associate than, for instance, with a first-time trading partner in Sri Lanka or Liechtenstein.

Certain central issues must, however, be dealt with in any international sales agreement regardless of the degree of familiarity between the parties or how comfortable they may be with each other. This is due to the direct relation of these issues to the ultimate price. Among these issues are the cost of the goods, freight, and insurance; the method of payment; and the associated questions of the timing of the passage of title to the goods and the transfer of the risk of loss. The importance of these matters is difficult to overstate: the factors of distance, language barriers, and general unfamiliarity between the parties to the international sales contract lead naturally to an increased concern with the allocation of basic rights and responsibilities. So universal is this concern, and of such a long-standing nature within international trade history, that certain commonly accepted **trade terms**, addressing these issues and clarifying them through usage, have evolved over time within the international trading community.[3]

There are a variety of recognized and accepted trade terms to provide for the differing patterns chosen by the parties to allocate responsibilities between themselves, but perhaps the most commonly used trade term today is the "C.I.F." designation. C.I.F. stands for "cost, insurance, and freight;" the term is a shorthand expression for the international sales contract under which the seller quotes a price which is inclusive of the cost of the goods (which will, of course, reflect a large number of factors related to the production of the goods as well as the seller's profit margin), shipping charges, and a marine insurance policy providing at least minimum coverage.

In such an arrangement, the buyer is paying the insurance premium to insure the goods and cover risks during international sea carriage (although, in most instances, the seller will take the measures necessary to obtain this policy because of its greater familiarity with local insurers). Therefore, the use of the C.I.F. term implies that the risk of loss rests on the seller during inland transit, i.e., from the factory to the port of shipment. However, when the goods clear the ship's rail, the risk of their damage or destruction is then covered under the marine insurance policy (paid for by the buyer in the C.I.F. term) and the risk of loss passes to the buyer at that point. In legal terms, "title" to the goods (at best a fiction with limited utility) then passes to the buyer and, with it, the attendant risk of loss.

Other trade terms are frequently employed. F.A.S. ("Free Alongside Ship") implies that risk of loss will pass from the seller/exporter when the goods are delivered alongside a vessel, usually designated by the buyer. Thus, deliv-

---

[3] Attempts have been made to further standardize these trade terms by the publication of uniform trade term definitions. This work was undertaken in the Revised American Foreign Trade Definitions (RAFTD) of 1941 and subsequently by the International Chamber of Commerce (ICC) in the 1953 publication of "International Commercial Terms" (Incoterms) which has been periodically revised since that time. The Uniform Commercial Code also sets forth definitions of some of these terms and these are, in states which have adopted the UCC, binding as law although subject to express modification by agreement of the parties. The 1980 U.N. Convention on the International Sale of Goods Overseas—not yet adopted by the United States—will displace inconsistent UCC provisions in circumstances where the Convention applies.

ery under the F.A.S. term occurs before that under the C.I.F. term and the risks of damage or destruction of the goods in the onloading operation rest on the buyer. F.O.B. ("Free On Board") contemplates delivery of the goods by seller, usually onto a designated vessel where shipment has been arranged by the buyer. In most instances where the F.O.B. vessel term is used, risk of loss passes at ship's rail as under the C.I.F. term. C&F ("cost and freight") is similar in operation to C.I.F. but, under the former, the buyer will arrange for insurance during carriage, unlike the usual pattern in a C.I.F. arrangement. "Ex" terms (i.e., "ex-factory") can be used to designate a place of delivery from seller to buyer which is other than the location of the carrier—for instance, at the factory, or perhaps, at the ultimate destination of the goods.

Resolving International Trade Disputes

No contract—including one for an international business transaction—can be so tightly drawn that it is totally impervious to later disagreement; similarly, unforeseen changes in circumstances may make performance of the contract impossible or, perhaps, more difficult or expensive than originally contemplated by the parties. An international trader should, therefore, have a clear understanding of the means available to resolve such disputes if they should arise.

Judicial litigation is rarely the best means to resolve any business dispute: the costs associated with it (attorney's fees, court costs, and general expenses) will often offset any profit expected from the transaction. These factors are compounded in transnational litigation.

Difficulties often arise, in the first instance, in identifying a court with proper jurisdiction (power to adjudicate) over the subject of the action (subject matter jurisdiction) or the parties to the transaction (personal jurisdiction). In the United States, courts require a showing of "effects" within this country stemming from the defendant's actions or "minimum contacts" by the defendant with the United States before they will allow themselves to be used as the forum for international litigation. Establishing the existence of such effects or minimum contacts can be difficult. Their existence is indicated by a showing of any of the following:

1. The defendant is present within the territorial jurisdiction of the court.
2. The defendant is domiciled or resident in the court's jurisdiction.
3. The defendant is a citizen of the political unit creating the court.
4. The defendant, a "juridical person," (a corporation or partnership) exists by virtue of the laws of the state asserting jurisdiction.
5. The defendant has expressly or implicitly consented to the court's jurisdiction.
6. The defendant regularly carries on business within the court's jurisdiction.

7. The defendant engages in an activity outside the state which has a substantial, direct, or foreseeable effect within the state.[4]

Some courts have taken the view that even a showing of effects and contacts will not necessarily decide the issue of personal jurisdiction over foreign defendants. The court's discussion in the following case describes the limitations of the "effects" test and suggests other factors which should be considered in resolving personal jurisdiction issues. Many regard the reasoning of the court in *Timberlane* to be superior to that of the traditional "effects" test.

Timberlane Lumber Co. v. Bank of America
549 F.2d 597 (1976)

Timberlane Lumber Company, an American corporation with subsidiary corporations in Honduras, brought a Sherman Act antitrust suit against the Bank of America and several Honduran citizens alleging that the defendants had conspired to shut down the plaintiff's milling operations in Honduras so that the Bank (and its Honduran affiliates and customers) could monopolize Honduran lumber exports to the United States. Timberlane filed suit in a federal court in California, arguing that the illegal activities of the defendants in Honduras had effects in the United States sufficient to vest the American court with personal jurisdiction over the foreign defendants. The District Court dismissed the action for lack of jurisdiction, and the plaintiff appealed.

Choy, Circuit Judge:

. . . There is no doubt that American antitrust laws extend over some conduct in other nations. . . .

That American law covers some conduct beyond this nation's borders does not mean that it embraces all, however. Extraterritorial application is understandably a matter of concern for the other countries involved. Those nations have sometimes resented and protested, as excessive intrusions into their own spheres, broad assertions of authority by American courts. . . . Our courts have recognized this concern and have, at times, responded to it, even if not always enough to satisfy all the foreign critics. . . . In any event, it is evident that at some point the interests of the United States are too weak and the foreign harmony incentive for restraint too strong to justify an extraterritorial assertion of jurisdiction.

What that point is or how it is determined is not defined by international law. . . .

Even among American courts and commentators, however, there is no consensus on how far the jurisdiction should extend. The district court here concluded that a "direct and substantial effect" on United States foreign com-

[4] See American Law Institute, Tentative Draft No. 2, *Restatement of the Foreign Relations Law of the United States (Revised)*, §§401(3) and 441.

merce was a prerequisite, without stating whether other factors were relevant or considered. . . .

Few cases have discussed the nature of the effect required for jurisdiction, perhaps because most of the litigated cases have involved relatively obvious offenses and rather significant and apparent effects on competition within the United States. . . . It is probably in part because the standard has not often been put to a real test that it seems so poorly defined. . . .

Implicit in [the] observation . . . in several of the cases and commentaries employing the "effects" test, is the suggestion that factors other than simply the effect on the United States are weighed, and rightly so. As former Attorney General (then Professor) Katzenbach observed, the effect on American commerce is not, by itself, sufficient information on which to base a decision that the United States is the nation primarily interested in the activity causing the effect. "[A]nything that affects the external trade and commerce of the United States also affects the trade and commerce of other nations, and may have far greater consequences for others than for the United States." Katzenbach, *Conflicts on an Unruly Horse*, 65 Yale L.J. 1087, 1150 (1956).

The effects test by itself is incomplete because it fails to consider other nations' interests. Nor does it expressly take into account the full nature of the relationship between the actors and this country. Whether the alleged offender is an American citizen, for instance, may make a big difference; applying American laws to American citizens raises fewer problems than application to foreigners. . . .

American courts have, in fact, often displayed a regard for comity and the prerogatives of other nations and considered their interests as well as other parts of the factual circumstances, even when professing to apply an effects test. To some degree, the requirement for a "substantial" effect may silently incorporate these additional considerations, with "substantial" as a flexible standard that varies with other factors. . . .

[T]he antitrust laws require in the first instance that there be effect—actual or intended—on American foreign commerce before the federal courts may legitimately exercise subject matter jurisdiction under those statutes. . . .

[Also], there is the additional question which is unique to the international setting of whether the interests of, and links to, the United States—including the magnitude of the effect on American foreign commerce—are sufficiently strong, vis-à-vis those of other nations, to justify an assertion of extraterritorial authority.

It is this final issue which is both obscured by undue reliance on the "substantiality" test and complicated to resolve. An effect on United States commerce, although necessary to the exercise of jurisdiction under the antitrust laws, is alone not a sufficient basis on which to determine whether American authority *should* be asserted in a given case as a matter of international comity and fairness. In some cases, the application of the direct and substantial test in the international context might open the door too widely by sanctioning jurisdiction over an action when these considerations would indicate dismissal. At other times, it may fail in the other direction, dismissing a case for which comity and fairness do not require forebearance, thus closing the jurisdictional door too tightly—for the Sherman Act does reach some restraints which do not have both a direct and substantial effect on the foreign commerce of the United States. A more comprehensive inquiry is necessary. . . .

What we prefer is an evaluation and balancing of the relevant considerations in each case—in the words of Kingman Brewster, a "jurisdictional rule of reason". . . .

The elements to be weighed include the degree of conflict with foreign law or policy, the nationality or allegiance of the parties and the locations or principal places of business of corporations, the extent to which enforcement by either state can be expected to achieve compliance, the relative significance of effects on the United States as compared with those elsewhere, the extent to which there is explicit purpose to harm or affect American commerce, the foreseeability of such effect, and the relative importance to the violations charged of conduct within the United States as compared with conduct abroad. A court evaluating these factors should identify the potential degree of conflict if American authority is asserted. A difference in law or policy is one likely sore spot, though one which may not always be present. Nationality is another; though foreign governments may have some concern for the treatment of American citizens and business residing there, they primarily care about their own nationals. Having assessed the conflict, the court should then determine whether in the face of it the contacts and interests of the United States are sufficient to support the exercise of extraterritorial jurisdiction.

The comity question is . . . complicated. [Author's note: Generally speaking, "comity" is respect for another nation's sovereignty.] From Timberlane's complaint it is evident that there are grounds for concern as to at least a few of the defendants, for some are identified as foreign citizens. . . . Moreover, it is clear that most of the activity took place in Honduras, though the conspiracy may have been directed from San Francisco, and that the most direct economic effect was probably on Honduras. However, there has been no indication of any conflict with the law or policy of the Honduran government, nor any comprehensive analysis of the relative connections and interests of Honduras and the United States. Under these circumstances, the dismissal by the district court cannot be sustained on jurisdictional grounds.

We, therefore, vacate the dismissal and remand the Timberlane action. [In other words, it is not obvious that Honduran sovereignty will be offended by permitting this case to proceed, so this by itself is not reason enough to dismiss the case. The case is remanded to the district court for full consideration of the various factors discussed.]

★★★

Foreign Sovereign Immunities Act

Even in circumstances where the court would be willing to assert its jurisdiction over the defendant under the effects or the comity tests, it may be barred from doing so because of a personal immunity of the defendant. This bar is most often encountered where the defendant is a foreign state or state agency, a circumstance more frequently present today when many nations—especially those with centrally planned economies—are engaging directly in trading activities. The Foreign Sovereign Immunities Act, passed by Congress in 1976, modifies the absolute sovereign immunity which the common law had recognized but continues to limit a plaintiff's ability to recover a judgment from a foreign state or state agency. The act basically permits suits against foreign sovereigns where the claim arises from either:

1. commercial activity of the foreign sovereign in the United States;
2. activities in the United States related to the sovereign's commercial undertakings outside this country; or
3. commercial actions of the foreign sovereign outside the United States which have direct effects within this nation.

The act imposes additional limitations on the seizure of property of a foreign sovereign to satisfy any judgment which the plaintiff might ultimately obtain.

International Litigation: Other Concerns

In the domestic setting, obtaining service of summons over a proper defendant; obtaining evidence to support the claim through oral depositions, written interrogatories, and document production; and, ultimately enforcing the judgment against a recalcitrant defendant can be troublesome—in the international context, it can be overwhelming. To reduce these barriers to the prosecution of a valid claim, a series of international agreements have been reached which are intended generally to increase international cooperation in these respects.

The Hague Convention on Service Abroad of Judicial and Extrajudicial Documents in Civil or Commercial Matters was concluded in 1965 and became effective in the United States in early 1969. Under the procedure commonly used prior to this Convention, a party to a lawsuit in one country wishing to serve documents on a party in another would normally arrange for the court to transfer the instrument from the court to the foreign ministry which would then forward it through diplomatic channels to the foreign ministry of the receiving state. The latter would then send the document to a local court for subsequent service on the other party. To replace this cumbersome and formal procedure, the Hague Convention provides that each signatory state will maintain a Central Authority to process such papers and expedite their transmission.

Similarly, the Hague Convention on the Taking of Evidence Abroad in Civil or Commercial Matters of 1970 (effective in the United States in 1972) seeks to reduce the barriers raised by national laws to obtaining evidence for use in court and to streamline the discovery process in international litigation. Given the sensitivity of most governments to allowing the affairs of their citizens to be opened up to foreign inspection, resistance to the full implementation of this Convention has been comparatively strong. In part this is due to conservatism in matters of judicial discovery in European legal systems where very little pretrial discovery is permitted and where discovery, when it is allowed, is usually conducted by the judge and not by the private litigants. The Convention creates Central Authorities in each signatory nation through whom discovery requests ("Letters of Request") are channeled; it permits consuls to conduct some discovery procedures regarding their own nationals; and, finally, it allows the use of court-appointed commissioners for discovery purposes in limited circumstances.

The task of enforcing local judgments against parties in other nations has been eased considerably by a number of national statutes and international agreements which afford recognition to foreign court orders. Within the United States, a number of state legislatures have adopted the Uniform Foreign Money-Judgments Recognition Act which permits the enforcement of final foreign money-judgments in civil matters even if the judgment is subject to appeal. Such a judgment can be denied recognition, however, if it was obtained through a court lacking personal or subject matter jurisdiction; if it was procured through fraud or the defendant did not receive timely notice of the proceedings; if there was a prior, conflicting judgment or the parties had earlier agreed to arbitrate their disputes; or if the place of trial was "seriously" inconvenient and the court's power to proceed was premised solely upon personal jurisdiction over the defendant. In more general terms, recognition of a foreign judgment can be withheld whenever it appears it was rendered "under a system which does not provide impartial tribunals or procedures compatible with the requirements of due process of law."

Similarly, federal courts will generally enforce foreign judgments by the doctrine of comity where it is shown that the foreign court had competent jurisdiction and acted in a fair and impartial fashion, no fraud was committed against the defendant, and due notice of the proceeding was provided.

Moreover, international recognition of judicial judgments has been greatly enhanced by multilateral agreements such as the 1961 Hague Convention Abolishing the Requirement of Legalization for Foreign Public Documents (effective in the United States in 1981), which eliminate the necessity for diplomatic or consular legalization of foreign public (including judicial) documents. Other regional measures such as the Inter-American Convention on Extraterritorial Validity of Foreign Judgments and Arbitral Awards of 1975 promote the same objective.

Arbitration

In view of the special difficulties encountered in international court litigation, it is not surprising that the international business community has actively sought alternative methods of commercial dispute resolution.

Arbitration is a process whereby parties to a transaction agree (either within the terms of their basic agreement or subsequently) to submit any future disagreements and disputes to an impartial third party (which may consist of a single individual or a panel) for nonjudicial resolution. The decision of the arbitrator—termed an "award"—may, depending upon the agreement of the parties, be binding or nonbinding.

Arbitration within the international trading context has a long and colorful history. In a real sense, the commercial courts established by the *lex mercatoria* in medieval times had much of the flavor of arbitration, consisting as they did of a board of commercial experts who would hear and decide disputes in accordance with commercial custom, usage, and practice. Arbitration gained renewed popularity in the latter part of the nineteenth century when it was used in the public international law sphere to settle claims of the United States against the United Kingdom arising from the activities of Confederate men-of-war on the high seas, notably the *CSS Alabama*. So great was its appeal that a Permanent Court of Arbitration was established at the Hague in 1899. Arbitration is still used in international commercial circles as the preferred alternative to litigation in the national courts.

The advantages of arbitration are many. It is comparatively less expensive than court procedures and offers the parties the opportunity to select knowledgeable experts to decide the matter rather than turning it over to unknown judges who are typically "generalists." The use of arbitration provides a means to avoid overcrowded courts with their high costs, technical delays, and formalities. Perhaps a primary reason why commercial traders frequently resort to arbitration is the privacy which it affords and the assurance that the award will be based on commercial realities rather than theoretical legal concepts.

Arbitration is not, however, without some disadvantages. Arbitral panels generally do not have the power to compel the attendance of witnesses or the production of other information relevant to the case; the familiar institution of the jury trial is absent; the informality of the procedure can lead to an undesired degree of "looseness" in the process; and, because the arbitrators are generally not bound by the strict letter of the law, the final terms of the award may be somewhat difficult to forecast.

One of the major disadvantages of the arbitral process is the fact that the award is "unofficial" and presents special problem in enforcement. Traditionally, arbitral awards were enforced through a subsequent court judgment which upheld the award as a matter of contract between the parties. The use of the court to enforce arbitral awards deprived the procedure of many of its apparent advantages.

This concern has been greatly reduced through the widespread adoption of the United Nations Convention on the Recognition and Enforcement of Foreign Arbitral Awards, concluded at New York in 1958 and effective in the United States in 1970. This Convention provides, in essence, that arbitral awards issued in one country can be enforced in another upon the presentation of a duly authenticated original award, together with a copy of the agreement upon which it was based. The Convention reserves the right of the receiving state to refuse to recognize a foreign arbitral award in certain circumstances, such as the incapacity of the parties to the agreement, defects in the composition of the arbitral panel, or cases in which the terms of the award either exceed the scope of authority of the arbitral panel or violate the public policy of the receiving country. A similar multilateral agreement was concluded by the Organization of American States in 1975 with the adoption of the Inter-American Convention on International Commercial Arbitration and the Inter-American Convention on Extraterritorial Validity of Foreign Judgments and Arbitral Awards.

So frequent has been the resort to commercial arbitration by the international trading community in this century that several international organizations have sought to facilitate this means of dispute resolution by providing standard arbitral rules and procedures. Chief among these has been the International Chamber of Commerce (headquartered in Paris), the American Arbitration Association, and the United Nations Commission on International Trade Law (UNCITRAL). The arbitration rules adopted by these agencies typically address the procedure for arbitral proceedings, the composition of the arbitral tribunal and various aspects of the arbitral award.

The UNCITRAL rules are unique in several respects. These rules were developed by the Commission after a decade of effort to ensure their compatibility with all the world's legal cultures and to make them more acceptable in developing countries which, to a degree, distrusted and resented the imposition of legal rules and procedures from developed countries. Similarly, the 1965 Convention on the Settlement of Investment Disputes Between States and Nationals of Other States (effective in the United States in 1966) was drawn carefully to be "neutral" with regard to legal bias. This important Convention fills a gap in the international arbitral framework by providing a forum, the International Centre for Settlement of Investment Disputes (ICSID), for the resolution of disagreements in which one commercial associate is a private citizen and the other a sovereign state. The ICSID maintains a Panel of Conciliators and a Panel of Arbitrators to resolve disputes falling within its jurisdiction, which includes any legal dispute arising directly out of an investment where one party is a state which is a signatory of the Convention and the other party is a citizen of another signatory state.

More recently, additional arbitral agencies have been established. The Inter-American Commercial Arbitration Commission and the London Court of Arbitration both attest to the rising popularity of arbitration as a means of resolving international commercial disputes and the frequency with which international traders resort to this process.

National Regulation of the Export/Import Process

The impact of export trade transcends, of course, the private interests of the parties to the international sales contract. Concerns at the national level touch upon defense and security matters (especially in the export of high technology with military applications) and the depletion of national stocks of critical materials. Moreover, the volume and direction of flow of export sales are inextricably bound up in the general economic posture of a nation and thus bear directly on its overall pattern of foreign relations. Not surprisingly, almost all nations have responded to these factors by adopting broad regulatory schemes to control exports. The implementation of these programs will directly affect the international trader and the methods used in that trade.

In the United States, the power to regulate international trade is vested in the Congress under the provisions of the Commerce Clause of the federal Constitution. Congress has used this power repeatedly since the early days of the Republic and the trail of congressional legislation dealing with import and export matters continues into the present day. The Export Administration Act of 1979 is perhaps the most important piece of federal legislation impacting American export traders today.

Export Administration Act

The Act is a comprehensive scheme to regulate exports from the United States and, together with the regulations adopted pursuant to it, extends its controls in some instances to the re-export of certain American goods to third countries. In general terms, it provides for three broad types of required export licenses:

1. A general license authorizing exports—this type of license covers the vast bulk of American exports and is normally issued by the Office of Export Administration of the Department of Commerce without a formal application by the exporter
2. A qualified general license authorizing multiple exports
3. A validated license relating to a specific export.

The latter two types of export license will be required only when the exported goods are of a kind, or their destination is to a place, which disqualify them for export under the general license.

The Export Administration Regulations (found in the Code of Federal Regulations) round out, define, and implement the provisions of the 1979 act. They contain a Commodity Control List which will assist the exporter in identifying circumstances where a validated export license must be obtained and where a general license will not suffice. In most instances, this decision is a function of what commodity is going to which country. Some few nations (North Korea, Cuba, and Vietnam, among others) are virtually closed to American exports. These regulations also contain provisions relating to the export of technical data (as opposed to commodities, which are treated as a separate and distinct category for licensing purposes). The general license "GTDR" controls the export of technical data both in terms of destination and the degree of "public accessibility" to the information; a more liberal license, the general license "GTDA," allows technical data exports to virtually any destination if the data meets the regulations' standard of public availability. A 1985 amendment to the Export Administration Act also provides for a comprehensive operations license to govern exports from American corporations to offshore affiliates and subsidiaries. This type of license will have frequent use within transnational corporate systems.

The 1979 act has provisions which are directly related to defense and national security interests of the United States. Any new technology developed through research funding by the Department of Defense requires the consent of that Department before it can be exported; moreover, a 1985 amendment to the act calls upon the Commerce Department and the Department of Defense to merge the Militarily Critical Technologies List (maintained by the Department of Defense) with the Commodities Control List provided for in the Export Administration Regulations to make export control over such materials more efficient and less subject to gaps. In the foreign policy field, recent amendments to the Export Administration Act prohibit export controls on shipments of donated goods relating to basic human needs.

Where an exporter unsuccessfully seeks a required export license, an appeals procedure through the Department of Commerce is established in the 1979 act. It specifically allows court action against the Department where the desired license is denied in the statutory appeals process.

Although the Export Administration Act is the major source of export regulation in the United States, it is by no means the only one.[5] Export control provisions are also found in the Nuclear Non-Proliferation Act (1978) and Atomic Energy Act (1954) which govern the export of nuclear materials. The Arms Export Control Act, the Trading with the Enemy Act, and the International Emergency Economic Power Act also contain important export restrictions.

Export Incentives

United States export policy and legislation is not, however, totally negative. Important legislation has long been on the books to encourage increased export trade by manufacturers and suppliers in this country.

As early as 1918, Congress adopted the Webb-Pomerene Act to promote American export trade by granting limited exemptions to exporters from the application of U.S. antitrust laws, principally the Sherman and Clayton Acts. Congress acted in the belief that American traders could better compete in foreign markets if they were permitted to form associations capturing the benefits of economies of scale and greater efficiency; such associations, however, involved a danger of criminal or civil liability under American antitrust laws. The Webb-Pomerene Act, therefore, relieved export associations of this risk, but conditioned the exemption in important respects. Principally, such an association is prohibited by the act from en-

[5]Note, too, the impact of other federal legislation impacting on the conduct of international business. For instance, the Foreign Corrupt Practices Act controls bribery and other undesirable acts abroad. This act is considered separately in Chapter 21.

tering into any agreement which "artificially or intentionally" depresses commodity prices within the United States or which "substantially lessens competition within the United States, or otherwise restrains trade therein." Further, the benefits of the act (obtained by registration of the association with the Federal Trade Commission) are limited to associations formed for the export of commodities; transactions for services or technology are not protected. As a result of these limitations and lingering anxiety about possible antitrust liability, comparatively few Webb-Pomerene associations are registered with the FTC.

Export Trading Company Act

The failure of the 1918 legislation to promote greater American export trade, coupled with increasing U.S. trade deficits[6] in the mid- and late 1970s, created a sense of urgency in Congress to devise new and more effective means to encourage increased exports from this country, especially by small- and medium-sized companies historically underrepresented in international trade transactions. The legislative response was the Export Trading Company Act of 1982.

At the heart of this Act is its provision that:

. . . [N]o criminal civil action may be brought under the antitrust laws [of the United States] against a person to whom a certificate of review is issued [by the Secretary of Commerce] which is based on conduct which is specified in, and complies with the terms of, a certificate . . . which . . . was in effect when the conduct occurred.

This exemption is available to individual persons resident in the United States; partnerships or corporations created under state or federal law; and, significantly for antitrust purposes, "any association or combination, by contract or other arrangement" between or among any of these.

The Secretary of Commerce is empowered to issue the protective certificate of review whenever it is shown that the activities of the applicant company will not result in a "substantial lessening of competition or restraint of trade within the United States nor a substantial restraint of the export trade of any competitors of the applicant," and whenever the application demonstrates that these activities will not "unreasonably" impact the U.S. price of the goods or services exported by the company or constitute an "unfair method of competition" against the exporter's competitors. The Secretary may deny

[6]The United States never experienced a trade deficit—an excess of imports over exports—until 1971. Between 1971 and 1976, however, the American trade deficit rose to $5 billion, due largely to massive (and expensive) oil imports which amounted to $77 million in 1981 alone. By 1982, the deficit had risen to crisis proportions—$42 billion. See Hirschhorn, "A Shot in the Arm for American Exports," 69 A.B.A.J. 746 (1983) and *Economic Indicators, Joint Economic Committee of the Council of Economic Advisors*, 98th Cong., 1st Sess., 35–37 (May 1983).

the application for the certificate, however, unless the applicant shows that the goods or services will not be reimported back into the United States or consumed there.

The act's scope is comprehensive. It extends its antitrust protection to activities related to the export of goods and merchandise and (going beyond the reach of the Webb-Pomerene Act) to services. This latter category is defined to include services which are the subject of the transaction (as in transborder management agreements) and includes accounting, architectural, data processing, business, communications, consulting, and legal services, among many others. Also eligible for exemption from possible antitrust liabilities are "export trade services," i.e., international market research, product research and design, transportation, warehousing, insurance, and the like.

The Export Trading Company Act also contains important provisions which modify statutory impediments that separate the banking community from participation in international trade. Title II of the act (termed the Bank Export Services Act) permits banks to invest in export trading companies up to the statutory limit of 5 percent of their consolidated capital and surplus; further, they are also allowed to own such companies outright. These provisions are intended to marshall substantial capital to promote international trade. The absence of such funding has hobbled export trade in the past since many small- and medium-sized banks were reluctant to finance "speculative foreign ventures" over which they had little or no control.

The first certificates of review under the Export Trading Company Act were not issued by the Department of Commerce until late 1983 and it is perhaps too early to predict its utility in promoting international trade. The act is, nevertheless, proving itself quite popular in the international trading community.

Regulating Imports

Compared with the elaborate nature of export controls and incentives, the regulation of imports into the United States is relatively straightforward. The application of these import control laws can, however, be quite complex.

Under the Import-Export Clause of the federal Constitution, the power to levy import customs and duties rests exclusively with the federal government. Using federal power in this regard, the government has established a comprehensive system of tariff schedules which apply to goods entering the United States—the Tariff Schedules of the United States (TSUS). The TSUS will be applied by federal customs officials first, to classify the entering goods and then, to determine the applicable tariff rate to the goods so classified. The actual rate is, of course, set by the federal government, but it may do so subject to bilateral or multilateral restraints which it has assumed for example, a treaty with another nation may stipulate the tariff level or, more generally, the applicable tariff may have been negotiated within the framework of a multinational commitment, e.g., the General Agreement on Tariffs and Trade (GATT). In either event, the tariff generally must be paid before the goods are admitted into this country.

An important exception to this principle is the use of a Foreign Trade Zone. Established by federal law, these Zones (FTZs) are fenced-off, policed warehouses and industrial parks usually located near American ports of entry. Goods entering the port from abroad may be taken into the FTZ and stored there without paying any applicable tariff and with a minimum of formality and procedure. As long as the goods are warehoused within the FTZ, no duty is payable and the goods may be further processed, assembled, or finished. Only when the merchandise leaves the confines of the FTZ will the duty be imposed, frequently at a reduced rate. The FTZ has shown itself to be an effective device for encouraging additional international trade in the United States.

While import licenses are generally not required for imports into the United States, certain goods may be denied entry altogether. Such bans on importation may be applied against undesirable imports such as narcotics, pornographic material, or printed materials advocating the violent overthrow of the United States. Other import bans may be applied to prevent entry of automobiles which do not meet vehicle safety regulations or other products not meeting standards established to protect public health and safety. Products violating the patent, trademark, and copyright laws of the United States may also be excluded. Moreover, certain goods may be subjected to tariff increases to offset foreign government subsidies which unfairly reduce their U.S. market price, or to counteract a foreign producer's deliberate attempt to destabilize or destroy the product's domestic production in the United States. These "countervailing" and "antidumping" measures are considered again in this chapter with regard to the General Agreement on Tariffs and Trade (GATT).

Organizing For International Trade

The massive devastation of the Second World War touched millions of lives and left in its wake incalculable physical destruction on two continents. Another casualty of the war was the international trade infrastructure which had been growing slowly but perceptibly since the middle of the nineteenth century. One of the major tasks of reconstruction following 1945 was the recreation of a framework for international trade. The negotiations leading to the establishment of modern institutions of the international economic system during and immediately after World War II focused on those international economic exchanges that were regarded as the most important ones at that time: trade, money, and finance. These negotiations led to the General Agreement on Tariffs and Trade, the International Monetary Fund, and the International Bank for Reconstruction and Development. Global concentration on issues relating to trade, money, and finance resulted, conversely, in a certain inattention to issues surrounding primary products, technology, and foreign direct investment. These were not to be addressed internationally in a significant way until the late 1960s and early 1970s.

The United Nations Conference on Trade and Employment met in Havana in late 1947 and early 1948. Attended by more than 50 countries, the conference was boycotted by the Soviet Union and its satellite states. The goal of this conference was, in general terms, to promote the international exchange of goods through increased export activity. To achieve this general objective, the conference drafted the Havana Charter for an International Trade Organization (ITO) which encompassed a general outline for an international trade organization and, together with it, a code of conduct for international trade to be observed by states which would ratify the proposed treaty. Largely because of the Communist boycott, however, the proposed International Trade Organization never came into being.

The Havana initiative was not, however, without a measure of success. In anticipation of the creation of the International Trade Organization at Havana, almost two dozen countries had concluded a General Agreement on Tariffs and Trade (GATT) in late 1947, the essential purpose of which was to achieve a significant reduction of the general level of national tariffs and, further, to provide an institutional framework within which future tariff conflicts could be resolved. The GATT has, since its creation, shown itself to be of enduring significance in international economic and trade relations.

The GATT

The GATT achieves its overall objective of liberalized international trade by addressing a series of key issues regarding import restrictions. It requires that each signatory state extend "most favored nation" tariff rates to goods from other signatory nations and, further, obligates participating nations to afford "national treatment" to the imported goods from other signatory countries. Article III of the agreement provides:

The products of the territory of any contracting party imported into the territory of any other contracting party shall be accorded treatment no less favorable than that accorded to like products of national origin in respect of all laws, regulations and requirements affecting their internal sale, offering for sale, purchase, transportation, distribution or use.

The GATT prohibits discrimination by participating states through quantitative trade restrictions by providing that import quotas, if adopted at all by a state, shall be applied equally to all nations which are parties to the agreement. An even more ambitious objective of the GATT is the elimination of all prohibitions or restrictions (other than duties, taxes, or other charges) on imports and exports among the member nations.

In large measure, the GATT implements its goals of free trade through a series of published tariff schedules which are developed through an intricate negotiation process within the framework of the organization and which, once published, are binding on each of the participating states. In recognition of inevitable trade anomalies and in order to secure the willing participation and cooperation of member states in its tariff reduction program, the GATT provides special circumstances where unilateral exceptions to the schedules of tariffs may be made. The most well known of these relate to antidumping duties and countervailing subsidies.

If the products of one country are "dumped" into another at prices below their fair market value in the exporting country in an effort to disrupt or destroy the domestic production of those goods in the receiving nation, the GATT contemplates that the government of the receiving country may impose an "antidumping duty" in an effort to equalize the domestic price in those goods with the prevailing fair market price in the exporting country. Similarly, where the production of certain goods in the exporting state is heavily subsidized by the government of that nation (leading to a reduced export price for that product), the GATT permits the receiving state to impose a "countervailing duty" to bring the market price up to a competitive level.[7]

In its formative years, the GATT concentrated almost exclusively on measures to reduce tariff barriers to increase international trade. More recently, it has turned its attention to the reduction of nontariff barriers, such as unreasonably restrictive local standards and inaccessible national distribution systems, to further increase the volume of trade among nations.

The IMF

The International Monetary Fund (IMF), like the GATT, is intended to coordinate the activities of governments regarding international trade functions and does not primarily address the individual international trader. Growing out of discussions held at Bretton Woods, New Hampshire, late in the Second World War, the IMF was designed to speed international financial and economic reconstruction by providing an institutional structure

---

[7]Both of these GATT "escape clauses"—permitting the imposition of additional customs payments above the published tariff schedules to offset foreign governmental subsidies and private "dumping" activities—are codified in U.S. trade law. The U.S. Trade Agreements Act of 1979 permits the Secretary of the Treasury to impose antidumping and countervailing duties to correct the price imbalances flowing from such unfair practices. In both instances, however, the U.S. International Trade Commission must first investigate the matter and determine that the practice is materially injuring an American industry or is threatening it with harm that is not inconsequential, immaterial, or unimportant. Such an investigation can lead to very sophisticated economic analyses of the foreign practice. The definition of a governmental "subsidy" for purposes of imposing a countervailing duty can be troublesome. A direct cash subsidy is, perhaps, the clearest case, but what about whole or partial exemptions on property taxes for the warehouses where the goods are kept prior to export to the United States? What about government participation in the research and development of the exported product? Government support for labor relocation programs for the employees of the foreign company which produces the exported product? These were considered recently by the U.S. Court of International Trade in *Agrexco Agricultural Export Co., Ltd. v. U.S.*, 604 Fed. Sup. 1238 (1985).

within which intergovernmental loans would be used to stabilize currency exchange rates and, through a system of credits (termed "Special Drawing Rights" or "SDRs"), to enable member countries to borrow from the fund or from each other as a means of stabilizing their national currencies within the international monetary system. Affiliated with the International Monetary Fund is the International Bank for Reconstruction and Development (IBRD) which was founded to "assist in the reconstruction and development of territories of members by facilitating the investment of capital for productive purposes" and to "promote private foreign investment by means of guarantees or participations in loans and other investments made by private investors." The IBRD, located in Washington, D.C., is permitted under its charter to guarantee, participate in, or make loans to member states and to any business, industrial, or agricultural enterprise in the territories of a member state. The availability through the IMF and IBRD of massive amounts of financial credit was particularly significant in Western Europe during the immediate postwar years and has had, in addition, a very significant role in the industrial development of Asia and Africa in the last several decades.

Regulating the Transnational Corporation

In the early 1970s, a series of economic, political, and legal factors focused international attention on the role and impact of the **transnational corporation** (TNC) in global economic relationships.[8] Third World countries had experienced renewed political and economic strength as a result of the oil

---

[8] International usage differs regarding the proper terminology for the TNC. Most United Nations organs seem to prefer "transnational corporations" but the International Labour Organization (ILO) and the Organization for Economic Cooperation and Development (OECD) have opted for "multinational enterprise." Other variations include multinational corporation and transnational enterprise. These distinctions are not merely semantic: they mask deep disagreements about a legal definition of the TNC. A final, legal statement in this respect has not yet been achieved and the attempt to reach one has led to much delay in the formulation of the various international codes which address the TNC. The OECD Guidelines take this interesting approach to the matter:

A precise legal definition of multinational enterprises is not required for the purposes of the guidelines. These usually comprise companies or other entities whose ownership is private, state or mixed, established in different countries and so linked that one or more of them may be able to exercise a significant influence over the activities of others and, in particular, to share knowledge and resources with the others. The degree of autonomy of each entity in relation to the others varies widely from one multinational enterprise to another, depending on the nature of the links between such entities and the fields of activity concerned. For these reasons, the guidelines are addressed to the various entities within the multinational enterprise (parent companies and/or local entities) according to the actual distribution of responsibilities among them on the understanding that they will co-operate and provide assistance to one another as necessary to facilitate observance of the guidelines. The word "enterprise" as used in these guidelines refers to these various entities in accordance with their responsibilities.

Many of the codes considered in this chapter appear, with their texts, in *Legal Problems of Codes of Conduct for Multinational Enterprises*, Norbert Horn, ed. (Deventer, The Netherlands: Kluwer, B.V., 1980).

crisis of 1973–1974 and seized the opportunity to assert with increased vigor international programs to eliminate neocolonialist economic policies and practices in their relationships with industrialized states. International sensitivity to political abuses in developing countries became fixed on the TNC after the revelation of the roles of the Central Intelligence Agency and American TNCs in the downfall of socialist President Salvadore Allende of Chile. A conceptual framework for these growing concerns was provided when Jean-Jacques Servan-Schreiber published his influential study, *The American Challenge*,[9] which documented the management expertise and worldwide economic influence of American transnational corporations.

Codes of Conduct on Transnational Corporations

The international response to these developments was swift. A Resolution of the U.N. Economic and Social Council of July, 1972, called upon the Secretary General of the United Nations to establish a "Group of Eminent Persons" to study and evaluate allegations of TNC abuses, especially in the Third World. That report, while noting "the potential of multinational corporations," emphasized certain "undesirable effects" of TNC activities in host countries. Of special concern to the group was the impact of TNC operations on the sovereignty and power of the states in which they conduct their business; their influence on government policies in those states, which destabilized host country governments and induced intergovernmental confrontations; and their negative effects on local development in seeking short-term profits, often at the expense of long-term developmental needs of the local economy. The group further recommended a series of measures to address these concerns, chief among which was the establishment of a United Nations Commission on Transnational Corporations together with an associated United Nations Centre on Transnational Corporations. Both of these measures were subsequently implemented.

Among the first priorities of the new commission was the development of a United Nations Code of Conduct on Transnational Corporations, a proposal which is, over ten years later, still under study and negotiation in the United Nations. The UN Code of Conduct on TNCs, in its draft form, addresses key issues of TNC economic relations with the host country, including shared ownership of local affiliates of the TNC, the impact of TNC operations on national balance of payments, issues relating to the operations on national balance of payments, questions regarding the transfer of technology from the parent corporation to its local affiliates, TNC influence on employment and labor conditions in the local economy, and TNC efforts to protect consumers and the environment. While this code is still under consideration, it is virtually certain that it will be completed within the next

---

[9] J.-J. Servan-Schreiber, *The American Challenge* (New York: Atheneum, 1968).

several years. Issues touching upon the legal character of the code—whether it will be voluntary or have the full force of law[10]—and its application to state trading corporations of the socialist bloc nations have been particularly troublesome and account for much of the delay in concluding the code's terms.

Latin America showed no such hesitation in arriving at a regulatory code for TNCs. In 1976, the Commission of the Andean Pact adopted its Decision 24, the intent of which was to "strengthen local subregional sovereignty through a 'homeward-oriented' policy" and to introduce within the Andean subregion "a common regime controlling foreign investment and technology transfer." At the heart of the program imposed by Decision 24 was the requirement that foreign TNCs sell off, over a graduated period of time, a portion of their interests in their local corporate affiliates in order to insure progressively greater local control. Moreover, the decision prohibited new foreign direct investment in public utilities and in other important areas such as magazines and newspapers, television and radio stations, transportation companies, banks, and insurance companies. Economists have debated the effectiveness of this regulatory program and it has been subsequently liberalized to some extent. Nevertheless, the essential framework of the code demonstrates the intense emotion evoked by the TNC in South America.

Nor was the attempt to regulate the TNC confined to "Third World–controlled" organs of the United Nations or disgruntled countries "south of the border." In June 1976 the Organization for Economic Cooperation and Development (OECD)—consisting of the nations of Western Europe and the United States, Japan, and Canada—adopted its "Guidelines for Multinational Enterprises." The provisions of this instrument address virtually every aspect of transnational corporate relations with host nations.

The Guidelines require that TNCs conduct their operations in harmony with the general policy objectives of their host countries, giving "due consideration" to the economic and social policies of those nations regarding industrial development, environmental protection, the development of employment opportunities, and transfers of technology. Further, the Guidelines stipulate that TNCs should divulge corporate information necessary to coordinate their activities with host-country policies and programs and cooperate closely with local community and business interests. Moreover, TNCs are encouraged to permit the maximum degree of flexibility to their local affiliates and to employ, wherever reasonable, local nationals in managerial

---

[10] A debate over the level nature of codes on TNCs still exists. Almost all of them state that they are "voluntary" and are couched in hortatory terms. Still, it is clear that the code provisions have more legal weight than merely pious principles: they are, after all, formal undertakings by the sovereign governments which have agreed to them. See Hans W. Baade, "The Legal Effects of Codes of Conduct for MNEs," in *Legal Problems of Codes of Conduct for Multinational Enterprises*, p. 3, see note 8 above. Baade uses the expression "Zebra code" to suggest that some provisions of these instruments may in fact be binding as law, others not.

and decision-making positions within the corporate network. Additionally, TNCs are cautioned not to engage in improper business practices such as bribery and to refrain from political activities, including political contributions unless permissible under local law.

One of the more controversial provisions of the Guidelines is that of encouraging corporate disclosure of information to host governments with respect to the structure and organization of the TNC, the geographic areas of its operations and activities, information regarding volume of sales within this geographic area, data concerning new capital investment in the area, and the like.

Other terms of the Guidelines caution the TNC against anticompetitive acquisitions, predatory behavior toward competitors, unreasonable refusals to deal, and discriminatory pricing. Considerations of financing, taxation, and employment and industrial relations, together with science and technology issues, are also addressed within the terms of the Guidelines. The express intent behind each of these provisions is "to encourage the positive contributions which multinational enterprise can make to economic and social progress and to minimize and resolve the difficulties to which their various operations may give rise."

Significantly, the OECD instruments of 1976 explicitly acknowledge that the coordination of TNC operations with host-country concerns cannot be accomplished by a unilateral regulatory measure; host-country obligations to the TNC are also considered. Although the Guidelines have received the lion's share of notoriety, they represent but one facet of the OECD program in the field of TNC and host-country harmonization. Adopted simultaneously with the Guidelines was a formal Declaration of the OECD Council of Ministers requiring that host countries provide "national treatment" to TNCs:

". . . [M]ember countries should, consistent with their needs to maintain public order, to protect their essential security interests and to fulfill commitments relating to international peace and security, accord to enterprises operating in their territories and owned or controlled directly or indirectly by nationals of another Member Country . . . treatment under their laws, regulations and administrative practices, consistent with international law and no less favorable than that accorded in like situations to domestic enterprises. . . ."

Other international organizations with specialized fields of interest have also turned their attention to the transnational corporation. In 1977, the International Labour Organization adopted its Tripartite Declaration of Principles Concerning Multinational Enterprises and Social Policy. This instrument calls upon the TNCs to promote employment in the nations where they have operations and to cooperate with labor unions in this respect; to afford equality of opportunity and treatment to its foreign employees without regard to race, color, sex, religion, political opinion, national extraction, or social origin; to provide stability of employment and social security to its foreign employees; to avoid arbitrary dismissal procedures and to promote the training of the employees in its local affiliates; and to maintain favorable conditions and standards relative to wages, benefits, work conditions, safety, and health of these employees. Of paramount importance within the ILO Tripartite Declaration is the emphasis placed upon the right of local employees to organize labor unions and to collectively bargain with the TNC employer.

Similarly, the United Nations Commission on Trade and Development (the UNCTAD, headquartered in Vienna) has had a voice regarding TNC impacts on its areas of concern. The UNCTAD Set of Multilaterally Agreed Equitable Principles and Rules for the Control of Restrictive Business Practices is intended to secure the "creation, encouragement and protection of competition" and the "control of the concentration of capital and wealth, promotion of social welfare and consumer interests, and benefits to the trade and development of developing countries." This instrument is addressed primarily to unfair trade practices, attempts at monopolization, and restraints of trade in much the same manner as the more familiar American antitrust laws. The UNCTAD has also developed an international code of conduct on the transfer of technology which is designed to promote increased international transfers of technology, especially from the developed to the developing world, on fair and reasonable terms and without the intervention of restrictive or unfair business practices in this regard. Underlying this code is the fear on the part of many Third World leaders that transnational corporations will use their dominant market positions and economic power to withhold state-of-the-art technology from licensees in developing countries and will, morever, unfairly restrict the use, transfer, or resale of licensed technology.

In summary, these international codes serve to provide TNCs with better defined environmental and public interest objectives and standards with which to formulate policies and procedures in pursuit of their corporate purposes. In general terms, the codes oblige the TNC to adhere to national standards and policies and to cooperate with host countries by considering the impact of their activities on the welfare of the local population and environment. Most of these codes attempt to achieve this result by host-country monitoring of transnational corporate activities through the required disclosure of relevant information. Thus, the basic duty of TNCs under these codes is to respect and adhere to the laws and regulations of the host country and to use reasonable measures to blunt any detrimental effects arising from their activities for profit.

The New International Economic Order

These multilateral efforts to harness TNCs and harmonize their activities with social and economic aspirations of the countries where they operate should be seen in a larger context of global economic adjustments to accommodate the emerging interests of less developed countries. A number of initiatives—collectively known as the New International Economic Order (NIEO)—have asserted Third World views in economic, political, and legal matters; these are treated with increasing sensitivity on the international level. U.N. General Assembly Resolutions 3201 (Declaration on the Establishment of a New International Economic Order) and 3202 (Programme of action on the Establishment of a New International Economic Order), adopted on May 1, 1974, both address strategies to correct perceived imbalances in global economic relationships. Specific recommendations in these instruments address the core of traditional international business linkages:

Permanent local sovereignty over natural resources should be ensured; these resources should be available to serve the national interests of developing countries.

The operation of producers' associations to control primary commodities should be encouraged and enhanced.

Access to markets in developed countries should be improved.

The costs of insurance and reinsurance should be reduced through the growth of institutions in developing countries to service these markets.

Indigenous transportation networks should be improved in developing countries to raise their capability to support export/import trade.

These instruments also direct attention to Third World needs relative to development finance, special measures to increase industrialization, improved access to technology, and TNC regulation. Many of these principles were reinforced when, in December of 1974, the General Assembly adopted its Resolution 3281, the Charter of Economic Rights and Duties of States, providing that every nation has the right:

—to choose its own economic, social, and political system;

—to regulate foreign investment in its territory;

—to nationalize and expropriate foreign property within its borders, subject to a duty to pay "appropriate compensation."

These rights, with others set forth in the Charter, are the fundamentals of the economic platform of the NIEO.

The principles of the NIEO have not been universally accepted; nor has their articulation through U.N. Resolutions been afforded the status of binding international law on a wide basis. Whether these initiatives—and particularly their efforts to control the TNC—will prove economically sound or politically wise in the long run lies in the realm of speculation. It is beyond debate, however, that these measures are impacting on the methods of international business. They are perhaps the most dramatic development of this century in the evolution of international trade law.

Questions and Problems

1. In the typical case, the subsidiaries of a transnational corporation are themselves separate corporate entities. Shoulds the activities of the foreign subsidiary suffice to make the parent corporation subject to the jurisdiction of the local foreign court? What considerations would prompt the parent corporation to organize its subsidiaries as separate corporate entities? If a foreign corporation manufactures automobiles and sells these to an American subsidiary which then resells them through a distribution chain of separate corporations in the United States, is the foreign manufacturer subject to the jurisdiction of a local American court in an action for damages arising from negligence in the manufacture and design of the automobile? For a case allowing jurisdiction, see *Régie Nationale des Usines Renault v. Superior Court*, 208 Cal. App. 2d 702, 25 Cal. Rptr. 530 (1962); for a case denying jurisdiction, see *Velandra v. Régie Nationale des Usines Renault*, 336 F.2d 292 (6th Cir. 1964). How do you explain the different results?

2. Suppose the existence of a contract to sell widgets to a long-time customer in a neighboring city. What additional terms would you wish to add if the buyer was a first-time customer in England? In South Korea? What concerns do the added terms address?

3. In *Board of Trade of San Francisco v. Swiss Credit Bank*, the court held that the shipper's use of aircraft to transport goods did not strictly comply with the provision of the letter of credit stipulating ocean shipment. Does the manner of shipment make any difference if, in fact, they arrive on time and undamaged? What if the commercial invoices presented to the bank by the seller do not use the same unit of measurement for the goods as used in the letter of credit? The court in *Atari, Inc. v. Harris Trust and Savings Bank*, 599 F. Supp. 592 (N.D. Ill. 1984) said that this was not a basis on which to dishonor the letter of credit. How strict, then, is the doctrine of strict compliance?

4. It is normally important to an exporter that the letter of credit issued in payment for the goods be "irrevocable" so that the buyer/importer cannot cancel the letter after the seller has shipped under the contract. Must the term "irrevocable" be used in the letter of credit to make it so? Will words having the same significance make the letter "irrevocable"? If the letter of credit states that it "shall remain in force for a period of six (6) months," is it an irrevocable letter of credit for that period of time? *Conoco, Inc. v. Norwest Bank Mason City*, 767 F.2d 470 (8th Cir. 1985) held that such language made the letter of credit an irrevocable one.

5. Since the Foreign Sovereign Immunities Act preserves the immunity of sovereign states in important respects, how might a seller be protected against an assertion of this residual immunity from suit in the event of a disagreement? Can the foreign sovereign waive the immunity? How explicit must such a waiver be? See *Resource Dynamics International, Ltd. v. General People's Committee*, 593 F. Supp. 572 (N.D. Ga. 1984), which held that a contract clause specifying American law to be applied in the performance of the contract was an implied waiver of immunity under the Foreign Sovereign Immunities Act.

6. American courts will enforce foreign court money-judgments by comity if, in the terms of *Hilton v. Guyot*, 159 U.S. 113 (1895), the foreign legal system is "likely to secure an impartial administration of justice between the citizens of its own country and those of other countries." By what standard is the "impartiality" test of *Hilton v. Guyot* to be measured? What legal system will define "justice"? Do international standards exist by which these concepts can be defined? Does the rule of this case open the door to racial or cultural prejudice through the selective enforcement of foreign money-judgments?

7. Of what practical importance is the fact that most codes on TNCs do not have formal standing as law? In the *Badger* case, the foreign subsidiary of an American

TNC laid off substantial numbers of local employees without first consulting with their union as stipulated in the OECD Guidelines. Further, it failed to make severance payments required by local law, contending that it was financially unable to do so. The parent corporation disclaimed any liability to the workers on the grounds that the subsidiary was a separate corporate entity and solely responsible for its debts. Enormous pressure was mounted on the parent corporation by European organized labor and, significantly, by other TNCs. Eventually, the parent corporation paid the debt of the subsidiary. The case has been regarded by many as establishing the coresponsibility of parent and subsidiary corporations under the OECD Guidelines; others deny this result. See Blanpain, *The Badger Case and the OECD Guidelines for Multinational Enterprises* (Deventer, The Netherlands: Kluwer B.V., 1977).

8. The possibility of damage is not the only risk that passes to the buyer at ship's rail in a C.I.F. contract. In *Badhwar v. Colorado Fuel & Iron Corp.*, 138 F. Supp. 595 (S.D.N.Y. 1955), goods shipped under a C.I.F. contract from California to Bombay were delayed en route almost six months because of a labor strike on the West Coast, causing damage to the Indian buyer. Neither buyer nor seller was responsible for the delay or the consequent loss to the buyer. The court nonetheless held that the risk of this loss had passed to the buyer when the goods cleared ship's rail in California. Does fault play no role in allocating the risk of loss? What if a seller is responsible for delay or damage after the goods are unloaded? Will this make any difference in a C.I.F. contract?

C·H·A·P·T·E·R 21

CORPORATE SOCIAL RESPONSIBILITY AND BUSINESS ETHICS

In the 1960s the government began to direct some of its energy toward recognizing and treating a variety of social ills with which this country was afflicted. From 1963 to 1972, for example, Congress enacted the Environmental Protection Act, the Equal Pay Act, Title VII of the Civil Rights Act, the Occupational Safety and Health Act, the Equal Employment Act, and several laws to protect the consumer. These laws have as their purpose the resolution or control of a national problem. Each of them is regulatory in nature and imposes a burden on business; they add to the complexity of the legal environment in which business must operate.

By enacting such statutes Congress has, in effect, defined the role of the corporation as a member of society and has to a considerable extent mandated corporate participation in that society. It would thus seem that a corporation that obeys the law, pays its taxes, and meets the other requirements imposed by statutes would be viewed as a solid citizen, socially aware and socially responsive, but business is increasingly being asked to play an even greater role and assume a larger share of the responsibility for the general well-being of the community in which it does business. If the corporation is very large, the community is considered to be the entire country and the foreign nations with which the company deals. The concept that a corporation should shoulder such a burden is referred to as *corporate social responsibility*, now a vital concern of management at all levels.

This has not always been the case. Noted economist Milton Friedman feels very strongly that the goal of business should be to make money; social goals or business action based on social considerations should not be the concern of business. For the most part, however, it is no longer acceptable to maintain that the corporation's primary goal is to maximize profits for the shareholders.

Intertwined with the concept of social responsibility, perhaps inseparably, is the concept of business behavior referred to as *business ethics*. Both concepts involve what society, or certain segments of it, expect of business. While both social responsibility and ethical considerations are the concern of the key managers who determine the corporation's posture, the two concepts are distinguishable. Socially responsible or irresponsible behavior may be attributed to the corporation as a concern of the organization as a whole, while ethical or unethical business conduct can, in most cases, be attributed to individuals, people within the organization.

The ethics of those who occupy positions of authority in business have come under careful scrutiny during the last two decades. Much has been said and written about business ethics, with more attention given as each serious departure from ethical standards of conduct is brought to light. It remains a constant concern for business and the managers whose responsibilities include decision making as to what kind of business behavior is ethical and what kind is not.

Corporate Social Responsibility

Early Corporations

The corporation as a means of doing business, whereby several parties share a community of interest and join together to pursue a common purpose, is not a new concept. Many of the English ventures of the sixteenth and seventeenth centuries, such as the East India Company, the Russia Company, and the Hudson's Bay Company, were joint stock companies. Charters were issued by the sovereign to groups of merchants to extend the empire and promote trade in far-off lands. Very similar to the modern corporation, the joint stock company was conceived as a money-making venture. Members of the company and any who might be interested in a specific voyage or expedition were invited to invest and would hope to receive a return on their investment. The charters to such companies granted corporate status, monopoly privileges in the area to be exploited, and governmental powers to maintain some semblance of law and order and home rule. While profits for the stockholders were a distinct possibility, the dominant factor in granting charters was the public, or sovereign, interest in extending the empire. Nevertheless, the purpose of early ventures and the mission of those in control was to maximize profits with little concern for the "community" in which the company operated.

Early U.S. Corporations—The Public Purpose

Corporation charters were granted sparingly by the states until the 1830s with external regulation motivated by the necessity to protect the creditors of the corporation. The primary concern of the states was the extent to which limited liability would be enjoyed by the shareholders. The legislatures maintained firm control over business corporations, most of which were chartered to serve some public purpose or community interest, including transportation, water, insurance, and banking facilities. Even though private profit was the aim of early corporations, they served the public welfare and were considered by many to be a social mechanism involved with some form of social activity.

The Transition to Private Corporate Interests

In the 1870s and 1880s an increasing number of businesses, most associated with the growth of heavy industry, were incorporated to meet the demands of the shift from an agricultural to a manufacturing economy. Special legislative grants gave way to legislation more favorable to incorporation for nearly any kind of business or lawful enterprise. The concept of social responsibility remained relatively limited, with corporation statutes focusing primarily on internal corporate affairs and management. Political and social interests were subordinated to the corporate enterprise, the promotion of business, and the maximization of profits. External regulation by the state was considerably relaxed with internal management, free of interference by ownership (the shareholders), quick to fill the void. The profit motive became all-compelling and social responsibility was whatever corporate management wanted it to be. Perhaps this was not all bad—much of this country's greatness is attributable by some to the entrepreneurship of a few corporate giants. Nevertheless, it was soon to become evident that free enterprise, with profit by any means as its primary goal, would come under scrutiny as government began to assert itself with regulatory schemes in the public interest.

The Re-emergence of Government Control

Certain practices by industry in the late nineteenth century caused the government to have second thoughts about big business laissez-faire methods and to establish limited regulation. There was the recognition that the inherent nature of some industries so affected the public interest that the control of such companies could not be left completely in the hands of private owners. Prime examples were the banking, transportation, and utility industries.

Further, at about the same time, other companies engaged in more general types of commerce were taking advantage of the absence of regulation to engage in noncompetitive and predatory practices that had serious consequences for their competitors and customers alike. Large firms (oil and sugar, for example) increasingly entered into price-fixing and other agreements not to compete with one another in specified areas. The burgeoning railroads likewise took advantage of their near-monopoly power and charged what many, particularly the farmers, considered to be unreasonably high shipping rates.

Because of the abuses of power exercised by many types of business there was born the scheme of regulation that has since grown to blanket every facet of American business. Early measures taken by the federal government to regulate specific sectors of the economy were primarily intended to curb certain undesirable business practices. The Interstate Commerce Act of 1887 was directed at the railroads; the Sherman Act of 1890 was designed to break up, and prevent future, monopolies. By the 1920s and 1930s, the structure of corporations changed from ownership and control by a small group to ownership by many investors and control by professional managers. Profit maximization began to give way to a concern for the social implications of management's decisions. This change in the corporate structure, together with the fact that a pluralistic society had emerged, created an awareness that management's responsibilities extended beyond the shareholders to include all who contributed to the firm—the workers, customers, suppliers, creditors, competitors, and the community of which the corporation was a member. Social responsibility assumed increasing importance as a topic of discussion in the corporate boardroom.

Corporate Philanthropy

Becoming a full-fledged member of the community and assuming a socially responsive role often involved a contribution to worthy causes. Donations of corporate funds were early questioned by the shareholders as giving away of company profits without appreciable benefit to the company—any disbursement of corporate funds for philanthropy or other worthy public cause was considered to be a violation of the common-law rule that the profit motive was paramount in managing corporate affairs. This did not present much of a problem or affect the public interest when corporations were few and did not dominate the country's economy, but this changed as control of economic wealth passed from the hands of a few powerful entrepreneurs to what are today dominating corporations. No longer could the public look to the relatively few wealthy individuals for charitable donations to one cause or another. Corporations assumed many of the obligations of citizenship that earlier had been taken care of by individuals.

Management was called upon to justify charitable donations by showing that some benefit would accrue to the company. In a 1953 New Jersey case, the board of directors of a large corporation appropriated $1,500 from its treasury to be given to Princeton University for its maintenance. This action was challenged as an unauthorized donation by a group of stockholders, who maintained that the company's certificate of incorporation did not expressly authorize the contribution and that under common-law principles the company did not possess any implied or incidental authority to make charitable donations. The equity court, in a declaratory judgment action, found for the corporation, and the stockholders appealed. The New Jersey Supreme Court affirmed, stating in its opinion that:

[The donation] . . . was voluntarily made in the reasonable belief that it would aid the public welfare and advance the interests of the plaintiff as a private corporation and as part of the community in which it operates. We find that it was a lawful exercise of the corporation's implied and incidental powers under common-law principles and that it came within the express authority of the pertinent state legislation. . . . Clearly then, the appellants, as individual stockholders whose private interests rest entirely upon the well-being of the plaintiff corporation, ought not be permitted to close their eyes to present-day realities and thwart the long-visioned corporate action in recognizing and voluntarily discharging its high obligation as a constituent of our modern social structure. . . . A. P. Smith Mfg. Co. v. Barlow, Supreme Court of New Jersey, 98 A.2d 581 (1953).

Most states now specifically authorize such donations by statute.

Decades of Change—The 1960s and 1970s

The A. P. Smith case above is an example of how some shareholders viewed even modest contributions of corporate funds where direct benefit to the donor could not be measured in dollars and cents. There remained at that time vestiges of the profit maximization theory; the idea that business exists solely to provide goods and services to society and to produce maximum profits from year to year. The other extreme view is that business, since it contributes to so many of today's social concerns, should have the major responsibility for resolving most of society's problems, particularly in the areas of education, employment, civil rights, pollution, and conservation of resources. Somewhere between these extremes lies the role business can reasonably be expected to assume. During the 1960s, while corporations could retain their identity as economic entities, there was an increased awareness of the societal functions they could perform. The public began to expect more of business and indeed began to demand that it assume greater responsibilities. Several years ago, John D. deButts, former chief executive officer of American Telephone and Telegraph Co., wrote:

The corporation is now viewed as having a wide variety of responsibilities transcending the marketplace. Some of those responsibilities are responsibilities to society at large. Whether a business has social responsibility is, I know, a subject of widespread debate. But to my mind, it is a debate that continues long after the argument is over. Today, I know of no leader of business who sees his function as limited to the pursuit of profit. I know of none who does not realize that the business that for profit's sake ignores the impacts of its actions on society is not likely to make a profit very long.[1]

It is no longer enough that the corporation respond to the demands of the marketplace. Public expectations have risen to greater heights and the corporation is now being held accountable for its activities that have social consequences. Indeed, the company with foresight enough to anticipate the concerns of society and plan accordingly is invariably able to profit from its managerial foresightedness. The Department of Commerce Task Force on Corporate Social Performance had this to say about environmental assessment and planning:

Unanticipated change has frequently had adverse consequences for American industry. Shifts in consumer preferences, rising energy costs, equal employment opportunity for women and minorities, and environmental protection are just several developments that caught many companies unaware and unprepared in the 1960s and 1970s. In many instances, the results were costly. Settlement and litigation of class-action equal employment suits have cost American industry hundreds of millions of dollars, damaged the reputations of some companies, and in a number of instances, adversely affected productivity and morale. Compliance with environmental standards has been especially costly to manufacturing firms that neglected to plan for the future. And in the view of many impartial observers, the misfortunes that beset the American automobile in 1980 are at least partially the result of the industry's having failed in the mid-1970s to grasp fully the serious consequences that America's growing dependence on foreign oil could have on the industry.

Firms that have made serious efforts to anticipate the future have sometimes profited handsomely. The Whirlpool Corporation, for example, was one of the first manufacturers of washing machines to conclude that consumer acceptance of permanent press fabrics could affect manufacturers of washing machines. Whirlpool was the first major manufacturer to offer consumers washing machines designed to wash permanent press fabrics. PPG Industries was one of the first companies in the glass industry to appreciate the significance that consumer concerns about product safety could have for the glass industry. It was also one of the first in the business to offer consumers commercial safety glass for installation in residential sliding doors and storm doors. Minnesota Mining and Manufacturing Company (3M) began implementing its efforts to conserve energy in the 1960s. When world en-

---

[1]U.S. Department of Commerce, *Business & Society: Strategies for the 1980s*; Report of the Task Force on Corporate Social Performance (Washington, D.C.: U.S. Govt. Printing Office, 1980), p. ix.

ergy prices began their dramatic climb in 1973, 3M already had in place a comprehensive energy conservation program. Between 1973 and 1979, 3M reduced energy consumption in its manufacturing plants by 25 percent per unit of production; during the same period, it reduced annual energy consumption at its St. Paul, Minnesota, headquarters by 33 percent per square foot.

The growing realization that the external environment is becoming more complex, and that changes in the external environment have significant consequences for industry, has led many companies to devote more time and resources to assessing the external environment. A variety of approaches has been used. In some companies, the interests of the chief executive officer largely determine the issues that receive attention. In other companies, the executive committee or some other senior management committee may consider the effects that external developments are likely to have on their businesses. Some companies have solicited the views of the heads of their line and staff groups. Others have formed interdepartmental task forces to consider the effects that change will have on company operations.

Increasingly, though, major companies are moving to establish formal, ongoing institutionalized approaches that provide a focal point for the systematic consideration of how changes in the external environment are likely to affect their businesses. Whatever their differences, the approaches reflect a common resolve to explore thoroughly what the future holds and to consider carefully what actions ought to be taken.

General Electric Company pioneered the development of environmental assessment in the 1960s when it created a unit to analyze the long-term social and economic trends that would affect G.E.'s business. Ian Wilson, now of SRI International and for many years a member of G.E.'s Business Environment Study Group, lists five principles that should form the basis for the operations of an environmental assessment group: (1) it should be holistic in its approach to the future business environment, treating social, political, economic and technological trends as one; (2) it should be continuous, involving constant monitoring and modification of forecasts; (3) it should provide alternative futures based on alternative assumptions about the future; (4) it should stress the need for contingency planning for the various alternative futures that might occur; (5) it should be integrated into the company's decision-making process.

Wilson and others have emphasized the overriding importance of the fifth principle: environmental assessments that are not useful to decision-makers and that are not part of the normal decision-making process are largely a waste of time. The systems that have worked best in practice are those that have been tailored to meet the short-term decision-making needs and the long-term planning needs of the corporation.[2]

---

[2] Ibid., pp. 5–7.

In its 1971 report, "Social Responsibilities of Business Corporations," based on studies by Opinion Research Corporation during 1970, the Committee for Economic Development—an arm of the Department of Commerce made up of members from government and the private sector—stated that twice as many people think companies are not doing as much as they should to satisfy consumer needs at reasonable prices as those who believe business is doing a particularly good job for consumers. The most frequent complaint related to deceptive packaging and misleading marketing practices. Forty-nine percent of the public do not believe that corporations are doing as much as they should to improve the environment, and 80 percent favor closing plants that violate pollution regulations. In other specific areas of societal concern, a significant percentage of the public would assign to corporations the responsibility for hiring and training blacks and other disadvantaged groups; for contributing to support public education, health, and charities; and for helping to clean up and rebuild the ghettos in big cities. This would seem to be a clear indication that the public, to a significant degree, does not feel that corporations are sufficiently concerned about a wide spectrum of problems facing society.

Corporations have responded to the concerns expressed in the CED report of 1971. The Sun Company (formerly Sun Oil) established an Environmental Assessment Group consisting of its chief economist, an energy consultant, and a public issues consultant. Aetna Life and Casualty Company created a Public Policy Issues Analysis Department in 1978. PPG Industries has a Manager of Public Policy Research within its Department of Government and Public Affairs. American Telephone and Telegraph, parent company of the Bell System, has an Emerging Issues Group within its Planning Department. Hundreds of other companies have initiated similar systems. The titles appearing on company organization charts at various levels may be quite diverse, but a common thread can be identified. Each group is charged with considering how changes in the external environment will affect the business and how the business should plan for the change. While there is undoubtedly some element of predicting the future, the system devised by each company is designed to assist management; it is a part of the decision-making process.

Looking Ahead

The authors of the article from which the following predictions were taken are senior executives of Yankelovich, Skelly and White, Inc., one of the nation's largest social and market research firms.

The Economy: *Controlling inflation is the public's number one concern. We are finding, however, that the public's concern about the economy is widening to include concern about the need to increase productivity, technological growth, and innovation, and to regain our position of world-wide economic dominance. Indeed, Americans are now concerned about all aspects of economic revitalization. The traditional agenda for business—economic performance—will be a critical part of the broad agenda in the 1980s.*

Energy: *Energy will be an issue not only for the energy industry, but for all American industry. Our firm's work suggests growing public concern about industrial energy wastefulness. It suggests, too, public demand for American business to develop new energy sources and more energy efficient products, and for business to provide mechanisms for consumers to better cope with higher energy costs.*

Involuntary Threats to Health: *The public will insist that threats to health and safety which cannot be reduced by product avoidance be strictly controlled. Chemical and nuclear waste disposal are likely to be two of the major public health issues of the 1980s.*

Consumer Issues: *Consumer issues in the 1980s will be expressed increasingly as consumer rights. These will include the rights to adequate and truthful information, warranties, guaranties, and clear channel of redress.*

Protection of Privacy: *Privacy is perhaps the ultimate individual issue. The 1980s will witness concern not only at business incursions into customer privacy (involving, for example, information held in credit files and dissemination of information), but also concern about the privacy rights of employees.*

Beyond this basic set of issues for the 1980s, we would speculate that late in the decade we may witness rising interest in expanding business' role in solving social problems, especially at the local level. Currently, concerns about the poor and disadvantaged are muted by preoccupation with inflation, high taxes, and other issues that affect individuals. But policies to address today's economic concerns may result in fewer new social programs, leaving a gap between the needs of certain groups and society's apparent ability to fill that gap. Thus, we may find increasing emphasis on the role of business as problem solver of last resort.[3]

Deregulation

With modest beginnings in the Carter administration and continued efforts under that of President Reagan, deregulation is becoming an economic fact of life. The 1980 election was in some respects a mandate to curb government regulation, if not from the voters, from the government leaders who are antiregulation. Possible candidates for extinction or liberalization are EPA rules concerning new chemicals and pesticides; the EPA rule on lead as an additive to gasoline; Civil Rights Act guidelines to avoid discrimination in hiring and to protect against sexual harassment; and regulations protecting wildlife under the Endangered Species Act. Other proposals would af-

---

[3]Ibid., pp. 58–59.

fect occupational safety and health, clean air, consumer product safety, and food, drug and cosmetic regulation.

While deregulation may be looked upon by business as a giant step forward, there may be a *quid pro quo*. In its efforts to trim the budget, the Reagan administration has called upon the private sector to fill the breach left by reduced federal spending in such areas as assistance to the arts, education, and to the poor through various health and welfare programs. American business is being asked to become even more socially responsible. This may be the price it must pay for having its views given more favorable consideration by the administration.

Managing Social Responsiveness

Corporation owners—the stockholders—have little to say about the day-to-day operations of their companies. Management, whether of long-range policies or short-term plans, is vested in the chief executive officer and the board of directors. It is also true that, having accepted that profit maximization is no longer the only corporate purpose, managers are now free to depart from strict profit-only policies. However, the extent to which this is done by the upper echelons may itself be governed by personal profit motives. The pay received by executives is often tied to company performance, bottom-line profit or loss, with the expected perquisites of office—bonuses, stock options, and use of a corporate limousine for instance—hanging in the balance. Consequently, any manager who places more importance on curing the ills of society than on making a profit is putting his or her career in jeopardy. There is a middle course by which the interests of management and society can be balanced; finding the middle road of responding to social change while maintaining a healthy business can be difficult.

Suppose that Omega Company uses large amounts of a toxic chemical in its manufacturing process and each week must dispose of hundreds of gallons of hazardous, liquid waste. Not too many years ago Omega could simply have dumped the waste in any manner convenient and inexpensive to the company. Later, as concern for the environment grew, Omega might have assumed a degree of social responsibility and established a burial ground for its waste on its own property, another relatively convenient and inexpensive disposal method. Today, however, since residential development surrounds Omega, concern is being expressed about the long-range effects of Omega's disposal procedures. While no adverse effects have yet surfaced, Omega's management recognizes that a decision must be made. To do nothing might be considered socially irresponsible. To discontinue dumping on premises and have the toxic materials transported to an approved hazardous waste disposal site would be moderately socially responsible but expensive. To be completely responsible Omega would transport its wastes off-premises and, in addition, spend millions of dollars cleaning up the old, on-premises dump site. This latter course of action could be considered as very socially responsible but could also bankrupt the company and put hundreds of employees

"I've discovered he's insensitive, unscrupulous, and devoid of moral character . . . We were lucky to get him!"

The type of business may dictate the degree of social responsiveness.
Source: Reprinted by permission: Tribune Media Services.

out of work. In view of current environmental concerns Omega's decision would seem to be obvious. Profit at any social cost will have to give way, if the company survives, to socially acceptable performance. It may not be possible for Omega to balance competing interests.

Increasingly, management is being called upon to consider social issues when devising the company's strategic plan. Failure in the past to do so has resulted in substantial penalties, in money from high jury awards and reputation when an injury-causing or threatening product must be recalled. While the role of management has been mandated by statute in many areas, diligent compliance may not be enough. As public expectations rise, corporate management's master plan, made up of attainable short-term and intermediate goals, must be based on an awareness of the need to contribute to the solution of some of society's problems. With this awareness must be a willingness to make decisions and commit resources of all kinds—money, leadership, and expertise—to the resolution of the problems. The corporation cannot be all things to all elements of society and the environment. Nevertheless, while profit may remain the compelling motive for corporate existence, the survival of the American business system may depend upon how energetic and resourceful modern managers can be as they respond to society's needs.

Business Ethics

It is difficult to distinguish business ethics from social responsibility and to discuss each as a separate topic with relation to American business and how it ought to behave. It is useful, however, to view social responsibility as a concern of the corporation as an organization and business ethics, that is, the kind of behavior the public expects to encounter in the marketplace, as attributable to key decision-makers within the corporate hierarchy. It is true that corporations are more socially responsive today, either because to be so is statutorily directed or because of an awakening of the corporate social conscience. At the same time, during the past fifteen or so years, the esteem with which the public holds business and its leaders has decreased considerably. Several Harris Surveys indicated that, in 1966, 55 percent of the American people had a "great deal of confidence" in the leaders of major companies. By 1976 that percentage had dropped to 16 where it remained, unchanged, in 1981. In late 1981, the Gallup Poll asked people to rate twenty-four professions and occupations on whether "the honesty and ethical standards" of those in the field are "very high, high, average, low or very low." The findings follow.

The Public Perception of Honesty and Ethical Standards of Certain Professions and Occupations

	High or Very High	Average	Low or Very Low
Clergy	63%	28%	6%
Druggists	59	33	5
Dentists	52	38	7
Doctors	50	38	10
Engineers	48	35	5
College teachers	45	36	8
Police officers	44	41	13
Bankers	39	47	10
TV reporters, commentators	36	45	15
Newspaper reporters	30	49	16
Funeral directors	30	41	19
Lawyers	25	41	27
Stockbrokers	21	46	7
Senators	20	50	25
Business executives	**19**	**53**	**19**
Building contractors	19	48	27
Congressmen	15	47	32
Local officeholders	14	51	30
Realtors	14	48	30
Labor leaders	14	29	48
State officeholders	12	50	30
Insurance salespeople	11	49	36
Advertising practitioners	9	41	38
Car salespeople	6	33	55

Sources: Harris, Louis, *The Harris Survey* (New York: Tribune Company Syndicate, Inc., November 25, 1982) and *The Gallup Report*, September 1981, Report No. 192.

Why should business and its leaders be held in such low esteem? What kinds of things has business done to earn for itself such low marks in ethics and morality? If it is accepted that the corporation has become more socially responsible, it would perhaps follow that the profit motive is less compelling than it was some years ago, probably true with regard to the corporation as an entity. But big business is managed by people who suffer the same frailties as do other human beings. They may be driven by a desire to get ahead and may find it difficult when a decision may lead to higher profits while at the same time working a hardship on society. A product may be very profitable for its manufacturer but its use by consumers may lead to serious illness and human suffering. For example, it may not be unethical to manufacture cigarettes but it is quite unethical to market and advertise them as harmless and pleasurable.

What Are Business Ethics?

The word "ethics" is generally understood to refer to the study of whatever is right and good for humans; it deals with moral duty and obligation and the principles of conduct governing an individual or group. The term "business ethics" can be understood to apply to business practices and policies in light of some concept of human values. To focus simply on business efficiency and how it may contribute to profit making may ignore important moral or ethical values. The marketing of cigarettes or other products that may affect the quality of human life thus ceases to be solely a business issue. Consequently, business ethics may be viewed as involving the relation of business activities to the quality of the human environment.

Unethical practices and corruption are by no means unique to this time. John Law's Mississippi Scheme of the 1720s and the Teapot Dome Scandal two centuries later are not well-remembered today. They have been supplanted by alleged unethical business conduct involving such common names as Exxon, Lockheed, Northrop, and United Brands, firms that have admitted to making substantial payments to foreign officials to obtain lucrative contracts with a particular foreign country. Lockheed, for example, paid some $12 million to Japanese officials in 1973 and 1974 in order to sell twenty-one TriStar airplanes to Japan. United Brands paid a $1.25 million bribe to the former president of Honduras to reduce the tax on banana production in that country. In the United States, business practices that formerly were common ways of doing business became suspect and scandalous as a result of what former Vice-president Agnew called the "post-Watergate morality." The public's disillusionment with business ethics was increasingly expressed in the aftermath of Watergate as each new revelation of corporate wrongdoing surfaced and was aired by the media.

Although records reveal that during the period 1971 through 1980 hundreds of companies of all sizes were convicted of federal criminal offenses, during the same period, many thousands of others did not misbehave. Why some companies are exemplary and others get into frequent trouble is probably a function of the kind of corporate leadership involved: some firms may be predatory and devoid of a sense of ethics, which may filter down to all levels of management. In law-abiding and socially responsible firms, obedience to the law is demanded and standards of ethics are high. This too filters down from top leadership. In either case, the moral tone of an organization is set by those at the top.

In discussing ethics the focus is on the higher echelons of management, those who make policy, create standards, and set the example, because it is top management that ultimately bears the responsibility for poor judgment involving ethical considerations. It is also probably true that the lower levels take their direction from above and base their values on what they feel is mandated from the top—if management is less than completely ethical the employees may feel justified in acting in much the same way. This can present a dilemma for an employee. Suppose that an employee discovers that a company is engaging in unethical practices. Perhaps the company is processing and packaging contaminated food products, or is discharging contaminants into a stream. To what extent is the employee liable for the misconduct of the employer? Should the employee remain silent? Or should he or she reveal the unethical conduct and risk retaliation, possibly the loss of employment? The course of action chosen may depend upon how the employee views ethics.

The refusal of an employee to go along with what may be considered to be completely unethical conduct can pose a problem for those involved in the decision-making process. For example, in 1968 the B. F. Goodrich Company was awarded the contract to develop and manufacture the brakes for the A7D light attack aircraft. Early efforts by Goodrich personnel failed to produce a brake that would work effectively and that would meet military specifications and requirements. A four-disk brake had been developed that was completely inadequate. Numerous field tests resulted in near crashes caused by brake failure. Nevertheless, an engineer was directed to analyze the development and test data and to prepare a qualification report to the effect that the brake was satisfactory. Being unable to convince his superiors that what the company was doing was wrong, he refused to sign the qualification report and was forced to resign a good position. His strong stand was not in vain, however. Two days after his resignation B. F. Goodrich recalled the false qualification report and replaced the four-disk brake with an improved five-disk that worked well. The additional cost to the company was considerable, but many lives were probably saved.

In another case an employee of United States Steel Corporation believed that his company's tubular steel products, used by the oil and gas industry, were unsafe. He so advised his immediate superior and obtained little satisfaction. He next went to the vice-president in charge of sales and was discharged from his position, perhaps as a troublemaker. The product in question was subsequently discontinued and taken off the market; nevertheless, the employee lost his job and was unsuccessful in a tort action against his former employer. The Pennsylvania court in which the action was brought refused to recognize the tort of "wrongful discharge" for which damages were sought. *Geary v. United States Steel Corporation*, 456 Pa. 171, 319 A.2d 174 (1975).

Whether or not a wrongfully discharged employee may recover damages may depend upon the jurisdiction in which the action is brought. The following case indicates that in California an employee discharged for refusing to engage in illegal conduct may have more success in an action for "wrongful discharge."

Tameny v. Atlantic Richfield Co.

Supreme Court of California
164 Cal.Rptr. 839 (1980)

Plaintiff Tameny began working for Atlantic Richfield (Arco) as a relief clerk in 1960 and worked his way up to retail sales representative, the position he held when Arco discharged him in 1975. As a retail sales representative his duties included the management of relations between Arco and the various independent service station dealers (franchisees) in his assigned territory of Bakersfield. Plaintiff's complaint alleged that, beginning in the 1970s, Arco, its district manager, and others engaged in a combination "for the purpose of reducing, controlling, stabilizing, fixing, and pegging the retail gasoline prices of Arco service station franchisees." Such conduct, alleged plaintiff, would constitute a violation of the Sherman Antitrust Act, the California Cartwright Act, and a specific consent decree which had been entered in a federal antitrust action against Arco in 1971. Arco had been enjoined from "entering into or adhering to any agreement, arrangement or understanding with any distributor or dealer to fix, maintain, or stabilize prices at which any distributor or dealer shall sell gasoline," and from "coercing any of its distributors or dealers to adhere to (its) suggested retail price. . . ."

Plaintiff Tameny claimed that during the early 1970s he was pressured to threaten and cajole the dealers in his territory to cut their gasoline prices to a point at or below a designated level specified by Arco. Arco's personnel records indicated that Tameny was fired for "incompetence" and "unsatisfactory performance." Tameny claimed that the sole reason for his discharge was his refusal to commit the "grossly illegal and unlawful acts which defendants tried to force him to perform." Plaintiff filed his action seeking relief on five separate theories including three tort causes of action: wrongful discharge, breach of the implied covenant of good faith and fair dealing, and interference with contractual relations. Only the tort of wrongful discharge is considered here. When the trial court sustained Arco's demurrer, dismissed the complaint, and entered judgment for Arco, plaintiff appealed.

Tobriner, Justice:

. . . Under the traditional common law rule, codified in Labor Code section 2922, an employee contract of indefinite duration is in general terminable at "the will" of either party. Over the past several decades, however, judicial authorities in California and throughout the United States have established the rule that under both common law and the statute an employer does not enjoy an absolute or totally unfettered right to discharge even an at-will employee. In a series of cases arising out of a variety of factual settings in which a discharge clearly violated an express statutory objective or undermined a firmly established principle of public policy, courts have recognized that an employer's traditional broad authority to discharge an at-will employee "may be limited by statute . . . or by considerations of public policy." (*Petermann v. International Brotherhood of Teamsters* (1959) 174 Cal.App.2d 184, 188, 344 P.2d 25, 27 (discharge for refusal to commit perjury). . . .

Petermann v. International Brotherhood of Teamsters, supra, one of the seminal California decisions in this area, imposes a significant condition upon the employer's broad power of dismissal by nullifying the right to discharge because an employee refuses to perform an unlawful act. In *Petermann*, the plaintiff, who had been employed as a business agent by defendant union, brought a "wrongful discharge" action against the union alleging that he had been dismissed from his position because he had refused to follow his employer's instructions to testify falsely under oath before a legislative committee, and instead had given truthful testimony. Emphasizing that the employer's instructions amounted to a directive to commit perjury, a criminal offense, plaintiff maintained that the employer acted illegally in discharging him for refusing to follow such an order.

The *Petermann* court recognized that in the absence of contractual limitations an employer enjoys broad discretion to discharge an employee, but concluded that as a matter of "public policy and sound morality" the employer's conduct, as alleged in the complaint, could not be condoned. The court explained: "The commission of perjury is unlawful . . . . It would be obnoxious to the interests of the state and contrary to public policy and sound morality to allow an employer to discharge any employee, whether the employment be for a designated or unspecified duration, on the ground that the employee declined to commit perjury, an act specifically enjoined by statute. . . . The public policy of this state as reflected in the penal code sections referred to above would be seriously impaired if it were to be held that one could be discharged by reason of his refusal to commit perjury. To hold that one's continued employment could be made contingent upon his commission of a felonious act at the instance of his employer would be to encourage criminal conduct upon the part of both the employee and employer and serve to contaminate the honest administration of public affairs. . . ."

As the statement of facts set out above demonstrates, the present case closely parallels *Petermann* in a number of essential respects. Here, as in *Petermann*, the complaint alleges that the defendant employer instructed its employee to engage in conduct constituting a criminal offense. Plaintiff, like the employee in *Petermann*, refused to violate the law and suffered discharge as a consequence of that refusal. . . .

Moreover, California courts have not been alone in recognizing the propriety of a tort remedy when an employer's discharge of an employee contravenes the dictates of public policy. In *Nees v. Hocks* (1975), 272 Or. 210, 536 P.2d 512, for example, the Oregon Supreme Court upheld an employee's recovery of compensatory damages in tort for the emotional distress suffered when her employer discharged her for serving on a jury. Similarly, in *Harless v. First Nat. Bank in Fairmont* (W.Va.1978) 246 S.E.2d 270, the Supreme Court of West Virginia upheld a wrongful discharge action by a bank employee who was terminated for attempting to persuade his employer to comply with consumer protection laws, reasoning that "where the employer's motivation for (a) discharge contravenes some substantial public policy principle, then the employer may be liable to the employee for damages occasioned by the discharge," and concluding that the employee's cause of action "is one in tort and it therefore follows that rules relating to tort damages would be applicable." . . .

In the last half century the rights of employees have not only been proclaimed by a mass of legislation touching upon almost every aspect of the employer-employee relationship, but the courts have likewise evolved certain additional protections at common law. The courts have been sensitive to the need to protect the individual employee from discriminatory exclusion from the opportunity of employment whether it be by the all-powerful union or employer. . . . This development at common law shows that the employer is not so absolute a sovereign of the job that there are not limits to his prerogative. One such limit at least is the present case. The employer cannot condition employment upon required participation in unlawful conduct by the employee.

We hold that an employer's authority over its employee does not include the right to demand that the employee commit a criminal act to further its interests, and an employer may not coerce compliance with such unlawful directions by discharging an employee who refuses to follow such an order. An employer engaging in such conduct violates a basic duty imposed by law upon all employers, and thus an employee who has suffered damages as a result of such discharge may maintain a tort action for wrongful discharge against the employer.

Accordingly, we conclude that the trial court erred in sustaining the demurrer to plaintiff's tort action for wrongful discharge.

The judgment is reversed and the case is remanded to the trial court for further proceedings consistent with this opinion.

It has long been a commonly-held belief that white-collar misconduct goes largely unpunished. To a certain extent, and in many cases, this may be true. However, in an increasing number of cases top executives are being held accountable for the roles they play in leading their firms into impermissible situations. In 1969, Container Corporation of America and others in the corrugated container industry were found to have entered into price-fixing agreements in violation of Section 1 of the Sherman Act, discussed in Chapter 11. Criminal actions were brought against the executives of the corporations for their personal involvement and, in 1976, forty-seven of them were given jail terms and fines. The toughest sentence, sixty days in jail (later reduced) and a $35,000 fine, was handed out to R. Harper Brown, president of Container Corporation of America. Other industries and their officers have also been found guilty of various antitrust violations as the government steps up its campaign against corporate crime. Commenting in the Container Corporation case, U.S. District Judge James Parsons declared that the cost of price-fixing "is passed along to the ultimate consumer."

Codes of Ethics

During the past decade most large corporations have established codes of ethics or conduct or have drastically revised those already in existence. Some such codes have also been established on an industry-wide basis. The codes may be either general or specific but, in either case, are designed as guides for all levels of management and all employees in decision-making positions. ITT, for example, has a comprehensive statement of company policies and has had it translated into German for its German and Austrian subsidiaries. Allied Corporation (involved in the pollution of Virginia's James River with the chemical kepone) has a statement of proper business practices that must be read and signed each year by top executives. International Paper, involved in extensive antitrust litigation, has sponsored production of a film, "The Price," depicting the perils of price-fixing. The film has received wide acceptance as a training aid for thousands of companies and is used by many universities and colleges in their business programs.

Standard Oil's Code of Ethics is typical of efforts by top management to convey its ethical concerns to all employees.[4] It is contained in the Standard Oil Company of California's booklet titled: *Our Business Conduct . . . Principles and Practices.*

TO ALL EMPLOYEES:

Over the years, Standard Oil Company of California employees have established a record of unexcelled integrity in their business conduct and relationships. This exemplary record is fundamental to the Company's reputation for doing business worldwide in a fair and honest way. The business reputation of our employees and the Company is one of the most valuable assets we have and should be a source of pride to all those who helped achieve it. We value this reputation, and it is management's intention to ensure that it is maintained—even improved—in the years ahead.

This booklet summarizes the Company's policies on specific issues relating to business conduct. These policies are set forth in detail in the Company's Manual of Compliance Procedures and Guidelines.

It is, of course, the policy of the Company for all employees to comply fully with the law at all times in their conduct of the Company's business. However, the policy of the Company goes beyond this. Our business should be conducted not only in compliance with the legal rules, but voluntarily in accordance with the highest standards of business integrity and honest dealing. While community standards of ethics may vary at different times and

---

[4]Reprinted by permission of Chevron U.S.A., Inc. (Standard Oil Company of California).

different places, the strict standards of honesty and integrity are a basic and continuing cornerstone of our business in all areas and functions and at all times.

Company management takes the matter of corporate responsibility and business ethics very seriously, and it is our policy to foster cooperative and forthright relationships with employees, shareholders, dealers, suppliers, unions, local communities, customers and governments. Our Company realizes that its longterm success depends, to an important degree, on its responsiveness to society's evolving needs and expectations, to the creation of a climate of trust in our business dealings and to a work environment for its employees which assumes high ethical standards of conduct.

While management recognizes its obligations to establish and monitor standards of conduct for the entire organization, and to carry out its own responsibilities in a manner beyond reproach, all employees share this responsibility. The Company desires to create an environment that encourages and rewards individual initiative and achievement, not only in results, but also in how they are achieved. In the final analysis, the ethical conduct of a corporation depends on the understanding, judgment and actions of its employees. All employees are asked to review their respective roles in light of the principles set forth in this booklet and to give their full cooperation in conducting themselves according to the high standards expected by our Company.

George M. Keller
Chairman of the Board
September 15, 1981

The Foreign Corrupt Practices Act (FCPA)

At the international level, a code of conduct and ethics has been prescribed by statute. Prior to passage of the Foreign Corrupt Practices Act (FCPA) in 1977, the payment of bribes by foreign traders to various officials of the host country had been a traditional way of doing business. Businessmen from European countries have accepted it as a commercial way of life, sanctioned at least implicitly by their governments. The European attitude is that without well-placed payments to influential foreign officials, not a great deal of business would be accomplished. This may have been the case in the United States as well until the post-Watergate morality made the scene. Investigation by the Watergate special prosecutor and the Securities and Exchange Commission revealed that much of the financing of the Watergate break-in consisted of corporate funds that had been "laundered" in foreign countries. Much of this money was in the form of illegal campaign contributions. It evolved that some of the methods used to conceal illegal contributions were also used to hide the bribery of foreign officials.

In May 1976 the SEC's Report on Questionable and Illegal Corporate Payments and Practices advised the Senate that there was evidence of widespread misuse of corporate funds that threatened to undermine public confidence in the American system of capital formation. The SEC report also outlined the legislative and other responses that the Commission recommended to remedy the problems. Acting on these recommendations, Congress enacted into law the FCPA of 1977. Hearings on the bill revealed that there had been corrupt foreign payments by over 300 U.S. companies involving hundreds of millions of dollars and thus an urgent need for strong antibribery legislation.

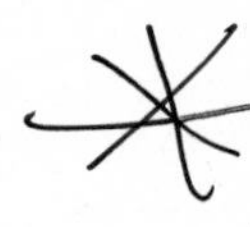

FCPA amends the Securities and Exchange Act of 1934 to (1) require that corporations maintain books and records that accurately and fairly reflect their transactions and design systems of internal control to assure that the assets of the corporation are used for proper corporate purposes; (2) prohibit the falsification of accounting records and deception of auditors; and (3) make criminal the payments of bribes to foreign officials. Responsibility for enforcement of FCPA's provisions is divided between the SEC and the Justice Department. Violations of the act by a company can result in a fine of not more than $1 million. Individual violators are subject to a fine of up to $10,000, imprisonment for up to five years, or both. Fines assessed against individuals may not be paid by the individual's company.

Reaction to FCPA has been mixed. A primary concern of the regulated corporations seems to be that American business will be at a distinct competitive disadvantage overseas and that this is bound to affect the balance of payments of the United States. Whether or not this is true remains to be seen.

Standards for Business Conduct

The Business Ethics Advisory Council, organized by the U.S. Department of Commerce, made the following statement on business ethics hoping to elicit response from business executives that would lead to higher ethical levels of business conduct. Somewhat philosophical and idealistic, it nevertheless defines the problem and urges top management to assume a large share of the responsibility for meeting the ethical obligations of a free enterprise system.

A Statement on Business Ethics and a Call for Action

The ethical standards of American businessmen, like those of the American people, are founded upon our religious heritage and our traditions of social, political, and economic freedom. They impose upon each man high obligations in his dealings with his fellowmen, and make all men stewards of the common good. Immutable, well-understood guides to performance generally are effective, but new ethical problems are created constantly by the ever-increasing complexity of society. In business, as in every other activity, therefore, men must continually seek to identify new and appropriate standards.

Over the years, American businessmen in the main have continually endeavored to demonstrate their responsiveness to their ethical obligations in our free society. They have themselves initiated and welcomed from others calls for the improvement of their ethical performance, regarding each as a challenge to establish and meet ever-higher ethical goals. In consequence, the ethical standards that should guide business enterprise in this country have steadily risen over the years, and this has had a profound influence on the performance of the business community.

As the ethical standards and conduct of American private enterprise have improved, so also has there developed a public demand for proper performance and a keen sensitivity to lapses from those standards. The full realization by the business community of its future opportunities and, indeed, the maintenance of public confidence require a continuing pursuit of the highest standards of ethical conduct.

Attainment of this objective is not without difficulty. Business enterprises, large and small, have relationships in many directions—with stockholders and other owners, employees, customers, suppliers, government, and the public in general. The traditional emphasis on freedom, competition, and progress in our economic system often brings the varying interests of these groups into conflict, so that many difficult and complex ethical problems can arise in any enterprise. While all relationships of an enterprise to these groups are regulated in some degree by law, compliance with law can only provide a minimum standard of conduct. Beyond legal obligations, the policies and actions of businessmen must be based upon a regard for the proper claims of all affected groups.

Moreover, in many business situations the decision that must be made is not the simple choice between absolute right and absolute wrong. The decisions of business frequently must be made in highly complex and ever-changing circumstances, and at times involve either adhering to earlier standards or developing new ones. Such decisions affect profoundly not only the business enterprise, but our society as a whole. Indeed, the responsible position of American business—both large and small—obligates each participant to lead rather than follow.

A weighty responsibility therefore rests upon all those who manage business enterprises, as well as upon all others who influence the environment in which business operates. In the final analysis, however, the primary moral duty to establish high ethical standards and adequate procedures for their enforcement in each enterprise must rest with its policymaking body—its board of directors and its top management.

We, therefore, now propose that current efforts be expanded and intensified and that new efforts now be undertaken by the American business community to hasten its attainment of those high ethical standards that derive from our heritage and traditions. We urge all enterprises, business groups, and associations to accept responsibility—each for itself and in its own most appropriate way—to develop methods and programs for encouraging and sustaining these efforts on a continuous basis. We believe in this goal, we accept it, and we encourage all to pursue its attainment.[5]

---

[5] U.S. Department of Commerce, Business Ethics Advisory Council, *A Statement on Business Ethics and a Call for Action* (Washington, D.C.: Government Printing Office, 1962).

Questions and Problems

1. In June 1976, the base price for a sixty-passenger, GMC school bus meeting Ohio safety standards was about $12,500. Despite questions regarding the safety of the vehicles and considerable publicity on the matter, little was done until new federal safety measures were developed. New features included rupture-proof fuel tanks, offset seating, emergency door, and special padded seats. These increased the cost of the bus by about $3,000. Assuming that the manufacturer had been forced to act to improve safety, could its handling of the situation be considered as socially responsible conduct?

2. In 1916, Henry Ford announced that the Ford Motor Company would, for the foreseeable future, pay no more special dividends but would use profits to expand the plant and production "to spread the benefits of this industrial system to the greatest possible number, to help them build up their lives and their homes." Two shareholders, the Dodge brothers, brought an action to compel Ford to pay a substantial dividend. Ford's surplus of assets over liabilities and capital stock at that time amounted to more than $110 million. Who will prevail, Ford or the Dodge brothers? At that time, to whom did Ford owe its primary obligation? (*Dodge v. Ford Motor Co.*, 170 N.W. 668, 1919.)

3. Ralph Nader, in a statement relative to his "Project on Corporate Responsibility," (directed primarily at General Motors) had this to say:

Ours is a corporate society. Corporations produce, process, and market most of the goods and services in the nation. They constitute the most powerful, consistent and coordinated power grid that shapes the actions of people in private and public sectors. Yet, far less is known about the actual operations of the giant corporations than any other institution in America, including the national security agencies.

Do you agree with him? Has GM become more responsible since 1969? What role has the federal government played in making GM a better citizen?

4. Page Airways, Inc., worldwide distributor of the Grumman Gulfstream II aircraft, found that in order to compete successfully in foreign markets it was necessary that bribes be paid to foreign governments and officials. Page did compete successfully by paying:

$200,000 to the President of the Republic of Gabon

$900,000 to the State Minister of Industrial Development of Sabah, Malaysia

$412,000 to the Republic of the Ivory Coast

A Cadillac Eldorado convertible to the Chief of State of Uganda.

These payments were disguised as sham transactions and paid to foreign entities as conduits to hide the true recipients and amounts. Discuss this way of doing business as a matter of economics and ethics. (*SEC v. Page Airways, Inc.*, Fed. Sec. L. Rep., Para. 96, 393, April 12, 1978.)

5. The Nestle Alimentana company of Switzerland manufactures and markets a powdered infant formula. It does a large volume of business in underdeveloped third world countries. Certain groups have urged Americans to boycott Nestle's products claiming that third world babies are being killed because uneducated, illiterate mothers are preparing the formula improperly and under unsanitary conditions. As Nestle's vice-president for marketing how would you respond to the accusations? What steps could you take to correct the problem if it is found to exist?

6. During the civil rights conflicts of the 1960s, civic leaders and others in Birmingham, Alabama, criticized business leaders of the community, especially those with U.S. Steel, for not taking more initiative in improving race relations. During a press conference the Chairman of U.S. Steel made these comments:

I do not either believe that it would be a wise thing for United States Steel to be other than a good citizen in a community, or to attempt to have its ideas of what is right for the community enforced upon that community by some sort of economic means. . . . When we as individuals are citizens in a community, we can exercise what small influence we may have as citizens, but for a corporation to attempt to exert any kind of economic compulsion to achieve a particular end in the racial area seems to me quite beyond what a corporation should do, and I will say also, quite beyond what a corporation can do.

Have corporate attitudes changed? In what areas might the predominant industry of a community (a "company town") make a contribution toward racial harmony?

7. It has been pointed out that most companies have codes of conduct or ethics to govern the business behavior of their key executives and others. However, enforcement of such codes is often lacking with many, if not most, executive wrongdoers going unpunished. In 1978, David Begelman resigned as president of Columbia Pictures after admitting that he had cashed checks made out to others and had misused company funds. He was fined $5,000 and put on three years' probation. Within a year he was hired as head of Metro-Goldwyn-Mayer Company and later became president of United Artists. If you were a stockholder in the two latter companies how would you feel about the hiring of Begelman? Would there be anything you could do about it?

8. A large food store chain and its president were indicted for violating Food and Drug Administration regulations by permitting food stored in warehouses to be contaminated by rodents. The corporation pleaded guilty to all counts, but the president pleaded not guilty, claiming in defense that while he was in overall charge of the company, he had delegated responsibility for eliminating the contamination, and his subordinates had failed him. To what extent should he be liable if he had been made fully aware of the continuing contamination? (*U.S. v. Park*, 421 U.S. 658, 1975.)

A · P · P · E · N · D · I · X A

THE CONSTITUTION OF THE UNITED STATES OF AMERICA

We the People of the United States, in Order to form a more perfect Union, establish Justice, insure domestic Tranquility, provide for the common defence, promote the general Welfare, and secure the Blessings of Liberty to ourselves and our Posterity, do ordain and establish this Constitution for the United States of America.

ARTICLE I

Section 1

All legislative Powers herein granted shall be vested in a Congress of the United States, which shall consist of a Senate and House of Representatives.

Section 2

The House of Representatives shall be composed of Members chosen every second Year by the People of the several States, and the Electors in each State shall have the Qualifications requisite for Electors of the most numerous Branch of the State Legislature.

No Person shall be a Representative who shall not have attained to the Age of twenty five Years, and been seven Years a Citizen of the United States, and who shall not, when elected, be an Inhabitant of that State in which he shall be chosen.

Representatives and direct Taxes shall be apportioned among the several States which may be included within this Union, according to their respective Numbers, which shall be determined by adding to the whole Number of free Persons, including those bound to Service for a Term of Years, and excluding Indians not taxed, three fifths of all other Persons. The actual Enumeration shall be made within three Years after the first Meeting of the Congress of the United States, and within every subsequent Term of ten Years, in such Manner as they shall by Law direct. The number of Representatives shall not exceed one for every thirty Thousand, but each State shall have at Least one Representative; and until such enumeration shall be made, the State of New Hampshire shall be entitled to chuse three, Massachusetts eight, Rhode Island and Providence Plantations one, Connecticut five, New-York six, New Jersey four, Pennsylvania eight, Delaware one, Maryland six, Virginia ten, North Carolina five, South Carolina five, and Georgia three.

When vacancies happen in the Representation from any State, the Executive Authority thereof shall issue Writs of Election to fill such vacancies.

The House of Representatives shall chuse their Speaker and other Officers; and shall have the sole Power of Impeachment.

Section 3

The Senate of the United States shall be composed of two Senators from each State, chosen by the Legislature thereof, for six Years; and each Senator shall have one Vote.

Immediately after they shall be assembled in Consequence of the first Election, they shall be divided as equally as may be into three Classes. The Seats of the Senators of the first Class shall be vacated at the Expiration of the second Year, of the second Class at the Expiration of the fourth Year, and of the third Class at the Expiration of the sixth Year, so that one third may be chosen every second Year; and if Vacancies happen by Resignation, or otherwise, during the Recess of the Legislature of any State, the Executive thereof may make temporary Appointments until the next Meeting of the Legislature, which shall then fill such Vacancies.

No Person shall be a Senator who shall not have attained to the Age of thirty Years, and been nine Years a Citizen of the United States, and who shall not, when elected, be an Inhabitant of that State for which he shall be chosen.

The Vice President of the United States shall be President of the Senate, but shall have no Vote, unless they be equally divided.

The Senate shall chuse their other Officers, and also a President pro tempore, in the Absence of the Vice President, or when he shall exercise the Office of President of the United States.

The Senate shall have the sole power to try all Impeachments. When sitting for that Purpose, they shall be on Oath or Affirmation. When the President of the United States is tried, the Chief Justice shall preside: And no Person shall be convicted without the Concurrence of two thirds of the Members present.

Judgment in Cases of Impeachment shall not extend further than to removal from Office, and disqualification to hold and enjoy any Office of honor, Trust or Profit under the United States: but the Party convicted shall nevertheless be liable and subject to Indictment, Trial, Judgment and Punishment, according to Law.

Section 4

The Times, Places and Manner of holding Elections for Senators and Representatives, shall be prescribed in each State by the Legislature thereof: but the Congress may at any time by Law make or alter such Regulations, except as to the Places of chusing Senators.

The Congress shall assemble at least once in every Year, and such Meeting shall be on the first Monday in December, unless they shall by Law appoint a different Day.

Section 5

Each House shall be the Judge of the Elections, Returns and Qualifications of its own Members, and a Majority of each shall constitute a Quorum to do Business; but a smaller Number may adjourn from day to day, and may be authorized to compel the Attendance of absent Members, in such Manner, and under such Penalties as each House may provide.

Each House may determine the Rules of its Proceedings, punish its Members for disorderly Behaviour, and, with the Concurrence of two thirds, expel a Member.

Each House shall keep a Journal of its Proceedings, and from time to time publish the same, excepting such Parts as may in their Judgment require Secrecy; and the Yeas and Nays of the Members of either House on any question shall, at the Desire of one fifth of those Present, be entered on the Journal.

Neither House, during the Session of Congress, shall, without the Consent of the other, adjourn for more than three days, nor to any other Place than that in which the two Houses shall be sitting.

Section 6

The Senators and Representatives shall receive a Compensation for their Services, to be ascertained by Law, and paid out of the Treasury of the United States. They shall in all Cases, except Treason, Felony and Breach of the Peace, be privileged from Arrest during their Attendance at the Session of their respective Houses, and in going to and returning from the same; and for any Speech or Debate in either House, they shall not be questioned in any other Place.

No Senator or Representative shall, during the Time for which he was elected, be appointed to any civil Office under the Authority of the United States, which shall have been created, or the Emoluments whereof shall have been encreased during such time; and no Person holding any Office under the United States, shall be a Member of either House during his Continuance in Office.

Section 7

All Bills for raising Revenue shall originate in the House of Representatives; but the Senate may propose or concur with Amendments as on other Bills.

Every Bill which shall have passed the House of Representatives and the Senate, shall, before it become a Law, be presented to the President of the United States; If he approve he shall sign it, but if not he shall return it, with his Objections to that House in which it shall have originated, who shall enter the Objections at large on their Journal, and proceed to reconsider it. If after such Reconsideration two thirds of that House shall agree to pass the Bill, it shall be sent, together with the Objections, to the other House, by which it shall likewise be reconsidered, and if approved by two thirds of that House, it shall become a Law. But in all such Cases the Votes of both Houses shall be determined by Yeas and Nays, and the Names of the Persons voting for and against the Bill shall be entered on the Journal of each House respectively. If any Bill shall not be returned by the President within ten Days (Sundays excepted) after it shall have been presented to him, the Same shall be a Law, in like Manner as if he had signed it, unless the Congress by their Adjournment prevent its Return, in which Case it shall not be a Law.

Every Order, Resolution, or Vote to which the Concurrence of the Senate and House of Representatives may be necessary (except on a question of Adjournment) shall be presented to the President of the United States; and before the Same shall take Effect, shall be approved by him, or being disapproved by him, shall be repassed by two thirds of the Senate and House of Representatives, according to the Rules and Limitations prescribed in the Case of a Bill.

Section 8

The Congress shall have Power to lay and collect Taxes, Duties, Imposts and Excises, to pay the Debts and provide for the common Defence and general Welfare of the United States; but all Duties, Imposts and Excises shall be uniform throughout the United States;

To borrow Money on the credit of the United States;

To regulate Commerce with foreign Nations, and among the several States, and with the Indian Tribes;

To establish an uniform Rule of Naturalization, and uniform Laws on the subject of Bankruptcies throughout the United States;

To coin Money, regulate the Value thereof, and of foreign Coin, and fix the Standard of Weights and Measures;

To provide for the Punishment of counterfeiting the Securities and current Coin of the United States;

To establish Post Offices and post Roads;

To promote the Progress of Science and useful Arts, by securing for limited Times to Authors and Inventors the exclusive Right to their respective Writings and Discoveries;

To constitute Tribunals inferior to the supreme Court;

To define and punish Piracies and Felonies committed on the high Seas, and Offenses against the Law of Nations;

To declare War, grant Letters of Marque and Reprisal, and make Rules concerning Captures on Land and Water;

To raise and support Armies, but no Appropriation of Money to that Use shall be for a longer Term than two Years;

To provide and maintain a Navy;

To make Rules for the Government and Regulation of the land and naval Forces;

To provide for calling forth the Militia to execute the Laws of the Union, suppress Insurrections and repel Invasions;

To provide for organizing, arming, and disciplining, the Militia, and for governing such Part of them as may be employed in the Service of the United States, reserving to the States respectively, the Appointment of the Officers, and the Authority of training the Militia according to the discipline prescribed by Congress;

To exercise exclusive Legislation in all Cases whatsoever, over such District (not exceeding ten Miles square) as may, by Cession of particular States, and the Acceptance of Congress, become the Seat of the Government of the United States, and to exercise like Authority over all Places purchased by the Consent of the Legislature of the State in which the Same shall be, for the Erection of Forts, Magazines, Arsenals, dock-Yards, and other needful Buildings;—And

To make all Laws which shall be necessary and proper for carrying into Execution the foregoing Powers, and all other Powers vested by this Constitution in the Government of the United States, or in any Department or Officer thereof.

Section 9

The Migration or Importation of such Persons as any of the States now existing shall think proper to admit, shall not be prohibited by the Congress prior to the Year one thousand eight hundred and eight, but a Tax or Duty may be imposed on such Importation, not exceeding ten dollars for each Person.

The Privilege of the Writ of Habeas Corpus shall not be suspended, unless when in Cases of Rebellion or Invasion the public Safety may require it.

No Bill of Attainder or ex post facto Law shall be passed.

No Capitation, or other direct, Tax shall be laid, unless in Proportion to the Census or Enumeration herein before directed to be taken.

No Tax or Duty shall be laid on Articles exported from any State.

No Preference shall be given by any Regulation of Commerce or Revenue to the Ports of one State over those of another: nor shall Vessels bound to, or from, one State, be obliged to enter, clear, or pay Duties in another.

No Money shall be drawn from the Treasury, but in Consequence of Appropriations made by Laws; and a regular Statement and Account of the Receipts and Expenditures of all public Money shall be published from time to time.

No Title of Nobility shall be granted by the United States: And no Person holding any Office of Profit or Trust under them, shall, without the Consent of the Congress, accept of any present, Emolument, Office, or Title, of any kind whatever, from any King, Prince, or foreign State.

Section 10

No State shall enter into any Treaty, Alliance, or Confederation; grant Letters of Marque and Reprisal; coin Money; emit Bills of Credit; make any Thing but gold and silver Coin a Tender in Payment of Debts; pass any Bill of Attainder, ex post facto Law, or Law impairing the Obligation of Contracts, or grant any Title of Nobility.

No State shall, without the Consent of the Congress, lay any Imposts or Duties on Imports or Exports, except what may be absolutely necessary for executing its inspection Laws: and the net Produce of all Duties and Imposts, laid by any State on Imports or Exports, shall be for the Use of the Treasury of the United States; and all such Laws shall be subject to the Revision and Controul of the Congress.

No State shall, without the Consent of Congress, lay any Duty of Tonnage, keep Troops, or Ships of War in time of Peace, enter into any Agreement or Compact with another State, or with a foreign Power, or engage in War, unless actually invaded, or in such imminent Danger as will not admit of delay.

ARTICLE II

Section 1

The executive Power shall be vested in a President of the United States of America. He shall hold his Office during the Term of four Years, and, together with the Vice President, chosen for the same Term, be elected, as follows:

Each State shall appoint, in such Manner as the Legislature thereof may direct, a Number of Electors, equal to the whole Number of Senators and Representatives to which the State may be entitled in the Congress: but no Senator or Representative, or Person holding an Office of Trust or Profit under the United States, shall be appointed an Elector.

The Electors shall meet in their respective States, and vote by Ballot for two Persons, of whom one at least shall not be an Inhabitant of the same State with themselves. And they shall make a List of all the Persons voted for, and of the Number of Votes for each; which List they shall sign and certify, and transmit sealed to the Seat of the Government of the United States, directed to the President of the Senate. The President of the Senate shall, in the Presence of the Senate and House of Representatives, open all the Certificates, and the Votes shall then be counted. The Person having the greatest Number of Votes shall be the President, if such Number be a Majority of the whole Number of Electors appointed; and if there be more than one who have such Majority, and have an equal Number of Votes, then the House of Representatives shall immediately chuse by Ballot one of them for President; and if no Person have a Majority, then from the five highest on the List the said House shall in like Manner chuse the President. But in chusing the President, the Votes shall be taken by States, the Representation from each State having one Vote; A quorum for this Purpose shall consist of a Member or Members from two thirds of the States, and a Majority of all the States shall be necessary to a Choice. In every Case, after the Choice of the President, the Person having the greatest Number of Votes of the Electors shall be the Vice President. But if there should remain two or more who have equal Votes, the Senate shall chuse from them by Ballot the Vice President.

The Congress may determine the Time of chusing the Electors, and the Day on which they shall give their Votes; which Day shall be the same throughout the United States.

No Person except a natural born Citizen, or a Citizen of the United States, at the time of the Adoption of this Constitution, shall be eligible to the Office of President; neither shall any Person be eligible to that Office who shall not have attained to the Age of thirty five Years, and been fourteen Years a Resident within the United States.

In Case of the Removal of the President from Office, or of his Death, Resignation, or Inability to discharge the Powers and Duties of the said Office, the Same shall devolve on the Vice President, and the Congress may by Law provide for the Case of Removal, Death, Resignation or Inability, both of the President and Vice President, declaring what Officer shall then act as President, and such Officer shall act accordingly, until the Disability be removed, or a President shall be elected.

The President shall, at stated Times, receive for his Services, a Compensation, which shall neither be encreased nor diminished during the Period for which he shall have been elected, and he shall not receive within that Period any other Emolument from the United States, or any of them.

Before he enter on the Execution of his Office, he shall take the following Oath or Affirmation:—"I do solemnly swear (or affirm) that I will faithfully execute the Office of President of the United States, and will to the best of my Ability, preserve, protect and defend the Constitution of the United States."

Section 2

The President shall be Commander in Chief of the Army and Navy of the United States, and of the Militia of the several States, when called into the actual Service of the United States; he may require the Opinion, in writing, of the principal Officer in each of the executive Departments, upon any Subject relating to the Duties of their respective Offices, and he shall have Power to grant Reprieves and Pardons for Offences against the United States, except in Cases of Impeachment.

He shall have Power, by and with the Advice and Consent of the Senate, to make Treaties, providing two thirds of the Senators present concur; and he shall nominate, and by and with the Advice and Consent of the Senate, shall appoint Ambassadors, other public Ministers and Consuls, Judges of the supreme Court, and all other Officers of the United States, whose Appointments are not herein otherwise provided for, and which shall be established by Law: but the Congress may by Law vest the Appointment of such inferior Officers, as they think proper, in the President alone, in the Courts of Law, or in the Heads of Departments.

The President shall have Power to fill up all Vacancies that may happen during the Recess of the Senate, by granting Commissions which shall expire at the End of their next Session.

Section 3

He shall from time to time give to the Congress Information of the State of the Union, and recommend to their Consideration such Measures as he shall judge necessary and expedient; he may, on extraordinary Occasions, convene both Houses, or either of them, and in Case of Disagreement between them, with Respect to the Time of Adjournment, he may adjourn them to such Time as he shall think proper, he shall receive Ambassadors and other public Ministers; he shall take Care that the Laws be faithfully executed, and shall Commission all the Officers of the United States.

Section 4

The President, Vice President and all civil Officers of the United States, shall be removed from Office on Impeachment for, and Conviction of, Treason, Bribery, or other high Crimes and Misdemeanors.

ARTICLE III

Section 1

The judicial Power of the United States, shall be vested in one supreme Court, and in such inferior Courts as the Congress may from time to time ordain and establish. The Judges, both of the supreme and inferior Courts, shall hold their Offices during good Behaviour, and shall, at stated Times, receive for their Services, a Compensation, which shall not be diminished during their Continuance in Office.

Section 2

The judicial Power shall extend to all Cases, in Law and Equity, arising under this Constitution, the Laws of the United States, and Treaties made, or which shall be made, under their Authority;—to all Cases affecting Ambassadors, other public Ministers and Consuls;—to all Cases of admirality and maritime Jurisdiction;—to Controversies to which the United States shall be a Party;—to Controversies between two or more States;—between a State and Citizens of another State;—between Citizens of different States;—between Citizens of the same State claiming Lands under Grants of different States, and between a State, or the Citizens thereof, and foreign States, Citizens or Subjects.

In all Cases affecting Ambassadors, other public Ministers and Consuls, and those in which a State shall be Party, the supreme Court shall have original Jurisdiction. In all the other Cases before mentioned, the supreme Court shall have appellate Jurisdiction, both as to Law and Fact, with such Exceptions, and under such Regulations as the Congress shall make.

The Trial of all Crimes, except in Cases of Impeachment, shall be by Jury; and such Trial shall be held in the State where the said Crimes shall have been committed; but when not committed within any State, the Trial shall be at such Place or Places as the Congress may by Law have directed.

Section 3

Treason against the United States, shall consist only in levying War against them, or in adhering to their Enemies, giving them Aid and Comfort. No Person shall be convicted of Treason unless on the Testimony of two Witnesses to the same overt Act, or on Confession in open Court.

The Congress shall have Power to declare the Punishment of Treason, but no Attainder of Treason shall work Corruption of Blood, or Forfeiture except during the Life of the Person attainted.

ARTICLE IV

Section 1

Full Faith and Credit shall be given in each State to the public Acts, Records, and judicial Proceedings of every other State. And the Congress may by general Laws prescribe the Manner in which such Acts, Records and Proceedings shall be proved, and the Effect thereof.

Section 2

The Citizens of each State shall be entitled to all Privileges and Immunities of Citizens in the several States.

A Person charged in any State with Treason, Felony, or other Crime, who shall flee from Justice, and be found in another State, shall on Demand of the executive Authority of the State from which he fled, be delivered up, to be removed to the State having Jurisdiction of the Crime.

No Person held to Service or Labour in one State, under the Laws thereof, escaping into another, shall, in Consequence of any Law or Regulation therein, be discharged from such Service or Labour, but shall be delivered up on Claim of the Party to whom such Service or Labour may be due.

Section 3

New States may be admitted by the Congress into this Union; but no new State shall be formed or erected within the Jurisdiction of any other State; nor any State be formed by the Junction of two or more States, or Parts of States, without the Consent of the Legislatures of the States concerned as well as of the Congress.

The Congress shall have Power to dispose of and make all needful Rules and Regulations respecting the Territory or other Property belonging to the United States; and nothing in this Constitution shall be so construed as to Prejudice any Claims of the United States, or of any particular State.

Section 4

The United States shall guarantee to every State in this Union a Republican Form of Government, and shall protect each of them against Invasion; and on Application of the Legislature, or of the Executive (when the Legislature cannot be convened) against domestic Violence.

ARTICLE V

The Congress, whenever two thirds of both Houses shall deem it necessary, shall propose Amendments to this Constitution, or, on the Application of the Legislatures of two thirds of the several States, shall call a Convention for proposing Amendments, which, in either Case, shall be valid to all Intents and Purposes, as Part of this Constitution, when ratified by the Legislatures of three fourths of the several States, or by Conventions in three fourths thereof, as the one or the other Mode of Ratification may be proposed by the Congress; Provided that no Amendment which may be made prior to the Year One thousand eight hundred and eight shall in any Manner affect the first and fourth Clauses in the Ninth Section of the first Article; and that no State, without its Consent, shall be deprived of its equal Suffrage in the Senate.

ARTICLE VI

All Debts contracted and Engagements entered into, before the Adoption of this Constitution, shall be as valid against the United States under this Constitution, as under the Confederation.

This Constitution, and the Laws of the United States which shall be made in Pursuance thereof; and all Treaties made, or which shall be made, under the Authority of the United States, shall be the supreme Law of the Land; and the Judges in every State shall be bound thereby, any Thing in the Constitution or Laws of any State to the Contrary notwithstanding.

The Senators and Representatives before mentioned, and the Members of the several State Legislatures, and all executive and judicial Officers, both of the United States and of the several States, shall be bound by Oath or Affirmation, to support this Constitution; but no religious Test shall ever be required as a Qualification to any Office or public Trust under the United States.

ARTICLE VII

The Ratification of the Conventions of nine States, shall be sufficient for the Establishment of this Constitution between the States so ratifying the Same.

AMENDMENT I [1791]

Congress shall make no law respecting an establishment of religion, or prohibiting the free exercise thereof; or abridging the freedom of speech, or of the press; or the right of the people peaceably to assemble, and to petition the Government for a redress of grievances.

AMENDMENT II [1791]

A well regulated Militia, being necessary to the security for a free State, the right of the people to keep and bear Arms, shall not be infringed.

AMENDMENT III [1791]

No Soldier shall, in time of peace be quartered in any house, without the consent of the Owner, nor in time of war, but in a manner to be prescribed by law.

AMENDMENT IV [1791]

The right of the people to be secure in their persons, houses, papers, and effects, against unreasonable searches and seizures, shall not be violated, and no Warrants shall issue, but upon probable cause, supported by Oath or affirmation, and particularly describing the place to be searched, and the persons or things to be seized.

AMENDMENT V [1791]

No person shall be held to answer for a capital, or otherwise infamous crime, unless on a presentment or indictment of a Grand Jury, except in cases arising in the land or naval forces, or in the Militia, when in actual service in time of War or public danger; nor shall any person be subject for the same offense to be twice put in jeopardy of life or limb; nor shall be compelled in any criminal case to be a witness against himself, nor be deprived of life, liberty, or property, without due process of law; nor shall private property be taken for public use, without just compensation.

AMENDMENT VI [1791]

In all criminal prosecutions, the accused shall enjoy the right to a speedy and public trial, by an impartial jury of the State and district wherein the crime shall have been committed, which district shall have been previously ascertained by law, and to be informed of the nature and cause of the accusation; to be confronted with the Witnesses against him; to have compulsory process for obtaining witnesses in his favor, and to have the Assistance of counsel for his defence.

AMENDMENT VII [1791]

In Suits at common law, where the value in controversy shall exceed twenty dollars, the right of trial by jury shall be preserved, and no fact tried by a jury, shall be otherwise reexamined in any Court of the United States, than according to the rules of the common law.

AMENDMENT VIII [1791]

Excessive bail shall not be required, no excessive fines imposed, nor cruel and unusual punishments inflicted.

AMENDMENT IX [1791]

The enumeration in the Constitution, of certain rights, shall not be construed to deny or disparage others retained by the people.

AMENDMENT X [1791]

The powers not delegated to the United States by the Constitution, nor prohibited by it to the States, are reserved to the States respectively, or to the people.

AMENDMENT XI [1798]

The Judicial power of the United States shall not be construed to extend to any suit in law or equity, commenced or prosecuted against one of the United States by Citizens of another State, or by Citizens or Subjects of any Foreign State.

AMENDMENT XII [1804]

The Electors shall meet in their respective states and vote by ballot for President and Vice-President, one of whom, at least, shall not be an inhabitant of the same state with themselves; they shall name in their ballots the person voted for as President, and in distinct ballots the person voted for as Vice-President, and they shall make distinct lists of all persons voted for as President, and of all persons voted for as Vice-President, and of the number of votes for each, which lists they shall sign and certify, and transmit sealed to the seat of the government of the United States, directed to the President of the Senate;—The President of the Senate shall, in the presence of the Senate and House of Representatives, open all the certificates and the votes shall then be counted;—The person having the greatest number of votes for President, shall be the President, if such number be a majority of the whole number of Electors appointed; and if no person have such majority, then from the persons having the highest numbers not exceeding three on the list of those voted for as President, the House of Representatives shall choose immediately, by ballot, the President. But in choosing the President, the votes shall be taken by states, the representation from each state having one vote; a quorum for this purpose shall consist of a member or members from two-thirds of the states, and a majority of all the states shall be necessary to a choice. And if the House of Representatives shall not choose a President whenever the right of choice shall devolve upon them, before the fourth day of March next following, then the Vice-President shall act as President, as in the case of the death or other constitutional disability of the President. The person having the greatest number of votes as Vice-President, shall be the Vice-President, if such number be a majority of the whole number of Electors appointed, and if no person have a majority, then from the two highest numbers on the list, the Senate shall choose the Vice-President; a quorum for the purpose shall consist of two-thirds of the whole number of Senators, and a majority of the whole number shall be necessary to a choice. But no person constitutionally ineligible to the office of President shall be eligible to that of the Vice-President of the United States.

AMENDMENT XIII [1865]

Section 1

Neither slavery nor involuntary servitude, except as a punishment for crime whereof the party shall have been duly convicted, shall exist within the United States, or any place subject to their jurisdiction.

Section 2

Congress shall have power to enforce this article by appropriate legislation.

AMENDMENT XIV [1868]

All persons born or naturalized in the United States, and subject to the jurisdiction thereof, are citizens of the United States and of the State wherein they reside. No State shall make or enforce any law which shall abridge the privileges or immunities of citizens of the United States; nor shall any State deprive any person of life, liberty, or property, without due process of law; nor deny to any person within its jurisdiction the equal protection of the laws.

Section 2

Representatives shall be appointed among the several States according to their respective numbers, counting the whole number of persons in each State, excluding Indians not taxed. But when the right to vote at any election for the choice of electors for President and Vice President of the United States, Representatives in Congress, the Executive and Judicial officers of a State, or the members of the Legislature thereof, is denied to any of the male inhabitants of such State, being twenty-one years of age, and citizens of the United States, or in any way abridged, except for participation in rebellion, or other crime, the basis of representation therein shall be reduced in the proportion which the number of such male citizens shall bear to the whole number of male citizens twenty-one years of age in such State.

Section 3

No person shall be a Senator or Representative in Congress, or elector of President and Vice President, or hold any office, civil or military, under the United States, or under any State, who, having previously taken an oath, as a member of Congress, or as an officer of the United States, or as a member of any State legislature, or as an executive or judicial officer of any State, to support the Constitution of the United States, shall have engaged in insurrection or rebellion against the same, or given aid or comfort to the enemies thereof. But Congress may by a vote of two-thirds of each House, remove such disability.

Section 4

The validity of the public debt of the United States, authorized by law, including debts incurred for payment of pensions and bounties for services in suppressing insurrection or rebellion, shall not be questioned. But neither the United States nor any State shall assume or pay any debt or obligation incurred in aid of insurrection or rebellion against the United States, or any claim for the loss or emancipation of any slave; but all such debts, obligations and claims shall be held illegal and void.

Section 5

The Congress shall have power to enforce, by appropriate legislation, the provisions of this article.

AMENDMENT XV [1870]

Section 1

The right of citizens of the United States to vote shall not be denied or abridged by the United States or by any State on account of race, color, or previous condition of servitude.

Section 2

The Congress shall have power to enforce this article by appropriate legislation.

AMENDMENT XVI [1913]

The Congress shall have power to lay and collect taxes on incomes, from whatever source derived, without apportionment among the several States, and without regard to any census or enumeration.

AMENDMENT XVII [1913]

The Senate of the United States shall be composed of two Senators from each State, elected by the people thereof, for six years; and each Senator shall have one vote. The electors in each State shall have the qualifications requisite for electors of the most numerous branch of the State legislatures.

When vacancies happen in the representation of any State in the Senate, the executive authority of each State shall issue writs of election to fill such vacancies; *Provided*, That the legislature of any State may empower the executive thereof to make temporary appointments until the people fill the vacancies by election as the legislature may direct.

This amendment shall not be so construed as to affect the election or term of any Senator chosen before it becomes valid as part of the Constitution.

AMENDMENT XVIII [1919]

Section 1

After one year from the ratification of this article the manufacture, sale, or transportation of intoxicating liquors within, the importation thereof into, or the exportation thereof from the United States and all territory subject to the jurisdiction thereof for beverage purposes is hereby prohibited.

Section 2

The Congress and the several States shall have concurrent power to enforce this article by appropriate legislation.

Section 3

This article shall be inoperative unless it shall have been ratified as an amendment to the Constitution by the legislatures of the several States, as provided in the Constitution, within seven years from the date of the submission hereof to the States by the Congress.

AMENDMENT XIX [1920]

The right of citizens of the United States to vote shall not be denied or abridged by the United States or by any State on account of sex.

Congress shall have power to enforce this article by appropriate legislation.

AMENDMENT XX [1933]

Section 1

The terms of the President and Vice President shall end at noon on the 20th day of January, and the terms of Senators and Representatives at noon on the 3d day of January, of the years in which such terms would have ended if this article had not been ratified; and the terms of their successors shall then begin.

Section 2

The Congress shall assemble at least once in every year, and such meeting shall begin at noon on the 3d day of January, unless they shall by law appoint a different day.

Section 3

If, at the time fixed for the beginning of the term of the President, the President elect shall have died, the Vice President elect shall become President. If a President shall not have been chosen before the time fixed for the beginning of his term, or if the President elect shall have failed to qualify, then the Vice President elect shall act as President until a President shall have qualified; and the Congress may by law provide for the case wherein neither a President elect nor a Vice President elect shall have qualified, declaring who shall then act as President, or the manner in which one who is to act shall be selected, and such person shall act accordingly until a President or Vice President shall have qualified.

Section 4

The Congress may by law provide for the case of the death of any of the persons from whom the House of Representatives may choose a President whenever the right of choice shall have devolved upon them, and for the case of the death of any of the persons from whom the Senate may choose a Vice President whenever the right of choice shall have devolved upon them.

Section 5

Sections 1 and 2 shall take effect on the 15th day of October following the ratification of this article.

Section 6

This article shall be inoperative unless it shall have been ratified as an amendment to the Constitution by the legislatures of three-fourths of the several States within seven years from the date of its submission.

AMENDMENT XXI [1933]

Section 1

The eighteenth article of amendment to the Constitution of the United States is hereby repealed.

Section 2

The transportation or importation into any State, Territory, or possession of the United States for delivery or use therein of intoxicating liquors, in violation of the laws thereof, is hereby prohibited.

Section 3

This article shall be inoperative unless it shall have been ratified as an amendment to the Constitution by conventions in the several States, as provided in the Constitution, within seven years from the date of the submission hereof to the States by the Congress.

AMENDMENT XXII [1951]

Section 1

No person shall be elected to the office of the President more than twice, and no person who has held the office of President, or acted as President, for more than two years of a term to which some other person was elected President shall be elected to the office of the President more than once. But this Article shall not apply to any person holding the office of President when this Article was proposed by the Congress, and shall not prevent any person who may be holding the office of President, or acting as President, during the term within which this Article becomes operative from holding the office of President or acting as President during the remainder of such term.

Section 2

This article shall be inoperative unless it shall have been ratified as an amendment to the Constitution by the legislatures of three-fourths of the several States within seven years from the date of its submission to the States by the Congress.

AMENDMENT XXIII [1961]

Section 1

The District constituting the seat of Government of the United States shall appoint in such manner as the Congress may direct:

A number of electors of President and Vice President equal to the whole number of Senators and Representatives in Congress to which the District would be entitled if it were a State, but in no event more than the least populous State; they shall be in addition to those appointed by the States, but they shall be considered, for the purposes of the election of President and Vice President, to be electors appointed by a State; and they shall meet in the District and perform such duties as provided by the twelfth article of amendment.

Section 2

The Congress shall have power to enforce this article by appropriate legislation.

AMENDMENT XXIV [1964]

Section 1

The right of citizens of the United States to vote in any primary or other election for President or Vice President, for electors for President or Vice President, or for Senator or Representative in Congress, shall not be denied or abridged by the United States or any State by reason of failure to pay any poll tax or other tax.

Section 2

The Congress shall have power to enforce this article by appropriate legislation.

AMENDMENT XXV [1967]

Section 1

In case of the removal of the President from office or of his death or resignation, the Vice President shall become President.

Section 2

Whenever there is a vacancy in the office of the Vice President, the President shall nominate a Vice President who shall take office upon confirmation by a majority vote of both Houses of Congress.

Section 3

Whenever the President transmits to the President pro tempore of the Senate and the Speaker of the House of Representatives his written declaration that he is unable to discharge the powers and duties of his office, and until he transmits to them a written declaration to the contrary, such powers and duties shall be discharged by the Vice President as Acting President.

Section 4

Whenever the Vice President and a majority of either the principal officers of the executive departments or of such other body as Congress may by law provide, transmit to the President pro tempore of the Senate and the Speaker of the House of Representatives their written declaration that the President is unable to discharge the powers and duties of his office, the Vice President shall immediately assume the powers and duties of the office as Acting President.

Thereafter, when the President transmits to the President pro tempore of the Senate and the Speaker of the House of Representatives his written declaration that no inability exists, he shall resume the powers and duties of his office unless the Vice President and a majority of either the principal officers of the executive department or of such other body as Congress may by law provide, transmit within four days to the President pro tempore of the Senate and the Speaker of the House of Representatives their written declaration that the President is unable to discharge the powers and duties of his office. Thereupon Congress shall decide the issue, assembling within forty-eight hours for that purpose if not in session. If the Congress, within twenty-one days after receipt of the latter written declaration, or, if Congress is not in session, within twenty-one days after Congress is required to assemble, determines by two-thirds vote of both Houses that the President is unable to discharge the powers and duties of his office, the Vice President shall continue to discharge the same as Acting President; otherwise, the President shall resume the powers and duties of his office.

AMENDMENT XXVI [1971]

Section 1

The right of citizens of the United States, who are eighteen years of age or older, to vote shall not be denied or abridged by the United States or by any State on account of age.

Section 2

The Congress shall have power to enforce this article by appropriate legislation.

A · P · P · E · N · D · I · X B

SHERMAN ACT (AS AMENDED) (EXCERPTS)

Section 1. Every contract, combination in the form of trust or otherwise, or conspiracy, in restraint of trade or commerce among the several States, or with foreign nations, is declared to be illegal. Every person who shall make any contract or engage in any combination or conspiracy hereby declared to be illegal shall be deemed guilty of a felony, and, on conviction thereof, shall be punished by fine not exceeding one million dollars if a corporation, or, if any other person, one hundred thousand dollars or by imprisonment not exceeding three years, or by both said punishments, in the discretion of the court.

Section 2. Every person who shall monopolize, or attempt to monopolize, or combine or conspire with any other person or persons, to monopolize any part of the trade or commerce among the several States, or with foreign nations, shall be deemed guilty of a felony, and, on conviction thereof, shall be punished by fine not exceeding one million dollars if a corporation, or, if any other person, one hundred thousand dollars or by imprisonment not exceeding three years, or by both said punishments, in the discretion of the court.

A · P · P · E · N · D · I · X C

CLAYTON ACT (AS AMENDED) (EXCERPTS)

Section 3. It shall be unlawful for any person engaged in commerce, in the course of such commerce, to lease or make a sale or contract for sale of goods, wares, merchandise, machinery, supplies, or other commodities, whether patented or unpatented, for use, consumption, or resale within the United States or any Territory thereof or the District of Columbia or any insular possession or other place under the jurisdiction of the United States, or fix a price charged therefor, or discount from, or rebate upon, such price, on the condition, agreement, or understanding that the lessee or purchaser thereof shall not use or deal in the goods, wares, merchandise, machinery, supplies, or other commodities of a competitor or competitors of the lessor of seller, where the effect of such lease, sale, or contract for sale or such condition, agreement, or understanding may be to substantially lessen competition or tend to create a monopoly in any line of commerce.

Section 4. Any person who shall be injured in his business or property by reason of anything forbidden in the antitrust laws may sue therefor in any district court of the United States in the district in which the defendant resides or is found or has an agent, without respect to the amount in controversy, and shall recover threefold the damages by him sustained, and the cost of suit, including a reasonable attorney's fee. . . .

Section 6. The labor of a human being is not a commodity or article of commerce. Nothing contained in the antitrust laws shall be construed to forbid the existence and operation of labor, agricultural, or horticultural organizations, instituted for the purposes of mutual help, and not having capital stock or conducted for profit, or to forbid or restrain individual members of such organizations from lawfully carrying out the legitimate objects thereof; nor shall such organizations, or the members thereof, be held or construed to be illegal combinations or conspiracies in restraint of trade, under the antitrust laws.

Section 7. No person engaged in commerce or in any activity affecting commerce shall acquire, directly or indirectly, the whole or any part of the stock or other share capital and no person subject to the jurisdiction of the Federal Trade Commission shall acquire the whole or any part of the assets of another person engaged also in commerce or in any activity affecting commerce, where in any line of commerce in any section of the country, the effect of such acquisition may be substantially to lessen competition, or to tend to create a monopoly.

No person shall acquire, directly or indirectly, the whole or any part of the stock or other share capital and no person subject to the jurisdiction of the Federal Trade Commission shall acquire the whole or any part of the assets of one or more persons engaged in commerce or in any activity affecting commerce, where in any line of commerce in any section of the country, the effect of such acquisition, of such stocks or assets, or of the use of such stock by the voting or granting of proxies or otherwise, may be substantially to lessen competition, or to tend to create a monopoly.

This section shall not apply to persons purchasing such stock solely for investment and not using the same by voting or otherwise to bring about, or in attempting to bring about, the substantial lessening of competition. . . .

Section 8. . . . [N]o person at the same time shall be a director in any two or more corporations, any one of which has capital, surplus, and undivided profits aggregating more than $1,000,000, engaged in whole or in part in commerce, . . . if such corporations are or shall have been theretofore, by virtue of their business and location of operation, competitors, so that the elimination of competition by agreement between them would constitute a violation of any of the provisions of any of the antitrust laws. . . .

A·P·P·E·N·D·I·X D

ROBINSON-PATMAN ACT (EXCERPTS)

Section 2. (a) It shall be unlawful for any person engaged in commerce, in the course of such commerce, either directly or indirectly, to discriminate in price between different purchasers of commodities of like grade and quality, where either or any of the purchases involved in such discrimination are in commerce, where such commodities are sold for use, consumption, or resale within the United States or any Territory thereof or the District of Columbia or any insular possession or other place under the jurisdiction of the United States, and where the effect of such discrimination may be substantially to lessen competition or tend to create a monopoly in any line of commerce, or to injure, destroy, or prevent competition with any person who either grants or knowingly receives the benefit of such discrimination, or with customers of either of them: *Provided*, That nothing herein contained shall prevent differentials which make only due allowance for differences in the cost of manufacture, sale, or delivery resulting from the differing methods or quantities in which such commodities are to such purchasers sold or delivered: *Provided, however*, That the Federal Trade Commission may, after due investigation and hearing to all interested parties, fix and establish quantity limits, and revise the same as it finds necessary, as to particular commodities or classes of commodities, where it finds that available purchasers in greater quantities are so few as to render differentials on account thereof unjustly discriminatory or promotive of monopoly in any line of commerce; and the foregoing shall then not be construed to permit differentials based on differences in quantities greater than those so fixed and established: *And provided further*, That nothing herein contained shall prevent persons engaged in selling goods, wares, or merchandise in commerce from selecting their own customers in bona fide transactions and not in restraint of trade: *And provided further*, That nothing herein contained shall prevent price changes from time to time where in response to changing conditions affecting the market for or the marketabilty of the goods concerned, such as but not limited to actual or imminent deterioration of perishable goods, obsolescence of seasonal goods, distress sales under court process, or sales in good faith in discontinuance of business in the goods concerned.

(b) Upon proof being made, at any hearing on a complaint under this section, that there has been discrimination in price or services or facilities furnished, the burden of rebutting the prima-facie case thus made by showing justification shall be upon the person charged with a violation of this section, and unless justification shall be affirmatively shown, the Commission is authorized to issue an order terminating the discrimination: *Provided, however*, That nothing herein contained shall prevent a seller rebutting the prima-facie case thus made by showing that his lower price or the furnishing of services or facilities to any purchaser or purchasers was made in good faith to meet an equally low price of a competitor, or the services or facilities furnished by a competitor.

(c) It shall be unlawful for any person engaged in commerce, in the course of such commerce, to pay or grant, or to receive or accept, anything of value as a commission, brokerage, or other compensation, or any allowance or discount in lieu thereof, except for services rendered in connection with the sale or purchase of goods, wares, or merchandise, either to the other party to such transaction or to an agent, representative, or other intermediary therein where such intermediary is acting in fact for or in behalf, or is subject to the direct or indirect control, of any party to such transaction other than the person by whom such compensation is so granted or paid.

(d) It shall be unlawful for any person engaged in commerce to pay or contract for the payment of anything of value to or for the benefit of a customer of such person in the course of such commerce as compensation or in consideration for any services or facilities furnished by or through such customer in connection with the processing, handling, sale, or offering for sale of any products or commodities manufactured, sold, or offered for sale by such person, unless such payment or consideration is available on proportionally equal terms to all other customers competing in the distribution of such products or commodities.

(e) It shall be unlawful for any person to discriminate in favor of one purchaser against another purchaser or purchasers of a commodity bought for resale, with or without processing, by contracting to furnish or furnishing, or by contributing to the furnishing of, any services or facilities connected with the processing, handling, sale, or offering for sale of such commodity so purchased upon terms not accorded to all purchasers on proportionally equal terms.

(f) It shall be unlawful for any person engaged in commerce, in the course of such commerce, knowingly to induce or receive a discrimination in price which is prohibited by this section.

A · P · P · E · N · D · I · X E

FEDERAL TRADE COMMISSION ACT (AS AMENDED) (EXCERPTS)

Section 5. (a) (1) Unfair methods of competition in or affecting commerce, and unfair or deceptive acts or practices in or affecting commerce, are hereby declared unlawful. . . .

A · P · P · E · N · D · I · X F

TITLE VII OF THE 1964 CIVIL RIGHTS ACT (AS AMENDED) (EXCERPTS)

Section 701. . . . (j) The term "religion" includes all aspects of religious observance and practice, as well as belief, unless an employer demonstrates that he is unable to reasonably accommodate to an employee's or prospective employee's religious observance or practice without undue hardship on the conduct of the employer's business. . . .

(k) The terms "because of sex" or "on the basis of sex" include, but are not limited to, because of or on the basis of pregnancy, childbirth, or related medical conditions; and women affected by pregnancy, childbirth, or related medical conditions shall be treated the same for all employment-related purposes, including receipt of benefits under fringe benefit programs, as other persons not so affected but similar in their ability or inability to work, and nothing in Section 703(h) of this title shall be interpreted to permit otherwise. This subsection shall not require an employer to pay for health insurance benefits for abortion, except where the life of the mother would be endangered if the fetus were carried to term, or except where medical complications have arisen from an abortion: *Provided*, That nothing herein shall preclude an employer from providing abortion benefits or otherwise affect bargaining agreements in regard to abortion. . . .

Section 703. (a) It shall be an unlawful employment practice for an employer—

(1) to fail or refuse to hire or to discharge any individual, or otherwise to discriminate against any individual with respect to his compensation, terms, conditions, or privileges of employment, because of such individual's race, color, religion, sex, or national origin or

(2) to limit, segregate, or classify his employees or applicants for employment in any way which would deprive or tend to deprive any individual of employment opportunities or otherwise adversely affect his status as an employee, because of such individual's race, color, religion, sex, or national origin.

(b) It shall be an unlawful employment practice for an employment agency to fail or refuse to refer for employment, or otherwise to discriminate against, any individual because of his race, color, religion, sex, or national origin, or to classify or refer for employment any individual on the basis of his race, color, religion, sex, or national origin.

(c) It shall be an unlawful employment practice for a labor organization—

(1) to exclude or to expel from its membership, or otherwise to discriminate against, any individual because of his race, color, religion, sex, or national origin;

(2) to limit, segregate, or classify its membership or applicants for membership, or to classify or fail or refuse to refer for employment any individual, in any way which would deprive or tend to deprive any individual of employment opportunities, or would limit such employment opportunities or otherwise adversely affect his status as an employee or as an applicant for employment, because of such individual's race, color, religion, sex, or national origin; or

(3) to cause or attempt to cause any employer to discriminate against an individual in violation of this section.

(d) It shall be an unlawful employment practice for any employer, labor organization, or joint labor-management committee controlling apprenticeship or other training or retraining, including on-the-job training programs to discriminate against any individual because of his race, color, religion, sex, or national origin in admission to, or employment in, any program established to provide apprenticeship or other training.

(e) Notwithstanding any other provision of this subchapter, (1) it shall not be an unlawful employment practice for an employer to hire and employ employees, for an employment agency to classify, or refer for employment any individual, for a labor organization to classify its membership or to classify or refer for employment any individual, or for an employer, labor organization, or joint labor-management committee controlling apprenticeship or other training or retraining programs to admit or employ any individual in any such program, on the basis of his religion, sex, or national origin in those certain instances where religion, sex, or national origin is a bona fide occupational qualification reasonably necessary to the normal operation of that particular business or enterprise, and (2) it shall not be an unlawful employment practice for a school, college, university, or other educational institution or institution of learning to hire and employ employees of a particular religion if such school, college, university, or other educational institution or institution of learning is, in whole or in substantial part, owned, supported, controlled, or managed by a particular religion or by a particular religious corporation, association, or society, or if the curriculum of such school, college, university, or other educational institution or institution of learning is directed toward the propagation of a particular religion.

(f) As used in this subchapter, the phrase "unlawful employment practice" shall not be deemed to include any action or measure taken by an employer, labor organization, joint labor-management committee, or employment agency with respect to an individual who is a member of the Communist Party of the United States or of any other organization required to register as a Communist-action or Communist-front organization by final order of the Subversive Activities Control Board pursuant to the Subversive Activities Control Act of 1950 [50 U.S.C. 781 et seq.].

(g) Notwithstanding any other provision of this subchapter, it shall be an unlawful employment practice for an employer to fail or refuse to hire and employ any individual for any position, for an employer to discharge any individual from any position, or for an employment agency to fail or refuse to refer any individual for employment in any position, or for a labor organization to fail or refuse to refer any individual for employment in any position if—

(1) the occupancy of such position, or access to the premises in or upon which any part of the duties of such position is performed or is to be performed, is subject to any requirement imposed in the interest of the national security of the United States under any security program in effect pursuant to or administered under any statute of the United States or any Executive order of the President; and

(2) such individual has not fulfilled or has ceased to fulfill that requirement.

(h) Notwithstanding any other provision of this subchapter, it shall not be an unlawful employment practice for an employer to apply different standards of compensation, or different terms, conditions, or privileges of employment pursuant to a bona fide seniority or merit system, or a system which measures earnings by quantity or quality of production or to employees who work in different locations, provided that such differences are not the result of an intention to discriminate because of race, color, religion, sex, or national origin, nor shall it be an unlawful employment practice for an employer to give and to act upon the results of any professionally developed ability test provided that such test, its administration or action upon the results is not designed, intended or used to discriminate because of race, color, religion, sex, or national origin. It shall not be an unlawful employment practice under this subchapter for any employer to differentiate upon the basis of sex in determining the amount of the wages or compensation paid or to be paid to employees of such employer if such differentiation is authorized by the provisions of section 206(d) of title 29.

(i) Nothing contained in this subchapter shall apply to any business or enterprise on or near an Indian reservation with respect to any publicly announced employment practice of such business or enterprise under which a preferential treatment is given to any individual because he is an Indian living on or near a reservation.

(j) Nothing contained in this subchapter shall be interpreted to require any employer, employment agency, labor organization, or joint labor-management committee subject to this subchapter to grant preferential treatment to any individual or to any group because of the race, color, religion, sex, or national origin of such individual or group on account of an imbalance which may exist with respect to the total number or percentage of persons of any race, color, religion, sex, or national origin employed by any employer, referred or classified for employment by any employment agency or labor organization, admitted to membership or classified by any labor organization, or admitted to, or employed in, any apprenticeship or other training program, in comparison with the total number or percentage of persons of such race, color, religion, sex, or national origin in any community, State, section, or other area, or in the available work force in any community, State, section, or other area.

Section 704. (a) It shall be an unlawful employment practice for an employer to discriminate against any of his employees or applicants for employment, for an employment agency, or joint labor-management committee controlling apprenticeship or other training or retaining, including on-the-job training programs, to discriminate against any individual, or for a labor organization to discriminate against any member thereof or applicant for membership, because he has opposed any practice made an unlawful employment practice by this subchapter, or because he has made a charge, testified, assisted, or participated in any manner in an investigation, proceeding, or hearing under this subchapter.

(b) It shall be an unlawful employment practice for an employer, labor organization, employment agency, or joint labor-management committee controlling apprenticeship or other training or retraining, including on-the-job training programs, to print or publish or cause to be printed or published any notice or advertisement relating to employment by such an employer or membership in or any classification or referral for employment by such a labor organization, or relating to any classification or referral for employment by such an employment agency, or relating to admission to, or employment in, any program established to provide apprenticeship or other training by such a joint labor-management committee, indicating any preference, limitation, specification, or discrimination, based on race, color, religion, sex, or national origin, except that such a notice or advertisement may indicate a preference, limitation, specification, or discrimination based on religion, sex, or national origin when religion, sex, or national origin is a bona fide occupational qualification for employment.

A · P · P · E · N · D · I · X G

NATIONAL LABOR RELATIONS ACT (AS AMENDED) (EXCERPTS)

Section 7. Employees shall have the right to self-organization, to form, join, or assist labor organizations, to bargain collectively through representatives of their own choosing, and to engage in other concerted activities for the purpose of collective bargaining or other mutual aid or protection, and shall also have the right to refrain from any or all of such activities except to the extent that such right may be affected by an agreement requiring membership in a labor organization as a condition of employment as authorized in section 8(a)(3).

Section 8. (a) It shall be an unfair labor practice for an employer—

(1) to interfere with, restrain, or coerce employees in the exercise of the rights guaranteed in section 7;

(2) to dominate or interfere with the formation or administration of any labor organization or contribute financial or other support to it: *Provided*, That subject to rules and regulations made and published by the Board pursuant to section 6, an employer shall not be prohibited from permitting employees to confer with him during working hours without loss of time or pay;

(3) by discrimination in regard to hire or tenure of employment or any term or condition of employment to encourage or discourage membership in any labor organization: *Provided*, That nothing in this Act, or in any other statute of the United States, shall preclude an employer from making an agreement with a labor organization (not established, maintained, or assisted by any action defined in section 8(a) of this Act as an unfair labor practice) to require as a condition of employment membership therein on or after the thirtieth day following the beginning of such employment or the effective date of such agreement, whichever is the later, (i) if such labor organization is the representative of the employees as provided in section 9(a), in the appropriate collective-bargaining unit covered by such agreement when made, and (ii) unless following an election held as provided in section 9(e) within one year preceding the effective date of such agreement, the Board shall have certified that at least a majority of the employees eligible to vote in such election have voted to rescind the authority of such labor organization to make such an agreement: *Provided further*, That no employer shall justify any discrimination against an employee for nonmembership in a labor organization (A) if he has reasonable grounds for believing that such membership was not available to the employee on the same terms and con-

ditions generally applicable to other members, or (B) if he has reasonable grounds for believing that membership was denied or terminated for reasons other than the failure of the employee to tender the periodic dues and the initiation fees uniformly required as a condition of acquiring or retaining membership;

(4) to discharge or otherwise discriminate against an employee because he has filed charges or given testimony under this Act;

(5) to refuse to bargain collectively with the representatives of his employees, subject to the provisions of section 9(a).

(b) It shall be an unfair labor practice for a labor organization or its agents—

(1) to restrain or coerce (A) employees in the exercise of the rights guaranteed in section 7: *Provided*, That this paragraph shall not impair the right of a labor organization to prescribe its own rules with respect to the acquisition or retention of membership therein; or (B) an employer in the selection of his representatives for the purposes of collective bargaining or the adjustment of grievances;

(2) to cause or attempt to cause an employer to discriminate against an employee in violation of subsection (a)(3) or to discriminate against an employee with respect to whom membership in such organization has been denied or terminated on some ground other than his failure to tender the periodic dues and the initiation fees uniformly required as a condition of acquiring or retaining membership;

(3) to refuse to bargain collectively with an employer, provided it is the representative of his employees subject to the provisions of section 9(a);

(4)(i) to engage in, or to induce or encourage any individual employed by any person engaged in commerce or in an industry affecting commerce to engage in, a strike or a refusal in the course of his employment to use, manufacture, process, transport, or otherwise handle or work on any goods, articles, materials, or commodities or to perform any services; or (ii) to threaten, coerce, or restrain any person engaged in commerce or in an industry affecting commerce, where in either case an object thereof is:

(A) forcing or requiring any employer or self-employed person to join any labor or employer organization or to enter into any agreement which is prohibited by section 8(e);

(B) forcing or requiring any person to cease using, selling, handling, transporting, or otherwise dealing in the products of any other producer, processor, or manufacturer, to cease doing business with any other person, or forcing or requiring any other employer to recognize or bargain with a labor organization as the representative of his employees unless such labor organization has been certified as the representative of such employees under the provisions of section 9: *Provided*, That nothing contained in this clause (B) shall be construed to make unlawful, where not otherwise unlawful, any primary strike or primary picketing;

(C) forcing or requiring any employer to recognize or bargain with a particular labor organization as the representative of his employees if another labor organization has been certified as the representative of such employees under the provisions of section 9;

(D) forcing or requiring any employer to assign particular work to employees in a particular labor organization or in a particular trade, craft, or class rather than to employees in another labor organization or in another trade, craft, or class, unless such employer is failing to conform to an order or certification of the Board determining the bargaining representative for employees performing such work:

Provided, That nothing contained in this subsection (b) shall be construed to make unlawful a refusal by any person to enter upon the premises of any employer (other than his own employer), if the employees of such employer are engaged in a strike ratified or approved by a representative of such employees whom such employer is required to recognize under this Act: *Provided further*, That for the purposes of this paragraph (4) only, nothing contained in such paragraph shall be construed to prohibit publicity, other than picketing, for the purpose of truthfully advising the public, including consumers and members of a labor organization, that a product or products are produced by an employer with whom the labor organization has a primary dispute and are distributed by another employer, as long as such publicity does not have an effect of inducing any individual employed by any person other than the primary employer in the course of his employment to refuse to pick up, deliver, or transport any goods, or not to perform any services, at the establishment of the employer engaged in such distribution;

(5) to require of employees covered by an agreement authorized under subsection (a)(3) the payment, as a condition precedent to becoming a member of such organization, of a fee in an amount which the Board finds excessive or discriminatory under all the circumstances. In making such a finding, the Board shall consider, among other relevant factors, the practices and customs of labor organizations in the particular industry, and the wages currently paid to the employees affected;

(6) to cause or attempt to cause an employer to pay or deliver or agree to pay or deliver any money or other thing of value, in the nature of an exaction, for services which are not performed or not to be performed; and

(7) to picket or cause to be picketed, or threaten to picket or cause to be picketed, any employer where an object thereof is forcing or requiring an employer to recognize or bargain with a labor organization as the representative of his employees, or forcing or requiring the employees of an employer to accept or select such labor

organization as their collective bargaining representative, unless such labor organization is currently certified as the representative of such employees:

(A) where the employer has lawfully recognized in accordance with this Act any other labor organization and a question concerning representation may not appropriately be raised under section 9(c) of this Act,

(B) where within the preceding twelve months a valid election under section 9(c) of this Act has been conducted, or

(C) where such picketing has been conducted without a petition under section 9(c) being filed within a reasonable period of time not to exceed thirty days from the commencement of such picketing: *Provided*, That when such a petition has been filed the Board shall forthwith, without regard to the provisions of section 9(c)(1) or the absence of a showing of a substantial interest on the part of the labor organization, direct an election in such unit as the Board finds to be appropriate and shall certify the results thereof: *Provided further*, That nothing in this subparagraph (C) shall be construed to prohibit any picketing or other publicity for the purpose of truthfully advising the public (including consumers) that an employer does not employ members of, or have a contract with, a labor organization, unless an effect of such picketing is to induce any individual employed by any other person in the course of his employment, not to pick up, deliver or transport any goods or not to perform any services.

Nothing in this paragraph (7) shall be construed to permit any act which would otherwise be an unfair labor practice under this section 8(b).

(c) The expressing of any views, argument, or opinion, or the dissemination thereof, whether in written, printed, graphic, or visual form, shall not constitute or be evidence of an unfair labor practice under any of the provisions of this Act, if such expression contains no threat of reprisal or force or promise of benefit.

(d) For the purposes of this section, to bargain collectively is the performance of the mutual obligation of the employer and the representative of the employees to meet at reasonable times and confer in good faith with respect to wages, hours, and other terms and conditions of employment, or the negotiation of an agreement, or any question arising thereunder, and the execution of a written contract incorporating any agreement reached if requested by either party, but such obligation does not compel either party to agree to a proposal or require the making of a concession: *Provided*, That where there is in effect a collective-bargaining contract covering employees in an industry affecting commerce, the duty to bargain collectively shall also mean that no party to such contract shall terminate or modify such contract, unless the party desiring such termination or modification—

(1) serves a written notice upon the other party to the contract of the proposed termination or modification sixty days prior to the expiration date thereof, or in the event such contract contains no expiration date, sixty days prior to the time it is proposed to make such termination or modification;

(2) offers to meet and confer with the other party for the purpose of negotiating a new contract or a contract containing the proposed modifications;

(3) notifies the Federal Mediation and Conciliation Service within thirty days after such notice of the existence of a dispute, and simultaneously therewith notifies any State or Territorial agency established to mediate and conciliate disputes within the State or Territory where the dispute occurred, provided no agreement has been reached by that time; and

(4) continues in full force and effect, without resorting to strike or lockout, all the terms and conditions of the existing contract for a period of sixty days after such notice is given or until the expiration date of such contract, whichever occurs later:

The duties imposed upon employers, employees, and labor organizations by paragraphs (2), (3), and (4) shall become inapplicable upon an intervening certification of the Board, under which the labor organization or individual, which is a party to the contract, has been superseded as or ceased to be the representative of the employees subject to the provisions of section 9(a), and the duties so imposed shall not be construed as requiring either party to discuss or agree to any modification of the terms and conditions contained in a contract for a fixed period, if such modification is to become effective before such terms and conditions can be reopened under the provisions of the contract. Any employee who engages in a strike within any notice period specified in this subsection, or who engages in any strike within the appropriate period specified in subsection (g) of this section shall lose his status as an employee of the employer engaged in the particular labor dispute, for the purposes of sections 8, 9, and 10 of this Act, as amended, but such loss of status for such employee shall terminate if and when he is reemployed by such employer. Whenever the collective bargaining involves employees of a health care institution, the provisions of this section 8(d) shall be modified as follows:

(A) The notice of section 8(d)(1) shall be ninety days; the notice of section 8(d)(3) shall be sixty days; and the contract period of section 8(d)(4) shall be ninety days;

(B) Where the bargaining is for an initial agreement following certification or recognition, at least thirty days' notice of the existence of a dispute shall be given by the labor organization to the agencies set forth in section 8(d)(3).

(C) After notice is given to the Federal Mediation and Conciliation Service under either clause (A) or (B) of this sentence, the Service shall promptly communicate with the parties and use its best efforts, by mediation and conciliation, to bring them to agreement. The parties shall participate fully and promptly in such meetings as may be undertaken by the Service for the purpose of aiding in a settlement of the dispute.

(e) It shall be an unfair labor practice for any labor organization and any employer to enter into any contract or agreement, express or implied, whereby such employer ceases or refrains or agrees to cease or refrain from handling, using, selling, transporting or otherwise dealing in any of the products of any other employer, or to cease doing business with any other person, and any contract or agreement entered into heretofore or hereafter containing such an agreement shall be to such extent unenforceable and void: *Provided*, That nothing in this subsection (e) shall apply to an agreement between a labor organization and an employer in the construction industry relating to the contracting or subcontracting of work to be done at the site of the construction, alteration, painting, or repair of a building, structure, or other work: *Provided further*, That for the purposes of this subsection (e) and section 8(b)(4)(B) the terms "any employer", "any person engaged in commerce or in industry affecting commerce", and "any person" when used in relation to the terms "any other producer, processor, or manufacturer", "any other employer", or "any other person" shall not include persons in the relation of a jobber, manufacturer, contractor, or subcontractor working on the goods or premises of the jobber or manufacturer or performing parts of an integrated process of production in the apparel and clothing industry: *Provided further*, That nothing in this Act shall prohibit the enforcement of any agreement which is within the foregoing exception.

(f) It shall not be an unfair labor practice under subsections (a) and (b) of this section for an employer engaged primarily in the building and construction industry to make an agreement covering employees engaged (or who, upon their employment, will be engaged) in the building and construction industry with a labor organization of which building and construction employees are members (not established, maintained, or assisted by any action defined in section 8(a) of this Act as an unfair labor practice) because (1) the majority status of such labor organization has not been established under the provisions of section 9 of this Act prior to the making of such agreement, or (2) such agreement requires as a condition of employment, membership in such labor organization after the seventh day following the beginning of such employment or the effective date of the agreement, whichever is later, or (3) such agreement requires the employer to notify such labor organization of opportunities for employment with such employer, or gives such labor organization an opportunity to refer qualified applicants for such employment, or (4) such agreement specifies minimum training or experience qualifications for employment or provides for priority in opportunities for employment based upon length of service with such employer, in the industry or in the particular geographical area: *Provided*, That nothing in this subsection shall set aside the final proviso to section 8(a)(3) of this Act: *Provided further*, That any agreement which would be invalid, but for clause (1) of this subsection, shall not be a bar to a petition filed pursuant to section 9(c) or 9(e).

(g) A labor organization before engaging in any strike, picketing, or other concerted refusal to work at any health care institution shall, not less than ten days prior to such action, notify the institution in writing and the Federal Mediation and Conciliation Service of that intention, except that in the case of bargaining for an initial agreement following certification or recognition the notice required by this subsection shall not be given until the expiration of the period specified in clause (B) of the last sentence of section 8(d) of this Act. The notice shall state the date and time that such action will commence. The notice, once given, may be extended by the written agreement of both parties.

Section 9. (a) Representatives designated or selected for the purposes of collective bargaining by the majority of the employees in a unit appropriate for such purposes, shall be the exclusive representatives of all the employees in such unit for the purposes of collective bargaining in respect to rates of pay, wages, hours of employment, or other conditions of employment: *Provided*, That any individual employee or a group of employees shall have the right at any time to present grievances to their employer and to have such grievances adjusted, without the intervention of the bargaining representative, as long as the adjustment is not inconsistent with the terms of a collective-bargaining contract or agreement then in effect: *Provided further*, That the bargaining representative has been given opportunity to be present at such adjustment.

(b) The Board shall decide in each case whether, in order to assure to employees the fullest freedom in exercising the rights guaranteed by this Act, the unit appropriate for the purposes of collective bargaining shall be the employer unit, craft unit, plant unit, or subdivision thereof: *Provided*, That the Board shall not (1) decide that any unit is appropriate for such purposes if such unit includes both professional employees and employees who are not professional employees unless a majority of such professional employees vote for inclusion in such unit; or (2) decide that any craft unit is inappropriate for such purposes on the ground that a different unit has been established by a prior Board determination, unless a majority of the employees in the proposed craft unit vote against separate representation or (3) decide that any unit is appropriate for such purposes if it includes, together with other employees, any individual employed as a guard to enforce against employees and other persons rules to protect property of the employer or to protect the safety of persons on the employer's premises; but no labor organization shall be certified as the representative of employees in a bargaining unit of guards if such organization admits to membership, or is affiliated directly or indirectly with an organization which admits to membership, employees other than guards.

(c) (1) Wherever a petition shall have been filed, in accordance with such regulations as may be prescribed by the Board—

(A) by an employee or group of employees or an individual or labor organization acting in their behalf alleging that a substantial number of employees (i) wish to be represented for collective bargaining and that their employer declines to recognize their representative as the representative defined in section 9(a), or (ii) assert that the individual or labor organization, which has been certified or is being currently recognized by their employer as the bargaining representative, is no longer a representative as defined in section 9(a); or

(B) by an employer, alleging that one or more individuals or labor organizations have presented to him a claim to be recognized as the representative defined in section 9(a);

the Board shall investigate such petition and if it has reasonable cause to believe that a question of representation affecting commerce exists shall provide for an appropriate hearing upon due notice. Such hearing may be conducted by an officer or employee of the regional office, who shall not make any recommendations with respect thereto. If the Board finds upon the record of such hearing that such a question of representation exists, it shall direct an election by secret ballot and shall certify the results thereof.

(2) In determining whether or not a question of representation affecting commerce exists, the same regulations and rules of decision shall apply irrespective of the identity of the persons filing the petition or the kind of relief sought and in no case shall the Board deny a labor organization a place on the ballot by reason of an order with respect to such labor organization or its predecessor not issued in conformity with section 10(c).

(3) No election shall be directed in any bargaining unit or any subdivision within which, in the preceding twelve-month period, a valid election shall have been held. Employees engaged in an economic strike who are not entitled to reinstatement shall be eligible to vote under such regulations as the Board shall find are consistent with the purposes and provisions of this Act in any election conducted within twelve months after the commencement of the strike. In any election where none of the choices on the ballot receives a majority, a run-off shall be conducted, the ballot providing for a selection between the two choices receiving the largest and second largest number of valid votes cast in the election.

(4) Nothing in this section shall be construed to prohibit the waiving of hearings by stipulation for the purpose of a consent election in conformity with regulations and rules of decision of the Board.

(5) In determining whether a unit is appropriate for the purposes specified in subsection (b) the extent to which the employees have organized shall not be controlling.

(d) Whenever an order of the Board made pursuant to section 10(c) is based in whole or in part upon facts certified following an investigation pursuant to subsection (c) of this section and there is a petition for the enforcement or review of such order, such certification and the record of such investigation shall be included in the transcript of the entire record required to be filed under section 10(e) or 10(f), and thereupon the decree of the court enforcing, modifying, or setting aside in whole or in part the order of the Board shall be made and entered upon the pleadings, testimony, and proceedings set forth in such transcript.

(e) (1) Upon the filing with the Board, by 30 per centum or more of the employees in a bargaining unit covered by an agreement between their employer and a labor organization made pursuant to section 8(a)(3), of a petition alleging they desire that such authority be rescinded, the Board shall take a secret ballot of the employees in such unit and certify the results thereof to such labor organization and to the employer.

(2) No election shall be conducted pursuant to this subsection in any bargaining unit or any subdivision within which, in the preceding twelve-month period, a valid election shall have been held.

Section 14. . . . (b) Nothing in this Act shall be construed as authorizing the execution or application of agreements requiring membership in a labor organization as a condition of employment in any State or Territory in which such execution or application is prohibited by State or Territorial law.

GLOSSARY

abuse of discretion The failure of a judge or administrator to use sound or reasonable judgment in arriving at a decision.

acceptance In contract law, the agreement of the offeree to the proposal or offer of the offeror.

action at law A suit in which the plaintiff is seeking a legal remedy (such as damages), as distinguished from an equitable remedy (such as an injunction).

action in equity A civil suit in which the plaintiff is seeking an equitable remedy, such as an injunction or decree of specific performance.

actual authority The express and implied authority of an agent.

adjudication The legal process of resolving a dispute.

adjudicatory power In administrative agency law, the right of an administrative agency to initiate actions as both prosecutor and judge against those thought to be in violation of the law (including agency rules and regulations) under the jurisdiction of the administrative agency—referred to as the quasi-judicial function of an agency.

administrative agency A board, commission, agency, or service authorized by a legislative enactment to implement specific laws on either the local, state, or national level.

administrative law Public law administered and/or formulated by a government unit such as a board, agency, or commission to govern the conduct of an individual, association, or corporation.

affirmative action In employment law, any voluntary or required program or action designed to remedy discriminatory practices in hiring, training, and promoting of protected class members. Such programs attempt to eliminate existing and continuing discrimination, to remedy lingering effects of past discrimination, and to create procedures to prevent future discrimination.

Age Discrimination in Employment Act (ADEA) A 1967 congressional enactment prohibiting all forms of employment discrimination based on age. Workers between the ages of 40 and 70 are protected from employer discrimination not based on a bona fide occupational qualification.

agency A relationship created by contract, agreement, or law between a principal and an agent whereby the principal is bound by the authorized actions of the agent.

agency shop or union shop provision A union security clause which requires an employer to discharge any employee who does not join a union or at least pay union dues within a specified time after hiring. Such a clause is permitted by the NLRA if employees are given at least 30 days after hiring to join the union or pay dues.

agent One who is authorized to act for another, called a *principal*, whose acts bind the principal to his or her actions.

airfreight International transportation by air from point of export of goods or merchandise subject to an international sales contract.

ally doctrine In labor-management law, the doctrine which permits a secondary boycott of an employer who is assisting the employer with whom the union has a labor dispute.

annual percentage rate The total of the items making up the finance charge, or cost of borrowing money or buying on credit, expressed as a yearly percentage rate that the consumer can use to "shop around" for the best credit terms.

answer In pleadings, the defendant's response to the plaintiff's complaint or petition.

apparent authority Authority created by the words or conduct of the principal that leads a third person to believe the agent has such authority.

appellant The party who appeals a decision of a lower court, usually that of a trial court.

appellee The party against whom an appeal is made (sometimes referred to as a *respondent*—a person who defends on an appeal).

arbitration The submission of a dispute to a third party or parties for settlement.

articles of incorporation A legal document, meeting the legal requirements of a given state, filed with a designated state official as an application for a certificate of incorporation.

articles of partnership The agreement of the partners that forms and governs the operation of the partnership.

assault The intentional movement or exhibition of force that would place a reasonable person in fear of physical attack or harm.

assault and battery Any intentional physical contact by a person on another without consent or privilege.

assignee The one to whom an assignment has been made.

assignment The transfer of rights or a property interest to a third person, who can receive no greater rights than those possessed by the transferor.

assignor The one who makes an assignment.

assumption of risk A person's full awareness and understanding of the risk connected with a particular activity, followed by that person's voluntary involvement in the activity. If the person is injured in the activity and sues a defendant for negligence, the defendant can use the plaintiff's assumption of risk as a defense. Also, assumption of risk is one of the few defenses that can be asserted in response to a strict liability claim involving injury caused by an allegedly defective product. However, assumption of risk can no longer be used as a defense against a workers' compensation claim.

award In arbitration proceedings, the decision or determination rendered by an arbitrator on a controversy submitted for settlement. In general usage, to grant, assign, or give by sentence or judicial determination. For example, the court *awards* an injunction; the arbitration *award* is equitable.

back to work order An injunction requested by the President under the Taft-Hartley Act prohibiting a lockout by the employer or a strike by the union for an 80-day period. If at the end of 80 days no settlement is reached, the lockout or strike can continue unless prohibited by emergency congressional legislation.

bankruptcy A court procedure by which a person who is unable to pay his or her debts may be declared bankrupt, have nonexempt assets distributed to his or her creditors, and thereupon be given a release from any further payment of the balance due on most of these debts.

battery The wrongful intentional physical contact by a person (or object under control of that person) on another.

beneficiary A person for whose benefit a will, trust, insurance policy, or contract is made.

benefit test A test through which the law determines whether a promise has consideration by seeing if the promisor has received an advantage, profit, or privilege in return for his or her promise.

bilateral contract A contract formed by the mutual exchange of promises of the offeror and the offeree.

bilateral mistake A mistake in which both parties to a contract are in error as to the terms of or performance expected under the contract. Also called mutual mistake.

bill of lading A document used in international sales contracts to evidence the shipper's receipt of the goods, the issuance of a contract of insurance during the period of transportation, and to serve as evidence of title (ownership) of the goods.

blue sky laws Laws enacted for the protection of investors that regulate the sales of stocks and bonds, and that also regulate other activities of investment companies related to such sales.

board of directors A body composed of persons elected by the corporation's shareholders and entrusted with the responsibility of managing the corporation.

bona fide occupational qualification (bfoq) An exception to otherwise illegal discrimination on the basis of religion, sex, or national origin. Where an essential element of a job requires certain qualifications (e.g., a drama role or a church position) to be present, Title VII permits such qualifications to be used as criteria for employment. Such cases are rather rare, however.

boycott In antitrust law, an agreement between two or more parties to not deal with a third party. When the purpose is to exclude a firm or firms from a market, such an agreement is per se illegal under Section 1 of the Sherman Act. In labor law, action by a union to prevent others from doing business with the employer. A primary boycott, directed at the employer with whom the union has a labor dispute, is usually legal. A secondary boycott, aimed at an employer with whom the union does not have a labor dispute, is usually an unfair labor practice.

breach of duty Failure to fulfill a legal obligation.

burden of proof The duty of a party to prove or disprove certain facts.

business necessity A legal defense to a *prima facie* case of discriminatory impact. The defendant must prove (1) the challenged employment practice is necessary to achieve a legitimate business objective, (2) the practice actually achieves such an objective, and (3) there is no other reasonably available method for accomplishing the objective without discriminatory effects.

bylaws The internal rules made to regulate and govern the actions and affairs of a corporation.

capacity The legal ability to perform an act—especially an act from which legal consequences flow, such as the making of a contract.

career tenure In effect, the guarantee of lifetime employment or for as long as the tenured person can function adequately.

case law Essentially synonymous with "common law."

cause of action A person's right to seek a remedy when his or her rights have been breached or violated.

caveat emptor In sales law, "let the buyer beware."

Celler-Kefauver Act A 1950 congressional enactment amending Section 7 of the Clayton Act. The act prohibits a firm from acquiring all or part of the stock or assets of another firm where, in any line of commerce in any section of the country, the effect of such acquisition may be substantially to lessen competition.

certificate of incorporation A document of a state that grants permission to do business in that state in the corporate form—sometimes called a *charter*.

certificate of origin A certificate issued to establish the national origin of goods, frequently used in international sales contracts to comply with the laws of the importing country which ban or otherwise limit imports from specified countries.

certification The process by which a union is selected by employees as their official bargaining representative. Certification via supervised elections protects the union from rival union challenges for a period of one year.

challenge for cause In jury selection, an objection to a prospective juror hearing a particular case, stating a reason that questions the impartiality of the juror.

circumstantial context In the process of statutory interpretation, a court's examination of the problem or problems that caused the enactment of the statute.

civil law As compared to criminal law, rules for establishing rights and duties between individuals whereby an individual can seek personal redress for a wrong committed by another individual. As compared to common law, codified rules reduced to formal written propositions as the law of a state or country. The written code serves as the basis of all decisions.

Civil Rights Act A comprehensive 1964 congressional enactment that prohibits discrimination in housing, public accommodations, education, and employment.

civil rights law That body of statutory and constitutional law defining and enforcing the privileges and freedoms belonging to every person in the United States. The objective of civil rights law is to secure equality of opportunity for all persons.

class action A legal proceeding initiated by one or more members of a similarly situated group or class of persons on behalf of themselves and other group members.

Clayton Act A 1914 congressional enactment to generally prohibit price discrimination by a seller of goods, exclusive dealing and tying of a seller's products, mergers and consolidations of corporations that result in a substantial lessening of competition or tend to create a monopoly, and certain interlocking directorates. The act also provides an exemption from the antitrust laws for the organization and normal activities of labor unions.

closed shop A union security clause requiring an employer to hire and retain only union members. Such a provision is an unfair labor practice.

collective bargaining agreement An agreement between an employer and a labor union regulating the terms and conditions of employment. Such an agreement becomes a binding labor contract when formally adopted by both the employer and a majority of employees in an appropriate bargaining unit.

commerce clause A clause contained in Article I, Section 8, of the U.S. Constitution, which permits Congress to control trade among the several states (and with foreign nations).

commercial contract A contract between two or more persons (merchants) engaged in trade or commerce.

common carrier A carrier that holds itself out for hire to the general public to transport goods.

common law Rules that have been developed from custom or judicial decisions without the aid of written legislation, and subsequently used as a basis for later decisions by a court—also referred to as judge-made or case law.

common stock A class of stock that carries no rights or priorities over other classes of stock as to payment of dividends or distribution of corporate assets upon dissolution.

community property A system of marital property ownership recognized in eight states under which property acquired after marriage (except by gift or inheritance) is co-owned by the husband and wife, regardless of which person acquired it.

comparative negligence The rule used in negligence cases in many states that provides for computing both the plaintiff's and the defendant's negligence, with the plaintiff's damages being reduced by a percentage representing the degree of his or her contributing fault. If the plaintiff's negligence is found to be greater than the defendant's, the plaintiff will receive nothing and will be subject to a counterclaim by the defendant.

compensatory damages A monetary sum awarded for the actual loss a person has sustained for a wrong committed by another person.

competition The condition of economic and noneconomic rivalry among firms for consumers' business.

complaint In an action at law, the initial pleading filed by the plaintiff in a court with proper jurisdiction. In an action in equity, it is frequently referred to as a *petition*.

concurrent jurisdiction Where more than one court of a different name or classification has the power to hear a particular controversy.

conflict of laws The body of rules specifying the circumstances in which a state or federal court sitting in one state shall, in deciding a case before it, apply the rules of another state (rather than the rules of the state in which the court is sitting).

conglomerate merger A merger between two companies which are not competitors and do not occupy a supplier-customer relationship.

conscious parallelism Uniformity of action by firms who apparently know their actions are uniform. Does not prove conspiracy under Section 1 of the Sherman Act, but is an extremely important factor in determining whether a conspiracy existed.

consent decree A court injunction, the terms of which are arrived at by agreement of the parties.

consent order An administrative agency order, the terms of which are arrived at by agreement between the agency and the charged party.

consideration In contract law, a detriment to the promisee or benefit to the promisor, bargained for and given in exchange for a promise.

constitutional law Those provisions of the state and federal constitutions that prescribe the structure and functions of the respective governments and the basic rights of and limitations upon these governments, as well as the courts' interpretation of these provisions.

consumer products Goods that are used or bought primarily for personal, family, or household purposes.

Consumer Product Safety Act A congressional enactment that created the Consumer Product Safety Commission, which has the responsibility of establishing and enforcing rules and standards to insure that products covered under the Act are safe for consumers' use.

consumerism The movement that has led to increased protection for the consumer and substantial burdens on the manufacturer and merchant.

contract An agreement that establishes enforceable legal relationships between two or more persons.

contract-bar rule Provision of the National Labor Relations Act prohibiting an election petition by a rival union while a valid collective bargaining agreement is in force, up to a maximum of three years. The parties to the agreement are similarly barred while the agreement is in force, but there is no maximum time. An existing contract does not bar an election if it (1) contains no stated duration *or* (2) is so skeletal in nature that it covers few subjects normally found in such agreements.

contract, combination, or conspiracy Express or tacit agreement required for a violation of the Sherman Act.

contributory negligence The fault (negligence) of a plaintiff, the result of which contributed to or added to his or her injury (used as a defense by a defendant against whom the plaintiff has filed a negligence action).

corporate stock Shares of stock, each representing an ownership interest in the business, issued by a corporation for the purpose of raising capital.

corporation An association of persons created by statute as a legal entity (artificial person) with authority to act and to have liability separate and apart from its owners.

corrective advertising Statements in advertising, placed by a firm acting under orders from an administrative agency (usually the Federal Trade Commission), which correct erroneous or misleading statements about its product that have appeared in earlier advertisements.

counterclaim A pleading by the defendant in a civil suit against the plaintiff, the purpose being to defeat or sue the plaintiff so as to gain a judgment favorable to the defendant.

counteroffer A proposal made by an offeree in response to the offer extended him or her, the terms varying appreciably from the terms of the offer. Such a proposal by the offeree constitutes a rejection of the offer.

course of employment The legal standard requiring that injuries covered by workers' compensation statutes be job-related or reasonably incidental to job duties. The injury must have at least some reasonable relation to an employee's work.

crime Any wrongful action by an individual or persons for which a statute prescribes redress in the form of a death penalty, imprisonment, fine, or removal from an office of public trust.

criminal conspiracy doctrine The legal view held until the mid-1800s that any combination of employees for effecting actions against an employer was illegal *per se.* Employers used this doctrine to stifle employee unions until the courts began to view unions as legal entities.

criminal law The law of crimes.

cross-elasticity of demand The extent to which the quantity of a commodity demanded responds to changes in price of a related commodity. Used to help courts define the relevant market.

cross-elasticity of supply The extent to which the quantity of a commodity supplied to the market responds to changes in the price of a related commodity. Utilized to help courts define the relevant market.

cumulative voting Where permitted, the procedure by which a shareholder is entitled to take his or her total number of shares, multiply that total by the number of directors to be elected, and cast the multiplied total for any director or directors to be elected.

damages The monetary loss suffered by a party as a result of a wrong.

Davis-Bacon Act A 1931 congressional enactment regulating wage rates for federally financed or assisted construction projects.

debenture In securities regulation law, a debt security; a written promise by a corporation to repay borrowed money. Usually refers to a corporate bond or promissory note that is not secured by specific assets of the firm (i.e., is not secured by a mortgage on corporate assets).

debtor A person who owes payment of a debt and/or performance on an obligation.

decedent A person who has died.

deceit A false statement, usually intentional, that causes another person harm.

deed The document representing ownership of real property.

de facto corporation A corporation not formed in substantial compliance with the laws of a given state but which has sufficiently complied to be a corporation in fact, not right. Only the state can challenge the corporation's existence.

default The failure to perform a legal obligation.

defendant The party who defends the initial action brought against him or her by the plaintiff.

defense Any matter which is advanced or put forth by a defendant as a reason in law or fact why the plaintiff is not entitled to recover the relief he seeks.

defined benefit pension plan A pension plan which specifies the amount of or method for computing benefits the employer contributes to the plan for each employee.

defined contribution pension plan A pension plan which specifically states either the amount of or the method for computing employer contributions to a company pension plan.

de jure corporation A corporation formed in substantial compliance with the laws of a given state; a corporation by right.

delegated powers The constitutional right of the federal government to pass laws concerning certain subjects and fields, thereby keeping the states from passing laws in these areas (sometimes referred to as *enumerated powers*).

delegation In contract law, the transfer of the power or right to represent or act for another; usually referred to as the delegation of duties to a third party, as compared to the assignment of rights to a third party.

delegation of authority In administrative law, a grant of authority from a legislative body to an administrative agency.

demurrer A pleading by a defendant in the form of a motion denying that plaintiff's complaint or petition states a cause of action.

de novo To start completely new. A trial *de novo* is a completely new trial requiring the same degree of proof as if the case were being heard for the first time.

detriment test A test through which the law determines whether a promise has consideration by seeing if the promisee, by entering into the contract, has thereby given up a legal right.

directed verdict A verdict that the jury is instructed (or directed) by the court to return in accordance with a motion by one of the parties that reasonable persons could not differ as to the result.

disaffirmance The legal avoidance, or setting aside, of an obligation.

discharge in bankruptcy A release granted by a bankruptcy court to a debtor who has gone through proper bankruptcy proceedings; the release frees the person from any further liability on provable claims filed during the proceedings.

disclaimer A provision in a sales contract which attempts to prevent the creation of a warranty.

discretionary powers The right of an administrative agency to exercise judgment and discretion in carrying out the law, as opposed to ministerial powers (the routine day-to-day duty to enforce the law).

discrimination Any failure to treat all persons equally, where no reasonable distinction can be made between those favored and those not favored.

discriminatory impact A legal test employed to determine violations of Title VII in the Civil Rights Act. Any employment rule or practice, although neutral on its face, which has an unequal impact on a protected class is considered discriminatory and in violation of Title VII. If the plaintiff proves such a discriminatory impact exists, a *prima facie* case of illegal discrimination is established, and the employer then bears the burden of proving business necessity.

disparagement of goods Making malicious and false statements of fact as to the quality or performance of another's goods.

diversity of citizenship An action in which the plaintiff and defendant are citizens of different states.

domestic corporation A corporation chartered or incorporated in the state in which the corporation is doing business.

due process The right of every person not to be deprived of life, liberty, or property without a fair hearing and/or just compensation.

duress The overcoming of a person's free will through the use of threat, force, or actions whereby the person is forced to do something he or she otherwise would not do.

duty to speak A legal obligation of one party to divulge information to another party.

economic duress The overcoming of a person's free will by means of a threat or other action involving the wrongful use of economic pressure, whereby the person is forced to do something he or she otherwise would not do.

edge effect The effect upon competition caused by the presence of a potential entrant having the ability and incentive to compete with established firms in the market, where that market is highly concentrated and the firms presently in the market perceive the presence of the potential entrant.

eminent domain The power of the government to take private property for public use by paying just compensation.

Employee Retirement Income Security Act (ERISA) A 1974 congressional enactment regulating the funding, managing, and membership rules of private pension and welfare plans. Provisions for protecting employee benefits and fairly allocating those benefits are also detailed in the act.

environmental impact statement The statement required by federal law that describes the effect of proposed major federal action on the quality of the human environment.

Environmental Protection Agency The federal agency charged with the responsibility for establishing and enforcing environmental standards and for continuing research on pollution and measures to eliminate or control it.

Equal Employment Opportunity Commission (EEOC) An independent federal administrative agency comprised of five presidentially appointed members responsible for enforcing Title VII of the 1964 Civil Rights Act and several other employment discrimination laws. The EEOC has authority to issue legally binding regulations, and to bring suit in federal court to enforce these laws.

Equal Pay Act A 1963 congressional amendment to the Fair Labor Standards Act prohibiting an employer from paying an employee of one sex less than an employee of the opposite sex where the two perform jobs (1) requiring "equal skill, effort, and responsibility," and (2) "under similar working conditions."

equal protection of laws A constitutional guaranty that no state government shall enact a law that is not uniform in its operation, that treats persons unfairly, or that gives persons unequal treatment by reason of race, religion, national origin, or sex.

equitable action An action brought in a court seeking an equitable remedy, such as an injunction or decree of specific performance.

exclusive dealing An agreement which commits a buyer to purchase a certain product only from one seller. These agreements, often called *requirements contracts*, can foreclose markets to competitors. Section 1 of the Sherman Act and Section 3 of the Clayton Act are applied in analyzing these actions.

executed contract A contract wholly performed by both parties to the contract, as opposed to an executory contract, which is wholly unperformed by both parties.

execution of a judgment The process by which a judgment creditor obtains a writ directing the sheriff or other officer to seize nonexempt property of the debtor and sell it to satisfy the judgment.

executive order An order by the president of the United States or governor of a state that has the force of law.

ex parte On one side only. For example, an *ex parte* proceeding is held on the application of one party only, without notice to the other party; and an *ex parte* order is made at the request of one party when the other party fails to show up in court, when the other party's presence is not needed, or when there is no other party.

experience rating The standard by which an employer's actual tax for unemployment insurance is determined. Employers with a record of stable employment pay less unemployment tax than ones with a record of higher employee turnover.

export license A license issued under government authority as permission for identified goods to be exported from the country issuing the license.

express authority Authority specifically given by the principal to the agent.

express contract A contract formed from the words (oral and/or in writing) of the parties, as opposed to an implied contract, which is formed from the conduct of the parties.

express warranty In sales law, a guarantee or assurance as to the quality or performance of goods that arises from the words or conduct of the seller.

externalities Third-party costs associated with producing a product that cannot be totally reflected in the product's price. Pollution is an externality borne by everyone in modern industrial societies.

Fair Labor Standards Act (FLSA) A 1938 congressional enactment regulating minimum wages, overtime, and child labor. Small businesses, managerial and professional employees, and state and local government workers are exempted from its mininum wage and overtime provisions. The FLSA is administered and enforced by the Labor Department's Wage and Hour Division.

false imprisonment The wrongful detention or restraint of one person by another.

fault Breach of a legal duty, sometimes used in lieu of the term *negligence*. The UCC definition is "wrongful act, omission, or breach."

featherbedding The union practice of forcing an employer to hire an employee for a job when there is no work to be done. An unfair labor practice.

Federal Communications Commission (FCC) A seven-member commission established in 1934 by congressional enactment of the Federal Communications Act. The commission is empowered to regulate all interstate communication by telephone, telegraph, radio, and television.

Federal Employers' Liability Act (FELA) A 1906 congressional enactment, reenacted in 1908 and amended in 1939, providing workers' compensation for employees of interstate railroads and airlines. It is not a no-fault system; employers are liable for an employee's injury only if the employer is negligent. The primary defense is comparative negligence.

Federal Employment Compensation Act (FECA) A congressional enactment providing a comprehensive workers' compensation system for civilian employees of the federal government. Similar to typical state workers' compensation laws.

federal law Rules of law derived from the U.S. Constitution, federal statutes and administrative agencies, and from cases interpreting and applying these rules.

federal preemption A legal principle which grants the Congress, the federal courts, and federal agencies exclusive authority in certain matters of law where the need for a uniform national body of law is great. Labor relations law, for example, is almost exclusively the domain of the federal government.

federal question A question presented by a case in which one party, usually the plaintiff, is asserting a right (or counterclaim, in the case of the defendant) which is based upon a federal rule of law—e.g., a provision of the U.S.

Constitution, an act of Congress, or ruling of a federal administrative agency.

Federal Trade Commission (FTC) A five-member commission established in 1914 by congressional enactment of the Federal Trade Commission Act. The commission enforces prohibitions against unfair methods of competition and unfair or deceptive acts or practices in commerce; it also enforces numerous federal laws (particularly federal consumer protection acts, such as "Truth in Lending" and "Fair Packaging and Labeling").

Federal Trade Commission Act A 1914 congressional enactment prohibiting unfair methods of competition and unfair or deceptive acts or practices in commerce.

fellow-servant rule Common-law defense that an employer is not responsible for injuries to an employee if they were caused by the negligence of a fellow employee.

felony A serious crime resulting in either punishment by death or imprisonment in a state or federal penitentiary, or where a given statute declares a wrong to be a felony without regard to a specific punishment.

fiduciary A position of trust in relation to another person or to his or her property.

finding of fact The process whereby from testimony and evidence a judge, agency, or examiner determines that certain matters, events, or acts took place upon which conclusions of law can be based.

firm offer In sales law, an irrevocable offer dealing with the sale of goods made by a merchant offeror in a signed writing and giving assurance to the offeree that the offer will remain open. This offer is irrevocable without consideration for the stated period of time, or if no period is stated, for a reasonable period, neither period to exceed three months.

forebearance The refraining from doing something that a person has a legal right to do.

foreign corporation A corporation chartered or incorporated in one state but doing business in a different state.

four-fifths rule An EEOC guideline for determining when a standardized employment test has a discriminatory impact or effect. If using the test causes the selection rate for any protected class to be less than 80 percent of that for the group with the highest rate, then the test is considered to have a discriminatory impact.

franchise (1) A business conducted under someone else's trademark or tradename. The owner of the business, which may be a sole proprietorship, partnership, corporation, or other form of organization, is usually referred to as the *franchisee*. The owner of the trademark or tradename, who contractually permits use of the mark or name, in return for a fee and usually subject to various restrictions, is ordinarily referred to as the *franchisor*. The permission to use the mark or name, which is part of the franchising agreement, is called a *trademark license*. (2) The term can also be used to refer to a privilege granted by a governmental body, such as the exclusive right granted to someone by a city to provide cable TV service in that city.

fraud An intentional or reckless misrepresentation of a material fact that causes anyone relying on it injury or damage.

garnishee A person who holds money owed to or property of a debtor subject to a garnishment action.

garnishment The legal proceeding of a judgment creditor to require a third person owing money to the debtor or holding property belonging to the debtor to turn over to the court or sheriff the property or money owed for the satisfaction of the judgment. State and federal laws generally permit only a limited amount of a debtor's wages to be garnished.

general duty clause An OSHA provision requiring employers to provide every employee a workplace free from recognized hazards causing or likely to cause death or serious bodily injury.

general intent In antitrust law, legal inference that a firm's actual conduct contributes to the acquisition or continuation of its market power. Usually proved by evidence of conduct that raises entry barriers.

good faith Honesty in fact on the part of a person in negotiating a contract, or in the carrying on of some other transactions.

goods Tangible and movable personal property (except for money used as a medium of exchange). Typical examples are automobiles, books, and furniture.

Green River ordinances State and municipal laws that regulate door-to-door sales on private premises. So called after the Green River, Wyoming, case in which such laws were held to be valid and enforceable.

group boycott In antitrust law, the express or implied agreement of two or more persons or firms to refuse to deal (buy, sell, etc.) with a third party. Such an agreement is usually illegal.

horizontal merger A merger of two competing firms at the same level in the production or distribution of a product.

horizontal price fixing Price fixing among competitors. *Per se* illegal under Section 1 of the Sherman Act.

hot cargo agreement A form of secondary boycott whereby a union and an employer agree not to do business with a third party for the purpose of coercing that party in a separate, unrelated labor dispute. Such an agreement is in violation of the NLRA.

implied authority Authority inferred for an agent to carry out his or her express authority and/or authority inferred from the position held by the agent to fulfill his or her agency duties.

implied contract A contract in which the parties' manifestation of assent or agreement is inferred, in whole or in part, from their conduct, as opposed to an express contract formed by the parties' words.

import license A license issued under government authority as permission for identified goods to be imported into the country issuing the license.

incorporation The act or process of forming or creating a corporation.

inference of discriminatory intent The legal presumption of the court that a Title VII violation exists even though there is no explicit intent to discriminate. If a plaintiff proves certain facts which make it logical to conclude an employer *intended* to discriminate, the court will find a *prima facie* case of discriminatory intent is present. The employer then has the burden of producing evidence that shows a legitimate, nondiscriminatory reason for its action.

injunction A decree issued by a court hearing an equity action either prohibiting a person from performing a certain act or acts or requiring the person to perform a certain act or acts.

inland freight Domestic transportation of goods from the point of manufacture or production to point of export.

insider trading The buying or selling of corporate securities of a particular firm by persons having business knowledge about such firm that is not available to the general public, with the expectation of making a personal profit in such transactions.

insolvency In bankruptcy law, the financial condition of a debtor when his or her assets at fair market value are less than his or her debts and liabilities.

intent requirement Judicial requirement that an alleged monopolist exhibit an *intent* to obtain or preserve a monopoly position. Such intent must be proved to exist in addition to overwhelming market power before Section 2 of the Sherman Act is violated.

interstate commerce The carrying on of commercial activities or the commercial transportation of persons or property between points lying in different states.

Interstate Commerce Commission (ICC) An eleven-member commission established in 1887 by congressional enactment of the Interstate Commerce Act regulating the licensing and rates of common carriers in interstate commerce.

investigative power In administrative agency law, the right of an administrative agency by statute to hold hearings, subpeona witnesses, examine persons under oath, and require that records be submitted to it in order to determine violations and to do research for future rule making.

involuntary bankruptcy Bankruptcy of a person upon petition of a certain number of creditors whose claims are statutorily sufficient in amount. [Note: This was changed by new Bankruptcy Law in 1979. Deletion makes it accurate.]

joint venture A pooling of resources by two or more firms to achieve a common objective.

judgment notwithstanding the verdict (judgment n.o.v.) The entry of a judgment by a trial judge in favor of one party even though the jury returned a verdict in favor of the other party.

judicial review The process by which the courts oversee and determine the legitimacy or validity of executive, legislative, or administrative agency action.

judicial self-restraint The philosophy that controversies must be settled, insofar as possible, in conformity with previously established principles and decisions.

jurisdiction of a court The right, by law, of a specific court to hear designated controversies.

justice The application of rules to arrive at what is recognized as a fair and reasonable result; also a title given to a judge.

laissez-faire doctrine The doctrine whereby business is permitted to operate without interference by government.

Landrum-Griffin Act A 1959 congressional amendment of the 1935 NLRA which established a bill of rights for union members, required public financial disclosures by unions and union leaders, and regulated election procedures for union officials by union members.

law Enforceable rules governing the relationship of individuals and persons, their relationship to each other, and their relationship to an organized society.

law merchant Rules and regulations developed by merchants and traders that governed their transactions before being absorbed by common law. These rules and regulations were developed and enforced by "fair courts" established by the merchants themselves.

legal entity An association recognized by law as having the legal rights and duties of a person.

legal environment A broad, imprecise term referring generally to those judicial, legislative, and administrative processes and rules that have particular application to the business world.

legal impossibility of performance An event that takes place after a contract is made, rendering performance under the contract, in the eyes of the law, something that cannot be done. Also referred to as objective impossibility, it legally discharges a party's obligation; it can be compared to subjective impossibility, which makes the contractual obligation more difficult to perform but does not discharge it.

legal rate of interest The rate of interest applied by statute where there is an agreement for interest to be paid but none is stated, or where the law implies a duty to pay interest irrespective of agreement. In the latter case, this may be referred to as a *judgment rate*, a rate of interest applied to judgments until paid by the defendant.

legislative history The history of the legislative enactment used by the court as a means of interpreting the terms of a statute. It consists primarily of legislative committee reports and the transcripts of committee hearings and floor debates.

letter of credit An agreement by the bank of a party to a sales contract (the buyer) to pay funds to the other party (the seller of goods) upon the presentation of stipulated documents. A letter of credit may be *revocable* (subject to withdrawal) or *irrevocable* (not subject to cancellation prior to a stated date). Used extensively in international trade.

lex mercatoria A body of principles governing commercial practices, first appearing in the Middle Ages, and based upon the international custom and practice of merchants. It is the predecessor of the U.S. Uniform Commercial. Code and the commercial codes of several modern civil law nations in Europe.

libel Written defamation of one's character or reputation.

limited partnership A partnership created under statute with at least one limited and one general partner. The limited partner's liability to third persons is restricted to his or her capital contributions.

liquidated damages In employment law, the additional amount of damages which an employer may be required to pay when the court finds it in willful violation of the FLSA provisions.

lobbying contract A contract made by one person with another under the terms of which the former agrees to represent the latter's interest before legislative or administrative bodies by attempting to influence their votes or decisions on legislative, quasi-legislative, or related proceedings.

lockout The withholding of employment by an employer as a means of coercing concessions from or resisting demands of employees.

long-arm statutes Laws that permit a plaintiff to bring a certain action and recover a judgment in a court in his or her home state against a defendant who resides in another state.

Magnuson-Moss Warranty Act A congressional enactment designed to prevent deceptive warranty practices, make warranties easier to understand, and create procedures for consumer enforcement of warranties. The act applies only to written warranties given in a consumer sales transaction and can be enforced by the Federal Trade Commission, Attorney General, or an aggrieved party.

marginal cost The cost of producing an additional unit of a product. In antitrust law, sales below marginal cost in some circumstances are viewed by courts as predatory.

market (1) An area over which buyers and sellers negotiate the exchange of a well-defined commodity. (2) From the point of view of the consumer, the firms from which he can buy a well-defined product. (3) From the point of view of a producer, the buyers to whom it can sell a well-defined product. Market definition is crucial in determining the relevant market share of firms under antitrust scrutiny.

market division arrangements Any concerted action among actual or potential competitors to divide *geographic* markets, to assign particular *customers*, or to market particular *products* among themselves so as to avoid or limit competition. Such market divisions are treated as *per se* violations of Section 1 of the Sherman Act.

market power The ability of a firm to behave in some way other than it could in a perfectly competitive market.

master In employment law, one who appoints or designates another to perform physical tasks or activities for him or her and under his or her control as to the manner of performance (sometimes designated employer).

maximum rate of interest A statutory limit on the amount of interest that can be charged on a given transaction.

mechanic's lien A statutory lien against real property for labor, services, or materials used in improving the real property.

merchant In sales law, a person who customarily deals in goods of the kind that are involved in a transaction, or who otherwise by occupation holds himself or herself out as having knowledge or skill peculiar to the goods involved in the transaction.

merger The purchase of either the physical assets or the controlling share ownership of one company by another. As a business combination, a merger can come under antitrust review if the Justice Department or the FTC have reason to believe it might lessen competition.

ministerial power In administrative agency law, the routine day-to-day administration of the law, as opposed to discretionary powers, which involve the power to exercise judgment in the rendering of decisions.

minor An infant; any person under the age of majority. In most states the age of majority is eighteen years; in some it is twenty-one.

misdemeanor Any crime less serious than a felony, resulting in a fine and/or confinement in a jail other than a state or federal penitentiary.

Model Business Corporation Act Uniform rules governing the incorporation and operation of corporations for profit recommended by the American Bar Association for enactment by the various states.

monopoly According to the economic model, a market having only one seller, high barriers to entry, and no close substitutes for the product being sold. The courts generally define a monopolist as a firm possessing such an overwhelming degree of market power that it is able to control prices or exclude competition.

National Labor Relations Act (NLRA) A 1935 congressional enactment regulating labor-management relations. This act (1) established methods for selecting a labor union that would represent a particular group of employees, (2) required the employer to bargain with that union, (3) prescribed certain fundamental employee rights, (4) prohibited several "unfair labor practices" by employers, and (5) created the National Labor Relations Board to administer and enforce the NLRA. Also known as the Wagner Act.

natural monopoly Unusual market structure resulting from unique characteristics of the product or service offered. Some goods (e.g., electricity) or services (e.g., local telephone system) require large capital outlays and/or require uniformity in delivery systems so that only one firm can efficiently provide them at a profit.

negligence The failure to exercise reasonable care required under the circumstances, which failure is the proximate or direct cause of damage or injury to another.

nolo contendere A plea by a defendant in a criminal prosecution that without admitting guilt subjects him to conviction but does not preclude him from denying the truth of charges in collateral legal proceedings.

nominal damages A monetary award by a court where there is a breach of duty or contract but where no financial loss has occurred or been proven.

Norris-La Guardia Act A 1932 congressional enactment (1) generally prohibiting federal courts from enjoining union activities in nonviolent labor disputes and (2) prohibiting yellow-dog contracts.

notice A fact that a person actually knows, or one he or she should know exists, based on all facts and circumstances.

nuisance Action by a defendant that impinges upon or interferes with the rights of others. The remedy for plaintiff is an injunction compelling abatement.

occupational disease A disease arising from, or incidental to, the usual and ordinary course of a person's employment.

Occupational Safety and Health Act (OSHA) A 1970 congressional enactment creating the Occupational Safety and Health Administration as part of the Labor Department, and requiring that agency to develop and enforce occupational safety and health standards for American industries.

ocean freight International transportation by sea from port of export of goods subject to an international sales contract.

offer In contract law, a proposal made by an offeror which manifests a present intent to be legally bound and expresses the proposed terms with reasonable definiteness.

offeree The person to whom an offer is made.

offeror A person who makes a proposal to another, with the view in mind that if it is accepted, it will create a legally enforceable agreement between the parties.

oligopoly A market structure in which a small number of firms dominate the industry.

open shop Any business in which union and nonunion workers can be employed indiscriminately. See right-to-work laws.

output contract An enforceable agreement for the sale of all the goods produced by a seller (the exact amount of which is not set or known at the time of the agreement) or all those produced at a given plant of the seller during the term of the contract; a contract in which the seller agrees to sell and the buyer agrees to buy all or up to a stated amount that the seller produces.

parens patriae suit A legal proceeding instituted in behalf of the citizens of a state by the state attorney general.

pari delicto Parties equally at fault.

partnership An association of two or more persons who by agreement as co-owners carry on a business for profit.

peremptory challenge The right to exclude a prospective juror without having to state a reason or cause.

performance Carrying out of an obligation or promise according to the terms agreed to or specified. In contract law, complete performance by both parties discharges the contract.

performance-oriented standards OSHA standards which state broad safety goals and leave the method of achieving those goals to individual employers.

per se rule Antitrust doctrine wherein certain types of group business behavior are inherently anticompetitive and are therefore automatically illegal. Horizontal price fixing and boycotts are examples of *per se* illegal activities.

personal property All property not classified as real property; "movables." May be tangible (e.g., cars and gasoline) or intangible (e.g., shares of corporate stock and other contractual rights).

picketing Posting of striking workers at entrances to a place of work affected by a strike for the purposes of discouraging nonstrikers from working, and publicizing the labor dispute. Such assembly must be conducted in a peaceful manner and must not disturb the public peace.

plain meaning rule The rule under which a court applies a particular statute literally, where it feels the wording of the statute is so clear as to require no interpretation (that is, no resort to outside factors).

plaintiff The party who initiates an action at law and who seeks a specified remedy.

police power The inherent power of a government to regulate matters affecting the health, safety, morals, and general welfare of its citizens; usually used to refer to such power possessed by the state governments, as distinguished from the federal police power.

precedent A rule of a previously decided case that serves as authority for a decision in a current controversy—the basis of the principle of *stare decisis.*

preemption The federal regulation of an area of law which is so complete that any state statutes or other regulations affecting that area are, as to such area, completely void.

preliminary negotiations In contract law, usually an invitation to a party to make an offer—not the offer itself but only an inquiry.

preponderance of the evidence The greater weight and degree of the credible evidence; this is the burden of proof in most civil lawsuits.

price discrimination Under the Robinson-Patman Act, the practice of charging different prices to different buyers for goods of like grade and quality.

price fixing Any action or agreement which tampers with the free market pricing mechanism of a product or service.

prima facie At first sight (Latin); on the face of it; a fact that will be considered as true unless disproved.

principal One who agrees with another (called an *agent*) that that person will act on his or her behalf.

private corporation A corporation formed by individuals, as compared to one formed by the government.

private law Rules that govern the rights and duties of an individual, association, or corporation to another.

privity of contract Relationship of contract; a relationship that exists between two parties by virtue of their having entered into a contract.

procedural law The rules for carrying on a lawsuit (pleading, evidence, jurisdiction), as opposed to substantive law.

promisee The person who has the legal right to demand

performance of the promisor's obligation. In a bilateral contract both the offeror and the offeree are promisees. In a unilateral contract only the offeree is the promisee.

promisor The person who obligates himself or herself to do something. In a bilateral contract both offeror and offeree are promisors. In a unilateral contract only the offeror is the promisor.

prospectus A document put out by a corporation that sets forth the nature and purposes of an issue of stock, bonds, or other securities being offered for sale, usually including additional financial data about the issuing corporation.

protected class (group) In civil rights law, any group of persons accorded specific legal protection from economic and social discrimination.

proximate cause The foreseeable or direct connection between the breach of duty and an injury resulting from that breach.

proxy An authorization by one person to act for another (used primarily by an individual who wants another to vote in his or her place at a shareholders' meeting because he or she cannot attend).

public corporation A corporation formed by the government, as distinguished from one formed by private parties.

public goods Those goods or services which cannot be provided by market mechanisms of price, demand, and supply. National defense, police and fire protection, and interstate highways are examples of such goods which are impractical to provide and price according to individual usage.

public law Rules that deal with either the operation of government or the relationship between a government and its people.

public policy Any conduct, act, or objective that the law recognizes as being in the best interest of society at a given time. Any act or conduct contrary to the recognized standard is illegal, even if there is no statute expressly governing such act or conduct.

punitive damages A monetary sum awarded as a punishment for certain wrongs committed by one person against another. The plaintiff must prove his or her actual out-of-pocket losses directly flowing from the wrong before punitive damages will be awarded.

qualified pension plan Any pension plan which meets Internal Revenue Service requirements for tax-exempt status.

quasi-contract A contract imposed upon the parties by law to prevent unjust enrichment, even though the parties did not intend to enter into a contract (sometimes referred to as an *implied-in-law contract*).

quasi-judicial The case-hearing function of an administrative agency.

quasi-legislative The rule-making power of an administrative agency.

quid pro quo Something given or received for something else.

ratification The affirmance of a previous act.

rational basis test The usual test applied by the courts in determining the constitutionality of a statute that is challenged on the ground that it violates the equal protection clause; under this test, if the classification of subject-matter in the statute is found to be reasonably related to the purposes of the statute, the statute is not a violation of the equal protection clause.

real property Land and most things attached to the land, such as buildings and vegetation.

receiver A person appointed and supervised by the court to temporarily manage a business or other assets for the benefit of creditors or others who ultimately may be entitled to the assets. The business or other property is said to be placed in *receivership*.

reciprocity Business practice whereby one firm buys from another only if the other buys from it. May be voluntary or coerced, and can violate Section 1 of the Sherman Act. Also, a merger creating a probability of reciprocity may violate Section 7 of the Clayton Act.

registration statement A document setting forth certain corporate financial and ownership data, including a prospectus, that is generally required by the S.E.C. to be filed with it before the corporation can offer its securities for sale.

regulatory law Essentially, the state and federal rules emanating from Congress, state legislatures, and administrative bodies that impose duties and restrictions upon business firms.

Rehabilitation Act A 1973 congressional enactment prohibiting federal agencies, employers having federal contracts exceeding $2,500, and federally subsidized programs from discriminating against qualified handicapped job applicants and employees.

rejection In contract law, a refusal by the offeree of proposal or offer of the offeror, such refusal being known to the offeror.

release The voluntary relinquishing of a right, lien, interest, or any other obligation.

relevant market In antitrust law, the geographic market area and/or product or products determined by a court or government unit to measure whether an antitrust violation has taken place.

remedy Generally, the means by which a right is enforced or a wrong is prevented; in a narrower sense, a court order addressed to the defendant, in proper circumstances, requiring the defendant to do a particular act requested by plaintiff (e.g., payment of damages) or to refrain from a particular act (e.g., prohibition of specified conduct on the part of defendant by the issuance of an injunction).

replevin A legal remedy that permits recovery of possession of chattels (personal property).

repossession The taking back or regaining of possession of property, usually on the default of a debtor. Repossession can take place peaceably (without breach of the peace) or by judicial process.

requirement contract An enforceable agreement for a supply of goods, the exact amount of which is not set or known at the time of the agreement but which is intended to satisfy the needs of a buyer during the term of the contract; a contract in which the seller agrees to sell and the buyer agrees to buy all (or up to a stated amount) of the goods that the buyer needs.

res In law a thing or things; property (corpus) made subject to a trust.

res ipsa loquitur The thing speaks for itself. In an action for negligence the plaintiff may allege that the act causing the injury or damage would not have happened but for the negligence of the defendant.

rescission In contract law, the cancellation of a contract by a court, the effect being as if the contract had never been made.

reserved powers The constitutional rights of states to pass laws under powers that are not specifically delegated to the federal government.

respondeat superior The doctrine under which a master or employer can be held liable for the actions of his or her subordinate.

restraint of trade Any contract, agreement, or combination which eliminates or restricts competition (usually held to be against public policy and therefore illegal).

reverse discrimination The unequal treatment of nonminorities arising from affirmative action programs. Subject to certain conditions, the courts permit such discrimination where court-ordered affirmative action is aimed at eliminating specific discriminatory practices or where affirmative action is strictly voluntary and temporary in nature.

revocation In contract law, the withdrawing of an offer by the offeror.

right-to-work laws Laws passed by state legislatures prohibiting closed shop, union shop, and agency shop clauses. Businesses in such states are free to hire union and nonunion employees.

Robinson-Patman Act A 1936 congressional enactment that substantially amended Section 2 of the Clayton Act, basically making it illegal for a seller in interstate commerce to so discriminate in price that the result would be competitive injury and prohibiting illegal brokerage fees, allowances, and discounts.

rule-making power The statutory right of an administrative agency to issue rules and regulations governing both the conduct and the activities of those within the agency's jurisdiction (referred to as an agency's *quasi-legislative function*).

rule of reason Antitrust doctrine adopted in *Standard Oil* and *American Tobacco* cases (1911) in judging Section 1 Sherman Act cases. Any business action or agreement whose *purpose* or *effect* is found to be substantially anticompetitive will unreasonably restrain trade and thus be illegal.

sale Passage of a title from a seller to a buyer for a price.

sanction A penalty used as a means of coercing obedience with the law or with rules and regulations.

scope of employment The range of activities of a servant for which the master is liable to third persons. These actions may be expressly directed by the master or incidental to or foreseeable in the performance of employment duties.

secondary party The drawer or indorser of an instrument.

secured party The lender, seller, or other person in whose favor there is a security interest.

securities In securities regulation law, primarily stocks and bonds; also includes such items as debentures, investment contracts, and certificates of interest or participation in profit-sharing agreements.

Securities Act of 1933 A federal statute establishing requirements for the registration of securities sold in interstate commerce or through the mails (prior to sale). The statute basically requires that pertinent financial information be disclosed to both the Securities and Exchange Commission and to the prospective purchaser. A misleading failure to make such disclosure renders directors, officers, accountants, and underwriters severally and jointly liable.

Securities and Exchange Commission A federal agency given the responsibility to administer and enforce federal securities laws.

Securities Exchange Act of 1934 A federal statute designed to strengthen the Securities Act of 1933 and expand regulation in the securities business. This Act deals with regulation of national stock exchanges and over-the-counter markets. Numerous provisions were enacted to prevent unfair practices in trading of stock, to control bank credit used for speculation, to compel publicity as to the affairs of corporations listed on these exchanges, and to prohibit the use of inside information. This act created the Securities and Exchange Commission (SEC).

security A type of instrument (bond or share of stock) that is issued in a bearer or registered form and that is most often bought, sold, or traded on recognized exchanges or markets. Securities are used in corporate financing by a corporation to acquire capital and by purchasers as investments.

separation of powers The result of the U.S. Constitution, which created and balanced the powers of three branches of government (executive, legislative, and judicial) by giving each separate duties and jurisdictions.

servant In employment law, one who performs physical tasks or activities for and under the control of a master (sometimes designated an *employee* of the master).

shareholder The owner of one or more shares of capital stock in a corporation.

shareholder agreement A binding agreement made prior to a meeting by a group of shareholders as to the manner in which they will cast their votes on certain issues.

shares of capital stock Instruments in the form of equity securities representing an ownership interest in a corporation.

Sherman Antitrust Act An 1890 congressional enactment that (1) made illegal every contract, combination in the form of trust or otherwise, or conspiracy in restraint of trade or commerce among the several states, and (2) made it illegal for any person to monopolize, or attempt to monopolize, or combine or conspire with any other person or persons to monopolize any part of the trade or commerce among the several states.

Simplified Employee Pension Plan A pension plan created by the Revenue Act of 1978 which allows employers to contribute up to 15 percent of an employee's income or $30,000, whichever is less, to an individual retirement account (IRA). Such a plan permits employees to change employers without losing previous pension benefits.

slander Oral defamation of one's character or reputation.

sole proprietorship A person engaged in business for himself or herself without creating any form of business organization.

sovereign immunity The doctrine that bars a person from suing a government body without its consent.

specific intent In antitrust law, the intent of a firm to achieve a monopoly position. Evidence of predatory actions such as below-cost pricing, stealing trade secrets, etc. can prove specific intent.

specific performance A decree issued by a court of equity that compels a person to perform his or her part of the contract where damages are inadequate as a remedy and the subject matter of the contract is unique.

standing The right to sue.

stare decisis Literally "stand by the decision"—a principle by which once a decision has been made by a court, it serves as a precedent or a basis for future decisions of similar cases.

Statute of Frauds The requirement that certain types of contracts be in writing (or that there be written evidence of the existence of the oral contract) in order for the contract to be enforceable in a lawsuit.

statute of limitations A law that sets forth a maximum time period, from the happening of an event, for a legal action to be properly filed in or taken to court. The statute bars the use of the courts for recovery if such action is not filed during the specified time.

statutory interpretation The process by which a court discovers or decides the meaning of a statute as it applies to a particular case.

statutory law Enforceable rules enacted by a legislative body.

stock Equity securities that evidence an ownership interest in a corporation; shares of ownership in a corporation.

strict liability A legal theory under which a person can be held liable for damage or injury even if not at fault or negligent. Basically, any seller of a defective product that is unreasonably dangerous is liable for any damage or injury caused by the product, provided that the seller is a merchant and the product has not been modified or substantially changed since leaving the seller's possession. This rule applies even if there is no sale of the product and even if the seller exercised due care.

strike A cessation of work by employees for the purpose of coercing their employer to accede to some demand. A strike is legal only if it consists of a complete work stoppage by a participating majority of employees for a legally-recognized labor objective.

Subchapter S corporation A corporation with only one class of stock held by twenty-five or fewer individual stockholders who all agree in writing that the corporation will be taxed in the same manner as a partnership.

subsidiary corporation A corporation that is controlled by another corporation (called a *parent corporation*) through the ownership of a controlling amount of voting stock.

substantial performance The doctrine that a person who performs his or her contract in all major respects and in good faith, with only slight deviation, has adequately performed the contract and can therefore recover the contract price less any damages resulting from the slight deviation.

substantive law The basic rights and duties of parties as provided for in any field of law, as opposed to procedural law, under which these rights and duties are determined in a lawsuit.

summary judgment A court's judgment for one party in a lawsuit, before trial, on the ground that there are no disputed issues of fact which would necessitate a trial. The court's conclusion is based upon the motion of that party, the pleadings, affidavits, and depositions or other documentary evidence.

summons A writ by a court that is served on the defendant, notifying that person of the cause of action claimed by the plaintiff and of the requirement to answer.

Taft-Hartley Act A 1947 congressional amendment of the 1935 NLRA which (1) prohibited certain "unfair labor practices" by unions, (2) outlawed closed shop agreements, (3) established the Federal Mediation and Conciliation Service for the purpose of assisting employees and unions reach compromises, (4) granted employers and unions the power to file lawsuits to enforce collective bargaining agreements, and (5) gave the president authority to intervene in industry-wide disputes when, in the president's opinion, the occurrence or continuance of the dispute would "imperil the national health or safety." This act is also known as the Labor-Management Relations Act.

tender An offer by a contracting party to pay money, or deliver goods, or perform any other act required of him or her under the contract.

tender offer In securities regulation law, an offer to buy a certain amount of a corporation's stock at a specified price per share; usually made with the intention of obtaining the controlling interest in the corporation.

testator (female, testatrix) A person who makes a will.

textual context The court's reading of a statute in its entirety rather than a single section or part; a principle of statutory interpretation.

title A person's right of ownership in property. The extent of this right is dependent on the type of title held.

Title VII That part of the 1964 Civil Rights Act which prohibits employment discrimination against individuals because of their race, color, religion, sex, or national origin. Employers, employment agencies, labor unions, and governmental units are subject to Title VII provisions if they (1) have fifteen or more employees and (2) engage in an activity affecting interstate or foreign commerce. Violation of Title VII can be proved by showing an explicit or implicit *intent* to discriminate or by showing that an employer's actions result in a discriminatory *impact* on a protected class.

title warranty In sales law, an assurance or guarantee given by the seller, expressly or impliedly, to the buyer that he or she has good title and the right to transfer that title, and that the goods are free from undisclosed security interests.

tort A noncontractual wrong committed by one against another. To be considered a tort, the wrong must be a breach of a legal duty directly resulting in harm.

tortfeasor A person who commits a noncontractual wrong (sometimes referred to as a *wrongdoer*).

tort of conversion One's unlawful interference with the right of another to possess or use his or her personal property.

trademark A distinctive mark, sign, or motto that a business can reserve by law for its exclusive use in identifying itself or its product.

trade term A standardized term of trade which serves as a shorthand expression of the agreement of the parties to a sales contract to allocate responsibilities, costs, and risks of damage to or loss of the goods.

transferee A person to whom a transfer is made.

transferor A person who makes a transfer.

transnational corporation A corporation created or headquartered in one country having a network of foreign affiliated (subsidiary) corporations which it controls through equity ownership or management devices.

treasury stock Shares of stock that were originally issued by a corporation and that subsequently were reacquired by it.

trespass In realty and personalty, the wrongful invasion of the property rights of another.

trial-type hearing The adjudicatory process by which administrative law judges determine the validity of administrative action. Similar in nature to a federal, nonjury civil trial.

trust Two or more companies that have a monopoly. In the law of property, a relationship whereby a settlor transfers legal ownership of property to a trustee to be held and managed for a beneficiary who has equitable title to the property.

trustee One who administers a trust.

trustee in bankruptcy A person elected or appointed to administer the estate of the bankrupt person.

tying agreement Any arrangement in which one party agrees to supply a product or service only on the condition that the customer also take another product or service. Such activity is scrutinized under Section 1 of the Sherman Act and Section 3 of the Clayton Act.

ultra vires Any acts or actions of a corporation that are held to be unauthorized and beyond the scope of the corporate business as determined by law or by the articles of incorporation.

unconscionable contract A contract or a clause within a contract which is so grossly unfair that a court will refuse to enforce it.

undisclosed principal In agency law, a principal whose identity and existence are unknown by third parties, leading them to believe that the agent is acting solely for himself or herself.

undue influence The overcoming of a person's free will by misusing a position of confidence or relationship, thereby taking advantage of that person to affect his or her decisions or actions.

unenforceable contract Generally a valid contract that cannot be enforced in a court of law because of a special rule of law or a failure to meet an additional legal requirement (such as a writing).

Uniform Commercial Code (UCC) Uniform rules dealing with the sales of goods, commercial paper, secured transactions in personal property, and certain aspects of banking, documents of title, and investment securities. Recommended by the National Conference of Commissioners on Uniform State Laws for enactment by the various states, it has been adopted by forty-nine states (and Louisiana has adopted parts of it).

Uniform Limited Partnership Act (ULPA) Uniform rules governing the organization and operation of limited partnerships recommended by the National Conference of Commissioners on Uniform State Laws for enactment by the various states. A Revised Uniform Limited Partnership Act (RULPA) was drafted in 1976. The RULPA has been adopted by 30 states; 19 states still follow the ULPA.

Uniform Partnership Act (UPA) Uniform rules governing the partnership operation, particularly in the absence of an agreement, recommended by the National Conference of Commissioners on Uniform State Laws for enactment by the various states.

unilateral contract An offer or promise of the offeror which can become binding only by the completed performance of the offeree; an act for a promise, whereby the offeree's act is not only his or her acceptance but also the completed performance under the contract.

unilateral mistake A mistake in which only one party to a contract is in error as to the terms or performance expected under the contract.

usage of trade Any practice or method repeated with such regularity in a vocation or business that it becomes the legal basis for expected performance in future events within that vocation or business.

usury An interest charge exceeding the maximum amount permitted by statute.

U.S. Code The full and complete compilation of all federal statutes.

validation requirement An EEOC guideline requiring an employer to prove that an otherwise illegally discriminatory employment test is legal. The employer must show the test predicts important work behavior relevant to the job or jobs for which applicants are being evaluated.

valid contract A contract that meets the four basic requirements for enforceability by the parties to it.

venue A designation of the right of the defendant to be tried in a proper court within a specific geographic area.

vertical integration Operation of a firm at more than one level in the chain of production and distribution of a product.

vertical merger A merger of two firms, one of which is a supplier or customer of the other.

vertical price fixing Price fixing between supplier and customer, relating to the price at which the customer will resell. *Per se* illegal under Section 1 of the Sherman Act.

vertical restraints of trade Any actions or arrangements made by firms operating at different levels of the distribution chain that harm competition. Vertical price fixing, tying and exclusive dealing arrangements, and reciprocity are examples of such restraints.

vesting right The legally enforceable right to certain pension benefits earned by an employee participating in a private pension plan. Such rights accrue even if there is no right to collect such benefits until a later date. ERISA regulates how private pensions may vest pension benefits to their employees.

vicarious liability The liability of a person, not himself or herself at fault, for the actions of others.

voidable contract A contract from which one or both parties can, if they choose, legally withdraw without liability.

voidable transfer In bankruptcy law, a transfer by a bankrupt debtor that can be set aside by a trustee in bankruptcy.

void contract A contract without legal effect.

voir dire The examination of prospective jurors by lawyers in a particular case to determine their fitness (i.e., to discover whether they have an interest in the outcome of the suit, a bias or prejudice against a party, or are otherwise unlikely to exercise the objectivity necessary in jury deliberations).

voluntary bankruptcy Bankruptcy based upon petition of the debtor.

waiver The voluntary giving up of a legal right.

warranty An assurance or guaranty, expressly or impliedly made, that certain actions or rights can take place, that information given is correct, or that performance will conform to certain standards.

warranty deed A deed with covenants, express or implied, that the title to real property is good and complete.

warranty of fitness for a particular purpose In sales law, an implied warranty imposed by law on a seller, who has reason to know of the buyer's intended use of the goods (where the buyer relies on the seller's skill and judgment), that the goods are suitable for the buyer's intended use.

warranty of merchantability In sales law, an implied warranty imposed by law upon a merchant seller of goods that the goods are fit for the ordinary purposes for which goods of that kind are used.

watered stock Shares of stock issued by a corporation for a consideration less than the par value or stated value of the stock.

wildcat strike A work stoppage initiated by a group of workers without the approval of a majority of employees in the bargaining unit. Such a strike is illegal and participating employees have no legal protection against discharge.

will A document by which a person directs the disposition of his or her property (estate) upon his or her death.

workers' compensation laws State statutory provisions calling for payments to employees for accidental injuries or diseases arising out of and in the course of employment. These payments, for medical expenses and lost income, are made regardless of whether anyone is at fault.

writ of certiorari What the appellant seeks by application to a higher court. An order issued by an appellate court directing a lower court to remit to it the record and proceedings of a particular case so that the actions of the lower court may be reviewed.

yellow-dog contract A contract by which an employer requires an employee to promise that he will not join a union, and that he can be discharged if he later joins a union. Such an agreement is illegal.

CASE INDEX

Cases appearing in boldface are summarized in the text.

SUBJECT INDEX